PLACE IN RETURN BOX to remove this checkout from your record.
TO AVOID FINES return on or before date due.

DATE DUE	DATE DUE	DATE DUE
AUG 2 5 2013	————	————
————	————	————
————	————	————
————	————	————
————	————	————
————	————	————
————	————	————

MSU Is An Affirmative Action/Equal Opportunity Institution

c:\circ\datedue.pm3-p.1

AFRICAN HISTORY

AFRICAN

edited, with introductions, by ROBERT O. COLLINS

HISTORY

TEXT AND READINGS

University of California, Santa Barbara

Random House New York

Library of Congress
Catalog Card Number 72–89480

Standard Book Number 394–30135–8

Manufactured in the United States of America by
Kingsport Press, Inc., Kingsport, Tennessee

Typography by Jack Ribik

First Printing
98765432

TO J. C. WHO "DARED TO DREAM TOMORROW MIGHT BE OURS."

PREFACE

During the past decade I have been continually frustrated in my search for suitable reading materials for moderately large classes of college and university students interested in the African past. Monographs are too expensive and too specialized. Articles in learned journals are not only inappropriate for the beginner but are virtually impossible to use in lecture courses with large numbers of competitive students. Recently, with the publication of numerous paperbound books, both general and specialized in content, the problem of selecting meaningful readings has become less acute. Unfortunately, the very nature of monographs and textbooks has failed to provide the firsthand accounts upon which the historian of Africa still depends for much of his knowledge of the African past. Without such examples he has been unable to demonstrate to the student the extent of the rich documentary materials that exist today for analysis and interpretation by scholar and student alike. The belief that Africa has no history because it has no records is still current today. If the present volume does not convince the skeptics, perhaps it will at least direct them to a wealth of sources that will help them to overcome their stubborn prejudices. Indeed, what follows is but a fragment of the immense volume of archival and published materials that await the historian and the student.

If my purpose has been to expose the student to the source materials of African history, my objective has been guided by two principles. First, I have sought to embrace the full time span of documentary records pertaining to Africa. Second, I have sought to cover the vast geographical sweep of sub-Saharan Africa. To achieve these two very ambitious objectives in a single and modest volume has required an eclectic, if not random, selection that betrays my own personal inclinations and interests. I have endeavored to choose documents that describe Africans and not just individuals who came to look or to rule. I have attempted to select passages from less-known accounts and descriptions as well as from the more standard authorities. I have tried, where possible, to obtain passages of sufficient length to make them meaningful to the inquiring student. Finally, I have prepared brief introductions to guide the beginner and to refresh the memory of the more experienced student.

I am most grateful indeed for the assistance of Eugene Titsworth, Ralph Herring, and Russell Chace in the preparation of the manuscript and to Nell Elizabeth Painter and Martin Legassick, whose suggestions and sympathy have immensely improved this volume and without whose support its appearance would still be many years away.

In order to make the selections more understandable to the beginner, I have frequently inserted explanatory material directly in the text, either in brackets or as a footnote, both followed by "ed." (editor). All other footnotes and bracketed material found in the various selections are the work of editors who have preceded me but whose efforts need not be duplicated or deleted.

I wish to express my appreciation to the many authors and publishers for permission to reprint the selections that are included herein.

December 1970
Robert O. Collins
Santa Barbara, California

CONTENTS

ix

Contents

AFRICAN HISTORY

ONE

WESTERN AND CENTRAL SUDAN

THE SAHARA AND SUDAN

Stretching from the Nile Valley westward to the Atlantic between the Sahara Desert to the north and the forest regions to the south is that broad belt of savanna grasslands known as the Sudan. These vast plains are populated by black peoples speaking many different languages, but the most important groups are the Wolof of the Senegal, the Mande-speaking peoples of the Upper Niger, the Voltaic peoples living south of the great bend of the Niger at the headwaters of the Volta rivers, the Hausa of northern Nigeria, and the Kanuri-speaking peoples living around Lake Chad. All are cultivators of Sudanic crops (millet, sorghum, watermelon, tamarind, kola, and sesame). Stimulated by the influence of alien cultures beyond the Sudan, these people created states that were frequently of vast dimensions and that had a complex form of political organization. One other group of western Sudanic peoples, the Fulani (also referred to variously as *Fellani, Fellata, Filani, Foulah, Ful, Fulbe, Peul,* and *Pallo*), were originally seminomadic people from the Senegal River area whose language was related to Wolof. From the seventh century, Berbers migrated southward from Morocco under Arab pressure into the Senegal Valley and beyond to the plains of the Futa Toro south of the Senegal. Here a process of acculturation took place; the Berber herdsmen adopted the Fulani language and intermarried with the Fulani cultivators along the river while retaining their predominantly nomadic way of life. Meanwhile, the Fulani cultivators continued their sedentary way of life in the towns of the Senegal. The pastoral Fulani prospered and followed their herds to the east, establishing themselves on land that was ill-suited to cultivation and developing a close relationship with the cultivators in every region. By the fourteenth century the Fulani had reached the region of Masina, and in the fifteenth century they first appeared among the Hausa of northern Nigeria. Smaller groups pressed on into Adamawa on the Nigerian-Cameroon border in the eighteenth century and expanded to Wadai in the nineteenth. The pastoral Fulani did not migrate alone, for their sedentary kinsmen invariably accompanied them. Better educated, politically more sophisticated, and possessing fanatical beliefs, the town Fulani played a decisive role in the foundation of theocratic states throughout the western Sudan during the Islamic renaissance of the late eighteenth and early nineteenth centuries.

From the rise of Pharaonic Egypt to the fall of Meroe in the fourth century A.D., Nile Valley civilizations have clearly influenced the development of western Sudanic culture. Some authorities go so far as to ascribe Nile Valley origins to West African peoples or at least to attribute the rise of civilization in the western Sudan to the importation of Egyptian institutions and ideas. Other scholars have refused to accept such a direct dependence on Nile Valley civilization, because the evidence is indeed circumstantial and tenuous. One must begin by distinguishing between influence and origin. Most authorities agree that Egyptian influence probably traveled west, but this does not mean that the West African peoples migrated from the Nile Valley. Indeed, there is an enormous amount of linguistic and agricultural evidence to indicate that blacks inhabited West Africa long before the rise of Pharaonic civilization in Egypt. Clearly, Egypt influenced West Africa, but although Nile Valley culture may have been imported by West Africans, it was molded, shaped, and frequently was entirely recast to meet particular needs. There was undoubtedly cultural borrowing, but western Sudanic civilization did not originate in Egypt or Kush. It was, rather, an independent creation of the Sudanic peoples, and the role of Nile Valley cultural ideas and institutions must not be exaggerated.

North Africa formed a second region of contact with the western Sudan. The Sahara has traditionally been regarded as a great barrier to communication, but in reality this territory has allowed peoples to travel back and forth. Inhospitable though it may be, its barren wastes have never totally prevented contact between Africa and the Mediterranean world. In Neolithic times the Sahara was not so arid and repellent but was inhabited by more varied forms of fauna and flora than are found there today. Rivers flowed from the highlands to the plains, creating shallow lakes around which lived extensive populations that hunted elephant, hippopotamus, and buffalo. Since that time the Sahara has deteriorated. The desiccation has resulted principally from climatic change, but the follies of man have clearly hastened the process. Fire, the ubiquitous goat, and the migration of cultivators

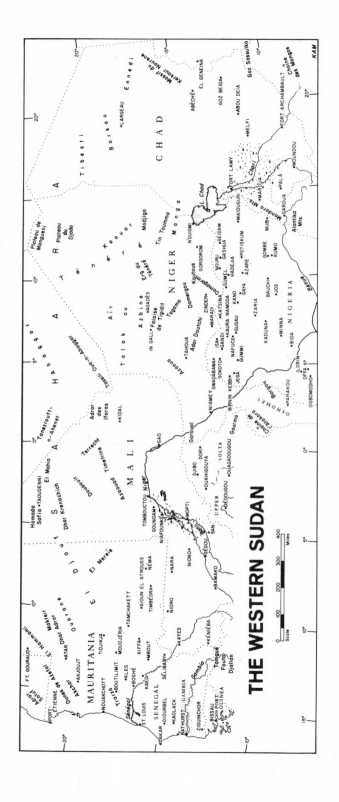

THE WESTERN SUDAN

have all contributed to the spread of the desert. Finally, the Sahara must not be regarded simply as a land of sand. There are thousands of square miles of *erg* (shifting sand), *hammada* (exposed bedrock), and *reg* (gravel and windblown sand), but some regions of the Sahara remain habitable by nomads while agriculturists continue to till the soil of its oases.

THE TRANS-SAHARAN TRADE

The great revolution of trans-Saharan travel came with the introduction of the camel in the first century A.D., even though trade had flowed across the desert for many millenniums before the birth of Christ. During Neolithic times (the Stone Age), human porters were undoubtedly used to carry trade goods between the North African littoral and the Sudan. Following the domestication of animals, bullocks were employed. (Under proper conditions and partly due to the fact that they move more slowly, these animals can go without water almost as long as camels.) The camel, which is well suited in terms of speed and endurance to desert travel, was introduced by the Romans in order to defend their towns in North Africa from desert raids. The caravan subsequently became a fixture of Saharan life for two millenniums; trans-Saharan trade developed rapidly until the desert was laced by caravan routes extending in all directions, intersecting at oases and crisscrossing in the middle of the desert (René Caillié, *The Trans-Saharan Caravan*). There were four principal routes— the Salima Trail from Cyrenacia to Wadai, the Bilma Trail or Garamantes Road from Tripoli to Kawar, the Gadàmes Road from Ghat to the Hausa country, and the Sijilmasa-Walata Road from Morocco to the Middle Niger and Upper Senegal (Antoine Malfante, *Tawat and the Western Sudan Trade*). Each of these routes represented a two months' journey, and each had long, waterless stretches between the oases. The prosperity of the Sijilmasa-Walata Road, the

greatest of the four, was founded on the gold of the Upper Niger that was exchanged for the salt of the Saharan oases of Taghaza and Taodeni. Timbuktu became the great entrepôt and southern terminus for this road, because its position on the Niger bend also gave it a strategic position in the east-west caravan routes traversing the Sudan.

THE ISLAMIZATION OF THE SUDAN

The baggage trains of Muslim merchants who made their way across the trans-Saharan caravan routes in search of gold in return for Mediterranean products represented the first currents of Islamization in West Africa. Although these merchants were Muslims, they did not seek to convert or to force their religion on the peoples of the western Sudan. Nevertheless, their presence in the towns and markets was observed and not infrequently imitated. Occasionally a Sudanic ruler professed Islam, but usually in addition to his traditional religion, not in displacement of it. The first attempt to disseminate Islam in the Sudan by force came from the Berber tribes that had joined the Murabitun movement. The Murabitun were the followers of Abd Allah ibn Yasin, who was brought from Mecca in 1036 by the Sanhaja Berber chief Yahya ibn Ibrahim to instruct his semipagan tribesmen in the true religion. Abd Allah ibn Yasin had little success, and after the death of his patron, Yahya, he and his small band of followers were driven to seek refuge in a *ribat,* or fortified fraternity, somewhere on the Atlantic coast of Mauritania. The ribat soon won fame for its holiness, and adherents flocked to it to learn Islam and to prepare for the *jihad,* or holy war against the infidels. They were called the Murabitun, or people of the ribat.

In 1042 Abd Allah ibn Yasin began his holy war to spread Islam among the pagan Berbers. He was spectacularly successful, and as his followers and victories increased, the Murabitun, or Almoravids (European corruption of the Arabic *al-Murabitun*), swept north to Morocco and across the Straits of Gibraltar into Spain to establish a powerful Muslim empire, where their rule was characterized by a puritannical drive to reform Islam. At first the energies of the Murabitun were completely taken up in Morocco, but in 1065 one of the Murabitun leaders, Abu Bakr, returned to the plains of the Sudan to carry the jihad against the Sudanic empire of the Ghana. After a long and difficult struggle, the capital of the Ghana, probably Kumbi, was captured, ending the long period during which this state had dominated the western Sudan. Its collapse led to the political triumph of Islam throughout the upland plains between the Senegal and the Niger, even though the political power of the Murabitun was short-lived.

GHANA

Ghana was the ancient state formed by the *Soninke* tribe of the Mande-speaking people and located in the Hawd region of the transitional plains lying between desert and savanna known as the Sahil. Geographically it is far removed from the modern Republic of Ghana, which adopted its name. With the introduction of iron-working techniques into the western Sudan about the time of Christ, the people of the Sudan were able to create new and more complex societies. Once they were equipped with iron, the Soninke were able to establish mastery over their neighbors. State building had begun, and under the influence of the trans-Saharan trade Ghana evolved from a tribe into an empire. Shortly after the introduction of iron, the camel enabled the trans-Saharan trade (and particularly the gold trade, which was controlled by Ghana) to expand. Gold was mined south of Ghana at the headwaters of the Niger, where Ghanaian merchants would secure it by means of the "silent trade," or dumb barter. When the merchants reached the

gold region, they beat big drums, then placed their trade goods on the ground and retired out of sight. The local Africans emerged from the mines and placed gold beside the trade goods. The Africans then withdrew and the merchants reappeared. If they were satisfied they took the gold, beating a drum to signify that the exchange had been completed. The gold was then taken to Kumbi, Awadaghast, or one of the other market towns, where it was exchanged for salt and Mediterranean products brought by the North African merchants. The Ghana, of course, received tax revenues from goods entering and leaving the empire.

Although historians traditionally refer to Ghana as a Sudanic state, *Ghana* was in fact the title of the ruler, and when Arabic writers use the term *Bilad Ghana* they mean the country of *the* Ghana. The kingdom, which probably was formed in the fourth or fifth century, remained a powerful and stable influence in the western Sudan until it was destroyed by the Murabitun. Although the Soninke were able to regain their independence after the death of Abu Bakr in 1087, when the Murabitun hegemony in the Sudan collapsed, they were never able to reassert their authority over the Mande-speaking tribes, and in 1224, one hundred years after the Soninke had thrown off Berber rule, another Mande-speaking dynasty, the *Susu,* established its rule in Ghana. During that same century, however, the Soninke and Arab merchants in the Sahil broke with the Susu and established themselves at Walata, one hundred miles to the north and beyond Susu control. Walata prospered, taking the trade from the towns of Ghana. Kumbi itself soon fell into disuse and ruin and was abandoned until its discovery in the twentieth century.

THE GROWTH OF ISLAM

The Murabitun had left no enduring political system in the Sudan. Although they had carried the holy war to the Sudan, their uncompromising and militant convictions were not as successful as the more peaceful, quiet penetration by Muslim merchants that had begun prior to the Murabitun movement. Thus the Murabitun may have accelerated the Islamization of the Sudan, but in the end the Muslim merchant, principally the Muslim Sudanese merchant, was primarily responsible for the spread of Islam beyond the Sahil. Here the market towns were the greatest centers of Islam, not only because of the presence of Muslim merchants but because the sedentary, intellectual life of the towns was more conducive to theological speculation and the transmission of religious ideas than was life in rural agricultural villages or among nomadic tribesmen. Djenné, one of the greatest trading cities, became Muslim in the late twelfth or early thirteenth century and rapidly grew to be the most famous Muslim metropolis in the western Sudan. Timbuktu, which was later to rival Djenné, owed its intellectual and religious life to Muslim missionaries and merchants. From the commercial towns Islam gradually spread to the ruling classes and became an imperial cult, but until the nineteenth century it had little impact on the cultivators, who continued to depend on their traditional religious beliefs and practices to resolve the great questions of man's relation to the universe. Thus Islam grew, but only as a class religion. Islam is a way of life, total and universal, but in the western Sudan its confined position within the framework of Sudanese society tended to neutralize its effects as a spiritual transformer.

THE SUDAN STATE SYSTEM

Although historians frequently have described the states of the western Sudan as "kingdoms" or "empires," they have in fact taken a term from European history and applied it to an African situation, thereby distorting the way in which Africans in the Sudan regarded their political organization. Two levels of political ac-

tion existed in the western Sudan: the local group and the ruling lineage. A kingdom was formed when a lineage was superimposed without damaging or undermining local authority. Thus ruling lineages might come and go, but the local villages remained governed by a clan head, a council of elders, or a village chief. So long as the local unit paid tribute, it was left to carry on its traditional way of life under its own laws and customs. Rulers of Sudanese states made no attempt to impose a bureaucracy or to legislate directly for the general welfare. Problems were solved at the local level with little interference from above. The state was, then, neither an expanded local community that had assimilated its neighbors nor a territorial unit that had grown by the addition of other territorial units. Rather, expansion came when one lineage head payed tribute to another lineage leader, the king, with the consequence that the extent of an empire could not be precisely defined by geographical delimitation, for lineages, and therefore empires, were forever expanding and contracting. Thus thousands of political groups, or lineages, coexisted within an empire, and because the emperor possessed no territorial sovereignty but only sovereignty over his people, there was generally no capital. The king or emperor retained allegiance partly by tribute, which his army exacted, and partly because of his spiritual qualities. Like the other social and occupational groups within the empire, kingship was a lineal occupation in which ritual and political functions were equally important. Thus the ritual role of the emperor transcended all lineages, and in this way he was responsible for the spiritual welfare of his subjects. Clearly, under such a system the Sudanic states possessed no cultural or ethnic homogeneity and no tribal boundaries. They consisted of an amorphous agglomeration of kin groups that had little in common but the recognition of a far-off suzerain with particular ritual powers. Within the empire there were tribute-paying units, but the local group was otherwise free to carry on its traditional political and social customs.

Such a political organization possessed very real structural weakness and instability. An empire, of course, could expand rapidly by receiving recognition from widespread lineage heads. An empire could disintegrate with equal rapidity when the superstructure collapsed, but the demise of the ruling lineage had very little effect on the mass of the Sudanese. In fact, the intrinsic organization of community life at the local level was left largely unimpaired as the superimposed empires rose and fell.

THE EMPIRE OF MALI

The fame of Ghana has tended to confuse history, for south of the Hawd region, where Ghana had known its glory, was the nucleus of what was to become a great empire, far surpassing Ghana in power and influence. The dynasty that founded Mali was one of a number of Mande chieftaincies, probably located in the hills on the right bank of the Upper Niger, upstream from the present-day city of Bamako. Historians have not been able to trace the exact evolution of Mali from independent family communities into a state, but the nucleus of the empire was probably in existence by the tenth century. The history of Mali begins with Sun Dyata, the Lord Lion, who defeated the Susu king in 1234 and plundered the ruined capital of Ghana six years later. Sun Dyata soon claimed allegiance of the vast Sudanic territories from the headwaters of the Niger to the Sahara in the north and the Senegal in the west. He himself was probably a pagan, but members of his family were Muslims.

The economic power of Mali was based on an agricultural economy that was supported by the profits of the flourishing gold trade. Mali's military power was invested in the great army of chain-mailed cavalry that carried the influence of the empire to the furthest corners of the western Sudan. The successors of Sun Dyata are, for the most part, just names until the accession of Sabakura in 1285. Sabakura was a freed slave who seized the throne and proved to be the strongest of all the kings. Under his militant rule Mali expanded to the Atlantic in the west and beyond the great bend of the Niger to Songhay territory in the east. After Sabakura the succession reverted to the legitimate line of rulers, who consolidated Sabakura's conquests. Mansa Musa (1312–1337) is the most famous of Mali kings, largely because of his ostentatious and lavish pilgrimage to Mecca in 1324–1325. Although his wild spending spree scattered gold from West Africa to Arabia and earned him undying fame by the chroniclers, Mansa Musa represented the golden age of Mali, during which the literature of the western Sudan reached its peak and Sudanic architecture, patterned after that of the south Mediterranean, flourished in all the great market towns of the Sudan. Religious schools in Timbuktu and Djenné achieved widespread fame for their erudition, and thus the demand for books and manuscripts became one of the principal items in the trans-Saharan trade.

Mali was a typical Sudanic state with a small core of feudal states administered directly by members of the royal family. Beyond these states the various chieftaincies continued to be ruled by the lineage heads, the traditional rulers, to whom the coming or fading away of the supreme ruler made little difference. When conquest brought other peoples into the empire, their rulers were recognized and their political and social customs were respected. The power of the *mansa,* or king, of Mali was based not on geographical realm but rather on the inheritance from his predecessors of a domain of clans, castes, and lineages. Mali was famous for its justice and security, and although little is known of the internal workings of the courts, virtually all Arab travelers attested to the existence of public security. The mansa himself was surrounded by an elaborate court ritual. He gave two types of audience, the first in the entrance to his compound and the second in a special open-air place surrounded by his council. The expenses of the court were met by taxes on crops and livestock, tribute from the dependent states, revenue from customs and tolls, and the spoils of war. Islam was an imperial cult but was little recognized or practiced outside the immediate entourage of the mansa. Although many of these rulers gained fame as a result of their extravagant pilgrimages to Mecca, neither Islamic law nor Islamic social custom was practiced in the Mali Empire. Nevertheless, the Muslim community of foreign merchants in the towns continued the Islamic tradition, so that many Islamic communities in West Africa attribute their conversion to missionaries from Mali (Ibn Battuta, *Mali*).

Following the death of Mansa Musa, this great empire, torn by dynastic rivalries and ruled by a series of incompetents and pretenders to the throne, gradually slipped into decline. Outlying dependencies attacked the empire, eroding away those vassals who sought to break their ties with a weak mansa. Although the mansas of Mali continued to exert their position as overlords well into the fifteenth century, by the sixteenth century Mali had been reduced to a petty chieftaincy on the Upper Niger and has changed little since that time. Like other Sudanic empires, Mali came and went, but for more than two centuries (1238–1468), Mali's hegemony over the far-flung plains of the western Sudan facilitated the movement of peoples and thus eradicated feelings of exclusiveness of language and custom. Throughout the western Sudan today one will find adjacent Mandingo, Soninke, and Fulani villages living in harmony, clearly the result of the intermingling and tolerance first experienced during the age of Mali.

THE SONGHAY

The Songhay live on the banks of the Middle Niger. Their origins are unknown, but they are a mixture of several immigrant peoples who moved up the Niger to settle in the region of Gao (Arabic: *Kawkaw*). Here a dynasty was founded known as the *Za* which, according to tradition, accepted Islam at the beginning of the eleventh century. Situated at the end of the Tilemsi Valley, which stretches northeastward into the Sahara, Gao was regularly visited by merchants from North Africa who introduced Islam to the Songhay. As in other regions of the western Sudan, Islam contributed to the unification of the Songhay by dissolving tribal differences and providing a cultural milieu that was shared by diverse peoples. For several centuries, however, Songhay was eclipsed by the expanding power of Mali to the west, and the Za rulers became tribute-paying vassals of the mansas of Mali. Toward the end of the thirteenth century a new dynasty called the Sonni or *Si* dynasty replaced the Za and sought to throw off the control of Mali. Under the leadership of Ali Kolon the Songhay were at first successful, but after continued and desultory warfare Mali was able to reassert its control and the Songhay remained a dependency of the rulers of Mali until the end of the fourteenth century.

With the decline of Mali the Songhay rulers began the process of empire building, particularly under Si Ali (1465–1492), the fifteenth ruler of the dynasty, who set out to make himself the master of the rich and populous region of the Upper Niger. In 1468 Timbuktu fell to the Songhay armies, and in 1473 Djenné was captured after a long siege. Si Ali's most formidable opponents were the Mossi states below the great bend of the Niger which, although defeated by Songhay forces, were never completely reduced or brought within the empire. Ali's empire was geographically divided into two parts. In the East was Songhay; in the west were the former dependencies of the empire of Mali. Neither Ali nor his successors ever really solved the problem of these two separate parts between which lay the desert, the Hombori Mountains, and the intractable Mossi states. Unlike most western Sudanic rulers, Ali did not favor Islam. Other kings in Ghana, Mali, or Songhay may not have been completely orthodox Muslims, but they were tolerant toward Islam and frequently sought to use it to their political advantage. Ali appears, however, to have purposely persecuted the *ulama,* the Islamic teachers and theologians, in order not to lose the critical support of the pagans in his kingdom.

In 1492 Ali died under mysterious circumstances, and his line fled into exile down the Niger. Power in Gao was seized by a man of Soninke origin, Muhammad Ture ibn Abu Bakr, who took the title *askiya.* Askiya Muhammad's first task was to eliminate any competitors to the throne and then to consolidate Ali's conquests. Unlike Ali, Askiya Muhammad sought to use the ulama, and he pandered to their vanity and supported them. Muhammad has been portrayed as a wise and beneficent ruler, just as Ali has been castigated for his ill treatment of pious and learned men. Muhammad fostered Timbuktu as a center of religious learning whose importance some authorities have exaggerated by reference to the "University of Sankore." Sankore was, in fact, the quarter of Timbuktu where the majority of the teaching clerics lived and held their classes, and although it was not organized in a single "university," the number of scholars and students there probably exceeded the number to be found in sixteenth-century Oxford or Paris. In spite of its growth under the Songhay, Timbuktu never replaced Djenné, either as a center of religious learning or as a market town. Protected by the network of canals that surrounded the city and supported by the agricultural populations beyond, Djenné was never plundered by Tuareg raiders or torn by internal disunity as was Timbuktu. At the age of eighty-five As-

kiya Muhammad, infirm and blind, was deposed and exiled to an island in the Niger. Although he was later set free, he died soon after in 1538, one of the most remarkable rulers to live during the period when remarkable men in Europe were also constructing states and founding empires.

ORGANIZATION OF THE SONGHAY EMPIRE

The Songhay Empire was organized in the traditional Sudanic state pattern, with various grades of occupational castes and lineages that were allowed to maintain their own traditions and customs so long as they acknowledged the Songhay rulers by the payment of tribute. Nevertheless, Songhay under the askiyas was more autocratic than the normal Sudanese state with its elaborate system of checks and balances. Askiya Muhammad, for instance, appointed members of his own family or court favorites to positions that would ordinarily have been given to vassal kings. Further, apart from these provincial officials there existed a central bureaucracy composed of the chief tax collector, the various military and naval chiefs, and an assortment of other officials who were in charge of the forests, lakes, and rivers, as well as relations with the Berber tribes of the Saharan fringe. As was the case with Mali, the security provided by the far-flung empire encouraged commerce and trade, which was supervised by special inspectors in the marketplaces and coordinated by a uniform system of weights and measures and currency. Even more than its predecessors, Songhay dominated the western Sudan as a vast and complex empire unequaled in extent or organization by any African state of that period except Kanem-Bornu to the east (Leo Africanus, *The Western Sudan in the Sixteenth Century*).

THE CENTRAL SUDAN

The central Sudan is that region stretching from the Middle Niger to Wadai with its focal point at Lake Chad, which, over the centuries, has been a center of cultural concentration and diffusion. Although there are legends telling of indigenous paleonigritic peoples in the region of Lake Chad, the history of the central Sudan begins with the So peoples, who moved south of the lake at the end of the tenth century and constructed towns where they developed the ceramic manufacture and bronze casting for which they are justly famous. Although they were continually exposed to invaders and immigrants alike, the So people managed to maintain their identity until the fifteenth century, when they were finally assimilated into the Bornu.

THE RISE OF KANEM-BORNU

In the ninth century the *Saifi* dynasty of Kanem was founded northeast of Lake Chad by black nomads called *Zaghawa*. The people of Kanem are called *Kanuri*, a name originally applied to a particular clan, but as other, non-Zaghawa were assimilated, the term "Kanuri" came to be widely, if imprecisely, applied to all the inhabitants of Kanem. Islam reached Kanem in the eleventh century, introduced by a holy man, Muhammad ibn Mani, and as in the western Sudan, its introduction not only increased the prestige of the dynasty but exposed the people of Kanem to the social, legal, and political ideas of a universal religion. By the thirteenth century Islam had become well established among the ruling class, and Kanuri Muslims even founded a hostel at Cairo for students from the central Sudan. Islam appears to have given Kanem the stimulus it required to become transformed from a group of disparate peoples under one leader to a powerful Islamic state capable of expansion and assimilation of pagan peoples. During the reign of Dunama I (1097–1150), Kanem began its expansion by gaining control of the desert caravan routes. Gradually the character of the Saifi kingship was changed. Chiefs of nomadic tribes became Sudanese monarchs and leaders of

a pastoral aristocracy became feudal lords with vassals in the Sudanic state pattern. During this time the basic structure of a Sudanese kingdom was formed, and it endured for the next seven centuries despite internal disruptions and external invasions.

Like Mali, Kanem consisted of a central core. The King of Kanem appointed members of his family as governors, and they administered their subjects directly. Beyond the heartland, vassals retained their own rulers, language, and cultural characteristics. The distinction between a subject of the central core and a vassal was determined by taxation—subjects were directly assessed and vassals simply payed a block tribute. Such a division was, of course, typical of the Sudanic kingdoms, but the nucleus of direct control was considerably larger than that of the Western Sudanic states, creating a more viable and lasting cultural group.

In the thirteenth century Kanem slipped into a decline that was precipitated by the religious conflicts between Muslims and pagans on the one hand and political rivalries within the royal family on the other. This time of troubles was known as the period of *Bulala* wars. The Bulala were a ruling class (actually a branch of the Saifi dynasty) that represented a pagan reaction against the Islamization of the Saifi kings. Throughout the thirteenth and fourteenth centuries the kings of Kanem struggled against the Bulala, until they were overcome and driven from Kanem at the end of the fourteenth century. For the next 125 years the Bulala ruled in Kanem, but the Saifi dynasty did not die. Retreating before the pressure of the victorious Bulala armies, the Saifi kings moved to Kaka in Bornu, southeast of Lake Chad, imposed their authority over the So towns, and sought to construct a new empire. Under Ali Ghazi ibn Dunama (1476–1503), the Bornu capital of Ngazargamu was established on the Yo River in 1484, and during the long reigns of his five successors Bornu grew in power and prosperity. Under Idris

Katagarmabe (1503–1526), the first great king of the sixteenth century, the armies of Bornu defeated the Bulala and reestablished the rule of the Saifi dynasty in Kanem. During each successive reign the Bulala were defeated and driven further to the east, their overthrow culminating in their demise during the glorious reign of the greatest of the kings of Kanem-Bornu, Idris ibn Ali—or, as he is better known, Idris Alawma (1570–1602). Not only did Idris Alawma drive the Bulala remnant from Kanem, but he, more than any other Saifi king, strengthened Islam in Kanem-Bornu so that it was no longer simply the religious cult of the aristocracy (Imam Ahmad ibn Fartuwa, *Idris Alawma and the Kanem Wars*).

Although the successors of Idris Alawma did not possess his ability, under them Kanem-Bornu enjoyed a long period of peace and prosperity that stretched well into the eighteenth century. To be sure, the empire was increasingly challenged by Tuareg raiders from the Sahara as well as by rebellious vassals, but not until the nineteenth century was Kanem-Bornu threatened by the rise of theocratic states to the west, at a time when its ability to withstand an alien assault had been jeopardized by a disastrous campaign that had been waged in the south.

HAUSALAND

The Hausa today form one of the largest linguistic groups in Africa. From the earliest times the Hausa have lived in walled towns (*birni*) situated in what is now northern Nigeria, within which dwelt a self-sufficient community that carried on trade and industry and utilized a large area of open land for cultivation. A Hausa state evolved when one town secured the acknowledgment of an ever-widening circle of hamlets, so that the original birni became a capital around which clustered a host of satellite villages. Political control within the town de-

pended on supervision of the religious cult, and much of early Hausa history can be explained by the struggles of immigrant groups to wrest control of the local cult. Unlike their neighbors to the east and west the Hausa never formed an empire, and their history consists of kaleidoscopic conflicts among numerous city-states. There were seven legitimate Hausa states—Gobir, Katsina, Zaria, Biram, Dawra (traditionally regarded as the founder states), Kano, and Rano. Each state possesses its own unique history preserved in its chronicles, and its people appear to have been more content to prosper economically through the labors of their cultivators, skilled craftsmen, and keen traders than to seek political unity (The Kano Chronicle, *Kings of Kano*).

COLLAPSE OF THE SONGHAY

In 1578 Ahmad al-Mansur, the Sadian Sultan of Morocco, turned his ambitions southward and prepared an army to seize the western Sudan, from which came the gold of Africa. By 1590 the Moroccan Army was ready and, under Judar Pasha, left Marrakech on October 16. Three months later Judar and his troops arrived at Karabara on the Niger. Well equipped with firearms and artillery, the Moroccans swept all before them and destroyed the Songhay armies on the battlefield of Tondibi, near Gao. Although the Songhay continued to harass the Moroccans, they no longer exerted hegemony over their vassals, who quickly asserted their independence. Nor were the Moroccans able simply to replace the Songhay. Powerful enough to destroy but not sufficiently strong to build, the Moroccans imposed themselves as a military caste that could control localized areas but that failed to hold together the great empire which the Songhay askiyas had been able to create and sustain. Without security, the western Sudan dissolved into chaos. Neighbor preyed upon neighbor and nomad pillaged cultivator. Famine and pestilence swept the land. Even the Moroccans exerted their own authority, ignoring the commands of their sultan 1,000 miles away across the Sahara. The Moroccan troops intermarried with the Sudanese and soon became acculturated to the manners and customs of the land even though they remained a distinct caste, called the *arma,* which lasted into the nineteenth century (Abd al-Rahman al-Sadi, *Songhay and the Moroccan Invasion*).

From the collapse of the Songhay at the end of the sixteenth century to the rise of the Islamic theocracies at the beginning of the nineteenth, the Sudan suffered two centuries of political disunity and social upheaval during which Islam fell into desuetude as the traditional religions reasserted themselves. Mali and Songhay were reduced to their heartlands, and the Hausa states remained as mutually antagonistic city-states. Not surprisingly, the trans-Saharan trade diminished as security and commerce declined, but the Muslim merchants, the *dyula,* continued to wander throughout the land, sharing in the life of the pagan environment and accommodating themselves to new circumstances, while at the same time keeping Muslim traditions alive during this long period of Islamic eclipse.

RENAISSANCE IN THE WESTERN SUDAN

The nineteenth century was a period of rebirth throughout the Muslim world and no less so in the western Sudan. There, on the vast grassland plains, Islam was revived by the alliance of the book and the sword. Ever since the collapse of the Murabitun, Islam in the Sudan had been carried forward by Muslim merchants and teachers who integrated themselves with the African community, accommodating Islam to the customs and traditions of the western Sudan. At the end of the eighteenth century, the Islamic revival produced a change in the charac-

ter of Islam in the western Sudan. The tolerant and accommodating ways of the past were replaced by an uncompromising and militant insistence upon adherence to the one true faith. Thus, as a result of the reform movements begun by the Islamic religious brotherhoods and spearheaded by whole tribes on the Saharan fringe that had been converted and convinced of the necessity of carrying on the jihad or holy war, Islam came to the nonbelievers of the south.

In the fifteenth and sixteenth centuries, Islamic missionaries had changed the religious attitudes of nomadic Saharan Berber tribes from spiritual indifference to a fanatical commitment to spread Islam. Thus whole tribes became clerical tribes, each member of which was prepared to extend Islam either by peace or war. Of even greater importance in the propagation of reformed Islam were the religious brotherhoods. Islamic religious brotherhoods or confraternities have their roots in Sufism, or Islamic mysticism, which taught, in contrast to the more legalistic, liturgical attitudes of more orthodox Muslims, that the way to god is through an emotional commitment. Sufism came to Morocco from Andalusia and thence pushed south into the western Sudan. Sufi mystics founded *zawiyas*—that is, retreats into the countryside where family and followers would come to partake of the *baraka,* or spirituality of the teacher. When the teacher, or holy man, died, his disciples went forth to found their own zawiyas, and in this way a holy family was born, with many branches and great influence. In the sixteenth century one such brotherhood, the *Qadiriyya,* was founded and gradually expanded in subsequent generations. Although at the opening of the nineteenth century the fraternity, or *tariqa* (Arabic for way—that is, way to God), played only a small role in West African Islam, nevertheless, during that century being a Muslim became synonymous with being a member of one of the religious brotherhoods, the Qadiriyya or the one that supplanted it in influence, the *Tijaniyya*. From the *turuq* (plural of tariqa) came the militant clerics who were determined to rupture the equilibrium between Africa and Islam by founding Muslim states that were ruled by theocratic leaders for the purpose of spreading Islam. Determined to stress the uniqueness of Islam and its incompatibility with the traditional worship of animistic cults, these clerics also created a political and social revolution in the western Sudan. The need to impose Islam required theocratic governments, and their creation brought forth a new aristocracy of devout Muslims that seized control and refused to tolerate loyalties that were divided between Islam and the pagan cults. The movement began on the plains of the Senegal, the Futa Jalon, and was spearheaded by Fulani clerics, the Tucolor, who founded several theocratic states in the last quarter of the eighteenth century (Sire Abbas Soh, *Abd al-Qadir in Senegalese Futa*). From these clerical clans came three of the most famous Islamic conquerors—Sheik Hamadu, al-Hajj Umar Tal, and Uthman, dan Fodio.

Uthman dan Fodio, born in 1754, was a Fulani cleric who was filled with revulsion at the way in which Muslims abiding in the Hausa states were treated by the pagan Hausa rulers and compromised with pagan practices. In 1774 he began his career as an itinerant preacher and soon sought to emulate the militant clerics of the Futa Jalon by issuing the call to the jihad in 1786 (Abd Allah ibn Muhammad, *The Hijra and Holy War of Shaykh Uthman dan Fodio*). By his words and deeds Uthman was reluctantly regarded as a subversive element in the land, and the Hausa king of Gobir sought to crush him. He failed, but in his failure he alienated the religiously indifferent pastoral Fulani, who soon became the shock troops of Dan Fodio's jihad. In 1804 the King of Gobir was at last defeated, and the Muslim forces under Dan Fodio's lieutenants gradually captured one Hausa state after another. By 1810 the Fulani jihad had triumphed everywhere except against Kanem-Bornu in the east, where the jihad was compromised and defeated by the devotion to Islam and the resistance of its great leader al-Kanami (Al-Kanami, *The Case Against the Jihad*, and Major Dixon Denham, *Bornu and Shaykh al-Kanami*). The Hausa states had become Muslim, but of even greater consequence, a new aristocracy, the Fulani, had replaced the traditional Hausa rulers. Uthman himself was never able to cast off the mantle of religious reform to assume that of ruler. He soon retired from public life, leaving by default the control of Hausaland to his more politically minded lieutenants, who had carved out states for themselves while spreading the word of God. Uthman appointed his son, Muhammad Bello, titular ruler over the eastern region with his capital at Sokoto, while Uthman's brother was the nominal ruler of the western region with his capital at Gwandu.

Despite Dan Fodio's deep convictions, the Fulani failed to inaugurate the new era of light and righteousness. In reality they simply exchanged places with the Hausa rulers, falling back on Hausa ceremonial and even adopting the well-defined social relationships of the feudal Hausa city-states. Although all the Fulani rulers recognized Muhammad Bello as suzerain and sent him tribute, they remained in practical control of their states. These were divided among the Fulani aristocracy into fiefs that were worked by slaves. Under such conditions slavery soon became the economic basis of the Fulani states—especially in the western Sudan, where slavery took a rather harsh form. Uthman dan Fodio died in 1817 and his tomb is today a place of pilgrimage, but perhaps his greatest legacy was the Islamic states of the Fulani clerics, Sheik Hamadu and al-Hajj Umar, who derived their inspiration to launch the holy war against the infidels directly from the success of Uthman dan Fodio.

At the beginning of the nineteenth century, Masina on the Upper Niger was controlled by the Mande-speaking, pagan *Bambara* chiefs. Among them was the Fulani cleric Sheik Hamadu (or Ahmadu), who had been with Dan Fodio in the early years and who obviously learned many of his techniques. Sheik Hamadu opened a school, and as his influence grew, the pagan Bambara kings began to persecute the Muslims. In retaliation Hamadu proclaimed a jihad, which swept the Bambara from control. By 1810 he was established as the undisputed master from the Black Volta in the south to Timbuktu in the north and from the Upper Senegal in the west to the Mossi country in the east (Ahmadu Hawpate Ba, *Shaykh Ahmadu and Masina*). Unlike Dan Fodio, Sheik Hamadu was able to control the Fulani. He eliminated those who refused to become Muslims and set up his state along strict theocratic lines. In fact, the state of Masina was the most genuine Islamic state in the western Sudan, in which the strict regulations against smoking, drinking, and dancing were hard on the fun-loving Sudanese. Sheik Hamadu died in 1844, and although his son and grandson were proclaimed rulers in Masina, they were ultimately overwhelmed by the all-conquering al-Hajj Umar. By 1862 their state had been incorporated into the empire of al-Hajj Umar.

Umar ibn Said Tal was born in the Futa Jalon in 1794. The son of a cleric, he received a religious education. He went to Mecca in 1826 and did not return to Senegalese Futa until 1845. In Mecca he founded a school, gathered followers, and soon began to expand eastward from the Futa Jalon. Umar's drive to the east was not entirely inspired by religion. Behind him the French were steadily pressing up the Senegal. Realizing he could not thwart the technical superiority of the French, Umar sought to incorporate the state of Masina in his empire. The assault on Masina, however, was his undoing.

Such a holy war could, of course, be justified only against infidels, but there was no question of the religious and reformist enthusiasm of Masina under Hamadu. Nevertheless, Umar ignored his religious scruples and attacked and overran Masina. In his later years he was continually absorbed by petty intrigues and court jealousies; he died at the height of his power (Mohammadon Alion Tyam, *The Life of al-Hajj Umar*). His son, Amadu Seku, managed to hold the state together until it was overwhelmed by the French advance. Amadu steadily retired before the French and died in Sokoto in 1898. His death represented the end of the domination of the western Sudan by militant clerics and the triumph of European technology, which added vast stretches of cartographic coloring to the maps of European empires.

PATTERNS OF EXPLORATION

Although Europeans had long inhabited the coast of West Africa, they had failed to penetrate the Sudan despite their knowledge of its gold and other products. Before European merchants could tap the potential markets of the interior of West Africa, a knowledge of what lay behind the periphery of the African coast was essential. This knowledge could, of course, be used to attack the actual sources of the slave trade in the hinterland, and not just that existing at the outlets on the coast. But in addition to the economic and humanitarian motives to open Africa was the widespread scientific curiosity of the eighteenth century, combined with the growing romanticism of the nineteenth, which sought to make funds available for the exploration of the unknown reaches of the globe. The explorations of Mungo Park (Mungo Park, *The Niger at Segu*), whose journals of his second expedition were published in 1815, created widespread enthusiasm in Britain, and a number of official expeditions were sent out to penetrate the coastal curtain, culminating in the two expeditions of

Hugh Clapperton, who reached Sokoto from the north in late 1822 and again from Badagri in the south in 1826. In 1830 the Lander Brothers completed the map of the Niger by canoeing from the Bussa Rapids where Mungo Park had drowned in 1805 to the Niger Delta, which Europeans had previously thought was a host of separate streams that they called collectively the Oil Rivers.

British merchants followed British explorers. Between 1832 and 1833, the Liverpool trader Macgregor Laird sponsored an expedition up the Niger to open direct trade with the country beyond the delta. Although Laird's attempt was not commercially successful, he was followed by John Beecroft, an agent from Fernando Po who represented a prominent Glasgow merchant. Between 1835 and 1850, Beecroft made numerous trips up the Niger and Cross rivers to keep legitimate trade alive and to acquire for himself a wide knowledge of the Africans of the Niger Delta. Once the interior had become known to Britain, however, and Laird and Beecroft had actually attempted to carry on legitimate trade, the British government agreed to cooperate to test Thomas Buxton's theories of Christianity, commerce, and civilization put forth in 1839 in his famous book, *The African Slave Trade and Its Remedy*. In 1841 the great Niger expedition was outfitted with the support of the British government as the vanguard of Christian, commercial civilization. The expedition, which consisted of traders, missionaries, and technicians, was a disastrous failure —one-third of the Europeans died within two months. The expedition was recalled, and for the next ten years the British government declined to participate in the opening of West Africa.

THE BEGINNINGS OF EUROPEAN RIVALRY

The return to a forward policy in West Africa arose out of two midcentury expeditions that encouraged Britain and France to try once again to establish their influence beyond the coastal forts. From 1850 to 1856, Heinrich Barth explored throughout the western Sudan from Adamawa to Timbuktu (Heinrich Barth, *Al-Hajj Bashir, Kukawa, and Timbuktu*). Barth was an acute and accurate observer, and his reports revived the interest in trade and diplomatic contact with the rich and populous regions of the western Sudan. In 1854 Dr. William Baikie led an expedition up the Niger to Lokoja and then up the Benue to Yola some 900 miles from the sea. The great significance of this voyage was that the members of the expedition regularly took quinine and not one of them died. Residence and travel in West Africa were now less restricted by the hazards of fever and death, and the beginning of European penetration was thus facilitated.

THE FRENCH INITIATIVE

Although the French had long sought to pursue a forward policy in the Senegal, French initiative was not crystallized until Captain Louis Faidherbe fashioned a real program of invasion and conquest of the western Sudan. After 1854 Faidherbe dispatched a succession of military expeditions into the interior, suppressed rebellions, and negotiated treaties to confirm French victories. The core of his policy was to cooperate with African states, always, of course, after demonstrating the superiority of French arms. Although Faidherbe left the Senegal in 1865, he set the pattern of French penetration, and a host of French merchants, explorers, and military expeditions followed to negotiate treaties and guarantee French rights. After 1874 the regions south of Cape Verde and below the Gambia were demarcated under French treaty rights. In 1887 Conakry was occupied, and the great push into the interior was undertaken to establish French presence in the Futa Jalon. Meanwhile, French forces were pressing ever eastward into the western Sudan. Bamako was occupied in 1883, and by

1893 the whole of the Upper Niger was brought under French control. In the following year Timbuktu was taken, and by 1896 the French had reached Say far to the east.

ESTABLISHMENT OF FRENCH COLONIAL ADMINISTRATION

Having conquered the Sudan, the French now had to rule it, and French historical tradition conditioned both the theory and the practice of French colonial rule in Africa. During the nineteenth century Frenchmen had either to choose or have forced upon them governments that reflected the two extremes of the French political tradition—revolutionary republicanism and Napoleonic authoritarianism. The changes that took place in metropolitan France were clearly reflected in the colonies. Thus the inhabitants of the Senegal communes were made citizens during the Second Republic, but in the Second Empire, which followed, these rights were given less consideration by the French military officers who governed in Senegal. After the creation of the Third Republic in 1871, these two political traditions blended together to form a paternalism that sought to modify authoritarian government by superimposing liberal ideas. In these political programs are found the seeds of the French policies of direct rule and assimilation for West Africa. Moreover, the conquest of French West Africa was undertaken by military officers who had been frustrated on the battlefields of Europe and who sought military glory in Africa by achieving victory over the well-organized and surprisingly militarily efficient African states of the western Sudan. Order, security, and regularity were required to ensure an acceptance of French rule by the peoples of the western Sudan, and the best way to accomplish these goals, they thought, was to impose a direct, authoritarian system and official hierarchy over all. Thus a great pyramidal administrative system

evolved. On the lowest level were the minor local authorities, who in time became officials appointed by the French commandant. Above them were the provincial and district officials, followed by the territorial governors. By 1902 governors had been appointed for the Senegal, Guinea, Ivory Coast, Dahomey, and the Sudan, from which the separate territories of Upper Volta, Niger, and Mauritania were taken in 1922. At the top of the pyramid was the Governor General at the great palace in Dakar, who was in turn responsible to the Minister of Colonies in France.

Alongside this elaborate and authoritarian structure survived the tradition of liberalism, expressed through the policy of assimilation, the defined purpose of which was to make French citizens out of colonial subjects. But French citizens could only be forged out of discipline and authoritarian tutelage, which meant forceful measures that were made respectable only by the fact that Africans were called upon to help fulfill the civilizing mission. Not surprisingly, the number of assimilated Africans remained incredibly small, a state of affairs bedeviled by the fact that French officials could never understand how and why anyone could possibly fail to see the advantages of becoming a Frenchman in outlook and culture.

WEST AFRICA BETWEEN THE WORLD WARS: FRENCH WEST AFRICA

French West Africa between World War I and World War II was dominated by two themes: the exploitation of Africa's manpower for service in French armies and the effort to make the colonies French by a revamping of earlier assimilationist policies. The first, the use of African troops in French armies, was a long tradition that went back to the early decades of the nineteenth century when a company of Wolofs was sent to Madagascar in 1828. Senegalese served in the Crimean War, the Mexican War, and the War of 1870. These early contingents consisted of volunteers, but in 1904 a system of conscription was inaugurated. World War I intensified recruitment so that by 1917 over thirty-one battalions of Senegalese were in action at the Somme and a total of 181,000 West Africans were serving France in Europe. Conscription continued after the war in spite of local resistance. In fact, the colonies themselves were required not only to contribute their most able-bodied men but to help finance their support in Europe. Although many French officials rationalized African conscription on the basis of the dubious assumption that the Africans became "civilized" during their sojourn in the army, the system was clearly designed to release French citizens in France from the defensive role that belonged to them and from which they alone benefited.

The second characteristic of French West Africa was the shift in emphasis away from the assimilation of Africans into French culture, which remained the ultimate objective, to a more immediate concern with the closer *association* between France and her African colonies. Economically as well as administratively the French African empire was to be centralized and developed to provide raw materials and markets for France. The effort to assimilate Africans into French culture was thus confined to a small élite bound to France by a knowledge of French language and traditions. This élite was granted political and civil privileges that were denied to the uneducated masses. Thus an African could become a Frenchman and reap the rewards of position and financial security. The results of assimilation, however, were ambiguous. On the one hand, French tolerance was affirmed by the belief that an African, given the opportunity, was capable of becoming French, but on the other, it was compromised by the fact that few assimilated Africans held responsible posts, thereby demonstrating that assimilation presupposed an underlying belief in the inherent inferiority of the African.

THE COMING OF INDEPENDENCE IN THE FRENCH SUDAN

The most eloquent opponent of France's strict assimilationist policies was Félix Eboué, a West Indian black who was governor of Chad (Félix Eboué, *Native Policy and Political Institutions in French Equatorial Africa*). Not only did he advocate decentralization of France's African empire but he supported General Charles de Gaulle and the Free French. Under Eboué's leadership a conference was held in Brazzaville in 1944, which was attended by Free French politicians and officials from French Black Africa. Although the conference affirmed African ties with France (the Brazzaville Conference, *The Political and Social Organization of the Colonies*), African representation in drawing up the postwar constitution for France was assured and ultimately led to the establishment of the French Union in which all Africans were citizens and greater authority was granted to territorial administrations. Thereafter, emergent African leaders, like Félix Houphouet-Boigny, Léopold Senghor, and Sékou Touré, exploited their new political status, but while Houphouet-Boigny and Senghor chose to remain within the French community, Sékou Touré defied General de Gaulle, and in the 1958 referendum his influence was decisive in securing an overwhelming vote for independence (Sékou Touré and Charles de Gaulle, *France and West Africa*). Within the next two years, all the former colonies of French West Africa became technically independent of France and, as in the former West African colonies of Great Britain, the struggle between the new African political leaders and the traditional rulers intensified (Al-Hajj Sir Ahmadu Bello, *Political Leader and Traditional Ruler*).

1 IBN BATTUTA

MALI

The celebrated Muslim traveler Ibn Battuta (1304–1368/9) traversed nearly the whole of the Muslim world and beyond during his many years of wandering. Born in Tangier, he made the first of his four pilgrimages to Mecca when he was twenty-one and thereafter traveled to East Africa and most of Asia, including China. He began his return from India in 1345, visiting Ceylon, Sumatra, Baghdad, and Cairo. He reached Fez in 1349 and in 1352 set out toward the Sudan, crossing the Sahara and traversing the kingdom of Mali (1238–1468). His description is one of the very few firsthand accounts of the customs practiced in Mali and Gao at that time.

AUDIENCES OF THE SULTAN OF MALI

Sometimes the sultan [of Mali] holds meetings in the place where he has his audiences. There is a dais in that place, situated under a tree, with three big steps called *penpi*. The dais is covered with silk and embellished with cushions, and above it is placed a parasol that looks like a silken dome. On the top of the parasol is a golden bird as big as a sparrow hawk. The sultan goes out by a well-used door in a corner of the castle. He holds his bow in his hand and wears his quiver on his back. On his head he wears a gold hat that is held in place by a band, also of gold. The ends of the hat are tapered like knives longer than a hand's span. Most often he is dressed in a red velvet tunic, made of either European cloth called *mothanfas* or deep pile cloth.

The singers come out in front of the sultan, and they hold *kanakir* (instruments whose name in the singular is doubtless *konbara,* which means lark) of gold and silver. Behind him are about 300 armed slaves. The sovereign walks patiently, advancing very slowly. When he arrives at the penpi, he stops and looks at those who are there. Then he slowly goes up onto the dais as the priest mounts his pulpit. As soon as the sultan is seated, drums are beaten, a horn is sounded, and trumpets blare. . . .

What I Found to Be Praiseworthy About the Conduct of the Negroes in Contrast to What I Found to Be Bad.

Among the good qualities of this people, we must cite the following:

1. The small number of acts of injustice that take place there [in Mali], for of all people, the Negroes abhor it [injustice] the most. Their sultan never pardons anyone guilty of injustice.

2. The general and complete security that is enjoyed in the country. The traveler, just as the sedentary man, has nothing to fear of brigands, thieves, or plunderers.

3. The blacks do not confiscate the goods of white men who die in their country, even when these men possess immense treasures. On the contrary, the blacks deposit the goods with a man respected among the whites, until the individuals to whom the goods rightfully belong present themselves and take possession of them.

4. The Negroes say their prayers correctly; they say them assiduously in the meetings of the faithful and strike their children if they fail these obligations. On Friday, whoever does not arrive at the mosque early finds no place to pray because the temple becomes so crowded. The blacks have a habit of sending their

From Ibn Battuta, *Ibn Batoutah,* trans. from the Arabic by C. Defremery and B. R. Sanguinétti (Paris, 1863), IV, 405–407, 421–424, 440–442. Trans. from the French by Nell Elizabeth Painter and Robert O. Collins. The bracketed material in this selection has been inserted by Professor Collins.

slaves to the mosque to spread out the mats they use during prayers in the places to which each slave has a right, to wait for their master's arrival. These mats are made from a tree that resembles the palm but that bears no fruit.

5. The Negroes wear handsome white clothes every Friday. If, by chance, one of them possesses only one shirt or a worn-out tunic, he at least washes and cleans it and wears it to the public prayers.

6. They are very zealous in their attempt to learn the holy *Quran* by heart. In the event that their children are negligent in this respect, fetters are placed on the children's feet and are left until the children can recite the *Quran* from memory. On a holiday I went to see the judge, and seeing his children in chains, I asked him, "Aren't you going to let them go?" He answered, "I won't let them go until they know the *Quran* by heart." Another day I passed a young Negro with a handsome face who was wearing superb clothes and carrying a heavy chain around his feet. I asked the person who was with me, "What did that boy do? Did he murder someone?" The young Negro heard my question and began to laugh. My colleague told me, "He has been chained up only to force him to commit the *Quran* to memory."

Some of the blameworthy actions of these people are:

1. The female servants and slaves, as well as little girls, appear before men completely naked. I observed this practice a great deal during the month of Ramadan [the ninth month and time of fasting in the Muslim year—ed.], for the usual custom among the Negroes is for the Commanders to break the fast in the sultan's palace and for each of them to be served by female slaves who are entirely nude and who bring the food to the number of twenty or more.

2. All the women who come into the sovereign's house are nude and wear no veils over their faces; the sultan's daughters also go naked. On the twenty-seventh night of the month of Ramadan, I saw about a hundred female slaves come out with the food for the sultan's palace, and they were nude. Two of the sovereign's daughters, who had been gifted with very large chests, accompanied the slaves and had no covering whatsoever.

3. The blacks throw dust and ashes on their heads to show that they are educated and as a sign of respect.

4. Negroes practice a sort of buffoonery when the poets recite their verses to the sultan, as described elsewhere.

5. Finally, a good number of the Negroes eat vultures, dogs, and asses. . . .

THE COPPER MINE

The copper mine is situated outside Takedda. Slaves of both sexes dig into the soil and take the ore to the city to smelt it in the houses. As soon as the red copper has been obtained, it is made into bars one and one-half handspans long—some thin, some thick. Four hundred of the thick bars equal a ducat of gold; six or seven hundred of the thin bars are also worth a ducat of gold. These bars serve as a means of exchange, in place of coin. With the thin bars, meat and firewood are bought; with the thick bars, male and female slaves, millet, butter, and wheat can be bought.

The copper of Takedda is exported to the city Couber [Gobir], situated in the land of the pagan Negroes. Copper is also exported to Zaghai [Dyakha—western Masina] and to the land of Bernon [Bornu], which is forty days distant from Takedda and is inhabited by Muslims. Idris, king of the Muslims, never shows himself before the people and never speaks to them unless he is behind a curtain. Beautiful slaves, eunuchs, and cloth dyed with saffron are brought from Bernon to many different countries. . . .

2 ANTONIUS MALFANTE

TAWAT AND THE WESTERN SUDAN TRADE

No details are known about the author of the following letter, written from Tawat (Tuat) in 1447 by Antonius Malfante and addressed to Giovanni Mariono in Genoa. Tawat was centrally located in the Sahara and was an important oasis on the road from Air, over which passed trade from the Hausa city-states of northern Nigeria.

After we had come from the sea, that is from Hono [Honein], we journeyed on horseback, always southwards, for about twelve days. For seven days we encountered no dwelling—nothing but sandy plains; we proceeded as though at sea, guided by the sun during the day, at night by the stars. At the end of the seventh day, we arrived at a *ksour* [Tabelbert], where dwelt very poor people who supported themselves on water and a little sandy ground. They sow little, living upon the numerous date palms. At this *ksour* we had come into Tueto [Tawat, a group of oases]. In this place there are eighteen quarters, enclosed within one wall, and ruled by an oligarchy. Each ruler of a quarter protects his followers, whether they be in the right or no. The quarters closely adjoin each other and are jealous of their privileges. Everyone arriving here places himself under the protection of one of these rulers, who will protect him to the death: thus merchants enjoy very great security, much greater, in my opinion, than in kingdoms such as Themmicenno [Tlemcen] and Thunisie [Tunis].

Though I am a Christian, no one ever addressed an insulting word to me. They said they had never seen a Christian before. It is true that on my first arrival they were scornful of me, because they all wished to see me, saying with wonder "This Christian has a countenance like ours"—for they believed that Christians had disguised faces. Their curiosity was soon satisfied, and now I can go alone anywhere, with no one to say an evil word to me.

There are many Jews, who lead a good life here, for they are under the protection of the several rulers, each of whom defends his own clients. Thus they enjoy very secure social standing. Trade is in their hands, and many of them are to be trusted with the greatest confidence.

This locality is a mart of the country of the Moors, to which merchants come to sell their goods: gold is carried hither, and bought by those who come up from the coast. This place is De Amamento [Tamentit], and there are many rich men here. The generality, however, are very poor, for they do not sow, nor do they harvest anything, save the dates upon which they subsist. They eat no meat but that of castrated camels, which are scarce and very dear.

It is true that the Arabs with whom I came from the coast brought with them corn and barley which they sell throughout the year at "f. saracen, la nostra mina." [1]

It never rains here: if it did, the houses, being built of salt in the place of reeds, would be destroyed.[2] It is scarcely ever cold here: in summer the heat is extreme, wherefore they are almost all blacks. The

From *The Voyages of Cadamosto and Other Documents on Western Africa in the Second Half of the Fifteenth Century,* trans. from the Italian and edited by G. R. Crone (New York: Cambridge University Press, 1937), pp. 85–90. Reprinted by permission of Cambridge University Press on behalf of *The Hakluyt Society.* In this selection the place names in brackets have been supplied by G. R. Crone.

[1] A *Saracen* was the Arab coin known as the *dinar*; *Mina* was a measure equalling approximately half a bushel. The "f." perhaps stands for "six."
[2] De la Roncière suggests that this is not a description of Tamentit but of Taghaza, where the houses were all built of rock salt.

children of both sexes go naked up to the age of fifteen. These people observe the religion and law of Muhammad. In the vicinity there are 150 to 200 *ksour.*

In the lands of the blacks, as well as here, dwell the Philistines [the Tuareg], who live, like the Arabs, in tents. They are without number, and hold sway over the land of Gazola [3] from the borders of Egypt to the shores of the Ocean, as far as Massa and Safi, and over all the neighbouring towns of the blacks. They are fair, strong in body and very handsome in appearance. They ride without stirrups, with simple spurs. They are governed by kings, whose heirs are the sons of their sisters—for such is their law. They keep their mouths and noses covered. I have seen many of them here, and have asked them through an interpreter why they cover their mouths and noses thus. They replied: "We have inherited this custom from our ancestors." They are sworn enemies of the Jews, who do not dare to pass hither. Their faith is that of the Blacks. Their sustenance is milk and flesh, no corn or barley, but much rice. Their sheep, cattle, and camels are without number. One breed of camel, white as snow, can cover in one day a distance which would take a horseman four days to travel. Great warriors, these people are continually at war amongst themselves.

The states which are under their rule border upon the land of the Blacks. I shall speak of those known to men here, and which have inhabitants of the faith of Muhammad. In all, the great majority are Blacks, but there are a small number of whites [i.e. tawny Moors].

First, Thegida,[4] which comprises one province and three *ksour*; Checoli,[5] which is as large.

Chuchiam,[6] Thambet [Timbuktu], Geni [Djenné], and Meli [Mali], said to have nine towns:

Thora [unidentified], Oden [Wadan], Dendi,[7] Sagoto [unidentified], Bofon [unidentified], Igdem [unidentified], Bembo,[8] all these are great cities, capitals of extensive lands and towns under their rule.

These adhere to the law of Muhammad.

To the south of these are innumerable great cities and territories, the inhabitants of which are all blacks and idolators, continually at war with each other in defence of their law and faith of their idols. Some worship the sun, others the moon, the seven planets, fire, or water; others a mirror which reflects their faces, which they take to be the images of gods; others groves of trees, the seats of a spirit to whom they make sacrifice; [9] others again, statues of wood and stone, with which, they say, they commune by incantations. They relate here extraordinary things of this people.

The lord in whose protection I am, here, who is the greatest in this land, having a fortune of more than 100,000 *doubles* [a billon coin], brother of the most important merchant in Thambet, and a man worthy of credence, relates that he lived for thirty years in that town, and, as he says, for fourteen years in the land of the Blacks. Every day he tells me wonderful things of these peoples. He says that these lands and peoples extend endlessly to the south: they all go naked, save for a small loin-cloth to cover their privates. They have an abundance of flesh, milk, and rice, but no corn or barley.

---

[3] Gazola (the *Gazula* of Idrisi) appears on many portolan charts, sometimes applied to a town, sometimes to a region. On the Pizigani chart of 1373 there is a cape, probably Cape Nun, called "Caput finis Gozole." It has been derived from the Berber people, the Guezulah, a branch of which inhabited the Sus; as used by Malfante it appears to be applied to the same area as "Sarra," or Sahara, of other contemporary writers.
[4] Takedda, five days' march west-south-west of Agadez.

[5] Possibly Es Suk (Tadmekka), north of Takedda at the head of the Tilemsi valley.
[6] Probably Gao.
[7] Dendi, probably the original home of the Songhai.
[8] Possibly Bamba, a town on the Middle Niger.
[9] Cf. Seligmann. "The Bambara have been little affected by Islam and retain their animistic beliefs and ancestor worship. Each village has its presiding spirit (*dasiri*) or divine ancestor, usually resident in a tree at which sacrifices are made and prayers offered by the *dugutigi* on all important occasions."

Through these lands flows a very large river [10] which at certain times of the year inundates all these lands. This river passes by the gates of Tambet, and flows through Egypt; and is that which passes by Carium.[11] There are many boats on it, by which they carry on trade. It would be possible, they say, to descend to Egypt by this river, were it not that at a certain spot it falls 300 cubits over a rock,[12] on account of which boats cannot go or return. This river flows at about twenty days' journey on horseback from here.

These people have trees which produce an edible butter,[13] of which there is an abundance here. I have seen them bearing it hither: it is as wonderful an unguent as the butter of sheep. The slaves which the blacks take in their internecine wars are sold at a very low price, the maximum being two *doubles* a head. These peoples, who cover the land in multitudes, are in carnal acts like the beasts; the father has knowledge of his daughter, the son of his sister. They breed greatly, for a woman bears up to five at a birth. Nor can it be doubted that they are eaters of human flesh, for many people have gone hence into their country. Neither there nor here are there ever epidemics.

When the blacks catch sight of a white man from a distance, they take to flight as though from a monster, believing him to be a phantom. They are unlettered, and without books. They are great magicians, evoking by incense diabolical spirits, with whom, they say, they perform marvels.

"It is not long since I was in Cuchia [Gao], distant fifty days' journey from here, where there are Moors," my patron said to me. "A heathen king, with five hundred thousand men, came from the south to lay siege to the city of Vallo. Upon the hill within the city were fifty Moors, almost all blacks. They saw that they were by day surrounded by a human river, by night by a girdle of flames and looked upon themselves as already defeated and enslaved. But their king, who was in the city, was a great magician and necromancer; he concluded with the besieger a pact by which each was to produce by incantation a black goat. The two goats would engage in battle, and the master of that which was beaten, was likewise to consider himself defeated. The besieger emerged victorious from the contest, and, taking the town, did not allow one soul to escape, but put the entire population to the sword. He found much treasure there. The town to-day is almost completely deserted save for a poverty-stricken few who have come to dwell there."

Of such were the stories which I heard daily in plenty. The wares for which there is a demand here are many: but the principal articles are copper, and salt in slabs, bars, and cakes. The copper of Romania [the Byzantine Empire], which is obtained through Alexandria, is always in great demand throughout the land of the Blacks. I frequently enquired what they did with it, but no one could give me a definite answer. I believe it is that there are so many peoples that there is almost nothing but is of use to them.

The Egyptian merchants come to trade in the land of the Blacks with half a million head of cattle and camels—a figure which is not fantastic in this region.

The place where I am is good for trade, as the Egyptians and other merchants come hither from the land of the Blacks bringing gold, which they exchange for copper and other goods. Thus everything sells well; until there is nothing left for sale. The people here will neither sell nor buy unless at a profit of one hundred per cent. For this reason, I have lost, Laus Deo!, on the goods I brought here, two thousand *doubles*.

---

[10] The Niger. It is to be noted that Malfante correctly implies that it flows eastwards, of which there was no certain knowledge till the end of the eighteenth century.

[11] Cairo. On the confusion between the Niger and the Nile.

[12] This appears reminiscent of the cataracts of the Nile.

[13] The Karité tree, the most characteristic of the Savannah. The butter is obtained from the kernel.

From what I can understand, these people neighbour on India.[14] Indian merchants come hither, and converse through interpreters. These Indians are Christians, adorers of the cross. It is said that in the land of the Blacks there are forty dialects, so that they are unable to understand each other.

I often enquired where the gold was found and collected; my patron always replied "I was fourteen years in the land of the Blacks, and I have never heard nor seen anyone who could reply from definite knowledge. That is my experience, as to how it is found and collected. What appears plain is that it comes from a distant land, and, as I believe, from a definite zone." He also said that he had been in places where silver was as valuable as gold.

This land is twenty-eight days' journey from Cambacies,[15] and is the city with the best market. It is twenty-five days from Tunis, from Tripoli in Barbary twenty days, from Trimicen [Tlemcen] thirty days, from Fecia [Fez] twenty days, from Zaffi [Safi], Zamor [Azamor] and Messa twenty days on horseback. I finish for the present; elsewhere and at another time, God willing, I will recount much more to you orally. I am always at your orders in Christ.

Your ANTONIUS MALFANT

---

[14] Probably Abyssinia, the kingdom of Prester John, which was regarded in the Middle Ages as one of the Three Indias.

[15] Probably Ghadames.

3 LEO AFRICANUS
THE WESTERN SUDAN IN THE SIXTEENTH CENTURY

Al-Hassan ibn Muhammad al-Wizaz al-Fasi was an Andalusian Moor born in 1493 of wealthy parents. The family was driven from Spain and settled in Fez, from which Al-Hassan made numerous journeys throughout North Africa and the western Sudan as judge, clerk, merchant, and diplomat. In 1518 he was captured by Christian corsairs off Tunisia, taken to Rome, and baptized Giovanni Lioni, from which the more popular Leo Africanus *was derived. His famous* The History and Description of Africa and the Notable Things Therein Contained, *which he wrote in Italian, was completed in 1526. The manuscript was published in 1550 in Ramusio's collection entitled* Voyages and Travels. *An English translation was published in London in 1600. Al-Hassan's description is the most authoritative one of the western Sudan between the writing of Ibn Battuta and the accounts of Heinrich Barth, the great mid-nineteenth-century Anglo-German explorer of the Sudan.*

A DESCRIPTION OF THE KINGDOME OF GUALATA [WALATA—ed.]

This region in regarde of others is very small: for it containeth only three great

From Leo Africanus, *The History and Description of Africa and the Notable Things Therein Contained,* trans. from the Italian by John Pory (1600) and edited by Robert Brown (London, 1896), pp. 821, 823–827, 829–830, 832–834.

villages, with certaine granges and fields of dates. From Nun it is distant southward about three hundred, from Tombuto [Timbuktu—ed.] northward fiue hundred, and from the Ocean sea about two hundred miles. In this region the people of Libya, while they were lords of the land of Negros, ordained their chiefe princely seate: and then great store of Barbarie-merchants frequented Gualata: but afterward in the raigne of the mighty and rich prince *Heli,* the said merchants leauing Gualata, began to resort vnto Tombuto and Gago,[Gao—ed.] which was the occasion that the region of Gualata grew extreme beggerly. The language of this region is called Sungai, [Songhay—ed.] and the inhabitants are blacke people, and most friendly vnto strangers. In my time this region was conquered by the king of Tombuto, and the prince thereof fled into the deserts, whereof the king of Tombuto hauing intelligence, and fearing least the prince would returne with all the people of the deserts, graunted him peace, conditionally that he should pay a great yeerely tribute vnto him, and so the said prince hath remained tributarie to the king of Tombuto vntill this present. The people agree in manners and fashions with the inhabitants of the next desert. Here groweth some quantitie of Mil-seed, and great store of a round & white kind of pulse, the like whereof I neuer saw in Europe; but flesh is extreme scarce among them. Both the men & the women do so couer their heads, that al their countenance is almost hidden. Here is no forme of a common wealth, nor yet any gouernours or iudges, but the people lead a most miserable life.

. . .

OF THE KINGDOME OF MELLI [MALI—ed.]

This region extending it selfe almost three hundred miles along the side of a riuer which falleth into Niger, bordereth northward vpon the region last described, southward vpon certaine deserts and drie mountaines, westward vpon huge woods and forrests stretching to the Ocean sea shore, and eastward vpon the territorie of Gago. In this kingdome there is a large and ample village containing to the number of sixe thousand or mo families, and called Melli, whereof the whole kingdome is so named. And here the king hath his place of residence. The region it selfe yeeldeth great abundance of corne, flesh, and cotton. Heere are many artificers and merchants in all places: and yet the king honourably entertaineth all strangers. The inhabitants are rich, and haue plentie of wares. Heere are great store of temples, priests, and professours, which professours read their lectures onely in the temples, bicause they haue no colleges at all. The people of this region excell all other Negros in witte, ciuilitie, and industry; and were the first that embraced the law of Mahumet, [Muhammad—ed.] at the same time when the vncle of *Ioseph* the king of Maroco [Yusuf ibn Tashufin—ed.] was their prince, and the gouernment remained for a while vnto his posterity: at length *Izchia* [Askiya Muhammad, 1493–1538—ed.] subdued the prince of this region, and made him his tributarie, and so oppressed him with greeuous exactions, that he was scarce able to maintaine his family.

OF THE KINGDOME OF TOMBUTO

This name was in our times (as some thinke) imposed vpon this kingdome from the name of a certaine towne so called, which (they say) king *Mense Suleiman* [Mansa Sulayman—ed.] founded in the yeere of the Hegeira 610, [1213–1214—ed.] and it is situate within twelue miles of a certaine branch of Niger, all the houses whereof are now changed into cottages built of chalke, and couered with thatch. Howbeit there is a most stately temple to be seene, the wals whereof are made of stone and lime; and a princely palace also built by a most excellent workeman of Granada. Here are many shops of artificers, and merchants, and especially of such as weaue linnen and cotton cloth. And hither do the Barbarie-merchants bring cloth of Europe. All the women of this region except maid-seruants go with their faces couered, and sell all necessarie victuals. The inhabitants, & especially strangers there residing, are exceeding rich, insomuch, that the king that now [in 1526—ed.] is, married both his daughters vnto two rich merchants.

Here are many wels, containing most sweete water; and so often as the riuer Niger ouerfloweth, they conueigh the water thereof by certaine sluces into the towne. Corne, cattle, milke, and butter this region yeeldeth in great abundance: but salt is verie scarce heere; for it is brought hither by land from Tegaza, which is fiue hundred miles distant. When I my selfe was here, I saw one camels loade of salt sold for 80. ducates. The rich king of Tombuto hath many plates and scepters of gold, some whereof weigh 1300. poundes: and he keepes a magnificent and well furnished court. When he trauelleth any whither he rideth vpon a camell, which is lead by some of his noblemen; and so he doth likewise when hee goeth to warfar, and all his souldiers ride vpon horses. Whosoeuer will speake vnto this king must first fall downe before his feete, & then taking vp earth must sprinkle it vpon his owne head & shoulders: which custom is ordinarily obserued by them that neuer saluted the king before, or come as ambassadors from other princes. He hath alwaies three thousand horsemen, and a great number of footmen that shoot poysoned arrowes, attending vpon him. They haue often skirmishes with those that refuse to pay tribute, and so many as they take, they sell vnto the merchants of Tombuto. Here are verie few horses bred, and the merchants and courtiers keepe certaine little nags which they vse to trauell vpon: but their best horses are brought out of Barbarie. And the king so soone as he heareth that any merchants are come to towne with horses, he commandeth a certaine number to be brought before him, and chusing the best horse for himselfe, he payeth a most liberall price for him. He so deadly hateth all Iewes, [Jews—ed.] that he will not admit any into his citie: and whatsoeuer Barbarie merchants he vnderstandeth haue any dealings with the Iewes, he presently causeth their goods to be confiscate. Here are great store of doctors, iudges, priests, and other learned men, that are bounti-

fully maintained at the kings cost and charges. And hither are brought diuers manuscripts or written bookes out of Barbarie, which are sold for more money than any other merchandize. The coine of tombuto is of gold without any stampe or superscription: but in matters of smal value they vse certaine shels brought hither out of the kingdome of Persia, fower hundred of which shels are worth a ducate: and sixe peeces of their golden coine with two third parts weigh an ounce. The inhabitants are people of a gentle and cherefull disposition, and spend a great part of the night in singing and dancing through all the streets of the citie: they keep great store of men and women-slaues, and their towne is much in danger of fire: at my second being there halfe the town almost was burnt in fiue howers space. Without the suburbs there are no gardens nor orchards at all.

. . .

OF THE TOWNE AND KINGDOME OF GAGO

The great towne of Gago being vnwalled also, is distant southward of Tombuto almost fower hundred miles, and enclineth somewhat to the southeast. The houses thereof are but meane, except those wherein the king and his courtiers remaine. Here are exceeding rich merchants: and hither continually resort great store of Negros which buy cloth here brought out of Barbarie and Europe. This towne aboundeth with corne and flesh, but is much destitute of wine, trees, and fruits. Howbeit here is plentie of melons, citrons, and rice: here are many welles also containing most sweete and holesome water. Here is likewise a certaine place where slaues are to be sold, especially vpon such daies as the merchants vse to assemble; and a yoong slaue of fifteene yeeres age is sold for sixe ducates, and so are children sold also. The king of this region hath a certaine priuate palace wherein he maintaineth a great number of concubines and slaues, which are kept by eunuches: and for the guard of his owne person he keepeth a sufficient troupe of horsemen and footmen. Betweene the first gate of the palace and the inner part thereof, there is a place walled round about wherein the king himselfe decideth all his subiects controuersies: and albeit the king be in this function most diligent, and performeth all things thereto appertayning, yet hath he about him his counsellors & other officers, as namely his secretaries, treasurers, factors, and auditors. It is a woonder to see what plentie of Merchandize is dayly brought hither, and how costly and sumptuous all things be. Horses bought in Europe for ten ducates, are here sold againe for fortie and sometimes for fiftie ducates a piece. There is not any cloth of Europe so course, which will not here be sold for fower ducates an elle, and if it be anything fine they will giue fifteene ducates for an ell: and an ell of the scarlet of Venice or of Turkie-cloath is here worth thirtie ducates. A sword is here valued at three or fower crownes, and so likewise are spurs, bridles, with other like commodities, and spices also are sold at an high rate: but of al other commodities salt is most extremelie deere. The residue of this kingdome containeth nought but villages and hamlets inhabited by husbandmen and shepherds, who in winter couer their bodies with beasts skins; but in sommer they goe all naked saue their priuie members: and sometimes they weare vpon their feet certaine shooes made of camels leather. They are ignorant and rude people, and you shall scarce finde one learned man in the space of an hundred miles. They are continually burthened with grieuous exactions, so that they haue scarce any thing remaining to liue vpon.

.   .   .

OF THE PROUINCE OF CANO
[KANO—ed.]

The great prouince of Cano stadeth eastward of the riuer Niger almost fiue hundred miles. The greatest part of the inhabitants dwelling in villages are some of them herdsmen and others husbandmen. Heere groweth abundance of corne, of rice, and of cotton. Also here are many deserts and wilde woodie mountaines containing many springs of water. In these woods growe plentie of wilde citrons and limons, which differ not much in taste from the best of all. In the midst of this prouince standeth a towne called by the same name, the walles and houses whereof are built for the most part of a kinde of chalke. The inhabitants are rich merchants and most ciuill people. Their king was in times past of great puissance, and had mighty troupes of horsemen at his command; but he hath since beene constrained to pay tribute vnto the kings of Zegzeg and Casena [Katsina—ed.]. Afterwarde *Ischia* the king of Tombuto faining friendship vnto the two foresaid kings trecherously slew them both. And then he waged warre against the king of Cano, whom after a long siege he tooke, and compelled him to marie one of his daughters, restoring him againe to his kingdome, conditionally that he should pay vnto him the third part of all his tribute: and the said king of Tombuto hath some of his courtiers perpetually residing at Cano for the receit thereof.

.   .   .

OF THE KINGDOME OF BORNO
[BORNU—ed.]

The large prouince of Borno bordering westward vpon the prouince of Guangara [Wangara—ed.] and from thence extending eastward fiue hundred miles, is distant from the fountaine of Niger almost an hundred and fiftie miles, the south part thereof adioining vnto the desert of Set, and the north part vnto that desert which lieth towards Barca. The situation of this kingdome is very vneuen, some part thereof being mountainous, and the residue plaine. Vpon the plaines are sundry villages inhabited by rich merchants, and abounding with corne. The king of this region and all his followers dwell in a certaine large village. The mountaines being inhabited by herdesmen and shepherds doe bring foorth mill and other graine altogether vnknowen to vs. The inhabitants in summer goe all naked saue their priuie members which they couer with a peece of leather: but al winter they are clad in skins, and haue beds of skins also. They embrace no religion at all, being neither Christians, Mahumetans, nor Iewes, nor of any other profession, but liuing after a brutish manner, and hauing wiues and children in common: and (as I vnderstood of a certaine merchant that abode a long time among them) they haue no proper names at all, but euery one is nicknamed according to his length, his fatnes, or some other qualitie. They haue a most puissant prince, being lineally descended from the Libyan people called Bardoa. Horsemen he hath in a continuall readinesse to the number of three thousand, & an huge number of footmen; for al his subiects are so seruiceable and obedient vnto him, that whensoeuer he commandeth them, they wil arme themselues and follow him whither he pleaseth to conduct them. They paye vnto him none other tribute but the tithes of all their corne: neither hath this king any reuenues to maintaine his estate, but ouely such spoiles as he getteth from his next enimes by often inuasions and assaults. He is at perpetuall enmitie with a certaine people inhabiting beyond the desert of Seu; who in times past marching with an huge armie of footemen ouer the said desert, wasted a great part of the kingdome of Borno. Whereupon the king of Borno sent for the merchants of Barbary, and willed them to bring him great store of horses: for in this countrey they vse to exchange horses for slaues, and to giue fifteene, and sometime twentie slaues for one horse. And by this meanes there were abundance of horses brought: howbeit the merchants were constrained to stay for their slaues till the king returned home conquerour with a great number of captiues, and satisfied his creditors for their horses. And oftentimes it falleth out that the merchants must stay three months togither, before the king returneth from the warres, but they are all that while maintained at the kings charges. Sometimes he bringeth not home slaues enough to satisfie the merchants: and otherwhiles they are constrained to awaite there a whole yeere togither; for the king maketh inuasions but euery yeere once, & that at one set and appointed time of the yeere. Yea I my selfe met with sundrie merchants heere, who despairing of the kings paiment, bicause they had trusted him an whole yeere, determined neuer to come thither with horses againe. And yet the king seemeth to be marueilous rich; for his spurres, his bridles, platters, dishes, pots, and other vessels wherein his meate and drinke are brought to the table, are all of pure golde: yea, and the chaines of his dogs and hounds are of golde also. Howbeit this king is extreamely couetous, for he had much rather pay his debts in slaues than in gold. In this kingdome are great multitudes of Negros and of other people, the names of whom (bicause I tarried heere but one moneth) I could not well note.

4 ABD-AL-RAHMAN AL-SADI
SONGHAY AND THE MOROCCAN INVASION

Abd-al-Rahman al-Sadi (1569–c. 1655) belonged to a leading family in Timbuktu and was a notary public in Djenné before being made Imam of Timbuktu. After 1629 he played an influential role in the affairs of the city. His Tarikh al-Sudan describes the origins of the Sonni dynasty of Songhay. The first ruler in this dynasty was Ali Kolon, who probably reigned late in the thirteenth century. The influence of Mali on Songhay fluctuated during succeeding generations until the Songhay empire was established under the fifteenth Sonni, Ali (1464–1492). Ali died mysteriously, and the throne of the Songhay was seized by one of Ali's generals, Muhammad Ture ibn Abu Bakr, a Soninke by origin, who took the title askiya. Ture consolidated Ali's conquests and became the greatest king of Songhay. He was eighty-five years old and blind when deposed in 1528; he died ten years later. The subsequent history of Songhay is marked by a series of fratricidal struggles that lasted until the coming of the Moroccans. In 1590 the Sadid Sultan of Morocco, Ahmad al-Mansur, sent an expeditionary force to the Sudan under Judar Pasha, consisting of 4,000 men. Judar defeated the Songhay army of Askiya Ishaq and occupied Timbuktu, but the Moroccans never were able to impose their control throughout the Sudan, which soon fell into anarchy and disorder.

THE ORIGINS OF THE SONNI

This is the story of the first Sonni, Ali Kolon. Employed in the service of the King of Mali, Ali and his brother, Salman-Nari, lived with this ruler. The two brothers were both sons of Za-Yasi Boi, and the name Salman, which was originally Sulayman, had been deformed by the barbarous language of the people of Mali.

The mother of Ali and the mother of Salman were two full sisters. Omma was the name of the mother of Ali Kolon; Fati was the name of the mother of Salman-Nari. Fati was the favorite wife of the father of the two princes. Despite many pregnancies, she never had any children, and as she no longer hoped to have any, she said to her husband, "Marry my sister Omma—perhaps she will give you the heir that I have not been able to produce."

From Abderrahman Ben Abdahah Ben Imran Ben Amir Es-Sadi, *Tarikh es-Soudan,* trans. from the Arabic by O. Houdas (Paris, 1898), II, 9–17, 22–24, 121–123, 215–225, 256–261. Trans. from the French by Nell Elizabeth Painter and Robert O. Collins. Reprinted by permission of Centre Universitaire des Langues Orientales Vivantes. Bracketed material has been inserted by Professor Collins.

Za-Yasi Boi followed his wife's counsel. He was not aware of the [Muslim] law forbidding the marriage of two sisters to the same husband. God willed that the two wives should become pregnant during the same night and equally that on the same night they each should give birth to a son. The two newborn children were placed on the ground in a dark room. Not until the next day were they washed, for custom dictated that when a child is born during the night, one must wait until the next day to wash him.

The first newborn child to be washed was Ali Kolon, and because of this fact he was considered the elder. The ablution of Salman-Nari followed and he was, for that reason, declared the junior.

When the two children were old enough to enter the service, the Sultan of Mali took them with him. At that time, in fact, these princes were his vassals, and the prevailing custom dictated that the sons of kings were compelled to serve their sovereign. (This custom continues to the present with all the sultans of the Sudan.) Some of these young men went back to their countries after having served for a certain time. On the other hand, some continued to stay with the sovereign until their death.

During the time that the two princes were at the court of the King of Mali, Ali Kolon would leave his residence from time to time to make a fruitful expedition, according to established custom, and would then return to his post. Ali Kolon, a very sensible man who was very intelligent and full of shrewdness and cunning, enlarged his circle of operations each day in order to get closer and closer to Songhay and to become acquainted with all the roads leading there. Then he conceived a plan to flee into this country and thus to make himself independent. Toward this end, he secretly prepared all the arms and provisions that he would need and hid them in places that he knew on the road to Songhay.

When he finished his preparations, Ali Kolon notified his brother and confided his secret designs to him. After having fortified their horses with choice feed so that they would not tire on the way, the two brothers left for Songhay. Upon being advised of their escape, the Sultan of Mali sent some men after the fugitives to kill them. Each time they were closely pressed, the two brothers turned around and fought their pursuers. In these battles, the fugitives always had the advantage, and they successfully regained their country without a single defeat.

When Ali Kolon had become king of the land of Songhay, he called himself Sonni and delivered his subjects from the yoke of the Sultan of Mali. After the death of Ali Kolon, his brother, Salman-Nari, succeeded him. Only during the reign of the great Kharijite tyrant, Sonni Ali, did the limits of the kingdom spread beyond the area of its capital. This prince gathered more troops and expended more energy than did those of his dynasty who had preceded him. He made expeditions and conquered provinces, and his fame spread to the east and to the west, as we will tell later on, if it pleases God. Ali

may be considered the last king of his dynasty, for his son Abu Bakr Dao, who ascended the throne after his father's death, ruled only a short time before his power was torn from him by Askiya al-Hajj Muhammad.

THE KING OF MALI, MANSA KANKAN MUSA

Sultan Kankan Musa was the first of the kings of Mali to take over Songhay. A pious and equitable prince, his virtue and courage were unequaled by any other King of Mali. He made the pilgrimage to the Holy Dwelling of God [Mecca] in the early years of the ninth century of the hijra, but God knows the exact date [1324–1325] better than anyone else.

The prince had with him an immense cortege and a considerable force of 60,000 men. Each time he mounted a horse, he was preceded by 500 slaves, each carrying a rod of gold worth 500 mitqals of gold [weighing about 6 pounds].

Kankan Musa set out toward Walata, in Awkar, and arrived at the present site of Tawat. He left a great many of his companions there who. had been struck during the journey with a foot disease that they called *touat*. The locality where they separated and where the sick people established their homes took the name of their disease.

The people of the Orient have related the journey of the prince in their annals; they indicated their surprise at the strength of his empire, but they did not describe Kankan Musa as a liberal and generous man; despite the extent of his empire, for he gave the sum of only 20,000 pieces of gold as alms to the two Holy Cities, whereas Askiya al-Hajj Muhammad set aside 100,000 pieces of gold for the same purpose.

After the departure of Kankan Musa on a pilgrimage, the people of Songhay were subjected to his authority. On his return, the prince passed through Songhay and had a mosque with a mihrab built just outside the city of Kagho [Gao], where he said Friday prayers. This mosque still exists today. In all the places he passed on Fridays, the prince customarily built mosques.

Then Kankan Musa took the road to Timbuktu. He took possession of the city and was the first sovereign to make himself master of it. He installed a representative of his authority there and had a royal palace built, called Madugu, meaning "palace of the king." In this area, still well known because of the palace, butcher shops have since been established. . . .

It has been said that Sultan Kankan Musa built the minaret of the great mosque of Timbuktu and that one of the princes of his dynasty, the Sultan of Mossi, during his reign headed a strong army and made a raid upon the city. Seized with terror, the people of Mali fled, abandoning Timbuktu to its assailants. Then the Sultan of Mossi entered the city and sacked, burned, and ruined it. Having killed all those he could get his hands on, he took away all the wealth he could find and returned to his country.

"Timbuktu has been sacked three times," said the very learned jurist, Ahmad Baba, "the first time by the Sultan of Mossi, the second by Sonni Ali, and the third by Mahmud ibn Zargun Pasha. This last devastation was less terrible than the first two." It is said that more blood was spilled during Sonni Ali's sacking than during the sacking of the Sultan of Mossi.

Toward the end of the domination of the princes of Mali, the Maghcharan Taureg [Saharan nomads] began their incursions against the city of Timbuktu. Headed by their sultan, Akil Akamalul, they ravaged the country on all sides and in every way. The inhabitants suffered great damages from these depredations. However, they did not take up arms to fight the enemy. It is said that a prince who is unable to defend his states is not worthy of allegiance. Thus the people of Mali had to abandon the area and return to their country. Akil took over Timbuktu and remained master there for forty years. . . .

DESCRIPTION OF DJENNÉ

This city is large and prosperous; it is rich and blessed by heaven. God has accorded all his favors to this land as though to do so were a natural and innate thing. The inhabitants of Djenné are benevolent, admirable, and hospitable. Even so, they are inclined by nature to be jealous of those who are successful in this world. If one of them obtains a favor or advantage, the others gather against him in a common feeling of hate, without letting any of this animosity show until that person is struck by bad fortune (May God preserve us from such an end!). Then each one displays by word and deed all the hate he has felt toward the misfortunate one.

Djenné is one of the great markets of the Muslim world. Merchants bringing salt from the mines of Taghaza and those with gold from the mines of Bitu meet there. These two marvelous mines have no equal in the entire universe. Everyone going to Djenné to trade reaps large profits and thus acquires fortunes whose amount can be known only by God. (May he be praised!)

Because of this city, caravans flock to Timbuktu from all the points of the horizon—from the east, west, north, and south. Djenné is situated to the southwest of Timbuktu, behind the two rivers [the Niger and the Bani], on an island formed by the [Bani] river. Sometimes the waters of the [Bani] river overflow (and come together); sometimes they fall back and separate, little by little. The high water comes in the month of August, and the waters go down in February.

In the beginning the city was built in a place called Zoboro; later it was moved to its present location. The ancient city was situated just to the south of the modern one.

Djenné is surrounded by a rampart that at one time contained eleven gates. Three of them have since been closed so that today only eight are left. When a person views the city from a certain distance outside the city, the trees are so numerous that he thinks he sees only a simple forest. However, once inside the city, he doubts that there is even a single tree in the area.

Djenné was founded by pagans in the mid-second century of the hijra of the Prophet. (The best salutations and benedictions be his!) The inhabitants were not converted to Islam until toward the end of the sixth century of the hijra. Sultan Konboro was the first to adopt Islam, and the inhabitants of the city followed his example.

When Konboro decided to enter the bosom of Islam, he gave the order to assemble the 4,200 ulema [Muslim scholars] then within the territory of the city. He abjured paganism in their presence and called upon them to pray that God would accord three things to Djenné: (1) that he who was chased from his country by injustice and misery would come live in Djenné and would find in exchange, by the grace of God, abundance and wealth, so that he would forget his old homeland; (2) that the city would be peopled by foreigners who were superior to its natives; (3) that God would deprive of their patience all those who came to sell their merchandise, so that they would become bored by staying in the place and would sell their packets at low prices, to the benefit of the inhabitants. Following these prayers the first chapter of the *Quran* was read, and the prayers were answered, as can be verified by seeing the city today.

As soon as he was converted to Islam, the sultan demolished his palace and replaced it with a temple intended for the worship of the almighty God—this is the present grand mosque. Konboro constructed another palace for the lodging of his court, and this palace is adjacent to the mosque on the east side. The territory of Djenné is fertile and populous; numerous markets are held every day of the week. This area allegedly is composed of 7,077 adjacent villages. . . .

ASKIYA MUHAMMAD TURE (1493–1538)

In the third year of the century [of the hijra], Askiya Muhammad returned from his pilgrimage and entered Kagho [Gao] in the last month of that year (July 31, 1497–August 30, 1497).

God favored the reign of Askiya Muhammad. He assured him great conquests and covered him with His bountiful protection. This ruler took over all the lands of the West, and his authority spread to the frontiers of the land of Bonduku as far as Taghaza and its dependencies. Askiya Muhammad subjected all these people by the sword and by force, as will be seen in the narrative of his expeditions. Everywhere God accomplished all that this sovereign desired, so that Askiya Muhammad was obeyed in all his states as loyally as he was in his own palace. There was great abundance everywhere and absolute peace reigned. Praise to Him who favors whom He wishes in the ways that please Him; He possesses the supreme good.

During the year 903 (August 1497–August 1498), Askiya Muhammad undertook an expedition against Naasira, the Sultan of Mossi. He took the blessed Sayyid Mur Salih-Ojaura with him, inviting him to give the necessary blessings so that this expedition would be a veritable holy war in the name of God. Mur did not refuse this order and explained to the prince all the rules relative to holy war. The Prince of the Believers, Askiya Muhammad, then asked the sayyid to be his messenger to the Sultan of Mossi. The sayyid accepted this mission. He went to the land of Mossi and submitted the letter of his master, summoning the sultan to embrace Islam.

The Sultan of Mossi unwittingly declared that he first wanted to consult his ancestors in the other world. Consequently, accompanied by his ministers, he went to the temple of the idol of the land. The sayyid went along in order to see how one went about consulting the dead. First, the customary offerings were made.

Then a very old man appeared. At the sight of him everyone lay prostrate, and the sultan announced the object of his journey. Answering in the name of the ancestors, the old man said, "I will never accept such a thing for you. On the contrary, you must fight to the last man until either you or they have fallen."

Then Naasira answered the blessed sayyid. "Return to your master and tell him that between him and us there can never be other than struggles and war." Left alone in the temple with the personage who had showed himself in the form of an old man, the sayyid questioned the man in these terms: "In the name of almighty God, I ask you to say who you are." "I am Iblis" [the devil], answered the pseudo old man, "I am leading them astray so that they will all die as infidels."

Mur returned to Askiya al-Hajj Muhammad and gave him an account of all that had taken place. "Now," he added, "your duty is to fight them." As soon as the sovereign had begun to fight the Mossi, he killed many of their men, devastated their fields, sacked their houses, and took their children prisoner. All those who were taken captive—men and women—were the object of divine benediction. In all the land, no other expedition had the character of a holy war made in the name of God.

THE COMING OF JUDAR PASHA TO THE SUDAN

Judar was short and had blue eyes. Following are the circumstances that led to his coming. A certain Ould-Kirinfil was one of the servants of the Prince of Songhay. His master, the sovereign Askiya Ishaq, son of Prince Askiya Daud, who was son of Prince Askiya al-Hajj Muhammad, was angry with Ould-Kirinfil and had sent him to be interned at Taghaza, which was part of the empire of the kings of Songhay and was administered by them.

Destiny had it that Ould-Kirinfil managed to escape from his confinement and succeeded in reaching the red [clay] city of Marrakech. He had planned to present himself to the sovereign of the land, Sultan Ahmad al-Mansur, but at that moment the sultan was in Fez, where he had gone to punish the sharif of that city. The sultan had the eyes of the insurgents put out, and a good number of them died of this punishment. (We belong to God and we must return to him.) Thus, he had acted with only temporal advantages in view. (May God preserve us from such a fate!)

Ould-Kirinfil stayed in Marrakech, and from there he wrote the Moroccan sovereign a letter informing him of his arrival and giving him news of the land of Songhay, whose inhabitants, he said, were in a deplorable situation because of the baseness of their nature. Thus, he strongly encouraged Ahmad al-Mansur to take over the country and to rescue it from the hands of its masters.

As soon as he had received this letter, the sultan wrote to Prince Askiya Ishaq announcing his intention to return to his land. He said that he was momentarily in Fez, far from his capital, but that if God wished, the askiya could be informed of his intentions by the document attached to the letter. In the document, Ahmad al-Mansur demanded, among other things, that the salt mine of Taghaza be given over to him—a mine that he, more than any other, had the right to possess because due to his efforts, the land had been protected from incursions of the Christian infidels [the Portuguese]. These dispatches were sent by messenger and arrived in the city of Kagho while the sovereign was still in Fez, in the month of Safar of the year 998 of the Prophet's flight (December 10, 1589–January 8, 1590). (The best of salutations and benedictions and benedictions upon him!) I myself saw the original of these documents. Then Ahmad al-Mansur returned to Marrakech. The snow fell so abundantly during the course of the trip that he nearly died. A great number of his people lost hands or feet from the effects of the cold, and they arrived in the capital in a most pitiable condition. (Let us ask God to save us from these trials.)

Not only did Prince Askiya Ishaq not consent to abandon the mine of Taghaza, but he answered in violent and abusive terms and sent javelins and two iron shoes along with his answer. As soon as this message reached him, Ahmad al-Mansur decided to send an army to the Sudan, and the following year—that is to say, the year 999 (November 1590)—he sent out an important army corps against Songhay that included 3,000 men in arms and as many horsemen as foot soldiers, accompanied by a double number of all sorts of followers, several sorts of workers, doctors and so on.

Judar Pasha was placed in command of this expedition. He had a dozen generals with him: Qaid Mustafa al-Turki, Qaid Mustafa ibn Askar, Qaid Ahmad al-Harusi al-Andalusi, Qaid Ahmad ibn al-Haddad al-Amri (chief of the constabulary), Qaid Ahmad ibn Atiya, Qaid Bu-Chiba al-Amri, Qaid Bu-Gheta al-Amri, Qaid Ammar al-Fata (the renegade), Qaid Ahmad ibn Yusuf (the renegade), Qaid Ali ibn Mustafa (the renegade). The latter was the first Moroccan chief invested with the command of the city of Kagho [Gao] and died at the same time as Mahmud ibn Zargun Pasha when the latter was killed at al-Hadjar. Two lieutenant generals commanded the two wings of the army: Ba-Hasan Friru (the renegade, the right wing) and Qasim Waradui al-Andalusi (the renegade, the left wing). Such were the generals and lieutenants who left with Judar.

The Moroccan prince [Ahmad al-Mansur] announced to his generals that the results of divination had shown that the land of Songhay should cease being dominated by the Sudanese and that his army should take over a certain part of their land. Then the army set out toward Songhay.

As soon as he got news of the departure of this army, Prince Askiya Ishaq brought together his generals and the principal people of his kingdom in order to consult them on the measures to be taken and to ask their opinions, but each time a judicious counsel was given, they hastened to reject it. God, in his foreknowledge, had thus decided that the kingdom should disappear and that the dynasty should perish. No one can reject what He has decided or obstruct His decisions. . . .

The Moroccan troops reached the Niger in the neighborhood of the town of Karabara. They stopped there, and Judar gave a great feast to celebrate their safe arrival at the river. The fact that the men arrived safe and sound was a portent that success would crown the efforts of their chief. This event took place on Wednesday, the fourth day of the month of Jumada II of the year 999 of the hijra (March 30, 1591), as stated above.

The army did not pass through the city of Arawan but rather passed to the east of it. On the road they encountered the camels of Abdallah ibn Qair al-Mahmudi. Judar took the number of camels he required, and then Abdallah left immediately for Morocco. He went to Marrakech and complained to Ahmad al-Mansur that he had been the victim of injustice. He was the first to announce the arrival of the Moroccan army at the Niger. The first person whom the ruler asked about was Ba-Hasan Friru. "Ba-Hasan," Abdallah answered, "is doing well perhaps." The sovereign asked of Qaid Ahmad ibn al-Haddad al-Amri and of Judar Pasha. Then he wrote Judar, instructing him to pay for the camels he had taken.

The Moroccans then resumed their march. They advanced toward the city of Kagho and met Askiya Ishaq on the road at a place called Tondibi, near Tonbodi. The Prince of Songhay [Askiya Ishaq] was at the head of 12,500 cavalrymen and 30,000 foot soldiers. The armies did not meet sooner because the people of Songhay could not believe the reports of the expedition and had awaited news of its arrival at the river.

The battle began on Tuesday, the seventeenth day of the month mentioned above (April 12). In the twinkling of an eye, the troops of the askiya were routed. Several notable persons perished in that battle; among the horsemen were the *Fondoko* Bubu Maryama (the former chief of Masina), the *Cha-Farma* Ali-Djauenda, the *Bintra-Farma* Osman Durfan ibn Bukar Kirin-Kirin (the son of Prince Askiya, named Al Hajj-Muhammad). He was very old at the time, and Askiya Ishaq had named him *Binka-Farma* when the Binka-Farma Muhammad Haika had died, as previously mentioned, on the expedition to Nemnatako.

On that day a great many of the foot soldiers died as well. When the army was defeated, the soldiers threw their shields on the ground and squatted on these improvised seats, awaiting the arrival of Judar's troops, who massacred them in this position because they could present no resistance. And that was because they must not flee in the case of a retreat by the regular army. The Moroccan soldiers stripped them of the gold bracelets they had on their arms.

Askiya Ishaq turned his horse's head and galloped away with the rest of his troops. Then he requested the people of Kagho to leave the city and flee to the other side of the Niger in the direction of Gurma. He sent the same recommendation to the inhabitants of Timbuktu, and continuing on his way without passing by Kagho, he arrived at Kurai Gurma in that state, where he camped with the remnants of his troops amid tears and lamentations. The group sorrowfully began to cross the river in boats. In the scuffle that took place, many people fell in the river and perished. Furthermore, such a quantity of wealth was lost that only God knows its value.

The people of Timbuktu could not leave the city and cross the Niger because of the obstacles they met and the difficulties of the situation. Only the Timbuktu *Mondzo,* Yahya-ould-Bordam, and the servants of the askiya who were there left the city and went to camp at Al-Kif-Kindi, a place near Tonga.

Judar Pasha continued with his army as far as Kagho. No one was left in the city except the *khatib,* Mahmud Darami (who was a very old man at that time), and the students and traders who had not been able to get out and flee. Khatib Mahmud went to the Moroccans and welcomed them, showing them deference and offering them generous hospitality. He had conferences and long meetings with Judar Pasha, during which he was treated with the greatest respect and consideration.

Judar expressed his desire to enter the palace of Askiya Ishaq. Consequently he sent for two witnesses, and when they arrived, he entered the palace with them, but after having resisted acknowledging their lack of wealth, and having examined everything, it seemed to him that the palace was, in fact, rather miserable.

Askiya Ishaq requested the pasha to negotiate with him. The pasha undertook to remit 100,000 pieces of gold and 1,000 slaves to the Moroccan sovereign, Ahmad al-Mansur. In return the pasha was to leave his country and take his army back to Marrakech. Judar replied that he [Askiya Ishaq] was only a docile slave and could not act without orders from the sovereign, his master. Then with the accord of the merchants of his country, he [Judar] wrote [to al-Mansur] in his name and in that of Qaid Ahmad ibn al-Haddad al-Amri, in an attempt to transmit these proposals, having taken care to say that the house of the chief of the ass drivers in Morocco was worth more than the palace of the askiya which he had visited. This letter was carried to its destination by Ali al-Adjimi, who was in charge of communications at that time.

Judar led his troops back to Timbuktu, where he awaited the response of the Sultan of Morocco. Unless I am mistaken, he stayed only seventeen days at Kagho. They arrived at Mosa-Benko on Wednesday, the last day of the month of Jumada II (April 24, 1591). They departed from there on Thursday, the first day of the month of Radjib (April 25). Then they camped for thirty-five days under the walls on the south side of Timbuktu.

The *Qadi* of Timbuktu, the jurist Abu Hafs-Umar (son of God's saint, the jurist), and Qadi Mahmud sent the Muezzin Yahma, to greet the pasha, but unlike Khatib Mahmud Darami, when the Moroccans had arrived at Kagho, Yahma did not offer the pasha the least hospitality. Judar was extremely annoyed by his reception. Nevertheless he [the pasha] sent all sorts of fruit, dates, and almonds, as well as a great deal of sugar cane. Then he had the qadi put on a coat of scarlet red cloth. Those with any common sense feared that nothing good was presaged by all this, and the facts soon confirmed their apprehensions.

The Moroccans entered the city of Timbuktu on Thursday, May 30, 1591. They covered the city in all directions and realized that the most flourishing quarter was that populated by the people from Gadàmes. Thus they chose it for their casbah, which they began to build after having expelled a certain number of the people of that quarter from their houses.

Then Judar let Hammu ibn Abd al-Haqq al-Diri out of prison and entrusted him with the functions of amir in the name of Sultan Ahmad al-Mansur. Both Rafi and Ahmad Nini-Bir died before his [Hammu ibn Abd al-Haqq al-Diri's] arrival. The pasha had sanctioned a delay of forty days in order for the officer in charge of communications to reach Marrakech and return.

When the Moroccan army arrived in the Sudan, it found one of the countries that God had favored most in wealth and fertility. Peace and security reigned everywhere in all the provinces, thanks to the sovereign—the very successful, the blessed, the Prince of the Believers, Askiya al-Hajj Muhammad ibn Abu Bakr, whose justice and strength spread every-where, so that his orders, which were effortlessly accomplished in his palace, were executed with equal facility in the farthest corners of the empire—from the frontiers of the land of Dendi to the frontiers of the land of al-Hamdiyya, and from the countries of the land of Bonduku to Taghaza and Tawat, as well as in the dependencies of these countries.

Everything changed at that moment. Danger took the place of security, misery replaced opulence, and trouble, calamity, and violence succeeded tranquillity. People destroyed each other on all sides, in all places, and in all directions. There was rapine and war. Neither life nor goods nor the condition of the inhabitants was spared. General disorder intensified and spread in all directions.

The first to give the signal for this violence was Sanba Lamdu, the Chief of Donko. He ruined the land of Ras al-Ma by taking possession of all the goods, by having a certain number of the inhabitants killed, and by reducing a great number of free men to slavery. His example was followed by the Zaghranians [of Zaghai], who devastated the lands of Bara and Dirma. The territory of Djenné was ransacked in the most horrible fashion by the idolatrous Bambara who, to the east as to the west, in the North as in the South, destroyed all the villages, pillaged the goods, and made concubines of free women and with them had children who were brought up in the religion of the Mages [pagans]. (May God preserve us from such calamities!) All these calamities were executed under the direction of Chaa-Kor of Qasim (the son of the Binka-Farma), Alu Zulail ibn Umar Kamzagho (the paternal cousin of the *Baghena-Fari* and of Bohom, the son of the Fondoko Bubu Maryama, of Masina). . . . .

These troubles endlessly continued and increased, whereas from the time that Prince Askiya al-Hajj Muhammad mounted the throne of Songhay, no chief of any region dared attack the sovereigns of the land [Songhay], because God had dispensed so much vigor, audacity, courage, and majesty to their force. Very much to the contrary, the prince went to attack these chiefs in their lands, and most often God accorded him the victory, as has been seen in the recitation of the history of Songhay.

The situation remained thus until the moment when the dynasty of Songhay drew to its end and its empire ceased to exist. At that moment faith was transformed into unbelief. All the things forbidden by God were overtly being practiced. The people drank wine and indulged in sodomy; adultery became so frequent that its practice seemed to have become legal. Without adultery there was no elegance and no glory; this popular feeling existed to such an extent that the children of sultans committed adultery with their sisters.

It is told that this moral corruption first took place at the end of the reign of the sultan, the just, the Prince of the Believers, Askiya al-Hajj Muhammad, and that his son Yusuf-Koi invented this type of debauchery. When the father learned of these practices, he became violently angry and cursed his son, asking God to deprive Yusuf of his virile member before he entered the other world. God answered that wish, and a disease made the young prince lose the organ of his virility. (May heaven preserve us from such a fate!) The malediction spread to the son of Yusuf, Arbinda, the father of the Bana-Kor, Yaqub, for he too lost his virile member toward the end of his life after an attack of the same disease.

Because of these abominations, God took revenge by causing the victorious Moroccan army to attack Songhay. He made the attack come from a very far-off country, and amid terrible suffering, the roots of this people were separated from the trunk, and the punishment they underwent was an exemplary one. . . .

The pasha's [Mahmud ibn Zargun Pasha] principal subordinate and most influential councillor at that time was Habib Muhammad Anbabu. The first act, taken after deliberation, was to announce to Timbuktu by public crier that the pasha would search all the houses of the city the next day and that any individual living in a house where arms were found would have only himself to blame for the fate awaiting him if he were found to possess weapons; only the homes of the jurists, children of Sidi Mahmud, would be exempt from the search.

Upon hearing this announcement, the whole population hastened to transport all its wealth to the houses of the jurists for safekeeping. The people thought, in fact, that if the pasha found money in any one of the houses during the search, he would take it unfairly and by violent means. Such was, in fact, the real objective of those [the pasha and his councillor] who had taken this measure.

The search took place the next day and all the houses were thoroughly investigated. After this operation the pasha announced by public crier that in the following days, all the inhabitants would have to meet in the Sankore mosque to pledge allegiance to Sultan Ahmad al-Mansur.

When everyone was assembled in the mosque, the people of Tawat, Fezzan, and Awjila were made to pledge allegiance. That procedure lasted all the first day, which was Monday, the twenty-second day of the sacred month of Muharram, the first month of the year 1002 (October 18, 1593). Then on Tuesday, the twenty-third day of the same month, the people of Walata and Ouadane had their turn.

"Now only the jurists have not yet sworn," said the pasha. "That will be tomorrow in the presence of everyone." The following day, when everyone was assembled in the mosque, the gates were closed and all the spectators were made to go out except the jurists, their friends, and their followers. Pasha Mahmud arrested them all on that day, which was Wednesday, twenty-fourth day of the month of Muharram of the year 1002 (October 20,

1593). Having made them prisoners in this way, the pasha ordered them to be led to the casbah in two groups. One group went to the casbah by crossing through the city, and the other group took a street that circled outside the city on the east side.

The persons who composed the second group were massacred on that day. As they were walking and reached the quarter of Zim-Konda, one of them, a *Wankore* [a resident of the Sankore quarter] named Andafo, seized the saber of one of the soldiers who was leading the group and struck him. Immediately the soldiers slaughtered fourteen of the prisoners.

Nine of the victims of this massacre belonged to great Sankore families: the very learned jurist Ahmad Muyaj, the pious jurist Muhammad al-Amin (son of the Qadi Muhammad ibn Sidi Mahmud), the jurist al-Mustafa (son of the jurist Masira Anda Umar), Muhammad ibn Ahmad Bir (son of the jurist Sidi Mahmud), Buzu ibn Ahmad Usman, Muhammad al-Mukhtar ibn Muya Akhar, Ahmad Bir ibn Muhammad al-Mukhtar (son of Ahmad, the brother of al-Fa Salha Takuni, who was the last son of the brother of Masira Anda Umar), Muhammad Siri ibn al-Amin (father of Sunna), Mahmud Kiraukurik (one of the inhabitants of the Kabir quarter), Yburhum Buyzuli al-Tawati, the shoemaker (one of the men of Koira-Kona), two Wankores, Andafo (who had provoked the catastrophe) and his brother, two hartani [serfs] belonging to the children of Sidi Mahmud, and finally Fadl and Chinun, both tailors.

A single individual of this group escaped the massacre—Muhammad ibn al-Amin Kanu. He was delivered from his bonds by the brother of Qaid Ahmad ibn al-Haddad al-Amri, who took the prisoner on his horse and carried him safe and

sound to his house. Learning of this catastrophe, Mahmud Pasha, who was still in the mosque, cried that he had not authorized this massacre and immediately sent orders that such a thing should not be repeated. . . .

The massacre of the prisoners took place near the house of Amraduchu, one of the hartani of the city of Timbuktu, and Amraduchu received the order to bury the bodies in his house. Jurist Ahmad Muyaj, jurist Muhammad al-Amin, and jurist al-Mustafa were buried in the same pit, and the very learned jurist Muhammad Bughyu took care of all the funeral ceremonies. Amraduchu then left Timbuktu in order to travel. He settled in the city of Chiki, where he lived until his death.

When the ascetic Sidi Abd al-Rahman learned of the event, he cried out, "Of all the members of this family, all were killed today with the exception of Muhammad al-Amin!" When he learned of the death of Fadl, he said, "Fadl has died in this affair, but he will have the supreme recompense."

Mahmud Pasha broke into the houses of the jurists and took from them all the money, goods, and furnishings—so much that only God knows the amount, for in addition to the possessions of the jurists, these houses contained the wealth deposited by the people for safekeeping.

The troops of the pasha pillaged all they could find and stripped men and women naked to search them. The troops then abused the women and took them and the men to the casbah, where they were kept as prisoners for six months. Mahmud Pasha wasted all the wealth he had seized and scattered it far and wide. He gave generously to his soldiers but sent nothing to Sultan Ahmad al-Mansur except 100,000 pieces of gold.

5 IMAM AHMAD IBN FARTUWA

IDRIS ALAWMA AND THE KANEM WARS

The state of Kanem was probably founded in the ninth century in the region northeast of Lake Chad by black Saharan nomads called Zaghawa. Between the eleventh and thirteenth centuries Islam was introduced and was accompanied by the political transformation of the chief of Kanem from a nomadic sheik to a Sudanese king, the mai, *with his capital at Njimi. During the reign of Dunama Dabalemi ibn Salma (1221–1259), the authority of the mai was strengthened, but his enthusiasm for Islam alienated the pagan branch of the ruling clan known as the* Bulala. *Thereafter, the kings of Kanem sought to crush the pagan Bulala, but in the fourteenth century this struggle intensified and the pagan reaction triumphed. Between 1384 and 1388, the mai abandoned Kanem to the Bulala and took refuge in Bornu, west of Lake Chad. Victorious, the Bulala established their capital at Gaw, north of Lake Fitri. Meanwhile, the former rulers of Kanem revived under Ali ibn Dunama (1476–1503), who established the kingdom of Bornu with its capital at Ngazargamu. Bornu flourished and reached its golden age during the reign of Idris ibn Ali (1570–1602), known as Idris Alawma. Idris Alawma was a great warrior king. He made the pilgrimage to Mecca, during which he learned the power of firearms and imported Turkish musketeers to consolidate his power in Bornu. He then launched the Kanem wars against the Bulala. In seven expeditions he defeated the Bulala but was never able to subdue them. In the end he acknowledged the independence of Kanem under its Bulala king and agreed upon a defined frontier between Bornu and Kanem. Ahmad ibn Fartuwa was the principal* imam *under Idris Alawma. His rich and detailed "A History of the First Twelve Years of the Reign of Mai Idris Alooma" and "The Kanem War of Idris Alooma" were first procured by Heinrich Barth in 1853 from the then* Wazir *of Bornu, al-Hajj Bashir. The selections in this section describe the pilgrimage, the return to Bornu, and the consolidation of the authority of Idris Alawma and are followed by excerpts from his fifth, sixth, and seventh expeditions to Kanem, which culminated in the peace treaty with the Bulala.*

So he made the pilgrimage and visited Tayiba, the Tayiba of the Prophet, the chosen one (upon whom be peace and the blessing of God), the unique, the victorious over the vicissitudes of day and night.

He was enriched by visiting the tomb of the pious Sahabe the chosen, the perfect ones (may the Lord be favourable and beneficent to them), and he bought in the noble city a house and date grove, and settled there some slaves, yearning after a plenteous reward from the Great Master.

From Imam Ahmad ibn Fartuwa, "A History of the First Twelve Years of the Reign of Mai Idris Alooma," in H. R. Palmer, *Mai Idris of Bornu, 1571–1583* (Lagos, 1926), pp. 11–13. Section describing Fifth Expedition from Imam Ahmad ibn Fartuwa, "The Kanem Wars," in H. R. Palmer, *Sudanese Memoirs* (Lagos, 1928), I, 48–51, 62–65, 67–69.

Then he prepared to return to the kingdom of Bornu. When he reached the land called Barak he killed all the inhabitants who were warriors. They were strong but after this became weak; they became conquered, where formerly they had been conquerors. Among the benefits which God (Most High) of His bounty and beneficence, generosity, and constancy conferred upon the Sultan was the acquisition of Turkish musketeers and numerous household slaves who became skilled in firing muskets.

Hence the Sultan was able to kill the people of Amsaka with muskets, and there was no need for other weapons, so that God gave him a great victory by reason of his superiority in arms.

Among the most surprising of his acts was the stand he took against obscenity and adultery, so that no such thing took place openly in his time. Formerly the people had been indifferent to such offences, committed openly or secretly by day or night. In fact he was a power among his people and from him came their strength.

So he wiped away the disgrace, and the face of the age was blank with astonishment. He cleared away and reformed as far as he could the known wrong doing.

To God belong the secret sins, and in His hands is direction, and prevention, and prohibition and sanction.

Owing to the Mai's noble precepts all the people had recourse to the sacred Sheria, putting aside worldly intrigue in their disputes and affairs, big or little.

From all we have heard, formerly most of the disputes were settled by the chiefs, not by the "Ulema."

For example, he stopped wrong doing, hatred and treachery, and fighting between Muslims, in the case of the Kuburi and Kayi. They had been fighting bitterly over their respective prestige, but on the Sultan's accession, he sternly forbade them to fight till they became as brothers in God.

Then again there was his leniency in his remarkable expedition to Gamargu and Margi and Kopchi and Mishiga and to the hills of Womdiu.

He also came to the people of the hills of Zajadu and the hills of N'garasa, called N'guma, who had allied themselves with the sons of Sultan Daud and his grandsons and relatives and made raids on the land of Bornu, killing men and enslaving women and children right down to the time of our Sultan (may God ennoble him in both worlds). He scattered their host, and divided them, but of the N'guma he spared all and established them in settlements under his direction as his subjects nor did they resist or become recalcitrant.

The tribe of N'gizim, the people of Mugulum, and the people of Gamazan

and others of the N'gizim stock who were neighbours were insolent and rebellious, till our Sultan went out to them with a large host, destroyed their crops, and burnt their houses in the wet season. Thus they felt the pinch of a ruined country, yielded to him obedience, and submitted to his rule.

He introduced units of measure for corn among these people by the power and might of God. The N'gizim who dwelt in the West, known as Binawa, would not desist from enslaving Muslims in their country and doing other evil and base actions. They kept seizing the walled towns of the Yedi as fortresses and places of refuge and hiding, using them as bases treacherously to attack the Muslims by day and night, without ceasing or respite. But when our Sultan ascended the throne, he and his Wazir in chief Kursu took counsel to stem the torrent of their guile and deceit, so that they left off their wickedness, and some followed the Sultan, others the Wazir Kursu, others various leaders who had waged "Holy War" with the Sultan.

To some the Sultan gave orders to settle, and devote their time to agriculture.

Again there is the record of the Sultan's dealings with the So whose home was in the East on the shores of the great lake of Chad. These people, known as Tatala, formerly perpetrated many iniquities and crimes. It is said that they took stores of water in gourds or other receptacles, and then with their weapons and shields, sallied forth to harry the towns of the Muslims, sometimes going two or three days distance on these forays.

But when the time of our Sultan came, he rebuked them with a stern rebuke, and chastised them with divers sorts of chastisement till they became downcast and ashamed. Many of their dwellings became desolate, empty, forlorn and deserted.

Know, my brethren, that in what we

have told you, we have failed to tell all. We have but told you a part of the story of the deeds of the early years of our Sultan's reign, with hand and pen. How can that be easy or possible for us, considering his actions covered most of that which is ordained in the Kura'an and Sunna concerning "Holy War" in the path of God, seeking the noble presence of God, and His great reward.

Thus we have cut short the recital of all his wars, in this brief compilation. As for his wars on the tribe of Bulala we will—please God—relate the Sultan's dealings with them in a separate work plainly and clearly and accurately, according to the accounts obtained, and following all the descriptions which have been given of the wars which our Sultan brought to an end by the might and power of God.

. . .

FIFTH EXPEDITION

So we arrived at Garku by slow stages. When we reached it and halted there, every man with great caution as had been ordered, the people began to cut down the thorn trees to protect the Sultan's camp, every man according to his share, according to the custom of our people which was initiated by our Sultan Hajj Idris (may God ennoble him in the time of his power).

When we halted with his army at any camp whatsoever, he used to order the people to divide up their camping place into sections so that every chief and captain should have his share of it, and should live in it, and make a fence for its enclosure. Thus the circumference of the "zariba" [fenced enclosure—ed.] was finished with great speed and rapidity. It comprised a large area, so great that everyone could find his share of dwelling space.

It was in this very town of Garku that fighting broke out at night between us and between our enemies. They rushed upon us unexpectedly though its perimeter was

fortified in the same way as other places.

In the building of these stockades, which the experienced thought and sound prudence of our Sultan had established, there was great advantage and usefulness. Firstly in that it obviated the need of tying up animals, so that they could be allowed to roam about in the midst of the camp. The horses and other animals also were unable to stray away. Then again it prevented thieves from entering for infamous and evil purposes, for they were frustrated and turned back. Again it prevented any one from leaving the camp on errands of immorality, debauch or other foolishness. Again when the enemy wished to force an entrance upon us either by treachery or open fighting he was obliged to stand up and occupy himself with the defences before he reached us. If we had taken many captives and much booty and put them inside, we could sleep restfully and the night hours were safe: also if the male or female slaves wished to run away from the camp, they were afraid to go out. The advantages of a stockade cannot be numbered.

There was no early warning that the Bulala would make a surprise attack on the Sultan's camp. Their onset only became known after the evening prayer. Some did not know until the night, and some did not even know until the enemy had entered the camp or had come close to it. Had there been a stockade there would not have been fighting and slaughter on this occasion between the Bulala and our Sultan Hajj Idris ibn Ali (may God ennoble him and bless him in his children and descendants for ever and ever by the grace of the Lord of creation, our master Muhammad the chosen, and his house, upon whom be blessing—Amen).

The Sultan went to Kanem four times before this journey in which there was fighting between us and them openly night and day. In this fighting he ravaged the three great and famous valleys until they were like vast empty plains: one of them the great town Ikima, the second the stockade of Aghafi, and the third the town of Ago.

When the Sultan laid waste these three valleys, there resulted to the inhabitants great misfortune, in that he laid waste the whole country. Then too the people who lived in Kanem were removed to the land of Bornu, including the people who lived at Kulu to the south and were riverain peoples. There did not remain in Kanem any branches of the tribes which went to Bornu. They did not however move to Bornu of their own will or desire, but impressed by the news of the conqueror, and the fear he inspired.

Had it not been for the Tubu, who wished to support Sultan Abdul Jalil and be his subjects, we had only gone to Kanem once.

God knows best the truth about character, and how He richly endowed Sultan Idris, by His grace, and abundant beneficence, and strengthened him, so as to be a terror to his many enemies, and, what time he gained the mastery over the Bulala Sultan, who relied on the Tubu, to go out to battle against them all.

Is it not stated in the account we have heard from our Sheikhs and elders who have gone before us that the Tubu attacked Sultan Dunama ibn Dabale, the son of Sultan Salma, son of Bikuru openly so that a state of war ensued, and lasted between the Tubu and Sultan Dunama for seven years seven months and seven days, raising fires of hate which lasted for all that time?

Thus we have heard from trustworthy sources; but there was no tribe of Bulala in those days.

We heard too from Wunoma Muhammad Al-Saghir ibn Tuguma in his life time, when he was telling us about the early Sultans (he was learned in ancient history) that the number of the horsemen of Sultan Dunama ibn Dabale was 30,000. Thus we heard from him, nor are we ignorant of, nor have we forgotten what he told us, since the day he told us.

But the war of Sultan Dunama ibn Dabale was with the tribe of the Tubu.

Whereas our Sultan fought the Bulala and Tubu and other people of different tribes, whose origin is unknown, and fought them all patiently, relying on God, and going forward trusting Him, till he vanquished them, and put them to flight. We shall talk of this plainly in what follows, if God wills.

The Bulala, after our Sultan had destroyed all their towns in the land of Kanem, even the town of Ikima and the stockade of Aghafi, wished to build up the old town of Ago and to return to it. They dwelt in it still, as we have heard. Whilst they were sojourning with the intention of settling there, they heard the news of our Sultan Hajj Idris, what time he came to Yisambu in the rainy season on a military expedition and halted in Dalli.

When they heard of his coming, they were afraid with a very great fear, and left the town of Ago; leaving it altogether and not returning to it. The people were amazed and stupefied throughout the villages and towns of Kanem, for they were certain that Sultan Hajj Idris ibn Ali would not cease from coming to Kanem so long as Sultan Abdul Jalil was there as ruler.

They therefore abandoned this town of Ago, and left it empty as the desert so that the troops of our Sultan should not surprise them there. Their women, however, daughters of the royal house, sent to Sultan Abdul Jalil and his army whom they knew were utterly cowed, to say that they did not love them and were bewildered. So the Bulala became even more terrified, and planned to build a stockade at Kiyayaka. In fact they built huts and sheds and found all that they needed as supports for these buildings.

We heard from trustworthy persons who had entered the country of Sultan Abdul Jalil that the towns of Yaki and Makaran and Kurkuriwa were inhabited.

would never move from this region. As the Poet says:

My master wept when he saw the road behind him, and felt that we should never find Kaisira. I said to him weep not, we will change the seat of power or we will die, and seek help from God.

Thus they built on the borders of this region which was contiguous to the river near the town of Kulu. They built at the town which had the largest perimeter, stockades on all sides but one, *i.e.,* the south. When they had finished building they set about moving the people so that the town should be filled.

Every one they saw in Kanem was sent to their new fortress, except the people of Tatalu, and Afaki near by, or those whose villages were afar off and difficult of access. As for the Tubu they removed them to the town of Kiyayaka mentioned above, as for instance the tribe of Kasharda. There were no Tubu tribes in the remotest parts of the land of Kanem which did not come in *en masse* without leaving anyone behind. All who came willingly or unwillingly built grass huts in which they dwelt with their families, until there was gathered together in the abovementioned place a great number of people. God (who is exalted) alone knows the number of them. They took their stores and grain supply as food. Between them and the people of the south there was made a pact of friendship and alliance and concord. Traders in foodstuffs were constant in coming and going between this region and the south to buy and sell. They sold food in exchange for cattle and clothes and other articles.

Trading did not cease between the Bulala and the owners of foodstuffs until the Emir of the Faithful camped at Garku, the Emir Hajj Idris ibn Ali (may God who is exalted ennoble him and bless him in his children and posterity until the end of the ages).

.   .   .

SIXTH EXPEDITION

On Wednesday they set out and at siesta time halted at Wurni; on Thursday about midday they set out and encamped at Labudu which was left on the Friday and a hasty march made to Kasuda; next day they went on to Buluji and spent the night there, while Sunday was spent at Bari. A halt was made at Ruru at noon on Monday, but the Sultan did not remain there longer than was necessary for the two o'clock and afternoon prayers, after which they rode on fast, halting only for the evening prayer at a pool called Kintak. They continued eastwards in the direction of the Kananiyya country in order to reach there by dawn and fare according as God had decreed for them. They travelled on continuously through the night, without halting for exhaustion or fatigue, until between a quarter and a third of the night was over. In this expedition of ours, since we set out from Fakara on the Friday we have mentioned, inclusive of the subsequent eleven days culminating on the Monday, we were not afflicted with exhaustion similar to that which befell us on this night. So greatly were we taxed, that some of us did not know in which direction to turn when praying unless guided by our camels in that direction; while others were unable to find their quarters although fully accustomed to their position. There were still others who, cut off from the main body, could not find their way back again. Such was the condition of some of our men on that night after the Sultan had emcamped. It is surely enough to show that the conditions of that journey were a foretaste of hell (as a matter of fact the word Jihad only receives its name on account of the strife and toil entailed in it). This was why our Sultan Al Hajj Idris (may God exalt his rank and abase his detractors and bless his children and issue for ever and ever) in setting out on this forced march on Monday, particularly avoided all drumming and ordered every soldier to take three days rations neither more nor less. He also laid emphasis on the fact that no fit infantry man should remain behind (Rajil is the singular of Rawajil and that is a foot soldier) and that no healthy horse, pack animal or camel should remain with the casualties at the base. He also ordered the various shieldbearers not to follow him but similarly to remain behind at the base. His aim was to concentrate around himself every fit man and beast. He mounted with the forces remaining in his hands, but before setting out appointed his deputy to take charge of the sick and baggage. This was Yuroma Yagha. The Sultan set out at the head of his army encamping at Ruru sometime after noon but only stayed there long enough to celebrate the two prayers, that of two o'clock and the afternoon prayer.

Then the force set out and travelled at a rapid pace so that the exhaustion we have referred to above overtook them. We continued on until we reached Siki (a well known place) or thereabouts, and there we spent the night. At dawn the Sultan divided the troops into three portions for the purpose of raiding, fighting, and plunder. His son Kaigama Abdul Jalil, he sent out with his Wazir Idris ibn Harun towards the south against the Kananiyya to proceed as far as Ririkmi and other cities. He sent his son Yarima Idris with the army known as the "Northern Force" which was under the command of Arjinoma and other northern captains, northwards to harass the Kananiyya and penetrate as far as their city Mai and others. They slaughtered a large number of the enemy and took captive many women and children. The Sultan himself had followed the course of the main road with the remaining troops and proceeded as far as Didi and other cities of the Kananiyya.

His troops worked great havoc among the enemy and carried off much property and about a thousand or more of their women and children. The fires of war having died down the Sultan turned his steps towards Ririkmi and there en-

camped towards evening. His senior captain Kaigama Abdul Jalil and the Wazir Idris ibn Harun had taken up their quarters at Ririkmi before the arrival of the Sultan as they had been detailed to raid it. They had taken a large store of booty. The senior commander Yarima Idris ibn Idris did not return with his army until after nightfall when he arrived with much loot having accounted for large numbers of the enemy.

Sultan Al Hajj Idris ibn Ali was at Ririkmi of good cheer and bright of eye; while discomfiture, rout, slaughter and despoilment fell upon his bellicose enemies who had persisted in hindering the free passage of Muhammadans. The troops were overjoyed and rejoiced at the victory of their Sultan over their rebellious and impious foe. The whole army spent the night at that town without taking any measures of defence; for they felt they had nothing to fear from the enemy, some of whom had been slain, others of whom had fled to a place of refuge and concealment.

Our troops ate their full there of mutton and goats' flesh; their tiredness left them; and they rested and slept the whole night through. When the dawn broke the Sultan gave the signal for departure and mounted, followed by his army, travelling westwards towards Ruru. They went on till the sun was declining and then halted in a place known as Kintak where there was a pond of water. There they stopped for a siesta, and celebrated the two o'clock and afternoon prayers after which they went on to Ruru without any of the captains, commanders, or body-guards remaining behind. The complement was complete even including the pack animals and camel drivers. They carried their booty along with them not forcing the pace but proceeding very slowly. When they reached the place on the frontier where our drum was beaten on our first expedition to Kanem on the occasion when we retraced our steps, our Sultan (the Commander of the Faithful Al Hajj Idris whom may God render victorious and whose children and grandchildren be blessed till the sounding of the Trumpet by the grace of the Lord of mankind, the Bringer of Good Tidings, the Eternal, the Seal of the Prophets, the Imam of the Pure, our Lord and Master Muhammad the Pure, and his descendant on whom be the mercy of God) halted, firmly reining in his horse near some tamarisk trees which I know are known far and wide. The people were dismayed at not rejoining the sick who were with the deputy commander Yuroma, but the Sultan was not minded to rejoin them on that day and dismounted under those trees, the tamarisks we mentioned, at the beginning of the book. Upon seeing this, the army bivouacked without delay, unsaddled both camels and horses, and constructed their quarters for the night as best they were able. They spent the night there cheerful and happy and free from fear of theft or attack together with the rich spoil we had taken.

They returned safely without the loss of a single man with the exception of those who were wounded or overcome at the first shock, but our infidel enemy's losses cannot be computed except after long search and investigation. That is because the warriors were killed at the first onset in the field of battle and overthrown, and all those who attempted to withstand our army were at once slain except those who prolonged their life by flight. Our armed patrols were unremitting in searching out fugitives in every place where we encamped, by search and investigation, and they killed our pagan prisoners by order of the Sultan. Not one of them was spared by the guards to remain in anyone's possession. One of the strangest things I have heard about our behaviour was that Kamkama Bamu, one of the Sultan's chief officers, put to death the youths and striplings who were not yet fully adult, in punishment of their evil deeds. Not one

survived except him whom God saved. The prisoners were slain there just as their companions had been slain on the field of battle. He who escaped, escaped; and he who died, died. The only survivors in our hands were the women and children.

After this, the Kananiyya rapidly became extinct. These were the people who only a short time before were puffed up with pride and insolence and considered themselves second to none. According to what I have heard, they were the most numerous tribe in Kanem, and it has been said that if any of their enemies angered them they used to set out with the whole of their people and attack the country of their adversaries without fear of living man, just as our Sultan does to his enemies. This was what emboldened them to deeds of evil and tyranny until they went to the length of openly opposing the armies of our Sultan by attacking and robbing them. They had no organisation of any sort and were led astray by their overweaning pride and insolence, until spoliation, slaughter, and destruction fell upon them, as we have described, and the country which our Sultan raided became so much scattered dust. These oppressors were exterminated from the face of the earth. This Tuesday came to them a day of deadly poison. May the dawn of the day be hateful to infidels and evildoers. So we have seen in the book of the creation of the world, what time punishment was inflicted on the people of Sodom because of their disobeying their prophet Lot. The Kananiyya took no heed of the fate of bygone scoffers and profited naught by the lessons of this changing life. As the proverbialist has said "He who does not learn in the school of the world's experience will not profit by the exhortations of the preacher, preach he never so long." But the Kananiyya of Kanem are people senseless and stupid, ignorant and stubborn, lacking in all qualities of intellect and common sense, and entirely devoid of organisation. Our reason for designating them by these three epithets, *i.e.,* Khurq, Humq, and Jahil, which are distinct in form but close in meaning, is because Khurq is a stronger term than Humq, and Humq is stronger than Jahil; for a senseless man (Akhraq) is one who cannot distinguish between what is beneficial and what is noxious and exhortation is entirely wasted on him, while the stupid man (Ahmaq) is one who will accept no service at all whether it be to his advantage or disadvantage and in this he resembles the senseless man. As regards the ignorant (Jahil) his case is simpler than that of the other two for, if he is adjured, he listens, and after listening, turns away from the advice to his own hurt. It is now time to return to the story of Ruru when we went to the great city called Birni. After encamping at Ruru on Thursday we only remained there three days and the whole of our army recovered from their fatigue and rested from their preparations.

.   .   .

SEVENTH EXPEDITION

We now return to the events which occurred on the seventh journey of the Sultan Aj Hajj Idris to Kanem. This great and just king and pious administrator of the lands of Islam and respecter of the rights of all Muhammadans, on setting forth for Kanem on this journey, after the destruction of the rebels, gave orders to his captains, commanders, and bodyguard and the remainder of his army to collect rations for the journey without delay. They did so. The Sultan set out from Gambaru in the month of Shawwal and encamped at Zantam; from there he passed on to Ghotuwa, then to Milu, Lada, Burkumwa, Ghawali, Milti, Bari, Gayawa, Malahe, Dagimsil and Hugulgul, in the neighbourhood of Dilaram, then to Ruru and on to Kasuda.

The Sultan stayed at Kasuda three or four days having previously sent Mala-galma Dalatu, chief of Miri, to Sultan Muhammad ibn Abdul Lahi to summon him to Sulu in the Kananiyya country with his people the Bulala. Dalatu left Kasuda on Saturday and was followed on Tuesday by the Sultan who travelled eastwards and halted at Siki Dananma to await the Sultan Muhammad Abdul Lahi. The Bulala Sultan arrived with his army headed by our messenger Malagalma Dalatu on Friday night and encamped in front of our Sultan's house. The troops were ordered to parade outside in full strength. Our Sultan and Sultan Muhammad ibn Abdul Lahi sat together in the same council. Many matters were discussed and the boundary was delimited between Bornu and Kanem, whereby we obtained Kagusti and the whole Siru district. This was made public to all and the commanders on both sides who were present at the proclamation heard it without dismay or opposition. Babaliya also was alloted to Bornu, but our Sultan granted them what remained of Kanem through his affection for Sultan Muhammad ibn Abdul Lahi. But for this he would not have given them an inch of territory in Kanem. I lay emphasis on this, because when our Sultan made his expedition to Kanem, and encamped at Ma'o, it was *he* who routed Abdul Jalil in three separate actions; firstly, at the town of Kirsila, then at Tusa or Gamira, and lastly at Aghafi. The Sultan remained there some time to await the arrival of his partisans and was joined by many of the troops of Abdul Jalil. Such captains and commanders as gave him their allegiance, he placed under the command of Sultan Muhammad ibn Abdul Lahi, having previously made them swear on the Kura'an that they would obey him and help him to victory. Having pronounced his friendly intentions towards Sultan Muhammad he gave him sway over the remaining territories of Kanem because of his affection for him. It was this affection alone which led him to alienate his territory.

Everyone of the Bulala whom he swore

in at Aghafi heard the speech of our Sultan which we have mentioned above and also the captains and commanders of the Bulala. After the settling of the frontiers of Bornu and Kanem the Sultan returned to Bornu.

Let us now resume the account of the treaty between ourselves and the Bulala entered into at Siki. When the conference took place between our Sultan and Sultan Muhammad ibn Abdul Lahi in front of the Sultan's house at Siki, everyone of the Bulala applauded, and sought pardon and swore by God that they would never again oppose our Sultan neither would they oppose their own Sultan Muhammad or his son. This they swore a second time after having sworn it previously to our Sultan.

Sultan Muhammad ibn Abdul Lahi and his people who had come with him then returned on Friday night, the night of the full moon, after obtaining a complete pardon, with their minds at ease after the terror which they had previously felt. We have heard from those who know the facts, that when the Bulala approached our Sultan's dwelling at Siki, they came into his presence invoking the protection of God, and humbly mentioning His name, and in such terror of their lives that they dismounted from their horses. The only one who felt no fear was their Sultan, Muhammad ibn Abdul Lahi in person, for he relied on the affection which our Sultan felt for him. When they had sworn an oath and received a free pardon from our Sultan, they were overjoyed, and praised God for escaping with their lives. On mounting to take their departure, they offered up thanks to God and returned with their sultan to the place from which they had come.

When Friday dawned, Chiroma Burdima arrived with the remaining commanders and chiefs of the Bulala. They were given audience of our Sultan on Saturday and clapped their hands and sought pardon as their predecessors had done on the previous day.

The Sultan ordered his Wazir Idris ibn Haruna to swear them on the Book of God, and they all took the oath without exception. Our Sultan gave orders that on the following day, a Saturday, every commander and captain was to parade fully equipped, each in a separate position, accompanied by his followers, grooms, and shieldbearers, since he intended to review them one after the other and wished to inspect them without confusion. On the appointed day the whole army in smart array took up their positions one by one in great number without overcrowding, for the Sultan to inspect them. On the Sunday, the Sultan did not inspect the shieldbearers and the Koyam, but did so on the next day. All our commanders and captains rejoiced at our increase of territory and at our eastward journey having come to a conclusion.

.   .   .

6 THE KANO CHRONICLE
KINGS OF KANO

The history of the Hausa is dominated by the growth of their city-states, which were formed in the eleventh and twelfth centuries as a result of an intermingling of the diverse peoples that wandered across the plains of northern Nigeria. The political unit of the Hausa was the birni, *or walled village, which became a city-state when one birni secured control over a wider circle of villages. At this point the village headman was made the city chief, the* sarki, *and was surrounded by an elaborate court and ritual. The birni of Kano remained a small settlement from the time that it was established in about 1000* A.D. *until about the fourteenth century, when it became a city-state and acquired a reputation as a manufacturing center. Nevertheless, Kano remained of little importance compared with the larger city-state of Katsina. The two city-states carried on an eighty-year war from 1570 to 1650, when both were attacked by the Jukun (or Kwararafa) from the south. Kano apparently strengthened its position in the eighteenth century and, despite the Fulani conquest in 1809, continued to be a manufacturing and commercial center throughout the nineteenth century.*

XIII. KANAJEJI, SON OF YAJI (A.H. 792–812. A.D. 1390–1410)

The thirteenth Sarki was Kanajeji. His father's name was Yaji. His mother's name Aunaka. He was a Sarki who engaged in many wars. He hardly lived in Kano at all, but scoured the country round and conquered the towns. He lived for some time near the rock of Gija. He sent to the Kwararafa and asked why they did not pay him tribute. They gave him two hundred slaves. Then he returned to Kano and kept sending the Kwararafa horses while they continued to send him slaves. Kanajeji was the first Hausa Sarki to introduce "Lifidi" [quilted armor—ed.] and iron helmets and coats of mail for battle. They were introduced because in the war at Umbatu the losses had been so heavy. He visited Kano and returned to Umbatu the next year, but he had no success in the war. He returned a second time to Kano, and again went out the following year. He again failed, but said, "I will not return home, if Allah wills, until I conquer the enemy." He remained at Betu two years. The inhabitants, unable to till their fields, were at length starved out, and had to give in to him. They gave him a thousand male, and a thousand female slaves, their own children. They also gave him another two thousand slaves. Then peace was made. The Sarkin Kano said: "No one shall again conquer Umbatu as I have conquered it, though

From "The Kano Chronicle," in H. R. Palmer, *Sudanese Memoirs* (Lagos, 1928), III, 107–109, 127–132.

he may gain spoil." In the following year the Sarki made war on Zukzuk and sat down in Turunku. The men of Zukzuk came out and defeated the Kano host, saying, "What is Kano! Kano is 'bush' " [primitive—ed.]. The Sarkin Kano went back to Kano in a rage and said: "What shall I do to conquer these men of Zukzuk?" The Sarkin Tchibiri said: "Re-establish the god that your father and grandfather destroyed." The Sarki said: "True, but tell me what I am to do with it." The Sarkin Tchibiri said: "Cut a branch from this tree." The Sarki cut off a branch. When it was cut, the Sarki found a red snake in the branch. He killed the snake, and made two *huffi* [slippers —ed.] with its skin. He then made four *dundufu* and eight *kuntakuru* [drums —ed.] from the branch. These objects he took to Dankwoi and threw them into the water and went home. After waiting forty days he came back to the water, and removed the objects to the house of Sarkin Tchibiri. Sarkin Tchibiri sewed the rest of the snake's skin round the drums and said to Kanajeji, "Whatever you wish for in this world, do as our forefathers did of old." Kanajeji said: "Show me, and I will do even as they did." The Sarkin Tchibiri took off his robe and put it on the *huffi* of snake's skin and walked round the tree forty times, singing the song of Barbushe. Kanajeji did as Sarkin Tchibiri did, and walked round the tree forty times. The next year he set out to war with Zukzuk. He encamped at Gadaz. The Sarkin Zukzuk came out and they fought; the men of Kano killed the Sarkin

Zukzuk. The Zukzuk men fled, scattered in ones and twos, and the chiefs of Zukzuk were killed. The Sarkin Kano entered Zukzuk and lived there close to the Shika eight months. The people gave him a vast amount of tribute. Because of this feat the song of Kanajeji was sung, which runs: "Son of Kano, hurler of the *kere,* Kanajeji, drinker of the water of Shika, preventer of washing in the Kubanni, Lord of the town, Lord of the land." Kanajeji returned to Kano. Among his great men of war were Berdi Gutu, Jarumai Sabbo, Maidawaki Babaki, Makama Toro, Dan Burram Jatau, Jakafada Idiri, Jambori Sarkin Zaura Bugau, Lifidi Buzuzu and Dan Akassan Goderi. He reigned twenty years.

XIV. UMARU, SON OF KANAJEJI (A.H. 812–824. A.D. 1410–1421)

The fourteenth Sarki was Umaru. His mother's name was Yatara. He was a mallam earnest in prayer. He was a pupil of Dan Gurdamus Ibrahimu and a friend of Abubakra. When he became Sarkin Kano his friend upbraided and left him and went to Bornu, where he remained eleven years. On his return to Kano finding Umaru still Sarkin Kano, he said to him: "O Umaru, you still like the fickle dame who has played you false, with whom better reflection refuses to be troubled. In time you will be disgusted, and get over your liking for her. Then regret will be futile even if you do regret." He preached to him about the next world and its pains and punishments. He reviled this world and everything in it. Umaru said, "I accept your admonition." He called together all the Kanawa, and said to them: "This high estate is a trap for the erring: I wash my hands of it." Then he resigned, and went away with his friend. He spent the rest of his life in regret for his actions while he had been Sarki. Hence he was called "Dan Terko." He ruled twelve years. In his time there was no war and no robbery. The affairs of Kano were put into the hands of the Galadima [Governor of the western provinces—ed.]. For this reason it was said of the Galadima Dana that he was the "Trusted guardian of the city, the dust-heap of disputes."

. . .

XLIII. MOHAMMA ALWALI, SON OF YAJI (A.H. 1195–1222. A.D. 1781–1807)

The forty-third Sarki was Mohamma Alwali, son of Yaji. His mother's name was Baiwa. As soon as he became Sarki he collected stores of "Gero" [millet—ed.] and "Dawa" [guinea corn—ed.] in case of war and famine. Nevertheless famine overtook him. His chiefs said to him, "Sarkin Kano, why do you refuse to give cattle to Dirki?" The Sarki said, "I cannot give you forty cattle for Dirki." They said, "What prevents you? If any Sarkin Kano does not allow us cattle for Dirki, we fear that he will come to some ill." Alwali was very angry and sent young men to beat "Dirki" with axes until that which was inside the skins came out. They found a beautiful Koran inside Dirki. Alwali said, "Is this Dirki?" they said, "Who does not know Dirki? Behold here is Dirki." Dirki is nothing but the Koran. In Alwali's time the Fulani conquered the seven Hausa States on the plea of reviving the Muhammadan religion. The Fulani attacked Alwali and drove him from Kano, whence he fled to Zaria. The men of Zaria said, "Why have you left Kano?" He said, "The same cause which drove me out of Kano will probably drive you out of Zaria." He said, "I saw the truth with my eyes, I left because I was afraid of my life, not to save my wives and property." The men of Zaria drove him out with curses. So he fled to Rano, but the Fulani followed him to Burum-Burum and killed him there. He ruled Kano twenty-seven years, three of which were spent in fighting the Fulani.

XLIV. SULIMANU, SON OF ABAHAMA (A.H. 1222–1235. A.D. 1807–1819)

The forty-fourth Sarki was Sulimanu, son of Abahama, a Fulani. His mother's name was Adama Modi. When he became Sarkin Kano, the Fulani prevented him from entering the palace. He went into the house of Sarkin Dawaki's mother. One of the remaining Kanawa said to Sulimanu, "If you do not enter the Giddan Rimfa, you will not really be the Sarki of city and country." When Sulimanu heard this he called the chief Fulani, but they refused to answer his summons, and said, "We will not come to you. You must come to us, though you be the Sarki. If you will come to Mallam Jibbrim's house we will assemble there." Sulimanu went to Jibbrim's house and called them there. When they had assembled, he asked them and said, "Why do you prevent me entering the Giddan Rimfa?" Mallam Jibbrim said, "If we enter the Habe's houses and we beget children, they will be like these Habes and do like them." Sulimanu said nothing but set off to Shehu-Osuman Dan Hodio [Dan Fodio—ed.] asking to be allowed to enter the Giddan Rimfa. Shehu Dan Hodio gave him a sword and a knife [1] and gave him leave to enter the Giddan Rimfa, telling him to kill all who opposed him. He entered the house, and lived there. All the Kano towns submitted to him, except Faggam, which he attacked. He took many spoils there. On his way back to Kano the chiefs of the Fulani said to him, "If you leave Faggam alone, it will revolt." So he divided it into two, and returned home. In his time Dabo Dan Bazzo raised a revolt. He dared to look for a wife in Sokoto and was given one. Sarkin Kano said, "What do you mean by looking for a wife at Sokoto?" So Dabo was caught and bound. His relations, the Danbazzawa,

however, came by night and cut his bonds, and set him free. He ran to Sokoto with Sulimanu following him. At Sokoto they both went before Dan Hodio. Dabo Dan Bazzo said, "I do not wish to marry your daughters, but I wish for a reconciliation between myself and your Sarki Sulimanu." So a reconciliation was made and they returned to Kano. Sulimanu sent the Galadima Ibrahima to Zaria to make war. Ibrahima conquered Zaria and took many spoils. He returned to Kano. Sulimanu was angry because of the Galadima's success, and had sinister designs against him when he died himself without having an opportunity of carrying them out. He ruled thirteen years.

XLV. IBRAHIM DABO, SON OF MOHAMMADU (A.H. 1235–1262. A.D. 1819–1846)

The forty-fifth Sarki was the pious and learned Ibrahim Dabo, son of Mohammadu, protector of the orphan and the poor, a mighty conqueror—a Fulani.

His mother's name was Halimatu. When he became Sarki he entered the Giddan Rimfa. Dabo made Sani Galadima. He, however, immediately tried to raise a revolt and incite all the towns to disaffection. The country Sarkis assembled and became "Tawayi" [rebellious —ed.] from Ngogu to Damberta, from Jirima to Sankara, and from Dussi to Birnin Kudu and Karayi. Dabo said, "I will conquer them, if Allah wills." He entered his house and remained there forty days praying to Allah for victory. Allah heard his prayers. He went out to hasten his preparations for war, and made a camp on Dalla Hill. Because of this he got the name of "The man who encamped on Dalla." He spent many days on Dalla,[2] and then returned home. He sent Sarkin Dawaki Manu Maituta to fight with Karayi. When the Sarkin Dawaki reached Karayi he sacked the town and returned to Dabo. Dabo said, "Praise be to God,"

---

[1] A flag was also given him as well as a knife and sword. He did not go to Sokoto, but sent a message. Had he gone himself, he would never have regained his position.

[2] Perhaps forty, I am not sure.

and prepared himself to go out to war. He went to Jirima and sacked that town and afterwards sacked Gasokoli and Jijita. Hence he was known as "Dabo, the sacker of towns." After he returned home he kept on sending out men to raid towns. He went in person to attack Dan Tunku and found him at Yan Yahiya. They fought. The Yerimawa ran away, and deserted Dan Tunku, who fled to Damberta, and thence, with Dabo following him, to Kazauri. When the Sarki reached the Koremma in pursuit he stopped, turned round again, and went back to Damberta, where he wrecked Dan Tunku's house. Dabo then returned home. Dabo was celebrated in the song:

The sacker of towns has come: Kano is your land, Bull Elephant, Dabo, sacker of towns.

When he went to war the trumpets played:

The sacker of towns is mounting.

He made war on Birnin Sankara and Birnin Rano, took the town of Rano, and lived in the house of Sarkin Rano. After this exploit he shaved his head. He never shaved his head except when he sacked a town. When the Kano towns saw that Dabo would not leave any town unconquered, they all submitted to him, and his power exceeded all other Sarkis. He had a friend whose name was Ango. When the Galadima Sini died, he made Ango Galadima, and as Galadima the latter reached great power through his pleasant manner and his persuasiveness. In Dabo's time there was no foreign war and people had food in plenty. Dabo conquered and spoiled Yasko. He had many war captains, a few among whom may be mentioned as: Berde, Kano Buggali, Sarkin Dawaki Manu, Sarkin Jarumai Dumma, Sulimanu Gerkwarn Karifi (he it was who killed Tunari, the son of Sarkin Sankara), Juli Kuda, Lifidi, Maidawaki Gawo and many others. These warriors of Dabo's time had no fear in war. When Dabo

mounted to go to war no such dust was ever seen, so many were his horses. The dust was like the Harmattan. Dabo was called "Majeka Hazo." His was a wonderful and brilliant reign, but we will not say any more for fear of "Balazi." He ruled Kano twenty-seven years and three months and nine days, his reign ending on the ninth of Safar.

XLVI. OSUMANU, SON OF DABO (A.H. 1262–1272. A.D. 1846–1855)

The forty-sixth Sarki was Osumanu, son of Dabo. His mother was Shekara. The first act of his reign was to build a house for Shekara at Tafassa with a big room the like of which was never seen before. Shekara was called "the mistress of the big room." Osumanu was a learned and good man and generous. He was called "The skin of cold water." The Galadima Abdulahi obtained in his time almost as much power as the Sarki, while Osumanu was like his Waziri. There was no war in his time except with Hadeijia. He built a house at Gogel and had a farm there. In his time mallams obtained great honour—among them Mallam Ba-Abseni, and others. In Osumanu's time Sarkin Dussi Bello revolted, but the Sarki enticed him to Kano and deposed him. Highway robbers were very numerous because Osumanu was so good-tempered and merciful. He could not bring himself to cut a man's hand off nor, because he was so pitiful, could he cut a robber's throat. He was called "Jatau rabba kaya." There was no Sarki like him for generosity. He ruled Kano nine years and ten months.

XLVII. ABDULAHI, SON OF DABO (A.H. 1272–1300. A.D. 1855–1883)

The forty-seventh Sarki was Abdulahi, son of Dabo. His mother's name was Shekara. When he became Sarki he set to work to kill all the robbers and cut off the hands of the thieves. He was called "Abdu Sarkin Yenka" because he was a strong-minded Sarki, ruthless, and victorious. He was quick to depose chiefs, but kept his word to his friends. He never stayed long in one place but went from town to town. In his time there was a very great famine, and the quarrel with Umbata grew big from small beginnings. The Sarkin Kano was eager to make war upon Umbatu. His first move was to attack Kuluki. Dan Iya Lowal of Kano died at Kuluki, whereupon the Sarki returned home himself, but sent Abdulahi Sarkin Dawaki Dan Ladan and his son Tafida to war in Zaria country. They went to Zaria together. This was in the time of Sarkin Zaria Abdulahi Dan Hamada. When they returned from Zaria it was not long before Dan Boskori made a descent upon Gworzo. The Sarkin Kano sent Sarkin Dawaki on ahead and followed himself personally to meet Dan Boskori Sarkin Maradi, west of Gworzo. A battle took place. The Kanawa ran away, deserting the Sarkin Dawaki Dan Ladan. Dan Boskori killed him. The Kanawa returned home in ones and twos. The Sarkin Kano was very angry. He gave orders that a house was to be built at Nassarawa for him to live in during the hot season; he also built a house at Tarkai for the war with Umbatu. He had a house at Keffin Bako where he lived almost two years because of Dan Maji the neighbour of Umbatu. He fought with Warji after the war with Kuluki, and took enormous spoil. No one knows the amount of the spoil that was taken at a town called Sir. The corpses of Warjawa, slaughtered round their camp, were about four hundred. The Sarki returned home. After a short time, the Sarki attacked Warji again, and once more took many spoils. Kano was filled with slaves. Abdulahi went to Sokoto, leaving his son Yusufu at Tarkai. While he was there Dan Maji came to attack Yusufu. A battle was fought at Dubaiya. The Kanawa fled and deserted Yusufu. Many men were slain and captured. After this Yusufu was made Galadima Kano, and hence acquired

much power. Abdulahi sent him to Dal from Tarkai to capture Haruna, the son of Dan Maji. Yusufu met Haruna at Jambo, and a battle took place. The Umbatawa ran away, deserting Haruna. Yusufu killed and took many men. It is said that about seven hundred were killed. Afterwards Yusufu tried to stir up rebellion and was deprived of his office and had to remain in chagrin and poverty till he was penniless. Abdulahi turned the Sarkin Dawaki Abdu out of his office and with him Makama Gadodamasu, Chiroma Diko, Dan Iya Alabirra, Galadima Abdul-Kadiri, and Galadima Yusufu. Abdulahi killed the Alkali Kano Ahmedu Rufaiyi, and degraded Maäji Sulimanu, Maji Gajere, and San Kurmi Musa. He deprived Mallam Dogo of his office of Waziri. The number of people that he turned out of office was countless. Hence the song—

Son of Ibrahim, a pick-axe to physic hard ground.

He sacked many towns. He made a new gate, the Kofan Fada. In his father's time it had been built up. He rebuilt the mosque and house of the Turaki Mainya early in his reign. They had been in ruins for many years. In his time Soron Giwa was built. At Woso he met Dan Maji in war. It was towards evening when the battle was fought. Dan Maji retreated. If it had not been that the light failed he would have been killed. Abdulahi attacked Betu, but failed. Abdulahi used to have guns fired off when he mounted his horse, till it became a custom. His chief men were:—Sarkin Yaki, called Mallam Dogo, Mallam Isiaka, Mallam Garuba, Sarkin Gaiya, Mallam Abdu Ba-Danneji, Alhaji Nufu, his friend Mallam Masu, Tefida his son, Shamaki Naamu, Manassara, Jekada of Gerko, and Dan Tabshi. Mallam Ibrahim was his scribe, and was made a Galadima. This man was afterwards turned out of office in the time of Mohammed Belo. Others were the Alkali

Zengi and Alkali Sulimanu. Abdulahi went to Zaria and sat down at Afira, and then at Zungonaiya. The Madawaki Ali of Zaria was in revolt against Sarkin Zaria. The Sarkin Kano made peace between them and returned home. In Abdulahi's time Salemma Berka became great. In the time of Mohammed Belo this man revolted and was degraded. In Abdulahi's time, too, the palace slaves became so great that they were like free men. They all rebelled in Mohammed Belo's time, but Allah helped Mohammed Belo to quell the rebellion. There were many great captains of war in Abdulahi's time, men without fear—so many of them that they could not be enumerated, but a few may be mentioned: Sarkin Yaki, Mallam Dogo and his son Düti, Jarumai Musa, Sarkin Bebeji Abubakr, Sarkin Rano Ali, Sarkin Gesu Osuman, Sarkin Ajura Jibbr. In this reign Sarkin Damagaram Babba came as far as Jirima and sacked Garun Allah. Sarkin Gummel Abdu Jatau came to Pogolawa to attack it. Sarkin Maradi Dan Boskori came to Katsina. Abdulahi went to meet him. They met at Kusada, but did not fight. For this reason the meeting was called "Algish Bigish Zuru Yakin Zuru," for they looked at each other and went back. There was also a fight between Barafia Sarkin Maridi and Sarkin Kano at Bichi.

Barafia ran away and Abdulahi took all the spoils. It is not known how many men were killed and slain. We do not know much of what Abdulahi did in the early part of his reign. He ruled Kano twenty-seven years and eight days, and died at Karofi on his way to Sokoto.

XLVIII. MOHAMMED BELO, SON OF IBRAHIM DABO (A.H. 1300–1310. A.D. 1883–1892)

The forty-eighth Sarki was Mohammed Belo, son of Ibrahim Dabo. His mother was Shekara. He was a very generous Sarki. He said to his friend Sarkin Fada Dan Gatuma, "You are Waziri Kano; I place in your hands the management of Kano." The Sarkin Fada was unrivalled as a settler of disputes. Belo was like his Wazir, and Sarkin Fada was like Sarki. When Sarki Fada died Mohammed Belo stretched out his legs because he saw that now he must become Sarki in earnest. He expelled the Galadima Ibrahim from his office and banished him to Funkui in Zaria, whence his name, "Galadima na Funkui." Belo gave the post of Galadima to his son Tukr, and his son Zakari was made San Turaki. Another son, Abubakr, he made Chiroma in place of Chiroma Musa.

·   ·   ·

7 SIRE ABBAS SOH
ABD AL-QADIR IN SENEGALESE FUTA

The celebrated genealogist Sire Abbas Soh was known throughout Futa Toro in the early part of this century for his knowledge of local traditions. He recounts the founding of the Muslim theocratic state in Senegalese Futa (in the present Republic of Senegal) in the last quarter of the eighteenth century, an event that later influenced Uthman dan Fodio in founding Hausaland. About 1776 the Torodbe, or Muslim clerical class in Senegalese Futa, overthrew the tyeddo, or warrior party, of the Denyanke and created a feudal theocratic elective state under the Almami, Abd al-Qadir. Abd al-Qadir was born in Futa Toro about 1728 and established his authority throughout Futa Toro by assigning fiefs to his followers during the jihad, or holy war, in return for their defense of Senegalese

Futa. Between 1796 and 1797 he fought the Damel *of Cayor with the intention of converting the* Wolof *to Islam. He failed, however, and in fact was taken prisoner. Abd al-Qadir was allowed to return, but because he was old and infirm, his authority diminished. His followers deserted him, and he was eventually defeated and killed in 1806 by the* Almami *of Bondu and his army. The elective principle, which was adopted to find a successor to Abd al-Qadir, as it had been early in Islamic civilization, led to political instability in Senegalese Futa and a host of ineffectual rulers whose weakness facilitated French penetration and control.*

The nightingales sang of his countenance, his piety, his superiority over the branches of the black [race] and the red [race], and God crowned his head: he who gives the faith to whom he wishes and maintains whom he wishes in unbelief is the most beautiful of crowns.[1]

When the members of the government and the population of the territory of Futa Toro recognized him [*Imam* Abd al-Qadir] as chief, he brandished the banner of holy war. He fought the *Ulad-Annaser* while on the expedition to Falo-Koli and broke their power. Then he began to collect a head tax from them that consisted of good horses and native utensils.

During the first decade of his reign he fought Sule-Bubu-Graysin in the village of Wali, as I have told before. He was defeated three times by Sule-Bubu, but Sule-Bubu died after the fourth battle, during which Abd al-Qadir and Ali-Mahmud Ali-Rasin were taken prisoner. Abd al-Qadir also fought the representatives of the dynasty of *Tengella* . . . near the village of Tuld, north of the [Senegal] river. They repulsed the imam twice. The third time, the imam defeated them and destroyed their village, where Dyadye-Konko and Amil-Konko were, with several other members of the family. In the

From Sire Abbas Soh, *Chroniques du Foûta Sénégalais,* edited by Maurice Delafosse (Paris, 1913), pp. 44–51, 54, 95–100. Trans. from the French by Nell Elizabeth Painter and Robert O. Collins. Reprinted by permission of LaRose Editions. Bracketed material in this selection was inserted by Professor Collins.
[1] This paragraph refers to the superiority of Abd al-Qadir over both the blacks and the Fulani, called the red people to distinguish them from the Negroes (ed.).

course of the last battle, *Samba-Anter,* Bokar-Sawa-Lamu, and Saboyi-Konko died. The families of this village [Tuld] were dispersed at that time. . . .

However, Dyadye-Konko and perhaps Amil-Konko began to make incursions into the territory of Futa Toro with *Banilsara* [pagan] armies. When this state of affairs threatened the people of Futa, they met with Ali-Sire-Buba-Musa in the village of Padalal and decided to bring Dyadye-Konko and Amil-Konko back to Futa in order to reestablish security and avoid misfortune for the people of Futa Toro. When they had been brought back, the imam assembled those of his vassals (with the exception of freemen) who declared themselves partisans of Islam. Recognizing the incontestable advantage they would have by conforming to the law established at Wali by Imam Abd al-Qadir, these vassals elected Dyadye-Konko imam of their canton, which was demarcated at that time. Subsequently, the people of Futa always would know abundance and the easy life, after having gone through considerably troubled times.

Then Imam Abd al-Qadir made war on the people of Bondu. His motive may be explained as follows. Imam Sega had invaded the village of the sheiks of the land of Bondu and had taken many of their children prisoner. Then the sheiks went to find Imam Abd al-Qadir to complain of this injustice, and Imam Abd al-Qadir sent a letter to Imam Sega ordering him to return the children to their families. However, Imam Sega refused so Imam Abd al-Qadir marched upon him. The two sides met near Fadiga, where Abd al-Qadir fought and cornered Imam Sega in his fortress of Dar-Lamin. Many of Imam Sega's men were killed in the course of this expedition, including fifteen men who were descendants of Malik Si.[2] Then Abd al-Qadir had Imam Sega brought to him, and when he arrived, Abd al-Qadir ordered that he be killed. Many among the men of Futa refused to execute this order; the only one who consented to execute it was Amar, son of Bela, son of Rasin, son of Samba, son of Pate, son of Mbaran, son of Silman, son of Ali, who passed on the order to one of his young servants named Sule-Musa, of the tribe of *Dyawe* of Mbumba, who killed him [Imam Sega] with one rifle shot. The ingenious wise man Mukhtar-uld-Buna was with him, and he said, "I was disgusted by the religion of the whites [the Moroccans] and I came to the blacks to learn their religion and abandoned the doctrine of the people who do not believe. But you, you have summoned this man under the safeguard of Islam. Why have you acted this way? (You are no better than the Moors.)" They did not discuss the reason with him for to do so would not have been a good thing, and Mukhtar-uld-Buna returned to the land of the Moors.

These wars took place during the first decade of the reign of Abd al-Qadir. After that, the blacks and the Moors submitted to his orders and his prohibitions, with the one exception of the *Trardya.* The imam sent their king, Aliyu-l-Kowri, a letter of this tenor.

From me, the Prince of the Believers, Abd al-Qadir the *Futanke,* to the King of the Trardya, Aliyu-l-Kowri. The aim of this letter is to let you know that Islam is the highest thing, that nothing is higher, and that it has demolished all things of the unbelief existing before it, save the consequences. I am sending you this letter so that you will send us five good horses, all

---

[2] Malik Si was the founder of a clerical family in Bondu in the seventeenth century. The head of this family had adopted the title of almami about 1775 (ed.).

saddled, to help us in the holy war that we are about to undertake. Salvation to him who follows the straight path and punishment to him who is in error and turns his back on the truth. May we and the holy servants of god be saved, with the mercy of God and his benedictions! Written by the pen of Sheik Sire, son of Sheik Hasan, son of Sheik Lamin in the village of Hayre and placed in the hands of Brahmin, son of Almaghfur of the tribe of the *Laghlal.*

When the letter arrived Aliyu-l-Kowri tore it up. Imam Abd al-Qadir attacked him in the year 1200 [1786–1787] and put the expositor Ahmadu, son of Sheik Hammad, son of Biran, son of Lord Abd Allahi, son of Lord Pate, son of Siwa, son of Lord Dyasa, commonly called the Tafsiru Ahmadu - Hammat - Kuro - Fatum - Atumane - Hammet - Pate - Biran - Musa, and so on, in command of this expedition.

When the troops of Futa were approaching, Aliyu-l-Kowri asked the wise men of his country the meaning of the word formed by the letters representing the date of the era of Muhammad. (May God spread his blessings over him and accord him salvation!) They told him: "bad year." He instructed them to reverse the order of the letters. Then they said: "bloody year." He concluded that this was an ill omen, and, in fact, the men of Futa killed him, and the imam [Abd al-Qadir] seized all the wealth found in the homes of the Trardya. Then the Futanke returned to his country.

After that he [Abd al-Qadir] denied the Moors access to the river, because they had killed certain Muslim notables and certain chiefs of the region who ruled the people of Futa, such as Sheik Sulayman-Bal, who disappeared, the expositor Ahmadu-Sambu of Dyaka, Malik-Tyayfal of Pate, and Ganne of Dyuade-Dyabi: May God have mercy on all those who were cruelly and unjustly killed!

When the Moors were convinced that there would be no security from attack by Futa Toro unless they paid tribute, they decided to take a number of presents to the imam in guise of taxes, such as excellent horses, and some utensils that the Moors make, and such a practice was continued until the time of Imam Muhammad, son of Imam Biran, for otherwise, the people of Futa would have taken over their country.

In the year 1210 [1796–1797] the imam (may the greatest God have mercy on him!) went as far as Bungoui, in the province of Cayor, to fight Damel Hammadi-Mangone.[3] The reason for this war was as follows. After the imam had come back from the Trardya, where he had fought Aliyu-l-Kowri (thanks to the expositor Ahmadu, son of Hammad, son of Abd Allahi, son of Pate, son of Siwa, son of Dyasa, who had commanded the expedition), the expositor Hamadi, son of Ibrahima, native of the village of Mbantu, had gone to the province of Cayor on the imam's orders to convert the inhabitants to Islam. They refused to obey his exhortations and made war on him for a long time for attempting to convert them, until, during the course of one year of that war, the sheik and expositor, Hamadi-Ibrahima, was treacherously killed by Damel Hammadi-Mangone, whose army took Hamadi-Ibrahima and his men by surprise while they were saying ritual prayers. All the members of Hamadi-Ibrahima's family were with him, including his two sons, Muhammad-Mudy-Taba and Muhammad-Halfi, each born of a different mother. Hamadi-Ibrahima had a wife who was originally from Hayre, by whom he had had a son named Muhammad-Mudy-Taba, who was the father of the wise professor Ibrahima-Muhammad-Mudy-Taka. Hamadi-Ibrahima also had another wife named Halfi, from the village of Fummi-Hara in the land of the *Dembube,* by whom he had a son named Muhammad-Halfi. The damel made prisoners of these two sons, then sent an order to the people of Hayre and

Fummi-Hara to come and collect the inheritance of the two wives of the deceased, who remained there without heirs.

When the damel's envoys arrived in the territory of Futa Toro, the blessed sheik, the perfect saint and sagacious Amar - Seydi - Yero - Buso - Demba - Ibrahima - Nyokor—such was his lineage on the paternal side—left at the same time as Sheik Abd Allahi, son of Lord Malik, son of Lord Birama, known by the name of Abd Allahi-Gaysiri, and they both went to find Imam Abd al-Qadir to ask him to pursue the damel, who had killed the expositor, Hamadi-Ibrahima. And so after these two people had exposed the whole affair to him, Imam Abd al-Qadir was brought to march against the damel.

The imam left in order to assure the triumph of religion and also because of the brotherly friendship that existed between him and the deceased, who belonged to nobility on both maternal and paternal sides of his family. His mother was Padel, daughter of Bubu, son of Malik, son of Rasin, son of Bubu, son of Hammay-Ali.

The imam thus began to fight the damel. Many of the notables of Futa were killed. This expedition was marked by the treachery and lack of loyalty of Ali-Dundu-Segele and the men of Boseya who accompanied him. They fled during the night, but the damel caught up with them because they were exhausted and hungry. The imam was taken prisoner the next day, after the death of the Prince of Dyolof, who accompanied him.

On their return, the men of Futa entrusted the administration of their country to Hammad, son of Sheik Lamin, son of Sheik Malik, son of Lord Haki, son of Bukar, son of Brahima, son of Nyokor, son of Brahima, son of Musa, son of Sulayman, who ruled justly during the brief duration of his functions, which were only purely administrative.

The great imam Abd al-Qadir was a prisoner of the rebels at Mbul and stayed there for a year, during which he was the

---

[3] Damel (chief) Hammadi-Mangone was Damel of Cayor and a chief of the pagan Wolof (ed.).

object of numerous marks of divine favor. . . .[4]

Sheik Muktar-Kudedye pronounced the decision before the people of Futa Toro that Imam Abd al-Qadir was incapable of exercising power. In pronouncing the destitution of the imam they relied on the facts that the imam had reached eighty years of age and that he had been a captive of the damel. The pretext was further cited that at the age of eighty years and being in the condition of serf of the people of Cayor as a result of his capture, the imam could not properly be a Prince of the Believers. A certain number of other persons supported the sheik's decision under the circumstances. . . .

Then the Governor of Ndar [St. Louis], Brière de l'Isle, arrived [in Futa] in the beginning of November, accompanied by the interpreter Hammad, son of Ndyay . . . and Usman-Sow.[5] They disembarked at Salde. Before the arrival of the governor and his above-mentioned companies at Salde, the people of Futa had elected an imam who was the wise professor and shrewd jurist, Muhammad, son of Ahmadu, son of Baka-Lik, son of Ahmadu, son of Sire, son of Ali, son of Abd Allali, son of Al-Hasan, son of Dowut, son of Ali, son of Fadl-al-Allah, of the village of Ogo, whose mother was Budu, daughter of Imam Sire, son of Ahmadu, son of Sire, son of Ali, son of Abd Allani, son of Al-Hasan, son of Dowut, of the village of Hayre, and they [the governor and his interpreter] came with him [Muhammad] to Dyaka. Abd al-Abu Bakr halted in this place, while the imam continued to Mbolo-Biran, where he stayed in the house of Almami Kana-Sire.

The above-mentioned governor of

Ndar sent them a letter to order them not to go as far as Lao because of the war that had taken place during the rainy season and the famine that had resulted from it. Their minds were divided (as to the answer they should give) and they tore up the letter and threw it on the ground. This action angered the governor of Ndar, who advanced a little to the east, then quickly went back and ordered them to retrace their steps. They refused.

Then the governor returned to Ndar, from which a column left that arrived at Nguy. The commander of this column, Colonel Reybaud, sent word to Abd al-Abu Bakr and Imam Muhammad to come to him. Abd al-Abu Bakr refused to come, but the imam came with the notables of Futa. The imam halted to the east of Nguy, in a place called Tulel-Dado. The colonel told them:

Abd al-Abu Bakr has refused to come, but I have already divided [the land] between you: [the land] extending to the east of Koylel-Tekke [will belong] to *Abd al-Abu Bakr*; Tyerno Muhammadu will be chief of Boseya; [the land extending] from Gunagol as far as Koylel-Tekke [will belong] to Ismail-Siley and [that] between Gunagol and Dodel [will belong] to Ibrahim, son of Imam Muhammad. We have given Abd al-Abu Bakr three months' grace; if he answers favorably and accepts a meeting with us so much the better, there will be peace; but if, after the grace period has passed, he perseveres in his attitude, we will expel him from Futa by force. And woe and woe again to the man who raises the dust of war between the beginning and the end of the period of grace.

As the imam was returning, the Almami of Rindyaw, Abbas, said [to him]: "We refuse you allegiance." Then the men of Futa returned, having deposed the imam.

During those same days the interpreter Hammad, son of Ndyay-An, went to the village of Galoya, as well as to the people of Futa. These people agreed to renounce the territorial limits that had been [previ-

---

[4] Abd al-Qadir was in fact imprisoned only a few months and was then released (ed.).

[5] Louis Alexandre E. G. Brière de l'Isle (1827–1896), Governor of Senegal from 1876 to 1881, was a disciple of Faidherbe, who was a previous Governor of Senegal and an exponent of French expansion toward the Niger, to be carried out by a bold scheme of railroad construction. His negotiation with Imam Muhammad constituted part of his forward program (ed.).

ously] fixed for the cantons of Futa and
wrote their names on a sheet of paper
[that was] presented to them by the interpreter Hammad. Then the interpreter
and Colonel Reybaud returned with the
column, accompanied by the *Lam* Toro
Samba and Ali-Buri-Ndyay, and the men
of Futa went back to their homes. These
events took place during the last days of
autumn, and Futa remained [without an
imam] during the following winter, summer, and autumn, and then during another winter and another summer.

When the autumn came [again], the
wise professor and shrewd jurist, Imam
Muhammad-Almami, son of the Almami
of Pate, Ahmadu-Muktar, the Black, son
of the *Tyerno* Demba, son of the Almami
Muktar (the magistrate mentioned in this
writing), son of Yero, son of Atumane,
son of Yusum, son of Samba, son of
Hamme, son of Bela, son of Al-Hasan,
son of Dyam-Lih, of the village of Pate,
whose mother was Ummu, daughter of
the Almami Siwa, son of Abu Bakr, son
of Siwa, son of Ndettye, son of Semta, son
of Biras, son of Ali, son of Dyam-Lih, also
from the village of Pate, was elected.

His election took place at the time in
the aforementioned autumn at harvest
time.

At that time, the telegraph poles, which
had been prepared by order [of the
French authorities] near Horé-Fondé and
Anyam-Barga, were burned by the people
of Boseya, who had at their head on that
occasion Ibra, son of Bukar, son of
Mahudu, son of Ali, son of Rasin, of the
village of Tyilon, who was accompanied
by the people from Tyilon. When they
wanted to burn the poles that were in the
village of Horé-Fondé, Imam Muhammad-Almami was opposed to it, and he
was upheld in this instance by the *Bummudy* Samba-Dyenada. Following this
incident, Saidu, son of Ndondi, son of
Samba, son of Demba-Nayel, from Asndi-
Balla, left to set the fire, but Imam
Muhammad Almami saw him and chased
him. Then Imam Muhammad-Almami

charged the inhabitants of the village of
Horé-Fondé with guarding the poles for
a salary, which the imam vouched for,
and which sum he collected from the public treasury of the adverse party [from the
treasury of the village of Tyilon]. There
were eight men [guards] each day and
eight men each night. On this occasion
part of what was remarkable with regard
to the imam's power and his blessed and
illustrious pen was plainly apparent.
Then he entrusted the guarding of the
poles to the *Bummudy* Samba-Dyenaba
and the *Bummudy* vouched for it [the
treasury of Tyilon] to him.

Subsequently, a column sent by the
Christians arrived, of which the Lam
Toro, Muhammad-Mbowba, was a part.
The column halted near Nguy and then
went into the canton of the Hebbiyabe
and began to ravage the village of Horé-
Fondé. Having burned Tyaski, the col-
umn invaded the village of Nere and took
a hundred prisoners or more. However,
Abd al-Abu Bakr hid himself in Damga.

The notables of Boseya realized the
gravity of the troubles [threatening the
country]; so these notables, particularly
*Ndondi-Samba-Dewa-Nayel, Hammadi-
Seydi-Daya, Ahmadu-Dewa-Yero, Amar-
Bakar,* and the *Tyerno* Molle Bubakar-
Abdul, chose [as imam] a man of the vil-
lage of Dyaba named Sire, son of Imam
Baba-Lih, son of the *Tatsiru-boggel* Ah-
madu, son of Samba, son of Demba, son
of Bubu, son of Dyam-Lih, whose mother
was Aysata, daughter of Bayla, son of
Sabbe, and Bubu, son of Moktar, son of
Musa, son of Yusufu, of the village of
Dyonto among the *Sillanabe*. Sire is best
known under the name of Imam Bubu-
Aba. These notables went with him to the
commander of the Christians' column
(which confirmed him as their imam).
Imam Bubu-Aba continued to serve these
functions until the final arrival of the
Christians and until they took possession
of the territory of Futa. Imam Bubu-Aba
was returned to power a second time, and
he retained this power until his death.

8 ABD ALLAH IBN MUHAMMAD

THE HIJRA AND HOLY WAR OF SHEIK UTHMAN DAN FODIO

Abd Allah ibn Muhammad (c. 1766–1828) was the younger brother of Sheik Uthman dan Fodio. A man of great learning, he served as his brother's wazir *after the declaration of holy war against Yunfa, the* Sarki *of Gobir. Uthman had begun his preaching against religious corruption and paganism in 1786, but not until Yunfa succeeded his father as Sarki of Gobir in 1802 did hostilities erupt. Yunfa marched against Uthman in February 1804, at which time Uthman made his* hijra, *or flight of the faithful, and from that time he regarded himself as God's chosen instrument to defeat the unbelievers and establish the pure religion throughout Hausaland. Uthman gathered his followers, mostly Fulani, at Gudu, and sent them, under the leadership of Abd Allah, against Yunfa and the army of Gobir. Yunfa was defeated, and thereafter the* jihad *was carried throughout the Hausa states until the Fulani acquired control over them. Overwhelmed by his success and unable to assert complete authority over his subordinates, Uthman retired from public life and appointed his son, Muhammad Bello, ruler of the eastern region, the capital of which was Sokoto. Uthman gave the western region to Abd Allah. The capital of this region was Gwandu, in Kebbi. Abd Allah recorded the hijra and the jihad in prose and verse in his* Tazyin al-Waraqat.

SECTION CONCERNING THE CAUSES OF OUR HIJRA, AND OUR HOLY WAR, AND VERSES ABOUT ITS BATTLES

Now when the kings and their helpers saw the *Shaikh's* community making ready their weapons, they feared that. Moreover, before that the numerousness of the community, and its cutting itself off from their jurisdiction had enraged them. They made their enmity known with their tongues, threatening the community with *razzias* [raids—ed.] and extermination, and what their breasts hid was worse than that. They began to forbid what they heard concerning the dress of the community, such as the turbans, and the order that the women should veil. Some of the community feared their threats, namely the people of our brother Abd al-Salam, and they emigrated before us to a place in Kebbi called Ghimbana.[1] Then the Sultan of Ghubir sent word to them, that

they should return, and they refused. Then that Sultan sent word to the *shaikh,* that he should travel to him, and we set out to (visit?) him. His intention was to destroy us, but God did not give him power over us, and when we went into his presence in his castle, he came towards us, we being three; the *shaikh,* myself, and Umar al-Kammawi,[2] the *shaikh's* friend. He fired his naphtha[3] in order to burn us with its fire, but the fire turned back on him, and nearly burnt him while we were watching him; and not one of us moved, but he retreated hastily. Then he turned back to us after a while, and sat near to us. We approached him, and spoke to him. He said to us: "Know that I have no enemy on the earth like you," and he made clear to us his enmity, and we made clear to him that we did not fear him, for God had not given him power over us. Then he said concerning that which God

From Abd Allah ibn Muhammad, *Tazyin al-Waraqat,* trans. from the Arabic and edited by M. Hiskett (Ibadan: Ibadan University Press, 1963), pp. 107–117. Reprinted by permission.

[1] Gimbama.

[2] "The Kammaite"; there is a Kamma in Bornu.
[3] Professor David Ayalon has shown that the term *naft* in the Arabic sources came to mean "gunpowder" or "firearm" and not "naphtha" as early as the fourteenth century, and continued to be used in this sense until the Ottoman conquest. . . .

had ordained him to say, such as I am not now able to relate. God kept him back from us, and we went away from him to our house, and none knew anything of that (affair) other than we ourselves. And the *shaikh* said to us, "Both of you conceal this, and pray God Most High on our behalf that we may never again meet with this unbeliever." He prayed for that, and we said "Amen" to it.

Then we returned to our country, and (the Sultan of Ghubir) dispatched an army after that against the community of Abd al-Salam, and it attacked them, and some of the Muslims were killed, and some were taken prisoner, and the rest of them scattered in the country of Kebbi. Now this increased him in pride and arrogance, and he, and those who followed him from among the people of his country, unbelievers and evil-doers, began to threaten us with the like of that until the Sultan sent word to the *shaikh* that he should go away from his community and leave them for a far place, he together with his family, alone. The *shaikh* sent word to him (saying) "I will not forsake my community, but I will leave your country, for God's earth is wide!" Then we made ready to emigrate, and he sent word to the *shaikh* that he should not leave his place. The *shaikh* refused, and we emigrated to a place on the far borders of his lands, in the desert places, called Qudu,[4] (with *damma* on the *qaf* and *dal*). Then (the Sultan) ordered the governors of his towns to take captive all who travelled to the *shaikh,* and they began to persecute the Muslims, killing them and confiscating their property. Then the affair came to the point where they were sending armies against us, and we gathered together when that became serious, and appointed the *shaikh,* who had previously been our *imam* and our *amir,* as our commander, in order that he might put our affairs in order, and I, praise be to

God, was the first who pledged obedience to him, in accordance with the Book [5] and the *sunna.* Then we built [6] a fortress there; after that we began to revenge ourselves upon those who raided us, and we raided them, and conquered the fortress [7] of Matankari,[8] then the fortress of the Sultan of Kunni.[9] Then the Sultan of Ghubir, Yunfa, came against us, having collected armies of Nubians and Touareg, and the Fulani who followed him such as none knows except God. The Commander of the Believers dispatched for us an army against him, and appointed me to command it. We met (Yunfa) in a place called Qurdam near to a stretch of water here called Kutu (spelt with *kaf* and *ta* taking the *damma* which gives one vowel the scent of another). God routed his armies by His favour and grace, and to Him be the praise, and the thanks. We took booty from their property, and we killed them, and drove them away. Then we returned to the *shaikh* safely, and I composed verses concerning this, which are:

I have commenced with the praise of God,
  and thanksgiving follows it
For the overcoming of the unbelievers
  gathered against us
To uproot Islam and the Muslims from
  their country;
But God is wider in grace!
Touareg, with Qubir, and Yunfa was their
  foolish one,
He mustered them, but God sees and
  hears.
And when they came to Ghunghunghi,[10]
  they destroyed what was in it,
By burning and laying waste, and captives

---

[4] The description "in the desert places" would fit with a place in the area of Barikin Daji.

[5] A reference to *Quran,* IV, 62.
[6] *Hafarna*—lit. "we dug": the reference is to the digging of earth to build the mud walls with which Sudanese towns are fortified.
[7] The word *hisn* as used by Abdullah probably means simply "walled town."
[8] There are seven places called Matankiri in the Sokoto area!
[9] Birnin Koni (?), in present French territory.
[10] Birnin Gungunge. A town in Kebbi.

were cut to pieces.

They searched out the thickets of Bajuwwi in which they slaughtered

Bands of nomads, and their property was gathered up.

This increased them in unbelief, and they increased in pride.

Upon (their horses) were saddle-cloths, their crests raised up,

And (they themselves) wore fine clothes which made them conceited.

Their horses paced haughtily, their spears couched.

Then I said, and my good omen was as a thing made certain to me

"*Sayunfa Yunfa*"; [11] he will return with disgrace.

We waited for them in intermediate places,

For three days, and another day made four.

Now when we saw their faint-heartedness in the face of our forces

We advanced towards them, the flag raised.

Someone said to us "They have gone towards Kutu, to westward of you.

In order to turn you back towards the east, and in order to gather together."

I said, "Escape! Do not let them get before us to our families."

On the tenth of Rabi—its full moon was rising,

We came to our families, and I passed by my house [12]

Without resting in it, while the people were slumbering,

And there were with me only a few who obeyed me

In setting out after fatigue, and (while) hunger was burning.

Now when we saw the dawn, its light shining,

We dismounted, and prayed until (the people) gathered.

Then we set out for Ghurdam, and our muster was complete

A little before midday, and the army was drawn up in battle order.

Then we drove away the forces of unbelief from their water source,

And they had thought that their army was as two of ours! Give heed!

They thought that the place of the thicket would overcome our army,

And that the hills were their helpers, (who would) be useful.

They fled towards them, then they lined up, and made their drums speak

While the (Muslim) army drew near, and followed (them)

Until (when) we saw each other, and came ever closer

They opened fire, and we opened fire on them, and they turned and dispersed,

And there was nothing, except that I saw that their waterless cloud

Had cleared away from the sun of Islam (which was) shining

By the help of Him who helped the Prophet against the foe

At Badr, with an army of angels gathered together.

And many a great man our hands flung down,

And axes cleft his head, split asunder.

And many a brave warrior did our arrows strike down,

And our swords; birds and hyenas cover him;

We drove them off in the middle of the day,

And they had nothing but the thicket for shelter in the darkness of the night.

And their Yunfa joined his midday and his evening prayers at Rima [13]

Performing them by signs, while the sun was rising.

To every side his army had scattered apart.

To the Day of Gathering Together [14] they will not be re-united!

They left to us, against their will, their wealth and their women.

---

[11] "Yunfa shall be driven away."
[12] At Gudu?

[13] The River Rima.
[14] I.e., the Day of Resurrection.

And God gives, and withholds!
And we are an army victorious in Islam,
And we are proud of nothing but that.
Tribes of Islam—and Turubbi is our clan
Our Fulani and our Hausa all united,
And among us other than these, certain
tribes joined together
For the help of God's religion—made up
the union.
And Turubbi are the maternal uncles of
the Fulani,
Brothers to the Arabs, and from Rumb.
Is they are sprung.
And Uqba is the ancestor of the Fulani
on the Arab side,
And from Turubbi their mother was Baj-
jumanghu: give heed!
Ask those who fought at Matankari about
them,
And at Kunni and Rima; the truth of the
affair will be heard.
O community of Islam, strive and wage
Holy War
And do not be weak, for patience comes
home to victory!
Your slain are in Paradise for ever,
And he who returns returns with glory
and wealth.
None can destroy what the hand of God
has built.
None can turn back the command [15] of
God if it comes.
God's promise has been completed and
the victory of His religion:
There remains nothing but thanks to
Him, and humble prayer.

　　Then after this *qasida* I composed
another *qasida* which I sent to my two
brothers Dadi and Zayd when they did
not emigrate with us, but remained
among the unbelievers. I warned them
about that, and informed them of what we
had achieved, urging them to emigrate,
and I said:

O who will convey from me to Dadi
And Zayd, and all who dwell in the

[15] Or "the affair."

towns,
Friends of the unbelievers, from fear of
loss of wealth,
And from hope of security from the cor-
rupt,
That there do not remain between the
Muslims and you
The signs of love.
You deserted the army of Islam openly,
Content to help the foe.
You forgot what you had read in the
Book.
For that reason you missed the straight
way.
Do not the verses *an yathqafukum,* [16]
Wala yalunakum [17] suffice you in this
aim?
Thus also *la tajid,* [18] *la yattakhidhuna* [19]
Up to *bura minkum;* [20] *yaibad* [21]
(These are) indeed comprehensive;
Wa lau kanu [22] and the commencement
Of *baraa* [23] therefore know the direction
of right!
We have no words for one who communi-
cates with them,
Their love is like a desert, that is apparent.

[16] *Quran,* LX, 2ff.: "If they come on you, they will
be enemies to you, and stretch against you their
hands, and their tongues, to do you evil, and they
wish that you may disbelieve."
[17] Ib., III, 114: "O believers, take not for your inti-
mates outside yourselves; such men spare nothing
to ruin you. . . ."
[18] Ib., LVIII, 22: "thou shalt not find any people who
believe in God and the Last Day who are loving to
anyone who opposes God and His Messenger, not
though they were their fathers, or their sons, or their
brothers, or their clan. . . ."
[19] Ib., LX, 1: "O believers, take not My enemy and
your enemy for friends. . . ."
[20] Ib., LX, 4: "You have had a good example in
Abraham, and those with him, when they said to
their people, 'We are quit of you, and that you serve,
apart from God'. . . ."
[21] There are several possible references: ib., XXIX,
56, is the most likely, "O my servants who believe,
surely My earth is wide. . . ." There is also a pun
on *wasia.*
[22] Ib., v, 84: "Yet had they believed in God, and the
Prophet and what has been sent down to him, they
would not have taken them as friends. . . ."
[23] Ib., IX, 1 f.: "An acquittal, from God and His Messenger unto the idolaters with whom you made
covenant. . . . God is quit, and His Messenger, of
the idolaters. So, if you repent, that will be better
for you; but if you turn your backs, know that you
cannot frustrate the will of God."

And do not ask concerning those who
have gone astray

Like he of the She Camel, the origin of
corruption.

He has turned back from greatness, hat-
ing religion.

He was their qudari,[24] and they were like
Ad

And indeed we are in a country in which

There is no rule other than that of God
over (His) servants.

The Commander of the Believers is our
commander,

And we have become, all of us, the people
of Holy War.

We fight in the way of god, always.

And we kill the unbelievers and the obstinate.

Ask concerning us, the place where we
clashed at Ghingha[25]

Matankari, Kunni in the days of the
fighting.

Ask the scoundrel of Qubir, Yunfa,

Was he not driven away from among the
nomads

When he had collected armies to cut off
religion

And cried out in the towns at every meeting place?

Upon them were ample suits of armour,

And beneath them excellent long-necked
horses.

They came slaying, and taking the Muslims prisoner, desiring corruption.

And we came upon them on Thursday

At Qurdam before midday, in the high
places;

And they had spitted meats around the
fire,

And gathered ready in tents

Fine vestments in a chest,

And all kinds of carpets, with cushions.

And do not ask about wheaten cake

Mixed with ghee and honey among the
provisions!

Nothing frightened them as they slept in
luxury

Save the tread of foot-soldiers and fine
horses.

They rose up, and made everything ready
for war.

Then they formed up in ranks according
to size.

Our banner began to draw near to them,

And it seemed to them like an ogre in
striped clothing.

We fired at them, and they fired naphtha.

Their fire became like ashes (and it was)

As if their arrows had no heads to them;

And as if their swords were in the hands
of inanimate things;

As if their lances were in the hands of the
blind.

They turned in flight, without provision,

And their army was scattered, and they
were thirsty,

Confused like young locusts.

We slew them, and collected all their
wealth

Which they had left strewn in the valley.

We killed Kabughi,[26] and also Namad-
ghi;[27]

Thus (also) Waru al-Qiyama[28] in the beginning (of the battle).

Thus (also) others like them one by one,
and all scoundrels,

And the most wretched of them was
Maghadi[29]

And Yunfa fled headlong,

Running before his horsemen, who fled in
disorder.

His clinging to the mane of his charger

Saved him from the death decreed.

The darkness of the night became fortresses for him.

He passed the night, without tasting the
taste of sleep.

His horsemen were (like) brides in garments of silk,

[24] It was Qudar who rashly slew the miraculous she-
camel sent by God as a sign to the Prophet Salih.
[25] Ginga. Barth mentions a "Ginnega" and a "Gin-
gawa," both towns of Kebbi.

[26] A notable of Gobir.
[27] A notable of Gobir.
[28] "Waru of the Resurrection" because he had slain
so many men! Alhaji Abubakar tells me that this
is not the same Waru who played a prominent part
in the Abd al-Salam incident.
[29] Magaji. A Hausa title—"mayor," "chief of a
town."

Sticking to their horses like tick(s).
They thought the thicket of Bajuwwi [30] palaces,
And cared nothing for thorns or prickles.
No sound clothing did they retain;
All was torn to rags in the low ground.
They will not return to fight us
In that place to the Day of Resurrection!
O deliver to Abu al-Hasan b. Ahmad [31]
A message, making clear the intention
That we will collect armies for Holy War
From the Niger even to Watadi [32]
Which will alight with their front at Ghazik [33]
While their two wings will cover Watafa up to Qaladi.[34]
They will cheer every man of honest heart,
And grieve every unbelieving heart.
Verily God will make his helpers victorious
Through a promise which comes from the Lord of men.
The promise of God is fulfilled in the victory of religion,
There is nothing for us but to give thanks for assistance.

Now when God had driven away the Sultan of Ghubir and his army, we began to raid them, while they did not raid us. This angered all the kings in Hausa, and humiliated them. Then they began to persecute the Muslims who were in their midst so that the Muslims fled to a far place. Then they fought them, and God gave us victory over the country of the Amir of Kabi, and we moved to (Kabi) about a month after the defeat of Yunfa. We then returned after about two months to the country of Ghubir, and we conquered certain towns in it which will be mentioned, if God wills, in the *qasida,* "The Army of the Conquests." Then the Commander of the Believers fitted out an army and gave me command over it against the fortress of the Amir of Ghubir, al-Qadawa.[35] We arrived there, and attacked them fiercely three times from all sides of the fortress. God did not enable us to conquer them at this time. We returned to the *shaikh* when we heard that the Touareg were raiding our families. Now I had been struck in my leg by an arrow at the time of the first battle, and God had made the matter easy for me to bear. When we reached the *shaikh,* he set out with all the community and the families until we arrived at a place called Thunthuwa.[36] The armies of Ghubir gathered together with their Touareg, and made them attack us by surprise. We did not hear them until they were upon us among our families. The community met them and suffered defeat, and more than can be numbered of its noble men suffered martyrdom, among them the standard bearer on that day, our brother Muhammad Sad b. al-Hasan, famous by the nickname of Sadar, and the Imam Muhammad Thanbu b. Abd al-Rahman, and Zayd b. Muhammad Sad, and others. Now on that day I was not able to rise up on account of the arrow wound in my leg, but when defeat came to us, I rose up lame and confronted the fugitives, chiding them. Some of them followed me until we came upon the first of the enemy, who were killing and taking booty. I formed those who were with me into ranks, and we fired one volley at them. They turned back towards their main body, and not one stood his ground. God by His power drove them off, and we followed them. News of this defeat reached the *shaikh,* and he mounted and followed us. He arrived, but God had driven off the enemy.

Then after that we set out until we came near to the fortress of al-Qadawa, and we besieged them for about a month.

[30] Bujaye, near Kwotto (?).
[31] A Touareg leader who fought against the Shehu (on the authority of Alhaji Abubakar Gumi).
[32] Said to be a lake called Wadadi in Gobir.
[33] Said to be a place in present French territory: Arziki (?).
[34] Galadi (?).

[35] Alkalawa. Oral tradition places this on the River Rima, near to the present Sabon Birni.
[36] Tsuntsuwa. Arnett places it S. of Alkalawa.

Then when hunger bore heavily upon the community we set out for the country of Zanfara,[37] and God enabled us to take it without fighting, and we reached it at the end of the (first) year of our *hijra*[38] in the month of Dhu al-Qada. When we had celebrated the Id al-Adha we made ready to escort the Amir of Kabi who had accepted Islam, he and those with him, and he followed our community until we returned with him to that place in which we had encamped, namely Sabun Ghari,[39] in order that I should bring him back to his place, and that we should then wage Holy War against the town of the Sultan of Kabi who had refused to follow. I prepared an army for this—the "Army of the Conquests." We set out with those who followed us, and the people of the country of the Sultan of Qumi[40] met us in battle, from their fortress called Kunda[41] towards the further side of his territories. And we left no fortress of his which we did not conquer. Then the Sultan of Qumi sought a truce from us. We granted him a truce in his fortress only, on condition that I, when I returned from raiding, should travel with him to the Commander of Believers.

Thus it happened, and God conquered for us more than twenty fortresses, among them the fortress of the Sultan of Kabi.[42] They will be enumerated in the poem. We returned in safety with booty, with praise to God. Before our return from raiding I said:

I remembered, (and remembrance moves one who is far away

To grief, and in remembrance blows the gentle breeze of love),

My companions have died in the Holy War and elsewhere,

And I am far from my *shaikh,* and grief has made me sleepless.

Who will convey from me to my sons and brothers,

To my family and to my neighbours and those who dwell with them,

The news that I and Danda[43] together with Ali[44] and our army,

And our horsemen in victory and glory and satisfaction,

Have conquered fortresses between Qunda and Kunduta,

More than twenty, with force and might. We made peace reluctantly with others than these.

They accepted Islam outwardly, and God knows what is within!

The three Kundas, Lima, Masu and Kulkulu[45]

And Zima Falam, the two forts of Dunka which have become ruined.

And Bandha and the two fortresses of Ghinbana, Rumu, Ghifuru

And the two forts of Maghadhin—Kada Matati in the desert places,

and Zawru, Ghaqi, Randali; then the big towns,

And Laylaba from which Kunduta fled away and escaped.

And on the twelfth of Muharram[46] we conquered

The big fortress, the fortress of Fudi,[47] who was led astray,

The Qudari of the Kabawa;[48] then he fled at noon

With his horsemen towards the north, among the hills,

And he left in that fortress wealth as if it

[37] The former state of Zanfara, lying S.E. of Gobir: roughly the area of present eastern Sokoto and western Katsina.
[38] The *hijra* commenced on 10 Dhu al-Qada 1218/21 February 1804, *InfM.* Abdullah therefore reached Zanfara at some time in February 1805.
[39] Sabon Gari. Brass sites this S. of Sherabi on the Gulbin Ka. The present Sabon Gari is on the W. bank of the Niger.
[40] Gumi.
[41] Brass locates this north of the River Jega (i.e. Zanfara).
[42] Namely, Birnin Kebbi.

[43] The name of his horse; *danda* is a horse which has white on at least four of the five points, head, and feet.
[44] Alhaji Abubakar thinks this was the name of Abdullah's servant.
[45] Possibly Kokilo, deserted in Barth's time.
[46] First month of Muslim year (ed.).
[47] The emir of Kebbi, Hodi, son of Tarana.
[48] The Kebbi people.

were Qarun's!

He took no provision for the wilderness.

Were it not for the net of the Sharia,

And the chain of manliness each of us
would have satisfied himself with what
(ever) he desired.[49]

Our army was called the "Army of the
Conquests," and all of us

Collected what he could of the booty of
the conquests.

Nothing grieved our hearts in religion,

Or in the world save the sadness of being
far away

And the loss of noble loved ones who followed one another

To the Gardens of Eternity at al-Qirari
and Thunthuwa.

Whenever I remember the *Imam* and his
party

Seas of rancour surge in my heart.

And if that makes Ghubir and the Touareg happy,

Then war has varied chances! Our place
of returning is not the same!

Those of them who were slain are in Hell
for ever,

And those who are in the Gardens of
Eternity are not their like!

Nevertheless, how many a day at Kunni,
Matankari,

And Ghurdam, and Tan Ghida [50] and the
day of Taghuwa,

And Rima, all, then Bumburmi after it,

And Buri [51] they tasted many kinds of destruction!

The army of our people marched to al-
Qadawa

And surrounded it, and war is an evil dispute!

You saw nought but angry and enraged
men

Cauterizing other's (wounds) when drawing out the arrows, or being cauterized.

By God, were it not for a deep ditch, and
a high building

They would have become as motes of dust
in a crack in a wall!

We went to them with our families and
our wealth.

We besieged them for a month, our huts
before their gates,

And there remained not a house between
Rima and their fortress.

But Mazum and Mazuzi [52] were not
ruined because of that.

They left for us their victuals and their
towns.

We were building huts between Zirwa [53]
and Tan Ruwa;

Many a day they came to us for the fight,
and retreated.

We fought them from the hill of Masu to
Danbawa; [53]

Many a time they came by night and then
dispersed,

And there was not one among them
turned for refuge in the same direction
as his companion!

And on another occasion they came upon
me while I was one of five,

Then they turned back, and they did not
obtain what their people desired.

Many times they came together, and
sometimes they came divided

From east and west. Then that which had
led them astray, failed them.

There was never an hour but a cry for help
caused our ears to ring;

Then we would meet them swiftly, without delay,

On close-cropped mares and tall close-
cropped stallions,

You would think it a yellow locust when
it rose up;

It was accustomed to morning raids.

You would imagine it, when it galloped,
to be above the hills, flying in the air.

When they saw that we were not wearied
in our Holy War

By killing and being taken prisoner, most
of them feared and ceased what they

---

[49] This suggests that there was some friction over
the division of booty according to the Sharia.
[50] Dan Gida.
[51] Bore, on the Gulbin-Sokoto, but deserted in
Barth's time.

[52] Possibly Mazoji. The sense of this line is obscure.
[53] Said to be villages in eastern Sokoto, in the district of Hammali.

had been doing.

And they fled to various countries, and
their community

Imitated the community of people who

were in Saba.[54]

To God be praise, first and last.

My poem is finished, and it is sweet to him
who relates it.

[54] Sheba, see *Quran,* XXXIV, 14.

9 AL-KANAMI
THE CASE AGAINST THE JIHAD

*In the late eighteenth century a Muslim cleric, Uthman dan Fodio, began to preach in
the Hausa state of Gobir against religious corruption and pagan practices. Although the
Sarki (King) of Gobir sought to counter the teachings of Uthman dan Fodio, he only
provoked him to declare a* jihad *or holy war against the unbelievers in 1802. Thereafter,
Uthman's Fulani followers defeated the Hausa armies, captured the Hausa city-states,
and replaced the Hausa rulers. In 1805 Uthman's lieutenants carried the* jihad *into the
Muslim state of Bornu, defeated the armies of the* mai, *or king, and convinced his
councillors to request assistance from Muhammad al-Amin ibn Muhammad Ninga, more
commonly known as Sheik al-Kanami. Al-Kanami was born in the Fezzan and studied
in Cairo and Medina; upon his return to Kanem, he won a great following as a result of
his piety, scholarship, and charisma. Rallying his army, he marched into Bornu, drove
out the Fulani, and recaptured Ngazargamu, the capital. During the war he wrote a series
of letters to Muhammad Bello, successor to Uthman dan Fodio, in an attempt to understand why the Fulani should attack fellow Muslims. Sheik al-Kanami continued to govern
Bornu until his death in 1835.*

Praise be to God, Opener of the doors
of guidance, Giver of the means of happiness. Prayer and peace be on him who
was sent with the liberal religion, and on
his people who prepared the way for the
observance of His law, and interpreted
it.[1]

From Thomas Hodgkin, *Nigerian Perspectives* (London: Oxford University Press, 1960), pp. 198–201.
Reprinted by permission.

[1] Further extracts from Muhammad Bello, *Infaq al-
maysur,* Whitting edition, London, 1951, pp. 124–7,
142–4, 150, and 157, translated by Mr. Charles
Smith. I am much indebted to Mr. Smith, not only
for his translation, but also for advice about the
historical significance of the whole lengthy al-
Kanami–Bello correspondence, from which these
brief extracts are taken. The interest of this correspondence lies in the light it throws on the relations
between the rulers of Sokoto and Bornu after the
Fulani *jihad;* on the methods of diplomacy of the
period; and on the political standpoints and characters of the two principals. Copies of nine letters
were published by Muhammad Bello in *Infaq al-
maysur,* one from al-Kanami to Bello, five from
Bello to al-Kanami, two from Uthman dan Fodio to
al-Kanami, and one from al-Kanami to Uthman.
Not all of Bello's letters appear to have been delivered. All belong to the period before 1813. The first
of the extracts translated here is taken from letter

No. 1 in *Infaq,* an early letter of al-Kanami, written
after the sack of Ngazargamu, the Bornu capital, by
the Fulani under Gwani Mukhtar and their subsequent expulsion by al-Kanami. The second extract
comes from letter No. 5 in *Infaq,* an apparently
much later letter from Bello, which counters arguments put forward by al-Kanami in No. 1. Mr.
Smith describes this letter as "a remarkable testimony to the literary leanings of Bello," and containing "evidence of his wide reading of the Islamic
classics."

The correspondence ranges over the main questions in dispute between Bello and al-Kanami, i.e.
between Sokoto and Bornu. Was the Fulani *jihad*
justifiable on accepted Muslim principles? That is
to say, was it conducted against states which were
in the strict sense "pagan" (*kafir*), and therefore *dar
al-harb,* not *dar al-Islam?* Was Bornu in fact such a
state? Were there appropriate precedents for such
a *Jihad?* (Muhammad Bello argued at length that
the actions of another reforming ruler, Muhammad
Askia of Gao, three centuries previously, were in
fact a precedent.) Was its real purpose the spreading of the frontiers of Islam, not of Fulani imperial
power? Had the *jihad* been conducted according to
the strict rules which ought to be applied in such
cases, or had there been excesses? Had the Fulani
been the aggressors, or had Bornu, by allying itself
with supposedly pagan Hausa governments, been
responsible for provoking the conflict? In the extracts quoted here the main issue under discussion
is whether Bornu at the time of the *jihad* could properly be described as a land of paganism (*dar kufr*).

From him who is filthy with the dust of sin, wrapped in the cloak of shame, base and contemptible, Muhammad al-Amin ibn Muhammad al-Kanami to the Fulani *"ulama"* and their chiefs. Peace be on him who follows His guidance.

The reason for writing this letter is that when fate brought me to this country, I found the fire which was blazing between you and the people of the land. I asked the reason, and it was given as injustice by some and as religion by others. So according to our decision in the matter I wrote to those of your brothers who live near to us asking them the reason and instigation of their transgression, and they returned me a weak answer, not such as comes from an intelligent man, much less from a learned person, let alone a reformer. They listed the names of books, and we examined some of them, but we do not understand from them the things which they apparently understood. Then, while we were still perplexed, some of them attacked our capital, and the neighbouring Fulani came and camped near us. So we wrote to them a second time beseeching them in the name of God and Islam to desist from their evil doing. But they refused and attacked us. So, when our land was thus confined and we found no place even to dwell in, we rose in defence of ourselves, praying God to deliver us from the evil of their deeds; and we did what we did. Then when we found some respite, we desisted, and for the future God is all-knowing.

We believe in writing; even if it makes no impression on you, it is better than silence. Know that if an intelligent man accepts some question in order to understand it, he will give a straightforward answer to it.

Tell us therefore why you are fighting us and enslaving our free people. If you say that you have done this to us because of our paganism, then I say that we are innocent of paganism, and it is far from our compound. If praying and the giving of alms, knowledge of God, fasting in Ramadan and the building of mosques is paganism, what is Islam? These buildings in which you have been standing of a Friday, are they churches or synagogues or fire temples? If they were other than Muslim places of worship, then you would not pray in them when you capture them. Is this not a contradiction?

Among the biggest of your arguments for the paganism of the believers generally is the practice of the amirs of riding to certain places for the purpose of making alms-giving sacrifices there; the uncovering of the heads of free women; the taking of bribes; embezzlement of the property of orphans; oppression in the courts. But these five charges do not require you to do the things you are doing. As for this practice of the amirs, it is a disgraceful heresy and certainly blameworthy. It must be forbidden and disapproval of its perpetrators must be shown. But those who are guilty of it do not thereby become pagans; since not one of them claims that it is particularly efficacious, or intends by it to associate anything with God. On the contrary, the extent of their pretence is their ignorant idea that alms given in this way are better than otherwise. He who is versed in the books of *fiqh* [Muslim theology—ed.], and has paid attention to the talk of the imams in their disputation—when deviation from the right road in matters of burial and slaughter are spoken of—will know the test of what we have said. Consider Damietta, a great Islamic city between Egypt and Syria, a place of learning and Islam: in it there is a tree, and the common people do to this tree as did the non-Arabs. But not one of the *"ulama"* rises to fight them or has spoken of their paganism.

As for uncovering the head in free women, this is also *haram* [forbidden —ed.], and the *Quran* has prohibited it. But she who does it does not thereby become a pagan. It is denial which leads to paganism. Failing to do something while believing in it is rather to be described as disobedience requiring immediate repentance. If a free woman has prayed with the head uncovered, and the time passes, but she does not repeat the prayer in accordance with what we know they say in the books of *fiqh,* surely you do not believe that her prayer is not proper because she has thereby become a pagan?

The taking of bribes, embezzlement of the property of orphans and injustice in the courts are all major sins which God has forbidden. But sin does not make anyone a pagan when he has confessed his faith. And if you had ordered the right and forbidden the wrong, and retired when the people did not desist, it would have been better than these present doings. If ordering and forbidding are confined within their proper limits, they do not lead to anything more serious. But your forbidding has involved you in sin, and brought evil on you and the Muslims in this world and the next. . . .

Since acts of immorality and disobedience without number have long been committed in all countries, then Egypt is like Bornu, only worse. So also is Syria and all the cities of Islam. There has been corruption, embezzlement of the property of orphans, oppression and heresy in these places from the time of the Bani Umayya [the Umayyad dynasty] right down to our own day. No age and no country is free from its share of heresy and sin. If, thereby, they all become pagan, then surely their books are useless. So how can you construct arguments based on what they say who are infidel according to you? Refuge from violence and discord in religion is with God. . . .

We have indeed heard of things in the character of the Shaikh Uthman ibn Fudi, and seen things in his writings which are contrary to what you have done. If this business does originate from him, then I say that there is no power nor might save through God, the most high, the most glorious. Indeed we thought well of him. But now, as the saying is, we love the Shaikh and the truth when they agree. But if they disagree it is the truth which comes first. We pray God to preserve us from being those of whom he said:

Say: "Shall we tell you who will be the greatest losers in their works?
Those whose striving goes astray in the present life, while they think that they are working good deeds." [2]

And from being those of whom he also said:

But they split in their affair between them into sects, each party rejoicing in what is with them. [3]

Peace.

[2] *Quran,* Sura 18, verses 103–4. This and the three following quotations from the *Quran* are taken from the English renderings of A. J. Arberry, in *The Koran Interpreted,* London, 1955.
[3] *Quran,* Sura 23, verse 55.

10 MUNGO PARK
THE NIGER AT SEGU

Before the nineteenth century, Europe's knowledge of the interior of West Africa was confused and fragmentary. The Europeans had learned from the Arabs that great cities existed in the western Sudan whose reputations for wealth seemed confirmed by the profits and goods of the trans-Saharan trade. The city of Timbuktu became synonymous with the mystery of unknown Africa in an age of Romanticism in Europe—a mystery that was deepened by Arab reports of a great river comparable with the Nile, on which were located several bustling and prosperous commercial centers. Yet no European had seen this river, its source, or its outlet. A few thought the river to be the source of the Nile. A more common assumption was that this river, the Niger, rose in the east and flowed westward, where its branches formed the Senegal, Gambia, and Jeba rivers. No one connected the Oil Rivers, which entered the Bight of Biafra, with the delta of the Niger. The mystery of the Niger stimulated not only scientific inquiry but also the idea that perhaps the river would turn out to be a highway into the commercial centers of the interior. Under the auspices of the African Association, a group of wealthy London men interested in geography and commerce, three expeditions were sent inland between 1788 and 1793. All three failed. A fourth was undertaken by a young Scottish doctor, Mungo Park, who marched into the interior from the Gambia River at the end of 1795. On July 20, 1796, he reached the Niger at Segu and described in his journal that dramatic moment when he saw the Niger flowing to the east. Park had opened the way to the western Sudan. He was one of the first to seek to exploit his discovery. In 1805 he returned to the Niger to follow the river to its mouth but was tragically drowned in the Bussa Rapids.

Departing from thence, we passed several large villages, where I was constantly taken for a Moor, and became the subject of much merriment to the Bambarrans; who, seeing me drive my horse before me, laughed heartily at my appearance.—He has been at Mecca, says one; you may see that by his clothes: another asked me if my horse was sick; a third wished to purchase it, &c.; so that I believe the very slaves were ashamed to be seen in my company. Just before it was dark, we took up our lodging for the night at a small village, where I procured some victuals for myself, and some corn for my horse, at the moderate price of a button; and was told that I should see the Niger (which the Negroes call Joliba, or *the great water*), early the next day. The lions are here very numerous: the gates are shut a little after sunset, and nobody allowed to go out. The thoughts of seeing the Niger in the morning, and the troublesome buzzing of musketoes, prevented me from shutting my eyes during the night; and I had saddled my horse, and was in readiness before daylight; but, on account of the wild beasts, we were obliged to wait until the people were stirring, and the gates

From Mungo Park, *Travels in the Interior Districts of Africa: Performed under the Direction and Patronage of the African Association in the Years 1795, 1796, and 1797* (London, 1799), pp.193–198.

opened. This happened to be a market-day at Sego, and the roads were every where filled with people, carrying different articles to sell. We passed four large villages, and at eight o'clock saw the smoke over Sego.

As we approached the town, I was fortunate enough to overtake the fugitive Kaartans, to whose kindness I had been so much indebted in my journey through Bambarra. They readily agreed to introduce me to the king; and we rode together through some marshy ground, where, as I was anxiously looking around for the river, one of them called out, *geo affilli* (see the water); and looking forwards, I saw with infinite pleasure the great object of my mission; the long sought for, majestic Niger, glittering to the morning sun, as broad as the Thames at Westminster, and flowing slowly *to the eastward*. I hastened to the brink, and, having drank of the water, lifted up my fervent thanks in prayer, to the Great Ruler of all things, for having thus far crowned my endeavours with success.

The circumstance of the Niger's flowing towards the east, and its collateral points, did not, however, excite my surprise; for although I had left Europe in great hesitation on this subject, and rather believed that it ran in the contrary direction, I had made such frequent inquiries during my progress, concerning this river; and received from Negroes of different nations, such clear and decisive assurances that its general course was *towards the rising sun,* as scarce left any doubt on my mind; and more especially as I knew that Major Houghton [who traveled inland from the Gambia between 1790 and 1791 to die near Nioro in the Republic of Mali —ed.] had collected similar information, in the same manner.

Sego, the capital of Bambarra, at which I had now arrived, consists, properly speaking, of four distinct towns; two on the northern bank of the Niger, called Sego Korro, and Sego Boo; and two on the southern bank, called Sego Soo Korro, and Sego See Korro. They are all surrounded with high mud-walls; the houses are built of clay, of a square form, with flat roofs; some of them have two stories, and many of them are whitewashed. Besides these buildings, Moorish mosques are seen in every quarter; and the streets, though narrow, are broad enough for every useful purpose, in a country where wheel carriages are entirely unknown. From the best inquiries I could make, I have reason to believe that Sego contains altogether about thirty thousand inhabitants. The King of Bambarra constantly resides at Sego See Korro; he employs a great many slaves in conveying people over the river, and the money they receive (though the fare is only ten Kowrie shells for each individual) furnishes a considerable revenue to the king, in the course of a year. The canoes are of a singular construction, each of them being formed of the trunks of two large trees, rendered concave, and joined together, not side by side, but end ways; the junction being exactly across the middle of the canoe; they are therefore very long and disproportionably narrow, and have neither decks nor masts; they are, however, very roomy; for I observed in one of them four horses, and several people, crossing over the river. When we arrived at this ferry, we found a great number waiting for a passage; they

looked at me with silent wonder, and I distinguished, with concern, many Moors among them. There were three different places of embarkation, and the ferrymen were very diligent and expeditious; but, from the crowd of people, I could not immediately obtain a passage; and sat down upon the bank of the river, to wait for a more favorable opportunity. The view of this extensive city; the numerous canoes upon the river; the crowded population, and the cultivated state of the surrounding country, formed altogether a prospect of civilization and magnificence, which I little expected to find in the bosom of Africa.

I waited more than two hours, without having an opportunity of crossing the river; during which time the people who had crossed, carried information to Mansong the King, that a white man was waiting for a passage, and was coming to see him. He immediately sent over one of his chief men, who informed me that the king could not possibly see me, until he knew what had brought me into his country; and that I must not presume to cross the river without the king's permission. He therefore advised me to lodge at a distant village, to which he pointed, for the night; and said that in the morning he would give me further instructions how to conduct myself. This was very discouraging. However, as there was no remedy, I set off for the village; where I found, to my great mortification, that no person would admit me into his house. I was regarded with astonishment and fear, and was obliged to sit all day without victuals, in the shade of a tree; and the night threatened to be very uncomfortable, for the wind rose, and there was great appearance of a heavy rain; and the wild beasts are so very numerous in the neighbourhood, that I should have been under the necessity of climbing up the tree, and resting amongst the branches. About sunset, however, as I was preparing to pass the night in this manner, and had turned my horse loose, that he might graze at liberty, a woman, returning from the labours of the field, stopped to observe me, and perceiving that I was weary and dejected, inquired into my situation, which I briefly explained to her; whereupon, with looks of great compassion, she took up my saddle and bridle, and told me to follow her. Having conducted me into her hut, she lighted up a lamp, spread a mat on the floor, and told me I might remain there for the night. Finding that I was very hungry, she said she would procure me something to eat. She accordingly went out, and returned in a short time with a very fine fish; which, having caused to be half broiled upon some embers, she gave me for supper. The rites of hospitality being thus performed towards a stranger in distress; my worthy benefactress (pointing to the mat, and telling me I might sleep there without apprehension) called to the female part of her family, who had stood gazing on me all the while in fixed astonishment, to resume their task

of spinning cotton; in which they continued to employ themselves great part of the night. They lightened their labour by songs, one of which was composed extempore; for I was myself the subject of it. It was sung by one of the young women, the rest joining in a sort of chorus. The air was sweet and plaintive, and the words, literally translated, were these. "The winds roared, and the rains fell. The poor white man, faint and weary, came and sat under our tree. He has no mother to bring him milk; no wife to grind his corn. *Chorus.* Let us pity the white man; no mother has he, &c. &c." Trifling as this recital may appear to the reader, to a person in my situation, the circumstance was affecting in the highest degree. I was oppressed by such unexpected kindness; and sleep fled from my eyes. In the morning I presented my compassionate landlady with two of the four brass buttons which remained on my waistcoat; the only recompence I could make her.

11 MAJOR DIXON DENHAM
BORNU AND SHEIK AL-KANAMI

Although Mungo Park had shown the way to the Niger, he drowned in the rapids near Bussa before completing his journey to the river's mouth. The next attempt to reach the Niger was undertaken by an expedition consisting of Dr. Walter Oudney, Major Dixon Denham, and Lieutenant Hugh Clapperton, R.N., who were authorized by the British government in 1822 to reach the Niger by crossing the Sahara along the well-established trade routes. Denham explored the country around Lake Chad, particularly the kingdom of Bornu, where he met Sheik al-Kanami. Oudney and Clapperton continued southwest toward the Niger. Oudney died, but Clapperton reached Kano and Sokoto. Here Sultan Muhammad Bello, successor to Uthman dan Fodio, refused to permit Clapperton to proceed to the river. Clapperton made his way back to Bornu and, accompanied by Denham, returned to England in 1825.

Feb. 16—Halted. Our visitors here were not very numerous, although we

From *Missions to the Niger,* edited by E. W. Bovill (New York: Cambridge University Press, 1966), II, 243–250, 289–291; III, 429–430. Reprinted by permission of Cambridge University Press on behalf of *The Hakluyt Society.*

were not above one hour's journey from the sheikh's residence, Kouka.[1] Various

[1] In the Kanuri language, as in Hausa, *kuka* means the baobab or monkey bread tree, *Adansonia digitata.* Barth, in whose time the town of Kuka had come to be called Kukawa, comments as follows: "Though the town of Kukawa has received its name

were the reports as to the opinion the sheikh formed of the force which accompanied Boo-Khaloom: all agreed, however, that we were to be received at some distance from the town, by a considerable body of troops; both as a compliment to the Bashaw, and to show his representative how well prepared he was against any attempt of those who chose to be his enemies.

One of the Arabs brought to me this day a Balearic crane; it measured thirteen feet from wing to wing.

Feb. 17—This was to us a momentous day, and it seemed to be equally so to our conductors. Notwithstanding all the difficulties that had presented themselves at the various stages of our journey, we were at last within a few short miles of our destination; were about to become acquainted with a people who had never seen, or scarcely heard of, a European; [2] and to tread on ground, the knowledge and true situation of which had hitherto been wholly unknown. These ideas of course excited no common sensations; and could scarcely be unaccompanied by strong hopes of our labours being beneficial to the race amongst whom we were shortly to mix; of our laying the first stone of a work which might lead to their civilization, if not their emancipation from all their prejudices and ignorance, and probably, at the same time, open a field of commerce to our own country, which might increase its wealth and prosperity. Our accounts had been so contradictory of the state of this country, that no opinion could be formed as to the real condition or the numbers of its inhabitants. We had been told that the sheikh's soldiers

were a few ragged negroes armed with spears, who lived upon the plunder of the Black Kaffir countries, by which he was surrounded, and which he was enabled to subdue by the assistance of a few Arabs who were in his service; and, again, we had been assured that his forces were not only numerous, but to a certain degree well trained. The degree of credit which might be attached to these reports was nearly balanced in the scales of probability; and we advanced towards the town of Kouka in a most interesting state of uncertainty, whether we should find its chief at the head of thousands, or be received by him under a tree, surrounded by a few naked slaves.

These doubts, however, were quickly removed. I had ridden on a short distance in front of Boo-Khaloom, with his train of Arabs, all mounted, and dressed out in their best apparel; and, from the thickness of the trees, soon lost sight of them, fancying that the road could not be mistaken. I rode still onwards, and on approaching a spot less thickly planted, was not a little surprised to see in front of me a body of several thousand cavalry drawn up in line, and extending right and left quite as far as I could see; and, checking my horse, I awaited the arrival of my party, under the shade of a widespreading acacia. The Bornou troops remained quite steady, without noise or confusion; and a few horsemen, who were moving about in front giving directions, were the only persons out of the ranks. On the Arabs appearing in sight, a shout, or yell, was given by the sheikh's people, which rent the air: a blast was blown from their rude instruments of music equally loud, and they moved on to meet Boo-Khaloom and his Arabs. There was an appearance of tact and management in their movements which astonished me: three separate small bodies, from the centre and each flank, kept charging rapidly towards us, to within a few feet of our horses' heads, without checking the speed of their own until the moment of their halt, while the

from the circumstance that a young tree of this species was found on the spot where the sheikh Mohammed el Kanemi . . . laid the first foundation of the present town, nevertheless scarcely any kuka is seen for several miles round Kukawa."

[2] Nevertheless, many of them might have seen Hornemann [who reached the Niger in 1800 but later died—ed.], and, as we have seen, there were a good many renegades wandering about northern Africa at this time.

whole body moved onwards. These parties were mounted on small but very perfect horses, who stopped, and wheeled from their utmost speed with great precision and expertness, shaking their spears over their heads, exclaiming, *"Barca! barca! Alla hiakkum cha, alla cheraga!* —Blessing! blessing! Sons of your country! Sons of your country!"* and returning quickly to the front of the body, in order to repeat the charge. While all this was going on, they closed in their right and left flanks, and surrounded the little body of Arab warriors so completely, as to give the compliment of welcoming them very much the appearance of a declaration of their contempt for their weakness. I am quite sure this was premeditated; we were all so closely pressed as to be nearly smothered, and in some danger from the crowding of the horses and clashing of the spears.[3] Moving on was impossible; and we therefore came to a full stop: our chief was much enraged, but it was all to no purpose, he was only answered by shrieks of "Welcome!" and spears most unpleasantly rattled over our heads expressive of the same feeling. This annoyance was not however of long duration; Barca Gana, the sheikh's first general, a negro of a noble aspect, clothed in a figured silk tobe, and mounted on a beautiful Mandara horse, made his appearance; and, after a little delay, the rear was cleared of those who had pressed in upon us, and we moved on, although but very slowly, from the frequent impediment thrown in our way by these wild equestrians.

The sheikh's negroes, as they were called, meaning the black chiefs and favourites, all raised to that rank by some deed of bravery, were habited in coats of mail composed of iron chain, which covered them from the throat to the knees, dividing behind, and coming on each side of the horse:[4] some of them had helmets, or rather skull-caps, of the same metal, with chin-pieces, all sufficiently strong to ward off the shock of a spear. Their horses' heads were also defended by plates of iron, brass, and silver, just leaving sufficient room for the eyes of the animal.

At length, on arriving at the gate of the town, ourselves, Boo-Khaloom, and about a dozen of his followers, were alone allowed to enter the gates; and we proceeded along a wide street completely lined with spearmen on foot, with cavalry in front of them, to the door of the sheikh's residence. Here the horsemen were formed up three deep, and we came to a stand: some of the chief attendants came out, and after a great many "Barca's! Barca's!" retired, when others performed the same ceremony. We were now again left sitting on our horses in the sun: Boo-Khaloom began to lose all patience, and swore by the Bashaw's head, that he would return to the tents if he was not immediately admitted: he got, however, no satisfaction but a motion of the hand from one of the chiefs, meaning "wait patiently"; and I whispered to him the necessity of obeying, as we were hemmed in on all sides, and to retire without permission would have been as difficult as to advance. Barca Gana now appeared, and made a sign that Boo-Khaloom should dismount: we were about to follow his example, when an intimation that Boo-Khaloom was alone to be admitted again fixed

---

[3] The manner of el Kanemi's welcome to the Mission, especially its display of armed strength, may have been partly due to the trouble there had been over the detention of his children in Murzuk. But it was chiefly due to the Europeans having arrived with an escort of foreign troops, who were unwelcome and of whom El Kanemi intended to rid himself as soon as possible.

[4] Suits of mail are still sometimes worn by the retainers of important Western Sudan chiefs. Their striking resemblance to the mail worn by the Crusaders led to the popular belief that these suits had survived from the Middle Ages. They are in fact modern and of African manufacture. In the thirties of the present century mail made from wire rings pinched together was being manufactured in Omdurman, and being sold to local notables at about £25 a suit. But the mail the Mission saw in Kuka had been made in Hausa, probably in Kano. "Some of the Kanem Negroes called the sheikh's Guard," wrote Denham, "were habited in Coats of Mail composed of Iron Chain work from sudan."

us to our saddles. Another half hour at least passed without any news from the interior of the building; when the gates opened, and the four Englishmen only were called for, and we advanced to the skiffa (entrance). Here we were stopped most unceremoniously by the black guards in waiting, and were allowed, one by one only, to ascend a staircase; at the top of which we were again brought to a stand by crossed spears, and the open flat hand of a negro laid upon our breast. Boo-Khaloom came from the inner chamber, and asked "If we were prepared to salute the sheikh as we did the Bashaw?" We replied "Certainly": which was merely an inclination of the head, and laying the right hand on the heart. He advised our laying our hands also on our heads, but we replied, "the thing was impossible! we had but one manner of salutation for any body, except our own sovereign."

Another parley now took place, but in a minute or two he returned, and we were ushered into the presence of this Sheikh of Spears.[5] We found him in a small dark room, sitting on a carpet, plainly dressed in a blue tobe of Soudan and a shawl turban. Two negroes were on each side of him, armed with pistols, and on his carpet lay a brace of these instruments. Firearms were hanging in different parts of the room, presents from the Bashaw and Mustapha L'Achmar, the sultan of Fezzan, which are here considered as invaluable. His personal appearance was prepossessing, apparently not more than forty-five or forty-six, with an expressive countenance, and a benevolent smile. We delivered our letter from the Bashaw; and after he had read it, he inquired "what was our object in coming?" We answered "to see the country merely, and to give an account of its inhabitants, produce, and appearance; as our sultan was desirous of

knowing every part of the globe." His reply was, "that we were welcome! and whatever he could show us would give him pleasure: that he had ordered huts to be built for us in the town; and that we might then go, accompanied by one of his people, to see them; and that when we were recovered from the fatigue of our long journey, he would be happy to see us." With this we took our leave.

Our huts were immediately so crowded with visitors, that we had not a moment's peace, and the heat was insufferable. Boo-Khaloom had delivered his presents from the Bashaw, and brought us a message of compliment, together with an intimation that our own would be received on the following day. About noon we received a summons to attend the sheikh; and we proceeded to the palace, preceded by our negroes, bearing the articles destined for the sheikh by our government; consisting of a double-barrelled gun, by Wilkinson, with a box, and all the apparatus complete, a pair of excellent pistols in a case, two pieces of superfine broad cloth, red and blue, to which we added a set of china, and two bundles of spices.

The ceremony of getting into the presence was ridiculous enough, although nothing could be more plain and devoid of pretension than the appearance of the sheikh himself. We passed through passages lined with attendants, the front men sitting on their hams; and when we advanced too quickly, we were suddenly arrested by these fellows, who caught forcibly hold of us by the legs, and had not the crowd prevented our falling, we should most infallibly have become prostrate before arriving in the presence. Previous to entering into the open court, in which we were received, our papouches, or slippers, were whipped off by those active though sedentary gentlemen of the chamber; and we were seated on some clean sand on each side of a raised bench of earth, covered with a carpet, on which the sheikh was reclining. We laid the gun and the pistols together before him, and

---

[5] "Among the Kanuri," wrote Sir Richmond Palmer, "a spear surmounted by a *trident* was the symbol of office of the principal chiefs."

explained to him the locks, turnscrews, and steel shot-cases holding two charges each, with all of which he seemed exceedingly well pleased: the powder-flask, and the manner in which the charge is divided from the body of powder, did not escape his observation; the other articles were taken off by the slaves, almost as soon as they were laid before him. Again we were questioned as to the object of our visit. The sheikh, however, showed evident satisfaction at our assurance that the king of England had heard of Bornou and himself; and, immediately turning to his kaganawha (counsellor), said, "This is in consequence of our defeating the Begharmis [people of Bagirmi—ed.]." Upon which, the chief who had most distinguished himself in these memorable battles, Bagah Furby (the gatherer of horses), seating himself in front of us, demanded, "Did he ever hear of me?" The immediate reply of *"Certainly"* did wonders for our cause. Exclamations were general; and, "Ah! then, your king must be a great man!" was re-echoed from every side. We had nothing offered us by way of refreshment, and took our leave.

I may here observe, that besides occasional presents of bullocks, camel-loads of wheat and rice, leather skins of butter, jars of honey, and honey in the comb, five or six wooden bowls were sent us, morning and evening, containing rice, with meat, paste made of barley flour, savoury but very greasy; and on our first arrival, as many had been sent of sweets, mostly composed of curd and honey.

In England a brace of trout might be considered as a handsome present to a traveller sojourning in the neighbourhood of a stream, but at Bornou things are done differently. A camel-load of bream, and a sort of mullet, was thrown before our huts on the second morning after our arrival; and for fear that should not be sufficient, in the evening another was sent.

We had a fsug, or market, in front of one of the principal gates of the town. Slaves, sheep, and bullocks, the latter in great numbers, were the principal live stock for sale. There were at least fifteen thousand persons gathered together, some of them coming from places two and three days distant. Wheat, rice, and gussub, were abundant: tamarinds in the pod, ground nuts, ban beans, ochroes, and indigo; the latter is very good, and in great use amongst the natives to dye their tobes (shirts) and linen, stripes of deep indigo colour, or stripes of it alternately with white, being highly esteemed by most of the Bornou women: the leaves are moistened, and pounded up altogether when they are formed into lumps, and so brought to market. Of vegetables there was a great scarcity—onions, bastard tomatoes, alone were offered for sale; and of fruits not any: a few limes, which the sheikh had sent us from his garden, being the only fruit we had seen in Bornou. Leather was in great quantities; and the skins of the large snake, and pieces of the skin of the crocodile, used as an ornament for the scabbards of their daggers, were also brought to me for sale; and butter, leban (sour milk), honey, and wooden bowls, from Soudan. The costumes of the women, who for the most part were the vendors, were various: those of Kanem and Bornou were most numerous, and the former was as becoming as the latter had a contrary appearance. The variety in costume amongst the ladies consists entirely in the head ornaments; the only difference, in the scanty covering which is bestowed on the other parts of the person, lies in the choice of the wearer, who either ties the piece of linen, blue or white, under the arms, and across the breasts, or fastens it rather fantastically on one shoulder, leaving one breast naked. The Kanemboo women have small plaits of hair hanging down all around the head, quite to the poll of the neck, with a roll of leather or string of little brass beads in front, hanging down from the centre on each side of the face, which has by no means an unbecoming appearance: they have sometimes strings of silver rings instead of the brass, and a large round silver ornament in front of their foreheads. The female slaves from Musgow,[6] a large kingdom to the south-east of Mandara, are particularly disagreeable in their appearance, although considered as very trustworthy, and capable of great labour: their hair is rolled up in three large plaits, which extend from the forehead to the back of the neck, like the Bornowy; one larger in the centre, and two smaller on each side: they have silver studs in their nose, and one large one just under the lower lip of the size of a shilling, which goes quite through into the mouth; to make room for this ornament, a tooth or two is sometimes displaced.

The principal slaves are generally intrusted with the sale of such produce as the owner of them may have to dispose of; and if they come from any distance, the whole is brought on bullocks, which are harnessed after the fashion of the country, by a string or iron run through the cartilage of the nose, and a saddle of nut. The masters not unfrequently attend the fsug with their spears, and loiter about without interfering: purchases are mostly made by exchange of one commodity for another, or paid for by small beads, pieces of coral and amber, or the coarse linen manufactured by all the people, and sold at forty gubka [7] for a dollar. . . .

EXTRACT

Bornou March 12 1823

On Monday the 17th Febry we made our entry into Kouka the present Capital of Bornou, altho' not the largest or most populous Town, but still it is the Capital. It has not been built above 8 years and is the work of an Usurper, if he may be so called, named Lameen el Kalmi, who built it after conquering the Country and

driving out the Fellatas a Tribe who had some Years before overthrown the ancient Sultans and then reigned in their place. El Kalmi an Arab of strong natural understanding & courage, had long resided in Kanem as a Fighi or writer of Charms & much respected for his abilities and Charity, he had sufficient address to raise an Army in Kanem to drive the Fellata from all the Bornou Country and when his Victorious Army whom the Natives of Bornou dared not oppose would have proclaimed him Sultan. He had magnanimity enough to refuse the Crown and not only place it on the Head of the remaining branch of the Ancient Sultans, but first doing homage himself he insisted on all his followers doing likewise—there was quite as much policy as magnanimity in this act of Kalmi's as by that means he gained the hearts of all the Bornou people, who were too numerous for him to have set at defiance; for several years he lived at Angornou, the largest and most populous of any in the Country, having at least 50,000 Inhabitants, while he established the Sultan at Birnie, a Town about 3 miles distant; 12 years ago he however determined on building Kouka which is about 18 miles N.W. of Angornou—His Kanem followers have here colonized and he is daily reconciling by the force of his Arms & otherwise the Shouans [Shuwa] or Arabs which are in his neighbourhood and already many of them have become Citizens of Kouka. These Shouans are of a fine dark copper colour with oval faces & acquiline noses; they seldom intermarry with the Negroes for each has an aversion to the color of the other—They were however always amongst Kalmi's bravest and most determined Enemies and the Measures he has taken to conciliate them will tend to give him more power than he ever possessed before—He can now bring 50,-000 Men into the Field most of them mounted, and if they are any thing like the 4000 that met us on our approaching the Town on the 17th they are a very formidable force for a Barbarian Ruler. His

---

[6] The Musgu, a pagan people of the Logone basin, who were much preyed on by powerful neighbours. They owed their survival to the impassable nature of their country which is much intersected by swampy waterways.

[7] *Gubka,* about a yard English.

Court is simplicity itself, as well as his manners, the dark avenues of his Mud Palace leading to his Apartment are lined with his Kanem Guards all plainly dressed in a Blue Tobe, or large Shirt, uncovered shaved heads with spears in their hands, round his person sit one or two of his principal Chiefs who on great occasions are clothed in the presents which the Bashaw may from time to time have sent him, two Negroe Slaves lay close behind him on a small Carpet with loaded pistols and a few fire arms, the only ones in his Country and of which he is uncommonly proud, are hung round the Walls—his dress is generally a Tobe of Soudan [?] or of Blue Linen with a Cashimere Turban—some of his horses are beautiful, and he has a body guard of Kanem Negroes all habited in Coats of Iron Chain with skull caps of Iron on their heads, who really ride beautifully and have a very warlike appearance . . . Kalmi has been most successful in overcoming all the neighbouring Negro States, several [8] Kerdi Kafir Nations have by his means embraced Mohomatanism.   By plundering them first, and demanding Tributes after, he has increased the consequence of the Bornou Sultan greatly. Beghermi has been a constant resource for him for the last 5 or 6 years as he has nearby annually made a most profitable expedition into that Country.   By these means he has been enabled to indulge the Sultan's natural propensity who with his Court revel in all the folly and Bigotry of their Ancestors—this has had the effect of alienating the affections of the mass of the people greatly from the reigning Family and fixing them on himself, who with the half only his successes bring him, which he retains the other half going to the Sultan, he builds Towns and distributes alms to 1000s of the Inhabitants—Kalmi has I am convinced at any time the power of overthrowing the Ancient Government

[8] These two terms are synonimous & mean unbelievers.

by a wave of his hand, but he is quite keen enough to know when that step should be taken, so as best to answer his Views.

.   .   .

Miram (princess in the Bornou language), now the divorced wife of the sheikh El Kanemy, was residing at Angala, and I requested permission to visit her.   Her father had built for her a house, in which she constantly resided; and her establishment exceeded sixty persons.   She was a very handsome, beautifully formed negress, of about thirty-five, and had imbibed much of that softness of manner which is so extremely prepossessing in the sheikh.   Seated on an earthen throne, covered with a turkey carpet, and surrounded by twenty of her favourite slaves, all dressed alike, in fine white shirts, which reached to their feet, their necks, ears, and noses thickly ornamented with coral, she held her audience with very considerable grace, while four eunuchs guarded the entrance; and a negro dwarf, who measured three feet all but an inch, the keeper of her keys, sat before her with the insignia of office on his shoulder, and richly dressed in Soudan tobes.   This little person afforded us a subject of conversation, and much laughter.   Miram inquired whether we had such little fellows in my country, and when I answered in the affirmative, she said *"Ah gieb!* what are they good for? do they ever have children?"   I answered, "Yes; that we had instances of their being fathers to tall and proper men."   "Oh, wonderful!" she replied: "I thought so; they must be better then than this dog of mine; for I have given him eight of my handsomest and youngest slaves, but it is all to no purpose.   I would give a hundred bullocks, and twenty slaves, to the woman who would bear this wretch a child."   The wretch, and an ugly wretch he was, shook his large head, grinned, and slobbered copiously from his extensive mouth, at this flattering proof of his mistresses's partiality. . . .

.   .   .

12 RENÉ CAILLIÉ
THE TRANS-SAHARAN CARAVAN

The French explorer René Caillié (1799–1838) was the first European to visit Timbuktu and return alive. Disguised as an Arab returning to Egypt, he made his way from the Rio Nunez to Djenné, whence he traveled by canoe down the Niger to Timbuktu. He found the mysterious city in 1828 to be a rather squalid, middle-sized Sudanic town with no sign of the great splendors described by Leo Africanus. *Leaving Timbuktu, Caillié crossed the desert from Arawan and Taghaza with a caravan of 1,400 camels taking slaves, gold, ivory, gum, and ostrich feathers to Morocco. After many harrowing adventures he reached Fez and then France, where his description shattered, but did not completely destroy, Europe's romantic image of Timbuktu as a magnificent and glamorous city.*

The caravan destined for el-Arawan, with which I had resolved to travel, was to set out on the 4th of May, at sun-rise. My host was up so early that morning as to allow me time, before my departure, to breakfast with him on tea, new bread, and butter. That nothing might diminish the agreeable impression which my stay at Timbuctoo had made upon me, I met, on departing, the host of Major Laing, who made me accept some new clothing for my journey.

Sidi-Abdallahi accompanied me to some distance from his house, and, at parting with me, he affectionately pressed my hand and wished me a good journey. This farewell detained me almost too long. To rejoin the caravan, which had already proceeded to a considerable distance, I was obliged, as well as three slaves who had also remained behind, to run a whole mile through the sand. This effort fatigued me so much, that, on reaching the caravan, I fell down in a state of insensibility; I was lifted up and placed on a loaded camel, where I sat among the packages, and though dreadfully shaken I was too glad at being relieved from the labour of walking to complain of my beast.

On the 4th of May, 1828, at eight in the morning, we directed our route to the

From René Caillié, *Travels through Central Africa to Timbuctoo and Across the Great Desert to Morocco, Performed in the Years 1824–28* (London: H. Colburn and R. Bentley, 1830), II, 88–97.

north over a sandy soil, almost moving, quite level, and completely barren. However, at the distance of two miles from the town, we met with a few shrubs resembling junipers, and some rather tall clusters of *mimosa ferruginea,* which yield a gum of inferior quality. The inhabitants of Timbuctoo send their slaves hither for fire-wood. The heat was most oppressive, and the progress of the camels was extremely slow; for, as they moved along, they browsed on the thistles and withered herbs, which they found scattered here and there on these plains. During this first day the slaves were allowed to drink at discretion, as I was. This conduct was doubtless very humane; nevertheless, I was soon shocked by an act of barbarity, which I had the misfortune to see too often repeated. A poor Bambara slave of twenty-five was cruelly treated by some Moors, who compelled him to walk, without allowing him to halt for a moment, or to quench his burning thirst. The complaints of this unfortunate creature, who had never been accustomed to endure such extraordinary privations, might have moved the hardest heart. Sometimes he would beg to rest himself against the crupper [hindquarters—ed.] of a camel, and at others he threw himself down on the sand in despair. In vain did he implore, with uplifted hands, a drop of water; his cruel masters answered his prayers and his tears only with stripes.

At Timbuctoo the merchants give the

slaves shirts, such as are worn in the country, that they may be decently covered; but on the route the Moors of the caravans, who are the most barbarous men I ever knew, take the good shirts from them and give them others all in rags.

At five in the evening the caravan, the camels of which amounted to nearly six hundred, halted in a ravine of yellow sand, which was, however, pretty solid. Here these animals found some herbage, and the spot appeared to me delightful. A slave, who was barely allowed time to take a drink of water, was ordered to look after our camels, and we thought of nothing but how to pass the night quietly; but before we laid ourselves down to sleep, we made our supper on a calabash of water, some dokhnou [dukhn: millet—ed.], and the bread which I had received from Sidi-Abdallahi; the bread being hard we soaked it in the water, into which we put a little butter and honey. This mixture was to us a delicious beverage. The slaves had for their supper some sangleh seasoned with butter and salt. These good-natured creatures were so kind as to offer me some of their meal.

On the 5th of May, at sun-rise, we resumed our journey. We still proceeded towards the north, upon ground similar to that over which we passed on the preceding day. A few stunted bushes were descried here and there, and also some salvadoras, which the camels devoured.

Towards noon we approached a less level region, where the ground was raised into slightly elevated mounds, all inclining in the direction from east to west. The heat was suffocating, on account of the east wind, which raised great clouds of sand: our lips were covered with it; our thirst became insupportable; and our sufferings increased in proportion as we advanced further in the desert. We fell in with two Tooariks [Tuaregs—ed.], who were going to el-Arawan, and whom we took to be the scouts of a troop of these marauders. Fortunately they were alone.

They were both mounted on one camel. On the left arm they had a leather buckler; by the side, a poniard; and in the right hand, a pike. Knowing that they should meet us in their route, they had brought no provisions with them, and trusted to the caravan for a supply. These robbers, who would have trembled at the slightest menace, if seriously made, took advantage of the terror which their name and the crimes of their tribe every where spread, and obtained whatever they demanded: in a word, the best of every thing was presented to them. On the one hand, there was a sort of rivalship in offering them whatever they chose to eat; on the other, to give them water, though it would be six days before we should come to any. At last, after they had staid with us three days, we had the satisfaction to see them depart, and to be delivered from their troublesome company.

At four in the evening we encamped to pass the night, during which we were oppressed by excessive heat, caused by a dead calm. The sky was heavy and covered with clouds which seemed immoveable in the immensity of space. Still the heat continued intense.

Before proceeding farther, I ought to inform the reader how I continued to make an estimate of the route. We travelled, at an average, about two miles an hour. At night we proceeded almost constantly in a northerly direction. Being afraid that my pocket compass would be noticed if I took it out to consult it, I judged of our course during the day by the sun; in the night, by the pole-star.

It is by this star that the Arabs are guided in all their excursions through the desert. The oldest caravan conductors go first, to lead the way. A sand-hill, a rock, a difference of colour in the sand, a few tufts of herbage, are infallible marks, which enable them to recognize their situation. Though without a compass, or any instrument for observation, they possess so completely the habit of noticing the most minute things, that they never go astray, though they have no path traced out for them, and though the wind in an instant completely covers with sand and obliterates the track of the camels.

The desert, however, does not always present the same aspect, or, consequently the same difficulties. In some parts I found it covered with rocks and gravel, which bore the traces of caravans that had passed long before. Besides, though the desert is a plain of sand and rock, the Arab commits few errors in crossing it, and is seldom wrong to the extent of half an hour in fixing the time of arrival at the wells. I ought not to omit to mention, that these wells are almost constantly found covered over, and that the first thing done on the arrival of a caravan is to clear away the sand.

On the 6th of May we resumed our march, at three in the morning, and continued our route to the north. Still the same soil, the same aridity, and the same uniformity, as on the preceding days.

The atmosphere was very heavy all day, and the heat excessive. It seemed as if we should have rain. The sun, concealed by clouds, appeared only at long intervals. But our prayers did not obtain from Heaven a drop of rain. In spite of all the prognostics no shower fell. The further northward we proceeded the more barren the country became. We no longer saw either thistles or salvadoras: sad consolations, where all nature wears so frightful an aspect! The plain had here the precise appearance of the ocean; perhaps such as the bed of a sea would have, if left by the water. In fact, the winds form in the sand undulating furrows, like the waves of the sea when a breeze slightly ruffles its surface. At the sight of this dismal spectacle, of this awful abandonment and nakedness, I forgot for a moment my hardships, to reflect on the violent convulsions which thus appeared to have dried up part of the ocean, and of the sudden catastrophes which have changed the face of our globe.

At eleven in the morning we halted. The heat was insupportable, and we seated ourselves beside some unhealthy looking mimosas, over which we extended our wrappers, for these shrubs being destitute of leaves afforded no shade of themselves. Under our tents thus formed, we had distributed to us a calabash of water, which was rendered tepid by the east wind. According to our custom, we threw into the water some handfuls of dokhnou. Finally, to relieve ourselves from every immediate care, we sent a slave to watch our camels, which were endeavouring to refresh themselves by browsing on some withered herbage. We then lay down to sleep on the sand, which at this place was covered with small stones. This was not done from indolence, but from consideration; for it was proper to wait for night to take advantage of the coolness, when we might travel more at our ease than during the day, in which the calms were sometimes more insupportable than the burning sun. During these calms I could not close my eyes, while the Moors slept soundly. The same kind of calm often prevails during the night, but then there is some compensation in the absence of the sun. In the inhabited countries, the night, or rather the latter part of the night, is always the most agreeable portion of the twenty-four hours. It is at day-break that the flowers exhale all their perfumes: the air is then gently agitated, and the birds commence their songs. Recollections, at once pleasing and painful, turned my thoughts to the south. In the midst of this frightful desert could I fail to regret the land which nature has embellished?

The caravans which traverse the desert are under no absolute commander; every one manages his camels as he pleases, whether he has many or few; some have fifteen, others six or ten; and there are individuals who possess not more than three; I have even seen some with only two, but these were very poor. Such persons join richer travellers and take care of their camels; in return, they are supplied with provisions and water during the journey.

The Moors always lay out the profits of their journeys in the purchase of camels, and none of them travel to Timbuctoo without possessing at least one. The camels do not advance in files, as they would do in our roads lined by hedges and cultivated lands. On the contrary they move in all directions, in groupes, or single, but in this journey their route is always between N.N.E. and N.N.W. Those which belong to one master keep together, and do not mix with strange camels; and I have seen as many as fifty grouped together in this way. A camel's load is five hundred pounds, and the carriage from Timbuctoo to Tafilet costs ten or twelve gold mitkhals,[1] which are paid in advance.

The camels which convey merchandise of light weight, such as ostrich feathers, clothes, and stuffs in the piece, have their loads made up with slaves, water, and rice; for, the load being paid for according to its weight, the proprietors of the camels, if that weight were not completed, would gain nothing by the carriage of merchandise more cumbersome than heavy. When the caravan stops, the groupes of camels are kept at the distance of two hundred paces from each other, to obviate the confusion which would arise if they were suffered to mix together.

When the Moors return to their country, they do not carry back merely ostrich feathers and ivory; but they take also gold, some more, and some less. I saw some who had as much as the value of a hundred mitkhals. This gold is generally sent to the merchants of Tafilet by their correspondents at Timbuctoo, in return for the merchandise sent by the former, and sold on their account by the latter. During our halts in the deserts, I often saw the Moors weighing their gold in little scales similar to ours, which are made in Morocco. The gold which is conveyed by these travelling clerks of the desert is carefully rolled up in pieces of cloth, with a label, on which are written

[1] The value of the gold mitkhal is about twelve francs, and the silver mitkhal about four.

the weight of the metal and the name of the individual to whom it belongs.

When night set in, we took our usual supper, consisting of water, bread, butter, and honey. Several Moors, with whom we were not acquainted, came and asked us for a supper; they then invited the two Moors who were of our party to share their mess of baked rice and butter. Though they knew that they had partaken of my provisions, yet they did not think proper to invite me, a proof, that notwithstanding all my efforts, there existed a feeling of distrust towards me. At sun-set a north breeze arose, which, though not very cool, was nevertheless very reviving, and enabled me to enjoy a little sleep.

About eleven at night we set out, still proceeding northward, and directing our course by the pole-star. The camels are so well acquainted with the desert that, as soon as they are loaded, they take, as if by instinct, the northern course. It would seem that they are guided by the recollection of the springs of water which are found in that direction. I really believe that a traveller, though alone, might safely trust himself to the guidance of his camel.

The night was hot and calm, and the clear sky was studded with stars. We had before us the great and the little wain which appeared very near the horizon. As I could not sleep, I amused myself by observing the courses of the stars; I saw in the east the remarkable groupe called the constellation of Orion; I watched it during nearly half its course, almost to our zenith. On the approach of day, the stars disappeared and seemed to sink into an ocean of sand.

The camels never accelerate their pace, which is naturally somewhat tardy. When they are in haste, they thrust forward their necks, the motion of which corresponds with that of their legs. They are led by men on foot, whose labour is so fatiguing, that it is necessary to relieve them every two hours.

The ground over which we travelled

during the night appeared to me to be even more barren than that which we had passed on the preceding days. For whole hours in succession we did not see a single blade of grass.

At eleven in the morning the heat became excessive, and we halted at a place where we found a few little banks of sand. A slave was sent to seek out a few bushes that might afford us shade, but no such thing was to be discovered. The reflection of the rays of the sun on the sand augmented the heat. It was impossible to stand barefoot on the sand without experiencing intolerable pain. The desert is here and there interspersed with a few hills, and we found at very distant intervals a little grass for the camels.

We had been the whole of the morning without drink, and as soon as our tents were pitched we slaked our thirst. Our water began to diminish in proportion as our thirst increased, therefore we did not cook any thing for supper, but merely drank a little dokhnou. About eleven at night we broke up our camp and proceeded northward: at seven in the morning we turned N.N.W.

At eleven o'clock on the 8th of May, the insupportable heat obliged us to halt on a spot as flat and barren as that at which we had stopped on the preceding day. We pitched our tents, and assembled beneath them. Some drink was distributed to us; and, as we had tasted none since five o'clock on the preceding evening, our thirst was very great. Though the water had received a bad taste from the leathern bag, it was nevertheless exceedingly grateful. I observed some ravens and vultures, the only inhabitants of these deserts. They subsist on the carcases of the camels that die and are left behind on the road. At half past six in the evening, after having refreshed ourselves with a glass of water and dokhnou, we proceeded on our journey. We travelled all night in a northerly direction. The camels, finding no pasture, went on without stopping.

About 8 o'clock on the morning of the 9th of May, we halted in a sandy plain, where we found a little grass for our poor camels. There we perceived at a distance the camels of el-Arawan.

In the morning, little before sun-rise, the Moors who accompanied me shewed me the spot where Major Laing was murdered [in 1826—ed.]. I there observed the site of a camp. I averted my eyes from this scene of horror, and secretly dropped a tear—the only tribute of regret I could render to the ill-fated traveller, to whose memory no monument will ever be reared on the spot where he perished.

Several Moors of our caravan, who had witnessed the fatal event, told me that the major had but little property with him when he was stopped by the chief of the Zawâts, and that he had offered five hundred piastres to a Moor to conduct him to Souyerah (Mogador). This the Moor refused to do, for what reason I was not informed, and I dared not inquire. They also spoke of the sextant, which I have mentioned above.

Having pitched our tents near some water, we could drink as much as we pleased. Rice was boiled for our dinner and we were somewhat indemnified for the privations we had undergone in the preceding days. At six in the evening we proceeded northwards over a very level sandy soil, on which were scattered a few solitary patches of vegetation. Though the sand has a tolerable consistency, yet not a tree was to be seen. Towards nine in the evening, we arrived at El-Arawan, another commercial entrepot. We encamped outside the city, and in the neighbourhood I observed several tents and camels, which I was told belonged to the caravan, waiting for the signal for departure. Our arrival was greeted by the howling of dogs, a circumstance which reminded me that I had seen none of those animals at Timbuctoo.

Being unaccustomed to riding on camels, I found myself extremely fatigued by the journey. The moment we stopped, I spread my wrapper upon the sand, and fell into a profound sleep. I did not find the heat so oppressive as it had been on the preceding days. I was roused to partake of an excellent couscous brought from the city.

13 HEINRICH BARTH
AL-HAJJ BASHIR, KUKAWA, AND TIMBUKTU

Heinrich Barth (1821–1865) was one of the greatest and most intelligent of the nineteenth-century African explorers. A German, he left Tripoli and crossed the Sahara in 1850 as a member of an English expedition to the Sudan. The commander, James Richardson, died, but Barth and another German, Adolf Overweg, visited Katsina and Kano, traveled to Bornu and its capital, Kukawa, explored Lake Chad, and reached the Benue River. Overweg died in 1852 and Barth continued alone to Sokoto and Timbuktu. He then returned to Bornu, crossed the Sahara, and reached England near the end of 1855. His journal contains immense information on the western Sudan that was collected from his precise and penetrating observations. Kukawa was built as the capital of Bornu in 1814 by Sheik al-Kanami but was destroyed in 1846 by the Sultan of Wadai in support of the titular mai *of Bornu. The Wadai forces were driven back by al-Kanami's son and successor, Umar (1835–1880), who rebuilt Kukawa as a twin town, the eastern part* (billa gediba) *of which was the seat of the ruler and was separated by an open space from the western part* (billa futela). *Umar confined himself to his palace and devoted himself to religious studies, leaving control in the hands of such* wazirs *as al-Hajj Bashir. Leaving Kukawa, Barth eventually made his way west to Timbuktu. Probably founded sometime in the eleventh century, Timbuktu seems to have remained only an insignificant settlement until the thirteenth century, when it became an emporium for trans-Saharan trade. Unlike Djenné, however, Timbuktu never became a real city-state and its heterogeneous population never achieved the unity of other Sudanic cities. Timbuktu was always dominated by outsiders—Mali, Songhay, Tuareg, Moors, Fulani. Nevertheless, its Sankore quarter was an important center of Negro Islamic learning. Timbuktu's reputation for scholarship lasted well into the nineteenth century and fired the imagination of Alfred, Lord Tennyson* (who won the poetry prize at Cambridge for his poem Timbuctoo) *and other romantics long after the city's greatness had passed.*

I have peculiar reason to thank Providence for having averted the storm which was gathering over his head during my stay in Bornu, for my intimacy with him [al-Hajj Bashir—ed.] might very easily have involved me also in the calamities which befell him. However, I repeat that,

From Heinrich Barth, *Travels and Discoveries in North and Central Africa from the Journal of an Expedition Undertaken under the Auspices of H.B.M.'s Government in the Years 1849–1855* (Philadelphia: J. W. Bradley, 1859), pp. 181–189, 447–450.

altogether, he was a most excellent, kind, liberal, and just man, and might have done much good to the country if he had been less selfish and more active. He was incapable, indeed, of executing by himself any act of severity, such as in the unsettled state of a semi-barbarous kingdom may at times be necessary; and, being conscious of his own mildness, he left all those matters to a man named Lamino, to whom I gave the title of "the shameless left hand of the vizier," and whom I shall have frequent occasion to mention.

I pressed upon the vizier the necessity of defending the northern frontier of Bornu against the Tawarek by more effectual measures than had been then adopted, and thus retrieving, for cultivation and the peaceable abode of his fellow-subjects, the fine borders of the Komádugu, and restoring security to the road to Fezzan. Just about this time the Tawarek had made another expedition into the border districts on a large scale, so that Kashella Belal, the first of the war-chiefs, was obliged to march against them; and the road to Kano, which I, with my usual good luck, had passed unmolested, had become so unsafe that a numerous caravan was plundered, and a well-known Arab merchant, the Sherif el Ghali, killed.

I remonstrated with him on the shamefully-neglected state of the shores of the lake, which contained the finest pasturegrounds, and might yield an immense quantity of rice and cotton. He entered with spirit into all my proposals, but in a short time all was forgotten. He listened with delight to what little historical knowledge I had of these countries, and inquired particularly whether Kanem had really been in former times a mighty kingdom, or whether it would be worth retaking. It was in consequence of these conversations that he began to take an interest in the former history of the country, and that the historical records of Edris Alawoma came to light; but he would not allow me to take them into my hands, and I could only read over his shoulders. He was a very religious man; and though he admired Europeans very much on account of their greater accomplishments, he was shocked to think that they drank intoxicating liquors. However, I tried to console him by telling him that, although the Europeans were also very partial to the fair sex, yet they did not indulge in this luxury on so large a scale as he did, and that therefore he ought to allow them some other little pleasure.

He was very well aware of the misery connected with the slave-trade; for, on his pilgrimage to Mekka, in the mountainous region between Fezzan and Ben-Ghazi, he had lost, in one night, forty of his slaves by the extreme cold, and he swore that he would never take slaves for sale if he were to travel again. But it was more difficult to make him sensible of the horrors of slave-hunting, although, when accompanying him on the expedition to Musgu, I and Mr. Overweg urged this subject with more success, as the further progress of my narrative will show. He was very desirous to open a commerce with the English, although he looked with extreme suspicion upon the form of articles in which the treaty was proposed to be drawn up; but he wished to forbid to Christians the sale of two things, viz., spirituous liquors and Bibles. He did not object to Bibles being brought into the country, and even given as presents, but he would not allow of their being sold.

. . .

Having now a horse whereon to mount, I rode every day, either into the eastern town to pay a visit to the sheikh or to the vizier, or roving around the whole circuit of the capital, and peeping into the varied scenes which the life of the people exhibited. The precincts of the town, with its suburbs, are just as interesting, as its neighborhood (especially during the months that precede the rainy season) is monotonous and tiresome in the extreme. Certainly the arrangement of the capital contributes a great deal to the variety of the picture which it forms, laid out as it is, in two distinct towns, each surrounded with its wall, the one occupied chiefly by the rich and wealthy, containing very large establishments, while the other, with the exception of the principal thoroughfare, which traverses the town from west to east, consists of rather crowded dwellings, with narrow, winding lanes. These two distinct towns are separated by a space about half a mile broad, itself thickly inhabited on both sides of a wide, open road, which forms the connection between them, but laid out less regularly, and presenting to the eye a most interesting medley of large clay buildings and small thatched huts, of massive clay walls surrounding immense yards, and light fences of reeds in a more or less advanced state of decay, and with a variety of color, according to their age, from the brightest yellow down to the deepest black. All around these two towns there are small villages or clusters of huts, and large detached farms surrounded with clay walls, low enough to allow a glimpse from horseback over the thatched huts which they inclose.

In this labyrinth of dwellings a man, interested in the many forms which human life presents, may rove about at any time of the day with the certainty of never-failing amusement, although the life of the Kanuri people passes rather monotonously along, with the exception of some occasional feasting. During the hot hours, indeed, the town and its precincts become torpid, except on market-days, when the market-place itself, at least, and the road leading to it from the western gate, are most animated just at that time. For, singular, as it is, in Kukawa, as well as almost all over this part of Negroland, the great markets do not begin to be well attended till the heat of the day grows intense; and it is curious to observe what a difference prevails in this, as well as in other respects, between these countries and Yoruba, where almost all the markets are held in the cool of the evening.

The daily little markets, or durriya, even in Kukawa, are held in the afternoon. The most important of these durriyas is that held inside the west gate of the billa futebe, and here even camels, horses, and oxen are sold in considerable numbers; but they are much inferior to the large fair, or great market, which is held every Monday on the open ground beyond the two villages which lie at a short distance from the western gate.

I visited the great fair, "kasuku lete-ninbe," every Monday immediately after my arrival, and found it very interesting, as it calls together the inhabitants of all the eastern parts of Bornu, the Shuwa and the Koyam, with their corn and butter; the former, though of Arab origin, and still preserving in purity his ancient character, always carrying his merchandise on the back of oxen, the women mounted upon the top of it, while the African Koyam employs the camel; the Kanembu with their butter and dried fish, the inhabitants of Makari with their tobes; even Budduma, or rather Yedina, are very often seen in the market, selling whips made from the skin of the hippopotamus, or sometimes even hippopotamus meat, or dried fish, and attract the attention of the speculator by their slender figures, their small, handsome features, unimpaired by any incisions, the men generally wearing a short black shirt and a small straw hat, "suni ngawa," their neck adorned with several strings of kungona or shells, while the women are profusely ornamented with strings of glass beads, and wear their hair in a very remarkable way, though not in so awkward a fashion as Mr. Overweg afterward observed in the island Belarigo.

On reaching the market-place from the town, the visitor first comes to that part where the various materials for constructing the light dwellings of the country are sold, such as mats; poles and stakes; the framework for the thatched roofs of huts, and the ridge-beam; then oxen for slaughter, or for carrying burdens; farther on, long rows of leathern bags filled with corn, ranging far along on the south side of the market-place. These long rows are animated not only by the groups of the sellers and buyers, with their weather-worn figures and torn dresses, but also by the beasts of burden, mostly oxen, which have brought the loads, and which are to carry back their masters to their distant dwelling-places; then follow the camels for sale, often as many as a hundred or more, and numbers of horses, but generally not first-rate ones, which are mostly sold in private. All this sale of horses, camels, &c., with the exception of the oxen, passes through the hands of the broker, who, according to the mode of announcement, takes his percentage from the buyer or the seller.

The fatigue which people have to undergo in purchasing their week's necessaries in the market is all the more harassing, as there is not at present any standard money for buying and selling; for the ancient standard of the country, viz., the pound of copper, has long since fallen into disuse, though the name, "rotl," still remains. The "gabaga," or cotton strips, which then became usual, have lately begun to be supplanted by the cowries or "kungona," which have been introduced, as it seems, rather by a speculation of the ruling people than by a natural want of the inhabitants, though nobody can deny that they are very useful for buying small articles, and infinitely more convenient than cotton strips. Eight cowries or kungona are reckoned equal to one gabaga, and four gabaga, or two-and-thirty kungona, to one rotl. Then, for buying larger objects, there are shirts of all kinds and sizes, from the "dora," the coarsest and smallest one, quite unfit for use, and worth six rotls, up to the large ones, worth fifty or sixty rotls. But, while this is a standard value, the relation of the rotl and the Austrian dollar, which is pretty well current in Bornu, is subject to extreme fluctuation, due, I must confess, at least partly, to the speculations of the ruling men, and principally to that of my friend the Haj Beshir. Indeed, I cannot defend him against the reproach of having speculated to the great detriment of the public; so that when he had collected a great amount of kungona, and wished to give it currency, the dollar would suddenly fall as low as to five-and-forty or fifty rotls, while at other times it would fetch as much as one hundred rotls, or three thousand two hundred shells, that is, seven

hundred shells more than in Kano. The great advantage of the market in Kano is that there is one standard coin, which, if a too large amount of dollars be not on a sudden set in circulation, will always preserve the same value.

But to return to the picture of life which the town of Kukawa presents. With the exception of Mondays, when just during the hottest hours of the day there is much crowd and bustle in the market-place, it is very dull from about noon till three o'clock in the afternoon; and even during the rest of the day those scenes of industry which in the varied panorama of Kano meet the eye are here sought for in vain. Instead of those numerous dyeing-yards or marina, full of life and bustle, though certainly also productive of much filth and foul odors, which spread over the town of Kano, there is only a single and a very poor marina in Kukawa; no beating of tobes is heard, nor the sound of any other handicraft.

There is a great difference of character between these two towns; and the Bornu people are by temperament far more phlegmatic than those of Kano. The women in general are much more ugly, with square, short figures, large heads, and broad noses with immense nostrils, disfigured still more by the enormity of a red bead or coral worn in the nostrils. Nevertheless, they are certainly quite as coquettish, and, as far as I had occasion to observe, at least as wanton also as the more cheerful and sprightly Hausa women. I have never seen a Hausa woman strolling about the streets with her gown trailing after her on the ground, the fashion of the women of Kukawa, and wearing on her shoulders some Manchester print of a showy pattern, keeping the ends of it in her hands, while she throws her arms about in a coquettish manner. In a word, their dress, as well as their demeanor, is far more decent and agreeable. The best part in the dress or ornaments of the Bornu women is the silver ornament which they wear on the back of the head, and which in taller figures, when the hair is plaited in the form of a helmet, is very becoming; but it is not every woman who can afford such an ornament, and many a one sacrifices her better interests for this decoration.

The most animated quarter of the two towns is the great thoroughfare, which, proceeding by the southern side of the palace in the western town, traverses it from west to east, and leads straight to the sheikh's residence in the eastern town. This is the "dendal" or promenade, a locality which has its imitation, on a less or greater scale, in every town of the country. This road, during the whole day, is crowded by numbers of people on horseback and on foot; free men and slaves, foreigners as well as natives, every one in his best attire, to pay his respects to the sheikh or his vizier, to deliver an errand, or to sue for justice or employment, or a present. I myself very often went along this well-trodden path—this high road of ambition; but I generally went at an unusual hour, either at sunrise in the morning, or while the heat of the midday, not yet abated, detained the people in their cool haunts, or late at night, when the people were already retiring to rest, or, sitting before their houses, beguiling their leisure hours with amusing tales or with petty scandal. At such hours I was sure to find the vizier or the sheikh alone; but sometimes they wished me also to visit and sit with them, when they were accessible to all the people; and on these occasions the vizier took pride and delight in conversing with me about matters of science, such as the motion of the earth, or the planetary system, or subjects of that kind.

.   .   .

The city of Timbuktu, according to Dr. Peterman's laying down of it from my materials, lies in 17' 37° N. and 3' 5° W. of Greenwich. Situated only a few feet above the average level of the river, and at a distance of six miles from the princi-

pal branch, it at present forms a sort of triangle, the base of which points toward the river, while the projecting angle is directed toward the north, having for its centre the mosque of Sankore. But, during the zenith of its power, the town extended a thousand yards further north, and included the tomb of the Faki Mahmud, which, according to some of my informants, was then situated in the midst of the town.

The circumference of the city at the present time I reckon at a little more than two miles and a half; but it may approach closely to three miles, taking into account some of the projecting angles. Although of only small size, Timbuktu may well be called a city—medina—in comparison with the frail dwelling-places all over Negroland. At present it is not walled. Its former wall, which seems never to have been of great magnitude, and was rather more of the nature of a rampart, was destroyed by the Fulbe on their first entering the place in the beginning of the year 1826. The town is laid out partly in rectangular, partly in winding streets, or, as they are called here "tijeraten," which are not paved, but for the greater part consist of hard sand and gravel, and some of them have a sort of gutter in the middle. Besides the large and the small market there are few open areas, except a small square in front of the mosque of Yahia, called Tumbutu-bottema.

Small as it is, the city is tolerably well inhabited, and almost all the houses are in good repair. There are about 980 clay houses, and a couple of hundred conical huts of matting, the latter, with a few exceptions, constituting the outskirts of the town on the north and northeast sides, where a great deal of rubbish, which has been accumulating in the course of several centuries, is formed into conspicuous mounds. The clay houses are all of them built on the same principle as my own residence, which I have described, with the exception that the houses of the poorer people have only one court-yard, and have no upper room on the terrace.

The only remarkable public buildings in the town are the three large mosques: the Jingere-ber, built by Mansa Musa; the mosque of Sankore, built at an early period at the expense of a wealthy woman; and the mosque Sidi Yahia, built at the expense of a kadhi of the town. There were three other mosques: that of Sidi Haj Mohammed, Msid Belal, and that of Sidi el Bami. These mosques, and perhaps some little msid, or place of prayer, Caillié must have included when he speaks of seven mosques. Besides these mosques there are at present no distinguished public buildings in the town; and of the royal palace, or Ma-dugu, wherein the kings of Songhay used to reside occasionally, as well as the Kasbah, which was built in later times, in the southeastern quarter, or the "Sane-gungu," which already at that time was inhabited by the merchants from Ghadames, not a trace is to be seen. Besides this quarter, which is the wealthiest, and contains the best houses, there are six other quarters, viz., Yubu, the quarter comprising the great market-place (yubu) and the mosque of Sidi Yahia, to the west of Sane-gungu; and west of the former, forming the southwestern angle of the town, and called, from the great mosque, Jingere-ber or Zangere-ber. This latter quarter, from the most ancient times, seems to have been inhabited especially by Mohammedans, and not unlikely may have formed a distinct quarter, separated from the rest of the town by a wall of its own. Toward the north, the quarter Sane-gungu is bordered by the one called Sara-kaina, meaning literally the "little town," and containing the residence of the sheikh, and the house where I myself was lodged. Attached to Sara-kaina, toward the north, is Yubu-kaina, the quarter containing the "little market," which is especially used as a butcher's market. Bordering both on Jingere-ber and Yubu-kaina is the quarter Bagindi, occupying the lowest situation in the town, and stated by the inhabitants to have been flooded entirely in the great inundation which took place in 1640. From this depression in the ground, the quarter of Sankore, which forms the northernmost angle of the city, rises to a considerable elevation, in such a manner that the mosque of Sankore, which seems to occupy its ancient site and level, is at present situated in a deep hollow—an appearance which seems to prove that this elevation of the ground is caused by the accumulation of rubbish, in consequence of the repeated ruin which seems to have befallen this quarter pre-eminently, as being the chief stronghold of the native Songhay. The slope which this quarter forms toward the northeastern end in some spots exceeds eighty feet.

The whole number of the settled inhabitants of the town amounts to about 13,-000, while the floating population during the months of the greatest traffic and intercourse, especially from November to January, may amount on an average to 5000, and under favorable circumstances to as many as 10,000.

[Dr. Barth made an excursion with the sheikh to Kabara, the harbor of Timbuktu, and they took up their residence at the desert camp already described.]

Notwithstanding trifling incidents which tended occasionally to alleviate the tediousness of our stay, I was deeply afflicted by the immense delay and loss of time, and did not allow an opportunity to pass by of urging my protector to hasten our departure; and he promised me that, as I was not looking for property, he should not keep me long. But, nevertheless, his slow and deliberate character could not be overcome, and it was not until the arrival of another messenger from Hamda-Allahi, with a fresh order from the sheikh to deliver me into his hands, that he was induced to return into the town.

My situation in this turbulent place now approached a serious crisis; but, through the care which my friends took of me, I was not allowed to become fully aware of the danger I was in [because of being a Christian—ed.]. The sheikh himself was greatly excited, but came to no decision with regard to the measures to be taken; and at times he did not see any safety for me except by my taking refuge with the Tawarek, and placing myself entirely under their protection. But as for myself I remained quiet, although my spirits were far from being buoyant; especially as, during this time, I suffered severely from rheumatism; and I had become so tired of this stay outside in the tents, where I was not able to write, that, when the sheikh went out again in the evening of the 16th, I begged him to let me remain where I was. Being anxious about my safety, he returned the following evening. However, on the 22d, I was obliged to accompany him on another visit to the tents, which had now been pitched in a different place, on a bleak sandy eminence, about five miles east from the town, but this time he kept his promise of not staying more than twenty-four hours. It was at this encampment that I saw again the last four of my camels, which at length, after innumerable delays, and with immense expense, had been brought from beyond the river, but they were in a miserable condition, and furnished another excuse to my friends for putting off my departure, the animals being scarcely fit to undertake a journey.

14 AHMADU HAMPATE BA
SHEIK AHMADU AND MASINA

Sheik Ahmadu was the son of a cleric who belonged to the Bari family of the Sangare clan of the Fulani of Masina. After being educated by his father, he wandered eastward in about 1805 and participated in the jihad *of Uthman dan Fodio. Returning to Masina he settled near Djenné, only to be expelled as a subversive. He moved to Sebera, where he opened a Quranic school and attracted a considerable following. The* Ardo *of Masina sought the help of his overlord, Da Dyara, the* Bambara *ruler of Segu, and Da sent an expedition against Ahmadu. Ahmadu declared a holy war and won a notable victory. He seized control in Sebera and rallied to his standard the Fulani, who were awaiting the opportunity to revolt against Bambara control. Ahmadu captured Djenné and established his capital at Hamdullahi in 1815. His state was organized on theocratic lines and, during its short existence, was the most strict Islamic state in West African history. In 1838 al-Hajj Umar visited Hamdullahi on his return journey but received a cool reception from Sheik Ahmadu. Ahmadu died in 1844, and control of Masina passed to his son, Ahmadu Seku II.*

In all of the Niger bend it was now known that Ahmadu Hammadi Bubu was

From Ahmadu Hampate Ba and Jacques Daget, *L'Empire Peul du Macina, 1818–1853* (The Hague and Paris: Mouton, 1962), I, 29–32, 59–65, 238–240, 246–247. Trans. from the French by Nell Elizabeth Painter and Robert O. Collins. Reprinted by permission. Material in brackets in this selection has been inserted by Professor Collins.

badly viewed by the chief and certain marabouts [holy men], notably those of Djenné. The antagonism, which grew daily, could not but degenerate into open conflict. The Muslim aims of Ahmadu Hammadi and his partisans were presented with such skill that all the believers who sincerely desired to see Islam spread could not reject a cause that seemed to them that of God himself. The marabouts of Djenné, eaten up with jealousy, concerted their efforts and asked the authorities of the city to expel Ahmadu from Runde Siru, which belonged to the chiefs of Djenné. "That Ahmadu Hammadi Bubu," they said, "gets bigger every day beneath our very eyes and we stand by watching, unperturbed by his rise. There is still time to check his rapid ascent. When he reaches the top, he will no longer be a man worth nothing, a straw that can be broken without danger. Then he will represent a threat to all those having a name and position in the country."

One of the chiefs of Djenné instructed Ahmadu to leave Runde Siru as he had come, with all those who wanted to follow him. But Ahmadu asked for a period of grace because of the interests he had in the country.

Meanwhile, a few of Ahmadu's *talaba* had gone to the market at Simay, a village in Derari, to take up a collection.[1] The Crown Prince of Masina, Ardo Guidado, son of the Ardo of Masina, Hamadi Dikko (1801–1810), was there. Seeing the pupils of Ahmadu pass, he said:

The marabouts of Runde Siru are beginning to acquire an importance that I hardly like at all. Let someone take a covering from one of his talaba by force so that I can sit on it and signify by this gesture to Ahmadu Hammadi Bubu that as long as there is an ardo alive in the land of Masina and its environs, a "quill-driver" will not command the territory. I want Ahmadu Hammadi Bubu to know that the role of a marabout should consist of blessing marriages, washing the dead, baptizing newborn infants, and especially of living on handfuls of food, begged here and there from door to door in the villages; but nothing more.

The courtisans chased the talaba and seized one of them. They beat him severely and tore off his cloak. After the

market, Ardo Guidado had word sent to Ahmadu Hammadi Bubu to leave Runde Siru immediately and to take only what belonged to him or else his cavalry would trample his fields and begging gourds.

After having worked ceaselessly for eight years to dispose the minds of the people in his favor, Ahmadu was no longer an obscure marabout who could be vexed and mistreated with impunity. He alerted his partisans and asked them to be ready for any eventuality. He declared to those present at Runde Siru, "God commands us to have no other master but Him. Now look, Segu and the ardos want to force us to obey their idols and themselves. They say that they are the masters of the land and that it will belong to them as long as they are living. In truth the earth belongs to no one but God, and He wills it to whomever He wishes." Then he took a blessed Nattal lance and armed one of his best *taliba*, Ali Guidado, from Taga in Sebera, with it.[2] This man was a sure partisan. He had left an immense fortune in livestock, lands, and watering places to dedicate himself to God and live under the orders of Ahmadu Hammadi Bubu, whose humble and sometimes difficult life he shared. Ahmadu said to his disciple:

Ali Guidado, go to the market of Simay; have a few talaba go with you. You will meet Ardo Guidado. On my behalf you will ask for the cloak of my pupil. If he refuses, repeat your request three times, invoking the name of God and the tradition of honest men. You will not let yourself be frightened by his cries or his threats. If he persists in refusing to give back the cloak, you will stab him with this lance; he will die.

Ali Guidado went to the market. Seeing Ardo Guidado stretched out on woolen coverlets in the midst of his courtisans, he turned to him and said, "I come to beg you in the name of my master, Ahmadu Hammadi Bubu, to give back the woolen

---

[1] Talaba, plural of taliba, meaning "one who seeks" —usually a student of divinity who has attached himself to a holy man and teacher (ed.).

[2] A nattal lance was one with a barbed head (ed.).

cover you took by force from one of his taliba last week." Ardo Guidado raged against Ali Guidado. The latter, unperturbed, reiterated his request a second and a third time. The prince, vexed to see a beggar resist him with such courage in public, became violently angry. He seized a saker and brusquely stood up, crying with all his might: "Get out of my sight, quick, quick! And go tell your master, who is far from being my own, that I will never return the cloak of his taliba. I've traded it for some hydromel. I know that will irritate him, but his anger means nothing to me. According to the *Quran,* hydromel is a shameful drink, but not so for my ancestors. Go tell your master to get out of Runde Siru or . . ." and Ardo Guidado addressed an indecent insult to Ahmadu Hammadi Bubu.

This outrage provoked Ali Guidado, who suddenly felt himself filled with supernatural strength similar to that with which God fills the hearts of those He chooses to accomplish heroic acts or to undergo painful tortures without weakening. Executing his perilous mission to the end, he leapt like a panther, emitted a fearful cry, and stabbed Ardo Guidado with his lance.

The prince received the blow in his stomach, staggered, and fell backward. The talaba were scattered throughout the market and surveyed the scene from afar. To spread panic and permit Ali Guidado to escape, they shouted war cries. The merchants, thinking the talaba were a group of brigands, dispersed. The courtisans, who could not believe their eyes, were dragged and jostled by the frantic crowd. Ali Guidado ran down the bank, threw himself into the little river of Simay, and swam to the other side, followed by all the talaba. They went back to Runde Siru and awaited the consequences of their attack.

Prince Ardo Guidado expired the same day. The news spread rapidly. The commentary varied, depending on whether one was for or against Ahmadu Hammadi

Bubu. Ardo Ahmadu, father of the victim, wanted to punish the marabout. He sent envoys to the *Da Dyara,* the King of Segu, to Gueladio Bayo Bubu Hambodedio, chief of *Kunari,* of Faramoso, the King of the Bubu, and to Musa Kulibali, King of *Monimpe.* "I ask for your support," he had them say to them. "The quill-driver of Runde Siru has dared to have my son assassinated. If his act remains unpunished, he will grow in the eyes of the inhabitants of the country and will undermine our prestige in the eyes of everyone. Worse than that, later he will force us to prostrate ourselves on the ground, like asses eating grass."

The notables of Djenné told Ahmadu to leave Runde Siru a second time, for they did not want to be confused with his partisans and to have to undergo retaliation for an act with which they had not been associated.

The Ardo of Sebera had promised Ahmadu hospitality in case he left Runde Siru and could find no place to live. Ahmadu asked the ardo if his promise still stood despite the serious incident at Simay. The ardo answered that not far from his residence, Soy, there was a place called Nukuma where Ahmadu could settle with his people when and as he liked. Ahmadu then made preparations and left Runde Siru for Nukuma, followed by all his talaba and partisans. He called upon those who could not meet him because they were far away to be ready for any eventuality. The father of Ali Guidado, frightened by the turn of events, wanted to deliver his son to Ardo Ahmadu to appease him [Ardo Ahmadu]; but the Ardo of Sebera opposed such an act, alleging that Ali Guidado had sought refuge in his territory and that honor forbade him to turn over a man to whom he had accorded hospitality.

The expulsion of Ahmadu Hammadi Bubu from Runde Siru by an ultimatum from the notables of Djenné, a city renowned as a spiritual center and Muslim metropolis, was considered by the faithful as a disloyal act that, contrary to the aim of the men of Djenné, had the effect of attracting more sympathy for Ahmadu. The latter, with Uthman and Ismail Sankoma, on one hand, and Imam Ismail of Gomitogo, on the other, had acquired the support of the following territories: Pondori, Dienneri, Derari, Sebera. But so long as he had not won Fakala to his cause, Ahmadu's situation remained precarious.

Ahmadu had reviewed several matters with the great marabout Alfa Yero. Afterward he had not broken with the family of this master. During his stay at Runde Siru, Ahmadu had not stopped helping the three sons of Alfa Yero—Mahmud, Bukari, and the youngest, Umar—all of whom were eminent marabouts and warriors at the same time.

Ahmadu Hammadi could enter relations soliciting their support without fear. The three brothers took to the field across Fakala and Femay. Because they were spiritual counselors and masters of the country and because they were aided by an intensive propaganda campaign, they succeeded in disposing the minds of the people in Ahmadu's favor. Mahmud Alfa Yero, who later became *Qadi* of Fakala and carried the title of *Alqali Fakala,* personally addressed his cousins, Alfa Samba Futa Ba (founder of the village of Poromain), Ahmadu Manti Ba, Almami Abdu Ba, and Ahmadu Daradia Ba, as well as the following notables whose support was indispensable: Abd al-Karim Dem, Ibrahima Kamara, Alfa Seydu, Hammadi Ali Futanke, Ahmadu Hammadi Koradie, Ahmadu Alqali Hafidji, called Hammadun Ba, and Ahmadu Diulde Kanne of Kuna. "The fetishes of all races have entered a pact with the ardos, and several armies, including that of Segu, are preparing to attack Nukuma. Ahmadu Hammadi Bubu must be able to find aid and protection among us." Such were the terms of his propaganda. The notables named above swore to defend Ahmadu Hammadi Bubu, who could then look with confidence toward the future. He organized his Quranic school like a veritable army of soldiers and waited. . . .

.   .   .

As a result of his rapid victory over the coalition, Ahmadu Bubu had won the adherence of all the Muslim groups to his party, whether Fulani, *Marka,* or *Bozo.* His name became a synonym for "powerful protector." On the other hand, the title of sheik that Uthman dan Fodio had bestowed on him permitted him to give the country a solid theocratic administration, for those who had rallied to his party had sworn allegiance to him and had placed themselves under his religious supervision. As soon as he was sheltered from internal and external intrigues, which are always possible and which he had to take into account during the first years of the Dina [state], Sheik Amadu brought together about a hundred marabouts and said to them:

I would not like to have the charge of administrating the Dina alone. Such power belongs only to God. You recognized me as your sheik, that is to say your spiritual guide. But all of us must unite our efforts to give the country a solid organization to take the place of the despotism of the ardos and of the other chiefs—an administrative and religious organism that will assure a better economic and social life for all.

After several months of work, the marabouts individually presented projects that Sheik Ahmadu examined attentively to the smallest detail. He called together forty authors who seemed to him the most objective and wise and gave them absolute power. Their assembly carried the name *Batu Mawde,* or grand council of consultative *madjilis.* Sheik Ahmadu asked the forty advisers to group themselves in commissions, by region of origin and without racial distinctions, in order to reexamine the projects that had been retained to make them conform with the essential laws of Islam. . . .

From among the forty, Sheik Ahmadu chose two trustworthy men to be his personal advisers. He did not present any project to the grand council for deliberation without having discussed all aspects of the project with the two men in private. In the beginning they sat with the other grand councillors, and Sheik Ahmadu called the two whenever he felt the need to do so. Finally, at his request, the two marabouts stayed beside him permanently. They came with their families to live at his house and were with him from the time he got up until the time he went to bed. . . .

.   .   .

The grand council was thus composed of forty members, of which thirty-eight sat in the room with seven doors and two remained in the house of Sheik Ahmadu. No one could be admitted to the body of the grand council unless he were forty years of age, married, and could show himself to be cultured and leading an irreproachable life. In case a grand councillor died, the replacement was chosen by Sheik Ahmadu from among sixty marabouts called arbiters. Then the grand councillors chose a new arbiter from among the marabouts of repute of Hamdullahi [the capital] or the rest of the country. The members of the grand council were required to reside in Hamdullahi. None of them could go more than a day's journey away without first having notified and received the consent of his colleagues. A member of the council who went on a journey was replaced by a marabout of his choice, designated from among the arbiters. The councillors were supported by the treasury. The arbiters could reside wherever they pleased; those who were settled in Hamdullahi enjoyed prerogatives almost equal to those of the grand councillors.

The grand council was charged with directing the country and had the highest authority in all matters. But the private council of Sheik Ahmadu could ask and even require that the grand council reverse a position it had taken. In case of conflict between the private council and the grand council, Sheik Ahmadu did *urwa* [a method of drawing straws of different lengths] and designated forty marabouts from among the sixty arbiters. The decision of this forty was final.

In the beginning Sheik Ahmadu sometimes had serious difficulties in gaining acceptance of his point of view because he lacked the power to cite legal texts to support him. In fact he never had had many books at his disposal, and the grand council included some marabouts who were older and more learned than he. This situation existed for seven years, until he had received, from the family of Uthman dan Fodio, four books treating command, the behavior of the prince, instructions for judges, and difficult passages of the *Quran*. The grand council examined the books they had received and found them to be in agreement with three criteria: the *Quran*, Sunna, and ijma.[3] From that time Sheik Ahmadu could refer to them whenever necessary. These books were conserved in a small building called *bait kitabu*, or house of the books, whose key was kept by Sheik Ahmadu himself. The books did not go out; people were required to consult them in the room with seven doors. Copyists transcribed passages or whole books for chiefs who needed them. Sheik Ahmadu had given each imam a little volume of instructions in which he forbade certain local practices that were not in conformity with Maliki *madhhab* and recalled certain Shiite practices. . . .[4]

.   .   .

[3] Sunna refers to Islamic custom or way of life, particularly the saying and doings of the Prophet. Ijma means "the collecting" and, in Muslim theology, the unanimous consent of the learned doctors (ed.).

[4] The Maliki madhhab, or rite, is one of the four schools of legal opinion in Sunni Islam. The Maliki school was predominant in North Africa. Shiite practices would, of course, be regarded as heretical (ed.).

In the empire of Sheik Ahmadu instruction was regulated, and whoever desired to open a school first had to present his qualifications. The grand council, by the intermediary of the *Sain* [messenger], supervised the schools and made sure that nothing was taught contrary to the *Quran,* Sunna, and ijma. In each capital of the provinces and cantons, Quranic schools existed whose masters received subsidies from the Dina, whereas other establishments received support as a result of public piety.

School age was fixed at seven years, according to Malikite rite. Boys and girls had to be sent to school if they lived in Hamdullahi or in a center designated by the state, *dude Dina.* The fathers of marabout families who did not send their children to school were cited before the notables' council, *batu Sahibe;* an adverse decision by this council constituted ostracism from society. Each marabout, recognized as such, free to open a school and to teach there, could not attempt to collect more than the fee fixed by the grand council for the literal and precise teaching of the *Quran.* This fee was 800 cowries per babz (that is, one-sixth of the *Quran*), which made 48,000 cowries for the whole *Quran.* The master of the school was authorized to have his pupils work, provided that their age and strength were taken into account. In addition he received 7 cowries per week for the youngest pupils. Rich families often sent milk, cows, or slaves to serve the marabout who taught their children, in exchange for their work. Wandering marabouts crossed the land to recruit pupils or simply to preach in order to expose children to religion in the hope that they would accept it. Some were sent by the great council or the provincial amirate; others came voluntarily.

Instruction culminated in an examination. When a pupil had finished learning the whole *Quran* by heart and his master was sure of him, a public meeting was organized. All the reciters of the *Quran* were invited and the presiding officer was chosen. The examination lasted an entire night. It was the wake of the *Quran.* The marabouts took places beside the masters, the relatives and friends formed a circle, and the pupil recited. The marabouts were attentive to confusions and bad pronunciation of the letters, inversion of the order of the verses, memory failures that necessitated the intervention of the marabout charged with prompting, errors that were corrected in time by the pupil, errors unnoted by the examiners and rectified by the pupil after a permitted stop, the endurance of the reciter, the quality of his voice, his age and bearing, and the aspect of his writing, among other things. The pupil who recited without error knelt before his master and terminated with the seven verses of the initial sura with which he had begun. Then the marabouts present bestowed upon the pupil the title of hafiz Kar.[5]

The father of the pupil received congratulations. He gave his child a reward in proportion to his fortune. Aunts, sisters, and the mother also gave presents to the new hafiz Kar. The master was not forgotten in the distribution. Whoever knew how to recite the *Quran* and knew all the conventional signs placed above and below the text could, at his own request, go to Hamdullahi to be heard by Sheik Ahmadu. One who emerged victorious from this second examination, more arduous than the first because of the quality and quantity of the audience, had his fortune assured. He could say: *Seku hadanike Kam*—"The Sheik has listened to me." Thus launched, the student could take courses in theology and law and, from the age of forty, he could become a teaching master or a statesman.

The *defu* was a great meal that the student's family gave for the schoolmasters of their child when he had finished the

[5] Sura is a term used exclusively for a chapter of the *Quran.* Hafiz Kar is a title bestowed on one who commits the *Quran* to memory (ed.).

first thirty suras of the *Quran*. The same feast was repeated more solemnly at the end of the last thirty suras, and relatives, friends, schoolchildren and all the village took advantage of it. This feast took place the day after the wake of the *Quran* and was a great family holiday.

Justice was administered according to Muslim law and the Malikite rite, but a good number of local customs that were not contrary to the letter of the *Quran* were considered to be canonical or were tolerated. In certain regions they were given the force of law. . . .

.   .   .

Al-Hajj Umar's journey in the Arab countries could not pass unnoticed for three reasons. The self-denial which he endured in order to give all his wealth to his master, Muhammad al-Ghali, was talked about everywhere. His great Muslim scholarship made him worthy of being cited, despite his color, as a remarkable doctor and a genius upon whom Islam in West Africa could depend. Finally, he held the title of *muqqadam* of the *Tijaniyya* order—the order that, although nearly the most recent, is gaining on the more ancient ones and is supplanting them in the East as well as in the West. If the impartial wise men welcomed and graciously assisted al-Hajj Umar, muqqadam of the Tijaniyya order, it was quite different with the doctors and masters of the congregations; the most rabid were the leaders of the *Qadiriyya* and *Taibiyya* brotherhoods. For seven months counterattacks were aimed at the Tijaniyya through al-Hajj Umar. Because they were unable to beat him in the domain of science, these adversaries tried to ridicule him because of the color of his skin.

Thus during the course of a scientific discussion, one of his malicious detractors said to al-Hajj Umar, "Oh knowledge, as splendid as you are, my soul is disgusted by you when you wrap yourself in black; you stink when you are taught by an Abyssinian." The crowd broke out in laughter. Al-Hajj Umar waited until the general hilarity had subsided before responding:

The envelope has never lessened the value of the treasure locked inside. Oh! Inconsistent poet, go no more around the Kaaba, the sacred house of Allah, for it is shrouded in black. Oh! Inattentive poet, read the *Quran* no longer, for its verses are written in black. Answer no more the call to prayer, for its first tone was given, under the orders of Muhammad our Model, by the Abyssinian Belal. Hurry and renounce your head covered with black hair. Oh! Poet who waits each day for the meal of the black night that will revive your forces spent by the whiteness of the day; may the white man of good sense excuse me, I am addressing myself only to you. Because you resort to satire to ridicule me, I refuse the competition. In my country, Takrur, as black as we may be, the art of vulgarity is cultivated only by slaves and buffoons. . . .

Then Sheik Muhammad al-Ghali communicated the secrets of the hexagram, the hidden symbol of the sect [Tijaniyya], to al-Hajj Umar and ordered him to return to his country. "Go sweep the country" was the order that al-Hajj Umar received from his master along with the titles of sheik and caliph of the Tijaniyya brotherhood.

Whatever sense commentators give to these words of command, "Go sweep the country," al-Hajj Umar encountered more pain than joy in following them. He would not only have to attack black paganism, but even more, he would have to ward off the blows, resulting from human rivalry, of the members of the Qadiriyya, Taibiyya, and other orders until the very end. Al-Hajj Umar had the habit of saying:

I have been given, I am given, and long after my death I will continue to be given all sorts of reputations. The marabouts are my most faithful detractors; they have attributed all the irregularities and all the moral faults to me; they have done everything to make me appear odious. I have had everything bad said of me except that I was "pregnant with a bastard." The biological impossibility for a man to give birth is the only reason I have been spared that calumny.

Some traditions do in fact make al-Hajj Umar a sublime sheik; some depict him as a sanguinary despot who burned and pillaged everything in his path. If slander is the ransom of greatness, then incontestably, al-Hajj Umar was a great man. When he left Medina, he firmly decided never to become a king or courtesan of a king (that is to say, an official marabout). The proof of this decision is found in this declaration attributed to him: "I have not kept company with kings and I do not like those who do."

Al-Hajj Umar, sheik of the Tijaniyya, journeyed to the lands of West Africa. He passed by Cairo where the savants of the celebrated university tried vainly to catch him in a mistake. This new success further augmented his prestige. A reputation for knowledge and piety preceded him but awakened the defiance of pagan kings and local marabouts. In Bornu al-Hajj Umar miraculously escaped the criminal plotting of the sultan, who gave the traveler one of his own daughters, Mariatu, who was to be the mother of Makki, Seydu, Aguibu, and Koreichi, to make up for his own abortive attempt. Finally the indefatigable pilgrim reached Sokoto, where Muhammad Bello, son of Sheik Uthman dan Fodio, succeeded his father as sultan.

Leaving Sokoto, al-Hajj Umar headed for Hamdullahi. He was accompanied by students, partisans, servants, women, and children—about a thousand people altogether. On the road, he initiated the inhabitants of the countries they crossed into the Tijaniyya belief and assured himself of their sympathy. Although he could not count on this allegiance to even the score with Atiq, at least his [al-Hajj Umar's] son, Ahmadu, when he fled the French in 1893, was cordially received in Hausaland.

At Hamdullahi, Sheik Ahmadu gave al-Hajj Umar the same welcome as he did on the occasion of his first passage. But Ahmad al-Bakkai [Sheik of the *Kunta*] had made arrangements and had given orders to all his vassals to create difficulties for the *Tukulor* pilgrim. The religious supremacy of the Kunta had everything to fear from a Fulani union between al-Hajj Umar and the *Sangare* [the family of Sheik Ahmadu]. When he discovered that al-Hajj Umar had arrived at Hamdullahi, Ahmad al-Bakkai sent him a very praiseworthy poem that ended with these words: "You are the most learned of the sons of slaves of whom I have ever been given to tell." This insidious fashion of insulting him irritated al-Hajj Umar, who answered by sending a harsh letter to the Kunta chief. The latter took a piece of paper and wrote at the top: "In the name of God the Clement and Merciful. Oh God! Pour out Your grace and accord salvation to our Lord Muhammad." In the middle of the page appeared the word "Greetings," and at the bottom appeared the word "End." When he had received this letter, Ahmad al-Bakkai understood that it was a spiteful puzzle intended for him. He showed it to one of his companions, the wise Abd al-Halim, of the *Ida* or *Ali*. "Sheik Ahmad al-Bakkai," said Abd al-Halim, "is calling you a *d'ahil* —that is to say, ignorant, without law." "On what do you base your interpretation of this puzzle?" [questioned al-Hajj Umar]. "On the following Quranic verse: 'The servants of the Benefactor are those who walk modestly on earth and who, challenged by those without laws, answer: Greetings.' " [6]

Al-Hajj Umar wrote a second letter that was more violent than the first and addressed it to Sheik al-Bakkai, who took a new sheet of paper and wrote only: "In the name of God the Clement and Merciful." Once again Abd al-Halim explained the meaning of this missive to al-Hajj

[6] The *Quran*, XXV, 63–64.

Umar. "Sheik al-Bakkai," he said, "thinks you are like Satan. He is basing his opinion on the tradition of the Prophet: The dog is chased away with a cudgel; Satan is a dog and the formula 'in the name of God the Clement and Merciful' is the cudgel that must be used to chase him away." Then Sheik Yerkoy Talfi, a disciple of Sheik al-Bakkai who was adept at handling al-Hajj Umar, said to him: "Do not continue this polemic with al-Bakkai—he will succeed in making you say foolish things and will depreciate you in the eyes of important people. Let me answer in your place. I know the eccentricities of my old disciple." Then Sheik Yerkoy Talfi composed a satirical poem that he entitled "To Make Bakkai Cry," because when he read it, he could not keep himself from crying.

Ahmadu Ahmadu often frequented the room where his grandfather stayed. But al-Hajj Umar never succeeded in caressing the child, who ran away everytime he saw his grandfather. One day Ahmadu Ahmadu, occupied with a game, did not notice the arrival of al-Hajj Umar. The latter grabbed him by the arm before he had time to flee and took him to Sheik Ahmadu, saying, "Oh Sheik Ahmadu, would you like to parley between my *nawli* [rival] and me?" Sheik Ahmadu took the hand of his struggling grandson, and when the child was calm, the sheik said to al-Hajj Umar, "The prayers that you formulated going around the Kaaba and in which you asked God to give you Hamdullahi will be answered of Ahmadu Ahmadu. How can you wish him to see you with pleasure? But let occur what can. Here is my grandson. I entrust him to you and repeat what I said a few years ago when you were present at his baptism." Al-Hajj Umar took Ahmadu Ahmadu's hand and said, "I repeat, Sheik Ahmadu, my first statement concerning our grandson."

15 MOHAMMADON ALION TYAM
THE LIFE OF AL-HAJJ UMAR

The Life of al-Hajj Umar *is a long eulogistic poem written in Fulani by Mohammadon Alion Tyam, who studied at Lao in present-day Senegal. He was one of Sheik Umar's earliest disciples (having joined him in 1846) and one of his most loyal followers. Umar ibn Said Tal was born in 1794 at Halwar in Senegalese Futa. The son of a cleric, he received a religious education and in 1826 set off on his pilgrimage to Mecca, where he was initiated into the* Tijaniyya tariqa *and was appointed* Caliph *of the Sudan. He extended the length of his return journey, residing in Bornu and Sokoto and then in Masina in 1838. He was expelled from Segu but finally settled at Dingiray, where the Futa Jalon, Bambuk, and Bondu regions join. He consolidated his power here between 1845 and 1850 and then proclaimed his* jihad *to spread his teachings and control over Futa Toro, Bambuk, and Karta. By 1854 the jihad was directed against French encroachment, in the face of which al-Hajj Umar turned eastward to establish his control over the Bambara kingdoms. Segu fell to his armies in 1861, and he then moved against the Islamic state of Masina. Despite his contempt for Ahmadu III, he was never able to justify his jihad against another Muslim state, and although his forces took Hamdullahi, he failed to impose his authority or* Tijani *ideas upon the Masinians, who supported a rival brotherhood, the* Qadiriyya.

Umar attempted to escape from Hamdullahi in 1864 but was pursued and lost his life in the struggle.

.   .   .

6. When he had reached his eighteenth year,
   he girded his loins, he prepared himself for combat against the soul, which is not
   an aid.

7. Iblis and all his companions, and this world,
   and the habits of the place, and the comrades who do not leave [you].

8. All that, he rejected it, he left it to make his way toward Allah alone, and that Envoy of Truth who does not add [to the divine prescriptions].

9. He sought acquaintance with Truth and all the laws;
   the divine prescriptions and those founded on the example of Ahmadu were known [by him].

.   .   .

30. When he had finished thirty and three years,
    then he made his preparations, that man who will not be weak.[1]

31. Then set out the servant [of Allah]; he crossed all the numerous lands
    of the Muslims, wending his way toward the great paganism that will not be converted.

32. From Futa toward Bondu, toward Futa Jalon,
    as far as Kangari, Kong, Hausaland, to the religion that does not grow old.

33. He spent seven months at Sokoto, until they were completely finished.
    He also stayed two months at Gwandu; that place was passed.

34. He arrived at Katchena [Katsina], turned his head toward the land of the Taureg, and bent his steps toward
    the Fezzan, toward Egypt, Jidda, where one is so near.

35. He came to the limits [of sacred territory], he stopped at the migat station [2] until he
    had answered [by reciting the Labbaika]; he said the Labbaika until he had entered Mecca.

.   .   .

60. . . . Then they returned toward the House of Allah; the pilgrimage was then tripled.

61. There the Differentiator became even more attached to our Sheik Muhammad al-Ghali, so as to seek that which has no end.

62. They left the Kaaba, went together toward Daiba [Medina],
    he went a second time to visit Ahmadu, the *zamzami* who tires not.

63. He found that the three years were up, ordered out by Sheik
    Al-Tijani, descendant of the Prophet who will be without fear [the day of judgment]:

64. "Hey, my disciple Muhammad al-Ghali, what keeps you

From Mohammadon Alion Tyam, *La Vie d'El Hadj Omar,* trans. from the Fulani by Henri Gaden (Paris: Institut d'Ethnologie, 1935), pp. 5–7, 12–19, 22–25, 107–120, 171–183, 194–200, 202–203. Trans. from the French by Nell Elizabeth Painter and Robert O. Collins. Reprinted by permission. Bracketed material in this selection has been supplied by Professor Collins.
[1] Umar ibn Said Tal left for Mecca in 1827. He died on February 12, 1864 at the age of 70 (ed.).

[2] Migat station is one of the places at which pilgrims to Mecca put on the ihram, or pilgrim's garment. The Labbaika is an invocation that is customarily recited during the pilgrimage to Mecca (ed.).

from going to Umar the Futanke
the thing that he seeks

65. the blessing and the *zikr* and all the
    secrets,
    and an authorization entirely [over
    the] whole; leave nothing aside."

66. He took him, he led him as far as
    the "garden" of Him
    who was made the best, so as to
    make him witness to a point that
    surpasses all.

67. Then he said to him [to the
    Prophet]: "Bear witness, I have
    given your *taliba,* according to
    the order of your descendant,
    and the taliba who never tires.

68. I have given him the blessing and
    the zikr entire and, at the same
    time
    a sound authorization, an *istikhara*
    that will not become obscure." [3]

69. Praise to Umar the Futanke, who
    loves [religion] and will not hate
    [it].
    Who is furnished with the heart of
    a man who has girded his loins,
    of a firm man who will not
    weaken.

70. As he had thought of staying [in
    Medina], then the superior [Mu-
    hammad al-Ghali] who never
    tires ordered him to return to the
    west: "Go sweep the country
    clean: [4]

71. All the affairs of this world and of
    the Other are in my hands. Yes,
    you, my taliba, listen and

remember well:

72. Here certainly [in my hands] as
    long as you do not mix with the
    kings of this world and their
    companions; listen and under-
    stand well."

73. The Differentiator said good-by to
    Daiba [Medina], set out toward
    Egypt; so that
    once again he could hear news of
    his people, to no longer worry.

74. There all the wise men of Cairo as-
    sembled to test him,
    the sheik who came from the lands
    [of the west], the savant who
    makes no mistakes,

75. because of what had been said of
    him [saying] that he understood
    all knowledge.
    They said that a man from the west
    was not worth [what was said of
    him] that he would
    be incapable.

76. When they sat down together, so
    many as to completely surround
    him, when they had cast their
    keen shafts, which do not fail to
    penetrate,

77. the universal [ram], with a black
    spot in mind, who understood all
    knowledge.
    Whoever pierced him [with a ques-
    tion], even then he did not stop
    short.

78. Until finally these prodigious men
    understood from the manner in
    which the sheik answered these
    profound, arduous questions,
    which are not easy.

79. Here is a wise man who has under-
    stood all he had read; here is a
    man who excels in profound
    comprehension; he is not mis-
    taken.

80. The Differentiator said good-by to
    Egypt, set off toward the Magh-
    rib,
    the western lands, toward Futa
    Toro, whence he came.

81. He marched hurriedly, he arrived

---

[3] Sheik Sidi Ahmad Al-Tijani requested Muhammad al-Ghali to initiate Umar into the religious
brotherhood (tariqa) of the Tijaniyya. Muhammad
al-Ghali not only initiated Umar into the Tijaniyya
tariqa but also gave him the authority of Caliph over
the land of the blacks. Zikr are acts of devotion
performed by Muslim holy men. A taliba is "one
who seeks"—a term that usually refers to a student
of divinity. The istikhara is a prayer for special
favor or blessing that, among the Tijani of Senegalese Futa, follows special and secret formulas provided by Sheik Sidi Ahmad al-Tijani and is known
only to the principal men of the order. Umar's
knowledge of these special istikhara enhanced his
prestige and authority in the western Sudan (ed.).
[4] That is, by means of the jihad (ed.).

at Fezzan. There
sorrows penetrated the heart of the
savant who does not worry,

82. because of the sickness of his
friend, an intimate confidant.
That place
is called Tidjrata, the name of the
place where they stayed.

83. There stayed [died] one of Allah's
saints, our Aliu,
the son of Saidu; the intimate
friend obtained that which has
no end.

84. May Allah pardon him, have pity
on him and pardon him
for the *baraka* [grace] of Him who
was made the best of the creatures and who committed no
sin.[5]

85. The Differentiator prepared himself, and set out for Tubu.
There he stopped, there he stayed
awhile, then once again continued on his way.

86. The Differentiator prepared to
march, heading for the land of
Sudan, dark, frightening, so that
they could cross them [the land]
again.

87. Finally he arrived in the land of
Bornu; he stopped.
The Sultan of Bornu contrived a
plot that miscarried.

88. He who is protected from behind
and from before and from all
sides and from above and from
below, to scheme against him,
certainly will not find it easy.

89. He readied men to go in the night
to he who commits
no injustice.
They were powerless to reach him,
by the protection of Allah for
whom nothing is impossible.

90. He sent still others in the day. And
these [were] strong men making

menacing gestures; then these
two as well were struck with
bewilderment and returned [to
the place whence they came].[6]

91. The Differentiator made preparations to turn his head toward
Gobir, went even farther,
went toward Gwandu, arrived at
Sokoto; there he stayed.

92. He found a just sultan, wise, powerful, who committed no injustice; they called him Muhammad Bello, a river that never
runs dry.[7]

93. He sheltered him, made him presents of hospitality without end,
because of the consideration between the finder and the found,
who were not without reputation.

94. This latter gladdened him, he softened him, he made easy
all his affairs, because a man of
great family and weight
does not humble.

95. To the point that they helped one
another within the limits fixed
by Allah and the *Sunnah*
because they were deep rivers that
do not run dry,·

96. of science and of holy war and of
the affairs of this world and the
Other.[8]
To the point that they intermingled
their pure names, which will not
be soiled.

.   .   .

105. When the sheik had spent seven
years at Sokoto, he made his

[6] Another tradition recounts that the Sultan of
Bornu welcomed al-Hajj Umar. He did provide him
with a wife, Mariatu, by whom the sheik had four
sons. Nevertheless, his miraculous escapes from
danger not only enhanced his prestige, but God
punished Bornu with four years of drought (ed.).
[7] Muhammad Bello was the son of Uthman dan Fodio, who led the Jihad against the pagans of northern Nigeria early in the nineteenth century (ed.).
[8] Sunnah refers to Islamic customs or way of life—
particularly the sayings and doings of the Prophet
(ed.).

[5] Tidjrata was the last oasis in the Fezzan on the
Bilma Trail leading to Bornu. Aliu was the brother
and companion of al-Hajj Umar (ed.).

preparations, he hurried in his march, he marched toward the west,

106. until he had entered Masina, until he had arrived in that city called Hamdùllahi; it was there he sojourned.

107. There Sheik Ahmadu gave him hospitality, not from affection, [but] from having seen his powers, which are without limit.[9]

.   .   .

109. When he had spent nine months in this city
named Hamdullahi, he made his preparations; that place too was passed.

110. Finally he arrived in the land of Segu, then he stopped
in that city of Sikoro, of great name, whose renown is undiminished.

111. There one named Tyefolo who would not convert [to Islam] had succeeded to power,
an infidel of dark heart, an evil man who would not change [his opinions].[10]

.   .   .

123. The King [*Almami*] of Futa Jalon treated him [Umar] with disdain, took no account [of him].
One named [Almami] Yahya, hostile to the power, was deposed.

124. The Sheik passed the season of the rains at Kumbi, it was com-

pletely finished, he was in perfect health,
finally he met there the Almami Abu Bakr, in front of whom he went.[11]

125. He welcomed Abu Bakr, who loves [religion] and was not hostile to him,
who had reflected on the Sheik's good qualities, who did not fail [to retain what they promised].

126. Almami Abu Bakr said to him: "Go down to that
place called Dyegunko, a place of light that will not become dark."

127. [Then] answered the sheik's appeal, the chosen Fulani, the patient ones untiring,
the supports of Allah and the Prophet who will not weaken.

128. There religions began to be reinforced, to be elevated until it [Dyegunko] was rendered luminous,
then the sheik knew that he had reached a place to stay and think out his plans.

129. When four rainy seasons had passed at Dyegunko, he set out to attempt to accomplish what he desired with all his heart.

130. Those who had made the exodus from Dyegunko toward Futa [Toro] and to
Dingiray, Nyoro, and Segu, pardon, [oh thou] who will never die,

131. All those among them who are dead! To those who are living, give your grace;
when their breath will come to an end, pardon, [oh thou] for whom nothing is impossible.

132. He left, he crossed Futa [Jalon]

[9] Al-Hajj Umar left Sokoto shortly after the death of Muhammad Bello in October 1837. He arrived the following year at the capital of the state of Masina, Hamdullahi, founded in 1815 by Sheik Ahmadu. Ahmadu was the son of a Muslim cleric who had assisted Uthman dan Fodio in Hausaland before setting up a Quranic school in Masina. Here he declared a holy war against the pagan rulers of Masina, defeated them, and established his authority (ed.).

[10] Al-Hajj Umar was expelled from Segu, whence he traveled to Kangaba (Mali) and thence to the Kaukan region of the Upper Niger, where he wandered for seven years preaching and initiating until settling at Dingiray (ed.).

[11] Almami Yahya was deposed by Abu Bakr in 1827. The author is mistaken here, for Almami Abu Bakr died in 1840 shortly before the arrival of Sheik Umar. His son and successor was installed at Dyegunko, two days' journey from Timbo in the Futa Jalon (ed.).

turning toward Gabu to Bokke,
to Salum; Baol also was reached.

133. He marched toward Cayor, toward
Dyellis and to our Walo, him of
Brak, having entered Toro at
Halwar he once again put his
foot to earth.

134. The going and the return of the pilgrimage of the sheik, the count
is

of twenty years complete; understand so as to remember
[this forgive, oh my listener].[12]

.   .   .

633. Each day the sheik preached a new
[sermon], he gave us innuendoes,
the project of peopling the village
of Kundyan was [thus] known.

634. Finally, one day, the sheik himself
got up,
he betook himself to the mountain,
then raised up a rock, which was
brought back [by him].

635. Immediately the army set out,
headed toward the mountain,
carried rocks on their heads until
they
formed piles: a rampart was drawn,
built up until it was entirely
finished.

636. The sheik sought *talaba* to people
the village;
responding to his call were good
and patient men in the pledging
of allegiance that they would not
break.

637. He asked Allah for all the happiness in this world and in the
Other for them;
whoever was entitled to his pardon
there turned toward paradise.

638. The sheik entrusted to Allah this
group that would not falter; the

sufa dyam was their chief; the
village was left behind.

.   .   .

645. He left there in the morning, proceeded to Gundguru. They
armed there and stopped.
They stayed there: the [people of]
Bondu came, saluted, and was
saluted in return.

646. The sheik said: "Hey, Bondu!
Raise up your country
so that it will assemble, you will fire
on Senudebu until it be utterly
destroyed.

647. Without that, emigrate, the land
has ceased to be yours;
it is the land of the European, existence with him will not be good."

648. Those who had accepted emigration did so safe and sound with
their goods.
Those who had refused to leave,
fire made them emigrate; they
cleared out [all the same].

649. The Differentiator said: "Hey,
Tyerno Haimut, accompany
them a little
so that they will be put well on the
road to Kuigui, and then you
will come back." [13]

650. They began to cry: "Ah! My
mother, ah! My small brother,
let us march!
Let us march, march! The world
is overturned! Where will we
go?"

651. The sheik left early from Gundguru, turned to Bulebane,
armed, dismounted; there too, he
stayed.

652. Muhammad Dyalo and Tyerno
Yero, they had taken some

---

[12] The wanderings of al-Hajj Umar took him over
most of Senegalese Futa and ended in Futa Toro in
1846. Thereafter al-Hajj Umar consolidated his position. He spread his tariqa among the lesser clergy
of the Futa Jalon, seeking to detach them from the
rival brotherhood, the Qadiriyya, and allegiance to
the almamis (ed.).

[13] In 1854 the forces of al-Hajj Umar invaded Bambuk and Bondu, where al-Hajj Umar sought to incite
the inhabitants to action against French encroachment and their outpost at Senudebu. The jihad was
now clearly directed against European penetration,
from which al-Hajj Umar urged the people to flee;
his forces frequently burned villages to force the
inhabitants to emigrate (ed.).

things from the column of those who deny Allah, they were then given to the sheik.[14]

653. Finally they were informed from the camps of the *Damel* [chief] of Carli;

they recrossed [the Senegal] and abandoned the river, which is solitary to the point that there would be no more animation.

.   .   .

657. They spent the day marching, until the evening, they arrived at Ndyawar.

They stopped there, passed the night; the morning there the departure was postponed.

658. There the sheik prayed the prayer of Korka when he had arrived [May 15, 1858].

When he left there, they arrived at Lobali; set down once again.

659. He left from there in the morning, he hurried the march until the evening, he came

to Horndolde, they stopped, spent the night, right away they were in a better state.[15]

660. There the *damga* came to greet the sheik.

He answered them: "Be praised, here friends who will not be hostile."

661. He said: "True friends, emigrate; the land has ceased to be yours.

It is the land of the European, your existence with him will not be correct."

662. Those who accepted and were resolute, were led safe and sound until they had arrived.

Those who left in hesitation and returned, Those, they were dis-

posed of.

663. The sheik sent a part of his house to Nyora. [capital of Karta] There he prepared himself to turn toward Futa, toward the true friends who would not weaken.

.   .   .

667. When he left from there, he dismounted at Horé-Fondé.[16]

There they stayed, there they camped, there new arrangements were made.

668. Futa came there, and Toro, to greet our sheik.

When he had returned their greetings, he told them that it was an emigration without delay.

669. The sheik said, "Leave, this land has ceased to be yours.

It is the land of the European, existence with him will never be good."

670. They answered, they said, "By understanding and consent." They returned.

Those having made firm resolution, when they arrived [at their homes], immediately [their] preparations were made.

671. The sheik put the masters of Futa at the head of the emigration.

They yielded, packed up, loaded, [their goods] the east was [their] point of direction.

672. Almami of Rindyao; Muhammad, him from Odedyi,

The son of Mahmud Ali, what they have said, Futa, certainly does not transgress it.

673. And Tyerno Salihu, son of Sire Haruna.

These are the men who showed themselves remarkable to the south of the river, the

[14] Muhammad Dyalo was a taliba from Futa Toro who appeared in Bondu in 1857 (ed.).
[15] In 1857 al-Hajj Umar besieged Medina, the capital of the small state of Khaso on the Senegal River. When the French captured Medina, Umar began his withdrawal to the east and urged the people to emigrate with him (ed.).

[16] In mid-July 1858, al-Hajj Umar returned to Senegalese Futa and the large village of Horé-Fondé. He then ordered the inhabitants of Senegalese Futa to emigrate eastward with him (ed.).

names that are not without reputation.

674. And Tyerno Mulay Abu Bakr, the
sheik, our saint.

All of them, when they were
united, respect grew to the point
of not being small.

675. From Futa to Nyoro, wherever
they stopped,

they were honored men, it was
holiday when they arrived.

676. Those who had stayed, stayed [be-
hind], groping in the search for
commandments. Name Tyerno
Fondu to a command that will
achieve [nothing]!

677. The sheik set out toward Toro.[17]

.   .   .

683. He turned toward Toro, he said:
"Emigrate, do not delay,

go out from where there is no religion, from where the Sunnah is
upside-down."

684. He began to tell them: "Emigrate,
the land has ceased to be yours.

It is the land of the European; your
existence with them will not succeed."

685. Those who had consented changed
their goods, procured

beasts of burden, made their packets.

As soon as the baggage was loaded,
they turned their heads toward
the east.

686. The sheik put our village of Halwar
at the head, he said:

"Rise up, go to Nyoro, the good
that never ends." [18]

687. The sheik learned that the *Dyum*
Samba had broken the understanding.

There the unique one went on

horseback to Gamadyi, where he
dismounted.

688. He said to the dyum [chief]: "What
are you saying, after having accepted what you had discussed?"

He said: "Make your packs." The
dyum made his pack, that was
loaded, then the sheik returned.

689. The sheik made his preparation,
said his good-byes to the dyum,
they set out

in the direction of the east. The
works of Allah were close.

.   .   .

694. The sheik talked with the men of
Haire; that they rise up and emigrate.

That was difficult, he made the
master of Haire move, then they
left.

695. He left Haire in the morning,
turned toward Golleta, they arrived, set down.

There they stayed because of
negotiations with Lao, they
passed on,

696. to m'Bumba. He arrived, there
they dismounted.

There their chief presented ex-
cuses, so they continued on farther.

697. The sheik mounted his horse, left
the village, then remembered.

He retraced his steps; he said:
"Bring my son so that I may go
farther."

698. Immediately the grandson of
Tyerno Baila was given to the
sheik.

The sheik set him on the hindquar-
ters of [his] horse, then they
went away.[19]

.   .   .

997. Ahmadu Ahmadu sent men once
again to our sheik.

---

[17] Almami of Rindyao, Muhammad Mahmud Ali
Dundu, Tyerno Mulay Abu Bakr, and Tyerno
Salihu Dya were all important and influential leaders in Senegalese Futa (ed.).
[18] Al-Hajj burned his birthplace, Halwar, to force
the Toro to follow him (ed.).
[19] Umar Tyerno Baila was Umar's commander at
Nyoro. He was married to a woman of [the]
m'Bumba who had returned to her family. Her child
was the one taken by Sheik Umar (ed.).

When they had arrived, they gave
him a letter, it was given back to
them.

998. The sheik said: "Read." They said:
"We cannot."
The sheik said: "Go back, let him
who is not incapable bring it."

999. When they had returned, he [Ah-
madu] sent others to our sheik.
Mudibbu Hammadi Ahmadu read
the [letter, it] was understood.

1000. They went back, he [the sheik] sent
these envoys with them
who have baraka [saintliness],
Khalidu, a good man, intelligent
who does not falter,

1001. and Muhammad, son of Tyerno al-
Hassan Baro [of Haire],
he was a savant who understood,
with a courageous tongue that
did not stutter.

1002. We went with them to Hamdu
[Hamdullahi]. When we ar-
rived,
immediately the country was called
together, assembled, the proof
was then given.

1003. Praise be to Muhammad al-Has-
san, your taliba [sheik].
Testimony was given about him in
Masina; this is not nothing.

1004. Verses of [the *Quran*] and traditions were cited and understood;
promises [of recompense in the
other world] and threats [of
punishment], historical recitations, all that was criticized

1005. before him [Ahmadu] until he
knew the work and he worked
until he had shed abundant
tears, recognizing what will
never be good [in his conduct].[20]

1006. We came back with his men to our
sheik,
the Pole and Mediator who is [such
that] whoever provokes
him would not be glad of it.

1007. Their marabout [holy man] stood
up, reading Ahmadu's letter;
finally he brought into [his
reading] bad examples, which
were not suitable.

1008. The sheik said: "Do not repeat
that. If you do it a second time,
I will cut off your head." This
argument was abandoned, they
passed on.

1009. When they returned, we were still
with them. We arrived,
immediately the land was called
together, met again; there they
repeated again [what had been
said].

1010. A letter [of the sheik] was read, a
stronger message than what had
preceded it,
from *Dohor* to the Maghrib, then
that was finished.

1011. The sheik said: "I appeal to justice.
If you accept,
you will mobilize your troops and
I will mobilize mine so that we
can submit together to the judgment when we will meet."

1012. He [Ahmadu] answered: "As you
will accept justice, I will accept
just the same.
All that is contrary to justice, you
will know that I would not accept it."

1013. We returned with his men until we
had arrived
[at the sheik's].
The letter was read, the discussion
was interrupted, and was aban-

---

20 When al-Hajj turned eastward, he attacked the
pagan Bambara kingdoms. The Muslim ruler of
Masina, Ahmadu Ahmadu (Ahmadu III, grandson
of Sheik Ahmadu who had received Umar in 1838),
succeeded to the throne in 1852 and was put to
death by Umar in 1862 after the fall of Hamdullahi.
Ahmadu Ahmadu foresaw the threat of Umar and
sought aid from the Bambara king, Ali, against
Umar on the condition that Ali accept Islam. In his
negotiations with Umar, Ahmadu Ahmadu claimed
that the Bambara king was a Muslim and was under
his protection. Umar sought to prove publicly the
false pretensions of Ahmadu by sending the mission
under Muhammad al-Hassan. The armies of al-Hajj
Umar took Segu, the Bambara capital, in 1861, and
al-Hajj Umar turned toward Masina and its ruler,
Ahmadu Ahmadu (ed.).

doned there.

1014. On Wednesday the prayer of Korka was prayed. He [the sheik] summoned the [warriors of] Segu [April 2, 1862].

Thursday the second prayer was prayed, preparations were made.

1015. He preached; he said: "An army." That very day

a veracious taliba proceeded to the engagement of fidelity, which he did not break.

.   .   .

1017. The sheik stayed at Sikoro seeking an army.

When they were many, the Mediator, the Pole that does not weaken made his preparations [to march against Ahmadu].

1018. There Madani Ahmadu [son] of our sheik was installed,

support of Allah and of the Prophet who does not tire.

1019. The sheik counted eight hundred [men], leaving him

these chosen talaba; the swearing of allegiance was not broken.

1020. On the eighth Thursday [April 10, 1862], they then set out,

the sheik of sheiks, who, emigrating for God, does not tire,

1021. toward Dika. He arrived, there they reassembled,

they camped there and waited until the soldiers were many.

.   .   .

1027. On Friday [May 9, 1862] Ahmadu made himself known to the savant who is not mistaken.

1028. There the unique one gave orders, told the columns to shoot to give the men courage; he was not presumptuous, he made no display . . .

1029. That day was Saturday [May 10, 1862], Ahmadu then set out early to meet him

at Tyayawal; they then grouped,

there they were put in order.[21]

1030. At the hour of dohor, when they would have said their prayers, they struck

so hard that they clashed. There acts were done that were not good.

1031. They came back to the sheik to the point of passing him. Those who have love of themselves

came to him and stopped; they thought that would not be settled.

.   .   .

1036. Ahmadu sent to Masina to have axes brought

so that a fence be made around them, so strong that they would not go out again.

1037. Look at their foolishness, one would think that they were dealing with cattle.

They did not know that the Mediator whom Allah has put as guide would not weaken.

1038. He was a great Pole, a saint who knew all the branches

of the science of Truth and Law and understood them,

1039. who has crossed the tributaries and still waters, the streams and the rivers;

who, reading this *hadra* [of Muhammed al-Ghali], drank there and was refreshed;

1040. who inherited from Ahmadu [the Prophet] his Sunnah complete,

who has followed the book and, when he has consulted it, does not wander lost.

1041. Having disciplined his heart when he vanquished [his] soul and all [his] members,

Iblis was stunned and reduced to

[21] Sheik Umar advanced rapidly toward Hamdullahi in May 1862. Ahmadu Ahmadu was at Djenné with his army, and to forestall Umar, he sent one of his uncles to request that Umar halt his march on Hamdullahi. In the afternoon of May 10, 1862, Ahmadu Ahmadu's forces attacked Umar's army from the south (ed.).

dust, his army dispersed.

1042. He braved the cold, he braved the heat and wind;

he was courageous, and when they brought the males [enemies] close, he did not lose his head.

1043. Finally, the night of Monday [May 11–12], the sheik ordered them to go meet them

the hypocrites; they went to meet in their turn, then came back.

1044. During the day of Wednesday [May 14] the sheik preached, drew their attention to

the promises [of recompense] and the threats [of eternal punishments];

the story [of the Prophet] and the maxims were exposed.

1045. "Hey! Be firm! Allah needs [our] passage farther on!"

The day of Thursday [May 15], they set out toward the village of Hamdu [Hamdullahi].

1046. When it was day, that was the day of Thursday, when he set out,

the sheik left to dwell in the village of Hamdu [Hamdullahi]; they did not impede him.

1047. There the sons of Futa swore allegiance to our sheik;

this pledge of allegiance until death, because of the promise [made] with Allah, they would not break [it].

1048. Then they got down from their horses, they began to say the zikr, they proceeded.

Ahmadu appeared, charged, was wounded, and then was taken to the back.

1049. All those who had made [their horses penetrate in our lines]; and their horses all remained there.

There victory came right through, Kaku was reached and passed! [22]

1050. Mahmud said, "What is this here?" They said, "This, it is Kaka; whoever goes past it does not stop from here to Hamdu [Hamdullahi]."

1051. Immediately he turned halfway around, he and his horse stayed there.

Then Futa was angry, scowled, and pursued. [23]

1052. Ahmadu, it was found that he had entered a canoe and fled; his army passed further up; scattered to the point of not assembling again.

.   .   .

1058. The sheik said to Alfa that he should pursue Ahmadu; he was pursued, reached, brought to Mopti, imprisoned [and was killed].

1059. The Masinians came there, repented, because they were powerless of the numerous cattle, horses, and lands, all was distributed.

1060. Some from among them [the Fulani] were sincere in repenting of the things they had done;

others, fastened tight to evil, swore that they would never go back.

1061. All the goods of the treasury, horses, captives, cattle, goats, sheep,

asses and gold, silver, clothes, salt, were acquired by the decision of justice.

.   .   .

22 Despite the fierce assaults by the army of Ahmadu Ahmadu, Umar's forces were able to defend themselves and throw back the Masinians. Ahmadu Ahmadu then decided to erect a zareba (thorn fence) around Umar's army in order to starve it into submission. Umar waited four days, during which he exhorted his troops and manufactured bullets to replace his exhausted supply of ammunition. On May 15 Umar's forces advanced on foot, holding their fire until they were within close range of the Masina infantry. Ahmadu Ahmadu had sent his cavalry to the rear, and his infantry was no match for Umar's musketeers. Despite valiant charges, the Masina infantry was defeated and Ahmadu Ahmadu was wounded (ed.).

23 Mahmud was a paternal uncle of Ahmadu Ahmadu. Upon reaching Kaka, where he was informed that the Masina army would not be reformed, he turned and charged Umar's advancing forces and was killed (ed.).

1110. There finished the battle of the
sheik against Masina.
Those who got away arrived, informed the sheik; then they felt
relieved.

1111. There the Masinians assembled,
beseiged the sheik who commits
no injustice [in Hamdullahi],
from all sides, until [the siege] was
very tight; the Muslims did not
get out.

1112. My sheik was closed up nine
months; they did not get out.

1113. So well that the investment was
very tight, the millet was
finished, the cattle killed,
the goats, sheep, asses, and horses,
so that finally they came to men.

1114. When he knew that it was a closed
question, immediately the Pole
sent Tijani to the Hake, so that
religion might regain its
strength.

1115. In Shaban, the night of Sunday the
twenty-eighth [February 6,
1864], then the sortie of the Generous One who commits no injustice was decreed by Allah.

1116. When they moved, those who were
ahead, when they arrived at the
gate, found a blazing fire; they
stopped.

1117. The Differentiator said, "What is
stopping you?" They answered,
"Fire." He said, "Go over it, no
one will be burned!"

1118. They went over it, all being preserved until they had crossed.
None of them was burned, even the
heat did not reach them.

1119. There went the one who was admitted on the pilgrimage that he had
accomplished;
the one who had received authorization emanating from the descendant whose reputation is
unsurpassed.

1120. A liar, tale bearer, spy, and envious
besides
and a cursed little woman having
informed them, My sheik was

pursued.

1121. That is, from Hamdullahi to the
mountain beyond,
they spent five nights; the end [of
the life of the sheik] was drawing
near.

1122. That day, the third of Ramadan,
during the day of Friday [Febru-
ary 12, 1864],
a great thing happened [whose
memory] will not disappear from
the villages of this world,

1123. near Deguembere, the best place in
our country.
There entered the Pole, whose
equal is not easy [to find],

1124. in that mountain, the best of all our
western mountains,
because of the last born of Adama,
of the son of Saidu who does not
commit injustice.

1125. He was with his chosen sons, those
Makki, Mahi, purified ones who
would not be dirtied.

1126. Muhammadu Sire and Ahmadu
Musa and
Abu Bakr Bambi and Saidi Korka,
who will not become bad,

1127. Demba Gueladyo and Samka Sada
and Ahmadu,
the Fulani from the highland, and
his sons, chosen men who would
not diminish in value,

1128. and Mahmud Bubu. Oh! Allah,
that I could have been included
among them, to be close by my
sheik, there where I would not
have been far away!

1129. Whoever has not had the means to
go to the cavern of Mount Hira,
maybe
go to Deguembere to visit, there he
will be beyond material cares.

1130. Oh! Allah, give me means to go
[there] to visit during my life,
because of the sheik of sheiks, so
that I may be beyond material
cares.

1131. Praise to my Master who protected
my sheik until he was safe,
until he was preserved from these

hypocrites who will not amend
their ways.

1132. You have lied, you have been
ashamed, you have not dared
look men in the face,

for not having been able to lean
over the [body of the] Pole who
causes no prejudice.

1133. Hey! People of Masina, you will la-
ment to the point of shrieking,

Woe to you! Weep these long tears
that will be limitless.

1134. Which way will you turn? Where
can you go? What is your hope?

You have caused bad actions to be
carried out, which will not
become good.

1135. The happiness of the other world
is forbidden you because you

have worked illicit deeds against
the great Pole who will not
shrink.

1136. Hey! Woe to you in this world and
in the Other,

when comes the day of resurrection, to enter the fire, to never
come out.[24]

1146. My sheik was the hut of this world,
you should know it, seventy
years; I add nothing.

1147. All the acts that Masina performed
against our sheik,

Tijani Ahmadu, certainly, has
avenged them to such a point
that they cannot be denied.

1148. Be praised, be blessed, be glorified,
[you] more than all the others
girded and pulled up tall, man
who does not weaken.

1149. All the sons of the sheik and the
talaba, it is they who must

imitate so as to avenge the offense
to the point that nothing is
missed [from their vengeance].

[24] Umar was besieged in Hamdullahi for eight
months from June 1863 to February 7, 1864, at
which time he escaped, but his troops, weakened by
privation, could not move rapidly and sought refuge
on a mountain. Here they repulsed the assaults of
the Masinians, who were joined by the Kunta under
Ahmad al-Bakkai. Continuing the retreat, Umar
reached Deguembere, but when he discovered that
he was being pursued, he sought refuge with his sons
and a few close followers in a cave within a mountain near Deguembere. "The cavern of Mount
Hira" is the cavern in the mountain near Mecca
where Muhammad received his first revelations.
According to one version, Umar then ordered his
army to flee to safety; another version states that a
brush fire reached the cave, ignited the powder, and
killed Umar and his companions. In any event his
death on February 12, 1864 is certain (ed.).

16 FÉLIX EBOUÉ

NATIVE POLICY AND POLITICAL INSTITUTIONS
IN FRENCH EQUATORIAL AFRICA

*Félix Eboué (1884–1944) became Governor General of French Equatorial Africa in 1940.
Originally from French Guiana, he was one of the most famous colonial administrators
in the French Empire and a leading figure at the French African Conference at Brazzaville
in 1944. He was best known for his policies of decentralization and his rejection of the
strict assimilationist policy in colonial administration. The eloquent definition of his
policies that follows was made in November 1941.*

From Jean de la Roche and Jean Gottmann, *La Fédération Française:* (Montreal: Editions de l'Arbre, 1945),
pp. 583–589. Trans. from the French by Nell Elizabeth Painter and Robert O. Collins. Reprinted by
permission.

French Equatorial Africa has reached a decisive moment in its existence. It is useless to look back on the errors of the past. We will do better to criticize and be sorry. The balance sheet of our good and bad points and the relative merits of the colonization plan that was imposed upon us have been made clear by long experience and by the lessons of the war, so that we can say in certainty what we should do and how it should be done.

Unfortunately, the implementation of progress cannot be as prompt as we would like. Although financial means are sufficient, at least, to make a start, personnel and material are lacking, and money does not always inspire their acquisition. The men have been mobilized, and we can buy only the surplus—the fools—left over by the devouring industries of war. This does not mean that all we can do is sit back and fold our arms; on the contrary, no opportunity to create will be neglected, and there is always opportunity for whoever is patient and decided. But lacking immediate manpower, we can act by taking advantage of the delay to find the best position from which to begin. Together we will set ourselves to this task. Together we will make sure that Equatorial Africa, instead of being served by France, as has too often been the case, will be prepared to serve France tomorrow.

As a first condition for this indispensable success, we must have at our disposal a native population that will not only be healthy, stable, and peaceful but that will increase in number and will progress materially, intellectually, and morally so that we will have the collaboration of leadership that is the contribution of the masses and without which development would never be more than just a word. If we do not obtain this cooperation, our only choice will be between absolute impotence (that is to say, ruin) or the settling in the colony of a foreign race that would take the place of the indigenous tribes. Pride forbids us the first choice; con-

science and elementary interest forbid the second.

Here then is the basic and urgent need dictated to us: to establish native society on bases that will push the colony forward on the road to prosperity. But this is not the need of the administration alone. If it is to be brought to a good end, all the leadership of the colony must participate. The whole of Equatorial Africa will have its own native policy; this policy, the expression of the will of all—industrialists, colonists, missionaries, traders, and civil servants—will survive any reign. When its results are measured in ten or twenty years, it will be recognized that it was not born of individual caprice but of the unanimous resolve of a team that, having drawn itself up to redeem and liberate France, decided to save French Equatorial Africa as well.

I use the word "save" advisedly. The colony is in danger, threatened in the interior, like a granary emptying itself out. Whether the cause is sought in the prolonged system of large concessions, in disorderly economic exploitation, in sometimes tactless proselytising, in the disregard of learning, or finally and especially in the neglect, or one could say the distrust, of native political and social leaders; the consequences are there, and we can put our finger on them: a population that, in one place, does not increase, and in another shrinks; a land incapable of furnishing the auxiliary and directive personnel that are absolutely indispensable to commerce, public works, and the administration; a mass, disintegrating and dispersing; voluntary abortion and syphilis spreading throughout a nascent proletariat; these are the evils inflicted all at once upon the colony by an absurd individualism.

I know very well that a more comprehensive and better executed system of medical and hygienic training, plus a more intensive system of general and moral education, would correct some of these vices. But the basic cause of the evil will remain untouched so long as a policy for the population is not defined and implemented once and for all. We will share the results of this policy together.

To attempt to make or remake a society (if not in our image, then at least according to our mental habits) is to court certain disaster. The native has behavior, laws, and motherland, which are not ours. We will not be the source of his happiness by following the principles of the French Revolution, which is our revolution, or by enforcing the Napoleonic Code, which is our code, or by substituting our civil servants for his chiefs, for our civil servants think for him, not as he does.

On the contrary, we insure his equilibrium by treating him as a person on his own—that is to say, not as an isolated and interchangeable individual, but as a human personage permeated by traditions, the member of a family, of a village and of a tribe, capable of progress within his milieu and probably lost if he is taken from it. We apply ourselves to the development of his sense of dignity and responsibility and his moral progress, and to his enrichment and his material progress; but we will do so within the framework of his natural institutions. If these institutions have been altered through our contact, we will reorganize them, of necessity in new forms, yet close enough to him to retain his interest in his country and his desire to prove himself before moving on. In a word, we will give back to the native what no man can relinquish without damage to himself; we will not give him an illusory gift, we will, at the same time, reconstitute his profound sense of life and his desire to perpetuate it.

OF POLITICAL INSTITUTIONS

Here Lyautey [1] shows us the way. Let him cite Lanessan,[2] his first master in

[1] Marshall Louis H. G. Lyautey (1854–1934) sought to establish French authority and introduce European economic development in colonial areas while respecting indigenous rights and customs (ed.).
[2] Jean-Louis de Lanessan was a governor-general of Indochina who was best known for his book *Principes de Colonisation* (ed.).

colonization: "In all countries there is leadership. For the European people who come there as conquerors, the great error is in destroying this leadership. Then the country, deprived of its framework, falls into anarchy. It is necessary to govern with the mandarin, not against the mandarin. Not being numerous enough, the European cannot act as his substitute, but control him." And Lyautey himself adds: "Therefore break no traditions, change no customs. In every society there is a leading class, born to lead, without which nothing is done. It must be in our interests."

Starting from such a principle, we must first confirm or reconfirm their recognition, and in all cases, promote native political institutions. Let one [principle—ed.] be well understood: there is no question of considering political custom as something set or immutable as museum objects. It is very clear that custom changes and will change, and that we are not here to sterilize it by fixing it. But we must understand its profound meaning and consider it as essential as the tradition that shaped it and feelings that gave birth to it. This tradition is that of the motherland. To strip the native of these two motors of human life is to rob him without retribution. It would be about as insane as taking his land, vineyard, cattle, and soup pot from the French peasant in order to make an ordinary factory worker, charged with handling the products of an industrialized countryside.

Furthermore, if we do not reconfirm the bases of native political institutions, these bases will themselves disappear and will give way to an uncontrollable individualism. And how will we be able to act on this collection of individuals? When I see impatient administrators seize, unmake, condemn, and remake chiefs and thus sap the strength of a traditional institution, I think that they do not reflect on what will happen when that institution, due to their faults, loses its efficiency along with its vital character. I could tell them this: the only means remaining to ward off the breakdown of natural command will be administration by native civil servants. Because the chief of a subdivision cannot directly watch each person he administers, he will have to use civil servants as intermediaries instead of the chiefs he will have lost. I leave it to each person to judge the best solution from his own experience. If an ambitious administrator pretends to do without chiefs and civil servants, at least to reduce them to the state of simple instruments in his hands—precise and punctual instruments—I am sure that he is fooling himself, but in any case, I am convinced that his successor would not have the same good fortune. The continuity of effort, whose prerequisite is the decisive superiority of a single administrator, would be compromised from the moment of his departure. He would have built his cathedrals on the sand.

I have just been speaking of chiefs. In truth, although native institutions are often monarchical, they are not always. The opposite is true. The nomadic tribes of the North, which live under a regime of organized anarchy, could be cited as an example. And even within a monarchical state, the chief does not represent the only political institution. His power is amended, attenuated, and shared by more than one principle and more than one institution. Nothing must be forgotten or rejected of all this. No constituted council will be omitted, no guardian ousted, and no religious taboo neglected on the pretext that it would be ridiculous, bothersome, or immoral. There is no question of denying or condemning what exists and what counts, but to lead it along the way to progress.

The institution of the chief, however, is most important, and we will take the most care with his person. A preliminary question is posed here: Who should be chief? I will not answer as I did in Athens: "The Best One." There is no best chief, there is a chief, and we have no choice. I have already spoken of the frequent mutations of the chiefs; they are deplorable and no less absurd. There is a chief designated by custom; the point is to *recognize him*. I use the term in the diplomatic sense. If we arbitrarily replace him, we divide the command into two parts, the official and the real; no one is fooled except us, and if we flatter ourselves for getting better results from *our chief*, we overlook, most of the time, that he himself obeys the *real chief*, and that we are dealing with dupes.

Chiefs are not interchangeable. When we depose them, public opinion does not; the chief preexists. This preexistence often remains unknown to us, and the most difficult thing for us is to discover the real chief. I want the governors and administrators henceforth to adhere to this tenet. Not only do I mean that power will no longer be given to a parvenu whose services must be repaid (are there not a hundred other ways to repay them?), but I want the legitimate chiefs to be searched out where our ignorance has let them hide and reestablished in their outward dignity. I know what will be said: that all that has disappeared, that it is too late, that poor incorrigibles will be found from whom nothing is to be had. I believe that this is not true; occult power subsists because it is traditional power. May it be discovered and brought out into the light of day, may it be honored and educated. Results are certain to be forthcoming.

17 THE BRAZZAVILLE CONFERENCE
THE POLITICAL AND SOCIAL ORGANIZATION OF THE COLONIES

The main purpose of the French African Conference held in Brazzaville (then the capital of French Equatorial Africa) in 1944 was to advise the new French government of the appropriate policies to be adopted in order to aid the progress of the French colonies in Africa. The conference, which was opened by General de Gaulle, passed several recommendations, among which was the encouragement of traditional institutions (as suggested by Félix Eboué in 1941—see the preceding section), economic development, and social reform. The conference specifically rejected the possibility of independence or self-government for the colonies.

The French African Conference of Brazzaville, before approaching the part of the general program that was proposed for examination, has thought it necessary to pose the following principle:

The aim of the work of civilization accomplished by France in the colonies, REJECTS ANY IDEA OF AUTONOMY, ALL POSSIBILITY OF EVOLUTION OUTSIDE THE BLOCK OF THE FRENCH EMPIRE; THE EVENTUAL CONSTITUTION, EVEN IN THE DISTANT FUTURE, OF SELF-GOVERNMENT IN THE COLONIES IS TO BE REJECTED.

POLITICAL ORGANIZATION OF THE FRENCH EMPIRE

The general program of the Brazzaville Conference summarizes the given aspects of the problem in these terms:

It is desirable that France's political power be exercised with precision and vigor in all the lands of her empire. It is also desirable that the colonies enjoy great administrative and economic liberty. It is also desirable that the colonized peoples sense this liberty themselves and that their sense of responsibility be formed and advanced little by little, so that they will be associated with the public function in their countries.

From *La Conférence Africaine Française, Brazzaville (30 Janvier 1944–8 Février 1944)* (Algiers: Ministère des Colonies, 1944), pp. 35–36, 38–41. Trans. from the French by Nell Elizabeth Painter and Robert O. Collins. Reprinted by permission. The bracketed material in this selection has been inserted by Professor Collins.

After having deliberated on the above problem at the meeting of February 6, 1944, the Brazzaville Conference adopted the following recommendation:

Recommendation:

The representation of the colonies in a new French Constitution, because of the complexity of the problems raised, can be studied in a useful manner only by a commission of experts designated by the government.

It is, however, apparent that the experts should retain the following principles to guide and orient their work:

1. IT IS DESIRABLE, EVEN INDISPENSABLE, THAT THE COLONIES BE REPRESENTED WITHIN THE BODY OF THE FUTURE ASSEMBLY, WHICH WILL HAVE AS ITS MISSION THE FRAMING OF A NEW FRENCH CONSTITUTION.

This representation must be adequate in relation to the importance of the colonies in the French Community, an importance that is no longer debatable after the services they have rendered to the nation during the course of this war.

2. It is indispensable that the representation of the colonies to the central power in the Metropole [France] BE ASSURED IN A FAR LARGER AND FAR MORE EFFECTIVE MANNER THAN IN THE PAST.

3. A priori, ANY PROJECT OF REFORM THAT ONLY INTENDS TO AMELIORATE THE SYSTEM OF REPRESENTATION EXIST-

ING ON SEPTEMBER 3, 1939: colonial deputies and senators in the metropolitan Parliament, Superior Council of Overseas France, APPEARS INADEQUATE AND DOOMED TO BE STERILE.

This is notably the case for the augmentations, which might be envisioned, of the number of colonial deputies and senators in the body of the metropolitan Parliament and for the granting of new seats to colonies that are not represented at the present time.

Whatever the case may be, the new organization to be created, colonial Parliament, or preferably, Federal Assembly, must fulfill the following prerequisites: AFFIRM AND GUARANTEE THE INTANGIBLE POLITICAL UNITY OF THE FRENCH WORLD—RESPECT THE LIFE AND LOCAL LIBERTY OF EACH OF THE TERRITORIES CONSTITUTING THE BLOC OF FRENCH COLONIES, or if there is the desire to use the term, despite the objections it might cause, the French Federation. To this end it is appropriate to define with a great deal of precision and rigor the allocation [of powers] to be reserved by the central authority or federal organ, on the one hand, and those recognized as belonging to the colonies, on the other.

5. The legislative sphere of the colonies, or, more concretely, the respective domains of law, edict, and decree, cannot be usefully determined until the decisions delineating the division of authority between the central power or federal organ and the divers territories are affected, WHICH, WE EMPHASIZE, WE DESIRE TO SEE GRADUALLY PROGRESS FROM ADMINISTRATIVE DECENTRALIZATION TO POLITICAL PERSONALITY. . . .

SOCIAL QUESTIONS

A. The element constituting colonial society. The respective places of Europeans and natives in colonization.

Respect of and progress in native life will be the basis of our whole colonial policy, and we must submit absolutely to the exigencies that this involves. Natives will not be considered as interchangeable nor subject to eviction or indiscriminate labor. Now colonies are essentially places of cohabitation of Europeans and natives. Although our policy is to be subordinated to the prosperity of the local races, we must also leave just place for European activity.

Before anything else, the conference must therefore define the role of the European in the colony. Only after having resolved this problem will there be means to confront the others.

Starting from these principles, and after having deliberated during the meeting of February 1st, 1944, the conference adopted the following recommendation:

Recommendation:

1. The Development of the INDIGENOUS POPULATIONS IS PREREQUISITE TO THE PROGRESS OF THE AFRICAN CONTINENT. The activities of Europeans and non-Africans in colonial territories must correspond to this prerequisite.

2. This progress of the African continent, such as it is conceived, CANNOT, HOWEVER, BE ASSURED IN THE NEAR FUTURE WITHOUT THE COLLABORATION OF A FAR GREATER NUMBER OF NON-AFRICAN PERSONS AND ACTIVITIES THAN AT THE PRESENT TIME. Consequently, precise appeal will be addressed to their necessary devotion, talent, and skill.

3. The recruitment of non-African persons and activities on the level of economic organization in the African territories DEMANDS THAT PRECISE CONDITIONS OF HEALTH, MORALITY, AND PROFESSIONAL COMPETENCE BE IMPOSED AT THE BEGINNINGS, and for certain territories and certain activities, financial means. These conditions will be adapted to the organization of each territory.

4. The exigencies indicated in the preceding propositions will be applicable only in the future. THE SITUATION OF EUROPEANS OR NON-AFRICANS PRESENTLY LIVING IN AFRICAN TERRITORIES

WILL REMAIN LEGALLY UNCHANGED. Their rights will not be subject to the imperative conditions of the plan and will be freely exercised within the limits of regulations of general interest only.

5. The most diverse professions possible should be progressively reserved for the natives. SOON THE GOVERNORS-GENERAL AND GOVERNORS WILL MAKE AN INVENTORY OF THE ACTIVITIES OPENED TO NATIVES AS THIS TAKES PLACE.

IT IS DESIRABLE, NOTABLY IN ALL AFRICAN COLONIES, THAT POSITIONS OF EXECUTIVE LEADERSHIP SHOULD BE HELD BY NATIVES, AS RAPIDLY AS POSSIBLE REGARDLESS OF THEIR PERSONAL STATUS.

This access to various positions, on an equal footing with European employees, must include equal pay for equal skills. Nevertheless, and for the present, positions of command and direction can admit only French citizens.

The rules applicable to each category of employment must not be considered as immutable and should be adapted to change, to the rate and measure that it takes place. For the moment, it appears that advancement by means of examination, whether giving access directly to the post or to the school concerned, should constitute the only means of recruitment of native employees.

6. EDUCATION OF NATIVES WILL BE DIRECTED TOWARD THIS PROGRESSIVE ACCESS TO EMPLOYMENT. Effort and excellent preparation will be the characteristic principles.

7. The exigencies of replacement, as well as the implementation of the work of reform proposed in all domains by the French African Conference of Brazzaville, indicate the necessity of carrying a massive recruitment program, as much for administrative positions as to satisfy the needs of the new colonial economy, as soon as the Metropole is liberated. THE COLONIES SHOULD BE ABLE TO COUNT ON THE YOUNG GENERATION OF THE RESISTANCE, WHICH WILL FIND JOBS OVER-SEAS WORTHY OF ITS VIRTUE AND EFFICIENCY.

The needs appear to be immense; therefore it is indispensable that A PLAN OF RECRUITMENT BE ESTABLISHED BY THE GOVERNMENT THAT WILL APPLY TO THE WHOLE OF COLONIAL ACTIVITIES AND INCLUDE AN ORDER OF PRIORITIES FAVORING CERTAIN ACTIVITIES; this order of priorities may vary according to the particular situation in each territory.

The preparation of the metropolitan candidates should be orientated. HIGH CULTURAL LEVEL AND A GOOD EDUCATION WILL BE ESSENTIAL for the candidates, who would be most usefully educated in ONE OR MANY UNIVERSITIES THAT WILL BEAR THE MARK OF THE COLONIAL IDEAL AND SERVE COLONIAL INITIATIVE. . . .

8. European activity in the colony WILL PREFERABLY BE UTILIZED IN THE ORGANS OF THE STATE, AND PUBLIC COLLECTIVITIES WILL BE CALLED UPON TO PLAY AN IMPORTANT ROLE. This requirement does not, however, exclude private initiative on the part of Europeans nor their profit, in the exercise of certain professions.

9. The European worker in the colonies should have AT LEAST EQUAL STATUS WITH A WORKER OF THE SAME CATEGORY IN THE METROPOLE.

B. Organization of Native Society. Traditional Institutions. Staffing.

Concerning this part of its study, the conference based its work on the acknowledgment that two elements exist within native society:

—on one hand, the masses, which remain faithful to their customary institutions;

—on the other hand, an élite that has grown up from contact with us.

Thus the problem consisted of finding the surest methods to have the native masses evolve in the sense of a greater and greater assimilation of the principles that constitute the common basis of French civilization, and more particularly, toward political responsibility. On the other hand, it was also desirable to give the native élite the opportunity to test its abilities as soon as possible against the hard realities of administration and command.

After having deliberated in a committee then in the plenary session of February 3rd, 1944, the conference adopted the following recommendation:

Recommendation:

Traditional political institutions SHOULD BE MAINTAINED, NOT AS AN END IN THEMSELVES, BUT AS A MEANS PERMITTING MUNICIPAL AND REGIONAL LIFE TO EXPRESS ITSELF WITH MAXIMUM STRENGTH FROM THE PRESENT TIME. THE ADMINISTRATION SHOULD follow and control the functioning of these institutions SO AS TO DIRECT THEIR EVOLUTION TOWARD THE RAPID ACQUISITION BY NATIVES OF POLITICAL RESPONSIBILITY. The principles formulated in the circular of November 8th, 1941, of Governor General Eboué, are suggested to the administrators as a sure and tested method to attain this result.

18 SÉKOU TOURÉ AND GENERAL DE GAULLE
FRANCE AND WEST AFRICA

The loi-cadre *of June 1956 established universal suffrage in French overseas territories and opened the path toward self-government in the territories, but African leaders often suspected that the* loi-cadre *was designed to fragment French West Africa and French Equatorial Africa. Sékou Touré (1922–   ), now President of the Republic of Guinea, was of this opinion. Following the failure of the Fourth Republic and the coming to power of General de Gaulle, France sought to redefine its policy toward its African colonies. The French hoped that as a result of the referendum of September 28, 1958 the ties between Africa and France would be maintained and that further wars of independence, such as had taken place in Algeria, would be avoided. Guinea was the only French African territory to vote for complete independence, and although the French accepted this decision and granted independence to Guinea in 1958, they did so with very bad grace. The following speeches were made by General de Gaulle and Sékou Touré in Conakry before the referendum.*

THE LOI-CADRE AND BLACK AFRICA

The Loi-Cadre constitutes an important event in the internal life of Africa and in its relations with France. It is the first of two contradictory wills: both use it to realize fundamentally opposed designs.

From Sékou Touré, *Expérience Guinéenne et Unité Africaine* (Paris: Présence Africaine, 1959), pp. 25–26, 28, 87–90, 95–100, 108. Trans. from the French by Nell Elizabeth Painter and Robert O. Collins. Reprinted by permission. The bracketed material in this selection has been inserted by Professor Collins.

Indeed, the period just after the war saw a reawakening of political consciousness, which required a situation in conformity with the noblest sentiments that had mobilized the African peoples within the camp of the anti-imperialist forces during the course of the last war: justice, equality, liberty for all.

These were the sentiments conveyed in the development of Africans' actions on the economic, social, political, and cultural planes. As you know, the African structure of our organization permits the

African of Senegal to be sensitive to the idea of homeland and the placing of African action within a framework, if not that of African nationality, at least within that of the African personality whose attributes no colonialist can deny. More and more this platform alarmed the partisans of the colonial regime who, after their failures in Indochina and North Africa, and being faced with important successes by dependent countries against their former Metropole on the way to their emancipation, realized the inevitable retreat of the forces of domination before the rising African nationalist movement. For those anxious to maintain French presence in the overseas territories, which they never ceased to confuse with the exercise of power on force and those established by force, *the Loi-Cadre should have as its direct consequence the breakdown of the federal structure of our countries and progressive isolation of the territories, which they hope to see bogged down in internal contradictions and oppositions that would shatter their united front.*

On the economic plane and especially the level of public offices, it was no longer possible to support a policy of assimilation without obliging France to treat its citizens and peoples from its underdeveloped possessions on an equal footing. *Thus when we speak of African realities in terms of advancement, reactionaries utilize these same realities to justify our backwardness, and for these reactionaries, the Loi-Cadre should be a frame definitively limiting our hope and our possibilities of evolutionary action.*

The second will, our own, considers the Loi-Cadre not as an end in itself but as a step toward the most complete autonomy, which will permit the country to associate itself freely with France and discuss problems on equal footings. This will does not want the Government Council to confine itself to this regime, but rather that the council transform it to better serve the cause of the people and their country. That is why, immediately after the constitution

of our Government Council, the first task was to define our line of action—the popular objectives to be reached. This line of action, in addition to safeguarding our acquisitions, in addition to defending African interests, essentially provides for complete decolonialization of all the country's structures. It is not possible to fight against colonialism while maintaining the structures favoring its system of exploitation and oppression. It is not possible, finally, to fight against colonialism without denouncing and destroying the causes that are at the base of the internal conflicts from which we have suffered so long. As you know, our movement, which controls practically all the organizations issuing from the Loi-Cadre regarding decolonialization, has indicated its absolute determination to defeat the colonial regime by concrete realizations. It considers colonial rule incompatible with African dignity and interests, as well with the persistence and development of French influence. . . .

·   ·   ·

That settled, *all ideas that lead to the designation of Africa in favor of separate states or territorial republics will be opposed by us with even more force, for in our eyes it would be the heritage of divisive colonialism.* Thus our insistence on the institution of a federal Executive must signify our will to adhere to the community with France, as a bloc having the same realities, the same hopes, the same problems. It is in this sense that we conceive of the constitutional revision. Our idea is not in the least that of separation from France, but the meaning of the confidence, of the love that we have for France—confidence and love that pass through Africa, that we wish as much as France to render beneficial to their association. . . .

The problem of the federal Executive has been the object of numerous commentaries, especially tendentious commentaries. For us it is not an end but simply a political *means* to consecrate and reinforce *African Unity*. The C.F.A. [Central French Africa] franc zone constitutes a single market and French West Africa and French *Equatorial Africa* are real entities. *To be for or against the federal Executive is, first of all, to declare oneself for or against African unity.*

THE SPEECH OF GENERAL DE GAULLE

I want first of all to say, in a word, to what degree I have been touched, for I must say it in public, by the sentiments whose magnificent testimony the population of Conakry has just offered me.

I must say that, in the expression of its sentiments, I notice, I distinguish a great deal of attachment to France and no reproach regarding her. There is no reason, in fact—and I would not be here if I were not convinced of it—there is no reason, in fact, for France to blush, nothing of the kind, for the work she has accomplished here with Africans. At every step, when we set foot on this land of Guinea, we see the realizations already accomplished by the communal work, and when we listen to the presidents of the assembly and of the Government Council of Guinea, we very much believe that we also see what the French culture, influence, doctrines, and passion have been able to contribute to revealing the quality of men who had it [such French qualities] naturally. This settled, I have, of course, listened to the words that have been pronounced here with the greatest attention, and they seem to me to ask General de Gaulle, the leader of France, to do here, to say here, what is necessary, to state clearly the things that must be made clear.

We believe, I have believed for many years and I have tested it when necessary, that the African peoples have been called to their free determination; I believe today that it was only a step, that they will continue their evolution and it is not I, it is not France, who will ever contest it [such a belief].

I also believe that we are in a land and

in a world where realizations are necessary if we want the humblest sentiments to have some sort of future. We are in a land and in a world where reality dominates, as it has always done. There is no policy that does not have feelings and reality as its bases. France knows this: Africa is new. Well! France also, France is always new; she has just proved it yesterday and I am here to say it.

The question between us, Africans and Metropolitans, is uniquely to know whether we want, the former and the latter, to put a Community into practice together for a duration that I have not determined, which will permit the development of what must be developed from the economic, social, moral, cultural points of view, and, if necessary, to defend our common liberties against whoever would attack them.

This Community is proposed by France; no one is forced to adhere to it. Independence has been spoken of, I say here louder than elsewhere that independence is at the disposition of Guinea. She can have it, she can take it on the 28th of September by saying "No" to the proposition made to her, and in that case I guarantee that the Metropole will set up no obstacles. Of course, she will take the consequences, but there will be no obstacles and your territory can do as it wants and under the conditions it wants, follow the road it wants.

If Guinea answers "Yes," it will be because freely, on its own, spontaneously, she accepts the Community proposed to her by France, and if France, on her side, says "Yes," for she too must say it, then the territories of Africa and the Metropole will be able to carry out this new work together, which will be made by the efforts of both, for the profit of the men who live there.

To this work, France will not refuse, I am sure of it in advance, on the condition, of course, that in other places, that understanding, that call, that are necessary to a people when there are efforts required,

I might even say sacrifices, particularly when that people is France, that is to say, a country that gladly responds to friendship and feelings and that responds in an opposite sense to the ill will that could oppose her.

This France, I am sure, will participate in the Community with the means that she has and despite the burdens she carries, and these burdens are heavy—the whole world knows it. They are heavy in the Metropole because of the great destruction she has suffered in two world wars for the salvation of liberty and the world and in particular for the salvation of the liberty of Africans. Then she has burdens in Europe, for she wants to make Europe, she wants to do it in the interest of those who live there and also, I think, in the interest of the continent in which I now find myself. France has burdens from a world point of view; she has them in North Africa. She must develop a difficult and unhappy territory in a way that would ensure equality of rights and equality of opportunity for all. She must develop, for the common good, the wealth contained in the Sahara.

All these burdens are considerable, but nevertheless, I believe that, on her side, the Metropole will say "Yes" to the Franco-African Community on the conditions that I indicated a while ago. If we do it together, Africans and Metropolitans, it will be an act of faith in a communal and humane destiny and it will also be, I believe very much, the way, the only way to establish a practical collaboration for the good of the men who are our responsibility. I believe that Guinea will say "Yes" to France, and then I believe the way will be open for us, where we can walk together. The way will not be easy; there will be many obstacles in the road of men of today and words will not change anything.

These obstacles must be surmounted, the obstacle of poverty must be overcome. You have spoken of the obstacle of indignity, yes, it is already largely overcome, it is necessary to completely overcome it;

dignity from all points of view, notably from the internal, national point of view. There are yet other obstacles that come from our own human nature, our passions, our prejudices, our exaggeration. These obstacles I think we will be able to surmount.

It is in this spirit that I have come to talk to you in this Assembly, and I have done it confidently, I have done it confidently because in short, I believe in the future made by the ensemble of free men who are capable of extracting from the soil and from human nature what is needed for men to be better and happier. And then I believe that an example must be set for the world, for if we disperse, all that there is of imperialism in the world will be upon us. Of course there will be ideologies like a screen, like a flag to go before it; it would not be the first time in the history of the world that ethnic and national interests march behind signs. We must be ready together for that also; it is our human duty.

I have spoken. You will think it over. I carry away from my visit to Conakry the impression of a popular sentiment that is entirely turned in the direction I would desire. I make the wish that the élites of this country take the direction that I have indicated and that I think responds to the deepest intentions of our masses, and having said that, I will interrupt myself, awaiting perhaps, if the event ever takes place, the supreme occasion to see you, in a few months, when things will be settled and when we will together publicly manifest the establishment of our Community. And if I do not see you again, know that the memory of my stay in this great, beautiful, noble city, working city of the future, this memory I will never lose.

Long live Guinea!
Long live the Republic!
Long live France!

SPEECH OF MR. SÉKOU TOURÉ

Dear Comrades:

This public conference is not an ordinary meeting. It is of the order of the decisive events that will follow the referendum of next September 28th.

Without mentioning the false problems whose creation has vainly been attempted since the debate on constitutional reforms was opened, without even taking account of the voluntary ambiguities created and the confusions engendered about these reforms, we will here, in all clarity, deal with the examination of concrete facts, the real elements to which the conditions of a durable and fruitful institutional reform are tied.

For a long time already, Africa, influenced in her homeland by French culture, has made its political options known; through all the great manifestations of the *R.D.A.* [*Rassemblement Démocratique Africain*], the former *Convention Africaine*, the *P.R.A.* [*Parti du Regroupement Africain*], the former *M.S.A.* [*Mouvement Socialist Africain*], the *Conseil Fédéral de la Jeunesse d' Afrique* or the *U.G.T.A.N.* [*Union Générale des Travailleurs de l'Afrique Noire*]; equally through such great assemblages as those of the *Anciens Combattants* [French Army veterans], Africa has already clearly defined the road she intends to follow to her Destiny. She has defined, on the African plane as well as the exterior plane, the nature of the political, economic, social ties that have made her lose her personality and that, if they are to continue, will maintain her in moral slavery.

What does Africa want? She wants to build. How? By using all her potential, all her means, all her strength, by declaring her originality and developing her personality more and more. In addition she intends, based on new relations with France, to build a great community in respect and dignity, liberty, reciprocal values of each of the members. On all occasions that has been the fundamental choice of Africa. We affirm this choice in full confidence because the motto of the French Republic affirms "Liberty," "Equality," "Fraternity" everywhere.

And also because the meaning of the principle desired to be given to colonialism was to lead Africa to her full and complete emancipation and because at a certain point in her evolution, this Africa would be permitted to determine freely her own course. But if we study history a little, we quickly realize that all the countries that are now free and independent nations acquired their right to nationhood, their independent status, at levels of evolution inferior to the level attained by the African peoples at present.

In fact, in comparison to Russia, China, the United States of America, and France, when it is said that we are backward peoples, it is true, in relation to these nations. But we would say—it is no less certain—that at the time when these nations were constituted, at the moment when they began to enjoy their independence, their economic, political, social, spiritual, cultural states were not, at that time, superior to the present state of African populations. Moreover, even if we had to go about nude, even if we had to remain without knowing how to read or write, our people, who are becoming conscious of their personality, would be able to develop respect for this personality. If a people, another people, wants, on the level of friendship, to link its destiny to ours, it must first recognize our personality and, taking off from this recognition, establish the main roads for a fruitful collaboration.

May they not therefore come to tell us: "You want to go too fast, you are not ready to govern yourselves." For if that were true, neither the France of Charlemagne nor the Russia of the Romanovs nor the India of today would have existed.

If it is thought that we want to go too fast, if we are accused of incompetency, it is truly because in spite of the historical realities, we are still considered the property of a Metropole, otherwise there would be no reason for recognition of the fact that Ghana, Liberia, and Togo have the capacity of nationhood at the same time.

We denounce this spirit because it is still, it is as always, the colonial spirit. It is not the spirit of the people of France, it is that of private interests and privileges, as dangerous for the destiny of France as for the destiny of Africa.

We have always said "Yes" to France and we will continue to say it, because we distinguish France from a Constitution and from certain men who want to make us their property, their instruments.

It must be known that in the several instances, when Africans, on the fronts of external battles, have accepted deprivations and even death, they did it for the Liberty of France, because in their eyes, the Liberty of France was confused with the Liberty of Africa.

They thought that in saving the independence of France they saved the independence of the people of Africa at the same time. It is the only meaning that the African combatants and the present-day fighting men have accorded and continue to accord to the sacrifices to which they have consented and to which they continue to consent for the flowering of our Community.

But today the essential problem is posed: the problem of constitutional reforms, the problem of the definition of a marriage between Africa and France. In Guinea we have always said: "If we want to destroy France in Guinea, we would not discuss it, for it is easier to destroy than to construct." If we wanted to carry on a struggle against France herself, we would discuss nothing; we would close ourselves up in a silence to plot and prepare the revolt, and no one would be able to stop such a revolt carried out in the interests of Africa herself.

We have not and we still do not want revolt. We have desired and still desire a revolution, a revolution that the peoples of Africa and the peoples of France owe themselves to carry out in respect of their common destiny, their linked interests. And for that, the people of France and the peoples of Africa must tell each other the

truth, the whole truth, not to please each other, but in order to see the great values through which peoples, linked in this way, necessarily develop beyond the present generation. In fact, if we have said of colonialism that we want no more of it, that does not mean that colonialism, beside its ill deeds, beside the injustice and discrimination that are part of it, has only negative aspects. For the acceleration of the Africans' self-awareness these sentiments of unity that animate us, these structures that we have inherited and that we have simply to reconvert so that they will fully serve the aspirations of the people, do not count for anything. Thus we want the colonialist to know of this fundamental reconversion so that the ties between Africa and France may be modified. In place of the ties of dependence that have led Africa to depersonalization, submission, and neurosis, we want ties of liberty, ties of dignity, ties of fraternal collaboration that, coming from the heart, reason, and our most evident interests, would permit us to give our marriage more solid bases, bases that would be respected by all and that, on the international plane, would be imposed as the foundation of a solidly constituted community.

This is what we say and what we will always say. We do not seek to please anyone, we only intend to declare what all of conscious Africa thinks, and the language held out to General de Gaulle is the language of the real Africa.

Review our speeches before the Assembly, review all the affirmations made in the name of Guinea; we have never concealed this basis of our thought.

And if one does not want to realize our preoccupations, we can choose another language that will also explain our thoughts. We remember the Constitution of April 19th, 1946, making the overseas territories, former colonies, associated territories. That first constitution was to have transformed the nature of our ties with France and raised us to the rank of nations—to the level of states freely associated with France. But we also remember that the R.P.F. [Rassemblement du Peuple Français] led the struggle against that constitution, saying that it went too far with the overseas territories.

It is common to refer to the Brazzaville Conference of 1944 as having laid the foundations for Franco-African collaboration, but conscious Africa knows that at Brazzaville collaboration was only admitted on the level of administration, whereas on the political level, the conference affirmed that even in the future, the transformation of the overseas territories into self-governing nations was not envisioned. In no case would such transformation be envisioned, and that was the keynote of Brazzaville. That keynote we have well remembered.

But we have confidence in General de Gaulle. Why?

Because he has symbolized resistance, the resistance that we are carrying out. He has said "No" to slavery; we too say "No" to slavery.

That is why, in history, he will remain a symbol for us, but we will tell him that his words do not have value only when they are pronounced in France. For us, these are universal principles, and if they mobilized the national consciousness of France, they will be able to mobilize the African natural consciousness.

We remember that at Brazzaville, in political matters, the possibility of our becoming an independent country freely associated with France was not even envisioned, even at the end of the road, no matter how long its duration. The Constitution of April 1946 was rejected by the same parties, by the same group of men that still contests our right to independence today. History has continued. The second Constitution, which was less favorable to us, was adopted by the referendum of October 13, 1946.

Even so, since 1946, relations between whites and blacks clearly have not improved. The truth must be told; even when a black man has confidence in a certain white man because he knows he is honest, because he knows he is human, because he knows he is his brother, because he knows that they both have linked interests, he does not think any the less that the basis of their association makes him, the black man, inferior and makes the white man legally superior. The same situation exists for the white man; even when he knows that a certain black man has positive worth, that he is honest, that he says what he thinks, or that he has such and such capabilities, that he is humane and just, he thinks nonetheless: "Help him to develop himself? That would be to put our privileges in jeopardy."

It is thus necessary to realize that today the white man cannot truly know if he is liked by the black man, as the black man cannot know if he is truly accepted by the white man, because they are both influenced by the judicial positions that make one of the countries a Metropole, which decides, and the other a colony, which must respond. And here are the elements of our present realities. We want to save our relationship; we want this relationship to begin with an objective appreciation of our identity, of our communion of ideas and action. We want our relationship essentially to take into account the dignity of one and the other.

As for us, the *R.D.A.,* we have always affirmed that we prefer a progressive white man to a reactionary black man.

Thus the problem is not a question of color. The whole of it is to know who, of the whites and the blacks, decides the respect of the liberty and dignity of peoples.

We have not, as certain people had hoped, taken a plebiscite on the person of General de Gaulle. We have to make a decision on the conditions of an association that binds the destiny of the people of France and the destiny of the people of Africa. . . .

All the political parties have shown the same desire for unity. Now the government, in its projected Constitution, has not taken that into account. It wants to divide Africa; it says: "Guinea will be a state, Ivory Coast will be a state, each territory will have its own personality, will make its own law." Although the market of West Africa is [already] too limited and although it should even include French Equatorial Africa in order to be a great economic and monetary whole, these parties want Guinea to be considered as a country separate from Senegal so that a custom post can be established along all the borders with Senegal, the borders with the Sudan [Mali], the frontiers with the Ivory Coast; this is what our French brothers, or European brothers living in Conakry, must know.

They want, under the cover of a constitutional reform and in light of the French political crisis, to shatter African unity, to reduce the potential of the political struggle of Africa, to make the African governments fail.

We consider this an attempt at colonial reconquest.

They have tried to create an agitated atmosphere among the Europeans. They have been told: "The 28th is the big day, all you can do is pack your bags, you will be thrown into the sea." Certain of the high-ranking personalities of the territory panicked and have spread false news in their turn in European circles.

A mysterious campaign is being carried out among the *Anciens Combattants* and the *Anciens Militaires Africans* with the hope of gaining a few votes. They must know that the *Anciens Combattants* and the *Anciens Militaires* have also a keen sense of duty to break the ties binding Africa together. These are vain battles that do not take the lessons of history into account.

We solemnly declare our choice without equivocation. It is for France, it will never be against France, but if the present government of France does not equally want to respect the dignity of Africa, we will say "Yes" to France, but we will say "No" to the Government, "No" to the Constitution.

It is for the French government to answer "Yes" or "No" to the aspirations of African unity, of the economical, social, administrative unity of Africa, to say "Yes" or "No" to Africa's demands for dignity, "Yes" or "No" so that a Franco-African Community be built on solid foundations. If the present government of France says "No" to our demands, the French people will remain close to our hearts, but we will answer "No" to the French government on September 28th.

19 AL-HAJJ SIR AHMADU BELLO
POLITICAL LEADER AND TRADITIONAL RULER

Al-Hajj Sir Ahmadu Bello (1909–1966) was a political and religious leader. Descendant of Uthman dan Fodio, he was both Sardauna *of Sokoto and Premier of the northern region of Nigeria until his death during the military coup d'état in January 1966. His autobiography reflects the dualism of his position as both a modern political leader and a traditional ruler. In this work, he translates some of the attitudes of northern separatism that are so strong today and so crucial for the future of Nigeria.*

From Al-Hajj Sir Ahmadu Bello, *My Life* (New York: Cambridge University Press, 1962), pp. 60–61, 228–230. Reprinted by permission.

During 1946 discussions were going on about a new Constitution for Nigeria. The Constitution at that time had been in existence since 1922: it had never been really satisfactory, even when it was first published, but no particular public interest had been taken in the matter until just before the war; then agitation was started against it. Oddly enough this was by Southern people, who were to some extent represented, though not at all adequately. Strong opposition should really have come from us Northerners, for we were not represented at all.

It seems inconceivable nowadays that this vast area and population had absolutely no say in the legislation or finances of the country for a quarter of a century. And yet that is the simple truth. In fact, the position was odder still, for even the Legislative Council could not enact legislation affecting the North, though they could pass a budget which affected it. They could ask questions about it, but they could not interfere in its organisation or policy. The fact that they did not want to do so probably permitted the system to continue for the length of time it survived.

The Governor personally, without advice or recommendation, could, and did, enact legislation affecting the Northern Provinces, as the Region was then called —that is, of course, the Governor of Nigeria; the Regions had Chief Commissioners until recently. To make it all fair and reasonable there were on the Legislative Council "the ten senior officers for the time being lawfully discharging the functions of Senior Residents in Nigeria," of whom some would inevitably be Northern officers. It was their duty and privilege to represent the Northern Provinces in Council; their intellectual ascendancy was apparently so great that they managed this without opening their mouths, save on the most formal motions. The Chief Commissioners were also members and they, it is true, were a little more vocal, but on the whole officials, apart from the Attorney-General, the Chief Secretary and the Treasurer, were not encouraged to break silence.

The small number of unofficial members did their best and spoke whenever they could on a variety of subjects. These men were mostly nominated and represented "areas," in much the same way as another member might represent, say, "shipping" or "mining." In spite of this, huge areas of even the Southern Provinces were left unrepresented. Needless to say, there was a very solid and substantial majority on the official side in the Council: this followed ordinary "Crown Colony" practice at that time.

· · ·

Some find our attitude to the Federation to be a little strange and to some it brings dismay and fear: maybe a disintegration of the Federation might arise from this state of mind? Earlier in this book you will have read of the 1953 crisis.[1] From that you will realise that disintegration was a sharp possibility just then. Behind this there was a long story of bickering and dissatisfaction between the Provincial administrations (as the Regions were in the first place) and the Nigerian Government in Lagos. Both were artificial and foreign, until the last decade, and both were run and staffed by British officers.

This feeling (though foreign bred) naturally communicated itself to us, but I must say categorically that, once the train of constitutional government was set in motion, the British Administration did their best to promote good relations. It is quite untrue to say that it was their influence that has created the present rifts and disagreements. Nevertheless, we discovered that the old British bickerings were not without reason and that, unless you fought hard, the Regions would certainly be left out and the central government would get away with most of the cake.

[1] The riots that erupted in Kano May 15–19, 1953, killing 36 and wounding 277, brought tribal and regional separation in Nigeria to a head and threatened to split the country in two (ed.).

That is why we are so keen on our Regional self-government. This is the only guarantee that the country will progress evenly all over, for *we* can spend the money we receive, and the money we raise, in the directions best suited to us. To show what I mean, you have only to consider the former backwardness of our educational and medical provision, compared with that of areas near Lagos. As I have suggested elsewhere, if it had not been for the Native Authorities the North would have been left completely standing in these and other important developments.

Eight years have passed from the last crisis and we see clearly now that Nigeria must stand as one and that, as things are, the existing external boundaries cannot readily be changed—nor can those of the Regions. But that does not necessarily bind us to the present *form* of Government at the Centre. Obviously we cannot be left with a vacuum there; for example, someone must look after foreign affairs, foreign trade, and defence, to name the more important: but who? As things are in the present constitution, the North has half the seats in the House of Representatives. My party might manage to capture these, but it is not very likely for the present to get any others: on the other hand, a sudden grouping of the Eastern and Western parties (with a few members from the North opposed to our party) might take power and so endanger the North.

This would, of course, be utterly disastrous. It might set back our programme of development ruinously: it would therefore force us to take measures to meet the need. What such measures would have to be is outside my reckoning at the moment, but God would provide a way. You can therefore see that the political future must rest on an agreeable give and take between the parties. So long as all respect the common purpose, all will be well.

And so, what about the future of the Emirs? You will have noticed in this book my insistence on the theme that the old Emirates were originally much more democratic than they were when the British left them, and that we have been doing our best since then to put things back; to ensure that the Chiefs are surrounded by a wide body of suitable councillors, mostly chosen by election, whose advice they *must* take.

We are also determined that they and their Administrations—and this, of course, applies also to the Conciliar Administrations—must accept the technical advice of the Regional Government and must at all times keep us in touch with the important events in their areas; that means especially anything likely to endanger the peace. Their areas must develop in step, each with each.

The immense prestige of their office is thus harnessed to the machine of modern progress and cannot, I am sure, fail to have a notable effect in bringing the country forward. To remove or endanger this prestige in *any way,* or even to remove any of their traditional trappings, would be to set the country back for years, and indeed, were such changes to be drastic, it might well need another Lugard to pull things together again. We must get away from the idea that they are effete, conservative, and die-hard obstructionists: nothing could be farther from the truth. I agree that there are one or two very elderly chiefs who probably do not fully appreciate all that is being done for their territories, but even these have progressive councils and their successors will be men educated and brought up to modern ideas.

.   .   .

THE GUINEA COAST

GEOGRAPHICAL FACTORS

Stretching from Dakar in the west to the Cameroons in the east, the West African coast forms a 2,000-mile belt of smooth beaches interspersed by river mouths and inlets forming mangrove swamps and quiet lagoons. Beyond are the rain forests, where the average rainfall ranges from thirty to over one hundred inches a year. In these well-watered forests, shifting cultivation is practiced to support a relatively dense, sedentary population. A minimal amount of group cooperation is required to clear the land and cultivate the corn, manioc, yams, and bananas, the staple crops of the coastal peoples. Beyond the coast the rainfall decreases, and the dense forests turn into parklands and the savanna of the western Sudan. Here the irregular, uneven rainfall supports fewer farmers and encourages pastoralism, which demands vast tracts of land and a sparse population compared with the forest belt further south. In the past, West Africa was more accessible from the north, across the Sahara and Sudan, than from the sea. Except for Dakar and Lagos, the coast of West Africa had few natural harbors and only three estuaries that offered sheltered anchorages—the Gambia, the Senegal, and the Niger. Landings along the rest of the coast had to be made through heavy surf or in mangrove swamps, beyond which lay the dark, brooding forests, penetrated only by narrow, tortuous footpaths that were suitable only for human porterage because the presence of the tsetse fly prohibited the use of animals. Malaria, yellow fever, and other tropical diseases struck down

the incomer until the discovery of pro-
phylactics in the nineteenth century.

THE PEOPLES OF THE WEST AFRICAN COAST

Despite these formidable and discouraging obstacles to outsiders coming from the
sea, the forest region has supported large
and prosperous African populations.
Many unsuccessful attempts have been
made to classify the peoples of West
Africa according to political, social, or
even physical typologies, but the only rational basis for comparison remains language. With few exceptions, the
inhabitants of the forest zone speak
related languages of what Professor
Greenberg has called the Niger-Congo
language family. In Senegal reside the
Wolof, Serer, Tucolor, and Susu, whereas
further down the coast there are a host of
small groups, chief among which are the
Temne, Vai, Bussa, and Kru. Further in
the interior, in the uplands where the
Senegal and the Niger rivers take their
rise, dwell the Mande-speaking peoples,
who have played such a prominent role
in the history of the western Sudan and
whose trade contacts with the forest regions have spread their influence to the
coastal peoples. In the Gold Coast to the
east live the Ashanti and Fanti, who are
Akan-speaking, and the less numerous Gã
and Ewe of the coast, who are not.
Dahomey is dominated by the Fon and
the Egba, and in the forest zone of Nigeria
live the powerful Yoruba in the west and
the Ibo in the east, both surrounded by
clusters of smaller groups.

THE STATELESS SOCIETIES

The history of the coastal regions of the
west, like those of East Africa, has polarized around stateless societies on the one
hand and well-organized African state
systems on the other. Along the lower
Ivory Coast, within the interior of Liberia,
and in parts of Guinea and Sierra Leone
live small, fragmented groups that never
developed the political organization
which characterized African state systems further to the east. The dense forests
of this region have traditionally hampered
movement, particularly between east and
west, whereas the rivers of the area provide no access from south to north. The
rainy season is long and continually renders communications difficult, if not virtually impossible. Thus, although the
density of the rain forest has hindered the
evolution of complex political organizations, it has provided a refuge for peoples
under pressure from the surrounding
states, mixing diverse groups and contributing to the proliferation of tribal
names that all but defy classification.
Nevertheless, these stateless societies
clearly are culturally related to the surrounding peoples, and although it is still
hopelessly confused, their history has undoubtedly been deeply influenced by the
well-recorded history of the Mande to the
north and the Akan to the east. Until
more adequate information is supplied by
comparative ethnographic studies, the
history of these stateless societies remains
a mosaic of tribal movements that have
split into smaller and smaller political
units.

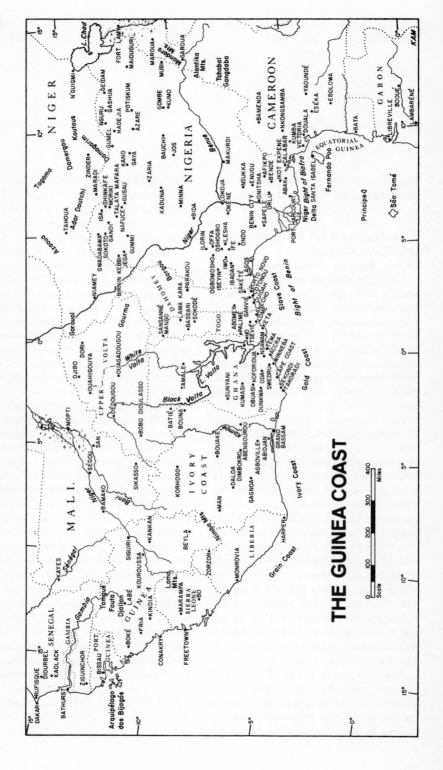

THE GUINEA COAST

THE FOREST STATES

Beyond the clusters of stateless societies huddled on the headland of West Africa, a series of forest kingdoms, whose sophisticated political and social organization enabled them to exert widespread cultural and economic influence, existed from the Ivory Coast to the Cameroons. Three factors have conditioned the rise and development of these states. The oldest and probably least-appreciated influence on the forest kingdoms was their contact with the Sudanic states to the north. The trade routes that spanned the Sahara did not always terminate in the great market towns of the western Sudan. Before the arrival of the Europeans in the fifteenth century, a well-established trade route connected the gold-bearing regions of the Gold Coast with the great Sudanic trading entrepôt of Djenné. Commercial centers were founded by Mande and Muslim traders south of the Mali Empire at Bobo Dioulasso, Kong, and even further south at Begho. The wanderings of these merchants almost certainly took them through the heart of Ashanti to the coast, where there may possibly have been a pre-European waterborne trade between the markets of the Gold Coast and the commercial centers of Benin and the Niger Delta. Thus, from the fifteenth to the nineteenth century, gold, kola nuts, and slaves were sent north in exchange for brassware, cloth, and salt—the products of the western Sudan and North Africa. The economic influence of the north was accompanied by political and cultural influences. Islam was carried further south, and groups of Mande warriors who came with the caravans to protect them remained behind to create small, centralized states. A similar northern influence penetrated south from Hausaland in northern Nigeria through Nupe and into the Yoruba state of Oyo. Like the rulers of Ashanti in the Gold Coast, the Yoruba claim a northern origin, though the evidence for this still consists mostly of myth, legend, and selected cultural

similarities to the inhabitants of the Sudan and the Nile Valley.

A second influence that shaped the forest kingdoms was the arrival of the Europeans and the development of the slave trade. Many authors have attributed the rise and growth in power of these states to the acquisition of European firearms in return for slaves, and the slave trade has been regarded by past historians of Africa as the sole and sufficient explanation for the rise and fall of the coastal states. Once equipped with guns, the Ashanti, the Fon, the Oyo, and the Benin were able to expand at the expense of their neighbors, founding kingdoms on the spiral of violence—slaves for guns, which led to more slaves for more guns. Certainly the European factor contributed to the growth as well as the ultimate decay of the forest states, but it is an increasingly unsatisfactory basis for the interpretation of their origins.

No history of the forest states can be properly understood without recognizing a third factor, the anatomy or internal dynamics of their political, social, and cultural institutions and the way in which these have precipitated historical change within the states. The manner in which the Ashanti confederacy was organized, the power of the hereditary nobility in Oyo, and the relative weakness of the hereditary class in Benin have, for example, played critical roles in the evolution of these kingdoms. So, too, have the relations of these states to the myriads of their less well-organized neighbors, as well as the development of culture and technology, conditioned the history of the forest states and placed the role of the slave trade in proper historical perspective. For important as it certainly was, the slave trade can no longer be regarded as the single driving force in the development of the forest states.

AKWAMU

In the early seventeenth century a federation of the Akan peoples living between the Volta and the Pra rivers was forged by leaders who may have been of Mande origin. Known as *Akwamu,* the state pressed southward to the sea, conquered the Gã, and sacked their capital, Accra, in 1677. Once having obtained a window on the sea, the ruler, the *Akwamuhene,* began to trade with the Europeans, acquiring an ever-increasing number of firearms with which he was able to expand eastward to Ouidah and westward to the frontiers of the Ashanti and the Fanti. In 1693 Akwamu was strong enough to capture Christiansborg castle from the Danes, reselling it to them several years later on favorable terms. By the eighteenth century, Akwamu was finally overextended and, in 1733, in a series of disastrous campaigns against the formidable armies of Akim, the warriors of Akwamu were defeated and the kingdom was reduced to a petty principality.

ASHANTI

Following the collapse of Akwamu, power shifted to the northwest, to *Ashanti,* which, like Akwamu, began a long period of expansion with the object of subordinating the coastal middlemen and establishing direct contact with the Europeans and the sea. At the end of the seventeenth century Osei Tutu (*c.* 1660–1712), who had been residing in Akwamu, was recalled to succeed his father. Osei Tutu had obviously learned much from Akwamu and, utilizing the economic and military techniques employed so successfully by the Akwamuhene, he welded the relatively weak Ashanti states into a powerful confederacy with its capital at Kumasi. Osei Tutu resolved the constitutional question by the institution of the Golden Stool. The stool represented all the spiritual (*sunsum*) and political power of the Ashanti peoples. All Ashanti owed unswerving loyalty to the stool, and, of course, to its custodian, the *ashantehene.* Once having acquired the allegiance of the other Ashanti chiefs, Osei Tutu set about the task of state build-

ing. He defeated the people of Doma to the west and between 1700 and 1701, reduced the people of Denkyera, whose position as middlemen had hindered Ashanti trade with the Europeans. Following the reign of Osei Tutu, the growth of Ashanti was momentarily checked in 1717 by the redoubtable people of Akim, but under Opoku Ware (1721–1750), the Ashanti confederacy was not only consolidated but became the greatest power in the Gold Coast. In the south, Akwamu, Wassaw, and even Akim were conquered, whereas in the north, the more distant kingdoms of Gonja and Dagomba were overcome. The successors to Opoku Ware, however, were unable to maintain the Ashanti Empire; Wassaw, Akim, and even the Fanti reasserted their independence to become troublesome tributaries that obstructed the flow of trade between the European forts and Ashanti. Osei Kojo (1764–1777) sought to revive the tarnished image of Ashanti but was only partially successful, for the Europeans increasingly assisted the coastal middlemen to resist Ashanti aggression, setting the pattern of conflict between European and Ashanti that was to dominate the nineteenth century.

Although the power of Ashanti to conquer its neighbors rested on the efficient use of trained military cadres that were equipped with firearms, the strength of the Ashanti confederacy was founded on the constitutional agreement represented by the institution of the Golden Stool whereby the custodian, the ashantehene, was invested with religious as well as political authority. The ashantehene was further supported by appointive officials, who formed a bureaucracy to manage financial and commercial affairs, and by military officers, who directed the armies. The Ashanti also possessed a legal system that was capable of wide application, which further helped to strengthen the ties between the members of the federation. The principal defect in the organization of Ashanti, however, was the difficulty of applying it successfully to non-Ashanti peoples who were conquered in battle. Thus, as Ashanti expanded, the subject peoples with no reverence for the Golden Stool were not assimilated and remained troublesome tributaries, always seeking to reassert their autonomy. Therefore, although by the end of the eighteenth century Ashanti controlled the heartland of the Gold Coast (150 miles wide and 90 miles deep), on every side there existed hostile elements—Muslim states to the north, European-connected states to the south.

THE KINGDOM OF DAHOMEY

During the great days of Akwamu, the *Fon,* who had previously inhabited the savanna lands east of the Volta River, invaded the forest regions to the south and established themselves around Allada and Ouidah on the coast. Later, as a result of dynastic quarrels, Fon princes returned north and founded Abomey during the early decades of the seventeenth century. At the time Osei Tutu was creating the Ashanti confederacy, the Fon of Abomey under Agaja (1708–1740) returned south, overran the small trading states of Ouidah and Allada, and extended the authority of Dahomey to the coast. Throughout the eighteenth century the kings of Dahomey sought to consolidate their absolute control while opposing Oyo incursions from Yorubaland to the east. By utilizing firearms that were acquired in the slave trade, the kings were able to employ these new means for political ends, building a highly centralized state in the hope of resisting the corrosive effects of the slave trade. Although they successfully created a sound internal administration, the kings of Dahomey were less successful in limiting the slave trade and were reluctantly participating in it by the mid-eighteenth century during the reign of Tegbesu (1740–1774). Relations with Oyo were no better. In 1726 the armies of Oyo defeated Agaja and captured Abomey, the capital of Dahomey. In the treaty of 1730 Dahomey was forced to concede tribute and a subordinate position to the *Alafin* of Oyo. Reduced to a tributary status, Dahomey continued to perfect its internal organization by using Oyo institutions and developing its own governmental institutions rather than squandering resources on fruitless military adventures. The end of the eighteenth century was characterized by a series of weak rulers and the decline of Dahomey's power until the accession of Adandozan (1797–1818) and his three successors—Gezo (1818–1853), Gelele (1858–1889), and Behanzin (1889–1894), strong and effective monarchs, who established the independence of Dahomey from Oyo and secured for Dahomey a dominant and prosperous position on the Slave Coast (Archibald Dalzel, *Dahomey and Its Neighbors;* Sir Richard Burton, *The Amazons*).

THE YORUBA KINGDOM OF OYO

Oyo rose to predominance among the forest kingdoms of Nigeria during the seventeenth century, when its armies subordinated the peoples of Yorubaland in western Nigeria to the rule of the Alafin of Oyo. The expansion of Oyo, spearheaded by its famous cavalry, continued during the eighteenth century until the suzerainty of the alafin extended from Benin to the borders of Togo. Like the other forest states, Oyo relied on the slave trade to provide an economic base for expansion, selling prisoners of war to European merchants in return for guns to equip its armies, but the ability to utilize this economic and military power clearly arose from the political and social organization of the state. The origins of Oyo are obscure, but Ife appears to have been its spiritual progenitor, as it was for Benin. The development of Oyo north and west of Ife near the present city of Ilorin took place under Alafin Shango, the fourth alafin after the traditional founder, Oranmiyan. Thereafter Oyo's armies sallied forth during every dry season to exact tribute from surrounding states. The alafin himself was elected by a council of local officials, or *obas,* who acknowledged, in theory at least, the spiritual authority of Ife. In theory the alafin possessed both absolute political and spiritual power in Oyo, but in fact his authority was circumscribed by numerous secular institutions, the paramount one being the council of obas, which could, and on occasion did, rid itself of an unpopular or tyrannical alafin.

As Oyo reached the height of its power in the eighteenth century, Yoruba colonies were established to the west, perhaps as a by-product of military expeditions, advancing the network of Yoruba trade. By 1800, however, the alafins of Oyo could no longer hold the state together. A disparity in power appeared between the southern regions, which had grown wealthy as a result of the slave trade, and the north, which remained the supplier. The Fon of Dahomey and the *Egba* were the first to break away, followed by Ilorin, who, with Fulani assistance, prevented horses and slaves from reaching Oyo and precipitated the long and destructive Yoruba wars that preoccupied Oyo until the coming of the British.

✕ THE KINGDOM OF BENIN

Although the founding of Oyo may have been contemporary with that of Benin, the verifiable history of Benin has given that state a primacy in the history of the south Nigerian kingdoms. The origins of Benin, like those of Oyo, are tied to Ife, from which came the spiritual authority of the Oba, the ruler of Benin. Under a series of warrior obas, Benin experienced a steady stream of Portuguese missionaries and merchants who traded in pepper and slaves, which were exchanged on the Gold Coast for gold. Trade brought increasing prosperity—pepper, slaves, and ivory in return for firearms, copper, and beads—and emissaries from Benin were sent to Lisbon while Catholic missionaries built churches and proselytized among the people of Benin.

The strength of both Oyo and Benin was attributable as much to political organization as to economic prosperity. The title of Oba of Benin was hereditary, however; that of Alafin of Oyo was not. A difference of even greater importance was that the chiefs of Oyo retained great power from the lineages that supported them, whereas the chiefs of Benin were not necessarily heads of lineages and consequently owed their position and power to the ruler more than to relatives or subjects. The emergence in Benin of a bureaucracy of nonhereditary, title-holding groups permitted a strong and able oba greater freedom than his counterpart, the Alafin of Oyo.

Beginning in the eighteenth century, Benin slipped into a long period of decline. Rivalries among the nobles were exacerbated by a century of warfare and the rise of Oyo. Moreover, the traders of Benin could no longer compete on favorable terms with the slave merchants of Dahomey or Oyo. Economically depressed and politically confused, Benin could no longer exert a paramount influence over its vassal states, and one by one they obtained their freedom. By the nineteenth century, both the size and influence of the kingdom had shrunk to that of a petty city-state (John Barbot, *Benin*).

EUROPEAN BEGINNINGS

During the Middle Ages European trade with Asia was confined to the eastern Mediterranean, where Muslim prohibitions restricted the operations of Christian merchants. At first the Italian city-states of Venice and Genoa dominated Europe's trade with the Levant, but during the fourteenth century Venetian merchants gradually eliminated their Genoese rivals, who were forced to seek new routes to the East. Genoa possessed skilled sailors, navigators, and geographers who were developing techniques to sail into the wind, a critical factor in the exploration of the Mauritanian coast, where ships returning to Europe must tack against steady northerly breezes. In the fourteenth century Genoese seamen, as well as Moors and Normans, reached the Canary Islands and sailed along the Saharan coast to Cape Bojador. These pioneering voyages were sporadic and unprofitable, however, so that a systematic exploration of the West African coast had to await the Portuguese expeditions of the following century.

Prince Henry of Portugal, called the Navigator, had learned in 1415 while Governor of Ceuta that North African merchants regularly crossed the Sahara to exchange salt and Mediterranean products for West African gold, and throughout the remainder of his life he organized the exploration of West Africa with deliberate, well-planned expeditions. The Portuguese hoped not only to outflank the Arabs in order to trade directly with the blacks of West Africa for gold but to convert the black inhabitants and enlist them in the crusade against Islam. Moreover, the circumnavigation of Africa would bring the Portuguese directly to the Orient, bypassing the traders of the Levant. The Portuguese reached the Azores in 1439 and Arguin in 1443, where a fort was later constructed. In 1460 Prince Henry died, and the exploration languished until 1469, when Fernao Gomes obtained a five-year monopoly of trade on the coast provided that he explore one hundred leagues of coast every year (Gomes Eannes de Azurara, *The Discovery of Guinea*). By 1475 Gomes had discovered the Gold Coast and had reached Fernando Po. The gold trade flourished, and in 1482 King John II of Portugal built a fort at São Jorge da Mina at the present Elmina (the mine) to facilitate Portugal's control of the trade. The profits of the trade helped to finance successive Portuguese expeditions, which succeeded in reaching India and the East Indies by the end of the century, thus diverting Portugal's interest in West Africa, except, of course, for the trade in gold and, later, slaves.

The Age of Exploration, of which the Portuguese expeditions along the West African coast were but a part, was largely a product of the growth of centralized states in Europe under national monarchs and of the rise of a merchant class interested in conducting overseas trade to obtain the products of Asia, Africa, and the New World. The object of these national monarchs and merchants was to monopolize world trade, thereby bringing power to the king and profits to the traders, but their mercantilistic policies and practices inevitably led them into national competition with European rivals. Clearly, mercantilism required control of the strategic forts, trading posts, and ports of call, but it also involved the exploitation of tropical resources to gain the greatest profit by creating large plantations worked by slave labor to produce valuable tropical crops. Thus the mercantilist policies of the European nation-states precipitated the competition for empire on a worldwide scale while contributing to the expansion of the slave trade to meet the demands of the plantations of the Americas.

Until 1598 Portugal was able to maintain the monopoly on the West African coast that had been granted by three papal bulls and the Treaty of Tordesillas of 1494, in which Castile and the Portuguese agreed to restrict themselves to their respective spheres of commercial exploitation—Castile in the New World and Portugal in Africa and Asia. There had, of course, been sporadic voyages by English and French interlopers, but it was not until the Dutch revolt from Spanish rule in 1572 that a European power set out on a conscious effort to destroy the Spanish and Portuguese commercial monopoly (*The Guinea Coast in the Sixteenth Century*). By 1610 the Dutch had driven the Portuguese out of the East Indies, and by 1642 all the Portuguese forts on the Gold Coast were under Dutch control. The Dutch, however, were not free from rivals for control of the gold trade, and the trade in slaves which was continually increasing to meet the voracious demands of the West Indian plantation owners for cheap labor. From the mid-seventeenth century, both England and France took active steps to foster a national trade, and in a century of intense and violent European competition, first the Dutch and then the French were eliminated by British sea power, leaving England in a preeminent commercial position on the West African coast. By 1785 British merchants controlled over half the slave trade (38,000 annually), compared with 20,000, 4,000, and 2,000 carried every year by the French, the Dutch, and the Danes, respectively (William Bosman, *Justice and Warfare at Axim*).

THE SLAVE TRADE

In traditional African society slavery was an established institution long before the arrival of the Europeans, but the slave was principally a domestic servant with rights and respect whose value depended more on the prestige that he accorded his master as a retainer than his economic value as a plantation field hand. Although he was not part of the kinship group, the slave in African society was accorded a position, frequently an influential one, that he never possessed in the New World. Moreover, slavery in Africa never involved many people except in regions where Islamic states had extended the trade in slaves or where a rudimentary plantation system, such as that existing in Dahomey, required cheap labor. Once the Africans had exhausted their supply of domestic slaves in exchange for European products, they acquired new sources of slaves by the extension of African warfare. Prisoners of war were captured in the interior and taken directly to the coast or, more usually, were passed through a series of African middlemen who kept the slaves in *barracoons* or stockades to await sale and shipment to the Americas. No one can accurately gauge the volume of the trade, but reasonable estimates place

the number at 9 to 12 million Africans landed in the New World between 1500 and 1900. Since approximately one-sixth perished during the Atlantic crossing, Africa lost well over 14 million persons during the four centuries of the trade (William Snelgrave, *The Slaves Mutiny*). The slaves were taken all along the coast from Senegal to the Cape but the greatest numbers came from the Gold Coast (present-day Ghana) and the Slave Coast (Togo, Dahomey, and Western Nigeria). In spite of the enormous total volume of slaves, they were never taken from Africa at a crippling rate—perhaps no more than 1 percent of the population was taken every year. Nevertheless, the young and the fit, mostly males between the ages of ten and thirty-five, were removed, whereas the old and the infirm remained. Clearly, the slave trade retarded orderly progress and development in West Africa by discouraging agricultural and industrial production. The skills and creativity of the West Africans were eroded away, nearly to die out.

THE AWAKENING OF THE EUROPEAN INTEREST IN WEST AFRICA

With few exceptions, Europeans during the first 300 years of contact with West Africa never developed any sustained interest in the interior. To them the coast represented a forest curtain behind which resided ferocious populations and tropical fevers that earned West Africa the reputation of "the White Man's Grave." Moreover, there seemed to be no reward in the interior to justify the risks of penetration. The earlier promises of gold and wealth had been better met elsewhere in the world—in the Orient and the Americas. The slave trade, it is true, brought handsome profits, but the system of African procurers and middlemen seemed adequate for the exploitation of Africa's human resources without direct intervention by Europeans. With the rise of empires, control of overseas territories was frequently justified on strategic grounds, but in West Africa any such political ends were easily met by controlling the coastal stations. Later Christian missionaries moved into the interior of West Africa to save souls for Christ, but the evangelical mission movement did not revive lagging European interest in West Africa until the nineteenth century. Perhaps the most important deterrent to European penetration was the unwillingness of the Africans themselves to allow Europeans into their midst. So long as the disparity between European and African technology was not great and European interest was checked by the rigors of the climate, the Africans had little difficulty in keeping out foreign interlopers.

During the eighteenth century, however, European interest in West Africa was revived by the rise of geographical curiosity and the melding of humanitarian motives to abolish the slave trade. In an age of encyclopedists, the dedication of men to the pursuit of knowledge of unknown quarters of the globe was not surprising. In 1788 the Association for Promoting the Discovery of the Interior Parts of Africa (more commonly known as the African Association) sponsored expeditions of exploration that were continued in the next century by its successor, the Royal Geographical Society. Although preliminary attempts by Ledyard, Lucas, and Houghton to reach the interior failed, Mungo Park arrived at the Niger River at Segu in 1796 and, in a second expedition begun in 1805, traveled down the Niger only to be drowned in the rapids at Bussa. Park's explorations whetted the English appetite for yet more information about the interior and cleared the way for a number of intrepid explorers, Laing, Bowdich, Clapperton, Lander, and René Caillié, all of whom made known to Europe the main outlines of West African geography.

Just as West Africa was being penetrated by the systematic expeditions of European explorers, the humanitarians in Britain focused public attention on the evils of the slave trade (Mercator Honestus, *A Defense of the African Slave Trade*). The abolitionist movement grew out of the interaction between the ideas of the Enlightenment, the rise of evangelical Christianity, and the desire of European and particularly British merchants to substitute "legitimate trade" for the slave trade. Led by Granville Sharp, Thomas Clarkson, and William Wilberforce, a campaign to prohibit the slave trade was organized in 1765. Seven years later slavery was declared illegal in England, and by an act of Parliament in 1807, British subjects were forbidden to engage in the trade. In 1833 slavery was abolished throughout the empire. The Royal Navy was sent to West African waters to enforce the Act of 1807, while British diplomats brought increasing pressure to bear on other nations to outlaw the trade in humans. Although British diplomacy had persuaded the principal European and American nations to declare the slave trade illegal by 1817, the West African Squadron was unable to capture the elusive slaving ships that continued to deliver slaves to the Americas. Disappointed at their failure to check the actual shipment of slaves, the British antislavery movement, now led by Thomas Buxton, turned to a more positive policy than that of repression. Allied with the evangelical Christians, many of whom were in the forefront of the abolitionist movement, and the ever-increasing number of British merchants who wished to expand "legitimate trade" to West Africa now that they were prohibited from engaging in that of slaves, Buxton changed the course of the abolitionist movement with the slogan, "Christianity, Commerce, Colonization." Writing in the 1830s, Buxton argued that the slave trade could not be eliminated unless an adequate substitute was provided. Thus, if legitimate trade were introduced by colonists, Europeans, and free slaves who were guided by the moral precepts of Christianity, the standard of civilization would be elevated and consequently slavery would wither away. In spite of the losses and expense of the West African Squadron and the declining economic importance of the West Indian plantations in British political life, the abolitionist movement, recharged by Buxton, kept Europe and particularly Britain committed to Africa when they might otherwise have lost interest in that continent as an exploitable land (Thomas Fowell Buxton, *The Principles of Abolition*).

COLONIZATION—SIERRA LEONE

A generation before Buxton's ideas gained widespread acceptance in the 1830s, the early members of the antislavery movement had proposed schemes of colonization as an instrument to combat the slave trade. In the 1780s a number of utopian colonization schemes were attempted. The most famous of these was evolved by Granville Sharp, whose plan called for the creation of a Province of Freedom, a colony to be located in Sierra Leone where American and British free blacks and Africans liberated from slave vessels could settle to create an outpost of Western Christian civilization. An initial shipment of blacks and white prostitutes was transported to Sierra Leone in 1787, but the expedition was badly organized and the settlement virtually ceased to exist. In 1791 the Sierra Leone Company was founded to develop trade in the interior of West Africa, the profits of which were to be used to meet the administrative expenses of the colony of former slaves. But trade with the interior did not develop. Moreover, the plain of Sierra Leone was ill-suited to agriculture. Relations between the settlers and the company were continually strained by misunderstandings, both financial and political. In 1794 the settlement was sacked by the French and probably never would have recovered if not for the abilities and leadership of Zachary Macaulay, governor from 1794–1799. Nevertheless, the Sierra Le-

one Company never proved to be a financial success, and after protracted negotiations, Sierra Leone was handed over to the British government as a crown colony. Under British rule the colony gradually grew as the West African Squadron delivered liberated Africans who slowly blended with black settlers from Nova Scotia, maroons, and black rebels from Jamaica to forge a Creole culture. Equipped with Western skills and converted to Christianity, the Sierra Leoneans turned increasingly to trade as their furtive attempts at agriculture failed. During this time they began to expand into the interior and along the coast and some returned to their original homelands, which they had last seen as slaves. At the outset the British authorities did not encourage their subjects to wander far from the colony, but under the administration of Governor Macaulay the influence of Sierra Leone was officially pushed into the hinterland. After his death in 1824, such influence continued informally and unofficially for another generation through trade, proselytization, and the urge of liberated Africans to return home. Thus in half a century, Sierra Leone had been transformed from a struggling settler community into a dynamic social force whose impact was felt far beyond the confines of the colony.

LIBERIA

If behind the founding of Sierra Leone lay a mixture of humanitarian, commercial, and diplomatic motives, the second important attempt at colonization in West Africa had few if any such motives. In 1816 the American Colonization Society was established, seemingly for humanitarian reasons, but in fact to deport a small and undesirable segment of the American population—the free blacks among the slave-owning communities of the Southern states. With the sympathy and support of the United States government, the first black settlers landed in Africa in 1821, to be followed by other settler communities sponsored by branches of the American Colonization Society. In 1839 these various communities were joined together in the Commonwealth of Liberia, and in 1841 J. J. Roberts became the first black governor. From the first the precise status of Liberia was ill defined, and after the United States had refused to define clearly its relationship with the settlers, the Liberians declared themselves a sovereign and independent republic in 1847. The Republic of Liberia grew slowly. By the 1860s the settler population probably numbered no more than 20,000, scattered in small enclaves along the coast and without any real means of cultural, political, or economic interchange with the peoples of the interior. Unlike the settlers of Sierra Leone, those of Liberia had no discernible influence in the other regions of West Africa (Theodore Canot, *Slaving in Liberia*).

SENEGAL

A third important colonization scheme in this period was undertaken by the French along the Senegal River. For two centuries French merchants had traded far up the river, and after the Napoleonic wars the restored monarchy set out to reestablish French influence on the Senegal, which had been momentarily eclipsed by the British seizure of St. Louis and Gorée. Although the French conceived bold and expansive schemes for agricultural plantations, these came to nothing and by the 1830s the only successful enterprise was the gum trade that was carried on by a chartered company. These failures convinced French officials that military conquest was a necessary prerequisite to orderly commerce, but until 1854 systematic attempts to organize a forward policy on the Senegal were frustrated by the formidable militant states of the interior. Nevertheless, these years were not without influence on subsequent French colonial policy, for during the Second Republic (1848–1851), inhabitants of the French settlements were accorded French citizenship, thus creating the nucleus of what the French came to regard as a colonial élite whose assimilation of French culture set the pattern for later colonial policies.

THE GOLD COAST

Throughout the eighteenth century the Ashanti enjoyed a succession of strong rulers who consolidated the confederation and sought to press forward to the sea by reducing the Fante middlemen to tribute-paying subjects and dealing directly with the Europeans themselves. But when the Ashanti pushed into the coastal region to challenge the Fante control of trade, the British at first supported the Fante. The wars with the Dutch and the French had been expensive, weakening what little influence, political or commercial, the two nations might exert over the coastal middlemen. Moreover, the commercial relationship between the Fante and the British merchants had long been well defined to their mutual advantage, a situation the European traders were loath to upset. However, the British soon regretted their choice. In 1806 the Fante were decisively defeated by the armies of the Ashantehene, and the British Governor, Colonel Torrance, capitulated and sought to create a new structure of relations with the formidable power of Ashanti. But the task was at once complicated by the abolition of the slave trade by the British in 1807. Abolition meant a severe dislocation of the means of economic support of the Ashanti state, which was now deprived of the medium for acquiring trade articles, particularly firearms, upon which its expansion depended. Thus the national interests of Britain and Ashanti became increasingly irreconcilable.

In 1821 the Company of Merchants, which had administered the Gold Coast forts, was dissolved, and Sir Charles Macarthy, Governor of Sierra Leone, became responsible for the government of the British settlements. Macarthy believed that only an extension of British rule could check the slave trade, and he now sought to initiate the forward policy in the Gold Coast that he had applied in Sierra Leone. He began by attempting to defeat the Ashanti, but when the British forces were defeated at Bonsaso in 1824 and Macarthy himself was killed, the policy of stopping the slave trade and furthering civilization and commerce by extending the responsibilities of the British government came to an end. British interests were confined to their coastal forts and perhaps would have disappeared altogether if British merchants had not taken over the forts by their control of the council that had been organized to administer them.

In 1830 George Maclean was sent out from London as president of the council. A personable and able man, Maclean slowly and almost imperceptibly began to extend British influence by acting as an unofficial mediator in local disputes between African chiefs. His purpose was to bring peace and order to the coast after the disruptions caused by earlier Ashanti invasions, thereby permitting the expansion of trade. As president of the council he possessed no legal authority to exercise jurisdiction over Africans who were not British subjects, and he succeeded more by the force of his personality and persuasion than by the limited authority of his official position. Maclean's policy triumphed in 1842 when a Parliamentary Select Committee recognized that his illegal dealings with the Africans of the Gold Coast had in fact conferred enormous benefits upon the Africans as well as the European traders. Consequently, in 1843 the British government resumed direct control over the Gold Coast, making the forts responsible to the Governor of Sierra Leone and permitting Maclean to make treaties, or "Bonds," regularizing the unofficial jurisdiction over the Africans that had previously been established by Maclean. Maclean died in 1847, and in 1850 the administration of the Gold Coast

was made independent from that of Sierra Leone, whose governor was too remote to take much interest in affairs farther down the coast. A full-fledged administration for the Gold Coast, however, required funds, which were to be raised from duties on trade. But adequate customs duties depended on a flourishing trade, which in turn depended on the cooperation of the coastal peoples and peaceful intercourse with Ashanti, neither of which proved possible. Although the coastal chiefs agreed to collect the taxes, resistance was so great that the revenue was less than expected and the prestige of the chiefs was further compromised in the eyes of their subjects. At the same time the Ashanti resented the growth of British control over those coastal peoples whom they regarded as members of rebellious states within the Ashanti sphere of influence. After many years of steadily deteriorating Anglo-Ashanti relations, the Ashanti armies, ostensibly to demand the return of refugees from Ashanti justice who had sought protection from the British, invaded the coast, raided with impunity, and brought trade to a standstill. The coastal people no longer believed in the power of Britain to protect them and British prestige collapsed. The initial reaction of the British government was to withdraw once again to the forts, but the political situation rapidly changed, and Britain was drawn once again into a final confrontation with Ashanti power.

Disputes with Ashanti over the claims to Elmina, precipitated by the sale of Dutch Gold Coast holdings to the British, the seizure of German missionaries by the Ashanti, and the Ashanti invasion of 1873, finally convinced the British government that Ashanti must be dealt with once and for all. In 1873 General Sir Garnet Wolseley and a force of British troops and African auxiliaries marched on Kumasi and defeated the Ashanti. The Ashantehene sued for peace, in return for which the Ashanti paid a large indemnity in gold and renounced suzerainty over the coastal peoples. Britain's ever-increasing interference in African affairs to check the slave trade and bring order to the interior had reached its logical conclusion. The extension of official British protection was not welcomed by the peoples of the Gold Coast, who were transformed from independent states to subjects of the British crown when an official British protectorate was declared over the Gold Coast in July 1874.

THE NIGER DELTA

East of the Slave Coast along the present-day littoral of the midwestern and eastern regions of Nigeria lay the great delta of the Niger River, a region that became one of the most important trading areas on the western African coast. Here the conduct of the slave trade created new, commercially oriented societies that evolved their own social and political institutions designed to carry on trade. Here Africans controlled all aspects of commercial exchange and required the European traders to abide by the commercial customs established in the market towns. Before the arrival of the Portuguese in the fifteenth century, Benin was the only important city-state in close proximity to the sea. East and south of Benin the indigenous social and political pattern was the small village, and under the impact of trade, some of these villages grew in subsequent centuries into commercial centers that were inhabited by powerful traders who wielded political as well as mercantile authority. Until the imposition of colonial rule in the late nineteenth and early twentieth centuries, each town remained independent of the others and no large-scale political unit emerged as in Yorubaland, Dahomey, or the Gold Coast.

Initially, the primary commodity in Portugal's trade with Benin was pepper, obtained through the coastal port of Gwato, but pepper was soon replaced by slaves for the plantation islands of São Thomé and Fernando Po. As the demand for slaves increased in response to the expansion of plantation economies in the New World, the delta villages became major suppliers and rivals of Benin. Such well-known Ijo market towns as Bonny (Captain Hugh Crow, *Bonny*), New Calabar, Brass, and Old Calabar were developed by the Efik traders, and the Itsekiri kingdom of Warri west of the Niger may have supplied a quarter of the slaves that entered the trade from all West African ports during the eighteenth century. Most of the slaves that passed through the delta towns were from the Ibo region on the eastern side of the Niger. Iboland itself was a large territory without any central authority to prevent the seizure and sale of slaves. During the centuries of trade in the delta the manner of exchange became precisely defined. A close commercial bond existed between the inland suppliers and the coastal middlemen, but the policy of the coastal middlemen toward the European traders was to isolate them in ships or old hulks moored in the river estuaries. Indeed most of the political difficulties in the delta arose from the determination of the middlemen to protect their inland sources of supply and the desire of Europeans to circumvent the coastal traders. In the trading towns, wealth was the usual key to political authority. For instance, among the Ijo a system of authority called house rule developed. A "house" consisted of a wealthy trader and his household, including family and domestic slaves. The exact authority of the head of the house differed from one town to another, but generally in the western delta it was superseded by more centralized monarchical rule. Differences among the city-states were not confined solely to degrees of political authority. In some towns, like New Calabar, slaves were easily assimilated into society. Through the house system they gained status as citizens and frequently rose to positions of power in the community. Elsewhere, among the Efik for instance, more rigid patterns of descent precluded the assimilation of slaves into society.

Thus the history of the delta city-states cannot be regarded simply in economic terms, for the political and social institutions they evolved clearly conditioned relations with the Europeans and particularly the British. The diffused political organization required British officials as well as traders and missionaries to deal with a multitude of local authorities so that individual treaties had to be made with every one, thus increasing British involvement and laying the groundwork for the ultimate imposition of imperial rule. Moreover, the delta is one of the richest palm oil areas in all West Africa, and when the British began to press for legitimate trade to replace the slave trade, palm oil could be easily substituted without upsetting the system of trade that had already been developed in slaves.

THE SLAVE COAST

Between the Gold Coast and the Niger delta, with its powerful middlemen traders and well-developed, commercially oriented city-states, lay the Slave Coast. Here the coast of Africa is one long sandbar behind which are lagoons into which flow the rivers of the upcountry. The history of the Slave Coast is one of fierce commercial competition between the various African states and of freewheeling trade and political dealing by the European powers and private traders in an attempt to obtain a monopoly. During the late seventeenth and early eighteenth centuries Abomey became a highly centralized state that established its predominance on the coast of Dahomey and contested European intrusion. The Fon of Abomey were supported in their drive to the coast by a group of Portuguese from Brazil, who had formed special relations with the African traders, and in the eighteenth century this group came to exert great influence on the Dahomey coast. To the east the Old Oyo Empire had been

able to assert fitful control over the southern Yoruba states, but with the decline of the empire these states broke away. Thus by the beginning of the nineteenth century, the Slave Coast was dotted with numerous states carrying on a precarious trade with many European merchants but always challenged by the growing power of Dahomey in the center.

LEGITIMATE TRADE

Along with the schemes of colonization, legitimate trade was regarded as an essential instrument in destroying the slave trade. Throughout the eighteenth century, trade in products had been discussed as a substitute for the slave trade and had been used as an argument in support of colonization schemes in Sierra Leone, Liberia, and Senegal. In the 1830s Thomas Buxton brought together many of these ideas when he urged the introduction of legitimate commerce along with colonization and Christianity in Africa. In the first half of the nineteenth century, Britain was becoming an industrialized nation and West Africa appeared a ready market for British-manufactured goods as well as a supplier of tropical products—pepper, peanuts, and palm oil—that were in ever-increasing demand in Europe. Despite the fact that West Africa in 1830 accounted for only a pitifully small percentage of Britain's exports, and the high European mortality rate discouraged British involvement, the opening of the interior of West Africa appeared to hold promise of profitable commercial trade, and the advance of Christian missionaries demanded the extension of European influence for humanitarian reasons.

THE MISSIONARY ADVANCE

The failure of the great British Niger expedition of 1841 did not deter the advance of Christian missionaries into West Africa. Although Catholic missionaries had accompanied the Portuguese explorers and had even resided at Benin, they made no serious attempt to spread the faith into the hinterland. The conversion of West Africa had to await the rise of evangelical Christianity among the Protestants of Western Europe and America, many of whom were closely associated with the abolitionist movement. At the beginning of the nineteenth century, well-financed religious groups in Europe provided the necessary funds to sustain missionary work in Africa. In 1806 the Church Missionary Society (CMS) sent its first major mission to Sierra Leone to work among the settlers and peoples of the hinterland for the purpose of founding an African church as an offshoot of the established Church of England. The Wesleyans followed in 1811, and in 1827 the Fourah Bay Institution (the first college in West Africa) was founded to train Africans for service in the church. Although by midcentury the number of converts in Sierra Leone numbered only 50,000, their influence ranged far beyond the colony. During the thirty years preceding the Niger expedition of 1841, numerous liberated Christian Africans returned to their homelands in Nigeria, where they preserved a Christian community and provided a nucleus for mission stations.

During the 1840s missionary activities steadily increased in West Africa. In 1844 the CMS established a mission at Abeokuta, to be followed shortly by a mission founded by the Wesleyans. The Baptists were active in the Cameroons after 1841 and in Nigeria after 1851. A Church of Scotland mission was established at Old Calabar in 1846. Further to the west the Bremen Society worked in Togo, and the famous Reverend Thomas Birch Freeman of the Wesleyan Missionary Society arrived at Cape Coast in 1837 and was active in expanding the Wesleyan movement on the Gold Coast, Nigeria, and the Slave Coast until his death in 1890. Clearly, the most important contribution of these missions was the creation of a new social class of mission-educated Africans who, whether they practiced Christianity or not, learned how to read and write European languages. Once equipped with this skill, they emerged during the latter part of the nineteenth century as an élite group that exerted widespread influence throughout West Africa. Until the 1870s the object of the missionaries in West Africa was to create an African Church staffed and led by Africans. Under the leadership of its great secretary Sir Henry Venn, the CMS supported its African missionaries (the famous Samuel Crowther, for example) and encouraged their efforts to control the church in Africa. After the 1870s, however, the change in European feeling toward Africa was clearly reflected in the missionary movement. Racial and patronizing attitudes accompanied the arrogant and opinionated young missionaries who arrived in Africa in the age of late Victorian imperialism and came to feel that all things African were absolutely unsuited to proper Christianity. But the church was not alone in this infectious, changing image of Africa.

THE CHANGING IMAGE OF AFRICA

The first European contacts with West Africa were not characterized by the rationalized racism of the nineteenth and twentieth centuries. Although African-European relations were clearly influenced by the slave trade, the Catholic Church affirmed the common humanity of both Africans and Europeans. In subsequent centuries the European image of Africa was formed by limited contacts in Africa and by much pseudo-scientific speculation, usually about race, in Europe. The luxuriant tropical growth of West Africa was conducive to visions of easy wealth that, in contrast to the Protestant ethic that civilization was a product of the hard work required to subdue a hostile environment, encouraged the belief among Europeans that the African was indolent and promiscuous in his soft environment. In reality, however, the West African environment was harsh, the soils leached, and the climate enervating. The African's Garden of Eden was a land of death to the Europeans, nearly half of whom died of fever during their first year on the coast. The immunity of the African to malaria appeared to support the many racist theories that grew out of eighteenth-century attempts to classify all animals and men. Most of these theories hopelessly confused race and culture, so that what began as social difference usually ended as cultural inferiority. In the latter part of the nineteenth century, the growing European image of African inferiority culminated in the corruption of Darwin's theories of evolution into the popular ideas that were expressed by the Social Darwinists in the phrase "survival of the fittest." From the European point of view the African clearly was not "fit," and therefore the European, as a member of a superior civilization, had the right, the duty, the white man's burden, to shape the lives of the Africans, who were "half devil, half child." Thus the equality, respect, and tolerance that had grown out of centuries of commercial contact between Europeans and Africans evaporated during the closing decades of the nineteenth century, the era of the new imperialists.

THE BEGINNINGS OF EUROPEAN RIVALRY

The return to a forward policy in West Africa arose out of two expeditions at midcentury that encouraged Britain and France to try once again to establish their influence beyond the coastal forts. From 1850 to 1856, Heinrich Barth explored throughout the western Sudan from Adamawa to Timbuktu. Barth was an acute and accurate observer, and his reports revived the interest in trade and diplomatic contact with the rich and populous regions of the western Sudan. In 1854 Dr. William Baikie led an expedition up the Niger to Lokoja and then up the Benue to Yola some 900 miles from the sea. The great significance of this voyage was that the members of the expedition regularly took quinine and not one of them died. Residence and travel in West Africa were now less restricted by the hazards of fever and death, and the beginning of European penetration was thus facilitated.

Two more decades were to elapse, however, before the real scramble for West Africa would take place. In the meantime the foundation was quietly being laid by the consuls, governors, residents, missionaries, and traders. The influence and authority that these agents acquired in West Africa between 1860 and 1890 were quite unofficial and were referred to by some authorities as "informal empire." The means by which informal empire was created and expanded was principally that of treaty making, supported occasionally by military action. Clearly, misunderstandings arose over treaty obligations, providing the men with numerous instant opportunities to extend their influence and that of the European countries they represented. For instance, under the governorship of J. S. Hill the colony of Sierra Leone was expanded at African expense as a result of attempts to control the trade routes to the interior on the one hand and of efforts to enforce former treaties in the Sherbro country on the other. Usually the British government supported Hill's forward course, largely because no one in London either understood or cared to inform himself of the intricacies of African diplomacy. Occasionally Hill, and others like him, would go too far or demand too much, at which point the British Treasury intervened. British initiative, however, was not left solely in the hands of its officials. Traders, missionaries, and residents all contributed to the expansion of British influence from the enclaves to which British interests had been confined for centuries.

Although the French were to take a more forward course in the Senegal under the leadership of Louis Faidherbe during this period, along the Slave Coast the aggressive Victor Régis had developed an important trade in palm oil. Because he was the quasi-official French representative, he dealt directly with the King of Dahomey. Régis was able to convince France to proclaim a protectorate over Porto Novo in 1861, but at that point French activity ceased, as all France's energies were required to meet the rising power of a resurgent Germany.

Although European initiatives in West Africa were informal and unorganized throughout the 1860s and 1870s, they deeply involved the governments of Britain and France at a time when events in these countries were bringing men with new attitudes and policies to the forefront of affairs. The "new imperialism" that played such a dominant role in shaping the African policies of Britain, France, Germany, and Italy in the late nineteenth and early twentieth centuries was an amalgam of many motives. The industrialization of Europe provided a new technology that gave the European occupiers an enormous superiority over African resistance. The outpouring of manufactured products required markets, and many argued that the vast non-European populations of the world were all potential buyers. Of course, the capital that industrialization had produced was always seeking profitable sources of investment, and although in fact little capital ever found its way to Africa or Asia by comparison with the Americas, the proponents of imperialism could not have foreseen that development. Economic considerations, however, can no longer be regarded as the driving force behind European imperialism in Africa. For there was also the argument, advanced by many, that the wealthy, "civilized" nations had a mission to bring the African out of darkness by investing him with Western culture, religions, and technology. Strategy too played a large role in the European occupation of Africa, although strategic factors were less prominent in West Africa than in eastern Africa

and the Nile Valley. Nevertheless, wars of conquest in West Africa did provide an outlet for disaffected individuals—the French army officer with little hope of promotion in Europe, the missionary, the explorer—and were frequently undertaken to preserve prestige as well as interests.

THE BERLIN CONFERENCE OF 1885

The scramble for Africa was begun not by the imperialism of a great European power but by the rivalry between Count Savorgnan de Brazza and Leopold II, King of the Belgians and sovereign of the Congo Free State. In 1876 Leopold organized the International African Association for the purpose of opening equatorial Africa to civilization. At first Leopold's association sent expeditions to East Africa, but when Henry Morton Stanley returned to Europe after his explorations in the Congo, Leopold organized the *Comité d'Etudes du Haut Congo,* ostensibly to carry out commercial and philanthropic work in the Congo but in reality to carve out a colonial empire. Not to be outdone, the French Committee of the International African Association sent de Brazza from Cabinda to the Congo, and from 1879 to 1882 de Brazza for the French and Stanley for King Leopold dashed about on their respective sides of the river, hastily signing treaties with chiefs. The schemes of Leopold and the French alarmed the British, who were not anxious to possess the Congo but by the same token were not anxious to see any other power control it. Feverish diplomatic activity followed. Britain sought to revive Portugal's ancient claims to the mouth of the Congo, while Leopold skillfully secured French and, indirectly through the French, German support. Seeing an opportunity to side with the French and to secure the support of the growing imperialist faction within Germany, Bismarck called for an international conference in 1884 to settle the

Congo question and to draw up rules regulating any European states that might seek to occupy African territory.

The Berlin Conference opened in November 1884 and was attended by all the European powers and the United States. The conference created a free trade zone in tropical Africa extending from 5 degrees north latitude to 19 degrees south latitude and embracing the mouths of three of the greatest rivers of Africa—the Niger, the Congo, and the Zambezi. Within this zone no taxes could be levied except as fair compensation and no power could concede monopolies or commercial privileges. Both the Congo and the Niger were to have freedom of navigation. In addition, the conference agreed to the requirements for occupation and laid down the guidelines for future partition among the powers. Finally, it recognized the sovereignty of the International African Association in the Congo, which as a "sovereign power," signed the General Act of the conference. The investiture of sovereignty, however, created an ambiguous situation in which the King of the Belgians was acting in a private capacity as the head of a private association that had in turn become a sovereign state. But this ambiguity was soon resolved by an amendment to the Belgian Constitution, and on July 1, 1885, the Congo Free State was proclaimed. With the Congo question settled and the rules for partition agreed upon, the European powers could now begin the scramble for Africa.

THE VARIETIES OF AFRICAN RESPONSE

Although the regenerated forces of European imperialism that confronted Africa after 1870 appeared theoretically irresistible, in fact African resistance was a vital factor in determining the pattern of colonial occupation. The African response took many forms, ranging from sullen acceptance to belligerent and unyielding opposition, but was always characterized by the failure of the Afri-

cans to act together to oppose the incomers. Occasionally an African leader like al-Hajj Umar would call for a *jihad* against the Europeans, or such uprisings as the Maji-Maji rebellion in German East Africa or the revolt of the Ndebele and the Shona in Southern Rhodesia rallied diverse groups by an appeal that transcended local loyalties, but such attempts were more the exception than the rule. As a result, the European imperialists were able to divide and to conquer, since many African states regarded the presence of European soldiers as a third force to be utilized in continuing the traditional conflicts among themselves. Consequently, Europeans were able to recruit African troops for their colonial armies, and the actual conquest, partition, and pacification were performed largely by African mercenaries.

In addition to African political disunity, which prevented united resistance against the invaders and allowed the recruitment of African soldiers for colonial armies, the overwhelming technological superiority of the Europeans enabled them to conquer and to occupy. The weapons developed during the nineteenth century and the skills evolved in their use gave the Europeans an advantage they had not hitherto enjoyed. Artillery (used now as an offensive weapon), the repeating rifle, and later the machine gun were dramatically more efficient than the old muzzle-loading guns employed by the Africans. Yet despite the awe-inspiring technical advantages possessed by the Europeans at the end of the nineteenth century, the Africans were still able to mount surprisingly formidable resistance, which conditioned the outcome of the European conquest and significantly affected the future administration of the resistors by their European rulers.

The fundamental purpose for which Africans resisted colonial encroachment was, of course, to maintain their independence. But independence from African rulers was frequently as important to some Africans as freedom from ill-defined European restrictions on African actions. In the Senegal, for instance, the long record of rebellion, replacement of rulers, and ever-shifting alliances grew out of a desire by African leaders to preserve their local autonomy whether the antagonist who threatened that autonomy was African or European. Thus, what appears to be a rapid conquest by European forces supported by their African allies invariably becomes a long drawn-out struggle to pacify and to win a measure of African acceptance of colonial rule (Sir Harry Johnston, *Jaja, Nana, and Resistance to British Control*).

RESISTANCE AND OCCUPATION

The French advance in West Africa was not confined to the western Sudan. In 1886 the French resumed direct control of their posts in the Ivory Coast, but attempts to extend French influence beyond Grand Bassam were frustrated by the absence of centralized African states. Resistance was local and required numerous military actions and innumerable negotiations. More often than not the resistance was exceedingly fierce because French presence, unlike that of the western Sudan, was direct, challenging every aspect of the African way of life. Opposition in the Ivory Coast was met by repression. Confiscation of weapons, deportations of resistance leaders, demands for porters, and a labor corvée for public works were all employed to establish French authority. Such measures were harsh and successful in breaking African opposition, but not without the use of continuous military and police action right up to the outbreak of World War I.

The pattern of French advance into the Ivory Coast was quite different from the British occupation of the Gold Coast to the east. A long and complex relationship had evolved between the British and the Ashanti. Although the Ashanti were prepared to accept British presence on the coast, they never reconciled themselves to their loss of control over the subsidiary African states outside the Ashanti Union. After two decades of deteriorating relations (the war of 1874 had been a futile attempt to resolve Anglo-Ashanti differences), the British declared a protectorate over Ashanti in 1895. The recalcitrant Ashantehene, Prempeh, was deported, and in 1900 the British Governor unwisely demanded the Golden Stool, in which the spiritual soul of the Ashanti people resided. The Ashanti rose in rebellion, which was subsequently crushed in 1901 by Britain's direct annexation and rule of Ashanti. In the meantime, the British had dispatched treaty-making expeditions to the north, and by 1898 numerous chiefs had placed themselves under British protection. Although these treaties established the present-day boundaries of Ghana, they also divided up communities and transgressed the traditional boundaries of older states, creating irredentism among the people and political problems for the later independent states of West Africa.

The Slave Coast provides the classic example of the mixed motives of imperialism—rival trading interests, competing diplomacy, and the use of naval patrols to establish European paramountcy. Before 1880, Britain was the only power that had actually laid claim to territory on the west coast of Africa from Accra to the Cameroons. Since the late 1860s the French had been strong competitors on the coast of Dahomey, and the Germans had become involved in Togo by a long tradition of missionary activity. Yet at no time before the partition had German trading interests urged the annexation of southern Togo, and the declaration of a protectorate arose more as an afterthought to the German acquisition of the Cameroons. Clearly, the annexation of the Cameroons and Togoland was conditioned more by the determination of the men on the coast to wrest advantages for their specific commercial interests than by any imperial conspiracy plotted in the European capitals. But as the British, French, and Germans staked out their coastal enclaves, it became clear that the first power that could penetrate into the hinterland, turn the flank of its neighboring rivals, and command the interior source of supply of trade goods would render the other shallow enclaves meaningless. The pattern of conquest for the partition of the interior of the Slave Coast was thus fixed, but the money gained from customs duties was patently insufficient to finance military expeditions against the powerful forces of Abomey in the interior. Only the home governments could provide the necessary resources to extend European control over Dahomey.

In 1890 Abomey still controlled Ouidah and was the fourth major trading power on the coast (after Britain, France, and Germany). Gradually, however, the French came to support the vassals of Abomey against their overlord and to channel the palm oil trade through French-controlled ports, creating a loss of trade and economic depression in Ouidah. The kings of Dahomey jealously guarded their independence, but by 1890 it was clear that France and Abomey could never resolve their antagonistic claims by any means short of war. At first the French hoped to establish King Behanzin as a loyal French ruler, protected by France but still exerting theoretical sovereignty. Behanzin, however, refused to become a French puppet. He was captured and exiled, and Abomey was carved up into small units, bringing to an end the most centrally organized state in all West Africa.

With Abomey secured, the way to Yorubaland and the Niger appeared open to the French, and they sought to challenge the vague British claims to the hinterland beyond Lagos. Whipped up by speeches in Parliament and the jingo press, the drive to establish control over the hinterland of the Slave Coast became a part of the Anglo-French contest throughout the world. In what was shortly to become Nigeria, the British initiative was taken by the Royal Niger Company. Since the late 1870s, Sir George Goldie Taubman had sought to monopolize the trade of the Niger Delta and the hinterland in order to eliminate French and German rivals. Between 1879 and 1884 Goldie's company, first called the United African Company and later the National African Company, bought out its rivals, which were worn down by the sharp competition of Goldie and his aggressive agents. By 1885 the company extended far inland, forestalling German initiative on the Niger by making advantageous commercial treaties with the Sultan of Sokoto. In 1886 Goldie obtained a royal charter for his company (now called the Royal Niger Company), investing it with administrative as well as commercial power, and in the following year a protectorate was proclaimed over territories whose rulers had signed treaties with the company's agents. From the delta upriver to Lokoja and beyond, Goldie created a virtual monopoly by any means, including administrative and judicial control, price wars, and the imposition of customs duties. Although Goldie's treaties with the Fulani sultans succeeded in keeping the French and Germans out of northern Nigeria, they were of little use south of the Niger, where in 1894 the French began to advance eastward toward Borgu. Goldie sent Captain (later Sir) Frederick Lugard to conclude a treaty with Borgu, placing it under British protection, but the company could hardly have continued to hold back the French without the aid of the home government. In 1897 the British government agreed to provide money and officers for a West African Frontier Force under Lugard, who was then able to hold his own against the French. In 1898 both Britain and France signed an agreement fixing the northern and western boundaries of Nigeria. The services of the Royal Niger Company were no longer needed to defend

British interests, and the charter was revoked in 1899. On payment of compensation, the British government took over the company's administrative and military assets.

ESTABLISHMENT OF BRITISH COLONIAL ADMINISTRATION

Although the British had proclaimed a protectorate over the Niger delta in 1885, there was no effective government—only loose courts of equity and a British consul who frequently found himself the unhappy arbiter between Goldie's company and the delta middlemen whom the Royal Niger Company was attempting to circumvent. The resistance of delta chiefs like Jaja of Opobo or Nana at Benin forced the representatives of the British government to remove any chief who hindered the plans of British subjects. Thus the traders of Brass, who assaulted the company's port at Akassa, were punished by a British punitive expedition just as Benin was crushed after it refused to trade with the British and allowed its people to attack the British consul who had come to mediate the dispute. Meanwhile in the West, in response to French control in Dahomey, the British governors of the Lagos protectorate pressed into Yorubaland. In 1892 Governor Gilbert Carter occupied Ijebu despite spirited resistance and in the following year trekked through Yoruba country drawing up treaties establishing British rule in Oyo, Ilorin, Ogbomosho, and Ibadan. The balance of power among the Yoruba was such that no one could win hegemony except the British, who could alter the balance in their favor by dealing separately with the divided Yoruba chiefs.

In 1900 Sir Frederick Lugard was entrusted with the task of establishing British administration in northern Nigeria. He first had to conquer and pacify the heartland of the Fulani Empire, Gwandu and Sokoto, and the great cities of the North. By 1903, in a series of campaigns, Lugard successfully crushed the Fulani resistance. His most important achievement, however, was the introduction of British control by the famous administrative practice of indirect rule (Lord Lugard, *Indirect Rule in Tropical Africa*). Lugard's forces had conquered a vast and populous land that possessed little in the way of immediately exploitable resources to pay for a vast superstructure of imperial rule. With only a £500,000 grant-in-aid from the home government and a handful of British officials, the obvious way to control the people was to rule through their traditional authorities and to utilize their elaborate hierarchy of officials for the day-to-day running of the government. Thus the amirs continued to rule the people, but always under the supervision of a handful of British officials who were attached to each of the courts. Thus began the famous system of indirect rule—a vague notion of trusteeship, guidance, and planned evolution that so captured the attention of colonial officials throughout the world that by 1920 this system was being applied and misapplied all over Africa by British colonial administrative officers (Mary Kingsley, *The Crown System in West Africa*).

THE PROBLEM OF COLONIAL ADMINISTRATION

Two important facts conditioned the growth of the problems that the colonial administration sought to resolve. First, colonial rule in West Africa did not mean a significant increase in the number of European colonizers so that the question of alienating African land to European settlers never became the issue it was later to become in eastern and southern Africa. Second, there was always the demand that the colonies be profitable for the mother country or at least not be a drain on the metropole. Clearly, such a demand almost inevitably conflicted with the interests of African society, and such conflicts were almost invariably resolved in favor of the ruler. Exploitation was an incontrovertible fact, not just a term of abuse.

Virtually all the problems of colonial administration had their origins in the Europeans' ignorance about the people they were governing and the resources of the land. Consequently, from the beginning to the twentieth century the French (followed by the British in the 1920s) commissioned scholars and officials to investigate the Africans and their problems. Such problems polarized around the administration of the law, the distribution of land, the collection of taxes, the conditions of labor, and the development of European educational institutions to produce Africans who would serve the administration and run the technical services. All these problems were directly related to the central question of authority—the institutions of political rule. The French were always experimenting to devise means of direct intervention in African political institutions in order to encourage the Africans to emulate the French pattern of administration. In contrast, the British increasingly sought to utilize native authorities, either hereditary or newly created, and encouraged them to rule with as little interference by British officials as possible. From the very beginning the "native problems" of the colonial territories can be traced to the subordination of African authority and the imposition of European rule in its place.

WEST AFRICA BETWEEN THE WORLD WARS: BRITISH WEST AFRICA

British West Africa between the wars was characterized by the expansion of an African élite, but one that was not so closely identified with British culture as were the Africans in the territories of France with the French. Before World War II the bulk of educational enterprise was left to the missions, which sought to use African languages in the lower grades, but even though the curriculum of advanced education was thoroughly British, it was not accompanied by the same ethnocentric judgments that dominated education in French West Africa (Sir Frederick Gordon Guggisberg, *The Education of the African*). Further, Christian missions were excluded from the Muslim population of northern Nigeria, so that education was drastically curtailed by the limited funds that the government could allocate for schools in that region.

Parallel to the growth of mission schools was the development of independent churches, particularly in southern Nigeria. When Europeans replaced African missionaries in the late Victorian age, African Christians resented the intrusion of European missionaries where in the past Africans had frequently performed outstanding service. Dissent took the form of groups of Africans who declared themselves administratively independent of the European churches, and once they no longer relied on Europeans for support they saw no reason why they themselves should not govern all aspects of their church organization and worship. Thus an increasing class of Western-educated Africans was obtaining experience in organizational techniques by running churches and social clubs. These same Africans were the first to demand a voice in running their government. The roots of nationalism in British West Africa can be traced directly to education and the growth of African organizations, whether church, social club, or labor union.

The growth of an educated class with its own organizations was sustained by the wealth gained from the cultivation of marketable produce—principally cocoa, peanuts, and the more traditional palm oil. Cocoa had been brought to the Gold Coast from Fernando Po in 1879, and by 1891 the first crop had been exported. Production expanded, and cocoa was grown all along the coast but particularly in Nigeria and the Gold Coast, where it was an effective element in providing funds for modernization and for the organizational techniques required by the development of cooperatives, controls, and long-range planning. Just as cocoa helped to revolutionize the economies of the forest coast, the peanut played a similar role in the economies of the savanna belt further north in Senegal, Gambia, the Sudan, and northern Nigeria. In addition to cocoa and peanuts, the efforts of the Europeans to exploit the colonies by the use of forced labor precipitated widespread social changes. Clearly, before the resources of West Africa could be developed, the necessary roads, rail lines, and other forms of infrastructure had to be constructed, and this was done by forced labor. Although attempts were made to justify forced labor as a traditional method that had been employed by African chiefs, there was in fact no moral justification; but without forced labor the means of modernization could probably never have been built. The use of forced labor took the able-bodied men from their community activities, often during the seasons when their presence was required in the fields, and the impact of groups of laborers moving around the territory to work on roads, dig in fields, or harvest farm produce loosened the ties of traditional society and almost created more social discord than economic gain.

RISE OF NATIONALISM IN WEST AFRICA

By the 1930s the old notions and practices of exploitation of the colonies were being modified and the European rulers realized that the value of West Africa could be taken advantage of only by substantial investment of social, industrial, and agricultural capital. Thus plans to organize development schemes were inaugurated, and although they remained relatively modest during the great depression and World War II, the postwar period saw a rapid expansion of roads, ports, schools, and government services. But just as the instruments and the will to develop were being fashioned by governments in Europe, the very magnitude of the problems of modernization outstripped the paternal attitudes and organizations of colonial administration in West Africa. To the Africans it became increasingly apparent that the colonial governments were expending their energies by hanging onto their power rather than initiating or keeping pace with the demands for modernization. Numerous African agencies existed through which dissatisfaction was channeled. New town associations, labor unions, and embryonic political parties began to agitate for an end to alien control at a time when the principles of the United Nations Charter were widely acclaimed by ruler and ruled alike. But the beginning of the end of colonial rule did not resolve the basic question of who was to possess final authority. At the time of conquest and pacification, the resistance was led by the traditional leaders, religious or secular, but with the growth of an educated élite that was trained to administer large-scale organizations, the authority of the hereditary rulers, supported and manipulated by the colonial administrations, was threatened. Alert to events beyond the African continent and equipped to use the techniques and apparatus of political organizations that had been developed in Europe, the African élite was ready to challenge both the traditional leaders and the colonial rulers for control. The success of this challenge has resulted in the creation of numerous independent African states out of the West African empires of the European powers (Nnamdi Azikiwe, *Nigeria and Independence*).

20 GOMES EANNES DE AZURARA
THE DISCOVERY OF GUINEA

Gomes Eannes de Azurara was the Royal Chronicler of Portugal during the time that Prince Henry the Navigator inaugurated the systematic exploration of the coast of West Africa. Although the dates of his birth and death remain unknown, Azurara was probably born in the province of Minho at the beginning of the fifteenth century. He appears to have obtained a post in the Royal Library during the brief reign of Dom Duarte (1433–1438), or shortly thereafter, as assistant to Royal Chronicler Fernão Lopez, whom he later succeeded. In 1453 he completed the Chronica de Guine, *which describes the Portuguese discoveries along the West African coast and which remains one of the earliest records of European activity in West Africa.*

.   .   .

So the Infant, moved by these reasons, which you have already heard, began to make ready his ships and his people, as the needs of the case required; but this much you may learn,· that although he sent out many times, not only ordinary men, but such as by their experience in great deeds of war were of foremost name in the profession of arms, yet there was not one who dared to pass that Cape of Bojador and learn about the land beyond it, as the Infant wished.[1] And to say the truth this was not from cowardice or want of good will, but from the novelty of the thing and the wide-spread and ancient rumour about this Cape, that had been cherished by the mariners of Spain from generation to generation. And although this proved to be deceitful, yet since the hazarding of this attempt seemed to threaten the last evil of all, there was great doubt as to who would be the first to risk his life in such a venture. How are we, men said, to pass the bounds that our fa-

From Gomes Eannes de Azurara, *The Chronicle of the Discovery and Conquest of Guinea*, trans. from the Portuguese by C. Raymond Beazley and Edgar Prestage (London: Hakluyt Society, 1896), I, 30–34, 39–43. Reprinted by permission of Cambridge University Press on behalf of The Hakluyt Society.
[1] Infant is the title of any legitimate son of a king of Spain or Portugal except the eldest. This reference is to the Infant Prince Henry (1394–1460), commonly known as "the Navigator," the third son of King João (or John) of Portugal. Cape Bojador is located at 26°15′ North latitude at the western end of the Atlas Mountains of Morocco (ed.).

thers set up, or what profit can result to the Infant from the perdition of our souls as well as of our bodies—for of a truth by daring any further we shall become wilful murderers of ourselves? Have there not been in Spain other princes and lords as covetous perchance of this honour as the Infant? For certainly it cannot be presumed that among so many noble men who did such great and lofty deeds for the glory of their memory, there had not been one to dare this deed. But being satisfied of the peril, and seeing no hope of honour or profit, they left off the attempt. For, said the mariners, this much is clear, that beyond this Cape there is no race of men nor place of inhabitants: nor is the land less sandy than the deserts of Libya, where there is no water, no tree, no green herb—and the sea so shallow that a whole league from land it is only a fathom deep, while the currents are so terrible that no ship having once passed the Cape, will ever be able to return.

Therefore our forefathers never attempted to pass it: and of a surety their knowledge of the lands beyond was not a little dark, as they knew not how to set them down on the charts, by which man controls all the seas that can be navigated. Now what sort of a ship's captain would he be who, with such doubts placed before him by those to whom he might reasonably yield credence and authority, and with such certain prospect of death before his eyes, could venture the trial of such a bold feat as that? O thou Virgin Themis, saith our Author, who among the nine Muses of Mount Parnassus didst possess the especial right of searching out the secrets of Apollo's cave, I doubt whether thy fears were as great at putting thy feet on that sacred table where the divine revelations afflicted thee little less than death, as the terrors of these mariners of ours, threatened not only by fear but by its shadow, whose great deceit was the cause of very great expenses. For during twelve years the Infant continued steadily at this labour of his, ordering out his ships every year to those parts, not without great loss of revenue, and never finding any who dared to make that passage. Yet they did not return wholly without honour, for as an atonement for their failure to carry out more fully their Lord's wishes, some made descents upon the coasts of Granada and others voyaged along the Levant Seas, where they took great booty of the Infidels, with which they returned to the Kingdom very honourably.

Now the Infant always received home again with great patience those whom he had sent out, as Captains of his ships, in search of that land, never upbraiding them with their failure, but with gracious countenance listening to the story of the events of their voyage, giving them such rewards as he was wont to give to those who served him well, and then either sending them back to search again or despatching other picked men of his Household, with their ships well furnished, making more urgent his charge to them, with promise of greater guerdons, if they added anything to the voyage that those before them had made, all to the intent that he might arrive at some comprehension of that difficulty. And at last, after twelve years, the Infant armed a "barcha" [bark or boat—ed.] and gave it to Gil Eannes, one of his squires, whom he afterwards knighted and cared for right nobly. And he followed the course that others had taken; but touched by the self-same terror, he only went as far as the Canary Islands, where he took some captives and returned to the Kingdom. Now this was in the year of Jesus Christ 1433, and in the next year the Infant made ready the same vessel, and calling Gil Eannes apart, charged him earnestly to strain every nerve to pass that Cape, and even if he could do nothing else on that voyage, yet he should consider that to be enough. "You cannot find," said the Infant, "a peril so great that the hope of reward will not be greater, and in truth I wonder much at the notion you have all taken on so uncertain a matter—for even if these things that are reported had any authority, however small, I would not blame you, but you tell me only the opinions of four mariners, who come but from the Flanders trade or from some other ports that are very commonly sailed to, and know nothing of the needle or sailing-chart. Go forth, then, and heed none of their words, but make your voyage straightway, inasmuch as with the grace of God you cannot but gain from this journey honour and profit." The Infant was a man of very great authority, so that his admonitions, mild though they were, had much effect on the serious-minded. And so it appeared by the deed of this man, for he, after these words, resolved not to return to the presence of his Lord without assured tidings of that for which he was sent. And as he purposed, so he performed—for in that voyage he doubled the Cape, despising all danger, and found the lands beyond quite contrary to what he, like others, had expected. And although the matter was a small one in itself, yet on account of its daring it was reckoned great—for if the first man who reached the Cape had passed it, there would not have been so much praise and thanks bestowed on him; but even as the danger of the affair put all others into the greater fear, so the accomplishing of it brought the greater honour to this man. But whether or no the success of Gil Eannes gained for him any genuine glory may be perceived by the words that the Infant spoke to him before his starting; and his experience on his return was very clear on this point, for he was exceeding well received, not without a profitable increase of honour and possessions. And then it was he related to the Infant how the whole matter had gone, telling him how he had ordered the boat to be put out and had gone in to the shore without finding either people or signs of habitation. And since, my lord, said Gil Eannes, I thought that I ought to bring some token of the land since I was on it, I gathered these herbs which I here present to your grace; the which we in this country call Roses of Saint Mary. Then, after he had finished giving an account of his voyage to that part, the Infant caused a "barinel" [2] to be made ready, in which he sent out Affonso Gonçalvez Baldaya, his cupbearer, and Gil Eannes as well with his "barcha," ordering him to return there with his companion. And so in fact they did, passing fifty leagues beyond the Cape, where they found the land without dwellings, but shewing footmarks of men and camels. And then, either because they were so ordered, or from necessity, they returned with this intelligence, without doing aught else worth recording.

.   .   .

I think I can now take some sort of pleasure in the narrating of this history, because I find something wherewith to satisfy the desire of our Prince; the which desire was so much the greater as the matters for which he had toiled so long were now more within his view. And so in this chapter I wish to present some novelty in his toilsome seed-time of preparation.

Now it was so that in this year 1441, when the affairs of this realm were somewhat more settled though not fully quieted, that the Infant armed a little ship, of the which he made captain one Antam

Gonçalvez, his chamberlain, and a very young man; and the end of that voyage was none other, according to my Lord's commandment, but to ship a cargo of the skins and oil of those seawolves of which we have spoken in previous chapters. But it cannot be doubted that the Infant gave him the same charge that he gave to others, but as the age of this captain was weaker, and his authority but slight, so the Prince's orders were less stringent, and in consequence his hopes of result less confident.

But when he had accomplished his voyage, as far as concerned the chief part of his orders, Antam Gonçalvez called to him Affonso Goterres, another groom of the chamber, who was with him, and all the others that were in the ship, being one and twenty in all, and spoke to them in this wise: "Friends and brethren! We have already got our cargo, as you perceive, by the which the chief part of our ordinance is accomplished, and we may well turn back, if we wish not to toil beyond that which was principally commanded of us; but I would know from all whether it seemeth to you well that we should attempt something further, that he who sent us here may have some example of our good wills; for I think it would be shameful if we went back into his presence just as we are, having done such small service. And in truth I think we ought to labour the more strenuously to achieve something like this as it was the less laid upon us as a charge by the Infant our lord. O How fair a thing it would be if we, who have come to this land for a cargo of such petty merchandise, were to meet with the good luck to bring the first captives before the face of our Prince. And now I will tell you of my thoughts that I may receive your advice thereon. I would fain go myself this next night with nine men of you (those who are most ready for the business), and prove a part of this land along the river, to see if I find any inhabitants; for I think we of right ought to meet with some, since 'tis certain there are people

---

[2] A barinel is a small vessel, characteristic of the type that sailed the Mediterranean (ed.).

here, who traffic with camels and other animals that bear their freights. Now the traffic of these men must chiefly be to the seaboard; and since they have as yet no knowledge of us, their gathering cannot be too large for us to try their strength; and, if God grant us to encounter them, the very least part of our victory will be the capture of one of them, with the which the Infant will feel no small content, getting knowledge by that means of what kind are the other dwellers of this land. And as to our reward, you can estimate what it will be by the great expenses and toil he has undertaken in years past, only for this end." "See what you do," replied the others, "for since you are our captain we needs must obey your orders, not as Antam Gonçalvez but as our lord; for you must understand that we who are here, of the Household of the Infant our lord, have both the will and desire to serve him, even to the laying down of our lives in the event of the last danger. But we think your purpose to be good, if only you will introduce no other novelty to increase the peril, which would be little to the service of our lord." And finally they determined to do his bidding, and follow him as far as they could make their way. And as soon as it was night Antam Gonçalvez chose nine men who seemed to him most fitted for the undertaking, and made his voyage with them as he had before determined. And when they were about a league distant from the sea they came on a path which they kept, thinking some man or woman might come by there whom they could capture; but it happened otherwise; so Antam Gonçalvez asked the others to consent to go forward and follow out his purpose; for, as they had already come so far, it would not do to return to the ship in vain like that. And the others being content they departed thence, and, journeying through that inner land for the space of three leagues, they found the footmarks of men and youths, the number of whom, according to their estimate, would be from forty to

fifty, and these led the opposite way from where our men were going. The heat was very intense, and so by reason of this and of the toil they had undergone in watching by night and travelling thus on foot, and also because of the want of water, of which there was none, Antam Gonçalvez perceived their weariness that it was already very great, as he could easily judge from his own sufferings. So he said, "My friends, there is nothing more to do here; our toil is great, while the profit to arise from following up this path meseemeth small, for these men are travelling to the place whence we have come, and our best course would be to turn back towards them, and perchance, on their return, some will separate themselves, or, may be, we shall come up with them when they are laid down to rest, and then, if we attack them lustily, peradventure they will flee, and, if they flee, someone there will be less swift, whom we can lay hold of according to our intent; or may be our luck will be even better, and we shall find fourteen or fifteen of them, of whom we shall make a more profitable booty." Now this advice was not such as to give rise to any wavering in the will of those men, for each desired that very thing. And, returning towards the sea, when they had gone a short part of the way, they saw a naked man following a camel, with two assegais in his hand, and as our men pursued him there was not one who felt aught of his great fatigue. But though he was only one, and saw the others that they were many; yet he had a mind to prove those arms of his right worthily and began to defend himself as best he could, shewing a bolder front than his strength warranted. But Affonso Goterres wounded him with a javelin, and this put the Moor in such fear that he threw down his arms like a beaten thing. And after they had captured him, to their no small delight, and had gone on further, they espied, on the top of a hill, the company whose tracks they were following; and their captive pertained to the number of these.

And they failed not to reach them through any lack of will, but the sun was now low, and they wearied, so they determined to return to their ship, considering that such enterprise might bring greater injury than profit. And, as they were going on their way, they saw a black Mooress come along (who was slave of those on the hill), and though some of our men were in favour of letting her pass to avoid a fresh skirmish, to which the enemy did not invite them,—for, since they were in sight and their number more than doubled ours, they could not be of such faint hearts as to allow a chattel of theirs to be thus carried off:—despite this, Antam Gonçalvez bade them go at her;

for if (he said) they scorned that encounter, it might make their foes pluck up courage against them. And now you see how the word of a captain prevaileth among men used to obey; for, following his will, they seized the Mooress. And those on the hill had a mind to come to the rescue, but when they perceived our people ready to receive them, they not only retreated to their former position, but departed elsewhere, turning their backs to their enemies. And so let us here leave Antam Gonçalvez to rest, considering this Chapter as finished, and in the following one we will knight him right honourably.

.   .   .

21 ANONYMOUS

THE GUINEA COAST IN THE SIXTEENTH CENTURY

This letter, which was written by an anonymous Portuguese pilot between 1535 and 1550 and sent to His Magnificence Count Rimondo della Torre, Gentleman of Verona, describes the rituals of kingship at Benin in present-day Nigeria and the physiognomy, food, eating habits, and slavery of the inhabitants of Guinea.

.   .   .

As your excellency knows, before I left Venetia, signor Hieronimo Gracastor ordered me, in his letters from Verona, to transcribe for him, as soon as I reached the Villa di Conde, from some notes which I had told your excellency I had with me, the whole of the voyage which we pilots made to the island of S. Thomé, when we went there to transport a cargo of sugar; together with all that happened during our voyage to this island, that seemed to him so wonderful and worthy

From G. B. Ramusio, *Navigationi e viaggi* (1550), I, 125–129, in *Europeans in West Africa, 1450–1560* (London: Longmans, Green and Co., Ltd., 1937), I, 145–153 (Vol. xiv in the Royal Commonwealth Society's Imperial Studies Series), trans. from the Italian and edited by John William Blake. Reprinted by permission.

of the study of a scholar. Your excellency also, on my departure, made the same request to me; and so, having arrived here, I began at once to write an account of the voyage in question, communicating also with some of my friends who took part in it.

Having read my account, and reflected upon it, I realised immediately that these writings of mine were not worthy of being read by such a great and distinguished man of science as signor Hieronimo— whose learning is proved by the books written for him which your excellency gave to me on my departure from Venetia; and I had almost decided to put my writings aside and let no one see them, when your further enquiry in regard to my obligation gave me courage, making me realise that, if I did not comply with your requests, which to me are like commands, I should appear unmindful of the many kindnesses and courtesies I have received from you, which are indeed infinite.

Then I decided rather to be regarded as rude and ignorant than as ungrateful and disobedient; and I am therefore sending you a few notes, which I made on other occasions, about the various people who live in the country north of Ethiopia: trusting that it will be understood that, as I am a sailor and not accustomed to writing, they are described simply and roughly, and that when they have been read, I beseech you to hide them, so that such mistakes as I have made, purely out of obedience to your wishes and not out of presumptuousness, will not cause you to curse me every time you read this.

The ships that set out to bring sugar from the island of San Thomé leave Lisbona, the capital of the kingdom of Portogello (called in ancient time Olissippo) 39 degrees above the equator, usually in the month of February (although some leave at all times of the year). They sail south-south-west as far as the Canarie Islands, called by the ancients the Fortunate Isles, and reach the island called Palme, 28^1/$_2$ degrees above the equator, which is part of the kingdom of Castiglia [Castile], 90 leagues from a promontory in Africa called Capo di Boiador. This island has an abundance of grapes, meat, cheese and sugar; and when they reach it they have covered 250 leagues, or 1000 miles.

This part is most dangerous, since the sea is very rough and is perilous at all times of the year, but particularly in December, and above all when the northeast wind blows, which comes straight across the sea and does not touch land anywhere.

From this island of Palme two routes may be taken. If the ships have been provisioned with salt fish (of which they take good care always to have enough), they go along by the island of Sal, which is one of the islands of Capo Verde, so called from one of the promontories of Africa. This island is 16^1/$_2$ degrees north of the equator, and is always reached towards the southwest. On reaching it, they have covered 225 leagues from the island of Palme. With a good wind this voyage can be accomplished in 6 or 8 days. This island is uninhabited, as it is barren, and the only animals to be found there are wild goats. Since the land is below sealevel, the sea rises in the lagoons and creeks whenever the weather is good; and as the sun, coming from the tropic of cancer, passes perpendicularly above it, the water soon dries and salt is formed. This happens in all the islands of Capo Verde, and also in the Canarie [islands], but more here than elsewhere; and it is for this reason that it is called the island of Sale. Then there is the island of Bona Vista, and not far from this the island of Maio, in which there is a lake more than two leagues long, and wide in proportion, full of salt dried by the sun, enough to fill a thousand ships. This salt is available to all, like the waters of the sea; and subjects of the kingdom of Portogallo pay nothing at all for it. In all the islands of Capo Verde, of which there are 10, the goats have three or four young at a time, every four months. The young kids are delicious to eat, and are fat and tasty. The goats drink sea water.

But if the ships which go to San Thomé have no salt fish, and wish to take provision on board, they make their way towards the African coast, to the river known as the river dell' oro [Rio do Ouro], above which runs the tropic of cancer, south-southeast. When they sight Africa, they have covered 110 leagues. Near this coast, if the weather is calm and the sea not rough, they leave nets in the sea for about four hours, or else drop long flexible lines with many hooks attached, with which they catch all the fish they need; but the lines cannot be let down for long in the water, since immediately fish of all kinds, large and small, swallow the hooks: *pagros,* which in Venetia you call *alberi, corui,* and *oneros,* which is a larger fish than *pagri*, very fat, and dark in colour. When they are caught, they are slit along the backbone and salted, and they make a very substantial food for sailors. On this voyage one sees an enormous number of fish called *tiburoni*, which are very large, like tunny, and have two rows of extremely sharp teeth. Greedy for food, they always follow every ship they see, swallowing everything that is thrown overboard; and for this reason they are easy to catch. But we Portoghesi do not allow them to be caught, although they taste good; as we believe that they are poisonous; although all the Castilian sailors on voyages to the *terra firma* of the West Indies catch and eat them. If the ships do not run into calm weather by way of the river dell' oro, they go along the coast towards Capo Bianco, to seek calm seas, and from there as far as Argin [Arguim]. One thing which it is useful to know is that the whole coast of Africa, starting from Capo del Boiador, that is, Capo della Volta (because those who sail to the islands of Canarie reach this cape of Africa, in 25²/₃ degrees, on their return, and turn back) is all low lying and barren as far as Capo Bianco, the position of which is 20¹/₂ degrees. They continue as far as Argin, where there is a large port, and a castle belonging to our king, with a population ruled over by one of his governors. This Argin is inhabited by Mori [Moors] and negroes, and the frontier dividing Berberia and the negro country is at this point.

But to return to our voyage. From the island of Sal, we went to the island of San Jacobo, or Capoverde. This is 15 degrees north of the equator, and a journey southwards of 30 leagues. This island is about 17 leagues long, and has a city on the coast with a great port, called *la Ribera grande,* because it is between two high mountains, and is reached by a large river of fresh water, whose source is about two leagues away. From the mouth of this river to the city there are vast groves on either bank of oranges, cedars, lemons,

pomegranates, figs of every kind, and for the last few years they have been planting palms which produce coconuts, or Indian nuts. All kinds of herbs grow well here, but their seeds are not good for sowing the following year, so each year they bring new plants cultivated in Spagna [Spain]. This city faces south, and is built of good houses of stone and chalk, in which numerous Portoghesi and Castigliani [Castilians] live; and there are more than 500 families. A corregedor, appointed by our king, lives there, and every year they elect two judges, one of whom supervises the harbour and navigational matters, the other dispensing justice among the people of the said island and the surrounding ones. This island is very mountainous and has many rough places barren of any trees; but the valleys are well cultivated. During the period of the tropic of cancer, that is, in June, it rains almost continuously, and the Portoghesi call it the moon of the rains [*la luna de las aquas*]. At the beginning of August they begin to sow grain, which they call *zaburro,* or, in the West Indies, *mehiz* [maize].[1] It is like chick pea, and grows all over these islands and all along the African coast, and is the chief food of the people. It is harvested in 40 days. They sow plenty of rice, and cotton, which flourishes well, and when gathered the people work this into different kinds of coloured material, which is marketed along the whole coast, that is, the negro country, and bartered among the negro slaves.

To understand the negro traffic, one must know that over all the African coast facing west there are various countries and provinces, such as Guinea, the coast of Melegete, the kingdom of Benin, the kingdom of Manicongo, six degrees from the equator and towards the south pole.

[1] This maize figured prominently in local Guinea trade. Portuguese ships, bound for the islands in the Gulf, São Thomé, O Principe and Annobon, in order to embark cargoes of slaves, were allowed by the royal ordinances to put into the ports of northern Guinea for the purpose of buying quantities of maize to feed the slaves they were to bring home.

There are many tribes and negro kings here, and also communities which are partly mohammedan and partly heathen. These are constantly making war among themselves. The kings are worshipped by their subjects, who believe that they come from heaven, and speak of them always with great reverence, at a distance and on bended knees. Great ceremony surrounds them, and many of these kings never allow themselves to be seen eating, so as not to destroy the belief of their subjects that they can live without food. They worship the sun, and believe that spirits are immortal, and that after death they go to the sun. Among others, there is in the kingdom of Benin an ancient custom, observed to the present day, that when the king dies, the people all assemble in a large field, in the centre of which is a very deep well, wider at the bottom than at the mouth. They cast the body of the dead king into this well, and all his friends and servants gather round, and those who are judged to have been most dear to and favoured by the king (this includes not a few, as all are anxious for the honour) voluntarily go down to keep him company. When they have done so, the people place a great stone over the mouth of the well, and remain by it day and night. On the second day, a few deputies remove the stone, and ask those below what they know, and if any of them have already gone to serve the king; and the reply is, No. On the third day, the same question is asked; and some-one then replies that so-and-so, mentioning a name, has been the first to go, and so-and-so the second. It is considered highly praiseworthy to be the first, and he is spoken of with the greatest admiration by all the people, and considered happy and blessed. After four or five days all these unfortunate people die. When this is apparent to those above, since none reply to their questions, they inform their new king; who causes a great fire to be lit near the well, where numerous animals are roasted. These are given to the people to eat, and he with great

ceremony is declared to be the true king, and takes the oath to govern well.

The negroes of Guinea and Benin are very haphazard in their habits of eating. They have no set times for meals, and eat and drink four or five times a day, drinking water, or a wine which they distil from palms. They have no hair except for a few bristly strands on top of the head, and none grows; and the rest of the bodies are completely hairless. They live for the best part of 100 years, and are always vigorous, except at certain times of the year when they become very weak, as if they had fever. They are then bled, and recover, having a great deal of blood in their system. Some of the negroes in this country are so superstitious that they worship the first object they see on the day of recovery. A kind of plant called melegete, very like the sorgum of Italia, but in flavour like pepper, grows on this coast. A kind of pepper also grows here, which is very strong, double the strength of the pepper of Calicut, and which because it has a small stem attached to it, is called by us Portoghesi *pimienta dal rabo,* that is, pepper with a tail. It is very like cubeb in shape, but has such a strong flavour that an ounce of it has the same effect as half a pound of common pepper; and as it is forbidden, there are heavy penalties for gathering it on this coast.[2] There is, nevertheless, a secret trade in it, and as it is sold in Inghilterra [England] at double the price of common pepper, our king, feeling that it would ruin trade in the larger quantity [of common pepper] which is taken every year from Calicut, decided that none should be allowed to trade in it. They also grow certain bushes with stems as long as beans, with seeds inside, which have no flavour; but the stem, when chewed, has a delicate ginger flavour. The negroes call them *unias,* and use them, together with the said pepper, when they eat fish, of which they are very

[2] King Manuel forbad the trade in Benin pepper in 1506.

fond. The soap made of ashes and palm oil, also forbidden by the said king, is very effective in whitening the hands, and so also is cloth made of flax, which is commonly used as soap.

All the coast, as far as the kingdom of Manicongo, is divided into two parts, which are leased [to European traders —ed.] every four or five years to whoever makes the best offer, that is, to be able to go to contract in those lands and ports, and those in this business are called contractors, though among us they would be known as *appaltadori,* and their deputies, and no others may approach and land on this shore, or even buy or sell. Great caravans of negroes come here, bringing gold and slaves for sale. Some of the slaves have been captured in battle, others are sent by their parents, who think they are doing their children the best service in the world by sending them to be sold in this way to other lands where there is an abundance of provisions. They are brought as naked as they are born, both males and females, except for a sheepskin cloth; and they have glass rosaries of various colours, and articles made of glass, copper, brass, and cotton cloths of different colours, and other similar things used throughout Ethiopia. These contractors take the slaves to the island of San Jacobo, where they are bought by merchant captains from various countries and provinces, chiefly from the Spanish Indies. These give their merchandise in exchange and always wish to have the same number of male and female slaves, because otherwise they do not get good service from them. During the voyage, they separate the men from the women, putting the men below the deck and the women above, where they cannot see when the men are given food; because otherwise the women would do nothing but look at them. Regarding these negroes, our king has had a castle built on the said coast, at Mina, 6 degrees north of the equator, where none but his servants are allowed to live; and large numbers of negroes come to this place with grains of gold, which they have found in the river beds and sand, and bargain with these servants, taking various objects from them in exchange; principally glass necklaces or rosaries, and another kind made of a blue stone, not lapis lazuli, but another stone which our king causes to be brought from Manicongo, where it is found. These rosaries are in the form of necklaces, and are called coral; and a quantity of gold is given in exchange for them, as they are greatly valued by all the negroes. They wear them round their necks as a charm against spirits, but some wear necklaces of glass, which are very similar, but which will not bear the heat of fire.

.   .   .

22 JOHN BARBOT
BENIN

John Barbot was an employee of English and French trading companies who made at least two voyages to West Africa between 1678 and 1682. He wrote the following account in French in 1682 and translated it into English; much of his material was derived from his journal of a voyage that began at La Rochelle, France, on October 22, 1678. At the time Barbot visited the Guinea Coast, the kingdom of Benin was one of the most powerful and effectively organized states of West Africa and was a center of the slave trade.

From John Barbot, *An Abstract of a Voyage to Congo River, or the Zair, and to Cabinde, in the Year 1700,* in Awnsham and John Churchill, *A Collection of Voyages and Travels* (London: Henry Linton and John Osborn, 1746), V, 367–370.

GOVERNMENT

The government of *Benin* is principally vested in the king, and three chief ministers, call'd great *Veadors*; that is, intendants, or overseers: besides the great marshal of the crown, who is intrusted with the affairs relating to war, as the three others are with the administration of justice, and the management of the revenue; and all four are obliged to take their circuits throughout the several provinces, from time to time, to inspect into the condition of the country, and the administration of the governors and justices in each district, that peace and good order may be kept as much as possible. Those chief ministers of state have under them each his own particular officers and assistants in the discharge of their posts and places. They call the first of the three aforemention'd ministers of state, the *Onegwa,* the second *Ossade,* and the third *Arribon.*

They reside constantly at court, as being the king's privy council, to advise him on all emergencies and affairs of the nation; and any person that wants to apply to the prince, must address himself first to them, and they acquaint the king with the petitioner's business, and return his answer accordingly: but commonly, as in other countries, they will only inform the king with what they please themselves; and so in his name, act very arbitrarily over the subjects. Whence it may well be inferr'd, that the government is intirely in their hands; for it is very seldom they will favour a person so far as to admit him to the king's presence, to represent his own affairs to that prince: and every body knowing their great authority, indeavours on all occasions to gain their favour as much as possible, by large gratifications and presents, in order to succeed in their affairs at court, for which reason their offices and posts are of very great profit to them.

Besides these four chief ministers of state, there are two other inferior ranks about the king: the first is composed of those they call *Reis de Ruas,* signifying in *Portuguese,* kings of streets, some of whom preside over the commonalty, and others over the slaves; some again over military affairs; others over affairs relating to cattle and the fruits of the earth, &c. there being supervisors or intendants over every thing that can be thought of, in order to keep all things in a due regular way.

From among those *Reis de Ruas* they commonly chuse the governors of provinces and towns; but every one of them is subordinate to, and dependent on the aforemention'd great *Veadors,* as being generally put into those imployments, by their recommendation to the king, who usually presents each of them, when so promoted to the government of provinces, towns or districts, with a string of coral, as an ensign or badge of this office; being there equivalent to an order of knighthood in *European* courts.

They are obliged to wear that string continually about their necks, without ever daring to put it off on any account whatsoever; and in case they lose it by carelessness, or any other accident, or if stolen from them, they forfeit their heads, and are accordingly executed without remission. And there have been instances of this nature, five men having been put to death for a string of coral so lost, tho' not intrinsically worth two-pence: the officer to whom the chain or string belong'd, because he had suffer'd it to be stolen from him, the thief who own'd he had stolen it, and three more who were privy to it, and did not timely discover it.

This law is so rigidly observ'd, that the officers so intrusted with a string of coral by the king, whensoever they happen to lose it, though it be taken from about their necks by main force, immediately say, *I am a dead man*; and therefore regard no perils though ever so great, if there be hopes of recovering it by force from those who have stolen it. Therefore I advise all sea-faring *Europeans,* trading to those parts, never to meddle with the strings of coral belonging to any such officers, not even in jest; because the *Black* that permits it, is immediately sent for to the king, and by his order close imprisoned, and put to death.

The same punishment is inflicted on any person whatsoever that counterfeits those strings of coral, or has any in his possession, without the king's grant.

That we have here call'd coral, is made of a pale red coctile earth or stone, and very well glazed, much resembling red speckled marble, which the king keeps in his own custody, and no body is allow'd as I have said, to wear it, unless honour'd by the prince with some post of trust in the nation.

The third rank of publick ministers or officers, is that of the *Mercadors,* or merchants; *Fulladors,* or intercessors; the *Veilhos,* or elders, imploy'd by the king in affairs relating to trade: all which are also distinguish'd from the other subjects not in office or post, by the same badge of a coral-string at their neck, given each of them by the king, as a mark of honour.

All the said officers from the highest to the lowest, being men that love money, are easily brib'd: so that a person sentenc'd to death, may purchase his life if he is wealthy in *Boejies,* the money of this country; and only poor people are made examples of justice, as we see is no less practised in *Europe:* yet it being the king's intention, that justice should be distributed without exception of persons, and malefactors rigidly punish'd according to the laws of the realm, the officers take all possible care to conceal from him, that they have been brib'd, for preventing the execution of any person condemn'd.

THE KING'S PREROGATIVE

The king of *Benin* is absolute; his will being a law and a bridle to his subjects, which none of them dare oppose; and, as I have hinted before, the greatest men of the nation, as well as the inferior sort, esteem it an honour to be call'd the king's slave, which title no person dares assume without the king's particular grant; and that he never allows but to those, who, as soon as born, are by their parents presented to him: for which reason, some geographers have thought, that the king of *Benin* was religiously ador'd by all his subjects, as a deity. But that is a mistake, for the qualification of the king's slaves, is but a bare compliment to majesty; since none of the natives of *Benin,* can by the law of the land, be made slaves on any account, as has been observ'd before.

The present king is a young man of an affable behaviour. His mother is still living, to whom he pays very great respect and reverence, and all the people after his example honour her. She lives a-part from her son in her own palace out of the city *Oedo,* where she keeps her court, waited on and serv'd by her proper officers, women and maids. The king her son uses to take her advice on many important affairs of state, by the ministry of his statesmen and counsellors: for the king there is not to see his own mother, without danger of an insurrection of the people against him, according to their constitutions. The palace of that dowager is very large and spacious, built much after the manner, and of the same materials as the king's, and those of other great persons.

The king's houshold is compos'd of a great number of officers of sundry sorts, and slaves of both sexes, whose business is to furnish all the several apartments with all manner of necessaries for life and conveniency, as well as the country affords. The men officers being to take care of all that concerns the king's tables and stables; and the women, for that which regards his wives and concubines: which all together makes the concourse of people so great at court, with the strangers resorting continually to it every day about business, that there is always a vast croud running to and fro from one quarter to another. It appears by ancient history, that it was the custom of the eastern nations, to have only women to serve them within doors, as officers in the king's houses. *David* being forced to fly before *Absalom* his son, and to leave *Jerusalem* his capital, to shelter himself in some of his strong cities beyond *Jordan*, left ten of his concubines for the guard of his palace.

The king being very charitable, as well as his subjects, has peculiar officers about him, whose chief imployment is, on certain days, to carry a great quantity of provisions, ready dress'd, which the king sends into the town for the use of the poor. Those men make a sort of procession, marching two and two with those provisions in great order, preceded by the head officer, with a long white staff in his hand, like the prime court officers in *England*; and every body is obliged to make way for him, tho' of never so great quality.

Besides this good quality of being charitable, the king might be reckoned just and equitable, as desiring continually his officers to administer justice exactly, and to discharge their duties conscienciously: besides that, he is a great lover of *Europeans*, whom he will have to be well treated and honoured, more especially the *Dutch* nation, as I have before observ'd. But his extortions from such of his subjects as are wealthy, on one unjust pretence or other, which has so much impoverish'd many of them, will not allow him to be look'd upon as very just.

He seldom passes one day, without holding a cabinet council with his chief ministers, for dispatching of the many affairs brought before him, with all possible expedition; besides, the appeals from inferior courts of judicature in all the parts of the kingdom, and audiences to strangers, or concerning the affairs of war, or other emergencies of state.

REVENUE

The king's income is very great, his dominions being so large, and having such a number of governors, and other inferior officers, each of whom is obliged, according to his post, to pay into the king's treasury so many bags of *Boejies*, some more some less, which all together amount to a prodigious sum; and other officers of inferior rank are to pay in their taxes in cattle, chicken, fruits, roots and cloths, or any other things that can be useful to the king's houshold; which is so great a quantity, that it doth not cost the king a penny throughout the year to maintain and subsist his family; so that there is yearly a considerable increase of money in his treasury. Add to all this, the duties and tolls on imported or exported goods, paid in all trading places, to the respective *Veadors* and other officers, which are also partly convey'd to the treasury; and were the collectors thereof just and honest, so as not to defraud the prince of a considerable part, these would amount to an incredible sum.

WARS

This prince is perpetually at war with one nation or other that borders on the northern part of his dominions, and sometimes with another north-west of his kingdom, which are all potent people, but little or not at all known to *Europeans*, over whom he obtains from time to time considerable advantages, subduing large portions of those unknown countries, and raising great contributions, which are partly paid him in jasper, and other valuable goods of the product of those countries. Wherewith, together with his own plentiful revenue, he is able, upon occasion, to maintain an army of an hundred thousand horse and foot; but, for the most part, he doth not keep above thirty thousand men, which renders him more formidable to his neighbours than any other *Guinea* king: nor is there any other throughout all *Guinea*, that has so many vassals and tributary kings under him; as for instance, those of *Istanna, Forcado, Jaboe, Issabo* and *Oedoba*, from whom he receives considerable yearly tributes, except from him of *Issabo*, who, though much more potent than all the others, yet pays the least.

ARMY

To speak now something of the soldiery in the king's pay. They generally wear no other clothes but a narrow silk clout about their middle, all the other parts of their body being naked; and are arm'd with pikes, javelins, bows, and poison'd arrows, cutlaces and bucklers or shields; but so slight, and made of small *Bamboos,* that they cannot ward off any thing that is forcible, and so are rather for show than for defence. Some, besides all these weapons, have also a kind of hooked bill, much of the form of those we use in *Europe,* for cutting of small wood whereof bavins and faggots are made, and some others have small poniards.

These soldiers are commonly distributed into companies and bands, each band commanded by its respective officer, with others of lower rank under him: but what is pretty singular there, those officers do not post themselves in the front of their troops, but in the very centre, and generally wear a scymitar hanging at their side, by a leather girdle fasten'd under their arm-pits, instead of a belt, and march with a grave resolute mien, which has something of stateliness.

The king's armies are compos'd of a certain number of those bands, which is greater or smaller, according to circumstances; and they always march like the ancient *Salij,* dancing and skipping into measure and merrily, and yet keep their ranks, being in this particular better disciplin'd than any other *Guinea* nation; however, they are no braver than the *Fida* and *Ardra* men, their neighbours westward, so that nothing but absolute necessity can oblige them to fight: and even then, they had rather suffer the greatest losses than defend themselves. When their flight is prevented, they return upon the enemy, but with so little courage and order, that they soon fling down their arms, either to run the lighter, or to surrender themselves prisoners of war. In short, they have so little conduct, that many of them are asham'd of it; their officers being no braver than the soldiers, every man takes his own course, without any regard to the rest.

The great officers appear very richly habited in the field, every one rather endeavouring to out-do another in that particular, than to surpass him in valour and conduct. Their common garment is a short jacket or frock of scarlet cloth over their fine clothes, and some hang over that an ivory quiver, lin'd with a tyger's skin, or a civet-cat's, and a long wide cap on their heads, like the dragoons caps in *France,* with a horse-tail pretty long hanging at the tip of it. Thus equipp'd, they mount their horses, to whose necks they commonly tie a tinkling bell, which rings as the horse moves. Thus they ride, with an air of fierceness, attended by a slave on foot on each side, and follow'd by many others, one carrying the large *Bamboo* shield, another leading the horse, and others playing on their usual musical instruments; that is, drums, horns, flutes; an iron hollow pipe, on which they beat with a wooden stick; and another instrument, the most esteemed among them, being a sort of large dry bladder, well swell'd with air, cover'd with a net, fill'd with peas and brass bells, and hung or tied at the end of a wooden handle, to hold it by.

When return'd home from a warlike expedition, every man delivers back to the king's stores, the quivers and arrows he has left. That store-house, or aresenal, is divided into many chambers; and immediately the priests are set to work to poison new arrows, that there may be always a sufficient stock for the next occasion.

Having observ'd what little courage there is in this nation, we shall not have much to say of their wars; nor is it easy to account for their becoming so formidable among their neighbours to the north and northwest, but by concluding those nations to be as bad soldiers as themselves, and not so populous; for there are other nations south and east of them who value not their power, amongst whom are the pirates of *Usa,* who give them no little disturbance, as has been hinted before.

THE KING APPEARING ABROAD

The king of *Benin* at a certain time of the year rides out to be seen by his people. That day he rides one of his best horses, which, as has been observ'd, are but ordinary at best, richly equipp'd and habited, follow'd by three or four hundred of his principal ministers and officers of state, some on horseback, and some on foot, arm'd with their shields and javelins, preceded and follow'd by a great number of musicians, playing on all sorts of their instruments, sounding at the same time something rude and pleasant. At the head of this royal procession, are led some tame leopards or tygers in chains, attended by some dwarfs and mutes.

This procession commonly ends with the death of ten or twelve slaves, sacrificed in honour of the king, and paid by the people, who very grosly imagine those wretched victims will in a little time after, return to life again, in remote fertile countries, and there live happily.

There is another royal feast, at a fixed time of the year, call'd the coral-feast, during which the king causes his treasure to be exposed to publick view in the palace, to shew his grandeur.

On that day the king appears in publick again, magnificently dress'd, in the second court or plain of his palace, where he sits under a very fine canopy, incompass'd by all his wives, and a vast croud of his principal ministers and officers of state, all in their richest apparel, who range themselves about him, and soon after begin a procession; at which time the king rising from his place, goes to offer sacrifice to his idols in the open air, and there begins the feast, which is attended with the universal loud acclamations of his subjects. Having spent about a quarter of an hour in that ceremony, he returns to his former place under the canopy, where he stays two hours, to give the people time to perform their devotions to their idols; which done, he goes home in the same manner he came thither, and the remaining part of that day is spent in splendid treating and feasting; the king causing all sorts of provisions and pardon-wine to be distributed among the people; which is also done by every great lord, in imitation of the prince. So that nothing is seen throughout the whole city, but all possible marks of rejoicings and mirth.

The king on that day also uses to distribute men and women slaves among such persons as have done the nation some service, and to confer greater offices on them; but for his jasper-stone and corals, which, with the *Boejies,* make the greatest part of his treasure, he keeps them to himself.

.   .   .

23 WILLIAM BOSMAN
JUSTICE AND WARFARE AT AXIM

William Bosman was the chief factor for the Dutch West India Company at Elmina Castle on the coast of the present Republic of Ghana. His A New and Accurate Description of the Coast of Guinea *consists of twenty letters written about 1700. Bosman may have borrowed some material from the Amsterdam geographer Olfert Dapper, whose* Description of Africa *had been published nearly twenty years earlier. Axim was one of the important trading towns on the Gold Coast.*

From William Bosman, *A New and Accurate Description of the Coast of Guinea,* in John Pinkerton, *A General Collection of the Best and Most Interesting Voyages and Travels in All Parts of the World, Many of Which Are Now First Translated into English* (London: Longman, Hurst, Rees, Orme, and Brown, 1808–1814), XVI, 404–405, 411–415.

· · ·

The government of the Negroes is very licentious and irregular, which only proceeds from the small authority of their chief men or Caboceros, and frequent wars are occasioned by their remiss government and absurd customs.

The difference betwixt the administration of the government of monarchies and commonwealths is here very great. Of the former, the power and jurisdiction being vested in a single person, I shall not say much at present; but shall only speak of the republics; amongst which that of Axim and Ante seeming the most like regular, I shall represent them as instances of the rest; though indeed the best of their governments and methods of administration of justice are so confused and perplexed, that they are hardly to be comprehended, much less, then, are they to be expressed with any manner of connexion on paper.

The government of Axim consists of two parts, the first whereof is the body of Caboceros, or chief men; the other the Manceros or young men. All civil or public affairs which commonly occur are under their administration; but what concerns the whole land, and are properly national affairs, as making of peace and war, the raising tributary impositions to be paid to foreign nations (which seldom happens), that falls under the cognisance of both parts or members of the government: and on these occasions the Manceros often manage with a superior hand, especially if the Caboceros are not very rich in gold and slaves, and consequently able by their assistance to bring over the other to their side.

Their distribution of justice is in the following manner:—If one of the Negroes hath any pretension upon another, he doth not go empty-handed, but loaded with presents of gold and brandy (the latter of which is here of a magnetic virtue), and applies himself to the Caboceros; after the delivery of which he states his case to them, desiring they will dispatch his cause with the first opportunity, and oblige his adversary to an ample satisfaction. If they are resolved to favour him highly, a full council is called immediately, or at farthest within two or three days, according as it is most convenient; and after having maturely consulted, judgment is given in his favour, and that frequently as directly opposite to justice as to any other reason than the received bribe.

But on the contrary, instead of favouring, are they incensed against the plaintiff, or have they received a larger bribe from his adversary, the justest cause in the world cannot protect him from judgment against him; or if right appear too plainly on his side, to avoid an ensuing scandal, they will delay and keep off a trial, obliging the injured person, after tedious and vain solicitations, to wait in hopes of finding juster judges hereafter, which perhaps does not happen in the course of his life, and so of consequence the suit devolves upon his heirs as an inheritance; who, whenever an opportunity offers, though thirty years after, know very well how to make use of it; as I myself have several times had such causes come before me, that one would be apt to think it were impossible they should remember so long, considering they want the assistance of reading and writing.

It sometimes falls out that the plaintiff, or perhaps the defendant, finding the cause given against him contrary to reason, is too impatient to wait to have justice done him, but makes use of the first favourable one of seizing such a quantity of gold or goods as is likely to repair his damage, not only from his adversary or debtor, but the first which falls in his way, if at least he does but live in the same city or village; and what he possessed himself of, he will not re-deliver till he receive plenary satisfaction, and is at peace with his adversary, or is obliged to it by force. If he be strong enough to defend himself and his capture, he is sure to keep it, and thereby engage a third person in the suit on account of the seizure of his effects for security, who hath his remedy on the person on whose account he hath suffered this damage; so that hence proceed frequent murders, and sometimes wars are thereby occasioned, but of this more hereafter.

.   .   .

The consultations with the Caboceros in conjunction with the Manceros principally relating to war, we shall at present touch upon.

When they are desirous of entering into a war, on account of ambition, plunder, or to assist other countries already engaged in a war, these two councils consult together: but otherwise the greatest part of their wars are chiefly occasioned by the recovery of debts, and the disputes of some of the chief people among them. I have formerly hinted something on this subject, with promise to proceed farther on it.

The firmest peace of neighbouring nations is frequently broken in the following manner:—One of the leading men in one country hath money owing him from a person in an adjacent country, which is not so speedily paid as he desires; on which he causes as many goods, freemen, or slaves to be seized by violence and rapine in the country where his debtor lives, as will richly pay him: the men so seized he claps in irons, and if not redeemed sells them, in order to raise money for the payment of the debt: if the debtor be an honest man and the debt just, he immediately endeavours by the satisfaction of his creditors to free his country-men: or if their relations are powerful enough they will force him to it: but when the debt is disputable, or the debtor unwilling to pay it, he is sure to represent the creditor amongst his own countrymen as an unjust man, who hath treated him in this manner contrary to all right, and that he is not at all indebted to him: if he so far prevails on his countrymen that they believe him, he endeavours to make

some of the other land prisoners by way of reprizal; after which they consequently arm on each side, and watch all opportunities of surprizing each other. They first endeavour to bring the Caboceros over to their party, because they have always some men at their devoir; next the soldiers: and thus from a trifle a war is occasioned betwixt two countries, who before lived in amity, and continues till one of them be subdued; or, if their force be equal, till the principal men are obliged to make peace at the request of the soldiers; which frequently happens, especially about sowing time, when all the warriors desire to return to till the ground; for in serving in the war without pay, and defraying all expences out of their private fortunes, they quickly grow tired; especially if they get no advantage of, and consequently no plunder by the enemy.

When the governors of one country are inclined to make war with those of another, perhaps on account that they make a better figure in their manner of living, or that they are richer; so that these have a mind to some of their effects: then they assemble together, in conjunction with the Manceros, who also give their advice, and being young, and puft up with hopes of plunder, are easily induced by the persuasions of the Caboceros; and the joint resolution is no sooner formed than every one prepares for war; and being got ready, make an irruption into the designed country, without giving the least notice or declaring war, urging much the same reasons with a present European potentate, "It is My royal will and pleasure, and for My glory." And thus they kill and pillage each other. The injured nation, to revenge this perfidious breach of peace, if not powerful enough of itself, hires another to assist it for less than 2,000l. sterling; for which price the best are here to be had, well armed and appointed for an engagement: so that, indeed, war is not here very dear, though at this cheap rate you cannot imagine the armies so formidable that are hired for such trivial wages: but plunder is their chief aim, instead of which they often get good store of blows, which prove all the perquisites to their mentioned wages. These wages they divide amongst the Caboceros and the Manceros; but the former manage the affair so cunningly, that the latter have not above four or five shillings each, or perhaps half that sum; for the leading men are sure to adjust the account so well in favour of themselves, that a mighty residue is not likely to be left to make a future dividend. But as for the plunder, though particularly appropriated to defray the expence of the war in the first place, and the remainder to be divided, yet every man seizes the first part thereof he can lay hold on, without any regard to the public: but if no booty is to be come at, the Manceros, like cats that have wet their feet, make the best of their way home, not being obliged to stay longer than they themselves please. Each is under a particular chieftain in a sort, though he can command only his slaves; a free Negro not owning his authority, or submitting even to their kings, unless compelled by their exorbitant power, without which they live entirely at their own pleasure: but if their leader is disposed to march up first towards the enemy, he may, but will not, be followed by many.

War, as I have twice before told you, is not so expensive as in Europe; our four years war with the Commanyschians (except the damage done to our trade) did not cost us in all six thousand pounds sterling: for which sum we had successively five nations in our pay. But I have formerly treated this subject so largely, that I need not say any more of it at present.

A national offensive war may very well be managed here with four thousand men in the field; but a defensive requires more. Sometimes the number of what they call an army does not amount to more than two thousand. From whence you may infer of what force the monarchies and

republics on the coast are, Fantyn [Fanti —ed.] and Aquamboe [Akwamu—ed.] only excepted; the first of which is able to bring an army of twenty-five thousand men, and the latter a much larger. But the inland potentates, such as Akim, Asiante, &c. are not to be reckoned amongst these, they being able to overrun a country by their numerous armies; though I cannot inform you any otherwise concerning those people, than what by hints we learn from the Negroes, who are not always to be believed. But as for the monarchies situate near us, I dare affirm, that though each of the two contending armies were composed of five or six several nations, they would not together make twenty-five thousand men; upon which account, joined to their cowardice, very few men are killed in a battle; and that engagement is very warm which leaves one thousand men upon the place; for they are so timorous, that as soon as they see a man fall by them, they run for it, and only think of getting safe home. In the last battle between the Commanyschians and those of Saboe, Acanni, Cabes Terra, and two or three other countries, I do not believe that one hundred men were killed, and yet the Commanyschians drove their enemies out of the field, and obtained a complete victory.

They are very irregular in their engagements, not observing the least shadow of order; but each commander hath his men close together in a sort of crowd, in the midst of which he is generally to be found; so that they attack the enemy man for man, or one heap of men against another; and some of their commanders seeing their brother-officer furiously attacked, and somewhat put to it, choose rather to run with the hare than hold with the hounds, and that frequently before they had struck one stroke, or stood so much as one brush; and their friends whom they left engaged certainly follow them, if in the least pressed, unless so entangled with the enemy that it is not for want of good will if they do not; but if no opportunity offers, though against their will, they get the reputation of good soldiers.

In fight, the Negroes do not stand upright against one another, but run stooping and listening, that the bullets may fly over their heads. Others creep towards the enemy, and, being come close, let fly at them; after which they run away as fast as they can, and, as if the devil were sure of the hindmost, get to their own army as soon as possible, in order to load their arms and fall on again. In short, their ridiculous gestures, stooping, creeping, and crying, make their fight more like monkeys playing together than a battle.

The booty which the commonalty chiefly aim at are the prisoners and ornaments of gold, and Conte de Terra; for some, especially the in-land Negroes, are so simple as to dress themselves in the richest manner possible on these occasions; wherefore they are frequently so loaded with gold and Conte de Terra, that they can scarcely march.

Common prisoners who cannot raise their ransom, are kept or sold for slaves at pleasure: if they take any considerable person, he is very well guarded, and a very high ransom put upon him; but if the person who occasioned the beginning of the war be taken, they will not easily admit him to ransom, though his weight in gold were offered, for fear he should in future form some new design against their repose.

The most potent Negro cannot pretend to be injured from slavery, for if he ever ventures himself in the wars, it may easily become his lot; he is consequently obliged to remain in that state till the sum demanded for his redemption is fully paid, which withal is frequently set so high, that he, his friends, and all his interest, are not sufficient to raise it; on which account, he is forced to a perpetual slavery, and the most contemptible offices. Some amongst them are so barbarous, that finding their hopes of a high ransom frustrated, they pay themselves by cruelly murdering the wretched prisoner.

Wars betwixt two despotical Kings, who have their subjects entirely at their command, are of a long duration, and frequently last several years successively, or till the utter ruin of one of them ends the dispute. They frequently lie a whole year encamped against each other without attempting any thing, a few diverting skirmishes excepted: only against rainy weather they each return home without molesting one another.

Though this is chiefly owing to their priests, without whose suffrage they are not easily induced to attempt a battle; they advise them against it, under pretence that their gods have not yet declared in favour of them; and if they will attempt it notwithstanding, they threaten an ill issue: but if these crafty villains observe that their army is much stronger than the enemies, and the soldiers well inclined to fighting, they always advise to attempt it; though with such a cautious reserve, that if it succeeds contrary to expectation, they never want an excuse to bring themselves off: the commanders or soldiers have done this or that thing, which they ought not to have done; for which reason the whole army is punished. In short, let the event prove how it will, the priest is infallibly innocent, and his character always maintains its own reputation.

I doubt not but I have sufficiently enlarged on their ridiculous wars, if I have not dwelt longer on them then they deserve; wherefore I shall relate the events which happened in my time, and apply myself to the description of their military arms.

The chief of these are musquets or carabins, in the management of which they are wonderfully dextrous. It is not unpleasant to see them exercise their army; they handle their arms so cleverly, discharging them several ways, one sitting, the second creeping, or lying, &c. that it is really to be admired they never hurt one another. Perhaps you wonder how the Negroes come to be furnished with fire-arms, but you will have no reason when you know we sell them incredible quantities, thereby obliging them with a knife to cut our own throats. But we are forced to it; for if we would not, they might be sufficiently stored with that commodity by the English, Danes, and Brandenburghers; and could we all agree together not to sell them any, the English and Zealand interlopers would abundantly furnish them: and since that and gun-powder for some time have been the chief vendible merchandise here, we should have found but an indifferent trade without our share in it. It were, indeed, to be wished that these dangerous commodities had never been brought hither, or at least, that the Negroes might be in a short time brought to be content with somewhat else in their room: but this in all appearance is never likely.

Next their guns, in the second place are their swords, shaped like a sort of chopping-knives, being about two or three hands broad at the extremity, and about one at the handle, and about three or four spans long at most; and a little crooked at the top. These sabres are very strong, but commonly so blunt that several strokes are necessary to cut off a-head: they have a wooden guard, adorned on one side, and sometimes on both, with small globular knobs, covered with a sort of skin, whilst others content themselves with bits of rope singed black with the blood of sheep or other cattle, with the additional ornament of a bunch of horse-hair, amongst people of condition thin gold plates are usual: to this weapon belongs a leather-sheath almost open on one side; to which, by way of ornament, a tiger's head, or a large red shell is hung; both which are valuable here. These sabres they wear when they go out at their left hip, hanging in a belt, which is girt about their waists for that end, or stuck in their Paan, which is round about their bodies, and comes betwixt their legs, that they may run the swifter; besides which, they are begirt with a bandalier belt, with about twenty bandaliers. They have a cap

on their heads made of a crocodile's skin, adorned on each side with a red shell, and behind with a bunch of horse-hair, and a heavy iron-chain, or something else instead of it, girt round their head. Thus appointed, with their bodies coloured white, our heroes look liker devils than men.

Their other weapons are first a bow and arrow; but these are not much in vogue amongst the Coast Negroes, those of Aquamboe alone excepted, who are so nicely dextrous in shooting, that in hare-hunting they will lodge their small fine arrows in what part of the hare's body is desired. These arrows have feathers at their head, and are pointed with iron. The Negroes of Awinee usually poison them; but on the Coast that pernicious custom is not practised, nor do they so much as know what poison is.

Next follow the Assagay or Hassagay [assegai, or slender hardwood spear tipped with iron—ed.], as some call them, which are of two sorts; the smaller sorts are about a Flemish ell [about 27 inches —ed.], or perhaps half an ell longer, and very slender, and these they cast as darts; the second, or larger sort, are about twice as long and large as the former, the upper part pointed with iron like a pike; some of them are covered for the length of one span or two, though in all manner of shapes. The Assagay serves them instead of a sabre, that having their shield in the left hand, they may the more conveniently dart the Assagay with the right, for they have always somebody or other to carry them after them.

Last of all are their shields, which serve only as a defensive covering of the body, and not to the offending any person. I have seen Negroes wonderously dextrous in the management of these shields, which they hold in their left hand, and a sabre in the right; and playing with both, they put their body into very strange postures, and so artificially cover themselves with the shield, that it is impossible to come at them. These shields, which are about four or five foot long, and three broad, are made of osiers; some of which are covered with gold leather, tigers' skins, or some other materials; some of them also have at each corner and in the middle broad thin copper-plates fastened on, to ward off the arrows and the light Assagayes, as well as the blows of the sabre, if they are good, though they are not proof against a musquet-ball.

I think these are all the weapons used amongst the Negroes, without I should tell you that some of them also are possessed of a few cannon; it is indeed true, but they use them in a very slovenly manner. The King of Saboe hath a very small number, with which he has been in the field, but he never made use of them. Some of them, after once firing them, have suffered the enemy to take them, as it happened to the Commanyschians; after which, those who took them were ignorant of the use of them; so that these monarchs' cannon only serves to shoot by way of compliment and salutation, of which the Blacks are very fond.

Promises create a debt; and at the beginning of this letter you have my word that it should conclude with the grandeur of their Kings; in pursuance of which, let us see wherein it consists.

The extent of their territories is so small, that some of them have not more land under their jurisdiction than a single captain or bailiff of a village, and bear the same name accordingly amongst the Negroes: for before the arrival of the Europeans in this country, no higher title was known amongst them than that of captain or colonel, with this only differ-ence, that the one was appropriated to a country, but the other to a village. But since their conversation with us, they, or rather we, make a distinction betwixt a king and a captain. The first word by which it was expressed, was Obin or Abin, which signifies captain in our language, but they always understood by it a commander of a country, town, or nation, for our masters of ships generally assume the same title; and by the same appellation would also be applied, without any distinction, to our director-general and chief of forts, if we did not better inform the natives of the difference. Kings are obliged in this country to preserve their power by dint of force; wherefore the richer they are in gold and slaves, the more they are honoured and esteemed; and without those, they have not the least command over their subjects; but on the contrary, would not only be obliged to pray, but pay their underlings to execute their commands. But if the goddess Fortune has endowed them with a rich share of treasure, they are naturally cruel enough to govern their people tyrannically, and punish them so severely in their purses for trivial crimes, that they cannot forget it all the remainder of their lives; and this is done with a seeming colour of justice; for the King, having any thing to charge on another, delivers the matter into the hands of the Caboceros, and submits it to their decision; who, knowing his mind, are sure to aggravate the crime as much as possible, and take care that their judgment be consonant to his royal will and pleasure.

. . .

24 WILLIAM SNELGRAVE
THE SLAVES MUTINY

William Snelgrave was an English slave trader on the Guinea Coast early in the eighteenth century. His account of the conduct of the slave trade describes events that occurred between 1720 and 1730. During this period the slave trade prospered, and slave mutinies on the ships became more common as the trade became dominated by independent traders who were probably more careless in their supervision of the slaves and who carried fewer crew members in relation to the size of their cargoes than did trading company vessels. The mutiny described by Snelgrave took place in 1727 when the author was trading at Ouidah, the principal trading center on what was then called the Slave Coast and is now Dahomey.

· · ·

The first Mutiny I saw among the Negroes, happened during my first Voyage, in the Year 1704. It was on board the *Eagle* Galley of London, commanded by my Father, with whom I was as Purser. We had bought our Negroes in the River of Old Callabar in the Bay of Guinea. At the time of their mutinying we were in that River, having four hundred of them on board, and not above ten white Men who were able to do Service: For several of our Ship's Company were dead, and many more sick; besides, two of our Boats were just then gone with twelve People on Shore to fetch Wood, which lay in sight of the Ship. All these Circumstances put the Negroes on consulting how to mutiny, which they did at four a clock in the Afternoon, just as they went to Supper. But as we had always carefully examined the Mens Irons, both Morning and Evening, none had got them off, which in a great measure contributed to our Preservation. Three white Men stood on the Watch with Cutlaces in their Hands. One of them who was on the Forecastle, a stout fellow, seeing some of the Men Negroes take hold of the chief Mate, in order to throw him over board, he laid on them so

From William Snelgrave, *A New Account of Some Parts of Guinea and the Slave Trade,* in Elizabeth Donnan, *Documents Illustrative of the History of the Slave Trade to America* (Washington, D. C.: Carnegie Institution, 1930), II, 353–361. Reprinted by permission.

heartily with the flat side of his Cutlace, that they soon quitted the Mate, who escaped from them, and run on the Quarter Deck to get Arms. I was then sick with an Ague [malaria—ed.], and lying on a Couch in the great Cabbin, the Fit being just come on. However, I no sooner heard the Outcry, That the Slaves were mutinying, but I took two Pistols, and run on the Deck with them; where meeting with my Father and the chief Mate, I delivered a Pistol to each of them. Whereupon they went forward on the Booms, calling to the Negroe Men that were on the Forecastle; but they did not regard their Threats, being busy with the Centry, (who had disengaged the chief Mate,) and they would have certainly killed him with his own Cutlace, could they have got it from him; but they could not break the Line wherewith the Handle was fastened to his Wrist. And so, tho' they had seized him, yet they could not make use of his Cutlace. Being thus disappointed, they endeavoured to throw him overboard, but he held so fast by one of them that they could not do it. My Father seeing this stout Man in so much Danger, ventured amongst the Negroes to save him; and fired his Pistol over their Heads, thinking to frighten them. But a lusty Slave struck him with a Billet [a round wooden bar—ed.] so hard, that he was almost stunned. The Slave was going to repeat his Blow, when a young Lad about seventeen years old, whom we had been kind to, interposed his Arm, and received the Blow, by which his Arm-bone was fractured. At the same instant the Mate fired his Pistol, and shot the Negroe that had struck my Father. At the sight of this the Mutiny ceased, and all the Men-Negroes on the Forecastle threw themselves flat on their Faces, crying out for Mercy.

Upon examining into the matter, we found, there were not above twenty Men Slaves concerned in this Mutiny; and the two Ringleaders were missing, having, it seems, jumped overboard as soon as they found their Project defeated, and were drowned. This was all the Loss we suffered on this occasion: For the Negroe that was shot by the Mate, the Surgeon, beyond all Expectation, cured. And I had the good Fortune to lose my Ague, by the fright and hurry I was put into. Moreover, the young Man, who had received the Blow on his Arm to save my Father, was cured by the Surgeon in our Passage to Virginia. At our Arrival in that place we gave him his Freedom; and a worthy Gentleman, one Colonel Carter, took him into his Service, till he became well enough acquainted in the Country to provide for himself.

I have been several Voyages, when there has been no Attempt made by our Negroes to mutiny; which, I believe, was owing chiefly, to their being kindly used, and to my Officers Care in keeping a good Watch. But sometimes we meet with stout stubborn People amongst them, who are never to be made easy; and these are generally some of the Cormantines, a Nation of the Gold Coast. I went in the year 1721, in the *Henry* of London, a Voyage to that part of the Coast, and bought a good many of these People. We were obliged to secure them very well in Irons, and watch them narrowly: Yet they nevertheless mutinied, tho' they had little prospect of succeeding. I lay at that time near a place called Mumfort on the Gold-Coast, having near five hundred Negroes on board, three hundred of which were Men. Our Ship's Company consisted of fifty white People, all in health: And I had very good Officers; so that I was very easy in all respects. . . .

After we had secured these People, I called the Linguists, and ordered them to bid the Men-Negroes between Decks be quiet; (for there was a great noise amongst them.) On their being silent, I asked, "-What had induced them to mutiny?" They answered, "I was a great Rogue to buy them, in order to carry them away from their own Country, and that they were resolved to regain their Liberty if possible." I replied, "That they had forfeited their Freedom before I bought them, either by Crimes or by being taken in War, according to the Custom of their Country; and they being now my Property, I was resolved to let them feel my Resentment, if they abused my Kindness: Asking at the same time, Whether they had been ill used by the white Men, or had wanted for any thing the Ship afforded?" To this they replied, "They had nothing to complain of." Then I observed to them, "That if they should gain their Point and escape to the Shore, it would be no Advantage to them, because their Countrymen would catch them, and sell them to other Ships." This served my purpose, and they seemed to be convinced of their Fault, begging, "I would forgive them, and promising for the future to be obedient, and never mutiny again, if I would not punish them this time." This I readily granted, and so they went to sleep. When Daylight came we called the Men Negroes up on Deck, and examining their Irons, found them all secure. So this Affair happily ended, which I was very glad of; for these People are the stoutest and most sensible Negroes on the Coast: Neither are they so weak as to imagine as others do, that we buy them to eat them; being satisfied we carry them to work in our Plantations, as they do in their own Country.[1]

[1] Africans commonly believed that white people were cannibals (ed.).

However, a few days after this, we discovered they were plotting again, and preparing to mutiny. For some of the Ringleaders proposed to one of our Linguists, If he could procure them an Ax, they would cut the Cables the Ship rid by in the night; and so on her driving (as they imagined) ashore, they should get out of our hands, and then would become his Servants as long as they lived.

For the better understanding of this I must observe here, that these Linguists are Natives and Freemen of the Country, whom we hire on account of their speaking good English, during the time we remain trading on the Coast; and they are likewise Brokers between us and the black Merchants.

This Linguist was so honest as to acquaint me with what had been proposed to him; and advised me to keep a strict Watch over the Slaves; For tho' he had represented to them the same as I had done on their mutinying before, That they would all be catch'd again, and sold to other Ships, in case they could carry their Point, and get on Shore, yet it had no effect upon them.

This gave me a good deal of Uneasiness. For I knew several Voyages had proved unsuccessful by Mutinies; as they occasioned either the total loss of the Ships and the white Mens Lives; or at least by rendring it absolutely necessary to kill or wound a great number of the Slaves, in order to prevent a total Destruction. Moreover, I knew many of these Cormantine Negroes despised Punishment, and even Death it self: It having often happened at Barbadoes [West Indies—ed.] and other Islands, that on their being any ways hardly dealt with, to break them of their Stubbornness in refusing to work, twenty or more have hang'd themselves at a time in a Plantation. However, about a Month after this, a sad Accident happened, that brought our Slaves to be more orderly, and put them in a better Temper: And it was this. On our going from Mumfort to Annamaboe, which is the principal port on the Gold Coast, I met there with another of my Owner's Ships, called the *Elizabeth*. One Captain Thompson that commanded her was dead; as also his chief Mate: Moreover the Ship had afterwards been taken to Cape Lahoe on the Windward Coast, by Roberts the Pirate, with whom several of the Sailors belonging to her had entered. However, some of the Pirates had hindered the Cargoe's being plundered, and obtained that the Ship should be restored to the second Mate: Telling him, "They did it out of respect to the generous Character his Owner bore, in doing good to poor Sailors."

When I met with this Vessel I had almost disposed of my Ship's Cargoe; and the *Elizabeth* being under my Direction, I acquainted the second Mate, who then commanded her, That I thought it for our Owner's Interest, to take the Slaves from on board him, being about 120, into my Ship; and then go off the Coast; and that I would deliver him at the same time the Remains of my Cargoe, for him to dispose of with his own after I was sailed. This he readily complied with, but told me, "He feared his Ship's Company would mutiny, and oppose my taking the Slaves from him:" And indeed, they came at that instant in a Body on the Quarter-deck; where one spoke for the rest, telling me plainly, "they would not allow the Slaves to be taken out by me." I found by this they had lost all respect for their present Commander, who indeed was a weak Man. However, I calmly asked the reason, "Why they offered to oppose my taking the Slaves?" To which they answered, "I had no business with them." On this I desired the Captain to send to his Scrutore, for the Book of Instructions Captain Thompson had received from our Owner; and he read to them, at my request, that Part, in which their former Captain, or his Successor (in case of Death) was to follow my Orders. Hereupon they all cried out, "they should remain a great while longer on the Coast to purchase more Slaves, if I took these from them, which they were resolved to oppose." I answered, "That such of the Ship's Company as desired it, I would receive on board my own; where they should have the same Wages they had at present on board the *Elizabeth,* and I would send some of my own People to supply their Places." This so reasonable an Offer was refused, one of the Men who was the Ship's Cooper telling me, that the Slaves had been on board a long time, and they had great Friendship with them: therefore they would keep them. I asked him, "Whether he had ever been on the Coast of Guinea before?" He replied no. Then I told him, "I supposed he had not by his way of talking, and advised him not to rely on the Friendship of the Slaves, which he might have reason to repent of when too late." And 'tis remarkable this very person was killed by them the next Night, as shall be presently related.

So finding that reasoning with these Men was to no Purpose, I told them, "When I came with my Boats to fetch the Slaves, they should find me as resolute to chastise such of them as should dare to oppose me, as I had been condescending to convince them by arguing calmly." So I took my leave of their Captain, telling him, "I would come the next Morning to finish the Affair."

But that very Night, which was near a month after the Mutiny on board of us at Mumfort, the Moon shining now very bright, as it did then, we heard, about ten a Clock, two or three Musquets fired on board the *Elizabeth.* Upon that I ordered all our Boats to be manned, and having secured every thing in our Ship, to prevent our Slaves from mutinying, I went my self in our Pinnace, (the other Boats following me) on board the *Elizabeth.* In our way we saw two Negroes swimming from her, but before we could reach them with our Boats, some Sharks rose from the bottom, and tore them in Pieces. We came presently along the side of the Ship, where we found two Men-Negroes holding by a Rope, with their heads just above water; they were afraid, it seems, to swim from the Ship's side, having seen their Companions devoured just before by the Sharks. These two Slaves we took into our Boat, and then went into the Ship, where we found the Negroes very quiet, and all under Deck; but the Ship's Company was on the Quarter-deck, in a great Confusion, saying, "The Cooper, who had been placed centry at the Fore-hatch way, over the Men-Negroes, was, they believed, kill'd by them." I was surprized to hear this, wondring that these cowardly fellows, who had so vigorously opposed my taking the Slaves out, a few hours before, had not Courage enough to venture forward, to save their Ship-mate; but had secured themselves by shutting the Quarter-deck door, where they all stood with Arms in their Hands. So I went to the fore-part of the Ship with some of my People, and there we found the Cooper lying on his back quite dead, his Scull being cleft asunder with a Hatchet that lay by him. At the sight of this I called for the Linguist, and bid him ask the Negroes between Decks, "Who had killed the white Man?" They answered, "They knew nothing of the matter; for there had been no design of mutinying among them:" Which upon Examination we found true; for above one hundred of the Negroes then on board, being bought to the Windward, did not understand a word of the Gold-Coast Language, and so had not been in the Plot. But this Mutiny was contrived by a few Cormantee-Negroes, who had been purchased about two or three days before. At last, one of the two Men-Negroes we had taken up along the Ship side, impeached his Companion, and he readily confessed he had kill'd the Cooper, with no other View, but that he and his Countrymen might escape undiscovered by swimming on Shore. For on their coming upon Deck, they observed, that all the white Men set to watch were asleep; and having found the Cook's Hatchet by the Fire-place, he took it up, not designing then to do any Mischief with it; but passing by the Cooper, who was centry, and he beginning to awake, the Negroe rashly struck him on the head with it, and then jump'd overboard. Upon this frank Confession, the white Men would have cut him to Pieces; but I prevented it, and carried him to my own Ship. Early the next morning, I went on board the *Elizabeth* with my Boats, and sent away all the Negroes then in her, into my own Ship: not one of the other Ship's Company offering to oppose it. Two of them, the Carpenter and Steward, desired to go with me, which I readily granted; and by way of Security for the future success of the Voyage, I put my chief Mate, and four of my under Officers (with their own Consent,) on board the *Elizabeth;* and they arrived, about five Months after this, at Jamaica, having disposed of most part of the Cargoe.

After having sent the Slaves out of the *Elizabeth,* as I have just now mentioned, I went on board my own Ship; and there being then in the Road of Anamaboe, eight sail of Ships besides us, I sent an Officer in my Boat to the Commanders of them, "To desire their Company on board my Ship, because I had an Affair of great Consequence to communicate to them." Soon after, most of them were pleased to come; and I having acquainted them with the whole Matter, and they having also heard the Negroe's Confession, "That he had killed the white Man;" They unanimously advised me to put him to death; arguing, "That Blood required Blood, by all Laws both divine and human; especially as there was in this Case the clearest Proof, namely the Murderer's Confession: Moreover this would in all probability prevent future Mischiefs; for by publickly executing this Person at the Ship's Foreyard Arm, the Negroes on board their Ships would see it; and as they were very much disposed to mutiny, it might prevent them from attempting it." These Reasons, with my being in the same Circumstances, made me comply.

Accordingly we acquainted the Negroe, that he was to die in an hour's time for murdering the white Man. He answered, "He must confess it was a rash Action in him to kill him; but he desired me to consider, that if I put him to death, I should lose all the Money I had paid for him." To this I bid the Interpreter reply, "That tho' I knew it was customary in his Country to commute for Murder by a Sum of Money, yet it was not so with us; and he should find that I had no regard to my Profit in this respect: For as soon as an Hour-Glass, just then turned, was run out, he should be put to death;" At which I observed he shewed no Concern.

Hereupon the other Commanders went on board their respective Ships, in order to have all their Negroes upon Deck at the time of Execution, and to inform them of the occasion of it. The Hour-Glass being run out, the Murderer was carried on the Ship's Forecastle, where he had a Rope fastened under his Arms, in order to be hoisted up to the Fore-yard Arm, to be shot to death. This some of his Countrymen observing, told him, (as the Linguist informed me afterwards) "That they would not have him to be frightened; for it was plain I did not design to put him to death, otherwise the Rope would have been put about his neck, to hang him." For it seems they had no thought of his being shot; judging he was only to be hoisted up to the Yard-arm, in order to scare him: But they immediately saw the contrary; for as soon as he was hoisted up, ten white Men who were placed behind the Barricado on the Quarter-deck fired their Musquets, and instantly killed him. This struck a sudden Damp upon our Negroe-Men, who thought, that, on account of my Profit, I would not have executed him.

The Body being cut down upon the Deck, the Head was cut off, and thrown overboard. This last part was done, to let our Negroes see, that all who offended thus, should be served in the same manner. For many of the Blacks believe, that if they are put to death and not dismembred, they shall return again to their own Country, after they are thrown overboard. But neither the Person that was executed, nor his Countrymen of Cormantee (as I understood afterwards,) were so weak as to believe any such thing; tho' many I had on board from other Countries had that Opinion.

When the Execution was over, I ordered the Linguist to acquaint the Men-Negroes, "That now they might judge, no one that killed a white Man should be spared:" And I thought proper now to acquaint them once for all, "That if they attempted to mutiny again, I should be obliged to punish the Ringleaders with death, in order to prevent further Mischief." Upon this they all promised to be obedient, and I assured them they should be kindly used, if they kept their Promise: which they faithfully did. For we sailed, two days after, from Anamaboe for Jamaica; and tho' they were on board near four Months, from our going off the Coast, till they were sold at that Island, they never gave us the least reason to be jealous of them; which doubtless was owing to the execution of the white Man's Murderer.

After the Captain [Messervy, of *Ferrers* galley] had told me this story, he desired me to spare him some Rice, having heard, I had purchased a great many Tuns to the Windward; where he had bought little, not expecting to meet with so many Slaves. This request I could not comply with, having provided no more than was necessary for my self, and for another of my Owner's Ships, which I quickly expected. And understanding from him, that he had never been on the Coast of Guinea before, I took the liberty to observe to him, "That as he had on board so many Negroes of one Town and Language, it required the utmost Care and Management to keep them from mutinying; and that I was sorry he had so little Rice for them: For I had experienced that the Windward Slaves are always very

fond of it, it being their usual Food in their own Country; and he might certainly expect dissatisfactions and Uneasiness amongst them for want of a sufficient quantity."

This he took kindly, and having asked my Advice about other Matters, took his leave, inviting me to come next day to see him. I went accordingly on board his Ship, about three a clock in the afternoon. At four a clock the Negroes went to Supper, and Captain Messervy desired me to excuse him for a quarter of an hour, whilst he went forward to see the Men-Negroes served with Victuals. I observed from the Quarter-Deck, that he himself put Pepper and Palm Oyl amongst the Rice they were going to eat. When he came back to me, I could not forbear observing to him, "How imprudent it was in him to do so: For tho' it was proper for a Commander sometimes to go forward, and observe how things were managed; yet he ought to take a proper time, and have a good many of his white People in Arms when he went; or else the having him so much in their Power, might incourage the Slaves to mutiny: For he might depend upon it, they always aim at the chief Person in the Ship, whom they soon distinguish by the respect shown him by the rest of the People."

He thanked me for this Advice, but did not seem to relish it; saying, "He thought the old Proverb good, that "The Master's Eye makes the Horse fat." We then fell into other Discourse, and among other things he told me, "He designed to go away in a few days:" Accordingly he sailed three days after for Jamaica. Some Months after I went for that place, where at my arrival I found his Ship, and had the following melancholy account of his Death, which happened about ten days after he left the Coast of Guinea in this manner.

Being on the Forecastle of the Ship, amongst the Men-Negroes, when they were eating their Victuals, they laid hold on him, and beat out his Brains with the little Tubs, out of which they eat their boiled Rice. This Mutiny having been plotted amongst all the grown Negroes on board, they run to the forepart of the Ship in a body, and endeavoured to force the Barricado on the Quarter-Deck, not regarding the Musquets or Half Pikes, that were presented to their Breasts by the white Men, through the Loop-holes. So that at last the chief Mate was obliged to order one of the Quarter-deck Guns laden with Partridge-Shot, to be fired amongst them; which occasioned a terrible Destruction: For there were near eighty Negroes kill'd and drowned, many jumping overboard when the Gun was fired.

This indeed put an end to the Mutiny, but most of the Slaves that remained alive grew so sullen, that several of them were starved to death, obstinately refusing to take any Sustenance: And after the Ship was arrived at Jamaica, they attempted twice to mutiny, before the Sale of them began. This with their former Misbehaviour coming to be publickly known, none of the Planters cared to buy them, tho' offered at a low Price. So that this proved a very unsuccessful Voyage, for the Ship was detained many Months at Jamaica on that account, and at last was lost there in a Hurricane. . . .

25 MERCATOR HONESTUS
A DEFENSE OF THE AFRICAN SLAVE TRADE

In July 1740, Mercator Honestus *(a pseudonym) had "A Letter to the Gentlemen Merchants in the Guinea Trade, Particularly Addressed to the Merchants in Bristol and Liverpool" published in the* Gentleman's Magazine.* *This letter argued against slavery and the slave trade and concluded with a request that some of the gentlemen who engaged in the trade should justify their participation. The following letter, written in reply to that challenge, presents the most common argument in defense of the slave trade—that life in Africa was so unbearable that Africans were better off removed from it, even if by bondage and servitude.*

Sir, The Guinea Trade, by the Mistake of some, or Misrepresentation of others, hath been charged with Inhumanity, and a Contradiction to good Morals. Such a Charge at a Time when private and publick Morals are laugh'd at, as the highest Folly, by a powerful Faction; and Self-interest set up as the only Criterion of true

From "A Defense of the African Slave Trade, 1740," *London Magazine,* 9 (1740), 493–494, in Elizabeth Donnan, *Documents Illustrative of the History of the Slave Trade to America* (Washington, D. C.: Carnegie Institution, 1930), II, 469–470. Reprinted by permission.
* Vol. X, p. 341.

Wisdom, is certainly very uncourtly: But yet as I have a profound Regard for those superannuated Virtures; you will give me Leave to justify the African Trade, upon those Stale Principles, from the Imputations of "Mercator Honestus"; and shew him that there are People in some boasted Regions of Liberty, under a more wretched Slavery, than the Africans transplanted to our American Colonies.

The Inhabitants of Guinea are indeed in a most deplorable State of Slavery, under the arbitrary Powers of their Princes both as to Life and Property. In the several Subordinations to them, every great Man is absolute lord of his immediate Dependents. And lower still; every Master of a Family is Proprietor of his Wives, Children, and Servants; and may at his Pleasure consign them to Death, or a better Market. No doubt such a State is contrary to Nature and Reason, since every human Creature hath an absolute Right to Liberty. But are not all arbitrary Governments, as well in Europe, as Africa, equally repugnant to that great Law of Nature? And yet it is not in our Power to cure the universal Evil, and set all the Kingdoms of the Earth free from the Domination of Tyrants, whose long Possession, supported by standing Armies, and flagitious Ministers, renders the Thraldom without Remedy, while the People under it are by Custom satisfied with, or at least quiet under Bondage.

All that can be done in such a Case is, to communicate as much Liberty, and Happiness, as such circumstances will admit, and the People will consent to: And this is certainly by the Guinea Trade. For, by purchasing, or rather ransoming the Negroes from their national Tyrants, and transplanting them under the benign Influences of the Law, and Gospel, they are advanced to much greater Degrees of Felicity, tho' not to absolute Liberty.

That this is truly the Case cannot be doubted by any one acquainted with the Constitution of our Colonies, where the Negroes are governed by Laws, and suffer much less Punishment in Proportion to their Crimes, than the People in other Countries more refined in the Arts of Wickedness; and where Capital Punishment is inflicted only by the Civil Magistrates. . . .

Perhaps my Antagonist calls the Negroes Allowance of a Pint of Corn and an Herring, penurious, in Comparison of the full Meals of Gluttony: But if not let him compare that Allowance, to what the poor Labourer can purchase for Tenpence per Day to subsist himself and Family, and he will easily determine the American's Advantage. . . .

Nevertheless, Mercator will say, the Negroes are Slaves to their Proprietors: How Slaves? Nominally: Not really so much Slaves, as the Peasantry of all Nations is to Necessity; not so much as those of Corruption, or Party Zeal; not in any Sense, such abject Slaves, as every vicious Man is to his own Appetites. Indeed there is this Difference between Britons, and the Slaves of all other Nations; that the latter are so by Birth, or tyrannical Necessity; the former can never be so, but by a wicked Choice, or execrable Venality.[1] . . .

---

[1] In December the *Gentleman's Magazine* (XI. 145–146, 186–188) contained a second article, brought forth by the letter of "Mercator Honestus," from inhabitants of the Leeward Islands. This refers to a controversy over the morality of the trade in which a negro, Moses Bon Saam, had taken part. The article distributed responsibility for the trade, first, on the African chiefs; secondly, on the English traders who bought in Africa; thirdly, on the people who protected the trade because of the gain in it or in the sugar trade which rested on it; lastly, on the planters, who would prefer white labor but could not get it. From this time forward the adherents of the trade were more and more frequently placed upon the defensive, being forced to consider not so much the economic contribution made to the nation by the slave trade as its ethical aspects. Their defense is in reality usually directed, as it is here, not to the trade but to the institution of slavery.

26 CAPTAIN HUGH CROW
BONNY

Hugh Crow (1765–1829) was an English sea captain and merchant who had long been engaged in the African slave trade. The following extract from his memoirs describes the kingdom of Bonny, which, at the end of the eighteenth century, was an important slave trading center in the eastern Niger River delta, a region known as the Oil Rivers. Bonny continued to trade in slaves during the nineteenth century but turned increasingly to the sale of palm oil.

The inhabitants of Bonny, when our author last visited that port, amounted to about 3,000. They are chiefly a mixture of the Eboe, or Heebo, and the Brass tribes; the latter deriving their name from the importation into their country, which lies to the northward and westward of Bonny, of a kind of European-made brass pans, known in the trade by the name of neptunes, and used for the making of palm oil and salt, with which last the countries in the interior have been supplied by the coast from the earliest times on record. The article is now largely imported from Liverpool, both to Bonny and Calabar. The Eboes, who are also from a neighbouring country, have already been spoken of as a superior race, and the inhabitants, generally, are a fair dealing people, and much inclined to a friendly traffic with Europeans, who humour their peculiarities. Their general honesty, when the loose nature of their laws, as respects Europeans, and the almost entire absence of the moral influence of religion amongst them, are considered, affords a favourable prognostic of what the negro character would be if placed under the restraints and precepts of an enlightened system of jurisdiction.

It is probable (and this opinion is entertained by Captain Adams and others) that Bonny, and the towns on the low line of the coast on either side of it were origi-

nally peopled from the Eboe country, and that before the commencement of the slave trade, if it then existed; the inhabitants employed themselves in the making of salt, by evaporation from sea water. The country, says Adams, for many miles into the interior is "a vast morass, heavily timbered, and unfit, without excessive labour, to produce sufficient food for a very scanty population; and as the trade in slaves increased, these towns, particularly Bonny, grew into importance. The king of New Calabar, in the neighbourhood, and Pepple, king of Bonny, were both of Eboe descent, of which also are the mass of the natives; and the number of the slaves from the Eboe country, which, throughout the existence of the British trade were taken from Bonny, amounted to perhaps three-fourths of the whole export. It is calculated that no fewer than 16,000 of these people alone were annually exported from Bonny within the twenty years ending in 1820; so that, including 50,000 taken within the same period from New and Old Calabar, the aggregate export of Eboes alone was not short of 370,000."

The Eboes, tho' not generally a robust, are a well-formed people, of the middle stature: many of their women are of remarkably symmetrical shape, and if white, would in Europe be deemed beautiful. This race is, as has been already remarked, of a more mild and engaging disposition than the other tribes, particularly the Quaws, and though less suited for the severe manual labour of the field, they are preferred in the West India colo-

From Hugh Crow, *The Memoirs of the Late Captain Hugh Crow of Liverpool* (London: Longman, Rees, Orme, Brown, and Green, 1830), pp. 197–201, 215–219, 227–228.

nies for their fidelity and utility, as domestic servants, particularly if taken there when young, as they then become the most industrious of any of the tribes taken to the colonies. Their skin is generally of a yellowish tinge, but varying to a jet black. Of the same tribe, and speaking the same language, are the Brechés, so called from the word Breché, signifying gentleman, or, like Hidalgo in Spanish, son of a gentleman. As these had seen better days, and were more liable than their countrymen, who are inclined to despond when sent on board ship, to take some desperate means of relieving themselves, and encouraging others to shake off their bondage, the masters of the slave ships were generally averse to purchasing them. The Brechés informed us, that in their country every seventh child of their class, when about six or seven years of age, undergoes the operation, to distinguish its rank, of having the skin of the forehead brought down from the hair, so as to form a ridge or line from temple to temple. This disfigurement gives them a very disagreeable appearance, and the custom is chiefly confined to the sons of great men, and our author never saw but one female so marked. But the Eboes and Brechés are tatooed with their country and family marks. The national tatoo of the commonalty consists of small thickly placed perpendicular incisions, or cuts on each temple, as if done with a cupping apparatus. These people are kind and inoffensive in their manners, but so fearful of the whites when first brought amongst them, that they imagine they are to be eaten by them; and while under this impression they would sometimes attempt to jump overboard, or destroy themselves in some other way, so that it was necessary to watch them narrowly. Their apprehensions, however, were to be overcome by mild treatment, and they soon became reconciled to their lot. Their mutual affection is unbounded, and, says our author, I have seen them, when their allowance happened to be short, divide the last

morsel of meat amongst each other thread by thread.

Besides the Eboes and Brechés, we received at Bonny negroes of several other nations, named Quaws, Appas, Ottams, and Brasses. The Quaws, (or Moscoes of the West Indies) are an ill-disposed people, whom the Eboes regard with great aversion, as they consider them cannibals in their own country; an assumption which their desperate and ferocious looks would seem to warrant. Their skins are blacker than those of the Eboes, and their teeth are sharpened with files, so as to resemble those of a saw. These men were ever the foremost in any mischief or insurrection amongst the slaves, and from time to time many whites fell victims to their fury at Bonny. They are mortal enemies to the Eboes, of whom, such is their masculine superiority, and desperate courage, they would beat three times their own number. The slave ships were always obliged to provide separate rooms for these men between decks, and the captains were careful to have as few of them as possible amongst their cargoes. The females of this tribe are fully as ferocious and vindictive as the men.

The Appas are a race of people so slothfully inclined, that they trust for a subsistence to the spontaneous productions of the earth, and rather than betake themselves to cultivation, will even eat grass and soil. The few of them whom our author knew were extremely indolent in their habits; and probably owing to this, and the coarseness of their usual food, their flesh was loose and soft, and their bodies feeble. They are however of a harmless disposition, and the Eboes take a great delight in tantalizing them.

The Ottam tribe are stout and robust, and of a deeper black than any of the other tribes at Bonny. Their bodies and faces are carved and tatooed in a frightful manner; they seem nevertheless to be a well-disposed good-tempered race, and are much liked by the Eboes. Besides these we sometimes got a few natives of

Benin, which is about 160 or 170 miles from Bonny. These resemble the Eboes, and it is probable were partly of the same nation. They are the most orderly and well-behaved of all the blacks. In their own country they are famous for the manufacture of a beautiful sort of table-cloth.

.   .   .

The kings of Bonny (there were two during our author's intercourse with the natives) although in many respects they appeared to exercise an absolute power, unrestrained by any fixed principles, may be properly termed the heads of an aristo-cratic government. This is evinced by their having a grand Palaver-house, in which they themselves presided, but the members of which, composed of the chiefs or great men, were convened and con-sulted on all matters of state emergency, and sometimes (as appears in the case of the illness of king Holiday's wife) in mat-ters relating to the domestic affairs of the kings themselves. The government, in-deed, may be said to combine three es-tates, the kings, the great men, and the feticheros, or priests; the last being proba-bly considered as instruments of popular subjection, whose influence over the peo-ple the two first consider it politic to toler-ate, if not to encourage. In some of the great kingdoms of the interior, as Ashan-tee, Aquambo, and Dahomy, the kings are absolute; but at Bonny, and many other parts of the coast, the monarchs ap-pear to hold a very mild and popular sway over their subjects; and whatever we find of apparent cruelty or barbarity in their conduct, or that of their head men, is at-tributable not to any wanton or uncon-trolled indulgence in a savage disposition, but to an accordance with those supersti-tious customs and ceremonies, sometimes ridiculous, and often horrible in the eyes of Europeans, which they have been taught, in common with their country-men, to consider as fit and necessary ei-ther for the purposes of justice, or the conciliation of their gods.

The revenues of the kings are derived from the duties on shipping and trade, contributions drawn from their subjects of all necessaries for their houshold, fines adjudged in criminal and civil cases, presents from Europeans, and from other less honorable sources. When paying for the negroes (says our author) the kings are sure to have two men on board to take the customs from the traders, which amounts to the tenth part, or "bar," as they call it. Besides the usual payment for firewood, water, yams, palm oil, and even for bury-ing ground, whether we made use of it or not, we were obliged to pay customs' du-ties on all these. With respect to the slaves, we had to pay for them a second time, for after the payment of the first purchase-money, we were called upon to pay what were called "work bars," a few days before the vessel sailed.

The body dress of the kings consists of shirts and trowsers, and like all the kings on the coast, they generally wear gold-laced hats. They are attended, when they board a ship, by a large retinue of serv-ants, one of whom carries a gold-headed cane, which, when sent off to a vessel by the king, serves as a note, or authority, when he is in want of any thing. "It is rather singular," says our author, "that although the two chiefs, Pepple and Holi-day, were relations and copartners in the throne, they could never agree: and I do not recollect having ever seen them together on board of any ship. Pepple was the superior, and maintained the ascend-ant over Holiday in a high degree." Their houses were only distinguished from those of their subjects by their being somewhat larger, detached, and more nu-merous, and being furnished in a superior manner, as many articles are imported for them from Europe. Bonny has long been celebrated for the size and construction of her canoes; and those of the king deserve notice. They are formed out of a single log of the capot, a species of cotton tree, which attains so enormous a size, that it is said that one was seen at Akim, which ten men could scarcely grasp. The canoes in general use, have about fifteen paddles on a side; but those of the king, which are superior vessels of the sort, carry, besides the rowers, as many as a hundred and fifty warriors, well furnished with small arms. They have also a long nine-pounder at each end of the canoe; and when they are equipped for war, with drums beating, horns blowing, and colours flying, they make a very dashing and formidable appearance. The kings often take excursions in their canoes, attended by about thirty stout men paddling, and a steersman. Several others are employed in playing some musical instrument, while others dance in the middle of the canoe. The rowers keep admirable time with their paddles, so that they drive through the water at a rapid rate, and appear to great advantage. Whenever king Pepple came off in his state canoe to the ship, all the traders, rich and poor, precipitately betook themselves to their canoes; and, on his coming on board, we always manned the side, and hoisted the colours.

Our author was not perhaps aware that Bonny owes its sovereignty to Benin, otherwise he would naturally have attributed the visit, which he records in the following passage, to that circumstance. "While I lay," he remarks, "at Bonny, on my last voyage, two large canoes arrived from Benin, full of presents, consisting of the manufactures and produce of the country, and with these came two remarkably fine looking men of from thirty to forty years of age, well formed, and about six feet high. Their look and manner were of a superior order, and they walked in a majestic style, followed by a retinue of servants. They were robed in a loose flowing dress; I found they spoke pretty good English, and I conversed with them on several occasions, particularly on the subject of the slave trade. They expressed their conviction that so long as there were lands to cultivate, and seas for ships to sail on, slavery would continue to exist. These men were near relations of King Pepple,

and had been sent to Bonny, as ambassadors by the king of Benin. They remained about a month feasting in their way, and then returned with their large canoes laden with presents. I never met with any black princes so sensible and well-informed as these men, or who had so noble and commanding an appearance."

. . .

The principal trade of Bonny, in our author's time, was in slaves; but since its abolition amongst the Britsh they have happily turned their attention to procuring and exporting palm oil. Ivory is rarely offered for sale, and only in small quantities and at dear rates, the elephants being probably fewer in the neighbourhood than on other parts of the coast. The slaves are procured from the interior, and much bustle takes place when the inhabitants are preparing their canoes for the trade. These vessels, which are large of the kind, are stored for the voyage with merchandise and provisions. "Evening," says Adams, "is the period chosen for the time of departure, when they proceed in a body accompanied by the noise of drums, horns, and gongs. At the expiration of the sixth day they generally return, bringing with them 1500 or 2000 slaves, who are sold to Europeans the evening after their arrival, and taken on board the ships." The Africans become domestic slaves, or are sold to Europeans, by losing their liberty in war, resigning it in famine, or forfeiting it by insolvency, or the crimes of murder, adultery, or sorcery. It may be inferred, too, without libelling the character of the Africans, that European cupidity has often led them to hunt their unoffending fellow-beings for the sole purpose of enriching themselves by the sale of their bodies! "The traders," our author further remarks, "have, in general, good memories, and some of them can reckon their accounts with as much expedition as most Europeans can with the aid of pen and ink. If they know the captain with whom they are dealing to be particular, they will generally calculate with accuracy; but, like many amongst ourselves, they will frequently overreach if they can, and although I have had occasion to remark upon their honesty, I must say, that many of them were in general restrained only by the dread of detection. Most of them, I must in strict justice add, are addicted to lying, and whatever be their probity amongst themselves, they do not make it a matter of conscience to take an advantage of strangers.

.   .   .

27 ARCHIBALD DALZEL
DAHOMEY AND ITS NEIGHBORS

During the latter part of the eighteenth century, the trader Archibald Dalzel spent nearly thirty years on the Guinea Coast, during four of which he was governor of Ouidah. Although his purpose in writing his well-known The History of Dahomey, an Inland Kingdom of Africa *was to demonstrate how savage the country was (thereby justifying the slave trade), he related the traditions or origins of Dahomey and described the rival neighboring kingdoms over which Dahomey was to establish its supremacy.*

The Dahomans were formerly called Foys, and inhabited a small territory, on the north-east part of their present kingdom, whose capital, *Dawhee,* lay between the towns of Calmina and Abomey, at about 90 miles from the sea-coast.

Early in the last century, Tacoodonou, chief of the Foys, having, at the time of his festivals, murdered a neighbouring prince, who was with him on a friendly visit, seized on his chief town, Calmina, and soon after made himself master of his kingdom.

Thus strengthened, he dared to wage war against a more powerful state, to the northward of Foy, and laid siege to Abomey, its capital; but meeting here with more resistance than he expected, he made a vow, if he should prove successful, that he would sacrifice Da, its prince, to the Fetische, or deity, whose succour he then implored.

At length, having reduced the town, and captured the unfortunate prince, he built a large palace at Abomey, in memory of his victory. And now it was that he fulfilled his vow, by ripping open the belly of his royal captive: after which he displayed the body on the foundation of the palace he was building; and carrying on the wall over it, he named the structure, when finished, Da-homy, or the house in Da's belly.

The conquest of Abomey happened about the year 1625; after which, Tacoodonou fixed his residence in that town, assuming the title of King of Dahomy. His subjects changed the name of Foys for that of Dahomans; and at the present hour, their former appellation, except amongst a few of the inland people, seems quite forgot.

Nothing further is related of Tacoodonou; nor, indeed, of his two immediate successors, Adahoonzou, and Weebaigah, except that the former ascended the throne about the year 1650, and the latter thirty years after.

From Archibald Dalzel, *The History of Dahomey, an Inland Kingdom of Africa* (London: T. Spilsbury and Son, Snowhill, 1793), pp. 1–7, 12–15.

It is not till the reign of Guadja Trudo, who succeeded Weebaigah in 1708, that any thing is precisely known about this extraordinary people. All before this time stands on the ground of tradition, which is ever more or less precarious, in proportion to the number of relators, and the frequency of the narration. Among the Dahomans, for reasons assigned in the Introduction, subjects of this nature are little known, and less discussed.

But when the active spirit of Trudo began to threaten the maritime states, his neighbours, it quickly attracted the attention of the Europeans, whom commerce had brought and settled amongst them. It was then that, by the assistance of writing, each transient fact was fixed, and scattered information collected into a body; it was then that tradition gave place to record, and legend to history.

Before we enter upon the memoirs of this enterprising and warlike Prince, it will not be improper to take a slight political view of the states around him, as they stood about the beginning of his reign, the better to form a judgment of the several transactions that are to pass in review before us.

In doing this, let us begin on the coast, with Coto or Quitta, to the west; which is a small kingdom, whose prince, about Bosman's time [late seventeenth century—ed.], resided at the village of Quitta, called also Coto and Verbun, and was at continual war with its neighbours, the Popoes, with various success.

Little Popo joins Quitta to the eastward. This is a small but very warlike kingdom, the remains of the Acras, who were driven out of their own territories on the Gold Coast, by the Aquamboes, in 1680. They were in alliance, at times, with Ardra, and fought her battles against Offra, and even Whydah itself. They were at continual war with the Quittas, which was fomented by the King of Aquamboe, for the purpose of directing the attention of both from his gold mines; and he managed this contention so cunningly,

that he suffered neither nation to prevail too much over the other. Indeed, during the dissensions at Aquamboe, in 1700, Popo prevailed, and drove the Quittas out of their country; but they were, somehow, reinstated not long after.

Both these countries are flat, the soil poor and sandy, with few trees, except palms and wild cocoas. They have, indeed, some cattle and fish, but most at Quitta; [1] so that this and Great Popo were then frequently obliged to the Whydahs for subsistence; from whom, though their enemies, they always found means to smuggle as much as they were in need of.

Great Popo joins to Little Popo. The country is more fertile; and the city, which is very large, is situated in a marshy lake at the mouth of the river Toree. This city is, from its situation, very strong; as a proof of which, when besieged by the Ardras, assisted by the French shipping, it was able to repulse them both with great loss. In 1682, this people was at war with both Quitta and Whydah; but, from prudential motives, they made a temporary peace with the latter, and obtained its assistance against the former. Some writers consider Quitta, Popo, and Whydah, as dismemberments of Ardra, with which kingdom, however, they are not more often at war, than they are with one another.

Whydah and Ardra were the two greatest maritime states in the neighbourhood of Dahomy; [2] rivals in trade, and consequently ever jealous of each other. The people of Whydah, at that time, are described as the most polite and civilized of any on the whole coast; those of Ardra being much more insolent and mercenary.

The country of Whydah is the very reverse of those already mentioned, being,

[1] At present, provision is more plentiful; they bring a number of fine cattle from the inland parts of Quitta.
[2] The trade here was very considerable, this being the principal part of all the Guinea Coast for slaves. In its flourishing state, there was above 20,000 negroes yearly exported, from this and the neighbouring places, to the several European plantations.

for beauty and fertility, almost beyond description; and, before the invasion of the Dahomans, was so populous, that one village contained as many inhabitants as a whole kingdom on the Gold Coast. It was reputed, that the Whydahs were able to bring into the field, two hundred thousand effective men.

The country of Ardra is no less beautiful than that of its neighbour; but this abounds with hill and dale, whereas the former is one uniform surface, one great park. Nor was this kingdom less formidable than Whydah, before the incursions of the Eyeos in the year 1698. Even at the time in question her power was very considerable; for we find, when invaded by Dahomy, her army consisted of more than fifty thousand men. Yet both these nations are branded by Bosman with pusillanimity, who tells us, they employed mercenary soldiers, such as the Aquamboes, or other Gold Coast negroes, to fight their battles: which we shall find to be true.

The capital of Whydah was then Xavier or Sabee, seven or eight miles from the beach; that of Ardra was a town of the same name, about twenty miles from the sea. This must be distinguished from another Ardra, or Alladah, which is also a great town on the road from Whydah to Calmina. As both these countries are particularly described in other parts of this work, it will be unnecessary to enlarge on the subject here. And with respect to the several small and independent states, interspersed amongst those we have already mentioned, such as Toree, Weemey, Offra, or Little Ardra, &c. it will be sufficient, in this place, to refer our readers to the map, for their respective situations; reserving their political connexions till they become of sufficient consequence to be taken notice of in our history.

Of the inland kingdoms, that to the west of Dahomy is called Mahee; that to the north-east, Eyeo. Snelgrave calls the former of these Yahoo; but as there was little of either of these known before the

reign of Trudo, their description properly belongs to the History. The Tappahs, to the north-east of Eyeo, were unknown in his time; and indeed till very lately, when they made themselves as formidable to the Eyeos, as these to all the southern nations.

Such were the states around Dahomy, and such their jarring and divided interests, about the time of the accession of Trudo; where a new scene opens, that displays to wiser nations, how soon a small state may become too formidable, and how necessary to their own preservation are those alliances, that maintain in equilibrio the balance of power.

The kingdom of Eyeo [3] lies many days journey to the north-east of Abomey, beyond a great and famous lake, the fountain of several large rivers that empty themselves into the Bay of Guinea. The people are numerous and warlike, and, what is here singular, their armies totally consist of cavalry; and as every savage nation has some cruel method of rendering themselves dreadful to their enemies, this people were said to have a custom of cutting of the privities of those they have slain in battle; and that no one dared, on pain of death, to take an enemy prisoner, that was not furnished with a hundred of these trophies.

The Eyeos are governed by a king, no less absolute than the King of Dahomy, yet subject to a regulation of state, at once humiliating and extraordinary. When the people have conceived an opinion of his ill government, which is sometimes insidiously infused into them, by the artifice of his discontented ministers, they send a deputation to him, with a present of parrots eggs, as a mark of its authenticity, to represent to him that the burden of government must have so far fatigued him, that they consider it full time for him to

[3] Called Oyeo, Okyou. Probably this may be the kingdom of Gago, which lies to the northward of Dahomy, eight or ten days journey. The Moorish aspirated sound of G being nearly like a hard H, as in the word *George*, spelt Jorje by the Spaniards, and pronounced Horké, or Horché; whence Gago may have been sounded Haho, Haiho, or Haiko.

repose from his cares, and indulge himself with a little sleep. He thanks his subjects for their attention to his ease; retires to his apartment, as if to sleep; and there gives directions to his women to strangle him. This is immediately executed; and his son quietly ascends the throne, upon the usual terms, of holding the reins of government no longer than whilst he merits the approbation of the people.

This seems to have been the first inland nation in this part of Africa, of which the Europeans had any intimation. Bosman speaks of an invasion of Ardra, in 1698, by a potent inland people, which could, from his description, be no other than the Eyeos. From him we learn, that some of the Ardras, who had been ill treated by their king, or his caboceers, flying to this inland prince for redress, he sent an ambassador to remonstrate with the King of Ardra on the subject, and to inform him, if his viceroys and other deputies did not govern the people more justly and tenderly, he should be obliged, however unwilling, to interfere. Ardra treated the monition with contempt, and put the ambassador to death; but the King of Eyeo took a dreadful revenge: his troops poured like a torrent [4] into Ardra; destroyed almost half the kingdom; and, what marks at once his severity and his justice, notwithstanding his general had obtained so signal a victory, he caused him to be hanged, on his return, because he had not brought with him the King of Ardra, who was the author of all this evil.

It was this nation that, shortly after the conquest of Ardra, made war on Trudo, at the instigation of several fugitive princes, whose fathers had been conquered and slain by the Dahomans. They entered Dahomy with an immense body of horse, amounting to many thousands.

Trudo immediately left Ardra; and, though he had none but infantry,[5] yet, these having fire-arms, as well as swords, he had some hopes that he might at least make a stand against them. He knew, however, that they were well mounted, and armed with bows, javelins, and cutting swords; that they were, besides, courageous, and had spread terror through the adjacent countries; he also knew, that he had to contest in an open country, where horse would have every advantage; yet all this could not damp his daring spirit. He marched boldly to face the enemy; and, on meeting them, supported such a fire from his musquetry as effectually affrighted the horses, so that their riders could never make a regular charge on the Dahomans. Notwithstanding this, their numbers were so great, and the dispute so obstinate, that, after fighting for four days, the troops of Dahomy were greatly fatigued, and all was in danger of being lost: at this critical moment a stratagem entered the mind of the king, worthy of the most enlightened general, and which has been several times practised, with equal success, in times both ancient and modern.

Trudo had in his camp great quantities of brandy, at that time one of the principal articles of the French trade to Guinea. This, with many valuable goods, he contrived to leave in a town, adjacent to his camp, and under favour of the night withdrew to a convenient distance. In the morning the Eyeos, seeing the enemy fled, secure of victory, began to burn and plunder the town, and to indulge themselves very freely with the treacherous liquor: this soon intoxicated, and spread the ground with the major part of their army. At this juncture, the Dahomans, who had timely intimation of the enemy's disorder,

---

[4] The Whydahs, say the Eyeos, invaded Ardra with ten hundred thousand horse; from which, without taking it literally, we may suppose the number must have been immense. We shall see, further on, the idea of the Dahomans about the number of an Eyeo army.

[5] There are few or no horses in Dahomy. Such as they have are very small; which indeed was the case with the inland countries, in Leo's time (about 1492), when good horses, from the north of Africa, were bought up at Gago, at a high price; perhaps with intention to improve the breed, and establish a numerous cavalry.

fell upon them with redoubled fury, destroyed a great number, completely routed the rest; and those that escaped, owed their safety to their horses.[6]

In this manner did Trudo happily clear his country of a very formidable enemy; but however he might consider himself victorious in the present instance, he knew there was every thing to be feared from the inroads of such a numerous nation, and that too a nation of horsemen. He, therefore, with a foresight that did him much honour, sent ambassadors with

[6] The Dahomans pretend, that in their flight, the terror and precipitation of the Eyeos was so violent, that great numbers tumbled into, and filled up part of the deep moat which surrounds Abomey, the rest making themselves a bridge of their bodies, to effect their escape.

many presents to the King of Eyeo, to avert his further anger; but, without depending too much on their success, he laid his plans, in case of another invasion. He knew that the Fetische of the Eyeos was the sea; and that themselves, and their king, were threatened with death, by the priests, if they ever dared to look on it: he therefore resolved, in case he should be defeated by them in a future battle, to repair with his people to the sea-coast for security, and leave the upland towns and country to their disposal; in which he knew they could not remain after they had destroyed the forage; and that all the damage they might otherwise do, to thatched houses and mud walls, would easily be repaired.

28 THOMAS FOWELL BUXTON
THE PRINCIPLES OF ABOLITION

Thomas Fowell Buxton (1786–1845) was one of England's leading nineteenth-century philanthropists. At the request of the great abolitionist William Wilberforce, Buxton assumed the leadership of the antislavery party in the House of Commons in May 1824. Buxton previously had been a champion of prison reform, and in March 1823 when the Antislavery Society was formed, he was a charter member. Taking up the cause of abolition, Buxton concerned himself with the statistics of slavery operations. He prepared documents containing irrefutable facts to present in the House of Commons and framed positive principles on which to base his attack on the slave trade and slavery in Africa. These principles were included in his famous book, The African Slave Trade.

It appears to me a matter of such peculiar moment that we should distinctly settle and declare the PRINCIPLES on which our whole intercourse with Africa, whether economic or benevolent, whether directed exclusively to her benefit, or mingled (as I think it may most fairly be) with a view to our own, shall be founded, and by which it shall be regulated, that I ven-

From Thomas Fowell Buxton, *The African Slave Trade* (New York: S. W. Benedict, 1840), II, 154–159, 163–168.

ture, though at the risk of being tedious, to devote a separate chapter to the consideration of them. The principles, then, which I trust to see adopted by our country, are these—
  Free Trade.
  Free Labor.

FREE TRADE
  Nothing, I apprehend, could be more unfortunate to the continent we wish to befriend, or more discreditable to ourselves, than that Great Britain should give

any color to the suspicion of being actuated by mercenary motives; an apology would thus be afforded to every other nation for any attempt it might make to thwart our purpose. We know, from the Duke of Wellington's dispatches, that the powers on the continent were absolutely incredulous as to the purity of the motives which prompted us, at the congress of Aix la Chapelle, to urge, *beyond everything else,* the extinction of the Slave Trade.[1]

In a letter to Mr. Wilberforce, dated Paris, 15th Sept., 1814, the Duke of Wellington says, "It is not believed that we are in earnest about it, or have abolished the trade on the score of its inhumanity. It is thought to have been a commercial speculation; and that, having abolished the trade ourselves, with a view to prevent the undue increase of colonial produce in our stores, of which we could not dispose, we now want to prevent other nations from cultivating their colonies to the utmost of their power."

And again, in another letter to the Right Honorable J. C. Villiers—

Paris, 31*st August,* 1814.

"The efforts of Great Britain to put an end to it (the Slave Trade) are not attributed to good motives, but to commercial jealousy, and a desire to keep the monopoly of colonial produce in our own hands."

The grant of twenty millions may have done something to quench these narrow jealousies, but still, the nations of the continent will be slow to believe that we are entirely disinterested. It should, then, be made manifest to the world, by some signal act, that the moving spring is humanity; that if England makes settlements on the African coast, it is only for the more effectual attainment of her great object; and that she is not allured by the hopes either of gain or conquest, or by the advantages, national or individual, political or commercial, which may, and I doubt not, will follow the undertaking. Such a demonstration would be given, if, with the declaration, that it is resolved to abolish the Slave Trade, and, that in this cause we are ready, if requisite, to exert all our powers, Great Britain, should couple an official pledge that she will not claim for herself a single benefit, which shall not be shared by every nation uniting with her in the extinction of the Slave Trade; and especially

First—That no exclusive privilege in favor of British subjects shall ever be allowed to exist.

Secondly—That no *custom-house* shall ever be established at Fernando Po [in the Gulf of Guinea—ed.].

Thirdly—That no distinction shall be made there, *whether in peace or in war,* between our own subjects and those of any such foreign power, as to the rights they shall possess, or the terms on which they shall enjoy them. In short, that we purchase Fernando Po, and will hold it for no other purpose than the benefit of Africa. I am well aware that these may appear startling propositions; I am, however, supported in them by high authorities; the suggestion as to the custom-house was made to me by Mr. Porter, of the Board of Trade; and that respecting neutrality in peace or in war, originated with the learned Judge of the British Vice-Admiralty Courts. Supported by his authority, I may venture to say that, though a novel, it would be a noble characteristic of our colony. As it is intended for different ends, so it would be ruled by different principles, from any colony which has ever been undertaken: it would have the distinction of being the neutral ground of the world, elevated above the mutual injuries of war; where, for the prosecution of a good and a vast object, the subjects and the fleets of all nations may meet in amity, and where there shall reign a perpetual truce.

---

[1] The Congress of Aix-la-Chapelle met in 1818 to arrange the withdrawal of the army of occupation from France. The British Foreign Minister, Lord Castlereagh, urged all nations to join in the abolition of the slave trade (ed.).

Let us look to the tendency of the proposition, that no custom-house shall be established at Fernando Po, or at the post to be formed at the junction of the Niger and the Tchadda: we might then hope that the history of these stations would be a counterpart to that of Singapore, which is described as having been, in 1819, "an insignificant fishing-village, and a haunt of pirates," but now stands as an eloquent eulogy on the views of its founder, Sir Stamford Raffles, proving what may be effected, and in how short a time, for our own profit and for the improvement of the uncivilized world, "by the union of native industry and British enterprise," when uncurbed by restrictions on trade.

FREE LABOR

I now turn to the second great principle, viz.—Free Labor.

It may be thought by some almost superfluous that this should be urged, considering that there is an Act of Parliament, which declares that "Slavery shall be, and is hereby utterly and for ever abolished *in all the* colonies, possessions, and plantations of Great Britain." But if ever there were a case in which this great law should be strictly and strenuously enforced, and in which it is at the same time peculiarly liable to be neglected or evaded, it is in the case of any possessions we may obtain in Africa. It is necessary to be wise in time, and never to suffer this baneful weed to take root there. Let us remember what it has cost us to extirpate it from our old colonies. It is remarkable that among the whole phalanx of antagonists to the abolition of West India Slavery, there was never one who was not, by his own account, an ardent lover of freedom. Slavery, in the abstract, was universally acknowledged to be detestable; and they were in the habit of pathetically deploring their cruel fate, and of upbraiding the mother-country, which had originally planted this curse among them; but prop-

erty had entwined itself around the disastrous institution, and we had to contend with a fearful array of securities, marriage settlements, and vested interests of all kinds. Again, bondage, it was said, had seared the intellect, and withered all that was noble in the bosoms of its victims. To have begun such an unrighteous system was an error, only less than that of suddenly eradicating it, and of clothing with the attributes of freemen, those whose very nature had been changed and defiled by servitude.

I firmly believe that much of all this was uttered in perfect sincerity; and yet, I feel the most serious apprehensions lest these wholesome convictions should evaporate before the temptations of a country, where land of the richest fertility is to be had for 1d. per acre, and laborers are to be purchased for 4l. per head. We know, not only that the Portuguese are turning their attention to plantations in the neighborhood of Loango, but that they have been bold enough to ask us to guarantee to them their property, that is their slaves, in these parts. This, together with certain ominous expressions which I have heard, convinces me that my apprehensions are not altogether chimerical; and I am not sure that we shall not once more hear the antique argument, that Negroes, "from the brutishness of their nature," are incapable of being induced to work by any stimulus but the lash: at all events, we shall be assured, that if we attempt to establish Free Labor, we shall assail the prejudices of the African chiefs in the tenderest points. If we do not take care, at the outset, to render the holding of slaves by British subjects in Africa highly penal, and perilous in the last degree, we shall see British capital again embarked, and vested interest acquired in human flesh. We shall, in spite of the warning we have had, commit a second time, the monstrous error, to say nothing of the crime, of tolerating slavery. A second time the slave-master will accuse us of being at least accomplices in his guilt;

and once more we shall have to buy off opposition by an extravagant grant of money.

The suggestion, then, that I make is, that we shall lay it down, as a primary and sacred principle, that any man who enters any territory that we may acquire in Africa, is from that moment "Free, and discharged of all manner of slavery," and that Great Britain pledges herself to defend him from all, civilized or savage, who may attempt to recapture him. That one resolution will do much to give us laborers—to obtain for us the affections of the population—to induce them to imitate and adopt our customs—and to settle down to the pursuits of peaceful industry and productive agriculture.

. . .

I will subjoin in the Appendix further proof on the authority of General Turner, Colonel Denham, and Major Ricketts, who also spoke from what they saw at Sierra Leone, as to the disposition of Africans to work for wages.

The Rev. W. Fox, missionary at M'Carthy's Island [off the Gambia—ed.] whom I have already quoted, says, "The Eastern Negroes, . . . come here and hire themselves as laborers for several months, and, with the articles they receive in payment, barter them again on their way home for more than their actual value on this island." In the journal of the same gentleman, just received, under date of April, 1838, he writes thus: "I have to-day paid off all the laborers who had been employed on the mission ground, and have hired about eighty more, with three overseers; *many others applied for work,* and I should have felt a pleasure in engaging them, but that I wished to keep the expenses within moderate bounds."

It thus appears that free labor is to be obtained in Africa, even under present circumstances, if we will but pay the price for it, and that there is no necessity at all for that system of coerced labor, which no necessity could justify. I am aware that I have trespassed on the patience of many of my readers, who require no arguments against slavery; but I have already expressed, and continue to feel, if there be danger anywhere in the plan for the cultivation of Africa, it lies in this point. And I wish the question of slavery to be definitively settled, and our principles to be resolved on, in such a way as shall render it impossible for us to retract them, before a single step is taken, or a shilling of property invested in the attempt to grow sugar and cotton in Africa.

I shall here introduce the consideration of two other points, which though they cannot precisely be classed as principles, yet are nearly akin to them, and deserve our very serious attention.

The proposal of a settlement in Africa, necessarily recalls to mind our vast empire in India: and, surely, no soberminded statesman would desire to see renewed, in another quarter of the globe, the career we have run in the East.

I entirely disclaim any disposition to erect a new empire in Africa. Remembering what has now been disclosed, of the affliction of that quarter of the globe, and of the horrors and abominations which every spot exhibits, and every hour produces, it would be the extreme of selfish cruelty to let a question so momentous be decided with an eye to our own petty interests; but there is another view of the case—it would also be the most extreme folly to allow ourselves to swerve one iota from its right decision, by any such indirect and short-sighted considerations.

What is the value to Great Britain of the sovereignty of a few hundred square miles in Benin, or Eboe, as compared with that of bringing forward into the market of the world millions of customers, who may be taught to grow the raw material which we require, and who require the manufactured commodities which we produce? The one is a trivial and insignificant matter; the other is a subject worthy the most anxious solicitude of the most accomplished statesmen.

It appears to me, however, that the danger of our indulging any thirst for dominion is rather plausible than real. In the first place, the climate there forbids the employment of European armies, if armies indeed formed any part of my plan, which they do not. I look forward to the employment, almost exclusively, of the African race. A few Europeans may be required in some leading departments; but the great body of our agents must have African blood in their veins, and of course to the entire exclusion of our troops.

2dly. In Asia, there was accumulated treasure to tempt our cupidity: in Africa, there is none. Asia was left to the government of a company: the African establishments will, of course, be regularly subjected to parliamentary supervision. Our encroachments upon Asia were made at a time, when little general attention was bestowed, or sympathy felt, for the sufferings and wrongs of a remote people. Now, attention is awake on such topics. India stands as a beacon to warn us against extended dominion; and if there were not, as I believe there are, better principles among our statesmen, there would be a check to rapacity, and a shield for the weak, in the wakeful commiseration of the public.

I may add, that, were the danger as great as some imagine, it would have disclosed itself ere this. The French have had for some time a settlement on the Senegal; the Danes on the Rio Volta; the Dutch on the Gold Coast; the Portuguese at Loango; the Americans at Cape Mesurado, and the English at Sierra Leone, in the Gambia, and on the Gold Coast; and I know not that there has been upon the part of these a desire manifested to raise an empire in Central Africa. Certainly, there has been none on the part of the British: on the contrary, I think there is some reason to complain that our government has been too slow, at least for the welfare of Africa, in accepting territory which has been voluntarily offered to us, and in confirming the treaties which have been made by our officers. We have been in possession of Sierra Leone not very far short of half a century; and I am not aware that it can be alleged that any injury has been thereby inflicted upon the natives.

Lastly. There is this consideration, and to me it seems conclusive—Granting that the danger to African liberty is as imminent as I consider it to be slight, still the state of the country is such, that, change as it may, it cannot change for the worse.

The other point to which I would call attention is, the encouragement which may be afforded to the infant cultivation of Africa, by promoting the admission and use of its productions. I shall not advert to the assistance which we may fairly expect from the Legislature in this respect, when the subject is brought under its consideration in all its important bearings; with the example of France and the United States before them, I cannot doubt that Government will introduce such measures as a liberal and enlightened policy will dictate. But individuals have it in their power to contribute largely to the encouragement of African produce, by a preference that will cost them little. Let them recollect that for centuries we were mainly instrumental in checking cultivation in Africa: we ransacked the whole continent in order to procure laborers for the West Indies. Is it, then, too much to ask, now when we are endeavoring to raise her from the gulf of wretchedness into which we have contributed to plunge her, that while she is struggling with enormous difficulties, we should force her industry and excite her to unfold her capabilities by anxiously encouraging the consumption of her produce?

29 THEODORE CANOT
SLAVING IN LIBERIA

Like many nineteenth-century slavers, Theodore Canot was a soldier of fortune and served under many flags. Although he had been brought up in Florence, Italy, he was educated by the captain of an American vessel. Canot had no religion, many vices, and few weaknesses.

By this time the sub-factory of New Sestros was somewhat renowned in Cuba and Porto Rico. Our dealings with commanders, the character of my cargoes, and the rapidity with which I despatched a customer and his craft, were proverbial in the islands. Indeed, the third year of my lodgment had not rolled over, before the slave-demand was so great that, in spite of rum, cottons, muskets, powder, kidnapping, and Prince Freeman's wars, the country could not supply our demand.

To aid New Sestros, I had established several *nurseries,* or junior factories, at points a few miles from the limits of Liberia. These "chapels of ease" furnished my parent barracoons [stockades—ed.] with young and small negroes, mostly kidnapped, I suppose, in the neighbourhood of the beach.

When I was perfectly cured of the injury I sustained in my first philanthropic fight, I loaded my spacious cutter with a choice collection of trade-goods, and set sail one fine morning for the outpost at Digby. I designed also, if advisable, to erect another receiving barracoon under the lee of Cape Mount.

But my call at Digby was unsatisfactory. The pens were vacant, and our merchandise squandered *on credit.* This put me in a very uncomfortable passion, which would have rendered an interview between "Mr. Powder" and his agent anything but pleasant or profitable, had he

From Theodore Canot, *Adventures of an African Slaver: Being a True Account of the Life of Captain Theodore Canot, Trader in Gold, Ivory, and Slaves on the Coast of Guinea* (Garden City, N. Y.: Garden City Publishing Co., 1928), pp. 330–334. Reprinted by permission of Albert & Charles Boni, Inc.

been at his post. Fortunately for both of us, he was abroad carousing with a king; so that I refused landing a single yard of merchandise, and hoisted sail for the next village.

There I transacted business in regular ship-shape. Our rum was plenteously distributed and established an *entente cordiale* which would have charmed a diplomatist at his first dinner in a new capital. The naked blackguards flocked round me like crows. I clothed their loins in parti-colored calicoes that enriched them with a plumage worthy of parrots. In five days nineteen newly "conveyed" darkies were exchanged for London muskets, Yankee grog, and Manchester cottons.

My cutter, though but twenty-seven feet long, was large enough to stow my gang, considering that the voyage was short, and the slaves but boys and girls; so I turned my prow homeward with contented spirit and promising skies. Yet before night, all was changed. Wind and sea rose together. The sun sank in a low streak of blood. After a while, it rained in terrible squalls; till finally darkness caught me in a perfect gale. So high was the surf and so shelterless the coast, that it became utterly impossible to make a lee of any headland where we might ride out the storm in safety. Our best hope was in the cutter's ability to keep the open sea without swamping; and accordingly, under the merest patch of sail, I coasted the perilous breakers, guided by their roar, till day dawn. But, when the sun lifted over the horizon—peering for an instant through a rent in the storm-cloud, and then disappearing behind the grey vapour—I saw at once that the coast offered no chance of landing our blacks at some friendly town. Everywhere the bellowing shore was lashed by surf, impracticable even for the boats and skill of Kroomen. On I dashed, driving and almost burying the cutter, with loosened reef, till we came opposite Monrovia; where, safe in the absence of cruisers, I crept at dark under the lee of the cape, veiling my cargo with our useless sails.

Sunset killed the wind, enabling us to be off again at dawn; yet hardly were we clear of the cape when both gale and current freshened from the old quarter, holding us completely in check. Nevertheless, I kept at sea till evening, and then sneaked back to my protecting anchorage.

By this time, my people and slaves were well-nigh famished, for their sole food had been a scant allowance of raw cassava. Anxiety, toil, rain, and drenching spray, broke their spirits. The blacks, from the hot interior, and now for the first time off their mother earth, suffered not only from the inclement weather, but groaned with the terrible pangs of sea-sickness. I resolved, if possible, to refresh the drooping gang by a hot meal; and, beneath the shelter of a tarpaulin, contrived to cook a mess of rice. Warm food comforted us astonishingly; but, alas! the next day was a picture of the past. A slave—cramped and smothered amid the crowd that soaked so long in the salt water at our boat's bottom—died during the darkness. Next morning, the same low, leaden, coffin-lid sky, hung like a pall over sea and shore. Wind in terrific blasts, and rain in deluging squalls, howled and beat on us. Come what might, I resolved not to stir. All day I kept my people beneath the sails, with orders to move their limbs as much as possible, in order to overcome the benumbing effect of moisture and packed confinement. The incessant drenching from sea and sky to which they had been so long subjected, chilled their slackened circulation to such a degree that death from torpor seemed rapidly supervening.

Motion, motion, motion, was my constant command; but I hoarded my alcohol for the last resource.

I saw that no time was to be lost, and that nothing but a bold encounter of hazard would save either lives or property. Before dark my mind was made up as to the enterprise. I would land in the neighbourhood of the colony, and cross its territory during the shadow of night.

I do not suppose that the process by which I threw my stiffened crew on the beach, and revived them with copious draughts of brandy, would interest the reader; but midnight did not strike before my cargo, under the escort of Kroo guides, was boldly marched through the colonial town, and safe on its way to New Sestros! Fortunately for my daredevil adventure, the tropical rain poured down in ceaseless torrents, compelling the unsuspicious colonists to keep beneath their roofs. Indeed, no one dreamed of a forced march by human beings on that dreadful night of tempest, else it might have gone hard had I been detected in the desecration of colonial soil. Still, I was prepared for all emergencies. I never went abroad without the two great keys of Africa— gold and firearms; and had it been my lot to encounter a colonist, he would either have learned the value of silence, or have been carried along, under the muzzle of a pistol, till the gang was in safety.

While it was still dark, I left the caravan advancing by an interior path to Little Bassa, where one of my branches could furnish it with necessaries to cross the other colony of Bassa San Juan, so as to reach my homestead in the course of three days. Meanwhile I retraced my way to Monrovia, and reaching it by sunrise, satisfied the amiable colonists that I had just taken shelter in their harbour, and was fresh from my dripping cutter. It is very likely that no one in the colony to the present day knows the true story of this adventure, or would believe it unless confessed by me.

30 SIR HARRY JOHNSTON
JAJA, NANA, AND RESISTANCE TO BRITISH CONTROL

Serious resistance to the encroachment of European power in West Africa was surprisingly slight. Two exceptions were the redoubtable Jaja, King of Opobo, and Nana, Governor of the Benin River region. Jaja was an ex-slave whose exceptional ability, ruthlessness, and instinct for survival enabled him to assume the title of head of the Anna Pepple House of Bonny * in 1863. He went on to establish the rival state of Opobo in 1869. By 1873 King Jaja had broken the power of Bonny and had made Opobo the most important state in the Niger delta (Oil Rivers) region. Although he had sent a contingent to help the British in their war with Ashanti in 1875, relations between Jaja and England steadily deteriorated. As the principal middleman of the delta, whose power and wealth depended on maintaining his strategic position between the source of palm oil and the European buyers, Jaja vigorously opposed free trade and strenuously sought to protect his source of supply by excluding European traders. The European merchants reacted by forming the African Association Limited to break the monopoly. The British government reacted by deporting Jaja to the West Indies in 1887. He was allowed to return in 1891 but died during the homeward journey.

Nana was even more vigorous than Jaja in his resistance to the British. In 1891 the British extended their control of the Oil Rivers protectorate to include the Itsekiri territory. The Itsekiri continued to regard Nana as their leader; moreover, he continued his trade monopoly on the Benin River and carried on a surreptitious slave trade. The British set out to break his monopoly and to open the river to traders. Nana resisted until he was overwhelmed by British reinforcements and his headquarters at Brohemie was captured. He was deported to the Gold Coast.

Sir Harry Hamilton Johnston (1858–1927) was one of England's leading amd most knowledgeable Africanists. Subsequent to his visit to Tunis in 1879 at the age of twenty-one, he made Africa the great interest of his life. He visited Angola and the Congo between 1882 and 1883 and Mount Kilimanjaro in 1884 and became a student of African languages, fauna, and flora. He admired Stanley and Livingstone and worked assiduously to promote British influence in Africa. He was appointed Vice-Consul of the Oil Rivers protectorate in 1885 and hastened British encroachment by subduing Jaja. In 1888 he was appointed British Consul to Portuguese East Africa, and in this capacity he repressed the Arab slave traders, made treaties, and declared the region that is now Malawi and Zambia a British protectorate. From 1891 to 1896 he served as the British Commissioner for South Central Africa and organized the administration of Nyasaland. In 1897 he was appointed Consul General of Tunisia and in 1899 was made Special Commissioner to Uganda. He was instrumental in adding about 400,000 square miles of the African continent to the British Empire. The following account of Jaja and Nana is, of course, from Johnston's point of view. We do not possess the reaction of his antagonists.

From *The Story of My Life* by Sir Harry H. Johnston, Copyright, 1923 by The Bobbs-Merrill Company, Inc., R. 1951 by J. G. Deedes, reprinted by permission of the publishers.
* A "house" was a small trading corporation that often was a quasi-political entity. In Bonny, a great deal of competition existed between two such houses—the Anna Pepple and the Manilla Pepple.

Whilst I was surveying the intricate network of streams between Calabar and the Cameroons, [the British—ed.] Consul Hewett was (very reluctantly) handing over to the Germans the erstwhile British possession of Cameroons Mountain and the Victoria township. When we both regained Old Calabar he was so ill he had to be carried on board a steamer and leave for England. He installed me as Acting Consul for the Bights of Biafra and Benin—the Oil Rivers, as we were beginning to call the vast Niger Delta, between Lagos and the Cameroons. I had now the opportunity of solving its knottiest problems which Hewett had envisaged but had lacked the physical health to disentangle and clear up. The most important of these difficulties was the position and rights of the chief settled near the mouth of the Opobo River—the famous Jaja.

Jaja had begun life as the slave of the King or one of the chiefs of Bonny. I could never ascertain decidedly what part of the Niger Delta had given him birth, but I think he was an Ibo, from Bende, and was sold as a slave when he was twelve years old. During the 'fifties and 'sixties he had become noteworthy by his ability. In the 'seventies he seems to have definitely settled down on the banks of the Opobo, a river which though it has several estuarine creek connections with the main Niger was derived from independent sources in the Ibo country. From being a trusted slave trading for his master Jaja rose to the position of an independent chieftain. The British war vessels visited his town occasionally; their commanders found him intelligent and hospitable, he gave them amusing entertainments and elaborate feasts. Among other extraordinary persons attracted to his "court" was an American Negress from Liberia: Emma Jaja Johnson, as she styled herself. I don't think she was ever a wife of Jaja: she was elderly and very plain. But she had become his secretary, after being governess to his children. Yet she looked into

his theory of dispute with the Consuls and told him he had no "case."

The point was this: Jaja, early in his history as an independent chieftain—for he had been recognized as such by Consul Livingstone [1] who made a treaty with him in 1873—wished to constitute palm oil and palm kernels throughout all his domain his own monopoly. He would farm the palm forests of the interior, be the sole seller of their oil products, and compensate the natives who brought in the oil or the kernels. He in fact would do all the trade; and as he had fixed a price at which the European merchants could buy these things from him, he resented the fluctuations in value of palm oil in the European market and the consequent occasional change of purchase price on the part of the merchants. After several years of disputes, he selected one firm with an agency at Opobo—Messrs. A. Miller Brothers of Glasgow—and sent all the oil to them.

No doubt the large and constant quantity he placed at their disposal compensated them for the slightly increased cost in the purchase; or they may have hoped that if the other firms had to abandon Opobo and they secured the monopoly they might bring Jaja to reason regarding the selling price. At any rate they had had in force a monopoly of oil purchase for some two years in the Opobo district, which materially increased the prosperity of their firm.

Amongst the questions to be solved was the area of Jaja's territory. If it were only ten square miles from the coast inland and could be fixed at that, it might have been better worth while to consider this ten square miles as being Jaja's personal property, his "farm," the produce of which he could dispose of as he pleased. But the Opobo River and its mouth with a "good" bar was the port for all the eastern portion of the Niger Delta, east of

[1] Charles Livingstone the brother of David who was given this consulate after the Zambezi Expedition.

Bonny and west of the Cross River (Old Calabar).

Jaja had been spending a proportion of his great wealth on the purchase of many rifles—it was said he had four thousand —and several small field pieces, and was from month to month making himself the great Chief of the eastern half of the Niger Delta. He was seeking to become the overlord of the vigorous Ibo people behind his swamps, and had begun to send armed men to form garrisons on all the river mouths between Opobo and the Cross River. In fact when I arrived at the Niger Delta in 1885 and took stock of the situation I decided there were two powerful native states with whom one had to deal carefully: The kingdom of Benin on the west—with its important coast viceroyalty under the chief Nana; and Opobo, under Jaja, to the east of the main river. I had no quarrel with Nana or Benin, perhaps because before I visited them I had settled the Opobo question; but Jaja represented the whole crisis of our Protectorate over southern Nigeria: our attempt to establish freedom of trade.

As soon as Consul Hewett had gone and I had attended to matters of pressing business at Old Calabar I went to Opobo in July, 1887. On the east bank of the estuary were five Liverpool firms, members of The African Association of Liverpool; on the west bank was one, Messrs. A. Miller Brothers of Glasgow. Jaja's chief town was on the west bank, several miles from its mouth. The five firms had been obstructed in commerce for a year or more because they wanted to trade direct with the native producers of the oil and not through Jaja, at Jaja's prices. The five firms in question belonged as I have said to The African Association of Liverpool. Miller Brothers in those days stood apart, independent of any League or Association, though they were credited with possessing an understanding with the Royal Niger Company. The firms of The African Association had a year or two previously brought out to Opobo

steam launches or little river steamers. They proposed sending these to the inland markets, near the plantations of oil palms, and therewith purchasing and transporting to the port at the mouth of the Opobo the palm oil and palm kernels of the interior beyond the mangrove swamps.

Jaja answered this movement by barring the way to navigation with booms slung across the river where it narrowed and digging narrow canals for the passage of his trading canoes; and when I had purposely struck into the worst of these booms and ordered its removal as an illegal bar to the navigation of the Niger rivers he further obstructed trade by threatening the Ibo and Kwo peoples with punishment if they should bring their oil for sale anywhere else than to his market places or (possibly) to Messrs. Miller Brothers' house.

Jaja looked upon Consul Hewett's departure as a moral victory: he considered he had driven him home and that it would be easy further to establish his position by giving a handsome entertainment to the British war vessels which might occasionally visit the river mouth and hear of the restiveness of the five firms excluded from the local trade. My arrival came as a disagreeable surprise, enhanced by my youthful appearance. At first he declined even to discuss the matter, telling me my "father," Consul Hewett, had gone home and that he could only resume the discussion when he returned. I showed him however one or two despatches from the Foreign Office asking for a full report on the Opobo difficulty and pointed out that they were addressed to me personally as Acting Consul. Moreover I had come to the Opobo River in a gunboat, the *Goshawk,* under Lieut.-Commander Pelly who stayed with me till the end of the controversy.

J. H. Pelly was what I used to call "an unmitigated trump." As his name is no longer in *Who's Who,* I fear he must be dead; for he won distinction later on in the

Persian Gulf which caused his name to be recorded in that compendium. He was short of stature, tight-lipped, twinkling-eyed, and very—quietly—determined. He was either a teetotaller or nearly so, and always spruce in his dress and tidy in his ship. He was no fool and required to be satisfied about the justice of any case in which he was asked to interfere. The *Goshawk* was a little, old-fashioned, slow-steaming gunboat, but he effected wonders with her. His officers and men seemed always in the pink of health and the best condition. He was the British Navy at its very best.

Captain Hand of the *Royalist* was the senior naval officer in command on the West African station and he met me in Opobo and lent me considerable assistance, making a journey with me under much discomfort and some danger to the verge of the Ibo country to satisfy himself that Jaja was really causing the alleged obstruction and monopoly in the palm oil trade. But without definite instructions from the Admiralty he would not undertake any coercive and punitory action, though he fully endorsed the views I expressed. Other coast business carried him away for a few weeks; and his departure having encouraged Jaja in the belief that there were divided counsels and a difference of opinion, the latter proceeded to more violent measures to enforce his monopoly of trade and obstruction to water passage through his territory. At last wishing to nip his scheme in two before he could assemble all his widely scattered forces and retire with them to the Ibo country, I applied to the Foreign Office for permission to bring matters to an issue and either persuade Jaja to go with me to the Gold Coast Colony and there have his case tried, or declare him to be at war with the British Government and then take action against him.

I waited at Bonny for the answer. In those days the ocean cable had only got as far toward the Oil Rivers as the mouth of the Bonny River, forty miles from Opobo. The creeks through which one had to pass between the two places were much too narrow or shallow for the passage of a gunboat or any ship; the journey could only be made by native canoes. I appreciated fully all the risks of being caught by Jaja's people and quietly "put away." But fortunately I had sometime previously made friends with the very civilized King of Bonny, who spoke and wrote English like an Englishman and dressed as we do. The kingdom of Bonny had once ruled over Opobo, and Jaja had been one of the king's slaves. Some unfortunate intervention of Consul Livingstone had recognized Jaja's independence and prevented Bonny administration of the affairs of Opobo. I managed however to enter into communication with the young king, whose great-grandfather had been converted to Christianity,[2] and he sent a State canoe of his own to fetch me and to take me back.

I despatched my telegram and a few hours afterwards—"very quick response!" I thought—received what I naturally took to be the answer: "Your action with regard to Jaja approved. Further instructions will be sent after communication with Admiralty."

Accordingly I returned to Opobo under the protection of King George Pepple and prepared for action. I summoned Jaja to a meeting at Messrs. Harrison's house (my headquarters) or, if he preferred it, on the beach outside, where I would read to him my decision and invite his acceptance. I gave him my word that if he *refused* my conditions he should be allowed to return to his town before any act of hostility took place.

He came, with many canoes and an armed escort of seven hundred warriors, each with a Snider rifle.

I reviewed the circumstances of this long struggle between him and the Consu-

---

[2] His conversion made a great sensation in Evangelical London in the 'forties, and Bonny in the main was the original of Dickens' "Borriaboola Gha."

lar authority and stated there was only one way of arriving at a solution, outside a resort to arms: that he should proceed to Accra on a mail-steamer with a few attendants, that I should accompany him; and there the case between us should be tried by a person to be appointed by the British Government. To every one's surprise he assented and went quietly on board H. M. S. *Goshawk.* I followed. The *Goshawk* took us to Bonny where we transferred ourselves to a mail-steamer which in two or three days landed us at Accra. Oddly enough, during our passage to Accra I noted "Jaja has never shown such friendliness toward me before. All through the daytime he is my constant companion. He will sit by my side while I am writing and amuse himself by looking over my sketch book and asking questions as to its contents. He occupies the Ladies' cabin on board the steamer, with his wife, Patience, and his housekeeper and amanuensis, Emma Jaja Johnson. He is further accompanied by a cook, a steward, three servants and one Accra carpenter."

To Jaja the sight of Accra (the first civilized town he had seen) was a source of wonderment and for a time distracted his thoughts from his own troubles; so much so that he intimated to the Administrator of the Gold Coast (Col. Frederick White) that if he were sentenced to be exiled from Opobo to Accra he would be quite content, being an old man. Either he had never looked much at the pictures of cities given in the English illustrated papers, or had judged Europe to exist on a wholly different plan to Africa.

Admiral Sir Walter Hunt-Grubbe, Naval Commander-in-Chief on the Cape of Good Hope and West African station, had been appointed to try Jaja for his breaches of treaty and to investigate his case generally, but he could not arrive immediately at Accra; so having much other business to attend, I went back to Opobo and Old Calabar. I returned to the Gold Coast at the close of November, 1887. Sir Walter Hunt-Grubbe gave Jaja a very fair trial, spent, indeed, several days beforehand mastering all the written and printed evidence. At the conclusion of his investigation he found the old man guilty on three counts of the breaches of treaty with which he was charged; on the fourth count the accusation was not fully proved. Jaja was therefore deposed, and no succeeding chief of Opobo was to be elected; Jaja was further sentenced to a banishment of five years from his country, and a choice of residence offered him—either in the British West Indies, St. Helena, Ascension, or Cape Colony. He chose St. Vincent in the Windward Islands.

Those of my readers who have long memories may remember that Lord Salisbury pardoned him after four years' residence at St. Vincent, that he was returning thence to Opobo, but fell ill on the voyage and died at one of the Canary Islands. His wealth, which must have been considerable, was secured to him, and during his exile the district of Opobo made him an allowance at the rate of £1000 a year. So that I do not think he could be regarded as harshly treated. And the quick result of my intervention was an enormous increase in Opobo trade, on the part of the natives as well as of the Europeans.

The settlement of this test case—a case watched from all points of the Protectorate coast—ended the tyranny of the "middle-man" which had been the great obstacle to a wide development of trade in the vast Niger Delta for a hundred years.

.   .   .

My final objective in the Delta before making preparations to return home on leave was a visit to the Benin River, to search for the unused balance of presents brought out for treaty-making by Consul Hewett, to enquire into the complaints of British traders, and if possible to visit Benin City and see the King of Benin. The gunboat which conveyed me thither from Old Calabar was to enter the Forcados mouth of the Niger and explore the various channels leading to the Benin River. The direct entrance to this estuary had a bad bar, and the discovery of the indirect approach by the Forcados mouth, the Warri and Sapele creeks (which in an eastern direction communicated with the main Niger) quite changed the commercial prospects of the Benin traders and accentuated the idea of getting into direct communication with the King of Benin who up till then had signed no treaty with us.

This remarkable native state in those days and later much inspired my curiosity. What was there in its geography and its people which should have generated its striking development of art in metal-working and design, and have made it the one powerful native state in the vicinity of the Niger Delta? One read of no similar kingdom in all southern Nigeria, Lagos, or the Cameroons. Benin had been of alluring fame since the fifteenth century, when it was visited by the Portuguese who were faithfully portrayed in their costumes and their armature of cross-bows and bell-mouthed guns by the Negro artists in bronze. When in the early part of the nineteenth century attempts were made to find the outlet of the Niger several of these explorations were commenced by way of Benin City. Yet access to Benin for several centuries had not been easy, geographically or politically. The Bini people proper inhabited the region between the Ovia River on the northwest and the Jamieson stream to the southeast; but east and south of the Jamieson River were the Sobo and Warri tribes which spoke dialects related to the Bini language and had probably been subject to Bini rule a century ago. The coast district west of the Benin River estuary was till about 1893 subject to the semi-independent rule of a Jekri or Ijo chief named Nana, usually called the Viceroy of the King of Benin.

Nana before 1888 was deemed to be a very truculent personage by the traders. I went to the coast settlements at the mouth of the Benin River to meet him in the winter of 1887–8, and found him different to the traders' descriptions: he was a fine-looking Negro, dressed in somewhat Muhammadan fashion in flowing garments. I investigated his complaints and found them in most cases justified. The trading houses came to an agreement with him and it was understood that the interior markets under Nana's control were open to them. Nana then gave me an invitation to come and see him at his town in the interior (Ogbobin?). I decided to trust myself to him, and accordingly was taken up to this place in a magnificently arrayed canoe. I was greatly astonished at its large buildings of white-washed clay, neatly thatched, its broad and well-swept streets and the good order of its population. I was lodged in a really comfortable house where he fed me with well-cooked meals, and in the afternoons and evenings entertained me with interesting and sometimes spectacular displays of athletic sports and dancing. It was almost like taking a part on the stage in a fantastic ballet. Hundreds of women dressed in silks and velvets and armed with large long-handled fans of horse-hide or antelope-hide executed elaborate and on the whole decorous dances. Perfect order was maintained. A full moon lit up the strange scenes which were also aglow with rosy light from the immense bonfires.

I have seldom enjoyed more any African experience than my visit to Nana: the comfort of my lodging, the good, well-cooked food, the ordered quiet; his politeness and regard for the value of time. He himself talked fairly fluently "Coast" English, so that intelligent conversation was possible with him. In addition he was a considerable African linguist in the tongues of the Niger Delta. He was greatly interested in my attempt to write down these languages; and far more intelligent in African philology than most of the white men (save missionaries) in the Niger Delta. I wished I had made his acquaintance a year earlier as he would have been a valuable adviser in Delta politics. Consequently it was with much surprise and disappointment that I learned some five years later of his having got into conflict with the Administration of south-ern Nigeria, possibly in connection with the Benin reluctance to open up treaty relations. The Protectorate Administration banished Nana from his "viceroyalty" for a number of years; but I fancy he was at length allowed to return, a broken man, and he is probably dead by now from old age. I hail him with friendliness across an interval of thirty-four years!

31 MARY KINGSLEY
THE CROWN COLONY SYSTEM IN WEST AFRICA

Mary Kingsley (1862–1900) was one of the most remarkable women travelers of Victorian times. A niece of the famous novelist Charles Kingsley, she first visited the West African coast in 1893, when she developed her method of traveling like an African trader, subsisting on local food and living among the people of the regions through which she passed. She traveled in Angola, the Belgian Congo, and the French Congo. She returned to West Africa in 1895, intending to travel up the Niger and Benue rivers. However, she changed her plans and proceeded up the Ogoué River in Gabon, after which she visited German Kamerun. Her Travels in West Africa *was first published in 1897 and was widely read. Both this book and her second book,* West African Studies, *were widely influential in changing the attitudes of European administrators toward their African subjects and laying the foundation for today's scientific anthropological study of Africa. Her sympathy, understanding, and enthusiasm for Africa and its inhabitants did much to make Europeans approach Africans with a willingness to understand them rather than simply to dismiss them as inferior savages.*

Wherein is set down briefly in what manner of ways the Crown Colony system works evil in Western Africa.

I have attempted to state that the Crown Colony system is unsuited for governing Western Africa, and have attributed its malign influence to its being a system which primarily expresses the opinions of well-intentioned but ill-informed officials at home, instead of being, according to the usual English type of institution, representative of the interests of the people who are governed, and

From Mary H. Kingsley, *West African Studies* (New York, 1899), pp. 267–275.

of those who have the largest stake in the countries controlled by it—the merchants and manufacturing classes of England. It remains to point out how it acts adversely to the prosperity of all concerned; for be it clearly understood there is no corruption in it whatsoever: there is waste of men's lives, moneys, and careers, but nothing more at present. By and by it will add to its other charms and functions that of being, in the early future, a sort of patent and successful incubator for hatching a fine lively brood of little Englanders, who will cry out, "What is the good of West Africa?" and so forth; and they will seem sweetly reasonable, because by then

West Africa will be down on the English rates, a pauper.

It may seem inconceivable, however, that the present governing body of West Africa, the home officials, and the English public as represented in Parliament, can be ill-informed. West Africa has not been just shot up out of the ocean by a submarine volcanic explosion; nor are we landing on it out of Noah's ark, for the thing has been in touch with Europe since the fifteenth century; yet, inconceivable as it may seem that there is not by now formulated and in working order a method of governing it suitable for its nature, the fact that this is so remains, and providentially for us it is quite easy of explanation without abusing any one; though no humane person, like myself for example, can avoid sincerely hoping that Mr. Kipling is wrong when he sings

Deep in all dishonour have we stained our garments' hem.
Yet be ye not dismayed, we have stumbled and have strayed.
Our leaders went from righteousness, the Lord will deal with them.

For although it is true that we have made a mess of this great feeding ground for England's manufacturing millions; yet there are no leaders on whom blame alone can fall, whom we can make scapegoats out of, who can be driven away into the wilderness carrying the sins of the people. The blame lies among all those classes of people who have had personally to deal with West Africa and the present system; and the Crown Colony system and the resolution of '65 are merely the necessary fungi of rotten stuff, for they have arisen from the information that has been, and has not been, placed at the disposal of our Government in England by the Government officials of West Africa, the Missionaries, and the Traders.[1]

We will take the traders' . blame first—their contribution to the evil dates from about 1827, and consists in omission—frankly, I think that they, in their generation, were justified in not telling all they could tell about the Coast. They found they could get on with it, keep it quiet and manage the natives fairly well under the system of Courts of Equity in the Rivers, and the Committee of merchants with a Governor approved of by the Home Government, which was working on the Gold Coast up to 1843. In 1841 there arose the affair of Governor Maclean, and the inauguration of the line of policy which resulted in the resolution of 1865. The governmental officials having cut themselves off from the traders and taken over West Africa, failed to manage West Africa, and so resolved that West Africa was not worth managing—a thing they are bound to do again.

The abuse showered on the merchants, and the terrific snubs with which the Government peppered them, did not make the traders blossom and expand, and shower information on those who criticised them—there are some natures that are not sweetened by Adversity. Moreover, the Government, when affairs had been taken over by the Offices in London, took the abhorrent form of Customs, and displayed a lively love of the missionary-made African, as he was then—you can read about him in Burton—and for the rest got up rows with the traders' best customer, the untutored African; rows, as the traders held, unnecessary in their beginning and feeble-handed in their termination. The whole of this sort of thing made the trader section keep all the valuable information to itself, and spend its en-

[1] In 1865 a Select Committee of the House of Commons considering British policy toward the coast of Guinea felt that Britain had acquired greater obligations than could be justified by her interests. The committee recommended that the administration of the Gold Coast, Lagos, and Gambia be united under the governor of Sierra Leone; that Britain decline to extend its rule or protection over African territories; and that Britain should urge Africans under British protection to prepare for self-government. The recommendations were adopted by the British government (ed.).

ergies in eluding the Customs, and talking what Burton terms "Commercial English."

Then we come to the contribution made by the Government officials to the formation of an erroneous opinion concerning the state of affairs in West Africa. This arose from the conditions that surrounded them there, and the way in which they were unable, even if they desired, to expand their influence, distrusted naturally enough by the trading community since 1865, held in continuously by their home instructions, and unprovided with a sufficient supply of men or money on shore to go in for empire making, and also villainously badly quartered—as you can see by reading Ellis's *West African Sketches.* It is small wonder and small blame to them that their account of West Africa has been a gloomy one, and such it must remain until these men are under a different system: for all the reasons that during the past have caused them to paint the Coast as a place of no value to England, remain still in full force—as you can see by studying the disadvantages that service in a West African Crown Colony presents to-day to a civilian official.

Firstly, the climate is unhealthy, so that the usual make of Englishman does not like to take his wife out to the Coast with him. This means keeping two homes, which is expensive, and it gives a man no chance of saving money on an income say of £600 a year, for the official's life in West Africa is necessarily, let him be as economical as he may, an expensive one; and, moreover, things are not made more cheerful for him by his knowing that if he dies there will be no pension for his wife.

Secondly, there being no regular West African Service, there is no security for promotion; owing to the unhealthiness of the climate it is very properly ordained that each officer shall serve a year on the Coast, and then go home on a six months' furlough. It is a fairly common thing for a man to die before his twelve months' term is up, and a still more common one

for him to have to go on sick leave. Of course, the moment he is off, some junior official has to take his place and do his work. But in the event of the man whose work he does dying, gaining a position in another region, or promotion, the man who has been doing the work has no reason to hope he will step into the full emoluments and honours of the appointment, although experience will thus have given him an insight into the work. On the contrary, it too often happens that some new man, either fresh from London or who has already held a Government appointment in some totally different region to the West African, is placed in the appointment. If this new man is fresh to such work as he has to do, the displaced man has to teach him; if he is from a different region, he usually won't be taught, and he does not help to develop a spirit of general brotherly love and affection in the local governmental circles by the frank statement that he considers West African officials "jugginses" or "muffs," although he freely offers to "alter this and show them how things ought to be done."

Then again the civilian official frequently complains that he has no such recognition given him for his services as is given to the military men in West Africa. I have so often heard the complaint, "Oh, if a man comes here and burns half a dozen villages he gets honours; while I, who keep the villages from wanting burning, get nothing;" and, mind you, this is true. Like the rest of my sex I suffer from a chronic form of scarlet fever, and, from a knowledge of the country there, I hold it rubbish to talk of the brutality of mowing down savages with a Maxim gun when it comes to talking of West African bush fighting; for your West African is not an unarmed savage, he does not assemble in the manner of Dr. Watts's ants, but wisely ensconces himself in the pleached arbours of his native land, and lets fly at you with a horrid scatter gun. This is bound to hit, and when it hits makes wounds worse than those made by a Maxim; in fact he quite turns bush fighting into a legitimate sport, let alone the service done him by his great ally, the climate. Still, it is hard on the civilian, and bad for English interests in West Africa that the man who by his judgment, sympathy, and care, keeps a district at peace, should have less recognition than one who, acting under orders, doing his duty gallantly, and all that, goes and breaks up all native prosperity and white trade.

All these things acting together produce on the local Government official a fervid desire to get home to England, or obtain an appointment in some other region than the West Coast. I feel sure I am well within the mark when I say that two-thirds of the present Government officials in the West African English Crown Colonies have their names down on the transfer list, or are trying to get them there; and this sort of thing simply cannot give them an enthusiasm for their work sufficient to ensure its success, and of course leads to their painting a dismal picture of West Africa itself.

I am perfectly well aware that the conditions of life of officials in West Africa are better than those described by Ellis. Nevertheless, they are not yet what they should be: a corrugated iron house may cost a heap of money and yet not be a Paradise. I am also aware that the houses and general supplies given to our officials are immensely more luxurious than those given to German or French officials; but this does not compensate for the horrors of boredom suffused with irritation to which the English official is subjected. More than half the quarrelling and discontent for which English officials are celebrated, and which are attributed to drink and the climate, simply arise from the domestic arrangements enforced on them in Coast towns, whereby they see far too much of each other. If you take any set of men and make them live together, day out and day in, without sufficient ex-

ercise, without interest in outside affairs, without dividing them up into regular grades of rank, as men are on board ship or in barracks, you are simply bound to have them dividing up into cliques that quarrel; the things they quarrel over may seem to an outsider miserably petty, but these quarrels are the characteristic eruption of the fever discontent. And may I ask you if the opinion of men in such a state is an opinion on which a sound policy wherewith to deal with so complex a region can be formed? I think not, yet these men and the next class alone are the makers of our present policy—the instructors of home official opinion.

The next class is the philanthropic party. It is commonly confused with the missionary, but there is this fundamental difference between them. The missionary, pure and simple, is a man who loves God more than he loves himself, or any man. His service (I am speaking on fundamental lines, as far as I can see) is to place in God's charge, for the glory of God, souls that, according to his belief, would otherwise go elsewhere. The philanthropist is a person who loves man; but he or she is frequently no better than people who kill lapdogs by over-feeding, or who shut up skylarks in cages; while it is quite conceivable to me, for example, that a missionary could kill a man to save his soul, a philanthropist kills his soul to save his life, and there is in this a difference. I have never been able to get up any respectful enthusiasm for the so-called philanthropist, so that I have to speak of him with calm care; not as I have spoken of the missionary, feeling he was a person I could not really harm by criticising his methods.

It is, however, nowadays hopeless to attempt to separate these two species, distinct as I believe them to be; and they together undoubtedly constitute what is called the Mission party not only in England but in Germany. I believe this alliance has done immense harm to the true missionary, for to it I trace that tendency to harp upon horrors and general sensationalism which so sharply differentiates the modern from the classic missionary reports. Take up that noble story of Dennis de Carli and Michael Angelo of Gattina, and read it through, and then turn on to wise, clear-headed Merolla da Sorrento, and read him; you find there no sensationalism. Now and again, when deeply tried, they will say, "These people live after a beastly manner, and converse freely with the Devil," but you soon find them saying, "Among these people there are some excellent customs," and they give you full details of them, with evident satisfaction. You see it did not fundamentally matter to these early missionaries whether their prospective converts "had excellent customs" or "lived after a beastly manner," from a religious standpoint. Not one atom—they were the sort of men who would have gone for Plato, Socrates, and all the Classics gaily, holding that they were not Christians as they ought to be; but this never caused them to paint a distorted portrait of the African. This thing, I believe, the modern philanthropist has induced the modern missionary only too frequently to do, and the other regrettable element which has induced him to do it has been the apathy of the English public, a public which unless it were stirred up by horrors would not subscribe. Again the blame is with England at home, but the harm done is paid for in West Africa. The portrait painted of the African by the majority, not all, but the majority of West African mission reports, has been that of a child, naturally innocent, led away and cheated by white traders and grievously oppressed by his own rulers. I grant you, the African taken as a whole is the gentlest kind of real human being that is made. I do not however class him with races who carry gentleness to a morbid extent, and for governmental purposes you must not with any race rely on their main characteristic alone; for example, Englishmen are honest, yet still we require the police force.

The evil worked by what we must call the missionary party is almost incalculable; from it has arisen the estrangement of English interests, as represented by our reason for adding West Africa to our Empire at all—the trader—and the English Government as represented by the Crown Colony system; and it has also led to our present policy of destroying powerful native States and the power of the African ruling classes at large. Secondarily it is the cause of our wars in West Africa. That this has not been and is not the desire of the Mission party it is needless to say; that the blame is directly due to the Crown Colony system it is as needless to remark; for any reasonable system of its age would long ere now have known the African at first hand, not as it knows him, and knows him only, at its headquarters, London, from second-hand vitiated reports. It has, nowadays, at its service the common sense and humane opinions of the English trade lords as represented by the Chambers of Commerce of Liverpool and Manchester; but though just at present it listens to what they say—thanks to Mr. Chamberlain—yet it cannot act on their statements, but only querulously says, "Your information does not agree with our information." Allah forbid that the information of the party with whom I have had the honour to be classed should agree with that sort of information from other sources; and I would naturally desire the rulers of West Africa to recognise the benefit they now enjoy of having information of a brand that has not led to such a thing as the Sierra Leone outbreak for example, and to remember in this instance that six months before the hut tax there was put on, the Chambers had strongly advised the Government against it, and had received in reply the answer that "The Secretary of State sees no reason to suppose that the hut tax will be oppressive, or that it will be less easy to collect in Sierra Leone than in Gambia." Why, you could not get a prophetic almanac into a second issue if it were not based on truer knowledge than that which made it possible for such a thing to be said. Nevertheless, no doubt this remarkable sentence was written believing the same to be true, and confiding in the information in the hands of the Colonial Office from the official and philanthropic sources in which the Office believes.

32 SIR FREDERICK GORDON GUGGISBERG
THE EDUCATION OF THE AFRICAN

Sir Frederick Gordon Guggisberg (1869–1930) was appointed Governor of the Gold Coast in 1919. He had been Director of Surveys, Southern Nigeria, since April 1, 1910 and was made Acting Survey-General of Nigeria in 1912. In mid-1914 it was proposed that he be made Director of Public Works in the Gold Coast colony. However, he went on leave in 1914 before filling this post and was never recalled. He subsequently returned to the Gold Coast full of interest and enthusiasm and guided by a spirit of idealism regarding Africa's future. His main object was "the general progress of the people of the Gold Coast towards a higher state of civilization, and the keystone of the progress is education." One of his first acts as Governor was to appoint a committee to study the educational system of the colony. Shortly thereafter the committee drafted, in collaboration with the Education Department and the missions, a master plan for education in the Gold Coast, which provided the foundation for the educational policy that made the modernization of the Gold Coast possible and subsequently made the independence of Ghana a reality.

NECESSITY FOR BETTER EDUCATION OF THE AFRICAN

Wherever one turns in the Gold Coast one meets the same demand—a better education for Africans than our present schools are capable of providing. Apart from the fact that the people themselves are clamouring for a better education, the future of the country demands it. In the Government Service alone the need is urgent; the development of the country is progressing so rapidly that we can no longer afford the proportionately larger number of Europeans required to deal with the work, for their long leave, their steamer-passages, and the higher rates of salary due to their employment in what can never be a "White Man's Country" are prohibitive. Government has definitely adopted the

From Brigadier-General Sir Frederick Gordon Guggisberg, *The Keystone* (London, 1924), pp. 5–12.

policy of employing Africans in appointments hitherto held by Europeans provided that the former are equally qualified in education, ability, *and character,* but progress in carrying out this policy is slow owing to the scarcity of suitably qualified Africans. When, besides the need of Government, that of the European firms —mercantile, banking, and professional —is considered, it is apparent that there is a great field for the employment of well-educated Africans throughout the country.

More important still is the demand of the educated African of the existing literate classes for an education and training that will fit him to take a greater share in the development of his own land. We have not to look far for the reason. To begin with, the southern portions of the Gold Coast have been in closer contact with European civilization for a far longer period than any other of Britain's West African colonies. In the second place, our great agricultural wealth and trade are far greater in proportion to our size and population than those of almost any other tropical unit of the British Empire. Our financial resources have, in comparison with our area, enabled us to cover the country with communications far more completely than has yet been found possible in countries possessing an equally productive soil and greater population. The annual increase of trade has naturally been accompanied by a steady increase of wealth until to-day we are far richer per head of the population than any of our neighbours. Now, prosperity brings a desire for the better things of life, and when this desire is heightened by the knowledge brought by the steady development of elementary education it is not surprising that there is to-day a rapidly increasing demand for better conditions of living, better sanitation, good water supplies, hospitals and dispensaries, and all the other benefits of modern civilization.

To comply with all these demands, to cope with rapidly changing conditions, Government acting by itself will make insufficient progress; its efforts must be supplemented by African enterprise. Government's duty at present is to lay the foundations of development in every direction, to organise the departmental machinery necessary for dealing with each system, and to provide such European staff as the revenue permits; while at the same time it must prepare, organise, and bring into being a system of schools where Africans can obtain the better and higher education that will fit them to enter the various trades and professions, both in the public service and in private enterprise.

This question of providing facilities for better education and training bristles with difficulties. There is, as I have said, a universal demand by the people. To comply hastily with this demand at the present moment would be fatal, for the simple reason that we have not got an educational staff sufficiently trained to carry out the work efficiently. To do it inefficiently would be to start on the wrong road, a road along which we should have ultimately to retrace our steps; to trust the future of the race to insufficiently trained leadership in education would be far worse than having no education at all. This, then, is our immediate task—the provision of well-trained teachers, instructors, and professors from among the Africans. Until we have done that we shall not be able to improve our present system of elementary education sufficiently to enable full use to be made of the secondary schools that we propose to start. Nor will the Africans themselves, who from time to time have initiated schemes for the provision of higher education by private enterprise, be able—no matter what funds they may raise—to carry out their intentions in a manner conducive to the ultimate success of their country without more and better trained teachers of their own nationality.

Higher education by itself will not solve the problem of the country. It must be accompanied by a better system of training in handicrafts, agriculture, and all those trades that go to provide for the necessities of a community; for although higher education may be the brain of a country, its productive capacity is its heart. Of what use is the brain if the heart ceases to beat? The education of the brain and the training of the hand, *each accompanied by the moulding of the mind,* must proceed together if success is to be sure.

The moulding of the mind! That is too important a subject to deal with here; it deserves—and receives in this booklet—a chapter to itself.

I am well aware of the belief held by some critics—and who has not heard it enunciated?—that the African is not capable of exercising those qualities that will be conferred on him by higher education. Now, whatever may be my own belief

—and I believe my African friends know what that is—there are two sides to every question, so I am going to examine the contention of these critics dispassionately and ask them four questions.

Firstly, have the critics ever considered that character-training—the essential factor in every branch of education but the all-essential factor in higher education—had hitherto been omitted from the African's curriculum, at any rate in Africa? If they have not thought of this, may I ask them to reconsider their belief in the light of what is written in the next chapter? If they persist in their belief, then they deny that a human being can rise from a lower to a higher plane of development and it does not appear to me that they receive the support of history.

Secondly, are they aware that the African races, in spite of the lack of educational facilities, of character-training, have produced men who have distinguished themselves in various walks of life, many intellectually, a number morally? America, where they have long studied the question of African education, has furnished many examples, even under the heavy handicap of "white" opposition to after-employment. Our own African and West Indian colonies furnish others, sufficiently numerous to warrant the belief that, had character-training been in their school curriculum, success would have been wider and more complete.

Thirdly, are the critics aware of the immense field in Africa for the employment of Africans, and if so are they deliberately going to turn men who have an earnest desire for intellectual advancement—and some of whom have shown that they can benefit by it—into a race of malcontents by confining them to the subordinate work of trades and professions?

And lastly, do the critics honestly believe that we have the right to deny the African the chance of proving that his race is capable of doing what other races have done in the past? If so, they have forgotten that Britain stands where she does to-day by giving her peoples and her opponents alike a "sporting chance."

When all is said and done, however, it is to future generations of Africans that we must leave the task of proving that the belief of the critics of their race is wrong, of justifying the confidence placed in them by British Governments of to-day; the present generations, except in isolated instances, cannot do so—they have not had the opportunity of receiving an education and a character-training that fits them for the task.

Other critics have it that, in advocating the provision of a higher education locally for Africans, we are deliberately inviting political troubles in the Gold Coast. Surely the absolute contrary is the case. If politics are to come—and come they must if history is of any value as a guide—surely the safeguard *against* trouble is the local education of the many, accompanied by character-training, rather than the education in Europe of a few, an education that invariably lacks character-training and that more often than not results in bad European habits replacing good African characteristics? If secondary education is not introduced to fill the gap between the English University-trained African and the semi-literate product of our primary schools, we shall be continuing our present system of providing the easy prey of the demagogue that the late Lord Cromer warns us against.

Another criticism is, that in educating Africans to fill higher appointments in the Government service we shall be deliberately interfering with European employment in the Gold Coast. This is a short-sighted view. I have already pointed out that the development of the country necessitates an annual increase in staff. No Government in the world could afford proportionately, the immense financial burden of European salaries, passages and long furloughs that would fall on the Gold Coast if this increase was to consist of Europeans only. Apart from that, the married European with children has not and never will have a real home life in West Africa, whereas there is a great field of employment for him in the good climates of the Dominions. It will be many long years before Africans are fit to fill the higher appointments in the Government service; in the meantime there is ample room for both.

Let there be no mistake, however, about the time of transition of the African peoples from primitive to modern civilization, no false hopes about the rapidity with which they will fit themselves to stand alone. There is no short cut to success; that can only be reached by hard and steady work, by a sustained effort that will try the race as it has not been tried before. A good education and character-training are all that the Government can provide; application, work, and an honest determination to prove himself worthy are the African's share in the general task.

It has been said that we must go slow, that we must not force education on the people. With regard to the last point there is no question of forcing; one has only to see the crowd of applicants for admission surrounding the primary schools of this country at the beginning of every term. As for going slow, we are going too slow. Although it is perfectly true that the races of the Gold Coast are now in a phase through which every other race has had to pass since time immemorial, yet every century sees a quicker rate of advance made by the primitive peoples of the world. Therefore, although we may draw lessons from the past experience of other nations, it is essential that we should move faster, quicker even than the educational authorities did in the days of our youth.

Taking advantage of such lessons as can be dug out of the buried history of the Gold Coast, watching carefully for pitfalls on the road along which we are travelling to-day, striving to see through the mists of the future, we must prepare carefully the better and the higher education of the local races—and their character-training. In no other way shall we fit them to absorb European civilization unhurt—and it is my belief that in no other way shall we keep them permanently the loyal and worthy members of our Empire that they now are.

33 LORD LUGARD
INDIRECT RULE IN TROPICAL AFRICA

Frederick Dealtry Lugard (1858–1945) served in the Indian Army before arriving in East Africa in 1888. Thereafter, he was instrumental in establishing the British presence in Nyasaland, Uganda, and Nigeria. In 1900 he was appointed High Commissioner in Northern Nigeria. As Governor of Northern and Southern Nigeria (1912–1913), he united the two provinces in 1914 and served as the Governor General of Nigeria from 1914 to 1919. He was later appointed to several international commissions with interests in Africa, but he is perhaps best known for the development and implementation of the administrative policy known as "indirect rule." Not only did indirect rule become identified with British colonial rule throughout Africa but it became widely accepted by British colonial officials both in London and overseas "first as a useful administrative device, then that of a political *doctrine, and finally that of a religious dogma."* * *The fundamentals of indirect rule as a method for ruling subject peoples were presented by Lord Lugard in his discussion of the relations between native rulers and the British staff.*

The system adopted in Nigeria is therefore only a particular method of the application of these principles—more especially as regards "advanced communities," and since I am familiar with it I will use it as illustrative of the methods which in my opinion should characterise the dealings of the controlling power with subject races.

The object in view is to make each "Emir" or paramount chief, assisted by his judicial Council, an effective ruler over his own people. He presides over a "Native Administration" organised throughout as a unit of local government. The area over which he exercises jurisdiction is divided into districts under the control of "Headmen," who collect the taxes in the name of the ruler, and pay them into the "Native Treasury," conducted by a native treasurer and staff under the supervision of the chief at his capital. Here, too, is the prison for native court prisoners, and probably the school. . . . Large cities are divided into wards for purposes of control and taxation.

The district headman, usually a territorial magnate with local connections, is the chief executive officer in the area under his charge. He controls the village headmen, and is responsible for the assessment of the tax, which he collects through their agency. He must reside in his district and not at the capital. He is not allowed to pose as a chief with a retinue of his own and duplicate officials, and is summoned from time to time to report to his chief. If, as is the case with some of the ancient Emirates, the community

is a small one but independent of any other native rule, the chief may be his own district headman.

A province under a Resident may contain several separate "Native Administrations," whether they be Moslem Emirates or pagan communities. A "division" under a British District Officer may include one or more headmen's districts, or more than one small Emirate or independent [1] pagan tribe, but as a rule no Emirate is partly in one division and partly in another. The Resident acts as sympathetic adviser and counsellor to the native chief, being careful not to interfere so as to lower his prestige, or cause him to lose interest in his work. His advice on matters of general policy must be followed, but the native ruler issues his own instructions to his subordinate chiefs and district heads—not as the orders of the Resident but as his own—and he is encouraged to work through them, instead of centralising everything in himself—a system which in the past had produced such great abuses. The British District Officers supervise and assist the native district headmen, through whom they convey any instructions to village heads, and make any arrangements necessary for carrying on the work of the Government departments, but all important orders emanate from the Emir, whose messenger usually accompanies and acts as mouthpiece of a District Officer.

The tax—which supersedes all former "tribute," irregular imposts, and forced labour—is, in a sense, the basis of the whole system, since it supplies the means to pay the Emir and all his officials. The district and village heads are effectively supervised and assisted in its assessment

From Frederick Dealtry Lugard, *The Dual Mandate in British Tropical Africa* (London: William Blackwood and Sons Ltd., 1926), pp. 200–207, 209–218. Reprinted by permission.
* Lord Hailey, "Some Problems Dealt with in 'An African Survey,'" *International Affairs,* March–April 1939.

[1] By the term "independent" in this connection is meant "independent of other native control."

by the British staff. The native treasury retains the proportion assigned to it (in advanced communities a half), and pays the remainder into Colonial Revenue.

There are fifty such treasuries in the northern provinces of Nigeria, and every independent chief, however small, is encouraged to have his own. The appropriation by the native administration of market dues, slaughter-house fees, forest licences, &c., is authorised by ordinance, and the native administration receives also the fines and fees of native courts. From these funds are paid the salaries of the Emir and his council, the native court judges, the district and village heads, police, prison warders, and other employees. The surplus is devoted to the construction and maintenance of dispensaries, leper settlements, schools, roads, court-houses, and other buildings. Such works may be carried out wholly or in part by a Government department, if the native administration requires technical assistance, the cost being borne by the native treasury.

The native treasurer keeps all accounts of receipts and expenditure, and the Emir, with the assistance of the Resident, annually prepares a budget, which is formally approved by the Lieut.-Governor.

In these advanced communities the judges of the native courts administer native law and custom, and exercise their jurisdiction independently of the native executive, but under the supervision of the British staff, and subject to the general control of the Emir, whose "Judicial Council" consists of his principal officers of State, and is vested with executive as well as judicial powers. No punishment may be inflicted by a native authority, except through a regular tribunal. The ordinances of government are operative everywhere, but the native authority may make by-laws in modification of native custom—e.g., on matters of sanitation, &c.—and these, when approved by the Governor, are enforced by the native courts.

The authority of the Emir over his own people is absolute, and the profession of an alien creed does not absolve a native from the obligation to obey his lawful orders; but aliens—other than natives domiciled in the Emirate and accepting the jurisdiction of the native authority and courts—are under the direct control of the British staff. Townships are excluded from the native jurisdiction.

The village is the administrative unit. It is not always easy to define, since the security to life and property which has followed the British administration has caused an exodus from the cities and large villages, and the creation of innumerable hamlets, sometimes only of one or two huts, on the agricultural lands. The peasantry of the advanced communities, though ignorant, yet differs from that of the backward tribes in that they recognise the authority of the Emir, and are more ready to listen to the village head and the Council of Elders, on which the Nigerian system is based.

Subject, therefore, to the limitations which I shall presently discuss, the native authority is thus *de facto* and *de jure* ruler over his own people. He appoints and dismisses his subordinate chiefs and officials. He exercises the power of allocation of lands, and with the aid of the native courts, of adjudication in land disputes and expropriation for offences against the community; these are the essential functions upon which, in the opinion of the West African Lands Committee, the prestige of the native authority depends. The lawful orders which he may give are carefully defined by ordinance, and in the last resort are enforced by Government.

Since native authority, especially if exercised by alien conquerors, is inevitably weakened by the first impact of civilised rule, it is made clear to the elements of disorder, who regard force as conferring the only right to demand obedience, that government, by the use of force if necessary, intends to support the native chief. To enable him to maintain order he employs a body of unarmed police, and if the occasion demands the display of superior force he looks to the Government—as, for instance, if a community combines to break the law or shield criminals from justice—a rare event in the advanced communities.

The native ruler derives his power from the Suzerain, and is responsible that it is not misused. He is equally with British officers amenable to the law, but his authority does not depend on the caprice of an executive officer. To intrigue against him is an offence punishable, if necessary, in a Provincial Court. Thus both British and native courts are invoked to uphold his authority.

The essential feature of the system (as I wrote at the time of its inauguration) is that the native chiefs are constituted "as an integral part of the machinery of the administration. There are not two sets of rulers—British and native—working either separately or in co-operation, but a single Government in which the native chiefs have well-defined duties and an acknowledged status equally with British officials. Their duties should never conflict, and should overlap as little as possible. They should be complementary to each other, and the chief himself must understand that he has no right to place and power unless he renders his proper services to the State."

The ruling classes are no longer either demi-gods, or parasites preying on the community. They must work for the stipends and position they enjoy. They are the trusted delegates of the Governor, exercising in the Moslem States the well-understood powers of "Wakils" [governors—ed.] in conformity with their own Islamic system, and recognising the King's representative as their acknowledged Suzerain.

There is here no need of "Dyarchy," for the lines of development of the native administration run parallel to, and do not intersect, those of the Central Government. It is the consistent aim of the British staff to maintain and increase the prestige of the native ruler, to encourage his initiative, and to support his authority. That the chiefs are satisfied with the autonomy they enjoy in the matters which really interest and concern them, may be judged by their loyalty and the prosperity of their country.

Comparatively little difficulty, it may be said, would be experienced in the application of such a system to Moslem States, for even if their rulers had deteriorated, they still profess the standards of Islam, with its system of taxation, and they possess a literate class capable of discharging the duties I have described. No doubt the alien immigrants in the northern tropical belt afford better material for social organisation, both racially and through the influence of their creed, than the advanced communities of negro stock which owe nothing to Islam, such as the Baganda, the Ashantis, the Yorubas, the Benis, and others. But the self-evolved progress in social organisation of these latter communities is in itself evidence that they possessed exceptional intelligence, probably more widely diffused among the peasantry than would be found among those over whom an alien race had acquired domination. They too had evolved systems of taxation and of land tenure, and had learnt to delegate authority. The teaching of missions through many decades had in most cases produced a class who, if their energies were rightly directed to the service of their communities instead of seeking foreign outlets, would form a very valuable aid in the building up of a "Native Administration." That these communities are fully capable of adopting such a system has been proved in recent years in South Nigeria.

They have not produced so definite a code of law, or such advanced methods of dispensing justice, as the Koran has introduced, and they lack the indigenous educational advantages which the use of Arabic and the religious schools have conferred on the Moslem. On the other hand, many—especially the Baganda—have benefited greatly by the Christian schools, and a wider range of knowledge, including English. Some of their chiefs—notably Khama of Bechuana, and several of those in Uganda—have been remarkable men. Among many of these communities the chiefs exercise an influence different in its nature from that accorded to an alien ruler, and based on superstitious veneration.

The limitations to independence which are frankly inherent in this conception of native rule—not as temporary restraints to be removed as soon as may be, but as powers which rightly belong to the controlling Power as trustee for the welfare of the masses, and as being responsible for the defence of the country and the cost of its central administration—are such as do not involve interference with the authority of the chiefs or the social organisation of the people. They have been accepted by the Fulani Emirs as natural and proper to the controlling power, and their reservation in the hands of the Governor has never interfered with the loyalty of the ruling chiefs, or, so far as I am aware, been resented by them. The limitations are as follows—

1. Native rulers are not permitted to raise and control armed forces, or to grant permission to carry arms. To this in principle Great Britain stands pledged under the Brussels Act.[2] The evils which result in Africa from an armed population were evident in Uganda before it fell under British control, and are very evident in Abyssinia to-day. No one with experience will deny the necessity of maintaining the strictest military discipline over armed forces or police in Africa if misuse of power is to be avoided, and they are not to become a menace and a terror to the native population and a danger in case of religious excitement—a discipline which an African ruler is incapable of appreciating or applying. For this reason native levies should never be employed in substitution for or in aid of troops.[3]

On the other hand, the Government armed police are never quartered in native towns, where their presence would interfere with the authority of the chiefs. Like the regular troops, they are employed as escorts and on duty in the townships. The native administration maintains a police, who wear a uniform but do not carry firearms.

2. The sole right to impose taxation in any form is reserved to the Suzerain power. This fulfils the bilateral understanding that the peasantry—provided they pay the authorised tax (the adjustment of which to all classes of the population is a responsibility which rests with the Central Government)—should be free of all other exactions whatsoever (including unpaid labour), while a sufficient proportion of the tax is assigned to the native treasuries to meet the expenditure of the native administration. Special sanction by ordinance—or "rule" approved by the Governor—is therefore required to enable the native authority to levy any special dues, &c.

3. The right to legislate is reserved. That this should remain in the hands of the Central Government—itself limited by the control of the Colonial Office, as I have described—cannot be questioned. The native authority, however, exercises very considerable power in this regard. A native ruler, and the native courts, are empowered to enforce native law and custom, provided it is not repugnant to humanity, or in opposition to any ordinance. This practically meets all needs, but the native authority may also make

---

[2] The Brussels Act of 1890, to which Great Britain was a signatory, restricted the importation of arms to Africa, but the clauses were in fact largely evaded (ed.).

[3] This rule does not seem to have been enforced in Kenya. "Administrative chiefs, in order to assert and maintain their authority, have found it necessary to form bands of armed retainers, to whom they accord special privileges which are found to be oppressive."

rules on any subject, provided they are approved by the Governor.

4. The right to appropriate land on equitable terms for public purposes and for commercial requirements is vested in the Governor. In the Northern Provinces of Nigeria (but not in the South) the right of disposing of native lands is reserved to the Governor by ordinance. In practice this does not interfere with the power of the native ruler (as the delegate of the Governor) to assign lands to the natives under his rule, in accordance with native law and custom, or restrict him or the native courts from adjudicating between natives regarding occupancy rights in land. No rents are levied on lands in occupation by indigenous natives. Leases to aliens are granted by the Central Government.

If the pressure of population in one community makes it necessary to assign to it a portion of the land belonging to a neighbour with a small and decreasing population, the Governor (to whom appeal may be made) would decide the matter. These reservations were set out in the formal letter of appointment given to each chief in Northern Nigeria.

5. In order to maintain intact the control of the Central Government over all aliens, and to avoid friction and difficulties, it has been the recognised rule that the employees of the native administration should consist entirely of natives subject to the native authority. If aliens are required for any skilled work by the native administration, Government servants may be employed and their salaries reimbursed by the native treasury. For a like reason, whenever possible, all non-natives and natives not subject to the local native jurisdiction live in the "township," from which natives subject to the native administration are as far as possible excluded. This exclusive control of aliens by the Central Government partakes rather of the nature of "extra-territorial jurisdiction" than of dualism.

6. Finally, in the interests of good gov-

ernment, the right of confirming or otherwise the choice of the people of the successor to a chiefship, and of deposing any ruler for misrule or other adequate cause, is reserved to the Governor.

.   .   .

The habits of a people are not changed in a decade, and when powerful despots are deprived of the pastime of war and slave-raiding, and when even the weak begin to forget their former sufferings, to grow weary of a life without excitement, and to resent the petty restrictions which have replaced the cruelties of the old despotism, it must be the aim of Government to provide new interests and rivalries in civilised progress, in education, in material prosperity and trade, and even in sport.

There were indeed many who, with the picture of Fulani misrule fresh in their memory, regarded this system when it was first inaugurated with much misgiving, and believed that though the hostility of the rulers to the British might be concealed, and their vices disguised, neither could be eradicated, and they would always remain hostile at heart. They thought that the Fulani as an alien race of conquerors, who had in turn been conquered, had not the same claims for consideration as those whom they had displaced, even though they had become so identified with the people that they could no longer be called aliens.

But there can be no doubt that such races form an invaluable medium between the British staff and the native peasantry. Nor can the difficulty of finding any one capable of taking their place, or the danger they would constitute to the State if ousted from their positions, be ignored. Their traditions of rule, their monotheistic religion, and their intelligence enable them to appreciate more readily than the negro population the wider objects of British policy, while their close touch with the masses—with whom they live in daily intercourse—mark them out as destined to play an important part in the future, as they have done in the past, in the development of the tropics.

Both the Arabs in the east and the Fulani in the west are Mohamedans, and by supporting their rule we unavoidably encourage the spread of Islam, which from the purely administrative point of view has the disadvantage of being subject to waves of fanaticism, bounded by no political frontiers. In Nigeria it has been the rule that their power should not be re-established over tribes which had made good their independence, or imposed upon those who had successfully resisted domination.

On the other hand, the personal interests of the rulers must rapidly become identified with those of the controlling Power. The forces of disorder do not distinguish between them, and the rulers soon recognise that any upheaval against the British would equally make an end of them. Once this community of interest is established, the Central Government cannot be taken by surprise, for it is impossible that the native rulers should not be aware of any disaffection.[4]

This identification of the ruling class with the Government accentuates the corresponding obligation to check malpractices on their part. The task of educating them in the duties of a ruler becomes more than ever insistent; of inculcating a sense of responsibility; of convincing their intelligence of the advantages which accrue from the material prosperity of the peasantry, from free labour and initiative; of the necessity of delegating powers to trusted subordinates; of the evils of favouritism and bribery; of the importance of education, especially for the ruling class, and for the filling of lucrative posts

[4] Soon after the establishment of British rule in Northern Nigeria more than one "Mahdi" arose, and obtained a fanatical following, but in every case the Fulani Emir actively assisted in suppressing the disturbance. In the Sudan thirteen Mahdis arose between 1901 and 1916. The Germans in East Africa, in order to check the spread of Islam, encouraged pig-breeding.

under Government; of the benefits of sanitation, vaccination, and isolation of infection in checking mortality; and finally, of impressing upon them how greatly they may benefit their country by personal interest in such matters, and by the application of labour-saving devices and of scientific methods in agriculture.

Unintentional misuse of the system of native administration must also be guarded against. It is not, for instance, the duty of a native administration to purchase supplies for native troops, or to enlist and pay labour for public works, though its agency within carefully defined limits may be useful in making known Government requirements, and seeing that markets are well supplied. Nor should it be directed to collect licences, fees, and rents due to Government, nor should its funds be used for any purpose not solely connected with and prompted by its own needs.

I have throughout these pages continually emphasised the necessity of recognising, as a cardinal principle of Britsh policy in dealing with native races, that institutions and methods, in order to command success and promote the happiness and welfare of the people, must be deep-rooted in their traditions and prejudices. Obviously in no sphere of administration is this more essential than in that under discussion, and a slavish adherence to any particular type, however successful it may have proved elsewhere, may, if unadapted to the local environment, be as ill-suited and as foreign to its conceptions as direct British rule would be.

The type suited to a community which has long grown accustomed to the social organisation of the Moslem State may or may not be suitable to advanced pagan communities, which have evolved a social system of their own, such as the Yorubas, the Benis, the Egbas, or the Ashantis in the West, or the Waganda, the Wanyoro, the Watoro, and others in the East. The history, the traditions, the idiosyncracies, and the prejudices of each must be studied by the Resident and his staff, in order that the form adopted shall accord with natural evolution, and shall ensure the ready co-operation of the chiefs and people.

Before passing to the discussion of methods applicable to primitive tribes, it may be of interest to note briefly some of the details—as apart from general principles—adopted in Nigeria among the advanced communities.

Chiefs who are executive rulers are graded—those of the first three classes are installed by the Governor or Lieut.-Governor, and carry a staff of office surmounted for the first class by a silver, and for the others by a brass crown. Lower grades carry a baton, and are installed by the Resident, or by the Emir, if the chief is subordinate to him. These staves of office, which are greatly prized, symbolise to the peasantry the fact that the Emir derives his power from the Government, and will be supported in its exercise. The installation of an Emir is a ceremonial witnessed by a great concourse of his people, and dignified by a parade of troops. The native insignia of office, and a parchment scroll, setting out in the vernacular the conditions of his appointment, are presented to him. The alkali (native judge) administers the following oath on the Koran: "I swear in the name of God, well and truly to serve His Majesty King George V. and his representative the Governor of Nigeria, to obey the laws of Nigeria and the lawful commands of the Governor, and of the Lieut.-Governor, provided that they are not contrary to my religion, and if they are so contrary I will at once inform the Governor through the Resident. I will cherish in my heart no treachery or disloyalty, and I will rule my people with justice and without partiality. And as I carry out this oath so may God judge me." Pagan chiefs are sworn according to their own customs on a sword.

Native etiquette and ceremonial must be carefully studied and observed in order that unintentional offence may be avoided. Great importance is attached to them, and a like observance in accordance with native custom is demanded towards British officers. Chiefs are treated with respect and courtesy. Native races alike in India and Africa are quick to discriminate between natural dignity and assumed superiority. Vulgar familiarity is no more a passport to their friendship than an assumption of self-importance is to their respect.[5] The English gentleman needs no prompting in such a matter—his instinct is never wrong. Native titles of rank are adopted, and only native dress is worn, whether by chiefs or by schoolboys. Principal chiefs accused of serious crimes are tried by a British court, and are not imprisoned before trial, unless in very exceptional circumstances. Minor chiefs and native officials appointed by an Emir may be tried by his Judicial Council. If the offence does not involve deprivation of office, the offender may be fined without public trial, if he prefers it, in order to avoid humiliation and loss of influence.

Succession is governed by native law and custom, subject in the case of important chiefs to the approval of the Governor, in order that the most capable claimant may be chosen. It is important to ascertain the customary law and to follow it when possible, for the appointment of a chief who is not the recognised heir, or who is disliked by the people, may give rise to trouble, and in any case the new chief would have much difficulty in asserting his authority, and would fear to check abuses lest he should alienate his supporters. In Moslem countries the law is fairly clearly defined, being a useful combination of the hereditary principle, tempered by selection, and in many cases in Nigeria the ingenious device is maintained of having two rival dynasties, from each of which the successor is selected alternately.

[5] "The Master said: The nobler sort of man is dignified but not proud; the inferior man proud but not dignified. The nobler sort of man is easy to serve yet difficult to please. In exacting service from others he takes account of aptitudes and limitations."

In pagan communities the method varies; but there is no rigid rule, and a margin for selection is allowed. The formal approval of the Governor after a short period of probation is a useful precaution, so that if the designated chief proves himself unsuitable, the selection may be revised without difficulty. Minor chiefs are usually selected by popular vote, subject to the approval of the paramount chief. It is a rule in Nigeria that no slave may be appointed as a chief or district headman. If one is nominated he must first be publicly freed.

Small and isolated communities, living within the jurisdiction of a chief, but owing allegiance to the chief of their place of origin—a common source of trouble in Africa—should gradually be absorbed into the territorial jurisdiction. Aliens who have settled in a district for their own purposes would be subject to the local jurisdiction.

.   .   .

There are some who consider that however desirable it may be to rule through the native chiefs of advanced communities, such a policy is misplaced, if not impossible, among the backward tribes. Here, they would say, the Resident and his staff must necessarily be the direct rulers, since among the most primitive peoples there are no recognised chiefs capable of exercising rule. The imposition of a tax is in their view premature, since (they say) the natives derive no corresponding benefit, and learn to regard the District Officer merely as a tax-collector. Moreover, refusal to pay necessitates coercive expeditions—scarcely distinguishable from the raids of old times. To attempt to adapt such methods—however suitable to the Moslem communities—to the conditions of primitive tribes, would be to foist upon them a system foreign to their conceptions. In the criticisms I have read no *via media* is indicated between those who are accounted to rank as advanced communities, entitled before long to independence, and direct rule by the British staff.

Let us realise that the advanced communities form a very minute proportion of the population of British Tropical Africa. The vast majority are in the primitive or early tribal stages of development. To abandon the policy of ruling them through their own chiefs, and to substitute the direct rule of the British officer, is to forgo the high ideal of leading the backward races, by their own efforts, in their own way, to raise themselves to a higher plane of social organisation, and tends to perpetuate and stereotype existing conditions.

We must realise also two other important facts. First, that the British staff, exercising direct rule, cannot be otherwise than very small in comparison to the area and population of which they are in charge.[6] That rule cannot generally mean the benevolent autocracy of a particular District Officer, well versed in the language and customs of the people, but rule by a series of different white men, conveying their orders by police and couriers and alien native subordinates, and the quartering of police detachments in native villages. Experience has shown the difficulty in such conditions of detecting and checking cases of abuse of office, and of acquisition of land by alien and absentee native landlords. There is a marked tendency to litigation, and the entire decay of such tribal authority as may previously have existed.

The changed conditions of African life is the second important fact for consideration. The advent of Europeans cannot fail to have a disintegrating effect on tribal

[6] What a thoroughly efficient system of direct rule means, may be seen in the "new territories" of Hong-Kong. In the matter of land alone, 40,000 acres are divided into 350,000 separate lots, classified and described in 87 bulky volumes, which for working purposes are condensed into 9. 24,000 receipts for rent are issued yearly, the average value being 1s. The preparation of the annual rentroll, and the collection of the rents, are tasks of some magnitude.—Hong-Kong Land Reports.

authority and institutions, and on the conditions of native life. This is due in part to the unavoidable restrictions imposed on the exercise of their power by the native chiefs. They may no longer inflict barbarous and inhuman punishments on the individual, or take reprisals by force of arms on aggressive neighbours or a disobedient section of the community. The concentration of force in the hands of the Suzerain Power, and the amenability of the chiefs to that Power for acts of oppression and misrule, are evidence to primitive folk that the power of the chiefs has gone. This decay of tribal authority has unfortunately too often been accentuated by the tendency of British officers to deal direct with petty chiefs, and to ignore, and allow their subordinates to ignore, the principal chief. It has been increased in many cases by the influx of alien natives, who, when it suited them, set at naught the native authority, and refused to pay the tribute which the chiefs were given no means of enforcing, or acquired lands which they held in defiance of native customary tenure.

But the main cause of the great change which is taking place in the social conditions of African life is to be found in the changed outlook of the African himself. There is, as a writer in 'New Europe' says, "something fantastically inconceivable about the policy of keeping the forces and ideas of the modern world out of Africa," and it is the negation of progress "to fasten down upon the African his own past. . . . Over most of tropical Africa the old order of tribal society is dead, dying, or doomed." He is apparently speaking of East Africa. His views were strongly endorsed by the Governor, Sir P. Girouard—than whom few have shown a greater insight into problems of native administration. In his report on East Africa for 1909–10, Sir P. Girouard enumerates the various agencies which are "breaking down the tribal systems, denationalising the native, and emancipating him from the rule of his chief." "There are not

lacking," he writes, "those who favour direct British rule; but if we allow the tribal authority to be ignored or broken, it will mean that we, who numerically form a small minority in the country, shall be obliged to deal with a rabble, with thousands of persons in a savage or semi-savage state, all acting on their own impulses, and making themselves a danger to society generally. There could only be one end to such a policy, and that would be eventual conflict with the rabble."

From every side comes the same story. "For fifteen years," says Mr. Wilson, writing of Nyasaland, "I have watched the tribal system breaking up—nothing could infuse new life into it." And with the rapid changes the native character has deteriorated. Stealing and burglary are rife, and the old village discipline and respect for chiefs has gone. In the West we find the mine manager with his wife and flower-garden established in a district which only a few years ago was the inaccessible fastness of a cannibal tribe. Ladies in mission schools teach nude savage children the elements of geography and arithmetic. The smattering of knowledge and caricature of the white man's ways acquired by these children react on their village, and upset tribal customs and authority. A few years ago one would find communities in which no individual had ever been twenty miles from his home. To-day the young men migrate in hundreds to offer their labour at the mines or elsewhere, and return with strange ideas. Some perhaps have even been overseas from West to East Africa during the war.

The produce of the village loom, or dye-pit, or smithy, is discounted by cheap imported goods, and the craftsman's calling is not what it was. Traders, white and black, circulate under the *pax Britannica* among tribes but recently addicted to head-hunting, and bring to them new and strange conceptions. The primitive African is called upon to cope with ideas a thousand years in advance of his mental and social equipment. "He cannot proceed leisurely along the road to progress. He must be hurried along it, or the free and independent savage will sink to the level of the helot and the slave."

Here, then, in my view, lies our present task in Africa. It becomes impossible to maintain the old order—the urgent need is for adaptation to the new—to build up a tribal authority with a recognised and legal standing, which may avert social chaos. It cannot be accomplished by superseding—by the direct rule of the white man—such ideas of discipline and organisation as exist, nor yet by "stereotyping customs and institutions among backward races which are not consistent with progress." [7]

The first step is to hasten the transition from the patriarchal to the tribal stage, and induce those who acknowledge no other authority than the head of the family to recognise a common chief. Where this stage has already been reached, the object is to group together small tribes, or sections of a tribe, so as to form a single administrative unit, whose chiefs severally, or in Council as a "Native Court," may be constituted a "Native Authority," with defined powers

[7] Debate on Colonial Office vote; 26th April 1920.

over native aliens, through whom the district officer can work instead of through alien subordinates. His task is to strengthen the authority of the chiefs, and encourage them to show initiative; to learn their difficulties at first hand, and to assist them in adapting the new conditions to the old—maintaining and developing what is best, avoiding everything that has a tendency to denationalisation and servile imitation. He can guide and control several such units, and endeavour gradually to bring them to the standard of an advanced community. In brief, tribal cohesion, and the education of the tribal heads in the duties of rulers, are the watchwords of the policy in regard to these backward races. As the unit shows itself more and more capable of conducting its own affairs, the direct rule, which at first is temporarily unavoidable among the most backward of all, will decrease, and the community will acquire a legal status, which the European and the native agent of material development must recognise. "The old easy-going days, when the probity of the individual was sufficient title to rule, are gone. . . . Intelligent interest, imagination, comprehension of alien minds—these are the demands of to-day."

34 NNAMDI AZIKIWE
NIGERIA AND INDEPENDENCE

Born in eastern Nigeria and educated in America, Nnamdi Azikiwe (1904–   ) was editor-in-chief of the West African Pilot, *one of the leading nationalist newspapers in West Africa, from 1937 to 1945. Long a champion of an independent Nigeria, Azikiwe became one of Nigeria's leading statesmen and was the first President of the Federal Republic. The selections that follow are representative of Azikiwe's ideas as nationalist, party leader, and statesman. The first speech, on the subject of freedom for Africa, was delivered at a rally in Trafalgar Square, London, on December 4, 1949, after the shooting of twenty-one coal miners at Enugu. The miners had staged a slowdown strike in the erroneous belief that back pay had been withheld from them. When the police entered the mine to secure the dynamite stored there, the miners feared that the officers had been sent to break the strike. They rioted and were shot. The news of the massacre was received with great horror all over Nigeria, and riots erupted in Calabar, Onitsha, and Port Harcourt. The second selection is from an address delivered in the Rex Cinema in Enugu, on February 14, 1953, during a rally convened under the auspices of the Enugu branch of the National Council for Nigeria and the Cameroons (NCNC). There Azikiwe presented the history and aims of the NCNC. The third address was delivered at the Carlton Rooms in the Maida Vale of London, on July 31, 1959, under the auspices of the London branch of the NCNC. As Premier of eastern Nigeria and National President of the NCNC, Azikiwe discussed Nigeria's relations with her neighbors and expressed the hope for a United States of Africa.*

In the United Kingdom, there were formal "debates" in the House of Commons about the shootings. What interested some of the Members of Parliament was the effect of the disturbances on the shipment of groundnuts to Britain. Some Africans lobbied them, not realizing that the debate on this subject had closed fifteen minutes before the lobby. In the House of Lords, dyed-in-the-wool imperialists took the opportunity of advertising that they were not politically dead but were passing through a stage of suspended animation so far as colonial affairs are concerned. They gave the impression of being less interested in the killing of mere natives than in the audacity of the United Nations in meddling with what they termed the domestic affairs of Great Britain. Said Lord Listowel, who hitherto had been regarded by some misguided Africans as a friend of the 'colonials' when he was a Labour back-bencher back in the days of Churchill: "We have sole responsibility for formulating the policy pursued in these territories and for choosing the right method of putting our policy into effect. We cannot allow any outside authority to usurp a function which we regard as essential to sound and progressive administration. It is our duty, in judging policy, to consider first the welfare of the indigenous inhabitants and to reject the counsel of the United Nations Assembly when in our opinion it conflicts with their interest. . . . Indeed it would

be a dereliction of our duty to the peoples of the Colonies if we were to offer to share our present responsibility with the representatives of other countries. . . . Our reasons for not wishing to throw the colonies into the arena of debate at Lake Success are that criticism there is often warped by anti-British or anti-Colonial prejudice and too infrequently directed to serving the genuine interests of colonial peoples."

The reaction from abroad has been very enlightening. Two hundred thousand workers in Eastern Germany protested against the shooting. Three million Czech trade unionists registered protests against this evidence of man's inhumanity to man. The National Union of Furnishing Trade Operators demanded the resignation of those responsible for the shooting. British Guiana workers were prevented from holding a rally to register their protest. A delegate from Poland at Friday's meeting of the United Nations General Assembly at Flushing Meadow, demonstrated that the statement of Lord Listowel was far-fetched and that it was necessary that the "colonial idol" should be destroyed in view of the "awakening of dependent peoples" and the "bloody disturbances in Nigeria."

It is a tragedy that a country which produced Thomas Clarkson and William Wilberforce is now telling the world that it is not prepared to be accountable to a world organization for its colonial administration, because in the words of its delegate at the United Nations it would mean "to put back the hands of the clock by committing colonial peoples to policies

From Nnamdi Azikiwe, *Zik: A Selection from the Speeches of Nnamdi Azikiwe* (New York: Cambridge University Press, 1961), pp. 48–51, 70–74, 179–182. Reprinted by permission.

in the formulation of which they have no say and which the United Kingdom regards as misguided." Since when, may I ask, has the British Government consulted us or respected our opinion in the formulation of colonial policy? What a brazen piece of smug hypocrisy! If it were left to the average Nigerian, we would rather have the United Nations exercising trusteeship over us if Britain thinks that shooting down our workers in cold blood is the correct way of exercising a protectorate over our people. . . .

The people of Nigeria cannot continue to accept as their destiny the denial of human rights. We, too, have a right to live, to enjoy freedom, and to pursue happiness like other human beings. Let us reinforce our rank and file in the fight for freedom, no longer suffering in silence and whining like a helpless dog, but striking back with all the force at our command when we are struck, preferring to suffer the consequences of pressing forward our claim to a legacy of freedom, than to surrender our heritage to despoilers and usurpers. Be of good cheer, my compatriots. The struggle for African freedom may be long and gloomy, but behind the cloud of suffering and disappointment loom the rays of hope and success on the distant horizon. So long as we are undaunted and are determined to be a free people, the fire of freedom shall not be extinguished from our hearths, we shall march forward towards our national emancipation. So long as we refuse to believe that we are doomed to be the serfs and peons of others, our continent shall be redeemed, and we shall have a new life and enjoy it abundantly.

We have friends in unexpected places: genuine and sincere friends. Freedom is within our grasp. Shall we let it slip away? Shall we relapse into the dungeon of fear and the servitude of hesitation? Let us no longer quake or doubt about our capacity to enter into our rightful heritage. Why not deal one blow in a gamble for national liberty? Let there be no mistake about our future. We are determined to discard the yoke of oppression. We shall be free. History is on our side. In this hour of national peril, Nigeria expects every patriot to stand firm in the cause of justice and righteousness. God knows we hate none but we love our country. Long live Nigeria and the Cameroons.

If you knew the history of your party you would realize that it is a child of circumstance born to discharge a patriotic duty which others shirked. If you knew the philosophy which animates the various activities of this party you would appreciate the constructive role you are playing in our national history. If you knew the structure of your party you would concede the good faith of those who are working unceasingly in order to enhance efficiency in the organization and administration of your party. Armed with these incontrovertible facts, you would be mentally equipped to resist the subtle suggestion that is constantly made to the effect that the NCNC is a rabble of political adventurers, that it has no policy, that its leaders are intellectually inferior not only to the party rebels but to leaders of the Action Group, that it seeks power in order to introduce the spoils system of American politics into Nigeria.[1]

Let me give you a gist of the historical origins of the NCNC. Unlike other political parties, the NCNC did not begin spontaneously as a political party. Early in 1942, a dozen thinkers formed themselves into what they ultimately called the Nigeria Reconstruction Group. They met every Sunday morning at 72 King George Avenue, at Yaba, which was my residence. They discussed political, social and economic problems which affected contemporary Nigeria and sought answers to them. Most of the members of

[1] The Action Group was the political party of the western region of Nigeria, dominated by the Yoruba. It was founded in 1951 under the leadership of Obafemi Awolowo in opposition to the NCNC but was subsequently outlawed (ed.).

this group were connected with the Yaba Higher College and its associated institutions. Their sole aim was to apply scientific methods in the solution of practical problems.

In course of their researches and discussions, they began to feel that a national front organization was necessary to act as a mouthpiece for expressing the aspirations of Nigerians in various walks of life. The aims of such a national front were stated to be the immediate improvement of social conditions and eventually the bringing about of far-reaching social progress which should include the exclusion of foreign exploitation and the establishment of self-government in Nigeria. Such aims could not be attained by only one section of the community working independently but must be faced by a front constituted of men and women who wished to see the setting up of an independent Nigeria. It was believed that only by agreement on practical measures of common action, whilst making allowance for differences of conviction, could Nigeria attain this desirable goal.

Representatives of the Nigeria Reconstruction Group then exchanged views with officials of the Nigerian Youth Movement, which was then under the leadership of Mr. Ernest Ikoli. They did the same with representatives of the Nigerian National Democratic Party, under the leadership of Herbert Macaulay. The Nigerian Youth Circle was also contacted and ideas were exchanged with its leaders in the persons of Messrs. H. O. Davies and J. M. Udochi. Having contacted other organizations, like the Nigeria Union of Teachers, the Union of Young Democrats, certain trade unions and tribal organizations, the NRG requested all of them to form a federation which would be an All-Nigerian National Congress.

In the meantime, a youth rally was organized to take place at the Ojukoro Farm of E. J. Alex-Taylor in November, 1943. Hundreds of youths stormed this suburban estate and a most impressive ag-gregation of nationalists demonstrated the possibilities of a Nigerian nationalist front. The thought was unanimous that the Nigerian Youth Movement should spearhead this front and so the NRG joined in suggesting that the Movement should summon a representative meeting of various organizations with a view to crystallizing the national front which was the dream of most nationalists. After six months of vacillation and inaction, the Nigeria Union of Students decided to assume responsibility for summoning such a meeting, which took place on August 26, 1944, in the Glover Memorial Hall, Lagos, under the chairmanship of Duse Mohamed Ali.

Subsequently, it was decided to adopt NCNC as the name of the new national front and Herbert Macaulay was elected its first President, with your humble servant as General Secretary. It is pertinent, at this stage, to give you the names of the thinkers who, without any political ambitions and without any thought of personal gain, sowed the seed which has now germinated to become the NCNC. They are as follows: T. O. Na Oruwariye, M. O. Balonwu, B. O. S. Adophy, T. E. E. Brown, S. I. Bosah, M. E. R. Okorodudu, E. E. Esua, E. C. Erokwu, Henry Collins, C. Enitan Brown, A. I. Osakwe, O. K. Ogan and Nnamdi Azikiwe.

The philosophy of the NCNC is linked with its aims and objectives. If you turn to the NCNC Constitution, which was originally framed by a committee composed of Herbert Macaulay, E. E. Esua, Dennis C. Osadebay, A. O. Omage, Glory Mordi and your humble servant, you will see that the aim is to disseminate ideas of representative democracy and parliamentary government by means of political education. Specifically, the objectives of the NCNC are political freedom, economic security, social equality and religious toleration. On attaining political freedom, the NCNC looks forward to the establishment of a socialist commonwealth.

According to the NCNC Constitution, the objects of this organization are:

1. To extend democratic principles and to advance the interests of the people of Nigeria and the Cameroons under British mandate.
2. To organize and collaborate with all its branches throughout the country.
3. To adopt suitable means for the purpose of imparting political education to the people of Nigeria with a view to achieving self-government.
4. To afford the members the advantages of a medium of expression in order to secure political freedom, economic security, social equality and religious toleration in Nigeria and the Cameroons under British Mandate as a member of the British Commonwealth of Free Nations.

Under "Political Freedom" the NCNC hopes

5. To achieve internal self-government for Nigeria whereby the people of Nigeria and the Cameroons under British Mandate should exercise executive, legislative and judicial powers.
6. To secure freedom to think, to speak, to write, to assemble, and to trade.

The aims summarized as "economic security" were these:

7. To secure an irrevocable acknowledgement by government of the fundamental principle upon which the land system of Nigeria is based, namely, that the whole of the lands in all parts of Nigeria, including the colony and Protectorates (North and South), whether occupied or unoccupied, shall be declared Native Lands, and that all rights of ownership over all Native Lands shall be vested in the natives as being inalienable and untransferable to government without purchase, concession or gift.
8. To secure the control by local administrations of the means of production and distribution of the mineral resources of the country.
9. To protect Nigerian trade, products, minerals and commerce in the interests of the natives by legislating against trade monopolies so as to avoid the exploitation of the country and its people.
10. To protect the Nigerian working people by legislating for minimum wages for skilled and unskilled labour in addition to humanizing the conditions of labour in Nigeria and instituting and guaranteeing social security for the people of Nigeria.

The aims of "social equality" were the following:

11. To secure the abolition of all forms of discrimination and segregation based on race, colour, tribe or creed in Nigeria.
12. To secure for Nigeria and the Cameroons under British Mandate the establishment of a national system of free and compulsory education for all children up to the age of sixteen.
13. To secure that a reasonable number of scholarships is awarded to Nigerians for study.
14. To secure that free medical and surgical treatment shall be provided by the central and the local governments for all the people of Nigeria who are in need of such services and to secure that there shall be no discrimination on account of race, colour, tribe or creed.

Under "religious toleration" the NCNC aimed "to secure for the people of Nigeria and the Cameroons under British Mandate the freedom of worship according to conscience, and for all religious organizations the freedom and right to exist in Nigeria."

In connection with the relationship between Nigeria and the other African States, the need for economic, social and political integration has been mentioned. Since many views have been propounded on how the free African States can be linked the situation is rather confusing. Perhaps it may be pertinent for me to pursue this matter further in order not to leave any room for doubt or confusion.

Nigeria should co-operate closely with the other independent African States with the aim of establishing unity of outlook and purpose in foreign policy. The pursuing of this objective should make for better understanding among the African States and a realization of identity of interest among them. Moreover, it would advertise the importance of Africa in world affairs and help to heal the wounds that have been inflicted on this continent and which can be a basis of a revanche movement.

There are many schools of thought on how the African States should be aligned. One school favours a political union of African States now. Another school favours an association of African States on the basis of community of interests. Still another school favours an alignment of a rigid or loose character on a regional basis. Other schools develop this splendid idea further and there can be no doubt that more will be heard from other quarters.

My personal opinion is that there is great need for close cooperation between Nigeria and the other African States. The nature of such close co-operation need not delay sincere efforts to attain such a desirable goal, but we must be realistic in pursuing this matter lest we plunge the continent of Africa in a maelstrom of conflicting personal ambitions and interests.

I would suggest that Nigeria, in the first instance, should explore with its nearest neighbours the possibility of a customs union. This would lead to the abolition of tariffs between the two or more countries and would encourage "free trade" in areas which might ultimately turn into a common market. With a free flow and interchange of goods, Nigeria and its neighbours would come closer in their economic relationship which is very fundamental in human relations.

I would also suggest a gradual abolition of boundaries which demarcate the geographical territory of Nigeria and its neighbours. The experience of Canada and the United States has been encouraging and should be explored. Once travelling is freely permitted, other things being equal, people will forget about physical

frontiers and begin to concentrate on essential problems of living together.

I would suggest further that Nigeria should interest its neighbours in a joint endeavour to build international road systems which should link West African countries with East African territories, on the one hand, and North African countries with Central African territories, on the other. By encouraging the construction of *autobahn* systems across strategic areas of Africa, and by providing travelling facilities, in the shape of hotels, motels, petrolfilling stations, we should be able to knit the continent of Africa into a tapestry of free-trading, free-travelling, and free-living peoples.

I would finally suggest cultural exchanges on a wider scale than is practised at present. Students, dancers, artistes, traders and holiday-makers should be able to cross the frontiers of Nigeria and its neighbours with full freedom. They are usually the ambassadors of goodwill and they can help to produce the sense of one-ness which is so lacking in most of Africa at present. Given official support these ordinary folk would become the harbingers of a new era in Africa, because once a sense of one-ness has permeated the social fabric it facilitates the crystallization of common nationality, as the experience of Nigerian history vindicates.

I believe that economic and social integration will enable Nigeria and its neighbours to bring to pass the United States of Africa, which is the dream of African nationalists. It would be capital folly to assume that hard-bargaining politicians who passed through the ordeal of victimization and the crucible of persecution to win their political independence will easily surrender their newly-won political power in the interest of a political leviathan which is populated by people who are alien to one another in their social and economic relations. It has not been possible in Europe or America, and unless Africa can show herself different from other continents, the verdict of history on this score will remain unchallenged and unaltered.

Lest there should be any mistaken notion of my stand on the alignment of interests of African States, may I reiterate that I firmly believe in the attainment of an association or union of African States either on a regional or continental basis in the future. I would regard such a future as not within the life-time of the heroes and heroines who have spearheaded the struggle for freedom in Africa, these four decades. But I honestly believe that social and economic integration would so mix the masses of the various African territories into an amalgam of understanding that the objective might be realizable earlier than we expected.

In other words, the prerequisites of political integration in Africa are the economic and social integration of African peoples. Otherwise, we shall be precipitating a crisis which will find African leaders jockeying among themselves for leadership of peoples who are not only alien to each other but are unprepared for such a social revolution. This would be disastrous to the ideals of Pan-Africanism which all of us, as sincere nationalists, have been propagating all these years. It means going the way of Europe, which gave top priority to political integration before social and economic integration, only to disintegrate into unimportant nation-states after the Peace of Westphalia in 1648.

The role of Nigeria in world politics can inspire respect if, in addition to creating a healthy relationship, she either spearheads or associates herself actively in the movement to revive the stature of man in Africa. This implies the downright denunciation of the spurious theory of racial inferiority which has no scientific basis. Nigeria should not hesitate to consider it as an unfriendly act for any State in Africa to proclaim or to practise this dangerous doctrine of racialism.

We can revive the stature of man in Africa by associating Nigeria actively with all progressive movements which are busily engaged not only in demolishing racial bigotry but also in spreading knowledge of the fundamental equality of the races of mankind. Nigeria should use its good offices to persuade African States which practise racial snobbery to mend their ways, and Nigeria should dissociate itself from organizations which condone the practice of race prejudice by their members.

The existence of colonies in Africa can no longer be justified in the light of science and history. It should be the manifest destiny of Nigeria to join hands with other progressive forces in the world in order to emancipate not only the people of Africa but also other peoples of African descent from the scourge of colonialism. Science has demonstrated that no race is superior to another. History has shown that no race is culturally naked. That being the case, Nigeria should be in the vanguard of the struggle to liberate Africans from the yoke of colonial rule.

May I at this stage refer to the reported plan of France to use the Sahara Desert as a site for testing its atomic bombs? I am not concerned in this lecture about the desirability or otherwise of using the atomic bomb as an instrument of war, but I am deeply concerned that a European State, which rules millions of Africans as colonial people, should calculatedly endanger the lives of millions of African people in a mad attempt to ape the Atom Powers.

The leaders and people of Nigeria are already reacting and I do not hesitate to warn France, with respect and humility, as I did in November 1958, when I first called the attention of the world to this attempt by France to perpetrate an atrocity against the peoples of Africa, that we will regard this Sahara test not only as an unfriendly act, but as a crime against humanity, in view of the dangers of radioactive fall-out and in view of the effect of the Sahara Desert on the climate of Nigeria.

EASTERN AFRICA

THE LAND OF PUNT

Although traders from Arabia, Persia, and India probably visited the coast of eastern Africa during the millenniums before Christ, the ancient Egyptians were the first to record their voyages. They made frequent and regular journeys down the Red Sea to the land of Punt, which is usually identified with the modern coast of Somalia south of Cape Guardafui. Here they traded Egyptian products for incense, myrrh, spices, and gold. Perhaps even in periods of great mercantile activity, such as during the reign of Queen Hatshepsut (c. 1520–1480 B.C.), Egyptian merchant captains were carried by the northeast monsoon farther south to the Tanganyika coast or beyond that to northern Mozambique.

THE ZANJ

The next surviving description of the East African coast is the *Periplus of the Erythraean Sea,* a commercial handbook compiled by a supercargo in the first or second century in which he describes the commerce and important trading ports of the Indian Ocean. From India ships reached East Africa with cotton cloth, grain, oil, and ghee, while from the Mediterranean world Graeco-Roman ships brought copper, tin, iron, and wine. In exchange for these goods the traders obtained cinnamon, frankincense, ivory, and tortoise shell. With the exception of Ptolemy's *Geography,* the East African section of which appears to be a description of the fourth century, little is known of the coast until the narratives of Arab travelers after the tenth century A.D. By this time the inhabitants were unmistakably Bantu migrants who had pressed northward up the coast during the preceding centuries and settled in the commercial ports. The Arabs called them the *Zanj* (the Blacks). A non-Muslim people, they soon controlled the trading cities and provided the goods, whereas the carrying trade itself remained in non-African hands. Throughout this period trade appears to have increased. Slaves were now an important commodity along with the more traditional African products. The scope of the trade appears to have expanded with the volume as merchants from China and Indonesia joined those from India, Persia, and Arabia (Tuan Ch'eng-shih, *China's Discovery of Africa*).

The East African coast slowly became Islamized, principally by the example set by Muslim merchants who traded with the Zanj cities. On the one hand, the spread of Islam to East Africa may be regarded as part of the larger process of Islamization that was taking place in the Indian Ocean region. On the other, conversion to Islam coincided with a period of prosperity founded on the expansion of trade, which had derived its stimulus from the growing Sofala gold trade. For centuries gold mined by African peoples in the interior of Central Africa (modern Rhodesia) had been taken to Sofala on the coast and then carried to Asia and the Middle East. By the fourteenth century, this trade had reached its height and with it the commercial prosperity of the coast. Kilwa was able to monopolize much of

the gold trade and consequently flourished, but the other city-states—Mombasa, Mogadishu, Pemba, and others north of Kilwa—all benefited from the general expansion of trade (João de Barros, *The Founding of Kilwa*).

The development of town life among the Zanj population was encouraged by the economic growth of the coastal trade and stimulated by frequent and regular contacts with foreign traders. As the Zanj adopted Islam, they applied the organization of Islamic states to suit their own circumstances. This acculturation, which included intermarriage, did not, however, result in the suppression of African culture but rather in a synthesis of the Muslim, Arabic ways of the traders and the ritualistic, Bantu-speaking customs of the Zanj to form the Swahili culture that dominates the East African coast today (Ibn Battuta, *The East African Coast in 1331*).

The prosperity of the coast did not last. By the end of the fifteenth century many of the city-states, particularly Kilwa, were in decline. No single reason can account for the decline of Kilwa, and the scholar must rely on intelligent speculation from the meager evidence. Clearly, Kilwa suffered from the problem of succession, as did most Muslim states. Intrigue and struggle for the sultanate undermined the power of the state as a succession of weak and debauched sultans undid the work of more competent predecessors. Moreover, the gold trade itself slipped into decline during the fifteenth century as the interior of Central Africa was convulsed by a new wave of Bantu migrants that later swept

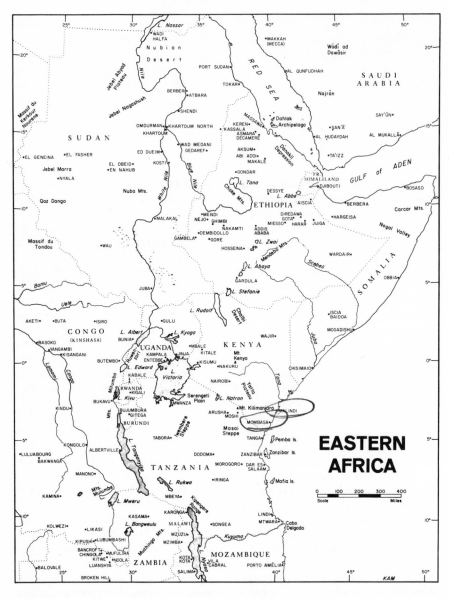

EASTERN AFRICA

Scale: 0 100 200 300 400 Miles

up the coast from Mozambique and Nyasaland, upsetting the trade routes to the interior, attacking the city-states, and diverting commerce. Finally, the "Zanj Empire" about which nineteenth-century writers wrote was in fact a myth, for each of the city-states jealously guarded its independence and frequently made war on rival towns. This inability to weld the competing cities into a unified empire left them easy prey for the Portuguese who

suddenly arrived on the East African coast.

THE PORTUGUESE

In April 1498 Vasco da Gama cast anchor in Mombasa harbor. Forty years after the death of Prince Henry, Portuguese explorers had achieved his dream of discovering a seaway to India and the Orient. The aim of Portugal and her explorers was to monopolize the trade of the Indian

Ocean and the East Indies, and in this grand Portuguese design East Africa was regarded principally as a way station to the East. Although the Portuguese were astounded to find a culture in East Africa as sophisticated as their own, they were able to establish their control by their technological superiority in the possession of firearms. Portuguese control was thus established by force and violence and assisted by the rivalries among the Zanj states. Some city-states, like Malindi, cooperated with the Portuguese and flourished as a result. Others, like Mombasa, opposed the invaders and suffered from Portuguese efforts to suppress their rebellious subjects. The Portuguese viewed their occupation of East Africa as only part of the larger crusade against the Muslims, and resistance was crushed in the name of Christ and the extension of His heavenly dominion. The result was a rule that was more bloody, tyrannical, and oppressive than it was peaceful, prosperous, and tolerant. But if the Portuguese were able to dominate, they made little attempt to establish systematic government on the coast and no attempt to administer the interior. Even Christian missionaries had few successes, and Portuguese endeavors to Christianize the coast left no lasting impression in East Africa. To the Portuguese, East Africa remained a revictualing station en route to the Orient. Portuguese settlers did not come to East Africa and the numbers of Portuguese on the coast never numbered more than a few hundred at any time (Duarte Barbosa, *The East Coast of Africa at the Beginning of the Sixteenth Century*).

OMAN AND EAST AFRICA

The Portuguese monopoly could not long remain unchallenged. At the end of the sixteenth century, Turkish expeditions appeared on the coast as part of the Ottoman holy war against the Christians. More formidable were the *Wazimba,* a militant Bantu people who swept up the coast at the end of the sixteenth century, destroying many of the cities before their defeat at Malindi (João dos Santos, *The Wazimba*). Although both the Turks and the Wazimba were successfully driven off, the Portuguese failed to repulse the assaults of rival Europeans and Arabs from Oman in southeast Arabia. Throughout the seventeenth century, the Portuguese steadily lost their Far Eastern trading posts to the Dutch, the English, and the French. While Europeans struck at the heart of the Portuguese Empire in the Orient, the Omani Arabs assaulted Portuguese posts on the East African coast. In the mid-seventeenth century, the energetic Imam of Oman, Nasir ibn Murshid, drove the Portuguese from the Persian Gulf. His subsequent campaign in East Africa and that of his successor, Saif ibn Sultan, must be regarded as an extension of that holy war. By the end of the seventeenth century, the Omani sultans had broken Portuguese power in East Africa. Under the leadership of Saif ibn Sultan, the Omani Arabs had taken Mombasa in 1698 and Pemba and Kilwa the following year.

Triumphant, Saif ibn Sultan did not remain in East Africa; instead, he appointed Arabian governors to rule over the East African city-states. Many of these rulers were soon united under the Governor of Mombasa, Muhammad ibn Uthman al-Mazrui, the head of the powerful Mazrui family, who gradually placed his relatives in key positions in numerous city-states. Soon members of the family controlled much of the East African coast, and although they nominally acknowledged the suzerainty of the Imam of Oman, they ruled in fact as independent sultans until the nineteenth century.

Throughout the seventeenth and eighteenth centuries, the Zanj city-states had steadily declined in power and prosperity. Destruction by the Portuguese, rebellions against them, and devastation by Turks, Wazimba, and Omani Arabs clearly precipitated the decay of the city-states.

Moreover, the sixteenth and seventeenth centuries saw a general decline throughout the Muslim world. The rise of the Ottoman state had shifted the center of Islam from Mesopotamia to Asia Minor, and shortly afterward the eastern Muslim states were overrun by Mongol invaders. In these dismal centuries, Islam lost much of its earlier driving force at a time when European powers appeared to monopolize the commerce of the Indian Ocean. The absence of commerce meant that fewer emigrants arrived from Asia; East Africa became a cultural backwater of decrepit towns controlled by members of the Mazrui family who devoted their energies to squabbling among themselves. Even the 200 years of Portuguese occupation left little mark, and one must certainly agree with the judgment of the German historian Justus Strandes:

Portuguese rule in East Africa was the rule of alien conquerors, based on force and destined to yield to greater strength when it appeared. It [the Portuguese period] had no lasting influence whatsoever on the country, and East Africa today would appear the same even if there had been no Portuguese period in her past.*

SAYYID SAID

In 1806 Said ibn Sultan succeeded to the Imanate of Oman. Known as Sayyid Said, he set about to regenerate the power of Oman, which had steadily declined during the undistinguished reigns of his father and grandfather in the eighteenth century. For twenty years Sayyid Said consolidated his rule in Oman, reorganizing the disorderly taxes, encouraging commerce, and enforcing order. While Sayyid Said was bringing peace and stability to southeast Arabia, equally important events were taking place in East Africa and the Indian Ocean. In 1810 the French Mascarene Islands—Ile de France

---

* J. Strandes and J. Wallwork (trans.), *The Portuguese Period in East Africa* (Nairobi: East African Literature Bureau, 1961), p. 320.

and Bourbon, now called Mauritius and Réunion, respectively—were captured by the British as part of their campaigns against Napoleonic France. Throughout the latter half of the eighteenth century, the French developed large sugar plantations on these islands, utilizing slaves taken from the East African coast. Like all commerce in East Africa, the slave trade had been in decline until it was revived by the demands of the French for slave labor to work their plantations on the Mascarenes. Once the British had occupied the islands, however, they set about to end the slave trade as part of Britain's larger campaign against the trans-Atlantic trade. Having learned from its experiences in attempting to curtail the American slave trade that slaving was best terminated at its source, the British government urged Sayyid Said, the titular ruler of East Africa, to prohibit the carrying of slaves. Unfortunately, Sayyid Said could hardly enforce his own claims to the East African towns against the virtually independent Mazrui sultans, let alone restrict a trade from which his subjects derived considerable profit. But in 1833 Sayyid Said did agree to forbid the trade between his Muslim subjects and any Christian power and subsequently signed a treaty with Captain Moresby of the Royal Navy. Not only did the Moresby Treaty solve the problem of the slave trade to the Mascarenes, but in return Sayyid Said received British friendship and support, which permitted him to reassert his claims to East Africa. Putting Oman in order, the Sayyid sailed to Mombasa in 1828 to enforce his suzerainty. This was no easy task, for despite their fraternal squabbles and harsh rule, the Mazrui successfully defied Sayyid Said, who in the end and after four military expeditions was forced to resort to diplomacy before breaking their power. By 1836, however, Omani troops had garrisoned the great stronghold at Mombasa, Fort Jesus, and Sayyid Said had firmly established his authority over the city.

Within a year the whole coast acknowledged his suzerainty, and Sayyid Said became the first ruler to control the East African coast from Mogadishu to the Rouvuma River. Sayyid Said ruled East Africa and Oman for another twenty years, and at the time of his death in 1856, he had not only restored the authority of the Imam of Oman in East Africa but had also refashioned and welded together the city-states into an absolute monarchy that owed allegiance to no one but himself. In addition to the peace and stability he created on the coast, Sayyid Said founded Zanzibar as his capital, to which he moved from Oman. He developed the island as a religious and political center and introduced clove plantations, which soon provided Zanzibar with its principal export. Finally, to expand trade and commerce he encouraged political and commercial dealing with Europe and America. In 1833 Sayyid Said made a commercial treaty with the United States, and until the outbreak of the Civil War the Americans continued to dominate Zanzibar's legitimate trade.

Sayyid Said was a strong and able ruler who sought to expand and develop commerce and trade, including the slave trade when that was possible. In doing so, however, he excited the interests of the European powers, not only by the profits to be made from trade with the West but even more because of the European humanitarian desire to suppress the slave trade. From such humanitarian beginnings the European presence in East Africa was soon to grow into an imperial adventure.

KUSH

The land stretching southward from the second cataract of the Nile at 22 degrees north latitude to Lake Albert near the equator is known as the Sudan. In its full sense the term embraces the *Bilad as-Sudan* ("Land of the Blacks") of the medieval Muslim geographers, which extended across Africa from the Red Sea to the Atlantic. This was the land where Arab and African cultures met and mingled. From that name the modern "Sudan" is derived. In the following pages the name "Sudan" is used in the restricted sense of the Sudanese territories acquired by Egypt in the nineteenth century that now constitute the Republic of the Sudan.

Our earliest knowledge of the Sudan takes us back some 5,000 years beyond the beginnings of the first dynasty in Egypt. The Sudan, or at least the northern Sudan, called Nubia, was inhabited by a homogeneous Kushitic culture to which were added in the subsequent millenniums groups of Negroid people from the south and Kushitic peoples migrating from Libya. From the invasions of the Pharaohs of the twelfth dynasty (2000–1788 B.C.), Egypt set out to colonize Nubia; in the New Kingdom (1580–1050 B.C.), Nubia was divided into two vice-royalties—Wawat in the north with headquarters at Aswan, and Kush in the south with headquarters at Napata (Merowe). Clearly, the Egyptian occupation of Nubia left an indelible imprint on Kush and the towns became centers of Egyptian culture where Egyptian law, medicine, art, and religion flourished; but Kush was not completely Egyptianized and the Nubians continued to practice their own customs and to make their own arts and crafts, which differed from the Egyptian-made products. By the eighth century B.C. Kush had grown in power, and as Egypt to the north became disrupted by civil war, the governors of Kush became independent kings. Under Kashta and his son Pianki (751–716 B.C.), Kush conquered Egypt and united the whole of the Nile Valley under the hegemony of its kings. The great days of Kush, however, were short-lived, for while Kush was establishing its control of the Nile Valley, the Assyrians were making themselves masters of the Middle East. Armed with iron weapons and under the leadership of Esar-haddon, the Assyrians invaded Egypt in 671 B.C. and defeated Taharqa, the King of Kush. In subsequent campaigns the Kushite armies were pushed back up the Nile to the safety of Nubia. The great days of Kush were over.

The story of Kush after the retreat from Egypt is one of gradual political and economic retrenchment in the face of growing competition from its neighbors and of social and cultural transformation. For as Egypt increasingly came under the influence of alien invaders, the cultural center of Kush shifted southward. In the seventh century B.C. the capital was moved from Napata to Meroe † near Shandi, although the center of religious life continued to be the temple of Jabal Barkal at Napata. This move inspired a Meroitic renaissance as Meroitic gods replaced those of Egypt, Meroitic writing became distinct from Egyptian, and Meroe became a civilization in its own right. For several centuries Meroe flourished as a trade center with ties to states as far distant as China and India, but at present there is little conclusive evidence to prove that Meroe was an industrial state with an iron-based economy or that it was the center for the transmission of iron technology to other parts of sub-Saharan Africa. Nevertheless, there is little doubt that Meroe remained a viable and at times creative civilization well into the Christian era, with periods of prosperity that were marked by intense building activity and widespread trade with Egypt and the East. Despite this prosperity, however, Meroe's power was gradually being undermined by the increasing desiccation of the northern Sudan and the arrival of new groups of people from the southwest that hastened the decline of Kushitic culture. Then about 350 A.D., the King of Aksum marched into the Nile Valley from Ethiopia, sacked Meroe, and demolished Kush (Ezana, *The Destruction of Kush*). The royal family is believed to have followed the trade routes to the west, where they were swallowed up by

† Not to be confused with Merowe near Napata.

the vastness of the savanna that stretches to the Atlantic. Although it was destroyed, Kush had made its contribution to history by preserving Nubian-Egyptian culture long after the culture of Egypt had vanished and by using this culture as the foundation of its own more distinctly African civilization.

THE CHRISTIAN KINGDOMS

Little is known of the history of the Upper Nile prior to the introduction of Christianity in the sixth century. The country was inhabited by a people called Nubas or Nobatae, who grouped themselves into the kingdoms of Maqurra in Nubia and Alwa with its capital at Soba on the Blue Nile upstream from the modern city of Khartoum. Christianity was introduced in the Sudan as a definite missionary effort on the part of the Church of Egypt. In 543 A.D. the Byzantine empress Theodora sent off a missionary, Julian, to convert the Nubians. He worked with success in Maqurra and on his return to Constantinople was succeeded by Theodore, Bishop of Thebais, who continued the work until 551. In 569 a third missionary, Longinus, arrived to guide the spread of Christianity, converting the King of Alwa. Christianity was received with great enthusiasm in the Nile Valley and was accompanied by a spate of church building whose ruins today dot the banks of the Nile from Dunqula to Sennar. Following the departure of Longinus, little is known of Maqurra and Alwa until the coming of the Arabs in 639.

Exploding from the desert of the Arabian peninsula in the seventh century, the Arab armies swept westward along the North African littoral and up the Nile. Between 651 and 652, a well-equipped expedition marched on Dunqula, the capital of Maqurra, and laid siege to the town. The King of Maqurra sued for an armistice, and a peace was established according to which the king paid an annual tribute in slaves while the Arabs gave presents of grain and other goods. Both Arabs and Nubians agreed not to settle in the territory of the other. This arrangement, sometimes called the Treaty of Dunqula, appears to have set the pattern of Arab-Sudanese relations until the thirteenth century. During these centuries relations between Arab Egypt and Christian Sudan remained peaceful. The Arabs restricted themselves to limited trade and the Nubians were determined to prevent the permanent settlement of Arabs in Nubia.

THE COMING OF THE ARABS

While Egypt remained under Arab control there was peace between Egypt and Maqurra, but when Egypt came under Mamluk rulers, conflict erupted. To rid themselves of troublesome subjects, the Mamluks encouraged the Arab Bedouins in Egypt to move southward and indulge their propensity to pillage the frontiers of Maqurra. The Bedouins were followed by regular Mamluk military expeditions, and although Maqurra fought back, the corrosive effect of Bedouin raids and Mamluk invasions weakened the authority of the king so that by the mid-fourteenth century, internal security had dissolved into anarchy. The country was now open to Arab immigration, and once the Bedouins learned that the lands beyond the Aswan Reach were capable of supporting their flocks and herds, they poured into the Sudan, intermarrying with the Nubians and settling down beyond the authority of the Mamluk government in Egypt. The Arabs did not overwhelm Maqurra, but rather infiltrated, dissolving Nubian culture and Christianity, and then wandered off to the east and to the west with their herds. South of Maqurra the Kingdom of Alwa continued to resist the Arab encroachment, principally because the Arab tribes could never combine to overcome Alwa, which, unlike Maqurra, had not been subjected to generations of corrosive raids. Steadily, however, Arab infiltration weakened Alwa until suddenly in 1504 an alliance of the Rufaa Arabs with a mysterious people, the Funj, forever put an end to the Kingdom of Alwa.

THE FUNJ

The Funj are one of the greatest mysteries of the African continent. They first appeared in 1504 when, in alliance with the Arabs, they defeated the forces of Alwa and established their own capital at Sennar. Although there are numerous conflicting theories that the Funj were from the Upper Nile, were Bulala from Bornu, or were exiles from Eritrea or even the Yemen, they were most likely a Negroid people of Hamaj descent from the Blue Nile. Under a dynasty of kings they controlled the Middle Nile in a loosely knit confederation with few common institutions and little centralization. The Arab tribes preserved much of their autonomy by paying tribute, although the Abdallab Arabs, whose chiefs resided at Qarri on the main Nile north of Khartoum, retained a unique position as the principal vassals of the Funj. Founded on the famous Black Horse cavalry, Funj power reached its heights in the seventeenth century (James Bruce, *Shaykh Adlan and the Black Horse Cavalry of Sennar*). The court itself was a melting pot of pagan Africa with Arab, Muslim elements. Arabic was spoken by the upper class and Islam was practiced by many members of the Funj aristocracy, but the acceptance of Arab culture and religion remained at best only a veneer. In the latter half of the seventeenth century, the Funj kings relied increasingly on slave troops, who took the place of the Funj aristocracy. At first the rulers could depend on the loyalty of their slave army, but by the eighteenth century their authority had been gradually undermined by *wazirs,* who reduced the kings to puppets. Without a powerful ruler, the Funj kingdom declined as aristocrats and slave commanders indulged themselves in petty wars and court intrigue in a kaleidoscopic competition for control of the hapless king. Upon the approach of Muhammad Ali's troops from Egypt in 1821, the last wazir was murdered, his supporters fled, and the titular king, Badi IV, submitted and was pensioned off into the limbo of history.

THE SOUTHERN SUDAN

Beyond the Funj kingdom in the remote regions of the southern Sudan lives a large group of peoples that speak Nilotic languages. The origins of the Nilotes are unknown, but one authority has suggested that they were a small group of agriculturalists that came from the west and settled in the Bahr al-Ghazal region of the southern Sudan, where they acquired, one knows not how or where, the techniques for domesticating cattle. Once equipped with a cattle complex, the Nilotes began to migrate from their cradleland in the Bahr al-Ghazal during the fifteenth century. The Dinka and the Nuer did not move far, wandering off to the northeast to the swamplands around Lake No and the Bahr al-Jabal. A second group, the Luo-speaking Nilotes, pressed south up the Nile to northern Uganda. Before reaching their destination the Luo split, with one group reversing its movement and marching northward through the Bahr al-Ghazal. During their march several smaller groups splintered off to remain in the Bahr al-Ghazal or, as in the case of the Anuak, to cross the Nile and settle in the upper reaches of the Sobat. The Luo remnant, under the leadership of Nyikang, pressed on to occupy the northern bank of the White Nile from Fashoda to Lake No, where their successors founded the Shilluk kingdom in the sixteenth century. Meanwhile, further south the Luo invaders of Uganda pressed on into Bunyoro-Kitara, where their *Bito* clans replaced the *Chwezi* aristocracy as rulers of the interlacustrine Bantu.

The Nilotes were not the only African inhabitants of the southern Sudan. At the beginning of the nineteenth century, groups of *Azande* were moving up the valley of the Mbomu and by midcentury had consolidated themselves along the Congo-

Nile watershed. During their expansion from their homeland far to the west the Azande, under their aristocratic chiefs the Avungara, had developed an efficient military organization, as had the neighboring Mangbettu people, which either assimilated non-Azande or drove them before the advancing Azande armies (Georg Schweinfurth, *King Munza*). Ever expansionist, the Azande continued to press northeastward, where they would have inevitably collided with the equally militant Nilotes if alien powers had not intervened in the southern Sudan.

The *Turkiya* ‡

In 1820 Muhammad Ali, the Turkish Viceroy of Egypt, decided to conquer the Sudan. He was lured southward by tales of gold and the need to recruit slaves for his army. Commanded by his son Ismail, Muhammad Ali's troops defeated the *Shayqiya,* who sought to oppose the advance near Kurti, and marched triumphantly on up the Nile to Shendi (John Lewis Burckhardt, *Shendi*). By May 1821, Ismail reached the juncture of the White and the Blue Niles, crossed the river, and proceeded to Sennar where Badi IV surrendered, ending the long drawn-out death agony of the Funj kingdom. While Ismail was marching unopposed up the Nile, Muhammad Ali sent a second expedition to conquer the regions of Kordofan and Darfur, west of the Nile. Under the command of Muhammad Ali's son-in-law, Muhammad Bey Khusraw, the *daftardar* (treasurer), the army assembled at ad-Dabba, marched southwest across the Bayuda, and routed the army of the Fur sultan at Bara to add Kordofan to Muhammad Ali's growing empire.

The new administration of the Sudan began very favorably. The conquest had

‡ The period of Egyptian-Turkish rule in the Sudan. The alien invaders of the Sudan in the nineteenth century were the Turkish-speaking rulers of Egypt. Ethnically, few were Turks, and fewer were Egyptians as we know them today.

been carried out with very little bloodshed, at least in the Nile Valley, and Ismail could begin his government with no past obstacles or former obligations. Unfortunately, however, Muhammad Ali had conquered the Sudan to exploit it, and the subsequent actions of his officials confirmed this policy. Taxes were instituted at a crushing rate, and the demand for slaves threatened to strip the petty chiefs of their retinues, upsetting the social structure in the Sudan. The result was a rebellion that began with sporadic attacks on Egyptian troops and culminated in the assassination of Ismail and his guard at Shandi in November 1822. Upon the death of Ismail, the daftardar was hastily ordered from Kordofan to the Nile to lay waste to the Nile Valley with fire and sword and brutally to stamp out the ill-coordinated and poorly armed Sudanese rebels. By 1824 the revolt was over. The daftardar returned to Egypt and Uthman Bey took over the administration of the Sudan with two objects in mind—to repress rebellion and to collect the taxes. Although Uthman Bey founded Khartoum at the juncture of the Blue and the White Niles, his policies did nothing to restore the Sudan. Soon an epidemic accompanied the economic depression, and even the army was drifting into anarchy when Uthman died in 1825.

Ali Khurshid Agha succeeded Uthman Bey in 1826, and his administration marks the turning point in Egyptian relations with the Sudanese. Ali Khurshid Agha first enticed the cultivators back to their lands with letters of amnesty and promises not to repeat the oppressive practices of the past. He then convened a council of notables to devise an equitable system of taxation and confirmed the appointment of Abd al-Qadir wad az-Zayn to act as liaison officer between the administration and the Sudanese and to attempt to associate the Sudanese more closely with the administration. Trade was encouraged and the caravans were protected. Khartoum was developed and settlers were given tracts of land and privileges. Khurshid returned to Cairo in May 1838. He had successfully rescued the Sudan from anarchy and transformed it into a peaceful and prosperous country and fully deserved the honors that were heaped upon him by a grateful Muhammad Ali.

Ahmad Pasha Abu Widan was appointed Khurshid's successor. He carried on the policies and schemes of development of his predecessor, but upon his death in 1843 the Sudan relapsed into twenty years of stagnation precipitated by the vacillating policies of the viceroys in Cairo. Concerned about the power that Abu Widan had concentrated in his own hands, both Muhammad Ali and his successor, Muhammad Said, sought to decentralize administration in the Sudan, weakening the authority of the governors general by means of short tenures. Between 1843 and 1862 eleven governors general sat at Khartoum, many of whom did not exercise authority over the governors of the outlying provinces.

In 1863 Ismail Pasha succeeded his uncle as Viceroy of Egypt and set out to transform Egypt from a petty, oriental state into a modern, westernized empire. He constructed schools, hospitals, and palaces. He expanded and modernized the army. His greatest achievement was the Suez Canal, and clearly the Sudan would not be left out of his grandiose projects. Three themes dominate Ismail's reign in the Sudan: the expansion of Egyptian territory, the fight against the slave trade (if for no other reason than to attract European and American capital), and the use of European, Christian administrators to carry out these objectives. The first drive to the south was led by Samuel White Baker, in whose person all three of Ismail's objectives were combined (Sir Samuel Baker, *Khartoum and the Nilotic Slave Trade*). Baker left Khartoum in February 1870 at the head of a mammoth expedition. He pushed through the swamp regions of the Nile, known as the *sudd,* and by 1873 he had occupied Equatoria, broken the power of the slave raiders along the Nile, and forced the inhabitants to acknowledge the rule of the khedive. In the same year the Egyptian flag flew as far south as Fatiko, near the Albert Nile. On Baker's return, Ismail appointed Charles George Gordon to continue the task of consolidating and expanding Egyptian rule in equatorial Africa. Gordon served in Equatoria from 1874 to 1877, during which time he consolidated the work of Baker and established effective Egyptian administration in Equatoria.

Ismail did not, however, confine his plans for expansion to the Nile. In 1865 the Red Sea ports of Suakin and Massawa were ceded to Egypt, bringing about several abortive attempts by Egyptian forces to penetrate into Abyssinia. Checked in the east, Ismail had greater success in the interior regions of the southern Sudan, the Bahr al-Ghazal. Ever since a passage through the Nile swamps had been found between 1839 and 1840, powerful commercial firms had established vast and complex trading networks in the Bahr al-Ghazal in order to carry on the ivory and slave trade. By the 1860s az-Zubayr Rahma Mansur, a northern Sudanese trader, had achieved a predominant position among the traders. He controlled most of the trading stations scattered throughout the Bahr al-Ghazal and was supported by a vast slave army that had been employed to round up the slaves and escort them to markets in the north. In 1871 Ismail sought to end the slave trade and annex the Bahr al-Ghazal to the Egyptian Sudan by sending a military expedition to crush the slavers. Under the leadership of az-Zubayr, however, the slavers rallied their private armies and defeated the Egyptian forces. In December 1873 the khedive, happy to make the best of a bad job, appointed az-Zubayr as the Egyptian governor of the Bahr al-Ghazal. The recognition of az-Zubayr allowed the

slavers to continue their nefarious trade, but in return Egypt had acquired nominal sovereignty over the Bahr al-Ghazal.

In February 1877 Gordon was appointed Governor General of the whole Sudan. One of his principal tasks was to implement the Anglo-Egyptian Slave Trade Convention, which provided for the termination of the sale and purchase of slaves in the Sudan by 1880, and he set out with his accustomed energy to break the slave trade. He lightened taxes, fired corrupt officials, issued a stream of reform legislation, and personally led the campaign against the slavers. But Gordon was illiterate in Arabic, impulsive, and a fanatical Christian in a fanatically Muslim land. He soon alienated not only the bureaucracy but all the very numerous and wealthy interests that derived their power from slaving. Suddenly, in 1879, the khedive's financial position collapsed. He could no longer pay the interest on the capital that he had borrowed from European bankers to modernize Egypt, and after cleaning out the spare cash in the treasury, Ismail sailed away to a gilded exile in a palace on the Bosporus. With the khedive gone, his own resources fast drying up, and the many groups of Sudanese bitterly hostile, Gordon resigned. He was succeeded by Rauf Pasha, a more pliant and mediocre man. With a weak governor general at Khartoum, the bureaucracy demoralized, and deep discontent running through the land, Muhammad Ahmad proclaimed himself Mahdi on June 29, 1881.

THE END OF THE TURKIYA

The Mahdist Revolution in the Sudan was the result of widespread Sudanese dissatisfaction with Egyptian rule and coincided with the collapse of the khediviate in Egypt and the subsequent British occupation. British officials in Egypt were too preoccupied to restore order and to protect the interests of the European bondholders. Nor were they concerned about the Sudan, which, with an ineffectual governor general, drifted without direction or determination in the face of the rising dissatisfaction. The Sudanese found a spokesman for their discontent in the Mahdi, Muhammad Ahmad, a religious mystic and holy man living the life of a religious ascetic on Aba Island in the White Nile south of Khartoum. He regarded himself as a reformer, a *mujaddid,* a renewer of the Muslim faith, whose duty was to purge Islam of the corruption introduced during the Egyptian regime and to return it to the pure form practiced by the Prophet. The Mahdi was to guide the Muslim community as its Imam, or leader—the successor to Muhammad, the Prophet of God. The Mahdi appealed, of course, to the pious men, whose position in the Sudanese community was very influential. But the slave traders, who came mostly from settled riverain tribes, also rallied to the Mahdi's cause, not out of religious piety but in the hope of overthrowing the government and restoring the slave trade. His staunchest supporters, however, came from the Baggara Arabs, the cattle nomads of Kordofan and Darfur, who simply sought to rid themselves of the government and the burden of taxes.

The administration in Khartoum replied to the Mahdi's call to arms with a series of military expeditions that were annihilated, partly by the incompetence of their commanders but principally by the zeal of the Mahdi's followers. Victory followed victory for the Sudan, culminating in the disastrous defeat at Shaykan of a large military expedition of 10,000 men under Colonel Hicks, formerly of the Indian Army. The Hicks expedition was the final effort of which the Egyptian Army was capable. Its destruction left the Mahdi master of the lands west of the Nile and convinced the British authorities in Cairo that the Sudan should be abandoned. To effect the Egyptian evacuation, or at least report on how to carry it out, Gordon returned to the Sudan for the third time. He arrived at Khartoum in February 1884 and quickly realized that both evacuation and negotiation with the Mahdi were out of the question. The city was soon besieged, and in spite of Gordon's heroic and skillful leadership and the appearance of a British relief expedition, Khartoum was taken by assault on January 26, 1885 and Gordon was killed. The Turkiya was over.

ETHIOPIA

Several centuries before the birth of Christ, immigrants from the flourishing kingdoms of southern Arabia crossed the Red Sea to settle in the fertile highlands of the Ethiopian Plateau. The colonists brought with them not only the technical skills employed to terrace, dike, and irrigate the land but a sense of social and religious organization that evolved some time during the second century B.C. into the city and Kingdom of Aksum in northern Ethiopia. Aksum flourished, prospering in the trade with Arabia to the south and east and with Greece and Rome to the north and west, and gradually expanded along the Red Sea and Blue Nile by means of powerful armies, which the wealth of Aksum could afford. During the fourth century A.D., Aksum appears to have reached its golden age under Ezana, who unified Ethiopian Aksum, conquered the Yemen, and destroyed the decrepit Kingdom of Kush. Of more lasting importance than his expansion of empire, however, was Ezana's conversion to Christianity in approximately 333 A.D. Monophysite Christianity became the state religion and gradually spread among the pagan peoples, facilitating the integration of the diverse groups within the kingdom. Not only did the monasteries that sprang up in Aksum become the cultural repositories of the Kingdom, but the clergy interwove religious innovations into the traditional fabric of Ethiopian life.

Throughout the fifth and sixth centuries, Aksum continued her vigorous trading with Byzantium, Persia, India, and

Ceylon. Emeralds, gold, incense, and spices were traded in her markets for the goods of the Orient and the merchandise of the Mediterranean (Cosmos Indicoplenstes, *Trade in Ethiopia*). However, trade and the political power it engendered were gradually disrupted by rivals on the periphery of the kingdom. In Arabia, Aksumite hegemony in the Yemen was destroyed by the Persians in the last decade of the sixth century, while depredations from the Beja of the Red Sea hills threatened Aksum from the north. The corrosive effects of these attacks could not, in themselves, have forced Aksum into decline had not the rise of Islam and the Muslim depredations of the seventh and eighth centuries isolated the kingdom, which thereafter turned in upon itself.

Although the rulers of Aksum reasserted their control along the Red Sea coast in the ninth and tenth centuries, as a result of their attempts to include the Agau, a supposedly Jewish people of the interior, the forces of Queen Gudit of Agau defeated the Aksumites and drove their king to Shoa. Little is known of Queen Gudit's successors, but not until about 1270 did Yekuno Amlak regain the Aksumite throne for the Solomonid dynasty (which claimed its origins from Solomon), move the capital to Shoa, and introduce Amharic as the language of the court. Thereafter, his successors were preoccupied with the consolidation of the empire throughout the Ethiopian highlands, in which Christian evangelism played an important role, while waging war against the Muslims on the frontiers. By the fifteenth century Ethiopia had assumed its modern shape, but the political organization of the kingdom proved inadequate to control such a vast area or to weld its diverse peoples into a common whole. Consequently, the same problems—traditional internal conflicts and the Muslim threat—remained to challenge the empire in modern times.

To maintain its position in the face of hostile tribesmen from within and the threat of Muslim states from without, Ethiopia appealed to the Christian powers of the West, particularly the Kingdom of Portugal, for assistance in driving back the Muslim sultanate of Adal. Between 1520 and 1525 a Portuguese embassy visited Ethiopia but failed to conclude an alliance (Françisco Alvarez, *The Land of Prester John*). Despite the lack of Portuguese support, the emperor reopened the conflict with the sultanate of Adal during the second quarter of the sixteenth century. Assisted by the power of the Ottoman Turks and led by the Muslim reformer Ahmad ibn Ibrahim al-Ghazi, who regarded himself as having been divinely appointed to conquer Christian Ethiopia, the Muslims swept all before them until Portuguese reinforcements arrived in 1541, checked the Muslim advance, and killed Ahmad in 1543. Thereafter Emperor Galawdewos successfully ended the Muslim occupation but failed to reassert the unity of old Ethiopia. In the south the Galla drove into Harrar, while within the empire the Falasha, Agau, and Sidama were in constant revolt.

Harried by Muslims from without and revolts from within, Emperor Susneyos (1607–1632) converted to the Church of Rome and permitted Roman Catholic missionaries to campaign against Monophysite Catholicism in the hope of receiving Christian military assistance from Europe (Father Lobo, *Portuguese Missionaries in Ethiopia*). Unhappily, religious strife soon degenerated into civil war between the emperor and the conservative leaders of the traditional religion. Unable to stem the tide of popular reaction, Susneyos abandoned his hope for a European alliance and returned to the Ethiopian Coptic Church just before his death in 1632. The reconversion of Susneyos, however, was but a momentary check in the long decline of the empire. Thereafter the spread of Islam, the growth of Galla power, and the endemic internal rebellions eroded the authority of the emperors. In the latter half of the seventeenth century, Emperor Fasiladas retired to Gondar in the heartland of the *Amhara,* where he established the first permanent capital. Although it was relatively secure, Gondar was too isolated for the emperors to control the far-flung territories beyond the Amhara area. During the eighteenth century the empire of Ethiopia disappeared. The Galla chiefs ousted the Christian Amhara chiefs and assumed control, although the Solomonid dynasty continued to provide petty kings for the principality of Gondar. Only the Monophysite Christian Church remained to provide a sense of unity throughout the fragmented empire.

In the mid-nineteenth century, Ethiopia consisted of numerous autonomous warlords ruling Christian peoples that spoke different languages and practiced divergent customs. In the 1840s one such warlord, Karsa, acquired control of Amhara, Gojjom, Tigre, and Shoa and persuaded the *abuna,* or head of the church, to install him as Theodorus II, King of Kings and Emperor of all the Ethiopians. Thereafter, Theodorus set out to consolidate his rule. Autonomous chiefs were defeated and rebellions were decisively crushed. The capital was moved from Gondar to Magdala, but here Theodorus acted with ever-greater capriciousness and his behavior became increasingly neurotic. Affronted by Queen Victoria's failure to answer his letters, he incarcerated British representatives, who were released only by a British military expedition that captured Magdala in 1868. Theodorus committed suicide. Although the British quickly withdrew, they had demonstrated the weakness of Ethiopia and aroused the interest and cupidity of the other European powers.

Upon the death of Theodorus, Johannes IV, the former Prince of Tigre, acquired the throne in 1872 after several years of struggle and ruled until his death in 1888 during the battle of Al-Gallabat

against the Mahdists from the Sudan. His successor, Menelik, Prince of Shoa and one of the most remarkable rulers in African history, found himself beset from without by Italian efforts to establish a predominant influence in Ethiopia and from within by the centrifugal designs of princes, warlords, and chiefs that always appeared in Ethiopia upon the death of an emperor. The Italian threat proved the more serious, and in 1896 an Italian army marched into Ethiopia to the place where Menelik had gathered a great host to repel the invaders. The two armies met at the village of Adua in March 1896. The Italian Army was overwhelmingly defeated and the Italian sphere of influence was reduced to Eritrea and the coastal port of Massawa. Ethiopia remained triumphantly independent.

Having thrown back the foreign invaders, Menelik skillfully played one European power against another in order to acquire assistance to expand the empire within Ethiopia itself. Equipped with European arms, he annexed Wallamo Galla, the Beni Shangul, Kaffa, and carried the emperor's authority as far south as Lake Rudolf. Nevertheless, Menelik's death in 1913 precipitated numerous intrigues against his successor, Lij Jasu, who openly espoused Islam, denounced his Solomonid ancestry, and claimed descent from the Prophet Muhammad. This flagrant advocacy of Christian Ethiopia's most ancient and traditional enemy deeply angered the Christian princes of Shoa, who marched on the capital, Addis Ababa, and in 1916 elevated Menelik's daughter Zanditu to the throne. Ras Tafari, the future Haile Selassie, became regent and the active ruler of the empire. As his influence grew he set out to bring Ethiopia into the modern world, and by 1930, when he assumed the title of emperor on the death of the Empress Zanditu, he had already set Ethiopia on a new and difficult course to break its traditional isolation from the world beyond the highlands.

BANTU AND KUSHITE IN EAST AFRICA

Perhaps before and probably no later than the arrival of the Bantu on the East African coast from south-central Africa, a second body of Bantu cultivators reached the great lakes in the interior of eastern Africa. Here in the salubrious upland heart of Africa the Bantu settled, tilled the fertile soils surrounding the lakes, and came in contact with Kushitic peoples from southwest Ethiopia. The nature of these first contacts between Bantu and Kushite is unknown, but in subsequent centuries Kushitic pastoralists appear to have moved into the lake region and superimposed their culture upon the sedentary Bantu. Oral traditions indicate several such groups of Kushitic peoples, the last being the famous *Hima* pastoralists under kings of the Chwezi clan. As Hima kings, the Chwezi established their authority over the Bantu agriculturalists and ruled a kingdom called Kitara, which embraced much of the area of modern Uganda. Their capital was at Bigo on the Katonga River. The Hima clearly formed a pastoral aristocracy that the Bantu treated with respect and deference.

THE NILOTES

At the end of the fifteenth century a third group, the Nilotes, entered the lake region of eastern Africa from the north, the southern Sudan. The Nilotes are a Negroid people who may have followed the dispersion of Sudanic crops from the Niger region of West Africa eastward into the Nile Basin. Here the Nilotes remained as a small group of cultivators until they developed pastoralism. How the Nilotes acquired cattle remains unknown. Perhaps they borrowed the techniques necessary for a pastoral complex from the Kushites. Perhaps they developed other techniques independently of other peoples. But once the Nilotes learned to subsist on pastoral nomadism, they began to expand and to move. One group, whose modern descendants are the Dinka and the Nuer, moved only a short distance,

settling by the great swamps of the Nilotic Sudan. A second group pressed east and south from the region between Lake Rudolf and the Nile into Kenya, where they met Kushitic peoples that were gradually assimilated but from whom the Nilotic nomads acquired numerous cultural traits. Today these Nilotes form an elongated funnel stretching from the Kenya-Sudan border west of Lake Rudolf southward to the Tanzania frontier and are represented by such famous tribes as the *Masai*, the *Nandi*, and the *Karamojong*. A third group of Nilotes, the Lwo-speaking peoples, marched from their cradleland in the Bahr al-Ghazal province of the southern Sudan south up the Nile and into Kitara. Here they drove out the Hima pastoral aristocracy and their Chwezi kings, settled among the Bantu, adopted Bantu speech, and established dynasties of rulers over Kitara, now called Bunyoro-Kitara, from the Bito clans of the Lwo. Although the Lwo became Bantuized, their Bito clans formed new political nuclei around which grew kingdoms.

The impact of the Lwo, however, did not stop at the limits of Kitara. The Hima pastoralists, whom the Lwo had driven out, settled in northwest Tanzania, southwest Uganda, and Burundi, where they introduced the idea of chieftainship and even resurrected kingdoms. Thus the Lwo invasions into northern Uganda not only created new chieftainships but stimulated political evolution beyond the limits of Lwo expansion.

Buganda is the outstanding example of the evolution of chieftainship. In the sixteenth century Buganda was but a small tributary state of the great feudatory kingdom of Bunyoro-Kitara. At the end of the sixteenth century, Buganda broke away from Bunyoro-Kitara and not only managed to maintain its independence but, in its confined state, developed a more homogeneous and centralized society than the sprawling structure of Bunyoro ever achieved. When Buganda began to expand in the seventeenth century, the conquered clans were not simply confirmed in their positions of authority; rather, new chieftainships were created for the conquered clans by the appointment of rulers who were *Baganda,* loyal to the Buganda king, the *kabaka,* and controlled from the central capital. Thus, in the seventeenth and eighteenth centuries Buganda developed a bureaucratic system under the absolute control of the kabaka, who monopolized the trade with the coast and exposed Buganda to external influences. Equipped with a centralized, efficient administration and alert to the outside world, by the nineteenth century Buganda had eclipsed Bunyoro as the predominate power in Uganda (Sir Apolo Kagwa, *Court Life in Buganda*).

The remaining area of eastern Africa never developed states like those of the coast or the lakes. In western Tanzania, Unyamwezi, a multiplicity of small units existed that never coalesced into a whole but tended to divide and proliferate. Even further south, between the Rufiji and Rouvuma rivers, the Bantu peoples remained hunters or fishermen or shifting cultivators—scattered, chiefless, anonymous. Even in eastern Kenya the presence of Nilotic peoples did not result in state building. In the lake regions the Lwo were the invaders; in Kenya the Bantu must be regarded as the incomers. For before the Bantu reached the Kenya highlands, groups of Nilotic pastoralists moved south from the Rudolf Basin, thus coming in contact with Kushitic peoples and adopting many Kushitic customs. The *Nandi* settled near Mt. Elgon as early as the sixteenth century and were followed by other Nilotic peoples, culminating with the *Masai.* Later, Bantu migrants, like the *Kikuyu,* pressed into the area, settling around the fringe of the Nilotic core and in turn adopting many Kushitic-Nilotic customs. Although people like the Masai, Kikuyu, and Nandi were tribes or even nations, they never developed the centralized political structure that characterized the kingdoms further west.

Until the middle of the nineteenth century, the interior of East Africa remained undisturbed by outside influence. There had, of course, long been contact between the Africans of the interior and the coast, but trade remained in the hands of the Africans, the greatest traders of whom were the *Nyamwezi,* the *Yao,* and the *Kamba,* who monopolized the hinterland trade throughout the first half of the nineteenth century. Moreover, trade among the peoples of the interior was carried on in peace and even in times of war by the women. During the second quarter of the nineteenth century, however, the interior beyond the East African coast was penetrated by an ever-increasing number of non-Africans. In 1825 two Khojas from Surat, India, arrived at the Unyamwezi country, and by 1842 caravans of coastal Arabs had reached Lake Tanganyika. Others followed, and in 1852 an Arab caravan traversed the African continent from the east coast to Benguela on the Atlantic Ocean.

The Arabs pressed into the interior principally in search of ivory. Slaves, of course, were of value to the traders, particularly as porters to carry the ivory out of Africa, but in these early years of the caravan trade, slaves were regarded as a secondary item. However, as the ivory regions became exhausted as Africans and Arabs sought to meet the growing world demand, the interests of the traders shifted to slaves. In this sense the slave trade grew out of the ivory trade. The main source of supply was near the lakes in western Tanzania, where the village was the largest political unit and the inhabitants possessed no strong, centralized political organization to oppose the Arabs. Occasionally the Arabs themselves would capture the Africans, but more frequently they would induce an African chief to raid his neighbors (who were probably his rivals) and hand over the captives in return for Arab possessions and trade goods. Slave raids produced yet more raids, resulting in the great increase of intertribal warfare, depopulated areas, and misery and desolation for those who were left behind in the smoking villages or pillaged fields. The march to the coast was the worst experience for a slave. It took generally three months, during which the slaves were roped or chained together. The recalcitrant Africans wore heavy yokes, and those who resisted were shot or left to starve. Once the slaves reached the coast they were placed in *barracoons,* or stockades, and then packed into the Arab dhows for the three-day crossing to Zanzibar. In Zanzibar the slaves were sold at the great market and shipped to Arabia, Persia, or beyond. Again they were packed in dhows that cruised north along the coast and then dashed to ports in the Red Sea, South Arabia, or the Persian Gulf. Those who survived the long and terrifying journey were sold to Muslim masters, and their lot improved considerably. For in contrast to the dehumanizing plantation slavery of the Americas, in the Middle East slaves were employed principally as domestic servants. Thus, many slaves were well-treated and respected members of the family whose relationship with their masters was regulated by the *Quran.* Many slaves in Zanzibar, for instance, were permitted to sell their own produce and to hold slaves in their own right.

The slave trade expanded because it was profitable and because Sayyid Said, the ruler of Zanzibar, provided a favorable climate for the growth of commerce, including slaves. He encouraged Banyans from India to settle in his domains, and they were soon the principal source of capital to finance the interior trade. Sayyid Said himself promoted expeditions to the mainland, and thus it was no coincidence that caravans began to penetrate into the interior during his reign. Despite the profits from his own commercial ventures, however, his chief sources of revenue remained the export and import duties on Zanzibar's main commodity—slaves.

As the slave trade expanded in East Africa, so too did Europe's and particularly Great Britain's interest in the country. Although some Victorian writers eloquently described East Africa's potential wealth, early British interest was fundamentally humanitarian and scientific. The development of the slave trade in East Africa therefore resulted in a European reaction against it led by Britain, who had championed the fight against the West African slavers. The great British humanitarian David Livingstone was also one of the foremost explorers of East Africa. Emotionally less powerful but intellectually more stimulating, however, was the scientific search for the source of the Nile. For whereas David Livingstone marched through East Africa as a great missionary general directing the attack on the slave trade, men like Richard Burton, John Hanning Speke, and Henry Morton Stanley were in Africa to solve the riddle of the Nile.

Burton and Speke set out in 1857 from Bagamoyo "for the purpose of ascertaining the limits of the sea of Ujiji" in the interior and to determine whether the lake was the source of the Nile. They had been attracted to East Africa by adventure and the Nile quest, which had been aroused by the preliminary explorations of German missionaries—Ludwig Krapf, J. Rebmann, and J. Erhardt—employed by the Church Missionary Society, the British Anglican missionary organization. The German missionaries had made numerous journeys into the interior from their coastal mission stations and had traced their explorations on a map published in Europe by Erhardt in 1856. Burton and Speke reached Lake Tanganyika in February 1858, traveled to the northern end of the lake, and found, to their disappointment, that the Ruzizi River flowed into the lake and thus could hardly be a headwater of the Nile. The two explorers returned to Tabora, from where Speke marched northward alone to the shores of Lake Victoria. He jumped to the conclusion that Lake Victoria was the source of the Nile and upon his return to England organized a second expedition with Captain A. J. Grant. Speke and Grant set out for Lake Victoria in 1860. They skirted the western shore of the lake, sojourned in Buganda and Bunyoro, and continued on down the Nile to Cairo, returning to London in 1863 (John Hanning Speke, *Unyamwezi and Uganda*). Although Speke asserted that the Nile question was settled, others remained unconvinced. Speke and Grant had not circumnavigated Lake Victoria; it might, in fact, be many lakes. Moreover, they had not followed the Nile from Victoria, but rather went overland, meeting the Nile far to the north at Gondokoro. The skeptics maintained that the river that flowed out of Lake Victoria might be but a tributary of the main Nile stream. No, the Nile question was not settled, but the controversy and the explorers' accounts were widely followed in England and focused British attention on East Africa.

Speke died tragically in 1863. Two years later, after the explorations of Sir Samuel Baker near Lake Albert had only deepened the mystery of the Nile source, Sir Roderick Murchison announced that Britain's foremost explorer, David Livingstone, would return to Africa to ascertain Africa's watersheds and resolve the problem of the Nile source. In 1866 Livingstone set out for Africa a third time. Twice before he had spent long years in Africa on epic journeys; from 1853 to 1856 he had traversed the continent and from 1858 to 1863 he had sought to find a high road into central Africa by way of the Zambesi River. Now Livingstone returned to Africa, more famous than ever and more possessed of the spiritual quality that the Arabs call *baraka,* to find God, as well as the source of the Nile, through Africa. For five years Livingstone wandered alone in East Africa, while the world wondered. His letters about the conditions of the slave trade and the havoc caused to African society by the

raiders were decisive in launching the great campaign against the slave trade. But such reports were punctuated by long silences, which soon elicited efforts to relieve if not rescue the good doctor. In 1871 the New York *Herald* sent its star reporter, Henry Morton Stanley, to Africa to find Livingstone. In November of the same year the two men met at Ujiji and Stanley provided Livingstone with the resources to continue his explorations. After two additional years of wandering in the interior, even Stanley's supplies were lost or exhausted, and, sick and failing, Livingstone died, as he wished, near the village of Chitambo on May 1, 1873.

Although Livingstone's last journey had ignited the antislave trade crusade in Britain, it had only confused the Nile question. For Livingstone had mistaken the upper Congo River, known as the Lualaba, for the Nile. Stanley resolved to piece together this geographical puzzle once and for all, and under his expert but ruthless leadership a large expedition plunged into Africa in 1874. In three years' hard marching he circumnavigated Lake Victoria, proving it to be one body of water, and then in like manner confirmed that Lake Tanganyika has no outlet. Then he and his men journeyed down the Lualaba-Congo to the Atlantic Ocean, establishing that it had no relation to the Nile. Stanley returned to Zanzibar in 1877. The Nile question was all but settled. Subsequently Europeans and an American explored lakes Albert and Albert Edward and the short stretch of the Victoria Nile, filling in the brief gaps that Stanley's continental explorations had neglected.

While Stanley was in the interior solving the geographical questions raised by previous explorers, on the coast the humanitarian forces of the antislave trade crusade, aroused by Livingstone, stood ready to halt that trade. For years the British government had sought to attack the slave trade by restricting it to the dominions of the Sultan of Zanzibar, but this policy was not completely successful. Although British squadrons patrolled East African waters, the commanders frequently could not determine whether a slave cargo was legally passing between Zanzibar and the sultan's domain in South Arabia or illegally bound for some other port. In 1873 the British government realized its failure, abandoned the policy of restriction, and sought to force the Sultan of Zanzibar, Barghash ibn Said, to abolish the trade. Sir Bartle Frere was sent to Zanzibar to negotiate with the sultan, and when negotiations failed, the British Navy enforced British policy by seizing the slavers and threatening war on Zanzibar. Barghash gave way and agreed to end the trade.

To his credit Barghash enforced the antislave trade treaty more rigidly than the British had ever expected. He was, of course, supported by British power, which probably prevented his overthrow by the powerful slaving interests on the coast, but his coercion was successful (Salim al-Mazrui, *The Sultan and Mombasa*). The seaborne trade was virtually halted, and when Arab traders tried to evade Barghash's decrees by marching slaves northward for sale in Somaliland, Barghash in 1876 forbade the conveyance of slaves on the mainland of Africa itself. For many years thereafter a surreptitious slave trade continued in East Africa and an occasional slave dhow slipped by British patrols bound for Arabia, but in fact as well as in theory, the British humanitarians had triumphed in East Africa as they had triumphed in West Africa. The Zanzibar slave trade was broken and European interest in East Africa was now aroused. Perhaps the legitimate commerce of Britain and Europe could replace that of human chattels.

PARTITION OF EAST AFRICA

Although the efforts of the Sultan of Zanzibar to curtail the slave trade fulfilled the requirements of British policy, the extent

of his rule in the interior remained ill-defined, and this breach in his authority enabled the international powers to divide up East Africa amongst themselves. Ironically, however, the partition of East Africa was begun not by a European but by an African power. In preparation for a thrust into the interior the Khedive of Egypt attempted in 1875 to extend his empire by acquiring ports on the coast of Somaliland that were loyal to the Sultan of Zanzibar. Although Barghash was powerless to eject the Egyptian invaders, his British allies were not, and British pressure at Cairo forced the khedive to recall his forces. The first attempt to contest the sultan's authority on the African mainland had failed.

No sooner had the Egyptian expedition withdrawn, however, than a flock of European concessionaires swarmed like flies around the sultan, their appetites whetted by the rapid increase in East African trade in the 1870s and the weakness of the sultanate, which the Egyptian invasion had so glaringly exposed. Before his energies were turned to the Congo, King Leopold of the Belgians promoted several expeditions to East Africa, which ostensibly were in the cause of science but in reality were the probable forerunners of political claims. Not to be outdone, the French Chamber of Deputies supported an expedition that reached Lake Tanganyika in 1879, when its leader died. But the French and Belgian interest in East Africa never developed beyond these tentative probings, and the serious challenge to the sultan's authority was left to the Germans. Numerous German explorers had wandered under their own impetus in various and widely separated parts of East Africa, but not until the appearance of Carl Peters in Usagara, behind Bagamoyo, was German enterprise in Africa given an imperial direction. Peters was one of Germany's more unsavory advocates of German colonial expansion. He had founded the Society for German Colonization in 1884 and went out to East

Africa for the express purpose of acquiring territory for the German Empire. Although reluctant to embark on imperial adventures, Bismarck, the German Chancellor, was quite prepared to use the work of German explorers in Africa in order to strengthen his domestic position in Germany and his international policy in Europe. He therefore supported Peters' claims in East Africa and declared a German protectorate over Usagara, where the Sultan of Zanzibar had always exercised jurisdiction and through which passed his strategic caravan route to the west. Barghash protested but to no avail, and this time the British government did not rush to the sultan's rescue. It was one thing for the British to push around a petty Oriental potentate; it was quite another to attempt to tamper with the wishes of the new and vigorous German Empire. The partition of East Africa was now begun in earnest.

Ever since 1882, when the British had occupied Egypt, they had welcomed German diplomatic support of the International Debt Commission for the administrative and financial reforms in the lower Nile Valley. In 1885 the Gladstone government still required German support in Egypt and elsewhere. Moreover, Gladstone himself welcomed Germany's appearance in Africa as a partner in the task of civilizing the continent. Consequently, not only did the British refrain from defending the sultan, but they even used their influence at Zanzibar to convince him to give way to German demands. Barghash had little choice. In December 1885 he recognized the German protectorate and signed a treaty giving the Germans commercial privileges and easy access from the port of Dar es Salaam to their protectorate in the interior. But the loss of Usagara was only the beginning. In the following year a commission composed of representatives of Britain, France, and Germany ascertained the limits of the sultan's territory on the East African mainland. Britain

and Germany agreed to recognize his authority along the coast but divided East Africa into spheres of influence. The German sphere stretched south of a line drawn from Tanga on the coast to 1 degree south latitude on the eastern shore of Lake Victoria and thence along that line to the west. The British sphere lay to the north.

Although the Anglo-German Agreement of 1886 had demarcated the respective spheres of Britain and Germany along the coast and beyond in the immediate hinterland, the agreement did not establish a western limit, so that the rear of each sphere was open to encroachment by the other; and as both British and German companies sought to exploit their spheres, the rivalry intensified for control of the interlacustrine Bantu kingdoms of the great lakes. British hopes to acquire predominant influence in Uganda rested with the Imperial British East Africa Company (IBEA), founded by Sir William Mackinnon in 1888 to carry on trade and commerce and even to administer the British zone. On the urging of the British government, the company decided in 1889 to push into the interior in order to secure the Bantu kingdoms of Uganda within the British sphere. The IBEA, however, was not alone in the field. Carl Peters set out ostensibly to rescue a fellow German, Emin Pasha, who was beleaguered on the Upper Nile, and at the same time to claim Uganda as a German protectorate. Peters arrived too late to relieve Pasha, who was already on his way to the coast accompanied by a British relief expedition under Henry Morton Stanley. However, in February 1890, Peters arrived in Uganda before the representatives of the IBEA and signed a treaty with Mwanga, the Kabaka of Buganda, placing Buganda under German protection. But Peters' victory was short-lived. Throughout the spring of 1890 negotiations between the governments of Great Britain and Germany continued and on July 1, 1890, culminated successfully in an agreement commonly called the Heligoland Agreement, whereby the British government, in return for Uganda and the vital sources of the Nile River, conceded the strategic island of Heligoland in the North Sea. The partition of East Africa was complete; the arduous task of pacification could now begin.

RESISTANCE

The partition of East Africa was but the prelude to occupation, and the demarcation of the respective spheres of Britain and Germany did not automatically result in African acquiescence to the imposition of European rule. Neither consulted nor advised, the East African peoples generally opposed the invaders until they were overwhelmed by the technological superiority of the Europeans. The Africans did not want European overrule, even if it meant all the manifold and humane benefits that Western science and technology could provide. They resented Western interference in their traditional way of living and only submitted after a decade of forceful resistance.

The Germans were the first to experience African resistance. In 1888 the coastal Arabs and their African allies, led by Bushiri of Pangani, rebelled against the German East Africa Company. Although the revolt was crushed by German troops under Captain Hermann von Wissmann, the Imperial German Government was determined to intervene directly and took over the administration of the protectorate from the company. Gradually the German administration spread out from the coast into the interior, playing on the divisions among the African tribes and crushing resistance with their superior weapons. But having conquered the African peoples, the Germans had equal difficulties keeping them subservient. In July 1905 the Maji-Maji Revolt erupted in the Matumbe Hills northwest of Kilwa. The Maji-Maji Revolt was the most serious challenge to German control. Once again the technological superiority of the

German weapons was decisive, but only after heavy fighting that resulted in large numbers of casualties on both sides. By 1907 the revolt had been brought under control and the Germans turned their energies to the economic development of the protectorate. The Africans had been pacified—beaten into a reluctant acceptance of German rule (Ruhanantuka, *Flight of the Ekirimbi*).

To the north the British, like the Germans, also had to crush African resistance before their occupation was complete. Although Uganda had been reserved for Britain after the Heligoland Agreement of 1890, the task of occupation was left to the Imperial British East Africa Company. When the company representative, Captain F. D. Lugard, arrived in Uganda in 1890, the Kingdom of Buganda was divided among rival religious factions— Protestants, Catholics, pagans, and Muslims—each competing for control. The rival Christian parties were followers of the European Protestant and Catholic missionaries who had answered the invitation of the *Kabaka* Mutesa. In 1877 Mutesa had requested Christian missionaries for Buganda, not so much because he was concerned to learn the teachings of Jesus Christ, but to offset the growing influence of the Muslim powers, particularly Egypt to the north, which, under Khedive Ismail, was relentlessly extending its control up the Nile Valley. Largely through the force of his personality, Lugard was able to convince Mutesa's successor, Mwanga, to transfer suzerainty to the IBEA. He then rallied the Christian parties in Buganda and drove the Muslims into exile before setting out to the west, where he signed treaties with the chiefs of Toro and Ankole and recruited 500 Sudanese troops in Equatoria who were formerly in the employ of the Khedive of Egypt but had been abandoned when Emin Pasha evacuated the province. With his force considerably augmented by the Sudanese troops, Lugard returned to Kampala, where in 1892 he intervened between the feuding Catholic and Protestant parties to resolve the religious wars that had divided the Baganda. Although Lugard imposed a semblance of stability on Buganda, his military operations had been expensive and commercially unprofitable. Consequently, the Directors of the IBEA decided to withdraw from Uganda, precipitating a great outcry from missionary and imperial groups in England who sought to include Uganda within the empire. Lugard himself returned to England to lead the campaign for the retention of Uganda and aroused such interest within the country that in 1894 the British government agreed to take over Uganda from the IBEA and set about the task of pacifying the territory. During numerous arduous campaigns from 1893 until 1900, British forces occupied Bunyoro, stamped out revolt in Buganda, and crushed a mutiny by the overworked Sudanese troops whom Lugard had enlisted. Although the campaigns of pacification had placed a great drain on British resources, by 1900 Uganda was thoroughly pacified and the introduction of administration could begin. The British had next to turn their attention to Sayyid Mahammad Abdille Hasan, who opposed European encroachment into Somaliland until sufficient forces were massed after World War I to crush him (Mahammad Abdille Hasan, *The Sayyid's Reply*).

ADMINISTRATION

The administration of German East Africa was characterized by concentration on economic development (which left few men and little money to provide services for the Africans) and exploitation by both government and private investors of the latent resources of the territory. In 1892 sisal was brought from Florida, flourished, and today remains Tanzania's principal export. Coffee and cotton plantations were established, and roads, rail lines, and the famous Amani Biological and Agricultural Institute were con-structed to make the economic achievements possible. The administration itself was in the hands of a governor. The territory was divided into districts usually administered by officers seconded from the German Army, and their methods frequently reflected their military background. The Sultan of Zanzibar had administered his coastal regions through *walis* in the towns and *akidas* in the countryside who supervised *jumbes,* or headmen, in the villages, and the Germans simply adopted this system for the coast. Thus, when local authorities were unable to control the laborers induced to work on the plantations of the northern hinterland, akidas were appointed by the Germans. Similarly, they placed akidas in the more sparsely populated south. But throughout the vast region of the interior the traditional chiefs were either tacitly accepted or formally recognized by the Germans.

British East Africa was divided and administered as two separate territories: the East African protectorate, later known as Kenya, and the Uganda protectorate. From the first the Uganda protectorate was regarded as the more important; the East African protectorate was considered only as a passage to the rich and productive territories around the great lakes. Before Uganda could be developed, however, a cheap means of transport would have to link the interior with the coast, and throughout the 1890s the Uganda railway was pushed up from Mombasa until it reached Lake Victoria in 1903. Unhappily the railway proved a costly venture, and the economic exploitation of British East Africa was required to pay for such a heavy capital investment. The Governor of the East African protectorate, Sir Charles Eliot, consequently encouraged the immigration of European and South African settlers to East Africa. Not only would the technically knowledgeable Europeans transform the subsistence economy, but by example they would introduce the Africans to the "benefits" of Western civilization. Between 1903 and 1904, several hundred Europeans settled on large farms in the Kenya highlands on land that the Kikuyu regarded as their traditional territory. The colonists not only required land but needed labor to work it, and they at once demanded that the government institute means to recruit African labor for the European farms and plantations. Thus, while the economy expanded and the railway began to pay for itself, the seeds of racial tension were planted in the fertile soil of the highlands of Kenya (Lord Delamere, *White Man's Country*).

At first the 1914 war was not expected to spread to East Africa, but on the outbreak of hostilities the outnumbered Germans, under their great guerilla leader, General Paul von Lettow-Vorbeck, sought to wage a long drawn-out campaign that would drain allied resources from the western front in Europe. Von Lettow-Vorbeck succeeded brilliantly, occupying many thousands of British, Indian, and South African troops who, at the time of the armistice in 1918, had still failed to force von Lettow-Vorbeck and his African and German troops to surrender. Although the British were ultimately victorious and acquired German East Africa as the Tanganyika mandate of the League of Nations, the war had created great economic problems in all the territories. In Tanganyika itself the British Governor, Sir Donald Cameron, introduced a system of indirect rule—that is, administration through the traditional African leaders and hereditary authorities. Indirect rule was in striking contrast to the very direct control of the Germans, which had destroyed many indigenous institutions of authority, and although British officials not infrequently had to rediscover African leaders or their descendants and install them in positions of authority, in coastal areas where the Arabs and Germans had obliterated the tribal leaders, the people regarded the government-appointed chiefs much as they had re-

garded the akidas. In the interior, however, where German administration had been less thorough, indirect rule functioned more rationally, even though many of the new-found chiefs proved to be unsuited or adopted a bureaucratic mentality toward their people. The benefits of indirect rule are still hotly debated among scholars, but at least it did provide for African participation, no matter how minimal, in the process of governing.

If British rule in Tanganyika was characterized by attempts to include Africans in the administration, in Kenya it had to devote its energies to protecting the Africans from the designs, for good or evil, of non-Africans. Following World War I the Kenya settlers demanded increasing participation in the government in return for their loyal services during the war. Ironically, the greatest opposition against the settlers came not from the Africans but from the Indian community. Indian traders had long been active on the coast, and their numbers were increased by those Indian laborers brought over to construct the Uganda railway who had refused repatriation to India. As petty traders they ventured into areas of East Africa where Europeans, because of the diminutive returns, were unwilling to risk capital. Thus, not only were Indian merchants responsible for opening far-off places in East Africa to world commerce, but their low standard of living gave them an economic edge over the Europeans. The British settlers, of course, were determined to protect their economic advantage, but to justify their privileged position they argued that Europeans, and Europeans only, should be entrusted with the responsibility for protecting African interests. The settlers employed this argument to further their own political ambitions for participation in the government of Kenya, but the British Colonial Office turned the argument around to declare in 1923 that African interests were paramount and were to be protected—not, however, by the European settler community, but by British civil servants of the Colonial Office (The Devonshire White Paper, *The Indians in Kenya*). The decision had momentous results, for Kenya never acquired self-government by a European minority (as did Rhodesia), and until the Africans themselves won the right to govern their own affairs the officials of the British Colonial Office continued to carry out the role of imperial trustee.

Since Uganda possessed few Europeans and Indians, the administration was more concerned with the Africans and particularly the relations of Buganda to the other interlacustrine kingdoms. As in Tanganyika, colonial administration in Uganda sought to include African participation in government through the institution of a legislative council. When the council was established in 1921, however, the Baganda chose not to participate, preferring to deliberate matters pertaining to Buganda in their own parliament, the *Lukiko,* which they completely controlled, rather than in a legislative council for the whole of the Uganda protectorate, where they would be outvoted. Thus the legislative council remained remote from the most powerful and active kingdom in Uganda, creating the impression that the government cared little for the welfare of Buganda.

NATIONALISM

World War II prepared the way for the rise of nationalism in East Africa and a greater emphasis on economic development. In all three territories plans were drafted during the war for development projects, and although all were not successful (such as the disastrous failure of the Tanganyika groundnut scheme), the progress in economic development in the postwar period was generally encouraging. Constitutional development, however, was complicated by the emergence of African nationalism which in Kenya erupted in the more violent form of Mau Mau.

The origins of Mau Mau are obscure, but the object of this secret society was clear—to drive the Europeans out of Kenya. Mau Mau was virtually a Kikuyu movement, and from 1952 until 1955 the society spread terror in Kenya by its acts of violence to African and European alike. Fundamentally, the movement was a reaction to British rule and the paternalism, no matter how benevolent, which dismissed a whole people as irresponsible. For half a century relations between Kikuyu and the Europeans were a tragic tale of frustration on the one hand and misunderstanding on the other. Although the rebellion was crushed, the Mau Mau did accomplish their goal by driving home the realization that it would be Africans who would ultimately rule in Kenya. And to the credit and foresight of the British, their officials pushed forward constitutional advance in a series of complex constitutions and elections in which the Africans, through two political parties, the Kenya African National Union (KANU) and the Kenya African Democratic Union (KADU), emerged as the most powerful force. Led by Jomo Kenyatta, African demands soon proved irresistible. The Europeans and Asians accepted, with reluctant grace, their position as minority groups, and on December 12, 1963, Kenya attained its independence.

Although constitutional development in Uganda was not opposed by the European community, the separate status of Buganda retarded political advance. When the British sought to bring Buganda into the process of constitutional development in Uganda as a whole, they were opposed by the kabaka, who was subsequently exiled in 1952. Without the kabaka, however, constitutional change could hardly go forward, and after long and difficult negotiations he returned to Uganda and agreed to revise Buganda's position to permit its political participation in the Uganda National Assembly. Under the leadership of A. M. Obote, the

Uganda Peoples Congress won control of the Assembly in the elections of April 1962, resulting in independence the following October.

Of all the three East African territories, Tanganyika presented the fewest obstacles to independence. Under the leadership of Julius Nyerere, the Tanganyika African National Union (TANU) was organized in 1954, and following a program of gradual advancement toward self-government that was marked by cordial relations between TANU and British officials, Tanganyika achieved independence on December 9, 1961.

THE MAHDIST STATE

After the fall of Khartoum the Mahdists quickly secured control of all the Sudan except for a few enclaves on the northern, eastern, and southern frontiers. The Mahdi regarded the fall of Khartoum as but the beginning of holy war throughout the Muslim world, but he never lived to carry out this larger design. On June 22, 1885, he died of the plague, six months after his greatest victory at Khartoum. The death of the Mahdi brought to a head all the underlying tensions of the revolutionary movement. The three groups— the pious men, the riverain tribes from which came the slave traders, and the Baggara—now became bitter rivals in the struggle for control of the Mahdist state. From the first the Baggara appeared the strongest of the three groups, and their support of their kinsman, Khalifa Abd Allahi, was decisive in his selection as the Mahdi's successor. Khalifa Abd Allahi at once set out to secure his position. He neutralized his riverain rivals as well as the Mahdi's relatives, the Ashraf, whose influences had steadily diminished after their kinsman's death. He then appointed his Baggara supporters to key positions in the Mahdist Army. Once the threat to his rule was overcome, the Khalifa sought to extend the holy war beyond the borders of the Sudan, but after several years of campaigning on the frontiers of Egypt,

Ethiopia, and Equatoria, his forces had made few gains but many losses. In 1889 the Mahdist Army, while advancing into Egypt, was crushingly defeated at Tushki, ending the Khalifa's attempts to carry Mahdism to the Muslim lands of the Middle East. Moreover, conditions in the Sudan after 1889 precluded any attempt to renew the holy war. A sequence of poor harvests in 1889 and 1890 brought famine and epidemic, aggravated by the large and unproductive standing armies on the frontiers and exacerbated by the decision of the Khalifa to bring the Baggara nomads from their western grazing lands to settle in Omdurman, the capital of the Mahdist state, situated across the White Nile from the ruined Khartoum. Ever since he had succeeded the Mahdi, the Khalifa had found himself surrounded by the riverain tribes that had never reconciled themselves to his rule. He now sought to bring the Baggara to Omdurman as a counterweight, or a tribal standing army, to secure his position. Although they were reluctant to leave their beloved plains, the Baggara obeyed and came to settle in the capital. Unhappily they failed from the very beginning to play the role the Khalifa expected of them. Wild and unruly, they never proved an effective instrument of government. Moreover, they were unproductive in times of famine and flaunted their privileged position before the settled cultivators, who, with their literary and religious traditions, rightly regarded the Baggara as ignorant and uncouth interlopers. Once again the riverain tribes, joined by the Mahdi's kinsmen, sought to seize power, but the Khalifa was able to put down the revolt and break the political power of the rebels. By 1892 peace and prosperity had returned to the Sudan, and the position of the Khalifa was never more secure. Gradually the Khalifa sought to transform the state into an Islamic monarchy, intending that the succession should pass to his son. More and more he himself retired from public view, defended by a bodyguard (*mulazi-*

miyya) that was, in effect, a reliable and powerful standing army. To be sure, his rule was autocratic, but as the threat of an Anglo-Egyptian power loomed on the northern horizon there was a gradual consolidation of Sudanese support for the regime and a widespread feeling that any invasion from the north would be an attempt to interfere with Sudanese independence.

EUROPEAN POWERS ON THE UPPER NILE

After the fall of Khartoum in 1885, the British government had neither reason nor desire to conquer the Sudan. Ten years later it had both. This great sea change in British policy was the result of Britain's determination to remain in Egypt. In 1882 the British occupation was regarded as temporary—until order throughout the country was restored and reforms were undertaken. Unfortunately, the task of regenerating Egypt required a British presence longer than any British government, whether Conservative or Liberal, had originally contemplated. By 1890 the British had decided to remain in Egypt, not only to complete their task of modernization but to defend the Suez Canal—the lifeline of the empire to the East. But once the decision to remain in Egypt had been made, British officials in both Cairo and London had to secure their position in Egypt, and since the life of Egypt depends on the Upper Nile, Britain's position had to be secured in the Sudan as well. At first there was no cause for alarm. The Mahdists, who controlled the Sudan, had neither the technological skills nor the interest to obstruct the flow of the Nile waters on which the life and stability of Egypt depended, but in 1889 European nations that possessed the capabilities to cut off the river flow sought to advance into the Nile Valley. Clearly, the British would have to ward off their European competitors by diplomacy, and failing that, by the outright military conquest of the Sudan.

The first threat came from the Italians, who in 1889 sought to slip into the Nile Valley from their sphere of influence in Abyssinia. The second threat came from the Germans in 1890, whose explorers were moving toward the headwaters of the Nile, the central African lakes. Lord Salisbury, the British Prime Minister, resolved both dangers by diplomacy, defining the German sphere in the Anglo-German (Heligoland) Agreement of 1890 and the Italian sphere in the Anglo-Italian Treaty of 1891, so that both nations were denied access to the Nile Valley. However, in keeping the Germans out Salisbury had unwittingly let King Leopold in by providing him with a way to the Nile. But if Leopold was to become a long-standing irritation in Salisbury's Nile policy, the French soon became a very real and powerful threat.

France had always opposed the British occupation of Egypt and never lost an opportunity to try to force the British to leave. French interests in Egypt stretched back to Napoleon's abortive occupation in 1799 and had been carried on throughout the nineteenth century by French traders and scholars who were foremost in the study of Pharaonic Egypt's great monuments and ruins. When France had been invited to join with Britain in the task of restoring order in Egypt in 1882 she had refused, only to find herself excluded from Egypt and resentful of the British occupation all the more because of her own indecisiveness. Thus in 1883, after the French were abruptly rebuffed for suggesting Anglo-French negotiations to effect a British withdrawal, French officials seriously began to consider forcing the British to evacuate Egypt. The instrument to accomplish such a bold stroke in the face of British power was the French Fashoda expedition.

The Fashoda expedition was conceived in 1893 with the purpose of marching from French possessions on the coast of western Africa, across the continent, to the Shilluk village of Fashoda on the

White Nile in territory that was at that time under Mahdist influence. Once astride the Nile the French, with their technical capabilities, could threaten to construct barrages and dams if the British did not acquiesce in withdrawal from Egypt. Like many other French projects during the partition of Africa, the Fashoda expedition had a heroic, cartographic sweep, but few seem to have considered the dangers of a head-on collision with Britain on the Upper Nile. Almost from the inception of the plan the British government knew of the Fashoda expedition. As with the Germans and the Italians, the British sought to exclude the French by diplomacy, first by leasing the southern Sudan to Leopold of the Belgians, thereby blocking a French advance to Fashoda, and second by offering territory in West Africa to keep the French out of the Nile Valley. The French forced Leopold to repudiate the first project, while haughtily rejecting the second. The race to Fashoda was on.

In the center of all this activity the Italian position in Ethiopia suddenly collapsed, enabling both the British and the French to make gains. On March 1, 1896, the Italian Army, advancing into Ethiopia, was destroyed by the Ethiopian Army under King Menelik. Not only was this battle a significant victory by a technologically backward people over a European invader, but the Italians, in their distress, appealed to the British for a demonstration in the Sudan to relieve Mahdist pressure on their position at Kassala. Clearly, an advance into the Sudan from the Anglo-Egyptian outpost of Wadi-Halfa could hardly have saved the Italians at Kassala some 700 miles away, but the British Cabinet saw the Italian pleas for support as an opportunity to acquire Sudanese real estate without objections from the other European powers. Thus in 1896 Anglo-Egyptian forces advanced to Dunqula and began to prepare for a final advance to Omdurman. But the French were as quick to profit from Ital-

ian misfortune as the British, thus replacing the Italians as the most influential Europeans at the court of Menelik. In 1897 France secured the emperor's dubious support for a French expedition to Fashoda from the east and by the beginning of 1898 was inexorably closing in on its goal. After several abortive attempts, a French expedition under Faivre reached the mouth of the Sobat in June and planted the French flag but was forced to retire by the heat, fever, and lack of supplies. In the west Marchand was more determined. Moving up the rivers and crossing over the Congo-Nile watershed, he and his men made their way through the swamps of the Nile and reached Fashoda in July, six weeks after Faivre's furtive visit to the east bank.

Although Marchand had beaten the British to Fashoda, the powerful and well-supplied Anglo-Egyptian forces were not far behind. Advancing up the Nile in 1898 under the command of General Kitchener, they swept all before them, defeating the Mahdist Army at the Atbara and moving to Omdurman, where, on September 2, 1898, the great army that the Khalifa had assembled was destroyed on the plains of Karari outside the city. Five days later Kitchener and a strong flotilla headed south up the White Nile toward Fashoda. Here, in a dramatic confrontation with Captain Marchand, Kitchener demanded that the French retire. Marchand refused. The great Fashoda crisis was on.

The immediate reaction in both Britain and France was to fight, and although today it appears absurd for the two great liberal powers to have plunged into war for possession of the desolate swamps of the Upper Nile, it must be remembered that Fashoda was a symbol of two imperial designs of sweeping proportions and that the fate of far-off lands from West Africa to the Far East would be determined by the outcome of the crisis. The British prepared for war, but unhappily for the French, France could not.

Deserted by her allies, torn by the Dreyfus Affair, and with her navy in deplorable condition, France was in no position to make war. Marchand was recalled, and the French recognized British influence throughout the Upper Nile. This influence, however, did not go unchallenged. In their diplomatic maneuvering to check the French, the British had leased a large portion of the Bahr al-Ghazal to the Congo Free State in 1894. Leopold now revived these rights, and only after many years of frustrating negotiations and numerous near clashes between British and Congolese forces did Leopold finally agree to withdraw upon his death. In 1909 he died. Six months later the last of his territory in the Nile Valley was handed over to the English authorities. The Upper Nile basin, from its source to its mouth, was at last securely British.

THE ANGLO-EGYPTIAN CONDOMINIUM

The defeat of the Mahdist state created complex legal and diplomatic problems for the British. The reconquest of the Sudan had been undertaken on British initiative and with British financial and military support, yet the Sudan was the former territory of Egypt and had been retaken in her name. But no Englishman, in 1898 or later, was prepared to return the Sudan to the maladministration of the Egyptians against whom the Sudan had first rebelled. Yet to attach the Sudan to the British Empire would be a gross injustice to Egypt's historical claims. The result was the condominium—an ingenious device whereby sovereignty was conferred jointly in the Khedive of Egypt and the British Crown. Within the Sudan, however, the supreme military and civil command was vested in a governor general nominated by the British government and appointed by the Khedive. The result was not a true condominium (joint partnership) but an administration dominated by British officials and served by Egyptian officials. Nevertheless, so long as Britain controlled Egypt, the Anglo-Egyptian condominium in the Sudan worked smoothly, but after the independence of Egypt had been won, the British and Egyptians in the Sudan became bitter rivals.

Although the battle of Karari brought about the collapse of the Mahdist state, dangers to the new administration appeared on every side. For a decade local risings of Mahdists in the northern Sudan, as well as rebellions of those who claimed to be the Mahdi's successors, were crushed. Even more difficult was the establishment of British rule in the southern Sudan, where the Nilotes opposed the British as they had done all alien invaders. Over a generation passed before the southern Sudan accepted imperial rule and the transformation of traditional customs resulting therefrom. The administration of the Sudan at first consisted of military personnel and later of civilians from Oxford and Cambridge who joined the Sudan Political Service and, although it was always a relatively small group (no more than 150 administrative officers at any one time), the administration developed an esprit de corps that was the envy of both the Colonial Service and the Indian Civil Service. The primary task of the administration was to establish order and win over Sudanese acquiescence for alien, Christian rule. Taxes were light, education was practical, and the basic infrastructure—railroads, steamers, and communications—was constructed to provide the foundation (particularly in the Gezira region between the White and the Blue Niles) of large-scale economic development. Under the leadership of Kitchener and Sir Reginald Wingate, his successor as Governor General, the Sudan gradually cast off its dependence on Egypt and quietly developed ever-increasing independence.

The future course of events in the Sudan was conditioned by the assassination of Sir Lee Stack, commander of the Egyptian Army (*Sirdar*) and Governor General of the Sudan, in Cairo in 1924. His murder by Egyptian nationalists convinced the British officials in the Sudan of their own anti-Egyptian attitudes. In retaliation the British removed Egyptians from the Sudan, forcibly when necessary, and although British officials in London refused to terminate the condominium, for all practical purposes Egyptian participation in the Sudan ceased to exist. Moreover, Stack's assassination created a crisis between the rulers and the ruled. Rather than turn to the small number of Western-educated Sudanese, British officials fell back on their more conservative fathers, the traditional leaders and the hereditary chiefs. As previously mentioned, this technique of ruling through tribal leaders was known as indirect rule and was regarded as a preliminary stage in the political development of African peoples. In reality, indirect rule frequently resulted in the appointment of authorities who were regarded as servants of the government and not of the people, while the officials themselves adopted a paternalism toward the chiefs that turned to scorn for their sons who were educated and oriented to the West (Sir John Maffey, *British Rule in the Sudan*).

In the late 1930s new forces appeared in the Sudan. The Anglo-Egyptian Treaty of 1936 permitted the return of Egyptians to the Sudan, and although they never regained the ground lost after their expulsion in 1924, their presence was increasingly felt in the rise of Sudanese nationalism. During the early 1920s embryonic Sudanese nationalists, such as Abd al Latif and members of the White Flag League, had sought to rally support against the British. At best they were naïve and at worst confused, but their program collapsed in the face of British resistance and was not revived until the formation of the Graduates' General Congress, consisting of educated Sudanese who represented a national consciousness and not simply the more limited, tribal concerns of their fathers. Supported both

morally and with money by the Egyptians, the Congress asserted in 1942 that it spoke for all Sudanese nationalists and raised difficult constitutional questions on the future of the Sudan. Preoccupied by the threat of German and Italian advances into the Middle East, the Sudan government brusquely refused to recognize the claims of the Congress. The result was a split between the extremists, known as the Ashiqqa, and the moderate elements who grouped themselves under the Umma. The Umma was supported by the Mahdists. The Ashiqqa was supported by the patronage of Sayyid al-Mirghani, the leader of the Khatmiyya *tariqa* (traditional religious rivals of the Mahdists). The alliances between the Umma and the Mahdists and the Ashiqqa and the Khatmiyya evoked all the bitter memories of the past and revived the feuds between the riverain peoples of the Nile and the wild Baggara nomads of the west. The hatreds and suspicions that were aroused soured Sudanese politics for years, bringing independent parliamentary government into disrepute.

However, the British officials of the Sudan government did not ignore the stirrings of the new Sudanese elite and in 1944 set up an Advisory Council to consult with the governor general, which was followed in 1947 by a Legislative Council with even greater powers of legislative initiative. The Egyptians regarded such unilateral actions with great suspicion, but after the coup d'état in Egypt in 1952 the military government sought to come to an accommodation with all the Sudanese political parties, and with the essential support of the Sudanese was able to force favorable amendments to a draft self-government statute that was put forward by the Sudanese Government. Without the confidence of the Sudanese the British gave way, and according to the amended self-government statute elections were held that resulted in the triumph of the pro-Egyptian former Ashiqqa leader, Ismail al-Azhari, and his

Khatmiyya supporters, who formed the hard core of the National Unionist Party.

Ismail al-Azhari was elected Prime Minister in January 1954. His principal task was to determine the future of the self-governing Sudan, whether as an independent country or an autonomous part of Egypt. Although Azhari had campaigned in 1953 on the slogan of "the unity of the Nile Valley," the possibility of tying the Sudan to Egypt became increasingly remote. Anti-Egyptian riots by Umma supporters in 1954, followed by the revolt of the Equatorial Battalion in the southern Sudan, convinced Azhari that any declaration of the Sudan as part of Egypt would have resulted in civil war. Thus in 1955, as the full effect of responsible government was brought home to him, Azhari abandoned his earlier campaign promises and, on January 1, 1956, unilaterally declared the Sudan an independent republic.

35 ANONYMOUS

PERIPLUS OF THE ERYTHRAEAN SEA

Probably written about 100 A.D. at Alexandria, "The Periplus of the Erythraean Sea" was a merchant's guide to the Red Sea and Indian Ocean ports. It is generally accepted as the earliest firsthand account of the East African coast to have survived to the present.

· · ·

From Tabai after 400 stades sailing is a promontory towards which the current runs, and the market-town of Opone. . . . It produces cinnamon, both the *aroma* and *moto* varieties, as well as the better sort of slaves, which are brought to Egypt in increasing numbers, and much tortoise-shell of better quality than elsewhere.

Voyages from Egypt to all these further market-towns are made in the month of July, that is *Epiphi*. The ships are usually fitted out in the inner [Red Sea] ports of Ariake and Barugaza; and they bring the further market-towns the products of these places: wheat, rice, ghee, sesame oil, cotton cloth (both the *monache* and the *sagmatogene*), girdles, and honey from the reed called *sakchari*. Some make voyages directly to these market-towns, others exchange cargo as they go. The country has no sovereign but each market-town is ruled by its own chief.

After Opone the coast veers more towards the south. First there are the Small and Great Bluffs of Azania and rivers for anchorages for six days' journey southwestwards. Then come the Little and the Great Beach for another six days' journey, and after that in order the Courses of Azania, first that called Sarapion, the next Nikon, and then several rivers and other anchorages one after the other, separately a halt and a day's journey, in all seven, as far as the Pyralaae Islands and the island called Diorux [the Chan-

From "The Periplus of the Erythraean Sea," in G. S. P. Freeman-Grenville, *The East African Coast: Select Documents from the First to the Earlier Nineteenth Century* (Oxford: Clarendon Press, 1962), pp. 1–2. Reprinted by permission of the Clarendon Press, Oxford.

nel]. Beyond this, slightly south of southwest after a voyage of two days and nights along the Ausanitic coast, is the island of Menouthesias some 300 stades from the land. It is flat and wooded. There are many rivers in it, and many kinds of birds and the mountain tortoise. There are no wild animals at all except the crocodile, but they never attack men. In this place there are small sewn boats and dug-outs, which they use for fishing and for catching tortoise. In this island they fish in a peculiar way with wicker baskets, which they fasten across where the tide goes out.

Two days' sail beyond the island lies the last mainland market-town of Azania, which is called Rhapta, a name derived from the small sewn boats [ραπτων πλοιαριων]. Here there is much ivory and tortoise-shell.

Men of the greatest stature, who are pirates, inhabit the whole coast and at each place have set up chiefs. The Chief of the Ma'afir is the suzerain, according to an ancient right which subordinates it to the kingdom which has become the first in Arabia. The people of Mouza hold it in tribute under his sovereignty and send there small ships, mostly with Arab captains and crews who trade and intermarry with the mainlanders of all the places and know their language.

Into these market-towns are imported the lances made especially for them at Mouza, hatchets, swords, awls, and many kinds of small glass vessels; and at some places wine and not a little wheat, not for trade but to gain the goodwill of the barbarians. Much ivory is taken away from these places, but it is inferior in quality to that of Adulis, and also rhinoceros horn and tortoise-shell, different from that of India, and a little coconut oil.

And these, I think, are the last of the market-towns of Azania on the mainland lying to the right of Berenice; for after all these places the ocean curves westwards and runs along the regions of Ethiopia, Libya and Africa, stretching out from the south and mingling with the western sea.

36 EZANA
THE DESTRUCTION OF KUSH

During the eighth century B.C., *the land south of Aswan known as Kush established its independence from Egypt and, by the mid-seventh century* B.C., *had asserted its hegemony over lower Egypt. Driven from Egypt by the Assyrians, the kings of Kush retreated to Nubia, where they continued to rule over the middle Nile for another thousand years, preserving their own unique Egyptian-Nubian culture. Soon after the retreat from Egypt, the capital of Kush was moved from Napata southward to Meroe near Shendi, where Kush was increasingly exposed to the Negroid cultures farther south and west. Kush passed on to these people the iron-working technology that had been developed at Meroe in the centuries before Christ. In the Christian era, Kush slipped into a gradual decay that ended in 350* A.D. *when the King of Aksum, Ezana, destroyed Meroe and sacked the decrepit riverain towns. Ezana recorded his destruction of Kush in one of the longest inscriptions to have survived from the Aksumite kingdom of Abyssinia.*

1. By the power of the Lord of Heaven, Who in heaven and upon earth is mightier than everything which exists,

2. Ezana, the son of Ella Amida, a native of Halen, king of Aksum and of

3. Hemer (Himyar), and of Raydan, and of Saba, and of Salhen, and of Seyamo, and of Bega, and of

4. Kasu (the Meroites), King of Kings, the son of Ella Amida, who is invincible to the enemy.

5. By the might of the Lord of Heaven, Who hath made me Lord, Who to all eternity, the Perfect One,

6. reigns, Who is invincible to the enemy, no enemy shall stand before

The inscription is found in L. P. Kirwan, "A Survey of Nubian Origins," *Sudan Notes and Records*, 20 (1937), 50–51. Reprinted by permission of the publisher and the Royal Geographical Society.

me, and after me no enemy shall follow.

7. By the might of the Lord of all, I made war upon Noba, for the peoples had rebelled and

8. had made a boast of it. And "they (the Axumites) will not cross the river Takkaze (Atbara)," said the peoples

9. of Noba. And they were in the habit of attacking the peoples of Mangurto, and Khasa, and Barya, and the blacks,

10. and of making war upon the Red peoples. And twice and thrice had they broken their solemn oaths, and had

11. killed their neighbours mercilessly, and they had stripped bare and stolen the properties of our deputies and messengers which I had

12. sent to them to inquire into their

thefts, and had stolen from them
13. their weapons of defence. And as I
had sent warnings to them and
they would not harken to me, and
they refused to cease from their evil
deeds,
14. and then betook themselves to flight,
I made war upon them. And I rose
in the might of the Lord of the
15. Land, and I fought with them on the
Takkaze (Atbara), at the ford of
Kemalke. Thereupon they took
flight, and would not
16. make a stand. And I followed after
the fugitives for twenty and three
days,
17. killing some and making prisoners
others, and capturing spoil wherever I tarried. Prisoners and
18. spoil my people who had marched
into the country brought back to
me. Meanwhile I burnt their
towns, both those built of bricks
and those
19. built of reeds, and my soldiers carried
off its food, and its copper, and its
iron, and its
20. brass, and they destroyed the statues
of their houses (i.e. temples), and
the treasuries of food, and the cotton trees, and
21. cast them into the River Seda (Nile).
28. And I came to Kasu (Meroe) and I
fought a battle and made prisoners
of its people at

29. the junction of the rivers Seda and
Takkaze. And the day after I arrived I sent out
30. to raid the country, the army
Mahaza, and the army Hara, and
Damawa, and Falha and Sera
31. upstream of Seda (i.e. towards the
modern Khartoum), and the cities
built of bricks and those of reeds.
The names of the cities
32. built of bricks were Alwa (near Khartoum) and Daro. And they killed,
and captured prisoners, and cast
people into the water. . . .
34. . . . And after that I sent the army
of Halen, and the army of Laken
35. . . . down the Seda (i.e. north of the
junction of the Nile with the Atbara) against the towns of the Noba
which are made of reeds—4
36. towns—Negus—I. The towns built
of bricks which the Noba had
taken
37. were   Tabito—I—and   Fertoti—I.
And my peoples arrived at the
frontier of the Red Noba and they
returned safe and sound,
38. having captured prisoners and slain
the Noba and taken spoil from
them by the might of the Lord of
Heaven.
39. And I planted a throne in that
country at the place where the Rivers Seda and Takkaze join. . . .

37 COSMAS INDICOPLEUSTES
TRADE IN ETHIOPIA

The Christian Topography *of Cosmas Indicopleustes was written in 547* A.D., *when the
Mediterranean world was just entering the Middle Ages. Cosmas attempted to establish
that the world is flat by citing Greek authors and the Scriptures. Cosmas himself did visit
Ethiopia, and his work is one of the few accounts that describe a barren period in East
African history.*

From Cosmas Indicopleustes, *The Christian Topography of Cosmas, an Egyptian Monk,* trans. and edited by
J. W. McCrindle (London: Hakluyt Society, 1897), pp. 49–54.

If one measures in a straight cord line the stages which make up the length of the earth from Tzinitza to the west, he will find that there are somewhere about four hundred stages, each thirty miles in length. The measurement is to be made in this way: from Tzinitza to the borders of Persia, between which are included all Iouvia,[1] India, and the country of the Bactrians, there are about one hundred and fifty stages at least; the whole country of the Persians has eighty stations; and from Nisibis to Seleucia[2] there are thirteen stages; and from Seleucia to Rome and the Gauls and Iberia, whose inhabitants are now called Spaniards, onward to Gadeira, which lies out towards the ocean, there are more than one hundred and fifty stages; thus making altogether the number of stages to be four hundred, more or less. With regard to breadth: from the hyperborean[3] regions to Byzantium there are not more than fifty stages. For we can form a conjecture as to the extent of the uninhabited and the inhabited parts of those northern regions from the Caspian Sea, which is a gulf of the ocean. From Byzantium, again, to Alexandria there are fifty stages, and from Alexandria to the Cataracts thirty stages, from the Cataracts to Axomis, thirty stages;[4] from Ax-

omis to the projecting part of Ethiopia, which is the frankincense country called Barbaria, lying along the ocean, and not near but at a great distance from the land of Sasu which is the remotest part of Ethiopia, fifty stages more or less; so that we may reckon the whole number of stages at two hundred more or less; and thus we see that even here the divine scripture speaks the truth in representing the length of the earth to be double its breadth; *For thou shalt make the table in length two cubits and in breadth one cubit,* a pattern, as it were, of the earth.

The region which produces frankincense is situated at the projecting parts of Ethiopia, and lies inland, but is washed by the ocean on the other side. Hence the inhabitants of Barbaria, being near at hand, go up into the interior and, engaging in traffic with the natives, bring back from them many kinds of spices, frankincense, cassia,[5] calamus,[6] and many other articles of merchandise, which they afterwards send by sea to Adule, to the country of the Homerites, to Further India, and to Persia. This very fact you will find mentioned in the Book of Kings, where it is recorded that the Queen of Sheba, that is, of the Homerite country, whom afterwards our Lord in the Gospels calls the Queen of the South, brought to Solomon spices from this very Barbaria, which lay near Sheba on the other side of the sea, together with bars of ebony, and apes and gold from Ethiopia which, though separated from Sheba by the Arabian Gulf, lay in its vicinity. We can see again from the words of the Lord that he calls these places the ends of the earth, saying: *The Queen of the South shall rise up in judgment with this generation and*

---

[1] This would mean the country of the Huns.
[2] Nisibis, the capital of Mygdoniia, was, after the time of Lucullus, considered the chief bulwark of the Roman power in the East. It was an ancient, large, and populous city, and was for long the great northern emporium of the commerce of the East and West. It was situated about two days' journey from the head waters of the Tigris in the midst of a pleasant and fertile plain at the foot of Mount Masius. The Seleucia here referred to was situated on the Tigris about 40 miles to the north-east of Babylon, from the ruins of which it was mainly constructed: just as, afterwards, its own ruins served to build Ctesiphon. Next to Alexandria, it was the greatest emporium of commerce in the East.
[3] Far northern regions (ed.).
[4] Axomis (Auxume in Ptolemy) is the modern Axum, the capital of Tigre. In the early centuries of our era it was a powerful State, possessing nearly the whole of Abyssinia, a portion of the south-west Red Sea coast and north-western Arabia. It was distant from its seaport, Adule, which was situated near Annesley Bay, about 120 miles, or an eight days' caravan journey. It was the chief centre of the trade with the interior of Africa. The Greek lan-

guage was understood and spoken, both by the court and the numerous foreigners who had either settled in it or who resorted to it for trading purposes. . . . Christianity was introduced into Axum in the fourth century by Oedisius and Frumentius, the latter of whom was afterwards appointed its first bishop. Sasu, which is next mentioned, is near the coast, and only 5° to the north of the equator.
[5] A kind of cinnamon (ed.).
[6] Reed used as a pen (ed.).

shall condemn it, for she came from the ends of the earth to hear the wisdom of Solomon—Matt. xii, 42. For the Homerites are not far distant from Barbaria, as the sea which lies between them can be crossed in a couple of days, and then beyond Barbaria is the ocean, which is there called Zingion. The country known as that of Sasu is itself near the ocean, just as the ocean is near the frankincense country, in which there are many gold mines. The King of the Axomites accordingly, every other year, through the governor of Agau,[7] sends thither special agents to bargain for the gold, and these are accompanied by many other traders—upwards, say, of five hundred—bound on the same errand as themselves. They take along with them to the mining district oxen, lumps of salt, and iron, and when they reach its neighbourhood they make a halt at a certain spot and form an encampment, which they fence round with a great hedge of thorns. Within this they live, and having slaughtered the oxen, cut them in pieces, and lay the pieces on the top of the thorns, along with the lumps of salt and the iron. Then come the natives bringing gold in nuggets like peas, called *tancharas,* and lay one or two or more of these upon what pleases them—the pieces of flesh or the salt or the iron, and then they retire to some distance off. Then the owner of the meat approaches, and if he is satisfied he takes the gold away, and upon seeing this its owner comes and takes the flesh or the salt or the iron. If, however, he is not satisfied, he

[7] The Agau people is the native race spread over the Abyssinian plateau both to east and west of Lake Tana. . . .

leaves the gold, when the native seeing that he has not taken it, comes and either puts down more gold, or takes up what he had laid down, and goes away. Such is the mode in which business is transacted with the people of that country, because their language is different and interpreters are hardly to be found. The time they stay in that country is five days more or less, according as the natives more or less readily coming forward buy up all their wares. On the journey homeward they all agree to travel well-armed, since some of the tribes through whose country they must pass might threaten to attack them from a desire to rob them of their gold. The space of six months is taken up with this trading expedition, including both the going and the returning. In going they march very slowly, chiefly because of the cattle, but in returning they quicken their pace lest on the way they should be overtaken by winter and its rains. For the sources of the river Nile lie somewhere in these parts, and in winter, on account of the heavy rains, the numerous rivers which they generate obstruct the path of the traveller. The people there have their winter at the time we have our summer. It begins in the month Epiphi of the Egyptians and continues till Thoth,[8] and during the three months the rain falls in torrents, and makes a multitude of rivers all of which flow into the Nile.

The facts which I have just recorded fell partly under my own observation and partly were told me by traders who had been to those parts.

[8] From July to September.

38 TUAN CH'ÊNG-SHIH
CHINA'S DISCOVERY OF AFRICA

Although China had long had contacts with the world beyond her frontiers, intercourse with the countries beyond Asia was encouraged during the T'ang Dynasty (618–907 A.D.) by a long period of peace and the cosmopolitan outlook of China's rulers. The selection below is from the Yu-yang-tsa-tsu, *a general book of knowledge, written by the Chinese scholar Tuan Ch'êng-shih (d. 863 A.D.).*

It is, however, in the T'ang period that the first definite information appears in Chinese sources on the countries beyond India, and what is to the point here, on Africa. There is a curious work, written by the scholar Tuan Ch'êng-shih, who died in A.D. 863, called the *Yu-yang-tsa-tsu.* This book was published in the *Chin-tai-pi-shu* by Mao Chin (1598–1657). The antiquity of the text is guaranteed by the *Hsin T'ang-shu,* by Ou-yang Hsiu, completed in 1060, which has an abridged extract of it. From the chapter in which a number of exotic plants are described, it is clear that part of his information is derived from priests of *Fu-lin,* that is Ta-ch'in or the Roman Orient and Magadha in India. Hirth has called attention to this text; in his translation, however, there are a few curious errors which make a new translation necessary.

The text runs: "The country of Po-pa-li is in the southwestern sea. (The people) do not eat any of the five grains but eat only meat. They often stick a needle into the veins of cattle and draw blood which they drink raw, mixed with milk. They wear no clothes except that they cover (the parts) below their loins with sheepskins. Their women are clean and of proper behaviour. The inhabitants themselves kidnap them, and if they sell them to foreign merchants, they fetch several times their price. The country produces only ivory and ambergris.[1] If Persian

merchants wish to go into the country, they collect around them several thousand men and present them with strips of cloth. All, whether old or young draw blood and swear an oath, and then only do they trade their products. From olden times on they were not subject to any foreign country. In fighting they use elephants' tusks and ribs and the horns of wild buffaloes as lances and they wear cuirasses [2] and bows and arrows. They have twenty myriads of foot soldiers. The Arabs make frequent raids upon them."

What is this country? Hirth first identified it with Berbera, on the Somali coast. This identification is confirmed by an important notice in a work about which we shall have to say a little more presently. It is the *Chu-fan-chih,* written by Chao Ju-kua, a Commissioner of foreign trade at Ch'üan-chou in Fukien province. It was completed in 1226. About one-third of its contents is drawn from an earlier work, the *Lingwai-tai-ta,* written by Chou Ch'ü-fei in 1178. This book has a note on a country called Pi-pa-lo which runs as follows:

"The country of Pi-pa-lo has four chou (departmental cities) and for the rest (the people) are all settled in villages which each try to gain the supremacy over the others by violence. They serve Heaven and do not serve the Buddha (presumably meaning that they are Mohammedans). The country produces many camels and sheep and they have camels' meat and

From J. J. L. Duyvendak, *China's Discovery of Africa* (London: Arthur Probsthain, 1949), pp. 12–15, 22–24. Reprinted by permission.
[1] A substance used in perfumes (ed.).

[2] A piece of close-fitting armor for protecting the breast and back; it was originally made of leather (ed.).

milk as well as baked cakes as their regular food. The country produces dragon's saliva (ambergris), big elephants' tusks, and big rhinoceros horns. Some elephants' tusks weigh more than 100 catty [3] and some rhinoceros horns more than 10 catty. There is also much putchuk, liquid storax gum, myrrh, and tortoise-shell which is extremely thick, and which (people from) other countries all come to buy. 'Among the products there is further the so-called camel-crane (i.e. the ostrich, called by the Persians *ushturmurgh* and by the Arabs *teir-al-djamal,* both meaning "camel-bird"), whose body to the crown is 6 or 7 feet high. It has wings and can fly, but not to any height.' Among quadrupeds there is the so-called *tsu-la* (giraffe), striped like a camel and in size like an ox. It is yellow in colour. Its front legs are 5 feet high and its hind legs are only 3 feet. Its head is high up and is turned upwards. Its skin is an inch thick. There is also a mule with red, black, and white stripes wound as girdles around the body. Both (these kinds) are animals of the mountain wilds. They are occasional variations of the camel. The inhabitants are fond of hunting and from time to time they catch them with poisoned arrows."

The *Hsin T'ang-shu,* as I said, reproduces part of the notice on Berbera of the *Yu-yang-tsa-tsu.* It also has a short entry on another African territory, which so far as I am aware has not been noticed in this connection, viz. on Ma-lin, that is Melinda. The text says: "South-west from Fu-lin (that is the country of the Roman Orient of which 'Ch'ih-san,' Alexandria, is indicated as the western border), after one traverses the desert for two thousand miles is a country called Ma-lin. It is the old P'o-sa. Its people are black and their nature is fierce. The land is pestilentious and has no herbs, no trees, and no cereals. They feed the horses on dried fish; the people eat *hu-mang;* the

---

[3] A unit of weight used in China that is generally equal to 1¹/₃ pounds avoirdupois (ed.).

hu-mang is the Persian date. They are not ashamed of debauching the wives of their fathers or chiefs, they are (in this respect) the worst of the barbarians. They call this: to seek out the proper master and subject. In the seventh moon they rest completely (i.e. Ramadan). They (then) do not send out nor receive (any merchandise) in trade and they sit drinking all night long."

. . .

There is a short note on Ts'eng-po, identified with Zanguebar, which is not particularly interesting, and one on K'un-lun Ts'eng-ch'i which deserves our attention. It is in the section dealing with countries on the sea.

" 'K'un-lun Ts'eng-ch'i is in the southwestern sea. It is adjacent to a large island in the sea. There are regularly great p'êng birds. When they fly they obscure the sun for a short time. There are wild camels, and if the p'êng birds meet them, they swallow them up. If one finds a feather of the p'êng bird, by cutting the quill, one can make a water-jar of it.

The products of the country are big elephants' tusks and rhinoceros' horns.'

In the west 'there is an island in the sea on which there are many savages. Their bodies are black as lacquer and they have frizzled hair. They are enticed by (offers of) food and then captured' and sold 'as slaves to the Arabic countries, where they fetch a very high price. They are employed as gate-keepers, and it is said that they have no longing for their kinsfolk.' "

There can be little doubt that the island mentioned is Madagascar. The p'êng bird is the legendary rukh, and perhaps it was the presence of the now extinct dodo which is at the origin of the story that it was found there. Marco Polo says that it can swallow an elephant. Yule explains the story of the quills as the fronds of the raphia palm; Ferrand identifies it with the use made of the *langana* (Malgash), a big bamboo, about 15 centimeters in diameter and 2 meters long, in which the knots have been perforated with the exception of the one at the end, so as to turn it into a water vessel. These *langana* are particularly used by the coast tribes of Madagascar.

The capturing of slaves brings up an interesting question. Chou Ch'ü-fei inserts another sentence: "thousands of them are sold as foreign slaves."

It is certain that some of these slaves came to China. Foreign slaves were designated by various names. K'un-lun-nu, K'un-lun slaves is one of them. The word *k'un-lun* has had an interesting history. Used early on as the name of the fabulous mountains in the West, the home of Hsi-wang-mu, the word originally seems to mean the round vault of the sky, in which as it were, these gigantic Tibetan mountains seem to lose themselves. Etymologically, it is certainly connected with the binom *hun-lun,* "chaos." The K'un-lun mountains are also identified with the Anavatapta mountain and the Sumeru in India, well known in Buddhist literature. Now the Chinese have applied the term *k'un-lun* to the peoples, mostly of the Malay race, whom they found at the ends of the earth. At first chiefly confined to the races of the South-West, later, as the geographic knowledge of the Chinese expanded, the same term was applied to the native races of the countries around the Indian Ocean, including the Negroes.

We also find Seng-chih-nu, slaves from Seng-chih, which undoubtedly is the same as Ts'eng-ch'i, as transcription of Zanggi, the general Arabic word for Negroes. In the name of the country K'un-lun Ts'eng-ch'i (k'i), we may therefore recognize the country of the blacks, Zanzibar, prefixed by the appellation K'un-lun, a curious, though perhaps accidental, reminder of the Malay origin of the inhabitants of Madagascar.

Slaves are further called: *kuei-nu,* "devil-slaves," *yeh-jen,* "wild men," *hei-hsiao-ssŭ,* "black servants," *fan hsiao-ssŭ,* "barbarian servants," or *fan-nu,* "barbarian slaves." These names may sometimes have designated Malay slaves in general, but often they undoubtedly refer to Negro-slaves. We hear about them quite early: the priest Tao-an is called K'un-lun-tzŭ, "the K'un-lun," or the Ch'i-tao-jen, "the lacquered monk," because he was so dark in spite of his being a northern Chinese. The later consort of Emperor Chien-wen of the Chin dynasty was nicknamed "K'un-lun" by the courtiers, because she was tall and of a dark colour. The *P'ing-chou-k'o-t'an* writes: "In Kuang-chou most of the wealthy people keep devil-slaves. They are very strong and can lift (weights of) several hundred catties. Their language and tastes are unintelligible. Their nature is simple and they do not run away. They are also called 'wild men.' Their colour is black as ink, their lips are red and their teeth white, their hair is curly and yellow. There are males and females (*N.B.:* the term for animals is used). They live in the mountains (or islands) beyond the seas. They eat raw things. If, in captivity, they are fed on cooked food, after several days they get diarrhoea. This is called 'changing the bowels.' For this reason they sometimes fall ill and die; if they do not die one can keep them, and after having been kept a long time they begin to understand people's language, although they themselves cannot speak it. There is one kind of wild men near the sea who can enter the water without blinking their eyes. They are called 'K'un-lun slaves.' "

That the slave-trade, whether of Negroes or other tribes of the Indian Ocean was pretty extensive also appears from a notice in the *Ling-wai-tai-ta:* "The people of Chan-ch'eng (Champa) buy male and female slaves; and the ships carry human beings as cargo." Chao Ju-kua adds that a boy was priced at 3 taels of gold or the equivalent in aromatic wood. Slaves were also used on board ships for mending a leaky ship from the outside under water.

There is a strange pathos in the thought of these melancholy, silent, black slaves, who were supposed to have no longing for their home, in medieval China, used as doorkeepers.

39 JOÃO DE BARROS
THE FOUNDING OF KILWA

In 1532 João de Barros became factor (agent) of the India House in Lisbon and thus had access to all the documents and correspondence of Portuguese officials who were under the authority of the Viceroy of the Indies. He does not indicate whether the Chronica dos Reyes de Quiloa *was written in Arabic or was translated therefrom.*

The Arabic version was presented in 1877 to the British Consul at Zanzibar, Sir John Kirk, by Sultan Sayyid Barghash. The author is unknown, but from clues in the text, G. S. P. Freeman-Grenville concludes that the author was born in 1499 and that his family came from Malindi. The chronicle may have been composed about 1520.

The two accounts are presented below for comparison.

DE BARROS' VERSION

According to what we learn from a Chronicle of the Kings of this town, a little more than seventy years after the towns of Mogadishu and Barawa were built, which, as we have already seen, were the first towns on this coast, and nearly four hundred years after the era of Muhammad, there reigned in the town of Shiraz, which is in Persia, a Moorish King named Sultan Hocen.

At his death he left seven sons. One of these, named, Ale, was held in little esteem by his brothers, because he was begotten by his father by one of his slaves of Abyssinian race, whereas their mother was descended from the Princes of Persia. But whatever he may have lacked by reason of his origin, he made up for it in character and wisdom. In order to escape the scorn and ill treatment of his brothers, he resolved to find a new place to dwell in, where he might live with better fortune than he had amongst his own people. He was already married, and gathered together his wife, sons, family and some other people, who wished to follow him in the enterprise, and embarked in two ships at the island of Ormuz, and, because of the reports of gold to be found on the coast of Zanzibar, came thither.

From G. S. P. Freeman-Grenville, *The Medieval History of the Coast of Tanganyika, with special reference to recent archaeological discoveries* (London: Oxford University Press, 1962), pp. 75–78, 84–86. Reprinted by permission.

ARABIC VERSION

Chapter One: The first man to come to Kilwa and found it, and his descent from the Persian kings of the land of Shiraz.

Historians have said, amongst their assertions, that the first man to come to Kilwa came in the following way. There arrived a ship in which there were people who claimed to have come from Shiraz in the land of the Persians. It is said there were seven ships: the first stopped at Mandakha; the second at Shaughu;[1] the third at a town called Yanba; the fourth at Mombasa;[2] the fifth at the Green Island (of Pemba); the sixth at the land of Kilwa; and the seventh at Hanzuan. They say all the masters of these six ships were brothers, and that the one who went to the town of Hanzuan was their father. God alone knows all truth!

I understand from a person interested in history, whom I trust, that the reason for their leaving Shiraz in Persia was that their Sultan one day dreamed a dream. He was called Hasan (sc. Husain) ibn Ali: he was the father of these six men and the seventh of those who left. In his dream he saw a rat with an iron snout gnawing holes in the town wall. He interpreted the

[1] Mandhakha has not been identified, nor Shaughu; Yanba could be Jambe (Yambe) Island, off Tanga harbour, but, if so, the list is out of order.
[2] The text has the Arabic word, which strictly is Mafia, but Mombasa seems more logical if the list is in order since the next place mentioned is certainly Pemba. Hanzuan, the last place named is presumably Yohana in the Comoro Islands.

Having come to the settlements of Mogadishu and Barawa, as he was of Persian origin and belonged to a sect of Mahamed which, as we have previously seen, was different from that of the Arabs, and as his intention was to found his own settlement of which he could be lord, and not be the subject of any other person, he sailed down the coast until he came to the port of Kilwa. Seeing from the situation and position of the land, which was surrounded by water, that he could live secure from the insults of the Kafirs, who inhabited it, he bought it from them at the price of some cloth, and, because, of the reasons he gave them, they crossed over to the mainland. After this, when they had abandoned the place, he began to fortify it, not only against them, in case they showed any malice, but also against various Moorish towns in the neighbourhood and against some Moors who inhabited certain islands called Songo and Xanga,[3] and who ruled the land up to Mompana about twenty leagues from Kilwa. As he was a wise man and of great courage, in a short time he fortified himself so that the place became a noble settlement, to which he gave the name it now bears. He began to rule over his neighbours, and sent his son, a goodly young man, to rule over the island of Monfia and other islands nearby. His descendants, who succeeded him, called themselves kings, as he did.

dream to prophesy the ruin of their country. When he had made certain that his interpretation of the dream was correct, he told his sons. He convinced them that their land would not escape destruction, and asked their advice. They said they left their decision to God and his Prophet (may he be exalted!), and to their father.

Their father said he intended to leave the land and go to another. His sons retorted: How can we go? Will the amirs and wazirs and the council agree to your departure, which involves the breaking of the cord that binds the kingdom together? He answered his sons and said: I have a stratagem by which we can escape. Tomorrow I shall summon all of you and the wazirs and amirs and the council. He said to his eldest son: I shall insult you before them all. When you have heard me show anger, strike me as though you were filled with rage. I shall grow angry on that account, and shall make it an excuse to leave the land. In this way, if God wills, we shall be able to depart.

Next day he summoned all his sons, and all the wazirs, amirs and the council, and they consulted together about the matters for discussion before them. The father spoke abusively of his eldest son, who thereupon struck him before them all. His father was angry and said: I will not remain in a land where I have been insulted like this. And the rest of his sons and all the people said: We will avenge you on your son and kill him. He answered: I am not satisfied. And they said: What will you? He replied: Only leaving this land will satisfy me.

And they all agreed to leave with their sultan. He got ready with his household and some of his amirs, wazirs and subjects. They took the road to the ports, and, embarking in seven ships, set sail. So they travelled under God's guidance to the lands of the Swahili coasts, where the ships dispersed, each going to the place already mentioned. It is strong evidence that they were kings in their own country,

[3] Both of these islands are in the Kilwa creek.

and a refutation of those who deny it.
God alone knows all truth!

When they arrived in the ship which
went to Kilwa, they found it was an island
surrounded by the sea, but that at low
water it was joined to the mainland so
that one could cross on foot. They disembarked on the island and met a man who
was a Muslim, followed by some of his
children. It is said his name was Muriri
wa Bari. They found there one mosque
said to be the one he is buried in, and
which is called Kibala.[4]

They asked the Muslim about the
country and he replied: The island is ruled
by an infidel from Muli,[5] who is king of
it; he has gone to Muli to hunt, but will
soon return. After a few days the infidel
returned from Muli and crossed to the
island at low tide. The newcomer and he
met together, and Muriri acted as interpreter. The newcomer to Kilwa said: I
should like to settle on the island: pray sell
it to me that I may do so.

The infidel answered: I will sell it on
condition that you encircle the island with
coloured clothing. The newcomer agreed
with the infidel and bought on the condition stipulated. He encircled the island
with clothing, some white, some black,
and every other colour besides. So the
infidel agreed and took away all the clothing, handing over the island and departing
to Muli. He concealed his real intention
of returning with troops to kill the newcomer and his followers and to take their
goods by force. The Muslim warned the
purchaser and said: He is very fond of this
island and will undoubtedly return to despoil you and yours of all your possessions
and kill you. You must find some stratagem to be safe from his evil intention.

So they set themselves to the task and
dug out the creek across which in former

[4] The term means the niche in a mosque which indi-
cates the direction of Mecca, and in Swahili the
north, since Mecca is northwards from the coast.
[5] The word evidently means mainland as distinct
from an island. It has been shown that the word
derives from Avestic through Pehlevi.

times men passed at low tide between the mainland and the island. The tide filled it and did not recede again. Some days later the infidel came from Muli to the point from which he was wont to cross. He saw the tide was up; and waited in the usual way for it to ebb until he could cross; but the water remained up and did not go down at all. Then he despaired of seizing the island and was sorry at what he had done. He went home full of remorse and sorrow.

The first king of the land was Sultan Ali ibn al-Husain ibn Ali surnamed Nguo Nyingi. And this was in the middle of the third century after the flight of the Prophet-Peace upon him! This king ruled Kilwa and then went to Mafia, for the island pleased him. He put in charge of it his son Muhammad ibn Ali, who was known as Mkoma Watu.

After his death he was succeeded by his son Ale Bumale, who reigned 40 years. As he had no sons, his nephew, Ale Busoloquete, inherited Kilwa, being the son of his brother who was in Mafia. He did not remain in power for more than four years and a half.

Muhammad ibn Ali ruled for two and a half years, and after his death his third brother Bashat ibn Ali succeeded him. He was the first independent king of Mafia after his father died. He ruled four and a half years and then died.

The first man to come to Kilwa ruled forty years. After his death Ali ibn Bashat ibn Ali ruled for four and a half years. He took precedence over his paternal uncles Sulaiman ibn Ali, al-Hasan ibn Ali and Daud ibn Ali. When he died his uncle Daud ibn Ali ruled in his stead for two years. Then he went to Mafia to visit his father's grave. He liked Mafia and settled there, and gave his kingdom to his son Ali ibn Daud ibn Ali ibn al-Husain. He was the last of the seed of the first man to come to Kilwa. God knows best!

Chapter Two: The disturbance in the affairs of the kingdom of Kilwa and the Matamandalin.

These, the people of Shagh, fought a great war with the people of Kilwa, and conquered the country.[6] They took over the government and appointed to rule one of themselves named Khalid ibn Bakr.

He (Ale Busoloquete) was succeeded by Daut, his son, who was driven out of Kilwa in the fourth year of his reign by Matata Mandalima, who was king of Xanga and his enemy, and Daut took refuge in Monfia, where he died. Matata left in Kilwa his nephew, named Ale Bonebaquer, who after two years was driven out by the Persians of Kilwa. In his place they put Hocen Soleiman, a nephew of the

[6] The people of Shagh were probably inhabitants of Songo Mnara Island (ed.).

deceased Daut. He reigned sixteen years. . . .

(Sc. al-Hasan ibn Sulaiman reigned sixteen years) and was succeeded by Ale Bem Daut, his nephew, who reigned sixty years, and was succeeded by his grandson of the same name.

The inhabitants rose against him be-

After two and a half years the people of Kilwa united to depose him and banish him from the country. They expelled him without injuring him in any way, and made him return to his own land.

Then al-Hasan ibn Sulaiman ibn Ali the founder of Kilwa ruled for twelve years. The Matamandalin attacked for a second time and conquered the country. And they set up a man named Muhammad ibn al-Husain al-Mandhiri, who reigned for twelve years, and the name of the Matamandalin was mentioned in the Friday prayers. All these things happened after the flight of Sultan al-Hasan to the land of Zanzibar.

Then the people of Kilwa gathered together to get rid of the Matamandalin. They agreed that the matter of setting up a king was not one for their sons, but that they would depute it to them to do it for them. So they called all the young men together and said: Are you content that your king should have been deposed? They all answered together: No! Then they said to the young men: Make up your minds and swear allegiance to the son of your king.

So a thousand young men met, and did as they were asked: they swore allegiance to the sultan's son. Then they went to the house of the Amir (sc. Muhammad ibn al-Husain) and seized him and put him in fetters. Then they sent the young men with their king with a message to his deposed father the sultan who had fled to Zanzibar, so that he might come and receive the land from his son. He returned from Zanzibar in six ships; and, when he arrived at Kilwa, the Amir broke out and went down to the strand to oppose him. Then the young men slew the Amir. Thus he took control of the country and ruled for fourteen years before he died.

cause he was a wicked man, and threw him alive into a well, after he had reigned six years.

They put in his place his brother Hasan Ben Daut, who reigned for twenty-four years.

After him there reigned Soleiman for two years. He was of royal descent. The inhabitants cut off his head because he was a very bad king.

He was succeeded by al-Hasan ibn Daud ibn Ali the founder of Kilwa, and at that time he was seventy years of age. And he reigned over his kingdom seventy years more. (End of Ch. II).

40 IBN BATTUTA
THE EAST AFRICAN COAST IN 1331

The celebrated Muslim traveler Ibn Battuta (1304–1368/9) traversed nearly the whole of the Muslim world and beyond during his many years of wandering. Born in Tangiers, he made the first of his four pilgrimages to Mecca when he was twenty-one; thereafter, his passion was to "travel throughout the earth," never twice by the same road. His second journey took him through southern Iraq and southwest Persia, then to Tabriz and north-western Mesopotamia. He subsequently traveled along the Red Sea, down the East African coast, and returned via the Persian Gulf. His fourth journey took him to Constantinople and from there to India, where he arrived in September 1333. He resided in India for several years in the service of the Sultan, traveling to China on the latter's behalf in 1342. Ibn Battuta then returned to the West, visiting Andalusia and the western Sudan. The account of this intelligent and perceptive observer provides an invaluable picture of the East African coast in 1331.

I travelled from the city of Adan by sea for four days and arrived at the city of Zaila, the city of the Barbara,[1] who are a

From *The Travels of Ibn Battuta*, A.D. *1325–1354*, trans. and edited by H. A. R. Gibb (New York: Cambridge University Press, 1962), II, 373–382. Reprinted by permission of Cambridge University Press on behalf of *The Hakluyt Society*. In this selection inserts bracketed into the text are those of H. A. R. Gibb.

[1] Zaila, on a sandy spit on the Somali coast due south of Aden, was included at this time in the Ethiopian kingdom of Awfat or Ifat. . . .

By the term *Barbara* the Arabic geographers apparently mean the Hamitic tribes who are neither Abyssinian (*Habash*) nor negroes (*Zinj*), and more especially the Somalis, although Ibn Battuta here includes them among the negroes. . . .

people of the negroes,[2] Shafiites in rite. Their country is a desert extending for two months' journey, beginning at Zaila and ending at Maqdashaw. Their cattle are camels, and they also have sheep which are famed for their fat. The inhabitants of Zaila are black in colour, and the majority of them are Rafidis.[3] It is a large city with a great bazaar, but it is in the dirtiest, most disagreeable, and most stinking town in the world. The reason

[2] Arabic *Zinj* or *Zanj*, a term ultimately derived from Persian or Sanskrit, probably in the language of the seamen of the Persian Gulf.
[3] I.e., Shiites, probably of the Zaidi sect.

for its stench is the quantity of its fish and the blood of the camels that they slaughter in the streets. When we arrived there we chose to spend the night at sea in spite of its extreme roughness, rather than pass a night in the town, because of its filth.

We sailed on from there for fifteen nights and came to Maqdashaw, which is a town of enormous size.[4] Its inhabitants are merchants possessed of vast resources; they own large numbers of camels, of which they slaughter hundreds every day [for food], and also have quantities of sheep. In this place are manufactured the woven fabrics called after it, which are unequalled and exported from it to Egypt and elsewhere. It is the custom of the people of this town that, when a vessel reaches the anchorage, the *sumbuqs,* which are small boats, come out to it. In each *sumbuq* there are a number of young men of the town, each one of whom brings a covered platter containing food and presents it to one of the merchants on the ship saying "This is my guest," and each of the others does the same. The merchant, on disembarking, goes only to the house of his host among the young men, except those of them who have made frequent journeys to the town and have gained some acquaintance with its inhabitants; these lodge where they please. When he takes up residence with his host, the latter sells his goods for him and buys for him; and if anyone buys anything from him at too low a price or sells to him in the absence of his host, that sale is held invalid by them. This practice is a profitable one for them.

When the young men came on board the vessel in which I was, one of them came up to me. My companions said to him "This man is not a merchant, but a doctor of the law," whereupon he called out to his friends and said to them "This

is the guest of the qadi." There was among them one of the qadi's men, who informed him of this, and he came down to the beach with a number of students and sent one of them to me. I then disembarked with my companions and saluted him and his party. He said to me "In the name of God, let us go to salute the Shaikh." "And who is the Shaikh?" I said, and he answered, "The Sultan," for it is their custom to call the sultan "the Shaikh." Then I said to him "When I am lodged, I shall go to him," but he said to me, "It is the custom that whenever there comes a jurist or a sharif or a man of religion, he must first see the sultan before taking a lodging." So I went with him to the sultan, as they asked.

Account of the Sultan of Maqdashaw.[5] The sultan of Maqdashaw is, as we have mentioned, called only by the title of "the Shaikh." His name is Abu Bakr, son of the shaikh Omar; he is by origin of the Barbara and he speaks in Maqdishi, but knows the Arabic language. One of his customs is that, when a vessel arrives, the sultan's *sumbuq* goes out to it, and enquiries are made as to the ship, whence it has come, who is its owner and its *rubban* (that is, its captain), what is its cargo, and who has come on it of merchants and others. When all of this information has been collected, it is presented to the sultan, and if there are any persons [of such quality] that the sultan should assign a lodging to him as his guest, he does so.

When I arrived with the qadi I have mentioned, who was called Ibn al-Burhan, an Egyptian by origin, at the sultan's residence, one of the serving-boys came out and saluted the qadi, who said to him "Take word to the intendant's office and inform the Shaikh that this man has come

---

[4] Mogadishu was founded in the tenth century as a trading colony by Arabs from the Persian Gulf, the principal group being from al-Hasa. . . .

[5] The various Arab tribes occupied different quarters in Mogadishu (hence presumably its expansion), but recognized the supremacy of the tribe of Muqri, who called themselves Qahtanis, i.e. south-Arabians, and furnished the qadi of the city. The sultanate seems to have emerged only towards the end of the thirteenth century, and the most noted of its sultans was this Abu Bakr b. Fakhr al-Din.

from the land of al-Hijaz." So he took the message, then returned bringing a plate on which were some leaves of betel and areca nuts. He gave me ten leaves along with a few of the nuts, the same to the qadi, and what was left on the plate to my companions and the qadi's students. He brought also a jug of rose-water of Damascus, which he poured over me and over the qadi [i.e. over our hands], and said "Our master commands that he be lodged in the students' house," this being a building equipped for the entertainment of students of religion. The qadi took me by the hand and we went to this house, which is in the vicinity of the Shaikh's residence, and furnished with carpets and all necessary appointments. Later on [the serving boy] brought food from the Shaikh's residence. With him came one of his viziers, who was responsible for [the care of] the guests, and who said "Our master greets you and says to you that you are heartily welcome." He then set down the food and we ate. Their food is rice cooked with ghee, which they put into a large wooden platter, and on top of this they set platters of *kushan*.[6] This is the seasoning, made of chickens, fleshmeat, fish and vegetables. They cook unripe bananas in fresh milk and put this in one dish, and in another dish they put curdled milk, on which they place [pieces of] pickled lemon, bunches of pickled pepper steeped in vinegar and salted, green ginger, and mangoes. These resemble apples, but have a stone; when ripe they are exceedingly sweet and are eaten like [other] fruit, but before ripening they are acid like lemons, and they pickle them in vinegar. When they take a mouthful of rice, they eat some of these salted and vinegar conserves after it. A single person of the people of Maqdashaw eats as much as a whole company of us would eat, as a mat-

ter of habit, and they are corpulent and fat in the extreme.

After we had eaten, the qadi took leave of us. We stayed there three days, food being brought to us three times a day, following their custom. On the fourth day, which was a Friday, the qadi and students and one of the Shaikh's viziers came to me, bringing a set of robes; these [official] robes of theirs consist of a silk wrapper which one ties round his waist in place of drawers (for they have no acquaintance with these), a tunic of Egyptian linen with an embroidered border, a furred mantle of Jerusalem stuff, and an Egyptian turban with an embroidered edge. They also brought robes for my companions suitable to their position. We went to the congregational mosque and made our prayers behind the *maqsura*.[7] When the Shaikh came out of the door of the *maqsura* I saluted him along with the qadi; he said a word of greeting, spoke in their tongue with the qadi, and then said in Arabic "You are heartily welcome, and you have honoured our land and given us pleasure." He went out to the court of the mosque and stood by the grave of his father, who is buried there, then recited some verses from the Quran and said a prayer. After this the viziers, amirs, and officers of the troops came up and saluted him. Their manner of salutation is the same as the custom of the people of al-Yaman; one puts his forefinger to the ground, then raises it to his head and says "May God prolong thy majesty." The Shaikh then went out of the gate of the mosque, put on his sandals, ordered the qadi to put on his sandals and me to do likewise, and set out on foot for his residence, which is close to the mosque. All the [rest of the] people walked barefoot. Over his head were carried four canopies of coloured silk, with the figure of a bird in gold on top of each canopy.[8] His gar-

---

[6] *Kushan* is probably a term of the Persian Gulf seamen for seasonings of meat and vegetables, resembling curries, served with rice. The origin may be related to Persian *gushtan,* glossed as "meats and fruit pulps."

[7] The enclosure in the congregational mosque reserved for the ruler.

[8] Ibn Battuta does not call these by the name of the ceremonial parasol, *jitr,* the use of which had been

ments on that day were a large green mantle of Jerusalem stuff, with fine robes of Egyptian stuffs with their appendages underneath it, and he was girt with a waist-wrapper of silk and turbaned with a large turban. In front of him were sounded drums and trumpets and fifes, and before and behind him were the commanders of the troops, while the qadi, the doctors of the law and the sharifs walked alongside him. He entered his audience-hall in this disposition, and the viziers, amirs and officers of the troops sat down in a gallery there. For the qadi there was spread a rug, on which no one may sit but he, and beside him were the jurists and sharifs. They remained there until the hour of the afternoon prayer, and after they had prayed it, the whole body of troops came and stood in rows in order of their ranks. Thereafter the drums, fifes, trumpets and flutes are sounded; while they play no person moves or stirs from his place, and anyone who is walking stands still, moving neither backwards nor forwards. When the playing of the drum-band comes to an end, they salute with their fingers as we have described and withdraw. This is a custom of theirs on every Friday.

On the Saturday, the population comes to the Shaikh's gate and they sit in porticoes outside his residence. The qadi, jurists, sharifs, men of religion, shaikhs and those who have made the Pilgrimage go in to the second audience-hall, where they sit on platforms prepared for that purpose. The qadi will be on a platform by himself, and each class of persons on the platform proper to them, which is shared by no others. The Shaikh then takes his seat in his hall and sends for the qadi, who sits down on his left; thereafter the jurists enter, and the principal men amongst them sit down in front of the

Shaikh, while the remainder salute and withdraw. Next the sharifs come in, their principal men sit down in front of him, and the remainder salute and withdraw. If they are guests, they sit on the Shaikh's right. Next the shaikhs and pilgrims come in, and their principal men sit, and the rest salute and withdraw. Then come the viziers, then the amirs, then the officers of the troops, group after group, and they salute and withdraw. Food is brought in; the qadi and sharifs and all those who are sitting in the hall eat in the presence of the Shaikh, and he eats with them. If he wishes to honour one of his principal amirs, he sends for him, and the latter eats with them. The rest of the people eat in the dining-hall, and the order of eating is the same as their order of entry into the Shaikh's presence. The Shaikh then goes into his residence, and the qadi, with the viziers, the private secretary, and four of the principal amirs, sits for deciding cases among the population and petitioners. Every case that is concerned with the rulings of the Divine Law is decided by the qadi, and all cases other than those are decided by the members of the council, that is to say, the viziers and amirs. If any case calls for consultation of the sultan, they write to him about it, and he sends out the reply to them immediately on the reverse of the document as determined by his judgment. And this too is their fixed custom.

I then sailed from the city of Maqdashaw, making for the country of the Sawahil [Coastlands], with the object of visiting the city of Kulwa in the land of the Zinj people. We came to the island of Mambasa, a large island two days' journey by sea from the Sawahil country.[9] It has no mainland territory, and its trees are the banana, the lemon, and the citron. Its people have a fruit which

---

apparently introduced by the Fatimid caliphs of Egypt and spread to all parts of the Muslim world. But apart from the fact of the four "canopies" (*qibab*), it is difficult to see how these differed from the parasols, especially as the latter too were often surmounted by the figure of a bird.

[9] *Sahil*, literally "coastland," meant in maritime usage a port serving as an entrepôt for the goods of its hinterland . . . Mombasa is separated from the mainland only by a narrow strait, but Ibn Battuta apparently means that it is two days sailing time from the "Coastlands" properly so called, i.e. the trading ports to the southward.

they call *jammun,* resembling an olive and with a stone like its stone. The inhabitants of this island sow no grain, and it has to be transported to them from the Sawahil. Their food consists mostly of bananas and fish. They are Shafiites in rite, pious, honourable, and upright, and their mosques are of wood, admirably constructed. At each of the gates of the mosques there are one or two wells (their wells have a depth of one or two cubits), and they draw up water from them in a wooden vessel, into which has been fixed a thin stick of the length of one cubit. The ground round the well and the mosque is paved; anyone who intends to go into the mosque washes his feet before entering, and at its gate there is a piece of thick matting on which he rubs his feet. If one intends to make an ablution, he holds the vessel between his thighs, pours [water] on his hands and performs the ritual washings. All the people walk with bare feet.

We stayed one night in this island and sailed on to the city of Kulwa, a large city on the seacoast,[10] most of whose inhabitants are Zinj, jet-black in colour. They have tattoo marks on their faces, just as [there are] on the faces of the *Limis* of Janawa.[11] I was told by a merchant that the city of Sufala[12] lies at a distance of half a month's journey from the city of Kulwa, and that between Sufala and Yufi, in the country of the Limis, is a month's journey; from Yufi gold dust is brought to Sufala.[13] The city of Kulwa is one of

the finest and most substantially built towns; all the buildings are of wood, and the houses are roofed with *dis* reeds. The rains there are frequent. Its people engage in *jihad,* because they are on a common mainland with the heathen Zinj people and contiguous to them, and they are for the most part religious and upright, and Shafiites in rite.

Account of the Sultan of Kulwa. Its sultan at the period of my entry into it was Abul-Muzaffar Hasan, who was called also by the appellation of Abul-Mawahib, on account of the multitude of his gifts and acts of generosity. He used to engage frequently in expeditions to the land of the Zinj people, raiding them and taking booty, and he would set aside the fifth part of it to devote to the objects prescribed for it in the Book of God Most High. He used to deposit the portion for the relatives [of the Prophet] in a separate treasury; whenever he was visited by sharifs he would pay it out to them, and the sharifs used to come to visit him from al-Iraq and al-Hijaz and other countries. I saw at his court a number of the sharifs of al-Hijaz, amongst them Muhammad b. Jammaz, Mansur b. Lubaida b. Abu Numayy, and Muhammad b. Shumaila b. Abu Numayy, and at Maqdashaw I met Tabl b. Kubaish b. Jammaz, who was intending to go to him. This sultan is a man of great humility; he sits with poor brethren, and eats with them, and greatly respects men of religion and noble descent.

An anecdote illustrating his generosity. I was present with him on a Friday, when he had come out [of the mosque] after the prayer and was proceeding to his residence. He was accosted by a poor brother, a Yamanite, who said to him "O Abul-Mawahib;" he replied "At your service, O faqir—what do you want?" The man said, "Give me those robes that you are wearing." He said "Certainly I shall give you them." The man said "Now," and he said "Yes, now," went back to the mosque and into the khatib's chamber, where he dressed in other garments, and having taken off those robes

---

[10] Kilwa (*Kulwa* is not otherwise attested), Quiloa of the Portuguese chronicles, now Kilwa Kisiwani in Tanganyika (8° 57′ S., 39° 34′ E.), 340 miles south of Mombasa. . . .

[11] *Limi* is a variant form of *Lamlam,* applied by the Arab geographers to the (supposedly cannibal) tribes of the interior. Janawa was the name given to the country of the pagan tribes south of the Muslim lands in West Africa, which passed into Portuguese and thence into English as Guinea.

[12] Sofala, at 20° 10′ S., 34° 42′ E., was the southernmost trading station of the Arabs in Africa, founded by colonists from Mogadishu.

[13] Yufi is the kingdom of Nupe in West Africa. This confusion between the gold dust of the Niger and the mined gold ore of Sofala and the assumption of a connection between them are probably due to some misunderstanding on Ibn Battuta's part.

he called to the poor brother "Come in and take them." So the faqir came in, took them, made a bundle of them in a kerchief, placed them on his head and went off. The population were loud in their gratitude to the sultan for the humility and generosity that he had displayed, and his son, who was his designated heir, took the clothing from the poor brother and gave him ten slaves in exchange. When the sultan learned of the gratitude expressed by the people to him for that action, he too ordered the faqir to be given ten head of slaves and two loads of ivory, for most of their gifts consist of ivory and it is seldom that they give gold. When this worthy and open-handed sultan died (God have mercy on him), he was succeeded by his brother Daud, who was of the opposite line of conduct. When a petitioner came to him he would say to him "He who gave is dead, and left nothing behind to be given." Visitors would stay at his court for many months, and finally he would make them some small gift, so that at last solicitors gave up coming to his gate.

41 DUARTE BARBOSA
THE EAST COAST OF AFRICA AT THE BEGINNING OF THE SIXTEENTH CENTURY

Duarte Barbosa was a Portuguese royal commercial agent whose account of the East African Coast concerns the years 1500 to 1518, the beginning of the Portuguese period. He describes the towns of the coast before the major impact of Portuguese control and influence had altered their character and affected their prosperity.

SOFALA

Having passed the Little Vciques, for the Indies, at xviii leagues from them there is a river which is not very large, whereon is a town of the Moors called Sofala, close to which town the King of Portugal has a fort. These Moors established themselves there a long time ago on account of the great trade in gold which they carry on with the Gentiles of the mainland: these speak somewhat of bad Arabic (garabia), and have got a king over them, who is at present subject to the King of Portugal. And the mode of their trade is that they come by sea in small barks which they call zanbucs (sambuk), from the kingdoms of Quiloa, and Mombaza,

From Duarte Barbosa, *A Description of the Coasts of East Africa and Malabar in the Beginning of the Sixteenth Century,* trans. by Henry E. J. Stanley (London: Hakluyt Society, 1866), pp. 4–15, 19–21.

and Melindi; and they bring much cotton cloth of many colours, and white and blue, and some of silk; and grey, and red, and yellow beads, which come to the said kingdoms in other larger ships from the great kingdom of Cambay [India—ed.], which merchandise these Moors buy and collect from other Moors who bring them there, and they pay for them in gold by weight, and for a price which satisfies them; and the said Moors keep them and sell these cloths to the Gentiles of the kingdom of Benamatapa who come there laden with gold, which gold they give in exchange for the before mentioned cloths without weighing, and so much in quantity that these Moors usually gain one hundred for one. They also collect a large quantity of ivory, which is found all round Sofala, which they likewise sell in the great kingdom of Cambay at five or six ducats [1] the hundred weight, and so also some amber, which these Moors of Sofala bring them from the Vciques. They are black men, and men of colour—some speak Arabic, and the rest make use of the language of the Gentiles of the country. They wrap themselves from the waist downwards with cloths of cotton and silk, and they wear other silk cloths above named, such as cloaks and wraps for the head, and some of them wear hoods of scarlet, and of other coloured woollen stuffs and camelets, and of other silks. And their victuals are millet, and rice, and meat, and fish. In this river near to the sea there are many sea horses, which go in the sea, and come out on land at times to feed. These have teeth like small elephants, and it is better ivory than that of the elephant, and whiter and harder, and of greater durability of colour. In the country all round Sofala there are many elephants, which are very large and wild, and the people of the country do not know how to tame them: there are also many lions, ounces, mountain panthers, wild asses, and many other animals. It is a country of plains and mountains, and well watered. The Moors have now recently begun to produce much fine cotton in this country, and they weave it into white stuff because they do not know how to dye it, or because they have not got any colours; and they take the blue or coloured stuffs of Cambay and unravel them, and again weave the threads with their white thread, and in this manner they make coloured stuffs, by means of which they get much gold.

KINGDOM OF BENAMATAPA

On entering within this country of Sofala, there is the kingdom of Benamatapa, which is very large and peopled by Gentiles, whom the Moors call Cafers. These are brown men, who go bare, but covered from the waist downwards with coloured stuffs, or skins of wild animals; and the

[1] A ducat was a gold coin of varying value (ed.).

persons most in honour among them wear some of the tails of the skin behind them, which go trailing on the ground for state and show, and they make bounds and movements of their bodies, by which they make these tails wag on either side of them. They carry swords in scabbards of wood bound with gold or other metals, and they wear them on the left hand side as we do, in sashes of coloured stuffs, which they make for this purpose with four or five knots, and their tassels hanging down, like gentlemen; and in their hands azagayes, and others carry bows and arrows: it must be mentioned that the bows are of middle size, and the iron points of the arrows are very large and well wrought. They are men of war, and some of them are merchants: their women go naked as long as they are girls, only covering their middles with cotton cloths, and when they are married and have children, they wear other cloths over their breasts.

ZINBAOCH

Leaving Sofala for the interior of the country, at xv days journey from it, there is a large town of Gentiles, which is called Zinbaoch; and it has houses of wood and straw, in which town the King of Benamatapa frequently dwells, and from there to the city of Benamatapa there are six days journey, and the road goes from Sofala, inland, towards the Cape of Good Hope. And in the said Benamatapa, which is a very large town, the king is used to make his longest residence; and it is thence that the merchants bring to Sofala the gold which they sell to the Moors without weighing it, for coloured stuffs and beads of Cambay, which are much used and valued amongst them; and the people of this city of Benamatapa say that this gold comes from still further off towards the Cape of Good Hope, from another kingdom subject to this king of Benamatapa, who is a great lord, and holds many other kings as his subjects, and many other lands, which extend far inland, both towards the Cape of Good Hope and towards Mozambich. And in this town he is each day served with large presents, which the kings and lords, his subjects, send to him; and when they bring them, they carry them bareheaded through all the city, until they arrive at the palace, from whence the king sees them come from a window, and he orders them to be taken up from there, and the bearers do not see him, but only hear his words; and afterwards, he bids them call the persons who have brought these presents, and he dismisses them. This king constantly takes with him into the field a captain, whom they call Sono, with a great quantity of men-at-arms, and amongst them they bring six thousand women, who also bear arms and fight. With these forces he goes about subduing and pacifying whatever kings rise up or desire to revolt. The said king of Benamatapa sends, each year, many honourable persons throughout his kingdoms to all the towns and lordships, to give them new regulations, so that all may do them obeisance, which is in this manner: each one of the envoys comes to a town, and bids the people extinguish all the fires that there are in it; and after they have been put out, all the inhabitants go to this man who has been sent as commissary, to get fresh fire from him in sign of subjection and obedience; and, whoever should not do this is held as a rebel, and the king immediately sends the number of people that are necessary to destroy him, and these pass through all the towns at their expense: their rations are meat, rice, and oil of sesame.

RIVER ZUAMA

Leaving Sofala for Mozambich, at forty leagues from it, there is a very large river, which is called the Zuama; and it is said that it goes towards Benamatapa, and it extends more than 160 leagues. In the mouth of this river there is a town of the Moors, which has a king, and it is called Mongalo. Much gold comes from Benamatapa to this town of the Moors, by this river, which makes another branch which falls at Angos, where the Moors make use of boats (almadias), which are boats hollowed out from a single trunk, to bring the cloths and other merchandise from Angos, and to transport much gold and ivory.

ANGOY

After passing this river of Zuama, at xl leagues from it, there is a town of the Moors on the sea coast, which is called Angoy, and has a king, and the Moors who live there are all merchants, and deal in gold, ivory, silk, and cotton stuffs, and beads of Cambay, the same as do those of Sofala. And the Moors bring these goods from Quiloa, and Monbaza, and Melynde, in small vessels hidden from the Portuguese ships; and they carry from there a great quantity of ivory, and much gold. And in this town of Angos there are plenty of provisions of millet, rice, and some kinds of meat. These men are very brown and copper coloured; they go naked from the waist upwards, and from thence downwards, they wrap themselves with cloths of cotton and silk, and wear other cloths folded after the fashion of cloaks, and some wear caps and others hoods, worked with stuffs and silks; and they speak the language belonging to the country, which is that of the Pagans, and some of them speak Arabic. These people are sometimes in obedience to the king of Portugal, and at times they throw it off, for they are a long way off from the Portuguese forts.

MOZAMBIQUE ISLAND

Having passed this town of Anguox, on the way to India, there are very near to the land three islands, one of which is inhabited by Moors, and is called Mozambique. It has a very good port, and all the Moors touch there who are sailing to Sofala, Zuama, or Anguox. Amongst these Moors there is a sheriff, who governs them, and does justice. These are of the language and customs of the Moors of Anguox, in which island the King of Portugal now holds a fort, and keeps the said Moors under his orders and government. At this island the Portuguese ships provide themselves with water and wood, fish and other kinds of provisions; and at this place they refit those ships which stand in need of repair. And from this island likewise the Portuguese fort in Sofala draws its supplies, both of Portuguese goods and of the produce of India, on account of the road being longer by the mainland.

Opposite this island there are many very large elephants and wild animals. The country is inhabited by Gentiles, brutish people who go naked and smeared all over with coloured clay, and their natural parts wrapped in a strip of blue cotton stuff, without any other covering; and they have their lips pierced with three holes in each lip, and in these holes they wear bones stuck in, and claws, and small stones, and other little things dangling from them.

ISLAND OF QUILOA

After passing this place and going towards India, there is another island close to the mainland, called Quiloa, in which there is a town of the Moors, built of handsome houses of stone and lime, and very lofty, with their windows like those of the Christians; in the same way it has streets, and these houses have got their terraces, and the wood worked in with the masonry, with plenty of gardens, in which there are many fruit trees and much water. This island has got a king over it, and from hence there is trade with Sofala with ships, which carry much gold, which is dispersed thence through all Arabia Felix, for henceforward all this country is thus named on account of the shore of the sea being peopled with many towns and cities of the Moors; and when the King of Portugal discovered this land, the Moors of Sofala, and Zuama, and Anguox, and Mozambique, were all under obedience to

the King of Quiloa, who was a great king amongst them. And there is much gold in this town, because all the ships which go to Sofala touch at this island, both in going and coming back. These people are Moors, of a dusky colour, and some of them are black and some white; they are very well dressed with rich cloths of gold, and silk, and cotton, and the women also go very well dressed out with much gold and silver in chains and bracelets on their arms, and legs, and ears. The speech of these people is Arabic, and they have got books of the Alcoran, and honour greatly their prophet Muhamad. This King, for his great pride, and for not being willing to obey the King of Portugal, had this town taken from him by force, and in it they killed and captured many people, and the King fled from the island, in which the King of Portugal ordered a fortress to be built, and thus he holds under his command and government those who continued to dwell there.

ISLAND OF MOMBAZA

Passing Quiloa, and going along the coast of the said Arabia Felix towards India, close to the mainland there is another island, in which there is a city of the Moors, called Mombaza,[2] very large and beautiful, and built of high and handsome houses of stone and whitewash, and with very good streets, in the manner of those of Quiloa. And it also had a king over it. The people are of dusky white, and brown complexions, and likewise the women, who are much adorned with silk and gold stuffs. It is a town of great trade in goods, and has a good port, where there are always many ships, both of those that sail for Sofala and those that come from Cambay and Melinde, and others which sail to the islands of Zanzibar, Manfia, and Penda, which will be spoken of further on. This Mombaza is a country well supplied with plenty of provisions, very fine sheep, which have round tails, and many cows,

[2] Mombaza.

chickens, and very large goats, much rice and millet, and plenty of oranges, sweet and bitter, and lemons, cedrats, pomegranates, Indian figs, and all sorts of vegetables, and very good water. The inhabitants at times are at war with the people of the continent, and at other times at peace, and trade with them, and obtain much honey and wax, and ivory. This King, for his pride and unwillingness to obey the King of Portugal, lost his city, and the Portuguese took it from him by force, and the King fled, and they killed and made captives many of his people, and the country was ravaged, and much plunder was carried off from it of gold and silver, copper, ivory, rich stuffs of gold and silk, and much other valuable merchandize.

MELINDE

After passing the city of Mombaza, at no great distance further on along the coast, there is a very handsome town on the mainland on the beach, called Melinde, and it is a town of the Moors, which has a king. And this town has fine houses of stone and whitewash, of several stories, with their windows and terraces, and good streets. The inhabitants are dusky and black, and go naked from the waist upwards, and from that downwards they cover themselves with cloths of cotton and silk, and others wear wraps like cloaks, and handsome caps on their heads. The trade is great which they carry on in cloth, gold, ivory, copper, quicksilver, and much other merchandise, with both Moors and Gentiles of the kingdom of Cambay, who come to their port with ships laden with cloth, which they buy in exchange for gold, ivory, and wax. Both parties find great profit in this. There are plenty of provisions in this town, of rice, millet, and some wheat, which is brought to them from Cambay, and plenty of fruit, for there are many gardens and orchards. There are here many of the large-tailed sheep, and of all other meats as above; there are also oranges, sweet and sour. This King and people have always been

very friendly and obedient to the King of Portugal, and the Portuguese have always met with much friendship and good reception amongst them.

ISLAND OF SAN LORENZO

Opposite these places, in the sea above the Cape of the Currents, at a distance of eighty leagues, there is a very large island, which is called San Lorenzo, and which is peopled by Gentiles, and has in it some towns of Moors. This island has many kings, both Moors and Gentiles. There is in it much meat, rice, and millet, and plenty of oranges and lemons, and there is much ginger in this country, which they do not make use of, except to eat it almost green. The inhabitants go naked, covering only their middles with cotton cloths. They do not navigate, nor does any one do so for them; they have got canoes for fishing on their coast. They are people of a dark complexion, and have a language of their own. They frequently are at war with one another, and their arms are azagayes, very sharp, with their points very well worked; they throw these in order to wound, and carry several of them in their hands. They are very well built and active men, and have a good method of wrestling. There is amongst them silver of inferior quality. Their principal food is roots, which they sow, and it is called yname,[3] and in the Indies of Spain it is called maize. The country is very beautiful and luxuriant in vegetation, and it has very large rivers. This island is in length from the part of Sofala and Melinde three hundred leagues, and to the mainland there are sixty leagues.

PENDA, MANFIA, AND ZANZIBAR

Between this island of San Lorenzo and the continent, not very far from it, are three islands, which are called one

[3] Root in the form of a gourd, composed of two bulbs, which grow one above the other, the larger one below the smaller one. It is cut into slices and eaten instead of bread. It throws out very large leaves, without fruit. . . .

Manfia, another Zanzibar, and the other Penda; these are inhabited by Moors; they are very fertile islands, with plenty of provisions, rice, millet, and flesh, and abundant oranges, lemons, and cedrats. All the mountains are full of them; they produce many sugar canes, but do not know how to make sugar. These islands have their kings. The inhabitants trade with the mainland with their provisions and fruits; they have small vessels, very loosely and badly made, without decks, and with a single mast; all their planks are sewn together with cords of reed or matting, and the sails are of palm mats. They are very feeble people, with very few and despicable weapons. In these islands they live in great luxury, and abundance; they dress in very good cloths of silk and cotton, which they buy in Mombaza of the merchants from Cambay, who reside there. Their wives adorn themselves with many jewels of gold from Sofala, and silver, in chains, ear-rings, bracelets, and ankle rings, and are dressed in silk stuffs: and they have many mosques, and hold the Alcoran of Mahomed.

PATE

After passing Melinde, and going towards India, they cross the Gulf (because the coast trends inwards) towards the Red Sea, and on the coast there is a town called Pate, and further on there is another town of the Moors, called Lamon; all these trade with the Gentiles of the country, and they are strongly-walled towns of stone and whitewash, because at times they have to fight with the Gentiles, who live in the interior of the country.

BRAVA

Leaving these places, further on along the coast is a town of the Moors, well walled, and built of good houses of stone and whitewash, which is called Brava. It has not got a king; it is governed by its elders, they being honoured and respectable persons. It is a place of trade, which has already been destroyed by the Portuguese, with great slaughter of the inhabitants, of whom many were made captives, and great riches in gold, silver, and other merchandise were taken here, and those who escaped fled into the country, and after the place was destroyed they returned to people it.

·   ·   ·

KINGDOM OF PRESTER JOHN

Leaving these towns of the Moors and entering into the interior of the country, the great kingdom of Prester John is to be found, whom the Moors of Arabia call Abexi;[4] this kingdom is very large, and peopled with many cities, towns, and villages, with many inhabitants: and it has many kings subject to it and tributary kings. And in their country there are many who live in the fields and mountains, like Beduins: they are black men, very well made: they have many horses, and make use of them, and are good riders, and there are great sportsmen and hunters amongst them. Their provisions are flesh of all kinds, milk, butter, and wheaten bread, and of these things there is a great abundance. Their clothes are of hides because the country is wanting in cloths; and there is a law amongst them by which certain families and ranks of persons may wear cloths, and the rest of the people may wear only hides well dressed and tanned. Amongst them there are men and women who have never drunk water, but only milk, which greatly supports them, and quenches the thirst, on account of its being more healthy and substantial, and there is great abundance of it in the country. These people are Christians of the doctrine of the blessed Saint Bartholomew, as they say; and their baptism is in three kinds, of blood, fire, and water: that is to say, that they circumcise themselves, and mark themselves on the temples and forehead with fire, and also in water, like the Catholic Christians. Many of them are deficient in our true faith, because the country is very large, and whilst in the principal city of Babel

4 Habeshy, Abyssinian.

Melech, where Prester John resides, they may be Christians, in many other distant parts they live in error and without being taught; so that they are only Christians in name.

BABEL MELECH

In the interior of this country is the great city of Babel Melech, where Prester John holds his residence. The Moors call him the great King of the Habeshys: he is Christian, and lord of many extensive countries and numerous people, with whom he makes subject many great kings. He is very rich, and possesses more gold than any other prince. This Prester John holds a very large court, and he keeps many men at arms continually in his pay, whom he takes about with him. He goes out very rarely from his dwelling; many kings and great lords come to visit him. In this city a great feast takes place in the month of August, for which so many kings and nobles come together, and so many people that they are innumerable:

and on this day of the feast in August they take an image out of a church, which is believed to be that of Our Lady, or that of St. Bartholomew, which image is of gold and of the size of a man; its eyes are of very large and beautiful rubies of great value, and the whole of it is adorned with many precious stones of much value, and placing it in a great chariot of gold, they carry it in procession with very great veneration and ceremony, and Prester John goes in front of this car in another gold car, very richly dressed in cloth of gold with much jewellery. And they begin to go out thus in the morning, and go in procession through all the city with much music of all sorts of instruments, until the evening, when they go home. And so many people throng to this procession, that in order to arrive at the car of the image many die of being squeezed and suffocated; and those who die in this wise are held as saints and martyrs; and many old men and old women go with a good will to die in this manner.

42 FRANCISCO ALVAREZ
THE LAND OF PRESTER JOHN

Father Francisco Alvarez (d. c. 1540) was chaplin to the Portuguese mission that was led by Don Rodrigo de Lima and that visited Ethiopia during the years 1520 to 1525. At that time Abyssinia was still known as the land of Prester John, the legendary priest-king whose dominions were thought to be in Ethiopia and whose Christian subjects Portugal was anxious to support against the Muslims of Arabia and the Persian Gulf as part of the continuing Portuguese crusade against Islam.

At a day's journey from this church of Imbra Christo are edifices, the like of which and so many, cannot, as it appears to me, be found in the world, and they are

From Father Francisco Alvarez, *Narrative of the Portuguese Embassy to Abyssinia During the Years 1520–1527,* trans. and edited by Lord Stanley of Alderley (London: Hakluyt Society, 1881), pp. 122–126, 240–245.

churches entirely excavated in the rock, very well hewn. The names of these churches are these: Emanuel, St. Saviour, St. Mary, Holy Cross, St. George, Golgotha, Bethlehem, Marcoreos, the Martyrs. The principal one is Lalibela. This Lalibela, they say, was a King in this same country for eighty years, and he was King before the one before mentioned who was named Abraham. This King ordered these edifices to be made. He does not lie in the church which bears his name, he lies in the church of Golgotha, which is the church of the fewest buildings here. It is in this manner: all excavated in the stone itself, a hundred and twenty spans in length, and seventy-two spans in width. The ceiling of this church rests on five supports, two on each side, and one in the centre, like fives of dice, and the ceiling or roof is all flat like the floor of the church, the sides also are worked in a fine fashion, also the windows, and the doors with all the tracery, which could be told, so that neither a jeweller in silver, nor a worker of wax in wax, could do more work. The tomb of this King is in the same manner as that of Santiago of Galicia, at Compostella, and it is in this manner: the gallery which goes round the church is like a cloister, and lower than the body of the church, and one goes down from the church to this gallery; there are three windows on each side, that is to say, at that height which the church is higher than the gallery, and as much as the body of the church extends, so much is excavated below, and to as much depth as there is height above the floor of the church. And if one looks through each of these windows which is opposite the sun, one sees the tomb at the right of the high altar. In the centre of the body of the church is the sign of a door like a trap door, it is covered up with a large stone, like an altar stone, fitting very exactly in that door. They say that this is the entrance to the lower chamber, and that no one enters there, nor does it appear that that stone or door can be raised. This stone has a hole in the centre which pierces it through, its size is three palms.[1] All the pilgrims put their hands into this stone (which hardly find room), and say that many miracles are done here. On the left hand side, when one goes from the principal door before the principal

chapel, there is a tomb cut in the same rock as the church, which they say is made after the manner of the sepulchre of Christ in Jerusalem. So they hold it in honour and veneration and reverence, as becomes the memory to which it belongs. In the other part of the church are two great images carved in the wall itself, which remain in a manner separated from it. They showed me these things as though I should be amazed at seeing them. One of the images is of St. Peter, the other of St. John: they give them great reverence. This church also possesses a separate chapel, almost a church; this has naves on six supports, that is, three on each side. This is very well constructed, with much elegance: the middle nave is raised and arched, its windows and doorways are well wrought, that is, the principal door, and one side door, for the other gives entrance to the principal church. This chapel is as broad as it is long, that is, fifty-two spans broad, and as many in length. It has another chapel, very high and small, like a pinnacle, with many windows in the same height: these also have as much width as length, that is, twelve spans. This church and its chapels have their altars and canopies, with their supports, made of the rock itself, it also has a very great circuit cut out of the rock. The circuit is on the same level as the church itself, and is all square: all its walls are pierced with holes the size of the mouth of a barrel. All these holes are stopped up with small stones, and they say that they are tombs, and such they appear to be, because some have been stopped up since a long time, others recently. The entrance of this circuit is below the rock, at a great depth and measure of thirteen spans, all artificially excavated, or worked with the pick-axe, for here there is no digging, because the stone is hard, and for great walls like the Porto in Portugal.

. . .

The church of St. Saviour stands alone, cut out of a rock; it is very large. Its

---

[1] *Palmo,* measure of four inches.

interior is two hundred spans in length, and a hundred and twenty in width. It has five naves, in each one seven square columns; the large one has four, and the walls of the church have as much. The columns are very well worked, with arches which hang down a span below the vaulted roof. The vaulted roofs are very well worked, and of great height, principally the centre one, which is very high. It is of a handsome height; most of the ends are lower, all in proportion. In the principal height of these naves there is much tracery, such as . . . , or keystones, or roses, which they put on the vaults, on which they make roses and other graceful works. On the sides it has very pretty windows, with much tracery, long and narrow in the middle. Within and without, these are long, like the loopholes of a wall, narrow without and wide within; these are wide both within and without, and narrow in the middle, with arches and tracery. The principal chapel is very high, and the canopy over the altar is very high, with a support at each corner. All this is made from the rock itself. In the other naves they do not deck the chapels and altars with canopies like the high altar in its grandeur. The principal door has at each side many and large buttresses, and the door commences with very large arches, and goes on narrowing with other arches until they reach a small door, which is not more than nine spans high and four and a half wide. The side doors are in this manner, only that they do not commence with so much width, and they end with the width of the principal door. On the outside part of this church are seven buttresses with arches, which are twelve palms distant from the wall of the church, and from buttress to buttress an arch, and above the church, on these arches, a vault constructed in such manner that if it were built of pieces and soft stone it could not be straighter nor better constructed, nor with more work about it. These arches outside may be about the height of two lances. There is not any variation in the whole of this rock in

which this church stands; it all looks like one block of marble. The court or cloister which the church has round it is all worked with the same stone. It is sixty palms wide at each end, and in front of the principal church door quite a hundred palms. Above this church, where it should be roofed, there are on each side nine large arches, like cloisters, which descend from the top to the bottom, to the tombs along the sides, as in the other church. The entrance to this church is by a descent through the rock itself, eighty steps cut artificially in the stone, of a width that ten men can go side by side, and of the height of a lance or more. This entrance has four holes above, which give light to the passage above the edges. From this rock to the enclosure of the church is like a field; there are many houses, and they sow barley in it.

.   .   .

On the 4th day of the month of January Prester John sent to tell us to order our tents, both that of the church and our own, to be taken from this place to a distance of about half a league, where they had made a large tank of water, in which they were to be baptized on the day of the Kings, because on that day it is their custom to be baptized every year, as that was the day on which Christ was baptized. We took thither a small tent for resting in and the church tent. The next day, which was the vigil of the day of the Kings, the Prester sent to call us, and we saw the enclosure where the tank was. The enclosure was a fence, and very large, in a plain. He sent to ask us if we intended to be baptized. I replied that it was not our custom to be baptized more than once, when we were little. Some said, principally the ambassador, that we would do what His Highness commanded. When they perceived that, they came back again with another message to me, asking what I said as to being baptized. I answered that I had been already baptized, and should not be so again. They still sent word that if we did not wish to be baptized in their tank, they would send us water to our tent. To this the ambassador replied that it should be as His Highness ordered. The Franks and our people had arranged to give a representation of the Kings, and they sent to tell him of it. A message came that it pleased him, and so they got ready for it, and they made it in the inclosure and plain close to the King's tent, which was pitched close to the tank. They gave the representation, and it was not esteemed, nor hardly looked at, and so it was a cold affair. Now that it was night they told us to go to our tent, which was not far off. In all this night till dawn a great number of priests never ceased chaunting over the said tank, saying that they were blessing the water, and about midnight, a little earlier or later, they began the baptism. They say, and I believe that such is the truth, that the first person baptized is the Prester, and after him the Abima, and after him the Queen, the wife of the Prester. They say that these three persons wear cloths over their nakedness, and that all the others were as their mothers bore them. When it was almost the hour of sunrise, and the baptism in fullest force, the Prester sent to call me to see the said baptism. I went and remained there till the hour of tierce, seeing how they were baptized; they placed me at one end of the tank, with my face towards Prester John, and they baptize in this manner.

The tank is large, the bottom of it in the earth, and it is cut very straight in the earth, and well squared; it is lined with planks, and over the planks waxed cotton cloth is spread. The water came from a rivulet through a conduit, like those to irrigate gardens, and it fell into the tank through a cane, at the end of which was a bag that was full; because they strain the water which falls into the tank; and it was no longer running when I saw it: the tank was full of blessed water, as they said, and they told me that it contained oil. This tank had five or six steps at one end, and about three fathoms in front of these steps was the dais of Prester John, on which he

sat. He had before him a curtain of blue tafetan, with an opening of about a span, by which those who were baptized saw him, because he was with his face to the tank. In the tank stood the old priest, the master of the Prester, who was with me Christmas night, and he was naked as when his mother bore him (and quite dead of cold, because it was a very sharp frost), standing in the water up to his shoulders or thereabouts, for so deep was the tank that those who were to be baptized entered by the steps, naked, with their backs to the Prester, and when they came out again they showed him their fronts, the women as well as the men. When they came to the said priest, he put his hands on their head, and put it three times under the water, saying in his language: "In name of the Father, of the Son, and of the Holy Spirit," he made the sign of the cross as a blessing, and they went away in peace. (The "I baptize thee," I heard him say it.) If they were little people they did not go down all the steps, and the priest approached them, and dipped them there. They placed me at the other end of the tank, with my face looking to the Prester, so that when he saw the backs, I saw the fronts, and the contrary way when they came out of the tank. After a great number of baptized persons had passed, he sent to call me to be near him; and so near that the Cabeata did not stir to hear what the Prester said, and to speak to the interpreter who was close to me: and he asked me what I thought of that office. I answered him that the things of God's service which were done in good faith and without evil deceit, and in His praise, were good, but such an office as this, there was none in our Church, rather it forbade us baptizing without necessity on that day, because on that day Christ was baptized, so that we should not think of saying of ourselves that we were baptized on the same day as Christ; also the Church does not order this sacrament to be given more than once. Afterwards he asked whether we had it written in books not to be baptized more than once. I replied,

Yes, that we had, and that in the Creed, which was made at the Council of Pope Leon, with the three hundred and eighteen bishops, about which at times His Highness had questioned me, it was said: "Confiteor unum baptisma in remissionem peccatorum." Then they said to me that such was the truth, and so it was written in their books; but what were they to do with many who turned Moors and Jews after being Christians and then repented, and with others who did not believe well in baptism, what remedy would they have? I answered: For those who do not rightly believe, teaching and preaching would suffice for them, and if that did not profit, burn them as heretics. And so Christ spoke, and St. Mark wrote it: "Qui crediderit et baptizatus fuerit salvus erit, qui vero non crediderit condemnabitur." And as to those who turned Moors or Jews, and afterwards of their own free will recognised their error, and asked for mercy, the *Abima* would absolve them, with penances salutary for their souls, if he had powers for this, if not, let them go to the Pope of Rome, in whom are all the powers. And those who did not repent, they might take them and burn them, for such is the use in Frankland and the Church of Rome. To this there came the reply, that all this seemed to him good, but that his grandfather had ordained this baptism by the counsel of great priests, in order that so many souls should not be lost, and that it had been the custom until now; and he asked if the Pope would concede to the Abima to hold these powers, and how much it would cost him, and in how much time could they come. I answered him that the Pope desired nothing except to save souls, and that he would esteem it fortunate to send to him, the Abima, with such powers, and that it would only cost him the expenses of the journey, which would not be much, and also the letters of his powers: and that they could go and come through Portugal in three years: and by the road of Jerusalem, that I did not know it. To this there

came no answer except that I might go in peace to say mass. I said it was no longer time for saying mass, that midday was long passed. So I went to dine with our Portuguese and the Franks.

This tank was all closed in and covered over with coloured tent cloths, so well that more could not be said, and so well arranged, with so many oranges and lemons, and boughs suspended and so well disposed, that the boughs, oranges, and lemons appeared to have grown there, and that it was a well ordered garden. The large tent which was over the tank was long and . . . , and above covered with red and blue crosses of the fashion of the crosses of the order of Christ. This day, later in the afternoon, Prester John sent to call the ambassador and all his company. The baptism was already ended, and His Highness was still within his curtain where I left him. We entered there, and he at once asked the ambassador what he thought of it. He replied that it was very good, although we had not got such a custom. The water was then running into the tank, and he asked if there were here Portuguese who could swim. At once two jumped into the tank, and swam and dived as much as the tank allowed of. He enjoyed greatly, as he showed by his looks, seeing them swim and dive. After this he desired us to go outside and go to one end of the enclosure or circuit; and here he ordered a banquet to be made for us of bread and wine (according to their custom and the use of the country), and he desired us to raise our church tent and the tent we were lodging in, because he wished to return to his quarters, and that we should go in front of him because he was ordering his horsemen to skirmish in the manner in which they fight with the Moors in the field. So we went in front of him, looking at the said skirmish. They began, but soon there came such heavy rain that it did not allow them to carry out the skirmish which they had begun well.

43 JOÃO DOS SANTOS
THE WAZIMBA

"Ethiopia Oriental," by Father João dos Santos, is one of the most complete sources of written information on the peoples living in southeastern Africa in the late sixteenth century—Bantu, Arab, and Portuguese. Dos Santos resided at Sofala and traveled to the interior stations of Sena and Tete between 1586 and 1590, when the marauding Wazimba were sweeping through the region northward out of Central Africa.

Opposite the fort of Sena, on the other side of the river, live some Kaffirs, lords of those lands, good neighbours and friends of the Portuguese, and always most loyal to them.[1] It so happened at the time I was there that the Muzimba Kaffirs, of whom I previously made mention, who eat human flesh, invaded this territory and made war upon one of these friendly Kaffirs, and by force of arms took from him the kraal in which he resided and a great part of his land, besides which they killed and ate a number of his people. The Kaffir, seeing himself thus routed and his power destroyed, proceeded to Sena to lay his trouble before the captain, who was then André de Santiago, and to beg for assistance in driving out of his house the enemy who had taken possession of it. The captain, upon hearing his pitiful request, determined to assist him, both because he was very friendly to us and because he did not wish to have so near to Sena a neighbour as wicked as the Muzimba.

Therefore, having made all necessary preparations for this war, he set out, taking with him a great number of the Portuguese of Sena with their guns and two pieces of heavy cannon from the fort. On arriving at the place where the Muzimbas were, they found them within a strong double palisade of wood, with its ramparts and loopholes for arrows, sur-

rounded by a very deep and wide trench, within which the enemy were most defiant. André de Santiago, seeing that the enterprise was much more formidable than he had anticipated and that he had brought with him but few men to attack so strong an enemy and his fortress, fixed his camp on the bank of a rivulet which ran by the place, and sent a message to the captain of Tete, Pedro Fernandes de Chaves, to come to his assistance with the Portuguese of Tete and as many Kaffir vassals of his fort as he could bring.

Pedro Fernandes de Chaves immediately prepared to go to the assistance of André de Santiago, and assembled more than a hundred men with their guns, Portuguese and half-castes, and the eleven vassal chiefs. They all crossed to the other side of the river and proceeded by land until they were near the place where the Muzimbas had fortified themselves. These had information of their approach, and greatly feared their arrival. For this reason they sent out spies secretly upon the road, that when they approached they might see them, and report concerning the men who were coming. And learning from these spies that the Portuguese were in front of the Kaffirs in palanquins and hammocks and not disposed in order of battle, they sallied out of their fortress by night secretly, without being heard by André de Santiago, and proceeded to conceal themselves in a dense thicket at about half a league's distance, through which the men of Tete would have to pass. When they were thus stationed the Portuguese came up nearly half a league in advance of the Kaffirs of their company,

From Friar João dos Santos, "Ethiopia Oriental," in George McCall Theal, *Records of South-Eastern Africa, Collected in Various Libraries and Archive Departments in Europe* (London, 1898), VII, 293–304.
[1] Sena is located on the Zambezi River, in Portuguese Mozambique (ed.).

quite unsuspicious of what might befall them in the thicket. Just as they were entering it the Muzimbas fell upon them suddenly with such violence that in a short time they were all killed, not one surviving, and when they were dead the Muzimbas cut off their legs and arms, which they carried away on their backs with all the baggage and arms they had brought with them, after which they returned secretly to their fortress. When the chiefs reached the thicket and found all the Portuguese and their captain dead, they immediately turned back from the place and retreated to Tete, where they related the lamentable event that had occurred.

At the time that preparations for this war were being made there was a friar of St. Dominic preaching at Tete, named Nicolau do Rosario, a native of Pedrogão, a man who had reached perfection in many virtues. The captain Pedro Fernandes and the Portuguese of Tete begged this friar to accompany them on the expedition, to receive confessions and administer the sacraments to those who required them. To this the father acceded, thinking that in doing so he was serving our Lord and showing friendship to the Portuguese, and therefore he accompanied them. In the ambush he was severely wounded, and seizing him yet alive the Muzimbas carried him away with them to put him to death more cruelly afterwards, which they did upon arriving at their fortress, where they bound him hand and foot to a tree and killed him with their arrows in the most cruel manner. This they did to him rather than to others because he was a priest and head of the Christians, as they called him, laying all the blame for the war upon him and saying that Christians did nothing without the leave and counsel of their cacis. And in this manner the father met his death with great constancy, never ceasing to preach in a loud voice and profess the faith of Christ, as I shall relate more in detail in another place.

These Zimbas, or Muzimbas, do not adore idols or recognise any God, but instead they venerate and honour their king, whom they regard as a divinity, and they say he is the greatest and best in the world. And the said king says of himself that he alone is god of the earth, for which reason if it rains when he does not wish it to do so, or is too hot, he shoots arrows at the sky for not obeying him; and although all these people eat human flesh, the king does not, to seem different from his vassals.

All these Kaffirs as a rule are tall, well-proportioned, and very robust. The arms they carry are battle-axes, arrows, assagais, and large shields with which they entirely cover themselves. These shields are made of light wood covered with the skins of wild animals which they kill and eat. They are in the habit of eating the men they kill in war, and drinking out of their skulls, showing themselves in this boastful and ferocious. If any of the Kaffirs of their tribe fall ill or are severely wounded in war, to save themselves the trouble of tending them they kill and eat them. They are addicted to many other brutalities similar to these, which I leave for the sake of brevity.

After the Zimbas had put Father Nicolau to death they rested during the remainder of that sad day, and on the night that followed they celebrated their victory and success, playing upon many cornets and drums, and the next day at dawn they all sallied out of their fortress, the chief clothed in the chasuble that the father had brought with him to say mass, carrying the golden chalice in his left hand and an assagai in his right, all the other Zimbas carrying on their backs the limbs of the Portuguese, with the head of the captain of Tete on the point of a long lance, and beating a drum they had taken from him. In this manner, with loud shouts and cries they came within sight of André de Santiago and all the Portuguese who were with him, and showed them all these things. After this they retired within their fortress, saying that what they had done to the men of Tete who had come to help their enemies, they would do to them, and that it was the flesh of those men that they were about to eat.

André de Santiago, who was waiting for Pedro Fernandes de Chaves with much anxiety, and who knew nothing of what had taken place, was greatly shocked, as also were all the other Portuguese, at this most horrible and pitiful spectacle, for which reason they decided to retreat as soon as night came on. In carrying this decision into execution they were in so great a hurry to reach the other side of the river that they were heard by the Muzimbas, who sallied out of their fortress and falling upon them with great violence killed many of them on the bank of the river. Among the slain was André de Santiago, who died as the valiant man he was, because it being within his power to escape he did not do so, but remained fighting and defending his companions on the bank, where he killed a great number of the Muzimbas before he was killed by them.

Thus these robbers and fierce Muzimbas killed one hundred and thirty Portuguese and half-castes of Tete and Sena and the two captains of these forts. This they accomplished with very little loss on their side, with their usual cunning, as they always took the Portuguese unawares, when they were unable to fight. This took place in the year 1592.

Great sorrow was felt at the death of Father Nicolau, whom all looked upon as a saint, and for all the Portuguese who lost their lives in this most disastrous war, both because some of them were married and left wives and children at these rivers, and because the Zimbas were victorious, more insolent than before, and were within fortifications close to Sena, where with greater audacity they might in the future do much damage to the Portuguese who passed up and down these rivers with their merchandise. For these reasons

Dom Pedro de Sousa, captain of Mozambique, determined to chastise these Zimbas, conquer them, and drive them from the vicinity of Sena. To do this he proceeded to the rivers of Cuama from Mozambique in the following year, 1593, accompanied by some soldiers from the said fortress, with whom he reached Sena.

After obtaining information of the condition of the Zimbas, he commanded all the necessary preparations to be made for this war, and assembled nearly two hundred Portuguese and fifteen hundred Kaffirs, with whom he crossed to the other side of the Zambesi and proceeded by land to the fortress of the Zimbas, where he formed a camp at the same place that André de Santiago had formed his. Then he commanded that the various pieces of artillery which he had taken with him for the purpose should be fired against the wall of the fortress, but this had no effect upon it, as it was made of large wood, strengthened within by a strong and wide rampart which the Zimbas had constructed with the earth from the trench.

Dom Pedro, seeing that his artillery had no effect upon the enemy's wall, determined to enter the fortress and take it by assault, and for this purpose he commanded part of the trench to be filled up, which was done with great difficulty and danger to our men, as the Zimbas from the top of the wall wounded and killed some of them with arrows. When this part of the trench was filled up, a number of men crossed over with axes in their hands to the foot of the palisade, which they began to cut down, but the Zimbas from the top of the wall poured so great a quantity of boiling fat and water upon them that nearly all were scalded and badly wounded, especially the naked Kaffirs, so that no one dared go near the palisade, because they were afraid of the boiling fat and through fear of certain iron hooks similar to long harpoons, which the Zimbas thrust through the loopholes in the wall and with which they wounded and caught hold of all who came near and pulled from within with such force that they drew them to the apertures, where they wounded them mortally. For this reason the captain commanded all the men to be recalled to the camp to rest, and the remainder of that day was spent in tending the wounded and the scalded.

The following day the captain commanded a quantity of wood and branches of trees to be collected, with which huge wickerwork frames were made, as high as and higher than the enemy's palisade, and he commanded them to be placed in front of the wall and filled with earth that the soldiers might fight on them with their guns, and the Zimbas would not dare to appear on the wall or be able to pour boiling fat upon the men cutting down the palisade. When this stratagem of war was almost in readiness, another peaceful or cowardly device was planned in the following manner. The war had lasted two months, for which reason the residents of these rivers, who were there rather by force than of their own free will, being away from their homes and trade, which is their profession, and not war, pretended to have received letters from their wives in Sena relating the danger they were in from a rebel Kaffir who they said was coming with a number of men to rob Sena, knowing that the Portuguese were absent, for which reason they ought immediately to return home. This false information was spread through the camp, and the residents of Sena went to the captain and begged him to abandon the siege of the Zimbas and attend to what was of greater importance, as otherwise they would be compelled to return to their homes and leave him.

Dom Pedro, seeing their determination and believing the information said to be given in the letters to be true, abandoned the siege and commanded the men to pass by night to the other side of the river and return to Sena, but this retreat could not be effected with such secrecy as to be unknown to the Zimbas, who sallied out of their fortress with great cries, fell upon the camp, killed some men who were still there, and seized the greater part of the baggage and artillery, that had not been taken away.

With this defeat and disappointment the captain returned to Sena, and thence to Mozambique, without accomplishing what he desired; and the Zimba's position was improved and he became more insolent than before. Nevertheless he offered peace to the Portuguese of Sena, saying that he never wished to be at war with them, and always desired their friendship and commerce, but that the Portuguese had unjustly made war upon him, without his having done them any injury, and that he had killed them in just defence, as he was compelled to do. Peace was conceded to him, I fancy, on account of the benefit that would result from it to the Portuguese of this river. The affairs of the country were in this condition when I left it to proceed to Mozambique.

A Muzimba Kaffir of the tribe of which I spoke in the last chapter, who was lord of a little kraal and had a few vassals, but who was most ambitious of human honour, meditating upon the means by which he might become a great lord and renowned in the world, decided that for this purpose it would be expedient to sally out of his country with an armed force and destroy, rob, and eat every living thing that came in his way. This his diabolical intention he made known to his vassals and other Muzimbas of the same tribe, to whom his design did not appear objectionable, because as they are usually addicted to idleness, robbery, and cannibalism, by it they had an opportunity offered to them of satisfying their cruel and depraved inclination. Their course of action having been decided upon and arranged, they sallied forth from their country and commenced expending their fury upon their neighbours; and they traversed all the kingdoms of Kaffraria, proceeding constantly towards the east.

Through these lands they marched, destroying and plundering all they found, and devouring every living thing, not only men, women, and children, but cattle, dogs, cats, rats, snakes, and lizards, sparing none except Kaffirs who came to them and wished to accompany them on this expedition, whom they admitted into their army. In this manner they assembled more than fifteen thousand warriors, with whom they laid waste all the lands they traversed, so that they appeared to be a cruel scourge and punishment that God chose to send to Kaffraria.

Having reached the island of Kilwa, which is close to the mainland and peopled by Moors, they saw that they could not enter it because of the sea by which it was surrounded. They therefore formed a camp upon the mainland, opposite the island, and besieged it for several months, devouring all the animals and crops that the Moors possessed upon the mainland, so that nothing from it could reach the island.

Meantime a Moor of the said island, moved by greed and ambitious of honour, proceeded secretly one night to the mainland, where the Muzimbas were stationed, by a ford, well known to him, where one could cross at low tide. On reaching the camp, he informed the Kaffirs who met him that he came from the island and wished to speak to the chief captain of the army upon a matter of great importance. Being taken by them and presented to the captain, he said: "Powerful captain, you must know that I am a native of this land and a resident of the island of Kilwa that you are besieging, and I know for certain that very soon you will be lord of it and will punish the people for not recognising you as the great lord that you are, and obeying you as is right. I, knowing this, have come to offer you the obedience that is your due, and further I wish to lead you into the island of Kilwa with all your army, by the ford by which I have come, which is well known to me, upon condition that you

will spare the lives of my relatives who are in the place and divide with me the spoils and riches which you seize in the island, and also that you will bestow upon me the lands there that I shall point out to you, as this is of little consequence to you and of great importance to me." The Zimba replied that he was well pleased, and that if he would lead him into the island with all his men, as he said he would do, he promised to perform what he desired.

Upon this all were disposed in order to cross the ford, and the Moor led them to it, going in front to show them the way. Thus they all reached the island after midnight, and seized the Moors who were asleep and unsuspicious of the treachery being enacted or of what was about to happen. The Muzimbas killed the greater number without any resistance, and the remainder they took prisoners and ate gradually while they remained there, so that they killed and ate more than three thousand Moors, men and women, among whom many were very beautiful and delicate; and they plundered the whole town of Kilwa, in which they found great spoils and riches. Of the Moors only those escaped who had time to flee to the thickets on the island, where they remained in hiding until the Muzimbas returned to the mainland, after which they went back to the town, which in former years was a most noble one, the residence of the kings of all that coast, and even at the present time the ruins of the vast and sumptuous mosques and dwelling-houses give proof of its former grandeur.

When the Muzimbas had nothing more to do in the island their captain sent for the Moor who had conducted them to it by the ford, who was yet alive with all his relatives, as the captain had commanded them to be guarded, not wishing any of them to be put to death as the others had been. When they were all assembled before him he turned to the Moor and said: "I do not wish, nor am I satisfied, that a creature as wicked as thou art should live any longer, as thou wert so cruel that for thy own interest thou deliveredst thy country and thy compatriots into the hands of their enemies." And turning to the Kaffirs he said: "Take this wicked man and all his family who are here present and bind them hand and foot and throw them into the sea to be eaten by the fishes, as it is not proper that any one belonging to so wicked a race should live, nor do I wish you to eat them, as their flesh must be poisonous." This command was forthwith carried into execution, a sentence which surely was not that of a barbarian such as this man was, but of a wise man, and which shows with what reason Alexander the Great said that he profited by the treachery of those who delivered cities to him, but that he hated the traitors.

When this war of Kilwa was thus concluded the Muzimba returned to the mainland by the same ford by which he had entered the island when he was guided by the Moor.

After Kilwa was destroyed, the Zimba continued his journey along the coast until he reached that part of the mainland which is opposite the island of Mombasa, where he fixed his camp on the shore and determined to enter the island as he had entered Kilwa, but he could not immediately do so, as at the same time four Turkish galleys from the straits of Mecca, of which I shall give more detailed information later on, had put in there. These Turks defended the entrance of the island against him and fought with him on many occasions, killing a number of men with their artillery fired from two galleys that they had stationed in the passage by which the Zimba wished to enter.

This contest was continued for several days, until it happened that Thomé de Sousa arrived from India with a powerful fleet to oppose these same galleys, and finding them in this strait he fought with them and captured them with all that they carried, taking the Turks who were in them prisoners, and also ravaged the is-

land of Mombasa. All this was accomplished in sight of the Muzimbas who were on the mainland, who marvelled much to see the wonders performed by the Portuguese, for which reason the Muzimba chief said that the Portuguese were the gods of the sea and he god of the land, and forthwith sent an ambassador to Thomé de Sousa to say that he was a friend of the Portuguese and did not wish to be at war with them, and that as they had completed their work with such honour he also wished to perform his, which had already occupied him a long time, and which was to enter the island and kill and eat every living thing he should find in it. This design he immediately carried into execution with the consent of the Portuguese, and entering the island he searched all the palm groves and thickets in it, where he found many Moors hiding, who had escaped from the town, of whom he killed and ate all he could seize. When this was done Thomé de Sousa with his fleet returned victorious to India, as I shall relate farther on, and the Zimba returned to the mainland and proceeded on his journey, marching with his army towards Melinde.

The king of Melinde was greatly alarmed by the intelligence he received of the approach of the Muzimbas, knowing the ruin they had caused in Kilwa and Mombasa; nevertheless he placed great confidence in the valour of Matheus Mendez de Vasconcellos, who was then captain of this coast, and was at the time in Melinde with only thirty Portuguese soldiers and merchants, who were prepared to defend the town until they died in combat. The Zimbas reached Melinde with great insolence and boastfulness, as men who had never feared any nation, and attacked the town with great fury. Although our soldiers killed many of them with their guns, some of them succeeded in entering at different parts of the wall, which was low, and were already almost masters of a rampart, while a fierce combat was raging on all sides. At this moment more than three thousand Kaffirs called Mosseguejos, friends of the king, came to the succour of Melinde. These Kaffirs, knowing how hard pressed their friend the king of Melinde was by the arrival of the Muzimbas, had come to succour and assist him.

These Mosseguejos are most valiant men, who love war, of whom I shall give more detailed information farther on.

Arriving then at this point of the combat, they attacked the Muzimbas in the rear with such courage and force that in a short time they assisted in defeating and putting them to flight. And as these Muzimbas were strangers and had committed so many barbarities and killed so great a number of people upon the roads and in the countries through which they had passed, the same was done to them in their flight, all that were found being put to death; only the chief and about one hundred men escaped, and these returned the same way they had come, keeping in one body, without again separating, until they were once more in their own country.

Thus was destroyed in the town of Melinde, by the help of the Mosseguejos, the host of Muzimbas that had sallied out of the land which extends along the river of Sena, and reached Melinde, which is a journey of about three hundred leagues, without encountering any resistance or finding any who could meet them in battle, but on the contrary the kraals and lands were abandoned when it was known that this cruel army of cannibals was about to pass through them.

What I have said here concerning the Kaffirs who inhabit the interior appears to me sufficient for the present. And as we began by describing the peculiarities of the river of Luabo, we should follow the river Quilimane until we reach the shore of the sea, saying something of its inhabitants.

44 GASPAR BOCARRO
FROM TETE TO KILWA

Gaspar Bocarro appears to have been the first European to travel overland from Tete on the Zambezi to Kilwa in 1616 through what is now the southern interior of Tanzania. The account of this journey appears in Extractos da Decada, *by Antonio Bocarro, Keeper of the Archives and Chronicler of India at Lisbon from 1631 to 1649. In his official capacity, Bocarro had access to official correspondence from East Africa and India. The* Extractos *were dedicated to Philip III of Portugal (1621–1640) but were not actually printed by the Royal Academy of Sciences at Lisbon until 1876. Gaspar Bocarro may have been related to Antonio Bocarro. Gaspar performed the journey to ensure the safe passage of African silver to Portugal.*

At the time when Diogo Simoës sent the silver to His Majesty by means of the religious of Saint Dominic, who perforce had to pass by the fortress of Moçambique, and to go from thence to India, there were in the rivers of Cuama [1] certain persons dissatisfied with Diogo Simoës, who said openly that the Captain of Moçambique ought to seize the silver and send it on his own orders to His Majesty; and some wrote that this should be done.

From Sir John Gray, "A Journey by Land from Tete to Kilwa in 1616," in *Tanganyika Notes and Records,* 25 (1948), 40–45. Reprinted by permission of the Tanzania Society, Dar es Salaam.

[1] The name given at this date to the country in the region of the Zambesi delta.

When Diogo Simoës heard this, he was very angry. For this reason Gaspar Bocarro, a man of noble birth, brought up in the household of the Marquis of Ferreira, who had spent many years in these rivers, offered to make the journey by land from Tete [2] to the coast of Melinde [3] so that he could put Moçambique out of his way, and from the coast pass to Ormuz [4] and from there make his way by land to Spain,[5] and deliver the silver, which Diogo Simoës had given to him, to His Majesty: which journey he would make at his own expense, so as to serve the said lord: and he also would lend two thousand cruzados [6] to help to maintain the fort at Chicove,[7] for which no provision had come from India.

Diogo Simoës was pleased, accepted his offer, and received the said money, which Gaspar Bocarro gave him for the maintenance of the fort; then he delivered to him two frasilas [8] of silver ore, in one of which there was a small stone of pure silver, which appeared to have been smelted, but was pure in origin: (he also gave him) authenticated papers and credentials, so that he might deliver all to His Majesty. When this had been arranged and concluded, Gaspar Bocarro provided himself with necessaries for his very long and risky journey.

Gaspar Bocarro left Tete in March, 1616, taking in his company ten or twelve of his slaves. He crossed to the other side of the River Zambeze and made his way through the lands of Bororo. After two days' journeying he reached the village of Inhampury, where he bought a thousand bracelets of copper wire, which are made by the Cafres of this village, because they have plenty of copper there. These bracelets serve as money for petty expenses on all these roads in Cafraria. Bocarro gave Inhampury a present of some garments and beads, which came to seven cruzados. They left there and slept at Baue, a village of the same Inhampury, where one of his wives lived, to whom he gave another present, which was worth three cruzados. Thence they made their way for three days through thickets and desert land to Danda, a town subject to Muzura, who is the biggest Cafre Lord in all the lands of Bororo. To the governor of this town Bocarro gave cloths and beads, which were worth two cruzados. After this they slept at Bunga, a large village, subject to Muzura, where he gave the governor one cruzado's worth of cloth and beads. Thence Gaspar Bocarro sent Muzura word of his coming and sent ahead of him a present, which the Cafres call "the mouth," consisting of cloth and beads, which were worth five cruzados. On reaching the town, in which he dwelt and which is called Marauy, he went to see Muzura and gave him garments, and beads, and silk cloths, which were worth seventy cruzados. He also gave him his bed which included the hangings, a bolster of damask, and linen sheets, because it was a heavy weight to carry such a bed on the shoulders for such a long journey. Muzura gave Bocarro two tusks of ivory, which were worth eighteen cruzados, and a black woman, and food during the fifteen days that he stayed there (and he also gave) to all his people plenty of millet, rice, hens, capons, cows and figs, and he also gave him three Cafres, who were his subjects and were to act as guides and to guard them safely when passing through his lands.

With these three guides Bocarro left

---

[2] A town about 270 miles up the Zambesi, where at this date there was a fort.

[3] In contemporary Portuguese letters and chronicles the coast between Cape Delgado and Cape Guardafui is usually referred to as "the coast of Malindi." . . .

[4] An island at the entrance to the Persian Gulf, which was at this date in the possession of the Portuguese.

[5] Portuguese historians call the period 1580–1640 "the Spanish captivity," it being the period during which their country was ruled by the kings of Spain. At this date Philip III of Portugal (1598–1621) was also Philip IV of Spain.

[6] The cruzado was valued at 400 reis. . . . at the beginning of the seventeenth century 400 reis were worth about 5s. 4d.

[7] On the banks of Zambesi above Tete.

[8] The frasila weighed 35–36 English pounds.

Muzura and slept at Moromba, a town of Muzura. He gave the governor thereof, who was called Inhamocumba, garments and beads, which were worth two cruzados, and he gave Bocarro three more Cafres to accompany him and to be his guides. Near this town of Moromba is the great river Manganja,[9] or lake which looks like a sea, from which flows the river Nhanha,[10] which enters the Zambesi below Sena,[11] where it is called the river of Chiry.[12] From Moromba Gaspar Bocarro set out with this three additional guides, and made his way alongside this river Nhanha, and slept on its shore, and on the following day crossed over to the other side in vessels belonging to the native Cafres.[13] (Then) he made his way North and slept at the town of Caramboe, a son of Muzura, to whom Bocarro gave garments and beads which were worth seven cruzados. Thence he dined at a village called Mocama and slept at another village called Mogombe, to the governor of which he gave cloths and beads which were worth one cruzado. There he slept on the confines of the lands of Muzura's son.

From here onward begin the lands which are called Manguro, and are subject to Chicoave, who is a friend and quasi-vassal of Muzura, for he is afraid of him. He began to make his way through these lands and slept at the village of Machambe, to whom he gave cloths and beads which were worth two cruzados. From there he slept at the village of Muzunguira, to whom he gave bracelets and beads which were worth one cruzado.

From there he slept at the town, in which dwelt Chicoave, the lord of these lands. Before he came to him he gave him in advance for "the mouth" one hundred bracelets, one cloth, and some beads, which were worth seven cruzados. When he spoke with this Cafre, he gave him another present, which was worth seven cruzados, and the Cafre gave him a tusk of ivory, which was worth three cruzados. Muzura sent this Cafre a present so that he might give the road and guides to Bocarro, and he gave him his son, who thenceforward accompanied him together with the other guides of Muzura. Thence he crossed a river called Ruambara, which he crossed in boats. After leaving the town of Chicoave he slept at the village Chipanga and after at the village of Changuessa, to whom he gave a cloth and a bundle of beads. Thence he slept in an uninhabited place and on the following day at the village of Mauano, to whom he gave a cloth and a necklace of beads. Thence slept at a village called Rupapa, the lord of which was Quitenga, to whom he gave three cloths and twenty bracelets. From there he slept in a thicket and on the following day proceeded along the river Rofuma [14] to the village of Muangongo, to whom he gave fifty bracelets, two necklaces of beads, a machira,[15] and a cloth. He ferried Gaspar Bocarro and all his people in his boat to the other bank of the river and accompanied them for three days.

The lord of the lands, which extend from this river Rofuma as far as the salt sea, is Manhanga. Leaving this river Bocarro slept at the house of Darama, to whom he gave six bracelets and a few beads. Thence he slept at the village of Davia, to whom he gave twenty bracelets and a necklace of beads. From there he slept in the town in which dwells Manhanga, the lord of these lands. Before he came to him, Bocarro sent in advance to

[9] "Manganja" appears to be a Portuguese corruption of some Bantu word which has "nyanja" (cf. Note 10) as one of its roots. Manganja is clearly identifiable with Lake Nyassa.
[10] Apparently the common Bantu word "nyanja" meaning an expanse of water such as a lake.
[11] A town about 150 miles up the Zambesi, where at this date the Portuguese had a fort.
[12] *Sc.* the Shire, which flows out of Lake Nyassa and joins the Zambesi a little below Sena.
[13] Bocarro evidently made his crossing in the upper reaches of the Shire very close to its exit from Lake Nyasa, but never actually reached that lake.

[14] *Sc.* the Rovuma.
[15] "A sort of cloak or upper garment worn by the Cafres."

acquaint him as to his coming, and sent as "the mouth" two hundred bracelets and a machira. When he came to him, he gave him a further six hundred bracelets. Muzura likewise sent this Cafre a hundred bracelets, and a machira, and a black girl, so that he might make the roads through his lands free to Bocarro. He (sc. Manhanga) gave Bocarro a tusk of ivory and sent to Muzura a present of garments, which had come there from the coast of Melinde,[16] because this Cafre is obedient to Muzura. Here Muzura's three guides returned, and also the three guides of Inhamocumba, the governor of Moramba, and also Chicoave's son. From here Bocarro travelled onwards with guides, who were given to him by Manhanga and to whom he gave forthwith twenty bracelets. They made their way for seven days through country, which was uninhabited, because it had been destroyed by the Zimbas, who passed that way making war. At the end of seven days they reached the village of Chiponda, brother of Manhanga, to whom he gave fifty bracelets and a machira; and he (sc. Chiponda) gave him a small tusk of ivory; and he also gave him another Cafre to act as his guide and to accompany him on the road from there to the seashore, to whom Bocarro gave twenty bracelets. From there they made their way for four days through desert lands, and at the end of that time came to the village of Ponde, to whom they gave a few beads. Thence they went to the village of Morengue, to whom they gave a machira and a few beads. Thence they travelled through desert land for four days and came to Bucury, a village of

[16] Probably from Kilwa Kisiwani.

Moors,[17] where they slept. The next day they came to the shore of the salt sea at the hour of midday. From there they embarked and passed over to the island of Quiloa,[18] which is opposite to the shore, where were the factor and other Portuguese, who made Bocarro their guest.

The inhabited lands along this road abound in foodstuffs, that is to say, millet, rice, fruits, hens, sheep, cows and goats, all of which are cheap. Gaspar Bocarro spent fifty three days on the road and also spent more than one hundred and fifty cruzados in presents and for his own food and for the food which he gave to the people who accompanied him on the road. Though Gaspar Bocarro spent fifty three days on the road with all his servants, they (sc. the servants) were able to return from Quiloa to Tete, travelling light, in no more than twenty-five days.

At Quiloa Bocarro took ship for his voyage to Ormuz. On reaching Mombaça he heard that the roads in Persia were being obstructed by the Shah, and the land was at war. Therefore he decided to return to Moçambique and thence to the rivers of Cuama, where he arrived safely.

I have written all the details of this journey, the names of the villages and the lands, and their lords, and the expenses incurred by Gaspar Bocarro, because, if any one in time to come wishes to make this journey, the adventurer, who makes it, may know about the road and the expense.

[17] Like other Portuguese chroniclers Bocarro used the word Moor (Mouro) to distinguish the coast inhabitant of mixed Arab and African blood from the pure Arab from Asia.
[18] Kilwa Kisiwani was at this date ruled by a "Moorish" Sultan, who was independent of the Portuguese, but was on friendly terms with them.

45 FATHER LOBO
PORTUGUESE MISSIONARIES IN ETHIOPIA

Father Jeronimo Lobo (1593–1678) left Portugal for Goa, India, in 1622. After residing in India for a year, during which he completed his studies in divinity, he received letters from Ethiopia proclaiming that the Emperor of Ethiopia had been converted to the Church of Rome and desired Roman Catholic missionaries. Father Lobo was among the eight Jesuit priests who were selected to go to Ethiopia and administer to the emperor. At the time, Ethiopia was in constant revolt; after an appropriate flirtation with Roman Catholicism, the emperor returned to the Coptic (Egyptian Christian) Church in 1632.

I continued two years at my residence in Tigre [in northern Ethiopia—ed.], entirely taken up with the duties of the mission, preaching, confessing, baptising, and enjoyed a longer quiet and repose than I had ever done since I left Portugal. During this time one of our fathers, being always sick, and of a constitution which the air of Abyssinia was very hurtful to, obtained a permission from our superiors to return to the Indies. I was willing to accompany him through part of his way, and went with him over a desart, at no great distance from my residence, where I found many trees loaded with a kind of fruit, called by the natives Anchoy, about the bigness of an apricot, and very yellow, which is much eaten without any ill effect. I therefore made no scruple of gathering and eating it, without knowing that the inhabitants always peeled it, the rind being a violent purgative; so that, eating the fruit and skin together, I fell into such a disorder as almost brought me to my end. The ordinary dose is six of these rinds, and I had devoured twenty.

I removed from thence to Debaroa, fifty-four miles nearer the sea, and crossed in my way the desart of the province of Saraoe. The country is fruitful, pleasant, and populous. There are greater numbers of Moors in these parts than in any other province of Abyssinia; and the Abyssins of this country are not much better than the Moors.

From Father Jerome Lobo, *A Voyage to Abyssinia*, translated by Samuel Johnson (London: A. Bettesworth and C. Hitch, 1735), pp. 125–131.

I was at Debaroa when the persecution was first set on foot against the Catholics. Sultan Segued, who had been so great a favourer of us, was grown old, and his spirit and authority decreased with his strength. His son, who was arrived at manhood, being weary of waiting so long for the crown he was to inherit, took occasion to blame his father's conduct, and found some reason for censuring all his actions; he even proceeded so far as to give orders sometimes contrary to the emperor's. He had embraced the Catholic religion, rather through complaisance than conviction or inclination; and many of the Abyssins, who had done the same, waited only for an opportunity of making public profession of the ancient erroneous opinions, and of re-uniting themselves to the church of Alexandria. So artfully can this people dissemble their sentiments, that we had not been able hitherto to distinguish our real from our pretended favourers; but as soon as this prince began to give evident tokens of his hatred, even in the life-time of the emperor, we saw all the courtiers and governors, who had treated us with such a shew of friendship, declare against us, and persecute us as disturbers of the public tranquillity; who had come into Ethiopia with no other intention than to abolish the ancient laws and customs of the country, to sow divisions between father and son, and preach up a revolution.

After having borne all sorts of affronts and ill-treatments, we retired to our house at Fremona, in the midst of our country men, who had been settling round about us a long time, imagining we should be more secure there, and that, at least during the life of the emperor, they would not come to extremities, or proceed to open force. I laid some stress upon the kindness which the viceroy of Tigre had shown to us, and in particular to me; but was soon convinced that those hopes had no real foundation, for he was one of the most violent of our persecutors. He seized upon all our lands, and advancing with his troops to Fremona, blocked up the town. The army had not been stationed there long before they committed all sorts of disorders; so that one day a Portuguese, provoked beyond his temper at the insolence of some of them, went out with his four sons, and wounding several of them, forced the rest back to their camp.

We thought we had good reason to apprehend an attack; their troops were increasing, our town was surrounded, and on the point of being forced. Our Portuguese therefore thought, that without staying till the last extremities, they might lawfully repel one violence by another; and sallying out, to the number of fifty, wounded about threescore of the Abyssins, and had put them to the sword, but that they feared it might bring too great an odium upon our cause. The Portuguese were some of them wounded, but happily none died on either side.

Though the times were by no means favourable to us, every one blamed the conduct of the viceroy; and those who did not commend our action, made the necessity we were reduced to of self-defence an excuse for it. The viceroy's principal design was to get my person into his possession, imagining, that if I was once in his power, all the Portuguese would pay him a blind obedience. Having been unsuccessful in his attempt by open force, he made use of the arts of negociation, but with an event not more to his satisfaction. This viceroy being recalled, a son-in-law of the emperor's succeeded, who treated us even worse than his predecessor had done.

When he entered upon his command, he loaded us with kindnesses, giving us so many assurances of his protection, that, while the emperor lived, we thought him one of our friends; but no sooner was our protector dead, than this man pulled off his mask; and quitting all shame, let us see that neither the fear of God nor any other consideration was capable of restraining him, when we were to be distressed. The persecution then becoming general, there was no longer any place of security for us in Abyssinia; where we were looked upon by all as the authors of all the civil commotions; and many councils were held to determine in what manner they should dispose of us. Several were of opinion, that the best way would be to kill us all at once; and affirmed, that no other means were left of re-establishing order and tranquillity in the kingdom.

Others, more prudent, were not for putting us to death with so little consideration; but advised, that we should be banished to one of the isles of the lake of Dambia, an affliction more severe than death itself. These alledged, in vindication of their opinions, that it was reasonable to expect, if they put us to death, that the viceroy of the Indies would come with fire and sword to demand satisfaction. This argument made so great an impression upon some of them, that they thought no better measures could be taken than to send us back again to the Indies. This proposal, however, was not without its difficulties; for they suspected, that when we should arrive at the Portuguese territories, we would levy an army, return back to Abyssinia, and under pretence of establishing the Catholic religion, revenge all the injuries we had suffered.

While they were thus deliberating upon our fate, we were imploring the succour of the Almighty with fervent and humble supplications, intreating him, in the midst of our sighs and tears, that he would not suffer his own cause to miscarry; and that however it might please him to dispose of our lives, which we prayed he would assist us to lay down with patience and resignation, worthy of the faith for which we were persecuted, he would not permit our enemies to triumph over the truth.

Thus we passed our days and nights in prayers, in affliction and tears, continually crowded with widows and orphans that subsisted upon our charity, and came to us for bread, when we had not any for ourselves.

While we were in this distress, we received an account that the viceroy of the Indies had fitted out a powerful fleet against the king of Mombaza, who, having thrown off the authority of the Portuguese, had killed the governor of the fortress, and had since committed many acts of cruelty. The same fleet, as we were informed, after the king of Mombaza was reduced, was to burn and ruin Zeila, in revenge of the death of two Portuguese Jesuits who were killed by the king in the year 1604. As Zeila was not far from the frontiers of Abyssinia, they imagined that they already saw the Portuguese invading their country.

The viceroy of Tigre had enquired of me, a few days before, how many men one India ship carried; and being told that the compliment of some was a thousand men, he compared that answer with the report then spread over all the country, that there were eighteen Portuguese vessels on the coast of Adel; and concluded, that they were manned by an army of eighteen thousand men. Then considering what had been achieved by four hundred, under the command of Don Christopher de Gama, he thought Abyssinia already ravaged, or subjected to the king of Portugal. Many declared themselves of his opinion, and the court took its measures with respect to us from these uncertain and ungrounded rumours. Some were so infatuated with their apprehensions, that they undertook to describe the camp of the Portuguese, and affirmed that they had heard the report of their cannons.

All this contributed to exasperate the inhabitants, and reduced us often to the point of being massacred. At length they came to a resolution of giving us up to the Turks, assuring them that we were masters of a vast treasure; in hope, that after they had inflicted all kinds of tortures on us, to make us confess where we had hid our gold, or what we had done with it, they would at length kill us in rage for the disappointment. Nor was this their only view, for they believed that the Turks would, by killing us, kindle such an irreconcilable hatred between themselves and our nation, as would make it necessary for them to keep us out of the Red sea, of which they are entirely masters: so that their determination was as politic as cruel. Some pretend, that the Turks were engaged to put us to death as soon as we were in their power.

46 JAMES BRUCE
SHEIK ADLAN AND THE BLACK HORSE CAVALRY OF SENNAR

James Bruce of Kinnaird (1730–1794) spent the early part of his life in study and travel. He was appointed British Consul in Algiers, but determined to seek the source of the Nile, which had baffled men for centuries, he visited Ethiopia in 1769. Here he found the origins of the Blue Nile. Although Pedro Paez had arrived at the same source over 150 years before in 1618 and although that source was but the beginning of one branch of the Nile River,

Bruce's Travels to Discover the Source of the Nile, 1768–73 *stimulated others to the Nile origins. Moreover, his narrative of his travels remains one of the few eighteenth-century descriptions of Ethiopia and the Funj kingdom of Sennar in the Sudan. The Funj were a mysterious people whose origins are unknown but who suddenly appeared on the Blue Nile in 1504 and established their capital at Sennar. Having been converted to Islam, the Funj asserted their hegemony over the middle Nile and reached the height of their power in the seventeenth century. At the time Bruce visited Sennar in 1772, the Funj kingdom was in decline, yet the Black Horse Cavalry of Sheik Adlan appeared to the traveler as impressive as its reputation.*

It was not till the 8th of May I had my audience of Shekh Adelan at Aira, which is three miles and a half from Sennaar; we walked out early in the morning, for the greatest part of the way along the side of the Nile, which had no beauty, being totally divested of trees, the bottom foul and muddy, and the edges of the water, white with small concretions of calcareous earth, which, with the bright sun upon them, dazzled and affected our eyes very much.

We then struck across a large sandy plain, without trees or bushes, and came to Adelan's habitation; two or three very considerable houses, of one storey, occupied the middle of a large square, each of whose sides was at least half of an English mile. Instead of a wall to inclose this square, was a high fence or impalement of strong reeds, canes, or stalks of dora (I do not know which), in fascines strongly joined together by stakes and cords. On the outside of the gate, on each hand, were six houses of a slighter construction than the rest; close upon the fence were sheds where the soldiers lay, the horses picqueted before them with their heads turned towards the sheds, and their food laid before them on the ground; above each soldier's sleeping-place, covered only on the top and open in the sides, were hung a lance, a small oval shield, and a large broad-sword. These, I understood, were chiefly quarters for couriers, who,

From James Bruce, *Travels to Discover the Source of the Nile, 1768–73* (Edinburgh: Archibald Constable and Co., and Manners and Miller, 1813), VI, 359–365.

being Arabs, were not taken into the court or square, but shut out at night.

Within the gate was a number of horses, with the soldiers barracks behind them; they were all picqueted in ranks, their faces to their masters barracks. It was one of the finest sights I ever saw of the kind. They were all above sixteen hands high, of the breed of the old Saracen horses, all finely made, and as strong as our coach horses, but exceedingly nimble in their motion; rather thick and short in the forehand, but with the most beautiful eyes, ears, and heads in the world; they were mostly black, some of them black and white, some of them milk-white, foaled so, not white by age, with white eyes and white hoofs, not perhaps a great recommendation.

A steel shirt of mail hung upon each man's quarters, opposite to his horse, and by it an antelope's skin, made soft like shamoy, with which it was covered from the dew of the night. A head-piece of copper, without crest or plumage, was suspended by a lace above the shirt of mail, and was the most picturesque part of the trophy. To these was added an enormous broad-sword, in a red leather scabbard; and upon the pummel hung two thick gloves, not divided into fingers as ours, but like hedgers gloves, their fingers in one poke. They told me, that, within that inclosure at Aira, there were 400 horses, which, with the riders, and armour complete for each of them, were all the property of Shekh Adelan, every horseman being his slave, and bought with his money. There were five or six (I know not which) of these squares or inclosures, none of them half a mile from the other, which contained the king's horses, slaves, and servants. Whether they were all in as good order as Adelan's I cannot say, for I did not go further; but no body of horse could ever be more magnificently disposed under the direction of any Christian power.

Adelan was then sitting upon a piece of the trunk of a palm-tree, in the front of one of these divisions of his horses, which he seemed to be contemplating with pleasure; a number of black people, his own servants and friends, were standing around him. He had on a long drab-coloured camblet gown, lined with yellow sattin, and a camlet cap like a head-piece, with two short points that covered his ears. This, it seems, was his dress when he rose early in the morning to visit his horses, which he never neglected. The Shekh was a man above six feet high, and rather corpulent, had a heavy walk, seemingly more from affectation of grandeur, than want of agility. He was about sixty, of the colour and features of an Arab, and not of a Negro, but had rather more beard than falls to the lot of people in this country; large piercing eyes, and a determined, though, at the same time, a very pleasing countenance. Upon my coming near him, he got up; "You that are a horseman," says he without any salutation, "what would your king of Habesh give for these horses?" "What king," answered I, in the same tone, "would not give any price for such horses, if he knew their value?" "Well," replies he, in a lower voice, to the people about him, "if we are forced to go to Habesh, as Baady was, we will carry our horses along with us." I understood by this he alluded to the issue of his approaching quarrel with the king.

We then went into a large saloon, hung round with mirrors and scarlet damask; in one of the longest sides, were two large sofas covered with crimson and yellow damask, and large cushions of cloth of gold, like to the king's. He now pulled off his camlet gown and cap, and remained in a crimson sattin coat reaching down below his knees, which lapped over at the breast, and was girt round his waist with a scarf or sash, in which he had stuck a short dagger in an ivory sheath, mounted with gold; and one of the largest and most beautiful amethysts upon his finger that ever I saw, mounted plain, without any diamonds, and a small gold ear-ring in one of his ears.

"Why have you come hither," says he to me, "without arms and on foot, and without attendants?" *Yagoube.* "I was told that horses were not kept at Sennaar, and brought none with me." *Adelan.* "You suppose you have come through great dangers, and so you have. But what do you think of me, who am day and night out in the fields, surrounded by hundreds and thousands of Arabs, all of whom would eat me alive if they dared?" I answered, "A brave man, used to command as you are, does not look to the number of his enemies, but to their abilities; a wolf does not fear ten thousand sheep more than he does one." *Ad.* "True; look out at the door; these are their chiefs whom I am now taxing, and I have brought them hither that they may judge from what they see whether I am ready for them or not." *Yag.* "You could not do more properly; but, as to my own affairs, I wait upon you from the king of Abyssinia, desiring safe conduct through your country into Egypt, with his royal promise, that he is ready to do the like for you again, or any other favour you may call upon him for." He took the letter and read it. *Ad.* "The king of Abyssinia may be assured I am always ready to do more for him than this. It is true, since the mad attempt upon Sennaar, and the next still madder, to replace old Baady upon the throne, we have had no formal peace, but neither are we at war. We understand one another as good neighbours ought to do; and what else is peace?" *Yag.* "You know I am a stranger and traveller, seeking my way home. I have nothing to do with peace or war between nations. All I beg is a safe conduct through your kingdom, and the rights of hospitality bestowed in such cases on every common stranger; and one of the favours I beg is, your acceptance of a small present. I bring it not from home; I have been long absent from thence, or it would have been better." *Ad.* "I'll not refuse it, but it is quite unnecessary. I have faults like other men, but to hurt, or ransack strangers, was never one of them. Mahomet Abou Kalec, my brother, is, however, a much better man to strangers than I am; you will be lucky if you meet him here; if not, I will do for you what I can, when once the confusion of these Arabs is over."

I gave him the Sherriffe's letter, which he opened, looked at it, and laid by without reading, saying only, "Aye, Metical is a good man, he sometimes takes care of our people going to Mecca; for my part, I never was there, and probably never shall." I then presented my letter from Ali Bey to him.[1] He placed it upon his knee, and gave a slap upon it with his open hand. *Ad.* "What! do you not know, have you not heard, Mahomet Abou Dahab, his Hasnadar, has rebelled against him, banished him out of Cairo, and now sits in his place? But, don't be disconcerted at that; I know you to be a man of honour and prudence; if Mahomet, my brother, does not come, as soon as I can get leisure I will dispatch you." The servant that had conducted me to Sennaar, and was then with us, went forward close to him, and said, in a kind of whisper, "Should he go often to the king?" "When he pleases; he may go to see the town, and take a walk, but never alone, and also to the palace, that, when he returns to his own country, he may report he saw a king at Sennaar, that neither knows how to govern, nor will suffer others to teach him; who knows not how to make war, and yet will not sit in peace." I then took my leave of him; but there was a plentiful breakfast in the other room, to which he sent us, and which went far to comfort Hagi Ismael for the misfortune of his patron, Ali Bey. At going out, I took my leave by kissing his hand, which he submitted to without reluctance.

"Shekh," said I, "when I pass these Arabs in the square, I hope it will not disoblige you if I converse with some of them out of curiosity?" *Ad.* "By no means, as much as you please; but don't let them know where they can find you at Sennaar, or they will be in your house from morning till night, will eat up all your victuals, and then, in return, will cut your throat, if they can meet you upon your journey."

I returned home to Sennaar, very well pleased with my reception at Aira. I had not seen, since I left Gondar, a man so open and frank in his manners, and who spoke, without disguise, what apparently he had in his heart; but he was exceedingly engaged in business, and it was of such extent that it seemed to me impossible to be brought to an end in a much longer time than I proposed staying at Sennaar. The distance, too, between Aira and that town was a very great discouragement to me. The whole way was covered with insolent, brutish people; so that every man we met between Sennaar and Aira produced some altercation, some demand of presents, gold, cloth, tobacco, and a variety of other disagreeable circumstances, which had always the appearance of ending in something serious.

---

[1] Ali Bey was an eighteenth-century Mamluk ruler of Egypt (ed.).

47 JOHN LEWIS BURCKHARDT
SHENDI

John Lewis Burckhardt (1784–1817) was born in Lausanne and was educated at several European universities. As an employee of the Association for Promoting the Discovery of the Interior Parts of Africa, he traveled in Asia Minor, Egypt, and the Sudan. At the end of 1813 Burckhardt crossed the Nubian Desert and arrived in 1814 at Shendi, the important caravan center and market town on the Middle Nile. He continued his journey eastward from Shendi to Sawakin on the Red Sea. Burckhardt died from dysentery in Cairo in October 1817 at the age of thirty-three.

Shendi in 1814 was ruled by Nimr Muhammad Nimr (1785–1846) of the Jaaliyin Arabs. Nimr spent his youth in exile among the Batahin and then returned to Shendi, where he was declared mek, or king, in 1802. He ruled Shendi until 1822, when he opposed the invasion of the forces of Muhammad Ali of Egypt by assassinating the viceroy's son and commander of the invading army, Ismail. Punitive expeditions from Egypt forced Mek Nimr to flee from Shendi; he took up exile on the Ethiopian frontier, where he became a redoubtable warlord until his death in 1846. His descendants were granted amnesty in 1865 and subsequently returned to Shendi.

Next to Sennaar, and Kobbe (in Darfour), Shendy is the largest town in eastern Soudan, and larger, according to the report of the merchants, than the capitals of Dongola and Kordofan. It consists of several quarters, divided from each other by public places, or markets, and it contains altogether from eight hundred to a thousand houses. It is built upon the sandy plain, at about half an hour's walk from the river; its houses are similar to those of Berber; but it contains a greater number of large buildings, and fewer ruins. The houses seldom form any regular street, but are spread over the plain in great disorder. I nowhere saw any walls of burnt bricks. The houses of the chief, and those of his relatives, contain courtyards twenty feet square, inclosed by high walls, and this is the general description of the habitations of Shendy. The government is in the hands of the Mek; the name of the present chief is Nimr, i.e. Tiger. The reigning family is of the same tribe as that which now occupies the throne of Sennaar, namely, the Wold Adjib, which, as far as I could understand, is a branch

of the Funnye. The father of Nimr was an Arab of the tribe of Djaalein, but his mother was of the royal blood of Wold Adjib; and thus it appears that women have a right to the succession. This agrees with the narrative of Bruce, who found at Shendy a woman upon the throne, whom he calls Sittina (an Arabic word, meaning our Lady). The Mek of Shendy, like the Mek of Berber, is subject to Sennaar; but, excepting the purchase money paid for his government, on his accession, and occasional presents to the king and vizier [1] of Sennaar, he is entirely independent, and governs his district, which extends about two days journey farther to the south, quite at his own pleasure.

Before the arrival of the Mamelouks in Dongola, Mek Nimr had been for many years in continual warfare with the Arabs Sheygya, who had killed several of his relatives in battle, and, by making inroads into his dominions with large parties of horsemen, had repeatedly laid waste the whole western bank of the river. The Sheygya made peace with him, in order more effectually to oppose the Mame-

From John Lewis Burckhardt, *Travels in Nubia* (London: J. Murray, 1822), pp. 247–256, 263–266.

[1] The vizier of Sennaar, of the Adelan family, is said to be the real master there, while the king has a mere shadow of authority.

louks, when his own brother, to whom the command of the western bank had been entrusted, declared against him, and they have now carried on war for several years, with little success or loss on either side, as they are separated from each other by the river, and can never pass it but in small parties.

The government of Shendy is much to be preferred to that of Berber: the full authority of the Mek is not thwarted by the influence of powerful families, which in these countries tends only to insecurity, nor has he adopted that system of rapacity which makes Berber so justly dreaded by strangers. His absolute power is owing to the diversity of Arab tribes inhabiting Shendy, none of which is strong enough to cope with his own family and its numerous branches. The largest of these tribes are the Nimrab, Nayfab, and Djaalein, the greater part of whom still lead the Bedouin life. The most respectable class of the inhabitants of Shendy are the merchants, amongst whom are great numbers of foreign settlers from Sennaar, Kordofan, Darfour, and Dongola: the last are the most numerous, and they occupy an entire quarter of the town, but their nation is less esteemed than any other. They are reproached with inhospitality, and their avarice has become proverbial; the broker business, which is almost exclusively in their hands, has added to the odium of their name, so that an Arab of Shendy considers it as an insult to be called a Dongolawy, a name here considered as equivalent to that of Jew in Europe.

Commerce flourishes at Shendy, because the Mek does not extort any taxes from the merchants, which many people assured me he dared not do from his fear of the vizier of Sennaar. I am not able to judge how far this may be true; but the fact is, that caravans pay nothing whatever by way of duty; they generally make up a small present to the Mek, in order to enjoy his particular protection, and add something further for one of his brothers,

who is a principal man in the place. Our party of Ababdes sent him a small parcel of soap and sugar, of which my quota amounted to half a dollar. I did not hear of any subordinate offices in the government of Shendy, and the Mek seems to unite all the branches of authority in his own person. His relatives are the governors of villages; and his court consists of half a dozen police officers, a writer, an Imam, a treasurer, and a body-guard, formed principally of slaves. The character of the people is much the same as that of the inhabitants of Berber. They are kept in some order, it is true, by the Mek; but wickedness and injustice govern all their conduct, for they know that the law can do little more than endeavour to prevent crimes, and that it very seldom punishes them. Nightly robbers, drunken people who have assaulted strangers, thieves detected in the market, &c. &c. are often carried before the Mek, but he is generally satisfied with imprisoning them for two or three days; and I did not hear a single instance of his having ordered any person to be put to death, or even flogged, although such crimes as I have mentioned were committed daily during my stay at Shendy. The delinquents were permitted to return quietly to their homes, on paying a small fine to the Mek and his people. I was told that at Kordofan thieves are always punished with death.

Debauchery and drunkenness are as fashionable here as at Berber; the latter, I think, is even more common. No night passed without my hearing the loud songs of some Bouza meeting, though our quarter, that of the Dongolawy, who are too avaricious to be addicted to these vices, was one of the quietest. At Berber public women were constantly seen in the street; at Shendy I very seldom met any of them, though within the inclosures of the houses they are almost as numerous as at Berber.

The dress, habits, and manners of the inhabitants of Shendy are the same as those of the places last described, and appear to prevail as far as Darfour, and

Sennaar. I observed more well-dressed people at Shendy than at Berber, and clean linen was much oftener seen. Gold being a very current article in the Shendy market, the women have more frequently golden rings at their noses and ears than those of Berber; the people also possess more wealth. It is not uncommon to see a family possessed of a dozen slaves, acting as servants in the house, and labourers in the field.

The people of Shendy, like those of Berber, are shepherds, traders, and husbandmen. Agriculture, however, seems to be little thought of by the inhabitants themselves, being chiefly left to the Arab peasants of the vicinity; the cultivable soil in the neighbourhood of the city is narrow; but to the north and south of it are some fine arable plains. Water-wheels are common; they are erected generally on those parts of the high banks, which the most copious inundations of the river cannot overflow; by means of them the cultivators raise one winter-crop; but they are too lazy to bestow the labour necessary for watering the soil a second or third time, as is done in the most elevated parts of Upper Egypt, where also the river very seldom rises high enough to overflow the banks. Dhourra [millet—ed.] is the chief produce; Dokhen and wheat are sown in small quantities, the former for the consumption of the western traders who visit Shendy, the latter almost exclusively for the families of the great. Large quantities of onions, some red pepper (brought from Kordofan), Bamyes, chick-peas, Meloukhye, and Tormos,[2] are always found in the market either green or dried. During the inundation some water-melons and cucumbers are sown, but for the use only of the Harem of the Mek.

The cattle are very fine; and the inhabitants say that their size and quality continue to increase, in proportion as you ascend the river. I saw no domestic animals that are not common in Egypt. Elephants are first met with at Abou Heraze, two or three days to the north of Sennaar; and they have never been known to pass to the northward of that district, which is bounded by a chain of mountains six or eight hours in breadth, reaching close to the river. I was told that tigers are frequently seen in the Wadys east of Shendy. In the mountains of Dender, a district towards the Atbara, and six or eight journies south-east of Shendy, the giraffa is found. It is hunted by the Arabs Shukorein and Kowahel, and is highly prized for its skin, of which the strongest bucklers are made. I frequently saw mountain-goats of the largest size brought to the market of Shendy; they have long horns bending to the middle of the back; their flesh is esteemed a great dainty. They call them Areal, a name given in Syria to the red deer. In Upper Egypt they are called Teytal and in Syria Beden. They are caught by the Djaalein Bedouins in nooses, in the same manner as they catch ostriches, which are also very common in this neighbourhood. The ostrich-feathers however are inferior to those of the western deserts. Those most esteemed in Egypt are from Kordofan and Darfour, which the caravans from the latter place bring to Siout. The Djaalein peasants bring the feathers to the market in bundles, good and bad together, and exchange them for Dhourra. Their price, when I was at Shendy, was about one-tenth of what they would bring at Cairo, where the best kinds, in 1812, sold at two hundred and eighty piastres per pound. The Pasha of Egypt has lately included them among the articles monopolized by him.[3]

[3] The trade in ostrich-feathers is one of the most complicated in the markets of Africa: at Cairo the feathers are assorted into several different qualities, and parcels are made up by the Jews, (who alone understand the trade well,) containing portions of every kind. Each parcel of ten pounds weight must contain one pound of the finest and whitest sort, one pound of the second quality, also white, but of a smaller size, and eight pounds of the sorts called

[2] In Egypt, the meal of the Tormos is used as a substitute for soap in washing the head and body.

The hippopotamus is not common at Shendy, though it occasionally makes its appearance there; during my stay there was one in the river in the vicinity of Boeydha, which made great ravages in the fields. It never rose above water in the day-time, but came on shore in the night, and destroyed as much by the treading of its enormous feet, as it did by its voracity; the people have no means of killing them. At Sennaar, where hippopotami are numerous, they are caught in trenches, slightly covered with reeds, into which they fall during their nightly excursions. It is generally said that no musketball can bring them to the ground, unless they are hit in the vulnerable spot, which is over the ear. The whips called Korbadj, which are formed of their skins, are made at Sennaar, and on the Nile, above that place; the skin, immediately after being taken off, is cut into narrow strips, about five or six feet in length, gradually tapering to a point: each strip is then rolled up, so that the edges unite, and form a pipe, in which state it is tied fast and left to dry in the sun. In order to render these whips pliable, they must be rubbed with butter or grease. At Shendy they are sold at the rate of twelve or sixteen for a Spanish dollar; in Egypt, where they are in general use, and the dread of every servant and peasant, they are worth from half a dollar, to a dollar each. In colder climates, even in Syria, they become brittle, crack, and lose their elasticity.

Crocodiles are very numerous about Shendy. I have generally remarked that these animals inhabit particular parts of the Nile, from whence they seldom appear to move; thus, in Lower Egypt, they have entirely disappeared, although no reasonable cause can be assigned for their not descending the river. In Upper Egypt, the neighbourhood of Akhmim, Dendera, Or-

ment, and Edfou, are at present the favourite haunts of the crocodile, while few are ever seen in the intermediate parts of the river. The same is the case in different parts of Nubia towards Dongola. At Berber nobody is afraid of encountering crocodiles in the river, and we bathed there very often, swimming out into the midst of the stream. At Shendy, on the contrary, they are greatly dreaded; the Arabs and the slaves and females, who repair to the shore of the river near the town every morning and evening to wash their linen, and fill their waterskins for the supply of the town, are obliged to be continually on the alert, and such as bathe take care not to proceed to any great distance into the river. I was several times present when a crocodile made its appearance, and witnessed the terror it inspired; the crowd all quickly retiring up the beach. During my stay at Shendy, a man who had been advised to bathe in the river, after having escaped the small-pox, was seized and killed by one of these animals. At Sennaar crocodiles are often brought to market, and their flesh is publicly sold there. I once tasted some of the meat at Esne, in Upper Egypt; it is of a dirty white colour, not unlike young veal, with a slight fishy smell; the animal had been caught by some fishermen in a strong net, and was about twelve feet in length. The Governor of Esne ordered it to be brought into his court-yard, where more than an hundred balls were fired against it without effect, till it was thrown upon its back, and the contents of a small swivel discharged at its belly, the skin of which is much softer than that of the back. Fish are very seldom caught by the Arabs at Shendy. Nets appear to be unknown, but children often amuse themselves in angling with hooked nails.

The produce of the fields of Shendy and its neighbourhood is not sufficient for the supply of the population, the wants of which are much increased by the continual arrival of caravans. Dhourra is imported principally from Abou Heraze, in the route to Sennaar. A caravan of more

Jemina, Bajoca, Coda, and Spadone, the last of which is black, and of little value. The market-price of white sorted feathers is at present (1816) two hundred and eighty piastres per rotolo, or pound, or two thousand eight hundred piastres, each parcel of ten pounds.

than three hundred camels arrived from thence with Dhourra during my stay at Shendy, and the price, which, on our arrival, was at the rate of one dollar for twelve measures, fell to twenty measures per dollar. The price of grain varies almost daily, the market being affected by the arrival of every caravan of traders, who always buy up a considerable quantity for the food of the slaves and camels. The Mek also monopolizes the corn-trade as much as he can. At Abou Heraze and Sennaar, Dhourra is said to be in great plenty: forty measures being sold for a dollar. This grain is of the same shape and size as that of Shendy and Upper Egypt; but it is of an ash gray colour; it is said to be less nourishing, and of course is less esteemed than the other.

Horses are more numerous here than at Berber. The Mek, it is said, can raise within Shendy itself from two to three hundred horsemen. According to the custom of the Eastern Arabs, the Djaalein Bedouins ride mares in preference to stallions; but the latter are preferred by the inhabitants of the town. The Mek's brother, Ras Saad ed Dyn, had a horse for which he had given in the southern districts thirteen slaves; it surpassed in beauty any other horse I ever remember to have seen. At a public festival on the occasion of the circumcision of one of Mek Nimr's sons, all the horsemen of Shendy met, and accompanied the family of the chief through the town, their horses prancing about. They appeared to me but very indifferent horsemen; none attempted any of the manoeuvres for which the Mamelouks are so famous; they contented themselves with galloping backwards and forwards, nor did I see one bold rider amongst them. It is in this cavalry, however, that the Mek places his chief strength, and it decides the fate of all the battles he is obliged to fight with his enemies. The saddles, and bridles, as well as the stirrups, in which they place the great toe only, are the same as those used at Berber and by the Arabs Sheygya, who appear to be as celebrated for their horsemanship in this country as the Mamelouks once were in Turkey. Mek Nimr has about twenty firelocks, which he has either bought or taken from Egyptian traders; with these he arms his favourite slaves, but few of them have courage sufficient to fire them off, and there are none who dare take an aim by placing the gun against the shoulder. The sight of it alone generally frightens the enemy, and so far it fully answers their purpose, for it is always the wish of both parties to finish the battle with as little bloodshed as possible, because the law of retaliation is in full force amongst these Arabs. Several of Mek Nimr's musquets are either broken, or so much rusted, as to make them unserviceable, and nobody could be found to clean and mend them. Having been seen one day cleaning my gun, I was supposed to be skilful in this art, and serious proposals were made to me, to enter into the Mek's service as gunsmith. He offered me one male and two female slaves, and as much Dhourra as I might want for their maintenance; and it was with difficulty that I could persuade the slaves who made me the proposal in the name of their master, that I knew nothing of the business of a gunsmith. Travellers in these countries ought to avoid showing their capacity in the most trifling things that may be of use or afford pleasure to the chiefs, who will endeavour to force them into their service. Not having succeeded in prevailing upon me to remain, the Mek wished at least to have my gun. He sent for it, and kept it for several days; and upon my urgent entreaties to have it returned to me, he sent me four Spanish dollars, ordering his slaves at the same time to carry me several dishes of bread and meat from his own kitchen. Upon complaining to some of the inhabitants of this treatment, they replied, that having now eaten of the Mek's food I had become his friend, and that it would therefore be a disgrace to me to make any difficulty in parting with my gun. I was very sorry to lose it, especially when I considered in what countries I still intended to travel; but in my present circumstances four dollars were not be despised. Seeing no chance therefore of either getting back my gun, or obtaining a higher price for it, I accepted the Mek's four dollars with many professions of thanks.

It will appear very singular that firearms are not more frequently met with here, as they may so easily be imported. But the fact is, that traders are afraid to carry them, lest they should excite the cupidity of some or other of the chiefs; and it is not to be supposed, that until they are more numerous, they can be taken to market like other goods, or be paid for at a regular price. To the country people, who seldom visit the towns where traders make any stay, a musquet is an object of the greatest terror, and will frighten away dozens of them. A Djaalein Arab, who had some ostrich-feathers to sell, came one day to the house where I lodged, to barter with my companions for his feathers. The moment he espied my gun standing in the corner of the room, he got up, and desired it might be removed, for that he did not like to remain near so deadly an instrument.

.   .   .

On the great market days, which are every Friday and Saturday, several thousands of people resort to Shendy from the distance of three or four days; the greater part of whom bring cattle for sale. Judging from the individuals I saw in the market, all these Arabs appear to be entirely of the same race, excepting only that the true Djaalein Bedouins who come from the eastern desert are much fairer-skinned than the inhabitants of the banks of the Nile, which arises probably from their taking greater care not to mix in concubinage with the Negro race. I was much struck with the physiognomy of many of these Djaaleins, who had exactly the countenance and expression of features of the Bedouins of eastern Arabia; their beards are even shorter, and thinner.

Some individuals of a tribe of Djaalein who border, to the south, upon the Shukorye, appeared at the market with hats on their heads, made of reeds; they were high and pointed, with broad brims, and were tied under the chin with a leather thong. They are worn both by men and women.

About four or five hundred camels, as many cows, a hundred asses, and twenty or thirty horses, were on sale on the great market-days. Every merchant then takes his stand in one of the open shops, or in the open market, and exposes part of his merchandize; for even the richest traders are not ashamed of trafficking in the minutest detail. The Egyptian, Souakin, Sennaar, and Kordofan merchants form separate corps, in the midst of which is a great circle of slaves, thus exposed for sale. The country people bring to market mats, baskets, ox hides, and other skins, coarse pottery, camel saddles, wooden dishes, and other articles of their own manufacture, &c. About a dozen shoemakers, or rather sandal-makers, from the country, work for these two days in the market, and will make a pair of sandals at an hour's notice. The works in leather are very prettily done. The leather is tanned with the Garadh or pulse of the acacia; the Bedouins about Sennaar are said to be the most skilful in its preparation. Leather sacks are likewise sold here; they serve for the transport of every kind of baggage and merchandize, excepting Dhourra, gum arabic, and salt, which are carried in baskets. Many blacksmiths repair to Shendy from the country; they make and sell the small knives generally worn among these people. The knives are about eight inches long, and are worn in a leather scabbard tied over the left elbow: they are two-edged, like those worn by the Berabera.

The market is so crowded, and the dust and heat are so great, during the mid-day hours, which is the favourite time for transacting business, that I was unable to remain in the market-place many hours together, and always left one of my companions in charge of the little I had to sell. In different parts of the place are stationed peasants with jars of water, which they sell to the thirsty, at the rate of a handful of Dhourra for as much water as two persons can drink. Several of the Fakys [holymen—ed.] have water-cisterns in the courtyards of their houses, which are always kept full, and at which every one may drink gratis. Many of them have likewise small chapels annexed to their dwellings. There is no mosque in the whole place.

The only artizans I saw at Shendy were blacksmiths, silversmiths, who work very coarse ornaments for the women, tanners, potters, and carpenters. If a house is to be built, the owner, his relatives, and slaves, with a few labourers, execute the masonry, and the carpenter is only called in to lay the roof and make the doors. Like the Bedouins of the desert, these Arabs are their own artizans upon all ordinary occasions.

There are no weavers at Shendy, but all the women and grown up children, and many of the men, are seen with a distaff constantly in their hands, spinning cotton yarn, which they sell to the people of Berber. The distaff, Mugzil, resembles that used in Egypt and Syria. Cotton is cultivated in this neighbourhood, and is a general produce of all the countries on the banks of the Nile, although nowhere in any great quantity, except at Damer and about Sennaar.

The wholesale trade at Shendy is principally conducted through the agency of brokers. Most of these are Dongolawy, who seem, in general, to be the most acute and intelligent traders of this part of the country. A caravan no sooner arrives, than every merchant's house is crowded with brokers; but the avidity and parsimony of all parties are too great to allow them to bring their transactions to a speedy conclusion. Even after the bargain is made, each party endeavours to cheat the other before the goods are delivered and the money paid. In addition to this, every attempt to enter into an engagement of any importance becomes known all over the place, and the jealousy of the traders often prevents its taking place. No merchandize has its fixed price; there is no such thing as a price current; every one sells according to the prospect he has of cheating the buyer and bribing the broker. The purchase money, or, in cases of barter, its equivalent in merchandize, is almost always immediately paid down; the longest credit I have witnessed is a couple of days; and it is evident, on the termination of every commercial transaction, that the buyer and seller reciprocally entertain suspicions of each other's honesty. To oblige a debtor to settle his accounts, recourse is generally had to the slaves of the Mek, who act as police officers; but a man who is unprotected, and without friends, is sure to lose the greater part of his goods, if he allows them to go out of his hands without immediate payment.

48 JOHN HANNING SPEKE
UNYAMWEZI AND UGANDA

John Hanning Speke (1827–1864) arrived in Zanzibar with Richard Burton in 1856 for the purpose of finding the inland sea of Ujiji in East Africa. During the expedition the two explorers reached Lake Tanganyika, and while Burton was recovering from an illness at Tabora, Speke wandered off to the north, where he saw the waters of Lake Victoria. Speke jumped to the conclusion that he had discovered the source of the Nile. To prove this assumption, he returned to East Africa in 1860 and, accompanied by J. A. Grant, traversed the Unyamwezi country of what is now western Tanzania and visited Uganda on the west and the northern shore of Lake Victoria. He was the first European to visit the powerful interlacustrine kingdom of Buganda, and his reports of the richness of the country and the prospects for "Christianity, Commerce, and Civilization" encouraged others to follow. Speke and Grant reached Gondokoro on the Upper Nile in 1863. They had contributed much to Europe's geographical knowledge of the interior of eastern Africa but had failed to resolve completely the question of the Nile source.

U-n-ya-muezi—Country of Moon—must have been one of the largest kingdoms in Africa. It is little inferior in size to England, and of much the same shape, though now, instead of being united, it is cut up into petty states. In its northern extremities it is known by the appellation U-sukuma—country north; and in the southern, U-takama—country south. There are no [written—ed.] historical traditions known to the people; neither was anything ever written concerning their country, as far as we know, until the Hindus, who traded with the east coast of Africa, opened commercial dealings with its people in slaves and ivory, possibly some time prior to the birth of our Saviour, when, associated with their name, Men of the Moon, sprang into existence the Mountains of the Moon. These Men of the Moon are hereditarily the greatest traders in Africa, and are the only people who, for love of barter and change, will leave their own country as porters and go to the coast, and they do so with as much zest as our country-folk go to a fair. As far back as we can trace they have done this, and they still do it as heretofore. The whole of their country ranges from 3000 to 4000 feet above the sea-level—a high plateau, studded with little outcropping hills of granite, between which, in the valleys, there are numerous fertilising springs of fresh water, and rich iron ore is found in sandstone. Generally industrious—much more so than most other ne-

groes—they cultivate extensively, make cloths of cotton in their own looms, smelt iron and work it up very expertly, build tembes to live in over a large portion of their country, but otherwise live in grass huts, and keep flocks and herds of considerable extent.

The Wanyamuezi, however, are not a very well-favoured people in physical appearance, and are much darker than either the Wazaramo or the Wagogo, though many of their men are handsome and their women pretty; neither are they well dressed or well armed, being wanting in pluck and gallantry. Their women, generally, are better dressed than the men. Cloths fastened round under the arms are their national costume, along with a necklace of beads, large brass or copper wire armlets, and a profusion of thin circles, called sambo, made of the giraffe's tail-hairs bound round by the thinnest iron or copper wire; whilst the men at home wear loin-cloths, but in the field, or whilst travelling, simply hang a goat-skin over their shoulders, exposing at least three-fourths of their body in a rather indecorous manner. In all other respects they ornament themselves like the women, only, instead of a long coil of wire wound up the arm, they content themselves with having massive rings of copper or brass on the wrist; and they carry for arms a spear and bow and arrows. All extract more or less their lower incisors, and cut a ∧ between their two upper incisors. The whole tribe are desperate smokers, and greatly given to drink.

On the 24th, we all, as many as were left of us, marched into the merchants'

From John Hanning Speke, *Journal of the Discovery of the Source of the Nile* (Edinburgh and London: Willam Blackwood and Sons, 1863), pp. 84–88, 273–279.

depot, S. lat. 5° 0′ 52″, and E. long. 33° 1′ 34″, escorted by Musa, who advanced to meet us, and guided us into his tembe, where he begged we would reside with him until we could find men to carry our property on to Karague. He added that he would accompany us; for he was on the point of going there when my first instalment of property arrived, but deferred his intention out of respect to myself. He had been detained at Kaze ever since I last left it in consequence of the Arabs having provoked a war with Manua Sera, to which he was adverse. For a long time also he had been a chained prisoner; as the Arabs, jealous of the favour Manua Sera had shown to him in preference to themselves, basely accused him of supplying Manua Sera with gunpowder, and bound him hand and foot "like a slave." It was delightful to see old Musa's face again, and the supremely hospitable, kind, and courteous manner in which he looked after us, constantly bringing in all kind of small delicacies, and seeing that nothing was wanting to make us happy. All the property I had sent on in advance he had stored away; or rather, I should say, as much as had reached him, for the road expenses had eaten a great hole in it.

Once settled down into position, Sheikh Snay and the whole conclave of Arab merchants came to call on me. They said they had an army of four hundred slaves armed with muskets ready to take the field at once to hunt down Manua Sera, who was cutting their caravan road to pieces, and had just seized, by their latest reports, a whole convoy of their ammunition. I begged them strongly to listen to reason, and accept my advice as an old soldier, not to carry on their guerilla warfare in such a headlong hurry, else they would be led a dance by Manua Sera, as we had been by Tantia Topee in India. I advised them to allow me to mediate between them, after telling them what a favourable interview I had had with Manua Sera and Maula, whose son was at that moment concealed in Musa's tembe. My advice,

however, was not wanted. Snay knew better than any one how to deal with savages, and determined on setting out as soon as his army had "eaten their beef-feast of war."

On my questioning him about the Nile, Snay still thought the Nyanza was the source of the Jub river,[1] as he did in our former journey, but gave way when I told him that vessels frequented the Nile, as this also coincided with his knowledge of navigators in vessels appearing on some waters to the northward of Unyoro. In a great hurry he then bade me good-bye; when, as he thought it would be final, I gave him, in consideration for his former good services to the last expedition, one of the gold watches given me by the Indian Government. I saw him no more, though he and all the other Arabs sent me presents of cows, goats, and rice, with a notice that they should have gone on their war-path before, only, hearing of my arrival, out of due respect to my greatness, they waited to welcome me in. Further, after doing for Manua Sera, they were determined to go on to Ugogo to assist Salem bin Saif and the other merchants on, during which, at the same time, they would fight all the Wagogo who persisted in taking taxes and in harassing their caravans. At the advice of Musa, I sent Maula's son off at night to tell the old chief how sorry I was to find the Arabs so hotheaded I could not even effect an arrangement with them. It was a great pity; for Manua Sera was so much liked by the Wanyamuezi, they would, had they been able, have done anything to restore him.

· · ·

Next day, after crossing more of those abominable rush-drains, whilst in sight of the Victoria Nyanza, we ascended the most beautiful hills, covered with verdure of all descriptions. At Meruka, where I put up, there resided some grandees, the

[1] The Jub is the largest river known to the Zanzibar Arabs. It debouches on the east coast north of Zanzibar, close under the equator.

chief of whom was the king's aunt. She sent me a goat, a hen, a basket of eggs, and some plantains, in return for which I sent her a wire and some beads. I felt inclined to stop here a month, everything was so very pleasant. The temperature was perfect. The roads, as indeed they were everywhere, were as broad as our coach-roads, cut through the long grasses, straight over the hills and down through the woods in the dells—a strange contrast to the wretched tracks in all the adjacent countries. The huts were kept so clean and so neat, not a fault could be found with them—the gardens the same. Wherever I strolled I saw nothing but richness, and what ought to be wealth. The whole land was a picture of quiescent beauty, with a boundless sea in the background. Looking over the hills, it struck the fancy at once that at one period the whole land must have been at a uniform level with their present tops, but that, by the constant denudation it was subjected to by frequent rains, it had been cut down and sloped into those beautiful hills and dales which now so much pleased the eye; for there were none of those quartz dykes I had seen protruding through the same kind of aqueous formations in Usui and Karague; nor were there any other sorts of volcanic disturbance to distort the calm quiet aspect of the scene.

From this, the country being all hill and dale, with miry rush-drains in the bottoms, I walked, carrying my shoes and stockings in my hands, nearly all the way. Rozaro's "children" became more and more troublesome, stealing everything they could lay their hands upon out of the village huts we passed on the way. On arrival at Sangua, I found many of them had been seized by some men who, bolder than the rest, had overtaken them whilst gutting their huts, and made them prisoners, demanding of me two slaves and one load of beads for their restitution. I sent my men back to see what had happened, and ordered them to bring all the men on to me, that I might see fair play. They, however, took the law into their own hands, drove off the Waganda villagers by firing their muskets, and relieved the thieves. A complaint was then laid against Nyamgundu by the chief officer of the village, and I was requested to halt. That I would not do, leaving the matter in the hands of the governor-general, Mr. Pokino, whom I heard we should find at the next station, Masaka.

On arrival there at the government establishment—a large collection of grass huts, separated one from the other within large enclosures, which overspread the whole top of a low hill—I was requested to withdraw and put up in some huts a short distance off, and wait until his excellency, who was from home, could come and see me; which the next day he did, coming in state with a large number of officers, who brought with them a cow, sundry pots of pombe [beer—ed.], enormous sticks of sugar-cane, and a large bundle of country coffee. This grows in great profusion all over this land in large bushy trees, the berries sticking on the branches like clusters of holly-berries.

I was then introduced, and told that his excellency was the appointed governor of all the land lying between the Katonga and the Kitangule rivers. After the first formalities were over, the complaint about the officers at Sangua was preferred for decision, on which Pokino at once gave it against the villagers, as they had no right, by the laws of the land, to lay hands on a king's guest. Just then Maula arrived, and began to abuse Nyamgundu. Of course I would not stand this; and, after telling all the facts of the case, I begged Pokino to send Maula away out of my camp. Pokino said he could not do this, as it was by the king's order he was appointed; but he put Maula in the background, laughing at the way he had "let the bird fly out of his hands," and settled that Nyamgundu should be my guide. I then gave him a wire, and he gave me three large sheets of mbugu, which he said I should require, as there were so many watercourses to cross on the road I was going. A second day's halt was necessitated by many of my men catching fever, probably owing to the constant crossing of those abominable rush-drains. There was no want of food here, for I never saw such a profusion of plantains anywhere. They were literally lying in heaps on the ground, though the people were brewing pombe all day, and cooking them for dinner every evening.

After crossing many more hills and miry bottoms, constantly coming in view of the lake, we reached Ugonzi, and after another march of the same description, came to Kituntu, the last officer's residence in Uddu [a province of Buganda—ed.]. Formerly it was the property of a Beluch named Eseau, who came to this country with merchandise, trading on account of Said Said, late Sultan of Zanzibar; but having lost it all on his way here, paying mahongo, or taxes, and so forth, he feared returning, and instead made great friends with the late king Sunna, who took an especial fancy to him because he had a very large beard, and raised him to the rank of Mkungu. A few years ago, however, Eseau died, and left all his family and property to a slave named Uledi, who now, in consequence, is the border officer.

I became now quite puzzled whilst thinking which was the finest spot I had seen in Uddu, so many were exceedingly beautiful; but I think I gave the preference to this, both for its own immediate neighbourhood and the long range of view it afforded of Uganda [Buganda—ed.] proper, the lake, and the large island, or group of islands, called Sese, where the king of Uganda keeps one of his fleets of boats.

Some little boys came here who had all their hair shaved off excepting two round tufts on either side of the head. They were the king's pages; and, producing three sticks, said they had brought them to me from their king, who wanted three charms or medicines. Then placing one stick on the ground before me, they said, "This one is a head which, being affected by dreams of a deceased relative, requires re-lief;" the second symbolised the king's desire for the accomplishment of a phenomenon to which the old phalic worship was devoted; "and this third one," they said, "is a sign that the king wants a charm to keep all his subjects in awe of him." I then promised I would do what I could when I reached the palace, but feared to do anything in the distance. I wished to go on with the march, but was dissuaded by Nyamgundu, who said he had received orders to find me some cows here, as his king was most anxious I should be well fed. Next day, however, we descended into the Katonga valley, where, instead of finding a magnificent broad sheet of water, as I had been led to expect by the Arabs' account of it, I found I had to wade through a succession of rush-drains divided one from the other by islands. It took me two hours, with my clothes tucked up under my arms, to get through them all; and many of them were so matted with weeds, that my feet sank down as though I trod in a bog.

The Waganda all said that at certain times in the year no one could ford these drains, as they all flooded; but, strangely enough, they were always lowest when most rain fell in Uganda. No one, however, could account for this singular fact. No one knew of a lake to supply the waters, nor where they came from. That they flowed into the lake there was no doubt—as I could see by the trickling waters in some few places—and they lay exactly on the equator. Rising out of the valley, I found all the country just as hilly as before, but many of the rush-drains going to northward; and in the dells were such magnificent trees, they quite took me by surprise. Clean-trunked, they towered up just as so many great pillars, and then spread out their high branches like a canopy over us. I thought of the blue gums of Australia, and believed these would beat them. At the village of Mbule we were gracefully received by the local officer, who brought a small present, and assured me that the king was in a nervous state of excitement, always asking after me. Whilst speaking he trembled, and he was so restless he could never sit still.

Up and down we went on again through this wonderful country, surprisingly rich in grass, cultivation, and trees. Watercourses were as frequent as ever, though not quite so troublesome to the traveller, as they were more frequently bridged with poles or palm-tree trunks.

This, the next place we arrived at, was Nyamgundu's own residence, where I stopped a day to try and shoot buffaloes. Maula here had the coolness to tell me he must inspect all the things I had brought for presentation to the king, as he said it was the custom; after which he would hurry on and inform his majesty. Of course I refused, saying it was uncourteous to both the king and myself. Still he persisted, until, finding it hopeless, he spitefully told Nyamgundu to keep me here at least two days. Nyamgundu, however, very prudently told him he should obey his orders, which were to take me on as fast as he could. I then gave Nyamgundu wires and beads for himself and all his family round, which made Maula slink farther away from me than ever.

The buffaloes were very numerous in the tall grasses that lined the sides and bottoms of the hills; but although I saw some, I could not get a shot, for the grasses being double the height of myself, afforded them means of dashing out of view as soon as seen, and the rustling noise made whilst I followed them kept them on the alert. At night a hyena came into my hut, and carried off one of my goats that was tied to a log between two of my sleeping men.

During the next march, after passing some of the most beautifully-wooded dells, in which lay small rush-lakes on the right of the road, draining, as I fancied, into the Victoria Lake, I met with a party of the king's gamekeepers, staking their nets all along the side of a hill, hoping to catch antelopes by driving the covers with dogs and men. Farther on, also, I came on a party driving one hundred cows, as a present from Mtesa to Rumanika, which the officers in charge said was their king's return for the favour Rumanika had done him in sending me on to him. It was in this way that great kings sent "letters" to one another.

49 SIR SAMUEL BAKER
KHARTOUM AND THE NILOTIC SLAVE TRADE

Born into a wealthy British family, Samuel White Baker (1821–1893) settled in Ceylon, where he established an agricultural colony and devoted himself to hunting. Thereafter he traveled widely, principally for the purpose of making hunting trips. Anxious to participate in the search for the Nile sources, he and his beautiful Hungarian wife, Florence Ninian von Sass (d. 1916), arrived in Cairo in 1861 and traveled up the Nile to spend a year in the Sudan hunting along the Abyssinian frontier. In 1862 they reached Khartoum, where they intended to prepare for an expedition to the upper White Nile. At that time, Khartoum was the capital of the Egyptian Sudan. The city had steadily increased in size and had become an outpost of Europe and the Middle East on the periphery of tropical Africa, through which passed the slaves who had been taken from the Nile tributaries far to the south. The Bakers proceeded slowly up the Nile, met Speke and Grant returning from their exploration of the Nile sources at Lake Victoria, and then pressed on to Bunyoro. They discovered Lake Albert in 1864.

From Sir Samuel White Baker, *The Albert N'Yanza: Great Basin of the Nile* (London: Macmillan, 1879), pp. 7–16.

Khartoum is situated in lat. 15° 29′, on a point of land forming the angle between the White and Blue Niles at their junction. A more miserable, filthy, and unhealthy spot can hardly be imagined. Far as the eye can reach, upon all sides, is a sandy desert. The town, chiefly composed of huts of unburnt brick, extends over a flat hardly above the level of the river at high-water, and is occasionally flooded. Although containing about 30,000 inhabitants, and densely crowded, there are neither drains nor cesspools: the streets are redolent with inconceivable nuisances; should animals die, they remain where they fall, to create pestilence and disgust. There are, nevertheless, a few respectable houses, occupied by the traders of the country, a small proportion of whom are Italians, French, and Germans, the European population numbering about thirty. Greeks, Syrians, Copts, Armenians, Turks, Arabs, and Egyptians, form the motley inhabitants of Khartoum.

There are consuls for France, Austria, and America, and with much pleasure I acknowledge many kind attentions, and assistance received from the two former, M. Thibaut and Herr Hansall.

Khartoum is the seat of government, the Soudan provinces being under the control of a Governor-general, with despotic power. In 1861, there were about six thousand troops quartered in the town; a portion of these were Egyptians; other regiments were composed of blacks from Kordofan, and from the White and Blue Niles, with one regiment of Arnouts, and a battery of artillery. These troops are the curse of the country: as in the case of most Turkish and Egyptian officials, the receipt of pay is most irregular, and accordingly the soldiers are under loose discipline. Foraging and plunder is the business of the Egyptian soldier, and the miserable natives must submit to insult and ill-treatment at the will of the brutes who pillage them *ad libitum*.

In 1862, Moosa Pasha was the Governor-general of the Soudan. This man was a rather exaggerated specimen of Turkish authorities in general, combining the worst of Oriental failings with the brutality of a wild animal.

During his administration the Soudan became utterly ruined; governed by military force, the revenue was unequal to the expenditure, and fresh taxes were levied upon the inhabitants to an extent that paralysed the entire country. The Turk never improves. There is an Arab proverb that "the grass never grows in the footprint of a Turk," and nothing can be more aptly expressive of the character of the nation than this simple adage. Misgovernment, monopoly, extortion, and oppression, are the certain accompaniments of Turkish administration. At a great distance from all civilization, and separated from Lower Egypt by the Nubian deserts, Khartoum affords a wide field for the development of Egyptian official character. Every official plunders; the Governor-general extorts from all sides; he fills his private pockets by throwing every conceivable obstacle in the way of progress, and embarrasses every commercial movement in order to extort bribes from individuals. Following the general rule of his predecessors, a new governor upon arrival exhibits a spasmodic energy. Attended by cavasses and soldiers, he rides through every street of Khartoum, abusing the underlings for past neglect, ordering the streets to be swept, and the town to be thoroughly cleansed; he visits the marketplace, examines the quality of the bread at the bakers' stalls, and the meat at the butchers'. He tests the accuracy of the weights and scales; fines and imprisons the impostors, and institutes a complete reform, concluding his sanitary and philanthropic arrangements by the imposition of some local taxes.

The town is comparatively sweet; the bread is of fair weight and size, and the new governor, like a new broom, has swept all clean. A few weeks glide away, and the nose again recalls the savoury old times when streets were never swept, and filth once more reigns paramount. The town relapses into its former state, again the false weights usurp the place of honest measures, and the only permanent and visible sign of the new administration is the *local tax.*

From the highest to the lowest official, dishonesty and deceit are the rule—and each robs in proportion to his grade in the Government employ—the onus of extortion falling upon the natives; thus, exorbitant taxes are levied upon the agriculturists, and the industry of the inhabitants is disheartened by oppression. The taxes are collected by the soldiery, who naturally extort by violence an excess of the actual impost; accordingly the Arabs limit their cultivation to their bare necessities, fearing that a productive farm would entail an extortionate demand. The heaviest and most unjust tax is that upon the "sageer," or water-wheel, by which the farmer irrigates his otherwise barren soil.

The erection of the sageer is the first step necessary to cultivation. On the borders of the river there is much land available for agriculture; but from an almost total want of rain the ground must be constantly irrigated by artificial means. No sooner does an enterprising fellow erect a water-wheel, than he is taxed, not only for his wheel, but he brings upon himself a perfect curse, as the soldiers employed for the collection of taxes fasten upon his garden, and insist upon a variety of extras in the shape of butter, corn, vegetables, sheep, &c. for themselves, which almost ruin the proprietor. Any government but that of Egypt and Turkey would offer a bonus for the erection of irrigating machinery that would give a stimulus to cultivation, and multiply the produce of the country; but the only rule without an exception is that of Turkish extortion. I have never met with any Turkish official who would take the slightest interest in plans for the *improvement* of the country, unless he discovered a means of filling his private purse. Thus in a country where

Nature has been hard in her measure dealt to the inhabitants, they are still more reduced by oppression. The Arabs fly from their villages on the approach of the brutal tax-gatherers, driving their flocks and herds with them to distant countries, and leaving their standing crops to the mercy of the soldiery. No one can conceive the suffering of the country.

The general aspect of the Soudan is that of misery; nor is there a single feature of attraction to recompense a European for the drawbacks of pestilential climate and brutal associations. To a stranger it appears a superlative folly that the Egyptian Government should have retained a possession, the occupation of which is wholly unprofitable; the receipts being far below the expenditure, "malgré" the increased taxation. At so great a distance from the sea-coast and hemmed in by immense deserts, there is a difficulty of transport that must nullify all commercial transactions on an extended scale.

The great and most important article of commerce as an export from the Soudan, is gum arabic: this is produced by several species of mimosa, the finest quality being a product of Kordofan; the other natural productions exported are senna, hides, and ivory. All merchandise both to and from the Soudan must be transported upon camels, no other animals being adapted to the deserts. The cataracts of the Nile between Assouan and Khartoum rendering the navigation next to impossible, the camel is the only medium of transport, and the uncertainty of procuring them without great delay is the trader's greatest difficulty. The entire country is subject to droughts that occasion a total desolation, and the want of pasture entails starvation upon both cattle and camels, rendering it at certain seasons impossible to transport the productions of the country, and thus stagnating all enterprise. Upon existing conditions the Soudan is worthless, having neither natural capabilities nor political importance; but there is, nevertheless, a reason that first prompted its occupation by the Egyptians, and that is in force to the present day. *The Soudan supplies slaves.*

Without the White Nile trade Khartoum would almost cease to exist; and that trade is kidnapping and murder. The character of the Khartoumers needs no further comment. The amount of ivory brought down from the White Nile is a mere bagatelle as an export, the annual value being about £40,000.

The people for the most part engaged in the nefarious traffic of the White Nile are Syrians, Copts, Turks, Circassians, and some few *Europeans.* So closely connected with the difficulties of my expedition is that accursed slave-trade, that the so-called ivory trade of the White Nile requires an explanation.

Throughout the Soudan money is exceedingly scarce and the rate of interest exorbitant, varying, according to the securities, from thirty-six to eighty per cent.; this fact proves general poverty and dishonesty, and acts as a preventive to all improvement. So high and fatal a rate deters all honest enterprise, and the country must lie in ruin under such a system. The wild speculator borrows upon such terms, to rise suddenly like a rocket, or to fall like its exhausted stick. Thus, honest enterprise being impossible, dishonesty takes the lead, and a successful expedition to the White Nile is supposed to overcome all charges. There are two classes of White Nile traders, the one possessing capital, the other being penniless adventurers; the same system of operations is pursued by both, but that of the former will be evident from the description of the latter.

A man without means forms an expedition, and borrows money for this purpose at 100 per cent. after this fashion. He agrees to repay the lender in ivory at one-half its market value. Having obtained the required sum, he hires several vessels and engages from 100 to 300 men, composed of Arabs and runaway villains from distant countries, who have found an asylum from justice in the obscurity of Khartoum. He purchases guns and large quantities of ammunition for his men, together with a few hundred pounds of glass beads. The piratical expedition being complete, he pays his men five months' wages in advance, at the rate of forty-five piastres (nine shillings) per month, and he agrees to give them eighty piastres per month for any period exceeding the five months advanced. His men receive their advance partly in cash and partly in cotton stuffs for clothes at an exorbitant price. Every man has a strip of paper, upon which is written by the clerk of the expedition the amount he has received both in goods and money, and this paper he must produce at the final settlement. The vessels sail about December, and on arrival at the desired locality, the party disembark and proceed into the interior, until they arrive at the village of some negro chief, with whom they establish an intimacy. Charmed with his new friends, the power of whose weapons he acknowledges, the negro chief does not neglect the opportunity of seeking their alliance to attack a hostile neighbour. Marching throughout the night, guided by their negro hosts, they bivouac within an hour's march of the unsuspecting village doomed to an attack about half an hour before break of day. The time arrives, and, quietly surrounding the village while its occupants are still sleeping, they fire the grass huts in all directions, and pour volleys of musketry through the flaming thatch. Panic-stricken, the unfortunate victims rush from their burning dwellings, and the men are shot down like pheasants in a battue, while the women and children, bewildered in the danger and confusion, are kidnapped and secured. The herds of cattle, still within their kraal or "zareeba," are easily disposed of, and are driven off with great rejoicing, as the prize of victory. The women and children are then fastened together, the former secured in an instrument called a sheba, made of a forked pole, the neck of the prisoner fitting into the fork, secured by a cross piece lashed behind; while the wrists, brought together in advance of the body, are tied to the pole. The children are then fastened by their necks with a rope attached to the women, and thus form a living chain, in which order they are marched to the head-quarters in company with the captured herds.

This is the commencement of business: should there be ivory in any of the huts not destroyed by the fire, it is appropriated; a general plunder takes place. The trader's party dig up the floors of the huts to search for iron hoes, which are generally thus concealed, as the greatest treasure of the negroes; the granaries are overturned and wantonly destroyed, and the hands are cut off the bodies of the slain, the more easily to detach the copper or iron bracelets that are usually worn. With this booty the *traders* return to their negro ally: they have thrashed and discomfited his enemy, which delights him; they present him with thirty or forty head of cattle which intoxicates him with joy, and a present of a pretty little captive girl of about fourteen completes his happiness.

But business only commenced. The negro covets cattle, and the trader has now captured perhaps 2,000 head. They are to be had for ivory, and shortly the tusks appear. Ivory is daily brought into camp in exchange for cattle, a tusk for a cow, according to size—a profitable business, as the cows have cost nothing. The trade proves brisk; but still there remain some little customs to be observed—some slight formalities, well understood by the White Nile trade. The slaves and two-thirds of the captured cattle belong to the trader, but his men claim as their perquisite one-third of the stolen animals. These having been divided, the slaves are put up to public auction among the men, who purchase such as they require; the amount being entered on the papers (serki) of the purchasers, to be reckoned against their

wages. To avoid the exposure, should the document fall into the hands of the Government or European consuls, the amount is not entered as for the purchase of a slave, but is divided for fictitious supplies—thus, should a slave be purchased for 1,000 piastres, that amount would appear on the document somewhat as follows:—

Soap	50	Piastres.
Tarboash (cap)	100	
Araki	500	
Shoes	200	
Cotton Cloth	150	
	1,000	

The slaves sold to the men are constantly being changed and resold among themselves; but should the relatives of the kidnapped women and children wish to ransom them, the trader takes them from his men, cancels the amount of purchase, and restores them to their relations for a certain number of elephants' tusks, as may be agreed upon. Should any slave attempt to escape, she is punished either by brutal flogging, or shot or hanged, as a warning to others.

An attack or razzia, such as described, generally leads to a quarrel with the negro ally, who in his turn is murdered and plundered by the trader—his women and children naturally becoming slaves.

A good season for a party of a hundred and fifty men should produce about two hundred cantars (20,000 lbs.) of ivory, valued at Khartoum at £4,000. The men being paid in slaves, the wages should be *nil,* and there should be a surplus of four or five hundred slaves for the trader's own profit—worth on an average five to six pounds each.

The boats are accordingly packed with a human cargo, and a portion of the trader's men accompany them to the Soudan, while the remainder of the party form a camp or settlement in the country they have adopted, and industriously plunder, massacre, and enslave, until their master's return with the boats from Khartoum in the following season, by which time they are supposed to have a cargo of slaves and ivory ready for shipment. The business thus thoroughly established, the slaves are landed at various points within a few days' journey of Khartoum, at which places are agents, or purchasers waiting to receive them with dollars prepared for cash payments. The purchasers and dealers are, for the most part, Arabs. The slaves are then marched across the country to different places; many to Sennaar, where they are sold to other dealers, who sell them to the Arabs and to the Turks. Others are taken immense distances to ports on the Red Sea, Souakim, and Masowa, there to be shipped for Arabia and Persia. Many are sent to Cairo, and in fact they are disseminated throughout the slave-dealing East, the White Nile being the great nursery for the supply.

The amiable trader returns from the White Nile to Khartoum; hands over to his creditor sufficient ivory to liquidate the original loan of £1,000, and, already a man of capital, he commences as an independent trader.

Such was the White Nile trade when I prepared to start from Khartoum on my expedition to the Nile sources. Every one in Khartoum, with the exception of a few Europeans, was in favour of the slave-trade, and looked with jealous eyes upon a stranger venturing within the precincts of their holy land; a land sacred to slavery and to every abomination and villainy that man can commit.

50 GEORG SCHWEINFURTH
KING MUNZA

During his second sojourn in Africa, the botanist and traveler Georg Schweinfurth (1836–1925) spent three years (1868–1871) in the Upper Nile hinterland. His travels and work were a major contribution to European knowledge of the southern Sudan and the northeast Congo. He describes his visit to the powerful Munza, king of the Mangbettu people who inhabited the valley of the upper Uele River on the eastern reaches of the Congo basin.

As we approached the huts, the drums and trumpets were sounded to their fullest powers, and the crowds of people pressing forward on either hand left but a narrow passage for our procession. We bent our steps to one of the largest huts, which formed a kind of palatial hall open like a shed at both ends. Waiting my arrival

From Dr. Georg Schweinfurth, *The Heart of Africa,* trans. by Ellen E. Frewer (New York: Sampson Low, Marston, Searle, and Rivington, 1874), II, 40–52.

here was one of the officers of state, who, I presume, was the master of the ceremonies, as I afterwards observed him presiding over the general festivities. This official took me by the right hand, and without a word conducted me to the interior of the hall. Here, like the audience at a concert, were arranged according to their rank hundreds of nobles and courtiers, each occupying his own ornamental bench and decked out with all his war equipments. At the other end of the building a space was left for the royal throne, which differed in no respect from the other benches, except that it stood upon an outspread mat; behind this bench was placed a large support of singular construction, resting as it seemed upon three legs, and furnished with projections that served as props for the back and arms of the sitter: this support was thickly studded with copper rings and nails. I requested that my own chair might be placed at a few paces from the royal bench, and there I took up my position with my people standing or squatting behind me, and the Nubian soldiers forming a guard around. The greater number of the soldiers had their guns, but my black squires, who had never before been brought face to face with so mighty a potentate, subsequently confessed to me that their hearts beat fast, and that they could not help trembling to think how a sign from Munza could have brought all our limbs to the spit.

For a considerable time I had to sit waiting in expectation before the empty throne. My servants informed me that Munza had attended the market in his ordinary costume, but that he had been seen to hasten home to his private apartments, where he was now undergoing a process of anointing, frizzling, and bedizening at the hands of his wives, in order that he should appear before me in the imposing splendour of his state attire. I had thus no other alternative than patiently to abide my time; for what could be more flattering to a foreign guest than for a king to receive him in his costliest toilet?

In the interval of waiting there seemed a continuous uproar. The fitful beating of kettle-drums and the perpetual braying of horns resounded through the airy building until it shook again, and mingling with the boisterous strains rose the voices of the assembled courtiers as they whiled away the time in loud and eager conversation. There was no doubt that I was myself the main cause of their excitement; for although I sat with my back to the majority, I could not be otherwise than quite aware that all eyes were intently fixed upon me. All, however, kept their seats at a respectful distance, so that I could calmly look about me and note down my observations of what I saw.

The hall itself was the chief object that attracted my attention. It was at least a hundred feet in length, forty feet high, and fifty broad. It had been quite recently completed, and the fresh bright look of the materials gave it an enlivening aspect, the natural brown polish of the woodwork looking as though it were gleaming with the lustre of new varnish. Close by was a second and more spacious hall, which in height was only surpassed by the loftiest of the surrounding oil-palms; but this, although it had only been erected five years previously, had already begun to show symptoms of decay, and being enclosed on all sides was dark, and therefore less adapted for the gathering at a public spectacle. Considering the part of Africa in which these halls were found, one might truly be justified in calling them wonders of the world; I hardly know with all our building resources what material we could have employed, except it were whalebone, of sufficient lightness and durability to erect structures like these royal halls of Munza, capable of withstanding the tropical storms and hurricanes. The bold arch of the vaulted roof was supported on three long rows of pillars formed from perfectly straight tree-stems; the countless spars and rafters as well as the other parts of the building being composed entirely of the leaf-stalks of the wine-palm (*Raphia vinifera*).[1] The floor was covered with a dark red clay plaster, as firm and smooth as asphalt. The sides were enclosed by a low breastwork, and the space between this and the arching

[1] This palm is found in every bank-forest in the Monbutto country, and its leaves vary from 25 to 35 feet in length: the midrib of the leaf (rhachis) is of a bright brown colour, and furnishes the most popular building material throughout Central Africa.

roof, which at the sides sloped nearly to the ground, allowed light and air to pass into the building. Outside against the breastwork stood crowds of natives, probably the "great unwashed" of the Monbuttoo, who were unable to obtain places within, and contented themselves with eagerly gazing through this opening at the proceedings. Officials with long sticks went their rounds and kept order among the mob, making free use of their sticks whenever it was necessary; all boys who ventured uninvited into the hall being vigorously beaten back as trespassers.

I had probably been left for an hour, and was getting lost in the contemplation of all the wonders, when a louder sound of voices and an increasing clang of horns and kettle-drums led me to suppose that there was an announcement of the approach of the king; but, no, this was only a prelude. The sovereign was still being painted and beautified by the hands of his fair ones. There was, however, a fresh and increasing commotion near the entrance of the hall, where a number of ornamental weapons was being arranged. Posts were driven into the ground, and long poles were fastened horizontally across them; then against this extemporized scaffolding were laid, or supported crosswise, hundreds of ornamental lances and spears, all of pure copper, and of every variety of form and shape. The gleam of the red metal caught the rays of the tropical noontide sun, and in the symmetry of their arrangement the rows of dazzling lance-heads shone with the glow of flaming torches, making a background to the royal throne that was really magnificent. The display of wealth, which according to Central African tradition was incalculable, was truly regal, and surpassed anything of the kind that I had conceived possible.

A little longer and the weapons are all arranged. The expected king has left his home. There is a running to and fro of heralds, marshals, and police. The thronging masses flock towards the entrance, and silence is proclaimed. The king is close at hand. Then come the trumpeters flourishing away on their huge ivory horns; then the ringers swinging their cumbrous iron bells; and now, with a long firm stride, looking neither to the right nor to the left, wild, romantic, picturesque alike in mien and in attire, comes the tawny Caesar himself! He was followed by a number of his favoured wives. Without vouchsafing me a glance, he flung himself upon his unpretending chair of state, and sat with his eyes fixed upon his feet. Mohammed had joined the retinue of his royal friend, and took up his position opposite me on the other side of the king on a stool that was brought for his accommodation. He also had arrayed himself in a suitable dress in honour of the occasion, and now sat in the imposing uniform of a commander of Arnauts.

I could now feast my eyes upon the fantastic figure of the ruler. I was intensely interested in gazing at the strange weird-looking sovereign, of whom it was commonly reported that his daily food was human flesh. With arms and legs, neck and breast, all bedizened with copper rings, chains, and other strange devices, and with a great copper crescent at the top of his head, the potentate gleamed with a shimmer that was to our ideas unworthy of royalty, but savoured far too much of the magazines of civic opulence, reminding one almost unavoidably of a well-kept kitchen! His appearance, however, was decidedly marked with his nationality, for every adornment that he had about him belonged exclusively to Central Africa, as none but the fabrications of his native land are deemed worthy of adorning the person of a king of the Monbuttoo.

Agreeably to the national fashion a plumed hat rested on the top of his chignon, and soared a foot and a half above his head; this hat was a narrow cylinder of closely-plaited reeds; it was ornamented with three layers of red parrots' feathers, and crowned with a plume of the same; there was no brim, but the copper crescent projected from the front like the vizor of a Norman helmet. The muscles of Munza's ears were pierced, and copper bars as thick as the finger inserted in the cavities. The entire body was smeared with the native unguent of powdered camwood, which converted the original bright brown tint of his skin into the colour that is so conspicuous in ancient Pompeian halls. With the exception of being of an unusually fine texture, his single garment differed in no respect from what was worn throughout the country; it consisted of a large piece of fig bark impregnated with the same dye that served as his cosmetic, and this, falling in graceful folds about his body, formed breeches and waistcoat all in one. Round thongs of buffalo-hide, with heavy copper balls attached to the ends, were fastened round the waist in a huge knot, and like a girdle held the coat, which was neatly-hemmed. The material of the coat was so carefully manipulated that it had quite the appearance of a rich *moiré antique*. Around the king's neck hung a copper ornament made in little points which radiated like beams all over his chest; on his bare arms were strange-looking pendants which in shape could only be compared to drumsticks with rings at the end. Halfway up the lower part of the arms and just below the knee were three bright, horny-looking circlets cut out of hippopotamus-hide, likewise tipped with copper. As a symbol of his dignity Munza wielded in his right hand the sickle-shaped Monbuttoo scimitar, in this case only an ornamental weapon, and made of pure copper.

As soon as the king had taken his seat, two little tables, beautifully carved, were placed on either side of his throne, and on these stood the dainties of which he continually partook, but which were carefully concealed by napkins of fig bark; in addition to these tables, some really artistic flasks of porous clay were brought in, full of drinking water.

Such was Munza, the autocrat of the Monbuttoo, with whom I was now

brought face to face. He appeared as the type of those half-mythical potentates, a species of Mwata Yanvo or Great Makoko, whose names alone have penetrated to Europe, a truly savage monarch, without a trace of anything European or Oriental in his attire, and with nothing fictitious or borrowed to be attributed to him.

He was a man of about forty years of age, of a fair height, of a slim but powerful build, and, like the rest of his countrymen, stiff and erect in figure. Although belonging to a type by no means uncomely, his features were far from prepossessing, but had a Nero-like expression that told of *ennui* and satiety. He had small whiskers and a tolerably thick beard; his profile was almost orthognatic, but the perfectly Caucasian nose offered a remarkable contrast to the thick and protruding negro lips. In his eyes gleamed the wild light of animal sensuality, and around his mouth lurked an expression that I never saw in any other Monbuttoo, a combination of avarice, violence, and love of cruelty that could with the extremest difficulty relax into a smile. No spark of love or affection could beam forth from such features as his.

A considerable time elapsed before the king looked directly at the pale-faced man with the long hair and the tight black clothes who now for the first time appeared before him. I held my hat in my hand, but no greeting had as yet taken place, for, observing that everyone kept his seat when the king entered the hall, I had done the same, and now waited for him to address me. The wild uproar of the cannibals still continued, and Munza, sitting in a careless attitude, only raised his eyes now and then from their fixed stare upon the ground as though to scan the whole assemblage, but in reality to take stray glances at my person, and in this way, little by little, he satisfied his curiosity. I could not help marvelling at the composure of this wild African, and wondering where in the world he could

have learnt his dignity and self-posses-
sion.

At length the monarch began to ask me
some questions. They were fluently translated into the Zandey dialect by the chief
interpreter, who always played a principal
part in our intercourse with the natives.
The Niam-niam [Azande—ed.] in their
turn rendered the sense to me in Arabic.
The conversation, however, was of the
most commonplace character, and referred neither to the purpose of my coming nor to the country from which I came.
Munza's interrogations brought to my
mind the rough reception afforded to
Reinhold Forster, the companion of the
renowned Captain Cook, by Frederick the
Great, who bluntly asked him if he had
ever seen a king? "Yes, your Majesty,"
was the answer, "several; two tame and
three savage." Munza appeared extremely anxious to keep up to an Oriental
measure the principle of *nil admirari*;
nothing could disturb his composure, and
even at my subsequent visits, where there
was no state ceremonial, he maintained a
taciturnity nearly as resolute.

My servants now brought forth the
presents I had brought and spread them
at the king's feet. These consisted, in the
first place, of a piece of black cloth, a
telescope, a silver platter, and a porcelain
vase; the silver was taken for white iron,
and the porcelain for carved ivory. The
next gift was a real piece of carved ivory,
brought as a specimen to show the way
in which the material is employed; there
was a book with gilt edges, a gift which
could not fail to recall to my mind the
scene in which Speke describes Kamrasi's
first lesson in the Bible; then came a double mirror, that both magnified and reduced what it reflected; and last, though
by no means least, was a large assortment
of beads of Venetian glass, including
thirty necklaces, composed of thirty distinct pieces, so that Munza was in possession of more than a thousand separate
beads. The universal principle followed
by the Nubians forbade that any presents

of firearms should be made to native rulers. Munza regarded all these offerings
with great attention, but without committing himself to any audible expression of
approval. Not so his fifty wives, who were
seated on stools arranged behind his
throne; they gave frequent half-sup-
pressed utterances of surprise, and the
double mirror was passed admiringly
from hand to hand, its contortions elicit-
ing shouts of delight.

There were fifty of these ladies present:
they were only the most intimate, or wives
of the first rank, the entire number of
court ladies being far larger. Except in the
greater elegance of their attire, they departed in no way from the fashion of the
country, the description of which must be
deferred for the present.

After a time Munza turned his attention to his refreshments. As far as I could
distinguish them, they consisted of lumps
of plantain-meal and tapioca piled on
leaves, of dried plantains, and of a fruit
which to my surprise I immediately
recognised as the cola-nut of the west.
From this rosy-shelled kernel the king cut
a few slices, and chewed them in the intervals of smoking his tobacco. His pipe, in
the shape of an iron stem six feet long, was
handed to him by a chibbukchak, who
was in attendance for that purpose. Very
remarkable was the way in which Munza
smoked. To bring himself into the correct
position he threw himself far back in his
seat, supported his right elbow on the
arm-rest, put one leg across the other, and
with his left hand received the pipe-stem.
In this attitude he gravely took one long
inhalation, then, with a haughty gesture,
resigned his pipe to the hands of his attendant and allowed the smoke slowly to
reissue from his mouth. It is a habit
among Turks of rank to smoke thus by
taking only two or three inhalations from
a pipe handed to them by their servants;
but where, again, may I ask, could this
cannibal prince have learnt such a custom?

To my request for a cola-nut the king

responded by graciously passing me a specimen with his own hand. Turning to Mohammed, I expressed my surprise at beholding this fruit of the far west amongst the Monbuttoo; I told him of its high value as a spice in Bornoo, where it is worth its weight in silver, and I went on to say that it confirmed my impression that the Welle was identical with the river of Baghirmy, called the Shary, and that this nut accordingly came to me like a key to a problem that I was seeking to solve. Then again addressing Munza, I made him understand that I knew the fruit, and pointing in the direction of Lake Tsad, I told him that there it was eaten by the great people of the country. I hoped in this way to induce him to give me some information on the subject; but he had made up his mind to be astonished at nothing, nor could I ever even on future occasions draw him into a geographical discussion. All that I could learn was that the cola-nut grew wild in the country, and that it was called "nangweh" by the natives, who were accustomed to chew it in the intervals of their smoking.

The performances that had been prepared for our entertainment now commenced. First of all a couple of hornblowers stepped forward, and proceeded to execute solos upon their instruments. These men were advanced proficients in their art, and brought forth sounds of such power, compass, and flexibility that they could be modulated from sounds like the roar of a hungry lion, or the trumpeting of an infuriated elephant, down to tones which might be compared to the sighing of the breeze or to a lover's whisper. One of them, whose ivory horn was so huge that he could scarcely hold it in a horizontal position, executed rapid passages and shakes with as much neatness and decision as though he were performing on a flute.

Next appeared a number of professional singers and jesters, and amongst them a little plump fellow, who acted the part of a pantomime clown, and jumped about and turned somersaults till his limbs looked like the arms of a windmill; he was covered from head to foot with bushy tufts and pigtails, and altogether his appearance was so excessively ludicrous that, to the inward delight of the king, I burst into a hearty fit of laughter. I called him a court fool, and in many respects he fully deserved the title. I hardly know why the Nubians should have drawn my attention, as though to something quite new, to the wooden Monbuttoo scimitar that he wore in his girdle. His jokes and pranks seemed neverending, and he was permitted to take liberties with every one, not excepting even Munza himself; and amongst other tricks he would approach the king with his right hand extended, and just as Munza had got hold of it, would start backwards and make off with a bound. A short time before he appeared, some freshly baked ears of maize, the first of the season, had been laid before me; of this delicacy the fool, with the most comical gestures, made me comprehend that he wished to partake; I therefore took up some detached grains, and threw them, one by one, into his open mouth; he caught them with a snap, and devoured them with such comical grimaces, that the performance called forth a roar of applause from the whole assembly.

The next episode consisted of the performances of a eunuch, who formed a butt for the wit of the spectators. How Munza had come into possession of this creature, no one seemed to know, and I could only learn that he was employed in the inner parts of the palace. He was a fat grotesque-looking figure, and when he sang looked exactly like a grunting baboon; to add to the oddity of his appearance, Munza, as though in mockery of his Nubian guests, had had him arrayed in a red fez, and thus he was the only one in all the immense concourse of natives who had anything foreign in his attire.

But the most important part of the programme was reserved for the end: Munza was to make an oration. Whilst all the audience remained quietly seated on their stools and benches, up jumped the king, loosened his coat, cleared his throat, and commenced his harangue. Of course I could not understand a single word, and a double interpretation would have been worse than useless: but, from what I could see and hear, it was evident that Munza endeavoured to be choice and emphatic in his language, as not only did he often correct himself, but he made pauses after the sentences that he intended to be impressive, to allow for the applause of his auditors. Then the shout of "Ee, ee, tchupy, tchupy, ee, Munza, ee," resounded from every throat, and the musical instruments caught up the strain, until the uproar was truly demoniacal. Several times after this chorus, and as if to stimulate the tumult, Munza uttered a stentorian "brrr—" [2] with a voice so sonorous that the very roof vibrated, and the swallows fled in terror from their nests in the eaves.

The kettle-drums and horns now struck up a livelier and more rhythmical strain, and Munza assumed a new character and proceeded to beat time with all the solemnity of a conductor. His *bâton* was something like a baby's rattle, and consisted of a hollow sphere of basket-work filled with

[2] It may interest the reader to learn that in the Shamane prayers "brrr—" is synonymous with "hail," and I have little doubt that it here meant some sort of applause, as it was always the signal for the repetition of the hymn in celebration of the glories of Munza.

pebbles and shells, and attached to a stick.[3]

The discourse lasted full half an hour, during which time I took the portrait of the king. . . . Hunger at length compelled me to take my leave of the sovereign and retrace my steps to the camp. At parting Munza said to me, "I do not know what to give you in return for all your presents; I am sorry I am so poor and have nothing to offer you." Fascinated by his modesty and indulging the idea that it was only a preface to a munificent gift worthy of royalty, I replied, "Don't mention that: I did not come for what I could get; we buy ivory from the Turks, and pay them with yellow lead and white iron, and we make white stuffs and powder and guns for ourselves. I only ask for two things: a pig (*Potamochoerus*) and a chimpanzee."

"You shall certainly have them," said Munza; but I was thoroughly deceived, and, in spite of my repeated reminders, neither pig nor chimpanzee ever appeared.

As I left the hall the king commenced a new oration. As for myself, I was so thoroughly fatigued with the noise and tumult, that I was glad to spend the remainder of this memorable day quietly in my tent.

[3] A similar contrivance is used on the river Gabon on the West Coast.

51 SALIM AL-MAZRUI
THE SULTAN AND MOMBASA

Only one example of a long and illustrious poetic tradition, Utendi wa al-Akida *was written by Abdallah ibn Maseed ibn Salim al-Mazrui (1797–1894). This heroic poem concerns the conflict between al-Akida, the* Wali *(Governor) of Mombasa and the Sultan of Zanzibar, Sayyid Barghash. Acting on the complaints of the people of Mombasa, the sultan deposed al-Akida, who was finally driven from Fort Jesus in 1875 with the assistance of two British men-of-war.*

From Abdallah ibn Maseed ibn Salim al-Mazrui, "Utendi wa al-Akida," in Lyndon Harris, *Swahili Poetry* (Oxford: Clarendon Press, 1962), pp. 131, 133, 135, 137, 139, 141, 143. Reprinted by permission of the Clarendon Press, Oxford.

First in the Name of God   if you want
the truth   the Swahili country
is no place for us to live in.

Ruler, our ruler   ruler born in our
country   how could anything be
withheld   from him that he could
not seize?

But the year is not good   it is like a
day of awakening   to sorrow and
repentance   listen, brethren.

It is a year beginning unluckily   and
ending with deception   a year of
much trouble   as you will see for
yourselves.

It came in with strife   want of friendliness   and destruction of souls
all, I say, without cause.

In these last days of the good old world
a subject cannot be allowed   to
quarrel with his Sultan   and go unpunished.

The tale of Bakhashweini   I will relate
exactly   understand that its beginning   is the strife that you know of.

The Wali was a man   beloved by the
people   a man in whom the Sultan
had great confidence.

But there is no ruler   who is loved by
all   there is sure to come an evil
person   who seeks to do him ill.

And so Muhammad   was slandered to
the Sultan   and the friction increased   until discord flared up.

Our great lord sent   his special minister   to investigate the reports
that had reached him.

When the ship arrived   it brought the
reply   there was nothing more to
say   the Sultan was angry.

The man in the ship   was Muhammad
b. Suleiman   the Sultan's envoy
he it is who was on board.

When he landed at the Customs   and
came up the steps   all the Kilindini
people   followed him in a crowd.

The elders of the town   told Said (the
Sultan)   al-Akida is a bad man
it is better to beware of him.

He asked, What is the matter?   What
has he done?   Whatever (he may

have done) in his own home Dauani
he cannot deal threateningly with me.

The elders were silent   not knowing
what to think   they kept on hesitating   till the great man was annoyed.

He asked them what was the matter
what had they to say   Say what you
have to   and I will consider it.

We have only one thing to say   Our
wish is this   that you take away
from us the trouble   that has come
upon us.

What Bakhashweini deserves   is
known to God Almighty   may the
Lord God curse him   and deliver us
all from him.

The Sultan's command   was to go to
the Court   five and fifty   soldiers were waiting there.

The Wali was sent for   he came in a
rage   when he arrived he saw how
it was   and sat down in his place.

He was handed a letter   which he
took hurriedly   he grasped it
and tore it open.

When he opened it   he saw the order
which had been written   that he
should leave the Fort   and live
there no more.

Then he spoke   with his tongue and
said   I am going for the keys
and I will bring them all here.

He went off, I tell you   he went off
arrogantly   just after midday
and barricaded himself within.

He sent forth the Khalifa   Go and
capture Mustafa   face death itself
to bring him to me.

Go quickly, sergeant   and arrest the
Baluchis [1]   then tell him (Mustafa)
Shishi anti, it is Arabic.

Go, Al-Adwan   my brave lion   I
have none like you   among all my
soldiers.

So shall I remove doubt   entirely from
my heart   I will seize the Baluchis
women as well as men.

Then spoke al-Adwani   al-Akida,

---

[1] An inhabitant of Baluchistan (ed.).

what is the matter?   Grieve not so
much   I will take the Baluchis.

I will seize the Baluchis   and put them
in chains   in the cell of Wadi
Mataka   there will I put them.

He set off to do so   going in a hurry
when he got there (he found him) eating rice   and Mustafa was en-
chained.

Rifles were fired   some people hid
themselves   As the Jemadari
crouched down   he was hit by a
bullet.

Alas this destruction   we are a famous
people   but because we are divided
(lit. in two ranks)   that is why we
are destroyed.

Ramadhani Kazabeka   these are the
things you wanted   there is no escape from them now   for they have
come upon us.

Mustafa was imprisoned   he was almost slain by the sword   but God
protected him   and he was put in
a cell.

The people of Bakhashweini   called
out in the Fort   Who is it today?
who is it?   Who (dares) to approach
us?

Never, never   far be it from me
I will prefer death   rather than be
forced out (of the Fort).

I will not agree to come out   to force
me out will be difficult   even
though you may collect riches   I
will not accept them.

I was born in the Fort   The Kilindi
folk   and all who are in the town
I am familiar with them all.

I ask the people of Mombasa   Why
should war come?   When you are
all entangled   you are all involved
in trouble.

Tell Sheikh Suud   the son of the Sai-
yids   because so much is involved
he can by no means disentangle affairs.

For he is as my father   the husband
of my mother   he has spun this web
around me   until I have been
deposed.

He left to go to Mgau   and I thought
nothing of him   not realizing he
was bent on mischief   going to tell
tales.

He involved me in discord   and it
stuck hard   so that I had nothing
to say   that I could make up before
the Sultan.

I appeared before the Sultan   without
getting my intention   like a corrupt
slave   who had done wrong.

I grieve for my efforts   in striving with
people   when lo a pot (of trouble)
very big indeed was being brewed for
me.

I said to myself   I will not leave Zanzibar   and I saw that I was in danger   of losing Mombasa.

When I was in Zanzibar   I thought I
would not come   I will not return
(but) I came   and I reached Mombasa.

I am expecting some people   they are
elders of the town   but they do not
come to me   I would give them
money (if they came).

I would grant them a share   of what
God gave to me   I should give it to
my companions   for them to use.

When I get the townspeople   it would
be for me a matter of questioning
like Rambi Saji   so great is my anger.

Salimu make ready   so that we may
die like men   even if it be by daylight   fear not, it is all the same.

Let Salimu stay right there   that is
where I am coming   let me fly
round him like a bat   till he knows
not where to go.

Muhammad remained   in the Fort
with the crowd   of men and women
and refused to open the gate.

There went to him groups   of good
and honourable men   (to beg him)
to cease from his folly   but he
refused their counsel.

Muhammad declared   I will not go
back on what I have decided   about
the gate have no doubt   I am not

the one to open it.

He drove them from the Fort   the poor Baluchis   in humiliation and sorrow   they were scattered about the villages.

The news spread   and reached Zanzibar   The Sultan pondered   how to get him out by a trick.

After a few days   there came good gifts   and a pledge of peace then he came out of the Fort.

After the day's round   there arrived Seif the Sour   with his akida Mataru   and an army of soldiers.

And Muhammad realized   that this is war indeed   without doubt he will be captured   unless he defends himself.

He said I must   get the town on my side   I will not rejoice the enemy and consent to be tricked.

Bakhashweini proclaimed   that of the soldiers of the Fort   none must remain in the town   after the setting of the sun.

He had a consultation   with his brothers and other faithful men   they spoke boastfully   and this is what they said.

We have placed the cannons in position our guns are set   only he who is a fool   will dare to come to us.

Every sensible man   even though he be strong   would be only a fool to come upon us so.

For this is a great loss   which follows along with great gain   and I call upon all Muslims (lit. the family of the Mother of Cities)   to come and join us here.

Do not think it is like Gaeti   who was not equal to death   I tell you without hiding anything   I will certainly face it.

You will see regiment upon regiment on the highway like smoke   Do not think this is boasting   what I am telling you.

Everyone who is first   with moaning and anguish   with twenty-four

pounds of chains   that is what I shall put him in.

To every man who is my enemy   I shall change into a leopard for him it is because he does not know me that he trifles with me.

This is how they talked   Muhammad and his brother   and all who followed along with them   were of the same mind.

But this is a gamble   and those who sleep must not sleep   they must keep watch   till the morning comes.

He opened the gate   (and said) what I say is no lie   I have no need of idle words   all I want I shall do.

He poured out his carriers   saying, Today is the day   Do not think there is a journey ahead   for we are going into the town.

What I say is true   the road was filled with smoke   we saw hosts of men and lo they were the enemy.

Now look after yourselves   it is not night but day   let us go forth like noblemen   let there be no running away.

They were like locusts   and they destroyed the town   and they behaved with violence   intent on evil.

An Englishman arrived   and gave him good advice   and he said I will not listen   to anything you say to me.

The European was vexed   and said to him sharply   You do not like my words   not one do you hear.

The Admiral spake   Now what advice should we give in Zanzibar   about what should be done?

I will arrange for gunboats   to creep up by sea   he has chosen evil and he must suffer for it.

I shall attack him with shell   but I shall not aim to hit   the shot shall pass as a sign   perhaps he will give up.

He took it in jest   the Fort had no sign (of damage)   those inside rejoiced and blessed their good fortune.

Another shell came over   and hit the
target   and it caused great damage
and lives were lost.
He lowered the flag   hoisting another
at once   to show them a signal
that we have surrendered.
The firing ceased   the young men
made ready   and came ashore to
look   and entered the Fort.
Muhammad came out   his heart was
very cold   I want your promise
Admiral, that you will do something
for me.
I want you to stand surety for me   and
leave me in the Fort   or if we go to
the Sultan   when we arrive intercede for me.
The Admiral explained   If I go to the
Sultan   and you are not in my
hands   that would be wrong.
Let us go on board   and sail at once
when we get to the Sultan   I shall
find something to say.

They went down to the shore   and
went on board   when they reached
Zanzibar   he told him not to worry.
He went ashore   and went to the Sultan   (who was told) Muhammad is
inside   Sir, I have brought him to
you.
We have come according to promise
do not refuse my request   he is under arrest   and now I ask pardon
for him.
What you ask has been granted   and
I will follow your counsel   you have
got   him   out   of   the   difficulties
which surrounded him.
Do not keep him in Zanzibar   I foresee danger there for him   for he is
a mischievous person   and will
harm my subjects.
Now I have come to the end   my tale
is finished   I have said all there is
to say   and there is nothing left to
say.

52 RUHANANTUKA
FLIGHT OF THE EKIRIMBI

The Bahima *were the cattle owners and warriors of the Ankole kingdom in what is now
Uganda, and poetry was part of their traditional way of life.   The poem that follows
concerns the flight of a group of Bahima, the* Ekirimbi, *from Karagwe in the early years
of the twentieth century.   The poem was composed by one of them, Ruhanantuka, and
although it appears to be a description of battle, no actual fighting took place between the
Ekirimbi and the German authorities who opposed their move.*

1. I Who Give Courage To My Companions!

2. I Who Am Not Reluctant In Battle
   made a vow!

3. I Who Am Not Reluctant In Battle

made a vow at the time of the preventing of the elephants [1] and with
me was The Tamer Of Recruits;

4. I Who Am Not Loved By The Foe
   was full of anger when the enemy
   were reported.

From H. F. Morris, *The Heroic Recitations of the
Bahima of Ankole* (Oxford: Clarendon Press, 1964),
pp. 52, 54, 56, 58, 60, 62, 64.   Reprinted by permission of the Clarendon Press, Oxford.

[1] I.e. at midnight, at which time it is often necessary
to prevent the elephants from destroying the crops.

5. I Who Am Vigilant called up the men at speed together with The Pain Bringer;

6. I found The Giver Of Courage in secret conference.

7. I Whose Decisions Are Wise, at me they took their aim and with me was Rwamisooro;

8. I Who Overthrow The Foe returned to the fight as they attacked us.

9. I Who Am Nimble withstood the bullets together with The Lover Of Battle;

10. I Who Am Invincible appeared with The Infallible One.

11. I Who Grasp My Weapons Firmly was sent in advance to Ruyanja together with The Overthrower;

12. I Who Seek No Avoidance Of Difficulties drew my bow.

13. I Who Do Not Tremble prepared to shoot together with The One Who Draws Tight His Bow;

14. I Who Crouch For The Attack, they brought me back for my sandals together with The Tall One;

15. I Who Do Not Disclose My Plans fought furiously and with me was The Brave One;

16. I Who Do Not Miss The Mark crossed over noiselessly together with The Spear Thrower.

17. I Who Am Not Reluctant In Battle was with The One Eager For Plunder;

18. I Who Attack On All Sides appeared with The One Who Exhausts The Foe.

19. I Who Move Forward To The Attack took the track of the Ekirimbi together with The Bringer Of Sorrow;

20. I Who Am In The Forefront Of The Battle tracked them down at Migyera together with The One Who Depends Not On The Advice Of Others.

21. At Kashaka, my rattle bell rang out and with me was Rwamisooro;

22. At Rubumba, I found their courage deserting them.

23. I Whose Aid Is Sought was assailed by bullets which left me unscathed and with me was The Fortunate One;

24. I Who Stand Firm In Battle defeated them utterly and so did The One Who Needs No Protection.

25. I Who Am Clear Headed faced the spears together with The Ceaseless Fighter;

26. I Who Am Agile came up alongside them and with me was Katwaza.

27. I Who Am Eager For Battle made a vow on an anthill [2] with The Tamer of Recruits;

28. I Who Am Not Disobeyed broke my bow in my impatience.

29. I Who Retaliate, they singled me out as I was fighting along with The Infallible One;

30. I Who Am Vigilant enticed them out from their camps and so did Katemba.

31. I Who Am Praised, with The Saviour Of The Warriors, gathered them together from whence they had fled;

32. I Who Attack Unprovoked was feared in the fight and so was Katemba.

33. I Who Fight Alone strove with men swift of foot and so did Katemba;

34. I Who Am Eager For Battle, with The One Who Seeks No Help, captured a slave girl.

35. I heard your cries, You Who Seek No Help;

36. I Who Encourage My Companions,
37. I Who Fight Unceasingly, with The Seeker Of The Foe, carried off all their cattle.

38. At Karambi, I and The Scourge Of The Warriors rejected the counsels of the middle-aged; [3]

[2] It was customary for an anthill to be adapted as a platform for chiefs to stand or sit on.
[3] Presumably because the advice given was one of caution.

39. At Rufunda, they sent me off and I outpaced them.

40. I Who Am Not Rejected came to their aid along with The Fortunate One;

41. I Who Am Eager To Attack was refreshed by the battle and so was He Who Draws Tight His Bow.

42. I Who Am Capable, with Rugumba, attacked the enemy in their flight and with us was The Scatterer Of The Foe;

43. I Who Depend Not On The Advice of Others fell upon them unexpectedly.

44. I Who Prepare For Battle pushed my way to the enemy's rear and with me was The Bringer of Sorrow;

45. I Who Am Moved To Anger attacked the enemy host together with Runyamosho.

46. I The Angry One fought with great fury and so did He Who Is Of Steel;

47. He Who Is Not Disobeyed, along with Rwamisooro, stood fast beside me;

48. I Who Am Second To None, they could not pass me by as they sought me.

49. } I Who Go To War, I Who Am Agile and He Who Is Led To Battle,

50. He Whose Appearance Is Pleasing, He Who Presses To The Battle's Fore, He Who Gets Ready To Shoot,

51. He Who Is Truculent and He Who Swells The Number Of The Warriors gave the foe no pause for breath.

52. I Who Am Agile, with Rwamisooro, passed over to the band of twenty; [4]

53. At Rushojwa, I had refused to leave and so had The Tamer Of The Recruits;

54. At Rugomerwa, we set off and they returned there.

55. I Who Do Not Miss The Mark outstripped those who were well armed together with The One Eager For Plunder;

56. I Who Incapacitate The Foe stood firm in the marketplace.

57. I Who Am Not Put To Flight passed on to the battle at Rufunza and so did Katemba;

58. I Who Do Not Tremble set to work with my spear.

59. At Kanyabihara, I turned them back with the spear together with The Tracker;

60. At Ibaare, I got before them to the cattle and He Who Draws Tight His Bow was with me;

61. I Who Do Not Ask For Help stood fast in the narrow way.

62. I Who Am Not Alarmed By The Footsteps Of The Plunderers with The One Unyielding Before Heroes,

63. I Who Am Agile completed the warriors' numbers.

64. I Who Surprise The Foe went ahead of those not yet in the fight and so did He Who Is Led To Battle;

65. I Who Do Not Despise Myself found them in flight.

66. I Who Am Invisible drove them off at dawn with The Pain Inflicter On Warriors;

67. I Who Fight Alone, my swiftness took me into the enemy's midst.

68. I Who Fight Alone, it took me into their midst along with Katemba;

69. I Who Devote Myself To Battle was wearied by the use of the bow;

70. I Who Am Well Armed with The One Who Is Not Disobeyed,

71. I Who Go To War, when I looked back, they stood motionless.

72. Without thought for myself, I gathered the warriors from Misheenyi and with me was He Who Frustrates The Foe;

73. I Who Cannot Be Dissuaded From Battle drove off the enemy hosts.

---

[4] Warriors fought in small groups of ten or twenty or so.

74. I Who Fight Alongside My Comrades scattered the foe and He Who Is Agile was with me;
75. I Who Am Hot For Battle overcame their artillery along with The Scourger.
76. I Who Do Not Lose Heart vanquished the rifles of the Baziba [5] and so did The Overthrower;
77. I Who Do Not Disclose My Plans stood fast with The Infallible One;
78. I Who Go To War pressed on to the fore of the battle.
79. I Who Have The Scars Of Battle, with The Overthrower, crossed over the bodies slain by The Vehement Assailant;
80. I Who Am Eager For Battle returned home undefeated.
81. At Kanshengo, I was amongst crowds and with me was The Tamer Of Recruits;
82. I told The Giver Of Courage the secrets of fighting and also The One Who Plants His Spear Firmly.
83. I, with The One Who Is Quick To Vanquish, made a vow in the royal enclosure;
84. I Who Drive The Foe Before Me visited Big Boots [6] and with me was The Irresistible One.

[5] Strictly speaking, the Baziba are the inhabitants of the small chieftainship of Kiziba in the north of Bukoba District, Tanganyika, but the Banyankore often apply the word indiscriminately to all inhabitants of this district.

[6] The nickname of Big Boots was given to Nuwa Mbaguta, the Enganzi of Ankole from about 1894 till 1937, on account of the large boots which he was in the habit of wearing.

53 MOHAMMED ABDILLE HASAN
THE SAYYID'S REPLY

Between 1895 and 1899, Sayyid Mohammed Abdille Hasan, commonly known as the Mad Mullah, urged the Muslim Somali of Berbera to reform. In 1899 he and his followers retreated inland from Berbera, where Sayyid Mohammed forced his reforming tenets on the Somali and declared a jihad, *or holy war, against the infidels or those who refused to accept his teachings. Between 1901 and 1904, British and Ethiopian expeditions failed to curtail his operations. He moved for a time into Italian Somaliland, but in 1909 he was back in British territory and remained in virtual control of the hinterland until sufficient British forces were released by the conclusion of World War I to crush him. Throughout his long struggle against the British, Sayyid Mohammed employed poetry as an effective instrument to counter British charges against him. As a master of invective, ridicule, and scorn, he defended himself in poems such as the one that follows.*

1. Concerning your plea "Do not incite the Ogaadeen against us" I also have a complaint.
2. The people of the Ethiopian region [1] look for nothing from you,
3. So do not press my claim against them.
4. Do not claim on my behalf the blood money which they owe me.
5. I will myself seek to recover the property and the loot which they have seized.
6. Were I to leave a single penny with them my pledge would be perverted.

From Mohammed Abdille Hasan, "The Sayyid's Reply," in B. W. Andrzejewski and I. M. Lewis, *Somali Poetry and an Introduction* (Oxford: Clarendon Press, 1964), pp. 74, 76, 78, 80, 82. Reprinted by permission of the Clarendon Press, Oxford.
[1] Mainly of the Ogaadeen clan.

7. What I claim from you is only what you yourself owe me;

8. Since you are the government the responsibility is yours,

9. Can you disclaim those whom you tricked into attacking me?

10. Do they not swim in the prosperity which they have gained from what they devoured of mine?

11. Do they not drive their livestock from the valley of 'Aado to the west?

12. What did they seek from the lands between Burao and your stations?

13. Had you a pact with them by God and by consent?

14. Or did thirst drive them mad? Fools easily lose their way.

15. And afterwards was it not into your pockets that you poured the wealth?

16. Did you not enter the amounts of the booty in your printed books and cash ledgers?

17. And have you not openly admitted this in the full light of day?

18. Are not these spoils laden upon you as upon a burden-donkey?

19. That is my statement: if you are honest with me what can you answer?

20. What profit will you gain by denial? I have clearly established my case.

21. Concerning your plea: "Do not incite the Ogaadeen against us" I also have a complaint.

22. As to your statement "We have not seen the sailing ship" [2] I also have a complaint.

23. Why are you tiring yourself out,[3] working your wiles?

24. Do you not get weary with pointless talk?

25. Who rules the sea and controls the sails and holds of ships?

26. The Italians are your followers, the foundlings whom you drive with you;

27. Had they not been led by you they would not have come to Dannood,

28. They would not have sent an expedition to Doollo and 'Iid;

29. They would not have sent their armies against me.

30. They would not have harassed me with assaults at daybreak.

31. I had no issue with the Italians until you summoned them to your aid.

32. It was you who intrigued and plotted with them;

33. It was you who said "Join us in the war against the Dervishes;"

34. And they did not say "Leave us, and stop conspiring with us;"

35. Did you never tire of these evil machinations?

36. Was it not through these schemes that the landings at Obbia took place?

37. Did they not greatly aid you with their arms and supplies?

38. You fools, those who attacked yesterday on your side

39. Will they not strike at me from the back if we fight tomorrow?

40. Will they be prevented from attacking me, by disclaiming their bond with you? [4]

41. It is you who lead to pasture these weaker infidels;

42. Can I distinguish between you and your livestock?

43. As to your statement "We have not seen the sailing ship," I also have a complaint.

44. As to the raiders of whom you talk, I also have a complaint.

45. It is you who have oppressed them and seized their beasts,

46. It is you who took for yourselves their houses and property,

47. It is you who spoilt their settlements and defiled them with ordure,

48. It is you who reduced them to eating the tortoise and beast of prey;

49. This degradation you brought upon them.

50. If they (in turn) become beasts of prey and loot you

[2] Here the Sayyid refers to his claim that one of his dhows had been intercepted by the British.
[3] Lit. "Why are you dying, running fast with deceit?"

[4] Lit. "Will they become fenced off by (the words) '(You) are not my company (or allies)?'"

51. And steal small things from the clearings between your huts,
52. Then they were driven to this by hunger and famine;
53. Do not complain to me and I will not complain to you.
54. If you do not accept my statement,
55. And unless your servants confuse you with lies,
56. That I harboured them, or that I sent them against you,
57. Bring me clear evidence; otherwise it is you who are guilty of the sin.
58. As to the raiders of whom you talk, I also have a complaint.

59. Concerning your demand "Turn aside from the Warsangeli," I have a complaint.
60. If they prefer you, then they and I shall be at variance:
61. It is not in my nature to accept people who cringe to you.
62. But if they are Dervishes, how can I turn aside from them?
63. Do you also share their ancestry from Daarood Ismaaiil? [5]
64. Are you trying to steal towards me through my ancestor's genealogy?
65. Of late have you not turned them into gazelles,[6] (fugitive and homeless)?
66. Have you not seen how they loathe you?
67. For have you not seized their shops

and stored their goods in your houses?
68. Have you not set fire to their ships so that smoke rose from them?
69. You, with your filthy genitals, have you not hanged their men?
70. They soon found out that you would have no mercy on them.
71. You are against both worship and the Divine Law.
72. You are building a mat partition between them and the streams of Paradise and Heaven.
73. You are casting them into the raging fury and fumes of Hell.
74. Do they not see how deceitful you are?
75. Or are they well pleased with your prevarication?
76. Will they be divorced from their womenfolk and wives? [7]

77. Concerning your demand "Return the camels," I have a complaint.[8]
78. I also have suffered damage and loss;
79. You threw me on the ground and skinned my knee,
80. It was you who snatched the camels as they grazed,
81. It was you who scattered the white-turbanned army,
82. It was I who was first hammered at Gallaadi and experienced your bitterness;
83. A fool understands nothing, but the warning did not elude me.
84. The tethering rope with which you bound Iise [9] was meant for me,

[5] Daarood Ismaaiil, the eponymous ancestor of the Daarood clans to which the Sayyid belongs and which include the Warsangeli. The Sayyid refers to the fact that while the Warsangeli are of one blood with him, the British have no connexion with them, and therefore in Somali values, no claims upon their loyalty.
[6] Lit. "Did you not turn them into Speke's gazelles (*deero*) and Soemering's gazelles (*'awl*)." In our interpretation gazelles symbolize here living in deserted places, away from human habitations, in constant fear and always on the move. We have also heard of another possible interpretation of this line: the Sayyid apparently refers to the internal split which occurred among the Warsangeli, when those who sided with him would no longer associate with those who opposed him. The two different species of gazelle mentioned in this line live in separate herds.

[7] This passage is very obscure. Literally it means: "Are they divorcing their womenfolk, they have divorced their wives?" Most probably this amounts to a rhetorical question "Are they becoming apostates from Islam?" According to oral traditions the Sayyid declared that marriages of those men who refused to follow him became void on the legal grounds of apostasy from Islam. Their wives were therefore automatically divorced and were bound to leave them.
[8] The reference here is to livestock seized from the clans friendly to the British by the Sayyid's forces.
[9] Iise was the captain of the dhow referred to in line 22 and allegedly captured by the British.

85. And unless he is released at once there will be no peace in the world.
86. I uttered a cry, asserting my rights, so that I may not be wronged;
87. Do not expect generosity from me: yet shall we make a bargain?
88. And shall we agree to what is in our mutual interest?
89. Or fall upon each other? God knows who is the oppressed.
90. Oh, leave trickery behind and decide today, now!

54 SIR APOLO KAGWA
COURT LIFE IN BUGANDA

In an attempt to improve on the description of the Baganda *by a missionary, the Reverend John Roscoe,* Sir Apolo Kagwa (d. 1927), Regent and Prime Minister of Buganda, wrote* The Customs of the Baganda *in Luganda in 1918 during the early part of the reign of Kabaka* Daudi Chwa. *In this work Kagwa recalls the enthronement of Kimera in 1910 and the pomp and ceremony of the courts of the kabakas (kings) of Buganda.*

The next morning Kibale, Mpewo clan, and Nakatanza, Lugave clan, came to the palace and knocked at the door of the king's house. At eight o'clock a council was held by the provincial chiefs to lay plans for the enthronement. Mugema, who tied the knot in the king's barkcloth on the right shoulder, demanded the right to tie the one on the left shoulder. This caused a disagreement in the council. It was finally settled against Mugema by the men of the royal family. Then the chiefs went to the royal palace.

Kabumba, of the Lugave clan, brought the carpet and Kiini, of the Mamba clan, the tanner, brought the skins of lions, leopards, hyenas, and cows. Apolo Kagwa escorted the king and his sister, Djuma Katebe. He headed the procession, carrying the king's spears and shields. He marched at the right of the king because he is next to the king and insures his peace. At the palace gate

From Sir Apolo Kagwa, *The Customs of the Baganda,* trans. by Ernest B. Kalibala and edited by May Mandelbaum Edel (New York: Columbia University Press, 1934), pp. 63–67, 170–173. Reprinted by permission.
* John Roscoe, *The Baganda* (London: Macmillan, 1911).

Mugema led the king to the throne and placed him on it. He then placed the barkcloth on the king and knotted it on the right shoulder, as an indication that the king was the owner of the country. He laid a calfskin over the barkcloth because Kimera wore a calfskin. Then he said, "You will perform all the acts and duties befitting a king."

The Kasudju knotted a barkcloth on the king's left shoulder which meant, "You are His Majesty who rules over all other officials and men." On top of this he put a leopard skin meaning, "A king is the leopard; the common people are squirrels." Then he too said, "You will perform all the acts and duties befitting a king."

Kakinda, of the Kobe clan, brought a differently decorated barkcloth and this was placed over all the other ceremonial robes. This was several yards long and was wrapped from the right shoulder around the body and back again.

Then the Mukwenda, Sabagabo, brought a shield and two spears and handed them to the king. This meant that the king would overthrow his enemies. Kadjubi tied a string of sparkling beads about the king's left arm as a memorial to Wanyana, saying, "You are Kimera." Segulu, of the Lugave clan, put a bracelet on the king's right hand to show that he among the princes was the king elect. Namutwe, assistant Sekibobo, handed a bow and arrow to the king to assure him of his jurisdiction over the subjugated Basagala. Those who remember Greek history know that there was a king who had a slave remind him about his victory over the Athenians at all his meals (sic!).

Kaima by virtue of his office of chief in charge of the weapons brought a bow and arrow to the king. Then Masembe came and stood before the king with a milk jar. Mugema introduced him, saying, "This is your head herdsman who takes care of Namala's cow from which your great-great-grandfather, Kimera, drank his milk." Then the king touched the jar and Masembe took it away. Sebalidja, the head shepherd, brought a brass milk jar, and handed it to Mpiŋga, who had been Kimera's shepherd. Mpiŋga introduced him to the king, saying, "When milking my cow Mbulide, given me by Kimera, I use this jar."

Luboyera, of the Butiko clan, brought a beer jar known as Mwendanvuma, saying, "This is the jar in which I make your beer." Kalinda presented the type of jar in which the king's drinking water is kept, saying, "This is your water jar."

Semwaŋga and Kabogoza, Ŋoŋge clan, the barkcloth makers, brought a mallet, saying, "This is the mallet upon which your barkcloths are made." Segirinya, Ŋgo clan, brought the iron tool used in engraving the crown and royal stick. He presented this to the king, saying, "This is omuindu.[1] I use it to adorn your crown and to fashion your walking sticks." Walukaga, of the Kasimba clan, a blacksmith, brought a hammer, saying, "With this I make the spear with which you conquer." Mutalaga, of the Nvuma clan, another blacksmith, brought a dagger. He

gave it to Kasudju, who gave it to the king saying, "Whoever rebels against you, you will destroy with this dagger."

Then Mugema introduced the chief royal drums, known as Mudjaguzo. Kaula, of the Lugave clan, brought the drumsticks and Kasudju gave them to the king. The king beat the drum. Kimomera, of the Butiko clan, the assistant drummer, gave the king another pair of drumsticks and the king beat on another drum known as Namanyonyi.

Muyandja, of the Nyonyi clan, brought an axe and said, "This is your axe Naŋkuŋga that builds your boats." Omusoloza,[2] of the Nyonyi clan, presented the king with two pieces of firewood, and said, "These two pieces of wood keep the fire in Gombolola, whence you obtain the ashes to smear yourself for war."

This ended the introductory ceremony. Several others followed.

Sekaiba, of the Mbogo clan, came covered with a barkcloth known as "Throne" and carried the king on his shoulders for about twenty feet, while the princesses and the huge crowd that had assembled paid homage to the enthroned king. They shouted and gave the yells of their clans. Then the prime minister with a shield and two spears escorted the king to his dwelling house. Here the relatives of the king offered him gifts. They came in order, his grandfather, then his aunts, his sisters, brothers and the other princes. They were required to stand at the end of the carpet and introduce themselves formally.

After that another group of kinsmen came. This comprised the children of the princesses. They adorned their heads in the proper fashion and came singing beautiful melodies. The king gave them a bull and bade them farewell. His mother's relatives also offered gifts, and introduced themselves. Before the conclusion of the ceremony his grandfathers of the Ŋoŋge clan, the grandfathers of

---

[1] A stick with branches.

[2] Tax-collector.

Tcwa I of the Ŋgeye clan, and those of Kimera of the Nsenene clan, in the order named, introduced themselves.

.   .   .

The men who served the various chiefs on their estates were mostly young men. It was they who were the most energetic and successful in the looting campaigns the king ordered from time to time against the neighbors. When the booty was brought home the chief selected that which pleased him most from among the loot of his subordinates, and so became a rich man. The king might show favoritism and assign his favorite chiefs to frequent and lucrative campaigns.

This custom may have had something to do with the Baganda ignorance of trading. They were used to use force to get anything they desired, or else to receive it from the king as a gift. Those who were appointed to the various estates cultivated them by means of the peasants, who moved wherever they pleased. They very commonly went to the estate of a newly appointed chief who they thought might be honored with presents and booty. This meant that there was very great instability, the great mass of the peasantry shifting about and chiefs long established being left alone with their wealth.

.   .   .

The following account gives an idea of the pomp of the King of Buganda and of his power in governing. When the king was about to appear, that is, to open the parliament [the Buganda parliament or *lukiko*—ed.], there was an overwhelming display. All people who were in their houses remained indoors; those in the street kneeled down; and all the drums, trumpets, and every sounding instrument was used to proclaim his majesty's approach. There was a band of executioners who walked near his majesty, ready to imprison and if necessary to kill any person who was found guilty of any sort of offense. When a verdict was passed in the

parliament, the guilty person was quickly enveloped in a multitude of ropes; even if he tried to plead for mercy, it was impossible that his majesty should hear him because he was almost choked to death.

There were many who, in order to gain recognition, told lies about other chiefs, so that they might lose their offices. It was not until Mutesa [1856–1884—ed.] that that kind of system was done away with. When one person accused another, the king sent for the accused person and told him that such and such a thing had been said about him. Mutesa was against people who told him untruths. He demanded the truth of the accused. If the man was guilty and told the truth, he was soon acquitted. If he lied and witnesses were produced who certified as to his guilt, he was finally killed.

When the king walked for exercise, there were many people about him. If he came to a place where there was no road, the people soon made one for him. During his journeys, all doorkeepers were required to carry their doors with them. When the king rested, they enclosed him with the doors and guarded him. To understand the kingly power it should be said that he was a law unto himself, an absolute monarch. The following were the king's palace officers.

Kauta	Chef
Seruti	Butler
Kaula	Drummer
Nsandja	King's priest, who guarded all his horns
Banda	Potter
Omukweya	King's head carrier during the journeys
Omusoloza	Man in charge of fire wood.

There was also the executioner's division. All these and many other petty divisions made up the king's household and contributed to his pomp. Sabakaki was the title of a person who was the head of the king's palace, including the division of the king's pages. He was promptly obeyed in everything he said. In the division of the king's pages there were about one thousand young men appointed by various chiefs to serve his majesty in the palace. They were under a chief named Sabawali.

Next to the king came his prime minister. He too was honored. When his drums sounded, all chiefs hurried to his palace to go with him to the king's court. The prime minister walked very slowly to give the people a chance to join him. When he reached the court he sat down to render judgment. When the king appeared to open the court, the prime minister presented the cases. Those who appealed to his majesty were given a chance to present their own cases. The prime minister had two assistants to help him dispose of the cases. One assistant was in Maseŋgere and the other in Gombolola in the outer royal court. The communication between his majesty and the prime minister was carried on by means of constant messengers, a man and a woman from the prime minister and a messenger from the king. The prime minister's messengers kept the king acquainted with what was going on in the country at large and the king's messenger kept the prime minister informed of the latest decisions or suggestions or new decrees issued by the king. Oftentimes there was concerted action, for they respected each other. If the king wished to do anything or to order something from his estates, the word went through the prime minister. The prime minister's messenger working with the king's messenger were certain to bring anything from any part of the country, but one without the other could do nothing.

All chiefs, high or low, when they visited the capital, brought news, or something to give to the king. First they reported to the prime minister and got his assent. All secrets to be told the king went through the prime minister, and vice versa. When the king decided to appoint another prime minister, he stopped the prime minister's reception of all important and secret messages. Instead he designated Kimbugwe, the king's twin guard, to receive information concerning state affairs pending the appointment of the new prime minister. When the new prime minister was to be charged with state affairs, . . . the king stood outside the parliament house with his scepter; a group of chiefs selected as candidates faced him. Then the king gave his scepter to the man he designated as prime minister, saying, "Go and judge my Buganda country." The newly appointed chief repeated the oath of allegiance, saying, "I shall render justice." After which he left and entered his official residence and the king returned to his palace. The prime minister never gave thanks or knelt down as did other chiefs.

All Saza [county—ed.] chiefs were equally powerful in their respective counties. No messenger of whatever nature could travel in a county without a Saza chief's messenger to accompany him. If the king's and the prime minister's messengers were sent to Muwemba to assist Mukwenda in buying cows for the king, they couldn't bring anything unless they had with them a Saza chief's messenger. They were regarded as thieves. This is one point to show how well Buganda was governed. The Baganda, as far back as can be remembered, have been an obedient and well-governed people, respecting their king, chiefs, and country. This may account for the respect and encouragement with which the British Government has consented to regard the native system of government.

55 LORD DELAMERE
WHITE MAN'S COUNTRY

Hugh Cholmondeley (1870–1931), Lord Delamere, was born in Cheshire, England, edu-
cated at Eton, and first visited the Kenya highlands in 1897 while on a hunting trip.
Captivated by the region, he returned and settled in Kenya in 1903. As the leading pioneer
of white settlement in East Africa, Lord Delamere devoted the remainder of his life to
making the Kenya highlands a white man's country. In the two letters that follow, he
discusses two principal interests of the European settler in East Africa: land and the Indian
immigrants, both of which became a persistent source of tension between the Africans and
the Europeans. The Europeans contested African claims that the land occupied by white
settlers rightfully belonged to the Africans but at the same time feared economic competi-
tion from Indian traders.

September 2nd, 1903
NAIROBI

At the present time, for an agricultural farmer with a small capital, the staple product is potatoes. They grow extremely well here for several years *without* manure. The crop varies between two to ten tons to the acre. Through freights from Nairobi to the South African ports run three pounds a ton. Prices there vary from £8:10:0 to £13:10:0 a ton.

This harvest some settlers are sending potatoes direct through to Johannesburg and expect good results. Last season (there are two in a year) all the crop practically was sent to the South African ports and to Zanzibar, Mozambique, &c., and realised good prices. The only difficulty is getting the potatoes to market.

All the men worth their salt at present in the country are writing home to their relations and friends to join them. There are four settlers within short distance of Nairobi who have lately got out their brothers. Now these are men practically without capital and they evidently think it good enough. There are three dairy farmers not far from Nairobi who are doing well chiefly with native cows, although there are now two or three bulls in the country.

From Elspeth Huxley, *White Man's Country: Lord Delamere and the Making of Kenya* (London, 1935), I, 108–110, 206–208. By permission of author, Chatto & Windus, and Frederick A. Praeger.

A man called Sandbach Baker who was formerly a Manchester cotton merchant and went broke gambling on cotton is one of the dairy farmers. His wife told Lady Delamere the other day that if she had sufficient cows she could sell 1000 lbs. of butter a month in Nairobi and Mombasa. Of course that is only a small thing, but it is an opening for one or two at the present time. As soon as we can get a refrigerating plant going, which I think will be very shortly, there should be as good a sale for butter and cheese as from New Zealand. The drawback to cattle is the danger of occasional outbreaks of rinderpest.

Another opening in a small way at present, and later for export, is fruit. There is only one man in the country at present who grows fruit to any extent, because settlers go in for potatoes which bring a quick return. He grows excellent apples, plums, greengages, Japanese plums, strawberries, &c., and gets rid of the small amount he can grow in the country without trouble, and there is a demand for considerably more. Fruit at present of course fetches more or less fancy prices, but that would hardly continue when any amount was grown.

With potatoes to keep a man going, coffee promises a certain high return with the cheap land and labour procurable. Several settlers are at present growing it as fast as they can. It grows *extraor-*

dinarily well and badly cleaned coffee in the parchment has been valued at 70 to 80 shillings a hundredweight. I am sure that there is a fortune in coffee for a man who is willing to lay out a little money or who chooses to start small and work hard himself. Coffee at its high price is not touched by freight, and for good class coffee which we can certainly grow here there is an unlimited market in London. I have gone carefully into coffee estimates with settlers here and I am sure it is a first rate speculation, absurdly easy to grow—grows here like a weed.

I believe myself that money is to be made out of sheep. Grazing land, which is said by New Zealanders and others to be first class, can be hired on a 99 years' lease (which will almost certainly be convertible some day into freehold) up to 10,-000 acres at a ha'penny an acre per annum. I intended to write a pamphlet for publication but my eyes have been giving me a lot of trouble lately and I have been unable to do more than begin it.

I have got my 100,000 acres of land but not at the place I originally intended, but I think at a better, though a little further from the coast. I have been unable to get a freehold but have got a 99 years' lease at ¹/₂ d. an acre per annum. My own opinion is that land will carry four or five sheep to the acre, but one cannot tell till one tries.

Besides coffee, tobacco and cotton appear to offer a good return.

Cotton has been produced (only in experimental plots) which has been valued by the Oldham Chamber of Commerce at 6d. a pound, or a penny more than middling American on the same day. With land and labour as cheap as they are, this should give a good return.

At present there is *no* one in the country with *any* capital except myself and some of the coast merchants, so none of these things are being developed except on a small scale, but it must be remembered that directly money is made land is sure to go up largely in value. At the

present time the land here seems to me absurdly cheap. A South African who has had much experience was here the other day and said he wouldn't take 20 acres in South Africa for one here. My own opinion is that there is a fortune for any of the early-comers that are worth anything. Of course, if markets and so on were all fixed, land could not be got at the price, or anything like it.

       .   .   .

August, 1907

Personally I can imagine no argument [he wrote] which is capable of justifying unchecked immigration of Asiatics into a country which we all of us hope may some day be part of a United South Africa, a great white colony stretching from the Cape to the Zambesi and governed for His Majesty by a true Afrikander bond.

Supposing that Indian immigration is allowed into South Africa it must carry with it that freedom which is one of the boasts of the British Empire. Indian colonists must be allowed to enter freely into competition in all trades and to hold land there. There is therefore only one choice before the Imperial Government. To choose whether South Africa is to be a colony of men of our own race holding the same ideals of civilisation and religion as ourselves, or whether it is to become an Asiatic colony peopled by a race whose civilisation is decadent and at its best stopped short of European civilisation, whose ideals and religion are totally different from our own and above all a people who undoubtedl , d I think naturally, look forward to a o when they can throw off the yoke of their white conquerors. . . .

In all new countries the backbone of the country is the small man, the white colonist with small means, but there is no place for him in a country when once the Asiatic is there. I have some years' experience myself of the newest of the colonies of the Crown in Africa and I know from personal observation and knowledge that every two or three Indians in the country mean the loss of a white colonist. There is no place for the small white man arriving in the country. All the vegetable growing for the towns is done by Indians, all the butchers with one or two exceptions are Indians, all the small country stores are kept by Indians and most of the town shops, all the lower grade clerks are Indians, nearly all the carpentry and building is done by Indians. They thus fill all the occupations and trades which would give employment to the poorer white colonists, especially those arriving new in the country.

That is what Indian immigration means in the early days of a very new country in Africa. It means that if open competition is allowed the small white colonist must go to the wall.

What is the next stage in the history of a country which has once allowed Asiatic immigration to get a foothold? The small man having been pretty well squeezed out, planters and farmers employ Indian labour, and then comes the stage that Natal has reached to-day when the Asiatics are as numerous as the white colonists and when they own large areas of land and businesses all over the country. White colonists will not go to a country which is filled with Asiatics, and the Asiatics go on increasing.

This shows again that it lies with the Imperial Government to-day to say whether Africa is to become a white daughter colony or an Asiatic granddaughter colony, to use an expression of Mr. Winston Churchill's.

And what does Indian immigration mean to the native? Because surely in Africa, in his own country, his rights both at the present time and in the future should be safeguarded. Admitting that at present he is lazy and relatively so well off that work has no particular attraction for him, will it always be so? Increasing as they do owing to cessation of wars and other benefits of civilisation, will they not be forced by circumstances into the life of

the country and have to work for a living like European or Asiatic? And is his birthright, the right to work for a living in his own land, to be taken away from him? Is it only Europeans who are affected by Asiatic competition? I should say that the Indian took the place of the African quite as much as that of the European.

And later on will it not be worse, when the African has been brought by education and training to a point where he will be able to take positions of trust and responsibility? Are these all to be taken away beforehand and given to the Asiatic? And to put the matter on a higher plane. Should not the African be protected from the decadent civilisation of India and from the influence of its Hindu religion? Is it desirable that such religions should be introduced among the African natives who are like children and capable of easily absorbing impressions?

Is the introduction of Hindu rites and practices among the natives of Africa to be calmly viewed by all the great missions which have hundreds of earnest men teaching the ideals of our own religion to the natives all over Africa?

I am fain to admit that all civilisation has a deteriorating effect on a certain proportion of natives, but in the case of the evils caused by contact with Europeans, wise laws can be enacted to prevent such evils. I submit that no government of Europeans can make laws to check the evils arising from the mixture of African and Asiatic, because the average European is incapable of understanding the mind of the Asiatic, nor can laws be enforced except by public opinion.

This I consider one of the greatest evils of Asiatic immigration into a country governed by Europeans—that owing to a lack of understanding of the Asiatic and the impossibility of getting European police capable of dealing with Asiatic crime, Asiatic police have to be employed, and only those who have seen the methods of bribery and corruption of Indian police, even when dealing with their own people, know the harm done by allowing Indian police to have control over natives.

Time after time I have heard a native say they have been stopped by an Indian policeman and when I asked them how they got away they always said, "Oh, of course I gave him something."

I earnestly hope that the very powerful missionary organisations in Africa will take this matter up. It is a thing to be remembered that public opinion sooner or later asserts itself among our own people to do the right thing by the people of the country.

56 THE DEVONSHIRE WHITE PAPER
THE INDIANS IN KENYA

In Kenya, as in South Africa, Indian immigrants were regarded with suspicion and even hostility by the European community. After World War I, Indians in Kenya began to demand equal representation with the Europeans on the Legislative Council, the end of segregation, and the right to acquire land in the highlands. Both the Indians and the European settlers sent delegations to London to plead their respective causes. In presenting their case to the Colonial Secretary, the Duke of Devonshire, both sides stressed their desire to maintain native interests. In this way both sides, but particularly the European deputation led by Lord Delamere, who emphasized the virtues of British as against Indian traditions in guiding the Africans, overplayed their hand by providing a welcome way of escape for the British government, which in 1923, in a White Paper issued by the Colonial Secretary, the Duke of Devonshire, promptly proclaimed that the interests of the African were paramount in Kenya. Kenya was not in the future to become another Rhodesia.

GENERAL STATEMENT OF POLICY

The general policy underlying any decision that may be taken on the questions at issue must first be determined. It is a matter for satisfaction that, however irreconcilable the views of the European and Indian communities in Kenya on many points may be, there is one point on which both are agreed, namely, the importance of safeguarding the interests of the African natives. The African population of Kenya is estimated at more than 2¹/₂ millions; and according to the census

From *Indians in Kenya Memorandum* (London: Her Majesty's Stationery Office, 1923), pp. 9–12. Reprinted by permission.

of 1921, the total numbers of Europeans, Indians and Arabs in Kenya (including officials) were 9,651, 22,822 and 10,102 respectively.

Primarily, Kenya is an African territory, and His Majesty's Government think it necessary definitely to record their considered opinion that the interests of the African natives must be paramount, and that if, and when, those interests and the interests of the immigrant races should conflict, the former should prevail. Obviously the interests of the other communities, European, Indian or Arab, must severally be safeguarded. Whatever the circumstances in which members of these communities have entered Kenya, there will be no drastic action or reversal of measures already introduced, such as may have been contemplated in some quarters, the result of which might be to destroy or impair the existing interests of those who have already settled in Kenya. But in the administration of Kenya His Majesty's Government regard themselves as exercising a trust on behalf of the African population, and they are unable to delegate or share this trust, the object of which may be defined as the protection and advancement of the native races. It is not necessary to attempt to elaborate this position; the lines of development are as yet in certain directions undetermined, and many difficult problems arise which require time for their solution. But there can be no room for doubt that it is the mission of Great Britain to work continuously for the training and education of the Africans towards a higher intellectual moral and economic level than that which they had reached when the Crown assumed the responsibility for the administration of this territory. At present special consideration is being given to economic development in the native reserves, and within the limits imposed by the finances of the Colony all that is possible for the advancement and development of the Africans, both inside and outside the native reserves, will be done.

His Majesty's Government desire also to record that in their opinion the annexation of the East Africa Protectorate, which, with the exception of the mainland dominions of the Sultan of Zanzibar, has thus become a Colony, known as Kenya Colony, in no way derogates from this fundamental conception of the duty of the Government to the native races. As in the Uganda Protectorate, so in the Kenya Colony, the principle of trusteeship for the natives, no less than in the mandated territory of Tanganyika, is unassailable. This paramount duty of trusteeship will continue, as in the past, to be carried out under the Secretary of State for the Colonies by the agents of the Imperial Government, and by them alone.

FUTURE CONSTITUTIONAL EVOLUTION

Before dealing with the practical points at issue directly connected with the claims of Indians, it is necessary, in view of the declaration of policy enunciated above, to refer to the question of the future constitutional evolution of Kenya.

It has been suggested that it might be possible for Kenya to advance in the near future on the lines of responsible self-government, subject to the reservation of native affairs. There are, however, in the opinion of His Majesty's Government, objections to the adoption in Kenya at this stage of such an arrangement, whether it take the form of removing all matters affecting Africans from consideration in the Council, or the appointment of the Governor as High Commissioner for Native Affairs, or provision for a special veto by the Crown on local legislation which touches native interests; and they are convinced that the existing system of government is in present circumstances best calculated to achieve the aims which they have in view, namely, the unfettered exercise of their trusteeship for the native races and the satisfaction of the legitimate aspirations of other communities resident in the Colony.

His Majesty's Government cannot but regard the grant of responsible self-government as out of the question within any period of time which need now to be taken into consideration. Nor, indeed, would they contemplate yet the possibility of substituting an unofficial majority in the Council for the Government official majority. Hasty action is to be strongly deprecated, and it will be necessary to see how matters develop, especially in regard to African representation, before proposals for so fundamental a change in the Constitution of the Colony can be entertained. Meanwhile, the administration of the Colony will follow the British traditions and principles which have been successful in other Colonies, and progress towards self-government must be left to take the lines which the passage of time and the growth of experience may indicate as being best for the country.

PRACTICAL POINTS AT ISSUE
Turning now to the practical points at issue arising directly out of the claims of Indians domiciled in Kenya, these may be considered under the following heads—

Representation on the Legislative Council
Representation on the Executive Council
Representation on Municipal Councils
Segregation
Reservation of the Highlands for Europeans
Immigration

REPRESENTATION ON THE LEGISLATIVE COUNCIL
(a) *Elective System*—In no responsible quarter is it suggested that the Indians in Kenya should not have elective representation upon the Legislative Council of the Colony. The point at issue is the method whereby such elective representation should be secured. There are two alternative methods—

(i) A common electoral roll

(ii) Communal franchise

Under the former system, Kenya would be divided up into a given number of constituencies, in each of which European and Indian voters on the roll would vote together at an election for candidates of either race, and the qualifications for admission to the voters' roll would be the same for Europeans and for Indians. Under the latter system, European and Indian constituencies would be demarcated independently, not necessarily coinciding in number or boundaries; the qualifications for admission to the voters' roll would not necessarily be the same for the two communities; and while Europeans would vote in the European constituencies for European candidates, Indians would vote in the Indian constituencies for Indian candidates.

As a variant of the former system, there is the common electoral roll with reservation of seats. This arrangement would involve the setting apart of a certain number of seats in a given constituency for candidates of a certain race; for example, in a constituency returning three members, with two seats reserved for Europeans and one for Indians, the two European candidates and the one Indian candidate highest in the poll would be elected, irrespective of the position in the poll of other candidates of either race.

The common electoral roll for all British subjects and British protected persons, with reservation of seats, was proposed in the Wood-Winterton report, and it was further suggested that the qualifications for voters should be such as to admit, if possible, ten per cent of the domiciled Indians to the register.

For the common electoral roll it is claimed that it would bridge the gap between the Europeans and Indians by giving a candidate of one race an incentive to study the needs and aspirations of the other race. Further, Indian sentiment, both in India and Kenya, strongly favours the common electoral roll, even though a communal franchise exists in India itself.

A communal franchise secures that every elector shall have the opportunity of being represented by a member with sympathies similar to his own, a consideration which in other Colonies has led the domiciled Indians to press for its adoption; it is well adapted to the needs of a country such as Kenya; no justification is seen for the suggestion that it is derogatory to any of the communities so represented, and it is believed that, so far from having a disruptive tendency, it would contract rather than widen the division between races in Kenya.

So far as Africans are concerned, a communal franchise provides a framework into which native representation can be fitted in due season.

From the point of view of the Indian residents themselves, this system permits of a far wider franchise being given than would be the case if a common electoral roll were introduced, and this alone should render it acceptable to all supporters of the Indian claims who have at heart the political development of the Indian people.

Finally, it allows of the immediate grant of electoral representation with a wide franchise to the other community in Kenya which is ripe for such institutions, the Arabs of the Coast.

These considerations were weighed before the Wood-Winterton report was drawn up; the recommendation then made turned largely on the desire to meet Indian feelings so far as conditions in Kenya would admit. The result of the reference to opinion in Kenya of the recommendation that a common electoral roll should be adopted, even though combined with a reservation of seats, was to show that the advantages claimed for the common electoral roll would in practice have been illusory. In the special conditions existing in Kenya it is clear that no candidate, European or Indian, could stand as an advocate of the interests of the other race without sacrificing the support of his own. If elections were to be fought on racial lines, as they undoubtedly would have been in Kenya, the main advantage claimed for the common electoral roll, namely, the bringing of the races nearer together, would be lost.

Having regard to all the circumstances, His Majesty's Government have decided that the interests of all concerned in Kenya will be best served by the adoption of a communal system of representation.

57 SIR JOHN MAFFEY
BRITISH RULE IN THE SUDAN

In 1924 the White Flag League was founded by Ali Abd al-Latif for the purpose of driving the British from the Sudan and uniting Egypt and the Sudan under the Egyptian monarchy. In June the White Flag League demonstrated and Abd al-Latif was arrested. In August the cadets of the military school demonstrated in Khartoum. In November, after the assassination of Sir Lee Stack, Governor General of the Sudan, the Eleventh Sudanese Battalion mutinied in Cairo and was annihilated by British artillery. Although crushed, the Sudanese revolt brought a conservative reaction on the part of the British rulers. The overwhelming number of Sudanese tribesmen and leaders remained steadfastly loyal. The British repaid this devotion with confidence, but they viewed with alarm the new class of Western-educated Sudanese that had sympathized with the rebellion. To check the Sudanese élite, whose liberalism could not be reconciled with the authoritarianism of imperial rule, the British sought to enlist the traditional tribal authorities in the task of governing and isolating the élite. Such a policy coincided with the colonial policy of indirect rule, which was then being hailed as the key to stable advancement of dependent peoples. Sir John Maffey (1877–1969) served in the Indian civil service from 1899 to 1924 and was Governor General of the Sudan from 1926 until 1933, when he became Permanent Undersecretary of State for the Colonies. He was made first Baron of Rugby in 1947.

From Sir John Maffey, *Minute by His Excellency the Governor General,* January 1, 1927 (Sudan Gov't Archives, Civil Secretary's Archives, January 9, 1933). Reprinted by permission of the Ministry of Interior.

The granting of powers to native magistrates and sheikhs is more in keeping with the prime principle [devolution of authority to tribal chiefs], but here again unless such machinery stands on a true native and traditional basis it is off the main drive. Advisory Councils cropped up as a possible means to our end but the proposal was not well received and I think there were good grounds for hesitation. Later on in certain intelligentsia areas, when we have made the Sudan safe for autocracy, such Councils may be innocuous or even desirable. Also Advisory Councils to Chiefs would be in keeping with the broad principle. Otherwise Advisory Councils contain the seeds of grave danger and eventually present a free platform for capture by a pushful intelligentsia.

If the encouragement of native authority in the true sense of the Milner formula is our accepted policy, before old traditions die we ought to get on with the extension and expansion in every direction, thereby sterilizing and localising the political germs which must spread from the lower Nile into Khartoum.

Under the impulse of new ideas and with the rise of a new generation, old traditions may pass away with astonishing rapidity. It is advisable to fortify them while the memories of Mahdism [revolt and control of the Sudan by the Mahdists, 1885–1898—ed.] and Omdurman are still vivid and while tribal sanctions are still a living force. The death of two or three veterans in a tribe may constitute a serious break with the past.

Such anxiety on my part may seem farfetched to those who know the out-lying parts of the Sudan. Perhaps it is, for I realize the wide range of differing conditions. But I have watched an old generation give place to a new one in India and I have seen how easily vague political unrest swept over even backward peoples simply because we had allowed the old forms to crumble away. Yet the native states in India remain safe and secure in the hands of hereditary rulers, loyal to the King Emperor, showing what we might have done if we had followed a different course. We failed to put up a shield between the agitator and the bureaucracy.

Political considerations are still easy in the Sudan. But nothing stands still and in Khartoum we are already in touch with the outposts of new political forces. For a long time the British Administrative Officer in the Sudan has functioned as "Father of the People." In many places he will for a long time so continue. But this cannot last. The bureaucracy must yield either to an autocratic or to a democratic movement and the dice are loaded in favour of the latter. If we desire the former, the British Officer must realize that it is his duty to lay down the role of Father of the People. He must entrust it to the natural leaders of the people whom he must support and influence as occasion requires. In that manner the country will be parcelled out into nicely balanced compartments, protective glands against the septic germs which will inevitably be passed on from the Khartoum of the future.

Failing this armour we shall be involved in a losing fight throughout the length and breadth of the land. . . .

FOUR

THE KINGDOM OF CONGO

In the fourteenth century the son of a chief of the small chiefdom of Bungu, located near Boma on the north bank of the lower Congo, conquered the plateau of Congo south of the river, taking the title *mani Kongo* and establishing his capital at Mpemba, the present-day town of San Salvador in northern Angola. The kingdom of the mani Kongo was expanded steadily as a result of the conquest of the neighboring chiefdoms, and even territories beyond to the east, southeast, and south recognized the overlordship of Congo and would send tribute and presents to the king. North of Congo, however, the African states of Tyo near Stanley Pool and Loango in the Kwilu Nyari basin maintained their independence. The Kingdom of Congo was divided into districts composed of numerous villages. The districts were governed by officials who were both appointed and removed by the king. These district officers carried out administrative duties and acted as judges. All the districts were either integrated into one of the six provinces—Soyo, Mpemba, Mbamba, Mpanga, Mbata, and Nsundi —or were dependent directly on the king. The provinces were ruled by governors who were also removable at the king's pleasure. In addition, there were officials with more specialized functions—such as the *mani lumbu,* who was responsible for the king's quarters in the capital. These officials possessed titles and formed a powerful aristocracy. At the apex of the Congo's political organization was the king, chosen after 1540 from the descendants of Affonso I by an electoral college of a dozen members. The king himself was protected by a permanent bodyguard, but war was carried out by the army, which was recruited by means of the instruction given by every territorial official to the headmen of his villages to rendezvous with all able-bodied men. The army lived off the land and could not therefore remain in the field for long. Consequently, a war was usually decided by a single battle, characterized by a general melee rather than by use of tactics or strategy. The government derived its income from taxation paid in raffia cloth, ivory, hides, and slaves. There were also the royal fisheries of Luanda Island, which provided shells used as currency whose value could be controlled by royal officials. Clearly, the Kingdom of Congo possessed a degree of centralization that few African states could match. Nevertheless, the very source of centralization, the king, proved the state's greatest weakness, for an ineffectual ruler would reduce the power of the state. Moreover, the conflicts over succession led to constant factionalism, strife, and intrigue, and the failure to establish clear rules for succession sapped the strength of the Congo just as it weakened many other African states (Olfert Dapper, *The Kingdom of Congo*).

THE COMING OF THE PORTUGUESE

In 1482 the first Portuguese caravels were sighted off the mouth of the Congo River, known to the Portuguese as Zaire, the name immortalized in the great Por-

tuguese epic poem the *Lusiad* for the mighty river emptying into the Atlantic from the center of Africa. In 1485 the Portuguese under the leadership of Diogo Cão returned, leaving four missionaries at the court of the mani Kongo in exchange for four nobles who sailed back with Cão to Portugal. The Portuguese came back again in 1487, and at that time Nzinga Kuwu, King of the Congo, sent a Congolese ambassador with a number of younger men to Portugal to request missionaries and technicians. After four years, the Congo embassy returned accompanied by missionaries and artisans. A church was constructed at Mpemba, the capital was christened San Salvador, and the king was baptized João I. The royal family and most of the nobility accepted Christianity as well. Although the king reverted to paganism after 1494, the queen mother and a son Affonso remained Catholic. Indeed, the religious rivalry reflected the opposition between two political factions in the struggle for the royal succession.

In 1506 Nzinga Kuwu died, and the rivalry between the pagan and Catholic groups erupted into open warfare in which Affonso defeated the pagan faction and was crowned king (Rui de Aguiar, *King Affonso I*). Affonso was not only devoutly Catholic but was in favor of increasing European influence. Consequently, contacts between Portugal and Congo developed rapidly between 1506 and 1512, and annual expeditions from Portugal carried priests, schoolteachers, artisans, and technicians to the Congo. Young Congolese were sent to be edu-

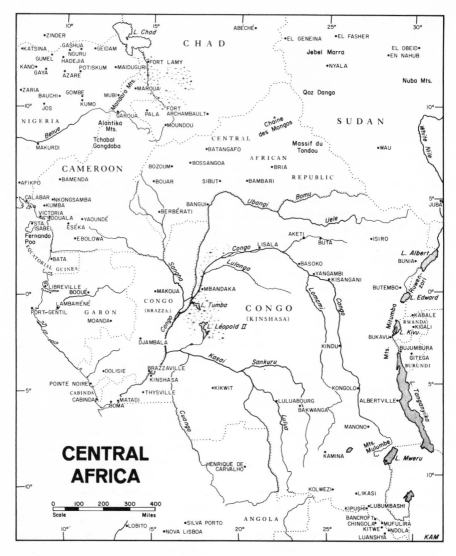

CENTRAL AFRICA

cated in Portugal, and what seemed to be a mutually advantageous relationship was beginning. Unhappily, cooperation between Congo and Portugal was soon beset by numerous obstacles. First, the Portuguese traders at São Tomé hampered the exchange of goods and detained envoys between the Congo and Portugal in order to protect their trade monopoly. Second, some of the technicians proved undesirable and unmanageable, compelling Affonso to request that an official be sent from Lisbon with special jurisdiction over the Portuguese in Congo. Third, in

1512 Simão de Silva arrived with instructions, or *regimento,* to carry out the Christianization and Lusitanization of the Congo. The regimento proved a failure. Affonso accepted many of the suggestions while refusing others, but in the long run the failure of the regimento must be attributed to the real difficulties blocking cultural change on such an ambitious scale and the immediate greed of local Portuguese traders. For a fundamental paradox conditioned Portugal's relations with the Congo that was never resolved and, in the end, greatly contributed to the collapse of the Congo kingdom; namely, that although they were willing to help Congo, the Portuguese wanted to exploit the country, and although they recognized Congo as an equal, they sought to limit its sovereignty. All the Portuguese in the Congo were inexorably drawn into the struggle to control the rapidly expanding trade in slaves, which soon compromised the more altruistic motives of the King of Portugal, and although Affonso also tried to limit the slave trade, he became increasingly powerless to do so. By 1526 the king's power throughout the country was being undermined by slave traders working with provincial officials. When he sought to restrict the European traders to the capital, they continued their raiding and trading through agents known as *pombeiros*. By 1530, 4,000 to 5,000 slaves were being exported annually, thus draining the kingdom of its vitality.

Just as Portuguese traders were eroding away the power of the mani Kongo, the Portuguese government determined to prevent Congo from communicating with other powers. In 1532 and 1539 two embassies sent by Affonso to the Vatican were blocked in Lisbon, and Portugal did all in its power to restrict Congolese relations with other European states. By the end of Affonso's reign the dream of collaboration between Congo and Portugal had vanished. The Portuguese traders acted independently, and the king was powerless to control them. In 1545 Affonso died, and with the support of the local Portuguese, Dom Diego I, grandson of Affonso, was placed on the throne (Filippo Pigafetta and Duarte López, *The Successors to Affonso I*). His succession, however, did little to change the pattern of Congo affairs conditioned by the coming of the Portuguese and fixed in Affonso's reign. The slave trade, the Portuguese factions, and the fitful efforts to educate and convert the Congolese continued for another dismal century.

The reign of Dom Diego was character-

ized by his unsuccessful attempts to control the white traders on the one hand and his more successful efforts to maintain his rule over his own people on the other. Supported by Portuguese traders at San Salvador, Diego was persuaded to go to war against the São Tomé traders, who were now dealing directly with the king's vassals and subjects. Diego's forces, however, were utterly routed, leading ultimately to the establishment of the colony of Angola. Although beaten by the São Tomé faction, Diego was able to enforce the ban on Portuguese traders going inland, but the pombeiros continued to carry out the wishes of the Portuguese traders. Diego was more successful at defeating internal rebellion, and in the spring of 1550 a plot by his principal rival was crushed. Nevertheless, his efforts to maintain internal security were always compromised by his failure to bring the white traders under close supervision and control (Monsignor Confalonreri, *São Tomé and the Slave Trade*).

THE JAGA INVASION

Diego died in 1561, and the Portuguese intervened to place Affonso on the throne. Affonso, however, was killed and was succeeded by numerous weak kings until 1568, when the *Jaga* fell on the kingdom. Erupting from the Kwango region to the south and east, the Jaga destroyed the Congolese Army and drove the king into exile on an island in the Congo River. Appealing for Portuguese assistance, the Governor of São Tomé, Francesco de Gouvea, rallied the Congolese and with his harquebuses drove the Jaga from the kingdom in 1571. Although Gouvea virtually occupied the country until 1576, the centralized Congo state continued to be racked by revolts, foreign invasion, and internal discontent, resulting in near anarchy. The Jaga meanwhile established states to the east and south and from them continued to raid the Congo (Andrew Battell, The *Jaga*).

THE LAST OF THE CONGO KINGDOM

After the expulsion of the Jaga and the retirement of Gouvea, the King of Congo sought to reestablish his authority and to disengage himself from the Portuguese. Alvare I and his successor, Alvare II, were not entirely successful in maintaining their independence against attempts by Portugal, and later Spain, to restrict their freedom. Internally they were never able to re-create the centralized Congo of Affonso I and were continually hindered by internal revolts and intrigue. (Alvare II and Alvare III, *Relations Between the Kingdom of Congo and the Papacy*). Throughout the first half of the seventeenth century, the Congolese kings were unable to reassert their authority, having lost the support of the people and their chiefs while squabbling among themselves in endless disputes over succession. In 1641, however, Garcia II came to the throne. He was to rule for twenty years, during which he succeeded in checking the disintegration of authority but was unable to establish internal peace. The slave trade (now amounting to about 15,000 slaves a year), as well as a series of natural calamities, complicated Garcia's attempts to extend his authority. The reigns of Garcia and his successor, Antonio I, were the last stand of the Congolese kings. Upon the death of Antonio in 1665 the kingdom dissolved forever into anarchy, with faction against faction, province against province, and village against village. When the kingdom was actually reunited in 1710, the king had lost all power, possessing only an empty title as a derisory memento of past greatness.

KING LEOPOLD'S CONGO

The disintegration of the Congo eliminated the last vestiges of Portugal's control, and although Portuguese slave traders continued to drain off the human resources of the Congo and the Portuguese crown continued to claim sovereignty over the region, Portuguese influence remained negligible. When Henry Morton Stanley arrived at the mouth of the Congo River in 1878, he found no trace of the Portuguese past in the Congo. Stanley's exploration of the Congo basin and his epic journey down the river excited the interest of King Leopold II of Belgium, who had taken an active interest in Africa since 1876 (Henry Morton Stanley, *The Great Rainforest of the Congo*). Leopold was eager to open up the Congo and in 1879 sent Stanley back up the river to make treaties with the chiefs that would transfer their sovereignty to the *Comité d'Études du Haut Congo*, which was organized by Leopold. Between 1879 and 1884 Stanley founded twenty-two stations and concluded over 300 treaties, firmly establishing the rights of the *Comité d'Études du Haut Congo* to the south bank of the river, while the French explorer de Brazza was laying claim to the territories along the north bank for France (Paul du Chaillu, *Trade in Gabon*).

Leopold's principal problem was to secure international recognition for the treaties concluded by Stanley, and after much skillful diplomacy and luck the king managed to convince the great powers at the Berlin Conference of 1885 to recognize the International Association of the Congo (formerly the *Comité d'Études du Haut Congo*) as a sovereign power. Called the *Etat Indépendant du Congo,* or more commonly, the Congo Free State, Leopold's Congo embraced nearly one million square miles of territory, dwarfing the old Kingdom of Congo by comparison. Although it was created by an international conference, which could theoretically "uncreate" the *Etat Indépendant du Congo,* in reality the Congo Free State was an absolute monarchy under the sole control of Leopold II. Although he established three departments (Foreign Affairs and Justice, Finance, and Interior) and a resident governor general in the Congo, the king himself managed the affairs of his state until just before his death in 1909.

The creation of the Congo Free State provided an outlet for Leopold's energies and abilities, but although the ownership of nearly one million square miles of African real estate was a sop to his megalomania, it taxed his private fortune. By 1889 Leopold had spent over 31 million francs of his own fortune to establish his rule throughout the Congo basin and administer its territory. This sum was, of course, quite insufficient to rule the Congo, and a series of loans and grants from the Belgian government followed in 1887 and 1890. Gradually, as Leopold and his agents desperately sought to make the Congo pay its way, the Free State exploited the ivory and rubber resources of the Congo. Farming out huge tracts of territory to private concessionaires, the king even formed his own company in 1896 to exploit 112,000 square miles of land called the *Domaine de la Couronne.*

The king's determination to make the Congo pay soon produced profitable results. In fifteen years he is estimated to have extracted nearly $15 million in profits on 11,345 tons of rubber, in addition to sums paid by concessionaires for the right to exploit other regions of the Congo. Ruthlessly driven to collect rubber at the expense of their fields and families, the Congolese, of course, were the ones who made these profits possible. Atrocities, hardships, and violence accompanied the Congo administration's lust for rubber, creating a wide discrepancy between the humanitarian aims professed at the founding of the state and the later malpractices (Edgar Canisius, *Rubber Collecting in the Congo*). As early as 1893 critics began to question Leopold's rule in the Congo, and, led by E. D. Morel, a British journalist and humanitarian, the criticism became so acute that in 1903 the British demanded an international inquiry on the strength of reports by Roger Casement, their consul at Boma. Bowing to the demands of the great powers, Leopold appointed a commission in 1904 to investigate. Although evidence was sup-

pressed, the report could not hide the fact that the lofty principles of the Berlin Act had been forgotten and that if Leopold's regime was not tyrannical, it was certainly most harsh indeed. The Report of the Commission of Inquiry did not still the clamor against Leopold's rule, however, and in November 1908 the Belgian Parliament took over the Congo, paying its king 50 million francs in addition to the 45 million francs that were paid for the beautification of Belgium and annuities for the royal family.

THE BELGIAN CONGO

When Belgium took over the Congo Free State in 1908, she had no experience or tradition of colonial rule, and her colonial policy was shaped more to deal with the immediate problems of administration and development than the political future of the Congo. Practical considerations thus determined the main lines of Belgian policy, clearly reflected in the basic law of the colony, the *Carte Coloniale,* which made no reference to the political status of the Congo. Since Belgium had been forced to take over the Congo by the maladministration of Leopold, the Congo must therefore be administered to prevent such atrocities in the future. Moreover, Belgium had to give evidence that she was doing something for the Africans. These philanthropic themes fitted Belgian attempts to exploit the mineral resources of the Congo, which were first being tapped at the end of Leopold's rule. The development of the great mines of the Congo has led some to conclude that the Belgians sought to develop the economic potential of the Congo while neglecting the needs and services of her inhabitants. This picture, however, is inaccurate, for the mineral wealth permitted development of social and health services second to none in colonial Africa.

Belgium's administration of the Congo was never marked by a large influx of European settlers (*colons*), and those who did come were equipped with large resources and capital. Thus the European settlers in the Congo never became sufficiently numerous to demand control of the government. But as the number of European settlers remained small, the growing urbanization marked by improvement in services to Africans resulted in nearly a quarter of the Congolese living in towns. The administration of the Congo was the responsibility of the Minister of Colonies, who issued the orders for his representative in the Congo—the Governor General. The Minister of Colonies in turn was advised by a council of nominated members, so that in fact the Congo was ruled by a small number of men—experts who scorned the political aspects of governing and steadfastly kept Belgian politicians out of Congo affairs.

The predominant characteristic of Belgian policy was economic development. As a heritage from the Congo Free State, the economic policy guided all others so that over 50 percent of the wage-earning population was involved in 3 percent of the commercial enterprises, which in turn held over 86 percent of the capital investment. Labor policy was designed to provide a stable labor force for industry without depleting the rural areas. Those Africans who were permitted to go to the industrial areas were educated and trained to become highly skilled technicians. The "stabilized labor policy," however, required careful control of the movements of Africans, which was frequently annoying if not oppressive. As a counterpart to industrialization, the administration in the Congo sought to create a peasant agriculture in an effort to increase African agricultural output. Such schemes were not always successful in the face of the shifting cultivation practiced by Africans in the Congo. Education under Belgian rule was guided by two principles. As in the British territories, instruction was given first in the vernacular, unlike the French colonies, where all instruction was carried out in French. Moveover, the emphasis of education in

the Belgian Congo was practical. Education was designed to create a useful class of craftsmen or agriculturalists to provide the administration with clerks and industry with technicians and artisans. Unlike the French and British colonies, no attempt was made to develop an African élite trained to occupy the higher administrative and political posts. Thus the education did not identify the Congolese with Belgium but concentrated on manual training. Many generations of Africans in French and British territories had passed through universities before the Congo possessed an institution of higher learning (Le Pétillon, *Native Policy in the Belgian Congo*).

THE COMING OF INDEPENDENCE

Belgian rule in the Congo was thus a form of paternalism that tempered the technical training of the African with political suppression. The placid conditions that such a policy created were rudely disrupted in 1959 by widespread rioting in Léopoldville. Spurred on by the sentiments for independence expressed during and after World War II and excited by the example of other African territories that had received their independence, the African demand for a greater say in the administration of the Congo was not surprising (Patrice Lumumba, *Crisis of Confidence*). Unfortunately, no political élite or quasi-political organization existed through which this discontent could be constructively channeled into a nonviolent transfer of authority. Receiving little support either from the Western powers, which were beginning the process of dismantling their African empires, or from the Belgian people themselves, the small group of men who controlled the Belgian administration in the Congo precipitously promised elections and ultimate independence. The Congolese replied with demands for immediate independence, supported by rioting and violence, and the Belgian government had the choice of administering by force or granting the demands for independence. At the Congo Round Table Conference held in January 1960, the Belgians capitulated, agreeing to grant immediate independence to the Congo. Thus the Congo raced toward independence led by an army with no Congolese officers and possessing only a handful of Congolese with university training to advise the new government. On June 30, 1960, the Congo became independent, the celebrations of which were tempered by warnings and grim forebodings on the future of tropical Africa's largest state.

THE ARRIVAL OF THE BANTU IN SOUTHERN AFRICA

Although the Bantu arrived in southern Africa approximately at the beginning of the Christian era, Bushmen, or Khosian-speaking peoples, and scattered bands of pygmies had long inhabited the plains and plateaus south of the Congo rain forest. These were Stone Age peoples, hunters and gatherers, who retired before the advancing Bantu or sought refuge in isolated pockets bypassed by the Bantu immigrants. Moving down the spine of Africa, the vanguard of the Bantu probably reached the plateau country south of Lake Tanganyika a few hundred years before the birth of Christ, to be followed by additional migrants in subsequent centuries. The pattern of migration may have been that of the ravaging band of hunter-warriors moving far and fast without many women and children and settling where they pleased. More likely, the movement of the Bantu was conditioned by their shifting cultivation, in which groups would settle, slash, and burn the vegetation and carry on cultivation for a few years until the soil was exhausted, thus forcing them to move on. Equipped with iron implements, the Bantu carried iron-working techniques southward and brought central and southern Africa into the Iron Age. Always pressing south-

ward, the Bantu crossed the Zambezi and settled on the plateau of Mashonaland in what is now Rhodesia. By 1000 A.D. the Bantu were south of the Limpopo.

ZIMBABWE

Sometime around 1000 A.D. dry stone construction was begun on the Mashonaland plateau, and the foundations of the impressive ruins at Zimbabwe were probably built in the eleventh century. Contemporaneous with the stone construction was the increased gold mining activity to satisfy the demands of Arab traders from the East African coast. During the subsequent centuries a thriving Bantu civilization developed in Mashonaland, during which Great Zimbabwe was completed. Comprising an acropolis of a massive defensive fortification, the structure contains intricate passageways and rooms. The acropolis appears to have been the original building, but as late as the eighteenth century an elliptical or great enclosure was constructed with embankments and a conical tower below the acropolis in the valley. All the great walls and buildings were built of cut stone fitted without mortar and dominated by the tragic solitude of the uninhabited valley. Indeed, Zimbabwe demonstrates such a high level of technological advancement that many of the Europeans who first saw the site in the nineteenth century refused to consider its construction by an African people. As a result, numerous theories were developed to explain its existence. Some argued that Zimbabwe was built by Phoenician sailors. Others have attributed the ruins to southern Arabian origins or even, incredibly, early Portuguese adventurers. In 1929 Caton-Thompson investigated the Zimbabwe ruins and conclusively demonstrated that they were of Bantu origin. Although a few authorities continue to question where and how the Bantu acquired the Zimbabwe technology, all are in agreement that the Bantu built Zimbabwe.

THE MWANAMUTAPA

During the centuries during which the Zimbabwe ruins were being constructed, new Bantu migrants continued to pour into the Rhodesian plateau, changing the ethnographic character of the region. The Sotho people probably crossed the Zambezi as early as the eleventh or twelfth century and remained for several hundred years until they were pushed south of the Limpopo into the northern Transvaal by the invasion of the *Shona* in the fifteenth century. The origins of the Shona are unknown, but they are a Bantu people that probably came, like other Bantu, from the north down the eastern highlands. The early Shona invaders consisted of related clans, such as the *Karanga, Zezuru,* and *Rozvi.* The Rozvi appear to have been a dominant clan, whose King Mutota led the Shona nation on a military expedition south from Zimbabwe to the Matopo Hills in the mid-fifteenth century, subjugating the autochthons. He then turned northward to make his headquarters just south of the Zambezi, taking the name *mwana mutapa* (master pillager).* During the next half-century Mutota and his son Matope led a succession of conquests that spread the borders of Rozvi influence from the Zambezi to the Limpopo and from the Indian Ocean to the Kalahari Desert. This was the short-lived empire of the mwanamutapa. By the end of the fifteenth century the empire began to fall apart. Matope tried to divide the administration of the confederation among brother, sons, and trusted vassals, but within a decade the southern provinces had broken away under their Rozvi ruler, a grandson of Mutota named Changa, who adopted the Arabic title amir and became the changamir. Overextended communications, political intrigue within the ruling circles, and lack of cultural and ethnic homogeneity were factors too strong for the mwanamutapa to over-

come. For another generation the mwanamutapa struggled in a series of wars to reassert his position over his rebellious vassals, principally the Rozvi. He failed and died about 1530 at the time of Portuguese penetration up the Zambezi.

The first European visitor to the mwanamutapa was the Portuguese *degredado* (outcast) Antonio Fernandez. In 1514 he reached the capital of the mwanamutapa and reported that the gold of Sofala originated in the land of the mwanamutapa. Consequently, for another half-century the Portuguese sought to establish direct contact with the interior. Sena was occupied by Portuguese troops in 1531 and a few years later Tete was founded. After 1550 a Portuguese trader resided at the court of the mwanamutapa as a free-lance adviser to the ruler. Ten years later the Jesuit Goncala da Silveira reached the mwanamutapa, but was murdered on suspicion that he was simply spying so that the Portuguese could conquer the empire. Francisco Barreto sought to avenge Silveira's death, but his expedition was unsuccessful. Only in 1574, when Vasco Fernandes Homem marched from Sofala into the empire, did the Portuguese learn that the gold fields of the mwanamutapa could not be worked economically without machinery. Portugal subsequently lost interest in the interior until late in the nineteenth century, when the scramble for Africa had begun (Manuel de Faria e Sousa, *The Kingdom of the Monomotapa*).

Meanwhile the plateau south of the Zambezi was invaded by groups of wandering warrior peoples like the Jaga coming from the Kasai or the more terrifying Zimba, who roamed unchecked throughout the shrunken state of the mwanamutapa in the 1590s. In 1628 mwanamutapa Kapararidze unsuccessfully sought to rally the Shona nation to drive out the Arab and Portuguese traders. With Portuguese help a puppet chief was installed and was maintained with Portuguese support until his death in

---

*The title *mwana mutapa* was frequently associated with his kingdom and was known to the Portuguese as monomotapa or, more correctly, mwana mutapa.

1652. By this time the "mwanamutapa" had become a nominal title, which was brought to an end by the return of the Rozvi in the last part of the seventeenth century. At first, Rozvi relations with the mwanamutapa remained friendly, but at the end of the seventeenth century the ruling changamir swept northward and established his hegemony throughout Mashonaland. Here the Rozvi ruled, occupying the stone forts in the south, including Great Zimbabwe, and even building new stone enclosures. Their work, however, never reached the quality of the mwanamutapa, and their political and economic organization never rivaled that of the earlier period. Gold production declined, the Rozvi appearing content to raid rather than to develop.

THE LUNDA STATES

Southern Rhodesia was not the only area in Central Africa in which state systems developed. To the northwest of Zimbabwe beyond the Zambezi River in the savanna regions below the Congo rain forest, complex states developed from the unification of a number of villages. The largest and most comprehensive was the Lunda Empire and its offshoots the Kingdom of Kazembe and the Yeke kingdom. The Lunda Empire began from a nuclear territory north of its present location in the Kasai. From there small groups of villages broke off and settled in outlying areas to meet the demands of an increasing population. Nevertheless, the villages maintained relations with one another through the notion of perpetual kinship among their leaders, so that by the sixteenth century Lundaland was already a loose but single political unit. Subsequent Lunda rulers unified these villages either by sending royal emissaries to receive the submission of local headmen or, when necessary, by conquest. The Lunda continued to expand into Angola, Katanga, Northern Rhodesia, and other territories where people did not recognize kinship ties with the Lunda. At first small groups of Lunda adventurers would migrate to these areas and assume political control through the prestige associated with their name, the superiority and adaptability of their political system, and their own aggressive spirit. Political control by Lunda chiefs was later followed by large migrations of Lunda subjects. Thus the main agent for establishing Lunda hegemony was not military might but political skill. Indeed the Lunda did not even have a regular standing army but depended entirely on irregular forces.

The foundation of the Lunda political structure was the village and its surrounding land. Villages were ruled by a council of elders and a hereditary headman who could be deposed only by the king. The villages were organized into groups according to the ties of perpetual kinship among their headmen. These groups of headmen were ruled by an elder, or *mbay,* and were grouped into districts under a *cilool.* The cilool was responsible for collecting taxes from his district for the king, and any report of dishonesty or inefficiency on the part of the cilool would bring a royal official called a *yikeezy* to supervise his activities. The central government was comprised of the king and his titleholders. The king's authority came from his power to nominate or dismiss officials and to create new titles. Tribute was paid to the king once a year and was the cement that held the empire together, for the provinces were free to do as they pleased so long as tribute was paid. The whole political structure of the Lunda Empire rested on the twin mechanisms of political succession and perpetual kinship. Each new official inherited the personal status as well as the office of his predecessor. In this way the political structure was divorced from the real descent structure and was not tied to any principle of descent in particular. Such a system could be diffused without necessitating any changes in the existing social structure, thus enabling many divergent cultures to be assimilated. Even after military defeat the local rulers were retained in honored and respected positions.

THE KINGDOM OF KAZEMBE

In the middle of the eighteenth century, a Lunda group migrated to the Lualaba and under its king, Kazembe, carved out a virtually independent Lunda state that embraced the territories from Lake Tanganyika to the Lualaba and to the south of Lake Bangweulu. Although the Kingdom of Kazembe was a state of the Lunda Empire, it remained the strongest Lunda kingdom until 1850, bringing security to the local population of the southern Katanga but also heavy taxation, some unwarranted cruelty by Lunda governors, and a restriction on the freedom of many formerly independent clans (Father Pinto, *The Kingdom of the Kazembe*). The kingdom, which succeeded because of the great prestige of the Lunda political system, has been remembered for its trade contacts with the Portuguese on the East African coast (P. J. Baptista, *The Kazembe*).

THE BEGINNINGS OF ANGOLA

At the beginning of the sixteenth century, the small chiefdom of Ndongo was founded by a wealthy smith who imposed himself as king with the title of *ngola* on the people north of the Cuanza River. By mid-century successive ngola had expanded the kingdom north to the Dande River, and in 1556 it became independent from Congo. From the early years the ngola appeared to have desired contacts with the Portuguese to enrich themselves by trade and to enhance their prestige. From the 1540s traders visited Kabasa, the capital of Ngola, and finally, in response to the requests of the Nadambi ngola, the Portuguese court sent four Jesuit priests to Kabasa under the leadership of Paul Dias de Novais. The party arrived in May 1560, but negotiations over missions and trade languished. In 1565 Dias was sent back to Portugal to secure mili-

tary assistance for the ngola, and in the following year he returned, determined to obtain a trade monopoly in Angola. With the assistance of the Jesuits Dias was granted a *donatario,* or feudal grant with all its rights and responsibilities. In 1571, by the terms of this grant, he received the lands south of the Cuanza but agreed to colonize Angola at his own expense (Filippo Pigafetta and Duarte López, *Paulo Diaz de Novais in Angola*).

In February 1575 Dias appeared off the island of Luanda with 400 men. He settled first on the island and then moved to the mainland, where he constructed the town of Luanda. Dias was convinced that huge silver mines existed in the interior in the territory of the ngola and was determined to seize the mines. Dias marched against the Ndongo forces in 1579, plunging Angola into forty years of continual skirmishes, raids, plunder, and pillage that finally ended with the defeat of the ngola after the Jaga had joined the Portuguese as allies. By 1622 the Portuguese appeared to have triumphed, but Nzinga, the new queen of Ndongo, renewed the war and the struggle continued (Giovanni Cavazzi, *Queen Anna Nzinga*).

The Portuguese efforts to expand the colony were hindered by the clash of entrenched interests. The Jesuit priests wanted a theocracy and the Portuguese soldiers and conquistadores sought only to profit from the trade in slaves, whereas the home government vacillated and was ineffectual in establishing its authority. The colony itself was populated largely by exiles, convicts, and criminals—hardly the type to bring the culture of Europe to Angola. In 1641 the Dutch allied themselves with the African powers opposing the Portuguese and captured Luanda, but their occupation was brief. In 1648 Salvador de Sá y Correa arrived with a fleet from Brazil, retook Luanda, and brutally crushed the African chiefs who had supported the Dutch. In 1656 Queen Nzinga made peace with the Portuguese, maintaining her independence but abandoning

Ndongo territory west of the Lukala River. Although the peace between the Portuguese and Nzinga was kept until her death in 1663, thereafter the Angolan settlers steadily expanded, their ambitions checked only by the power of the African states in the interior. By the end of the century the colony of Angola controlled over 50,000 square miles between the Dande and the Cuanza rivers inland to the Kwango and from Benguela all the way to the southern tip of the highlands.

The Portuguese divided Angola into *presidios* (captaincies), in which the military commander was the absolute ruler. As an absolute despot he controlled the chiefdoms that were formerly ruled by the old vassal chiefs of the ngola, or by settled Jaga chiefs, or by previously independent chiefs. All were now vassals of the commanders of the presidios, whose principal policy was to exploit the Africans to the fullest extent without precipitating rebellion. In addition, the three towns of Luanda, Masangano, and Benguela were ruled by town councils. (That of Luanda, the *camara,* was particularly powerful.) Responsibility for the colony lay with the governor, who acted on orders from Portugal but had to consult closely with officials and the camara. Everyone in Angola was involved directly or indirectly in the slave trade, and little distinction was made between traders and officials. Graft and corruption characterized official life, drawing the colonists into the slave trade with its spiral of violence as they urged expansion, war, and conquest in order to acquire slaves. During the eighteenth and nineteenth centuries Angola stagnated as none sought to exploit any but human resources. At the same time it became a predatory state in its quest for slaves. For the African, life in Angola was one of terror and misery.

So deeply entrenched a system could not be easily uprooted, and although the rise of humanitarian interests in the nineteenth century forced Portugal to abolish the slave trade in 1836, the decree was ignored and was not fully enforced until 1845—and then only by a British naval squadron. Abolition soon followed in 1858, but the spirit of slavery in Angola died hard, continuing into the twentieth century under different names. Thus after 300 years and in spite of the claims of Portuguese occupation regarding the ability of the Portuguese to adapt themselves to Africa and the Africans, in 1850 Angola was a land whose population had been plundered in return for a few crumbling fortresses, with scarcely any visible signs of Christianity or European civilization.

THE BEGINNINGS OF MOZAMBIQUE

In March 1498 Vasco da Gama anchored in Mozambique harbor and then sailed on up the East African coast to India. Vasco da Gama was followed by other Portuguese expeditions, which culminated in that of Don Francisco de Almeida, who sailed into Mozambique in 1505 with twenty-two ships and 2,500 soldiers and sailors, forced the ruler to acknowledge the suzerainty of Portugal, and then continued northward to establish Portuguese control over the city-states of East Africa. By 1507 the Portuguese had abandoned the pretense of rule through the local chiefs and established direct control over Mozambique, which soon became the center of Portuguese authority in southeastern Africa. Nevertheless, Mozambique, which is located on the tip of an African headland that juts into the Indian Ocean, remained chiefly a revictualing station on the sea road to India. Portuguese ships called here, and the small Portuguese community looked more to the sea than inland to the interior of Africa. Further south, however, Sofala became the center from which Portuguese traders and adventurers moved into the interior. Sofala had been occupied in 1505, and in the following year Diogo de Alcaçova reported that Sofala derived its wealth from the interior kingdom of the mwanamutapa. Although Antonio Fernandes reached the capital of the mwanamutapa in the sixteenth century, it was not until the Arabs began to drain off the gold trade that Portugal decided to protect the trade by intervention in the hinterland beyond their coastal settlements. Accordingly, in 1531 Portuguese troops occupied Sena on the Zambezi River and a few years later established Tete further upstream, not far from the capital of the mwanamutapa. Troops and traders were soon followed by Jesuits, but after the expedition of Vasco Fernandes Homem failed to find easily worked gold mines, few Portuguese ventured into the hinterland. Thereafter, until the nineteenth century, Portugal lost interest in the interior, leaving it to the half-caste settlers who lived in barbarian isolation on their estates and a few missionaries who competed for converts at Sena, Tete, and the court of the mwanamutapa (Antonio Suarez, *The Conversion of the Monomotapa*).

COLONIZATION AND SETTLEMENT

Portuguese attempts to colonize Mozambique and Angola were confined to sending *degradados,* beggars, thieves, assassins, and political exiles to Africa, for the industrious Portuguese never seriously considered going to the colonies. There were no white women and no attempt was made to attract them, so that a large half-caste population appeared, which in Mozambique created the *prazo* system in Zambezia. The *prazeros* were wild half-castes who carved feudal estates for themselves in the Zambezi Valley. A typical prazero was Antonio Vicente da Cruz, known locally as Bongo (Charles Livingstone, *The Prazeros*). Illiterate, thieving, cruel, barbarous, and a drunkard, he was a sufficiently powerful baron to defeat a Portuguese army numbering over 1,000 men that was sent against him in 1850. Gradually, by the end of the nineteenth century, the prazeros were ousted from

Zambezia in favor of Portuguese *colonos,* colonists who would work and develop the land and the chartered companies that were given exclusive rights to trade and exploit mineral resources. Neither solution was a great economic success, but both were better than the prazo system. As for the Africans, they were no worse and probably no better off than they had been under the prazeros.

In Angola colonization took much the same form as in Mozambique, and except in Luanda and Benguela, the Portuguese lost their identity. In 1845 Benguela had 600 houses, 38 white men, and one white woman (Hermenegildo Capello and Roberto Ivens, *Benguella in 1877*). By 1900 the white population of the whole colony was less than 9,000. Poverty, immorality, and degradation are perhaps the most accurate terms to describe Angola and Mozambique in the nineteenth century.

MISSIONARY EFFORTS

The Christianizing of Africans had been a cardinal policy of Portuguese expansion since the days of Henry the Navigator. Portugal's historic combat with the Moors invested it with a traditional mission to implant the faith among the heathen, while the insularity of Portugal conditioned its Catholicism with a narrow and provincial outlook. Vasco da Gama's remark, "I seek Christians and spices," was not mere rhetoric, and the most Catholic of nations regarded with pride its mission to carry Christ to Africa. Unhappily, the performance of Portuguese missionaries never matched the visions of its statesmen, and Portugal lamentably failed to Christianize Africa. The climate certainly took its toll of priests, who were never numerous, and many of them had come to Africa not for Christ but to seek their own fortunes and to satisfy their passions. But the principal reason for the failure of Portugal's missionaries was that they offered nothing to the African but a disembodied doctrine, of which many of the disciplines and disciples were distinctly distasteful. Where were the superior advantages of European civilization that went with this faith? In the slave trade, in armed incursions into the interior, in the examples of Portuguese traders who were more African than European? By the mid-nineteenth century Mozambique had only six missionaries, and the long involvement of the Jesuit missionaries of Angola in the slave trade was a mockery of their evangelization. By 1850 only five missionaries were left in the colony. Although the numbers of Catholic missionaries increased in the twentieth century and even Protestants were allowed to proselytize, neither group has yet understood the basic requisite of spreading Christianity in Portuguese Africa. If the African is to be drawn into a Christian community, he must be treated with Christian dignity and understanding.

SLAVE TRADE, SLAVERY, AND CONTRACT LABOR

Portuguese participation in the slave trade was neither worse nor better than that of other nations, the only distinction being that Portugal was one of the first to participate and one of the last to give it up. Portugal exploited the African not because he was African but because he was exploitable. Between 1680 and 1836 over 2 million slaves, acquired from African chiefs, from pombeiros, in wars against tribes, and as the refugees from intertribal strife, were taken out of Angola. Slaves were held in barracoons on the coast before being carried to Brazil. Probably 10 to 20 percent died during the middle passage. By the mid-nineteenth century the slave trade was largely curtailed by the British Navy, but slavery remained until 1869, when it was officially abolished. In fact, abolition meant little, and what had formerly been slavery was now euphemistically called forced labor, obligation labor, or contract labor. Although colonial officials later argued that the African could best be "civilized"

through work, there is not much evidence to support this rationale.

REVIVAL OF PORTUGUESE INTEREST

The European exploration, scramble, and partition of Africa stimulated new Portuguese interest in its African colonies, symbolized by the Colonial Act of 1895. The new era was characterized by efforts to consolidate the administration, devise a new native policy, and develop the resources of the colonies. The task of consolidating the administration was to execute in Africa the legislation that was drawn up in Lisbon. Although the Liberal government that took power in Portugal introduced humanitarian reforms, such reforms had little effect. The attitude of the governors was frequently opposed to liberal legislation and, for the most part, the European population of the colonies remained indifferent to proposals for the emancipation of Africans. Finally, many laudable projects died for want of trained personnel to execute them.

During this period the concept developed among Portuguese colonial officials that the African was a child who must be brought up slowly to civilized adulthood. No attempt was made to understand the African or his culture, which was dismissed by pious platitudes and conventional superficialities that in the end made the native problem less complex but more burdensome. From this attitude arose the practices of assimilation and miscegenation. If an African Europeanized himself (or, more correctly, became a black Portuguese), he would be accepted without prejudice so that a Portuguese could take an African wife or mistress without shame. Thus, although it never became official colonial policy, miscegenation was invested with moral dignity and equalitarian significance.

PORTUGUESE AFRICA IN THE TWENTIETH CENTURY

The interest in the African colonies that was aroused in Portugal at the end of the nineteenth century could not be sustained, and by the 1920s Angola and Mozambique had once more relapsed into the lassitude that had characterized their earlier centuries of rule. This condition did not last, however, and under the regime of Antonio Oliveira da Salazar, great efforts were made to turn Angola and Mozambique into assets for the mother country. Salazar first sought to whip up enthusiasm for the colonies by recalling the great maritime traditions of the golden age of Portuguese expansion mixed with historic traditions of Lusitanian overseas policy. The colonial mystique was compounded out of the cartographic sweep of Portuguese holdings, the heroic literature of the Portuguese epic poet Camoëns, and the lure of the hidden riches of the colonies for the profit of Portugal and her subjects. The Portuguese Empire was to be a far-flung, pan-Lusitanian community held together by the spiritual bonds of Portuguese culture.

The greatest task facing Portugal was to convert this vision into reality. The foundations of the new colonial administration were laid down in the Colonial Act of 1930, which sought to unify and center the administration of the colonies at Lisbon, to nationalize the economies of the colonies, and to emphasize the sovereignty of Portugal. The colonies became provinces of Portugal and the administration in the colonies was revised to conform to that of the metropole. A governor general supervised each colony and was responsible for the administration and operation of government. He had extensive powers, which were executed by the governors over the districts into which the colony was divided. The key men were the local administrators, who combined the judicial, executive, and legislative authority all in one. Under this pyramidal administrative organization the African was under the closest possible control—peace and calm were preserved but enterprise and initiative were discouraged and restricted.

Out of the authoritarian purpose and mystique of the Salazar regime evolved a policy of assimilation of the Africans, which, in the past, had been but mere expediency. The purpose of the policy was to eliminate the African as a separate element so that his identity would become completely Portuguese. As one Portuguese official put it:

Our whole policy has been and continues to be to improve the cultural, economic and social level of the Negro, to give him opportunities, to drag him from his ignorance and backwardness, to try to make him a rational and honorable individual worthy of the Lusitanian community.

The policy was based on legislation first fashioned in 1926 and reinforced in 1929, 1933, and 1950. Nevertheless, assimilation remained but a dream. In spite of its humanitarian language and its proposals for social and economic service, the policy was little more than an attempt to preserve the status quo. In 1950 only 30,000 assimilados existed in Angola out of a population of 4 million, and only 4,353 were registered in Mozambique out of a population of 2.5 million. Any policy designed for the population as a whole that affects less than .5 percent can hardly be described as a success, in spite of the fact that, in this case, the long and traditional acceptance of the African and the products of miscegenation favored assimilation. The very poverty of Portugal herself worked against assimilation. Education, which was clearly the main instrument for making the Africans Portuguese, remained selective and open to only a few. Medical services were limited and frequently discriminatory. Christianity, like education, was a cornerstone of Portuguese civilization, and yet the number of priests and converts remained small in spite of the protection and encouragement of the state. Moreover, if the goal of the Portuguese was assimilation, it could be acquired only through work. Although slavery and forced labor had gone or had been ameliorated, the attitude that produced them had changed little. The African was still regarded as a lazy child who must be disciplined, and the best way to instill discipline was through labor. Thus a system evolved to coerce the Africans to labor, but the recruitment and contracts were often abused by the government itself, no less than by companies. In an expanding economy the need for labor was so great that such abuses were tolerated by the home government, but the failure to eliminate corruption or the system itself hardly convinced the Africans of the value of Portuguese culture.

PORTUGAL'S COLONIES IN FERMENT

The poverty of Portugal's policies in Africa was first glaringly exposed by the forces of nationalism that swept through the continent in the mid-twentieth century. First the Sudan and Ghana, next the French territories, and then the Belgian Congo and Nigeria all experienced the rise of African nationalist groups whose determined opposition, both violent and nonviolent, to colonial rule led inexorably to self-government and independence. The Portuguese colonies of Angola and Mozambique could hardly have remained immune from the nationalism on their borders. Sparked by the granting of independence to the Congo in 1960, Angolan nationalism collided with the more determined nationalism of Portugal. Proud of her long, if inept, colonial rule and convinced of her mystical role as a governing power, Portugal was intent on remaining in control of her colonies. Violence was met by force, but supported from camps in the Congo, Angolan nationalists continue to remain in the field despite attempts by Portuguese military forces to crush them. The Portuguese are determined to retain their African holdings. The first Europeans to arrive in Africa, the Portuguese will probably be the last to leave.

THE RETURN OF THE SOUTHERN BANTU

At the beginning of the nineteenth century, Central Africa was invaded by the northward march of Ngoni into the highland areas from the Limpopo to Lake Tanganyika. Between 1785 and 1789 a Ngoni chief, Dingiswayo, united the independent sections of the Ngoni peoples, including the Zulu, which occupied the present-day lands of Natal. In the early nineteenth century, Shaka obtained power in one of the regiments that Dingiswayo had organized for conquest, managed the death of Dingiswayo, and made himself chief. The people he ruled became known as the Zulu. Through the military despotism he founded and by the use of his Spartan military society, Shaka sought to impose his authority on other Ngoni, subjugating some and driving others away. Fleeing from Shaka, one group of Ngoni crossed the Limpopo and laid waste to Mashoaland in their northward march to the Zambezi. Another Ngoni group, the Ndebele (also known as Matabele), led by Mzilikazi, settled on the high veld north of the Limpopo and raided far and wide over the lands between the Kalahari Desert and eastern Nashonaland. (Robert Moffat, *Mzilikazi*). Meanwhile, in 1835 the main group of Ngoni crossed the Zambezi and moved on through th highlands west of Lake Nyasa as dissident segments splintered in all directions—north into Tanzania, east to the Rufiji and Ruvuma rivers, and west through the territory of the Bemba and Bisa to what is now Zambia. During their march the Ngoni pillaged and ravaged the inhabitants of Trans-Zambezia, including the remnants of the Maravi (Malawi) confederacy (A. C. P. Gamitto, *The Maravi*), disrupting their social and political patterns and making easier the European conquest that soon followed.

The Ngoni chiefs created their states by adding the conquered to the original Ngoni nucleus, but frequently the Ngoni were a minority and took wives from subject tribes, the Ngoni language thus giving way to that of the non-Ngoni mothers. Not all the Ngoni, however, lost their identity. By 1840 Mzilikazi's Ndebele established themselves north of the Matopo Hills, where the previous Ngoni groups had broken the resistance of the indigenous inhabitants, who, like the Shona, were reduced to tribute-paying vassals, whereas others were assimilated by the Ndebele. Thus the Ndebele retained their own language and customs under Mzilikazi's autocracy. By 1870, when Lobengula succeeded Mzilikazi, the Ndebele had fashioned the strongest state in Central Africa, with a highly centralized political organization supported by a powerful and well-trained army.

THE LOZI KINGDOM

Northwest of the Ndebele in Barotseland the Lozi had occupied the floodplain of the upper Zambezi. From about 1833 to 1835, however, the Kololo, another Ngoni group fleeing from Shaka, moved north and west under the leadership of Sebitwane, crossed the Zambezi, and defeated the Lozi. So long as Sebitwane lived, he was able to control Barotseland, but his successors soon lost the confidence of their subjects, and under Njekwa, the Lozi threw off Kololo domination. Njekwa and his successors continued to expand the Lozi kingdom until, under Lewanika, the Lozi exerted control over the peoples of the upper Zambezi.

DAVID LIVINGSTONE

David Livingstone set out for Africa in 1840 as a medical missionary for the London Missionary Society. He established himself at Kuruman in Bechuanaland, but he soon began to look for new sites for mission stations in the north. His passion for exploration grew out of his missionary investigations, and in 1849 he crossed the Kalahari Desert. Determined to range even further afield, he set out in 1853 to march north to the Zambezi and with the help of the Kololo chief,

Sekeletu, pressed on up the river and overland to Luanda, which he reached in 1854. He remained in Luanda but soon plunged back into Africa, traversed the continent, and emerged at Quilemane on the east coast in 1855.

Livingstone returned to England a famous man, and he used his fame to open an attack on the slave trade that he had seen both in Angola and on the lower Zambezi. In order to end the slave trade, Livingstone advocated new forms of commerce and Christianity to develop "civilization" in Africa. Not only did his explorations encourage others to seek answers to the many geographical riddles of Africa (foremost among them being the source of the Nile), but Livingstone himself returned to Africa to ascend the Zambezi, which he hoped would be a "highroad" into the interior. From 1859 to 1863 he and his companions of the government-sponsored expedition pressed up the Zambezi and Shire rivers. Although he was frustrated by the rapids at Tete, Livingstone was successful in discovering Lake Nyasa and the Shire highlands, but his expedition was a failure in its principal objective—to open a way to Central Africa. Nevertheless, in spite of its failure, Livingstone's Zambezi expedition made a profound imprint on the public mind in England. The expedition's tragic record, its revelation of new and fertile country, and its discovery of how to cut the slave trade at its source fired the public imagination and inspired a host of missionary societies to establish themselves on the fringes of Central Africa—Lake Nyasa and the Shire highlands.

MISSIONARY BEGINNINGS IN CENTRAL AFRICA

Livingstone's example inspired missionary societies in England and France to press into Central Africa to end the slave trade and to introduce Christianity and European commerce. The Universities' Mission to Central Africa (UMCA) was a direct response to Livingstone's appeal.

It failed. The UMCA first established itself in the Shire highlands, but as a result of the deaths of several of its members and the lack of African response, it soon transferred its operations to Zanzibar. Even the advance of the London Missionary Society further west from Kuruman to Inyati at the borders of Matabeleland was stalled. Malaria and the geographical obstacles to penetration checked the efforts of the missionary societies.

The death of Livingstone in 1875 revived missionary interest in penetrating into Central Africa, and the *Société des Missions Evangéliques de Paris* sent a mission to Mashonaland led by François Coillard in 1877. Barred from Matabeleland by Lobengula, Coillard founded his first mission at Sefula on the edge of the Barotse plain, and under the patronage of the great Lozi chief Lewanika expanded his work among the Lozi. In 1893 Coillard was followed by the Methodist missionaries under Arthur Baldwin, who founded stations among the Lozi on the Nkala River. While Coillard's French Protestants and Baldwin's Methodists were carrying on in the west, the Free Church and the Established Church of Scotland sent missionaries to Lake Nyasa, where they were joined by a Scottish commercial concern, the Livingstonia Central Africa Company, in an attempt to end the slave trade by a mixture of Victorian commerce and Christianity. Finally, in 1890, the last of the early mission societies, the Roman Catholic White Fathers, entered Central Africa from its stations in the north, in Uganda and Tanganyika, and established a station at Mambwe between lakes Nyasa and Tanganyika.

Although few in number, the European missionaries had a profound effect on Central Africa. In general, they acted independently of either European or African control. They maintained their own supply routes to the coast and even acted as traders with the African population. They tried, not infrequently by force, to impose their own concept of law and order and even sought to extend political authority over the Africans. Few of the missionaries, no matter how consciously they tried, could abstain from meddling in African politics. In return, the missionaries brought Christianity to Central Africa. Perhaps more important, they brought the beginnings of modernization in the form of hospitals, schools, and European products, which dramatically changed the life of the Africans who inhabited Central Africa.

THE DEFENSE OF TRANS-ZAMBEZIA

The influx of British missionaries into Central Africa, particularly Nyasaland, became of increasing concern to the Portuguese, who possessed long-standing and traditional pretensions to the hinterland beyond the East African coast. Consequently, after 1880 the Portuguese government sought to reassert its claims. At the same time the British, heeding the pleas of the Scottish missionaries for protection, refused to recognize Portugal's sovereignty in those parts of the interior that were neither occupied by Portugal nor operating under Portuguese jurisdiction. To support the missionaries, the British government sent a consul, Henry Hamilton (later Sir Harry) Johnston, to watch over British interests in Nyasaland and to take responsibility for British relations with the African chiefs. Johnston's appointment, however, only served to stimulate countermeasures by the Portuguese. After 1884 Portuguese officials made efforts to extend their real authority to Nyasaland and in 1887 even obtained the recognition of Portuguese sovereignty by several African chiefs. Elsewhere the Portuguese sought to hinder the passage of goods and equipment to the African Lakes Company on Lake Nyasa. These supplies included guns and ammunition to carry on the war against the Arab slave traders in Nyasaland, which effort, of course, could not be separated from the endeavors of the Scottish missionaries and traders to consolidate their control.

Meanwhile, in Britain the representatives of the missionaries and traders urged the British government to declare Nyasaland a protectorate. They combined the usual arguments of the economic and strategic value of Nyasaland with the prospect of losing the Africans to Catholicism if the Portuguese succeeded in making good their claims to the interior. Although the British government expressed sympathy for the position of the missionaries and provided moral support for the campaign of the African Lakes Company against the slave trade, a succession of British foreign secretaries refused to declare a protectorate over Nyasaland. By 1889 the issue clearly remained in doubt.

CECIL RHODES

The British missionaries who led the advance into Central Africa were shortly followed by British trading firms. The African Lakes Company was the vanguard of British interests in Nyasaland, whereas south of the Zambezi in Mashona and Matabeleland the extension of the British Empire had become the personal mission of Cecil John Rhodes. Rhodes came from England in 1871 at the age of eighteen in order to preserve his health. He first tried cotton growing, but when diamonds were discovered in Griqueland he set out for the diggings. Rhodes made his initial capital by selling food and equipment to the miners and then began to buy up the small individual claims. In 1880, in partnership with Alfred Beit, he amalgamated these small holdings into the huge DeBeers Consolidated Mining Company. Rhodes used his wealth to carry out his political ambitions. He had a passionate faith in the destiny of Englishmen to carry the torch of Anglo-Saxon civilization throughout Africa and the world and wanted to open new territory for English settlers to colonize and to civilize. Such territory lay beyond the Boer

republics of the Orange Free State and the Transvaal. The boundaries of these republics had been fixed by the Pretoria Convention, but the Boers sought to extend their control north of the Limpopo and west of the Transvaal, an action that would, of course, frustrate Rhodes' dream of empire in the north. In 1887 Paul Kruger, President of the Transvaal, sent Piet Grobler to the Matabele capital at Bulawayo to obtain permission for the passage of Boers beyond the Limpopo. Although he concluded a treaty with Lobengula in 1887, Grobler was later killed, and Rhodes' representatives at Bulawayo subsequently won over Lobengula to sign a treaty granting Rhodes mineral rights in Matabeleland. Once armed with the consent of Lobengula to enter Matabeleland, Rhodes sought a royal charter for his company in order to acquire administrative as well as commercial powers in Central Africa.

In the past the British government had been quite reluctant to extend its responsibilities to Central Africa, whether Nyasaland or Mashonaland. Protectorates were expensive and offered little hope of immediate return, but if a commercial company agreed to undertake the onerous financial and administrative burden in return for commercial exploitation, the British government welcomed such assistance to maintain British interests in the region. Thus, when Rhodes arrived in London in 1889, enormously rich and politically successful, he offered to pay for the colonization and administration of Bechuanaland and Matabeleland and to push telegraph and rail lines northward. He further agreed to obtain for Britian the territory north of the Zambezi, including Nyasaland. The British Prime Minister, Lord Salisbury, agreed to let Rhodes expend his fortune for the extension of the British Empire. Rhodes' company was chartered as the British South African Company, with authority to colonize and govern the territories north of the Limpopo. In addition, Rhodes agreed to support the activities of Harry Johnston in Nyasaland.

NYASALAND AND NORTHEASTERN AND NORTHWESTERN RHODESIA

Between 1889 and 1890 Johnston traveled up the Shire Valley and along Lake Nyasa, making treaties with African chiefs and encouraging the British missionaries and traders. His efforts were rewarded in 1890 when Lord Salisbury sent a gunboat to Mozambique and ordered the Portuguese to remove their troops from Mashonaland and the Shire highlands. Portugal submitted, and Harry Johnston returned in 1891 as "Her Majesty's Commissioner and Consul General to the territories under British influence to the north of the Zambezi" with instructions to declare a British protectorate over the Shire highlands, thereby frustrating the designs of Portugal. With the assistance of Alfred Sharpe and the well-known African explorer Joseph Thomson, he negotiated a host of treaties with chiefs between Lake Nyasa and Mweru that could be used to support British claims if challenged by European rivals. While Johnston was extending the British Empire in the Shire Valley and Lake Nyasa, Rhodes' representative, Frank Lochner, obtained the signature of Lewanika, the Lozi king, to a treaty forfeiting control of Barotseland and its mineral rights to the British South Africa Company. Although Lewanika did not appreciate the full extent of his action, the Lochner treaty gave the company a claim to rule in western Trans-Zambezia and to exploit the rich copper deposits. Thus in 1891 Trans-Zambezia was divided into three protectorates: Nyasaland (known as the British Central African Protectorate), northeastern Rhodesia, and northwestern Rhodesia. Johnston governed both Nyasaland and northeastern Rhodesia from Zomba in the Shire highlands, while agents of the British South Africa Company administered the land of the Lozi,

Barotseland (northwestern Rhodesia). By employing Sikh soldiers recruited in India, Johnston was able to pacify and consolidate British administration in Nyasaland. He believed that tropical Africa "must be ruled by whites, developed by Indians, and worked by the Blacks." He therefore encouraged the settlement of European colonists and introduced Asians to organize the commercial life of Nyasaland. Meanwhile, the British South Africa Company gradually took over the administration of northwestern Rhodesia and, by governing directly, eclipsed the Lunda state of Kazembe and the Ngoni state under Mpexeni. By 1901 all the inhabitants of the lands north of the Zambezi were British subjects governed by the agents of the British South Africa Company.

THE CREATION OF SOUTHERN RHODESIA

Having extended British influence into Barotseland and northeastern Rhodesia, Rhodes was determined to occupy Matabeleland and Mashonaland. Despite the agreements and treaties he had signed with prospectors and Rhodes' agents, Lobengula retained undisputed control of the lands between the Limpopo and the Zambezi. His fearsome and powerful Ndebele *impis,* or raiding parties, ranged widely over Central Africa, exacting tribute and submission to Lobengula. Rhodes sought to break Lobengula's control of the Mashona plateau by sending in settlers who would consolidate British control against any attempts either by the Portuguese to press inland from the east or by the Boers to come from the south in the hope of discovering gold. Led by Colonel Leander Starr Jameson and guided by the great hunter Frederick Courtney Selous, the specially selected pioneer column guarded by some 500 company policemen marched into Matabeleland, bypassed Lobengula's capital of Bulawayo, and pressed northward to found Fort Salisbury in the heart of Mashonaland. Declaring Mashonaland British, the pioneers were soon joined by other white Europeans, who forcefully acquired *Shona* lands.

Mashonaland never fulfilled the expectations of the settlers. Its soil was unsuited to intensive farming or grazing, and workable gold deposits were not discovered. Moreover, the expense of transporting goods from South Africa was exorbitantly expensive, making the position of the settlers virtually untenable. Consequently, the pioneers began to press into Matabeleland, where they hoped to find the gold and grazing they had failed to discover in Mashonaland. Lobengula and his Ndebele opposed the probings of the settlers. They feared that the white prospectors would take their land, and they resented the protection the Europeans gave to the Shona, whom the Ndebele considered their traditional vassals. In 1893 a large Ndebele impi raided Mashonaland, pillaging not only the Shona but the farms and livestock of white farmers. Several Africans were killed but no whites lost their lives, although the inhabitants of Fort Victoria were terrorized by roaming Ndebele warriors. Jameson, who was charged with administering the colony, ordered the impi to leave. When it tarried, the settlers attacked the Ndebele, driving them back to Bulawayo. Although the British government refused to encourage aggressive action, the settlers, supported by the British South Africa Company's mounted police, advanced into Matabeleland late in 1893. After several skirmishes and a few desultory battles, Bulawayo was captured and Lobengula was driven to the north, where he died in 1894. His followers made peace. This ended the Ndebele's first revolt, but not their resistance.

Although various assurances concerning their treatment had been given by Jameson at the time of their surrender, the Ndebele soon found themselves herded into reserves where the soil was the least fertile and water scarce, their best land having been taken by the settlers. The settlers also seized Ndebele cattle as reparations and forced the Ndebele to work on their farms so that they could pay the taxes imposed by the administration. Humiliated and resentful, the Ndebele were attracted to the leaders of a revitalized religious cult who used their widespread following to unite the Ndebele and Shona peoples behind a mass revolt against white rule in 1896. At first only the Ndebele rebelled, but their success in destroying European farms and besieging European towns led the Shona to rise in the north. The company and settlers fought back on two fronts to regain their undisputed control of Rhodesia. In July the Ndebele were crushingly defeated but fought on from the safety of the Matopo Hills until Cecil Rhodes personally persuaded the Ndebele chiefs to surrender and accept the rule of the British South Africa Company (Ndansi Kumalo, *The Matabele Rebellion*). In the north the Shona rebellion dragged on until the following year before the chiefs were captured and the Shona warriors were hunted down. By the end of 1897 the white settlers had demonstrated their superiority, Rhodesia had been conquered and occupied, and the settlers began to govern themselves under the paternal rule of the British South Africa Company, theoretically as a colony of the British Empire. Although the superior military power of the British almost ensured their defeat, the Ndebele-Shona uprising forced Rhodes to acquiesce to many of the demands of the Ndebele chiefs before they would surrender. Moreover, the limited success achieved by the united Ndebele people was not forgotten by subsequent nationalist leaders.

CENTRAL AFRICA UNDER COLONIAL RULE

Controlled by the British South Africa Company, following the pacification the Rhodesias were carved up into large reserves (usually of the least desirable land) for the Africans, while well-watered land near the railway was alienated for European settlement. The policy of the company was to segregate Africans and Europeans, assuming that those Africans who "squatted" on European lands or who sought employment on the farms or in the cities were temporary residents. To control the movements of Africans, "passes" or identification certificates were issued and laws were passed to maintain segregation. Although the number of Europeans in Nyasaland was never so great as in the Rhodesias, the alienation of land followed a similar process, so that the Africans soon found themselves paying rent on land where they had possessed security of tenure.

Once the white settlers had acquired large land holdings, they required labor to work their farms. As in East Africa, the settlers argued that the employment of Africans presented a "civilizing influence" and persuaded the government to institute means to force the Africans to work for the settlers. This was usually accomplished by taxing the Africans, who were then forced to labor for the Europeans in order to earn the wherewithal to pay their taxes. In Nyasaland tax defaulters' huts were burned or their wives seized as hostages. In Southern Rhodesia the company pressed the chiefs to supply labor for the European farms. Thus gradually throughout Central Africa the Africans offered their labor for European services to acquire cash for taxes and new wants.

Soon the European settlers began to form themselves into pressure groups— local chambers of commerce or planters' associations—to demand representation in the legislative councils of the colonial administration. Although the settlers were accorded a certain amount of satisfaction, in Northern Rhodesia and Nyasaland their demands for increasing authority were resisted by the colonial administrators, who were frequently the only defenders of African rights. In Southern Rhodesia, however, the white settlers had possessed a large say in governing the colony from its inception, and in 1907 they obtained a majority of seats in the legislative council and urged the company to administer the country on their behalf.

Although the Africans had been forced to submit to European rule, they continually protested their subordinate role. Throughout the Rhodesias and Nyasaland the principal means of protest were African separatist churches, where millennial preachers sought to lead their followers to the kingdom beyond colonialism and promised an independent, tax-free Africa. Perhaps the most influential was John Chilembwe of Nyasaland, who openly opposed the measures that he regarded as intolerable for the Nyasas. He spoke out against taxes and protested the use of African troops to fight Europe's wars. Establishing a chain of churches and schools, he led his followers in an unsuccessful rising against British rule in Nyasaland in 1915. Although he failed, Chilembwe had made it perfectly clear to those who cared that in Central Africa the Africans were not happy under British rule. In Northern Rhodesia, the African Watch Tower or Kitawala movement acted as a similar organization of discontent, which spoke of the end of the world and the destruction of colonial rule. Although not openly rebelling, the Watch Tower movement continued to offer a millennarian solution to the economic, political, and social subordination to European colonial rule.

CENTRAL AFRICA BETWEEN THE WARS

Following World War I and the influx of veterans to Central Africa, white settlers in each of the territories sought greater control. In Southern Rhodesia the settlers had voted in favor of home rule in 1922, and in the following year the British government formally annexed the colony, ending the rule of the British South Africa Company. Permitted to rule their own internal affairs, the settlers sought to frame racial policies designed to meet the interests of the settler community. Thus in the Land Apportionment Act of 1930, Africans were prohibited from living in European areas, except singly or in specific locations. Beyond in the reserves, pressure on the land continued to mount at an alarming rate. In 1931 half of the 96 million acres of Southern Rhodesia were controlled by 50,000 whites, whereas about a million Africans possessed rights to 28 million acres. Yet without African labor, Central Africa could not have been developed. The Africans dug for minerals and harvested the tobacco crop that provided Southern Rhodesia with capital for development but nevertheless remained second-class citizens. Dr. Godfrey Huggins (later Lord Malvern), Prime Minister of Southern Rhodesia from 1933 to 1953, was the creator of the "two pyramid" scheme of racial development based on strict segregation, which was enforced by the "pass" laws (Lord Bledisloe, *Native Policy in Rhodesia, 1938*).

During the years before World War II the settlers of Central Africa sought to amalgamate the Rhodesias and Nyasaland. In 1936 representatives of the settler community met at Victoria Falls and agreed to work toward that end. Although Huggins and others urged amalgamation, a royal commission sent to study the matter found that liberal Europeans and Africans opposed any arrangement that would allow settlers to rule the protected peoples of Northern Rhodesia and Nyasaland. The issue was deferred.

While the south fell increasingly under the control of its European settlers, Northern Rhodesia was dramatically transformed by the beginning of a great mining industry. After 1924 the development of the rich copper deposits created mining towns that attracted both European and African labor. New towns sprang up; the industry boomed, survived the depression, and during World War II brought great wealth to Northern Rhodesia. Yet the growth of the copper belt

created as sharp a pattern of discrimination as that experienced in the agricultural south.

THE STIRRINGS OF AFRICAN NATIONALISM IN CENTRAL AFRICA

Despite the bitter opposition of African leaders, the two Rhodesias and Nyasaland were at last forged into a federation in which there was to be a partnership between white and black. There were, to be sure, great economic advantages in the federation of Central Africa, but politically it meant the entrenchment of white rule throughout Nyasaland and Northern Rhodesia as well as in the south. In the autumn of 1953, the federation was made official, but ironically, instead of ensuring white domination, it hastened the time when Nyasaland and Northern Rhodesia would govern themselves.

In 1958 nationalists from all over Africa met at Accra to attend the first All-African Peoples' Conference. Both Hastings Banda and Kenneth Kaunda attended and departed determined to break up the Central African Federation and struggle for independence by force if necessary. Throughout 1959 tension and militant agitation swept through Nyasaland and Northern Rhodesia. Mission buildings were burned, property was destroyed, and police were stoned. Discontent escalated into open violence, which was stopped only by the appearance of Rhodesian troops in Nyasaland and the arrest of Banda. Nevertheless, the violence marked only the beginning, not the end of African nationalism. Banda, leading his new Malawi Congress Party, and Kaunda, with his United National Independence Party, soon won victory in the elections, toppling in the process the structure of the Central African Federation and leading to the complete independence of Northern Rhodesia, called Zambia, and Nyasaland, known as Malawi, in 1964.

58 OLFERT DAPPER
THE KINGDOM OF CONGO

Olfert Dapper (1636–1689) was a Dutch geographer who wrote one of the best seventeenth-century accounts of Africa. He acquired his information firsthand from Dutchmen who had traded and fought along the coast of western Africa. He describes in this selection three critical periods in the history of the kingdom of Congo: the introduction and impact of Christianity, the invasion of the Jaga, and the rebellion of the Count of Soyo at the time when the kingdom was disintegrating. The introduction of Christianity into the kingdom of Congo was one of the most fascinating but futile experiments in European-African relations. In 1568 the Jaga crossed the Kwango River, defeated the Congolese army, and destroyed the capital of San Salvador. Although their origins are still unknown, the Jaga probably had some connection with the Luba-Lunda peoples of the interior. The Jaga were cannibals but not savages, for after sacking the kingdom of Congo, they retired to the south and east, where they founded states. Located at the mouth of the Congo River, Soyo was one of the six provinces of the kingdom of Congo that was ruled by a governor who was originally removable at the king's pleasure, but after 1491 the office became hereditary in the lineage of the then-ruling governor, who later took the Portuguese title of count.

CHRISTIANITY IN THE CONGO

Before the Portuguese entered the land of Congo, the inhabitants were extremely idolatrous, and each one fabricated a god to his own fancy. The Congolese adored dragons, serpents of a prodigious girth, billygoats, tigers, and other ferocious beasts, imagining that the honors they accorded them would stop them from doing harm. Birds, grass, trees, even the skins of animals filled with straw were the object of their cult. Their religious ceremonies consisted of genuflections and prostrations. They covered their heads with dust and offered to the idols whatever was most precious to them. Finally, about two centuries ago, Christianity (or at least a semblance of the Christian religion) was introduced into the kingdom.

In the year 1484 Dom João II, the Portuguese king who sponsored the discoveries of the coasts of Africa and the route to India, had a fleet equipped under the leadership of Diogo Cão, who, having ar-

From Olfert Dapper, *Description de l'Afrique* (Amsterdam: Wolfgang, Weesekerge, Boom, and Van Someren, 1686), trans. by Nell Elizabeth Painter and Robert O. Collins, pp. 355–358. Material in brackets has been supplied by Professor Collins.

rived at the mouth of the Zaïre [Congo] and having learned from the signs made by the few Negroes whom he met on the coast that there was a powerful king in the interior, sent some of his people to him. But seeing that they did not come back, he took with him four Congolese who seemed intelligent and promised to bring them back in fifteen moons. The King of Portugal looked kindly upon these foreigners, and having had them taught the language and religion, he sent them back with presents under the same pilot. When he was once again anchored at the mouth of the Zaïre, Diogo Cão sent one of these Negroes to the King of Congo to beg him to send back his Portuguese to him because he had brought back the Congolese, as he had promised.

During their stay in that land, the Portuguese had so put themselves in the good graces of the Count of Soyo, the uncle of the king, and had impressed him with such a great horror of idolatry and such a vivid interest in our mysteries that the prince went to find his nephew, the king, and strongly encouraged him to abandon pagan superstitions and to embrace Christianity. Because the king was half-convinced, he asked Diogo to bring Cacuta, one of the four Negroes who had been with him in Portugal, so that, acting as his ambassador, Cacuta would ask King Dom João for priests to instruct his people. Cacuta learned Portuguese and Christianity so well that he was baptized with his followers. He left King João, after having received a thousand signs of friendship, and brought back with him priests, images, crosses, and other church ornaments, whose novelty was received by the Negroes with great admiration and pleasure.

The first to receive baptism in the country were the Count of Soyo and his son, who were baptized on Christmas Day of the year 1491. The count was given the name Emmanuel and his son was named Anthony. The king, his wife, and the younger of their children did the same and took the names of the House of Portugal. Thus, the king was named João, the Queen Eleonor, and their son Affonso. A great many people of both sexes followed the example of their princes, and since then the Portuguese have expended much effort to banish pagan idolatry among these people. That is why they established several posts for schoolmasters who would teach reading, writing, and the principles of religion and that is why they support many Portuguese and mulatto priests who celebrate the mysteries according to the ceremonies of the Latin Church. But even though the majority of these Negroes outwardly profess to be Christians, the greater number are still idolatrous in their hearts and secretly worship false gods, tigers, leopards, and wolves, imagining that in this way they will escape feeling the effects of their fury. They are straightforward hypocrites who act like Christians only in the presence of Europeans and who have more respect for their king than they do for the true God. Those who live around the churches and under the gaze of the Portuguese have their marriages blessed by the priest, but they are not willing to go very far to seek

this benediction; furthermore, even those who receive it do not in the least admit to the condition under which it is given, and they take as many concubines as they can feed.

The Negroes of Soyo are Christians of the same strength; they all have two strings in their bows—the Catholic religion and paganism, and when the saints do not answer their prayers, they invoke the fetishes. Yet to see them all covered with crosses and rosaries one would take them for sanctimonious people. Many churches and many Negro and mulatto priests are found in their province. When the Count of Soyo goes to mass, he dresses himself superbly and wears golden chains and collars of coral. He marches pompously to the sound of drums and horns, surrounded by guards among whom there are five or six musketeers who fire from time to time and others who carry flags and are followed by a great crowd of people.

Between 1644 and 1647, at the request of the King of Congo, the Pope sent a mission of Capuchins from Sicily and Cabis to that country. As the Capuchins entered Soyo, the count kept a few of them, and the others spread throughout the kingdom of Congo. The Negroes of the province of Oando [Luanda] are good Christians, according to what they say; at least great care is taken to make good Catholics of them. There are churches, Negro schoolmasters, and priests who baptize and say mass.

THE JAGA INVASION, c.1570

During the time of Alvarez I, successor and son-in-law of Dom Diogo, the last prince of the old family of the kings of Congo, the Jagas of Ansico and Angola brought the kingdom close to ruin. These Jagas are people without faith, king, or religion—wandering nomads of the plains, or rather robbers of the open road, like the Arabs. First they crossed the province of Mbata and put it all in blood and flames.[1] Then they came to camp on the plain before San Salvador. They defeated Dom Alvarez in an ordered battle and forced him to retreat into the city with great losses. But the prince, not feeling safe within the walled city, abandoned his capital to be pillaged and fled to a small island called *Ilhas das Cavallas,* because horses are found there. He took with him a great many Portuguese and the principal lords of the land. As masters of the city, the barbarians reduced it and the churches to ashes and took a great many men prisoners and subsequently killed and ate them. During these disasters, the land was uncultivated and the peasants hid themselves in the forests and mountains; consequently, food became so expensive that a slave worth ten crowns was sold for a loaf of bread. Most of the peasants died of hunger and the others sold themselves to the Portuguese, who shipped them to the island of São Tomé. Thus princes of the blood and lords of the kingdom found themselves reduced to the condition of slaves. Of those who sought refuge on the island, nearly all died of sickness because of the stench of the air. The king contracted dropsy, from which he never fully recovered, and which left him with swollen legs for the rest of his days.[2]

Seeing no other remedy for his miseries, the king finally resolved to send an ambassador to Portugal to implore King Dom Sebastian to send help, which he agreed to do, preparing a regiment of six hundred men. When several gentlemen and volunteers had joined the group, the captain of the squadron, Francisco de Gouvea, set out for Africa. Having called at the island of São Tomé and having furnished themselves with arms and provisions, they went to get the King of Congo, his men, and a few horses that were found on the

Ilhas das Cavallas. They immediately put down on dry land. There were several battles between the Jagas and the Portuguese, in which the barbarians suffered more and fled, frightened by the discharges of the muskets and the noise and fire of the cannon. Even so, one-and-one-half years were needed to clear the country of these brigands and to reestablish the King of Congo to his kingdom. Put back on his throne, this prince was so grateful to the King of Portugal, his benefactor, that he sent him an ambassador to thank him and to ask for priests to reestablish Christianity in the lands belonging to him. He gave them letters in which he offered to become a vassal of the Portuguese crown and to pay an annual tribute in slaves, but Dom Sebastian graciously refused and sent him a very obliging response in which he addressed him as brother and said that he would be satisfied if only he would constantly preserve the Christian religion. After four years had passed and Francisco de Gouvea saw that he was no longer necessary in Congo, he left several Europeans who had come there with him and returned to Portugal.

WAR BETWEEN THE KING OF CONGO AND THE COUNT OF SOYO

The Count of Soyo is the most powerful vassal of the King of Congo, but he is not the most faithful or the most subject. Because the forest of Findemguolla encompassing his states serves as a strong bulwark and renders him nearly inaccessible to a great army, this count no longer wants to recognize the King of Congo as his sovereign and believes that he should be given the status of an ally. This was the count who, at the instigation of the Portuguese, set fire to the stores of the Dutch East India Company; but when the States-General [of the Netherlands] made themselves masters of Luanda São Paulo in the year 1643, he was obliged to reestablish these stores.

[1] Mbata was the eastern province of the kingdom of Congo (ed.).
[2] Probably edema or swelling caused by an abnormal accumulation of fluid in the interfibrillar tissue (ed.).

In the year 1636, a war took place between the King of Congo, Dom Alvarez II by name, and the Count of Soyo. Having raised troops and received a reinforcement of eighty Portuguese commanded by the Governor of Luanda São Paulo, the king wanted to invade the lands of the count, but this invasion was not as easy as he had thought, because the people of Soyo set up an ambush in the woods, surprised him, cut his army to pieces, and took the king to their master as a prisoner. To buy back his freedom, the king was forced to cede divers lands to the count. Of these the most important was the principality of Mocato. The following year, the king wanted revenge and put a new army into the field but was defeated a second time. These two victories gratified the people of Soyo and their count, but the self-esteem of the Congolese was undiminished, and they blamed their misfortune on the imprudence of Dom Alvarez, who despised his enemy out of false bravado. Instead of overwhelming him with a multitude of countless soldiers, which he could have raised from his lands, Dom Alvarez attacked his foe with weak forces. Thus these two battles, instead of producing peace, sowed the seeds of a longer and more bloody war between these two princes in the year 1641, the occasion of which I will describe.

Dom Daniel de Silva, son of Dom Michel, Count of Soyo, seeing himself excluded from paternal succession by a powerful intrigue, retired into the lands of the Duke of Bamba [province of kingdom of Congo], where he was poorly received. In time, the enemies of Dom Daniel died, and he was recalled and reestablished himself in Soyo with the good wishes of all the people. Dom Daniel may have wanted revenge or he may have been using the bitterness between himself and the Duke [of Bamba] as a pretext to break away and become independent; in any case, Dom Daniel neglected to go pay homage and did not ask for confirmation from the King of Congo, saying that his birth and his free election by his subjects gave him sufficient right to the throne. Irritated by this disdain, the king invested Prince Dom Affonso, his son, with the principality of Mocato, which Dom Alvarez had ceded to Count Michel. Because Dom Affonso had raised troops to go and take possession of his new state, the Soyolese did the same. The two sides came to blows on April 29 of the year 1645. The royal army was cut to pieces, the prince and his principal chiefs were made prisoners, and, according to the custom of these barbarous people, all their heads were cut off and were carried triumphantly on the end of long poles, amid much dancing and jumping about. Only Prince Affonso was spared, by order of the count, his cousin, who treated him in a manner consistent with his rank.

One can imagine the state in which this defeat and capture put the King of Congo. The following year he gathered as many people as he could and put an army in the field that was so large that it seemed to flood the province of Soyo. He gave command to the Duke of Bamba who, followed by nearly all the nobility of the kingdom and three or four hundred mulattoes, approached the enemy's frontiers. However, the count's people, who were in ambushes scattered throughout the Findemguolla forest, charged them spontaneously and with so much valor that the general, the nobles, and the most courageous soldiers were left dead on the field; the others sought their safety in flight. Such a great loss reduced the King of Congo to the most trying extremes. He realized that he was no longer able to obtain his son's liberty by force of arms and that he would have to buy it with a fat ransom and cede new provinces to the count. The moment the prince was free, the Congolese could no longer suffer their vassals congratulating themselves on their victories and tried to seek all means imaginable to revenge themselves and ruin their vassals. Thinking that the Soyolese would be more afraid of a foreign militia than of his own, the king sent letters and ambassadors to Brazil to Count

Maurice, Governor of the States-General in the West Indies, with two hundred slaves and a good chain for the governor and other slaves for the counselors of state. Having been warned by this action, the Count of Soyo also sent three ambassadors. One ambassador went to Holland and the other two went to Maurice to beg him to remain neutral. The Dutch governor, who was allied to the princes, thought that the best course would be not to get involved but rather to preserve his position as mediator. That is why, after having written to his lieutenants in Congo and Angola to bring about a satisfactory peace between the two nations, he assembled their ambassadors and gave them presents for themselves and their masters. To the King of Congo he sent a red velvet coat with gold and silver braid, a coat of silk, and a beaver hat with a cord of gold and silk. To the Count of Soyo he sent a chain covered with silk embroidered in gold and silver, a coat, a beaver hat, and a saber whose shoulder belt was decorated with a silver fringe. Nevertheless, the King of Congo and the Duke of Bamba were not content. They sent new ambassadors to Count Maurice, who again gave them a warm welcome and sent them to Holland. They took letters from their master to the States-General, to Prince Frederic Henri, and to the intendants of the East India Company. These men were very black, robust, and agile, and in order to make themselves more supple, they rubbed themselves regularly with palm oil. They seemed to be born tightrope walkers and gladiators, for they knew how to do prodigious jumps and fence in a surprising manner. Some of the gentlemen of the States-General, having invited them to dinner, had the pleasure to see them demonstrate the manner in which the King of Congo sits on his throne and shows his majesty by profound silence. They also saw how the Negroes adore their prince, according to ancient pagan superstition.

59 RUI DE AGUIAR
KING AFFONSO I

Rui de Aguiar, a Portuguese missionary, worked in the Congo as Vicar-General during the second decade of the sixteenth century. The following description of the greatest King of Congo, Affonso I (Mvemba Nzinga), who ruled from 1506 to about 1545, is contained in a letter dated May 25, 1516 from Rui de Aguiar to King Manuel of Portugal. A genuine and devout convert to Christianity, Affonso sought to establish Catholicism and to carry out a program of westernization in the Congo. Only a shrewd and able king could have abandoned the traditional sanctions of divine kingship and introduced new customs to challenge the old without disrupting the kingdom or losing his throne.

This king, Dom Affonso, has nothing else in mind but Our Father and His

Rui de Aguiar to King Manuel of Portugal, May 25, 1516, in Willy Bal, *Le Royaume du Congo aux XVième et XVIième Siècles. Documents d'Histoire* (Kinshasa: Éditions de l'Institute National d'Études Politiques, 1963), pp. 71–72. Trans. by Nell Elizabeth Painter and Robert O. Collins. Bracketed material has been supplied by Professor Collins.

manifestations. He has presently ordered that every man in all his kingdom pay the tithe,[1] saying that the light must be carried in front and not behind.

In his quality as a Christian, Your Highness will know, it seems to me, that

[1] A tax, usually ten percent, for the support of the church (ed.).

he is not a man but an angel whom God has sent to this kingdom to convert it, according to the things he says and expresses. For I swear that he teaches us, and he knows the prophets and the gospel of Our Lord Jesus Christ and all the lives of the saints and all the things of our sacred mother the church better than we ourselves know them. I swear that such a sight would greatly astonish Your Highness. He says things so well phrased and so true that it seems to me that the Holy Spirit always speaks through him, for he does nothing but study, and many times he falls asleep over his books, and many times he forgets to eat and drink for talking of Our Lord, and he is so absorbed by the things of the Book that he forgets himself, and even when he is going to hold an audience and listen to the people, he speaks of nothing but God and His saints. He studies the sacred gospel, and when the priest finishes saying mass, he begins to preach to the people with great love and charity, asking these people and begging them, for the love of Our Lord, to convert and turn themselves toward God—so much so that his people are taken by amazement and we, even more so, by his virtue and the faith he has in Our Lord. And he does that every day, and he preaches, as I have described to Your Highness.

Your Highness will also know that he is very just and that he greatly punishes those who adore idols and that he burns them with their idols, and that he has, throughout his kingdom, ministers of justice to seize all those of whom it is learned that they possess idols or carry on sacrilege or any other bad actions touching our saintly Catholic faith. And again,

throughout his kingdom he has sent many men, natives of the country, Christians, who have schools and teach our saintly faith to the people, and there are also schools for girls where one of his sisters teaches, a woman who is easily sixty years old, and who knows how to read very well and who is learned in her old age. Your Highness would rejoice to see it. There are also other women who know how to read and who go to church every day. These people pray to Our Lord at mass and Your Highness will know in truth that they are making great progress in Christianity and virtue, for they are advancing in the knowledge of the truth; also, may Your Highness always send them things and rejoice in helping them and, for their redemption, as a remedy, send them books, for they need them more than any other things for their redemption.

I am not speaking [here] of the great love and friendship that the King of Congo has for Your Highness. I have heard him say, in fact, that he asked Our Lord not to let him die before having seen Your Highness. I also have heard him say that Your Highness was King of the Congo, and he, King of Portugal. These things he says often to whomever wants to hear them. By that, Your Highness will know that all that I say is very true, and if I write a lie to Your Highness, may God destroy me, body and soul. And may Your Highness remember the very great good that has begun and for that Our Lord will give him the retribution he deserves.

Done today, the twenty-fifth day of the month of May of the year MDXVI.

60 FILIPPO PIGAFETTA AND DUARTE LÓPEZ
THE SUCCESSORS TO AFFONSO I

Filippo Pigafetta (1533–1604) was an Italian writer and humanist. His popular Relatione del Reame di Congo *drew European attention to the kingdom of Congo. Pigafetta's informant was Duarte López (c. 1550–c. 1623), a merchant who visited the Congo on a trading voyage in 1578. In 1583 the King of Congo, Alvaro I, sent López as an ambassador to the pope with a mining concession for the Vatican in return for papal support to counter Portuguese influence. The pope refused the concession. In Rome López collaborated with Pigafetta on the* Relatione. *Whether or not he returned to the Congo is unknown.*

While these works undertaken in the service of God were being carried on [in 1543] and Christianity, still in its beginnings, was spreading in such a favorable way, it pleased God to call King Dom Affonso to him. The manner in which he died heightened the merits of his past life. His faith was great, he showed that his time had come and he spoke of the Christian religion with such favor that the cross and the true belief in Our Savior Jesus Christ were shown to be deeply ingrained in the depths of his heart. To Dom Pedro, his son and successor, he recommended principally the keeping of the Christian doctrine. The son followed the example of the father, for he maintained and defended the religion.

During his reign a greater number of boats began to navigate these waters and, by the order of the king, the island of São Tomé was populated with Portuguese. Up to that time the interior had been deserted; only the coasts were inhabited by a few navigators who frequented the neighboring regions. In time the island was well populated by Portuguese and people from other nations who came there with the authorization of the king. There was much trade. The people cultivated and planted, as has been said above. Then

From Filippo Pigafetta and Duarte López, *Description du Royaume du Congo et des Contrées Environnantes (1591)*, trans. and annotated by Willy Bal (Louvain: Editions Nauwelaerts, 1963), pp. 100–105. Trans. from the French by Nell Elizabeth Painter and Robert O. Collins. Reprinted by permission. Bracketed material has been supplied by Professor Collins.

the king sent a bishop to govern the Christians of the island and those of Congo. He arrived at São Tomé and then proceeded to the kingdom of Congo, where he took possession of his charge [1543].

When the bishop disembarked, the king and the whole population welcomed him with incredible joy. From the sea to the capital (that is, for a distance of one hundred and fifty miles), the king had the roads smoothed and widened. He even had them covered with mats, the people having received an order to take charge of a particular portion [of the road]. Thus the bishop never put his foot on a bit of ground that was not decorated. But even more admirable was the sight of the spaces bordering the road as well—the trees and hills, which were covered with men and women who ran to see the bishop, whom they took for a saint, an envoy of God. One would offer him lambs, another kids, another chickens, still another guinea fowl, game, fish and other food in such abundance that he did not know what to do with it and had to leave much behind him. In this way the great zeal and obedience of these new Christians were made known. The memorable event should be especially noted that countless men and women, girls, boys, old people of eighty years and more, came to meet him, throwing themselves across the road asking him for the water of holy baptism and making the singular signs of the true faith, not wanting to let him pass without having received it. Thus the bishop had to stop a great deal to satisfy them, and he had provided himself with water contained in certain containers, salt, and other necessities.

Let us now leave the narrative of the welcome made to the bishop by the populations of each region, the vivid manifestation of joy, as much general as particular, and speak of his arrival in the city of San Salvador. The priests, the king, and all the court came to meet him. He was led to the church in a procession; then after he had rendered grace to God, he was taken to the home set aside for him. Immediately he began to set the organization of the church and the clergy—monks and secular priests—in order. He gave rank of cathedral to the Church of the Holy Cross, which then had about twenty-eight canons and their chaplains, a musical director and chorus, an organ, church bells, and all the objects of worship.

But this bishop, in cultivating the vine of the Lord, now in the kingdom of Congo, now in São Tomé, coming and going with twenty days at sea each time, and always leaving his vicars on the spot, ended by dying. He was buried on the island of São Tomé.

Another bishop succeeded him in the Congo. He was a black man of the royal family whom King Affonso had first sent to Portugal, then to Rome. There he had learned Latin and Christian doctrine. He came back to the Congo, and shortly after having disembarked, while on his way to his bishopric of San Salvador, he died. After that the kingdom remained without a pastor for some years. Then the king died also; he had no children. His brother, Dom Francisco, succeeded him, but his reign was short [reign ended in 1545]. A fifth king mounted the throne. His name was Dom Diogo [1545–1565], and he was the closest to the royal line. He was a man with a noble soul, magnificent, ingenuous, of good judgment and wise counsel, and above all a guardian of the Christian faith. A great warrior as well, he conquered several neighboring countries in a few years. He liked the Portuguese very much and put aside the

traditional costume to dress himself in their manner. He sought to be pleasing in his dress as well as in the ornamentation of his palace. He was liberal and courteous and gave generously to his own people as well as to the Portuguese. He bought ornaments that pleased him at great expense, saying that rare things should belong to no one but kings. He wore a suit of clothes only two or three times and then gave it to his people. The Portuguese, who saw that he appreciated golden brocades, tapestries, and other precious things, brought them to him from Portugal, and thus tapestries, cloths brocaded in gold, and lordly ornaments of that nature began to be appreciated in the kingdom.

During the reign of this king there was a third bishop of São Tomé and Congo who was of Portuguese nationality. On the road and at the court of San Salvador he was welcomed with the habitual ceremonies. But the devil, who was very annoyed by the happy progress of the Catholic religion, began to sow the seeds of discord among the monks, secular priests, and the bishop. The discord grew from the long period of liberty—the many years when the people had had no pastor. Each of them considered himself not only a bishop but even more, and did not want to obey his prelate. This tendency gave rise to grave dissension, and serious scandal followed. The king, a faithful Catholic, always took the bishop's side, and to put an end to these troubles he sent some of the priests as prisoners to Portugal, others to São Tomé. Others went away of their own accord, taking their goods with them. For this reason, instead of progressing, the religion regressed by the fault of its own ministers.

But the enemy did not stop there. In addition he stirred up disturbances between the princes and their subjects. In fact, after the death of the king, three people declared themselves pretenders to the throne. The first was the son of the king. He only had the favor of a small number of people because they wanted someone else. He was put to death. Two others of royal blood were left. One of them was made king by his partisans with the support of the majority of the people but against the will of the Portuguese and a few lords who aimed at placing the third pretender on the throne. They went to the church to murder the one who had just been crowned, reasoning that if they killed him, the other contender would necessarily become king. But at the same time, those of the opposing party assassinated the one favored by the Portuguese, thinking that after his death their prince would no longer have any difficulty in taking possession of the kingdom, for there would no longer be any other possible pretender to the royal scepter. In this manner, at the same hour, in different places, the princes were murdered.

The people saw that because of these conspiracies and murders, there was no longer any legitimate pretender to the throne. Placing the blame for all these evils on the Portuguese, they turned on them. Those who were found on the spot were massacred. The priests and Portuguese living in other places were not touched.

As there was no one of royal blood left to place in power, a brother of the deceased King Diogo, Dom Henrique, was chosen. Intending to make war on the Anzincas,[1] Dom Henrique left Dom Alvaro behind as governor with the title of king. Dom Alvaro was a young man of twenty-five years and the son of the wife of Dom Henrique by another marriage. Dom Henrique died in the war a short time afterward [1567]. Dom Alvaro [1568–1587] was chosen and recognized as sovereign by the people, the ancient line of the kings of Congo thus having ended with Dom Henrique.

Dom Alvaro was a man of good judgment who combined authority with gentleness. He immediately calmed all the

[1] Probably the people of the kingdom of Ndongo in Angola, which seems to have recognized the suzerainty of the kingdom of Congo in the sixteenth century (ed.).

troubles of the kingdom. He reunited the Portuguese, the monks, and the laymen who had dispersed into the neighboring provinces following the past wars. Thanks to them his Catholic faith was well reconfirmed. He pardoned them, demonstrating that they had not been the cause of the evils of the past, which was clearly seen by all. He decided to furnish ample written information on these events to the King of Portugal and the bishop of São Tomé and had letters delivered to them by certain persons. The bishop had not dared risk a visit to the kingdom during the height of the disturbances. As soon as he received this news, he embarked for the Congo and used all his authority to calm the dissension and restore order to all the affairs concerning the divine cult and ministry of the priests. Shortly afterward he returned to his residence in São Tomé, where sickness ended his days. For the third time, these regions remained without a bishop.

The absence of a pastor meant that the Christian faith cooled somewhat in the heart of the king, as well as in the hearts of his lords and his people. All of them let themselves be drawn into carnal licentiousness—especially the king, led by other young men of his age who were his everyday companions, in particular by a lord named Francisco Bulamatari (which means "breaker of rocks"), who was one of his relatives. Because he was a great lord, he led a dissolute life already parted from Christian teaching. He declared publicly that to have only one wife was stupid and that it was better to go back to ancient custom. Thus, by this intermediary, the devil opened the door to the destruction of the temple of Christianity in this kingdom, which had up to then been built at the cost of so much trouble. This man divorced himself so much from the way of the truth that, from sin to sin, he abandoned the true faith almost entirely.

Meanwhile, he died, and as he was a noble lord, he was buried in the Church of the Holy Cross, although he was manifestly suspect and tainted with heresy. An extraordinary event took place, calculated to reconfirm the good in the holy faith and frighten the devil. At night, malicious spirits opened part of the roof of the Church of the Holy Cross where he was interred, making a great din heard by the whole city, and drew him out of the tomb and carried him off. The next morning the doors were found closed, the roof bro-

ken, and the sepulcher empty of his body.

This event was a warning intended to show the gravity of the fault that had been committed by the king and by those who followed him. But as there was still no bishop in the kingdom, the sovereign, who was young and unmarried, while remaining firm in his faith, persisted in carnal license until God inflicted severe punishment on him.

61 ANDREW BATTELL
THE JAGA

Andrew Battell (1565–1614) was an English sailor who was seized from a British privateer operating in South American waters and imprisoned at Luanda by the Portuguese authorities. After numerous adventures, Battell lived with the Jaga for twenty-one months; his account of these mysterious and warlike people is the most authoritative. Like the Funj of the Sudan, the origins of the Jaga are unknown. They probably had cultural connections with the Luba-Lunda peoples of the interior of Central Africa. In any event, they suddenly appeared in 1568, overran the kingdom of Congo, and destroyed the capital, San Salvador. Originally, the Jaga were probably small in number, but like the Zulu in the nineteenth century, they rapidly assimilated conquered peoples. Their military superiority was irresistible, and they roamed widely, spreading terror from the Congo River to the Cunene River. A few military units settled and founded states on the Kwango, Cuanza, and Cunene rivers.

In our second voyage, turning up along the coast, we came to the Morro, or cliff of Benguele,[1] which standeth in twelve degrees of southerly latitude. Here we saw a mighty camp on the south side of the river Cova.[2] And being desirous to know

From *The Strange Adventures of Andrew Battell of Leigh in Angola and the Adjoining Regions,* edited by E. G. Ravenstein and reprinted from *Purchas His Pilgrimes* (London: Hakluyt Society, 1901), pp. 19–35. Reprinted by permission of Cambridge University Press on behalf of *The Hakluyt Society.* Bracketed material in this selection was supplied by E. G. Ravenstein, except for footnote 36.
[1] The Morro, or bluff, of Old Benguella, in lat. 10° 48′ S., is a conspicuous headland, presenting a perpendicular cliff towards the sea, its summit being covered with cactus trees. Here Antonio Lopez Peixoto, a nephew of Paulo Dias, in 1587, had built a presidio, which was soon afterwards abandoned.
[2] The river Cuvo (Kuvu) enters the sea in 10° 52′ S.

what they were, we went on shore with our boat; and presently there came a troop of five hundred men to the waterside. We asked them who they were. Then they told us that they were the Gagas, or Gindes, that came from Sierra de lion [Serra Leoa],[3] and passed through the city of Congo, and so travelled to the eastward of the great city of Angola, which is called Dongo.[4] The great Gaga, which is their general, came down to the waterside

[3] *Sierra de lion,* or mountains of the lion, is of little help in identifying the origins of the Jaga, because there are many possible mountains of the lion (ed.).
[4] Ndongo is the name of the kingdom of Ngola (Angola). Its old capital was at Pungu-a-Ndongo, a remarkable group of rocks, popularly known as Pedras Negras.

to see us, for he had never seen white men before. He asked wherefore we came. We told him that we came to trade upon the coast. Then he bade us welcome, and called us on shore with our commodities. We loaded our ship with slaves in seven days, and bought them so cheap that many did not cost one real, which were worth in the city [of Loanda] twelve mil-reis.[5]

[In a marginal note, Purchas adds:

He, in discourse with me, called them Iagges, and their chief the great Iagge. I think he writ them Gagas for Giagas, by false spelling.]

AMONG THE JAGAS

Being ready to depart, the great Giaga staid us, and desired our boat to pass his men over the river Cova, for he determined to overrun the realm of Benguele, which was on the north side of the river Cova. So we went with him to his camp, which was very orderly, intrenched with piles of wood; we had houses provided for us that night, and many burthens [loads] of palm-wine, cows, goats and flour.

In the morning, before day, the general did strike his *gongo,* which is an instrument of war that soundeth like a bell, and presently made an oration with a loud voice, that all the camp might hear, that he would destroy the Benguelas, with such courageous and vehement speeches as were not to be looked for among the heathen people. And presently they were all in arms, and marched to the river side, where he had provided *Gingados.*[6] And being ready with our boat and *Gingados,* the general was fain to beat them back because of the credit who should be first.

We carried over eighty men at once, and with our muskets we beat the enemy off, and landed, but many of them were slain. By twelve of the clock all the Gagas were over.

Then the general commanded all his drums, *tavales,*[7] *petes, pongos,* and all his instruments of warlike music to strike up, and gave the onset, which was a bloody day for the Benguelas. These Benguelas presently broke, and turned their backs, and a very great number of them were slain, and were taken captives, man, woman and child. The prince, Hombian-gymbe, was slain, which was ruler of this country, and more than one hundred of his chief lords, and their heads presented and thrown at the feet of the great Gaga. The men, women and children that were brought in captive alive, and the dead corpses that were brought to be eaten, were strange to behold. For these Gagas are the greatest cannibals and man-eaters that be in the world, for they feed chiefly upon man's flesh [notwithstanding of their] having all the cattle of that country.

They settled themselves in this country and took the spoil of it. We had great trade with these Gagas, five months, and gained greatly by them. These Gagas were not contented to stay in this place of Benguela, although they lacked almost nothing. For they had great store of cattle and wheat, and many other commodities; but they lacked wine, for in these parts there are no palm-trees.

After the five months were expired they marched toward the province of Bambala,[8] to a great lord that is called Calican-samba, whose country is five days up into

---

[5] Real and milreis were Portuguese monetary units in use before 1911 after which they were superseded by the escudo (ed.).

[6] "Gingado," elsewhere spelt "Iergado," is evidently a misprint for *Jangada,* a Portuguese word meaning "raft." Such a raft is called *Mbimba,* and is made of the wood of the *bimba,* which is identical with the *Ambaj* of the Nile, and grows abundantly on the swampy banks of the rivers. Battell himself, at a critical point of his career, built himself such a *jangada.*

[7] *Tavale.* Mr. Dennet suggests that *tavale* corresponds to the *libala* of Loango, a word derived from the Portuguese *taboa* (table), for the instrument of this name consists of a board supported by two sticks of wood, and kept in its place by wooden pegs driven into the ground. The player beats this board with his two index fingers. A. R. Neves, *Mem. da Epediçao a Cassange,* p. 110, calls *tabalha* a drum, which is beaten to make known the death of a Jaga Cassange.

[8] Mbala or Embala merely means town or village. . . .

the land. In these five months' space we made three voyages to the city of San Paul, and coming the fourth time we found them not.

MARCH INTO THE INTERIOR

Being loth to return without trade, we determined to go up into the land after them. So we went fifty on shore, and left our ship riding in the Bay of Benguela to stay for us. And marching two days up into the country we came to a great lord which is called Mofarigosat; and coming to his first town we found it burnt to the ground, for the Gagas had passed and taken the spoil. To this lord we sent a negro which we had bought of the Gagas, and [who] lived with us, and bid him say that he was one of the great Gaga's men, and that he was left to carry us to the camp. This lord bade us welcome for fear of the great Gaga, but he delayed the time, and would not let us pass till the Gaga was gone out of his country. This lord Mofarigosat, seeing that the Gagas were clear of him, began to palter with us, and would not let us go out of his land till we had gone to the wars with him, for he thought himself a mighty man having us with him. For in this place they never saw [a] white man before, nor guns. So we were forced to go with him, and destroyed all his enemies, and returned to his town again. Then we desired him that he would let us depart; but he denied us, without we would promise him to come again, and leave a white man with him in pawn.

LEFT AS AN HOSTAGE

The Portugals and Mulatos being desirous to get away from this place, determined to draw lots who should stay; but many of them would not agree to it. At last they consented together that it were fitter to leave me, because I was an Englishman, than any of themselves. Here I was fain to stay perforce. So they left me a musket, powder and shot, promising this lord, Mofarigosat, that within two months they would come again and bring

a hundred men to help him in his wars, and to trade with him. But all was to shift themselves away, for they feared that he would have taken us all captives. Here I remained with this lord till the two months were expired, and was hardly used, because the Portugals came not according to promise.

The chief men of this town would have put me to death, and stripped me naked, and were ready to cut off mine head. But the Lord of the town commanded them to stay longer, thinking that the Portugals would come. And after that I was let loose again, I went from one town to another, shifting for myself within the liberties of the lord. And being in fear of my life among them I ran away, purposing to go to the camp of the Gagas.

HE JOINS THE JAGAS

And having travelled all that night, the next day I came to a great town which was called Cashil, which stood in a mighty overgrown thicket. Here I was carried into the town, to the lord Cashil. And all the town, great and small, came to wonder at me, for in this place there was never any white man seen. Here were some of the great Gaga's men, which I was glad to see, and went with these Gagas to Calicansamba, where the camp was.

This town of the lord Cashil is very great, and is so overgrown with *Olicondie* [*baobab*] [9] trees, cedars, and palms, that

[9] The baobab is indifferently called by Battell *alicunde, licondo, elicondi, olicandi.* or *alicunde,* all of which are corruptions of *nkondo,* by which name the tree is known in Congo. The Portuguese know this characteristic tree of the coast-land and the interior as *imbondeiro* (from *mbondo* in Kimbundu). Its inner bark yields a fibre known as *licomte,* is made into coarse cloth, and is also exported to Europe to be converted into paper. The wood is very light. The pulp of the fruit is refreshing, and was formerly esteemed as a remedy against fever and dysentery. The seeds are eaten. The shell (*macua*) is used to hold water (hence the popular name of Calabash tree). Ficalho distinguishes three species, viz., *Adansonia digitata,* Linn., the fruit of which is longish; *A. subglobosa,* bearing a bell-shaped fruit; *A. lageniformis,* yielding a fruit shaped like a cucumber. . . .

the streets are darkened with them. In the middle of the town there is an image, which is as big as a man, and standeth twelve feet high; and at the foot of the image there is a circle of elephants' teeth, pitched into the ground. Upon these teeth stand great store of dead men's skulls, which are [were] killed in the wars, and offered to this image. They used to pour palm oil at his feet, and kill goats, and pour their blood at his feet. This image is called Quesango,[10] and the people have great belief in him, and swear by him; and do believe when they are sick that Quesango is offended with them. In many places of this town were little images, and over them great store of elephants' teeth piled.[11]

The streets of this town were paled with palm-canes, very orderly. Their houses were round like a hive, and, within, hanged with fine mats very curiously wrought. On the south-east end of the town was a mokiso [*mukishi*] which had more than three tons of elephants' teeth piled over him.

From this town of Cashil I travelled up into the country with the Gagas two days, and came to Calicansamba, where the great Gaga had his camp, and was welcome to him. Among the cannibal people I determined to live, hoping in God that they would travel so far to the westward that we should see the sea again; and so I might escape by some ship. These Gagas remained four months in this place, with great abundance and plenty of cattle, corn, wine, and oil, and great triumphing, drinking, dancing, and banquetting, with man's flesh, which was a heavy spectacle to behold.

At the end of four months they marched towards the *Serras,* or mountains of Cashindcabar, which are mighty high, and have great copper mines, and

they took the spoil all the way as they went. From thence they went to the river Longa,[12] and passed it, and settled themselves in the town of Calango,[13] and remained there five or six months. Then we arose and entered into the province of Tondo,[14] and came to the river Gonsa [Coanza],[15] and marched on the south side of the river to a lord that was called Makellacolonge, near to the great city of Dongo. Here we passed over mighty high mountains, and found it very cold.

Having spent sixteen months among these cannibals, they marched to the westward again, and came along the river Gonsa, or Gunza, to a lord that is called Shillambansa,[16] uncle to the King of Angola. We burnt his chief town, which was after their fashion very sumptuously builded. This place is very pleasant and fruitful. Here we found great store of wild peacocks,[17] flying up and down the trees, in as great abundance as other birds. The old lord Shillambansa was buried in the middle of the town, and had a hundred tame peacocks kept upon his grave, which peacocks he gave to his *Mokeso,* and they were called *Angello Mokeso,*[18] that is, the Devil's or Idol's Birds, and were accounted as holy things. He had great store of copper, cloth, and many other things laid upon his grave, which is the order of that country.

From this place we marched to the westward, along the river Coanza, and came right against the *Serras* or mountains of Cambambe, or Serras de Prata.[19]

[10] Kizangu, in Kimbundu, means fetish. . . .
[11] The so-called fetishes (from *feitiço,* a Portuguese word meaning sorcery) are not idols, but charms and amulets, generally known as *nkissi, nkishi,* or *mukishi.* . . .

[12] The river Longa [Lungu] enters the sea in lat. 10° 20′ S.
[13] A soba Calungo is shown on the most recent maps as residing north of the river Longa.
[14] Perhaps we ought to read *Tunda,* the bush, the East. . . .
[15] The Gonsa or Gunza (Ngunza) of Battell is undoubtedly the Coanza. A river Ngunza enters the sea at Novo Redondo.
[16] *Shila,* nasty; *mbanza,* towns.
[17] According to Duarte López, the feathers of peacocks and of ostriches are used as a standard in battle. Hence, peacocks are reared within a fence and reserved for the king.
[18] *Njilo* (in Kimbundu), bird; *mukishi,* a charm.
[19] Cambambe (*Ka,* diminutive; *mbambi,* gazelle), a village on the north bank of the Coanza, below the

Here is the great fall of water, that falleth right down, and maketh a mighty noise that is heard thirty miles. We entered into the province of Casama,[20] and came to one of the greatest Lords, which was called Langere. He obeyed the great Gaga, and carried us to a Lord called Casoch,[21] which was a great warrior, for he had some seven years before overthrown the Portugals camp, and killed eight hundred Portugals and forty-thousand negroes, that were on the Portugals side. This Lord did stoutly withstand the Gagas, and had the first day a mighty battle, but had not the victory that day. So we made a sconce of trees after their fashion, and remained four months in the wars with them. I was so highly esteemed with the great Gaga, because I killed many negroes with my musket, that I had anything that I desired of him. He would also, when they went out to the wars, give charge to his men over me. By this means I have been often carried away in their arms, and saved my life. Here we were within three days' journey of Massangano, before mentioned, where the Portugals have a fort: and I sought means, and got to the Portugals again with merchant negroes that came to the camp to buy slaves.

---

falls formed by the river in forcing its way through the Serra de Prata. Silver, however, has never been found there (at least not in appreciable quantities), nor anywhere else in Angola or Congo. Still we are told that the King of Congo, in 1530, sent the wife of King Manuel two silver bracelets which he had received from one of his chiefs in Matamba, and that among the presents forwarded by Ngola Nbande, the King of Ndongo, to Paulo Dias in 1576, there were several silver bracelets, which the Regent of Portugal, Cardinal Henrique, had converted into a chalice, which he presented to the church at Belem. According to Capello and Ivens, silver ore is plentiful in Matamba, although they never saw any *in loco.*

[20] Battell's Casama is the wide province of Kisama (Quiçama), to the south of the Coanza.

[21] This Casoch (a misprint for Cafoch) is the Cafuxe (Cafuche) of the Portuguese, who defeated Balthasar de Almeida on April 22, 1594. On August 10, 1603, the Portuguese, led by Manuel Cerveira Pereira, retrieved this disaster.

MILITARY ORGANISATION OF THE JAGAS

There were in the camp of the Gagas twelve captains. The first, called Imbe Calandola, their general, a man of great courage. He warreth all by enchantment, and taketh the Devil's counsel in all his exploits. He is always making of sacrifices [22] to the Devil, and doth know many times what shall happen unto him. He believeth that he shall never die but in the wars. There is no image among them, but he useth certain ceremonies. He hath straight laws to his soldiers: for, those that are faint-hearted, and turn their backs to the enemy, are presently condemned and killed for cowards, and their bodies eaten. He useth every night to make a warlike oration upon an high scaffold, which doth encourage his people.

It is the order of these people, wheresoever they pitch their camp, although they stay but one night in a place, to build their fort, with such wood or trees as the place yieldeth: so that the one part of them cutteth down trees and boughs, and the other part carrieth them, and buildeth a round circle with twelve gates.[23] So that every captain keepeth his gate. In the middle of the fort is the general's house, intrenched round about, and he hath many porters to keep the door. They build their houses very close together, and have their bows, arrows, and darts standing without their doors; and when they give alarm, they are suddenly all out of the fort. Every company at their doors [gates?] keep very good watch in the night, playing upon their drums and *tavales.*

---

[22] Human victims are still sacrificed by the diviner when consulting departed spirits.

[23] Cavazzi gives a plan of a Jaga camp, or Kilombo. It is formed of a square stockade, having in its centre the quarters of the Commander-in-chief, within a triple hedge of thorns. Between the stockade, which has only a single gate, and the inner enclosure are the quarters of the six principal officers, including the Golambolo (*ngolo,* strength *mbula,* a blow), or Lieutenant-General, the Tendala, or Commander of the Rear-guard, and the Mani Lumbo (*lumbu,* a stockade), or Engineer-in-chief.

A RIVER OF GOLD

These Gagas told us of a river that is to the southward of the Bay of Vaccas,[24] that hath great store of gold: and that they gathered up great store of grains of gold upon the sand, which the fresh water driveth down in the time of rain. We found some of this gold in the handles of their hatchets, which they use to engrave with copper; and they called it copper also, and do not esteem it.

PALM WINE

These Gagas delight in no country, but where there is great store of Palmares, or groves of palms. For they delight greatly in the wine and in the fruit of the palm, which serveth to eat and to make oil. And they draw their wine contrary to the Imbondos.[25] These palm-trees are six or seven fathoms high, and have no leaves but in the top: and they have a device to go up to the top of the tree, and lay no hands on it, and they draw the wine in the top of the tree in a bottle.

But these Gagas cut the palm-trees down by the root, which lie ten days before they will give wine. And then they make a square hole in the top and heart of the tree, and take out of the hole every morning a quart, and at night a quart. So that every tree giveth two quarts of wine a day for the space of six and twenty days, and then it drieth up.

JAGA RAIDS

When they settle themselves in any country, they cut down as many palms as will serve them wine for a month: and then as many more, so that in a little time they spoil the country. They stay no longer in a place than it will afford them maintenance. And then in harvest-time they arise, and settle themselves in the fruitfullest place they can find; and do reap their enemy's corn, and take their cattle. For they will not sow, nor plant, nor bring up any cattle, more than they take by wars. When they come into any country that is strong, which they cannot the first day conquer, then their General buildeth his fort, and remaineth sometimes a month or two quiet. For he saith, it is as great wars to the inhabitants to see him settled in their country, as though he fought with them every day. So that many times the inhabitants come and assault him at his fort: and these Gagas defend themselves and flesh [26] them on for the space of two or three days. And when their General mindeth to give the onset, he will, in the night, put out some one thousand men: which do ambush themselves about a mile from their fort. Then in the morning the great Gaga goeth with all his strength out of the fort, as though he would take their town. The inhabitants coming near the fort to defend their country, being between them, the Gagas give the watchword with their drums, and then the ambushed men rise, so that very few escape. And that day their General overrunneth the country.

DRESS AND ORNAMENTS

The great Gaga Calando [27] hath his hair very long, embroidered with many knots of Banba [28] shells, which are very rich among them, and about his neck a collar of *masoes,*[29] which are also shells, that are found upon that coast, and are sold among them for the worth of twenty shillings a shell: and about his middle he weareth *landes,* which are beads made of the ostrich eggs.[30] He weareth a palm-cloth about his middle, as fine as silk. His body is carved and cut with sundry works, and every day anointed with the fat of

---

26 "Flesh" in the sense of encourage.
27 Calando should be Calandola.
28 Mbamba, a whelk or trumpet-shell.
29 Mr. Dennet suggests *msose,* a turritella, popularly known as screw-shell.
30 No ostriches are met with in Angola, and as to beads made of ostrich eggs, I can give no explanation.

24 Bahia das Vaccas, old name for Benguella Bay. . . .
25 The Imbondos are clearly the Nbundu of Angola, who draw the palm wine from the top, whilst the Jagas cut down the tree.

men. He weareth a piece of copper cross his nose,[31] two inches long, and in his ears also. His body is always painted red and white. He hath twenty or thirty wives, which follow him when he goeth abroad; and one of them carrieth his bows and arrows; and four of them carry his cups of drink after him. And when he drinketh they all kneel down, and clap their hands and sing.[32]

Their women wear their hair with high *trompes* full of bamba [*mbamba*] shells, and are anointed with civet.[33] They pull out four of their teeth, two above and two below, for a bravery. And those that have not their teeth out are loathsome to them, and shall neither eat nor drink with them. They wear great store of beads about their necks, arms, and legs; about their middles, silk cloths.

INFANTICIDE

The women are very fruitful, but they enjoy none of their children: for as soon as the woman is delivered of her child, it is presently buried quick [alive], so that there is not one child brought up in all this generation.[34] But when they take any town they keep the boys and girls of thirteen or fourteen years of age as their own children. But the men and women they kill and eat. These little boys they train up in the wars, and hang a collar about their necks for a disgrace, which is never taken off till he proveth himself a man, and bring his enemy's head to the General: and then it is taken off and he is a freeman, and is called *Gonso* or soldier.[35]

This maketh them all desperate, and forward to be free, and counted men: and so they do increase. In all this camp there were but twelve natural Gagas that were their captains, and fourteen or fifteen women. For it is more than fifty years since they came from Serra de Lion, which was their native country. But their camp is sixteen thousand strong, and sometimes more.

HUMAN SACRIFICES [36]

When the great Gaga Calandola undertaketh any great enterprise against the inhabitants of any country, he maketh a sacrifice to the Devil, in the morning, before the sun riseth. He sitteth upon a stool, having upon each side of him a man-witch: then he hath forty or fifty women which stand round about him, holding in each hand a *zevra* [zebra] [37] or wild horse's tail, wherewith they do flourish and sing. Behind them are great store of petes, ponges, and drums, which always play. In the midst of them is a great fire; upon the fire an earthen pot with white powders, wherewith the men-witches do paint him on the forehead, temples, 'thwart the breast and belly, with long ceremonies and inchanting terms. Thus he continueth till sun is down. Then the witches bring his *Casengula*,[38] which

---

[31] The practice of wearing such nose ornaments exists to the present day in Lunda, among the Bangala and other tribes.

[32] Marginal note by Purchas: "They use this ceremony in Florida."

[33] Civet-cats are numerous in this part of Africa.

[34] I am inclined to believe, from what we learn from Cavazzi and other missionaries, that only those children were killed which were born within the *Kilombo*. On the other hand, at the Court of the ferocious queen Jinga, we are told by Captain Füller, a Dutchman, that, on two days in 1648, 113 newborn infants born *outside* the camp were killed.

[35] *Ngunza,* according to Cordeira da Matta, means all-powerful; according to Bentley a herald, who speaks on behalf of a chief.

[36] Human sacrifices among the Jaga are even now [1900] of frequent occurrence. They are made at the installation of a Jaga, one year after his election (when the sacrifice and its accompanying banquet are intended to conciliate the spirit of Kinguri, the founder of the Dynasty), at his death, on the outbreak of war, etc. The ceremony witnessed by Battell was an act of divination. The soothsayer summons the spirit of Kinguri, who is supposed to foretell the results of any enterprise about to be undertaken. In 1567, the Jaga Ngonga Kahanga, of Shela, having been advised by his soothsayers that he would suffer defeat in a war he was about to enter upon against the Portuguese, declined the arbitration of the sword, and submitted voluntarily. The body of the victim is cooked with the flesh of a cow, a goat, a yellow dog, a cock and a pigeon, and this mess is devoured (ceremoniously) by the Jaga and his *makotas* (councillors).

[37] The handle of this switch contains a potent medicine, which protects the owner against death.

[38] Casengula, called Kissengula, was perhaps a trombash, for *sangula* means to kill at a long range.

is a weapon like a hatchet, and put it into his hand, and bid him be strong against his enemies: for his *mokiso* is with him. And presently there is a man-child brought, which forthwith he killeth. Then are four men brought before him; two whereof, as it happeneth, he presently striketh and killeth; the other two he commandeth to be killed without the fort.

Here I was by the men-witches ordered to go away, as I was a Christian, for then the Devil doth appear to them, as they say. And presently he commandeth five cows to be killed within the fort, and five without the fort: and likewise as many goats, and as many dogs, and the blood of them is sprinkled in the fire, and their bodies are eaten with great feasting and triumph. And this is used many times by all the other captains of their army.

BURIAL OF THE DEAD

When they bury the dead they make a vault in the ground, and a seat for him to sit.[39] The dead hath his head newly embroidered, his body washed, and anointed with sweet powders. He hath all his best robes put on, and is brought between two men to his grave, and set in seat as though he were alive. He hath two of his wives set with him, with their arms broken, and then they cover over the vault on the top. The inhabitants when they die are buried after the same fashion, and have the most part of their goods buried with them. And every month there is a meeting of the kindred of the dead man, which mourn and sing doleful songs at his grave for the space of three days, and kill many goats, and pour their blood upon his grave, and palm-wine also; and use this ceremony as long as any of their kindred be alive.[40] But those that have no kindred think themselves unhappy men, because they have none to mourn for them when they die. These people are very kind one to another in their health; but in their sickness they do abhor one another, and will shun their company.

---

[39] The Jagas are still buried sitting, and wives are sacrificed. In Ngois, likewise, the dead are occasionally buried in a sitting posture.

[40] These feasts are intended to secure the goodwill of the deceased, so that he may not injure the living. Human beings are occasionally sacrificed, in addition to goats and fowls.

---

62 ALVARE II AND ALVARE III, KINGS OF CONGO
RELATIONS BETWEEN THE KINGDOM OF CONGO AND THE PAPACY

After the Jaga attack had been subdued, the kings of Congo, Alvare I (1568–1587), Alvare II (1587–1614), and Alvare III (1614–1622) sought to reassert their authority and to disengage themselves from dependence on the Portuguese. Alvare I had sent Duarte López to Rome in 1583, hoping to enlist Vatican support against Portugal. In 1590 Alvare II allied himself against the Portuguese in Angola and in 1604 sought to make the Congo a papal vassal. The Vatican rejected this proposal but agreed to intercede with the King of Spain on behalf of Congo. The appointment of Monsignor Vivès inaugurated an era of close relations between Rome and San Salvador. Acting on the appeal of Alvare III for support, the Vatican remonstrated with the King of Spain to check Portuguese who invaded the Congo from Angola.

From J. Cuvelier and L. Jadin, *L'Ancien Congo d'après les Archives Romaines (1518–1640)* (Brussels: Académie Royale des Sciences d'Outre-Mer, 1954), pp. 329–331, 333–335, 348–351. Trans. by Nell Elizabeth Painter and Robert O. Collins. Reprinted by permission. Bracketed material has been supplied by Professor Collins.

ALVARO II TO POPE PAUL V SAN SALVADOR (CAPITAL OF THE KINGDOM OF CONGO) 27 FEBRUARY 1613

Dom Alvaro II by divine grace, augmenter of confession to the faith of Jesus Christ and defender of that same faith in these lands of Ethiopia, king of the very ancient kingdom of Congo, Angola, Matamba, Ocango, and of the Ambandu, and also of many other kingdoms and sovereignties that are subject to him this side and beyond the marvelous river Zaïre. Written from his royal city of San Salvador, the 27th of February 1613.

To the very Holy Father, Pope Paul V, at present head of the Church of God Our Lord.

He expresses the desire that he has to come personally to kiss the feet of His Holiness.

He acknowledges the reception of the letter from His Holiness, received in the year 1611. He thanks him for the title of Majesty, which was given to him in that letter, which was read from the pulpit by a father of Saint Dominic who was here at that time.

He expresses his thanks for the welcome made for Dom Antonio Manuel, his ambassador, who died in Rome.

Dom Antonio Manuel, not being able to be admitted as ambassador and thus unable to kiss the feet of His Holiness, having been taken away by death; the king not being able to come himself, nor send others at short notice, has chosen for his ambassador to Your Holiness Monsignor Jean-Baptiste Vivès, prothonotary of the number of participants and referendary [arbitrator] of the one and the other signature, so that with all the solemnity of ambassadors of kings, he may kiss the feet of His Holiness in his name, swear allegiance and express the joy which he feels about his elevation to the Sovereign Pontry. Monsignor Vivès will be able to take care of the business entrusted to D. Antonio Manuel. . . .

He chooses the Cardinal of Saint Cecilia as protector of his kingdom. If both should die, His Holiness may replace them as he sees fit.

He has been informed that the Portuguese in this country seek to bring about a division between himself and the King of Spain, so that the latter would be prompted to conquer the kingdom of Congo. For his own part, he has always shown friendship to this king and he has favored his subjects.

He has always treated the churches and priests well and has made sure that the tithes are paid. He has had the tithes collected by his servants in specie because foodstuffs could not be transported due to the size of the kingdom and could not be taken out of the villages. They have agreed on a certain number of measures of *Nzimbu,* the word that designates their money.

He has not received the brief mentioned in the letter.

He asks that by means of a brief, everyone would be prohibited, on pain of censure, from encroaching on the lands of his kingdom or taking possession of the mines. . . .

He asks for a brief in order to be able to defend himself against the attacks of the bishops. If he is not treated justly, may he notify them by a priest or cleric, because the bishop threatens to interdict him and deprive him of priests. This suggests to him that the Portuguese desire to conquer his kingdom. In the past pontiffs accorded very ample briefs, but these briefs were lost during the wars with the "Giacchi" [Jaga]. . . .

He is very badly treated by the Portuguese and the prelates. He is very ashamed of this. He hides it so that the pagan kings may not be glad of it and because he expects protection from Rome. If his authority is maintained these other kings may be converted.

He suffers many vexations because of the distance from the King of Portugal and because his business is sent to Portugal, where the relatives of the Portuguese who are in the Congo occupy certain offices.

The Christian religion is making no progress because there are no priests. . . . The foreign priests who come to the Congo have no preoccupation other than that of enriching themselves and returning to their countries; they take no interest in gaining souls for heaven. If religious personnel are sent, may they be like the "Mariani" [Monks of Mary], or Carmelites, who came during his father's time. They got very good results because of the example they set, their doctrine, and their charity.

As for the Dominican fathers requested from the King of Portugal, of the four he sent, two died during the course of the trip and the two who arrived at their destination are hardly useful.

They interfere in the foreign affairs of the kingdom and in the plans and duties of the king at their own bidding. May those fathers who will come in the future be ordered to keep to their own duties.

He begs that a brief be accorded the bishop giving him the faculty of dispensing with irregularities of notable persons wanting to be ordained and also the faculty to dispense with the impediment of consanguinity and affinity, with the order that the bishop not make difficulties in according them and not do so according to his own desires, but that he carry out what Your Holiness commands and what the king asks.

At the time of the first vacancy of the episcopal seat, there was much dispute and disorder among the members of the chapter. They abused themselves publicly at mass and in the offices in the presence of the king, imposing conflicting censures. If the situation had not been remedied, it would have become aggravated. The remedy (there was no other means) was to threaten them with expulsion from the kingdom. Then they calmed down.

He begs that remedies be found for other similar cases, for they take excessive liberties. The king asks that the vicar, who at that time did not conduct himself according to law, be sent away and another chosen by means of a brief that he requests and that the new one be of the best group and chosen from among those who are in agreement with him.

ALVARO III TO POPE PAUL V SAN SALVADOR, 25 OCTOBER 1617

Very Holy Father,

Myself, Dom Alvaro the Third, by divine grace, augmenter of the faith of Jesus Christ and defender of the faith in these lands of Ethiopia, king of the very ancient kingdom of Congo, Angola, Matamba, Ocanga, and of the Ambandu, here and beyond the marvelous river Zaïre [Congo], and of many other kingdoms and neighboring sovereignties, . . .

As the very humble and very obedient son of Your Holiness, I kiss his very holy feet in my name and of my royal person as well as in the name of all my kingdoms and states, I give him the allegiance due him as the universal pastor of the flock of Christ. I beg Your Holiness with all possible ardor to accept the above-said allegiance, which I have given and offered by the intermediary of my procurer, Dom Jean-Baptiste Vivès of Valencia. The prothonotary and referendary [arbitrator] of Your Holiness will remit it, according to the mode and manner which the other Catholic Kings are accustomed to in dealing with the apostolic Holy See. I give him all necessary faculties to pledge allegiance as well as to treat affairs in my name to Your Holiness and to all the Roman pontiffs, his successors. If for any reason he cannot do so, we would like Your Holiness and his successor to have the power to name other procurers in my name and in the name of my kingdoms. In this way the designs of King Dom Alvaro II, my lord and father whom God has, in His glory, taken up again. This is what he had in mind when he sent Dom Antonio Manuel, who died in Rome, to the apostolic Holy See. He entrusted letters to him, affairs to be discussed and commissioned him with an embassy. It is necessary that these projects be developed for the greater service of God and for the greater good of Christianity.

I reconfirm the instructions he gave and the business he negotiated, and I humbly beg Your Holiness to give orders so that old requests and those which more recently have been addressed to the above-named procurer, to be submitted by him to Your Holiness, may be examined. All these affairs are contained in instructions that I have sent, signed by my hand, which manifest that my goal is to promote the divine cult for the greater glory of God, the exaltation of His Church, the confusion of barbarians and pagans, and the consolidation of Catholics.

By other routes I have written to Your Holiness, to the Seignior Cardinal, protector of these kingdoms, and to the above-named procurer, my ordinary ambassador resident at that Roman court, Dom Jean-Baptiste Vivès.

In those letters I announced the death of King Alvaro II, my lord and father. I related that after his death, given my young age, the kingdom was put in the possession of Dom Bernard, my uncle, bastard half-brother of the above-named king, with the help of a few important people. But after less than a year, the kingdom, seeing the injustices done to me, scandalized by some disorders indicative of little Christian religion, took up arms against him without my knowing. This was under the command of Dom Antonio da Silva, Grand Duke of Mbamba, a province of the kingdom, and general of the kingdom, to whom the above-named king, my lord and father, before dying, had given over my person, as executor of his will. Dom Bernard was deprived of the kingdom and his life, and I was reestablished in power to the great joy of all, and I was recognized by all the states as their king and their universal lord.

I beg Your Holiness to deign to send many favors and spiritual graces to me and to all my subjects, to deign to let us rejoice in his letters, which will bring us many benefits and much honor, and the courage to resist the barbarous pride of paganism by which, from all sides of our kingdom, we are besieged.

We also beg Your Holiness to deign to receive us forever under the protection and defense of the apostolic Holy See and to make his Catholic Majesty, King Dom Philippe [of Spain], whom we greatly esteem and honor as our well-loved brother, favorable to us, recognizing the great benefits that I and all these kingdoms and this Christianity owe to his magnificence. These benefits have cost His Majesty great expenditures, which he has not ceased to make in favor of this Christianity whose culture he assures. Even so, we are under the weight of injustice on the part of his captains-general and governors who reside in Angola. They enter the lands belonging to our crown and make themselves masters there, as if it were enemy territory, without receiving any such orders from His Majesty. On the contrary, the king orders them in his instructions, which he gives them, to aid and serve us in all instances. They do not do this, having only their own interests in mind. They commit numerous unjust acts, making alliance with a nation of extremely barbarous men called Gindas and Ingas [Jagas], who live on human flesh.

May Your Holiness deign to find a remedy for this. I beg him to accord me his immediate protection.

May the Lord care for the very holy person of Your Holiness in the measure that his very humble and very obedient son desires. . . .

63 MONSIGNOR CONFALONRERI
SÃO TOMÉ AND THE SLAVE TRADE

By the donatarios* of 1486 and 1493, the Portuguese who had settled on the island of São Tomé had been granted the privilege of trading in slaves along the western coast of Africa. Although the donatario of 1493 was withdrawn in the regimento of 1512, the São Thomistas, under their Governor, Ferrão de Mello, acted quite independently of Portugal and used their strategic position between the kingdom of Congo and Europe to subvert Congolese-Lusitanian relations to their own advantage. Throughout the sixteenth century, the São Tomé party and its supporters carried on a vigorous trade in slaves, ignored the commands of the King of Portugal, and undermined the authority of the King of Congo. Their subversive activities did much to bring about the disintegration of the kingdom of Congo. The following description was probably compiled by Monsignor Confalonreri, who used the Relatione *of Pigafetta and López and the firsthand accounts of two Carmelite fathers who were missionaries in Congo and São Tomé from 1584 to 1587.*

THE WAY OF LIFE OF THE MERCHANTS WHO GO IN THESE REGIONS FOR COMMERCE AND THE GREAT ABUSES THERE ARE ON THE ISLAND OF SÃO TOMÉ CONCERNING THE SLAVES POSSESSED BY THE PORTUGUESE THERE

The Portuguese merchants in these countries have been reprimanded and corrected many times by diverse preachers secretly and publicly in lessons and in sermons. They are reproached for the numerous abuses and customs and sins that they practice and live in this land, and because there has been no evidence of change up to the present time, it is necessary to notify the church. . . . Where there are many Spaniards [Portuguese] in these areas, some are merchants and go to the Congo and other places to trade. They are of two types: some are called *pombeiros,* who go to the interior of the country and trade with pagans as well as with Christians. They buy and sell the

merchandise that they bring. They buy slaves whom they send to Congo (San Salvador) or to Pinda, and to others of their associates. The latter embark them on ships coming to the port of the island of São Tomé, where they take care of feeding them until the return of the slave owners. The others are inhabitants of the city of Congo or of the port of Pinda and have the job of receiving the slaves that the pombeiros send them. They own slaves, and they send those whom they trust into the interior of the country with merchandise to trade as the pombeiros do.

There are others living on the island of São Tomé and they are also of two sorts: some are inhabitants, but they are occupied only with feeding and receiving slaves, who are sent to them by the pombeiros up to the time they are embarked for Portugal, or else they keep the slaves until they come, according to what they have agreed upon between them.

Others live on the island and have sugar factories; many slaves cultivate the plantations.

Here the way of life will be described. The country is very hot and humid, but not, however, as much as is said. And this they take as a pretext to live with the greatest latitude and liberty in their persons, concerning (food) and so they all indiscriminately eat meat, on Fridays and

From J. Cuvelier and L. Jadin, *L'Ancien Congo d'après les Archives Romaines (1518–1640)* (Brussels: Académie Royale des Sciences d'Outre-Mer, 1954), pp. 152–156. Trans. by Nell Elizabeth Painter and Robert O. Collins. Reprinted by permission. Bracketed material has been supplied by Professor Collins.
* A royal grant of land or privileges.

on other fast days; Lent, they do not know what it is. . . .

The monks stayed a long time without eating meat on forbidden days, not giving up fasting, even though the bishop had commanded them not to fast and to eat meat, so much has this perverse custom been accepted. But they still do not do it because of their scruples, and they are still in good health and do not accord themselves other dispensations that were in vogue but that are illicit.

I will abstain here from discussing their trade, about which there is much to be said, particularly of their trickery and the exorbitant prices that they demand for their wares. There are very few of them who do not do everything possible for gain. From this these traders can become rich in two days, although this be counter to their conscience.

Similarly, their houses are full of Creoles who are the children of the whites and Negroes, and there are no other whites to whom the children could belong if not to them. Finally, because the major part of those who go in these lands are not people of pure blood (they are Jews, half-castes, mulattoes), as soon as they find themselves at liberty with no one to control them, they live as they please without performing the sacraments or giving signs of being good Christians, which would be necessary to do where the faith begins.

In particular, the pombeiros, who are those who go among the pagans, communally take with them three or four Negroes as slaves—those with whom they can do whatever they please—and at the end of the year there are that many Creoles. Besides that, years pass when they do not attend mass, or listen to a sermon, or go to confession, or carry out the other duties of a Christian. And what is even [worse], many of them go to the pagans without having confessed or taken communion or put their souls in order. . . .

The merchants [established] on the island of São Tomé and who live there have many plantations, from which they harvest much sugar and other products. . . . The person directing these plantations has a recreation house there and near it an enclosure, and in the interior of this enclosure are the slaves, men and women, who cultivate these plantations. They have their camps and in one line one hundred men slaves and in the other one hundred women slaves . . . [others are arranged] so that each man has a woman slave or two as concubines, and thus they live in concubinage, as though they were married in a cabin. The masters see this and not only do they not reprimand them but they are glad of it, because at the end of the year they have their lands cultivated and half again more slaves because of the births. Every Negress infallibly gives life to a black child each year. Besides this, the masters do not teach the doctrine or the faith to these slaves. They remain ignorant of such things as if they had stayed in their country and were pagans. The masters do not care about Sundays or holidays, and they neither hear mass nor confess. They do not even give the slaves the time necessary for that. They only care about one thing: that the slaves work the land and increase their number. The masters do not support them, giving them nothing to eat all week. The slaves have to procure their nourishment themselves, and thus it is necessary for them to work on Sundays and holidays to sustain themselves. When they are sick they are not given what is necessary. Finally, they are treated like so many cattle—even worse than that, because cattle are cared for where no account is taken of slaves at all. And all this was introduced to this island as though it were consistent with reason. On the island of Principe [in the Gulf of Guinea], conditions are the same. Neither sermons nor admonitions nor even the interventions of bishops I think could remedy or procure protection against these abuses, because they say that if the slaves did not have their concubines they would revolt or join with the blacks who are already in a state of rebellion and would no longer work. They say that it is good that each man slave has his woman slave and that it is necessary that they be united thus, because if these slaves married, they could no longer separate them. As for food, they say that their plantations would no longer be kept up if it were necessary to feed them. It is a surprising thing that such a great abuse exists that does not exist among the pagans or among the Turks. . . . A remedy must be found for this abuse, which offends all law, divine and human. Those who do it or permit it, being obliged to remedy it, are in a bad spiritual state. May great attention be paid. The prelates who go in these lands cannot do much unless they are aided by the king, who draws a great deal of profit from these islands, which are part of their patrimony. The ecclesiastics, who receive a payment from the king, also have the obligation to remedy these abuses, and it is not possible that such a Christian and Catholic king would not support them in these things, which he could easily remedy.

Of great importance for this end would be that the king pass a law for the slave trade, a law prohibiting all merchants from entering the interior to trade. The merchants would be established only at the ports where they embark or disembark. They are a great source of scandal and a hindrance to the conversion of souls, for how can one persuade them to hear mass and not to have a great many wives, when they see that the Europeans do the contrary.

It would also be a great remedy if slaves were prohibited to live in concubinage. . . . Slaves should be accorded one or two days so that they might be able to see to their own sustenance. At the least His Majesty should see that no one keeps male and female slaves together in the same cabin unless they are married. . . .

64 FILIPPO PIGAFETTA AND DUARTE LÓPEZ
PAULO DIAZ DE NOVAIS IN ANGOLA

The kingdom of Ndongo was probably founded at the beginning of the sixteenth century. The king took the title of ngola. *From 1519 on, the ngola sought to make contact with the Portuguese. In 1560 four Jesuit priests and a young nobleman, Paul Diaz de Novais, arrived at the capital of Kabasa. Diaz returned to Portugal in 1565 and sought to obtain a commercial monopoly of the silver mines that he believed were in the interior. He obtained a* donatario, *or land grant, from the Portuguese crown in 1571, allowing him to colonize Angola at his own expense and to receive land and a commercial monopoly. Diaz appeared off the island of Luanda with 400 men in February 1575. He moved into the interior in 1576 and began a long series of campaigns that culminated in a great victory in 1583 and the construction of the Fort of Masangano at the confluence of the Lukala and Cuanza. Diaz died in 1589.*

In the direction of the sea several lords are found who accord themselves the title of king but whose domains are tiny. There are no suitable ports on these

From Filippo Pigafetta and Duarte López, *Description du Royaume du Congo et des Contrées Environnantes (1591)*, trans. and annotated by Willy Bal (Louvain: Éditions Nauwelaerts, 1963), pp. 39–41,

44. Trans. from the French by Nell Elizabeth Painter and Robert O. Collins. Reprinted by permission. Bracketed material has been supplied by Professor Collins.

coasts. Already many times we have made mention of the kingdom of Angola. That is why it is now time to talk of it in more detail. We have said that in the past a governor of the King of Congo ruled this territory. This governor proclaimed himself king long before the conversion of the king [of Congo] to Christianity. In this way he usurped absolute power in the whole area under his administration, and then in time he conquered other neighboring territories so that he has now become a great and rich prince, hardly less powerful than the King of Congo, to whom he pays or refuses tribute as he pleases.

It came about that King João II of Portugal implanted the Christian faith in the Congo and that the king of this land converted [to Christianity]. Since that time the Lord [King] of Angola has always been his friend and, so to speak, his vassal, sending him a present every year. The people trade with each other. With the permission of the King of Congo, the Portuguese traded with the people of Angola at the port of Luanda. Slaves were brought there and were traded for various sorts of merchandise, and all were sent to the island of São Tomé. In this way the trade of Luanda was linked with that which was carried on in the island. First the boats landed at São Tomé before going to Luanda. Because the commerce continually increased, they began to send boats from Lisbon expressly for Angola. A governor was sent there [in 1575]; his name was Paulo Diaz de Novais. The trade belonged to him because his ancestors had discovered its beginnings. The King of Portugal, Dom Sebastian, awarded him the right to conquer thirty-three leagues of coast from the mouth of the Cuanza toward the south and in the interior all that he could conquer entirely at his expense for himself and his heirs. Diaz left with many boats and began a prosperous trade in Angola, always directing it from the already-mentioned port of Luanda where the boats were unloaded. Little by little he penetrated into

the interior and established himself in a village called Anzelle, one mile from the river Cuanza, for convenience and to get closer to his market in Angola. The traffic increased even more; the Portuguese as well as the Congolese freely brought the merchandise that they wanted to sell or trade to Cabaza, which is situated 150 miles from the sea and where the court of the Lord of Angola is to be found.

The Lord of Angola gave the order to massacre all the merchants and seize their wealth, on the pretext that they came to spy and invade his state. It is believed that in reality the Lord of Angola simply wanted to appropriate their goods, which were considerable, for himself. These people, whose business was trade, were merchants and had nothing to make war. The massacre took place the same year that King Sebastian suffered a defeat from the Berbers [1578].

Seeing this, Paulo Diaz took arms against the King of Angola. He assembled as many Portuguese as he could find in the region. With two canal barges and some other boats that were anchored in the Cuanza, he ascended the river, conquering both banks. By force of arms he subjugated many lords and rendered them vassals and friends.

Seeing that his vassals surrendered to Paulo Diaz, who was continually gaining ground, the King of Angola raised a great army to destroy the Portuguese. Then Paulo Diaz asked for help from the King of Congo, who sent reinforcements of 60,-000 men, led by one of his cousins, Dom Sebastian Manibamba, and a captain with 120 Portuguese soldiers who were in the region and whom he had hired for this campaign.

This army was to join the forces of Paulo Diaz in order to combat the King of Angola. When the army arrived at the river Bengo twelve miles from Luanda, the numerous embarkations caused the army to be late in coming. For this reason and because a good deal of time had been lost in trying to move so many men, the army ascended the river along the bank. Advancing in this way it encountered the troops of the King of Angola, whose mission was to prevent the Congolese penetration of the country. . . .

. . .

A few advances were made by each side. From the first battles the Congolese emerged victorious. In the combats that followed, the losses were equal on both sides. Already food had become short. Some men became sick and died. The army of the King of Congo dissolved as the soldiers returned to their homes.

Not being able to join the friendly army, Paulo Diaz marched at that moment. He passed the river and stopped at Lukala because this place, naturally fortified, could permit him to resist the King of Angola. Lukala is situated at the confluence of the Cuanza and the Lukala, 105 miles from the coast. A little upstream from the confluence, the two rivers are separated by just the distance of a shot of a harquebus and thus form a peninsula. At its end, where the two waterways meet there is a hill. Paulo Diaz occupied it and fortified it for more security. The place was not inhabited when he arrived. Now a small congregation of Portuguese has formed there.

From this place called Lukala, which Paulo Diaz occupied, one can go down the river as far as the sea in small boats. By land there are 105 miles to cover and the way is not dangerous. Not far from there are the mountains called Cambambe. An infinite quantity of silver is extracted from them. Diaz is still trying to conquer these mountains and that is why the people of Angola oppose him. They know as a fact that the Portuguese prize these mountains because of the numerous silver mines. Thus they apply more force to repulse the Portuguese. Fighting takes place in other areas as well because the Portuguese cross the river and make continual incursions into the territory belonging to the King of Angola.

65 GIOVANNI CAVAZZI
QUEEN ANNA NZINGA

Father Cavazzi was a Capuchin missionary, originally from Modena, who went to Angola in 1654. He returned to Rome in 1658 and, with Father Alamandini di Bologna, wrote the History of Ethiopia. *He returned to Angola in 1670. Queen Anna Nzinga came to the throne of Ndongo in 1623 after having poisoned her brother, the king. Thereafter, this able and determined woman began her long struggle against the Portuguese. She allied with the* Jaga *and induced Portuguese vassal chiefs to rebel. The Portuguese retaliated by proclaiming Aidi Kiluanji the rightful king of Ndongo in 1625. For the next fifteen years, Nzinga and the Portuguese fought indecisively for control of Angola until the Dutch, in their struggle against the combined empires of Portugal and Spain, captured Luanda in August 1641. Allied with the Dutch and the King of Congo, Garcia II, Nzinga's armies consistently defeated the Portuguese, destroying their field army in 1648 and besieging the fortress of Masangano. Masangano probably would have fallen had not the Dutch suddenly withdrawn. The Africans could not defend themselves against a strong Portuguese expeditionary force from Brazil under Salvador de Sa. After protracted negotiations Nzinga signed a peace treaty in 1656, by which she lost much territory but retained her independence. Peace prevailed between the Portuguese and Queen Nzinga until her death in 1663.*

In 1641 a Dutch fleet composed of twenty-two warships with good land troops appeared in the port of Luanda. The Portuguese defended Luanda so badly that the town was taken, along with a goodly part of the kingdom.

Having learned of these advantageous events, Queen Zingha [Nzinga] thought that the time had arrived for her to revenge herself against the Portuguese. She had always remembered in her heart how they had affronted her by proclaiming Ngola Arij [Aidi Kiluanji] the King of Dongo [Ndongo]. She sent them [the Dutch] ambassadors to congratulate them on their victories and to invite them to join their troops to hers so as to get rid of their common enemies once and for all. She assured them that she would be happy to have them as neighbors because she knew of their justice and politeness, whereas she could no longer bear the proud and haughty manner of the Portuguese.

The Dutch accepted these propositions with joy; these were offers that they had not expected. The King of Congo [Garcia II] entered the alliance so that the Portuguese found themselves attacked in three different places all at once. They faced them all. They had some advantages, but they were so closely pressed that they lost all the flat country and were besieged in their fortresses of Massangano, Muzzima, Cambamke, and Embacca, as well as in a few little islands in the Cuanza.

Queen Zingha had a few encounters with them that were not favorable to her. This made her think again. She wanted

to consult the demon about the outcome of the war she had entered. She did it because of a superstition that is common to the Negroes of that country. They use two cocks, one white and the other black. From the outcome of the combat, they judge whether the whites or the blacks will gain victory. Thus two cocks were prepared, one black and the other white, and they had them fight. They saw wonderful things. The black one always came out on top. Finally on the third day he pulled out all the white one's feathers and killed it.

For those people, the victory absolutely decided the outcome of the war and there were great celebrations. Without waiting any longer they went to attack the fortress of Massangano, but the queen's army was almost completely defeated. The Portuguese took a great many prisoners, and among them were the two sisters of Zingha, Cambo and Fungi, and it was only by luck that she herself escaped a trap that they had set for her.

This defeat did not discourage her but curbed her desire to attack such places and obliged her to decimate the countryside, which the Portuguese had carefully cultivated and which she made a desert.

It is true that she once surprised a few Portuguese troops and defeated them, taking a rather sizable number of prisoners. This made her think that she could surprise a frontier fort that the Portuguese had on the borders of one of her tributary vassals. She attacked it with a vigorous assault, and she was vigorously thrown back, losing part of her army on that occasion, so that comparing her losses with her gains, she found that the losses were infinitely more considerable than the advantages, despite the fact of the information she had of the Portuguese, even in the fortress of Massangano where her sister Fungi was prisoner.

From Giovanni Antonio Cavazzi, *Relation Historique de l'Ethiopie Occidentale,* trans. by J. B. Labat (Paris, 1732), pp. 80–86. Trans. from the French by Nell Elizabeth Painter and Robert O. Collins. Bracketed material has been supplied by Professor Collins.

That princess had been given the freedom of the town out of respect for her birth, and she abused it by winning over a large number of Negro subjects of the Portuguese and other discontented people. By means of presents and promises, she had them agree to seize one of the gates of the fortress and relinquish it to the troops of Zingha, who were to approach on a certain day with a new army that she had assembled. The treason was discovered, Fungi was tried and strangled, and her body was thrown in the river.

Meanwhile the war continued between the Portuguese and the Dutch, but the Dutch, having been defeated on several occasions, were so closely pressed by the victors that at the end they were forced to abandon the country and even the city of Luanda, which the Portuguese reentered and fortified better than it had been before.

Queen Zingha was deeply upset by the defeat of her allies. She could easily see that she missed the help of Europeans and would be exposed to all the vengeance of the Portuguese with even less hope of resisting, for the King of Congo had also made a settlement with them.

God took advantage of this misfortune to touch her and bring her back to herself. In her heart she had always kept some of the kind sentiments that she had had when she was outwardly a Christian. These good thoughts came to her, and she thought seriously of the crimes she had committed. She cried over them in secret, beginning to show signs of repentance. Here are some events that mastered her conversion.

Her army was in the province of On-nando, which it sacked. A priest named Dom Augustine Floris was taken and killed by one of the soldiers. This miserable cannibal, along with a few of his companions, resolved to eat the cadaver, but at the first cut he made to take a piece and eat it, it fell off dead stiff, which destroyed the desire of the others to taste such meat.

The queen was advised of this and was possessed by a very great fear of the judgments of God. She published an edict that forbade, under threat of very vigorous punishment, the killing of the priests of the whites. She even ordered that the sacred ornaments of the deceased should be conserved.

Dom Jerome Segueira, a priest in the Portuguese Army, was wounded and was taken in battle. She ordered that he be carefully taken care of and that all that had been taken from him be returned to him. She saw that he was well fed, and when he was cured, she permitted him to come and go at liberty in her camp. When he went out, whether on foot or carried in a hammock by the slaves whom she had given him, those who accompanied him cried out from time to time, "This is how we respect the Ganga, or the Priest of the God of the Catholics."

She did more than that. She permitted the building of a church to which she gave some carpets for decoration, as well as all that had been taken from the priest killed at Onnando. It is true that she never entered the church. She still had political reasons for not doing so, but every time she passed by it, she gave signs of the respect that she had for the Sovereign Master of the Universe, to whom it was dedicated.

66 MANUEL DE FARIA E SOUSA
THE KINGDOM OF THE MWANAMUTAPA

At the beginning of the fifteenth century, a group of patrilineal Bantu clans known collectively as the Karanga *occupied southwestern Rhodesia. They were organized under a dominant clan, the* Rozvi, *which, under the leadership of Mutota, sought to secure control of the whole of Central Africa from the Kalahari Desert to the Indian Ocean, between the Zambezi and the Limpopo rivers. Known as* Mwana Mutapa, *"the great plunderer," Mutota swept northward and established the center of the kingdom of the Mwanamutapa in northeastern Rhodesia. Mutota's son and successor, Matope, continued to expand the empire, but upon his death in about 1480, Changa, a Rozvi vassal, took the title of* changamir *and asserted his independence in southwestern Rhodesia. Although the empire of the Mwanamutapa was thus beginning to disintegrate within two generations of its founding, the kingdom continued to exist until the end of the nineteenth century. The Mwanamutapa had, in fact, been dominated by the Portuguese since the beginning of the seventeenth century. Manuel de Faria e Sousa (1590–1649), author of* Asia Portuguesa, *was regarded as one of the most learned men of his time. His description of the kingdom of the Mwanamutapa in 1569 is based on an account of the expedition of Francisco Barreto. Barreto was sent to avenge the murder of Father Gonçalo da Silveira, who had been killed by the Mwanamutapa at the instigation of Muslim traders at his court. At this time the Mwanamutapa were only beginning to confront the challenge of the Portuguese incomers.*

The empire of Monomotapa from the mouth of Cuama in the east runs two hundred and fifty leagues, is divided by the great river Zambesi, which falls into that of Chiri [Shire—ed.], running through the country of Bororo, where are many other large rivers, and on their banks many kings, some absolute, some subjects of Monomotapa. The greatest of the first is Mongas, bordering on Sena and the Zambesi, which falls into the sea between Mozambique and Sofala, to the south-east by four mouths: the first that of Quilimane, 90 leagues from Mozambique, the second Cuama, 25 to the southward, the third Luabo, 5 leagues lower, and the fourth Luaboel, 15 more to the south.[1] Between them are fruitful and large islands, whereof one is sixty leagues in compass. The river is navigable the same

number of leagues up to the town of Sena, inhabited by Portuguese, and as many more to Tete, a colony of theirs also. The richest mines are those of Masapa, called Aufur, the Ophir where the queen of Sheba had her riches, when she went to Jerusalem.[2] In these mines has been found a lump of gold worth twelve thousand ducats. It is not only found among stones, but grows up within the bark of several trees to the top where the branches spread.

The mines of Manchica and Butica are not much inferior to these. There are many others not so considerable. There are three fairs or markets, whither our people trade for this gold from the castle of Tete on the river Zambesi, 120 leagues from the sea: the first is Luane, four days' journey up the inland; the second Buento, farther distant; and Masapa the third, yet farther off. This gold was purchased for

From Manuel de Faria e Sousa, *Asia Portuguesa* (first published in Lisbon in 1666), trans. and reprinted by George McCall Theal in *Records of South-Eastern Africa, Collected in Various Libraries and Archive Departments in Europe* (London, 1898), II, 22–25.
[1] Leagues. A unit of measure varying from 2.4 to 4.6 miles (ed.).

[2] Some scholars have identified the gold mines of Rhodesia and the port of Sofala with the Biblical land of Ophir, whence came the gold for the Queen of Sheba (ed.).

cloth, glass beads, and other things of no value among us. At Masapa resides a Portuguese officer appointed by the commander of Mozambique, by consent of the emperor of Monomotapa, but upon condition not to go into the country without his leave upon pain of death. He is judge of the differences that arise there. There are churches of the Dominicans at Masapa, Bocuto, and Luanze.

The original number and time of the reign of the kings is not known; it is believed there were several in the time of the queen of Sheba, and that they were subject to her, for thence she had her gold. In the mountain Afur, near Masapa, are seen the ruins of stately buildings, supposed to be palaces and castles. In process of time the empire was divided into three kingdoms: Quiteve, Sabanda, and Chicanga, this last the most powerful, as possessing the mines of Manchica, Butua, and others. It is believed the blacks of Butua of the kingdom of Chicanga are those that carry the gold to Angola, because it is thought there are but one hundred leagues distance between those two places. This country bears rice and what we call Indian wheat, has abundance of all sorts of cattle, fowl, and gardening. Their chief care is pasturage and tillage. This empire is divided into twenty-five kingdoms, which are Mongas, Baroe, Manica, Boesa, Macingo, Remo, Chique, Chiria, Chidima, Boquiza, Inakanzo, Chiruvia, Condesaca, Daburia, Macurumbe, Mungussi, Anturaza, Chove, Chungue, Diza, Romba, Rassini, Chirao, Mocaranga, and Remo de Beza. There are many lordships that have not the title of kings.

The emperor has a great palace, though of wood; the chief apartments in it are three: one for himself, another for his wife, and a third for his menial servants. It has three doors into a court: one for the queen to go in and out at, another for him and the servants that attend his person and are sons of his noblemen, the third for his cooks, who are two great men and his relations, and the under-cooks who are also men of quality. None of these must be above twenty years of age, for till that age they do not believe they have to do with women, and if any do they are severely punished; after that time they are preferred to great employments. Those within doors are governed by a captain, and those without by another, as formerly in Spain.

The principal officers about the king are Ningomoxa, governor of the kingdoms; Macomoaxa, captain-general; Ambuya, great steward, to him it belongs when the Mazarira, or the king's principal wife, dies, to name another in her stead, but it must be one of the king's sisters or nearest relations; Inhantovo, the head musician, who has many under him, and is a great lord; Nurucao, captain of the vanguard; Bucurumo, which signifies the king's right hand; Magande, the chief conjuror; Netambe, the apothecary that keeps the ointments and utensils for sorcery; Nehono, chief porter. All these offices are executed by lords. There is no delicacy in cookery used; they only eat boiled and roasted; they eat the same as is usual with us, with the addition of mice, which they esteem as good as partridge or rabbit.

The king has many wives, only nine called great queens, which are his sisters or near relations, the others the daughters of nobles. The chiefest is called Mazarira, and mother of the Portuguese, who often present her, because she solicits their business with the king, and he sends no ambassador to them without some servants of hers; the second is Inahanda, that solicits for the Moors; the third Nabuiza, that lives in the same apartment with him; the fourth Navemba; the fifth Nemangore; the sixth Nizingoapangi; the seventh Negangoro; the eighth Nessani; the ninth Necarunda. Each of them lives apart, with as great state as the king, and have several revenues and kingdoms for their expense. As soon as one dies, another succeeds in place and name. They have power to reward and punish, as well as the king. Sometimes he goes to them, sometimes they come to him. There are many women waiting on them, of whom he makes use as he pleases.

The principal people of Monomotapa, and whereof the emperor is, are the Mocaranga, not warlike, nor furnished with any other arms but bows, arrows, and javelins. They have no religion nor idols, but acknowledge one only God, and believe there is a devil, that he is wicked, and they call him Muzuco. They believe their kings go to heaven, and call them Muzimos, and call upon them in time of need, as we on the saints. They speak of things past by tradition, having no knowledge of letters. They give ear to the doctrine of Christianity: the lame and blind they call the king's poor, because maintained by him with great charity, and if they travel the towns they go through are obliged to maintain and furnish them guides from one place to another: a good example for Christians.

Every month has its festival days, and is divided into three weeks, each of ten days; the first day is that of the new moon, and the festivals the fourth and fifth of each week. On these days they put on their best apparel, the king gives public audience to all, holding a truncheon [club —ed.] about three quarters of a yard long in each hand, as it were leaning upon it; they who speak to him lie prostrate; this lasts from morning till evening. If he is indisposed Ningomoxa stands in his place; nobody can speak to him or go to court on the eighth day of the new moon, because it is held most unlucky.

On the day the new moon appears, the king with two javelins runs about in his house as if he were fighting, the great men are present at this pastime, and it being ended, a pot full of Indian wheat, boiled whole, is brought, which he scatters about the ground, bidding them eat, because it is the growth of the earth; they know how to flatter, for every one strives to gather most, knowing that pleases him, and they eat it as savourly as if it were the greatest dainty.

Their greatest holy day is the first day of the moon of May, they call it Chuavo. On this day all the great men, which are a great number, resort to court, and there with javelins in their hands run about representing a fight. The sport lasts all day. Then the king withdraws, and is not seen in eight days after, during which time the drums never cease beating. On the last day he orders the nobleman he has the least affection for to be killed; this is in the nature of a sacrifice to his Muzimos or ancestors; this done, the drums cease, and every man goes home. The Mumbos eat man's flesh, whereof there is a public butchery. Let this suffice for the customs of this empire, for it would be endless to relate all.

67 ANTONIO SUÁREZ
THE CONVERSION OF THE MWANAMUTAPA

During the mid-fifteenth century, a vast empire that included most of what is now Rhodesia and part of Mozambique was created by Mutota and his son and successor, Matope. Known to the Portuguese as the Mwanamutapa, the empire of Mutapa began to disintegrate and finally broke up in the early sixteenth century during the successful revolt of a provincial chief, Changa. While Changa established an independent center of power at Zimbabwe in the south, the Mutapa empire in the northeastern part of the country contracted. Here the Mwanamutapa became increasingly dependent upon the Portuguese, whose influence was moving steadily up the Zambezi valley. Father Gonçalo da Silveira baptized the Mwanamutapa in 1560 but was assassinated soon thereafter. To avenge the death of Father da Silveira, the Portuguese sent punitive expeditions against the Mwanamutapa in 1572 and 1574. Although these expeditions failed to establish permanent Portuguese control, Portuguese influence in the seventeenth century reduced the Mwanamutapa to a puppet king. Upon the death of such a puppet king, Mavura, in 1652, the Mwanamutapa were baptized by Dominican missionaries, as described in the following account.

Dom Dominic Manamotapa, by the grace of God king and lord of Mocharanga, Boessa, BoronNo, Quiteve, Monghos, Inhaxamo, &c., make known to all to whom these presents shall come, that during the life of our father and lord the king Philip, we, being prince of these kingdoms, were brought up by the Religious of St. Dominic, to whose care the said king, our father, consigned us in the days of our early youth, and by them we were instructed and catechised and many times persuaded, until we desired to embrace the holy faith of Jesus Christ, and to receive the waters of holy baptism, and though we fervently desired the fulfilment of this our longing, being firmly convinced that this was the true path, in which the fathers walked; nevertheless we deferred the effect of our desire until such time and season as God our Lord should have done us the grace of bringing us to the actual possession of this our kingdom, wishing to imitate in this particular all that was done by the king our father, who being instructed and catechised in the doctrines of the holy faith, by Friar Emanuel Sardigna, of the said order of St. Dominic, would not receive holy baptism until he was in possession of his kingdoms, the Divine Majesty being after-

"Authentic testimony of the baptism of the emperor and king Manamotapa, signed by the said emperor, sealed with the royal seal, signed by his secretary and interpreter, and sent to the Father Provincial Friar Dionysio de Lancastro of the Portuguese province of the Order of Preachers." Trans. by Miss A. de Alberti in George McCall Theal, *Records of South-Eastern Africa, Collected in Various Libraries and Archive Departments in Europe* (London, 1898), II, 445–448.

wards pleased to call the said king our father to his holy glory on the 25th of May 1652, immediately the fathers of St. Dominic and the nobles of the kingdom, who were present at court, informed us of his death, and several of these religious, although they were assisting the vicar of the court in person, Friar Ignatius of St. Thomas and others in his company came to us in the place where we resided, many leagues distant from the court, such being the custom and usage of these kingdoms, and after they had arrived we immediately prepared to depart with all possible haste, fearing some disturbance upon our succession on the part of Caprasine the tyrant king, who for his oppressions was expelled from the kingdom, and whose turbulent risings have brought forth many evils to these realms, in particular the death of many of our Portuguese vassals and of several religious, during the space of three years that the rising lasted. Therefore, before setting forth from the retreat where we resided, we caused the captain of Dambarare to see that the Portuguese were in order and readiness for any event which might occur. Afterwards there came Friar Giovanni de Melo, to whom our father gave our person in charge to instruct and make learned in letters, which charge the said Father ever fulfilled with the utmost diligence and zeal, and therefore we hold him in great consideration and esteem, keeping him next our person in the place of a father, being confident that if in this our government he assists us with his good counsel and aid we shall govern it with the same peace and tranquillity with which it was ever governed by the king our father with the assistance of Friar Emanuel Sardigna. And treating with the said Friar Giovanni de Melo of grave matters, he did not fail to remind us that the time was now come to receive holy baptism, in order to procure the assistance of God our Lord in our government, which is what the said father places above everything. We were well pleased with his reminder, agreeing in every way with his wish that we should receive holy baptism, to which end we greatly desired to keep him in our company as far as the court, but it was not possible to gratify this wish, it being necessary that the said father should go to Dambarare in person to treat of different matters of great importance to our person. He therefore hastened his journey thither, and on arriving, in a few days he successfully dispatched the business with which we had charged him, and there also overcame the difficulties which might have deferred the fulfilment of our desire of receiving holy baptism, and returned directly to this court, in company with the Presentado Friar Salvador of the Rosary, and arrived at court on the 1st of July of the year aforesaid. We rejoiced greatly at his coming, great signs of joy being also shown by all the nobles of our court, who were all ready, owing to the zeal of the said fathers, to receive the waters of holy baptism. We omitted no occasion of encouraging the holy work of the said fathers, and hearing that some of our nobles showed some reluctance to receive the waters of holy baptism, we ordered them to be summoned to our presence, and making use of the doctrine learned from the said fathers, we made them an exhortation by means of which they were fully convinced and resolved to become Christians. The fathers did not fail, for many days following, in catechising the said nobles, and their instructions came to an end on the feast of St. Dominic. On this day we issued from our palace with great pomp, accompanied by all the no-

bles, the soldiers of the garrison, and by the aforesaid religious who walked on each side of our person. On arriving at their church, richly decorated and prepared with great magnificence, we prescribed the order in which the waters of baptism were to be administered, which was in this manner following: we caused Friar Giovanni de Melo to baptize us and the queen our consort, Friar Salvador of the Rosary being godfather and bestowing upon us the name of Dom Dominic, the day being consecrated to that saint, and upon the queen the name of Dona Louisa. Then we ordered the two chief nobles of our kingdom to be baptized, Inigomaxa receiving the name of Dom John, and Inevinga that of Dom Sebastian, and after these two Inhamapa was baptized by the name of Dom Ferdinand, and Inhamafunhe our friend by the name of Dom Peter, who five or six months before dreamed that a religious of St. Dominic was baptizing him and making him a Christian, as he himself related to us in the presence of the said fathers. All the above named are nobles of our kingdom, lords of many lands, and nearly related to ourself. This baptism was celebrated with great rejoicing, especially by those of our court, who with musical instruments and festive dances gave incredible signs of joy. The said fathers are continuing their religious and Christian office, by which it is held as certain that in a few days there will be another baptism of other nobles, who are all ready and disposed to receive holy baptism. From all that has been said it cannot be denied that glory and the greatest praise are due to the Order of St. Dominic and the friars thereof, who are ministers in these our realms. We have therefore commanded Antonio Suárez, interpreter and secretary in this our court, faithfully and well to draw up an authentic document with the royal seal, confirmed by which these presents may come to the Superiors of the said Order, that they may certify the same to the Most Serene Majesty of Portugal, our brother, that this kingdom may remain under his protection, and that he may be pleased to command the Superiors of the said fathers to recognise their labours and the great services they have rendered to God, his Majesty, and ourself, in these realms.

Given at our court of Zimbaoe, signed

by us and the aforesaid secretary, and sealed with the royal seal, the 14th of August 1652.

MANAMOTAPA, THE KING.
ANTONIO SUÁREZ,
Secretary and interpreter in the faith.

68 FATHER PINTO
THE KINGDOM OF THE KAZEMBE

Francisco José Maria de Lacerda e Almeida (d. 1798) was Governor of Sena (on the Zambezi River) when he was ordered to open a transcontinental route from Mozambique to Angola. His expedition reached the Kazembe *capital, where Lacerda died. A record of the expedition had been kept by its chaplain, Father Pinto. The kingdom of the Kazembe originated in the early eighteenth century when the* Lunda *adventurer, Nganda Bilonda, was invested with the title of* kazembe *and organized a state on the upper Lualaba. His successors expanded eastward, and under Kazembe III, or Lukwesa (c. 1760–1850), the kingdom reached its height, becoming the strongest of all Lunda states and embracing southern Katanga and parts of northeastern Zambia. Kazembe III had established trade relations with the Portuguese settlers around Tete. Although he refused to permit Lacerda's expedition to proceed westward, trade developed with the coast, and the Kazembe capital became a major terminus for routes to Kilwa and Tete.*

February 17, 1799—At 8 A.M. the Sana Muropúe returned to my house, and, in presence of all the whites, delivered a message from the Cazembe, that, as there was no more talk of Angola, he wanted the now superfluous presents intended for the Muropúe and the Mueneputo.[1] I put it to the vote of all: they were in a panic lest I should refuse: knowing the demand would be made, they augured the worst; some, for fear of being plundered and stripped, could not sleep at night. Lieut.-

Colonel Pedro Velasco (sic pro Nolasco) Vieira d'Araujo, the chief sergeant Pedro Xavier Velasco, and Antonio José da Cruz, were the only officers who did not show fear.

All being of one opinion, namely, that refusal would be dangerous, I was obliged to consent; but before doing so, I inquired of the Sana Muropúe what the Cazembe meant by such a claim; he replied it was all done in good friendship. I added that the presents should be put into his hands, not into those of the Fumo Anceva, as the latter had received a considerable gift in the name of our sovereign, and we did not know whether it had reached its destination. Moreover, that besides plundering what was given to his master, he robbed what the Cazembe sent to his friends and relatives (buenozes). But I insisted that in presence of the king the first present

From *Lacerda's Journey to Cazembe in 1798*, trans. and edited by Captain R. F. Burton, and *Journey of the Pombeiros P. J. Baptista and Amaro José Across Africa from Angola to Tette on the Zambeze*, trans. by B. A. Beadle (London: Royal Geographical Society, 1873), pp. 124–136.

[1] This was one of the strongest reasons for the transit not being allowed. The message was delivered by the apparent friend of the party, the Sana Muropúe, after the bully Fumo Anceva had been allowed to frighten them. All was perfectly *en règle*.

should be referred to. The Fumo Anceva changed colour, now denying that he had received the gift, then affirming that he had given up all to his master. The Sana Muropúe confirmed this last assertion, and relieved the Caffre whose guilt was evident; either to please the Cazembe who much affected his minister, or to draw him from a confusion which also fell upon all the nation (Murundas). Yet I persisted that the present gift should be reported before delivery, and to that purpose I sent the lieutenant, Antonio José da Cruz, who could not, however, find the Cazembe at home. The poor king has the *naïveté* to believe that over-zeal for his interests makes the Fumo Anceva, who is the greatest thief in his dominions, suffer from our false charges. I was therefore obliged to deliver the present without further ado, and without verifying the delivery of the former gift, a fact committed to paper and signed by all the party.[2] In the evening I began to inquire into the misdemeanour of Pedro Xavier Velasco.

18*th*–21*st*—There was drumming and dancing (tombocacao), which other Caffres of these parts call "Pembe-raçao,"[3] between Prince Muenebuto and his brother-in-law Chibuery, already alluded to on January 20th. The Cazembe was present with his usual dignity, but guarded by armed Caffres, as the prince danced with his large knife drawn in order to touch with it that of his father, a sign of honour and respect. The Cazembe, however, thus favoured only his son. The ceremony took place in the open space before the principal gate of the palace, a great crowd of people having instruments collected, and there also were our troops, for whom the Cazembe sent, and whose

discharge of musketry he himself directed. It was said that this fête was to celebrate his having closed once for all the Angola road, so as to increase his connection with Tete, whence their best things came. This was not confirmed, as they do not wish to break off with Angola.

I will now describe Muenebuto the prince, and his Murundas. Muenebuto is tall, good-looking, and well proportioned; his expression is pleasing, nay, almost always cheerful and smiling; he cares only for amusement, and his age—twenty years—permits nothing else. On the contrary, the Cazembe shows gravity and inspires respect; he also is tall, and well built, and his age may be about fifty. As he has many wives—the greatest sign of Caffre dignity—he becomes every year the father of two, three, or four children. He is very generous at times in giving slaves and pieces of cloth to his vassals, as well as to strangers and whites, when he is not set against them; and every day he sent the Muzungos money and different presents of provisions, captives, ivory or copper bars, in proportion to their offerings of cloth and beads, and according to his regard for them.

He is severe; death, or at least amputation of the hand, being the usual punishment. He is barbarous; every new moon he causes a Caffre to be killed by his medicine-man, and with the victim's blood, heart, and part of the entrails, they make up his medicine, always mixing it with oil. When these charms are prepared, they are inserted into the horns of various animals, and even into scrivellos, which are closed with stoppers of wood or cloth. These fetishes are distributed about his palace and courts; they are hung to the doors, and for fear of sorcery the king never speaks to any one without some of these horns lying at his feet.[4]

He holds assemblies of his chiefs, who are invited to drink pombe, or millet-beer,

[2] Those who have not travelled in Africa often wonder at all the importance attached to these trifling presents. But the fact is that without supplies the journey is brought to a dead stop, not taking into account the hardships and sufferings of return. The explorer, therefore, must fight for every cubit of cloth, and this is, perhaps, the severest part of his task.

[3] Native festivities, including drinking and cancan.

[4] Small horns of goats and antelopes are thus used in Unyamwezi, stuffed with thin iron wire; in Congo with strips of cloth.

which is mixed with other pulse or not, as each man's taste is. These drinkings begin with the full moon, and continue to the end; they commence daily at or before 1 P.M., and they last two hours. All those present drink as much as they please, but should any one vomit in the assembly, the wretch is instantly put to death. Though superstition-ridden, like all these people, the Cazembe is not so much so as are others. He visits no one in person, and never leaves his palace to walk; he has the name of being proud, but his people make him inconsistent.

The subjects (Murundas), who say that sixty years ago they came from the Western regions and established themselves in the lands of the conquered Vaciras (Messiras), are of the same nation as the Cazembe, whose rites and customs they follow.

Usually the men are tall, dark, well made, and good-looking; they tattoo (incise), but do not paint their bodies, nor do they jag their teeth. Their dress is a cloth extending from the waist to the knees, which are exposed by the garment being raised in front; it is girt by a leathern belt, 4 to 10 fingers broad. Their gala-dress is called "Muconzo;" it is of woollen or cotton, but it must be black. To make it they cut a piece 5$^1/_2$ fathoms, or a little less in length, and if it be too short they add a bit of the same quality; the breadth is 2$^1/_2$ hands, and if wider it is reduced to that size. It must be finished with a full edging, which increases it in all parts; this border is made of three strips of a different cloth, each 4 fingers broad. When the colour is red, for instance, the middle is white; it is yellow if the middle be red or white. Finally, they diversify these strips as they please, always taking care that the colour differs from the body or the principal part of the cloth. When putting on the "Muconzo," they cover the waist and legs, finishing at the front of the person with a great band of artificial pleats; and the larger it is, the grander is the garb. For arm-ornaments they use strings of fine beads like bracelets; their feet are covered with strung cowries, large opaque stoneware beads (pedras de côres), and white or red porcelains (velorios). Over their combed head-dresses, which are of many braids, large and small, they wear a cap (carapuça), covered with exquisite birds'-plumes; the locks are also striped (barradellas) with a certain clay, which, when dry, resembles the levigated sandalwood used by the Moors and Gentoos (Hindus); the stripes, however, are only on the crown and temples (molleira). Others rub their bodies upon the waist and upwards to the hair with a certain vermilion (vermelhao),[5] here common.

Such is the gala dress. Their every-day clothing is a little cloth, 1$^1/_2$ to 2 fathoms long, with or without a border of a single strip; others wear bark cloth, like the Muizas, or edgeless cotton; and finally, coarse native cotton (maxilas de Gondo),[6] as each one has or can afford.

As usual the women dress better than the men, as to the kind of cloth, which is of wool (collomanha) or similar stuff. They also use, like the males, strings of many sorts of beads, to cover their ankles, but they are not so fond of cowries or porcelain (velorio). Their coiffure is unlike that of the men; they cut off all the hair, leaving a little lock in the middle, which in time, growing long, serves to support a kind of diadem [ornamental headband—ed.]; the rest of the hair, when it grows, forming sundry lines of short braid. Their ordinary dress is extremely poor, consisting of one very small cloth. These women, who also can be sold by their husbands, lead the lives of slaves, doing all the labour of domestic slavery.

The Murundas,[7] like other peoples of

---

[5] It has previously been described as being wood-powder.
[6] The expression is fully explained in the diary of June 20–23. Dr. Kirk says that a "Maxila de garda" is a hammock of native cloth. "Maxila de Gondo" is a stuff so coarse that hammocks can be made of it. Hence Monteiro and Gamitto call the coarse cotton cloth made by the Marave, "Manxila."
[7] In the original misprinted "Mosundas."

this country, have no (practical) religion. They recognize the existence of a sovereign creator of the world, and call him "Reza," but they consider him a tyrant that permits his creatures' death. They have great veneration for their Azimos (murimos), or dead, whom they consult on all occasions of war or good fortune. The Caffre servants of any Moçaza,[8] or place in which a king is buried, have many privileges. The Azimos require offerings of provisions, as dough (massa), a food made of manioc flour, to stew with the porridge, which in the Brazil is called Angú; of quiriaça (any mess of meat, fish, or herbs), and of pombe, the millet-beer before described. They greatly respect what the oracle says to them. Their sons are circumcised between the ages of fourteen and eighteen,[9] and they affect polygamy, which they regard as their greatness, much wondering at the one-wife marriage of the whites.

Their unions are effected without ceremony: the would-be husband goes to the father or guardian of the girl, who may be quite a child, and with him arranges the dowry in cloths, which, if great, may reach a dozen. After this arrangement, called betrothal (roboracção), the payment being left to the bridegroom's convenience, they arrange a day for leading home the bride, who, until of nubile years, remains with her parents. Consummation is done thus: carried by the horse of some Caffre, and accompanied by her female relations and friends, beating drums, the bride is escorted to near the bridegroom's house, and when close to it they send him word that they bring his wife. This done, they drum and dance till some velorio beads are sent to them, after which they advance two paces or so, and stop till they get more. Thus, on his marriage-day, the

poor Caffre must not only strip himself, but also go out borrowing, to show that he has given all his own. Seeing nothing more come, they inspect the sum offered them, then they advance nearer, and at length they hand over the bride to the chief wife and her companions, and retire to their homes, leaving her in tears. As the Caffres may buy an unlimited number of spouses, even their slaves being wives to them, they choose one, and call her the great woman, and she is the most respected. Her peculiar duties are to preserve the husband's wardrobe and medicines, and to apply the latter when required; without using them no one goes to war, to hunt, or to travel, or, indeed, on any important business.

The funerals of these people are proportioned to the means of the deceased. Their pomp consists in the great cortége by which the body is borne to the grave, and in the quantity of food and drink expended upon the crowd of people, who sing and dance to the sound of drums. If the deceased be a king, he must carry with him all that he possesses, with slaves to serve him and women for his pleasures. Throughout his dominions robberies and disorder (cleirero) are allowed for ten or fifteen days, or even more. Their deadliest crimes are witchcraft, adultery, and theft. The first, and the most enormous, is always punished capitally; the second sometimes, but more often by mutilation of the hands, the ears, and the offending member. They are less severe with the women, as a rule, but some plaintiffs are not satisfied except by death. Although they cut off the thief's hands and ears, many wretches have exposed themselves to such mutilation.

The soil of this land is fertile, and would produce all that the people want; there are many kinds of food, but the principal is manioc. They eat it in dough, toasted and boiled and even raw; and they drink it in pombe with a little mixture of millet. Manioc flour for dough is easily made in the following way: after gathering

---

[8] Mussassa is a camp: here it must be the burial-place before called Mâxâmo.
[9] In Dahomey this rite is deferred often till the twentieth year, and then it becomes dangerous. I have repeatedly recorded my opinion that it is of African origin, borrowed by the Jews from the negroid race.

the root, they peel it, and soak it in a stream, for three days; on the fourth, when it is almost rotten, they dry it in the summer sun, or in winter over a fire which they light under the cots used for this purpose; and, finally, they pound it in a tree-trunk mortar. We may say that they are collecting and sowing this root all the year round, but the harvest is when provision is wholly wanting. At such times they dig up a small quantity to last for a few days, and in its stead they bury a few bits of stalk which act as seed. The rains are abundant and regular. Fruits are few, except bananas of many kinds: of live stock, poultry is the most plentiful and goats are rare. Game and fish suffice, but they cannot salt their provision, so to keep it they dry it with fire and smoke, making it unfit for us to eat. The black cattle is well flavoured, but only the king keeps them in certain places, to show his greatness: he does not eat their flesh, saying that they are Fumos [black in color—ed.], like himself; also he does not milk them, not knowing how, so the cows are almost wild. Here we find traces of the Metempsychosis theory.[10] With this idea the king sends his cattle as gifts to his guests, and when they die or are killed for injuring millet fields—these animals pasture by night and sleep by day—he divides the meat amongst his people, who, not considering them, like their king, great Fumos, eat them unscrupulously. Cow leather makes their girdles, that of other horned cattle their dress, and cows' blood enters into their medicines. Therefore they sent us only dead and skinned animals.

There may be many articles of trade, but it is now confined to two—ivory and slaves. A tusk of 32 lbs. to 48 lbs. costs 2 to 3 pieces of cloth, the piece being

$1^1/_2$ to 2 fathoms long, and ten couros.[11] The tusk of 80 lbs. to 96 lbs. is worth 5 to 6 pieces, with a little couro or velorio. There are copper bars sold for four common cloths, or pagnes (pannos de fato), or 40 to 50 couros; the small bars cost as a rule one cloth's worth of missanga. Uncut greenstone (malachite)[12] of different sizes is sold cheap, but the two latter articles are not indigenous.

22nd—The Sana Muropúe took away, in presence of all the whites, the gifts destined for the Muropúe and the Mueneputo, as was promised at our assembly on the 17th instant.

23rd—Having ordered Lieutenant Antonio José da Cruz, commandant of the troops, to chastise a soldier with forty blows, he not only disobeyed me, but he also falsely reported having carried out my orders.

February 24th to *March* 1st—The men, instigated by their officers, demanded an advance of three months' pay, which I sent to them without receiving any reply.

2nd–4th—I gave Pedro Xavier Velasco leave to go back to Tete, not only at his request, but because I wished to avoid the disgust shown by all the Expedition to the Cazembe, with whom, it is said, this arrangement of return had been made in anticipation of my desires. José Rodrigues Caleja, hearing this, wished to interfere and exceeding his duties as guide and Receiver of the Treasury, he addressed me a note in which, after a fashion, he made himself accessory to the command. As I took no notice of his false reasonings, he began to show me aversion and to seek his revenge.

5th—The manioc grown in the land which the Cazembe had offered to the whites (muzungos) on the 27th January was divided, but their carelessness prevented them sending their slaves (checun-

---

[10] Superficial observers often confound the highly philosophical and complicated theory of metempsychosis with the vulgar metamorphosis of the savage African. [Metempsychosis is the passing of the soul at death into another body either animal or human —ed.]

[11] From the context it would appear that these couros are some kind of bead.

[12] Monteiro and Gamitto mention malachite "malaquites," which the Cazembes call "chifuvia." I have seen fine copper from the Cazembe's country.

das) to receive the portion appertaining to them.

6th–9th—Loud murmurs arose about the Expedition arriving at the Cazembe's city—which it could not at once leave—during the early month of January, when the evils caused by the wet season and the country rendered a long rest necessary. As José Rodrigues Caleja, by declaring me to be the cause of the delay and of their consequent sufferings, showed signs of stirring up against me even the most indifferent, I assembled all the whites. They knew what were my reasons for wintering here, so I resolved that each should separately declare his opinion touching our inaction, whether it could have been avoided or not and how. I told the writer, or notary, to take the paper in which all had recorded their opinions, to draw it up in legal form, and to get their signatures. It was late when we separated, and the scribe was not skilled enough to draft the deed without the aid of others. He went to José Rodrigues Caleja, being of that party, and with him falsified not only Caleja's vote but also that of Vasco Joaquim Pires, as is proved in the forged paper. I was disregarded by Captain João da Cunha Pereira, and when I wished to punish him there and then he would not be arrested, nay, with threats he declared that His Excellency, the Captain-General of Mozambique, should not deprive him of his receivership, as had been done to Lieut. Manoel dos Santos Silva.

As I had little power, nothing was effected. I asked Gonçalo Caetano Pereira, the first guide, how to ascertain from Chinhimba and Mossindassaro the deficiency of the loads entrusted to them for carriage to the Cazembe's court. He replied, in the presence of many, that this must be done with the beneplacet of the king, whose vassals they were. Finding the answer reasonable, I entrusted to him the business, which he undertook promptly and with good will.

10th—Lieutenant Antonio José da Cruz, when ordered to attest in writing the refusal of Captain João da Cunha Pereira to submit to arrest yesterday, gave in his attestation which denied all that had happened.

11th–14th—Gonçalo Caetano Pereira, whom I had resolved to send on the 8th instant to the Cazembe in the matter of Mossindassaro and Chinhimba, when asked by José Rodrigues Caleja not to delay, excused himself by means of his Caffre Inharugue, saying that the latter did not wish to bear any message to the Cazembe. The most embarrassing thing is, that they try to lay the blame upon me, when at the same time they bar my road to the king, and they prevent the two Caffres obeying all my summons. At last I tried every effort to send some other person on this errand to the king, who deferred it till the morrow.

15th—Sending back to the Cazembe the messenger who had returned yesterday, I heard to-day that the king was pleased with my calling up and examining the two Caffres before mentioned. When they declined to obey my summons I reported the fact to the king, begging that his messenger would conduct them into my presence. He promised but he never performed, which I attributed to the intrigues of Caleja. This man, under colour of benefiting D. Francisca Josefa of Tete, whose niece he had married, declared that the late Governor de Lacerda, who had taken charge of that lady's venture, and whose death had caused the goods to be confused, had concealed by means of the Mossindassaro, six bales (moteros) [13] of cloth, and had changed the mark or mixed the articles, removing 150 pannos and two bags (guissapos) [14] of velorio beads. These he had wished to make over to D. Francisco's slave, Candeone, in order to exchange for ivory. And this was done with the knowledge of the gover-

[13] This is afterwards explained to be one-third of 456 cloths, that is to say, each 152 cloths.
[14] The word "guissapo" means a bag of bamboo rind or grass cloth. Monteiro and Gamitto speak of "um Quissápo, sacco feito de palma."

nor's managing man, whose duty it was to take charge of those articles, pretexting the report spread by José Rodrigues Caleja that the manager had wished to appropriate the said spoils. This trick of José Rodrigues Caleja's was very ingenious, for not only was that Caffre encouraged to conceal 912 more cloths (pagnes) of royal property, but Chinhimba, the other Caffre messenger, also took heart successfully to embezzle from the Crown 456 cloths, three bags (guissapos) of velorio, two ditto of (red) beads, and one of cowries.

16th–28th—José Rodrigues Caleja was always imposing upon them the necessity of giving the Cazembe time to prepare for our departure. The others being sick, I directed him to go with a "mouth" or parcel of cloth and to make preparations, at the same time reviving the matter of the two Caffres. The Cazembe received him well, and said that he knew—the winter now being over—that the Expedition would wish to return to Tete. As regards the defaulting Caffre, he said that the whites had allowed a long time to pass in silence, and had finally received everything. The first part of this reply could not have come from a Caffre, who all hold that the palaver (milando) never dies, nor wastes, but is kept up till "settled" from generation to generation. So I resolved either that the king had not said it, or had been taught to say it by José Rodrigues Caleja. The affair was not pushed further, because it was not advisable to call Chinimba to account until the appearance of Mossindassaro, who would hear of it from the Cazembe and conceal himself.

29th–30th—I gave the said Caffres some small quantity of clothing for which they asked, thus hoping to assemble them and to elicit something about the hidden goods.

31st—The Cazembe sent me the chair enclosed in his present (mirambo), begging me to have it lined with "cherves," which was done at once.

April 1st–7th—By an accidental fire eight of my slaves were burned in their own huts; many of the Expedition rejoiced thereat, and a certain José Thomaz Gomes da Silveira, openly wished that the accident had taken place in my house. I report this and other things, which do not exactly relate to the service of the Crown, both to carry out my instructions and to show the character of my subordinates.

8th–9th—The Cazembe forbade the whites, who had begun their cabals greatly to his disgust, all intercourse with him, thus avoiding their impertinences, and he wondered at our disunion.

10th—José Rodrigues Caleja, an old enemy of Lieutenant Manoel dos Santos e Silva, with whom he appeared friendly only when wishing to insult me, after visiting him in his sickness, declared to me that he wished for death, and that if he knew of anything to end his life he would take it.

11th–12th—I had some inklings that the crime charged upon Pedro Xavier Velasco was a mere imputation, and Lieutenant José Vicente Pereira Salema confessed that he had been intimidated to give false witness by José Rodrigues Caleja. I also learned that Captain João da Cunha Pereira, after his deposition, went to Pedro Xavier Velasco's quarters, and told him that I wanted to drink his blood, which was my reason for drawing up papers against him, but that no depositions made by himself or his colleagues would do him any injury.

13th—José Rodrigues Caleja convoked, in the house of Gonçalo Caetano Pereira, to debate over the affair of the 9th of March, all those of his party, viz., Captain João da Cunha Pereira, Lieutenant Manoel dos Santos e Silva, Captain José da Cruz, José Thomaz Gomes da Silva, Lieutenant José Vicente Pereira Salema, and Ensign José Joaquim Pires; they agreed to outrage me in that business, first by word and then by deed. The Lieut.-Colonel Pedro Nolasco Vieira de Araujo and the chief sergeant Pedro Xavier Velasco were sick, and not of the league.

I had no testimony whereby to convict them, thus they could insult me with impunity. The former of these two, however, came unexpectedly upon them, and the project fell to the ground. All this was told to me by Lieutenant José Vicente Pereira Salema, whom as the most timorous they sent to me with a paper of their requisitions.

14th–15th—José Rodrigues Caleja, who was in the habit of troubling me morning and evening, came early to report that messengers were expected from Tete to recall the troops, as there was great alarm of the French.

16th—José Rodrigues Caleja required me to assemble the members in order to determine how to sell the Crown stores remaining in the receiver's hands. My reply was that I had reasons for not convening any more of such assemblies. He went at once and wrote me a letter representing the loss that would result from taking the goods back to Tete. In view of all this trouble I at once ordered the stores to be valued.

17th—The effects were valued by the arbitrators at only double their cost-price at Tete, and the receiver, with sundry impertinences, demanded permission to sell them. I ordered them to be sold for the sums offered, finding that nothing more advantageous could be obtained.

18th–19th—I sent to compliment the Cazembe, who was then a great friend of mine; he sent back that he wanted to see me.

20th—I returned an answer to the Cazembe's message, declaring that I would call upon him personally.

21st—José Rodrigues Caleja, angry because, without consulting him, I had allowed Pedro Xavier Velasco to return to Tete, and because I would not be made the tool of his private enmities, did all he could to annoy me. He teazed me with requests to smuggle out the cloth required for our return march, as the Cazembe would never allow it, after once entering, to leave the country. Fearing his malice,

I appointed him and the guide, Gonçalo Caetano Pereira, to fix upon the quantity and the place. The former was settled, the latter they refused to tell me, pleading that, as we had travelled together, I—a chaplain—must know as much as they (the guides) did.

22nd–23rd—I again ordered the two aforesaid guides to tell me the "cache," and they refused.

24th—The Cazembe consented to receive me on the morrow, and to send a household officer to conduct me, as the Fumo Anceva wished all the whites to be purely dependent upon himself. José Rodrigues Caleja happened to be present, and, dissimulating his jealousy of my getting an audience when he had failed, begged me to forward the departure of the Expedition, which, depending upon the Cazembe, would easily be forgotten unless often brought to mind.

25th—After a short delay I was admitted to the Cazembe, who received my compliments kindly, responding briefly after the country fashion. This over, I earnestly prayed him to forward the time of our return; to which he also replied favourably. I then submitted to him that on reaching Tete there would be a difficulty in explaining to my superiors the prohibition of passing over to Angola; he bade me leave two members of the party to proceed there after our departure. The Fumo Anceva wrested this into a demand that each of the whites should leave behind one or two Cheundas.[15] Knowing that the slaves would be pawns for our future communication, and that the Caffres being scarce, and many of them sickly, the whites would not consent to the measure. I replied that when Catára and Chinimba had come with friendly messages to Tete, we had at once set out without hostages. Hearing me speak to the soldier-linguist in the Sena dialect, the Cazembe at once explained that he did not want hostages, but two persons to go to

[15] This, I presume, is "checunda"—a slave.

Angola. I could not reply to so sudden and unexpected a permission, so I told the king that the presents destined for the Muropúe and the Muenebuto having been given away, and the treasury being exhausted, my confusion prevented my returning an answer. The Cazembe at once said that he would manage about the presents, and that all I had to do was to look after the subsistence and the means of travel. I finally answered that the matter should be thought over. He then spoke of the opaque stoneware beads (pedras de côres) which he wanted from the whites, who still, he knew, had good things. I contented him as well as possible, and left deeply preoccupied about Angola. After my return, José Rodrigues Caleja, on hearing the affair, malignantly remarked, that if I had proposed Pedro Xavier Velasco as envoy to the Cazembe, he would soon close the road with a new prohibition; and much of the same kind to throw obstacles in my way.[16]

26th—José Rodrigues Caleja came, and insultingly showed me a paper in which the lieutenant-colonel Pedro Nolasco Vieira de Araujo and Pedro Xavier Velasco had complained of him, and charged him with being their informant. As if a secret between nine persons could be kept, especially when of the many councillors are Captain João da Cunha Pereira and Lieutenant José Vicente Pereira Salema, who do nothing but tittle-tattle. I tried to avoid a scandalous rupture, but from that day forward he did nothing but oppose me, wishing to commit all the goods to the Cazembe, and thus to frustrate the transit to Angola.

27th—The Fumo Anceva came from the Cazembe, refusing passage to Tete for Lieut.-Colonel Pedro Nolasco Vieira de Araujo, who wished to leave these bad men. I answered that he was not going, because I had not given him leave. This reply closed the Caffre's mouth. He doubtless had been taught to oppose this departure, though not by his friendship for the departer. It was José Rodrigues Caleja's plan, in opposing the going of the two Pedros, Nolasco and Velasco, to forewarn all those who might be useful to him at Tete, adding as many lies as possible, and well knowing that the thing first heard, though false, is generally credited in preference to truth.

Not satisfied by this mischief, that perverse man went with Lieutenant Antonio José da Cruz to the Cazembe, designing to traduce me and Pedro Nolasco, but the Cazembe, who hated his mutinous disposition, refused him access. He must indeed be a bad white man who is hated by Caffres. He reported to the Fumo Anceva that the Lieut.-Colonel Pedro Nolasco and the other whites had so well hidden many fine cloths and coloured stoneware beads (pedras pintadas), that these could be discovered only by opening their boxes. The Cazembe, despite his generosity, was persuaded to give this order, or the Fumo Anceva fabricated it. I sent for the lieutenant-colonel, Pedro Nolasco, to hear the message: he excused himself, but he could not prevent the search. I positively refused to sanction it in the case of other whites, knowing that the Fumo Anceva wanted only to enter the receiver's house and to carry off everything for his king.[17]

[16] This permission for two of the party to proceed to Angola was a sham, to see if any presents had been withheld, and to try the perseverance of the whites. The Cazembe must have thought unfavourably of the leader when he hesitated at once to reply—a thing ever to be avoided in Africa. The two soldiers were eventually left behind as was proposed, but they never, it need hardly be said, reached Angola. In 1806 the Angolan Pombeiros found one man still waiting for permission.

[17] There is a Fumo Anceva at every African court, who thinks only of recommending himself to the king by giving any amount of trouble to strangers. Of course it is a shallow, short-sighted policy, but nothing better can come from the negro's brain. It is, however, dangerous, and must be carefully watched, as it is calculated to cause disagreeables between the members of an expedition, and then everything goes to ruin.

69 P. J. BAPTISTA
THE KAZEMBE

In 1806 two pombeiros *(African traders), P. J. Baptista and Anastasio José, arrived at the capital of Kazembe and there met Lukwesa's successor, his son Kibangu Keleka, or Kazembe IV. After a prolonged residence at the capital, Kazembe IV permitted the pombeiros to complete their trans-African journey in 1810. The following excerpts are from Baptista's diary.*

[74th.] *Saturday, 20th*—Halted in the Cazembe's sister's farm, by her own order. At two in the morning, she sent for us, and we went inside her walls. She asked whence we came. We replied, from Angola and the court of Muropue, who had given us the guide. That we had come to speak with her brother King Cazembe, to get permission to go on to the town of Tette. She replied it was very good on the part of Muropue to send white people to speak with her brother; that none of Muropue's predecessors had done so; that it was a very great fortune for her brother Cazembe's heir to the State. She offered us a large she-goat, forty fresh fish, two bottles of a drink called "pombe," and six quicapos of dry mandioca flour. We presented her with thirty-two xuabos, a blue glass, and a "mozenzo" of a hundred white stones. She said she was much pleased with our gifts. We waited there that she might send notice of our arrival to her brother, King Cazembe, as it is obligatory on her part when travellers come to report them to her brother. With this end we waited six days at her farm, when the carriers came in search of us.

[75th.] *Saturday, 27th*—Got up and left the farm of Cazembe's sister at 7 A.M. Had no rain. We followed down the course of the Luapula. Passed a river of two fathoms' width, name unknown, which runs into the Luapula. During the

From *Lacerda's Journey to Cazembe in 1798,* trans. and edited by Captain R. F. Burton, and *Journey of the Pombeiros P. J. Baptista and Amaro José, Across Africa from Angola to Tette on the Zambeze,* trans. by B. A. Beadle (London: Royal Geographical Society, 1873), pp. 186–188.

journey we came to the farm of a black named Murumbo: we reached it at midday. We met no one, and marched with the sun on our right. We lodged in the houses of the farm, and saw nothing rare or important.

[76th.] *Sunday, 28th*—We got up at 2 A.M., and started from the farm of Murumbo. We marched down with the above-named river on our left. We passed two rivers, Lufubo and Capueje, which run into the above-named river. During the journey we came to the farm of a black named Gando, near a river called Gona, here we gave no presents. We reached it at six in the afternoon. We marched with the sun as before.

[77th.] *Monday, 29th*—At 5 A.M. we got up and started from the farm of Gando, near the river Gona. We passed two rivers, one called Belenje, the other's name not known; during the march we came to the place of a black named Canpungue. We reached this place at three in the afternoon, and met a good number of King Cazembe's people carrying firewood. We presented this black, Canpungue, with a chuabo of "Zuarte" or Indian cloth; he told us to continue our journey, as the Cazembe was expecting us.

[78th.] *Tuesday, 30th*—At seven A.M. we started from the place of the black, Canpungue—had no rain; we passed no river, and during the journey came to the place of a black named Luiagamára, of the Cazembe. Reaching this place at four in the afternoon, we lodged in the houses near a river called Canengua, narrow, and running into the river called Mouva, near which Cazembe's city is situated. We gave no present to the owner of this place; we halted there, and sent forward a day's notice of our arrival; we waited a little time, when the King Cazembe's messenger arrived, bringing us, as guest-gift, four murondos of a drink called "pombe," one hundred pieces of fresh meat, with some manioc flour for our consumption, and also a message from King Cazembe, asking us to remain at present where we were, that he would send for us later. Day breaking directly, and it being two o'clock in the morning, he sent for us by his chief, with orders that on our arrival near the walls of his chiefs (ancestors?), we should fire off all our guns, as a signal that we had arrived at his capital. He ordered us to lodge with one of his gatekeepers, named Fumo Aquibery. We did nothing respecting our journey on this day: he sent us for our people, however, some provisions, manioc flour, fish, fresh meat, and "pombe," she-goats, and meats already prepared; he said he would see us with great pleasure. When morning broke, he sent word for us to come and tell him what brought us there. We found him seated in the public highway, where he was accustomed to deliver his judgments to his people, surrounded by all the great potentates of his councils. He was robed in his silks and velvets, and had beads of various kinds on his arms and legs; his people surrounded him, and he had all his instruments of barbarous grandeur round about him. He sent to say that the guide who had come with us from his Muropue should speak. The guide said, "I bring you some white men here from the king they call Muenuputo; they come to communicate with you, King Cazembe; treat them well, without malice, and execute the wishes entrusted to them: grant them, King Cazembe, permission, together with some guide, who you may see able to conduct them, to go to the town of Tette, to deliver a letter to the Most Illustrious Governor of that town, they being entrusted with this mission in Angola,

whence they came. Muropue also strongly recommends you will do all necessary to despatch the travellers where they wish to go, and afterwards send them back to Muropue, in order that he may return them whence they came." The King Cazembe said that he esteemed it much, and not a little, his Muropue's having sent travellers from afar; that for a long time past he had entertained the idea of opening the road to Senna; that he was very pleased to see travellers from Muropue, none of whose predecessors had similarly acted before; that he would do all in his power—not only provide a guide, but go with us himself as far as the Warcamp, to fight the highwaymen and robbers who meet with and intercept people on the road coming to communicate with him, King Cazembe. We had gone with King Cazembe as far as a farm of his people, about half a league from Cazembe, with numerous troops to escort us on the road; after this, a perturbation spread among his people, who did not wish to fight, so the attempt was frustrated; we returned to the farm with him against his wish. He began to cast out his chiefs; he cut the ears of some, others he mulcted in slaves and manilhas (bracelets); and on the second month he handed us over to his chief named Muenepanda to accompany us with more people. On our reaching a desert-lodging called Quipire, he turned back, saying that the town of Tette was a long way off; that the force he (Muenepanda) had to oppose to the potentates he might meet on the road was very small; that he did not wish to run any risk. We returned with him, and after waiting another half month, the black, named Nharugue, belonging to Gonçalo Caetano Pereira arrived, and we started and marched in his company till we reached this town of Tette.

King Cazembe is very black, a fine, stout young man, with small beard, and red eyes; he is very well accustomed to white traders, who come to his court to buy and sell such articles as seed, manioc flour, maize, millet, haricot beans, a good many "canas" (sugar-cane?), and fish which the people catch in the river near there called Mouva. Ivory comes from the other side the river Luapula, and is brought as tribute by the people; green stones (malachite) are found in the ground, called "catanga"; traders from the Muizas people come and buy ivory, in exchange for tissues and merchandise; another nation, named Tungalágazas, brings slaves and brass bracelets, cowries, palm-oil, and some goods which King Cazembe has, come from the Cola (Angola?), a land of Muropue, also fine large beads. There is a good deal of salt in that part, which they get from the ground; there is also another kind of rock-salt which is brought as tribute from the salt district, on the road to Muropue's territory, called Luigila, where he has a chief and a relation, named Quibery, who takes account of the Salina, and sends tributes of salt to his Muropue, besides buying it of the travellers who come from Muropue. I have made no entry of the rainy days we stopped, or of those when we were detained by sickness. I saw nothing more at the Court of King Cazembe which I have forgotten to write; I saw nothing but that already stated.

70 A. C. P. GAMITTO
THE MARAVI

A. C. P. Gamitto (1806–1866) was second in command of the Monteiro expedition that set out to open a transcontinental route from Mozambique to Angola between 1831 and 1832—an abortive mission that Lacerda similarly had failed to accomplish a generation before. The Maravi *described by Gamitto are one of the principle groups in the modern state of Malawi, which takes its name from the former chiefdoms of the Maravi west of Lake Nyasa. The Maravi claim to have originated in Lubaland, and although the Portuguese believed that the Maravi built a great empire, the probability is that no one chief became paramount, as was the case in the kingdom of the* Kazembe.

     .   .   .

The territory occupied by these people is one of the largest in this part of Africa. Its inhabitants, who are in continual warfare among themselves, are the subjects of a great number of small chiefs or princes who are forever trying to destroy one another; this is one reason for the poor opinion that foreigners hold of this country in

From A. C. P. Gamitto, *King Kazembe and the Marave, Cheva, Bisa, Bemba, Lunda, and Other Peoples of Southern Africa, Being the Diary of the Portuguese Expedition to that Potentate in the Years 1831 and 1832,* trans. by Ian Cunnison (Lisbon: Junta de Investigações do Ultramar, 1960), I, 63–73. Reprinted by permission.

spite of its size and population. The land, properly known today by the name of Marave, is bounded in the west by the Shombwe stream, which divides it from the Cheva; and in the east by the Mukakamwe torrent, which separates it from the Portuguese dominions of Tete district which extend on the left bank of the Zambezi as far as the Lupata. In the north, the boundary is with the Bororo and the Maganja; and in the south the boundary is the Zambezi, which divides it from the Munhaes of Monomotapa and the Portuguese territory of the district mentioned.

The part which we traversed, which is not its widest part, would be about 59 leagues. Its length from north to south comprises a very great extent, but not knowing how much I am unable to calculate the total area. In the east, north and south these people border Portuguese lands.

Formerly this region was divided into two dominions, Munhaes and Maraves; and today these people have taken various names. Those referred to above are prope˙ly the Marave; Bororos are those who dwell on the left bank of the Zambezi and are bordered by the territory of Quelimane and on the west by the Shire. Between these and the Lupata are the Maganjas. And from the north to the coast at Cape Delgado are the Makwa. West of the Marave, as far as the river Luangwa, live the Cheva, and to the east of these and near the mouth of that river are the Senga and between these and the Portuguese territories of the left bank of the Zambezi are the Mogoa. East of the Makwa, and on the shores of the river or lake Nyanja, are the Yao or Nguru. All these people today are totally independent of each other, and each is known by its own name. Nevertheless it is beyond dispute that all are of the same Marave race, having the same habits, customs, language, etc.

This country is of very vast extent, and according to my information there are many impassable regions in it, because of the bad treatment received from the savage inhabitants, and the thick forests covering it. The Nguru are of ferocious appearance, and do not agree to penetration by strangers into their land beyond the western margin of the aforesaid lake or river. It is only there that commerce with them takes place.

II

It is still not known whether the Lake Marave of the geographers, called Nyanja-Mukulu (Rio Grande) by the Blacks, and Rio Nyanja by the Portuguese, has

communication with the sea. It seems certain however that it forms a mighty river which has its mouth on the Zanzibar coast, being perhaps the Koavo, which debouches opposite Kilwa. It seems it was visited by the early Portuguese,[1] but I have no information that it has been visited by any European traveller, but only by Moors and Blacks who have gone there from Mozambique to trade, and Bisa who are today the merchants of those regions. From all of these I have received the following unanimous information.

The river Nyanja-Mukulu, or great Nyanja, has an extraordinary breadth. Embarking in canoes to cross it, it is necessary to sleep two nights on islands, with which it is sprinkled, before arriving on the third day in the afternoon on the opposite shore: a distance which, according to my calculation, must be about nine leagues. It has a strong easterly current. The many islands it contains, some of which are very large, are for the most part inhabited, those on the west by the Marave, and those on the east by the Yao or Nguru. This is the story that mer-

[1] Father Manoel Godinho, in his Voyage from India to Portugal by Land in 1663, says as follows:

"The road from Angola to India by land is not yet discovered; but it certainly will be, and the passage will be easy, because from Angola to Lake Zachaf (which is in the middle of Ethiopia and is fifteen leagues broad, although its length is not yet known) is less than 250 leagues. Cosmographers put this lake at 15° 50', and according to a map I have seen, made by a Portuguese who went many years to the kings of Monomotapa, Manica, Butua and others of Kaffraria, this lake is not far from the Zimbawe, or court, of Mesura or Marabia. There issues from it the river Aruvi which flows into the Zambezi above our fort of Tete. And also the river Chire which, cutting through many lands, and latterly through those of the Rondo, joins the river Cuama below Sena. This assured I now say: he who would make this journey from Angola to India by way of Mozambique, crossing the interior of Kaffraria, should ask for the said Lake Zachaf, and on finding it, descend by the rivers to our forts of Tete and Sena and from there to the Quelimane delta; from Quelimane by land and sea to Mozambique, and from Mozambique to Goa in a month. That there is such a lake is stated not only by the Kaffirs, but also by Portuguese who already went there, navigating up the rivers and who, for lack of funds, have not yet discovered this route."

chants who have been there generally give.

There is another river called by the Africans Nyanja-Panono, or little river, and which the Portuguese call Nyanja-Pequeño. I cannot say if it comes out of the Rio Grande, from which at some places it is several days away.

On this point, and on the matter of its shores being inhabited by Marave and Yao, I can affirm nothing positively, because these were not things I observed.

To this information on the two Nyanjas we may add what is read in the diary of the march made to Kazembe in 1798 by Dr. Lacerda, "On September 21st he found himself in the village of the Fumo Mouro-Achinto, situated 10° 20' 35" lat. S., and 39° 10' 0" long. E. of Lisbon according to observations made on the sun and two eclipses of Jupiter's satellites: and he mentions that he was told there that to the north, between the Sukuma nation which reaches the banks of the Shire or Nyanja, and the Bisa, lay the Bemba nation: and that the lands to the south were peopled by the Lamba and Ambo, and that these two nations do commerce with the Africans in the neighbourhood of Zumbo."

I have said already that the Bisa today have no land of their own, it having been conquered by the Muembas, who are probably the Bemba (Uemba) mentioned above. As to the Shire being the same as the Nyanja, we add nothing to what is already stated.

It would not be difficult to confirm the truth about the Nyanja Grande if a small expedition left the Sena Rivers, another left Mozambique and another left the isles of Cape Delgado, without military equipment but with all possible trade goods, each taking a man capable of making an exact description to satisfy the aims of the exploration. It would be best to leave from these three points, making arrangements to communicate and inform each other of discoveries made, because in this way, if one or two of them miscarried

through various obstacles (of which the main is the desertion of Kaffirs who have to be taken as carriers), one of them would probably arrive at its destination and this would be enough. All should be ordered to make for the River, and there buy canoes in sufficient number to provide transport for all, or a part, and navigate downstream to its mouth. A craft appropriate to the task would have to be sent from Mozambique to where its mouth is supposed to be, in order to bring them back. This should be easy and would involve little expense.

I calculate the width of the great Nyanja at nine leagues because, according to my information, it has a strong current; therefore the canoes have to go obliquely and so they have to spend three days on a journey which, with a slow current, they could do in half the time. The same width in slightly different circumstances takes longer.

The best season for such an exploration would be spring, and it should not begin before the end of April or even May.

The Portuguese rule in Cape Delgado by right, but by the neglect which this territory has suffered it has been left to the Arabs of the Imam of Muscat to profit by all its commerce; this they do mainly through contraband, without the Portuguese government of the district having the power to embarrass them; and so they monopolise the trade and take all the profits. As this is another subject I shall keep what I have to say for another memorandum on Portuguese East Africa; but just now I felt it was necessary to explain about these explorations.

III

In the middle of Marave land is a small area occupied also by some Marave who are known as Chupeta; and their district has the same name. Although they have the same habits, etc., they live quite independently. Each village has a supreme chief, who belongs to the family composing it, and who recognises no political superior: it is better to let oneself be annihilated or destroyed completely, than to give obedience to another. In case of a dispute or outbreak of war between two chiefs, which is very frequent, the members of the two villages fight one another but it never finishes with the first fight. He who weakens retreats and gets another one to help him, and thus the two factions grow incessantly to the point where often all the chiefs are eventually involved in the contest. On each occasion, the quarrel is brought to an end by the appointment of arbitrators to judge the matter, which may be nothing more than the purloining of a millet stalk. Often enough war breaks out again if the guilty party does not agree to pay an indemnity which appears too exorbitant, or if the innocent party is not satisfied with it. In such cases when fighting has been heavy, the quarrel is brought to an end and the condemned party pays war damages to the satisfaction of all the chiefs who helped the winning side, who assess all the damage since the start of the fighting. It usually happens that the lives of all those who died are indemnified if there are deaths on only one side; but if both sides lost lives, then deaths on the losing side are discounted. These payments go to the profit of the chiefs of both sides and are usually made in livestock, i.e. cattle, sheep and goats, or in slaves.

These people are much more warlike and industrious than other Marave, but are also bigger liars and thieves. The land of the Chupeta is flat, with few trees, and those that exist are very small. Hence they lack firewood, and use instead millet stalks, dry shrubs, and particularly cattle dung which they are careful to keep dry. They have peat, but do not know its use. They keep many cattle, sheep and goats, and in other respects they are like the Marave.

IV

The climate in summer—i.e. May to September—is agreeable, being mild rather than hot. In the rains the sun is burning.

In general, Marave country is much cut about with rivers and has plenty of water; and there are many mountain ranges and hilly districts which the people prefer for their dwellings: in the valleys, they have few villages, and these they use as keeps or outposts. Generally the gardens are on the hills and slopes, and as I mentioned they inhabit one of the hilliest regions of East Africa. I saw no navigable rivers on my march.

V

The population of this country is enormous, although the populated districts are smaller than the deserted ones. If the chiefs were united they would constitute a respectable nation. The Marave busy themselves for the most part with agriculture, from which they gain their livelihood. Weavers, smiths, and basket makers, and those that practise other trades, do so mostly for amusement rather than as a way of life. They have also a large number of lazy people and highway robbers.

VI

Government is despotic and hereditary, succession going to sister's son, and never to brother's son; if there is none, then the dead man's brother succeeds. A Fumo or Mambo is rarely recognised before months, or even years, have elapsed in civil war, brothers and kinsmen fighting one another until one side is triumphant and, having the advantage, supplants all the others. It is from these continual wars and expulsions that the sale and killing of prisoners and outlaws, who are all themselves Marave, result. The chief of the nation has the title Unde; his orders are executed without question or delay in all the dominions in which he is obeyed; but no important matter is decided without being heard by a council composed of elders, or of those in whom he has equal trust. On rare occasions this council meets in secret session; it gathers usually under a great tree in the Muzinda (the name of the village in which the Mambo or Fumo resides), against whose trunk Unde sits back with the council about him; round the council are seated the people who want to listen to the case. The spectators who do not belong to the council often speak and are heard as if they belonged to it. When the subject has been talked over, Unde declares that he agrees with the council's deliberations, or amends them, as he thinks fit. The councillors always follow Unde's opinion if they know it beforehand; and if any speak against it, it is because they do not know it; for as soon as it is known, everyone assents. But Unde usually opens the council. The village in which he lives is called Muzinda-a-Unde.

The whole of Marave country is divided into territories or provinces governed by Mambos, and these are subdivided into districts whose chiefs are the Fumos. Both are hereditary and succession takes place in the same way as for Unde. Neither he nor the Mambos and Fumos wear insignia of any kind to mark them off from other Marave; they usually go dressed in a skin or a Nyanda, a kind of cloth, not woven but made from the inner bark of certain trees. The form and process of government is the same throughout the Marave. Alliances are of short duration, and often broken; any new interest may persuade Mambos and Fumos to change their allies, or become neutral or hostile. These changes often occur when they are in the process of negotiating with their allies. The wars, in which they are at most times involved, often start from bagatelles. All affairs can be judged by arbitrators, but if they are not satisfied, they litigate before the authorities, appealing from one Fumo to another, and then to the Mambo; but at times, if they are not satisfied with the judgment of the Mambo in council, they have resort to arms, and this gives rise to a small war which may spread. This happens sometimes, but not very often.

When the Fumos are at war, the Mambos to whom they are subordinate do not interfere, and at the end receive the tribute due to them. If one of the Fumos is killed, his place is usurped by his enemy, who pays the Mambo and receives recognition and rules in peace as if he were the legal heir. This happens in all ranks. The Marave authorities are Unde, the paramount chief of the nation; and the Fumos and Mambos in their districts and provinces, who all exercise in them the same arbitrary power. All legislation is traditional. In judgments and sentences they look to sentences already given in similar cases, which custom has made law: all the same, some judgments are invariable and do not change, as those relating to sorcery, adultery, theft and homicide, the most important being directed against sorcerers and adulterers. They have no statute law.

VII

The strength of these people consists in their great number. They know no elements of attack or defence apart from courage. Although continually engaged in small civil wars, the result in no way alters the general state of the nation because the victor is always a Marave and is subject to the same laws and customs. When Unde is attacked, a rare enough eventuality, the whole nation takes up arms without regard to age, as many as can manage; those unable to fight take to the hills and forests with everything they possess. The number of fighting men is great, but there is no discipline or military plan. In time of peace there are no standing armies, but when war breaks out, people gather in groups, called Mangas, of which the Mambos or Fumos of the districts they belong to are the leaders. If they are large, each one acts on its own; if they are small, two or more may join together. The word Manga, though used by the Portuguese in this part of Africa, is certainly African, and has no other meaning than a column or group of armed men. Perhaps the Portuguese adopted it from them.

As Unde is nearly always in a safe place with a large population, he is seldom subject to a close attack; but he engages in frequent distant wars, and only gets notice of them when they are over or nearly so.

As they have no formal military organisation into armies, so they have no recruitment; but in each Muzinda there is a big drum called Ngoma which can be heard a great way off, and which is used as a call to arms when the enemy is expected or imminent or when the spies or Sopozos, who are distributed around the roads to get news from travellers, come and give information that armed men are near. At the sound of the alarm, there come armed as many as belong to the district under the Muzinda; and in the next district also the alarm is sounded, and people gather, and so on successively until all are up in arms. Warriors arm themselves and maintain themselves at their own cost during a war, and this they do mainly by pillage.

There is no other way of calling up, and no way of finding out if anyone capable of fighting is missing, even if he is one of those obliged to turn out. But it is only those who are totally incapable of fighting who fail to present themselves, because the hope of plunder moves them all.

VIII

Their legs are their only defensive weapons and they put them to good use. Offensive arms are bows, poisoned arrows, spears, axes and knives. The bow is carried in the left hand with the spear, the arrows being in a leather quiver called Mutumba. The bow is Uta, the spear Dipa, the arrow Miseve, the axe Bazo and the knife Shisu. Axe and knife are worn in the belt, one on each side. The arrows have very small heads, but are entirely barbed; they are inserted into canes which they use for shafts in such a way that when an arrow hits its mark the head enters the body and the shaft falls, and

within two hours the poison has taken effect and has killed. But if a certain kind of oil, called by the Portuguese "Frei Pedro" and by the Africans Mafuta, is used upon it, no harm results. I do not know the composition of this antidote—it was not divulged.

Africans come with it for sale, but much of it is not genuine, and the only way to be sure is to see the effect it produces. This syrup was discovered by a Portuguese friar of that name in Zumbo [a town 600 miles up the Zambezi River —ed.], who found it to be a swift and efficacious anti-toxin. It is from Zumbo that this discovery has spread to all parts.

They say that among other things the poison contains certain substances considered essential—crocodile gall, hippopotamus brain, a kind of kapok, and the sap of some grasses. The effect produced is to stop the circulation of the blood, making it coagulate immediately.

The Marave are completely ignorant of any military operational planning, and of the division of armies into corps, and the formation of lines for defense and attack. On the contrary, the crowds march against the enemy as a body and as soon as they see him they become completely disorganized, utter the Tunguro cries and start letting off their arrows at random, without revealing themselves or leaving the shelter of the trees which defend them. There is no command, every warrior fights as he likes and because it appears the safest thing for him to do he attends mainly to his self-preservation. They use the spear only to finish off the wounded, and the axe and knife only to cut heads off the dead bodies. As superstition is at the base of all their beliefs, the Mambos and Fumos propagate the notion that the safety and prosperity of their lands depend upon their being sorcerers, and so they are all thought to be; they are feared and respected by their people and by strangers alike. The higher they stand in the hierarchy, the more they seek to inculcate the superiority of their medicines, of which they boast. The most important thing is to have in one's dominions under one's protection the most renowned magicians, to whom the public attributes supernatural powers by means of their Mankwaras, or magic. Nothing is done which has not the approval of the magic.

The Ganga or Surjao is the one who divines and makes the supposed magic or divination. The latter term may be a corruption of the Portuguese word Cirurgião.[2]

In times of war it is the Gangas who go in front of the Mangas, much attired with feathers, bones, tails of various animals, horns, etc. etc. They make long speeches in which they exhort the warriors to trust their medicines, because they are efficacious and infallible, and assert that they alone will be able to conquer the enemy.

The Marave place complete faith in these charlatans. If the outcome is fortunate, the Gangas attribute it entirely to themselves; and if it is adverse they blame someone for the breach of the elaborate taboos they impose, which consist usually in abstinence from certain foods, from cohabitation with someone of the other sex, etc. When they fight the Portuguese, these try first to procure the death of the Ganga who is reckoned infallible. This obtained, victory is not far ahead, because resistance then is weak, since they think that the Europeans have better magic than they, which it would be useless to resist. But in an internecine war this does not happen; all avoid shooting at the Ganga for fear that if they killed or wounded him they would be lost for his blood would fall upon the man who spilt it and the Muzimos would thus have to take vengeance.

[2] Surgeon. (Trans.).

IX

The Mambos or Fumos, according to their rank, receive Chipatas, or presents for safe conduct, from all traders passing through their lands; fees, or costs, for hearing and judging cases; Mouths (Muromos) and tribute from the land, etc. The only way they spend this is by sharing it out among the people about them, and the more liberal they are, the greater the number of followers, the larger the Muzindas, the stronger their cause and the greater their power. They spend it also in making new houses for their wives, and in paying the debts they contract; these are all personal expenses. But apart from them the Fumos pay tribute to the Mambos to whom they are subordinate, and the Mambos pay to Unde.

The Chipata, or safe-conduct, is a tribute which has to be paid in merchandise to the Mambos and Fumos through whose country one passes. Its size should correspond to the category of chief to whom it is made and to the wealth of the person making the payment. The safe-conduct gives right of transit and obliges the authorities on the land to guarantee the life and property of the merchants. There is no sure rule about the value of this tribute; the traveller can only learn from practice. Nearly always the chiefs ask for more, however much is given, and it is always necessary to take this into account when the Chipata is made up.

The Muromo, a word signifying mouth, is the fee for asking to speak to an African authority, and this cannot be done without first presenting something, this being the "morsel for the mouth," whose value should be relative to the nature of the business or discussion desired. There is no set price.

.   .   .

71 CHARLES LIVINGSTONE
THE PRAZEROS

David Livingstone (1813–1873) was the greatest Christian missionary-explorer of the nineteenth century. Between 1853 and 1856 he traveled overland from Kuruman, the mission station of his father-in-law, Robert Moffat, to the Victoria Falls, which he was the first white man to see, and thence to Luanda and back across Africa to the mouth of the Zambezi River. His Missionary Travels and Researches *aroused great enthusiasm in Victorian England for the opening of the interior of Central Africa to Christianity and commerce. With the support of the Royal Geographical Society and the assistance of the British government, Livingstone returned to Portuguese East Africa in 1859 with a large expedition that included his brother, Charles, and that aimed to establish the Zambezi as a highway into the interior. The Zambezi proved unnavigable beyond Tete, but Livingstone's descriptions of the slave trade and the Prazeros of Zambezia continued to excite humanitarian and commercial interests in England.*

By the eighteenth century, a group of half-caste Portuguese had carved out for themselves great feudal estates in Zambezia. These Prazeros *were warlords beyond the reach of any authority, African or European, and dominated vast areas. From the profits of their plantations and the slave trade they equipped large private armies that terrorized the countryside. The Portuguese were unable to root out the* Prazo *system until the 1890s. A typical* Prazero *was Antonio Vincente da Cruz, commonly known as "Bonga." Like his brother, Mariano, he was an illiterate, thieving, cruel, barbarous drunkard.*

On reaching Mazaro, the mouth of a narrow creek which in floods communicates with the Quillimane River, we found that the Portuguese were at war with a half-caste named Mariano, *alias* Matakenya, from whom they had generally fled, and who, having built a stockade near the mouth of the Shire, owned all the country between that river and Mazaro. Mariano was best known by his native name Matakenya, which in their tongue means "trembling," or quivering as trees do in a storm. He was a keen slave-hunter, and kept a large number of men, well armed with muskets. It is an entire mistake to suppose that the slave-trade is one of buying and selling alone, or that engagements can be made with laborers in Africa as they are in India; Mariano, like other Portuguese, had no labor to spare. He had

From David and Charles Livingstone, *Narrative of an Expedition to the Zambesi and its Tributaries; and of the Discovery of the Lakes Shirwa and Nyassa, 1858–1864* (New York: Harper and Brothers, 1866), pp. 26–30, 38–43.

been in the habit of sending out armed parties on slave hunting-forays among the helpless tribes to the northeast, and carrying down the kidnapped victims in chains to Quillimane, where they were sold by his brother-in-law Cruz Coimbra, and shipped as "Free emigrants" to the French island of Bourbon. So long as his robberies and murders were restricted to the natives at a distance, the authorities did not interfere; but his men, trained to deeds of violence and bloodshed in their slave forays, naturally began to practice on the people nearer at hand, though belonging to the Portuguese, and even in the village of Senna, under the guns of the fort. A gentleman of the highest standing told us that, while at dinner with his family, it was no uncommon event for a slave to rush into the room pursued by one of Mariano's men with spear in hand to murder him.

The atrocities of this villain, aptly termed by the late governor of Quillimane a "notorious robber and murderer," became at length intolerable. All the Portuguese spoke of him as a rare monster of inhumanity. It is unaccountable why half-castes, such as he, are so much more cruel than the Portuguese, but such is undoubtedly the case.

It was asserted that one of his favorite modes of creating an impression in the country, and making his name dreaded, was to spear his captives with his own hands. On one occasion he is reported to have thus killed forty poor wretches placed in a row before him. We did not at first credit these statements, and thought that they were merely exaggerations of the incensed Portuguese, who naturally enough were exasperated with him for stopping their trade and harboring their runaway slaves; but we learned afterward from the natives that the accounts given us by the Portuguese had not exceeded the truth, and that Mariano was quite as great a ruffian as they had described him. One expects slave-owners to treat their human chattels as well as men do other animals of value, but the slave-trade seems always to engender an unreasoning ferocity, if not bloodthirstiness.

War was declared against Mariano, and a force sent to take him; he resisted for a time, but, seeing that he was likely to get the worst of it, and knowing that the Portuguese governors have small salaries, and are therefore "disposed to be reasonable," he went down to Quillimane to "arrange" with the governor, as it is termed here; but Colonel da Silva put him in prison, and then sent him for trial to Mozambique. When we came into the country his people were fighting under his brother Bonga. The war had lasted six months, and stopped all trade on the river during that period. On the 15th of June we first came into contact with the "rebels." They appeared as a crowd of well-armed and fantastically-dressed people under the trees at Mazaro. On explaining that we were English, some at once came on board and called to those on shore to lay aside their arms. On landing among them we saw that many had the branded marks of slaves on their chests, but they warmly approved our objects, and knew well the distinctive character of our nation on the slave question.[1] The shout at our departure contrasted strongly with the suspicious questioning on our approach. Henceforth we were recognized as friends by both parties.

At a later period we were taking in wood within a mile of the scene of action, but a dense fog prevented our hearing the noise of a battle at Mazaro; and on arriving there immediately after, many natives and Portuguese appeared on the bank.

Dr. Livingstone, landing to salute some of his old friends among the latter, found himself in the sickening smell and among the mutilated bodies of the slain; he was requested to take the governor, who was very ill of fever, across to Shupanga, and just as he gave his assent, the rebels renewed the fight, and the balls began to whistle about in all directions. After trying in vain to get some one to assist the governor down to the steamer, and unwilling to leave him in such danger, as the officer sent to bring our Kroomen did not appear, he went into the hut, and dragged along his excellency to the ship. He was a very tall man, and as he swayed hither and thither from weakness, weighing down Dr. Livingstone, it must have appeared like one drunken man helping another. Some of the Portuguese white soldiers stood fighting with great bravery against the enemy in front, while a few were coolly shooting at their own slaves for fleeing into the river behind. The reb-

[1] Toward the close of the eighteenth century, a small group of high-principled Englishmen organized a campaign against slavery and the slave trade. Outraged by the horror and injustice of the trade, the abolitionists were convinced of its moral wrongness, and through their influence slavery was declared illegal in England in 1772. In 1807 an act of Parliament prohibited British subjects from engaging in the African slave trade, and finally in 1833 another act abolished slavery throughout the British Empire. Thereafter Britain used its diplomatic and military power to persuade other nations to abandon the trade (ed.).

els soon retired, and the Portuguese escaped to a sand-bank in the Zambesi, and thence to an island opposite Shupanga, where they lay for some weeks, looking at the rebels on the main land opposite. This state of inactivity on the part of the Portuguese could not well be helped, as they had expended all their ammunition and were waiting anxiously for supplies; hoping, no doubt, sincerely that the enemy might not hear that their powder had failed. Luckily, their hopes were not disappointed; the rebels waited until a supply came, and were then repulsed after a three and a half hours' hard fighting. Two months afterward Mariano's stockade was burned, the garrison having fled in a panic; and as Bonga declared that he did not wish to fight with this governor, with whom he had no quarrel, the war soon came to an end. His excellency meanwhile, being a disciple of Raspail, had taken nothing for the fever but a little camphor, and after he was taken to Shupanga became comatose.[2] More potent remedies were administered to him, to his intense disgust, and he soon recovered. The colonel in attendance, whom he never afterward forgave, encouraged the treatment. "Give what is right; never mind him; he is very (*muito*) impertinent;" and all night long, with every draught of water, the colonel gave a quantity of quinine: the consequence was, next morning the patient was cinchonized and better.

.   .   .

Bonga, the brother of the rebel Mariano, and now at the head of the revolted natives, with some of his principal men, came to see us, and were perfectly friendly, though told of our having carried the sick governor across to Shupanga, and of our having cured him of fever. On our acquainting Bonga with the object of the expedition, he remarked that we should suffer no hinderance from his people in our good work. He sent us a present of rice, two sheep, and a quantity of firewood. He never tried to make any use of us in the strife; the other side showed less confidence by carefully cross-questioning our pilot whether we had sold any powder to the enemy. We managed, however, to keep on good terms with both rebels and Portuguese.

Being unable to take the steamer up the shoal channel along which Senna stands, we anchored at Nyaruka, a small hamlet of blacks, six miles below, and walked up to Senna next morning. The narrow winding footpath, along which we had to march in Indian file, lay through gardens and patches of wood, the loftiest trees being thorny acacias. The sky was cloudy, the air cool and pleasant, and the little birds, in the gladness of their hearts, poured forth sweet strange songs, which, though equal to those of the singing birds at home on a spring morning, yet seemed, somehow, as if in a foreign tongue. We met many natives on the road. Most of the men were armed with spears, bows and arrows, or old Tower muskets; the women had short-handled iron hoes, and were going to work in the gardens; they stepped aside to let us pass, and saluted us politely, the men bowing and scraping, and the women, even with heavy loads on their heads, courtesying—a courtesy from bare legs is startling!

Senna is built on a low plain, on the right bank of the Zambesi, with some pretty detached hills in the background; it is surrounded by a stockade of living trees to protect its inhabitants from their troublesome and rebellious neighbors. It contains a few large houses, some ruins of others, and a weatherbeaten cross, where once stood a church; a mound shows the site of an ancient monastery, and a mud fort by the river is so dilapidated that cows were grazing peacefully over its prostrate walls. This grieves not the villagers, for its black garrison was wont to keep within doors when the foe came near, leaving the merchants to settle the

[2] François Vincent Raspail (1794–1878), French chemist and revolutionary (ed.).

strife as best they could; and they therefore consider that the decay of the fort has not caused them to be any more helpless than they were before.

The few Senna merchants, having little or no trade in the village, send parties of trusted slaves into the interior to hunt for and purchase ivory. It is a dull place, and very conducive to sleep. One is sure to take fever in Senna on the second day, if by chance one escapes it on the first day of a sojourn there; but no place is entirely bad. Senna has one redeeming feature: it is the native village of the large-hearted and hospitable Senhor H. A. Ferrão. The benevolence of this gentleman is unbounded. The poor black stranger passing through the town goes to him almost as a matter of course for food, and is never sent away hungry. In times of famine the starving natives are fed by his generosity; hundreds of his own people he never sees except on these occasions; and the only benefit derived from being their master is, that they lean on him as a patriarchal chief, and he has the satisfaction of settling their differences, and of saving their lives in seasons of drought and scarcity. His father, a man of superior attainments, was formerly the Portuguese governor of Senna, and acquired a vast tract of rich country to the southward, called Chiringoma, in a most honorable manner; but the government ordered it to be split up, and reserved two leagues only for the heir, apportioning the rest in free grants to emigrants; the reason assigned for the robbery was that "it would never do for a subject to possess more land than the crown of Portugal." The Landeens soon followed, took possession of the whole, and spoiled the spoilers.

Senhor Ferrão received us with his usual kindness, and gave us a bountiful breakfast. During the day the principal men of the place called, and were unanimously of opinion that the free natives would willingly cultivate large quantities of cotton, could they find purchasers. They had in former times exported largely both cotton and cloth to Manica and even to Brazil. "On their own soil," they declared, "the natives are willing to labor and trade, provided only they can do so to advantage: when it is for their interest, blacks work very hard." We often remarked subsequently that this was the opinion of men of energy; and that all settlers of activity, enterprise, and sober habits had become rich, while those who were much addicted to lying on their backs smoking invariably complained of the laziness of the negroes, and were poor, proud, and despicable. We dined with another very honorable Portuguese, Major Tito A. d'A. Sicard, who quoted the common remark that Dr. Livingstone's discovery of the Kongone Bar had ruined Quillimane; for the government had proposed to abandon that fever-haunted locality, and to found a new town at the mouth of the Kongone. It was not then known that householders in the old village preferred to resign all offices rather than remove. The major had a great desire to assist Dr. Livingstone in his enterprise; and said that when the war was past he would at once take up his goods to Tette in canoes; and this he afterward most generously did. While returning to Nyaruka, we heard a bird like a nightingale pouring forth its sweet melody in the stillness of the evening.

72 HERMENEGILDO CAPELLO AND ROBERTO IVENS
BENGUELLA IN 1877

Two officers of the Portuguese Royal Navy, Hermenegildo Capello and Roberto Ivens, led an expedition to Central Africa during the years 1877–1880 that produced the first survey of the Bié region and the upper reaches of the Okovanggo River. In 1884 they were sent once more into the interior by the Portuguese government in order to discover a trans-African route connecting Angola and Mozambique and to assert Portuguese rights in Central Africa at a time when other European nations, particularly Great Britain, were challenging Portuguese claims.

In latitude 12° 34' 17" of the southern hemisphere and longitude 13° 22' 30" east of Greenwich, lies upon the west coast of Africa, at the bottom of a spacious bay, the ancient and well-known city of Benguella.

The capital of a vast territory, it possesses as subdivisions the districts of Dombe Grande and Dombe Pequeno, Egito, Novo Redondo, Catumbella, Quillengues, Caconda, &c.; embracing an approximate area of 15,000 square miles of the southern portion of the Portuguese province.

Its custom-house revenues amount, at the present day, to some 25,000£. A delegation of the central government, the seat of which is at Loanda, its administration is entrusted to an official, who can only be appointed by the government of the mother country.

A traveller, on arriving there, may, in the course of a day's wandering about the city and its environs, get a general impression of the place, which the following narrative must, to a certain extent, reproduce.

A sufficiency of houses, among which rise the public buildings, somewhat larger than the rest, without any pretension to elegance, but spacious, clean, and set in

right lines in broad streets, bordered with trees, and connected together by garden-ground, constitute the commercial ward, properly so called, where the authorities and numerous merchants have their habitations.

A custom-house, a hospital, barracks, a palace (the residence of the governor), and a fortress on the seashore, where, in the evening, the tired wayfarer can breathe the pure air of the ocean, observe the splendid spectacle of the setting of a tropical sun, and watch the waves as they roll into the beautiful bay, closed in at the south-west by a lofty mount called the *Sombrero,* constitute the most remarkable features of the landscape, and form altogether an agreeable picture.

Scattered here and there, the observer will note a good many isolated establishments, where the most important business of Benguella is carried on. The aspect of these buildings is singular and antiquated. In the foreground appears the classical wooden balcony, either blackened by time or painted blue, surrounded by massive benches piled up with every kind of cotton goods, striped stuffs, beads, caps, and mirrors; the whole crowned by well-ordered rows of bottles containing various liquors, all of them articles of a nature to excite the cupidity and warm the imagination of the aborigines. On penetrating farther in, the curious traveller will find spacious store-houses, where the first object that meets his eye, suspended from a beam, is

From Hermenegildo Capello and Roberto Ivens, *From Benguella to the Territory of Yacca: Description of a Journey into Central and West Africa,* trans. by Alfred Elwes (London: Sampson Low & Co., 1882), pp. 10–19.

the old wooden balance, supported by eight ropes, with square scales. These magazines are full of the most varied products of the interior, among which prominently figure wax, india-rubber and ivory; and waiting their turn at the weighing-machine, stands a numerous band of natives, who, lank, bony, and emaciated, suck at the long and traditional calumet, the while their roving glances are turned incessantly to the coveted European goods.[1]

This quarter of the town has other features of a less agreeable character. These are tortuous lanes, lined with miserable huts, amidst which are vast enclosures, called *quintaes,* surrounded by walls of a sufficient height to intercept the heat and light, within which are frequently huddled together some hundreds of negroes who have travelled from the interior. The utmost disorder and squalor exist in these enclosures. Calcined stones upon which are still standing the earthen pipkins that have been used for cooking the recent meal; wretched old rags serving as beds; gourds scattered all over the place among tobacco-pipes, bows, and assagais; the inevitable black glass bottle, with a small cord round the neck, by which it is suspended in the long country-basket called a *muhamba;* two or three dozen negroes in the garb of our first parents, with long tresses reeking with oil and *tacúla* (a vermilion powder obtained by triturating tiny morsels of the trunk of an acacia), lying asleep in every direction, are the more salient objects which distinguish these habitations of the natives' ward. And if we throw in some five or six hundred Ban-dombes, Bailundos, Bihenos, and Ganguellas, promenading the streets, with skins hanging from their girdles, some far gone in intoxication, others well upon the road, talking, gesticulating, shrieking; if we frame in the town with a belt of thin and wiry vegetation; draw a line of blue mountains at some twenty to

twenty-five miles' distance from Benguella, and set the whole in a clear, grey atmosphere, we shall have the general aspect presented by this celebrated city on one of its busy market-days.

The effluvia emanating from this accumulation of black humanity, from monstrous head-dresses anointed with rancid oil, from reeking pipes, and the fumes of *aguardente,*[2] must be taken into account to make our sketch complete, and which, out of a feeling of delicacy, we have reserved for the close, though the aroma thus created is perhaps the first thing which strikes the recently arrived traveller from Europe.

Shortly after sunset the profoundest silence falls upon the place, broken only by the occasional tramp of a couple of natives carrying their master in a *muchila,*[3] through the deserted streets, or a group or two of aborigines, directing their steps towards the *quintaes,* where the reflection of ruddy light hints at the preparation of some meal.

The darkness is, otherwise, complete; the silence interrupted only in the manner we have stated, or by the occasional roar or howl of a wild beast, followed by the barking of the dogs, becomes, in the intervals, supreme; until the obscurity is gradually dissipated, the terrors of the night begin to vanish, and within an incredibly short time one of nature's most brilliant aspects, the break of day, entrances the observer.

The earth reacquires all its brightness and freshness, and dons its verdant mantle; the birds fill the air with melodious song; the limpid atmosphere and soft temperature invite the traveller abroad, and the general stir of humanity recommences.

The negro is on foot, armed with his fishing-tackle; the trader opens his store; the women proceed to their washing-places; the thirsty souls, rousing them-

---

[2] Any strong, distilled alcoholic liquor (ed.).
[3] A sort of elongated chair, suspended from a pole, having a rectangular tester, from which curtains fall all round.

[1] A calumet is a highly decorated ceremonial pipe (ed.).

selves from their beds of foul rags, where they have been shivering with cold, shuffle off to the neighbouring tavern, there to imbibe the fiery *aguardente.*

The climate of Benguella is mild during a great part of the year; still, it must not be considered as fine, and is very far from being the best on the coast. The improvements effected during these latter years, the irregularity of the rains since 1870, and the more restricted gathering of the natives within its precincts, in consequence of the diversion of many of them to the mart at Catumbella, somewhat more to the northwards, are the causes of the alteration in climatic circumstances; so that Benguella finds, mainly among the merchants and traders there established, numerous advocates of its salubrity.

Still, the fact remains that there are many victims to various fevers, but as the dead cannot offer an opinion upon the subject, the causes which brought about their end are soon forgotten amid the hurry and absorption of trade. The Bandombes, who are always seen about Benguella, are almost exclusively the inhabitants of a good part of the district. Long accustomed to dealing with Europeans, they are of infinite service to the latter, chiefly as regards transport, for they are not much given to trade.

The language spoken in the town is very different to the *n'bunda* of Loanda, and is known by the name of *n'bundo* [4] of the Bihé, which is understood in the neighbouring districts and in the regions extending eastward as far as the Ganguellas, where it begins to undergo alterations in consequence perhaps of the introduction of *lulundo* words and phrases.

The life of a European in Benguella is purely and exclusively a commercial one. The caravans which come in, the tidings which arrive, the products that are brought forward, the prices made through the competition of others, and his negotiations with the natives absorb every mo-

ment of daylight. It is no uncommon thing for the latter, after haggling, for two or three hours with a merchant, suddenly to break away and carry the rest of the troop with them, to seek a more liberal purchaser elsewhere.

In the Benguella market, where the trade is in the hands of the Portuguese, almost all the important products of the interior of Africa are exposed to view, and ivory, wax, walrus's teeth, *abbuda* (unicorn) horns, gums, resins, *licomte,* [5] skins, feathers, india-rubber, and canes appear in considerable quantities, and are bartered for arms, powder, cotton goods, and other similar products.

The Bihenos, the great African traders, are, not unnaturally, the chief habitués of the market, as they are exactly upon the line which connects this city with the inland producers. On completing their transactions, they carry off with them their European wares, travelling in caravans into the interior, where they again exchange their purchases in still remoter regions.

These men know how to drive very hard bargains, and having learned how much is to be gained by competition among the Europeans, they have gone on constantly raising the standard of value until they have succeeded in establishing the following prices upon the sea-board:

One pound of ivory	
standard	6s. 9d.
medium	6s. 1d.
small	4s. 0d.
One pound of wax,	
clean	0s. 9^{1}/2d.
A quarter hundred-	
weight of india-rubber	38s. 3d.
A panther's skin	9s. 0d.

In times not so very remote, travellers or *aviados,* as they were called, were despatched by firms established on the coast into the interior; and inland traders, gen-

---

[4] A dialect of the *lu-nano* language, generally denominated *quinbundo* (*t'chinbundo*).

[5] Fibre of the *Adansonia digitata* [the monkey bread tree—ed.].

erally styled *funantes,* still make their way thither on their own account.

The marts in the interior that were most frequented by these enterprising men were: *Alucusso,* one of the earliest travellers to which was Candimba (Gonçalves), a Portuguese from the main, recently deceased: *Garanganja; Canunguessa* and *Catanga,* to the west of Bangueolo, frequently visited by José Alves, and recently by the sons of Major Coimbra, Tiberio and others; *D'jengi,* the valley of the Zambese, and finally *Liniani* for many years frequented by Silva Porto, that old and honoured Portuguese citizen, long established at the Bihé in Belmonte, and whose journeys are so well known that his itineraries may be seen traced upon many maps published abroad, where the name of the veteran traveller figures so justly, as a testimony of his merit.

We spent with this old gentleman several agreeable hours, during which he had the kindness to read to us the most important portions of his diaries, containing facts which though now no longer new, had all the charm of novelty then. They proved in the most conclusive manner how great was the industry of this bold traveller in collecting data that he might some day turn to account, notwithstanding the difficulties which his business as a trader entailed upon him, amid peoples hotly opposed at that period to the advance of any European, and frequently at open hostility to himself.

It was this Portuguese who had the honour to meet, in the heart of Africa, with David Livingstone during his first journey across the continent, and whose friendly services the celebrated English explorer could not at the time accept.

In this place we may also name as worthy of special mention, a remarkable Portuguese *funante,* João Baptista Ferreira, who for many years scoured the country, and was well known for the boldness and venturesomeness of his journeys, until, some years ago, they terminated in

his destruction at the hands, it is surmised, of some petty sovereign of the interior or of the Arabs, either Janima Mericani or Sheik Abed-ben-Salim in the north.

He was the first European who, as it would appear, starting from Benguella, arrived at the dominions of the Cassongo Calombo, and became acquainted with Imbarri, the residence of Tibu-tib, Sheik Hamed-ben-Mohammed; subsequently crossing the Samba, passing through Quilemba, and penetrating nearly to Niangué.

Tired of wandering about the Garanganja, and presuming this region to be in great part commercially explored, João Baptista began to turn his attention to the Samba, where, during one of his journeys, he was informed that there existed in the territory of Ulua, to the east of the Lunda do Muata-Janvo, a track which would lead him to the markets of the north, which abounded in ivory.

Adventurous and fearless, he determined at once to follow it, notwithstanding the objections raised by his native followers, and towards the close of 1870 and beginning of 1871 he entered Cassongo's territory in company with a son of Major Coimbra who, two years later, elected to reveal to José Alves this identical route.

After rendering important services to Cassongo, João Baptista returned to the coast, in order to procure a further supply of goods, as had been arranged with the king, and subsequently return to his dominions with a view to barter.

José Alves, however, started on the same occasion, and Coimbra having, as above mentioned, undertaken to guide him by a track known at that time only to himself, the former accepted the offer, and the two great traders met one another in the coveted territory in 1874.

Nowadays the travellers or *aviados* of European houses are few. The death of some, the flight of others, have so disenchanted the merchants on the coast with the system of sending goods into the interior, that they have given it up almost entirely, so that the trade at this present time is almost exclusively carried on by the natives themselves, working on their own account.

The time of our departure now drew near, and after a sojourn of a fortnight in Benguella, the Portuguese expedition was in readiness to start upon its journey into the interior.

73 ROBERT MOFFAT
MZILIKAZI

Chief of the Khumalo Nguni and one of Shaka's most trusted generals, Mzilikazi defied Shaka's authority about 1821 and marched up to the highveld of the Transvaal, where he settled with his followers. None of the tribes of the Transvaal could stand against Mzilikazi's regiments, and between 1825 and 1834 prisoners from defeated Sotho-speaking tribes swelled the ranks of Mzilikazi's people, evolving into the Ndebele* nation. The Ndebele nation crystallized along the lines of a typical Nguni military state but soon found itself under assault from half-caste Korana and Griqua peoples from the south who were equipped with firearms. Mzilikazi was able to defeat the half-caste Africans, but in 1837 Boer commandoes successfully defeated the Ndebele and convinced Mzilikazi to take his people north across the Limpopo River to the upland pastures of Rhodesia. The Ndebele rapidly recovered in their new home, and their state developed under their king until his death in 1868.

A pioneer missionary and the father-in-law of David Livingstone, Robert Moffat (1795–1883) went to South Africa on behalf of the London Missionary Society in 1817. In 1825 he settled at Kuruman, where he lived and worked for nearly half a century. He first visited Mzilikazi in 1829 and established a profound influence over the Ndebele monarch. Mzilikazi probably found in the stern, uncompromising missionary the qualities of a father figure that he had not experienced in his youth since the execution of his own father, Mashobane, by the Khumalo overlord, Zwide. Mzilikazi's devotion to Moffat was repaid, and the two shared a deep, lifelong friendship.

. . . Umbate and two of his relations, whom he wished to introduce to my notice, remained behind till a late hour. One of these appeared to be a man of superior intellect, and put rather striking questions on the subjects which I had brought before the attention of the great man. The stillness of a serene night, far from the

From Robert Moffat, *Missionary Labours and Scenes in Southern Africa* (London: J. Snow, 1842), pp. 539–546.
* Ndebele is frequently spelled Matabele.

dance and war song, which echoed from the neighbouring hills, inspired confidence in these chieftains, who spoke in whispers, as if afraid that their king should hear their liberty of speech. Umbate repeated to his friend much that he had heard from me on the road about divine things. Though extremely cautious in their remarks, it was evident that they were not insensible of the rigours of the despotism under which they lived. I had been struck with the fine, open countenances of many of the warriors, who, though living amid the bewildering mazes of ignorance and superstition, debased, dejected, and oppressed under the iron sceptre of a monarch addicted to shedding blood, possessed noble minds; but, alas! whose only source of joy was to conquer or die in the ranks of their sovereign. The following morning was marked by a melancholy display of that so-called heroism which prefers death to dishonour. A feast had been proclaimed, cattle had been slaughtered, and many hearts beat high in anticipation of wallowing in all the excesses of savage delight; eating, drinking, dancing, and singing the victors' song over the slain, whose bones lay bleached on the neighbouring plains. Every heart appeared elate but one. He was a man of rank, and what was called an Entuna, (an officer,) who wore on his head the usual badge of dignity. He was brought to head-quarters. His arm bore no shield, nor his hand a spear; he had been divested of these, which had been his glory. He was brought into the presence of the king, and his chief council, charged with a crime, for which it was in vain to expect pardon, even at the hands of a more humane government. He bowed his fine elastic figure, and kneeled before the judge. The case was investigated silently, which gave solemnity to the scene. Not a whisper was heard among the listening audience, and the voices of the council were only audible to each other, and the nearest spectators. The prisoner, though on his knees, had something dignified and noble in his mien. Not a muscle of his countenance moved, but his bright black eyes indicated a feeling of intense interest, which the moving balance between life and death only could produce. The case required little investigation; the charges were clearly substantiated, and the culprit pleaded guilty. But, alas! he knew it was at a bar where none ever heard the heart-reviving sound of pardon, even for offences small compared with his. A pause ensued, during which the silence of

death pervaded the assembly. At length the monarch spoke, and, addressing the prisoner, said, "You are a dead man, but I shall do to-day what I never did before; I spare your life for the sake of my friend and father"—pointing to the spot where I [Moffat—ed.] stood. "I know his heart weeps at the shedding of blood; for his sake I spare your life; he has travelled from a far country to see me, and he has made my heart white; but he tells me that to take away life is an awful thing, and never can be undone again. He has pleaded with me not to go to war, nor destroy life. I wish him, when he returns to his own home again, to return with a heart as white as he has made mine. I spare you for his sake, for I love him, and he has saved the lives of my people. But," continued the king, "you must be degraded for life; you must no more associate with the nobles of the land, nor enter the towns of the princes of the people; nor ever again mingle in the dance of the mighty. Go to the poor of the field, and let your companions be the inhabitants of the desert." The sentence passed, the pardoned man was expected to bow in grateful adoration to him whom he was wont to look upon and exalt in songs applicable only to One to whom belongs universal sway and the destinies of man. But, no! holding his hands clasped on his bosom, he replied, "O king, afflict not my heart! I have merited thy displeasure; let me be slain like the warrior; I cannot live with the poor." And, raising his hand to the ring he wore on his brow, he continued, "How can I live among the dogs of the king, and disgrace these badges of honour which I won among the spears and shields of the mighty? No, I cannot live! Let me die, O Pezoolu!" His request was granted, and his hands tied erect over his head. Now my exertions to save his life were vain. He disdained the boon on the conditions offered, preferring to die with the honours he had won at the point of the spear—honours which even the act that condemned him did not tarnish—to exile and poverty among the children of the desert. He was led forth, a man walking on each side. My eye followed him till he reached the top of a precipice, over which he was precipitated into the deep pool of the river beneath, where the crocodiles, accustomed to such meals, were yawning to devour him ere he could reach the bottom! This was a sabbath morning scene such as heathenism exhibits to the view of the Christian philanthropist, and such as is calculated to excite in his bosom feelings of the deepest sympathy. This magnanimous heathen knew of no hereafter. He was without God and without hope. But, however deplorable the state of such a person may be, he will not be condemned as equally guilty with those who, in the midst of light and knowledge, self-separated from the body, recklessly rush into the presence of their Maker and their Judge. We have often read of the patriotism of the Greeks and Romans, and heard that magnanimity of soul extolled which could sacrifice honour, property, and life itself, for the public good, rather than become the vassals of a foe, and live divested of the poor trappings of human glory; if this be virtue, there are, even among Africa's sons, men not inferior to the most illustrious of the Romans. The very monarch who was thus influenced by the presence of the Christian missionary, needed only to ask his warriors, "Who among you will become a sacrifice for the safety of the state, and the country's good?" and his choicest men would have run upon the thick bosses of the enemy's buckler.

Moselekatse's [Mzilikazi—ed.] conduct in this affair produced a strange impression among his people, some of whom regarded me as an extraordinary being, who could thus influence one more terrible to them than the fiercest lion of the forest. His government, so far as I could discover, was the very essence of despotism. The persons of the people, as well as their possessions, were the property of their monarch. His word was law, and he

had only to lift his finger or give a frown, and his greatest nobles trembled in his presence. No one appeared to have a judgment of his own; none dared negative an opinion breathed by his sovereign. When any were permitted to approach his person, they crouched softly, muttering his great names. Messengers from the distant out-stations of his dominions were constantly arriving. These laid down their shields and spears at a distance, approached, and then kneeled about thirty yards from his royal person; and when it was his pleasure to receive the communication, it was conveyed by one of his chiefs in waiting. Some of these brought the news of the attacks of lions on some parts of his distant herds, but no one presumed to be the reporter without bringing the head and paws of the animal which had dared to assail the possessions of its mighty namesake.

Although his tyranny was such, that one would have supposed his subjects would execrate his name, they were the most servile devotees of their master. Wherever he was seated, or wherever he slept, a number of sycophants, fantastically dressed, attended him, whose business was to march, jump, and dance about, sometimes standing adoring his person, then manoeuvring with a stick, and vociferating the mighty deeds of valour performed by himself and Machobane. The same things are repeated again and again, often with a rapidity of articulation which baffles the understanding of their own countrymen. After listening many times, I was able, with the assistance of one of these parasites, to pick up the following expressions: "O Pezoolu, the king of kings, king of the heavens, who would not fear before the son of Machobane, mighty in battle! Where are the mighty before the presence of our great king? Where is the strength of the forest before the great Elephant? The proboscis is breaking the branches of the forest! It is the sound of the shields of the son of Machobane. He breathes upon their faces; it is the fire among the dry grass! His enemies are consumed before him, king of kings! Father of fire, he ascends to the blue heavens; he sends his lightnings into the clouds, and makes the rain to descend! Ye mountains, woods, and grassy plains, hearken to the voice of the son of Machobane, king of heaven!" This is a specimen of the sounding titles which incessantly meet the ear of this proud mortal, and are sufficient to make the haughty monarch believe that he is what the terror of the name of Dingaan convinced him he was not; for, notwithstanding all his vain boasts, he could not conceal his fears of the successor of the bloody Chaka, against whose iron sway he had rebelled.

It may be necessary to notice here, very briefly, the origin of this great man. When a youth his father was the chief of an independent tribe. His people were attacked by one more powerful, and routed. He took refuge under the sceptre of Chaka, who was then rendering his name terrible by deeds of crime. Moselekatse, from his intrepid character, was placed at the head of a marauding expedition, which made dreadful havoc among the northern tribes; but, instead of giving up the whole of the spoils, he made a reserve for himself. This reaching the ears of Chaka, revenge instantly burned in the tyrant's bosom, who resolved to annihilate so daring an aggressor. Moselekatse was half prepared to take flight, and descend on the thickly peopled regions of the north, like a sweeping pestilence. He escaped, after a desperate conflict with the warriors of Chaka, who killed nearly all the old men, and many of the women. His destructive career among the Bakone tribes has been noticed; but dire as that was, it must have been only a faint transcript of the terror, desolation, and death, which extended to the utmost limits of Chaka's conquests. Though but a follower in the footsteps of Chaka, the career of Moselekatse, from the period of his revolt till the time I saw him, and long after, formed an interminable catalogue of crimes. Scarcely a mountain, over extensive regions, but bore the marks of his deadly ire. His experience and native cunning enabled him to triumph over the minds of his men, and made his trembling captives soon adore him as an invincible sovereign. Those who resisted, and would not stoop to be his dogs, he butchered. He trained the captured youth in his own tactics, so that the majority of his army were foreigners; but his chiefs and nobles gloried in their descent from the Zoolu dynasty. He had carried his arms far into the tropics, where, however, he had more than once met with his equal; and on one occasion, of six hundred warriors only a handful returned, who were doomed to be sacrificed, merely because they had not conquered, or fallen with their companions. Abject representatives came, while I was with him, from the subjugated tribes of the Bamanguato, to solicit his aid against a more distant tribe, which had taken their cattle. By means like these, it may be said, "He dipped his sword in blood, and wrote his name on lands and cities desolate." In his person he was below the middle stature, rather corpulent, with a short neck, and in his manner could be exceedingly affable and cheerful. His voice, soft and effeminate, did not indicate that his disposition was passionate; and, happily for his people, it was not so, or many would have been butchered in the ebullitions of his anger.

The above is but a faint description of this Napoleon of the desert,—a man with whom I often conversed, and who was not wanting in consideration and kindness, as well as gratitude. But to sympathy and compassion his heart appeared a stranger.

74 NDANSI KUMALO
THE NDEBELE REBELLION

Defeated and bitterly discontented over the loss of land and cattle, the Ndebele rebelled in March 1896, when the military resources of the British South Africa Company were preoccupied in the Jameson Raid in the Transvaal. Over a hundred Europeans were killed in the revolt, and the remainder were besieged until a relief force under Major Plumer reached Bulawayo. The Ndebele rebels were then defeated by the superior fire power of Maxim guns and driven into the Matopo Hills, where Cecil Rhodes personally arranged the surrender of the principal Ndebele Ndunas (chieftains) and their followers.

So we surrendered to the white people and were told to go back to our homes and live our usual lives and attend to our crops. But the white men sent native police who did abominable things; they were cruel and assaulted a lot of our people and helped themselves to our cattle and goats. These policemen were not our own people; anybody was made a policeman. We were treated like slaves. They came and were overbearing and we were ordered to carry their clothes and bundles. They interfered with our wives and our daughters and molested them. In fact, the treatment we received was intolerable. We thought it best to fight and die rather than bear it. How the rebellion started I do not know; there was no organization, it was like a fire that suddenly flames up. We had been flogged by native police and then they rubbed salt water in the wounds. There was much bitterness because so many of our cattle were branded and taken away from us; we had no property, nothing we could call our own. We said, "It is no good living under such conditions; death would be better—let us fight." Our King gone, we had submitted to the white people and they ill-treated us until we became desperate and tried to make an end of it all. We knew that we had very little chance because their weapons were so much superior to ours. But we meant to fight to the last, feeling that even if we could not beat them we might at least kill a few of them and so have some sort of revenge.

I fought in the rebellion. We used to look out for valleys where the white men were likely to approach. We took cover behind rocks and trees and tried to ambush them. We were forced by the nature of our weapons not to expose ourselves. I had a gun, a breech-loader. They—the white men—fought us with big guns and Maxims and rifles.

I remember a fight in the Matoppos when we charged the white men. There were some hundreds of us; the white men also were many. We charged them at close quarters: we thought we had a good chance to kill them but the Maxims were too much for us. We drove them off at the first charge, but they returned and formed up again. We made a second charge, but they were too strong for us. I cannot say how many white people were killed, but we think it was quite a lot. I do not know if I killed any of them, but I know I killed one of their horses. I remember how, when one of their scouts fell wounded, two of his companions raced out and took him away. Many of our people were killed in this fight: I saw four of my cousins shot. One was shot in the jaw and the whole of his face was blown away—like this—and he died. One was hit between the eyes; another here, in the shoulder; another had part of his ear shot off. We made many charges but each time we were beaten off, until at last the white men packed up and retreated. But

From Margery Perham, *Ten Africans* (London: Faber and Faber Ltd., 1963), pp. 72–75. Reprinted by permission of Northwestern University Press and Faber and Faber Ltd.

for the Maxims, it would have been different. The place where we have been making the film is the very place where my cousins were killed.

We were still fighting when we heard that Mr. Rhodes was coming and wanted to make peace with us. It was best to come to terms he said, and not go shedding blood like this on both sides. The older people went to meet him. Mr. Rhodes came and they had a discussion and our leaders came back and discussed amongst themselves and the people. Then Mr. Rhodes came again and we agreed at last to terms of peace.

So peace was made. Many of our people had been killed, and now we began to die of starvation; and then came the rinderpest and the cattle that were still left to us perished. We could not help thinking that all these dreadful things were brought by the white people. We struggled, and the Government helped us with grain; and by degrees we managed to get crops and pulled through. Our cattle were practically wiped out, but a few were left and from them we slowly bred up our herds again. We were offered work in the mines and farms to earn money and so were able to buy back some cattle. At first, of course, we were not used to going out to work, but advice was given that the chief should advise the young people to go out to work, and gradually they went. At first we received a good price for our cattle and sheep and goats. Then the tax came. It was 10s. a year. Soon the Government said, "That is too little, you must contribute more; you must pay £1." We did so. Then those who took more than one wife were taxed; 10s. for each additional wife. The tax is heavy, but that is not all. We are also taxed for our dogs; 5s. for a dog. Then we were told we were living on private land; the owners wanted rent in addition to the Government tax; some 10s., some £1, some £2 a year. After that we were told we had to dip our cattle and pay 1s. per head per annum.

Would I like to have the old days back? Well, the white men have brought some good things. For a start, they brought us European implements—ploughs; we can buy European clothes, which are an advance. The Government have arranged for education and through that, when our children grow up, they may rise in status. We want them to be educated and civilized and make better citizens. Even in our own time there were troubles, there was much fighting and many innocent people were killed. It is infinitely better to have peace instead of war, and our treatment generally by the officials is better than it was at first. But, under the white people, we still have our troubles. Economic conditions are telling on us very severely. We are on land where the rainfall is scanty, and things will not grow well. In our own time we could pick our own country, but now all the best land has been taken by the white people. We get hardly any price for our cattle; we find it hard to meet our money obligations. If we have crops to spare we get very little for them; we find it difficult to make ends meet and wages are very low. When I view the position, I see that our rainfall has diminished, we have suffered drought and have poor crops and we do not see any hope of improvement, but all the same our taxes do not diminish. We see no prosperous days ahead of us. There is one thing we think an injustice. When we have plenty of grain the prices are very low, but the moment we are short of grain and we have to buy from Europeans at once the price is high. If when we have hard times and find it difficult to meet our obligations some of these burdens were taken off us it would gladden our hearts. As it is, if we do raise anything, it is never our own: all, or most of it, goes back in taxation. We can never save any money. If we could, we could help ourselves: we could build ourselves better houses; we could buy modern means of travelling about, a cart, or donkeys or mules.

75 LORD BLEDISLOE
NATIVE POLICY IN RHODESIA, 1938

The Bledisloe Commission was a Royal Commission appointed in 1938 under the chairmanship of Lord Bledisloe to investigate the feasibility and desirability of closer association between Northern and Southern Rhodesia and Nyasaland. The commission found the differences in the aims of the racial policies to be of very great importance. By this time, Southern Rhodesia's policy of strict racial segregation was closer to that of South Africa than to the policies of the other two territories. The commission recommended the formation of a territorial council to study the possibility of economic coordination.

SOUTHERN RHODESIA

392. In Southern Rhodesia native policy is more complicated by reason of the more extended development of white settlement. In the absence of any official statement of policy, we venture to quote certain passages from a public speech which the Prime Minister made in the Colony on the 30th March, 1938, to an audience composed largely of natives, and which he brought to our notice shortly after our arrival in Salisbury:

In common with several other African States, the most important question in Rhodesia is the regulation of the relations between Europeans and natives. For nearly four centuries African administrators and statesmen have found this matter so beset with difficulties that for the most part they have shelved it. Meanwhile it has steadily grown more acute. Because of the presence of the white man the Bantu is, with accelerating speed, lifting himself out of his primitive conditions. His inter-tribal wars have been prohibited, and his once frequently recurring epidemics checked. His numbers are increasing. Tribes once separated by traditional animosities are developing the idea of racial unity—an idea fostered by the development of Bantu newspapers and the publication of books in their own dialects. The Bantu is resolved to learn, and within as yet undetermined limits, is capable of learning. To forbid him opportunities is contrary to natural justice, but are we to allow him to develop and in the course

From *Rhodesia-Nyasaland Royal Commission Report* (Bledisloe Report) (London: H.M. Stationery Office, 1939), pp. 170–175. Reprinted by permission.

of time, because his requirements are so small, gradually to oust the European?

While there is yet time and space, the country should be divided into separate areas for black and white. In the native areas the black man must be allowed to rise to any position to which he is capable of climbing. Every step of the industrial and social pyramid must be open to him, excepting only—and always—the very top. For what can be done we may point to Uganda, for what must be avoided we may look at Haiti and Liberia. The senior administrative officer must be white. The native may be his own lawyer, doctor, builder, journalist or priest, and he must be protected from white competition in his own area. In the European areas the black man will be welcomed, when, tempted by wages, he offers his services as a labourer; but it will be on the understanding that there he shall merely assist, and not compete with, the white man. If he wishes to stop in his own area, let him. The two races will develop side by side under white supervision, and help, not hinder, each other's progress. The interest of each race would be paramount in its own sphere.

The policy I suggest enables the two races to live side by side to the benefit of both.

393. The policy as a whole is based on the Land Apportionment Act, the main features of which we have already described. In order to ensure to the natives security of tenure in the land available to them, the native reserves themselves are vested in a Board of Trustees, and no portion of them can be alienated without the approval of the Secretary of State for Dominion Affairs. In the area set aside for

purchase by individual natives (the "Native Purchase Area") no person other than an indigenous native may hold or occupy any land. The natives have therefore fixity of tenure of the land available to them.

394. The native lands comprise some 30 per cent. of the total land area of the Colony, but it may be anticipated that a considerable portion of the Unassigned Area (some 19 per cent. of the total) will eventually be added to that presently available to the natives. Certain disadvantages attach to the native lands. For example, as map No. 5 annexed to this Report will show, they are widely scattered in comparatively small patches and are not, generally speaking, well served by communications. Of 1,350 miles of railway approximately only 60 miles traverse native land, and the position as regards main road communications is little better. It was contended by certain of our witnesses specially interested in native welfare, and possibly with some justification, that in many cases the native lands are inferior in respect of both soil and rainfall, and that, judged from the standpoint of the present density of the native population, without taking into account the possibilities of its increase, they are inadequate. In our opinion the position in this respect has been materially aggravated by wasteful methods of cultivation and by over-grazing, resulting in excessive soil exhaustion and erosion. This the Government is now attempting to check by education and demonstration in more approved methods of husbandry.

We realise that it is impossible to say with confidence, at the present time, that the land set aside is or is not sufficient to provide for the reasonable needs of the native. Until all the reserves have been dealt with, both by the development of irrigation and water conservation schemes, where practicable, and by the adoption of a more prudent and economical system of husbandry, and until it has been possible to replace the present herds of inferior cattle by smaller numbers of improved stock, it is admitted that the land at present available cannot with any certainty be said to be sufficient. It is, however, claimed that the land potentially available for natives should prove adequate, when proper steps have been taken for its maintenance and proper treatment, to provide for their reasonable needs.

We do not regard ourselves as qualified, without a much more detailed examination of the subject on the spot, to express a definite opinion on the general question whether the natives in Southern Rhodesia will in the long run prove to have been adequately provided for in the matter of land. We feel justified in concluding, however, that in so far as there may be defects in this respect, these are due to mistakes in the past, when the necessity of providing for prospective native requirements was not so clearly appreciated as it is to-day. The record of the Colony in recent years shows that genuine efforts are being made to meet the land requirements of the native.

395. As regards the political aspects of native policy in Southern Rhodesia, we have described how in 1937 provision was made for the constitution of Native Civil Courts and the establishment of Native Councils. These Native Courts and Councils represent a delegation of power from the Central Government to Chiefs or Headmen selected by that Government. This presents a marked contrast to the principle of "indirect rule" in Nyasaland and Northern Rhodesia, under which the government of the natives is (within the narrow limit of the functions so far assigned to the Native Authorities) carried on by the traditional tribal authorities. This difference in approach to the native problem is explained largely by the view current in Southern Rhodesia that, as a result of the rebellions of 1896 and 1897, and of forty years of subsequent direct rule, it is impracticable to build up a system of native administration based on tribal discipline.

396. The present social policy of Southern Rhodesia as regards the native areas is progressive. We have, in our review of the social services commented upon the absence of any systematised attempt, prior to 1936, to provide medical facilities for natives in the reserves. Since then the Medical Department has addressed itself to the problem with energy, and has successfully initiated an excellent scheme for the extension of medical services. In the spheres of education and agriculture a considerable advance has been made in the course of the last ten years. In the former respect the missions, as in Northern Rhodesia and Nyasaland, have played a noteworthy part, the main work of primary education being entrusted to them. In the agricultural sphere the Government is making determined efforts to arrest the deterioration of the soil by improved methods of cultivation and rotation of crops, and to expand and render more productive the cultivable areas in various ways, especially by water conservation and irrigation. The steps being taken to reduce the numbers of native cattle in order to limit the ill effects of over-grazing appear to be causing concern in some reserves, and care will be needed to see that the objects of such measures are fully understood.

397. The provision of medical services and schools for natives in the European areas is not being overlooked by the Government and other interested agencies. Native labour in the mining and other industrial centres is housed in compounds provided by the employers, in conformity with the practice in other African countries. In most cases, especially where the compounds are provided by the larger industrial companies, the natives are better fed and cared for than when living in their villages. The standard, however, varies. In the larger towns Africans are confined to urban locations provided by the municipalities. The conditions in some of these (especially the lack of recreative facilities and the terms charged for ac-

commodation) leave room for improvement and amendment. The Government is setting a commendable example in the relatively high standard of housing, sanitation and amenities provided in its model native villages at Highfield, near Salisbury, and Luveve, near Bulawayo. In establishing such model villages proximity to the towns is an important consideration.

398. The Pass Laws of Southern Rhodesia are of a complicated nature. The following are their main provisions. As regards *indigenous natives* they require that adult males, with certain special exceptions, shall carry a registration certificate. In the principal towns every native is compelled to have, in addition to the registration certificate, one of the following:

(a) a pass to seek work in the town; or
(b) a certificate to show that he is employed within the town; or
(c) a certificate signed by a Native Commissioner to the effect that he is earning a living in the town by lawful means; or
(d) if he is employed outside the town, a written permit from his employer; or
(e) a visiting pass.

Section 14 (1) of the Natives Registration Act, 1936, provides that any native who is found in a town without being in possession of one of these documents shall be guilty of an offence. The provisions of this sub-section do not apply to wives and minors living with their families, but this does not free such persons from liability to be challenged by the Police, and this feature of the system is much disliked by the natives.

No native living on his employer's premises in a town, or living in a native location, may be absent therefrom between 9 P.M. and 5 A.M. without a written permit. Every native who is seeking employment in, or visiting, a "proclaimed" township must, if he wishes to remain for the night within the township, spend the hours of darkness in a township hostel. No township had been so proclaimed down to the date of our visit.

Non-indigenous natives are subject to the same requirements, as regards both the registration certificate and the special town passes. In addition, adult males, unless they are employed under a contract of service entered into outside the Colony which provides for their return on the completion of their service, are required to possess either a "visiting pass" or a pass to seek work in the Colony. This requirement applies to non-indigenous male natives throughout the Colony, and not only in the towns.

399. Under the Agreement [1] relating to Migrant Native Labour signed at Salisbury in August, 1936, male natives of Northern Rhodesia and Nyasaland entering Southern Rhodesia are required to possess certificates in a form adequate for identification purposes. Upon presentation of this proof of identity such immigrants are furnished with Southern Rhodesia certificates of registration, of a colour different from those issued to indigenous natives of the Colony. Where there exists no doubt that a native has previously been registered in the Colony, this certificate of registration is issued by the Pass Officer at the point of entry. In other cases particulars are forwarded to the Native Foreigners Identification Bureau, the native receiving a temporary Protection Pass until his identity has been verified, after which a registration certificate can be issued by the Pass Officer in the district where he intends to seek work.

400. The economic prospects of the native in the European areas are limited owing to the policy of segregation. In these areas no career is open to natives, the pursuit of which would adversely affect the opportunities of employment, or the standard of living, of Europeans. Native unskilled labour is, however, indispensable for the economic prosecution of any industrial enterprise, and the native is therefore free to offer his services as a worker on the condition that he shall merely assist, and not compete with, the European.

This policy finds expression in an agreement made under the Industrial Conciliation Act, 1934, between the parties constituting the Industrial Council of the building industry. This agreement, which applies in the areas of, and immediately around, the principal European centres, stipulates that no employee shall receive wages at less than certain rates. The object of this provision is to prevent the under-cutting of European skilled labour in the areas in question by the employment of less highly paid Africans. This legislation does not specifically disentitle the native to be employed as a skilled labourer, provided that he is paid at the same rate as the European; but where it is put into practice it operates to the exclusion of the native from employment in the industry to which it applies, since employers who are compelled to pay a specified rate of wages will obviously prefer to employ the more efficient European worker. Pending the development of opportunities within the native areas, this limitation of employment is calculated to act as a deterrent to the development by the native of his efficiency as a skilled worker. A further handicap is imposed by the limitation of opportunities for the employment of natives in clerical and other subordinate posts in the central Government service. Employment in similar capacities in the native areas is however open to them without restriction.

[1] This Agreement [is] usually referred to as the "Salisbury Agreement."

76 PAUL DU CHAILLU
TRADE IN GABON

Paul Belloni du Chaillu (1831–1903) spent eight years in Africa—four as a trader and four as a naturalist and explorer. During his travels between 1856 and 1859, he explored Gabon, Congo (Brazzaville), and areas that are now in the Spanish colony of Rio Muni, hitherto unknown to Europeans. As a trader he well knew the methods of commerce then in use in equatorial Africa, as well as the role of the African trader in the systems of controlled barter and exchange with European traders along the coast and in the interior.

. . . Each of these tribes assumes to itself the privilege of acting as go-between or middle-man to those next to it, and charges a heavy percentage for this office; and no infraction of this rule is permitted under penalty of war. Thus a piece of ivory or ebony may belong originally to a negro in the far interior, and if he wants to barter it for "white man's trade," he dares not take it to a market himself. If he should be rash enough to attempt such a piece of enterprise his goods would be confiscated, and he, if caught, fined by those whose monopoly he sought to break down, or most likely sold into slavery.

He is obliged by the laws of trade to intrust it to some fellow in the next tribe nearer to the coast. He, in turn, disposes of it to the next chief or friend, and so ivory, or ebony, or bar-wood, passes through probably a dozen hands ere it reaches the factory of the trader on the coast.

This would seem to work against the white trader by increasing the price of products. But this is only half the evil. Although the producer sold his ivory, and though it was resold a dozen times, all this trade was only a *commission* business with no advances. In fact, the first holder has *trusted* each successive dispenser with his property without any equivalent or "collateral" security. Now, when the last black fellow disposes of this piece of ebony or ivory to the white merchant or

From Paul Belloni du Chaillu, *Explorations and Adventures in Equatorial Africa* (London: J. Murray, 1861), pp. 10–16.

captain, he retains, in the first place, a very liberal percentage of the returns for his valuable services, and turns the remainder over to his next neighbour above. *He,* in turn, takes out a commission for *his* trouble and passes on what is left; and so, finally, a very small remainder—too often nothing at all—is handed over to the poor fellow who has inaugurated the speculation or sent the tusk.

Anyone can see the iniquity of this system, and the fatal clog it throws on all attempts at the building up of a legitimate commerce in a country so rich in many products now almost indispensable to civilized nations. The poor interior tribes are kept by their neighbours in the profoundest ignorance of what is done on the coast. They are made to believe the most absurd and horrid stories as to the ferocity, the duplicity, and the cunning of the white traders. They are persuaded that the rascally middle-men are not only in constant danger of their lives by their intercourse with the whites, but that they do not make any profit on the goods which they good-naturedly pass on to a market; so that I have known one of these scoundrels, after having appropriated a large share of the poor remainder of returns for a venture of ivory, actually, by a pitiful story, beg a portion of what he had handed over to his unsuspicious client. Each tribe cheats its next neighbour above, and maligns its next neighbour below. A talent for slandering is, of course, a first-rate business talent; and the harder stories one can tell of his neighbours below the greater profit he will make on his neighbour above.

The consequence is that the interior tribes—who own the most productive country—have little or no incentive to trade, or to gather together the stores of ivory, bar-wood, ebony, &c., for which they get such small prices, and these at no certain intervals, but often after long periods, even years elapsing sometimes before a final settlement is found convenient. Thus they are discouraged, and perforce remain in their original barbarism and inactivity.

The trade in slaves is carried on in exactly the same way, except that sometimes an infraction of trade-laws, or some disturbance on account of witchcraft, causes a war between two tribes in the commission business, when, of course, each side takes all it can of the opposite and ships them direct to the coast—to the barracoons or slave-depôts, of which I shall have something more detailed to say farther on.

There are, however, other obstacles to the prosecution of a regular commercial enterprise even by the shrewder among the negroes. It is not permitted that any member of a tribe shall get into his hands more than his share of the trade. It occurred some years ago to a shrewd Mpongwe fellow that in trade transactions honesty might be the best policy, and he followed the suggestion so well that presently both the whites and the interior natives threw a very considerable trade into his honest hands. But no sooner was this observed than he was threatened with poisoning, accused of witchcraft, and such a hullaballoo raised about his ears that he was forced to refuse the trade offered him, and, in a measure, retire from business to save his life.

More recently still, there were three or four men in the river who had obtained by long good conduct quite a character for honesty, and also, in consequence, got a good deal of business. At last a captain came for a load of bar-wood, and declared that he would trust only the three or four men in question, to the bitter disappointment of other traders. The vessel was

quickly filled and departed; and there arose a great "palaver"—the Mpongwe cant for a quarrel—in which the kings and chiefs and all the disappointed trading fellows met together at Glass Town—the residence of my honest friends—to advise about such an outrage. The men were called up for trial. They had been educated at the American mission, and knew how to write; and the charge made against them now was that they had written to the white man's country to say that there were no good men in Gaboon but themselves.

To this the accused shrewdly replied that the white men would not believe men who should thus praise themselves.

But reply was useless. They were threatened that if they took the next ship that came, the malcontents would "make a boondgi," or work a spell of witchcraft upon them, and kill them. Fortunately, in this case, the honest fellows had learned at the mission not to fear such threats; and the French commander for once stepped in and protected them against their envious fellows, so that for this time, on the West Coast of Africa, honesty seems likely to get its reward.

Again, through the anxiety of white traders to secure "trade," there has sprung up along the coast an injurious system of "trust." A merchant, to secure to himself certain quantities of produce *yet to come down* from the interior, gives to such black fellows as he thinks he can depend upon advances of trade goods, often to very considerable amounts. In this way, on the Gaboon and on the coast, often many thousand dollars' worth of goods are in the hands of natives, for which no consideration has been received by the white trader, who meantime waits, and is put to trouble and expense, and thinks himself lucky if he does not eventually lose a part of his investment.

This system of "trust," as it is called, does great injury to the natives, for it tempts them to practise all sorts of cheats, for which they are sharp enough—indeed, much too shrewd often for the white man.

Of course, *his* only dependence lies in the knowledge of his black debtor that if he cheats too badly his future supplies will be stopped entirely. But the practice develops all kinds of overtrading as well as rascality—negroes seldom hesitating to contract to supply much greater quantities of produce than they can hope to procure during a season.

Even the slave-trade, I found, on my visit to Cape Lopez, is burdened with this evil of "trust," and some of the Portuguese slavers, I was told, get preciously cheated in their advances on shipments of slaves sold "to arrive," but which do not come to hand.

I have heard the negroes called stupid, but my experience shows them to be anything but that. They are very shrewd traders indeed; and no captain or merchant who is a new hand on the coast will escape being victimized by their cunning in driving a bargain.

Say that to-day the good ship *Jenny* has arrived in the river. Immediately every black fellow is full of trade. The ship is boarded by a crowd of fellows, each jabbering away, apparently at random, but all telling the same story.

Never was there such dearth of ivory, or whatever the captain may want!

Never were the interior tribes so obstinate in demanding a high price!

Never was the whole coast so bare!

Never were difficulties so great!

There have been fights, captain!

And fever, captain!

And floods, captain!

And no trade at all, captain!

Not a tooth!

This point settled, they produce their "good books," which are certificates of character, in which some captain or other white trader who is known on the coast vouches for the honesty—the great honesty and entire trustworthiness—of the bearer. It is not worth while for a fellow to present himself without a certificate, and the papers are all *good,* because when "the bearer" has cheated he does not apply for a "character." Now these certificates help him to cheat. When he finds the need of a new set of papers, he conducts himself with scrupulous honesty towards two or three captains. These, of course, "certify" him, and then he goes into the wildest and most reckless speculations, upheld by the "good books," which he shows to every captain that comes.

Now, while they are pretending that nothing is to be bought, that there is no ivory on the coast, all this time the lying rascals have their hands full, and are eager to sell. They know the captain is in a hurry. The coast is sickly. The weather is hot. He fears his crew may fall sick or die, and he be left with a broken voyage. Every day is therefore precious to him; but to the black fellows all days are alike. They have no storage, no interest account, no fever to fear, and, accordingly, they can tire the captain out. This they do. In fact often, if they have an obstinate customer to deal with, they even combine and send all the trade a day's journey up river, and thus produce a fair show of commercial scarcity. At last, when high prices have been established, when the inroads of fever on his crew or the advance of the season have made the poor captain desperately willing to pay anything, the ivory comes aboard, and the cunning black fellows chuckle.

Even then, however, there are tedious hours of chaffering. A negro has perhaps only one tooth to sell, and he is willing —as he must live on this sale for a long period of idleness—to give much time to its proper disposal. He makes up his mind beforehand how much more he will ask than he will eventually take. He brings his tooth alongside; spends the afternoon in bargaining, and probably takes it back ashore at dusk, to try again the next day; till at last, when he sees he cannot possibly get more, he strikes the trade. I have known several days to be spent in the selling of a single tooth or a single cask of palm-oil.

Of course the captain protests that he is not in a hurry—that he can wait—that they shan't tire *him* out. But the negroes know better; they know the fatal advantage their climate gives them.

When it is supposed that a captain or trader will return to the coast no more after his present voyage, then he is properly victimized, as then the native has no fear of future vengeance before him; and I have known many individuals who, by the system of "trust," were all but ruined—getting scarce any return at all.

It is much to be wished that white traders would combine to put down at least this abuse. But until the spread of commerce shall break down the scoundrelly system of middle-men in this land, there will be no really prosperous trade there. And this will not happen till the merchants themselves visit the headquarters whence the produce is brought, and until the rude tribes shall be somewhat civilized by lengthened contact with the whites. At present things are in a state of utter disorganization, and the "trust" abuse seems a real necessity. For so hardly and often have the interior tribes been cheated of all returns for their wares, that now they have come to demand at least part payment in advance; and, of course, this advance is exacted of the white trader on the coast, to lure whom great rumours are spread through the tribes of teeth of a marvellous size lying ready for purchase, &c. Too often, when an advance has been made for a specific purchase—of a tooth, say— it is, after all, seized for some intermediate party's debt on its way down, and thus the poor trader is again victimized.

So eager are the Mpongwe for trade that they have even set up a regular coasting business. Every considerable negro trader owns several canoes; but his great ambition is to buy or build a larger vessel, in which he may sail along the coast, and, getting goods on trust from white merchants, make his regular voyage, or establish his little factory on some out-of-the-way point on the shore. The splendid harbour of the Gaboon has made them tolerably fearless on the water, and their rage for trade leads them to all manner of adventures.

Their coasting-vessels are only large boats, but I have seen some of so considerable size as to hold conveniently eight to ten tons. To make one of these they cut down an immense tree, sharpen it at the ends, then burn out the interior, guiding the fire so as to burn the heart of the tree and leave them the shell they need. For this hull, which is then scraped smooth, and otherwise finished and strengthened, they next make masts and sails, the latter being of matting, and then they are ready for sea. These cockle-shells stand the wind and sea remarkably well, as is evident when the squally and blustery weather of this country is considered, and when we know that they make voyages from the Gaboon as far as Cape St. Catherine's south, and as far as Banoko and Cameroon north.

The start for one of these voyages is a great occasion. Guns are fired, and the people shout and wish a pleasant voyage; and the lucky vessel is received at her port of destination with similar ceremonies.

The great aim of a Mpongwe trader, however, is to get "trust" from a white man, with authority to go off up or down the coast and establish a factory. Then there is double rejoicing. But the poor white trader is generally sadly victimized; for his agent goes to some spot where he thinks he can get ivory and other trade and settles down. Then, first, he mostly picks out the best and most valuable of the goods with which he has been intrusted, and secretes these for his own use. His next step is to buy himself some slaves and to marry several wives; all which being accomplished, it is at last time to think of the interests of his principal. Thus, after many months, perhaps he makes returns on his sales, or perhaps he fails altogether to make returns, if he thinks he can cheat so far with impunity.

These fellows understand all the dialects spoken on the coast, as well as English, French, Spanish, and Portuguese.

On their voyages, as they go poorly provisioned, and depend more on luck than real skill, they often suffer extreme hardships, but they are seldom drowned.

The chief product of the Gaboon country is its ivory. This is said to be the finest on the western coast. It produces also bar-wood, a dye-wood, from which is obtained a dark red dye, and ebony, the last taken from the great forests of this wood which abound near the head-waters of the Gaboon River. I have seen very large sticks brought thence, but the supply is not yet large. The bar-wood tree is found in great plenty along the shores of the river and its numerous tributary creeks. It is also found on the Moondah and Danger rivers. Copal is another product of this country, but it is of inferior quality, and is not sought.[1]

Ivory comes down the river from the interior by inland journeys in great quantities. Upwards of 80,000 pounds are taken from the Gaboon River yearly when home prices are good; for the ruling prices here are so high that traders cannot buy to advantage unless the home demand is very brisk. I suppose that the country from Banoko to Loango furnishes in brisk years at least 150,000 pounds of ivory.

But however important may be these commercial resources of the Gaboon country, I am convinced that the people will never prosper till they turn their attention more to agricultural operations, for elephants must finally disappear. This, indeed, is the great evil of all the nations of Western Africa. The men despise labour, and force their women and slaves to till the fields; and this tillage never assumes the important proportions it deserves, so that the supply of food is never abundant; the tribes, almost without exception, live from hand to mouth, and, with a fertile soil, are half the time in a state of semi-starvation.

---

[1] Copal is a resinous substance exuded from various tropical trees that is used in making varnishes and lacquers (ed.).

77 HENRY MORTON STANLEY
THE GREAT RAINFOREST OF THE CONGO

Sir Henry Morton Stanley (1841–1904) was a famous journalist who was commissioned by his employer, James Gordon Bennett, owner of The *(New York)* Herald, *to march into the interior and find Dr. David Livingstone, whose whereabouts were unknown. Stanley's subsequent meeting with Dr. Livingstone at Ujiji in 1871 brought him greater fame, and upon the death of Livingstone in 1873, Stanley returned to Africa to resolve the geographical riddle of the sources of the Nile and Congo rivers, which Dr. Livingstone had failed to untangle. Stanley circumnavigated Lake Victoria, proving that John Hanning Speke had been correct in his assumption that Lake Victoria was a single lake and the source of the Nile. Stanley then circumnavigated Lake Tanganyika, proving that Sir Richard Burton had been wrong—the lake had no outlet and was thus divorced from the Nile system. Finally, Stanley struck west through the great tropical rainforest of the Congo basin to make his way down the Lualaba/Congo River to the Atlantic. His descriptions of the rainforest did much to confirm the image of Africa that was common throughout the Romantic and Victorian eras—that the continent was indeed the heart of darkness—mysterious, brooding, remote, and terrifying.*

From Henry Morton Stanley, *Through the Dark Continent* (New York: Harper and Brothers, 1878), pp. 130–133, 136–140.

On the 6th November we drew nearer to the dreaded black and chill forest called Mitamba, and at last, bidding farewell to sunshine and brightness, entered it.

We had made one mistake—we had not been up early enough. Tippu-Tib's heterogeneous column of all ages were ahead of us, and its want of order and compactness became a source of trouble to us in the rear.[1]

We, accustomed to rapid marching, had to stand in our places minutes at a time waiting patiently for an advance of a few yards, after which would come another halt, and another short advance to be again halted. And all this time the trees kept shedding their dew upon us like rain in great round drops. Every leaf seemed weeping. Down the boles and branches, creepers and vegetable cords, the moisture trickled and fell on us. Overhead the wide-spreading branches, in many interlaced strata, each branch heavy with broad thick leaves, absolutely shut out the daylight. We knew not whether it was a sunshiny day or a dull, foggy, gloomy day; for we marched in a feeble solemn twilight, such as you may experience in temperate climes an hour after sunset. The path soon became a stiff clayey paste, and at every step we splashed water over the legs of those in front, and on either side of us.

To our right and left, to the height of about twenty feet, towered the undergrowth, the lower world of vegetation. The soil on which this thrives is a dark-brown vegetable humus, the debris of ages of rotting leaves and fallen branches, a very forcing-bed of vegetable life, which, constantly fed with moisture, illustrates in an astonishing degree, the prolific power of the warm moist shades of the tropics. The stiff clay lying under this mould, being impervious, retains the moisture which constantly supplies the millions of

tiny roots of herb, plant, and bush. The innumerable varieties of plants which spring up with such marvellous rapidity, if exposed to the gale, would soon be laid prostrate. But what rude blast can visit these imprisoned shades? The tempest might roar without the leafy world, but in its deep bosom there is absolute stillness. One has but to tug at a sapling to know that the loose mould has no retentive power, and that the sapling's roots have not penetrated the clays. Even the giants of the forest have not penetrated very deeply, as one may see by the half exposed roots; they appear to retain their upright positions more by breadth of base than by their grasp of earth.

Every few minutes we found ourselves descending into ditches, with streams trending towards the Kunda River, discharged out of leafy depths of date-palms, Amoma, Carpodinae, and Phrynia. Climbing out from these streams, up their steep banks, our faces were brushed by the broad leaves of the Amomum, or the wild banana, ficus of various kinds, and climbing, crawling, obstructing lengths of wild vines.

Naturally our temper was not improved by this new travelling. The dew dropped and pattered on us incessantly until about 10 A.M. Our clothes were heavily saturated with it. My white sun-helmet and puggaree appeared to be weighted with lead. Being too heavy, and having no use for it in the cool dank shades, I handed it to my gun-bearer, for my clothes, gaiters, and boots, which creaked loudly with the water that had penetrated them, were sufficient weight for me to move with. Added to this vexation was the perspiration which exuded from every pore, for the atmosphere was stifling. The steam from the hot earth could be seen ascending upward and settling like a grey cloud above our heads. In the early morning it had been so dense that we could scarcely distinguish the various trees by their leafage.

At 3 P.M. we had reached Mpotira, in

[1] A well-known and powerful Swahili trader who built up a large commercial empire in the eastern Congo and western Tanzania in the 1870s and 1880s (ed.).

the district of Uzimba, Manyema, twenty-one miles and a half from the Arab depot on the Lualaba.

The poor boatmen did not arrive until evening, for the boat sections—dreadful burdens—had to be driven like blunted ploughs through the depths of foliage. The men complained bitterly of fatigue, and for their sake we rested at Mpotira.

The nature of the next two days' experiences through the forest may be gathered by reading the following portions of entries in my journal:

"*November* 8. N. ¹/₂ W., nine miles to district of Karindi, or Kionga, Uregga.

"We have had a fearful time of it to-day in these woods, and Bwana Shokka, who has visited this region before, declares with superior pride that what we have experienced as yet is only a poor beginning to the weeks upon weeks which we shall have to endure. Such crawling, scrambling, tearing through the damp, dank jungles, and such height and depth of woods! . . . Once we obtained a side-long view from a tree on the crown of a hill, over the wild woods on our left, which swept in irregular waves of branch and leaf down to the valley of the Lualaba. Across the Lualaba, on the western bank, we looked with wistful eyes on what appeared to be green grassy plains. Ah! what a contrast to that which we had to endure! It was a wild and weird scene, this outlook we obtained of the top of the leafy world! . . . It was so dark sometimes in the woods that I could not see the words, recording notes of the track, which I pencilled in my note-book. At 3.30 P.M. we arrived in camp, quite worn out with the struggle through the intermeshed bush, and almost suffocated with the heavy atmosphere. Oh for a breath of mountain air!"

"*November* 9, 1876. N. ¹/₂ W., ten and a half miles' march to Kiussi, Uregga.

"Another difficult day's work in the forest and jungle. Our Expedition is no longer the compact column which was my pride. It is utterly demoralized. Every man scrambles as he best may through the woods; the path, being over a clayey soil, is so slippery that every muscle is employed to assist our progress. The toes grasp the path, the heads bear the load, the hand clears the obstructing bush, the elbow puts aside the sapling. Yesterday the boatmen complained so much that I organized all the chiefs into a pioneer party, with axes to clear the path. Of course we could not make a wide road. There were many prostrate giants fallen across the path each with a mountain of twigs and branches, compelling us to cut roads through the bush a long distance to get round them. My boatbearers are utterly wearied out."

.   .   .

From Kiussi, through the same dense jungle and forest, with its oppressive atmosphere and its soul-wearying impediments, we made a journey of fourteen miles to Mirimo. Four streams were crossed, all trending westward to the Lualaba, the two principal being the Rugunsi and Rumuna rivers. Mirimo is a populous settlement, and its people are good-natured.

The boatmen did not arrive at all on this day, the obstacles having been too great, but on the 12th, about noon, they appeared, utterly disheartened at the delays which had deprived them of their food and rest.

On the 13th we moved to Wanekaman-kua, crossing *en route* the Kariba River and two small streams.

Our next march was to Wane-Mbeza, in Uregga, eight miles in a north-westerly direction. We crossed the Kipembwé, a river 40 yards wide, deep and swift, which flows westward.

Uregga, it appears, occupies a broad belt of country lying north-east and south-west. Its people know nothing of the immediate settlements contiguous to them, and though within twenty miles of the Lualaba, many adult males at Wane-Mbeza had never seen it. They have been imprisoned now for some five or six generations within their almost impenetrable forest fastnesses, and the difficulty of travelling, and the danger that would be incurred unless they united in strong bands, are the causes of their knowing nothing of the world outside, and the outside world knowing nothing of them.

The Wangwana began at this place to murmur loudly, while the boatmen, though assisted by a dozen supernumeraries and preceded by a gang of pioneers, were becoming perfectly savage; but the poor fellows had certainly cause for discontent. I pitied them from my soul, yet I dared not show too great a solicitude, lest they should have presumed upon it, and requested me either to return to Nyangwé or to burn my boat.

Even Tippu-Tib, whom I anxiously watched, as on him I staked all my hopes and prospects, murmured. Sheikh Abdullah was heard to growl ominously, and Bwana Ibrahim was particularly severe in his remarks upon "the pagans' forest." The evil atmosphere created sickness in the Arab escort, but all my people maintained their health, if not their temper.

At this camp we parted from Bwana Shokka and his 300, who were about to penetrate some eight or ten marches more to the north-east to Tata country. I have a suspicion that "Tata" is not a proper name, but that it simply signifies "farther in."

On the 15th we marched six miles and a half to Wane-Kirumbu. From this village, which, like all the villages that we had passed, crowned a hill, we obtained the most extended view we had enjoyed since entering the forest. Towards the north and north-east the outlook was over a jumble of forest-clad hills separating narrow and deep valleys. The view was indeed most depressing and portentous.

Our march, short as it was, was full of incidents. The constant slush and reek which the heavy dews caused in the forest through which we had travelled the last ten days had worn my shoes out, and half

of the march I travelled with naked feet. I had then to draw out of my store my last pair of shoes. Frank was already using his last pair. Yet we were still in the very centre of the continent. What should we do when all were gone? was a question which we asked of each other often.

The faces of the people, Arabs, Wangwana, Wanyamwezi, and the escort, were quite a study at this camp. All their courage was oozing out, as day by day we plodded through the doleful, dreary forest. We saw a python 10 feet long, a green viper, and a monstrous puff-adder on this march, besides scores of monkeys, of the white-necked or glossy black species, as also the small grey, and the large howling baboons. We heard also the "soko" or chimpanzee, and saw one "nest" belonging to it in the fork of a tall bombax. A lemur was also observed; its loud harsh cries made each night hideous.

The path presented myriapedes, black and brown, 6 inches in length; while beetles were innumerable, and armies of the deep brown "hot-water" ants compelled us to be cautious how we stepped.

The difficulties of such travel as we had now commenced may be imagined when a short march of six miles and a half occupied the twenty-four men who were carrying the boat sections an entire day, and so fatigued them that we had to halt another day at Wane-Kirumbu, to recruit their exhausted strength.

The terrible undergrowth that here engrossed all the space under the shade of the pillared bombax and mast-like mvulé was a miraclē of vegetation. It consisted of ferns, spear-grass, water-cane, and orchidaceous plants, mixed with wild vines, cable thicknesses of the *Ficus elastica,* and a sprinkling of mimosas, acacias, tamarinds; llianes, palms of various species, wild date, *Raphia vinifera,* the elais, the fan, rattans, and a hundred other varieties, all struggling for every inch of space, and swarming upward with a luxuriance and density that only this extraordinary hothouse atmosphere could nourish. We had certainly seen forests before, but this scene was an epoch in our lives ever to be remembered for its bitterness; the gloom enhanced the dismal misery of our life; the slopping moisture, the unhealthy reeking atmosphere, and the monotony of the scenes; nothing but the eternal interlaced branches, the tall aspiring stems, rising from a tangle through which we had to burrow and crawl like wild animals, on hands and feet.

About 9 A.M. Tippu-Tib and the Arabs came to my hut at Wane-Kirumbu. After a long preamble, wherein he described the hardships of the march, Tippu-Tib concluded by saying that he had come to announce his wish that our contract should be dissolved!

In a moment it flashed on my mind that a crisis had arrived. Was the Expedition to end here? I urged with all my powers the necessity for keeping engagements so deliberately entered into.

"It is of no use," Tippu-Tib replied, "to have two tongues. Look at it how you may, those sixty camps will occupy us at the rate we are travelling over a year, and it will take as much time to return. I never was in this forest before, and I had no idea there was such a place in the world; but the air is killing my people, it is insufferable. You will kill your own people if you go on. They are grumbling every day more and more. This country was not made for travel; it was made for vile pagans, monkeys, and wild beasts. I cannot go farther."

"Will Tippu-Tib then return to Nyangwé, and break his word and bond? What will all the Arabs at Nyangwé, Mwana Mamba, and Kasongo's say when they hear that Tippu-Tib, who was the first Arab to penetrate Rua, proceeded only a few days with his friend, and then returned?"

"Show me a man's work, and I will do it."

"Well, look here, Tippu-Tib. The land on the west bank of the Lualaba is more open than this, and the road that Mtaga-moyo took to go to the Lumami is on that side. Though the land is more open, I hear that the people are worse there than on this side. However, we are not Mtaga-moyo, and they may behave better with us. Let us try the other side.

"Now, I will give you choice of two contracts. Accompany me to the river, and wait while I transport my people across, and I will give you 500 dollars; or accompany me twenty marches farther along the west bank, and I will give you 2600 dollars. At the end of that time, if you see your way clear, I will engage you for another journey, until I am quite satisfied that I can go no farther. Provisions will be given your people until we part, and from that point back to Nyangwé."

For two hours I plied him with arguments, and at last, when I was nearly exhausted, Tippu-Tib consented to accompany me twenty marches farther, beginning from the camp we were then in. It was a fortunate thing indeed for me that he agreed to this, as his return so close to Nyangwé in the present dispirited condition of my peoples' minds would have undoubtedly ensured the destruction of all my hopes.

78 EDGAR CANISIUS
RUBBER COLLECTING IN THE CONGO

In 1885 King Leopold II of Belgium became sovereign of the Congo Free State and set out to establish the state's authority throughout the Congo basin and beyond. The task soon absorbed the king's private resources, and despite loans from Belgium, by the early 1890s the Congo Free State was on the verge of bankruptcy. It was saved from financial collapse by the rubber industry. King Leopold leased vast territories of the Congo to concessionaire companies while exploiting the royal domain with his own agents. Soon rubber was exported from the Congo in ever increasing quantities, to the profit of the companies and the king. Unhappily, rubber could be collected only by employing brutal and repressive methods against the Africans who derived no profit from tapping the vines and collecting the sap and consequently had no wish to work. The atrocities that were perpetrated to force the Africans into the forest to tap the vines soon caused an international scandal and ultimately resulted in the transfer of the Congo Free State to Belgium. Edgar Canisius was a young American who joined the service of the Congo Free State in 1896 and was stationed in the Province Orientale. *After completing his tour of duty, he joined the* Société Anversoise du Commerce au Congo *and, as an agent of that concessionaire company, he was able to describe at first hand the methods employed to collect rubber.*

There are, or were, in the immediate vicinity of N'Dobo about a dozen villages, the people of which were obliged to bring in rubber every fifteen days. On these occasions the natives crowded into the post, each village in charge of a "capita," or headman, whose most important duty it was to ensure that the demanded amount of rubber was collected. These capitas usually belonged to tribes settled in other districts of the State, and were as a general rule, armed with muskets of the gas-pipe variety, although some had breech-loaders. They were paid by the company, but the villagers were expected to supply them with food, and this Mr. "Capita" was never remiss in deciding should be of the best and of sufficient quantity.

The natives carried to the muster small baskets supplied by the post, and supposed to be full of rubber. When all had arrived, the people were ranged by the capitas according to their villages. The agent, who had their names inscribed in

From Edgar Canisius, "A Campaign Amongst Cannibals," in Captain Guy Burrows, *The Curse of Central Africa* (London: R. A. Everett & Co., 1903), pp. 74–80.

a book kept for the purpose, then called the people forward, first by villages, then individually. As each man stepped up I noticed that he carried, attached to his neck by a cord, a small disc of metal evidently cut from the zinc lining of a packing-case, and that each disc bore a number corresponding with that entered in the book opposite the man's name. The soldiers having ranged the people in lines, each man with his basket before him, the agent proceeded to verify the individual numbers—not without some difficulty, however, for the natives by some means or other frequently get their "tags" mixed, and much time and a fearful amount of shouting and gesticulation are required, on the part of both natives and white man, to set matters right.

As each man or boy presented his basket, the agent carefully inspected the quantity of rubber it contained, and paid the bearer accordingly in *mitakos*—pieces of brass wire about six inches long, the estimated value of which at N'Dobo was about a half-penny. I calculated that the rubber was paid for at the rate of rather less than one penny per pound, which certainly could not be considered excessive in view of the fact that at that time the product in Europe was fetching from two to three shillings a pound. Those natives who had brought in quantities which the agent deemed insufficient were ordered to one side, and as soon as the entire village had been thus inspected and paid, these delinquents were seized by some of the "soldiers" attached to the post, thrown upon the ground, and soundly flogged. Some received twenty-five lashes, others fifty, but I have occasionally seen even 100 lashes administered, the instrument used being the "chicotte," a heavy whip of hippopotamus hide. This proceeding—inspection and eventual punishment—was repeated until all the villages had been dealt with. Then the natives started off for their jungle homes, usually at a sharp trot, apparently only too glad to escape with life from a place which no doubt they looked upon much as the Belgians' forefathers regarded the torture-chambers to which they were oftimes led by their Spanish masters. They, of course, carried with them their baskets and their *mitakos,* which they did not want but were forced to accept. The manager of the post had accumulated perhaps no less than a thousand pounds of rubber at the cost of about £4 sterling, including presents to the chiefs and capitas. Thus was rubber "gathered" twice each month at N'Dobo.

I found that it was usual to "tag" not all, but only three-fourths or so of the male villagers. Those "tagged" at once became mere slaves to the company, for rubber-making occupied all their time, the victim having to search far and wide for the giant vines from which the sap is extracted. They were not even fed by their taskmasters, their only remuneration being merchandise or *mitakos* distributed in ridiculously small quantities, as already described.

The cruel flogging of so many men and boys would probably have had a peculiar effect upon a new-comer, but I was in a measure case-hardened. My experience in the State service during three years had made me familiar with many such, and worse incidents of Congolese life. For instance, at the Government post where I was for a long time stationed, a man had died as the result of an exceptionally severe castigation at the hands of a white official, and elsewhere I had seen blood drawn from the backs of women.

At N'Dobo I found many brick houses and magazines in course of construction under the direction of an ex-architect and builder. At that time, it was evident, the company's officials at Mobeka entertained keen hopes that the fierce and hitherto intractable Budjas of the interior were about to tumble over each other in their eagerness to bring in rubber—an idea which proved very erroneous, as will later be seen.

The Brazilian rubber-gatherer has no reason to envy the people engaged in a similar occupation in the wilds of Africa, for his work in comparison is a mere picnic. The great rubber-trees of the Amazonian forest yield to him their precious sap after but a few blows of the axe, and fill the bucket of the collector without entailing upon the latter any necessity of raising himself above the ground. Nor does the extraction of a few quarts of sap deprive him of another supply from the same source later on.

Not so, however, with the Congolese rubber-gatherer. In the African jungle the sap is drawn from a giant creeper (often six inches in diameter at the base), which, shooting upward towards the life-giving light of heaven, twists about the surrounding vegetation—its rivals in the struggle for existence. After reaching the crown of the highest monarch of the forest (often a hundred feet above the ground), the vine rises still further until it is bent back by its own weight to the topmost branches of its original support. Then it climbs along these branches, and those probably of half-a-dozen other great trees, until the machete of the rubber-gatherer cuts short its career.

The Congo native, when about to

gather rubber, generally goes with his fellow-villagers far into the jungle. Then, having formed a rough, shelterless camp, he begins his search for the creepers. Having found one of sufficient size, he cuts with his knife a number of incisions in the bark, and, hanging a small earthenware pot below the vine, allows the sap to slowly trickle into it. Should the creeper have been already tapped, the man must climb into the supporting tree at more or less personal risk and make an incision in the vine high above the ground where the sap has not been exhausted; and here he will remain, perhaps the whole of the day, until the flow has ceased. Not unfrequently the natives slumber on their lofty perches, and, falling to the ground, become victims to the white man's greed. Few Africans will imperil their lives in rubber-gathering unless under compulsion. The natives, if pressed for time, as they usually are in the Congo in consequence of the threats of the white man and the fear of the Albinis of the soldiers and the muskets of the capitas, cut down long lengths of the giant creepers and then subdivide them to make the sap ooze out more quickly.

Of late, the people have been compelled to so frequently tap the vines that the latter soon dry up and die. Each tribe has only a limited extent of forest which it can call its exclusive domain, and it consequently very frequently happens, when their own "bush" is worked out, that natives from one village penetrate the territory of the other in defiance of tribal usage. Such an invasion is naturally resented by their neighbours, who, equally pressed no doubt by circumstances and the white man, are themselves experiencing difficulty in making up the quota of rubber definitely fixed for each village, and a deficient production of which may entail dire punishment and even death. In consequence, disputes arise between villages which heretofore, perhaps for quite a long period, have been at peace; and then come wars, involving more or

less loss of life, destruction and cannibalism. Natives, I may add, have often come to me with bitter laments over the disappearance of their brothers after accidents when rubber-gathering, or the attacks of leopards or hostile tribesmen.

The coagulation of the sap is effected in a variety of ways. In some regions, the natives smear the latex over their chests, and with their hands rub it until a small ball is formed. This process is repeated until the ball is the size of a small walnut. These balls have often a reddish hue, the result of the powdered camwood with which the natives usually smear their bodies. In other parts, the juice is poured into a pot in which is boiling water, and is then allowed to boil until all the water has evaporated and the rubber forms a kind of cake over the bottom of the pot. This product, when brought to the stations, is cut into fine strips and hung upon battens in a drying-shed for several months. In the Province Orientale the natives generally pour the sap into an oblong form of box, made of flat-sided sticks laid upon the ground. The heat of the sun is utilized to coagulate the sap, a thin layer of latex being poured on the top from time to time until the whole forms a solid mass of rubber some fifteen to twenty inches long, eight inches wide, two or three inches thick, and weighing from eight to ten pounds. After reaching the stations, these slabs are cut into small strips or *vidoles* (fingers), and then placed in sheds to dry upon shelves made of poles.

I have seen it stated in official documents, and in books written by persons represented to have travelled through the African forests, that there are regions where the jungle is literally a tangled mass of rubber-vines. Such stories are ridiculous, for nowhere does the creeper exist in such luxuriance; like all tropical jungle vegetation, it is scattered over large areas with many other similar plants, which may belong to the same genus but are not the true rubber-vine. On an acre of jungle one rarely finds two trees of a kind, and the same may be said of the large creepers, or lianas, with which the tropical bush abounds.

That the stock of rubber-vines in those parts of the Congo which have been worked for any length of time is being rapidly exhausted is evidenced by the ever-increasing difficulty experienced in inducing the natives to exploit it. Wherever I have been in this vast territory, always excepting, of course, the Budja country, which has never been much

worked, the natives bitterly bemoaned the scarcity of the rubber-producing lianas, and piteously begged to be allowed to perform other service than rubber-gathering. In some places they brought in large quantities of "false rubber," a resinous matter much resembling caoutchouc, from which, indeed, when freshly-made, it cannot be easily distinguished. In the course of drying, however, the false rubber assumes a glossy appearance, unlike that of the genuine article.

79 L. PÉTILLON
NATIVE POLICY IN THE BELGIAN CONGO

In his speech before the Government Council of the Belgian Congo in Leopoldville on July 18, 1955, Governor General L. Pétillon outlined a revised native policy, according to which the Belgians hesitantly agreed to begin to train Africans for a greater role in the administration of the colony. The tardy awakening of Belgian colonial policy is in striking contrast to the relatively mild demands of Patrice Lumumba put forth in his book, Le Congo, *a portion of which is the subject of the following selection.*

THE TASK OF THE OLD CHIEFS
In their great majority, the traditional chiefs are elements of value; even among those who lack education, there are those who enjoy great prestige; many of them establish, in a satisfactory manner, the contacts between the European administration and the populations whose resources, needs and aspirations they know. They are among the most precious collaborators that Belgium has on African soil. They have worked under often difficult circumstances, executing orders whose scope exceeded their understanding, in a spirit of trusting submission. Therefore, we have decided that it was

necessary to compensate them in relation to the importance of their responsibilities, present and future, and have just raised their salary.

Far be it from me to minimize their merit or to slight the importance of their services. But we have to admit that except for a very small number, they are rooted in the tradition that they personify, and envision only with reserve and anxiety an order of things different from that over which they preside. It is up to us to make them, and especially their successors, understand that we wish only that their institutions develop in such a way as to make of them instruments of progress.

Moreover, the ever-increasing multiplicity and the diversity of the tasks of the chief call for the creation of administrative machinery and, as far as possible, the

From *Belgium's Policy in the Belgian Congo* (New York: Belgian Government Information Center, 1956), pp. 18–22, 26–27. Reprinted by permission of the author.

separation of the executive and judicial powers. The collection of duties and taxes, the preparation of the cadastral survey (plan of commune), the registration of the vital statistics, the administration of public thoroughfares, the execution of social works, the setting up and running of the record office of the provinces require a specialized and trained personnel. Besides, the chief no longer has the peace of mind nor the necessary time to fulfill his function of judge; therefore, whenever custom permits, he must be relieved of this obligation.

TRAINING THE ELITE FOR ADMINISTRATIVE TASKS

That is why we thought that, in order to instruct the future rural authorities and their assistants in their tasks, it was necessary to create a system of instruction which might give an authentic administrative and civic training to the sons of chiefs and notables and to all the young natives called upon to exercise a function in their rural milieu.

Furthermore, it is not exclusively a matter of specialized instruction; the pupils must be assured a solid general training which will permit them eventually to request other functions or to attempt other activities. But it is deemed necessary that this program be organized in the very districts where the functions taught are to be exercised, in order to inculcate in their officials a spirit of healthy regionalism and to familiarize them with the tangible aspects of public office.

Two levels of education are planned, corresponding to the minor and the responsible positions. These schools will be directed by an experienced member of the territorial service, assisted by a pedagogue chosen from the teaching personnel.

A first step has been envisaged for the near future: three schools of administration will be opened in the provinces for which the need is the most pressing: Equator, Kasaï and the East Province.

At the same time we shall anticipate an adaptation of the program of the existing secondary schools, especially as regards civic formation, in such a way as to permit their pupils to become oriented in communal occupations, if they so desire.

2. To encourage or increase the participation of the populations in public life also implies that it is necessary to confer upon the districts communal autonomy to the extent that the formation and popular control of those whom they administer would allow.

To be autonomous, is above all to control one's own finances.

Through a series of measures that your Permanent Delegation has recently approved, the legislator will allow additional quotas in the duty to be increased from 40 to 70% and will authorize the creation of non-compensatory taxes. It is a first step towards fiscal autonomy.

COMMUNAL DOMAIN

Besides, it is necessary that the districts possess a domain. The assignment to the advanced centers of the lands in their jurisdiction had already been decided. The Royal Decree of December 19, 1949 for the center of the Katanga and the projected decree of the Cities were resolutely conceived in this view.

The existence of a private domain calls for strict regulations and the capacity to extract from them the benefit that a prudent administration would authorize. This problem must be initiated and resolved without particular apprehension.

The setting up of assets and the creation of receipts to tend to financial autonomy without contrivances would necessitate the total suppression of imposed works not having an educational nature, in such a way that the obligations which the districts met by means of a noncompensated manpower may henceforward have to be paid for with their money. Shortly, it will also be an accomplished fact.

However, we must see to it that the

burdens of the native communities are bearable.

The maintenance of the road network of local interest such as it was conceived up to now might exceed the means of most people. Therefore, the State undertook on its own account a part of the expense since the beginning of this year; besides, we have placed under study, to be applied starting next year, a reclassification of the roads reducing the proportion of those which we call "of local interest."

Furthermore, the development of the communal administration will considerably increase public expenses. It was, therefore, fitting to provide, a priori, that each district be able to fulfill its tasks properly, and to conceive of an adequate system of subsidization until, after a long initial period which is beginning, complete financial autonomy can be foreseen and instituted. That is why the system of subsidies has been re-examined and will in the future be based on new principles which will go into effect in 1956. We are expecting notably a simplification of the duties of the territorial administrator as manager of the credits of the Colony, more faithful respect for financial soundness, a calmer management of the coffers of the chefferies,[1] an activity becoming more and more predominantly that of native authorities.

But, it will not suffice for native communities to manage their ordinary receipts and expenses from day to day. As every public administration, they will have to be able to proceed with community investments and with the equipment that our reform calls for. Communities, like men, need starting capital. Therefore, the districts are authorized to contract loans under certain conditions.

The National Savings Bank, which collects the available funds of the richest communities, is normally indicated to lend to the poorest the funds which they

[1] A chefferie is a community under the administration of a local chief.

need. Later, it will be necessary to establish an institution which would have a statute similar to the Communal Bank of Belgium, founded on the principle of the coöperatives. The first step will be accomplished without difficulty; the scope that the credit will have, and which will be the reflection of the desired evolution, will tell us when the establishment of an autonomous organism is justified.

3. It thus appears that we intend henceforward to substitute a regime of guardianship for the paternalism that we have practiced up to the present: the representatives of European authority will only continue to intervene as animators, advisers and inspectors.

A balance must be established between the two elements which serve as counterweights for the liberal administration of the communities: popular control on one side, European guardianship on the other. Proportionately, as the first falters, it is essential that the second be more closely exercised. One should not have any illusions in this regard: a careful guardianship will have to compensate for the insufficiency of popular control for a long time to come. Nevertheless, is it to be expected that it will ever disappear entirely since, as everywhere, the local powers here remain subordinate to the higher instances of authority?

As the decree of July 14, 1952 on the political organization of Ruanda-Uruandi already provides, the action of territorial authority will be exercised a priori, by means of councils and a posteriori, by means of veto. The text which is submitted to you specifies the duties and the powers of the authority in this respect: the success of the new regime evidently depends in large measure on the tact with which the administrator of the territory and his assistants exercise their tutelary function. Just as they will have to remain vigilant toward the backward communities and be uncompromising when, as must be anticipated, abuses develop, so they must be discreet and unobtrusive, when the communal authorities merit their confidence.

COOPERATION ON A HIGHER PLANE

The third point with which our plans deal is to create a favorable climate for collaboration on the higher plane of the Belgo-Congolese community.

For the cities, we have visualized a regime which makes allowances for the duality in fact which exists between the African and the European cities, a duality which dominates and tempers administrative unity in all that concerns the general interest and towards which we wish to tend more and more.

For still more evident reasons, it is inconceivable that on the level of the native communities of the interior, the assemblies be homogeneous for still a long time. But it is necessary, here also, to anticipate a level of coordination and of cooperation of the local administrations, on the one hand with those which surround them, on the other hand with the European population.

That will have to be accomplished with the flexibility desirable, in creating mixed councils in the territories and the districts, councils whose essential and local competency will have to be within the range of understanding and capacity of the men who compose them. There would be certain danger in the beginning, to create these organs abstractly and to impose them everywhere with the same methods. It will therefore be necessary that the local authorities experiment with a theory, adapted to the necessities of each region, in several places judiciously chosen, and put it to the test.

The program that I outlined in 1952 would thus be realized, little by little, as a foundation, on which is to be constructed later—the last step of our reform—the pyramid of the Territorial and District Councils, crowned by the Provincial and Government Councils.

. . .

NATIVES TO ACQUIRE REAL ESTATE

We have been, the very first in this respect, to burn with impatience, realizing how much this delay would retard the progress of the native middle class and, more generally, the installation of one of the most innovative measures and one most likely to bring about profound changes, that has been applied in recent times.

For, its economic and social scope will be considerable. "To grant to the Congolese," as the texts proclaim, "the enjoyment of all the real estate rights provided by written law," is to confer upon them the possibility of becoming title holders of actual guaranteed rights, to use them freely and conveniently within the limits which only the law may fix; to settle and mortgage their heritage economically; to have recourse to mortgage credit.

But it was certainly necessary to yield to the evidence and admit the reasons which the heads of service brought forth to justify the impossibility of going more quickly. It is not, indeed, without infinite precautions that one can put into effect, in an immense territorial area, a precise system or organization of real estate rights, with all the legal, economic and social implications that it embodies at a time when nothing was yet provided for in this domain, when all the indispensable opinions remained to be gathered, the collaboration to be obtained and the specialized personnel to be recruited.

Oddly enough, in the centers where the problem was most urgent, it was necessary to organize the cadastral survey, set up the administration and train the personnel.

In large measure, the difficulties are today surmounted and resolved in the following manner.

The Office of the African Cities— whose cooperation has been sought in the settlements where it is established because of its related activities and its more flexible organization—is charged with the surveying and the demarcation of boundaries of the lands placed at its disposal; it will do this according to a plan and an order decided by mutual agreement between the Administration and itself. The conditions and the methods of this collaboration have been agreed upon in the belief that the Office will give the maximum of efficiency to the accomplishment of its task.

For the lands other than those of the Office, we shall go forward, starting from the basis which we have. In the chief provincial towns, the urbanistic studies are advanced enough to permit land development, if not by districts, at least by blocks limited by public thoroughfares; there, the Cadastral Service will establish its land developments and will proceed with the surveying and parceling according to the directions of the town-planners. Besides, the land developments would be best completed with the means and personnel that the local authorities have at their disposal; the parcels of land will be delimited provisorily and sold or rented without guarantee of area.

This work—I am sketching here only the outstanding features—will be executed everywhere with the maximum of precision that circumstances will permit, if it is not perfect, the excuse will be found in the will which animates us not to wait and in the obligation to resign ourselves sometimes to the "almost" when one cannot do better.

As for the administration of the real estate domain, it will be assured, according to the case, either by the Colony, or by the native communities as soon as they will have become owners of their land grants.

We shall have thus done the maximum that is necessary and sufficient to satisfy urgent necessities, to resolve in a practical way the problem of accession of natives to private real estate property.

Henceforward and everywhere where they will usefully desire it, the Congolese people will be in a position to acquire real estate, fully and completely, to dispose of it prudently, to exhaust all its economic possibilities and, notably through mortgage credit, to have recourse to a new efficient and flexible means of amplifying their activities and giving a more competitive luster to their enterprises.

80 PATRICE LUMUMBA
CRISIS OF CONFIDENCE

The following selection is taken from the book originally entitled Le Congo, Terre d'Avenir, Est-Il Menacé?, *written by Patrice Lumumba (1925–1961) before he became the first Premier of the Congo and before he was committed to the needs of a Congolese national consciousness and pan-Africanism. Moderate in tone and in demands, Lumumba criticizes the Belgian leaders for their failure to understand, let alone appreciate, Congolese nationalism.*

Ever since the Belgians first came to Africa, the Congolese have shown themselves to be docile, obedient and grateful to their mentors. Their confidence has been put to the test for over seventy-five years.

From Patrice Lumumba, *Congo, My Country,* trans. by Graham Heath (London: Pall Mall Press, 1962), pp. 160–166. Reprinted by permission of Frederick A. Praeger and Pall Mall Press.

The social peace which reigns in the Congo and which foreigners call the "Belgian Miracle in Africa," is a dazzling sign of good administration and of the high morale of the native population.

The first stage of the colonisation has been completed: the stage of the conclusion of treaties, construction of roads, liberation of the people, etc. After these three-quarters of a century of hard work, of groping steps which have now led to success, the people of the colony put forward a confident and dignified plan to leave this stage, which has been out-dated by the course of development, and to enter stage two.

Will Belgium disappoint them? I do not think so, because there is no valid reason to justify such a refusal and because Belgian policy as a whole is sincerely moving towards the steady emancipation of the Congolese under Belgian trusteeship.

What is this *second stage?* It is the stage of *integration* (not of assimilation which involves the absorption of one people by another) of the *democratisation of the country* and of the *Africanisation of the leadership.*

This integration is the task of our rulers, in whom I have every confidence. In this book, I have mentioned some transitional stages which may facilitate the immediate advancement of the Belgian Africans.

In their co-existence with the Whites, the Africans are greatly worried, not by the fact of living alongside them, but by the idea that they may never be able to attain complete emancipation and liberty whilst under European domination.

Hence the African's dream of independence does not arise from hatred for the Whites or a desire to drive them out of Africa, but simply from the wish to be not merely a free man but also a citizen in the service of his country and not perpetually in the service of the European. He believes, moreover, that, even if he is able to obtain complete emancipation un-

der white domination, it will only come after centuries, because the European will hamper that emancipation by all sorts of tricks and political schemes, and that the Blacks will therefore be kept in a state of inferiority as long as possible. Finally, he believes that once the country becomes independent, the emancipation of the inhabitants will be much more rapid than it would have been under the system of tutelage and colonialism.

"We shall certainly have difficulties at the beginning—like every other nation— but we shall overcome them thanks to the help of the Europeans to whom we shall appeal and who will come, in this case, not to dominate us but to help us and to serve Africa. With these Europeans we shall always maintain neighbourly and fraternal relations."

This is what the Africans think in their heart of hearts.

This general impression prevailing among the Congolese, which they do not pass on to Europeans for fear of reprisals—a fear which is often imaginary—arises out of the following considerations:

Since the European occupation began, some eighty years ago, no African in the Congo has been accepted for any post —even the lowest—of European officer grade in the administrative services, the law and the army, even if he has had a full secondary education and studied philosophy for several years. (I am leaving out of account the two Congolese from Leopoldville who recently finished their studies in Belgium and the native priests.) A European (I refer here to temporary officials, some of whom have had no secondary education) is *always* superior to an African even if the latter has studied longer and hence is better educated.

There are, in fact, some cases of this kind.

Except for the priests and the two or three Congolese who have studied in Belgium, no native, however competent, occupies the post which is his due and which he could have occupied long ago or could take over now *if the leading administrative posts were Africanised.* Even if he holds a responsible position, he does not have the same prestige as a European official. He is only a minor assistant, always dependent on a European official.

As a justification for refusing him the position which should by rights be his, the African will be told that he does not hold the European secondary education certificate or some other academic document, or that he must go to university, even though everyone cannot go to university even in Europe or America; or, if he is employed in the Government Service, he will have to wait twenty, twenty-five or thirty years before getting to the rank of chief clerk, Grade I, assistant drafting officer or assistant territorial officer, although a short three- or five-year course would be amply sufficient to give a really capable person the competence to do the work of a territorial officer or drafting officer. Many people can do these jobs long before completing five, ten, fifteen or twenty years of service.

Example: A Congolese with six years of secondary education is at present taken on in the rank of a clerk, third class. He must have a minimum of eighteen years' service (with good reports and regular promotion) in order to enter the grade of chief clerk, first class; to become an assistant territorial officer or assistant drafting officer, he must serve for a further three years, making a total of twenty-four years. Thus, it is only after twenty-four years of good and loyal service that a Congolese with a certificate of secondary education can take his place among the European officers, just when he has reached the end of his career or is about to do so.

At the moment when the Congolese is admitted to the lowest grade in the European hierarchy, a European who has had the same education (secondary) and who was initially engaged in the rank of area officer or drafting officer, will, after the same period of service of twenty-four years, be a director or head of some department.

And yet the same Congolese could very well carry out the duties of a territorial officer or drafting officer immediately on recruitment, or at least after a normal probationary period; there is no need for him to wait for this excessively long period of twenty-four to thirty years.

The fact that Ruanda-Urundi, a territory which has been under Belgian mandate since 31st August 1923, is more favourably situated than the Congo from the administrative point of view is not without influence on the Congolese.

"Whereas Ruanda-Urundi, which had the great good fortune to be placed under international trusteeship in 1923, is taking giant strides towards autonomy, we Congolese, who have been under the *same Belgian administration* for more than three-quarters of a century—much longer than Ruanda-Urundi—are far behind our neighbour. In Ruanda-Urundi, the position of the chiefs and underchiefs has been *enhanced,* their authority is respected and there are two kings, but, in the Congo, the authority of the native chiefs is reduced to the point where they are no longer real chiefs in the etymological sense of the word but mere V.I.P.s, government servants working under the authority of territorial officers and agronomists." That is the authentic view of the Congolese on this matter.

There is a contradiction in methods, particularly between the political principles enunciated by the Government and the higher authorities in all their official statements on colonial policy, and the application of those principles—sometimes in a contrary sense—*by the executive* officers. Some lower-grade officers apply these principles in a reactionary fashion *whenever* they are not personally in favour of a particular measure planned and enacted by their superiors for the benefit of the African.

These contradictions have created, and are still creating, a most regrettable confusion in the minds of the Congolese who draw the illogical conclusion that "The Government is scheming and intriguing with its officials to hoodwink us. The Government promises us this or that, enacts its laws and regulations and makes spectacular speeches, but the Government officials go in the other direction; perhaps they have received secret instructions. Even at school in Europe, they are taught to be cunning in dealing with the Blacks. Before they come to Africa, they are told that they must always live a long way away from the Blacks. This is proved by the sharp line of demarcation between the European and African quarters. The so-called green belts which separate the European and African quarters are barricades but, in order to fool us, they plant trees and flowers there to look like nursery gardens. If what they tell us is true, it should be put into practice by the high-ups and by the lower-ranking officials."

Let me explain: If, for example, the Governor General gives instructions to European officials, advising them to behave towards the natives with all due correctness, and if no change takes place in the behaviour of a large number of these officials, so that the Africans still do not obtain satisfaction, the latter follow this train of reasoning: "It is inconceivable that a minor official can ignore the instructions and recommendations given by the Head of the colony. As these instructions do not always give the results which we expect them to give, we doubt their sincerity. The policy is designed to trick us."

When some Congolese find difficulty in obtaining a loan from the Colonial Advancement Fund to purchase a decent dwelling, they reason as follows: "They don't want us to have nice houses to suit our taste. They refuse us loans so as to compel us indirectly to live in the houses of the African Townships Department, houses which are not to the taste of most people but for which funds are provided without any hesitation. All this is so that

the Blacks shall not have houses of the same taste and style as those of their 'masters' (the Whites)."

When the "King's Fund" [1] does not give the satisfaction which Congolese families expect, their reaction is the same: "Our dear King has seen with his own eyes that we are poor and badly housed and he has SENT money to enable us to have decent dwellings. The Whites have misappropriated this money and are using it for projects which are of benefit only to them. We are being deceived."

I note that quite a number of settlers (though there are exceptions) hesitate or even protest sometimes whenever the Government or the high-ups decide on the smallest increase in salaries or confer some benefit on the Congolese in the economic or social sphere or elsewhere.

There is an impression that anyone, be he minister, governor-general, governor, administrator, or mere official, in the public or private sector, who concerns himself actively with native interests and interracial relations and lives in close contact with the Africans, often ends up by being looked at askance by the others, *simply* because he takes a greater interest in the advancement of native society and has no axe to grind. Thus there are some people who pay dearly for espousing the cause of the natives and who forfeit sympathy in many quarters.

This idea can be illustrated by a few notable examples: "M. Jungers, who, in the opinion of the Congolese, was the first Governor General to advocate, in his historic speech to the Government Council in 1952 (the last Council over which he presided at the end of his term of office), the establishment of the Belgo-Congolese Community and the total assimilation of the Congolese *immatriculés*, was hotly

[1] *King's Fund: Fonds du Roi*—instituted on 18th October, 1955 by King Baudouin to promote social welfare in the Congo. The number of beneficiaries from the Fund in 1955 was 777 on a budget of about £60,000; in 1958 it provided for 2,608 beneficiaries from a budget of more than £4,600,000.

criticised, regarded with disapproval in some quarters and described as a *madman* by certain organs of the Press" (I have irrefutable proof of this in the form of Press articles) "because he was bold enough to express progressive ideas in front of people with conservative ideas."

Then Governor General Pétillon, who won the approval and appreciation of the protagonists of African advancement, was frowned on by a considerable number of people because of his moving speech at the opening of the Government Council of 1955, dealing with human relations between Whites and Blacks, and also because of the authorisation which he gave to the Blacks to enter public premises which had previously been reserved for Europeans only.

One section of the Press threw back at M. Pétillon the idea which he had put forward in his speech that "Anyone who disagrees with the policy of the Government is respectfully asked to pack his bags," and invited the Governor General "to pack his bags."

I still recall the tension which prevailed in the Congo following the decision of the Governor General to allow the Congolese entry to public premises. Fortunately, this tension was eased when the Africans, with great reasonableness, withdrew from these places voluntarily.

I must add that a number of public premises were, and still are, glad to welcome Congolese.

"M. Buisseret continues to be the object of malicious partisan criticism, not because he is administering the Colony badly but because he attaches a great deal of importance to the social factor; because he never ceases to preach and defend the principle of equal rights and equal prestige; because he invites the Africans to come and discuss their problems in Belgium instead of confining them to the Congo and leaving all matters which concern them to be decided on the spot; because he wants to "go quickly" with the Africans instead of crawling along at a snail's pace and slowing up the emancipation of the natives by excessive delays; and because he introduced state education for the Congolese. But the establishment of state education for Europeans (the Royal Athenaeums) roused no protests; protests only come when Africans are concerned, and yet this education is giving great satisfaction to Congolese parents. The reason why protests are made against this education is that French is taught from the first year of the primary school. The curriculum is similar to that of the European schools, so that the Africans will soon have enough education to compete with the Europeans. There is opposition to M. Buisseret because he has won the hearts of the Congolese who regard him not as a Minister, a Belgian, a Catholic, a Liberal, a Socialist or a Communist, but a sincere FRIEND of the Blacks, just as they do in the case of all other Belgians who champion their cause. Some people are afraid that the unanimous liking which the Congolese of all shades of opinion, Protestants, Catholics and pagans, show for a Liberal Minister, and their great confidence in him, will lead all the Africans of the Congo to become Liberals; but this is completely false, since the African masses are not interested in the label—Liberal, Catholic, Socialist or Communist,—but in their *material, intellectual and moral welfare.* We will turn to anyone who can secure these benefits for us, or help us to obtain them, and we ignore questions of dogma or freemasonry, which are of little interest to us as they will bring us no material advantages. Finally, there is opposition to M. Buisseret because he wants the Blacks to advance instead of leaving them as servants of the Whites." These opinions have been expressed to me by ninety per cent of the Congolese, and I do not wish to make any comment on them.

SOUTH AFRICA

EUROPEAN BEGINNINGS AT THE CAPE

Although the Portuguese were the first Europeans to round the Cape of Good Hope, their contact with South Africa and its inhabitants remained slight and hostile. The Orient was the destination of the Portuguese captains, who soon learned that a wide sweep far from land through the storm-tossed waters off the Cape was the best route to East Africa and India. Occasionally, homeward bound ships put in at the Cape to revictual, but after *Khoikhoi* (Hottentot) pastoralists—who, with the *San* (Bushmen), inhabited southern Africa—killed the Viceroy of India, Francisco d'Almeida, at Table Bay in 1510, the Portuguese tended to sail clear of the Cape to more secure anchorages along the coasts of eastern and western Africa. At the end of the sixteenth century, the Portuguese monopoly of the Indian trade was challenged by English and Dutch merchants venturing into eastern waters. In 1580 Sir Francis Drake rounded the Cape of Good Hope, and in 1591 James Lancaster landed at Table Bay. The Dutch were not far behind. In 1595 Cornelis de Houtman circumnavigated the Cape on his way to Java, soon to be followed by the organized expeditions of the newly founded Dutch East India Company. Since their goal was the East Indies, neither the British nor the Dutch ever displayed much interest in East African ports, preferring to sail south of Madagascar and directly across the Indian Ocean. Thus the Cape became the last and consequently an important landfall for Dutch and English captains, and as early as 1619 an Anglo-Dutch station at Table Bay was proposed by the Dutch East India Company. Nothing came of the proposal, however, since English interest soon shifted to India and the seaway to the Asian subcontinent that swung south of the hazardous coast of the Cape of Good Hope.

The Dutch, however, continued to require a refreshment station in southern Africa, and after the shipwreck of the Haarlem in 1647 had dramatized this need, Jan van Riebeeck arrived at Table Bay in 1652 on instructions from the Dutch East India Company. He built a fort, planted a vegetable garden, and sought to obtain cattle and sheep by barter in order to supply the company's ships (Jan van Riebeeck and Z. Wagenaar, *Of the Native Tribes of South Africa*). The results were at first disappointing. The station failed to provide adequate foodstuffs or livestock so that the company, hoping to stimulate production, began to offer land grants for settler farming in 1657. Settlers, however, were restricted to company servants, and certain crops and prices were strictly regulated. As a result, the growth and transformation of the Cape from a commercial outpost to a colony of free settlers remained imperceptible until the last quarter of the seventeenth century, when colonists were recruited from Holland and given free passage and free land. Thereafter, the number of colonists steadily increased. By 1707 there were over 1,600 free burghers at the Cape, producing more food than could be consumed internally or sold to the company for revictualing. Economic difficulties were compounded by settler discontent over the favoritism displayed by Governor Willem Adrian van der Stel, and although the company agreed to recall him, the directors blamed the political unrest on the colonists and terminated their assistance to immigrants from Holland. Thereafter, the growth of the free burgher population was determined more by natural increase than by immigration, weakening the settlers' links with Europe on the one hand and placing greater reliance on slaves to meet the farmers' labor requirements on the other.

Slaves had been present in the Cape colony almost since its inception, but the company practice of fixing prices on farm commodities encouraged the colonists to employ slave labor in order to produce crops cheaply enough to make a profit. The first slaves were not taken from the indigenous Khoikhoi population but were obtained from the traditional slave markets of West Africa and occasionally from Madagascar and the East Indies. The number of imported slaves increased steadily throughout the early decades of the eighteenth century, and since slave labor was three times cheaper than that of European farmhands and more manageable, white settlement was given no encouragement by either settlers or company. As the decades passed, the institution of slavery was not only accepted as the proper relationship between white man and black, but was regarded as necessary to the colony's economy, and the slave population, by importation and internal increase, soon came to outnumber the free burghers.

SOUTH AFRICA

Scale	0	100	200	300	400
				Miles	

KAM

Despite the presence of English, Danish, Swedish, and even French Huguenots among the colonists, the various European nationals were gradually assimilated during the eighteenth century and the character of the colony remained predominately German and Dutch. There was no restriction on the teaching of national languages, but the company insisted that Dutch be taught. However, the Dutch language that was used and invariably taught in the colony was more the vernacular of Dutch seamen than the language of the great cultural centers of Holland. When infused with elements from French, German, English, and African languages, South African Dutch gradually evolved into the Afrikaans language of today. The unifying force of South African Dutch, the inevitable social intercourse, intermarriage, and the pervasive influence and popularity of the Dutch Reformed Church (which was Calvinist in theology and fundamentalist in practice) produced not only a homogeneous settler class but one whose isolation from the rapid and profound changes taking place in seventeenth- and eighteenth-century Europe contributed to the development at the Cape of a unique white settler community.

THE EUROPEAN ADVANCE INTO THE INTERIOR

At the same time that the Europeans were evolving a distinctive folk nation, they were also challenging the indigenous societies of the Cape—the San and the

Khoikhoi. Perhaps because of their lack of centralized institutions, but certainly because of their propensity for cattle rustling, the San were relentlessly driven from the frontier by Europeans and Khoikhoi alike. The more numerous Khoikhoi fared little better, however, and their society steadily disintegrated in the face of European presence and disease. Like the San, many Khoikhoi retired to the frontiers of white settlement, where they conducted limited trade. Others remained behind in a servile capacity, adopting European customs while forgetting their own. Within the European community the dearth of white women soon resulted in a mixed class of "Cape Coloured" people—the products of the intercourse between white settlers and nonwhite slaves and indigenous peoples, which came to occupy a unique and not undistinguished place in the colony. By the eighteenth century, the black Africans no longer remained a threat to European expansion from the Cape.

The European advance into the hinterland followed the search for cattle pasturage. At the beginning of the eighteenth century, cattle raising became widely practiced by those farmers who, regarding Cape Town and its officials with deep suspicion, moved into the interior. In addition, the inability of the local market to absorb agricultural produce, as well as the steady increase in population, always producing more foodstuffs than could be consumed, encouraged more farmers to become frontier cattlemen, particularly as Khoikhoi resistance dissipated in the interior. Thus throughout the eighteenth century, a slow but steady stream of colonists, comprising a substantial part of the population increase, moved away from the administrative authority at Cape Town.

The colonists first went northward along the western coastal belt until they were blocked by the arid regions of Namaqualand. A second and more popular route took them along the southern coast, across the Hottentot Holland Mountains, and then eastward. In 1745 the importance of this eastward advance was acknowledged when the Cape authorities established a magistrate at Swellendam. Later, pioneers continued up over the mountains to the plateau, spurred on by company land grants of 600 acres. The promise of land encouraged the pioneers and drove them on, thus creating a pastoral people, accustomed to isolation, self-reliant, contemptuous of authority, and intensely individualistic. Not surprisingly, these Boers, as they came to be called, were difficult people to govern, and the company's failure to check their dispersion produced only contempt for its authority (Andrew Sparrman, *The Boers*). In the end the company was forced to extend its control, thereby acknowledging the expansion it had vainly sought to prevent. In 1778 Governor van Plettenberg established the eastern boundary of the colony at the Great Fish River, hoping that such a demarcation would act as a barrier not only to the Boers but also to the Bantu, with whom the colonists were coming in contact for the first time.

The Boers were not the only group to disperse. Bands of Cape Coloureds, acculturated to white society but unable to find a place within it, drifted north to the Orange River and then eastward along its course at the same time that the Boers were pressing on to the Great Fish River. Here on the Orange River the Griqua, as these Cape Coloureds were known, established several small states not unlike the abortive Boer frontier republics except that the European missionaries exerted considerable influence within them.

Thus in 150 years the revictualing station of the Dutch East India Company had grown from a small commercial outpost into a colony half again as large as England and Wales and inhabited by some 15,000 European colonists. Cape Town was the company's headquarters and Table Bay was its port. Beyond this administrative capital were the agricultural areas of the coastal belt where, despite the monopolistic practices of the company, the settlers prospered from the produce of their farms. Finally, in the remote regions of the coast and on the interior plateau lived the pastoral population, which was difficult to rule in its isolation from the organized state, the established church, and the formal education of the settled regions around Cape Town. Despite differing national origins, the members of the European population had attained a homogeneous character and culture unique and even distinct from its Netherlands origins. Everywhere the Europeans employed slaves and menial laborers from the indigenous population. As a product of interracial intercourse, a third group of people with mixed blood had emerged to form the Cape Coloured folk. At the end of the eighteenth century, however, two new elements were soon to appear that changed dramatically, if not tragically, the course of South African history—the Bantu and the British.

THE BANTU

The first to appear were the Bantu. Although their initial appearance south of the Limpopo remains uncertain, they probably had arrived there by the end of the first millennium and certainly by the fifteenth century. By 1800 the two principal divisions of the South African Bantu—the *Nguni* and the *Sotho-Tswana* —had established numerous independent chieftaincies among whom the *Xhosa* had pressed westward to the Great Fish River. At this point the river formed an uncertain frontier between the volatile Bantu societies on the one side and the restless Trekboers on the other, and the clash of cultures soon led to open disputes all along the eastern frontier. Differing conceptions of land tenure and political authority combined with outright competition for control to precipitate numerous Kaffir (as the Bantu were called) wars throughout the last quarter of the eight-

eenth century (Thomas Pringle, *Boer Meets Bantu*). These frontier wars were fought mainly by the colonists themselves, who would hastily band together to repel Bantu raiders and seize their land and cattle. Occasionally, the authorities at Cape Town assisted the colonists, but the declining fortunes of the Dutch East India Company, which declared bankruptcy in 1794, did not enable its officials to provide adequate protection from the Xhosa raiders who remained in disputed territories. Infuriated at its failure to defend them, the colonists on the Zuurveld frontier rebelled against company rule in 1795 and established their own government at Graaff-Reinet. The burghers of Swellendam quickly followed their example in June 1795 and the colony broke into three parts.

THE BRITISH

The revolt at Swellendam coincided almost to the day with the arrival at Table Bay of nine British men-of-war. The great confrontation between Britain and France during the wars of the French Revolution and the Napoleonic Wars had drawn the British to South Africa. The Cape was still the halfway port between Europe and the eastern empires of Britain and France. Throughout the eighteenth century, Britain and France had struggled for supremacy in the East, and the outbreak of war in Europe only intensified this conflict for trade and dominion in the Orient. In the past the Cape had been in Dutch hands, but now the Dutch East India Company was in liquidation, Holland was dissolved, and the Cape was about to fall within the French sphere of influence. With the sanction of the Prince of Orange, whom the French had driven from the Netherlands into exile in England, a British naval force set sail for South Africa to secure the Cape against French annexation. After a short struggle the company officials capitulated on June 11, 1795, and the rule of the Dutch East India Company in South Africa came to an end.

In this way the British came to South Africa—at first as temporary rulers, representatives of the Prince of Orange, guardians of the passage to India. Although the Cape was restored to the Batavian Republic (the former kingdom of the Netherlands) after the Peace of Amiens in 1803, after the resumption of war in Europe the British returned and occupied Cape Town in 1806. This time the British did not retire, and as part of the European peace settlements concluded at Vienna in 1815, the Netherlands formally ceded the Cape to Great Britain.

Thus the British and the Dutch were brought together in South Africa. At first their relationship was that of ruler and ruled, but the arrival of British settlers introduced a distinct element into the homogeneous European society of South Africa. The political predominance of the British, as well as their Olympian preference for the English language and their intense national pride, prevented their being absorbed into the South African European community as readily as the French and the Germans had been assimilated earlier. At the same time, the British were never sufficiently numerous to absorb in turn the Cape Dutch, whose traditions and characteristics were as sharply delineated as their own. Briton and Boer were to discover that they possessed many common sentiments that might serve as the basis for cooperation and friendship. They were also to find, however, that the great strengths of their traditions and the divisive nature of their respective individualities hindered the inclusion of both groups into a larger white community of southern Africa.

BRITISH RULE AT THE CAPE: SLAVERY, MISSIONARIES, AND ENGLISHMEN

British rule at the Cape was not unwelcome during the early stages of first occupation. The new government began with the advantage of its predecessor's unpopularity. It abandoned the system of commercial monopoly, stimulated trade, and enjoyed the prosperity of a war economy. On the frontier, however, the British were less successful, proving to be every bit as vacillating as the company and nearly as unpopular. The second British occupation began less auspiciously than the first, yet the rulers and the ruled found they had much in common. The Europeans at the Cape were a conservative people, as were their British rulers. At first both the institutions and personnel of government remained virtually unchanged, and there was little interference with the customs and traditions of the Boers. In spirit the Cape remained a Dutch colony, and there was no policy of deliberate Anglicization. Even on the frontier the popularity of the government reached unprecedented heights when the Xhosa were finally driven from the Zuurveld to satisfy the insatiable land hunger of the white settlers at the expense of Xhosa needs for pasturage. In fact, cooperation between the Dutch and the British might very well have grown into confidence and acceptance if not for their different attitudes toward and treatment of the black South Africans.

In 1807 Great Britain abolished the slave trade throughout her empire, and although attempts were made to evade the law, the supply of slaves to the Cape dwindled to insignificance, and the European population, bolstered by the arrival of English immigrants, soon outnumbered the slaves. Diminished in number, the slaves increased in value along with the solicitude of the owners for their welfare. As an institution, slavery at the Cape had always been comparatively free from the abuses that prevailed on the slave plantations of the Americas. In fact, the abolition of the slave trade aroused little opposition at first but was ultimately to create much ill feeling. For without slaves, the farmers became increasingly dependent on the labor of free Khoikhoi or Cape Coloureds, and in the master-employer and servant-employee relations were the origins of exploitation that precipitated the righteous indignation of the English missionaries.

The early nineteenth-century missionaries were the religious by-products of the eighteenth-century Enlightenment. Just as the philosophes conceived of the natural rights of *all men,* so too did the missionaries preach the equal rights of *all men* before God. The disparity between the theory and practice of this doctrine as applied to the blacks of South Africa was self-evident to the English missionaries, particularly Dr. John Philip of the London Missionary Society, who soon came to regard themselves as protectors of their people against their Boer employers. But to the farmers suffering from a shortage of labor in the years after abolition, the mission stations became an annoying if not subversive sanctuary for unemployed blacks. It was not a difference between a specifically Dutch and a specifically British conception, for as British settlers came to South Africa they quickly adopted the farmers' point of view. But the missionaries were mostly British and the farmers were mostly Dutch, and consequently the issue sowed the seeds of future bitterness between Briton and Boer.

The preaching of the missionaries found its secular counterpart in the law, which was applied equally by British magistrates to both white men and black. But if the white colonists could not accept equality before God, they were not likely to accept equality before man. Thus, in one incident, when a frontiersman was summoned to court for maltreating a black servant, he resisted arrest and was shot to death. His friends vainly sought to raise the frontier in retaliation and revolt, but the rebels were seized and seven ringleaders were hung at Slachter's Nek. Although this frontier incident was relatively unimportant at the time (since most Boers appear to have agreed with British rule and its enforcement), Slachter's Nek became a vivid symbol of British oppres-sion in the 1870s and its victims martyrs against British tyranny. The memory of Slachter's Nek has since remained a constant source of division between Briton and Boer.

The Slachter's Nek affair coincided with a change in the attitude of the British rulers toward the Cape colony. Until 1814 British occupation of the Cape remained uncertain; it merely checked innovations in government and discouraged British colonists from settling in South Africa. After the peace of 1815, however, immigration was actively encouraged, not only to relieve postwar unemployment in Britain but to place settler farmers on the Zuurveld frontier as a bulwark against the Bantu. Consequently, in 1819 the British government made available free passage and land on the frontier to parties of English immigrants that would settle in the Zuurveld, and in 1820 some twenty ship-loads arrived at Algoa Bay. From there the immigrants scattered over the Zuur-veld and beyond, and by 1821 nearly 5,000 English men, women, and children had arrived in the Cape colony. Although English settlers comprised only one-seventh of the European population, an active policy of Anglicization soon followed their arrival in the colony. The gradual substitution of English for Dutch as the official administrative and judicial language began in 1822. The judicial system of the colony was remodeled to conform to the English pattern. The old Burgher Senate ceased to exist, and even the Dutch rix-dollar was replaced by the British pound sterling. Clearly, the intention of the government was to make the Cape a British colony, administered by a central-ized Anglicized British bureaucracy in the spirit of the Tory reaction of the 1820s. Although the Dutch inhabitants under-stood conservative government, they would not willingly abandon their language and traditions, to which they were deeply attached. Humiliated, the Boers soon had cause for even greater discontent.

The old established farmers of the western Cape met their labor requirements principally by the use of slaves. The eastern frontiersmen, however, possessed few slaves and were dependent for labor on Khoikhoi and Cape Coloured folk. These eastern farmers continually complained of the difficulties of securing labor and the depredations of those Khoikhoi who preferred to remain unemployed rather than labor on settler farms. The farmers therefore sought to impose checks on Khoikhoi freedom of movement by enacting vagrancy laws and legislation designed to force the blacks to labor on white farms. The English missionaries vigorously objected against this discriminatory legislation. Their object was to convert the Khoikhoi into landowners who were both equal before the law and in a position to bargain freely for their labor.

The struggle between the farmers and the missionaries was long and bitter, but in 1828 the missionaries triumphed with the passing of the famous Fiftieth Ordinance, which canceled the legislation restricting Khoikhoi freedom and secured the legal equality of the free black inhabitants of the Cape colony. Among the farmers in general, but among the eastern frontiersmen in particular, the passage of the Fiftieth Ordinance aroused great resentment. To them the ordinance meant scarcity of labor, the weakening of the white man's authority, and an invitation to vagrancy. But the effects of the ordinance went even further. It exacerbated the hostile feelings against the missionaries and brought into focus the fundamental differences between the missionaries' conception—a conception beginning to be widely accepted in Britain—of equal rights for all men, black, or white, and the view of the pioneer farmer who refused to admit such equality now or in the future. Once opened, the great gulf between the indiscriminate idealism of Exeter Hall and the intolerant but not unkindly pragmatism of the frontiersman could not easily be bridged.

THE GREAT TREK

The emancipation of the slaves in 1834 contributed to the growing resentment of the Boer farmers. Not only did the slave owners object to the legislation concerning the use of freed slaves passed in preparation for emancipation, but they were furious with the inadequate compensation paid for these slaves. Moreover, all claims had to be presented in London, where payment was to be made partly in cash and partly in bonds at 3.5 percent, so that many farmers, having no option but to sell their claims to agents, received only a small fraction of the value of their property. Humiliated by the regulations of emancipation and forced to take a considerable financial loss, the farmers received in return no law against vagrancy and little security against possible depredations by liberated slaves. To make matters worse, relations with the Bantu deteriorated into war on the frontier.

In 1834 the Bantu invaded the colony—burning, looting, and killing Europeans. The Governor, Sir Benjamin D'Urban, rushed troops to the frontier. In a short, sharp struggle the Bantu were defeated and driven back and D'Urban sought to push the frontier eastward to the Kei River in the expectation of annexing the territory and granting the land to the frontier burghers both as compensation for their losses and as farms for their land-hungry sons. Although the D'Urban policy was popular in the colony, it was vigorously opposed by the missionaries and by their philanthropic supporters in London. D'Urban was overruled by the colonial secretary, Lord Glenelg, who had no intention of compensating the frontier burghers for damages incurred in a war that, in his opinion, the Bantu had ample justification for beginning. Frustrated at every turn within the colony and desperate for land, the Boers began to look beyond the boundaries of the colony for freedom from British control and for expansive farms to give their numerous sons. The Great Trek soon followed

(Anna Elizabeth Steenkamp, *The Great Trek*).

In one sense the Great Trek was but a continuation of the migration eastward from Cape Town, which had scattered European farmers over the interior plateau as far as the Great Fish River. Unlike the random, haphazard movements of the eighteenth century, however, the trek was undertaken only after considerable organization and planning. In 1834 three reconnaissances were made—one to Damaraland in what is now Southwest Africa, one to the Zoutpansberg in the northern Transvaal, and one to Natal. These investigations discovered good, thinly populated land to the northeast, and in the following year the first of two parties of Voortrekkers departed. The first group was destroyed by the Bantu; the second was decimated by fever. Undeterred, the main body of emigrants crossed the Orange River in 1836 just as the *Mfecane* had spent its terrible force.

THE MFECANE

The Nguni-speaking Bantu had inhabited Zululand and Natal since the sixteenth century. Here on the fertile grasslands between the Drakensberg Mountains and the sea the Bantu population rapidly increased; land became scarce, and intertribal fighting intensified as the eighteenth century came to a close. To compete effectively in these wars, the Nguni borrowed the use of age-regiments* from the neighboring *Sotho,* making warfare more efficient but also more intense. During this time of turmoil Shaka, the son of a chief of a small tribe known as the Zulu, began to train his followers in new methods of warfare, employing the short-stabbing spear, the assegai, for the traditional throwing spear, so that his warriors not only retained their weapons but could maneuver in close formation (Henry Francis

* Groups of young men of approximately the same age who, having passed through the initiation ceremonies together, remained together as a military unit.

Fynn, *Shaka*). By conquering neighboring tribes his forces increased, and by 1818 Shaka had become the dominant power in Zululand. Introducing the conception of total war, Shaka's victorious armies swept all before them, precipitating hordes of refugees northward where, by imitating Zulu military tactics, they absorbed the local inhabitants before breaking up into sections to found kingdoms in Zambia, Malawi, and Tanzania. Other Bantu tribes fled westward from Shaka's depredations into the high plateau country beyond the Drakensberg Mountains, which was inhabited by the Sotho-speaking Bantu.   Destruction, upheaval, and death followed as tribes turned into wandering, pillaging hordes, that fought desperately with invaders and inhabitants alike and turned the plateau beyond the Orange River into a deserted land infested with bands of leaderless men, known indiscriminately as *Mantatees*, who preyed on the starving refugees of war. Two remarkable leaders soon emerged, however, to lead their people out of the chaos in Sotholand and to establish states in the upper Zambezi and the hill country of the upper Orange River. Sebetwane led his tribe, called the *Kololo,* to Barotseland, where he established a short-lived empire, while Moshweshwe founded a kingdom in Basutoland by bringing together the remnants of many tribes (Andrew Geddes Bain, *The Ngwaketse Defeat the Kololo*).

Refugees from Zulu armies were not the only peoples on the move. In 1821 one of Shaka's generals, Mzilikazi, defied his king and fled into the Transvaal with a section of the Zulu Army that came to be known as the Ndebele (or Matabele). Sweeping through the Transvaal, Mzilikazi's forces decimated the Tswana tribes, incorporating their young men into the Ndebele age-regiments. Meanwhile, in Zululand itself Shaka had become increasingly despotic, and after the deprivations that he had made his people undergo upon the death of his mother, he was assassinated by two of his brothers, one of whom, Dingane, made himself king of the Zulu. But the death of Shaka did not end the great upheavals of the South African Bantu—known as the Mfecane (the crushing)—which continued on into the decade of the Great Trek. Nevertheless, by 1830 the Mfecane had destroyed or driven away the Bantu inhabitants of wide areas of Natal, Trans-Orangia, and the Transvaal, while concentrating relatively dense populations in Basutoland and the coastal plains between the colonial frontier and Natal. The high veld of the interior of South Africa did not long remain empty, for soon the great ox-drawn wagons of the Voortrekkers appeared on the quiet grasslands.

BANTU AND BOER

One after another the Voortrekkers crossed the Orange River, traveling usually in small parties and dispersing to search out the land and graze their cattle. The only serious opposition came from Mzilikazi and his Ndebele, but Mzilikazi was ultimately defeated by Potgeiter in 1837 and headed north across the Limpopo River to establish his people in modern Rhodesia.. Potgeiter and his followers remained behind to claim the high veld by right of conquest and to settle down to enjoy the fruits of victory. Meanwhile, the majority of the trekkers under the leadership of Pieter Retief turned eastward, crossed the Drakensberg Mountains, and appeared in Natal, where they requested permission from Dingane to settle. Dingane was at once alarmed by the appearance of the Voortrekkers and was determined to be rid of them. After agreeing to permit the Boers to enter Natal, he ordered Retief and his companions massacred at the royal enclosure. The murder of Retief precipitated a dramatic struggle between Bantu and Boer for control of Natal, the turning point of which was the Boer victory over Dingane's forces at the Battle of the Blood River on December 16, 1838. Dingane made peace

and promised to withdraw his people north of the Tugela River, but his defeat and willingness to evacuate divided the Zulu. One of Shaka's brothers, Mpande, refused to follow Dingane, placed himself under Boer protection, and defeated Dingane at the Battle of Magongo in February 1840. The Boers, however, were the principal winners of strife among the Zulu who, outgunned and divided, could no longer compete successfully for control in Natal.

BRITISH POLICY IN SOUTH AFRICA: ANNEXATION OR ABANDONMENT

Although the Great Trek had done much to resolve the difficulties that the Boers had faced in the Cape colony, it created more problems for the British government than it had solved for the Boers. On the one hand the Boers were British subjects, owing allegiance to the Crown, which was ultimately responsible for them, yet the British government was reluctant to incur the great expense of administering the vast and unproductive land into which the Boers had fled. On the other hand, if the Boers were left to create their own independent states, as they had already done in Natal, another European power might gain influence in southern Africa, endangering the route to India and undermining the fundamental purpose for British presence at the Cape. Moreover, the Boers regarded the Bantu with implacable hostility, and conflict between them, which seemed inevitable, would keep South Africa in turmoil, threaten the Cape colony, and require heavy military expenditure on punitive expeditions. If the Cape colony could not dominate frontier policy, the colonial government would undoubtedly have to intervene with military force. The dilemmas of South Africa were not easily resolved, and British policy vacillated wildly between ruling and abandoning the interior regions. As a result, all parties were ultimately alienated and British influence in South Africa was greatly diminished.

The Great Trek immediately presented the British with these great issues. No sooner had the Boers arrived in Natal than they declared an independent republic, to the alarm of the British authorities who were concerned for the defense of the route to India and the consternation of British philanthropists who were angered by Boer expropriation of Bantu land and cattle. In 1842 a British force was sent to occupy Port Natal, and although it was besieged by the Boers, British reinforcements arrived and the republican government collapsed. In 1845 Natal was officially annexed to the Cape colony, and many Boers trekked back over the Drakensberg Mountains to the high veld. Here on the plateau the Boers could disperse over a much wider area than was possible in the comparatively restricted region of Natal. The Boers possessed two centers—one at Winburgh south of the Vaal and the other at Potchefstroom north of the river—but their dearth of political experience, their resolute individualism, and their impatience with restraint, all the products of the isolated life on the frontier of the Cape colony in the eighteenth century, mitigated against the development of settled government. Winburgh and Potchefstroom possessed loose links with the Natal republics, but when Natal was annexed, the ties disappeared and the Boer communities on the plateau fragmented into detached units.

At first the British authorities tried to bring about order without expense to the interior by recognizing the authority of the chiefs in the hope that they could maintain control over black and white in their territories in return for a small British subsidy and British protection. Thus agreements were signed with the Griqua Chief Adam Kok and with Moshweshwe of the Basuto in 1843, but the policy soon appeared bankrupt. No Boer was about to submit to black authority, and British forces had to be rushed to the defense of Adam Kok in 1844. Then the British

authorities tried another device. Governor Maitland sought to resolve the conflict between black and white by segregating the land into that portion over which the chief would exercise his direct authority and those portions where powerful white settlers would be under the control of a British resident. Although the system worked well at first, it was soon undermined by the insatiable demands of the Boers for land and ended in yet another frontier war that dragged on until December 1847.

Having failed to resolve frontier conflict by recognizing and protecting the indigenous authorities, Sir Harry Smith, the new Governor, tried outright annexation. Dashing madly from the Cape to Natal, he annexed the eastern frontier and the whole area between the Orange and the Vaal rivers. The Boers were furious. They had trekked into the interior to escape British control and now found it suddenly imposed upon them. They rebelled but were soon overpowered by British forces who reinstated British officials in Trans-Orangia.

Although Sir Harry Smith's precipitate annexations seemed to have resolved the problem of frontier control, his policy had neither the resources to support it nor authorization from London. His representative in Bloemfontein, Major H. D. Warden, sought to reconcile the incompatible interests of Boer, Griqua, and Bantu, and in this effort was dependent only on the good will of the white farmers who had already been alienated. Not surprisingly he failed, and although Boer rebellions against the government were suppressed, the British government was prepared to abandon its attempts to control the wild interior of South Africa. The fluctuations of British policy reflected the important changes occurring within mid-nineteenth-century Britain. Philanthropic humanitarianism went into decline after the emancipation of the slaves in 1834. Moreover, in the free trade atmosphere of the times, colonies were regarded a burden to be avoided if possible and abandoned at the first opportunity. Even the indignation that was aroused at the thought of leaving Bantu alone to face Boer was giving way to a cynical acceptance of the historical inevitability that concern for distant natives was a sentimental luxury Britain could no longer afford. In 1852 the Sand River Convention was signed, granting independence to the Transvaal, to be followed in 1854 by the Convention of Bloemfontein, creating an independent Orange Free State. The fragmentation of South Africa begun by the Great Trek now seemed complete.

The British might reluctantly abandon the interior, but they could not forget it. The independent Boer states simply did not have the resources to maintain order on their frontiers without resorting to violence and intimidation against their non-European neighbors. Without cooperation and coordination, characteristics that ran counter to Boer attitudes, these same states would remain permanently insecure before the mass of Bantu tribes. Moreover, the dearth of resources prevented both security and education for the Boers, which might have produced a more enlightened approach toward race relations than the primitive assumptions derived from their simplistic religion and the wild land they inhabited. Just as the British could not control the Boers except by force, so too the Boers failed to live with the Bantu except by violence (James Chapman, *The Boers and Their Attack on the Kwena*). By 1858 war had broken out between the Orange Free State and the Basuto, but the Free State could not maintain its forces in the field and was forced to ask the British Governor at the Cape, Sir George Grey, to arbitrate peace. Unable to remain aloof from conditions in the interior, Grey sought to avoid outright annexation by creating a federation of white states. But even federation required a greater commitment than any British government wished to assume. Grey's policy was repudiated, and without imperial overrule, by 1863 frontier affairs had degenerated once again into war with

the Basuto. Although the forces of the Orange Free State successfully exhausted Basuto resistance, they stirred the powerful supporters of Moshweshwe in England to protest against the breakup of Basutoland before the Boer invasion. Reluctantly the British government gave way and permitted Governor Wodehouse to annex Basutoland and defend it with British troops. Elsewhere on the frontier the British authorities continued to encroach upon the traditional powers of the chiefs in their efforts to establish control (*The Governor and the Tembookies*). Thus, despite its official determination to limit its commitments, the British government became increasingly involved in the interior, where a new factor suddenly appeared to further complicate relations among Briton, Boer, and Bantu.

THE DISCOVERY OF DIAMONDS

In 1867 diamonds were discovered in Griqualand West in an area disputed by the Orange Free State, the Transvaal, the Griquas, and the *Tswana* tribes. The discovery not only coincided with the revival of the scheme for federation but led to the annexation of yet another interior region by the British government. But it was not the glint of profits from the diamond diggings that alone determined the government's occupation of the diamondiferous area. Clearly, the British did not wish to see a major shift in population from the Cape to an unsettled land on the frontier in Griqualand West or the turbulent mining population free from the restraints of British authority. The philanthropists did not wish to see the Griqua fall under Boer domination, and of course no British government would want the riches of the Kimberley mines to strengthen the Orange Free State. In 1871 Griqualand West was unceremoniously added to Britain's expanding empire in South Africa.

The discovery of diamonds led to greater changes in South African life than the transfer of Griqualand West to imperial control. The diamonds could not be excavated without large amounts of capital, which soon poured into South Africa, transforming the country from a rural to a mining economy. The social effects of the mining industry were far-reaching. Diamond mining required large numbers of laborers who were recruited from the Bantu population and left their homes to work in the mines. The use of migrant labor not only resulted in serious social and economic adjustments in the tribal homelands but brought the Bantu increasingly within the white-dominated economy of South Africa. Here in the mines the men of many tribes found a common identity and a common enemy.

The annexation of the diamond mines provided yet another reason for Britain to try once again to establish a confederation of white states in South Africa. A confederation would ensure British influence while relieving Britain of the expense of administration. Unfortunately, the annexation of Griqualand West had further alienated the Boers of the Orange Free State, who not surprisingly felt that they had been unjustly deprived of their rightful claims. To the north in the Transvaal the grievance over British rule in the diamond region was not nearly so acute, but there on the high veld dwelt the most conservative Boer farmers. Isolated, poverty-stricken, and devoid of education, they were firmly opposed to the racial egalitarianism implied by a British-dominated federation. Even in the Cape colony there was a strong minority against confederation, and when the British Colonial Secretary, Lord Carnarvon, sought to hold a conference in London, the interested parties refused to attend and the scheme collapsed.

THE FAILURE OF FEDERATION

Although Carnarvon pressed on with his plans for confederation, the problems of black and white in South Africa remained to frustrate them. In Zululand, Cetewayo, who had succeeded Mpande, had rebuilt the Zulu military system as it had been in the great days of Shaka and restored the Zulu as the most powerful Bantu state in South Africa. His intentions were not aggressive, but the mere presence of his formidable fighting machine posed a serious threat to the farmers of Natal and the Transvaal. Caught between the appeals for protection against the Zulu and the demands of philanthropic opinion in Britain to end Boer mistreatment of the Bantu, Carnarvon sought to force the pace of confederation by annexing the Transvaal. In April 1877 the Natal Secretary for Native Affairs, Theophilus Shepstone, appeared in the Transvaal, raised the British flag, and declared the end of Transvaal independence. The annexation was a disastrous blunder, arousing Boer national feeling and deepening antagonism and distrust between Briton and Boer. The annexation was not only a flagrant violation of solemn treaty obligations, but a tragedy, since the Transvaal Republic would probably have ultimately consented to confederation of its own volition. Instead, the opposition steadily increased, and protest followed protest. The British tried frantically to win Boer good will by breaking the threat of Zulu power, gratifying Boer grievances with Bantu land, and disassociating British policy from the pro-Bantu philanthropists in order to sweeten the bitter pill of annexation. The policy was as opportunistic as it was unsuccessful. The British forces sent into Zululand were annihilated at the Battle of Isandhlwana by Cetewayo's *impis* (regiments), and although British arms were ultimately victorious, Zulu power was broken, and Cetewayo was taken prisoner to Cape Town, the British had failed to win the Boers, while alienating the Bantu and their supporters. Driven to desperation the Boers rebelled, besieged the British garrison at Pretoria, and defeated British relief forces at the Battle of Majuba Hill. With both their policy and practice in ruins, the British had either to crush the Transvaal by overwhelming force or to reach a settlement. The British Prime Minister, William Ewart Gladstone, who had campaigned in Midlothian against the suppression of Boer freedom, agreed to negotiate, and in the Pretoria Convention the Transvaal regained its internal autonomy while recognizing in return only Britain's ultimate sovereignty, control of foreign affairs, and a British resident at Pretoria to advise on the Transvaal's policy toward the Bantu. Virtually independent, the Transvaal, together with the Orange Free State, had come to form the bastion of Boer nationalism and intransigence. Dutch heritage had been awakened, and the sense of Dutch nationhood became a powerful motive and inspiration in political action, ultimately to drive Briton and Boer into sharper antagonisms and hostility. Confederation had failed.

CECIL RHODES AND THE WAY TO THE NORTH

No longer checked by the restraints of British imperial policy, the Boers resumed their expansion to drive the Bantu from the frontiers and to seize their land. In the east the defeated and divided Zulu lost nearly half their land to Boer encroachment. In the west white freebooters interfered in the tribal disputes of the Tswana. In return for their assistance, various chiefs gave their whites land on which they established two petty republics that the Transvaal would certainly have absorbed had not the British government intervened to place the territory under imperial control and declare a protectorate over the tribes of Bechuanaland (John Mackenzie, *Bushman Land*). As in Natal and Basutoland, the imperial factor had once again been employed to check Boer expansion.

Bechuanaland itself was of little importance, but its strategic position in southern Africa was critical. Not only did the Bechuanaland protectorate prevent any land link between the Transvaal and their cultural kin and sympathizers in German Southwest Africa, but it provided a corridor to the north, the logical direction of European expansion toward the fertile uplands of Rhodesia and Zambia. The principal advocate for retaining the way into the interior beyond the Limpopo was Cecil Rhodes. Rhodes had come out to Africa for his health and drifted to the diamond fields where, by buying up small bankrupt claims, he was able to consolidate a host of petty holdings into profitable mines. Soon his De Beers Consolidated Mining Company controlled almost the whole South African diamond production and Cecil Rhodes had become a very wealthy man. He regarded money not as an end in itself but rather as a means to unite Africa, from the Cape to Cairo, under the British flag. He was determined to employ his vast financial resources to move more conservative men in the extension of British authority, sweeping aside the opposition with little concern for the morality of his means. Rhodes envisaged that the way north was to be pioneered by both Briton and Boer, who, working together in a united South Africa, would push the cause of civilization beyond the Limpopo. The African was to play only a minor role in this great drama, and although Rhodes frequently uttered philanthropic sentiments, he regarded the African either as an instrument to further his grand design or as an obstacle to be overcome.

THE DISCOVERY OF GOLD

Rhodes' hopes for a united South Africa in which Briton and Boer would participate together in the march to the north were compromised by the discovery of gold at Witwatersrand and destroyed by the Jameson raid. The discovery of gold in the Transvaal not only accelerated the industrialization of South Africa that had been begun by the discovery of the diamond mines but dramatically altered the balance of power in that area. Hitherto the Transvaal had been a poor and petty state that sooner or later would probably have been absorbed by the rich, populous, British-dominated Cape colony. Gold changed all that. Overnight the Transvaal became the richest of the white states, capable of amalgamating the others under the banner of Boer nationalism and possibly, in alliance with Germany, jeopardizing Britain's strategic position in the Cape and the world. Two principal obstacles, however, stood in the way of the Transvaal's efforts to carry out a forward course in southern Africa—the miners and Paul Kruger, President of the Transvaal.

The miners who came to dig Transvaal gold were not Boers. They were capitalists and mineworkers from Europe and America, but principally from Britain. They were a rough, tough lot, who had little use for the simple farmers of the Republic, whose symbol was Paul Kruger himself. Kruger had taken part in the Great Trek and had been reared as an honest, brave, God-fearing adult concerned with his duty and obligation to maintain the hard-won independence of his people. Unfortunately, he was also ill-educated and unable to understand either the world about him or the sophisticated English. In the end he proved ill-fitted to lead the Transvaal through the tumultuous period of social and economic change that Cecil Rhodes soon sought to turn to his own advantage in his efforts to build a united South Africa.

By the mid-1890s Rhodes had reached the height of his career, having marched steadily from success to success. In 1888 he had entered Cape politics and had managed to win over Jan Hofmeyr, leader of the Afrikaner Bond, which had originally been anti-British, to his idea of British and Boer cooperation in South Africa. Rhodes became Prime Minister of the Cape, in 1890, the same year that his British South Africa Company sent a pioneer column to acquire Mashonaland and eventually the rest of what is now Rhodesia. Financial success accompanied these political victories. His economic empire by this time included the largest diamond

business in the world, gold mines in the Transvaal, and the British South Africa Company with its growing colony in Rhodesia. More than ever Rhodes was ready to absorb an independent Transvaal into a united South Africa, single-handed if necessary. To Rhodes, Kruger's government appeared an anachronism against which the alien mine owners and workers, who had been denied the vote by the republican government, would turn if presented with an appropriate opportunity. Rhodes was determined to provide that opportunity.

THE JAMESON RAID AND THE BOER WAR

Aware of the discontent with Kruger's regime, felt by mine owners and miners alike, Rhodes planned to precipitate a revolt by the miners, who would seize the Rand mines until relieved by an armed column from the Bechuanaland protectorate, which would finish the overthrow of the Transvaal government. Joseph Chamberlain, the British Colonial Secretary, gave his blessing to the conspiracy, and the British High Commissioner at Cape Town approved. In December 1895 the plot was set in motion, only to end in dismal failure. The miners failed to rise and the raiders, led by Dr. Starr Jameson, were surrounded and forced to surrender. Rhodes resigned as Prime Minister of the Cape, his dream of a united South Africa in ruins, and rode north to put down the Bantu rebellion in Rhodesia, which had erupted when Jameson and his police withdrew from the territory in order to lead the raid into the Transvaal.

The greater consequence of the raid, however, occurred south of the Limpopo. For over a century the Boers had regarded the British with sullen suspicion at best and open hostility at worst. These fears now seemed confirmed and throughout South Africa there remained only bitterness, recriminations, and broken friendships in the aftermath of the Jameson raid (Jan Christiaan Smuts, *A Century of*

Wrong). The clash of interests appeared insoluble except by force, and in 1899 the British High Commissioner, Sir Alfred Milner, called on British arms to carry out what British diplomacy and duplicity had failed to accomplish. The Anglo-Boer War lasted longer and entailed far greater expense than anyone, Briton or Boer, had foreseen. British forces were at first defeated by the tough farmers who comprised the Boer commandos, and even after Lord Roberts and Lord Kitchener had occupied the towns of the Transvaal and the Orange Free State, Boer guerillas continued to resist in the countryside. In order to prevent their support of the guerillas the Boer population was methodically herded into concentration camps, where some 20,000 women and children died from disease and the unsanitary conditions existing in the camps. Unbeaten but without victory, both sides were overcome by war weariness, which ultimately brought them to the conference table, where a negotiated peace was signed at Vereeniging on May 31, 1902. The Boer republics lost their independence, but in return the Boers insisted that the blacks be denied the franchise. Both Briton and Boer then began to rebuild the devastated land with large sums from the British Treasury.

The task of reconstruction was directed with skill and efficiency by Lord Milner, who seized the opportunity to tie South Africa closely to Great Britain. He encouraged English settlers to immigrate to South Africa and hoped to Anglicize the Boers by expanding public education in the English language. To carry out this policy Milner first had to revive the Transvaal economy. Although Bantu labor had been sufficient during normal times, there was an acute shortage of laborers during the period of reconstruction, which Milner resolved by importing Chinese workers from Asia. Economically, the introduction of the Chinese was a great success, and the mines were soon back in production. Politically, however,

the arrival of Asians was intensely unpopular in South Africa and even more so in England. There the Liberals rallied to the cry of Chinese slavery, and when they came to power in 1906, members of the Liberal government hastily gave the former republics responsible government. The Chinese were subsequently repatriated, but the British government had surrendered its powerful position to influence the development of South African society.

THE UNION OF SOUTH AFRICA

Ironically, the combination of Milner's policy of Anglicization with the granting of responsible government by the Liberals produced results opposite from the intended objectives. Neither Milner nor his subordinates were in South Africa long enough to carry out their policy of Anglicization successfully, whereas the representative government granted by the Liberals enabled the Afrikaners † to acquire power in South Africa within a few years after their military defeat. Although the Afrikaners were at first determined to cooperate with the British, the increasing influence of Afrikaners in the political life of South Africa ultimately advanced Afrikaner culture and language, from which Afrikaner nationalism sprang as a common political movement.

Although the Boers had been conscious of their distinctiveness since the time of W. A. van der Stel, this feeling could not be called a national one for many generations. The Free State had many English-speaking citizens and many Boers to whom state boundaries meant little. The English language was generally spoken at Bloemfontein, even by many people of Dutch descent, and Free State farmers had farms and kinship ties in the Cape and Natal. This ease of intercourse with the British was less noticeable in the Transvaal, but here the Boers themselves were so deeply divided that national con-

† White South Africans of Boer extraction.

sciousness was slow to develop. Meanwhile, in the Cape Anglicization continued. Schools and churches were filled with British, and Dutch Reformed services were often conducted in English. Portraits of Queen Victoria were venerated even in farmhouses where English was not understood. The Cape Boers were led and represented by a squirearchy and by townsmen who were partly Anglicized and who deplored the Great Trek and all its consequences.

In the nineteenth century, particularly in the 1870s and 1880s, British policy in South Africa began to direct these diverse groups among the Boer population toward a common sentiment. The annexation of Basutoland and Griqualand West encouraged the process. The feeling that the Free State had been cheated of the diamond fields made the Boers aware that the Free Staters were their own people. The British annexation of the Transvaal, followed by the victory of Majuba and the granting of independence, fed the smoldering fires of Afrikaner nationalism, which blazed forth in the Boer War. Although a British subject, the Boer of the Transvaal regarded the British attack as an assault against his own land and his own people. In the Cape colony, Afrikaner nationalism was symbolized more by the fact that the Cape Boers were subject to an alien regime than by the vacillations of British policy on the frontier. English was the official language, and those who were not fluent in it were excluded from public life. Few Boers sat in the Cape Parliament or held positions in the civil service. To the simple Boer farmer the whole apparatus of the state appeared to be an alien institution imposed without consent from abroad. Boer resentment was first formalized by the creation of the Afrikaner Bond in the late 1870s. Under the leadership of Jan Hofmeyr, the Bond remained studiously loyal during the Boer War, though deeply sympathetic to the cause of the Afrikaners. The problem of language symbolized the political differences. To the Boer the Dutch language had become nearly as alien as English. Most literate Boers had difficulty expressing on paper their vernacular in the High Dutch, which, as a spoken language, was quite foreign, and after the mid-nineteenth century a movement was begun to promote Afrikaans as a written language. Rules of spelling and grammar were laid down and the language was formalized, so that by the end of the Boer War Afrikaans proved to be a fluent medium of communication and a powerful instrument for promoting Afrikaner nationalism.

The granting of representative government to the colonies provided the opportunity for Afrikaner nationalism, tempered in the crucible of war and given literary legitimacy, to seize political power. In the Transvaal a Boer party, the *Het Volk* led by Louis Botha and Jan Christiaan Smuts, won a large majority. In the Orange River colony, control passed into the hands of the Orangia Unie Party under J. B. M. Hertzog, and even in the Cape the strongly pro-British administration was defeated by the Afrikaner Bond, which installed the government of John Xavier Merriman. Although nationalist in sentiment if not in action, none of these Afrikaner parties was prepared to break with the British. To them, seeking equal recognition of their own culture did not necessarily mean refusal to collaborate with the British, and just as Jan Hofmeyr and his Afrikaner Bond cooperated with Cecil Rhodes in the 1890s, Smuts and Botha and even Merriman were prepared to create a Union of South Africa in association with the British. In 1909 the South Africa Act was passed by the British Parliament, and the diverse regions of South Africa were politically united. Many of the provisions of the act were similar to those that other dominions had adopted from the British Constitution: a Governor General, a Senate and a House of Assembly, a Cabinet of Ministers responsible to Parliament, a single Supreme Court, and a permanent civil service. The crucial issue was the franchise. The Transvaal was adamant against extending the franchise to nonwhites and even advocated removing the limited franchise of the coloreds and blacks in the Cape. In the end a compromise was agreed upon whereby the Cape franchise was retained but no nonwhite could vote in the former republics or sit in the Union Parliament. In addition the rural areas, which comprised the heartland of Boer conservatism, were given higher representation than the more cosmopolitan urban centers. Although protests were made to the British government by Cape Liberals, the British had had enough of South Africa. So long as the country was united and within the British Empire, the government was unwilling to jeopardize these gains by insisting on an extension of the franchise to the blacks. The draft constitution was accepted with few amendments, and except for the Cape franchise, the nonwhite remained without the vote in South Africa.

HOLISM AND HERTZOGISM

The force of Afrikaner nationalism became more visibly apparent soon after the creation of the Union of South Africa. In 1912 J. B. M. Hertzog broke with the South African National Party to form the National Party on the principle of South Africa first, the empire second, and the proposition that the "two separate streams" of Anglo and Afrikaner nationalism should flow apart. The National Party was not formally a republican or secessionist party, but Afrikaner aspirations were its driving force. The extremists in the party hoped to turn South Africa against Britain during World War I, but even Hertzog would not go that far, contenting himself with benevolent neutrality. In any event, he could not command sufficient support to defeat the Anglo-Afrikaner cooperation personified by the ruling South Africa Party, which,

after Louis Botha's death in 1919, came under the leadership of Jan Christiaan Smuts.

Smuts had originally been an Afrikaner Cape lawyer who emigrated to the Transvaal. There he became an aide to President Kruger (a Boer general) and a participant in the Peace of Vereeniging. During World War I he was a key member of the Commonwealth's Imperial War Cabinet and was later an architect of the League of Nations. Smuts attempted to apply the idealism of war and peace to the South African dilemma, and he envisaged an amalgam of Anglo-Afrikaner culture, which he called Holism, that would provide paternal leadership to the blacks while allowing South Africa to participate in the larger community of mankind beyond its borders. According to the philosophy of Holism, each race would develop its own distinctive characteristics and would acquire meaning only in its unique relationship to the whole community. Smuts' intellectual brilliance and his enormous prestige abroad tended to obscure the growing division between Briton and Boer that Holism sought to reconcile.

In 1924 Smuts and his South African Party were defeated by a coalition government led by Hertzog, but Hertzog did not have sufficient support, particularly among English-speaking workers, to press his policy of two separate streams to its logical conclusion. During and after World War I the Labor Party had become a powerful force in South African politics. Originally founded by English-speaking workers, the labor movement was increasingly influenced by landless Afrikaners who came to work in the mines. These poor white workers deeply feared the Bantu laborers, and as they came to dominate the trade unions, they sought to prevent the blacks, Cape Coloureds, and Indians from competing in the skilled labor market. The labor movement became the protector of the poor white, and after Smuts' government broke up the strikers who had seized the Rand mines in 1922 in opposition to proposals by the mining companies to open more jobs to the blacks, labor and the Afrikaner nationalists combined to defeat Smuts and to obstruct his hopes for Anglo-Boer cooperation in South Africa.

From 1924 until the outbreak of World War II, Hertzog and his coalition ruled South Africa. The basis of their policy was segregation of black and white, equality among whites, and sovereign independence for South Africa. The segregation of black and white was based on the assumption that the Bantu were intruders, permitted in South Africa by the white man's leave. Consequently, they could be segregated into settlements on the reserves, removed from the common voters' roll in the Cape, and eliminated from certain nonskilled jobs in favor of white workers. Indeed, Hertzog's "civilized labor" policy involved not simply the denial of certain jobs to nonwhites but the actual replacement by whites of those coloreds, Indians, and black Africans working as skilled laborers or on the railways and in the postal services. Although much of the legislation passed to implement this program was virtually unenforceable, the principles of segregation were legally defined, particularly in the crucial Native Trust and Land Act and the Representation of Natives Act of 1936, and were later to be refined by the practices of apartheid (Jan Hendrik Hofmeyr, *The Representation of Natives Act, 1936*).

While seeking to segregate black from white, Hertzog worked assiduously to make the Afrikaner equal with English-speaking whites. In 1925 Afrikaans officially became equivalent to English and took the place of High Dutch in South Africa. An official Afrikaans dictionary was commissioned, and in 1933 Afrikaans acquired religious legitimacy with the appearance of an Afrikaans translation of the Bible. The sense of inferiority that had often accompanied those who used colloquial Afrikaans gave way to increas-

ing pride and the stronger sense of national consciousness that went with it. Only in the field of Commonwealth relations did Hertzog refuse to force the issue of South African sovereignty. In fact, he seemed to accept the assurance of South African independence given at the Imperial Conference of 1926, as well as that given in the Statute of Westminster of 1931, which defined the dominions as equal and in no way subordinate one to the other. Great Britain had abandoned even theoretical power to rule, and although judicial appeals could still be taken to the Privy Council, constitutional sovereignty belonged strictly to South Africa. White South African nationalism had achieved this crucial goal within a generation after the Anglo-Boer War, and this achievement conditioned the internal struggle between Briton and Afrikaner for control.

THE TRIUMPH OF AFRIKANER NATIONALISM

The crisis of the world depression hit South Africa very hard, and before this great economic threat to national survival the smoldering issues of race and culture momentarily receded. Smuts even brought his South African Party into the Hertzog government in a grand coalition, entitled the United South African National Party, to rally the nation against economic decline. On the fringe of the United Party, which embraced the vast bulk of English- and Afrikaans-speaking voters, were two dissident groups, the Dominion Party, which hoped to resurrect direct ties with Britain, and the Nationalists, led by Dr. Daniel François Malan, who believed that Hertzog had sold out to Liberal British interests. Malan repudiated Holism and even Hertzog's segregation in favor of a nation ruled by the will of the Afrikaner folk. At the time, neither party appeared to be a threat to the great United Party, but the coalition was in fact a fair-weather government, which could not stand against the storms of war.

The outbreak of war revealed the deep divisions in South African society, which the United Party had temporarily obscured. To Smuts, the war was a world crisis in which South Africa should play its part in defeating Germany's bid for the mastery of Europe and the world. Hertzog, however, did not feel that the war concerned South Africa, and when the Parliament agreed by a very small margin to support the Allies, Hertzog resigned. As South African forces became increasingly committed during the war and Smuts once again began to participate in Allied war councils, the Afrikaner nationalists remained neutral at best and openly hostile to the Allies at worst. Gradually, the more moderate Afrikaner leadership gave way to the extreme nationalists—Malan at the Cape, Johannes Gerhardus Strijdom and Hendrik Frensch Verwoerd in the Transvaal, and Charles Swart in the Free State—who banded together in a political alliance to defeat Smuts and his United Party in 1948.

In 1948 the Nationalists campaigned on a policy of apartheid, or comprehensive apartness of black and white in South Africa. By the end of the war the basic institutions of Afrikaner nationalism had been consolidated in youth groups, cultural organizations, paramilitary militias, and even the trade unions to provide a strong political base from which to challenge the moderate ruling coalition. They attacked Smuts for devoting his time to international diplomacy while ignoring the problems that industrialization had created in South Africa, particularly the migration of black Africans to the cities. The demands of war had accelerated South African industrialization, which had been slowly recovering from the setback of the Great Depression. The discovery and extension of rich new gold fields stimulated demands for steel, cement, machinery, and a wide variety of manufactured products. New coal mines

were opened and the world demand for gems revived the diamond industry. Nor was the countryside unaffected by the rapid pace of industrialization. Everywhere black laborers left the reserves and Afrikaners abandoned marginal farms to drift into the cities, and around the white residential centers shanty towns sprang up to breed crime and disease in the slum conditions. The fundamental fact that large numbers of Africans were now present in the towns precipitated political reaction, which took its form in apartheid. Burglaries, assaults, and murders increased, as did the pressure of black workers for employment in jobs traditionally reserved for whites. Despite the success of the white trade unions in resisting this pressure, such unions could not allay the fears of white workers, particularly the Afrikaners who had recently arrived from the countryside. To them the National Party and apartheid had great appeal, and by the end of the war the unions were almost completely under Afrikaner control.

Apartheid was not new; its only claim to originality was its systematic application of old assumptions. The first of these was that individuals of Dutch origin who belonged to the Reformed Church had been singled out by God and placed above and separate from all nonwhites and non-Calvinist aliens. Second, the Afrikaans-speaking South African was unique in that he had no European mother country. Acting on these assumptions, the Nationalists argued that the voters must choose between (1) white rule, racial purity, and Christian civilization, or (2) gradual absorption by the black masses. Only apartheid, or separate existence, could prevent the assimilation and loss of white civilization in South Africa by black barbarism. Although the Nationalists did not precisely define how apartheid would work in practice, the electorate understood it to mean separation of the races into definite territorial reserves. The black would be removed to the reserves, where he could work out his own economic and political destiny while being permitted temporarily into the white man's towns so long as his labor was required. Certainly this doctrine reassured the white worker, concerned over the pressure from black labor, the rise of crime, riots, and the growing "truculence" of the black. The result was a slim victory for the Nationalists in 1948, which was soon confirmed in the subsequent elections of 1953 and 1958 as the opposition steadily diminished in size and power before the implacable logic of Afrikaner nationalism (M. D. C. de Wet Nel, *The Principles of Apartheid*).

Once in power, Malan and his successors began to reorganize South African life in accordance with their policies, and in the practice of apartheid new features of past segregation inexorably appeared. For the first time the Nationalists politically unified the scattered Afrikaner groups and brought together the Afrikaans' social and cultural organizations into a powerful and well-supervised organ of nationalist propaganda and control. Then the Nationalists began to apply apartheid. A host of apartheid legislation extended and systematized the practical segregation already in existence into a rigid and comprehensive separation. Everyone was required to carry a certificate of racial classification, and each race was restricted to the areas that it already occupied. The reserves were to be transformed into autonomous *Bantustans* ‡ in which the traditional life of the Bantu people would be revived and allowed to develop uninfluenced by European ideas and institutions (Nelson Mandela, *Verwoerd's Tribalism*). In 1956 even the Cape Coloured population lost the vote. But before this sweeping legislation could be enacted, the opposition, both black and white, was rigorously suppressed as the civil liberties of all the people were increasingly restricted. In Parliament only

‡ Autonomous geographical and political entities within South Africa in which the black Africans managed their own internal affairs.

a few lonely voices crying in the wilderness lashed out against apartheid and its implications (Helen Suzman, *Mrs. Suzman and Apartheid*). Those organizations that did not cooperate with the government were dissolved or banned. Indeed, the triumph of Afrikaner nationalism appeared fully confirmed when the final tie with Great Britain was broken by the Declaration of the Republic on May 31, 1961.

AFRICAN NATIONALISM AND RESISTANCE

Although white resistance to Afrikaner nationalism has proved to be the most troublesome, black African nationalism was potentially the most dangerous. Africans had formed one or more national organizations since the early part of the twentieth century, but firm, coordinated opposition against Afrikaner nationalism and apartheid did not emerge until 1949, when a group of African intellectuals led by Anton Lembede, Walter Sisulu, Oliver Tombe, and Nelson Mandela gained control of the African National Congress, which adopted their program of utilizing strikes, civil disobedience, and boycotts to force the government to abandon its discriminatory legislation. In 1952 this same group succeeded in making Albert J. Luthuli, a devout Christian, President of the African National Congress, and under his leadership the first systematic campaign against the Afrikaner government was undertaken. In cooperation with the South African Indian Congress, the African National Congress in 1952 called for a voluntary defiance of discriminatory laws, as a result of which some 8,000 people were arrested. Although the protest began peacefully, at the end of the year rioting occurred in several cities, and in 1953, when Parliament enacted severe penalties against the demonstrators, the passive resistance campaign terminated in failure.

In 1953 the Afrikaner Nationalist government returned to power with an even greater parliamentary majority, determined to broaden the application of apartheid while increasing the penalties against protest and resistance by its opponents. To combat the growth of apartheid, a national campaign was launched in 1955 in which the African National Congress joined with the South African Indian Congress, the South African Coloured People's Organization, the Congress of Democrats, and the multiracial South African Congress of Trade Unions to form a "Congress of the People," which adopted a "Freedom Charter" demanding equal rights for "all national groups and races." This attempt to enlist the nonwhite masses and the sympathy of the outside world was met by further repressive legislation and widespread arrests of the leaders, which summarily broke the campaign.

The failure of passive resistance and the campaign by the Congress of the People created new divisions within the African National Congress. The more radical members, led by Robert Sobukwe, argued that the alliance with the Indians, coloreds, and whites only weakened the African National Congress, whose nonviolent methods should be abandoned for whatever means were necessary to emancipate the black African majority of the South African population. In 1959 the radicals seceded from the African National Congress to found the Pan-Africanist Congress, and the rivalry between these two organizations has clearly helped to neutralize their effectiveness. Hoping to retain the initiative, the African National Congress planned a new campaign against the pass laws, only to be forestalled by the Pan-Africanist Congress, which called upon its followers on March 21, 1960, to turn in passes at police stations, thereby hoping to upset the machinery of justice and create labor shortages. At Sharpeville, near Johannesburg, the police shot into a crowd, killing 69 Africans and wounding 178. A week later, both the African National Congress and the Pan-Africanist Congress held a day of mourning in which some 30,000 Africans marched to the center of Cape Town. The government reacted swiftly and severely. The armed forces were mobilized, the African National Congress and the Pan-Africanist Congress were outlawed, and thousands of South Africans of all colors were arrested. The campaign was broken, but of even greater importance, the Africans were deprived of the last means of lawful opposition to the South African political system. The only alternative appeared to be underground resistance.

After 1960 three underground revolutionary movements emerged from the wreckage of the African National Congress and the Pan-Africanist Congress and, not surprisingly, reflected the parent organizations from which they had sprung. One, the Spear of the Nation, was an offshoot of the African National Congress that had been founded by Nelson Mandela with the hope that sabotage would lead to guerilla warfare and ultimately to the end of white supremacy. A second group, Poqo, was founded by former members of the Pan-Africanist Congress to destroy the whites by any means. A third organization, the African Resistance Movement, consisted mainly of white professional men and students committed to acts of violence in the hope of extracting concessions from the government. Thereafter, until 1963, hundreds of minor incidents of sabotage were carried out, mostly by the Spear of the Nation. Once again the government reacted repressively, banning these movements, passing still more restrictive legislation, and arresting the leaders. In mid-1963 Poqo was smashed, and in July, at a house at Rivonia, the leadership in Spear of the Nation was captured. By 1964 most of the saboteurs of the African Resistance Movement either had fled South Africa or were imprisoned.

Since 1964 there have been few active revolutionaries at large in the Republic of South Africa, but despite their absence the historic and tragic issues they represent remain to smolder below the placid surface of repressive Afrikaner rule in the Beloved Country.

81 JAN VAN RIEBEECK AND Z. WAGENAAR
OF THE NATIVE TRIBES OF SOUTH AFRICA

The first two governors of the Cape of Good Hope after it was annexed as a trading and revictualing station by the Dutch East India Company in 1652 were Jan van Riebeeck (governor, 1652–1662) and Z. Wagenaar (governor, 1663–1666). Among the documents that they wrote for their successors were the following descriptions of the Khoikhoi (Hottentot) population of the Cape.* At this time the Khoikhoi still retained their traditional organization of chiefdoms. This organization was soon disrupted by the alien influence of the Europeans, and the Khoikhoi became a landless population that existed in outlawry or in servitude to white masters. The chiefdoms were incorporated under the law of the Cape and were given some rights and partial protection only in 1828 as the result of missionary agitation on their behalf.

EXTRACTS OF MEMORANDUM LEFT BY COMMANDER J. VAN RIEBEECK, FOR THE INFORMATION AND GUIDANCE OF HIS SUCCESSOR Z. WAGENAAR

May 5. [The first paragraph merely refers to the several instructions and other papers explanatory of the objects of taking possession at the Cape. Then follow the several subjects here omitted, which are denoted by the following marginals, given in italics.]

Company's first object attained; in addition to other refreshments. A good prospect of fruit, particularly from the vines; also olives in time. The corn lands turn out much poorer than was supposed. Trade; and the condition of the Cape Tribes.

Coming now to the subject of the trade with these native tribes, the same is now, thanks to God! on a much better footing than ever, through the knowledge which we are gradually acquiring of various races of people in the interior, whose names, with their places of abode and mode of living are thus briefly stated, in order to convey a better idea of their circumstances. We have then, in the first place—

The GORINGHAICONAS,[1] of whom Herry has been usually called the Captain; these are strandloopers, or fishers, who are, exclusive of women and children, not above 18 men in number, supporting themselves, without the least live stock of any description, by fishing from the rocks along the coast, thus furnishing a great accommodation to the Company's people and freemen, and also rendering much assistance to those who keep house, by washing, scouring, fetching firewood, and other domestic work; and some of them placing their little daughters in the service of the married people, where they are clothed in our manner, but they must have a slack rein, and will not be kept strictly, such appears to be contrary to their nature; some of them, however, begin to be tolerably civilized, and the Dutch language is so far implanted among them, old and young, that nothing can any longer be kept secret when mentioned in their presence, and very little in that of the—

GORINGHAIQUAS, whose Chief is named Gogosoa, and who are the Capemans; they are, exclusive of women and children, about 300 men capable of bearing arms, supplied with about enough cat-

From D. Moodie, *The Record* (Cape Town: A. S. Robertson, 1838), I, 246–251, 290–293.
* Although these are the first reliable contemporary accounts of the Khoikhoi, others of the same period may be found in Isaac Schapera and B. Farrington (eds.), *The Early Cape Hottentots, 1688–1695* (Cape Town: Van Riebeeck Society, 1933), Vol. XIV.

[1] The Goringhaiconas and other tribes mentioned herein are all Hottentot peoples (ed.).

tle to provide for their own wants, but as they begin to be somewhat fond of mercantile gains, (coopmanachtige) they are rather increasing their stock, particularly as they have always been knowing enough, upon the approach of strangers from the interior with pretty good cattle, to act as brokers and guides to conduct the strangers to us; exchanging their leanest and worst cattle for the good, and then bringing those strangers to us, and insisting upon it that they have been the means of enticing and fetching them out of the interior, &c. in which manner they well know how to enrich themselves, becoming every day worse and more cunning; these are they who pretend that this Cape land has been theirs from all ages, and who, seeing that we were betaking ourselves to permanent agriculture, made war upon us in the year 1659, on account, according to their statements, of their harsh treatment by some of the free men; but on seeing, contrary to their expectation, that we, though assailed at the weakest, were not to be so easily driven away, and that, meanwhile, the chief or king of the Saldanhars, took the opportunity of that disturbed time, to form an alliance with us—which alliances they had always used every art to prevent, &c. they were induced two years ago to request and to conclude a peace with us, as also did—

The GORACHOUQUAS, or tobacco thieves, so called because they once stole, from the field, the tobacco belonging to some free men, and whose chief is named Choro. You have been in both their camps—they have, besides women and children, 6 or 700 men capable of bearing arms, and are fully 6 times as rich in cattle as the last mentioned tribe, and a few head are sometimes bought from them; but nothing of importance.

They have, since the war before mentioned, generally lived close to the Capemans, and about a day's journey to the N. E. behind the Leopards Hill, not far from, and as it would seem, under the wing of the Saldanhars; but this April both tribes

have come back to live at the foot of the Bosheuvel, under our protection, in consequence, as it would seem, of some difference which has arisen between them and the Saldanhars, who are the—

COCHOQUAS, consisting of two divisions, under 2 chiefs, or choquees, (which means kings) the first is named Oedasoa, a quiet man, whose wife—last year deceased—was sister of the interpreter Eva, who is also a niece of Herry, and has from her childhood been brought up in our house, and can speak Dutch almost as well as a Dutch girl, and we thus derive much service from her in translation, although she does lead us a dance now and then . . . and some things must be received from her with caution.

The other chief of the Saldanhars, or Cochoquas, is named Gonnoma, and is often some distance apart from Oedasoa. They have, together, several thousand men, and generally occupy the middle of the country opposite to us, under the African mountains, extending from near False Bay, quite to Saldanha Bay, but not always remaining in one place, and moving about for change of pasture. With which Oedasoa and Gonnoma we appear to have a very firm alliance, and with whom we carry on a good, indeed a constant trade in live stock—chiefly in sheep—but not so many horned cattle that we have ever been able to spare so many as now for the refreshment of the Company's shipping; they have helped however; but we have never procured any stock whatever, deserving of the name, from the—

LITTLE CHARIGURIQUAS, a people about as numerous as the Goringhaiquas, who chiefly reside between Saldanha Bay, and midway between Robben and Dassen Island—about 4 or 5 hours' walk from the sea coast, subject to Oedasoa, though they have rebelled against him; they were accustomed to be his stock keepers, but appropriated his cattle to their own use; and therefore they are not recognized by any of the Hottentoos as a people who have a Choeque or Hunque, that is a hereditary king or chief; they seem, however, to be able to take their own part, as it now begins to appear, through the fear which Oedasoa entertains for the—

NAMAQUAS, with whom the great Chariguriquas have sought and formed an alliance; this people have recently been found by us, after long search; they are very rich in cattle, and very tall in stature, almost half giants, dressed in fine prepared skins, as may be seen at full by the notes kept by our travellers, and inserted in our Journal under date the 11th March 1661; where it may also be seen that they are very favorably disposed towards us, and that they seem to be a people who carry on trade with other tribes residing further inland, and through whom the way is now in so far opened, that it is only now that we can properly begin to discover any thing better than cattle. Of these people, to all appearance, more will come to you than you can wish; and thus after 10 years toil we hope that we have opened for you a fortunate road to the North side of this Africa; whither, towards the end of September, another journey must be taken, in order to be enabled to cross the dry country (which at that season will probably be still moist after the rains) to the river upon which there is laid down, in Linschoten's map, a town (vaste plaets) called Vigiti Magna, and where there is a race of people quite different from the Hottentoos, of whom we have been hitherto treating, and to whom we shall also return, namely, to those whom we have found to be the richest, almost all of whom reside to the Eastward, along the East coast of Africa, where they sometimes show themselves in some bays, as we can discover from their own statements.[2] We have only begun to know them well during the last two years, and they are the—

CHAINOUQUAS, whose Choque or King is named Sousoa, with whom we are upon very good, and rather firm terms of friendship, and who have since that time bartered to us a great number of cattle, and a good many sheep also. They are able to supply us abundantly, and on taking leave of us last year promised to come back with a still larger quantity; we sincerely trust that you may, on the Company's account, enjoy the fortunate result, and also that, as we are given to expect by the accounts of all the Hottentoos, you may be soon visited by the—

HEUSAQUAS, from whom a messenger was last year at the fort, with intelligence that his Chief also intended to come to visit the Sourye (that is the Lord of the Land, the name by which I have been generally known,) of the Dutch, with money and cattle, to try to procure, like his friends, the Chainouquas, a share of our merchandize, which will be a most desirable event, as they are very rich in cattle, and have a strong liking for the consumable tobacco, and for certain red beads in the Company's stores, for which the cattle are procured from those people at a very cheap rate. The Hottentoos who live near us, speak in high terms of this tribe, saying that now that Sousoa is gone, they will come with such great herds of cattle, that the merchandize will fall short. This, however, need not be feared, but hoped for, *item,* also for the arrival of the—

HANCUMQUAS, who, according to the hopes held out to us, and from all that we have been able to learn, are the greatest and most powerful of all the race of greasy Hottentoos, living in houses, which like their's, are covered with mats, but of a very large size, and living permanently on the same spot, where they cultivate and dry a certain plant which they call *Dacha,* this they chew and eat, and consequently become very light-headed, as in India from opium, and this is the reason why they are so eager for the strongest tobacco. The Chiefs of this tribe appear to be Chiefs over all the other Choques or

[2] Jan van Linschoten (1563–1611), a Dutch traveler, spent nine years in the Portuguese service in the East Indies and wrote a detailed account of the Indian Ocean. His *Voyages* was an important contribution to sixteenth-century Europe's knowledge of Africa and Asia (ed.).

Kings, being entitled Choebaha, which seems to mean Emperor, or at least Upper King, or Lord over all the others.

Those now who reside further than this Chief Lord of the Hottentoos, though of the same race, and much richer in cattle than all those who live on this side of this supreme Chief, are named first, the— CHAMAQUAS, and next them the OMA-QUAS, ATIQUAS, HOUTUNQUAS, and CHAUQUAS, all subsisting like the Han-cumquas, besides their countless herds of cattle, by Dacha plantations, living on fixed spots, in large mat huts, dressed in skins like all the Hottentoos, and also equally greasy, &c.

After those, are said to begin, though beyond the river Vigiti Magna, and in an Easterly direction, another race of people, called by all the before mentioned Hotten-toos—

CHOBOQUA or COBONA, residing in fixed houses constructed of wood, clay, and other materials, but at the same time maintaining themselves by cattle, and wearing clothes, whom we conjecture to be the people of Monomotopa, as Eva would often persuade us, and that—as we have also been informed, through her interpretation, by the said Sousoa—there is Chory or gold and white gems among those Choboquas, of which he has promised to bring proofs, and also some one of that people. We trust that you may, for the good of the Company, experience the success of this, and procure some further account of the people of whom the messenger from the HEUSAQUAS told us, that they keep lions as tame as we keep dogs, and among whom it is said that the gold and the white gems are to be found. I trust that diligent inquiry will afford us further knowledge upon all these matters, either through their own people coming to us, or through our men, who are sufficiently well disposed to visit them, as the roads have, through the alliances formed with the several tribes of the race of Hot-tentoos, become so safe that our people have nothing to look for, in any quarter, but the most friendly reception. In conse-

quence of this, had I remained here, we fully intended, as soon as the rains were over, and at the commencement of the dry season, to send out a party of volunteers to try whether we could not find out the said Choboquas, as we last year, as before mentioned, found the long sought Nama-quas.

Jealousy of the Saldanhars. But there is no doubt that Oedasoa, who is the greatest among the natives who live near to the Cape, is as jealous upon this matter, as were the Capemans formerly, when we were endeavoring to become better acquainted with him; and equally fearful of falling into less esteem, in proportion to the extent of our discoveries; this may be fully relied upon, as we have already begun to perceive it from Oedasoa's demeanor, but we have endeavored to remove his apprehension by friendly and affable treatment; and this course must of necessity be continued, for, upon any coolness with him, we can see no prospect of profit for the Company, and deem the preservation of friendship the preferable course; although he (just like the Goring-haiquas or Capemans, who long kept us in ignorance of him) has had in view precisely the same object as to the other tribes, in hoodwinking us, and leading us to believe that he was the greatest *heer* of this country.

But now, seeing that we have at length discovered the Namaquas, (a different, and as before observed, a more active race than the Hottentoos) and hearing that we have been well received by them, and that they have promised to come hither, whether he likes it or not—they having, however, first shown their inclination to be reconciled to him, and for that purpose offering to send 2 or 3 with our party to express their disposition for peace, and to settle old disputes with him (for the Namaquas did not dare to attack him here, for fear of our assisting him)—the said Oedasoa allowed himself to be in so far guided by us, that on the 21st March last year he sent 3 of his people to them as commissioners, in company with our party who went thither, and who were to act between the parties as mediators. This endeavour succeeded according to our wishes, and the result has been that they not only now leave each other unmolested on journeys, and in trading with us, but the Saldanhars may carry on a friendly intercourse and traffic with the said Namaquas, who are, as before observed, a different race from these Hottentoos, of much larger stature, clothed in fine well dressed skins without hair and using rushes (ruyge) at night to sleep on. Their own hair, although like that of the Caffers, is worn long, and plaited in an ornamental manner like locks, with many ornaments of copper, iron, and red beads; also, *caurys* and *bougys,* for which they are very eager, as well as for red caps, and for the red cloth of which to make them.

Hopes of Elephants' teeth among the Namaquas, and why. It would seem also that ivory is much more plentiful among them than among the Hottentoos, from the very thick bracelets of that article which they wear, and from the very singular plates of ivory which they wear over a finely dressed skin, worn as an apron. A specimen of each has been sent to our masters in Holland, and 2 such plates are in the office here; it may therefore happen that a trade in ivory and other articles may yet be opened with them, which were much to be desired for the relief of the Company's expenditure at this place.

Whereabouts the Namaquas are to be found by sea. From a calculation of the courses and distances travelled by our land parties, we are led to conjecture that those people reside not far distant from the coast, and near the bay called by Linschoten, *Angra das Voltas,* between the 29th and 30th parallel to the Northward; and had I staid here, I had it in contemplation, upon a favorable opportunity, to send a Cape galiot, or any small vessel that could be spared, to ascertain that point, as well as whether that bay might not be found suitable, in respect of anchorage, water, and other refreshments,

for Company's ships to touch at, when occasionally blown to leeward of the Cape by the S. S. E. gales in February and March, when the ships arrive from India, and when those winds are usually most severe; or in the event of ivory or other merchandize being found (which might be too bulky for conveyance by land) to place a trading station there, or otherwise, according to circumstances. I therefore bring the subject under your notice in order that you may, at a fitting opportunity, improve upon the suggestion in as far as you may deem it to be practicable, and serviceable to the Company; but the vessel must first be sent to Madagascar for rice and whatever else our masters have directed, or may hereafter direct to be done there.

Nothing more serviceable to the Company than peace with the Hottentoos. It being, above all things necessary, that you always endeavour to live in constant peace with the Hottentoos—one tribe as well as the other, not only that the roads may be every where safe, to facilitate further discoveries, but also that the tribes above named may always be able to come down without apprehension, with their cattle, for the refreshment of the crews of the Company's ships. To this object—in the first place, a more than usually liberal reception will much contribute, and especially if little squabbles occurring between our people—particularly the ship people —and them, be not too seriously taken up, but rather passed over occasionally, as if in ignorance, especially at first, or otherwise they would become so shy that they would fly inland with all they possess, making the other tribes so shy also, that they would keep away altogether; and you would thus find yourselves in a moment deprived, not only of the daily barter with the Saldanhars, but also of the trade with all the other tribes before named. The best advice, therefore, that I am able to give you in this matter is—that you keep your attention constantly fixed—steadfast as a wall, to this point: to live without any the slightest estrangement from your neighbours here, the Capemans or Go-ringhaiquas, and the tobacco thieves or Gorachouquas, as well as with Oedasoa, the king of the Saldanhars; which may be effected—besides the friendly treatment aforesaid—by keeping so sharp and strict a watch, by mounted and other guards, (already brought so far into order) over the Company's live stock, and that belonging to the freemen, that a fair opportunity of driving them off is never left open to the natives, without exposing their lives to danger. For, should they have even the least chance of success, they could not refrain from the attempt; and on this account a very close watch will be always required here. *Au reste,* that when they sometimes perceive some simple green horn from the ships going to some retired spot and rob him of his tobacco, bread, and brass, or iron buttons from his clothes, is not a matter of such mighty importance, but that it may be easily arranged. The quarrels also, which occur between them and the ship people, more than those who are resident here, and which proceed perhaps to the length of pelting each other with stones, ought not to be too gravely regarded, for, our men, who, when playing and wrestling (sto-eyende) with them, sometimes get a thump a little harder than they will bear, and are thus provoked to abuse them, and call them black stinking dogs, &c.—are themselves in a great measure the cause. For the natives fully understand these, and other Dutch words, and reply, that they are men as well as the Dutch, and so forth—so that I will add that our common people are often found, when out of our presence, to be the first cause of many disputes (questien) which are sometimes attended with trouble, in order to restore tranquillity among these natives; and this may be best accomplished by a show of injustice towards our own people, paying the others by a friendly promise of inflicting some kind of punishment on our men on board of their ships.

And although this course appears to many of our people somewhat improper, it is nevertheless most absolutely necessary, in order that we may live in peace and quiet; and I have therefore always pursued this line of conduct, and enforced it upon others; and whatever better course you may be able to adopt, cannot fail to be still more serviceable to the Company; for, in the event of disagreement, you will not be able to keep a single Hottentoo here or hereabouts; and therefore friendship, with those who have been herein named, should be kept in mind as one of the principal maxims; in which case the trade will not only continue to flourish more and more, but the roads also will be safe for travelling in every direction, to search for what has not been hitherto found; and, as before observed, the Directors [of the Dutch East India Company—ed.] and their Honors at Batavia will be thus best satisfied; for it may be seen from the public and private letters from both quarters, that journeys for the purposes of discovery are not disapproved, but expressly ordered to be prosecuted with every assiduity; and therefore—so far from dissuading you from continuing them at fitting seasons of the monsoon—I would most earnestly recommend their being prosecuted with vigor at the seasons before mentioned.

And to give out any lands beyond the Company's enclosure, is, on account of the attendant expense of protecting the freemen, quite unadvisable; even should they be disposed to live out there at their own risk, we have never dared to venture upon it, for they would instantly lose their cattle, and would be robbed of them, even by our best friends—unless indeed any one were mad enough, and rich enough to hazard his own capital—but with the Company's means—upon which all the farmers here have been set up—this would be entirely wrong, and ought never to be thought of; for the Hottentoos, upon seeing the least opportunity, could not abstain from stealing the cattle, as we have, at full length and breadth, explained to the Directors. And for the same reason I would not venture to sell cattle, even for ready money, to any one who was about to farm there, for he would forthwith lose them, and would then be troubling the Company for more.

The slaves here learn nothing but Dutch, and also the Hottentoos, so that no other language is spoken here, and if this can be continued it will be a desirable thing, as it always will keep the Portuguese and others from communicating with these tribes, so that they will be the less able to mislead them, &c. Herry and Doman live chiefly here at the fort, as interpreters or advocates, the first, as it were, for the tobacco thieves, and the other for the Capemans. They get their food and drink from us, and they should continue to be thus supported, to bind them to the Company, and to keep mischief out of their heads; though indeed, now that we are so well supplied with horses, I do not think that they will easily be inclined to undertake any thing against us, so long as good attention is paid to the mounted guard and the outposts.

How the interpreter Eva is retained and treated has been already mentioned, and verbally communicated. She acts chiefly for the Saldanhars, and others who come from a distance.

As I cannot but think that every thing has now been detailed at sufficient length, I do not know what more I can say, than to repeat briefly the most advantageous, and the chief rules to be attended to, for the service of the Company, namely,

1st. That you always endeavour to live, and trade, in peace with these tribes, at the same time and for the same purpose, to penetrate—by parties of volunteers— further and further into the interior.

2d. To have constantly in readiness sufficient refreshments for the shipping.

3d. The necessary increase of the stock of cattle and sheep, and also of pigs, &c.

4th. To keep up the cultivation of corn, and as far as practicable to extend it more

and more, for the purpose of provisioning this Residency, and that the less food may be required from abroad.

5th. The cultivation of the olive, as urgently recommended by the last letter from the Directors.

And now, trusting that I have sufficiently explained the objects of our Honorable Masters. I shall conclude by recommending you to the merciful protection of the Almighty, and by recommending to you the command and management of affairs here in the manner most serviceable to the Hon. Company. In the Fort the Goede Hope, adij 5th May Ao. 1662. JAN VAN RIEBEECK

EXTRACTS OF A MEMORANDUM LEFT BY COMMANDER Z. WAGENAAR, BY ORDER OF THE DIRECTORS, FOR THE INFORMATION OF HIS SUCCESSOR, MR. C. VAN QUAELBERGEN, &C.[3]

.   .   .

Respecting these aboriginal inhabitants. And although Mr. van Riebeeck has written very clearly upon every point, and in particular, has given so good a sketch of the disposition, character, and habits of these greasy Africans, commonly called Hottentoos, that I might be well excused from making any allusion to the subject, I shall, nevertheless, take a brief view of these savages, *en passant,* that I may let you know, by way of warning, from what kind among that people, the Company has to look for the greatest advantage in that very essential point, the cattle trade, (without which, there would be very little for us to do here,) and who, on that account, ought to be gratified and well treated in preference to others.

The said Hottentoos then, who usually reside inland within a space of 40 or 50 mylen to the east and north of this Afri-

[3] This memorandum is dated September 24, 1666 (ed.).

can Cape, and are in the habit of wandering from one place to another with their cattle, for the sake of pasture, are, (in so far as they are, for the greater part, known to us,) divided into 9 hordes, or assemblages of families, or rather of villagers, or members of the same kraal: they are named

Goringhaiconas, Goringhaiquas, Gorachouquas, Cochoquas, Charequriquas, Namaquas, Chainouquas, Heusequas, and *Hancumquas.*

The Cochoquas bring us the greatest number of cattle. Of all these tribes we procure the greatest quantity of live stock, chiefly sheep, from the Cochoquas, they live to the north, towards Saldanha Bay, whence their name of Saldanhars. They consist of two divisions, under separate *Choques* or Chiefs, Oudasoa and Gonnoma; they were formerly, with the kraals under their authority, so strong, that both together might have mustered three thousand men capable of bearing arms; but they were, some time ago, very much diminished and melted away by a sickness which prevailed among them. The others, who are nearer to us, and are in the habit of bringing their cattle close to us for good pasture, are the Goringhaiquas, or the Capemans, thus called because they at first made pretensions to a right of property in this Cape land; with the Gorachouquas, nicknamed the tobacco thieves; but at present both kraals, exclusive of women and children, can scarcely make out 800 men. The last, namely, the Gorachouquas, are however, much richer in cattle than the first, and bring us for sale, now and then, a lean ox or cow, or a few sheep equally lean; and although such supplies are of little use to us, we receive, notwithstanding, all they offer us, whether it be large or small, young or old, fat or lean.

What is commonly given for their cattle. Neither do we allow them to stand long waiting, but give instantly what they desire in exchange, such as copper in plates, or brass in bars, various kinds of beads, but chiefly a small blood red sort, or tobacco, the first thing they ask for; and when they have received for each cow, calf, or sheep, such a quantity of those articles of merchandize as has been long since brought into train, we give to each of them a dram (pimpeltje) of brandy, and occasionally, to such as bring us many, or very fine fat cattle, a little biscuit or boiled rice besides; and thus dismiss them well satisfied. In this, or in some such manner, it will be necessary to attract these strangers to us, and to keep the trade alive. But to sell them thin square bar iron, as the Cochoquas or Saldanhars would have recently wished, is by no means advisable, as they know how to beat it into *pickysers,* or sharp points for their arrows and assagais, and to harden it very tolerably; so that, should they again come to ask for this iron, you should, upon one pretence or other, decline supplying it.

The Goringhaiconas subsist in a great measure by begging and stealing. Among this ugly Hottentoo race, there is yet another sort called Goringhaiconas, whose chief or captain, named Herry, has been dead for the last three years; these we have daily in our sight and about our ears, within and without the fort, as they possess no cattle whatever, but are strandloopers, living by fishing from the rocks. They were at first, on my arrival, not more than 30 in number, but they have since procured some addition to their numbers from similar rabble out of the interior, and they now constitute a gang, including women and children, of 70, 80, or more. They make shift for themselves by night close by, in little hovels in the sand hills; in the day time, however, you may see some of the sluggards (*luyoerts*) helping to scour, wash, chop wood, fetch water, or herd sheep for our burgers, or boiling a pot of rice for some of the soldiers; but they will never set hand to any work, or put one foot before the other, until you have promised to give them a good quantity of tobacco or food, or drink. Others of the lazy crew, (who are much worse still, and are not to be induced to perform any work whatever,) live by begging, or seek a subsistence by stealing and robbing on the common highways; particularly when they see these frequented by any novices out of ships from Europe.

Bold attempt of these Hottentoos. This was evident enough last year, when some men were ordered to go to the wood to assist in dragging out some timber; for, the corporal of the party being a little way behind with two soldiers who were carrying the provisions, and being attacked by seven or eight of those thieves, scarcely 1/4 of a myl from the fort, stood up bravely in his own defence, not being inclined to part with his bread and cheese so cheaply; at last, however, he was so fearfully assailed from all sides with stones, that he was driven back and compelled to return to the fort with a bleeding pate.

In the same manner, shortly before, those vagabonds broke open a house at Salt River, belonging to a certain poor fisherman, and stole from it 200 guilders in cash, and all his little stock of tobacco, and food, and drink.

And although these, and similar daring acts require that an appropriate punishment should be inflicted upon those who commit them, or at least that this good for nothing gang should be denied a free access to the fort or the burgers' houses in the country, or entirely turned away from us; yet still we could not well dare to do so hitherto, for several reasons, but have winked at it all, and suffered it to pass unnoticed; for our masters in the Fatherland, in their letters from time to time, recommend to us nothing more earnestly than to deal with these men in a kind and peaceful manner; and not be too easily led to apply to them terms of opprobrium, still less to kick, push, or ill use them, upon every slight cause of offence, so that they may not acquire any dislike towards us. This was also the course followed by Mr. van Riebeeck, as you may see in several parts of the memoir left by him.

Who should one day be severely punished. But as, subsequently to his departure, this crew (*gespuys*) have not only (as before stated) increased in number, but have daily become more impudent and daring in the commission of every kind of mischief, we have deemed it as improper, as it is impossible, any longer to put up with such violence, breaches of the peace, and theft; but, ever since that time we have intended to have the first person that we can get hold of, who may be convicted of housebreaking or highway robbery, bound to a whipping post in front of the fort, and there to have his greasy hide so well rubbed down with good rods, that all his mischievous countrymen who might witness the punishment, should be frightened from the commission of the same offence; for to this it must come (would we live in peace and quiet) if we are annoyed by these *rappaille;* particularly because our honorable masters, upon our representations upon the subject, have been pleased to give their full approval and consent; but at the same time it will be much better and safer for us all if they will take a turn of their own accord, or if the greater part of the males could be induced to go away, without violence, than that the proposed punishment, or any kind of banishment should be resorted to. You will however be able to ascertain what may be hereafter the best course in this respect, with the aid of time and good counsel.

A close watch should also be kept on them. Meanwhile it will do no harm to keep a strict eye upon those idlers, while they are allowed to pass freely in and out, particularly now that all our soldiers are daily working upon the ditch of the new castle, and only 10 or 12 sick or lame men are on guard at the gate; for it has been seen already what these dirty creatures have dared to undertake against the Fort. It has been well apprehended and remarked by Commissioner Overtwater, (as you may see by the *memorie* he left here) that the maintenance of peace and concord with these tribes, should be attended by a proper degree of caution.

We also procure many cattle from the Chainouquas. For the last six years we have begun to be acquainted with the tribes who live to the Eastward, named the Chainouquas; and have always lived in perfect friendship with them, as we still do; they are very rich in cattle, for upon two missions which I sent to them in 1663 and 64, the first under fiscal Lacus, and the second under secretary Cretser, we procured 170 fine cattle and 400 sheep; and I would have sent a third party last year, but that we were then without tobacco, the merchandize chiefly in demand; we have however recently sent thither a party of 12 men under Mr. Cretser, and I hope that before my departure he may return with a good herd.

Which excites the jealousy of the Cochoquas. In consequence of Sousoa the chief of the Chainouquas not only inviting us into his country, but sending oxen to carry our provisions and merchandize; and of our availing ourselves of his invitation and assistance, the Saldanhars—and particularly the chief Oudasoa [*Oudasoa's proposal*]—conceived such a jealousy of them, that he came to the Fort and apprised us that he meant to make war upon Sousoa (who is since dead) as he could no longer suffer him to play the master every

where; and requesting, not only the aid of some troops, but that we would take charge of 2500 of his cattle during the war, promising to send us, in 3 or 4 days, 600 cattle in payment, and an equal number in the event of his getting the victory; but after mature consideration, it appeared to us that the proposal would lead to much embarrassment, and perhaps eventually to some dispute, and we civilly declined his offer, allowing him to go away rather dissatisfied. The Directors have fully approved of our conduct in this respect, as may be seen by their letter of Oct. 8, 1664, in which they state their desire, that we should not concern ourselves with the mutual disputes or wars of these inland tribes; which will serve as a rule for your guidance under similar circumstances. Meanwhile it would appear that Oudasoa still feels much vexed, for it is more than 2 years since he has been in the Fort.

The Namaquas recently discovered. Of the Namaquas whom we first discovered in 1661, and who are a very *robust* people; as also of the tribes bordering on them to the Eastward, and who are all very rich in cattle, I am unable to add any thing to the remarks of Mr. Van Riebeeck, as contained in his memoir, to which I will merely refer, and pass on to some thing else.

82 ANDREW SPARRMAN
THE BOERS

Andrew Sparrman was a Swede who studied medicine at the University of Uppsala and subsequently accompanied Captain James Cook to the Antarctic as assistant naturalist. Between 1772 and 1776 he traveled in Cape colony, and although he was primarily concerned with its fauna, he provided the first complete description of the character, manners, and attitude of the Boer settlers at the frontier. The following selection was written in January 1776.

From Andrew Sparrman, *A Voyage to the Cape of Good Hope from 1772 to 1776* (2nd ed.; London: Robinson, 1786), pp. 164–169.

All the colonists who follow the grazing business, and particularly those at *Agter Bruntjes-boogte,* lead an easy and pleasant life. One of these boors usually puts to his plough eight or ten of his fat, or rather pampered oxen; and it is hardly to be conceived, with what little trouble he gets into order a field of a moderate size; and in consequence of his feeding so great a number of cattle, how easily he can render it in the highest degree fertile. So that, always sure of a rich harvest from a soil not yet worn out, and ever grateful to the culture bestowed upon it, he may be almost said merely to amuse himself with the cultivation of it, for the bread he wants for himself and his family; while many other husbandmen must sweat and toil themselves almost to death, both for what they use themselves, and for that which is consumed by others, who frequently live in ease and indolence. By his extensive pastures, and by throwing a sufficient quantity of land into tillage, he rears a considerable number of horses, which frequently are used only a few days in a year, for the purpose of treading out and threshing his corn. With pleasure, but without the least trouble to himself, he sees the herds and flocks, which constitute his riches, daily and considerably increasing. These are driven to pasture and home again by a few Hottentots or slaves, who likewise make the butter; so that it is almost only with the milking, that the farmer, together with his wife and children, concern themselves at all. To do this business, however, he has no occasion to rise before seven or eight o'clock in the morning; and notwithstanding his having enjoyed his bed so long in the morning, he can afford, without neglecting any thing of consequence, to allow himself an afternoon's nap, which the heat of the climate renders more agreeable than it is in our northern regions.

That they might not put their arms and bodies out of the easy and commodious posture in which they had laid them on the couch, they have been known to receive travellers lying quite still and motionless, excepting that they have very civilly pointed out the road, by moving their foot to the right or left. Professor THUNBERG, who has had greater opportunities than I had of exploring the warmer *Carrow* districts, where the inhabitants were still more indolent, has given me an account much to the same purpose.

The leaning of their arms on the table at meal times, is a custom very common with the colonists, and considered by them as a very laudable one, and in this particularly I followed my host's example; but I could not sufficiently admire the inventive spirit of idleness, exhibited in the voluptuous posture in which they universally indulge themselves when they smoke their pipes. Sitting on a bench or a chair without elbows, with their backs moderately bent, they lay their left leg over their right knee, and upon the left knee again thus raised, they rest their left elbow, while with the hand on the same side they support their chin, or one of their cheeks, at the same time holding their pipes in their mouths. Their right hand is then at liberty to grasp the small of their left leg with, or else to convey now and then to their mouth a cooling draught of tea. Let the reader represent to himself several people sitting together in this posture, and he will readily conceive what an elegant figure they would make in a group. I never saw any of the fair sex, however, in a posture of this kind. Among a set of beings so entirely devoted to their ease, one might naturally expect to meet with a variety of the most commodious easy chairs and sofas; but the truth is, that they find it much more commodious to avoid the trouble of inventing and making them.

I remarked as a very singular circumstance, that a wealthy farmer at *Agter Bruntjes-boogte,* who had plenty of timber to sell, had nevertheless only a ricketty elbow-chair in his house, and a few scanty stools of the most simple construction, made of a single board, with four rough-hewn ill-shapen legs. What, however, was still more singular was, that notwithstanding that one of these stools had lost a leg, yet it was frequently made use of to the endangering of the person's limbs who sat upon it, without either the master of the house or any of his three sons, who were otherwise all alert enough at the chase, having ever once thought of mending it. Nor did the inhabitants of this place exhibit much less simplicity and moderation, or to speak more properly, slovenliness and penury in their dress than in their furniture; neither of which, therefore, were in any wise correspondent to the large flocks and herds possessed by these graziers, and the plentiful tables they could afford to keep in consequence of these possessions. The distance at which they are from the Cape, may, indeed, be some excuse for their having no other earthenware or china in their houses, but what was cracked or broken; but this, methinks, should not prevent them from being in possession of more than one or two old pewter pots, and some few plates of the same metal; so that two people are frequently obliged to eat out of one dish, using it besides for every different article of food that comes upon table.

Each guest must bring his knife with him, and they frequently make use of their fingers instead of forks. The most wealthy farmer here is considered as being well dressed in a jacket of home-made cloth, or something of the kind made of any other coarse cloth, breeches of undressed leather, woollen stockings, a striped waistcoat, a cotton handkerchief about his neck, a coarse calico shirt, Hottentot field-shoes, or else leathern-shoes, with brass buckles, and a coarse hat. Indeed it is not in dress, but in the number and thriving condition of their cattle, and chiefly in the stoutness of their draught-oxen, that these peasants vie with each other. It is likewise by activity and manly actions, and by other qualities, that render a man fit for the married state, and the rearing of a family, that the youth chiefly

obtain the esteem of the fair sex; none of whom likewise were ever known, for the sake of vying with each other in point of dress, to have endangered either their husband's property or their own virtue. A plain close cap, and a coarse cotton gown, virtue and good housewifery, are looked upon by the fair sex as sufficient ornaments for their persons; a flirting disposition, coquetry and paint, would have very little effect in making conquests of young men, brought up in so hardy a manner, and who have had so homely and artless an education, as the youth in this place. In short, one may here, if any where in the world, lead an innocent, virtuous, and happy life.

When in company with these plain artless husbandmen, I used frequently to start such questions and subjects of conversation, as tended to give them a proper sense of the happiness of their situation, and make them set a higher value upon it, than they perhaps had done before. Indeed, I thought I could not more properly or more agreeably employ the little Dutch I had learned, than in persuading the good people among whom I sojourned, to be content with their lot, and consequently to be happy. One day, when I was urging this point, I received the following pertinent, but kind reply, from a discreet sensible woman, who was daughter to an inferior magistrate at *Zwellendam,* and was married to a yeoman in this place.

"My good friend, said she, you talk like a prudent sensible man; I am quite of your opinion, and wish you every happiness that can attend you: why need you wander any longer up and down the world in quest of happiness? You find it here, and are welcome to enjoy it among us. You have already a waggon, oxen, and saddle horses; these are the chief things requisite in order to set up a farmer; there are yet uncultivated places enough in this neighbourhood, proper either for pasturage or tillage, so that you may choose out of an extensive tract of land the spot that pleases you best. Here are people enough, who will send you that part of their cattle to keep which they cannot conveniently look after themselves, on conditions that you shall have the young ones produced by them for your trouble. In this way, many young beginners have acquired a competency in a few years. With your knowledge of disorders and plants, you may render yourself serviceable to your neighbours, and now and then get a heifer or a calf. In short, I will venture to prophesy, that you will soon have cows and sheep in abundance. Yet there is still somewhat wanting, which is most essential to your happiness; this is, a prudent and discreet wife: take my advice and look about you, and I will take upon me to assure you, that you will not long be without one in this country."

This advice, so consonant to the voice of nature, and coming with such kind intention from the fair sex, could not but greatly affect me: it is remarkable, however, that the poor woman who gave it me, had herself a bad husband.

83 THOMAS PRINGLE
BOER MEETS BANTU

Thomas Pringle (1789–1834) was born in Scotland. Associated with various literary reviews as poet and editor, he emigrated from his homeland to South Africa in 1820 with the wave of British settlers and established his home in the Albany district of the Eastern Province. Finding the frontier too dull, he moved to Cape Town in 1822, where he became well known as the co-founder, with John Fairbairn, of the South African Commercial Advertiser, *as well as for the controversy surrounding the subsequent suppression of the publication for his outspoken comments on the autocratic actions of the governor, Lord Charles Somerset. Pringle returned to Britain in 1826 and a year later became Secretary of the Anti-Slavery Society. He published two volumes of poetry, the second of which included a description of his experiences in South Africa and some aspects of South African history. The following selection is taken from a republication of the prose section of this volume entitled* Narrative of a Residence in South Africa, *in which Pringle provides his interpretation of the first contacts between the southern Nguni and the whites.*

The term *Caffer,* like that of *Hottentot,* is entirely unknown in the language of the people to whom it is applied. It was originally a term of contumely (being the Arabic word *Cafir* or *Kafir,* signifying *Infidel*) employed, by the Moorish or Arabian inhabitants of the north-eastern coast, to designate the nations of South-eastern Africa who had not embraced the Mohammedan faith; and from them the term was adopted by the early European navigators. The appellation, though sometimes still applied in a more extensive sense, is generally used, in the Cape Colony, to denote the three contiguous tribes of Amakosa, Amatembu, and Amaponda; of whom the last may be considered identical with the Mambo, or what used to be called the Mambookie, nation. These three tribes, though governed by several independent chiefs, are decidedly one people; their language, manners, customs, and polity being essentially the same. The Amakosa, whose territory borders with the colony from the Winterberg

From Thomas Pringle, *Narrative of a Residence in South Africa* (London: E. Moxon, 1840), pp. 92–95.

to the coast, is the tribe with whom our intercourse, both in peace and war, has been far the most frequent.

The Caffers are a tall, athletic, and handsome race of men, with features often approaching to the European or Asiatic model; and, excepting their woolly hair, exhibiting few of the peculiarities of the negro race. Their colour is a clear dark brown. Their address is frank, cheerful, and manly. Their government is patriarchal; and the privileges of rank are carefully maintained by the chieftains. Their principal wealth and means of subsistence consist in their numerous herds of cattle. The females also cultivate pretty extensively maize, millet, water-melons, and a few other esculents; but they are decidedly a nation of *herdsmen*—war, hunting, barter, and agriculture, being only occasional occupations.

In their customs and traditions, there seem to be indications of their having sprung, at some remote period, from a people of much higher civilisation than is now exhibited by any of the tribes of Southern Africa; whilst the rite of circumcision, universally practised among them, without any vestige of Islamism, and several other traditionary customs greatly resembling the Levitical rules of purification, would seem to indicate some former connexion with a people of Arabian, Hebrew, or, perhaps, Abyssinian lineage. Nothing like a regular system of idolatry exists among them; but we find some traces of belief in a Supreme Being, as well as in inferior spirits, and sundry superstitious usages that look like the shattered wrecks of ancient religious institutions. Of their superstitions, the belief in sorcery is far the most mischievous, leading, in the same way as among the negroes on the west coast, to many acts of revolting oppression and cruelty.

The clothing of both sexes consists entirely of the skins of animals, rendered soft and pliable by a sort of currying. Their arms are the assagai or javelin, a short club, and a large shield of bullock's or buffalo's hide. The wars between the contiguous tribes above-mentioned, or the several clans with each other, are seldom very bloody, generally arising from quarrels relating to their respective pasture-grounds or the stealing of cattle, and bearing little resemblance to the ferocious mode of warfare recently pursued with such destructive effect by the Zoola [Zulu —ed.] nations. The females are seldom slain in their internal wars; and in their conflicts with the colonists, there are many well-known examples of their humanity towards females who had fallen into their hands. They are *barbarians,* but not *savages,* in the strict and proper sense of the term.

It is a curious and characteristic circumstance that the earliest notice upon record of intercourse between the Cape colonists and the Caffers, is an account of a marauding expedition by a party of the former against the latter. In 1701, a band of Cape-Dutch freebooters, under the name of traders or barterers, marched to the eastward, and after an absence of seven months returned with a large quantity of cattle and sheep, which they had obtained by plundering a nation called Cabuquas, or Great Caffers, (probably Tambuquas, *i.e. Amatembu,*) together with two kraals of Hottentots. In the attacks made upon these then remote tribes, numbers of the natives had been slaughtered. The facts are stated in a despatch sent to Holland in 1702 by the Governor and Council of the Cape of Good Hope, who, while they deplore "the intolerable and continued excesses of some of the free inhabitants, in committing acts of violence, with robberies and murders, and by these abominable means depriving those poor people of their subsistence," declare at the same time their inability to punish the delinquents.

The impunity thus enjoyed by the colonial freebooters (who consisted for the most part of the very refuse of Europe, disbanded soldiers from mercenary regiments in the Dutch service, and the like), led, as was to be expected, to the frequent renewal of similar marauding excursions. By this means, and by the gradual occupation of all the best parts of the country, the Hottentot race were, as we have seen, at length either extirpated, reduced to thraldom, or driven to the northern deserts. The Caffers, a more numerous and warlike people, and acting together in large masses, were not so easily overwhelmed. They appear to have successfully resisted on many occasions the attacks of the colonists; but, having only their slender missiles to oppose to the musket, they also often suffered dreadfully from their aggressions.

The Caffers had been for several generations gradually pressing upon the Hottentot race from the eastward. This is not only known from traditionary memorials, but is manifest from most of the names of the rivers west of the Kei being of Hottentot etymology. The Hottentot hordes do not appear to have been extirpated by them, but to have been partly pushed farther westward, and partly incorporated with their frontier clans. The Ghonaqua tribe, once numerous and powerful, consisted of a people of mixed Caffer and Hottentot lineage; and the dialect now spoken by the frontier Caffers partakes to a certain extent of the Hottentot *cluck,* a peculiarity not to be found among the tribes farther back.

The country between the Camtoos and Great Fish rivers was, up to 1778, partly occupied by the Ghonaqua tribes and other hordes of Hottentots still enjoying a precarious independence, partly by Caffer clans, intermingled with the Ghonaquas, and partly by European colonists, who, in defiance of the colonial regulations, had taken possession of the choicest spots they could find beyond the nominal boundary—then Camtoos River. In 1778, the Governor, Van Plattenberg, having, in the course of an extensive tour which he made into the interior, visited Bruintjes-hoogtè, and finding a considerable number of colonists occupying tracts

beyond the frontier, instead of recalling them within the legal limits, he extended the boundary (according to the ordinary practice of Cape Governors, before and since), adding, by a stroke of his pen, about 30,000 square miles to the colonial territory. It was at this period that the Great Fish River was first declared to be the colonial boundary on the east. The rights of the Ghonaquas and other independent Hottentot tribes within the extensive region thus acquired, do not appear to have occupied a single thought; the Boors were left to deal with them as they had dealt with their brethren already extinct: but with the more formidable Caffers the *form* of an agreement was observed. Colonel Collins relates that Colonel Gordon was sent in search of Caffers as far as the Keiskamma, and that he conducted "a few" to the Governor, who obtained their consent that the Great Fish River should thenceforth be considered the boundary between the two countries.

Who were "the few" that concurred in this agreement, it would be vain to inquire; but it is certain that the principal Caffer chiefs who had an interest in the affair refused to recognize it. Jalumba, then chief of the Amandanka clan of the Amakosa, endeavoured to maintain his ground in Bruintjes-hoogtè. "The *inhabitants,*" says Col. Collins, "reminded Jalumba (in 1781) of the recent treaty, and required his immediate departure. Their remonstrance having been disregarded, a commando assembled, by which the intruders were expelled with the loss of Jalumba and a great number of his followers. His son Dlodlo perished two years afterwards, in a similar attempt." Such is the colonial account of the affair; but Col. Collins, who derived his information entirely from the Boors and local functionaries, has not mentioned that on this occasion the expedition (of which Adrian Van Jaarsveld was the leader) plundered the Caffers of 5,200 head of cattle, which he divided "after consultation with the Veld-wagtmeester and corporals, amongst the commando." Nor was this the worst. We have got from Mr. Brownlee the Caffer account of the transaction, which is at least as much deserving of credit as the reports of the colonists who had enriched themselves with the spoils of the slaughtered Caffers; and from this it appears, that Jalumba and his clan were destroyed by a most infamous act of treachery and murder. The details may be found in the works both of Thompson and Kay. Vaillant, who spent a considerable time in this part of the country in the following year (1782), gives an account of the spirit of the frontier boors, and of the oppressions perpetrated upon the Caffers, that but too well accords with the story told by Mr. Brownlee, from Caffer tradition, of the massacre of the Amandanka. "A mulatto colonist," he says, "informed me that the report of this nation being barbarous and bloody was industriously circulated by the colonists, in order to justify the atrocious thefts they were daily guilty of towards them, and which they wished to have passed for reprisals. That they often formed pretences of losing cattle, purposely to make inroads into the Caffers' settlements, exterminating whole hordes without distinction of age or sex, carrying away their herds, and laying waste the country; this means of procuring cattle appearing much easier than the slow method of breeding them. In this manner, Hans assured me, twenty thousand head had been obtained the last year." After giving some details of particular atrocities reported to him, and making some very pertinent remarks upon the flagitious impunity enjoyed by these barbarous backsettlers, Vaillant states that when he expressed to one of them his surprise that the governor did not send down a troop of soldiers to arrest those who committed such acts in defiance of all authority, the Boor replied, that if such a thing were attempted, they would kill half the soldiers, and send them back salted by those that were spared, as an earnest of what they would do to any

authority that should dare to interfere with them! Such were the men who rose in arms in 1796, and again in 1815, against the British Government, in order to vindicate their right to rob and murder the natives without control!

Nearly about the same period, Zaka, the head of the Gunuquebi clan, with some other bands of the Amakosa, had obtained possession of the Zureveld, by purchasing with a large number of cattle permission to settle there from Kohla (called by the colonists Ruiter), who was then chief of the Ghonaqua Hottentots, the original possessors of the country. The colonists at the same time advanced into the Zureveld from the west. For a number of years the Boors and the Caffers occupied that district together, with their habitations and herds amicably intermingled; until, in 1786, some differences arising between them, the colonists called in the chief Islambi, the enemy of Zaka, to their assistance. The latter chief, being attacked simultaneously by the Boors on one side and by Islambi with 3000 warriors on the other, was defeated and slain; and his tribe (the Gunuquebi) were plundered by the confederates of almost the whole of their cattle, and driven by necessity to plunder the colonists for means of subsistence. The Boors, however, did not by this means accomplish their object. Kongo, the son of Zaka, having been soon afterwards joined by Maloo, Toli, Etoni, and several other chiefs at enmity with Islambi and Gaika, and by the remnant of the Amandanka under Olila the brother of Jalumba, the Gunuquebi, with their allies, re-established themselves in the Zureveld, in spite of the colonists, and plundered them in their turn of many cattle; and it is from the period of this struggle, and from the destruction of the Amandanka in Bruintjes-hoogtè, that the bitter animosity of the border tribes, formerly friendly, and their extensive depredations against the colonists, are to be dated.

In consequence of the representations

of the colonists, a large commando of Burgher militia was collected in 1793, to chastise the Caffers. This force, under the command of Mr. Maynier, landdrost of Graaff-Reinét, marched through the Zureveld, and penetrated into the Amakosa country, four days' journey beyond the Great Fish River, driving the natives everywhere before them into the woods, and capturing some herds of cattle; but without obtaining any decided advantage over the enemy, who, as soon as the commando retreated, returned to their former position. A treaty was at length concluded, leaving things precisely as they were, and in which, as Colonel Collins remarks, nothing was mentioned about the retreat of the Caffers from the disputed territory. In a report made to Government by the landdrost, Maynier, respecting the causes of this war, he observes, "that the excursions of the Boors into Cafferland for the purpose of hunting, the trade carried on between them and the Caffers, and the improper treatment which the latter had experienced from the former when in their service, were the principal occasions of the rupture."

In 1795, the colony was captured by the British arms; and the Boors of the Graaff-Reinét district having in the following year driven away their new magistrate, Mr. Bresler, the whole of the eastern province was thrown into a state of the utmost anarchy. Some of the Caffer chiefs were instigated by the colonists to attack the British troops who had been sent down by Sir James Craig to maintain order. Many of the Hottentots, as has been already noticed, availing themselves of the crisis, rose against their masters, and prevailed on the Caffer clans of the Zureveld to join them in plundering and driving out the frontier Boors, who were thus caught in the net of mischief they had themselves spread; and devastation and bloodshed continued to prevail for several years, during which much misery and many barbarities were reciprocally inflicted by both parties.

Such was the state of affairs on the eastern frontier in 1797, when Earl Macartney assumed the government, and Mr. Barrow was sent on a mission to Cafferland, of which he has given so interesting an account in his able work on the colony. The policy of the British government towards the native tribes at this period was unquestionably characterised by a spirit of justice and benevolence. The firm repression by Sir James Craig of an audacious attempt by the Boors of Bruintjes-hoogtè to obtain permanent possession of the country on the Kat and Koonap rivers; the testimony of Mr. Barrow on that subject; and the tone of Lord Macartney's proclamation of July 14, 1798, in establishing a fixed boundary for the colony, afford satisfactory evidence of the enlightened sentiments by which those Governors were actuated. But some great and lamentable mistakes were also then committed. The unjust and mischievous policy was adopted of treating with *one* Caffer chief instead of those who were far more directly interested in the question of boundaries; and this, notwithstanding that Gaika, while he stated truly enough that he was the chief first in *rank* on the frontier (for he was secondary to Hinza in the Amakosa tribe), carefully informed Mr. Barrow at the same time that those who held possession of tracts of country west of the Great Fish River, "were chiefs as well as himself, and entirely independent of him." No consideration was had to the claims of the Caffer chiefs in the Zureveld, who absolutely refused to accede to the treaty with Gaika or to leave the country, which they considered, and not without good reason, as their own both by purchase and conquest. Still less consideration appears to have been given to the yet more indisputable rights of the aborigines of the soil, the Ghonaquas, and other Hottentot hordes, to whom had originally belonged the large tract of country usurped so unscrupulously by Governor Plettenberg in 1778. The limits then assigned to the colony were now reclaimed without qualification, by the proclamation of Earl Macartney.

For the details of the policy pursued towards the Caffers for the twelve years which followed Mr. Barrow's embassy to Gaika, I must refer to the works of that writer and of Lichtenstein, and to the more recent publications of Thompson, Bannister, and Kay. The Gunuquebi clan, under Kongo, kept possession of the fastnesses of the Zureberg and the adja-

cent country, to the mouths of the Bushman and Sunday rivers. Islambi, who was at war with Gaika, had also crossed the Great Fish River, and fixed himself in the Zureveld. Their alliance with the insurgent Hottentots has been already mentioned. With the Boors they were sometimes at war, and sometimes living in precarious truce.

84 HENRY FRANCIS FYNN
SHAKA

Henry Francis Fynn arrived in South Africa in 1818 and six years later went to Port Natal as leader of an expedition of the Farewell Trading Company that was sent to open up the eastern coast. Soon after his arrival he visited Shaka, ruler of the Zulu state. Fynn's accounts of the events of this time and of Nguni history are the earliest and most reliable surviving record. Fynn remained at Port Natal and traded with Shaka and his successor, Dingane, until 1834, after which time he became an interpreter to Governor Benjamin D'Urban and British Resident for various southern Nguni chiefdoms. In 1852 he returned to the British colony of Natal, where he served as a magistrate and was regarded as an expert on native affairs. He never published the book based on his experience that he had intended to publish because he lost the original of his journal, but his writings have been preserved in the works of other travelers and annalists and in government reports. Fynn died in Natal in 1861.

I may at once state that the distance from the port to Shaka's residence was 200 miles. Our progress was exceedingly slow, each day's journey being arranged by Mbikwana [Shaka's uncle—ed.]. We afterwards found out that he had not taken us by a direct route, but to kraals of minor chiefs and some of the barracks of Shaka's regiments. Cattle-slaughtering occurred sometimes twice and thrice a day. Numbers of Zulus joined our column in order to relieve Mbikwana's peo-

ple of their burdens. We were struck with astonishment at the order and discipline maintained in the country through which we travelled. The regimental kraals, especially the upper parts thereof, also the kraals of chiefs, showed that cleanliness was a prevailing custom and this not only inside their huts, but outside, for there were considerable spaces where neither dirt nor ashes were to be seen.[1]

Frequently on the journey we saw large parties seated with grotesquely dressed men apparently lecturing in their midst,

From Henry Francis Fynn, *Diaries,* edited by James Stuart and Daniel McKinnon Malcolm (Pietermaritzburg, South Africa: Shuter & Shooter (Pty.) Ltd., 1950), pp. 70–80. Reprinted by permission. Except for two insertions in the texts delineated by brackets the notes are those of James Stuart and Daniel McKinnon Malcolm.

[1] One afternoon seeing a flock of vultures near us, I shot one and on going to pick it up found they were devouring dead bodies, of which there were five. They appeared to have been killed the day before. Author's MS.

and on several occasions saw individuals seized and carried off and instantly put to death. The grotesque characters we learned were "witch finders" whilst those singled out and put to death were said to be "evil doers." [2]

Messengers passed three or four times a day between Shaka and Mbikwana, the former enquiring about our progress and doubtless directing how we should proceed so as to fall in with his own preparations for our reception. We had thus dallied 13 days on the road in travelling 200 miles, when the locality of Shaka's residence was pointed out to us about 15 miles off. While encamped that night we saw much commotion going on in our neighbourhood. Troops of cattle were being driven in advance; regiments were passing near by and on distant hills, interspersed with regiments of girls, decorated in beads and brass with regimental uniformity, carrying on their heads large pitchers of native beer, milk and cooked food. The approaching scene we anticipated witnessing cheered us considerably that evening. Farewell and Petersen expressed extreme affection and attachment for one another, with mutual apologies for past small differences.

It was not until ten o'clock the following morning that a proposal was made about advancing. In about two hours we arrived at a ridge from which we beheld

an extensive and very picturesque basin before us, with a river running through it, called the Umfolozi.[3]

We were requested to make a stand under a large euphorbia tree, from whence, about a mile before us, we saw the residence of Shaka, viz: a native kraal nearly two miles in circumference.

While in this position, messengers went backwards and forwards between Mbikwana and Shaka. At length one came and desired Mr. Farewell and myself to advance, leaving Mr. Petersen and our servants and native followers, who were carrying Shaka's present, at the euphorbia tree. Mbikwana and about 20 of his followers accompanied us.

On entering the great cattle kraal we found drawn up within it about 80,000 natives in their war attire.[4] Mbikwana requested me to gallop within the circle, and immediately on my starting to do so one general shout broke forth from the whole mass, all pointing at me with their sticks. I was asked to gallop round the circle two or three times in the midst of tremendous shouting of the words, "*UJojo wokhalo!*" (the sharp or active finch of the ridge).[5] Mr. Farewell and I

---

[2] One day we arrived at a large kraal containing 190 huts, the barracks of one of Shaka's regiments. We had not been there many minutes before our attention was drawn to a party of 150 natives sitting in a circle with a man opposite them, apparently interrogating them. In reply, they each beat the ground with a stick and said, He-sa-gee! [*Yizwa Zhi! Editor.*] After they had been answering with the same word about an hour, three of them were pointed out and killed on the spot. This man, whom they called an *inyanga,* or as we should say a necromancer, was dressed in an ape skin cap; a number of pieces of different roots were tied round his neck; and a small shield and assegai were in one hand, and the tail of a cow in the other. He was an interpreter of dreams and thought capable of telling what has happened in any other part of the country, also if one has injured another by poison or otherwise. His decision is fatal to the unfortunate individuals pointed out by him. Author's MS.

[3] Evidently the Umhlathuze is meant, for the Umfolozi cannot be seen from the position the travellers had now got to. *Editor.*

[4] "On entering its gates we perceived about 12,000 men in their war attire, drawn up in a circle to receive us." The author here refers to warriors only, whereas in the text he includes regiments of girls, women, servants, etc., as well. *Editor.*

[5] Literally the words mean: Long tailed Finch of the Ridge, which implies that the person to whom the words are applied is quick and brave in attacking and overcoming his enemy. *Editor.*

It is customary for the principal warriors of each regiment, in their war dances, to dance forwards [i.e. each dances a pas-seul by rushing forwards, gesticulating as he does so with the shield and weapons he is carrying.—*Editor.*], when they are applauded by their own heroic names. They, therefore, on the occasion in question, considered I was adopting their own practice, hence cheered me by a phrase or name commonly found among their own heroes. On entering the kraal's gates . . . we were desired to gallop two or three times round, then twice more; then to return and bring the remainder of the party with us. We were desired to gallop four times more round the kraal and then stand all together about

were then led by Mbikwana to the head of the kraal, where the masses of the people were considerably denser than elsewhere. The whole force remained stationary, as, indeed, it had been since the commencement of the reception.

Mbikwana, standing in our midst, addressed some unseen individual in a long speech, in the course of which we were frequently called upon by him to answer "*Yebo,*" that is to affirm as being true all he was saying, though perfectly ignorant of what was being said.[6]

While the speech was being made I caught sight of an individual in the background whom I concluded to be Shaka, and, turning to Farewell, pointed out and said: "Farewell, there is Shaka." This was sufficiently audible for him to hear and perceive that I had recognised him. He immediately held up his hand, shaking his finger at me approvingly. Farewell, being near-sighted and using an eye-glass, could not distinguish him.[7]

Elephant tusks were then brought forward. One was laid before Farewell and another before me.[8] Shaka then raised the stick in his hand and after striking with it right and left,[9] the whole mass broke from their position and formed up into regiments. Portions of each of these rushed to the river and the surrounding hills, while the remainder, forming themselves into a circle, commenced dancing with Shaka in their midst.[10]

It was a most exciting scene, surprising to us, who could not have imagined that a nation termed "savages" could be so disciplined and kept in order.

Regiments of girls, headed by officers of their own sex, then entered the centre of the arena to the number of 8,000–10,000, each holding a slight staff in her hand. They joined in the dance, which continued for about two hours.

Shaka now came towards us, evidently to seek our applause. [The following from Bird's *Annals of Natal,* contributed by the author, describes the scene.] "The King came up to us and told us not to be afraid of his people, who were now coming up to us in small divisions, each division driving cattle before it. The men were singing and dancing and whilst so doing advancing and receding even as one sees the surf do on a seashore. The whole country, as far as our sight could reach, was covered with numbers of people and droves of cattle. The cattle had been assorted according to their colour. . . . After exhibiting their cattle for two hours, they drew together in a circle, and sang and danced to their war song. Then the people returned to the cattle, again exhibiting them as before, and, at intervals, dancing and singing. The women now entered the kraal, each having a long thin stick in the right hand, and moving it in time to the song. They had not been dancing many minutes, when they had to make way for the ladies of the seraglio [harem—ed.], be-

---

20 yards from a large tree at the head of the kraal. Author's note.

The probabilities are that Fynn began galloping alone, hence he was acclaimed, his prowess as a pioneer doctor having already become known, as stated in the text, and that in the succeeding gallops he was accompanied by Farewell. *Editor.*

[6] Evidently the King, but Shaka was so surrounded by his chiefs that we could not see him. Author's note.

[7] A speech in answer to Mbikwana's was then made by a chief opposite. Author's note.

[8] Mbikwana now made another speech. Author's MS.

[9] "and springing out from amidst the chiefs." Author's MS.

[10] In another MS. Fynn has: The whole body then ran to the lower end of the kraal, leaving us alone, with the exception of one man who had been hidden

in the crowd. This man proved to be a native of the Cape Frontier, who had been taken prisoner in a war between the Colonists and Kaffirs and sent to Robben Island. Captain Owen of the *Leven* had taken him as an interpreter to attend him during his survey of the Eastern coast. Afterwards the interpreter had been given over to Farewell on his voyage to St. Lucia Bay. There he ran off and sought protection with Shaka, who gave him the name of Hlambamanzi, denoting one who had crossed (swum) the water. Among the colonists he had been known by the name of Jacob Sumbiti. He spoke good Dutch.

Further particulars about this man will be found in Isaacs, *Travels and Adventures in Eastern Africa,* II, 251–58, 264–69; Owen, *Narratives of Voyages to Explore Shores of Africa, Arabia and Madagascar,* I, 59, II, 222. *Editor.*

sides about 150 others, who were called sisters. These danced in parties of eight, arranged in fours, each party wearing different coloured beads, which were crossed from the shoulders to the knees. Each wore a head-dress of black feathers, and four brass collars, fitting closely to the neck. When the King joined in the dance, he was accompanied by the men. This dance lasted half an hour. The order observed and the precision of every movement was interpreted to us by his interpreter, Hlambamanzi. He desired to know from us if ever we had seen such order in any other state, assured us that he was the greatest king in existence, that his people were as numerous as the stars, and that his cattle were innumerable. The people now dispersed, and he directed a chief to lead us to a kraal where we could pitch our tents. He sent us a sheep, a basket of corn, an ox, and a pot of beer, about three gallons. At seven o'clock, we sent up four rockets and fired off eight guns. He sent people to look at these, but from fear did not show himself out of his hut. The following morning we were requested to mount our horses and proceed to the King's quarters. We found him sitting under a tree at the upper end of the kraal decorating himself and surrounded by about 200 people. A servant was kneeling by his side holding a shield above him to keep off the glare of the sun. Round his forehead he wore a turban [11] of otter skin with a feather of a crane erect in front, fully two feet long, and a wreath of scarlet feathers, formerly worn, only, by men of high rank. Ear ornaments made from dried sugar cane, carved round the edge, with white ends, and an inch in diameter, were let into the lobes of the ears, which had been cut to admit them. From shoulder to shoulder, he wore bunches, five inches in length, of the skins of monkeys and genets, twisted like

the tails of these animals. These hung half down the body. Round the ring on the head,[12] were a dozen tastefully arranged bunches of the loury feathers, neatly tied to thorns which were stuck into the hair. Round his arms were white ox-tail tufts, cut down the middle so as to allow the hair to hang about the arm, to the number of four for each arm. Round the waist, there was a kilt or petticoat, made of skins of monkeys and genets, and twisted as before described, having small tassels round the top. The kilt reached to the knees, below which were white ox-tails fitted to the legs so as to hang down to the ankles. He had a white shield with a single black spot,[13] and one assegai. When thus equipped he certainly presented a fine and most martial appearance.

While he was dressing himself, his people proceeded, as on the day before, to show droves of cattle, which were still flocking in, repeatedly varying the scene with singing and dancing. In the meantime, we observed Shaka gave orders for a man standing close to us to be killed, for what crime we could not learn, but we soon found this to be a very common occurrence." [14]

Mr. Petersen, unfortunately, at this moment placed a musical box on the ground, and, striking it with a switch, moved the stop. Shaka heard the music. It seemed to produce in him a superstitious feeling. He turned away with evident displeasure and went back immediately to the dance.

Those portions of regiments which had

---

[11] This word, often applied to Zulu head-dresses and especially Shaka's, seems to us inaccurate. Zulus do not wear turbans. They wear headbands or circlets cut out or made of various skins or other substances. *Editor.*

[12] This clearly proves that Shaka wore a head-ring (*isicoco*). We have sometimes heard doubts expressed on this point by Europeans. Well-informed natives, however, believe the King to have worn a ring, without, in these latter days, being able to prove it. The only portrait of Shaka we know of which can claim to be authentic (that in Isaacs' *Travels and Adventures in Eastern Africa*, I, 58) leaves one in doubt, for the band there shown round the head may well be the circlet or headband known as *umqhele. Editor.*

[13] Somewhat oval in shape (seven inches by five inches) about the size of a man's open hand. It was midway down the shield and on the right-hand edge thereof. *Editor.*

[14] Bird, *Annals of Natal,* I, 77.

separated prior to the dance now returned from the river and from behind the adjoining hills, driving before them immense herds of cattle. A grand cattle show was now being arranged. Each regiment drove towards us thousands of cattle that had been allotted to their respective barracks, the colour of each regiment's cattle corresponding with that of the shield the men carried, which, in turn, served to distinguish one regiment from another. No cattle of differing colour from those allotted to a given regiment were allowed to intermix. There were many droves without horns, others with pendulous projections, four or six inches long, which covered a considerable portion of the animal. The cattle of the other droves had four, six, and eight horns apiece. This show of cattle continued till sunset, with dancing at intervals, when we proposed to pitch the tents we had brought with us. A man was ordered to point out a spot for the purpose. Greatly to Farewell's astonishment, this man proved to be Jacob, his interpreter, who had landed at St. Lucia the year previous when he, Farewell, lost his boats and the sailors therein were drowned. Jacob had been taken to Shaka, who immediately appointed him one of the sentries for guarding his establishment.

Two oxen were slaughtered for us. After dinner we prepared to retire, but messengers from Shaka requested us to go to him, with Jacob the interpreter.[15] I was

then led into the seraglio, where I found him seated in a carved wooden chair and surrounded by about 400 girls, two or three chiefs and two servants in attendance.

My name Fynn had been converted into Sofili by the people in general; by this, after desiring me to sit in front of him, he several times accosted me in the course of the following dialogue:

"I hear you have come from um-George, is it so? Is he as great a king as I am?"

Fynn: "Yes; King George is one of the greatest kings in the world."

Shaka: "I am very angry with you," said while putting on a severe countenance. "I shall send a messenger to um-George and request him to kill you. He sent you to me not to give medicine to my dogs." All present immediately applauded what Shaka had said. "Why did you give my dogs medicine?" (in allusion to the woman I was said to have brought back to life after death).

Fynn: "It is a practice of our country to help those who are in need, if able to do so."

Shaka: "Are you then the doctor of dogs? You were sent here to be my doctor."

Fynn: "I am not a doctor and not considered by my countrymen to be one."

Shaka: "Have you medicine by you?"

Fynn: "Yes."

Shaka: "Then cure me, or I will have you sent to umGeorge to have you killed."

Fynn: "What is the matter with you?"

Shaka: "That is your business to find out."

Fynn: "Stand up and let me see your person."

---

[15] The first meeting of Shaka with Farewell, Fynn, and the rest of the party was manifestly a unique and memorable occasion. Instead of the formal, stiff and constrained ceremonial customary at such a moment, Shaka, whose heart was mysteriously touched by the advent of British settlers to his shores, converted the occasion into a grand and dramatically planned festival. We cannot but think these warm-hearted exhibitions of regard should be attributed in the main to two influences seemingly trivial in themselves: (a) Jacob's previous lengthy contact with worthy officers of the Royal British Navy; (b) Fynn's discreet, courageous and humane bearing during the weeks he was striving to open up communication with Shaka. His spontaneous humanity straightway disarmed all suspicion and even caused him to be taken as typical of the race he belonged to. Thus, through the agency of Fynn

and Jacob, the British people henceforth began to stand in a favourable light. Shaka, despot though he was, one of the greatest the world has ever known, took them to his heart and, as will be seen, never failed to treat them as friends. More than this, the conviction then arrived at as to their friendliness has, after many sad and trying vicissitudes of later years, been honoured down to the present time. *Editor.*

Shaka: "Why should I stand up?"

Fynn: "That I may see if I can find out what ails you."

Shaka stood up but evidently disliked my approaching him closely. A number of girls held up lighted torches. I looked about his person and, after reflecting on the great activity he had shown during the day, was satisfied he had not much the matter with him. I, however, observed numerous black marks on his loins where native doctors had scarified him, and at once said he had pains in his loins. He held his hand before his mouth in astonishment, upon which my wisdom was applauded by all present. Shaka then strictly charged me not to give medicine to his dogs, and, after a few commonplace questions in which he showed good humour, I was permitted to retire for the night.[16]

Very few, if any, of the Zulu army had any sleep that night. Cattle were slaughtered in great numbers, and all the country round about was illuminated by the fires, around which the people sat in groups.

The following day had been appointed by Shaka for receiving our present, which, fortunately, had been well chosen by Farewell for presentation to so superior a chief as Shaka. It consisted of every description of beads at that time procurable in Cape Town, and far superior to those Shaka had previously obtained from the Portuguese at Delagoa. There was a great variety of woollen blankets, a large quantity of brass bars, turned and lacquered, and sheets of copper, also pigeons, a pig, cats and dogs. There was, moreover, a full-dress military coat, with epaulettes covered with gold lace. Though Shaka showed no open gratitude, we saw clearly that he was satisfied. He was very interested in the live animals, especially the pig, until it got into his milk stores where

it committed great havoc, and set all the women in the seraglio screaming for assistance. All this ended in the pig being killed.[17]

The showing of cattle and dancing continued during the day, whilst other regiments, which had come from a great distance, arrived and took part in the festivities. Among the articles we had brought were some Congreve rockets. These we kept back. On returning to our camp, as the evening was dark, we fired them off, having first informed Shaka, and asked him to order his people to look upwards. Their surprise was great; I, however, question if the showing of such wonders to ignorant natives is advisable after so short an acquaintance between white and black as ours had been. In conversation on our object in coming to Natal, this part of South Africa, Shaka showed great desire that we should live at the port. Each evening he sent for me and conversed with me through the Kaffir Jacob, the interpreter, for three or four hours.

On the first day of our visit we had seen no less than ten men carried off to death. On a mere sign by Shaka, viz: the pointing of his finger, the victim would be seized by his nearest neighbours; his neck would be twisted, and his head and body beaten with sticks, the nobs of some of these being as large as a man's fist. On each succeeding day, too, numbers of others were killed; their bodies would then be carried to an adjoining hill and there impaled. We visited this spot on the fourth day. It was truly a Golgotha, swarming with hundreds of vultures. The effects of this together with the scenes of death made Mr. Petersen decide at once to dissolve the partnership and leave for the Cape.

[16] I remained till ten o'clock when I left him with a promise that, agreeable to his request, I would remain with him a month after the departure of Messrs. Farewell and Petersen. Author's MS.

[17] The bringing of the live animals to Shaka was due to a suggestion by Shaka's uncle Mbikwana, who had returned with me to Natal to accompany us all to Shaka's residence. He asked us not to omit to take one of each species of domestic animals we had brought with us, among which was a pig. All were taken to the *isigodlo,* a seraglio, for the amusement of the women. Author's MS.

In the afternoon of the fifth day Shaka sent for me and requested me to proceed with some of his servants to a distant kraal where the chief Mupangazitha was very ill. I went and found him in high fever. I bled him, gave him medicine and caused him to be brought to a full perspiration. At midday on the following day he was able to report himself comparatively well.[18] As this captain was a great

18 Five days afterwards I heard of his final recovery. Author's note.

favourite with Shaka, my success gave him much pleasure.

.   .   .

On taking leave of the King on the following morning, Shaka presented Farewell and myself with five elephant tusks each and 40 head of cattle, and promised he would send out his soldiers to kill elephants for us. I accompanied Messrs. Farewell and Petersen a few miles, returned to Shaka by sunset and sat with him two or three hours in the evening.

85 ANDREW GEDDES BAIN
THE NGWAKETSE DEFEAT THE KOLOLO

The rise of the Zulu under Shaka set in motion a chain of movements and wars known as the Mfecane *or, in Sotho, the* Difaqane. *These events were not often recorded by eyewitnessess who had seen them, so that any accounts dating from this time are valuable. Only on the eastern frontier, where British forces accidentally came into collision with the* Taung, *and in the western borderlands, where missionaries and travelers were just arriving, were such eyewitness accounts possible. Some of the best known of these accounts are of the Battle of Dithakong, during which the Griqua, armed with guns and mobilized on horses, defeated a large army of raiders that had been set on a career of destruction and killing by the Zulu eruption. Three years after the Battle of Dithakong, while traveling north from Kuruman and Dithakong to the country of the* Ngwaketse, *Andrew Bain and John Burnet Biddulph found the Ngwaketse driven from their capital by more of these raiders. Although the raiders were known indiscriminately as* Mantatees *(after the leader of one group who, in fact, never crossed the Vaal River), those that Bain and Biddulph encountered were the* Kololo, *led by Sebetwane. After the defeat of the Kololo by the Ngwaketse, Sebetwane gradually moved northward and eventually established the state north of the Zambezi where David Livingstone met Sebetwane in 1851, shortly before the death of the Kololo leader.*

Andrew Geddes Bain (1797–1864) immigrated to South Africa from Scotland in 1816 and settled in Graaff Reinet. He was apparently the first to take out a license to trade across the Orange River when this requirement was imposed in 1825. The following year Bain made a trip northward with John Biddulph. The following extract is from a journal kept by Bain of this journey in 1826. He made numerous other trips, participated in public affairs in the Cape, built roads, and fought in the frontier war of 1835; he seems always to have been a figure of controversy. The Bain's Kloof Pass not far from Cape Town was named after him.

From *Journals of Andrew Geddes Bain, Trader, Explorer, Soldier, Road Engineer, and Geologist,* edited by Margaret Hermina Lister (Cape Town: Von Riebeeck Society, 1949), XXX, 51–53, 56–60, 64–71. Reprinted by permission of the Van Riebeeck Society, South African Library, Cape Town.

We pursued our journey & in about an hour more reached the valley of Silaqualaly [1] which we found literally strewed with human sculls, it having been the theatre of a bloody battle between the Bawanketzie & the Mantatees in which Makabba, the celebrated King of the former & father of the present monarch, was killed. The sight of the sculls did not impress us with a great idea of the humanity of the natives, & we were not void of apprehensions that our own might bleach in the same spot in a few days. We met a great number of natives of both sexes as we rode up the valley, but it was dark before we reached the springs.

This evening at 7 o'clock we reached Siloquilaly, the springs which supply the town of the same name, at present the capital of the Wanketsie Kingdom & situated a mile & a half to the eastward. We were scarcely span'd out before the King's 2 brothers waited on us to welcome us to their country & brought a large bag of thick milk, as much as 2 men could carry, part of which they poured out in their hands & tasted to shew that it contained no poison. They placed sentinels round our waggons to prevent the mob from injuring anything & told us that Sibigho, the King, would visit us as soon as the moon should rise, which would be about 9 o'clock. We gave each of them a piece of tobacco with which they appeared exceedingly well pleased.

At 9 the King made his appearance attended by 5 or 6 of his principal people. He greeted us in a very friendly manner but with very little ceremony &, taking his seat on the ground close by us, entered cordially into conversation with us. His appearance is very prepossessing & would alone point him out as the Chief among all his subjects. He is above the common size, well made, & features more approaching the European than the Bechuana or negro. He was dressed in a jack-

[1] Selokolela, near the present Kanye, BaNgwaketse Reserve, Bechuanaland Protectorate. Latitude 24 57. Biddulph's list.

alls Kabo, had his head wrapped in a large & beautiful snake's skin [2] & in his hand carried a handsome battle axe. On his legs, ancles & wrists he wore an unusual number of copper rings & bracelets of curious workmanship, some of which I was told were made by himself. [3]

As he had already testified his friendship for us by sending us a cow for slaughter & a large quantity of milk the moment we arrived at his place, we took the earliest opportunity of presenting him with some beads, a roll of tobacco, a tinder box & knife.

He said he was very glad we were come as he expected our assistance against the common enemy, the Mantatees, who killed his father & destroyed all their towns & had driven them about from place to place for the last 3 years. They were now living in miserable huts which he would be ashamed to shew us, instead of the comfortable dwellings they had been accustomed to. We told him we were sorry we were not in condition to contend with such formidable enemies as the Mantatees were represented to be, that our number was very small & besides they had not done us any harm; that we were peaceable people who had come to open a friendly trade with him & we trusted we might remain friends without espousing his cause against his enemies. "That cannot be," said he, "you have accepted of & given presents to us & we look upon you as our friends. If you are then what you pretend to be, you will join us

[2] "As an antidote against the headache with which he was troubled." *Ibid.*
[3] "Round his ancles were four rows of beads of virgin gold which he said he had taken from a Mantatee chief whom he had killed in battle." From Extract from Bain's Journal, *S.A. Quarterly,* 1830, and *G.T. Journal,* Oct. 27th, 1855, and Bain's letter to *The S.A.C. Advertiser,* Nov. 14th, 1826. In a note for the *Quarterly* extract Bain writes, "That was the first and only time that I have ever met with that precious metal among the savages of Southern Africa." The omission of gold beads from the list of ornaments mentioned in the original journal may be accounted for by the fact that Bain first saw Sebego by moonlight and firelight, and probably mistook gold for copper.

against the common enemy of mankind. It is but a month ago that they drove us hither, robbed us of our cattle & took possession of our town which they now occupy about one day's journey to the N.E. of this, & we are in daily expectation of being again attacked by them here." To prevent which he intended risking an engagement with them in a couple of days in which he hoped (in self defence) we would assist him.

In vain did we represent our inability to assist him, that some of our people were sick & none of them accustomed to fight; that we did not wish to be enemies with any nation & that our King, who is a Mighty Monarch, would certainly punish us should we interfere with other people's quarrels without his consent. "You are now," resumed he, raising himself a little from the ground, "in my dominions and consequently under my orders. Every respect shall be shewn you & you shall be treated as great Captains, as you certainly are, but it is my pleasure that you join us to eradicate from the face of the earth, the plunderers of this & all the neighbouring kingdoms before you can again return to your own country."

This he spoke in rather an authoritative tone which did not please us, so we begged the subject might be dropped for the present thinking we could devise some method of avoiding the disagreeable alternative he left us. We then changed the conversation & chatted together till 11 o'clock when he left us in very good humour, leaving some people with us to guard the waggons.

. . .

Augt. 22nd. This day we bought a good many elephants teeth from Sibigho without anything of consequence happening, except his telling us that we must prepare ourselves to join in the attack against the Mantatees, as we could not otherwise leave his dominions, for as long as we were here we would be a protection to him, but he wished to drive them entirely out of the country & then he would suffer us to go whenever we liked. This news rather disconcerted us as we were now entirely under his power. He had only to take possession of our oxen to secure us, which he hinted would be done if we did not resolve to join him. We again tried to laugh it off & succeeded in turning the conversation, but the respite was of very short duration.

At sunset the King & all the people left us except the guards who watched the waggons day & night, but in about 2 hours after Kooa, Malmanjana and three grave looking old men came with a message of great importance from Sibigho, which they said would require our immediate consideration. Their spies had brought them information that the Mantatees were preparing to attack them again & that the King had resolved to meet them, in which case it would be absolutely necessary that we should join them with a few muskets, which he did not doubt would put their enemies to the route. We had already urged every excuse that we could devise but to no purpose, so we now begged them to give us the night to think over the matter & they should have our answer in the morning.

Augt. 23rd. This morning Sibigho sent for us at sunrise, for which purpose we could easily guess. We found him as usual sitting under the large tree surrounded by his great folks. After a mutual pull of our noses, the two inverted dishes were brought & we were invited to drink a beverage called Bajalo or Beer made from the Caffer Corn. This stuff exactly resembled the sour wash with which in England pigs are supplied from the breweries but, out of compliment to the King, we were obliged to swig off a good draught & pronounce it *Munati* (excellent). It nearly turned Mr. Biddulph's stomach, but mine stood it tolerably well.

After sitting there a few minutes Sibigho, attended by his two brothers, who are his almost inseparable companions & councillors, & the other grave personages who formed the embassy to us the preceding evening, rose & beckoned to us to follow them, which we did, to the outskirts of the town where they all sat down on the ground bidding us follow their example. This party I suppose form the King's privy council, for we always found them consulted on every important occasion.

Sibigho then asked us if we had made up our minds, to which we replied in the affirmative. We had naturally considered his message of last night and found our only alternative was to join him with, at least, a seeming good will, in which case we would no doubt be well used during our stay, or be compelled to go, when we might not have that respect shewn us which we hitherto had had. We told him that we would join him, but as the Mantatees had done us no harm we would fire nothing but blank cartridges, & stipulated further that he should promise not to take more cattle from the enemy than they had plundered him of. They cheerfully consented to our terms though we had reason to doubt their sincerity. Their eyes glistened with joy & the whole party shouted with one impulse Sinkly! Munati! [4] (excellent! good!) & in the height of their transports nearly pulled our noses off our faces. Very few more words passed on this subject. He only told us his army was ready & they should march tomorrow morning.

.   .   .

Augt. 25th. The King requested one of us to come up to the Kraal to look out the oxen he had promised us to ride on, but we found they were not riding oxen but merely pack bullocks, which were of no use to us as we only wanted one for each of ourselves & people to ride on, knowing that we could not keep up on foot with the Wanketsie army. We were now put to our shifts; we had only one horse left & that very poor, & we dreaded the fatigue of the march. We proposed at first

that Mr. B. & myself should ride & walk alternately & the people would be forced to trudge it all the way, when one of them told us that one of our draught oxen was an excellent riding one, so Mr. B. had it saddled up for himself & I mounted the horse.

When everything was ready we could not help smiling at the ludicrous appearance which our little party made on this important occasion. Mr. Biddulph was mounted on his war ox with his double barrel on his shoulder & his boat cloak bound in front to prevent his falling forward, & I on my Rosinante with an old horse pistol (for I had only one) fastened to the bow of my saddle without a holster case. The rest of my thunder & lightning was contained in a trusty old fowling piece which I bore in proud pomp on my right knee. Behind us followed 3 Hottentots, each with a good musket on his shoulder, & next to them came our interpreters Ias & Poloholo, the one with a gun & the other with an old Blunderbuss which closed our rear. [5]

The cloaths of our people, from the length of the journey and the bushy country thro' which we had passed, were reduced to tatters &, waving gracefully in the wind, answered all the purposes of Banners. Thus Hudibrastically equipped did we sally forth to conquer a mighty & warlike people who had been for upwards of 3 years the scourge & dread of all South Africa.

When we reached the top of Golgotha we found the army waiting for us. They rose and greeted us with becoming acclamations of joy & we advanced at their head in company with Sibigho. We could not help admiring the good order & discipline which prevailed among those people & the alacrity with which the Chief's orders were executed.

Their dress consisted of a panther's hide thrown carelessly over the shoulders;

[4] Sentle! Monate!

[5] "Our mustachios would have done honour to any officer in the Cape Corps." Bain's letter to *S.A.C. Advertiser.*

a lynx's skin, suspended round the neck & cut in an oval form, covered the lower part of the body. A white tuft of goat's hair made up in the shape of a sun & a plume of ostrich feathers crowned their heads which, from the way they were covered with Sibilo & fat, a good deal resembled a steel helmet when exposed to the rays of the sun. Each had a shield of white ox hide, generally with a black or brown spot in the middle, to which were fastened 3 to 6 assagais. It is suspended from the Chacka or Battleaxe which they carry over their left shoulders & dangles at their backs, the shafts of the assagais being upwards & the blades fixed in a pocket at the bottom of the shield.

.   .   .

Augt. 27th. The bags being filled with water we started at sunrise in the same manner as yesterday morning, & only proceeded a short way when the usual halt & semicircle were made, only with the difference that we observed small parties of men at regular distances from the main body seated under the trees. They were now preparing for battle, not the Chase. All being assembled Sibigho rose & called out Hey! to which a sort of suppressed grunt or hem (a sound difficult to describe) was coughed out by all the men at once as a mark of attention to the speaker. He then said "Silence, warriors!" & the grunt was repeated. Then waving his assagais over their heads pronounced "Maroomo!"[6] (which literally signifies Assagais, but is used on such occasions, according to our interpreter, metaphorically to express that nobody shall throw one away without making sure of killing an enemy). A whistle of applause thrilled thro' the ranks which was [undecipherable] succeeded by a dead silence, leaving us gazing at one another in admiration & surprise.

He commenced his harangue in words (as I imperfectly gleaned from our inter-

preter) something to the following effect:

"Bawanketsie warriors! The honor of your country is now at stake & you are called upon to protect it. Long, long have the scum & dread of the earth had possession of our finest fields, driven us from our once flourishing towns & are still feeding on the fattest of our flocks & herds. They have killed your late king, my father, who was the love of his subjects & the dread of his enemies. Shall we longer live in continual fear of such a scourge? No! the time is now come when we must rid ourselves of them for ever, that we may again restore peace to the world & claim its admiration as we were wont to do.

Fortune has favoured us by sending the Makooas to our country just as we were preparing to strike this decisive blow; but let not the brunt of the battle fall on them. Their thunder & lightning will strike terror on the enemy, but on your bravery alone do I trust. The Macooa are great Captains and have passed thro' our enemies to visit us; let them be witnesses of your courage that the fame of your glory may reach the most distant nations.

The Mantatees are numerous as the locusts of the field, but let not that discourage you, for the Bawanketsie have the hearts of lions." Here he was interrupted by a whistle of applause & he again proceeded: "Yes, the Bawanketsie alone have stemmed the torrent of the Makarie[7] (Mantatees) which swept from the face of the earth our once powerful neighbours, the Bamorootzie[8] and Bakweenie,[9] whose very names are now almost forgotten. Let them no more enter the territories of the sons of Meleta[10] where they butchered

[7] Makgare, another name for Mmantatisi.
[8] BaHurutshe, a Tswana tribe who once owned the country round Zeerust, Transvaal. Skilled workers in iron. Kurrechane (Kaditshwene) their capital was a very large town. Campbell, in *Travels in South Africa*, London, 1822, gives an attractive picture of the tribe before it was destroyed by the Mmantatisi and MaTebele.
[9] BaKwena, Tswana tribe. Settled north of the BaNgwaketse.
[10] Moleta, father of Makabba II and grandfather of Sebego.

[6] Marumo.

my renowned sire, Makkabba. Yes, his glorious name must rouse our hearts to vengeance! Revenge! Revenge! Revenge!"

So saying, with his eyes gleaming fire & in a fine theatrical attitude, he twirled his battleaxe in the air amidst the shrill plaudits of his host.

. . .

At sunset we bivouaced in a thick wood at a short distance from the enemy's town & no fires were allowed to be lit until the King returned about midnight from reconnoitring the position. Few of the people, however, availed themselves of this privilege, as they had no game to grill & were doubtless fatigued with their day's march & the gastronomical exercises of the preceding night.

The King was, notwithstanding, always on his legs examining everything of consequence with his own eyes, & indeed we were astonished at the precautions, foresight & military skill used by this intrepid Chief, which indicated a practical knowledge of his profession that would not have disgraced any European general. He slept none the whole night but conversed privately with his Captains on the best method of attack. In vain did we request him to inform us of his plans, our knowledge of which we said might prevent a deal of confusion in the hurry of battle, but the wary Chief, perhaps doubting the sincerity of the part we would play from our lukewarmness in joining him at the beginning, merely replied with a smile: "There will be no confusion but always time to execute my orders when I give them." Then turning coolly round continued his conversation in a whisper to his friends who surrounded him.

Augt. 28th. At 4 o'clock this morning we resumed our march in perfect silence &, leaving the thicket, entered a beautiful open vale that leads to the town of Letubaruba, whose vicinity became evident by the numerous tracks of cattle taking [the] place of those of elephants, etc.

Here the King sat down and formed his favourite semicircular phalanx. By the glimmering light of the waning moon their white shields & plumes were alone perceptible along the inside of the crescent. After the usual preliminaries of calling to order, Sibigho rose &, in an animated speech of some length but of purport similar to that of yesterday, addressed his army, to which they frequently testified their approbation, not by noisy shoutings or clapping of hands, but their usual singular note whistled thro' their teeth. After the King had concluded, several Captains harangued them & each in his turn received the whistle of applause.

Orders were now given for the attack. One division, headed by a brother of the Chief, was dispatched thro' a defile to the left, to which two of our men were attached much against our will, as we wished to be all together. Our will, however, was not taken into consideration by the despotic Chief, he very coolly telling us that he knew what he was doing & it was our duty now only to obey his orders!

I must own that I felt a little melancholy that our people, who had hitherto served us so faithfully, should thus be taken from us perhaps never to see them more, for we were as yet perfectly ignorant of the nature of the warfare which we were destined to take such an active part in.

Every pass was quietly taken possession of before we, with the main body headed by his majesty, commenced our movement in breathless silence down the valley. My friend & self were dismounted, as Sibigho ordered our ox to be kept in the rear lest its bellowing on smelling the cattle of the town might, like the geese in the Roman Capitol, warn the inhabitants of the presence of their enemies. We passed thro' a small kloof &, on reaching its summit, the faint streaks of dawn now becoming visible dimly discovered to us the devoted town of Letubaruba at our feet. It is situated in a hollow valley surrounded on all sides by hills of inconsiderable height.

One glance at its situation shewed the wisdom of the general, for the Wanketzee white shields were now plainly perceptible in every outlet with a large body in their rear, so that it was impossible for any one to escape. Our orders were to remain steadfastly by the King & not to fire until a signal should be given from the party that our two men accompanied.

When I looked round on the scene before me I could scarcely persuade myself that it was reality, but only the "baseless fabric of a vision." A shot from the opposite side, reverberating among the hills like thunder, & a most hellish war whoop simultaneously uttered by the whole Bawanketzee host soon convinced me to the contrary. A sudden rush was made upon the town, warriors enough being left to guard every pass, & with their battleaxes in hand they butchered every unhappy wretch which the terrific sound of our musketry caused to emerge from their huts.

We kept up a brisk fire & doubtless the King thought we did great execution, but I had told our people by no means to kill any of the poor wretches except in self defence & therefore our balls passed over the town which was now on fire in several places. The shrieks of the women & children were most heart-rending, for wherever they turned they were met by a bloody battleaxe or the dreadful sound of our thunder.

Sibigho stood by us calmly looking on and giving directions to his numerous *aides du camp* about securing of the cattle, which seemed on the whole to be the only aim in storming the place. Very little resistance was offered on the part of the enemy as they were taken so aback as to be quite unprepared, which shews great improvidence in such a marauding people then living in an enemy country. When the cattle were driven out the confusion in the town became great on account of the thick clouds of dust & the smoke from the burning huts, for the whole town was now in flames, that in endeavouring to avoid the fury of the assailants they jumped thro' the burning element where, in all probability, they were met by an uplifted Chacka [ax—ed.] which cleft their scull in twain. One poor boy about 8 years of age, having lost his mother, came running towards us as if to seek protection & my blood freezes still in my veins when I think of his reception. Our interpreter, a Bechuana doubtless inured to scenes of blood, advanced in front of our line & clapping his blunderbuss to the child's head shot him dead on the spot.

The cattle being now secured & the enemy, who had the good fortune to escape the Bawanketze Chackas, clambered up the hills glad to get off with their lives, casting a desponding look behind on the town, now a heap of ashes, the greatest part of their cattle and effects in the hands of the conquering Bawanketzie.[11]

[The manuscript journal ends here, but the following extract supplies further information.]

EXTRACT FROM THE LETTER WRITTEN BY BAIN TO THE SOUTH AFRICAN COMMERCIAL ADVERTISER

The victory was complete and was ascribed entirely to us; and we were hailed as mighty gods (Moonris Zoora) and their deliverers from the scourge of the Mantatees. Our noses were pulled at such a rate that I really thought they would have sent us home without them. Had fortune turned against them I make no doubt they would have murdered us on the spot as the cause of it. The Bakwain country, as laid down by Burchell, as well as the Bankwet and several others which he

11 "The Bawankets did not follow the fugitives, but were content with the rich booty which consisted of at least 2,000 head of cattle and a vast number of shields, assegais and battle axes, and a few sheep." From fragment of manuscript of Bain's letter to *S.A.C. Advertiser.*

merely had from hearsay are quite incorrect. Litabaruba is situated in the 24th degree of S. Latitude and the 7th of East Longitude. Makabba, the late king of the Bawankets, gave the unfortunate Mr. Cowan an escort to this town and the Bakweens escorted him to a powerful nation lying to the north east, called the Maglazielies, from which they proceeded to a tribe described as being near the coast and having long hair. The Bakween and the Bawankets suppose that they were murdered by the long-haired people as the murderers are described as being exceedingly savage.

On our return to Siloqualali we entered in triumph—the women singing and shouting for joy on hearing of our success —and we found everything right about our wagons, which we left in charge of the guard set over them by the king.

They sent us 82 head of cattle as our share of the spoil which we declined accepting, telling them we had merely assisted them through motives of friendship. This rather displeased him [Sebego] and he did not afterwards show us so much respect as before, no doubt taking it as a great affront.

After a journey of two months, in which we were frequently in danger with all our cattle dying of thirst from the great scarcity of water, we arrived here [Graaff-Reinet] safely on the 19th ultimo.

86 ANNA ELIZABETH STEENKAMP
THE GREAT TREK

Anna Elizabeth Steenkamp was a member of the famous Retief family. Pieter Retief was the foremost of the Voortrekkers—those Boers who moved from the Cape Colony inland to the high veld of the Transvaal and the plains of Natal in the decade after 1835. The article written by Anna Steenkamp first appeared in Cape Monthly Magazine *in September 1876 and has since become one of the best-known manifestoes of the Great Trek. The reader should remember, however, that this account was written some forty years after the events.*

This record is written for the sake of my relations, children and grandchildren, now still residing in the interior, in order that they may know for what reason their parents and grandparents have forsaken their mother country, and what anxiety and anguish, grief and pain, destitution and distress, by reason both of foes and fire, have befallen us, and have been the cause of many a sad sigh and bitter tear; whilst, nevertheless, amidst these trying

Anna Steenkamp, "Record or Journal of Our Migration from Our Mother Country to Port Natal," *Cape Monthly Magazine,* September 1876. Reprinted in John Bird, *Annals of Natal* (Pietermaritzburg: P. Davis and Sons, 1888), I, 459—468.

circumstances, we were being guided and guarded by our faithful God, our Father.

The reasons for which we abandoned our lands and homesteads, our country and kindred, were the following:

1. The continual depredations and robberies of the Kafirs [black South Africans —ed.], and their arrogance and overbearing conduct: and the fact that, in spite of the fine promises made to us by our Government, we nevertheless received no compensation for the property of which we were despoiled.

2. The shameful and unjust proceedings with reference to the freedom of our slaves: and yet it is not so much their

freedom that drove us to such lengths, as their being placed on an equal footing with Christians, contrary to the laws of God and the natural distinction of race and religion, so that it was intolerable for any decent Christian to bow down beneath such a yoke; wherefore we rather withdrew in order thus to preserve our doctrines in purity.

3. But it is unnecessary to mention anything further just now about these questions, as I am aware that you are acquainted with these matters; but I shall rather relate to you what occurred to us on our expedition. Two bodies of people had left before us. The foremost were the Taljaards and Liebenbergs, among whom the first sad massacre was perpetrated by the great Kafir king (Masilikatzi).[1] At this battle, Potgieter with forty men defeated fully a thousand Kafirs, but we were ourselves not in that band. The rumours of this massacre, however, were the cause of our leaving the colony all the sooner, in order to hasten to the assistance of our brethren. The massacre committed by Masilikatzi took place on 2nd September, 1836. Another troop under the leadership of G. Maritz, as well as my aged father, François Retief, departed from the colony on 15th November, 1836, and I and my family had to stay behind, as my husband was very ill; but on 5th May, 1837, we also left the colony, alone with our children, servants, four wagons, and cattle. Our departure from Zeekoe River was accompanied with many troubles; for I had a sick husband and a sick child to attend to, and was myself suffering from a bad cold. The most difficult part of all still was, that we had to bury our lead and gunpowder under ground every day, and to send for them by night with a wagon. The reason of this was that we had a great deal of ammunition, and there was a prohibition against leaving with it. At length with great danger and much trouble we crossed the Orange River, and

there I offered my thanks to God, because thus far He had helped us. Then to our misfortune we arrived among the Bastards [people of mixed blood—white Europeans and black Africans—later known as Griquas—ed.], who received us very brutally, saying they had the right and orders to rob and despoil us of everything: for this tribe has since long ago been known to be the greatest thieves and robbers in the world. Our servants deserted us, and the girls, although weak and delicate, were obliged to lead and drive the wagons, nay even to drive the cattle on through all these ungovernable tribes. Our company was not increased: we were only with four wagons. Nevertheless we were cheerful, cherishing the hope of better days, consoling our hearts and longing for gladder times. We had, however, still to travel through two kinds of Bastards, the Korannas and Boschjesmans, with the loss of a number of our cattle and horses. With joy and gladness we reached the Riet River, and there we found a multitude of people, who were the first Christians whom we had seen on our long journey. Here we delayed twenty days on account of my husband being too ill to proceed further on the journey; but scarcely was he better than we set out with our four wagons. We then came into a desolate country, without any wood or manure (for fuel), where the grass was so high that we could hardly find the children and the cattle. Here also we had bitterly cold weather, and heavy rains.

At last we reached King Maroko, and the Kafirs came to meet us by hundreds, surrounding our four wagons like two walls. At the mission-house we delayed a little, and the great King Moshesh, with his servant and the clerk of Maroko, came to look if we had any slaves or apprentices by us, in order to take them away from us. After we left Maroko we had to experience severe trials, as we could find no road, and for that reason we had to wander hither and thither, and could find no one to show us the right way and give us

[1] Umsilikazi.

instructions; but we saw abandoned kraals and encampments, and our cattle died in great numbers; and above all we were in a country destitute of wood, but full of deserted kraals, and here and there heaps of bones of tribes murdered and destroyed by Masilikatzi. Here there was an abundance of game of all kinds.

At length after four months' travelling we reached Sand River; but as we were quite on the wrong road, my son rode forward on horseback to see whether he could find anybody to show us the way, and to our great joy he succeeded on 24th August, 1838, to meet people; and on 25th I was delivered of my youngest child. Herein I perceived the truth of the word of the Lord, that when our needs are sorest He is nearest. Nevertheless we had not yet found the formed company of which Maritz was the leader, nor my father; but three days after the birth of my child, 28th August, Commandant Potgieter proceeded on his journey with all his company, and then we all came together.

It was, however, still too troublesome for us to travel forward with so many people, and for that reason we were compelled to pass through a burning country, where we were in great anxiety lest our children should be burned. A number of our cattle, and of others whole herds, were burned. In the course of our journey we travelled through the country of two kinds of Bastards, Korannas and Bushmen (Maroko and Moshesh). Now we had to go through the country of the great Masilikatzi, but as his power had been broken by Mr. Maritz we had nothing to fear from him.

When we had left the Sikonyela behind us, we met Mr. Piet Retief in the neighbourhood of Drakensberg with the first emigrants, as well as my aged father, François Retief, and the Rev. Mr. Smit. This caused us great joy, as we had in the first some one to execute our existing laws, and in the last-mentioned a minister to give instruction in God's word, to administer baptism and the holy sacrament, so that our religious service flourished.

Every Sunday and every evening there were public services, and this made our journey through the wilderness pleasant, seeing that the Lord had not forsaken us.

Mr. Maritz had gone on with a part of the emigrants; but we soon after left, under the command of Mr. Retief, as far as the great Drakensberg; and from there Mr. Retief departed, with five men, for King Dingaan [Shaka's successor—ed.], to get the land from him, by purchase or by exchange, and in this he succeeded.

I must now relate to you something about Sikonyela. Whilst we remained on the Drakensberg, Sikonyela was found guilty of theft and robbery; for he had sent his people, on horseback, with guns and clothed, to Dingaan to steal cattle. We were not aware of this; but when Mr. Retief came to the king, the latter asking him whether he was not afraid to visit himself, as he had stolen his (the king's) cattle, Mr. Retief replied, "No; I have not done so." "Then," said the king, "you have fired on my people; they tell me it is the Malungus (white people) who have done so." After Mr. Retief had cleared himself of guilt, Dingaan entertained him in a friendly manner. This was mere hypocrisy, as you will see from the sequel.

Mr. Retief then started for the Bay. When he left King Dingaan, the latter gave him two chieftains and some of his people to see if any of his cattle were with Sikonyela. Mr. Retief then rode with the Kafirs and a portion of his men to Sikonyela, and found the cattle with him, and delivered them to the two chieftains to hand them over to the king.

With great difficulty we passed over the Drakensberg, and we encamped before the Great Tugela, when the emigrants under Mr. Maritz had collected together. Then the council resolved that Mr. Retief, after having convinced the king of the above-mentioned robberies, should go to acquire the land from him, which was done. He left us, accompanied by sixty-three men and three children, besides the "after-riders."

When Mr. Retief came to the king, the

latter willingly gave him, as he had found the cattle at Sikonyela's, the country from the Tugela to the Umzimvubu as a present, according to the contract which was afterwards found with the persons who were murdered. Nevertheless, all the friendliness of Dingaan proves that he intended carrying out a cruel and fearful murderous design, which he actually accomplished on 11th February, by the tyrannical murder of Mr. Retief and sixty-six other men; and on 17th February, the Kafirs attacked us also. Oh! dreadful, dreadful night! wherein so much martyred blood was shed; and two hundred innocent children, ninety-five women, and thirty-three men were slain, and hurled into an awful eternity by the assagais of those bloodthirsty heathens. Excluding the servants, the number was over four hundred souls. Oh! it was unbearable for flesh and blood to behold the frightful spectacle the following morning. In one wagon were found fifty dead, and blood flowed from the seam of the tent-sail down to the lowest. Ah! how awful it was to look upon all those dead and wounded. The following day we fled altogether to another encampment at Doornkop, between the Tugela and the Bushman's River. The massacre was perpetrated between Blaauwkrantz and Bushman's River. Mr. Maritz was at Doornkop with the first emigrants. The Kafirs came in in force in the daytime, but were gallantly repulsed and driven off by Mr. Maritz; and as the river was full, and the Kafirs had to go across, a large number was killed, so that the river ran as red as blood.

I must also tell you, my dear children, how it was that the Kafirs could so easily perpetrate the massacre that night. It was on account of disobedience and imprudence: the greater portion of the people were on the mission, and others engaged in buffalo-hunting; others, moreover, were on the road to the Drakensberg to assist their families in coming down: so that the Kafirs found the women and children quite alone, and sleeping peacefully. Mr. Retief had cautioned us at Doornkop

to remain by each other till he came back, as he was ill at ease. He also wrote to us afterwards that we should not separate from each other; but the trouble we had with the cattle obliged many to proceed down the river with their families in small troops. We were alone, feeling secure and contented. Mr. Retief left his wife at Doornkop with Mr. Smit, and the Kafirs did not come there.

The day after our arrival there, the wounded (the women and children who were left) came; some on foot, some on horseback, and a portion in wagons. Our field-commandant, Mr. Piet Greyling, carefully provisioned and strengthened our encampment. He also took back our cattle from the Kafirs; that is to say, our sheep, as the oxen were across the river, which was full.

The commandant had the dead buried and the wounded attended to. On all sides one saw tears flowing, and heard people weeping by the plundered wagons, painted with blood; tents and beds torn to shreds; pregnant women and little children had to walk for hours together, bearing the signs of their hasty flight. Oh! how weary and fatigued were those women and children, and how terrible it was to see unborn children rent asunder by the murderous Kafirs. When the women came up to us, they fell upon their knees and thanked God for their deliverance out of the hands of the cruel tyrant. In our encampment there was nothing but lamentation and weeping. Every day we had to bury the dead bodies of the wounded. This spectacle, and the terrible circumstances, cannot be described by my pen.

In April our encampment was at Blaauwkrantz. There Field-commandant Piet Uys arrived. He went out with a commando, and perished with ten other men on the 10th May, 1838. The men who betrayed us, Stubbs and Blanckenberg, also went out on a marauding expedition to the Bay at the same time that our commando left; but the Kafirs flew round and murdered seventeen Englishmen, a number of Natal Kafirs, and also Stubbs; so that our betrayers fell into their own toils.

Thereafter, our whole force was assembled at the Blaauwkrantz River. Oh! my children, to live in so large a "laager [encampment—ed.]" of a thousand wagons is hard, and it is also injurious to cattle. In July our laager went as far as Bushman's River. Listen now, my children, to my sad misfortunes.

On 2nd February your beloved younger sister died. On the 11th February the commission was murdered, amongst whom were my uncle Retief, his two sons, and other relations. On the 17th February the great massacre occurred. On the 10th May Piet Uys, with ten of his men, perished. On 23rd July your dear father died, and many other of our nearest relations and acquaintances. The last cases of death were probably caused by the dampness of our encampment, for nearly every day we had rain, and we could wear no shoes on account of the mud.

On the 10th August we were again attacked by the Kafirs at Bushman's River. Their bands were stretched out by thousands as far as the eye could see. It was a terrible sight to witness. I cannot describe their number, for one would have thought that entire heathendom had gathered together to destroy us. But thanks and praise are due to the Lord, who so wonderfully has rescued us out of the hands of our numberless and blcodthirsty foes, and granted us the victory. Their foremost band wore clothes and had the guns of the killed, and swarmed down upon us, whilst the others surrounded us. Our number of fighting men was considerably diminished, for a portion was with Maritz at Tugela, and another portion had gone ahead to Port Natal, so that our strength consisted of only two field-commandants and two field-cornets, with their men. The names of the field-commandants and field-cornets were Joachim Prinsloo, Jacobus Potgieter, Johannes du Plessis, and Johannes de Lange. Thirty

of Plessis' men and also a portion of Prinsloo's were with our cattle at the Drakensberg, so that we had only a few men capable of bearing arms at our laager, and the heathen had entirely overwhelmed us had God suffered them to do so. Now you may imagine, my dear children, in what a state of anxiety we women were when we beheld the onslaught of the enemy. The majority of the women consisted of widows and orphans. For we could not imagine that so few people would gain the victory; but the Lord strengthened us and weakened our enemy. They rushed down on us in a circle till almost within range of our guns. Then they attacked us at different points, so that our men were obliged to walk one behind the other to shoot down the enemy, now at one and then at another corner of the encampment. We had arranged our cannon so that they could not break into it. The Kafirs kept us busy for two days and two nights, and constantly fired at us, but not one of our men received any injury from their bullets, and seeing that a multitude of theirs were killed in that conflict, and that they were severely defeated, they left us with a war-song, and fired charges as far as we could hear them. The second day our men went in pursuit of them with the view of recovering our cattle, but the horses were too few and almost too famished in the encampment, so that they were obliged to return, and the enemy retained our cattle; but we thanked God for the preservation of our lives, with the exception of the loss of one man, who was murdered whilst with his sheep, and my faithful female slave who had fled from the encampment. After this occurrence we departed for Tugela, as Maritz wished his men to get out of the mountain. We remained together, however, for six months. In the meanwhile your brother, François Marthinus Hattingh, had left for the interior in order to collect a commando, and also to get horses in order to take away our cattle from the enemy, for there was famine among those who had been ruined by the enemy; but we assisted each other until we were entirely deprived of means of subsistence.

I was also married a second time to a stranger, a widower, named Thomas Engenaar Steenekamp. Mr. Maritz died; Mr. Retief had been murdered; Mr. Uys had been slain. All our leaders had been killed, and we were as sheep without a shepherd. On 10th November my son arrived with his uncle, Andries W. J. Pretorius, who was then by the general vote appointed head-commandant. He thereupon collected a commando, and had a fight with the Kafirs. Through God's blessing the Kafirs sustained a defeat, whilst a large number of them perished, and five of our men were killed. After the battle we left the Tugela in January, 1839, and arrived here at Pietermaritzburg. I must tell you what occurred to me on this last journey.

We left on the 20th January, and on the 23rd of the same month, my son, François Marthinus Hattingh, was killed by lightning during a violent thunderstorm, while he was with his cattle, at the age of twenty-eight years, and left a widow and two children behind to deplore his loss. Oh! what a blow it was for me and his whole family when he was snatched away by death. He was a peaceful man, respected and esteemed by everyone, and deplored by all. But the hand of the Lord doth what He willeth, and with death there is no respect of persons.

Since our arrival here we lived a whole year in laagers, and in the last of them a sad misfortune occurred to us. On the 28th August, 1839, at nine o'clock in the evening, our encampment caught fire through a little servant girl lighting a candle; and some had already gone to bed when the fire broke out, but we were still busy, teaching the children. Suddenly a cry was raised of "Kafirs!" and we did not think otherwise than that our enemies had put the encampment on fire. As soon as the first house stood in flames, all the rest caught fire. The laagers were plentifully supplied with lead and gunpowder; for our father, Steenekamp, alone had a barrel containing six hundred pounds of powder, and the other houses were full of the same article, so that it was very dangerous to remain within the encampment. I fled with my twelve children out of the gate, as I was afraid of the fire and of the reported Kafirs, and went as far as the first hollow; further I could not go. Afterwards the other women followed me, and there we remained until the fire was burned out. Then I received information who the persons were that had perished in the fire; and people also told me that my husband was amongst the number: but this message gave me no anxiety, as I thought that it was impossible that the whole of us should have our lives spared. That night I had still more terrible thoughts: it was, in short, like unto the Day of Judgment; and the words of St. Peter occurred to my mind, when he says: "The day of the Lord shall come as a thief in the night: in which the heavens and earth shall pass away with loud noises, and the elements shall burn and be destroyed; and the earth and the works which are within it shall be burnt." The most terrible part still of that night was to see when the gunpowder caught fire, and the pieces of the wagons around us flew about in all directions. As soon as the danger was passed, we betook ourselves again to the laager to assist the injured and bury the dead. When the first house caught fire, there were ten men to quench the flames, and when the gunpowder ignited three of them were killed, and the others severely injured. A trading wagon containing a large quantity of powder also caught fire. Two men attempted to save it, whereby one was so severely injured that he died immediately afterwards, and the other lived a short time. The gunpowder wagon was in the middle of the encampment. Two white children and two little Kafirs were burned to death in the house. The following day we found nine dead and twelve wounded, lying in the ashes. The heat was so intense that we could not take out the dead that night. Everything belonging to us was roasted and broiled: four wagons, nine "salted" fat oxen, as also fat, soap, salt, sugar, &c., were consumed, for we were wealthy, and provided with everything. Thirteen houses also were burned down. We had to sit by the fire the whole night, without clothing or bedding. Some of the wives and mothers were weeping, for they had seen their husbands and sons perishing in the fire. We, poor women and little children, had to struggle through many serious trials on account of the cold and the enemy, as we lay by night beside the houses; but to remain by so great a fire, wherein so many people were burned, was a still greater hardship; and the night was bitterly cold. In the morning of the following day, we bound the bones in a counterpane and buried them in a hole. There were three Steenekamps, two Potgieters, one Deventer, two children, and two Kafirs burned: and two Steenekamps severely injured, of whom my husband was one, but by God's goodness he recovered.

Here now, my dear children and friends, you may see with what sad misfortunes I had to struggle in my journey of twenty months before we had a home or a shelter. Shortly after the fire we were visited by measles, through which a great many deaths occurred. My old husband and myself had alone to provide for twenty-three children and grandchildren who were laid up, and who had to be attended by us, without house or tent, in only a wagon. Several days I was so weak through these exertions that I could hardly endure it; but God be praised, who has strengthened me in body, so as to bear the burdens which He has laid upon us; so then I was able to perform my duties.

For about two years after this we lived quietly, securely, and at peace with all the surrounding tribes, so that every one was again beginning to acquire the means of subsistence; for the country is very fertile, so that one could very well make a living, if not visited by wars or other misfortunes. But to our grief and sorrow the peace was again disturbed, and all our dreams of prosperity and happiness vanished; for on 6th May, 1842, Captain Smith [the commander of British forces—ed.] arrived in the bay of Port Natal, and on the 25th of that month he attacked us. He came along the shore of the sea with pieces of cable twisted round the axles of his gun-carriages. Here, also, my darlings, I wish you to see how the Lord has visibly assisted our men; for in spite of all the treachery displayed in this war, and all the heavy ordnance brought to bear against us, five men only were killed, whilst two were murdered by the Kafirs. Women and children were stripped of their clothes, and had to fly naked. Farms and lands were laid waste by the heathens, and again much cattle was taken from us by the Kafirs, so that we, through the unceasing thefts of the Kafirs, again fell into poverty. On 15th July, the first Cloete [British commissioner—ed.] arrived at Pietermaritzburg, and made peace with eleven persons, and fixed that day to be celebrated as a festival of happiness for us and for our children. On 9th May, 1843, the second Cloete arrived here, and we were fated to be deprived of the land which we had earned and bought: that was the satisfaction promised us.

But, my dear friends and children, I may finally mention, that if everything remains in the same unfortunate position as it is already, we shall be completely ruined; and it is possible that, after a few months, you will meet with very few of your kindred at Port Natal, for we are entirely impoverished, and wish to travel inland, if God grants us health and His blessing.

Your affectionate Mother and
Grandmother,
(Signed) ANNA ELIZABETH
STEENEKAMP
(*née* RETIEF).

87 JAMES CHAPMAN
THE BOERS AND THEIR ATTACK ON KWENA

Shortly after the British and the Transvaal Voortrekkers concluded the Sand River Convention in 1852, by which the British renounced any alliances with African peoples north of the Vaal River and agreed not to provide them with firearms, the Transvaalers attacked the Tswana state of Kwena, then ruled by Sechele. The attack had repercussions in the Ngwato state to the north. James Chapman was perhaps the only white non-Afrikander to see David Livingstone's quarters immediately after the destruction, because Livingstone himself was away at the time and never returned to them. Chapman's account is, therefore, of importance, in light of the extensive and partisan histories that followed the Boer attack. The argument might be advanced that Chapman had anti-Afrikander prejudices, but he did have a fairly intimate knowledge of Afrikander attitudes and way of life and had many friends among the Afrikanders.

James Chapman (1831–1872) traveled extensively in the western part of southern Africa in what is now Bechuanaland, South-West Africa, Zambia, and Rhodesia. In 1852 he almost forestalled Livingstone by three years in the discovery of the Victoria Falls, but African political disputes prevented his passage down the Zambezi. Chapman spoke Tswana and was a keen observer of the African political scene during his travels. He became a friend of Sir George Grey, Governor of the Cape, who acted as his patron. Chapman was elected a Fellow of the Royal Geographical Society in 1867, but by that time he was in poor health and was ruined financially. In 1870 he went to the diamond fields, where he died two years later.

On the 15th of October we were delighted to be under way, steering for Sechelli's Town, which, after several days' march through heavy sands and dense forests, in parts well stocked with game, we reached on the 28th. Wirsing and I proceeded to Sechelli's residence on horseback, riding forward the last stage through rugged glens and among rocky hills, never venturing to move faster than a walk. We found the chief at his residence, perched on a hillock composed of blocks of sandstone, loosely piled upon each other, a fit abode for baboons only.

Sechelli, chief of the Bakwains, a tribe mustering about 500 men, stands about 5 ft. 10 in. high, has a pleasing countenance, and is rather stout. He was dressed in

From James Chapman, F.R.G.S., *Travels in the Interior of South Africa, Comprising Fifteen Years' Hunting and Trading; with Journeys Across the Continent from Natal to Walvisch Bay, and Visits to Lake Ngami and the Victoria Falls* (London: Bell and Daldy; Edward Stanford, 1868), I, 112–124.

moleskin trousers, a duffel jacket, a wide-awake hat, and military boots. In address and behaviour Sechelli is a perfect gentleman. He can read and write, having learnt within the last few years, and is an accepted member of the Kuruman [mission station—ed.] church. He was instructed by Dr. Livingstone, who lived with him for four or five years. Sechelli is said to be very quick at learning, and anxious to substitute more civilized customs among his tribe in the place of their own heathenish practices. He is also said to be good-natured and generous. He presented us with a fat ox for slaughter, a custom prevailing among all the tribes that can afford it.

Sechelli at once pronounced us to be Englishmen; and having corroborated the intelligence we had already heard from Sekomi respecting his disasters, he apologised for not being able to receive us as he would like; but he entertained us with roast beef, sweet and sour milk, served in clean dishes, and with silver spoons, also with sweet earth-nuts; and while we were doing justice to his hospitality, a man stood fanning away the flies with a bunch of white ostrich feathers. His loss, he informed us, was sixty-eight men killed of his own tribe, besides a number of women, and between 200 and 300 children carried away captives. He lost, also, about 1500 head of cattle, and several thousand sheep and goats. For his cattle he seemed not to care so much, although his people were starving. He hoped to be able to replace them by the profits of huntings for ivory; but his people felt sorely the loss of their children. Ninety wagon-loads of corn had been carried off by the Boers, and the rest they had burnt in his town. Besides his own property, they had carried off several wagons, oxen, and other property belonging to English gentlemen at that time travelling to the lake.

From Sechelli we learnt that the war originated with Maselleelie, chief of the Batkatla tribe at Mabotoa, who had often been promised by the Boers that if he supplied them with a number of servants he would be exempted from further demands; but on giving one supply after another, still more was demanded, in spite of the promises made him. At length he refused, and became surly, thinking probably, with many others of the natives, that the late fever had so diminished the numbers of the Boers that he could successfully resist their authority. The Batkatla chief having ascertained, however, that the Boers intended to punish him, and being an arrant coward, fled to Sechelli for protection, it being a custom amongst those races that when one tribe flies to another and solicits protection it must be given; so that on the Boers demanding that Maselleelie should be delivered up, Sechelli refused, saying he "could not do it unless he was to cut open his own bowels and let them fall out."

Most of the people of Sechelli's tribe were out during the day grubbing for roots, their only food at present. Famine, "the meagre fiend," that "blows mildew from between the shrivelled lips," had already made great havoc among them. Several mothers had followed the Boers home, and, hiding themselves during the day, endeavoured at night to steal away their children; a few only had succeeded and returned.

On the 1st of November we obtained a guide from Sechelli to conduct us to the main road, our wagons having been brought since our own arrival up to his town. We accordingly departed, and at night overtook some emaciated Bakwains, roasting the roots they had gathered during the day. I ate one of these roots, but I thought I should have died from the effects it produced, creating a lather like soap, and blistering the inside of my mouth in a few minutes. I drank water to cure it, but that only aggravated the symptoms. The pain I suffered was at last allayed by putting some fat into my mouth.

Next day we travelled still south, and reached Kolobeng in the forenoon. This is the site of the town where Dr. Livingstone lived with the tribe. His house had been pillaged, and presented a melancholy picture of wanton destruction. The Boers had taken away everything that was valuable to them in the shape of furniture, utensils, and implements, and destroyed some hundreds of volumes of Sechuana Testaments, and other religious works and tracts, the leaves of which still lay scattered for nearly a mile in every direction. Even the window and door frames had been taken out, and the floor was strewed with bottles of valuable medicines, the use of which the Boers did not understand. The town where Sechelli was attacked, and which was burnt to the ground, a few miles from Kolobeng, presented a melancholy scene of desolation, bestrewn with the unburied carcases and bleaching bones of the natives who fell.

In the afternoon we started from Kolobeng, and, traversing the side of a very high mountain, the next day pushed on again.

.   .   .

By the fountain, and about some hundred yards from where I lay, stood a solitary but dense bush of the Waght-en-beetje (wait-a-bit) kind, and about ten minutes after, to my great surprise, about thirty savages, armed with spears, shields, and knobkerries, emerged from the bush. They came on, eyeing me with great suspicion, and inquiring whence I came; but on learning that I came from Sechelli's, they seemed satisfied; and from what I could understand they had heard of our being on the way from "Old Booy," whose wagon had preceded us a couple of days. Otherwise these fellows would probably have put an end to my travels, having been placed here by the chief for the purpose of cutting off spies or straggling parties of Boers.

The next day Wirsing and I left the wagons to follow, and proceeded on horseback to Mr. Edwards's station at Mabotoa, where, arriving in the afternoon, we were hospitably entertained with the first food we had eaten for three days, except a few gwarrie berries, which had made us sick. Having heard the news, and been shown all the damage done to Mr. Edwards's property by the Boer commando, we passed on to Mr. Inglis's station at Matebe, where we were also kindly received, and reached Vilgoen's place on the 5th of November, greatly to the astonishment of the Boers, who had long given us up as dead, and who overwhelmed us with inquiries about the movements of the natives, of whose attacks they were under great apprehension—wondering by what miracle we, having ventured to go to Sechelli's, had come away unhurt.

.   .   .

Having conveyed incidentally the results of some of my observations on the habits and manners of the Boers, I leave the reader to review in his own mind, as well as he is able to do from these inadequate notes, their past and present condition, and the degenerating tendency their daily course is taking. This arises partly from their nomadic life, their natural taste for that wild and roving state of existence in preference to any other, and their frequent collision and hostilities with the natives, for whom their hatred and contempt seems to have become quite inherent, and has been and is exaggerated in proportion as the tribes meet with sympathy from the Christian world.

It must I think be admitted, if such a man as Judge Watermeyer is an authority, that the first trekking of the Boers was not an act forced upon them by the British government, but the spontaneous inclination of a people fond of a roving life, and wishing to escape the control of law—a feeling which was already in operation during the time of their own Dutch government, and from the very beginning of the colony, and that in those days already inroads were made upon the territory of Hottentots and Kaffirs.

According to Judge Cloete, it will further be seen that the great impetus given to the trekking of the Dutch farmers commenced seriously after the merited condemnation to the gallows, by British authority, of some of their countrymen for acts of a criminal nature. These and other acts admit of no palliation. However much we may regret the necessity of such extreme measures, nobody will dare to dispute the legality of the punishments inflicted, which were only similar to many that have at various times occurred in England and Ireland, and which would very likely have been dealt more stringently upon rebellious Englishmen. The act of hanging the Boers on "Slagter's Nek" was a very painful necessity, but at the same time will never reflect dishonour on the British name, although it may excite pity for the sufferers, and their unfortunate relations who saw the sad end of their foolish and misguided countrymen.

It will probably not be denied that, on the part of the many Boers who have left the colony since [1835—ed.] the British administration, there were some *real* causes of complaint amongst many fancied grievances. Through a change of ministry in England, or a change of governors in the colony, it has happened that faith has not always been kept with some of the colonists, British as well as Boers, but it has been the peculiar failing of succeeding governors, as well as secretaries of state for the colonies, to upset, upon first coming into office, all the good work their predecessors have done.

Cases of unwarranted aggression on the part of Kaffirs towards the colonists have also transpired, such as may well wring the heart of many an honest farmer —English as well as Dutch. But even in these matters, when we come to look back into the first causes of things, and to review the many injustices that have been done to the native tribes of South Africa in the beginning, and take into consideration the unforgiving and unforgetting disposition (the great characteristic) of a savage, we cannot wonder at his persevering hatred towards the white man, however much we may pity the innocent, and, as it were, modern colonist, made the scapegoat for the sins of a former generation, and suffering grievously in the loss of their property and their friends at the hands of a savage and ruthless but, it has been asserted, in many respects still a noble enemy. The native races, it must in justice be allowed, have had cause for their hatred to the white man, and, as I have before remarked, a Kaffir may forget an injury for a time, but he never forgives. It is a national characteristic, and until their nationality is utterly destroyed this prominent feature will never be eradicated.

Vacillating as the government of this colony has ever been, there was one remarkable feature which had hitherto always pervaded British rule, and that was, the earnest solicitude it evinced for the welfare of the native tribes, as well as the desire it had shown to regain their confidence, and the inclination to redress their wrongs; but in one short year a blow was struck that has proved, as it will continue to prove, an injury to British subjects, a disgrace to a civilized and Christian gov-

ernment, and the bane to the British name in South Africa. A high commissioner, inexperienced in the affairs of the colony, in the person of Sir George R. Clerk, was entrusted to break up Her Majesty's government in the Sovereignty (now Free State)—a task which he is said to have performed with a tact and precision that did him great credit. This was in truth the greatest act of cruelty and injustice, not alone towards natives, but towards Europeans, that any government could have been guilty of, and was virtually equivalent to the discarding a great number of Her Majesty's faithful and loyal subjects! These men strongly remonstrated against the act, but too late, and their voices were too feeble. They indeed sent to England two delegates to represent their grievances, in the persons of Dr. Frazer and the Rev. A. Murray, jun., but it has never transpired satisfactorily in what the labours of these gentlemen resulted. It may be asserted that the orders Sir George R. Clerk received were imperative; but if he had represented the feelings of the people to the home government, and remonstrated with them, he would have done humanity a service, saved a jewel in the British crown, and gained honour for himself by advocating the retention of the Sovereignty. By leading people to believe that he was, if anything, in favour of retention, he misled them, so that they had no chance of remonstrating until the act was done; and this piece of injustice, unprecedented in the history of civilized nations, has not even been equalled by the Trans-Vaal Boers. From such humiliating injustice and pusillanimous behaviour on the part of a government to its own people—an act perpetrated by a government which, above all others, makes pretension to be the most humane and just towards its subjects, the protector of the oppressed, and the defender of the whole world against slavery—we must recoil in horror and hide our faces with shame. It is indeed a pity that the fair fame of our beloved sovereign should be compromised by a transaction which, to those who regard it from a distance, may seem of so trivial a nature, and should thereby receive in this colony an enduring blemish, brought about, we believe, by the misrule or misrepresentations of the individual or individuals employed to carry out this cruel and unwise policy.

Having alluded to the great change of feeling on the part of all the native tribes in South Africa—unfavourable to the English—I may mention that it is principally resulting from the injustice of the treaties made with the Boers, by which the natives are debarred from getting gunpowder and firearms (to them the *necessaries* of life as well as to the Boers), while every provision is made for the Boer getting as much as he requires. Native tribes within and out the colony, who are known only by their fidelity to Britain in her time of need, and were taught by us to fight against those very Boers who had rebelled against their queen and given so much trouble, are now spurned for their loyalty, and not alone spurned and discarded most ungraciously, but oppressed in the most arbitrary and ungrateful manner that ever a people were.

As soon as the tenor of the Sand River Treaty became known to the natives, and the subsequent abandonment of the Sovereignty, the news spread like wildfire from tribe to tribe, not alone along the whole border of British and Boer dominions, but even into the interior to the Bamanwato, Lake Ngami, and even to the Zambesi river, and meetings were held between the Griqua, Basutos, Barolong, Batlapies, Bakwain, Bahurutsi, Bamanwato, Baselika, and many other tribes: treaties were made between them for mutual protection and defence against the white man—Englishmen in particular— who seemed now to prove themselves the true oppressors of the black. By these treaties they are still bound to each other, nearly from one side of the continent to the other, and if any Kaffir war had unfor-

tunately broken out after this crisis, woeful would have been the consequences to the northern parts of this colony, and the Trans-Vaal and Free State in particular. As it was, many travellers were handled roughly, and, being questioned about the strange and dishonest policy of their government, were overwhelmed with shame. Much is due to the missionaries of Kuruman and other parts for the part they took, not in palliating or exculpating the policy of government (which they could not in justice do), but in seeking to alleviate the pain it inflicted, by expressing a conviction, prompted by their own hopes, that these proceedings would be disapproved of at home: they were, however, grievously disappointed. Time has, indeed, softened the feeling of the natives to a considerable extent, and much praise is due to the more enlightened and liberal rule of the present government, which has in many cases, by its acts, given the natives reason to hope for better days: and but for this some sad tragedy would have darkened the pages of modern South African history.

To return, however, to the Boers of the Trans-Vaal, on whose probable future, their prospects of an improved state of civilization, and the chances of a prosperous and useful career, I may perhaps be expected to say something. This I shall briefly enter upon, but with great diffidence, as it is a subject that ought much rather to come from one skilled in politics and prophecy than myself.

In the present state of society in the Trans-Vaal, it seems to me that as there are many ways (although sometimes uncertain) of easily attaining a livelihood and a competency, emigrants will find their way thither from the colony; but the treatment hitherto has been such as to exclude enlightened foreign immigration, and rather to encourage the introduction of disaffected Dutch farmers from the colony, many of whom have recently sold their farms there, and, with their flocks and servants, trekked into what they consider a free country (because exempt from British rule, which gives equal rights to white and black—an equalization which they cannot conceive to be just), where they can obtain a title to a 6000 acre farm for 2s. 6d. Beyond this, they give only encouragement to British deserters from Bloemfontein, or from Natal, because these are often useful as bricklayers, carpenters, or schoolmasters, and are compelled by their peculiar position to work for almost any terms offered to them, which generally consist of little more than their wretched food, a hut to sleep in, and concealment from their pursuers, if any should be in search of them. Hollanders were at one time in great favour with them; but since the defalcations of one or two, who imposed seriously upon the credulity of the Boers by representing themselves emissaries from the King of Holland, &c., they are utterly at a discount.

I have often thought that as European immigrants, and especially missionaries to the native tribes, have met with so much opposition from the Boers in these quarters, it is a pity that missionary societies, instead of quarrelling with the Boers in their endeavours to instruct the natives, have not rather turned their attention and their means to the advancement and instruction of the Boers themselves, who at the time I speak of had not one permanent clergyman amongst them, and generally no better schoolmaster than a British deserter fresh from the ranks to teach their progeny the *Dutch* language. In other countries missionaries have become willing martyrs to the Christian cause; and if the missionary societies had but taken half the pains to instruct the Boers first, and spent as much money in edifying and enlightening them during the last twenty years as they have done for the natives, they would now have reaped by this time a glorious harvest, not alone from the white populations thay had reclaimed from a retrograding state, but in the good fruit that that glorious harvest would

again have yielded. The Boers of the Trans-Vaal then would not only have by this time been perfectly civilized themselves, but many of them might have gone forth pioneers of civilization, carrying the Gospel into the dark regions, and have proved a blessing to South Africa, instead of carrying destruction and desolation through the land. Real Christianity infused into the bosom of the Boers would have done away with that feeling of superiority with which the white man is prone to look down upon the black races, their contempt for whom would thus be eradicated, and, as a necessary result, slavery in every form would be abolished. Until this is done, it appears to me that no real substantial improvement will take place. They must be taught to believe first. At present ninety out of every hundred will not believe that the soul of a black man is esteemed by the Creator equal to a white man's, and a feeling of this kind was manifested only a few days ago, even within the borders of this colony, when some white men declined sitting on a jury with men of colour; but the judge, though a descendant of a Dutch colonist himself, to his honour be it said, reproved them in a very laudable and becoming manner.

In the present unsettled state of the Trans-Vaal country, missionary influence will do great good if exerted first to promote the refinement of the Boers themselves, and soften down their peculiar prejudices. In this manner they will gain the confidence of the natives, and break that chain of alliance which, since the giving up of the Sovereignty, has been formed amongst the native tribes on their immediate borders. Their *real* position needs but, I am sure, to be made known to their fellow-countrymen and relations in the Cape (amongst whom we have so many noble examples of the great and powerful advantages of education), and they will, I feel confident, use their utmost exertions and influence amongst the many members of the Dutch Reformed Church, to whom they are bound by the ties of faith and relationship, to aid in promoting the education of the Trans-Vaal youths, by sending thither the necessary means, ministers, and teachers. In so fruitful a region, every description of farmers and mechanics can do well, and such people would find their way into a peaceable country, but that in the present state of things they are never certain of what they possess, for various reasons, which will have been gleaned throughout the perusal of this journal. Missionaries to preach to the Boers, and to instruct their children,

might make them in a few years all useful and intelligent members of society, and thus we might, at no distant period, hope to see these very men, now so narrow and selfish in their ideas, confer benefits upon the natives by teaching and instructing them, and sending missionaries from among themselves (as some of the native tribes have long done) into the dark regions beyond. In the hope that this may yet be their destiny, we may look forward trustfully to happy days for our expatriated fellow-colonists.

88 NEWSPAPER ACCOUNT
THE GOVERNOR AND THE TEMBOOKIES

This account, published in the newspaper Queenstown Representative, *is less important as an example of Cape frontier policy, whose twists and turns were highly complex and confusing at the time, than as a verbatim recording of the dialogue between white officials and Africans on the question of the role of the chieftain under European rule.*

Wednesday, November the 22nd, 1865, will be remembered by the Tembookies as long as they remain a people; for that day witnessed the deposition of their chiefs, the substitution of English for native law, and the abolition of the office of Tembookie agent. This startling revolution, which, however, only concerns the Tembookies within, and not those beyond the boundary of, the colony, was effected by the civil commissioner of the district, C. D. Griffith, Esq., who quietly declared that this was the will of the governor, and henceforth it would be law.

As soon as the civil commissioner received his final instructions from Capetown, he communicated with Inspector Gilfillan, of the Frontier Armed Mounted

"The Governor and the Tembookies," *Queenstown Representative,* November 1865. Reprinted in W. C. Holden, *The Past and Future of the Kaffir Races* (London, 1866), pp. 393–402.

Police, at present stationed at Glen Grey, who immediately sent messages to the different chiefs and head men, calling upon them to attend at Glen Grey, and receive a message from the governor. At first it was intended that the gathering should take place on last Saturday; but it was found that it would be impossible to get the people together so speedily, and Wednesday was the day ultimately fixed upon.

From the first streak of dawn, the people in all parts of the location were in motion, forming into companies under their respective chiefs and head men, mustering as imposing a force as possible, and hastening to the place of rendezvous. One of the first of the natives to arrive on the ground was the great chief—or perhaps it would be more correct to say chieftainess—Nonesi, who was attended by a goodly cavalcade, by several of the inferior chiefs, and by an umbrella bearer, who was busily engaged in shielding her sable majesty's delicate complexion from the rays of the sun, which on Wednesday were extremely fierce. As it is usual to describe the dresses worn by royal personages on great occasions, we may state, for the information of the curious, that Nonesi was attired in a sky-blue dress, which had evidently seen better days; a mantle, also of sky-blue, and also somewhat faded; a black riding hat, trimmed with brown ostrich feathers; and Balmoral boots. The royal petticoats were of white, rendered somewhat dingy by use; and, unless her Majesty's stockings were of the very hue and texture of her skin, we may safely affirm, from certain glimpses of the royal understandings with which the wind favoured us, that she wore none at all. The effect of Nonesi's somewhat magnificent "get-up" was slightly marred by the fact that she insisted on riding astride, instead of in the orthodox feminine fashion; but this gave a dash of piquancy to the affair which partially redeemed its want of dignity.

Very soon after the arrival of the great chief the plain in front of the old Mission station and school buildings began to swarm with life. Troop after troop of Kaffirs galloped up, all having some appearance of military discipline, and all armed with formidable knobkerries, with the exception of the head men and chiefs, who generally carried assagais. The majority of the natives were extremely well mounted, many of them, nevertheless, on mares that had recently foaled. The foals in these cases followed their dams, and, as they ran, set up a whinnying that, although dissimilar, in some way reminded those who listened to it of the cries of children parted from their mothers, and longing to reach them.

At one time, the scene was not only animated, but highly interesting. Nonesi, surrounded by her immediate followers, was engaged in earnest conversation; the troops of Kaffirs that had already arrived

were knee-haltering their horses; others were galloping up at full speed; while others again were pouring down a mountain pass at some distance from the station: those at the bottom of the pass appeared to be but a few inches in height, while their comrades at the top were mere dark specks thrown out into strong relief by the deep, dark, beautiful blue of the unclouded sky.

The footmen were not by any means as numerous as those who came on horseback; but they formed a goodly company nevertheless, and probably numbered five hundred men; of the horsemen there could not have been less than a thousand; and, by some people, this estimate was nearly doubled. For our own part, we think that a total of fifteen hundred natives will be somewhere near the mark. Of Europeans, there were, perhaps, five-and-twenty on the ground; but not one of them bore the slightest mark of authority, with the exception of Inspector Gilfillan, and one or two of his subordinates, who were in uniform.

At about half-past twelve o'clock, the civil commissioner took his seat in the porch of the church. He was supported by Inspector Gilfillan and Mr. Liefeldt—the latter acting as interpreter; the remaining Europeans grouped themselves about him; and the Kaffirs were invited to draw near. Nonesi, for whose accommodation a chair was provided, came first, and was speedily followed by her chiefs, counsellors, and people. The chiefs and counsellors sat on forms, placed right and left of Nonesi; the people, squatting on the ground, formed themselves into a huge semicircle, while at the rear of all were a few who stood upright to listen to the message of the great chief, the representative of their "mother," Queen Victoria.

To persons used only to meetings of whites, to crowds of English people, or of colonists, it was strange to observe the decorous silence, the apparent indifference of this crowd of half naked savages, who, armed with knobkerries as they all were, listened with perfect gravity and respect to the fiat that dethroned their chiefs, and at one blow declared unlawful all their cherished customs. The natural courtesy of these barbarians would put to shame half of the polished but constrained civilities of nations long accounted civilized, refined, and polite.

When all, chiefs and people, had taken their respective places, the civil commissioner, addressing the great multitude before him, said: "I have sent for you Tembookies, that I may make you acquainted with the governor's instructions as to your position in the Tembookie location on this side of the Indwe [River —ed.]. The governor's instructions to me are as follows: 'All chiefs remaining on this side of the Indwe are no longer to have any authority in their tribe.' "

At this portentous announcement there was a movement of surprise, slight almost as the motion of the leaves of the forest when touched by the softest breath of the summer wind; but this evidence of emotion almost instantly subsided, and a profound stillness took its place.

The civil commissioner went on: "I have to tell you also that all alike, chiefs and people, without exception, are to be dealt with under the colonial law, and treated in every respect as British subjects; and therefore all matters in dispute among you are to be decided by the magistrate in Queenstown, and not by your chiefs at all. This is the message which I have to communicate to you from the governor with regard to the position of those of you, whether chiefs or people, who choose to remain in the location on this side of the Indwe."

There was a long pause here; the people were still perfectly quiet; the chiefs apparently utterly indifferent to the whole matter. Nonesi, perplexed and thoughtful, took some long pulls at her pipe, and occasionally exchanged a few words in a low tone with her counsellors.

"And now, Nonesi," said the civil commissioner, addressing the great chief, "it is to you I speak. A complaint has been lodged with me by a Tembookie, who says that you sent some of your people to seize an ox of his, and had it slaughtered. You had no right to seize that man's property under any plea. Your customs are abolished. You have no authority to take anything belonging to any man without an order from a judge, or from a magistrate, or from a police officer. And those people who were sent by you to take the ox will have to appear in Queenstown, to answer the charge of robbing the man who was the owner of the ox. I want all the people to understand that it will be no excuse for them to say that they were sent by the chief to do any act contrary to the colonial law. The law will not recognise that as an excuse; and any man who commits a crime under any circumstances will be tried for it, and will suffer the penalty the law imposes. This is the message that I have to give you."

This announcement was succeeded by a long pause. At length an old man, in the thick of the crowd, exclaimed: "Your speech is about two or three matters. Cut them up and let us talk about them separately."

The civil commissioner: "I have explained that no one in the location has any right to exercise authority: that Nonesi did exercise authority; and was wrong in doing so."

An old man: "Who ate that man up?"

The civil commissioner: "I do not know; but you must understand that there can be no other chief but the governor in the colony. As you remain in the colony you must put up with colonial law, which is to recognise no other authority but that of the governor, and of the people he appoints to act under him."

A head man: "What is the cause of this sudden change? What have we done that we should be visited with the governor's anger?"

The civil commissioner: "All the chiefs agreed to accept the governor's terms, and go across the Indwe, and afterwards nearly all refused to do so; still I have not come here to answer any questions that you may put to me in this way, but simply to tell you what are the governor's instructions. If you have anything you wish to say to the governor, tell me, and I will represent it to him, and get his answer: but I will not argue with you."

Zenzwa, a chief, addressing the people, said: "You have heard what the magistrate has told you; and if you have anything to say against it, you had better go home and think it over, and then get ready your reply."

At this juncture, a long conversation took place between the principal Kaffirs as to whether they should reply at once, or delay their answer. Nonesi spoke with some energy, and her temper was plainly ruffled. Eventually the chief Lumko asked: "What offence are we guilty of, that such a thing as this should happen to-day? We have always thought, for years past, that we were under English rule; why are we thus treated?"

The civil commissioner: "I have told you that I cannot answer your questions. I have not come here to argue the matter, but to carry out the governor's instructions."

Umlanjane: "I cannot see my way through this. Mr. Griffith has come here to give us our new law, and why cannot we ask any questions?"

One of the crowd: "Why should our chiefs be taken from us? Why should they be deprived of their authority? We have lived a long time in the country. Some little chiefs and their people have gone away; but why then should authority be taken away from the chiefs who remain? This is the country of our fathers. The fathers of the chiefs were chiefs in the time of our fathers; and why, then, should we be so hardly treated?"

Nonesi: "I am an old chief, one of an old race. I was Umtirara's mother, and I belong to government. I have always been loyal. I was here under Warner; and when he left us he left his son behind.

When his son was going away, I tried to prevent it; but the governor would not listen. I am the mother of the great chief Queya; he is away from here, but I do not want to go away. I never agreed to cross the river; and it is not known to any one what I have done that the governor should be angry with me. Why, magistrate, do you speak in such a manner to me? If I have been guilty of any fault, let me know my fault, and then tell me that you will drive me over the river, or deprive me of my authority. I am a chief; why should I be less than a chief? Why should I be driven across the river? I am an old woman; I have been here since I was a child; I have brought up children here; and some of them have died before me, and their graves are here. I have been living with my own people in my own country, and have done nothing to make the governor deal so harshly with me. What have I done? The Tembookies are a large nation. My own people, the people over the river, and the people of Queya, my son, all consider themselves under the English government. Why, then, are we called together here to receive this particular report to-day? I have been loyal to the British Government always. I was loyal when other chiefs were fighting against it. In the time of the cattle slaughtering I was on the English side. I have all the country down to the Indwe, and have kept it loyal. I had always, till now, some one to look after me, and see that I was properly dealt with. When the governor took Warner away, I hoped that some one would be sent in his place; but no one is sent. We do not deny being under government; the Tembookies, wherever they may be, are, as we all know, under government. We do not wish it otherwise. Who among us said that we were willing to go over the river? I never agreed to go over. Some have crossed; others remain here. Those who have crossed the river were not sent across by me. I cannot say anything about them; they pleased themselves. That is all that

I have to say to-day—to ask the question why I am treated in this manner, and to deny that the Tembookies as a tribe ever agreed to cross the Indwe. I and all my people have been expecting a successor to Warner, and we are still looking for one to come after. Let some one follow Warner. I have said all now."

A native, addressing Nonesi, said: "Who is it that you are expecting in Warner's place? Where is the man?"

Nonesi: "I do not know the man; I am waiting for him."

The civil commissioner, turning to the chiefs, said: "You and your people are not to occupy any of the kraals vacated by those who have gone through the Indwe, without permission from me."

Nonesi: "There are no kraals empty in this part of the Tembookie country."

The civil commissioner: "I am not talking to you, Nonesi, alone, but to all the chiefs of your tribe."

Nonesi: "There may be vacant kraals, but I know nothing of them. Is not this place vacant now that Warner has gone?"

The civil commissioner: "Where there are vacant kraals, they are not to be occupied without my permission. I have not come here to answer any questions; but anything you may have to say I will take down, and send to the governor."

Nonesi: "There are no vacant kraals."

The civil commissioner: "Very well, then, it is all right."

Nonesi: "Who is to take Warner's place, and rule here on my ground?"

The civil commissioner: "There is no ground that belongs to you. It is government ground."

Nonesi: "I am the child of the government, but the ground is mine."

A Kaffir (to the crowd): "There is nothing to be done that will help us; but if you want to do anything at all, sit down and cry."

This terminated the conference on the principal business of the meeting, and the civil commissioner now called Carolus and Seelo to come forward. The men,

who were both decently dressed in European attire, having placed themselves in front of their brethren, the civil commissioner said: "Carolus and Seelo, you were both paid head men in the government service; and it has been reported to the governor that you objected to carry out the instructions of the agent residing with the Tembookies, and that you have also done all in your power to prevent the Tembookies from accepting the governor's offer of land beyond the colonial boundary. At the time you did this, you were drawing salaries as government servants; and because you did so, I am to tell you that you are no longer in the government service, and no longer to get government pay."

Carolus, whose tone and manner were both respectful and dignified, said: "I thank you, magistrate, for your words. I am thankful for what the government has done for us. We are all thankful; but there were head men and chiefs before the government paid us; and there will be head men and chiefs still, even if they are without pay."

The Chief Viezi: "I thank you, magistrate, for calling your children together that you may see them. We have been your children for a long time, and have always been under your protection; but you have come to say something to us that we do not understand. You say you take us under government rule. We thought we always were under government rule. Still, for what you have said, I thank you to-day with my hat in my hand; and I speak the word for all who are here. They have always wanted to belong to the government, and the governor has to-day kindly taken them under his protection, so that they may live properly under his rule! We cannot understand this thing, but we thank you! The Tembookies as a tribe have not crossed the river. Nonesi belongs to government. She stays with her tribe in Tembookie land. Those who have crossed the river are young men who had no huts and no land here, and wanted some. Nonesi always was the governor's, and will be so still. Her children were always your dogs, and will remain so."

The Chief Telle: "I have only a small word to say, which you may take as Nonesi's also. All the chiefs are here, and none have moved. Those who have moved are not held as chiefs, and have no land." Chief Telle said, "We want to know again what we have done to be treated as you are treating us to-day. There is one thing we want from the government: a magistrate to rule in Warner's place, and to be as he was. We thought the meeting to-day was to show us the new magistrate. Let him come. We wish to see him."

The civil commissioner terminated the meeting by telling the natives that he was very glad at having seen them all together, to hear what they had to say, and that they were at liberty to go home again.

As soon as Mr. Griffith left the place of meeting, the Tembookies broke up into scattered groups, who were speedily engaged in loud and animated conversation.

This, however, did not last long. In a very short time they began to catch and mount their horses; the different parties were formed under their chiefs and head men— chiefs and head men no longer, according to Sir Philip Wodehouse; and, in less than an hour, the whole of this numerous assemblage had dispersed, east, west, north, and south, and every Kaffir who had taken part in the meeting was out of sight, and Glen Grey was as quiet as though it had never witnessed a gathering of such great moment.

Two or three accidents happened in the course of the day. One Kaffir was thrown from his horse, but escaped with a severe shaking; a restive horse that seemed to have a great objection to being ridden, managed to fall in the course of the struggle with his owner, and singularly enough broke his neck—of course dying on the spot. Another horse was likewise accidentally killed, but under what circumstances we are unable to state.

89 JOHN MACKENZIE
BUSHMAN LAND

The eastern Tswana states—the Ngwato, Kwena, *and* Ngwaketse—*were scattered over the Kalahari Desert, a wilderness of scrub and thorns broken only by a few seasonal waterholes. The Kalahari was inhabited only by the* Sarwa, *a people of Bushman extraction, and the* Kgalagadi, *probably descendants of the earliest* Sotho *migrants to southern Africa. The following selection describes the relationship between the Tswana and the inhabitants of the desert.*

The Reverend John Mackenzie (1835–1899) spent most of his life as a missionary among the Tswana. Ordained in 1858, he left for South Africa later in that year and, after a time of uncertainty as to where he would take up mission work, settled at Shoshong, capital of the Ngwato state, in 1864. Between 1870 and 1871 he made a trip to Britain, where he wrote Ten Years North of the Orange River. *During a second term at Shoshong (1871–1876) and Kuruman (1876–1882), he became increasingly involved in the political aspects of British–South African–Tswana relationships. In 1883 and 1884 he returned to Britain to campaign for the annexation of Bechuanaland. In subsequent years he served briefly as the British Deputy Commissioner in southern Bechuanaland and as a political adviser and propagandist. In 1891 he retired from his position as pastor to a mission station for Negroes on the eastern Cape, where he died.*

. . . There are two distinct races held in subjection in this country, and we now met with specimens of both at every fountain. Those called Bakalahari are Bechuanas, whose tribes have been worsted in former contests, and who, not able to preserve their own independence, "khetha" or pay tribute to a powerful neighbouring chief [the state of the Bamangwato or Ngwato, a Tswana (Bechuana) people—ed.]. Like their rulers, these vassal-Bechuanas are not all of one tribe, nor do they all speak the same dialect of Sechuana. Within the memory of those now living, tribes once independent have been reduced to the condition of Bakalahari; while others who had been long Bakalahari, have been called, through the grace of their chief, to the privileges of citizenship, and appointed a place in the town of the tribe. The other subject race is that of the Bushmen, called Barwa by the Bechuanas in the south, and Masarwa by those in the north of the country. The relationship between the Bakalahari and their masters is much more friendly than that between the same masters and their Bushmen. The helplessness of the Bakalahari excites the contempt of their owners, and they are usually spoken of with the diminutive form of the word —Bakhalahatsane; but otherwise they are regarded as "bathu hela"—"like other people." The master therefore, knowing that he can trust to instincts and traditions similar to his own in the mind of the Bakalahari, sends his flocks and sometimes his herds to be taken care of by his vassals. The children of the Bakalahari luxuriate in goats' milk, while their father imagines himself considerably elevated in society as he gazes night and morning on

From John Mackenzie, *Ten Years North of the Orange River: A Story of Everyday Life and Work Among the South African Tribes* (Edinburgh: Edmonston and Douglas, 1871), pp. 128–139.

the cattle as they enter and leave their pen. When the owner of the stock now and then makes his appearance at the post, he speaks of the cattle as if they belonged to the Bakalahari; and when it is his intention to sell or to slaughter a certain animal he usually announces it, and sometimes even goes through the form of asking permission to do so, although all the cattle belong to himself. The pastoral instincts of the Bakalahari thus find full occupation, to the satisfaction of their lord, and to the advantage of the vassals. Then the master provides dogs for hunting—the ivory and ostrich-feathers, the furs and skins, to be his, the meat to belong to the Bakalahari. And when he visits the little settlement, it is usually with a little present of some tobacco or wild hemp for smoking, or a clasp-knife or a few beads, which he has purchased from a trader. He now receives the "tribute" of his vassals, staying with them a longer or shorter time according to his taste. As among Europeans, there are some Bechuanas who are happiest when "out of town" and in the hunting-field with their vassals. It is only at the positive command of the chief in time of disturbance that such Nimrods reluctantly return to their houses in the town.

But the Bushmen seldom secure much liking or consideration from their Bechuana masters. "Masarwa a bolotsana thata"—"Bushmen are great rascals," "Masarwa ki linoga hela"—"Bushmen are perfect snakes," are remarks often heard among the Bechuanas. The fact is, there is less in common between the two. Their allegiance is never so genuine, and while they yield tribute they hardly conceal their contempt for their masters. The Bushman is of use only in hunting. When his Bechuana master arrives he takes possession of the little huts, and receives all skins, etc., which the family have collected. And now they hunt every day in company, the Bushmen with their spears, bows and arrows, and dogs—their master with his spears, or, in recent years, with his gun. Woe betide the Bushmen should it be found out that they have hidden away part of the produce, or that, instead of keeping the skins for his master, the Bushman has ventured to make with some of them a mantle for himself or his wife! Thus Bushmen are continually on the alert for the arrival of their masters in the country; and should they cross the path and see his foot-mark on it, they are able to recognise it at once, and if possible will hasten home before him to hide that which must not meet the eye of their lord.

Looked at in this connection, it is not difficult to account for the well-known reluctance of Bechuana chiefs to allow traders and travellers to pass through their country. . . . While the Bamang-wato, in whose country I was travelling, participate in the advantages of the trade recently begun with Europeans, they have lost property to the value of many hundreds of pounds through the opening up of the waggon roads to the Lake and to the Zambese. Both roads lead through districts occupied by their vassals, and it is well known that the latter do not hesitate to keep back part of the produce from their masters, and barter with it themselves as soon as a European waggon makes its appearance. . . . It has been found impossible by the Bamangwato to stop this "contraband" trade. They began with severity, and put some of their vassals to death for daring to sell what belonged to their masters. But they found that severity did not answer their purpose, and so the masters now are in point of fact competitors with the European hunters and traders for the purchase of ivory and feathers from their own vassals. Of course they do not acknowledge that they occupy such a position, but the "presents" which they now give their vassals are every year more handsome, and the whole transaction assumes more the appearance of bar-

ter than the levying of tribute. In a few instances masters have intrusted their Bakalahari and Bushmen with guns. The latter take to this weapon at once. What with their skill in stalking, and their steady aim, they soon excel their master in its use. Public opinion is against putting such dangerous weapons into the hands of the "lower classes," as an unsafe proceeding. But as it is to the decided advantage of the masters it is increasingly practised.

It is very interesting to observe how this vassalage becomes all but impracticable, and melts away before the teachings of Christianity and the increasing intercourse which now obtains among tribes that were formerly isolated. The missionaries in the southern district of Bechuanaland did not preach directly against this system; but they taught that the love and mercy of God were toward all, and that God was no respecter of persons. It was the custom even in the olden time, and is still in heathen towns, that if a slave regarded himself as ill-used by his master, or thought that his life was in danger, he might flee to the chief, and cast himself upon his protection. If the master complained of was a favourite with the chief, he would formally reprove him, and persuade the slave to return to his service. But if a charge of cruelty was proved against a master with whom the chief had a quarrel, he would at once release the slave from his obligations to him, and provide for him another master. It can readily be seen that Christianity, finding the slave enjoying such an amount of liberty, would speedily secure for him more. Thus in the southern district, and especially where Christian churches exist, this vassalage exists in many cases more in name than in reality. In most cases, as long as the vassals remain with their masters they receive some kind of payment for their service; and when they go away, there does not seem to be any power which is able and ready to bring them back. It is one of the faults which the heathen prefer against the partially-Christianized district in the south, that there the "batlanka" or slaves are no longer under their masters' control, as in the times of undisturbed heathenism. Christianity thus quietly lets the oppressed go free, and breaks every yoke.

But while under this system of appeal to the chief, the lot of these vassals is just bearable in time of peace, it is beyond conception wretched in time of war. I do not mean war among themselves in the country; they are too poor to quarrel seriously, or for a long time: but they are deeply interested in all the political questions of the town, being part of the property of the head men—a quarrel among whom is often followed up in the country in a way which astonishes as it shocks the Christian man. The contest for the possession of certain villages of Bakalahari or Bushmen, is a fruitful source of strife in Bechuana towns. The vassals with all their belongings are the subject of litigation and endless jealousies; and it needs all the skill of a chief to settle these matters between greedy and plausible rivals. When a decision is come to, the poor people in the country are hastily "lifted" by the successful litigant, to be brought back again should he afterwards lose his case. When rival chiefs fight for supremacy in the same tribe, the condition of the harmless vassals is wretched in the extreme. They are then scattered and peeled, driven hither and thither, and mercilessly killed, as the jealousy, caprice, or revenge of their masters may dictate. It is quite fair in such a struggle to kill all the vassals, as it would be to lift the cattle, of him who cannot be displaced from his chieftainship. And so with the varying fortunes of a "civil war," the vassals might be attacked by both parties in turn.

Again, when one Bechuana tribe attacks another, the Bushmen and Bakalahari belonging to both are placed in the same category with cattle and sheep—they are to be "lifted" or killed as opportunity offers. In such cases, therefore, all Bakalahari and Bushmen flee into wastes and inaccessible forests, and hide themselves until the commotion is past.

We found an illustration of the terror and mistrust in which these people live, when we reached the fountain of Lotlakane. A "civil war" was still going on, in an intermittent fashion, between Macheng and Sekhome, for the chieftainship of the Bamangwato tribe. It mattered little to these serfs who the chief was to be; with them the important question was, to escape both parties while the strife was going on. And so for the first night we saw nobody at Lotlakane; but in the morning my men told me that there were footmarks of Bushmen all round our camp. They had come in the night to satisfy themselves that there were no Bamangwate in my party, before they ventured to come amongst us. How they distinguished as the men lay asleep between the two Bakwena whom I had hired from Sechele and Bamangwato, I know not; but their midnight inspection was held to be satisfactory, and next day several made their appearance at our waggon. It was affecting to witness the earnestness with which they asked if the Bamangwato were still fighting among themselves.

.   .   .

On all subjects lying within the range of the Bushman's observation you will meet with extreme shrewdness and intelligence. The Bushman has the most extensive knowledge of the *materia medica* of the country. If my own medicines were not available, I would trust myself sooner to the care of a Bushman than to any other native doctor. Nothing can exceed the skill and intelligence of the Bushman as a hunter, and an observer of the habits of the wild animals. And as to religion, if I am not greatly mistaken, the Bushmen are the most "superstitious" race in Southern Africa. The fact that they are so peculiarly dependent for subsistence upon what is beyond their control will

perhaps account for this. With other natives the chief season of praying and
necromancing begins when they have
sown their corn, and stand in need of rain.
But all seasons are the same to the Bushman. Therefore whilst he is most accomplished in everything belonging to his own
way of life, and by general consent the
guide and leader of every hunting party
of which he is a member, he constantly
seeks by charms and by spells to supply
his own deficiencies. Whether the European has bent his knee in prayer or not
before he springs to the saddle in the
morning of a hunt, the Bushman has not
failed to consult his "oracles." Approaching with mysterious and confident mien,
he announces to the hunters that if they
will only proceed in a given direction they
will find the game they seek. In short, he
has assumed the office of "seer" for the
party. He has been inquiring of his dice
or charms, and announces to you their
verdict with confidence. If you still hesitate, he explains to you that Morimo [god
—ed.] has told him where the game is,
and at the same time shakes the dice
which he carries round his neck. If you
smile, and say that these are merely bits
of ivory or bone, he assents at once, and
would readily dispose of them to you for
a few beads. But then at the earliest opportunity he would repair the deficiency,
and replace them by another set. The bits
of bone are nothing, he will admit, but
through them he "makes inquiry" of the
ex-human if not super-human. No party
of Bushmen would consent to take the
field without these charms. Whoever fan-
cies he is self-contained, and able in himself, without prayer, or without divining,
to cope with the difficulties of human existence, the Bushman in Bechuana-land is
not. I believe life to a Bushman without
this professed addressing something out
of and beyond himself would be complete
misery.

The relics of a tribal rite are also to be
found among these Bushmen. If you
point to the pierced cartilage of the nose,
he will explain to you that that was done

when he was introduced to Bushman
manhood. He here uses the word "rupa,"
which in Sechuana means the introductory ceremony of circumcision. This,
then, is to him what circumcision is to the
Bechuanas. You point to certain marks
on his face, or bits of wood on his hair,
or tied round his neck. These are medicines or charms to be taken in sickness,
or proximity to lions, or in other circumstances of danger. This is the fetichism
which is common throughout Africa at
the present time, as it was in Europe in
past ages, and which is not unknown in
our own day in rural districts of England
and Scotland. If you point to the dice, the
Bushman will say that they are "Lilo tsa
Morimo oa me,"—"Things of my God."
He will add, "Lia impuléléla mahuku,"
—"They tell me news." If he does not
know much Sechuana, he will point to
them and say, "Se se Morimo, se,"—
"This is God." As in the other cases, this
explanation is to be regarded in its connection with such views of Morimo as are
known to these Bushmen. The Bushman
means to say that what Morimo is to the
Bechuanas and to you his dice and charms
are to him. To affirm from such data that
the Bushmen have a definite notion of
Morimo (God) would be to say too much;
to say that their God is a bit of ivory or
bone would be equally incorrect; while to
affirm that they have no religion or superstition to distinguish them from the brutes
that perish is entirely false. . . .

In sleeping at the same fire with Bushmen or Bakalahari you are sure to be
roused twice in the course of the night, or
oftener, by the rising of one after the other
of your companions. Their first stretch-
ings, yawnings, and gruntings over, they
assume a sitting position in a row round
the fire, which they replenish with fresh
logs. Sometimes they fall asleep in this
position, and you see them nodding over
the flames. When they lie down again you
take notice that it is always in the opposite
position with reference to the fire from
that which they last occupied. Thus if
they had their backs to the fire before they

got up, they now turn their faces to it. Having no blanket or covering whatever, except a little skin mantle, which just covers their shoulders, it is only by repeated "turnings" that they are able to keep up heat in their bodies during the cold winter nights. Thus their bodies are always scorched and scarred, and generally "over-done" on both sides, by the fire at night. Before the day is fairly broken you again hear the yawning and other demonstrations—now in a louder tone. As the light increases the restless eye of the Bushman scans the heavens with a close scrutiny. On the ground also, as far as the eye can reach, he seems to notice every living thing. The process of roasting meat on the live coals now commences; and as this early breakfast goes on each one parenthetically mentions what he observes. At length one starts to his feet. What has he descried? After great effort you can just see "manong" or vultures in the distance sweeping over a certain spot. Seizing their weapons two or three men start at once in that direction; they hope to get there before the lion has finished the antelope or zebra, which has been his midnight meal. If they find the killer of the prey still at his repast, with a jackal venturing to approach the opposite end, while hyenas or younger lions bide their time at a distance—the Bushmen, who have been talking loudly as they approached, to give due notice of their arrival, now shout at the top of their voice, rattle their spears, break off decayed branches from trees, or shake their mantles, to frighten the lion and his courtiers, who retire into the adjoining thicket. Everything is now collected which is at all edible, and carried to the encampment. Should their visit be too late, and they find only bits of bone and hide and hoofs to reward them for their trouble, all these are collected and brought away; the vulture and the hyena or jackal finding little to pick up after the visit of the Bushman. Thus although Bakalahari object to lions in their vicinity, on account of the live stock which they are rearing for themselves and their masters, the Bushmen do not at all object to this proximity, for they have a good deal to gain from it, and if they only keep up a good fire at night in self-preservation they have nothing whatever to lose.

.   .   .

90 JAN CHRISTIAAN SMUTS
A CENTURY OF WRONG

First issued in Dutch in 1899 under the authorship of the State Secretary of the Transvaal Republic, F. W. Reitz, A Century of Wrong *was translated into English in 1900 and was published with a preface by W. T. Stead, himself an opponent of the Boers or Afrikanders. A biased and polemical account of nineteenth-century South African history, particularly the relations between the Afrikanders and the English, this book was in fact written by Jan Christiaan Smuts (1870–1950), then an official in the government of the Transvaal. Smuts was later a general in the Anglo-Boer War (1899–1902), and Prime Minister of South Africa (1919–1924, 1939–1948). As a member of the British Imperial War Cabinet in World War I and as one of the major architects of the League of Nations and the United Nations, Smuts acquired an international reputation. In spite of, or perhaps because of this reputation, Smuts was never able to implement the same universalistic ideas at home that he proclaimed abroad.*

From [Jan Christiaan Smuts] *A Century of Wrong*, issued by F. W. Reitz, State Secretary of the South African Republic, with a preface by W. T. Stead (London: Review of Reviews, 1900), pp. 89–98.

I have now reviewed all the facts connected with the history of our oppression and persecution during the past hundred years. The allegations I have made are not invented, but are based upon the statements of the most reliable witnesses, nearly all of them of British nationality; they are facts that have been declared incontestable before the tribunal of history. As far as the more recent occurrences since 1898 are concerned, I may state that I have had personal knowledge of all the negociations and questions at issue above referred to, and I can only declare that I have confined myself to facts; these will stand out in a much clearer light when the curtain is raised and the events of the last two years in this sorely afflicted part of the world are revealed.

In this awful turning point in the history of South Africa, on the eve of the conflict [the Anglo-Boer War—ed.] which threatens to exterminate our people, it behoves us to speak the truth in what may be, perchance, our last message to the world. Even if we are exterminated the truth will triumph through us over our conquerors, and will sterilise and paralyse all their efforts until they too disappear in the night of oblivion.

Up to the present our people have remained silent; we have been spat upon by the enemy, slandered, harried, and treated with every possible mark of disdain and contempt. But our people, with a dignity which reminds the world of a greater and more painful example of suffering, have borne in silence the taunts and derision of their opponents; indeed, they elected out of a sense of duty to remedy the faults and abuses which had crept into their public administration during moments of relaxed vigilance. But even this was ascribed to weakness and cowardice. Latterly our people have been represented by influential statesmen and on hundreds of platforms in England as incompetent, uncivilised, dishonourable, untrustworthy, corrupt, bloodthirsty, treacherous, etc., etc., so that not only the British public, but nearly the whole world, began to be-

lieve that we stood on the same level as the wild beasts. In the face of these taunts and this provocation our people still remained silent. We were forced to learn from formal blue books issued by Her Majesty's Government and from dispatches of Her Majesty's High Commissioner in South Africa that our unscrupulous State Government, and our unjust, unprincipled, and disorderly administration, was a continual festering sore, which, like a pestilential vapour, defiled the moral and political atmosphere of South Africa. We remained silent. We were accused in innumerable newspapers of all sorts of misdeeds against civilisation and humanity; crimes were imputed to us, the bare narration of which was sufficient to cause the hair to rise with horror. If the reading public believe a hundredth part of the enormities which have been laid at the door of our people and Government, they must be irresistibly forced to the conclusion that this Republic is a den of thieves and a sink of iniquity, a people, in fact, the very existence of which is a blot upon humanity, and a nuisance to mankind. Of the enormous sums which we are alleged to have spent out of the Secret Service Fund in order to purchase the good opinion of the world there has been no practical result or evidence, for the breath of slander went on steadily increasing with the violence of a hurricane. But our people remained silent, partly out of stupidity, partly out of a feeling of despairing helplessness, and partly because, being a pastoral people, they read no newspapers, and were thus unaware of the way in which the feeling of the whole world was being prejudiced against them by the efforts of malignant hate.

The practical effect has been that our case has been lost by default before the tribunal of public opinion. That is why I feel compelled to state the facts which have characterised the attitude of the British towards us during the Nineteenth century. Naboth's title to his vineyard must be cancelled. The easiest way of securing that object, according to the tortuous methods of British diplomacy, was to prove that Naboth was a scoundrel and Ahab an angel. The facts which have marked Ahab's career have been stated. I shall now proceed to draw my conclusions, which I submit must appeal irresistibly to every impartial and right-minded person.

During this century there have been three periods which have been characterised by different attitudes of the British Government towards us. The first began in 1806, and lasted until the middle of the century. During this period the chief feature of British policy was one of utter contempt, and the general trend of British feeling in regard to our unfortunate people can be summarised by the phrase, "The stupid and dirty Dutch." But the hypocritical ingenuity of British policy was perfectly competent to express this contempt in accents which harmonised with the loftiest sentiments then prevailing. The wave of sentimental philanthropy then passing over the civilised world was utilised by the British Government in order to represent the Boers to the world as oppressors of poor peace-loving natives, who were also men and brethren eminently capable of receiving religion and civilisation.

It may seem inexplicable that the Power which stood up boldly at the Treaty of Utrecht [1713—ed.] as the shameless champion of negro slavery was the very one which was celebrated in South Africa for its morbid love of the natives; the explanation, however, is that it was not so much love for the native that underlay the apparent negrophilistic policy as hatred and contempt of the Boer. As a result of this hatred of the Boer, disguised under the veneer of philanthropy in regard to the aborigines, the natives were employed as police against us; they were provided with arms and ammunition to be used against us; they were incited to fight us, and, wherever it was possible, they murdered and plundered us. In fact, our people were forced to bid farewell to the Cape Colony and all that was near and dear to them, and seek a shelter in the unknown wilderness of the North.

As an ultimate result of this hatred, our people had to pursue their pilgrimage of martyrdom throughout South Africa, until every portion of that unhappy country has been painted red with the blood, not so much of men capable of resistance as with that of our murdered and defenceless women and children.

The second period lasted until the year 1881. The fundamental principle then underlying British policy was no longer one of unqualified hatred. Results had already proved that hatred was powerless to subdue the Africander; it had, on the other hand, contributed largely to the consolidation of Africanderdom and to the fact that they spread over the whole of South Africa, thus forming the predominant nationality almost everywhere. In a moment of disinterestedness or absent-minded dejection England had concluded treaties with the Boers in 1852 and 1854, by which they were guaranteed in the undisturbed possession of certain wild and apparently worthless tracts of territory.

The fundamental sentiment which governed the policy of the second period was a feeling of regret at having made this mistake, coupled with the firm determination to set aside its results. These wild and useless tracts, which had been guaranteed to the Boers, appeared to be very valuable after the Boers had rescued them from barbarism, and opened them up for civilisation. It was felt that they ought to gleam amongst the jewels of Her Majesty's Crown, notwithstanding the obstacle in the treaties that had been concluded with the Boers. This was the concealed intention. As far as the means were concerned—they were, from the very exigency of inborn hypocrisy, partly revealed and partly concealed; the one differing from the other, as light from darkness. The secret means consisted in arming the Kaffir tribes against us in the most incredible manner, and in inciting them to attack us in violation of solemn treaties and promises. If this policy succeeded the real objects and means could be suppressed, and England could then come forward and pose openly as the champion of peace and order, and as the guardian angel of civilisation in this part of the world. The Republics could then be annexed under cover of these plausible pretexts. This policy failed as far as the Orange Free State was concerned, because the brave burghers of the neighbouring Republic succeeded, after great difficulty, in overcoming Moshesh [the great Basuto king —ed.], notwithstanding the fact that their arms and ammunition had been illegally stopped by the British Government. England was compelled in that case to confine itself to the protection of its "Basuto" tools. The British, however, succeeded in preventing the Boers from reaping the legitimate fruits of their victory, and in annexing the Diamond Fields— a flagrantly illegal act.

As far as the South African Republic is concerned, it was unfortunate that the burghers were not vigilant enough to foresee and prevent the crafty policy of the enemy. As the Transvaal Boers had subdued the most powerful Kaffir tribes, they never dreamt that the insignificant Kaffir wars in which they had been involved through English intrigue would have been seized as a pretext to annex their country to the British Crown. They had been remiss in not putting their full force into the field so as to bring these little wars to a speedy conclusion. And so the Magato and Socoecoeni campaigns were conducted in a protracted and half-hearted way, much to the satisfaction of Sir Theophilus Shepstone [Secretary for Native Affairs in Natal—ed.], and those who were at his back.

The Annexation was brought about. It was announced that the extension of Her Majesty's sway and protection over the South African Republic could alone secure unity of purpose and trade, as well as open out a prospect of peace and prosperity. In these words of Shepstone's proclamation we see in all its repulsive nakedness the hypocrisy which openly masqueraded in the guise of the disinterested and pitiful Samaritan, while its true and secret object was to inflict a fatal wound upon the burgher Republic.

The third period of our history is characterised by the amalgamation of the old and well-known policy of fraud and violence with the new forces of Capitalism, which had developed so powerfully owing to the mineral riches of the South African Republic. Our existence as a people and as a State is now threatened by an unparalleled combination of forces. Arrayed against us we find numerical strength, the public opinion of the United Kingdom thirsting and shouting for blood and revenge, the world-wide and cosmopolitan power of Capitalism, and all the forces which underlie the lust of robbery and the spirit of plunder. Our lot has of late become more and more perilous. The cordon of beasts of plunder and birds of prey has been narrowed and drawn closer and closer around this poor doomed people during the last ten years. As the wounded antelope awaits the coming of the lion, the jackal, and the vulture, so do our poor people all over South Africa contemplate the approach of the foe, encircled as they are by the forces of hatred and revenge, and by the stratagems and covetousness of their enemies. Every sea in the world is being furrowed by the ships which are conveying British troops from every corner of the globe in order to smash this little handful of people. Even Xerxes, with his millions against little Greece, does not afford a stranger spectacle to the wonder and astonishment of mankind than this gentle and kindhearted Mother of Nations, as, wrapped in all the panoply of her might, riches, and exalted traditions, she approaches the little child grovelling in the dust with a sharpened knife in her hand. This is no War—it is an attempt at Infanticide.

And as the brain of the onlooker reels,

and as his thoughts fade away into uneasy slumbers, there arises before him in a dream the distant prospect of Bantu children playing amongst the gardens and ruins of the sunny south around thousands of graves in which the descendants of the European heroes of Faith and Freedom lie sleeping.

For the marauding hordes of the Bantu are once more roving where European dwellings used to stand. And when the question is asked—why all this has happened? Why the heroic children of an heroic race, to which civilisation owes its most priceless blessings, should lie murdered there in that distant quarter of the globe? An invisible spirit of mockery answers, "Civilisation is a failure; the Caucasian is played out!" and the dreamer awakens with the echo of the word "Gold! gold! gold!" in his ears.

The orchids of Birmingham are yellow. The traditions of the greatest people on earth are tarnished and have become yellow.

The laurels which Britannia's legions hope to win in South Africa are sere and yellow.

But the sky which stretches its banner over South Africa remains blue. The justice to which Piet Retief appeals when our fathers said farewell to the Cape Colony, and to which Joachim Prinsloo called aloud in the Volksraad of Natal when it was annexed by England; the justice to which the burghers of the Transvaal entrusted their case at Paarde Kraal in 1880, remains immutable, and is like a rock against which the yeasty billows of British diplomacy dissolve in foam.

It proceeds according to eternal laws, unmoved by human pride and ambition. As the Greek poet of old said, it permits the tyrant, in his boundless self-esteem, to climb higher and higher and to gain greater honour and might until he arrives at the appointed height, and then falls down into the infinite depths.

Africanders, I ask you but to do as Leonidas did with his 300 men when they advanced unflinchingly at Thermopylae against Xerxes and his myriads, and do not be disturbed by such men as Milner, Rhodes, and Chamberlain, or even by the British Empire itself, but cling fast to the God of our forefathers, and to the Righteousness which is sometimes slow in acting, but which never slumbers nor forgets. Our forefathers did not pale before the terrors of the Spanish Inquisition, but entered upon the great struggle for Freedom and Right against even the mighty Philip, unmindful of the consequences.

Nor could the rack and the persecuting bands of Louis XIV tame or subdue the spirit of our fathers. Neither Alva nor Richelieu were able to compass the triumph of tyranny over the innate sentiment of Freedom and Independence in our forefathers. Nor will a Chamberlain be more fortunate in effecting the triumph of Capitalism, with its lust for power, over us.

If it is ordained that we, insignificant as we are, should be the first among all peoples to begin the struggle against the new-world tyranny of Capitalism, then we are ready to do so, even if that tyranny is reinforced by the power of Jingoism.

May the hope which glowed in our hearts during 1880, and which buoyed us up during that struggle, burn on steadily! May it prove a beacon of light in our path, invincibly moving onwards through blood and through tears, until it leads us to a real Union of South Africa.

As in 1880, we now submit our cause with perfect confidence to the whole world. Whether the result be Victory or Death, Liberty will assuredly rise in South Africa like the sun from out the mists of the morning, just as Freedom dawned over the United States of America a little more than a century ago. Then from the Zambesi to Simon's Bay it will be

"AFRICA FOR THE AFRICANDER."

91 JAN HENDRIK HOFMEYR

THE REPRESENTATION OF NATIVES ACT, 1936

Jan Hendrik Hofmeyr (1894–1948), son of Jan Hofmeyr, leader of the Afrikaner Bond, was one of South Africa's most brilliant minds and, in the fifteen years before his death, was the most prominent spokesman for the liberal philosophy in South Africa. A university graduate at the age of fifteen and principal of the University of the Witwatersrand at twenty-four, he became a minister in the fusion government of Prime Minister Hertzog and Jan Christiaan Smuts in 1934. Although he resigned temporarily from his Cabinet post in 1938, Hofmeyr was closely associated with Smuts during World War II and was widely regarded as his successor. Hofmeyr died, however, in the same year in which the Nationalist party defeated Smuts' United party (1948). The following speech, made by Hofmeyr during the debate on the second reading of the Representation of Natives Bill on April 6, 1936, is regarded as one of the great speeches of South African parliamentary history.

I regret that I cannot vote for this Bill. I can hardly make that vote a silent one, and, therefore, I must ask the indulgence of the joint sitting to give my reasons for that vote. Circumstances have prevented me from doing so at an earlier stage, as I had fully intended to do. Those circumstances kept me away from this joint sitting during the whole of the second reading debate, and during the discussion of nearly all the vital points in Committee. I had intended to vote and speak against the second reading. This Bill has emerged from the Committee practically the same as it was when read a second time. Therefore, I have no option but to vote and to speak against it now.

I used the word "regret" in all sincerity. I do very sincerely regret that I cannot, on this occasion, align myself with my leader, the Prime Minister's sincere desire to further the best interests of White men and Black in this country. I recognise that his knowledge and experience of Native affairs are far greater than mine, and that this Bill represents a life-work to him. I am most grateful indeed to him for his forbearance and his tolerance in this mat-

From "Third Reading of Representation of Natives Bills [J.S.1 and 2, 1936]," *Joint Sitting of Both Houses of Parliament, Union of South Africa, 13 February to 7 April 1936* (Cape Town: Hansard, 1936), cols. 1082–1091.

ter to an errant colleague. But for all that, there is a fundamental difference in this matter between my outlook and that which underlies this Bill. While that is so, I can do no other than oppose it, and I must do so regardless of what the political consequences for myself might be.

It is not the first time, Mr. Speaker, that a government of the Union has been divided on a franchise Bill. Five years ago the Prime Minister also introduced a franchise Bill for the enfranchisement of women. Two of his colleagues opposed that Bill at all stages. That Bill dealt with some 400,000 to 500,000 persons. This Bill deals with some 10,000 to 11,000 persons. But there is this further difference. By virtue of the seven points of coalition, those who entered into coalition specifically reserved to themselves the right to their own opinions in regard to this matter. The seven points contained this sentence—

This does not imply that an agreement has been attained in regard to the principle of separate political representation.

In the party programme again, that was stated to be a matter to be left to the individual party member. It was in that knowledge that some of us went into the present Government. It was with the knowledge of that fact that the country gave its endorsement to that Government. I claim today for myself that right to differ. But I want to make it very clear that in doing so I am neither directly nor by implication criticising anyone with whom I have been in agreement in the past but who today takes a different attitude from my own. I am merely asserting an individual right for myself.

I want to ask the joint sitting to view this Bill in its true setting. There is a right setting and a wrong setting in which this Bill can be viewed. Many hon. members have supported this Bill because they have viewed it against the background of its immediate predecessor, Bill No. 1. That is the wrong setting. The right setting in which to view this Bill is the two previous Bills of the Prime Minister, the Bill of 1926 and the Bill of 1929.[1] Those two Bills and this Bill represent a legitimate succession. The other Bill which I have mentioned, why, sir, that was left at the Prime Minister's doorstep by the hon. member for Roodepoort (Colonel Stallard) and by the hon. member for Zululand (Mr. Nicholls), and very gallantly adopted by him, fortunately only temporarily.

Let us look back upon those two Bills. The 1926 draft legislation provided for the representation of Natives on a communal basis to the extent of seven members in the House of Assembly. It provided for the representation in the House of Assembly of Natives in all provinces. It provided for the extension of Coloured representation to the north. It reconstituted the Native Council on a definite basis, making it a body meeting annually and giving it also legislative power. The 1929 Bill reduced the number of Native representatives in the Union House of Assembly from seven to three. It left the northern provinces to be represented in the House of Parliament only in

the Senate. The 1929 Bill, therefore, from the point of view from which I am speaking, marked a retrogression on the Bill of 1926.

This Bill marks a further retrogression on the Bill of 1929 and that is why I want the Bill to be viewed in its true setting. Let me mention four points.

In the first place this Bill, unlike its predecessors, creates what is virtually a colour bar in the Cape Provincial Council. The right hon. Senator Malan on Friday quoted a letter written by Onse Jan in 1909.[2] He might also have quoted the fact that Onse Jan at that time protested, amongst other things, against the creation of a colour bar in the Union House of Assembly. We are now going further and we are creating a colour bar in the Provincial Council.

In the second place we are laying down a definition of "Native" which is going to degrade an ever-increasing number of Coloured people and place them for ever among the ranks of Natives.

In the third place, this Bill not only provides for a separate Cape voters' roll but it also provides for the immediate removal of all existing voters to that roll. To me that seems in conflict with the spirit of the Act of Union. If we look at Section 35 of the Act of Union, we find that there are two sub-clauses. The one deals with existing qualifications and says that any change in those qualifications leading to a restriction shall not be made except by a certain procedure. Existing qualifications are entrenched, but there is laid down a method by which they may be altered. But the second sub-clause of the same section lays down absolutely and in definite terms that as a result of any such change of qualifications no single Native already on the voters' roll shall have his name taken from that roll and in this case no procedure is laid down for an amendment. I contend that in this new provision in this Bill we are acting against

[1] Earlier attempts by General Hertzog which did not get the necessary two-thirds majority of both Houses sitting jointly.

[2] Mr. J. H. Hofmeyr (Snr.), Leader of the Afrikaner Bond in the Cape.

the spirit of the Act of Union and I may say that I have very high authority for that statement of mine.

Then there is another point. It is now proposed to put up an entrenchment of a two-thirds majority not only against any deterioration in the Natives' position but also against any improvement in the Natives' position. The National Convention did not think such a double entrenchment necessary. Why not? Because the White man was put in the constitution into an impregnable position. They thought there was no necessity to protect the White man. They did not think it necessary to protect the White man against the possibility of his own generosity. Today we are asked to do both. I have heard one of my friends say that it is only just and fair that, if we give entrenchment on the one side, we should also give it on the other, and that reminded me of the first recorded definition of justice. "Justice is the interest of the stronger." I am afraid it is from that conception of justice that a good deal of the support of this Bill is derived. I think it is clear then that this Bill is less acceptable than its predecessors.

I shall be told, however, that there is another side of the account—that this Bill creates a Native Representative Council. Let us remember that the 1926 Bill put on a definite basis the Union Native Council, making it in some respects a weaker, in other respects a stronger body than the body which we are now creating, giving it legislative powers, which we are not doing today. But apart from that, I want to say that I have always had hopes for this Native Representative Council, but I have always realised that everything is going to depend on the attitude towards it of Government and Parliament, during the first critical formative years of its existence; and when I consider the spirit in which these changes which I have been mentioning have been brought in the present Bill, when I think of the attitude of mind which underlies them, when I know how it has been said again and again that this

Bill is only accepted for the present, when I realise that there will be powerful influences to make that Native Representative Council a futile body, then I find it difficult to maintain my hopes. I know that high hopes have been expressed during this session in regard to the Native Representative Council, but high hopes were also expressed in 1920 in regard to the Native Council created then. I find it difficult to discover ground for confidence that the hopes expressed at this time are not destined to similar discomfiture as were the hopes expressed in 1920. And so I again assert that this Bill is no more acceptable than its predecessors. It is called a compromise, but if we look back to 1926, then from the point of view of the Natives, it is the Natives who have done all the giving and none of the taking.

Let us see what this Bill does. The central feature is to give to the Natives an inferior, a qualified citizenship, a citizenship which has the marks of inferiority in clause after clause of this Bill and which bears the added stigma that whatever may be the advance of the Native in civilisation and education, to all intents and purposes, he is limited for all time to three members in a House of 153. That surely is a qualified, an inferior citizenship. May I make my own position clear? I am not one of those who would necessarily stand or fall by the ideal of common citizenship as an absolute thing. I do not go with the right hon. Senator Malan to that extent. If we were starting with a clean sheet, I think it would certainly be possible to devise a system of separate representation in separate assemblies which would be fair and just and sound. I am not saying that it is impossible to do so even today. But we are not starting with a clean sheet. We are starting with the existence of a vested right which has been in existence and which has not been abused for more than 80 years. And I want to say this, that once franchise rights have been given and exercised by a section of the community, then no nation save at the cost of honour and ultimate security should take away those rights without adequate justification. The Prime Minister, when he substituted this Bill for its predecessor, either in definite terms or by implication admitted that fact. He admitted that you could not take away franchise rights without justification and that there was no justification today for that absolute removal of the existing Cape Native franchise rights. This Bill does not absolutely remove franchise rights but it does replace those vested rights by an inferior, a qualified right. I contend that the same principle applies in this case, and I say that no nation save at the cost of honour or ultimate security can take away these rights without adequate justification.

Well, we are taking them away and we are replacing them by a qualified and inferior right. We have then to ask, what is the justification for this proposal? Attempts have been made to answer that question. Some have sought to find that justification in terms of high ethical or political principle. Some have used those blessed word phrases, segregation, trusteeship, the Native developing along his own lines. The Native developing along his own lines—that means for most who use the words the same as the Native being kept in his own place. Segregation—well, what a thing of shreds and patches this Bill makes of political segregation, just as my hon. friend over there pointed out, territorial segregation has become a thing of shreds and patches. And as for trusteeship, I would only say this: I have always regarded trusteeship as implying that at some stage or another, the trustee is prepared to hand over the trust to his ward. I have yet to learn that the European trustee in South Africa contemplates any such possibility. And that being so, I find it very difficult to reconcile the use of the word trusteeship in relation to a Bill for which it is claimed that it is going to make South Africa safe for European civilisation.

But we are also told that we can justify this Bill because once the political question is removed the Native will receive better treatment. There will be more sympathy with their development. I know that that is sincerely meant, but I know too that, in the case of many people, that is simply a conscience-salving argument which they are laying to their souls. I say that because I have sat for five years in the Transvaal Provincial Council. There was no question of Native political representation there. There was no such bogey, but I know how desperately difficult it was to get any consideration whatever for any question of Native development. Let me put it concretely—before long, we shall have to face up to the question of the inadequacy of Native education. I wonder how many after the first flush of enthusiasm over this Bill is passed, how many of those who support this Bill will be any more ready to repair the present inadequacy of Native education than they would have been if this Bill were not passed.

There is another justification adduced, and that is the justification of danger. We have heard so much, especially in the past, of the Cape Native vote being a danger. It is certainly not an immediate, urgent danger. In 1926 when the Prime Minister introduced a much more liberal Bill than this one there were 300,000 European voters on the roll of the Union and 16,500 Natives, but today there are 925,000 Europeans and 10,600 Natives. My department in 1933 and 1935 was instructed to do all in its power to get every qualified Native voter on to the rolls. In spite of that the figures dropped from 12,-715 to 10,628 today. Today there are only 14 constituencies in the Cape with more than 250 Native voters. There are only four with a more than 10 per cent Native electorate. Surely there is no immediate urgent danger. But we are told there is that danger in the uncertain future, that danger of which my colleague, the Minister of Mines, was speaking. It is the fear of that danger which is the only real justification which has been advanced in favour of the act of deprivation in this Bill. Well, here I agree with my hon. friend the member for Wonderboom (Mrs. Malherbe), who said a wise and timely word on Friday when she declared that no sound policy can be based on fear. No sound policy can be based on fear, and if that is the only justification for this Bill, the only justification for this act of deprivation, the fear of what may happen in an uncertain future, then, sir, I say there is no adequate justification.

Well, sir, I object to the Bill for that reason. I object to it also because I regard, as I have always done, the principle of communal representation as an unsound one, and a dangerous one not least of all from the point of view of the European in this country. Communal representation of different races implies a divergence of interests, and in South Africa there is no real ultimate divergence of interests between Europeans and non-Europeans. There is a far greater community of interests in this land. We have on both sides a contribution to make to the welfare of South Africa, and the weakness of this Bill, from my point of view, is that it emphasises the differences, it stimulates hostility, and it pays no regard to the ultimate community of interest. After all, sir, this principle of communal representation is no new one. It has been tried before, and verdicts have been pronounced upon it before. Here I have what the Donoughmore Commission wrote about it in regard to Ceylon—

Communal representation, they said, was devised with a view to assisting the development of democratic institutions in countries of different races and religions, and in the hope of eliminating the clash of those various interests during elections. Unfortunately, the experiment has not given the desired results, but has had, if anything, the opposite effect. The representatives of the various communities do not trust one another. The introduction of communal representation into the constitution with good intentions, has had unfortunate results.

A year after, the Hilton-Young Commission [of 1927—ed.] in regard to [the closer union of—ed.] East Africa wrote these words—

The surest foundation for a stable constitution is community of interests. The communal system where it has been tried has tended to accentuate differences and prevent the creation of a healthy political life.

The Simon Commission [of 1927—ed.] in regard to [the constitutional problem in—ed.] India similarly condemned it. They only allowed it to pass as a temporary expedient, in view of the deep religious cleavages in that unhappy land. What justification have we with these warnings before us for accepting and applying that system here? Surely we are deliberately accepting the worse course and incurring grave dangers for the future.

What, sir, is the chief objection to communal representation which emerges from these quotations? It is that it makes not for friendship, but for hostility. In the last resort, there is greater danger, there is more real cause for fear in this Bill than in anything we have today. By this Bill we are sowing the seeds of a far greater potential conflict than is being done by anything in existence today. Let me explain. To my mind, as I have always felt, the crux of the position is in regard to the educated Native. We have many educated and semi-educated Natives in South Africa. Many of them have attained to and many more are advancing towards European standards. They have been trained on European lines, they have been taught to think and act as Europeans. We may not like it, but there are the plain facts. Now what is the political future for these people? This Bill says that even the most educated Native shall never have political equality with even the least educated and the least cultured White or Coloured man. This Bill says to these educated Natives: "There is no room for you, you must be driven back upon your

own people." But we drive them back in hostility and disgruntlement, and do not let us forget this, that all that this Bill is doing for these educated Natives is to make them the leaders of their own people, in disaffection and revolt. No, the introduction of this principle in this Bill will not make for peace and safety but for hostility and conflict and strife. I would put it in this way. This Bill is a Bill the acknowledged aim of which is the self-preservation of the European. It starts out from fear, and its underlying conception is the interests of the stronger. I do not believe that, in those circumstances, you can attain self-preservation. I do not believe that you can, in this country, have a safe Native policy which is not based on consent. I do not believe that we can assure the future of White civilisation in South Africa, save with the consent and the goodwill of the non-European people.

When I hear the Christian principle of self-preservation invoked in connection with this Bill, then I am reminded of the eternal paradox that whosoever will save his life shall lose it. It has been said recently, and I think we all acclaim it, "that the spirit of inequality and subjection in which the Peace of Versailles was concluded could only lead to great trouble. We are passing through days of division and strife, we have had them for years, and they are the result of that peace." I can only hope that the same division and strife is not going to be the result of the spirit of inequality and subjection which is largely at the root of this Bill.

I said that this Bill is born largely of fear. I know people don't like that word. Let me be perfectly frank. It is a perfectly natural fear, it is a fear we all have whether we oppose or support this Bill. We have all got that fear of the White man being drowned in a Black ocean, and we have all got that fear of race mixture and miscegenation.

AN HON. MEMBER: A justified fear.

MR. HOFMEYR: No, it is an unreasoning fear, it is largely an illogical fear. Let

me put this to my friend. We are told that political equality must make for social equality, and, therefore, for race intermixture. We are told that in regard to the Natives, but many of those who tell us that in regard to the Native have no fear at all of political equality in regard to the Coloured man. There, apparently, political equality will not make for social equality. I do not believe that the principle applies necessarily in either case, and I shall say why. Because the facts show that you get most miscegenation where you have White and Black people side by side, and where the Black people are kept in subjection. You get least race intermixture in such countries where the development of the Black people is encouraged and their race consciousness, their pride and their self-esteem are stimulated.

Let me give you the facts in South Africa. Here in the Cape we have a measure of political equality, which we have not got in the rest of the Union. Now take the figures in regard to offences against the Immorality Act [of 1927—ed.] for the last three available years. The figures in the Cape, where you have political equality were 3.2 per 100,000 of the Native population. In the rest of the Union where you have no political equality, they were 6.4 per 100,000, or twice as many. I have taken out the figures in regard to crimes of violence with sexual intent. In the Cape the figure is .6 per 100,000 of the Native population. I am now dealing with crimes of violence with sexual intent, committed by Natives on Europeans, and the figure in the Cape is .6 per 100,000 of the Native population. In the rest of the Union the figures are 2.4 per 100,000.

MR. C. R. SWART: [3] That proves nothing.

MR. HOFMEYR: No, sir, the fear is an unreasoning fear but, it is there for all that, and we cannot get away from it. It is that fact together with the sentiment based on tradition that is to a large extent

[3] National Party.

behind this Bill. These are the facts that made the Prime Minister recede from the relative liberalism of the Bill of 1929 (which was) worse than the Bill of 1926, and made this Bill again worse than the Bill of 1929. And there is no finality. There is no more finality than there was in 1892, when Sir James Rose-Innes supported the Bill of that date because it might bring finality. That tide of reaction is still flowing forward. I know that those of us who are opposing that tide cannot hope to check it. The puny breastworks that we put up must be swept away, but I do believe that the mere putting up of those breastworks is going to accelerate the day when the tide will turn, as turn, I believe, it some day will.

Let me repeat then, I oppose this Bill. It is a Bill which replaces a vested right by a qualified and inferior citizenship, and which creates a system of communal representation. I oppose it because for that act of deprivation no adequate justification has been advanced. I oppose it because in that system of communal representation there are the seeds of hostility and strife, and I oppose it also be-cause of those forces of reaction behind this Bill which, if left unresisted, are inevitably bound to do us greater harm than anything can do us today. I know perfectly well that I am speaking against the feeling of the overwhelming majority of this House. I know I am speaking against the feeling of the great mass of the people of this country, I know how my remarks will be described as "academic" and quixotic and unrealistic. I am accustomed to that. I can see all the adjectives that will be used. But these are matters on which the future must be left to judge. I expressed the belief that the tide of reaction will turn, and I base that belief on what I know of what is going on in the minds of some at least of the younger people in South Africa, especially in the universities. I believe that there is also a rising tide of liberalism in South Africa. It is mostly the younger people who are in the forefront of that tide. It is they who are the custodians of our future. And whatever we may or may not do today, it is by them that the ultimate issues in connection with this matter will have to be decided.

92 M. D. C. DE WET NEL
THE PRINCIPLES OF APARTHEID

The Honorable M. D. C. de Wet Nel (1901–) is presently Bantu Commissioner General for the ethnic units of Venda and Tsonga (in the upper Transvaal); he was formerly Minister for Bantu Administration and Development in the South African government and a principal Cabinet spokesman for the ideal form of apartheid—separate development of black and white South Africans, including segregation of the Bantu peoples into their own states, called Bantustans, where they might run their own affairs and preserve their own culture. Wet Nel has a degree of Doctor of Philosophy from Pretoria University and was secretary of the Nationalist party between 1939 and 1948. The following selection is an extract from his speech in the House of Assembly on May 18, 1959, explaining National party policy during the debate on the second reading of the bill promoting Bantu self-government.

From *Debates of the House of Assembly (Hansard), Union of South Africa* (Cape Town: Hansard, 1959), CI, cols. 6006–6011, 6018–6024.

I want to say that it is my deep and honest conviction that we have reached the stage where serious attention should be devoted to actually giving the Bantu the opportunity to manage their own affairs; because that is one of the elementary and the most moral rights to which every person is entitled. It is the legacy demanded by every nation in the world, and the Bantu eagerly demands it just like the White man and every other nation. Every nation in the world finds its highest expression and fulfilment in managing its own affairs and in the creation of a material and spiritual heritage for its successive generations. We want to give the Bantu that right also. The demand for self-determination on the part of the non-White nations is one of the outstanding features of the past decade. Outside Africa more than a dozen non-White nations have already obtained their freedom. In Africa it is the greatest phenomenon of the time. There are a number of people in Africa who have already received their freedom, and others are on the way to receiving it. This desire to manage their own affairs exists in the hearts of the Bantu population, just as it exists in the hearts of all other nations in the world. It is therefore our duty to approach these matters soberly and realistically. It is no use putting our heads in the sand and pretending to see nothing. We have to face the real facts. These matters lie near to the soul of the nation, and no safety valve in the world can smother them forever. The late Dr. Malan described it very pithily in this House once when he said that one might just as well try to stop the Southeaster with a sieve as to suppress the national sentiments of a nation. That applies to the Bantu also.

I say we must approach these matters soberly and with clear minds. If we close our eyes to them we are heading for self-destruction and death. People who are reckless in that regard are committing treason to their own people and digging the grave of the nation. We hear so many provocative remarks about Bantu nationalism and Black nationalism, but it is my conviction that there is nothing of the kind. If it exists, then there is also something like White nationalism. But what does exist in fact is hatred on the part of the Black man for the White man. That is the monster which may still perhaps destroy all the best things in Africa. But I want to ask whether this monster has not to a large extent been created by the White man himself? The fact that he has ignored the existence of national enmities,[1] that he has ignored their own forms of government and that he has ignored their own cultural assets, has led to the growth of this monster, and that is the reason why we plead that this monster must not rear its head in South Africa. That is why we want to give them these opportunities.

Mr. Speaker, I want to say frankly that I believe in the existence of nationalism on the part of the Bantu population groups. We cannot deny it; it is there. Amongst the Zulus there is a feeling of nationalism which can serve as an example to more than one of us, but it is not a Bantu nationalism; it is their own racial nationalism, just as it exists amongst the White people of South Africa and of the world. I grant them that nationalism. If the White man is entitled to it, I ask what right we have to say that those people should not be entitled to it also? Let us be honest and fair. Moreover, nationalism is one of the forces which puts into motion the best things in the spirit of the human being. Nationalism is one of the forces which has led to the most beautiful deeds of idealism and sacrifice and inspiration. Should the Bantu not have it? It is the Nationalist who has learned to appreciate the cultural assets of other nations, and as someone once put it very strikingly, a Nationalist is the best citizen of the world. That is my belief in regard to this matter. For that reason I want to

[1] Entities?

say this. It will always be my task to respect these things of the Bantu, but to assist them to develop it as something beautiful and something which is in the interest of South Africa. It is our task to provide the opportunities for developing these matters, so that we may have co-operation instead of racial clashes. To think that we can solve this problem by lumping together in one community everything which is Bantu is nothing less than a crime towards the Bantu. One of the good things contained in this Bill is that it formally recognises these national units among the Bantu, and to give them the right and to encourage them to continue along this road of national development.

The question may be put in all fairness: Will it not be better, in the interest of South Africa, rather to continue building on the pattern we have now? I want to deal with a few considerations only.

In the first place, I stated the proposition that the overwhelming majority of the national groups in South Africa, including the Bantu, have rejected the ideal of a multi-racial community and have chosen separate development on their own. If we continued to build further on the present pattern, it would be nothing else but a negation of the will and the desires of the overwhelming majority of the population groups in South Africa, White as well as Bantu. In the second place we must be fair and honest and admit that the present state of affairs is very unsatisfactory to the Bantu and very uncertain for the Whites. If we continue building on the present pattern the position of the Whites will be very uncertain and the Bantu will not be satisfied. Let us remember that in this House there are three representatives who represent only the Bantu population of the Cape Province. The rest of the Bantu in South Africa are not represented in this House. Do hon. members want to tell me that the Bantu population takes no notice of that and that they are satisfied with it? It is

an injustice which rankles in the minds of the Bantu in the other parts of the country. That is one of the main factors which engenders a spirit of suspicion and doubt regarding the honesty and the fairness and the justice of the White man. It is a political state of affairs which can no longer be tolerated. If hon. members want to be fair and logical, they should ask that at least the rest of the Bantu population in South Africa should be represented in this House on an equal footing with those in the Cape Province, and if they do that, I ask: Where will it end? We would then be setting in progress the same process which is being experienced in Kenya, Nyasaland and Northern Rhodesia today. We just cannot foresee the results of it.

In the third place, it is my honest conviction that these Bantu population groups can best be guided on the road to progress if their whole development is Bantu orientated, which means that all the administrative bodies from the highest to the lowest should be linked up and the whole of the Bantu population should be concerned in them. It must form part of the whole structure. The present pattern was White orientated, because it was coupled to the White man. The result was that there was a flight from the Bantu community. The developed Native no longer sought the satisfaction of his ambition to develop amongst his own people, but in the White areas. Surely that is a very sad state of affairs. There was a migration going on, not only of migrant labourers from the Bantu areas, but also of educated people from the Bantu areas, that most essential material for building up of a community. In my opinion every nation in the world is entitled to benefit from the efforts of its best sons and daughters and a policy which is calculated to deprive them of it is immoral; it is human erosion. A policy like that cannot be tolerated. Such a policy is one of the chief causes of racial hatred.

In the fourth place, I am convinced in

my mind that the expansion of the present system will have the result that the White population of South Africa will be dominated by the political power of the Bantu population. If this pattern is extended logically in the future, I say that the White people will be dominated by the political power of the Bantu. Surely it must be a very stupid politician who cannot appreciate the logical consequences of this.

The present system of Bantu representation has really made no contribution in any way towards creating sound racial relations in South Africa. I challenge any person to deny that. All it has done is to increase racial tension. That is the only result which can today stand as a monument for those people, with few exceptions. If we extended the present system, what would the result be? It would create a racial hatred which South Africa simply cannot afford, because, in the course of years, we would then have a bitter struggle on the part of the White man to ensure that he is not ploughed under politically by the non-White groups of the population, but, at the same time, it must be remembered that if we accepted that principle today, then the Bantu would have to accept this Parliament as his Parliament, and he would then become involved in a struggle in which he would demand representation in this House on at least the same basis as the White man. That is the trouble which awaits South Africa, and I say that anybody who does not realise that, must be stupid. Mr. Speaker, if there are people who say that the Bantu will always be satisfied to be represented in Parliament by a few people, I say to them that they are living in a fool's paradise. No nation in the world would agree to it, and still much less the proud Bantu.

Reference has been made here to "White leadership with justice." Mr. Speaker, this whole outlook is so unrealistic and childishly naïve that it amuses one. It is pathetic. Show me one nation in our modern history which would be prepared to agree to such a thing. Even the Bushmen rejected it in respect to the Bantu. Do members of the United Party want to tell me that the proud Bantu would agree to it? They can go and tell that story to political baboons but not to intelligent people. It is a hallucination!

Mr. Speaker, the African states are giving their reply today to this issue with which we are dealing. We are getting an object lesson with regard to this same issue in various territories of Africa. Are we politically blind or politically deaf? Are we going to learn no lesson from that? In places like Kenya, Nyasaland and Northern Rhodesia we saw that the British Government was prepared to go very far in giving the Bantu, on this same sort of basis, a say together with the White man in the government of the country, and what were the results? Did it produce peace? No, it created greater dissatisfaction. On this very same basis, they wanted to give greater rights to the Native population of other territories, and the result was simply that those people, once they had been given these rights, demanded that the sole say should be in the hands of the majority of the people. They are not going to be satisfied with anything less than the sole say. Why then should South Africa be an exception? No, Mr. Speaker, this political pattern does not create racial peace, but racial tension; it does not produce harmonious relations but clashes; it does not produce confidence but fear; it does not bring peace but strife; it does not produce order but chaos.

Mr. Speaker, in the light of South Africa's fundamental choice and standpoint, on the basis of our experience extending over generations, having regard to the salvation of South Africa and the happiness of all groups of the population, there is only one way—the traditional way, the way which is embodied in this Bill which I am submitting to the House for its consideration.

I want to pause for a moment to deal with the recognition of Bantu homelands.

In the White Paper [Promotion of Bantu Self-Government—ed.] I put forward a few propositions which I do not want to repeat here, but I just want to make this submission again that in setting aside Bantu territories both before and after the establishment of Union, the object was not purely and simply to set aside land for them; the great object was to give that land to the various communities as their homelands. The object was not simply to set aside that land; the main object was to assist those communities with their development, to link them up with their land. This setting aside of land was undertaken not only by the British Government, but also by the Republican Governments. As from 1878 the Bantu territories of the Ciskei were deliberately demarcated by the British Government, and that was done in the region between the Great Fish and the Kei Rivers. The constituent parts of the present Transkei, with the retention of their identity as Bantu territories, were incorporated into the Cape Colony by means of a series of acts and proclamations as from 1879. In 1839 the Voortrekkers started with territorial demarcation in Natal, and that was continued by the British Government in 1843. Separate areas were demarcated and given to the Natal Native Trust in 1864. In 1897 Zululand proper, with the retention of its identity, was incorporated into Natal by legislation. In the Transvaal a start was made in 1853 with the granting of land to the tribes, and in 1881 a standing Native Location Commission started defining those areas. The republic of the Orange Free State, by means of grants and resolutions, also recognised Bantu areas. So, for example, in 1867, with a further extension in 1873, Witzieshoek was granted to two tribes, while in 1884 Thaba'Nchu was set aside for the Barolong. With the establishment of Union, the British Government kept the three large Bantu territories, Bechuanaland, Basutoland and Swaziland—which jointly represented one-third of the surface area of British South Africa, outside the Union and thereby indicated that these territories should be maintained as Bantu territories. After the establishment of Union the Union Government, by legislation, immediately entrenched as Bantu territories the areas which had been recognised by its predecessor as Bantu territories, and it did so by incorporating them in terms of the Native Land Act of 1913. But the Union Government did not leave it at that. Subsequently, a further 7,250,-000 morgen [a morgen is 2.116 acres —ed.] of land were released for systematic addition to the Bantu areas and since then nearly 5,000,000 morgen of land have been added. But I say again that the main task was neglected, and that is the development which should have accompanied that. In the case of the Transvaal, the Free State and Natal the main object was perfectly clear.

I just want to pause for a moment to deal with the aims which it was intended to achieve in setting aside Bantu areas. The main aim was to create homelands for the Bantu. In the case of the Cape Colony there was a two-fold policy. The first aim coincided with that of the Transvaal and Natal, and the other was to establish a number of small locations which were to serve as a means of breaking up the tribes, of introducing civilisation to the Bantu, and, as an historian put it, as labour reservoirs for the Whites. Here we really had a difference between the opinion of the people and that of the authorities, but the mass of the population in South Africa regarded these areas as the homelands of the Bantu and the Bantu accepted them as such.

One of the fine things that we are doing in this Bill is to give formal recognition to the various Bantu population groups. That is a desire that we find on the part of all the groups of the population. In the short time during which I have had some dealings with them, one of the questions which has been put to me everywhere is this: "Can't you give us recognition; why are you tearing us asunder?" In this Bill formal recognition is being given to the existence of those population groups, but particularly to the process of national development by and in the population groups themselves. I think by this time hon. members will concede that you cannot start a process of development by simply linking it up with the White man's way of life. That would be nonsensical. No process in which the Bantu's dignity is not acknowledged can form the basis on which development can take place, and in refusing to appreciate his own system of government and his own rights we slight the dignity of the Bantu himself. But hon. members will also concede a second thing, Mr. Speaker, and that is that that process cannot be started by creating an artificial unit, in other words, by bundling all the Bantu together in one common society, as many hon. members on the other side want to do, because there are only two bonds which bind them together: The first is their colour and the other is their hatred of the White man. But there is something greater than that, something higher than that which binds people together, and that is their spiritual treasures, the cultural treasures of a people. It is these fine things which have united other nations in the world. That is why we say that the basis of our approach is that the Bantu too will be linked together by traditional and emotional bonds, by their own language, their own culture, their national possessions. I am convinced that for this measure I shall receive the gratitude of the Bantu throughout South Africa.

This Bill also gives the various population groups their own territorial authorities. That is very important. Where there are no territorial authorities as yet, a Territorial Council will be established in the meantime, but I am convinced that within a year or two all these matters will be disposed of.

But the most important consideration is that this Bill makes it possible for the Governor-General to transfer his legislative powers systematically to those Territorial Authorities. Because of the nature of our national structure it is not possible today to see this in clear perspective, but I am convinced that once these Territorial Authorities have all been established, and these powers have been systematically transferred to them, we are going to achieve excellent results. This is an act of faith in the Bantu such as we have never had before in South Africa, and it is something which is going to satisfy him and for which he is already very grateful today. I readily concede that many of these things will take a little time before they can all be arranged and before all these powers can be granted, but once all the Territorial Authorities are in operation, it is my intention to review this whole matter and to see how we can best shape it in the interests of every population group and in the interests of the whole of South Africa. But the Bantu himself will have to help in extending this system. He will be called upon to extend it, and that is one of the fine principles contained in this Bill, because now it will no longer be the White man who will be doing these things; it will be the Bantu himself.

In the second place I want to mention another important aspect, and that is that we envisage that the Bantu will develop his own courts. Let me put it this way: The Bantu has developed a very fine legal system which ensures a high degree of justice. That is why it has also been recognised by the authorities, but the mistake that was made was that no attention was given to the question of allowing the courts to develop together with the development of the community. It was looked down upon and jeered at. After all, according to the United Party it was just a court conducted by barbarians. Mr. Speaker, that is not fair towards the Bantu; it is not reconcilable with the general development of the Bantu. That is why this Bill provides for special attention to be given to this matter so that it will become possible for them to administer their own system of justice. They will be assisted actively to extend their own courts, and I anticipate that the time will come when they themselves will have their own supreme court in their own territories with their own judges on the Bench. I propose to give very serious attention to this matter.

But this Bill goes further. It holds out this prospect that the Territorial Authorities are going to look after their own education. I just want to announce that the Department of Bantu Education is ready, as soon as the Bantu Territorial Authorities are in operation, to place a large portion of the education in the areas concerned directly under the Territorial Authorities. That will mean that the Territorial Authority will exercise authority and control over all the school boards and committees in this area. In exercising that control it will have in its hands the most important means of building up its community culturally and economically. Just think what it will mean to the Bantu if he himself exercises control over his education. Welfare work and social services will also be placed under them in due course. We shall see to it that it takes place on a sound basis.

Then I want to mention another important matter and that is that in due course the Native Trust Lands will be transferred to the Territorial Authorities, a very important decision. It must not be forgotten that the land which has been set aside for them—7,250,000 morgen—falls under the Native Trust. The Native Trust is responsible for the development of that land, etc. We now envisage transferring this land in due course to the Territorial Authorities. They will then be responsible for the proper conservation of the soil and its development, etc. I need only say this, Mr. Speaker, that when we look at the results which are being achieved at the present time, there can be no doubt that it would be in the interests of the Bantu

and of South Africa as a whole to entrust that task to the Natives. It is a question of faith. They would be responsible for the allocation of that land and all that type of thing. Let me just say this: There are very few things which have caused so much dissatisfaction amongst the Bantu as the fact that the land which was purchased at the time—I refer to the land which was promised to them at the time by General Hertzog and of which a portion was bought—was placed under the Native Trust and not directly under the chiefs. Throughout the whole of South Africa I have heard this reproach. Under the system which is now being introduced it will fall under the Territorial Authority, which is a responsible body. This is an important step forward.

Then I want to mention another important principle which is contained in this Bill. Formerly the Governor-General could appoint or dismiss any chief at will. He will now be obliged to consult the Territorial Authority. I admit that in the past the Governor-General has always consulted the tribe, but the responsibility is now going to rest with the Territorial Authority. In this way it is being given status, it is being given the status in its own territory which our Government has in the territory of the White man. That is the basic approach in connection with this matter.

But there is another important principle embodied in this legislation, and that is that for the first time official links are being instituted between the Bantu territories and the Natives in the cities. For the first time! I admit at once that here we are facing a very great problem. I readily admit that there are many Bantu in the White areas. But I also want to make this further submission that very large numbers of those Bantu were not born in South Africa. There are many of them whose home is Basutoland. Do you know, sir, that there are approximately 1,000,000 Sothos in South Africa? Large numbers of them were born in the Protectorate of Bechuanaland, and Swaziland is the home of a large section. Do not let us overlook that factor. That is a factor which will have to be faced squarely sooner or later. But that does not detract from the fact that there are also large numbers of our own Natives in the cities, and that is a very important problem. The question which is frequently asked is this: What is to be their future?

Let me first say this—and in this regard I want to be explicit and clear. It must be quite clearly understood by the United Party and by the whole world that those Natives will never become part of the White community; we are not going to follow a policy which is going to lead to a common society in South Africa. Let us be perfectly clear and explicit on that point. But in the second place, I want to make this statement that the vast majority of those people have never lost their links with their own territories. I personally made some pilot surveys and the Tomlinson Commission[2] made a large number of pilot surveys over the whole country, and it was found that easily 80 per cent, if not more, of those Bantu had always retained some link or other with the Bantu areas. We are not faced here with a problem of displaced persons. Our practical experience has been that although a Bantu has been in the city for years, for perhaps two or three generations, he still knows where his tribe is, and you will be surprised to know, sir, how readily he is absorbed again into his tribe. Why do hon. members come along and make a mountain out of a molehill? The fact of the matter is that links will now be created between the Bantu areas and those people in the cities. I have no doubt that it will have a very salutary effect. It will also have a salutary effect on the moral standards of those people. It must not be for-

gotten that as far as customs, etc. are concerned, the Bantu in the cities constitute rather a loose population, and in those places where the different ethnic groups are already separately housed and where we have given them non-official recognition, it has already been shown that a new ideal has been created for these people, where they have their own links and their own mother-tongue and when we restore to them those emotional links which are of so much value to every nation in the world. I have no doubt that in this way we are going to create a very fine link as far as the whole Native population is concerned.

Then I just want to say that in this process we should at least concede to the Bantu what the English people did not begrudge themselves. Let me just remind the House that the whole democratic system of the British nation was developed round the Royal house and the nobility. Let them deny it. It took years, but that is the position. Today every Englishman is proud of that democratic system. But it must not be forgotten that it is only since 1832 that that system has actually taken definite shape. Why then do we begrudge this same process to the Bantu? Here we have the same process. What is contained in this Bill is something that the Bantu understands, something that is integrated into his life.

But hon. members may ask perhaps why we do not carry on with this matter and leave alone the question of Natives' representation; why we do not allow the Natives' representatives to remain in this House; why we do not first complete the whole pattern and then consider thereafter whether we want to abolish the Native representation in this House. I just want to say that that is an attitude which can only be adopted by a person who has no knowledge at all of the Native. Any person who has taken the slightest trouble to make a study of the approach of the Bantu population to these matters, could never adopt such an attitude. Because in

[2] Appointed in 1948 by the Malan Government. Chairman: Professor F. R. Tomlinson of Pretoria University. [The commission was to consider the implementation of separate development—ed.]

connection with this political issue, they have an axiom which runs as follows, that the idea of two bulls in one kraal never works. The Native does not want it; to him it is unthinkable. To have two political processes which are diametrically opposed to each other and which try to destroy each other, is something which the Native simply cannot understand, and he would regard that as the greatest dishonesty on the part of the White man. Sir, there are Natives who have asked me to abolish the Native representation immediately. If we want to be honest, then we must take into account the approach of the Bantu himself, and then we cannot start such a process; we must adopt the course that is acceptable and understandable and honest towards the Bantu population, a course which in their eyes is not a conflicting policy but which they regard as an honest policy.

The question may be put to me: What does the Native population think about this matter? How do they feel? I just want to say that after the introduction of this Bill I made it my business to make its contents known to all the Bantu population groups throughout South Africa. More than 3,000 copies of the Bill and of the White Paper were distributed amongst them. The full contents were also published in the journal *Bantu,* more than 30,000 copies of which were distributed. What was the reaction? The reaction was this, that I have here a large number of telegrams from all parts of South Africa, from all the important Bantu population groups, from Cyprian, from Victor Poto, from Botha Sigcau, from the Venda chiefs, from the Ciskei, etc. I have had telegrams from the responsible groups in every territory conveying their gratitude and congratulations and telling me to go ahead with this. And do you know, sir, that I did not have a single letter or telegram of protest? Do you know where I came across a protest? A moment ago at the entrance to Parliament, where there is a placard bearing the words "no taxation without representation." The Black Sash!

MRS. BALLINGER: Hear, hear!

MR. DE WET NEL: I agree, but that is one of the great principles embodied in this Bill, because here it is envisaged that in the future they will impose their own taxes, and the time will come when all taxes in the Bantu areas will be imposed by the Bantu themselves. That is the only protest that I received. Everywhere the Bantu have acclaimed this as a new day and a new era which has dawned for the Bantu in South Africa. That is their approach to this matter.

The aims of this Bill could be briefly summarised as follows:

1. It gives expression to the racial pattern and the philosophy of life of the people of South Africa in respect to the colour question. It is the product of a deep and honest conviction which flows from historical experience and which is based on the Christian principles underlying the approach of our people, because we do not begrudge those people what we claim for ourselves.

2. It rests on the conviction that it will ward off those factors which may possibly plough the White man under, but at the same time it also creates the possibility for the Bantu to bring to the fullest fruition his personal and national ideas within his own population group. What we demand for ourselves, we do not begrudge the Bantu. Our approach is not simply negative but also positive.

3. It converts the Bantu development which was formerly instituted under the direction of the White man, into a development which will be anchored in the Bantu community itself, a development in terms of which all the factors of nation and community building will be actively placed in the service of each group of the Bantu population, on the same lines as in the case of the White man. In this way the material and spiritual growth of the Bantu population groups will be set in motion, so that they will also be able to

make a contribution to the eternal and lasting values of South Africa and of the world as a whole.

4. It lays the foundation of a form of government in which all population groups, on a basis of honour and mutual respect, can be informed and consulted about the great problems of South Africa and where everyone's efforts can be harnessed in a spirit of mutual trust for the welfare of South Africa.

5. It creates, I am convinced, a future of hope and expectation for all population groups in South Africa, a future of peace and security, not only for the White population of South Africa, but also for the Bantu population groups. Now every group will know in which direction it is moving. It removes the mists of doubt and uncertainty, which are the greatest cause of mistrust of the White man. Those mists of doubt and uncertainty have now disappeared. Everybody will know in which direction he is heading, and it is that certainty which gives man the greatest satisfaction.

6. I am deeply convinced that this is the only basis on which a great and happy South Africa can be built for all population groups.

93 NELSON ROLIHLAHLE MANDELA
VERWOERD'S TRIBALISM

Nelson Rolihlahle Mandela (1918–) is one of South Africa's foremost African nationalist leaders and is now serving a sentence of life imprisonment on Robben Island. The son of a Tembu chief, Mandela left the University of Fort Hare in 1940 and went to Johannesburg, where he became involved in the formation of the Youth League of the African National Congress (ANC), a radical "ginger-group" within South Africa's oldest African nationalist organization. When the ANC launched its passive resistance campaign in defiance of apartheid legislation, Mandela was Volunteer-in-Chief and was later elected to the National Executive of the ANC. Restrictions were subsequently placed on him by the government, and in 1956 he was arrested and was one of the defendants in the abortive treason trial (1956–1961). He rose to prominence in the white community in 1961, when South Africa declared itself a republic. Mandela went underground to organize a stay-at-home campaign and became known as the "Scarlet Pimpernel." While underground he also acted as one of the leaders of a sabotage group known as Umkhonto We Sizwe (Spear of the Nation). Many of the leaders of this group were arrested in 1963 at Rivonia and in 1964 some of them, including Mandela, were sentenced to life imprisonment.

During the 1950s, Mandela wrote a number of analytical articles on the South African situation, which have recently been collected into a book entitled No Easy Walk to Freedom, *edited by Ruth First.*

South Africa belongs to all who live in it, black and white.—Freedom Charter.

All the Bantu have their permanent homes in the Reserves and their entry into other areas

From Chapter 8, *No Easy Walk to Freedom,* by Nelson Mandela, © Nelson Mandela, 1965, Basic Books, Inc., Publishers, New York. Reprinted by permission of Basic Books, Inc. and Heinemann Educational Books Ltd.

and into the urban areas is merely of a temporary nature and for economic reasons. In other
words, they are admitted as work-seekers, not
as settlers.—Dr. W. W. M. Eiselen, Secretary
of the Department of Bantu Administration
and Development. (Article in *Optima,* March
1959)

The statements quoted above contain
diametrically opposite conceptions of this
country, its future, and its destiny. Obviously they cannot be reconciled. They
have nothing in common, except that
both of them look forward to a future of
affairs rather than that which prevails at
present. At present, South Africa does
not "belong"—except in a moral sense
—to all. Ninety-seven per cent of the
country is legally owned by members (a
handful of them at that) of the dominant
White minority. And at present by no
means "all" Africans have their "permanent homes" in the Reserves. Millions of
Africans were born and have their permanent homes in the towns and cities and
elsewhere outside the Reserves, have
never seen the Reserves, and have no desire to go there.[1]

It is necessary for the people of this
country to choose between these two alternative paths. It is assumed that readers
of *Liberation* [an anti-apartheid journal
—ed.] are familiar with the detailed
proposals contained in the Charter.

Let us therefore study the policies submitted by the Nationalist Party.

The newspapers have christened the
Nationalists' plan as one for "Bantustans." The hybrid word is, in many ways,
extremely misleading. It derives from the
partitioning of India after the reluctant
departure of the British, and as a condition thereof, into two separate states, Hin-
dustan and Pakistan. There is no real

[1] According to the 1951 census, trust land locations
and Reserves accounted for only $2^1/2$ million out of
a total African population of, at that time, $8^1/2$ million. A further $2^1/2$ million, nearly, were on European-owned farms. The rest were mainly in urban
areas.

parallel with the Nationalists' proposals,
for:

(a) India and Pakistan constitute two com-
    pletely separate and politically independent
    states.

(b) Muslims enjoy equal rights in India; Hin-
    dus enjoy equal rights in Pakistan.

(c) Partition was submitted to and approved
    by both parties, or at any rate fairly wide-
    spread and influential sections of each.

The Government's plans do not envisage the partitioning of this country into
separate, self-governing states. They do
not envisage equal rights, or any rights at
all, for Africans outside the Reserves.
Partition has never been approved of by
Africans and never will be. For that matter it has never really been submitted to
or approved of by the Whites. The term
"Bantustan" is therefore a complete mis-
nomer, and merely tends to help the Nationalists perpetrate a fraud.

Let us examine each of these aspects in
detail.

It is typical of the Nationalists' propaganda techniques that they describe their
measures in misleading titles, which
convey the opposite of what the measures
contain. Verwoerd called his law greatly
extending and intensifying the pass laws
the "Abolition of Passes" Act. Similarly,
he has introduced into the current parliamentary session a measure called the
"Promotion of Bantu Self-Government
Bill." It starts off by decreeing the abolition of the tiny token representation of
Africans (by Whites) in Parliament and
the Cape Provincial Council.

It goes on to provide for the division of
the African population into eight "ethnic
units" (the so-called Bantustans). They
are: North and South Sotho, Swazi,
Tsonga, Tswana, Venda, Xhosa, and
Zulu. These units are to undergo a
"gradual development to self-government."

This measure was described by the
Prime Minister, Dr. Verwoerd, as a "su-

premely positive step" towards placing Africans "on the road to self-government." Mr. De Wet Nel, Minister of Bantu Affairs, said the people in the Reserves "would gradually be given more powers to rule themselves."

The scheme is elaborated in a White Paper, tabled in the House of Assembly, to "explain" the Bill. According to this document, the immediate objects of the Bill are:

(a) The recognition of the so-called Bantu National Units and the appointment of commissioners-general whose task will be to give guidance and advice to the units in order to promote their general development, with special reference to the administrative field.

(b) The linking of Africans working in urban areas with territorial authorities established under the Bantu Authorities Act, by conferring powers on the Bantu Authorities to nominate persons as their representatives in urban areas.

(c) The transfer to the Bantu territorial authorities, at the appropriate time, of land in their areas at present held by the Native Trust.

(d) The vesting in territorial Bantu authorities of legislative authority and the right to impose taxes, and to undertake works and give guidance to subordinate authorities.

(e) The establishments of territorial boards for the purpose of temporary liaison through commissioners-general if during the transition period the administrative structure in any area has not yet reached the stage where a territorial authority has been established.

(f) The abolition of representation in the highest European governing bodies.

According to the same White Paper, the Bill has the following further objects:

(a) The creation of homogeneous administrative areas for Africans by uniting the members of each so-called national group in the national unit, concentrated in one coherent homeland where possible.

(b) The education of Africans to a sound understanding of the problems of soil conversion and agriculture so that all rights over and responsibilities in respect of soil in African areas may be assigned to them.

This includes the gradual replacement of European agricultural officers of all grades by qualified and competent Africans.

(c) The systematic promotion of a diverse economy in the African areas, acceptable to Africans and to be developed by them.

(d) The education of the African to a sound understanding of the problems and aims of Bantu education so that, by the decentralization of powers, responsibility for the different grades of education may be vested in them.

(e) The training of Africans with a view to effectively extending their own judicial system and their education to a sound understanding of the common law with a view to transferring to them responsibilities for the administration of justice in their areas.

(f) The gradual replacement of European administrative officers by qualified and competent Africans.

(g) The exercise of legislative powers by Africans in respect of their areas, at first at a limited scale, but with every intention of gradually extending this power.

It will be seen that the African people are asked to pay a very high price for this so-called "self-government" in the Reserves. Urban Africans—the workers, businessmen, and professional men and women, who are the pride of our people

in the stubborn and victorious march towards modernization and progress—are
to be treated as outcasts, not even "settlers" like Dr. Verwoerd. Every vestige
of rights and opportunities will be ruth-
lessly destroyed. Everywhere outside the
Reserves an African will be tolerated only
on condition that he is for the convenience
of the Whites.

There will be forcible uprooting and
mass removals of millions of people to
"homogeneous administrative areas."
The Reserves, already intolerably over-
crowded, will be crammed with hundreds
of thousands more people evicted by the
Government.

In return for all these hardships, in return for Africans abandoning their birthright as citizens, pioneers, and inhabitants
of South Africa, the Government promises them "self-government" in the tiny 13
per cent that their greed and miserliness
"allocates" to us. But what sort of self-
government is this that is promised?

There are two essential elements to self-
government, as the term is used and understood all over the modern world. They
are:

1. *Democracy.* The organs of government
   must be representative; that is to say,
   they must be freely chosen leaders and
   representatives of the people, whose
   mandate must be renewed at periodic
   democratic elections.
2. *Sovereignty.* The government thus
   chosen must be free to legislate and act
   as it deems fit on behalf of the people,
   not subject to any limitations upon its
   powers by any alien authority.

Neither of these two essentials is present in the Nationalist plan. The "Bantu
National Units" will be ruled in effect by
the commissioners-general appointed by
the Bantu Government, and administered
by the Bantu Affairs Department officials
under his control. When the Government
says it plans gradually increasing self-gov-

ernment, it merely means that more powers in future will be exercised by
appointed councils of chiefs and headmen. No provision is made for elections.
The Nationalists say that chiefs, not
elected legislatures, are "the Bantu tradition."

There was a time when, like all peoples
on earth, Africans conducted their simple
communities through chiefs, advised by
tribal councils and mass meetings of the
people. In those times the chiefs were
indeed representative governors. Nowhere, however, have such institutions
survived the complexities of modern industrial civilization. Moreover, in South
Africa we all know full well that no chief
can retain his post unless he submits to
Verwoerd, and many chiefs who sought
the interest of their people before position
and self-advancement have, like President
Lutuli, been deposed.

Thus, the proposed Bantu authorities
will not be, in any sense of the term, representative or democratic.

The point is made with pride by the
Bantu Affairs Department itself in an official publication:

The councillors will perform their task without
fear or prejudice, because they are not elected
by the majority of votes, and they will be able
to lead their people onwards . . . even though
. . . it may demand hardships and sacrifices.

A strange paean to autocracy, from a
department of a Government which
claims to be democratic!

In spite of all their precautions to see
that their "territorial authorities"—appointed themselves, subject to dismissal
by themselves and under constant control
by their commissioners-general and
their Bantu Affairs Department—never
become authentic voices of the people, the
Nationalists are determined to see that
even those puppet bodies never enjoy real
power of sovereignty.

In his notorious (and thoroughly dishonest) article in *Optima,* Dr. Eiselen

draws a far-fetched comparison between the relations between the future "Bantustans" and the Union Government, on the one hand, and those between Britain and the self-governing Dominions on the other. He foresees:

A cooperative South African system based on the Commonwealth conception, with the Union Government gradually changing its position from guardian and trustee to become instead the senior member of a group of separate communities.

To appreciate the full hypocrisy of this statement, it must be remembered that Dr. Eiselen is an official of a Nationalist Party Government, a member of a party which has built its fortune for the past half century on its cry that it stands for full untrammelled sovereignty within the Commonwealth, that claims credit for Hertzog's achievements in winning the Statute of Westminster, which proclaims such sovereignty, and which even now wants complete independence and a republic outside the Commonwealth.

It cannot be claimed, therefore, that Eiselen and Verwoerd do not understand the nature of a commonwealth, or sovereignty, or federation.

What are we to think, then, in the same article, when Dr. Eiselen comes into the open, and declares:

The utmost degree of autonomy in administrative matters which the Union Parliament is likely to be prepared to concede to these areas will stop short of actual surrender of sovereignty by the European trustee, and there is therefore no prospect of a federal system with eventual equality among members taking the place of the South African Commonwealth . . .

There is no sovereignty then. No autonomy. No democracy. No self-government. Nothing but a crude, empty fraud, to bluff the people at home and abroad, and to serve as a pretext for heaping

yet more hardships and injustices upon the African people.

Politically, the talk about self-government for the Reserves is a swindle. Economically, it is an absurdity.

The few scattered African Reserves in various parts of the Union, comprising about 13 per cent of the least desirable land area, represent the last shreds of land ownership left to the African people of their original ancestral home. After the encroachments and depredations of generations of European land-sharks, achieved by force and by cunning, and culminating in the outrageous Land Act from 1913 onwards, had turned the once free and independent Tswana, Sotho, Xhosa, Zulu, and other peasant farmers of this country into a nation of landless outcasts and roving beggars, humble "work-seekers" on the mines and the farms where yesterday they had been masters of the land, the new White masters of the country "generously presented" them the few remaining miserable areas as reservoirs and breeding-grounds for Black labour. These are the Reserves.

It was never claimed or remotely considered by the previous governments of the Union that these Reserves could become economically self-sufficient "national homes" for 9,600,000 African people of this country. The final lunacy was left to Dr. Verwoerd, Dr. Eiselen, and the Nationalist Party.

The facts are—as every reader who remembers Govan Mbeki's brilliant series of articles on the Transkei in *Liberation* will be aware—that the Reserves are congested distressed areas, completely unable to sustain their present populations. The majority of the adult males are always away from home working in the towns, mines, or European-owned farms. The people are on the verge of starvation.

The White Paper speaks of teaching Africans soil conservation and agriculture and replacing European agricultural officers by Africans. This is merely trifling with the problem. The root problem of the Reserves is the intolerable congestion which already exists. No amount of agricultural instruction will ever enable 13 per cent of the land to sustain 66 per cent of the population.

The Government is, of course, fully aware of the fact. They have no intention of creating African areas which are genuinely self-supporting (and which could therefore create a genuine possibility for self-government). If such areas were indeed self-supporting, where would the Chamber of Mines and the Nationalist farmers get their supplies of cheap labour?

In the article to which I have already referred, Dr. Eiselen bluntly admits:

In fact not much more than a quarter of the community (on the Reserves) can be farmers, the others seeking their livelihood in industrial, commercial, professional, or administrative employment.

Where are they to find such employment? In the Reserves? To anyone who knows these poverty-stricken areas, sadly lacking in modern communications, power resources, and other needed facilities, the idea of industrial development seems far-fetched indeed. The beggarly £500,000 voted to the so-called "Bantu Investment Corporation" by Parliament is mere eyewash: it would not suffice to build a single decent road, railway line, or power station.

The Government has already established a number of "rural locations"— townships in the Reserves. The Eiselen article says a number more are planned: he mentions a total of no less than ninety-six. Since the residents will not farm, how will they manage to keep alive, still less pay rents and taxes and support the traders, professional classes, and civil servants whom the optimistic Eiselen envisages will make a living there?

Fifty-seven towns on the borders of the Reserves have been designated as centres where White capitalists can set up industries. Perhaps some will migrate, and thus "export" their capital resources of cheap labour and land. Certainly, unlike the Reserves (which are a monument to the callous indifference of the Union Parliament to the needs of the non-voting African taxpayers), these towns have power, water, transport, railways, etc. The Nationalist Government, while it remains in office, will probably subsidize capitalists who migrate in this way. It is already doing so in various ways, thus creating unemployment in the cities. But it is unlikely that any large-scale voluntary movement will take place away from the big, established industrial centres, with their well-developed facilities, available materials, and markets.

Even if many industries were forced to move to the border areas around the Reserves it would not make one iota of difference to the economic viability of the Reserves themselves. The fundamental picture of the Union's economy could remain fundamentally the same as at present: a single integrated system based upon the exploitation of African labour by White capitalists.

Economically, the "Bantustan" concept is just as big a swindle as it is politically.

Thus we find, if we really look into it, that this grandiose "partition" scheme, this "supremely positive step" of Dr. Verwoerd, is like all apartheid schemes— high-sounding double-talk to conceal a policy of ruthless oppression of the non-Whites and of buttressing the unwarranted privileges of the White minority, especially the farming, mining, and financial circles.

Even if it were not so, however, even if the scheme envisaged a genuine sharing-out of the country on the basis of population figures, and a genuine transfer of power to elected representatives of the people, it would remain fundamentally unjust and dangerously unstable unless it were submitted to, accepted, and endorsed by all parties to the agreement. To think otherwise is to fly in the face of the principle of self-determination, which is upheld by all countries and confirmed in the United Nations Charter, to which this country is pledged.

Now even Dr. Eiselen recognizes this difficulty to some extent. He pays lip-service to the Atlantic Charter and appeals to "Western democracy." He mentions the argument that apartheid would only be acceptable "provided that the parties concerned agreed to this of their own free will." And then he most dishonestly evades the whole issue. "There is no reason for ruling out apartheid on the grounds that the vast majority of the population oppose it," he writes. "The Bantu as a whole do not demand integration, in a single society. This is the idea . . . merely of a small minority."

Even Dr. Eiselen, however, has not the audacity to claim that the African people actually favour apartheid or partition.

Let us state clearly the facts of the matter, with the greatest possible clarity.

NO SERIOUS OR RESPONSIBLE LEADER, GATHERING, OR ORGANIZATION OF THE AFRICAN PEOPLE HAS EVER ACCEPTED SEGREGATION, SEPARATION, OR THE PARTITION OF THIS COUNTRY IN ANY SHAPE OR FORM.

At Bloemfontein in 1956, under the auspices of the United African clergy, perhaps the most widely attended and representative gathering of African representatives, of every shade of political opinion ever held, unanimously and uncompromisingly rejected the Tomlinson Report, on which the Verwoerd plan is based, and voted in favour of a single society.

Even the rural areas, where dwell the "good" (i.e. simple and ignorant) "Bantu" of the imagination of Dr. Verwoerd and Dr. Eiselen, attempts to impose apartheid have met, time after time, with furious, often violent resistance. Chief after chief has been deposed or deported for resisting "Bantu authorities" plans. Those who, out of short-sightedness, cowardice, or corruption, have accepted these plans have earned nothing but the contempt of their own people.

It is a pity that, on such a serious subject, and at such a crucial period, serious misstatements should have been made by some people who purport to speak on behalf of the Africans. For example, Mrs. Margaret Ballinger, the Liberal Party M.P., is reported as saying in the Assembly "no confidence" debate:

The Africans have given their answer to this apartheid proposition but, of course, no one ever listens to them. They have said: "If you want separation then let us have it. Give us half of South Africa. Give us the eastern half of South Africa. Give us some of the developed resources because we have helped to develop them." (*S.A. Outlook,* March 1959)

It is most regrettable that Mrs. Ballinger should have made such a silly and irresponsible statement towards, one fears, the end of a distinguished parliamentary career. For in this instance she has put herself in the company of those who do not listen to the Africans. No Africans of any standing have ever made the proposals put forward by her.

The leading organization of the African people is the African National Congress. Congress has repeatedly denounced apartheid. It has repeatedly endorsed the Freedom Charter [a manifesto of ideals for future South African society drafted by African nationalists and their associates of other races—ed.], which claims South Africa "for all its people." It is true that occasionally individual Africans become so depressed and desperate at Nationalist misrule that they have tended to clutch at any straw to say: give us any little corner where we may be free to run our own affairs. But Congress has always firmly rejected such momentary tendencies and refused to barter our birthright, which is South Africa, for such illusory "Bantustans."

Commenting on a suggestion by Professor du Plessis that a federation of "Bantustans" be established, Mr. Duma Nokwe, secretary-general of the African National Congress, totally rejected such a plan as unacceptable. The correct approach, he said, would be the extension of the franchise rights to Africans. Thereafter a National Convention of all the people of South Africa could be summoned and numerous suggestions of the democratic changes that should be brought about, including the suggestion of Professor du Plessis, could form the subject of the Convention.

Here, indeed, Mr. Nokwe has put his finger on the spot. There is no need for Dr. Eiselen, Mrs. Ballinger, or others to argue about "what the Africans think" about the future of this country. Let the people speak for themselves! Let us have a free vote and a free election of delegates to a national convention, irrespective of colour or nationality. Let the Nationalists submit their plan, and the Congress its Charter. If Verwoerd and Eiselen think the Africans support their schemes they need not fear such a procedure. If they are not prepared to submit to public opinion, then let them stop parading and pretending to the outside world that they are democrats, and talking revolting nonsense about "Bantu self-government."

Dr. Verwoerd may deceive the simple-minded Nationalist voters with his talk of Bantustans, but he will not deceive anyone else, neither the African people, nor the great world beyond the borders of this country. We have heard such talk before, and we know what it means. Like everything else that has come from the Nationalist Government, it spells nothing but fresh hardships and suffering to the masses of the people.

Behind the fine talk of "self-government" is a sinister design.

The abolition of African representation in Parliament and the Cape Provincial Council shows that the real purpose of the scheme is not to concede autonomy to Africans but to deprive them of all say in

the government of the country in exchange for a system of local government controlled by a minister who is not responsible to them but to a Parliament in which they have no voice. This is not autonomy but autocracy.

Contact between the minister and the Bantu authorities will be maintained by five commissioners-general. These officials will act as the watchdogs of the minister to ensure that the "authorities" strictly toe the line. Their duty will be to ensure that these authorities should not become the voice of the African people but that of the Nationalist Government.

In terms of the White Paper, steps will be taken to "link" Africans working in urban areas with the territorial authorities established under the Bantu Authorities Act by conferring powers on these authorities to nominate persons as their representatives in urban areas. This means in effect that efforts will be made to place Africans in the cities under the control of their tribal chiefs—a retrograde step.

Nowhere in the Bill or in the various proclamations dealing with the creation of Bantu authorities is there provision for democratic elections by Africans falling within the jurisdiction of the authorities.

In the light of these facts it is sheer nonsense to talk of South Africa as being about to take a "supremely positive step towards placing Africans on the road to self-government," or of having given them more powers to rule themselves. As Dr. Eiselen clearly pointed out in his article in *Optima,* the establishment of Bantustans will not in any way affect White supremacy since even in such areas Whites will stay supreme. The Bantustans are not intended to voice aspirations of the African people; they are instruments for their subjection. Under the pretext of giving them self-government the African people are being split up into tribal units in order to retard their growth and development into full nationhood.

The new Bantu Bill and the policy behind it will bear heavily on the peasants in the Reserves. But it is not they who are the chief target of Verwoerd's new policy.

His new measures are aimed, in the first place, at the millions of Africans in the great cities of this country, the factory workers and intellectuals who have raised the banner of freedom and democracy and human dignity, who have spoken forth boldly the message that is shaking imperialism to its foundations throughout this great continent of Africa.

The Nationalists hate and fear that ban-ner and that message. They will try to destroy them, by striking with all their might at the standard-bearer and vanguard of the people, the working class.

Behind the "self-government" talks lies a grim programme of mass evictions, political persecution, and police terror. It is the last desperate gamble of a hated and doomed fascist autocracy—which, fortunately, is soon due to make its exit from the stage of history.

May 1959

94 HELEN SUZMAN
MRS. SUZMAN AND APARTHEID

Helen Suzman is the sole member of Parliament representing the Progressive party, which advocates a gradual evolution to a nonracial society. Her constituency is the wealthy Houghton district of Johannesburg. Mrs. Suzman was Assistant Statistician to the Accountants for the War Supplies Board from 1941 to 1944 and Part-Time Lecturer in Economic History at Witwatersrand University from 1944 to 1952. She is a member of the Council of the Institute of Race Relations. Mrs. Suzman's speech of January 28, 1965, which she made during the annual "no confidence" debate initiated by the opposition United party, follows.

Mrs. SUZMAN: Members on the Government side are always giving us impossible choices to make in South Africa. We have heard from the hon. Prime Minister that South Africa had to choose between being poor and White or mixed and rich; this afternoon we heard from the hon. Deputy Minister of Labour that South Africa has to choose between a shortage of labour and prosperity. Does it never occur to hon. members on the other side that these are not the only choices lying before this country? The country can be prosperous and does not have to suffer this shortage of labour. Indeed a little

From *Debates of the House of Assembly (Hansard), Fourth Session, Second Parliament, Republic of South Africa, 22nd January to 18th June 1965* (Cape Town: Hansard, 1965), XIII, cols. 195–205.

advanced planning would have seen to it that we would not suffer such a shortage of labour. What is more, I want to warn the hon. Deputy Minister that prosperity will disappear in South Africa and that we will have inflation unless steps are in fact taken, drastic steps, to overcome the shortage of labour.

I saw the hon. Deputy Minister of Labour in a new role this afternoon. Usually when one discusses job reservation, or any other of the methods that inhibit the full utilization of labour resources in South Africa, the hon. Deputy Minister comes along and defends the rights of the White workers in South Africa, proclaiming that people wish to undermine the standards which have been reached by White workers in South Africa, proclaiming that the removal of the industrial colour bar would spell doom for the White workers in South Africa. This afternoon, I am glad to say, the hon. Deputy Minister took a different line, a much more intelligent line; even if it was not completely accurate it showed that he is thinking on new lines.

The DEPUTY MINISTER OF LABOUR: We can deal with that further when we come to your motion.

Mrs. SUZMAN: I have got a lot in reserve for my motion as well. The hon. Deputy Minister and I will cross swords on that in due course, but I want to say that I am very glad to find this new pattern of thinking in the hon. Deputy Minister's mind, because he was trying to tell us to-day that in fact job reservation was not as serious as people were making out; that thousands upon thousands of Coloured workers were engaged in skilled trades in the Cape—which of course is true—but he forgot to add that there are other areas in the Cape Province where there are statutory barriers against the employment of Coloured workers in certain skilled trades, and most important, he forgot to remind us that although existing workers may continue in their skilled occupations in the Cape, new entrants to those occupations are in fact forbidden . . .

The DEPUTY MINISTER OF LABOUR: That is a very limited sphere, as you know.

Mrs. SUZMAN: It is true that it is limited, but it does exist. Then the hon. Deputy Minister gave figures which were accurate, but he used them in a misleading way. The hon. Minister told us, quite correctly, that 30 per cent of the workers in South Africa who are engaged in managerial, technical, administrative and other high standards of occupation are non-Whites. I think that figure comes from the Bureau of Statistics. But the hon. Deputy Minister did not tell us the other half of this equation and that is that Whites, who only represent 20 per cent of the total economically active population in South Africa (1960 figures) represent 70 per cent of the country's managerial, technical and skilled workers; the non-Whites representing 80 per cent of the country's totally economically employed population represent only 30 per cent of that higher class. These are equations that the hon. Minister should have given to the House for the sake of accuracy. What I am trying to point out is that 80 per cent of the working population, the non-Whites, represent only 30 per cent of any form of skilled workers, and this represents an imbalance in the country's economy.

Mr. F. S. STEYN: It may also be a question of ability.

Mrs. SUZMAN: Well, let us give them an opportunity to show whether they are less gifted. That is all I ask: equal opportunity. It is quite possible that the hon. member is right, but we do not really know if we deny them an equal opportunity to become skilled workers. We do not give them an equal opportunity because we do not give them the necessary education. There is no free education for non-Whites, and we do not allow them to enter skilled trades because they are not included in the definition of "employee." Therefore until the hon. member for Kempton Park is prepared to withdraw these very real barriers and restrictions to the full employment of non-White labour in this country, both he and I will be guessing in regard to the non-White's ability. But I say that the hon. member has less faith in the White workers than I have, because I am prepared to withdraw the superficial colour bar that protects the White worker, because I believe the White workers will be able to hold their own with non-White workers. Is the hon. member prepared to withdraw these restrictions? Is he prepared to allow the non-Whites to become apprentices, to join trade unions and get the necessary education? That will be the only way to see whether they can take full advantage of such opportunities. The hon. member of course is not prepared to commit himself on that. But I do commend the hon. Deputy Minister on the fact that at least he is not standing up defending the rights of White workers against the intrusion of non-Whites in their field.

I want to come back to the main trend of this no-confidence debate over the last three afternoons, and I must say that I have been profoundly depressed by what I have heard in this House. Both the Government and the official Opposition have been vieing with each other in pretending to be the main defenders of White supremacy, domination, in South Africa. The official Opposition now say that their policy is White leadership. It used to be White leadership "with justice." I am afraid I did not hear the words "with justice" uttered in this House over the past few days. I heard much talk about the maintenance of White leadership. They say that what they stand for is White leadership in the whole of South Africa. The Government on the other hand also claims to be upholding White leadership in South Africa, but with this difference: They claim White leadership over the whole of South Africa minus 13 per cent, and that 13 per cent of course represents the land allotment under the Land Acts for the Bantustans, for the Native reserves. In that 13 per cent of South Africa, the Government is prepared to set aside what it calls "White leadership," and at some distant time in the future it will be prepared to give independence to the Bantustans. On this basis the hon. member for Vereeniging (Mr. B. Coetzee) bluffs himself presumably, because he speaks with great sincerity, but he also imagines that he is bluffing the world that the Nationalist Party has a policy of non-discrimination and that indeed they are offering a fair *quid pro quo* to the non-Whites because they are giving them rights in 13 per cent of the country as against the deprivation of all rights in the White areas. The hon. member for Heil-

bron (Mr. Froneman) yesterday admitted that there is discrimination in the White areas of South Africa. He likened this to the discrimination suffered by immigrants who go to any country in the world. Well, I would like to find a country first of all which classifies persons born within its borders as "immigrants" and a country where immigrants who have been living there for one generation or two generations and are still classified as immigrants with no rights in the country where they are now living. In other words, all the Africans who have been in the so-called White areas of South Africa for two and three generations are in the mind of the hon. member for Heilbron still immigrants. But this he claims justifies the whole policy of the Government. The hon. member for Vereeniging had a vision in this House which he put across with his usual skill, of South Africa as the leading nation on the great Black continent of Africa, the leading light in Africa, in this Commonwealth of Nations. He was not very pleased for having to use the word "commonwealth," but at the moment he could not think of anything better. Now I ask him whether he can carry this vision a little further for us and tell us how he imagines this image measures up to the realities of the situation where South Africa is not welcome at international conferences held in the Black states of Africa, where she is denied air space and landing rights and airports throughout Africa, where South Africa has not got a single representative in any Black country in Africa and where South Africa is only prepared to accept diplomats from the rest of this Black commonwealth under the most stringent conditions. By virtue of what does the hon. member for Vereeniging bluff himself that South Africa is going to be the leading nation in Africa under such circumstances? Now the interesting thing about this vision is that it could indeed come to pass if South Africa made some very necessary adjustments in racial policies, and I want to put it to this

House that there has never been a time
when White South Africa could more
easily afford to make the necessary adjustments so as to make this country able to
take what I do believe is its rightful place
on the continent of Africa, as the leading
light on the continent of Africa, with
friendly neighbours and not hostile neighbours on our continent. I want to put it
to the Government that without any sort
of partnership policy there are still methods whereby it could in some way read-
just its position in the eyes of the rest of
Africa. I put it to the Government that
now is the time to do this in a position of
strength. Concessions which are made in
a position of weakness are of no use at all,
which is the main reason (I might add)
why the partnership policy of the Federation failed. It failed because that Government did not make concessions at a period
when the Government was in a position
of strength, but waited and only in the last
two years of the ten years of the Federation Government real concessions to partnership were made. For the first eight
years of partnership a policy indeed of
apartheid was practised. It was the old
Huggins policy of the partnership of the
man and his horse, with the man riding
on the back of his horse as his partner.
If the hon. member for Pinelands (Mr.
Thompson) would speak to Rhodesians,
they would tell him that during the last
two years when concessions were forced
on the Rhodesians, it was too late. By
then the Black man had lost all faith in
the White man's good intentions. Of
course in my opinion the Government
should go in a different direction, in the
interests of common justice, viz., a multi-
racial partnership in South Africa, a
country where merit and not colour
would be the yard-stick. But while I do
not expect the Government to go in this
direction it could still make very important adjustments which would help us in
our present position, and I want to tell the
Government what I mean by that. I mean
that the Government must stop some of

these devastating implementations of
policy which are going on at the present
time. Call a halt to them. After all it has
been ticking over very nicely gathering
White votes unto itself on the, shall I say,
paper policy that it has been presenting.
But now we are seeing the devastating
effect of the actual implementation of
these policies and I think the Government
should call a halt. I am not talking about
"petty apartheid," which really does not
interest me very much. I am not talking
about the sort of nonsense like the Adam
Faith-Dusty Springfield debacle [English
pop singers who wanted to perform before
integrated audiences and quarreled with
the South African government—ed.]
which makes us ridiculous in the eyes of
the civilized world because it is such a
ridiculous example of the Government's
obsession in regard to any sort of multi-
racial mixing. I am not talking about that
nonsense, although heaven knows those
incidents should never have occurred. I
am not talking about the removal of no-
tices which say "Whites only" or "non-
Whites only," which certain people think
would solve the trick right away. I am
not doing that because to me they are just
symbols of the deeper malaise of attempted separation. So what I propose
goes much further than that but it still
could be done and still could help this
country without, as I say, the Government having to throw overboard all its
prejudices. I am referring to the Government's senseless policy at the present
stage in regard to the devastating group
areas proposals, where one sees proposals
to make the whole of the Western Cape
bar small areas entirely White, spreading
alarm and despondency amongst thousands upon thousands of non-Whites, the
sort of group areas proposals for Durban,
for Johannesburg, for the Transvaal,
where one pattern evidences itself all the
way through: Get rid of the non-Whites,
out of the town, out of the suburbs, push
them across the river, onto the veld, miles
away outside the trading areas of our

towns. These are devastating instances of the implementation of this policy of apartheid which I believe is spreading despair among our indigenous non-Whites and is making it absolutely hopeless for South Africa to play her part on the continent of Africa. I believe the implementation of the Bantu Urban Areas Act should be called off. It is having a most far-reaching effect on the family lives of the Africans in our cities. The hon. the Leader of the Opposition called this Act "a gesture to apartheid." I want to tell him that it is very much more than a gesture to apartheid, irrespective of whether economic integration is going on apace. It is going on apace, but this does not mean that Africans are not feeling the effect of the implementation of apartheid.

Indeed, they are feeling it in a more and more critical way every year, because they are now being integrated as migratory workers and not as permanent workers, and that means that family life is more and more adversely affected, and it means that Africans coming to work for Whites are tied to specific employers and are unable to take jobs where they can better their position. They run the risk of endorsement out if they lose their jobs. Now, however many additional Africans come in to towns as evidence of integration, I can assure this House that the effect of the apartheid legislation is felt in stark reality and these are things which the Government should score out at this stage of the history of Africa. Otherwise we are sowing a legacy of hatred for ourselves which we may be able to weather but which I can assure the House our children will certainly not be able to weather. I think that the Government, apart from taking what I will call a positive and they will call a negative step of calling off the devastating effects of the implementation of the apartheid policy, should be willing to take a far more positive step in tackling the very real problem of poverty among the non-Whites in this country. That is the overriding problem, and it does not

matter whether one allows Africans to come into the urban areas or applies influx control in order, as it is said, to protect the urban Africans, if those Africans are going back to the rural areas to starve. The problem is one of unemployment and of poverty, and of course I believe that industrialization will solve that problem if the Government would only allow it to. But nevertheless these are the problems to which the Government is not paying sufficient attention, and these are the factors which are sowing bitter despair among the non-Whites. We heard the hon. the Minister of Bantu Administration painting one of his charming pictures of satisfied Africans in the tribal areas. He is always coming to us with examples of people enjoying themselves in the tribal areas. If it is not a man walking along in the track £1,000 with tucked in his moochi, it is another one cycling along with his Hansard [parliamentary debates—ed.] tucked under his arm. But the realities of the situation are those of poverty and unemployment in those areas, and of Africans living at subhuman standards of living and the break-up of family life. [Interjection.] The Chairman of the Bantu Affairs Commission should be the last person to ask me where that happens.

The industrialization in the rural areas that he speaks of is a farce. There are two factories in the Transkei, which is after all the only Bantustan which now exists. We do not know when the others will come about [no other Bantustans have yet been established—ed.]. There are two factories employing between 200 and 300 people. The border industries are mostly in the established industrial areas. As I pointed out last year, the Witwatersrand could easily be a border area in terms of the argument that you simply declare Soweto to be a Black area. But none of these areas touch the fringe of the vast poverty of the non-Whites in this country, and there is poverty in the urban areas as well, because the Government refuses to introduce minimum wage legislation, which I asked for in a motion in this House the year before last and which was rejected, and which the White trade unions are now asking for in South Africa because they are beginning to realize that the prosperity of the non-Whites is the corner-stone of the prosperity of the Whites, and that unless we expand the productivity and the consumer power of the non-Whites, our present prosperity is not going to be of any lasting duration. The figures I want to quote emanate from the manager of the Non-European Affairs Department of the Municipality of Johannesburg. In a recent survey—he delivered this paper in December 1964—he found that most families are living below the poverty line. The average family income was calculated in Johannesburg at R58 a month, and the average income earned by the head of the family was R42 a month; 48 per cent of all the families in Soweto, which is a huge African township, depend on the income of the head of the family, and the calculated minimum budget is R48 a month, and therefore unless the wives and children go out to work the majority of the families are at least R6 below the poverty datum line.

Mr. FRONEMAN: Nonsense!

Mrs. SUZMAN: I do not know how the hon. member for Heilbron (Mr. Froneman) substantiates his idea of what is really going on in the country. I am talking about figures taken out by a responsible official who is hardly likely to produce figures simply for my benefit. As long as important members like the hon. member for Heilbron—and he is important, *ex officio*—persistently ignore the realities of the situation in South Africa, I for one am filled with despair. I am not interested in which side of the House is going to maintain White domination. I only know that unless real and important changes are made in South Africa, the future of the White man in this country will not be ensured either by the Government party or by the Opposition, nor even by the Security Police of the hon. the Min-

ister of Justice. None of these things will help, because there are genuine underlying grievances and injustices in this country which are not being set right. Therefore I ask these necessary adjustments, and not because I want to set us right in the eyes of the outside world. That is not my basic reason, and not even because I want to meet Black demands, but simply because of the demands of natural justice. I can see no justification for denying people rights simply on the basis of the colour of their skins, for not allowing a man to live a family life just because he is an African; for not allowing an Indian to continue to run his shop which he has been running for 20 or 30 years, just because he is an Indian; and for not allowing Coloured folk to go on living in Kalk Bay or District Six simply because they are Coloured. I can see no justification for not educating people to take full advantage of their potentialities, simply because they are not White. Not only do I see no justification for this, but I consider it incredibly short-sighted of White South Africa not to realize what a legacy of resentment and hatred it is building up against the White man in South Africa. That is why I ask for what I believe to be very necessary adjustments in this country.

Now I want to say a few words to the hon. the Minister of Justice. I am sorry he is not in the House now, but I must say it. The Minister has told the country that he has restored law and order in South Africa.

Mr. FRONEMAN: He has not restored it; he has maintained it.

Mrs. SUZMAN: Well, in that case it means that there never was any unrest in this country. I understood that there was a state bordering on an emergency some time ago when we had to introduce the 90-day law [indefinite detention without writ of habeas corpus—ed.]. I want to say right away of course that I never believed that there was any justification for that law. I believe that our Police Force and our Special branch should be quite competent to handle any such manifestation of subversion, without recourse to any law as far-reaching as this 90-day law. I want to warn the Minister that I believe, as I said earlier this afternoon, that there will always be unrest in South Africa unless the basic injustices are set right. I believe that there are injustices and I will not adopt the ostrich-like attitude of people in this country who say there are no injustices, and that it is all only the work of agitators and communists, and that everything is fine. Everything is not fine as long as there is poverty and there are group areas and such things. But I want to come back to this question of the 90-day law and I want to say that I believe this law has done more harm than any other single law that has ever been passed. It is not a law which a Western civilized country requires to maintain law and order. That should be possible if the Government is governing with the consent of the majority of the people, and if the Government takes cognizance of the injustices before it is too late. I believe that this law should be not suspended but repealed. I was against its introduction and I am against its continuation on our Statute Book. I think the Minister should not only suspend it but should repeal it. It is a law which lends itself to abuse, which allows people to be subjected to standing interrogation for long periods, the sort of thing done by the Ogpu, standing for hours while being interrogated by teams of officers. It kept people in solitary confinement week after week, a devastating form of torture. [Interjection.] Of course, I am not in favour of sabotage, but

I can tell the hon. member that it is no use trying to stop sabotage unless one tackles the basic underlying reasons for it. The 90-day law should be repealed.

In the few minutes remaining to me I want to raise a final matter, again with the Minister of Justice, and that is the banning of Professor Roux and of Professor Simon under the new use to which he is putting his anticommunist law; in other words, the prohibiting of these men, because they were listed as communists, from teaching at our universities. [Interjections.] Professor Roux in fact has not been a member of the Communist Party since 1936, when he resigned from it. [Interjections.]

An HON. MEMBER: Solly Sachs also resigned.

Mrs. SUZMAN: Professor Roux wrote a book which is a standard text-book for students and he is now prohibited not only from teaching but from publishing his work or from continuing with his research in plant physiology. I think this is the most absurd banning order on a man of science who has contributed a great deal to South Africa. As far as Professor Simon is concerned, he remained a member of the Communist Party until it was banned in 1950, and to the best of my knowledge since that time he has taken no part in political activity and, indeed, he has broken no law, because if he had broken a law one wonders why the hon. the Minister of Justice has not hauled him, as well as Professor Roux, into the courts of law, where they can be dealt with under proper procedure, and not simply by arbitrary banning by the Minister of Justice. [Time limit.]

INDEX

Index